CRIMINOLOGY

THIRD EDITION

CRIMINOLOGY

THIRD EDITION

LARRY J. SIEGEL

UNIVERSITY OF LOWELL

WEST PUBLISHING COMPANY

ST. PAUL   NEW YORK   LOS ANGELES   SAN FRANCISCO

Cover Image	Gregg Kreutz, *Below the Manhattan Bridge* (1986), oil on canvas, 28" x 40", with permission of the artist. Private collection.
Cover Design	Paula Schlosser Design
Text Design	Laura Carlson
Copyediting	Solveig Tyler-Robinson
Artwork	Alice Thiede
Composition	Dahl and Curry
Indexing	Lois Oster

Photos 3 Karen R. Pruess/Taurus Photos, Inc., 5 Patricia Hollander Gross/Stock, Boston, 6 and 14 Historical Pictures Service, Chicago, 16 AP/WIDE WORLD PHOTOS, 23 The Bettmann Archive, 25 and 33 Historical Pictures Service, Chicago, 45 Gale Zucker/Stock, Boston, 54 UPI/Bettmann Newsphotos, 59 Cary Wolinsky/Stock, Boston, 67 Gale Zucker/Stock, Boston, 73 AP/WIDE WORLD PHOTOS, 75 courtesy of Freda Adler, 79 courtesy of Marvin Wolfgang, Bachrach Photographers, Inc. 79 courtesy of Paul Tracy, 81 Jerry Bernot/Stock, Boston, 95 AP/WIDE WORLD PHOTOS, 98 and 103 Historical Pictures Service, Chicago, 106 John Coletti/Stock, Boston, 112 AP/WIDE WORLD PHOTOS, 113 courtesy of Ronald Clarke, 123 Gale Zucker/Stock, Boston, 127 courtesy of C. Ray Jeffrey, 132 Irene Fertik/courtesy of Sarnoff Mednick, 136 AP/WIDE WORLD PHOTOS, 140 provided by Albert Bandura, 143 Michael Weisbrodt and Family/Stock, Boston, 149 courtesy of James Q. Wilson, 149 courtesy of Richard Herrnstein, 157 Michael Weisbrodt and Family/Stock, Boston, 164 Historical Pictures Service, Chicago, 167 Patricia Hollander Gross/Stock, Boston, 172 Owen Franken/Stock, Boston, 177 J. P. Laffont/Sygma, 187 Shirley Zeiberg/Taurus Photos, Inc., 189 Laima Druskis/Taurus Photos, Inc., 195 courtesy of Ronald Akers, 199 Frank Siteman/Stock, Boston, 201 courtesy of Travis Hirschi, 204 Eric Kroll/Taurus Photos, Inc., 206 courtesy of Edwin Lemert, 219 and 221 AP/WIDE WORLD PHOTOS, 225 Peter Menzel/Stock, Boston, 227 AP/WIDE WORLD PHOTOS, 233 UPI/Bettmann Newsphotos, 247 Mike Mazzaschi/Stock, Boston, 251 AP/WIDE WORLD PHOTOS, 254 UPI/Bettmann Newsphotos, 273 AP/WIDE WORLD PHOTOS, 276 Reuters/Bettmann Newsphotos, 289 Frank Siteman/Stock, Boston, 292 AP/WIDE WORLD PHOTOS, 301 Ira Berger/Woodfin Camp and Associates, 307, 311, 316, 323, 332 and 335 AP/WIDE WORLD PHOTOS, 351 Charles Gatewood/Stock, Boston, 360 UPI/Bettmann Newsphotos, 366 AP/WIDE WORLD PHOTOS, 375 Reuters/Bettmann Newsphotos, 387 and 392 AP/WIDE WORLD PHOTOS, 401 Spencer Grant/Taurus Photos, Inc., 405, 407, 417, 421 and 430 AP/WIDE WORLD PHOTOS, 434 UPI/Bettmann Newsphotos, 442 AP/WIDE WORLD PHOTOS, 453 Ellis Herwig/Taurus Photos, Inc., 463 UPI/Bettmann Newsphotos, 474 and 477 AP/WIDE WORLD PHOTOS, 480 UPI/Bettmann Newsphotos, 495 Ellis Herwig/Stock, Boston, 499 Historical Pictures Service, Chicago, 506 AP/WIDE WORLD PHOTOS

Library of Congress Cataloging-in-Publication Data

Siegel, Larry J.
  Criminology.

  Includes index.
  1. Crime and criminals. 2. Crime and criminals—United States. I. Title.
HV6025.S48   1989   364   88-20510
ISBN 0-314-45208-7

To

Andrew, Eric and Rachel Siegel

and

Therese J. Libby

CONTENTS

CHAPTER 6   PSYCHOLOGICAL AND BIOLOGICAL APPROACHES TO CRIME: TRAIT THEORY   123

Chapter 12   Economic Crimes: Organizational Criminality   311

Chapter 13   Public Order Crime   351

CLOSE-UPS

PREFACE

Criminology continues to be one of the most fascinating courses offered on college campuses today. What could be more important or interesting than a field of study which deals with events within our society, ranging from mass murder to insider trading, from crack use to child abuse? The field is extremely dynamic, constantly reshaped by major research studies, Supreme Court rulings and governmental policy changes. Therefore, this third edition of *Criminology* has kept pace with current knowledge on crime and criminality.

GOALS AND OBJECTIVES

A criminology course is normally a student's first opportunity to study the nature of criminal behavior. The text for use in such a course must be comprehensive, logically organized, easily understood, and reflective of major research efforts. Consequently, the goals of the third edition of *Criminology* are: first, to be as objective as possible, presenting the many diverse views that characterize criminology and reflect its interdisciplinary nature; second, to achieve a balance in presenting material, not allowing any single viewpoint to dominate its content; third, to be thorough, presenting the most important works in criminological literature; and fourth, to make the text interesting and readable, thus encouraging students to pursue further study in the field. This book analyzes criminology in depth by examining historical data, statistical information, journal articles, scholarly works, and government documents.

TOPIC AREAS

The book is divided into four main sections, each carefully structured to cover relevant material in a comprehensive, balanced, and objective fashion. Section I provides a framework for studying criminology. The first chapter defines the field and its most basic concepts: the essence of crime, component areas of criminology, and ethical issues which confront it. The second chapter reviews criminal law functions, processes, defenses, and reforms. The third and fourth chapters analyze various methods of acquiring crime data and what those data sources tell us about crime and criminality. The data reveals the relationships between race, age, gender, class and crime. Chapter 4 concludes with chronic offender concepts and their impact on crime and criminal justice.

Section II covers criminological theory within five chapters: why do people behave the way they do? Historical and contemporary theories cover rational choice and classicism, trait, social structure, social process, and social conflict. Appropriate discussions are included on recent attempts by criminologists to integrate different theories into a unified whole.

Section III is devoted to major forms of criminal behavior. Four chapters explore violent crime, common theft offenses, white-collar and organized crime, and public order crime.

Section IV focuses on the criminal justice system. The opening chapter is an overview of judiciary processes, legal concepts, and contemporary perspectives. The final three chapters cover the police, court, and correctional systems in detail.

— What Is New in This Edition? —

The most notable difference in this edition is an Epilogue which highlights the most important information contained throughout the text. Also, each chapter has undergone considerable updating and expansion. This is a detailed breakdown of new elements in each chapter:

In Section I, Chapter 1 (*Crime and Criminology*) contains updates on self-defense against crime; revises portions on ethical issues and today's criminology. Chapter 2 (*The Criminal Law and Its Processes*) contains new material on the history of the jury and the development of the law of vagrancy; gives the insanity plea area special attention as to how often defendants are actually found not guilty by reason of insanity. Chapter 3 (*Measuring Criminal Behavior*) now has sections on acquiring crime data, such as survey research, aggregate data research, observational research, and experimental studies; incorporates newer statistics on crime and victimization. Chapter 4 (*Patterns of Crime and Victimization*) focuses on the age/crime controversy; compares new information on the characteristics of victims and criminals and the lifetime likelihood of victimization.

In Section II, Chapter 5 (*Classical Criminology: Crime as Choice*) expands upon deterrence and the effectiveness of incapacitation; divides the review of research into aggregate, perceptual, panel and experimental sections; analyzes rational choice and routine activities theories. Chapter 6 (*Psychological and Biological Approaches to Crime: Trait Theory*) has additions on hormonal influences (e.g., PMS and crime), television and violence, and psychopathy and physical traits, including arousal theory; reconsiders the relationship between crime and IQ in light of the most recent evidence; reviews Wilson and Herrnstein's crime-as-choice theory as an attempt to integrate trait and choice theory. Chapter 7 (*Sociological Approaches: Social Structure Theory*) re-examines teenage gangs; integrates the social ecology theory of Bursik, Blau, Sampson, Messner, Byrne, and others; includes relative deprivation theory and the effects of urbanism; presents new evidence regarding the relationship between unemployment and crime; reviews results of the Head Start program. Chapter 8 (*Sociological Approaches: Social Process Theories*) provides updated material on control, labeling and learning theory; a major section on integrated theory analyzes the work of Weis, Elliott, and

Thornberry; also includes a section on crime prevention through family training. Chapter 9 (*Sociological Approaches: Social Conflict Theory*) now divides Marxist criminology into instrumental and structural areas; contemplates newly-emerging integrated Marxist theories such as those by Hagan, the Schwendingers, and Colvin and Pauly.

In Section III, Chapter 10 (*Violent Crime*) presents new material on violent crime trends and causes, date rape, rape and the macho male, stranger homicides, robbery victims, gun control, and terrorism. Chapter 11 (*Economic Crimes: Street Crime*) now discusses the crime of stooping and the section on fencing is reworked to include principles of Steffensmeier's *The Fence*. New material in Chapter 12 (*Economic Crimes: Organizational Criminality*) involves insider trading, the Boesky affair, illegal lobbying, management fraud, Braithwaite's theory of white collar crime, trends in the prosecution of white collar criminals, and the concept of corporate murder; organized crime sections are viewed in light of new federal enforcement practices. Chapter 13 (*Public Order Crime*) discusses current knowledge on the relationship between pornography and violent crime; changing patterns of drug use include cocaine and crack abuse; new sections also look at the drug trade as a business enterprise, the lifestyle of addicts, and the fight for control of the sex-for-profit industry. Chapter 14 (*Overview of the Criminal Justice System*) analyzes costs of the criminal justice system and the "wedding cake" model of justice; the section on legal control of the justice process reflects changes in the exclusionary rule.

In Section IV, Chapter 15 (*The Police*) explores problem-oriented policing, community policing, citizen self-help groups, and improved police effectiveness; sections on the police and the rule of law reflect changes in Fourth and Fifth Amendment cases. Chapter 16 (*The Judicatory Process*) reviews the death penalty, sentencing disparity, preventive detention, the courtroom work group, the effectiveness of plea bargaining, imposition of the sentence, and time served in prison; sections on legal control include discussion of *Batson v. Kentucky, Nix v. Whiteside, Heath v. Alabama*, and *Turner v. Murray*. Chapter 17 (*Corrections*) debuts innovative probation services including house arrest, electronic monitoring, and intensive probation supervision, as well as changes in inmate culture, private prisons, and private industry in prisons; changes in parole and recidivism rates are covered.

——— DISTINCTIVE FEATURES ———

This edition also has some distinct pedagogical features that should help students to better understand the study of criminology.

1. *Chapter Outlines.* Each chapter begins with an outline of subject headings. The material is thus concisely organized for the student and instructor.
2. *Photos, tables, and illustrations.* More illustrations, tables, and photographs are used throughout this edition. They help students visualize components of criminology and enhance the text material.
3. *Close-Ups.* Every chapter contains Close-Ups to illustrate important research, surveys, policies, academic ideas, or case studies. They are current, controversial, informative, and thought provoking. Each Close-Up is accompanied by discussion questions to stimulate classroom discussions.
4. *Summary.* Each chapter concludes with a summary of its most significant topics, issues and concepts. The student thus can concentrate on the chapter's material in a summarized form.
5. *Key Terms.* Following each chapter summary is a list of key terms used by professional criminologists. A good vocabulary helps the student become better acquainted with the field of criminology.

——— ACKNOWLEDGMENTS ———

Many people helped make this book possible. The author is grateful to those who reviewed the second edition and made suggestions, which were followed and appreciated: Thomas C. Calhoun, Western Kentucky University; Edna Erez, Kent State University; Denny E. Hill, Georgia Southern College; Alfred N. Himelson, California State University at Northridge; Pamela D. Mayhall, Pima Community College; Steven F. Messner, SUNY at Albany; Theodore P. Skotnicki, Niagara University; and Michael Wiatrowski, Florida Atlantic University.

Others who helped with material or advice were Bonnie Berry, James Black, Stephen Brodt, Edward Green, Dennis Hoffman, Alan Lincoln, Gerrold Hotaling, Joseph Jacoby, James McKenna, Paul Tracy, Charles Vedder, Sam Walker, David Friedrichs, Chris Eskridge, William Wakefield, Frank Cullen, Marty Schwartz, Chuck Fenwick, John Laub, Spencer Rathus, Bob Regoli, Marvin Zalman, James Fyfe, Lee Ellis, Lorne Yeudall, Darrell Steffensmeier, M. Douglas Anglin, Bob Langworthy, Jim Inciardi and Bruce Johnson. Special thanks also goes to James Garofalo and Anne Pastore at the Hindelang Research Center in Albany, New York; James Byrne at the Criminal Justice Research Center, University of Lowell; the staff at the Institute for Social Research, University of Michigan; Kristina Rose and Janet Rosenbaum of the National Criminal Justice Reference Service.

This work was guided by my acquisition editor Mary Schiller of West Publishing; this is the tenth volume we have done together! Mary Garvey Verrill, my production editor, must take the credit for putting together a beautiful publication. Best wishes to the students of criminology and their instructors, that they may find this field as exciting and fascinating as those who were involved with this project.

Larry J. Siegel

SECTION I

CONCEPTS OF CRIME AND CRIMINOLOGY

Section I of this book introduces students to the field of criminology and its most basic subject matter. It covers the concept of crime, the nature of law, and the extent of criminal behavior.

The first chapter provides an overview of criminology. Who are criminologists? What do they do? How do they perceive their field of study? Chapter 1 also discusses the various components of the field. Like many other academic disciplines, criminology contains various subdisciplines that practitioners can specialize in: victimology, penology, sociology of law, crime measurement, and so on. Students will learn that there is no unified view of criminology, but rather conflicting concepts of the field and its subject matter.

The section's second chapter focuses on the criminal law. It introduces the major components of the law: the definition of crimes, the concept of intent, and the defenses to criminal accusations. Students will find that simply engaging in an act that is outlawed by society may not mean a person has committed a crime. All the elements of criminal law must be considered before an action is labelled criminal.

The final two chapters review the various sources of crime data and discuss what they tell us about criminals and their victims. Chapter 3 reviews the methods used to measure crime and gives an overview of the extent of crime in the United States. Chapter 4 focuses on the individual characteristics of criminals and victims and evaluates the influence of important social traits—age, race, sex, economic status—on the likelihood of becoming a criminal or victim. Measuring criminal behavior patterns is the basis for criminological theory. The way crime is organized, its trends and patterns, has profoundly influenced the way criminologists view the causes of crime. The validity of criminological theory is bound up in the validity of crime measurement.

CHAPTER 1

CRIME AND CRIMINOLOGY

CHAPTER OUTLINE

INTRODUCTION

Consider the following events which have taken place in the past few years:

- The federal government investigated and prosecuted a group of Wall Street investment bankers and brokers for illegal insider trading. Some of those convicted had annual incomes of over $1 million and personal fortunes of over $100 million.
- Donald Harvey, a hospital aide in Cincinnati, was convicted of killing 24 patients. Privately, Harvey indicated that the actual death toll could be as many as 54.
- Police in Providence, Rhode Island, broke up a sex-for-profit ring. A number of the women involved were students at Brown University, one of the nation's most exclusive Ivy League schools.
- In New York City, three teenage boys were convicted of manslaughter in the death of Michael Griffith, a 23-year-old black man. Griffith was killed when he was struck by a car while trying to escape from a mob of white youths in the Howard Beach section of Queens. The racially motivated violence shocked a city long used to urban conflict.
- California correctional authorities attempted to release inmate Lawrence Singleton on parole; not a single community was willing to accept him as a resident. Singleton had served eight years for raping a teenage girl and cutting off her arms with a hatchet.

These incidents illustrate why crime and criminal behavior are topics which have long fascinated people. Crime touches all segments of society. Both the poor and desperate, as well as the wealthy and powerful, engage in criminal activity. Crime cuts across racial, class, and gender lines. It involves acts which shock the collective conscience of the nation, and acts which seem relatively harmless human foibles. Crimes may be committed among friends and family members; they can also involve absolute strangers.

Regardless of whether crime is shocking or pardonable, most people view it as a major social problem. Public opinion polls indicate that a majority of citizens believe that too little money is currently being spent on solving the crime problem; about 30 percent of Americans over age 18 own firearms, and 69 percent of these answered "yes" when asked if they would use them against a burglar in their home (see Close-Up entitled "Self-Defense Against Crime").[1]

This long-term concern about crime has encouraged the development of an academic discipline, **criminology,** which is the scientific approach to the study of the nature, extent, cause, and control of criminal behavior. **Criminologists** bring the scientific method to bear on the study of crime and justice. Unlike the general public, whose opinions about crime are colored by personal experiences, biases, and values, these well-informed and highly trained observers of social phenomena use established research methodologies to objectively examine issues relating to crime and its consequences.

This text reviews criminology and analyzes its major areas of inquiry. It focuses on the nature and extent of crime, causes of crime, crime patterns, and crime control. This chapter introduces criminology. How is it defined? What are its goals? What major issues face its practitioners? What ethical issues face those wishing to conduct criminological research?

WHAT IS CRIMINOLOGY?

Criminology has at its heart the study of social behavior and human interaction. In their classic definition, criminologists Edwin Sutherland and Donald Cressey state:

> Criminology is the body of knowledge regarding crime as a social phenomenon. It includes within its scope the processes of making laws, of breaking laws, and of reacting toward the breaking of laws . . . The objective of criminology is the development of a body of general and verified principles and of other types of knowledge regarding this process of law, crime, and treatment.[2]

Sutherland and Cressey's definition includes the most important areas of interest to criminologists: the study of crime as a social phenomenon; the development by society of a criminal law and its use to define crime; the causes of law violation; and the methods society uses to control criminal behavior. Also important is their use of the term *verified principles* to signify the use of the scientific method in criminology. Many people study crime without using established methods of scientific inquiry. These people are not criminologists but journalists, commentators, critics, social

CLOSE-UP

Self-Defense Against Crime

Many Americans have adopted elaborate self-defense mechanisms to make their homes, neighborhoods, and businesses safe from crime. A Victimization Risk Survey administered to over 21,000 people residing in about 11,000 households across the United States found that substantial numbers of Americans have taken at least one of three specific crime prevention measures to secure their homes or place of employment: installing a burglar alarm (7 percent); participating in a neighborhood watch program (7 percent); or engraving valuables with an identification number (25 percent). Other commonly used crime prevention techniques include: a fence or barricade at the entrance; a doorkeeper, guard, or receptionist in an apartment building; an intercom or phone to gain access to the building; surveillance cameras; window bars; warning signs; and dogs chosen for their ability to guard the house.

The survey found that the use of these measures was directly proportional to perception of neighborhood safety: people who feared crime the most were more likely to use crime prevention techniques. There were also specific social patterns in the use of crime prevention techniques. For example, family income seems to play an important role in the decision to adopt crime prevention—about half of all households with income of $50,000 or more reported using at least one measure, while only about 20 percent of households earning under $7,500 used prevention measures. Similarly, the probability of crime prevention measures being taken was greater if a person had some college education, owned a home rather than rented, and lived in an urban or suburban area rather than a rural environment.

Another self-protection mechanism which has become commonplace is purchase of a handgun. Douglas Smith and Craig Uchida interviewed 9,021 residents in Rochester, New York, Tampa–St. Petersburg, Florida, and St. Louis, Missouri, and found that gun ownership was highest among individuals who had been the victims of crime, who perceived police protection as inadequate, and who believed that the crime rate in their area and their chances of future victimization were on the increase. Smith and Uchida also linked gun ownership to household income and makeup. Male-dominated households were much more likely to contain guns than those which were solely female; those earning more than $30,000 were more likely to purchase guns than those earning less than $10,000.

These studies indicate that Americans fear crime and take elaborate measures to protect themselves from victimization. Do such measures actually work? A recent review by Gary Kleck found evidence that the use of private force was a more effective and immediate deterrent to crime than legal sanctions. Kleck found that each year between 1,500 and 2,800 accused felons are killed by gun-wielding civilians, and between 8,700 and 16,000 are wounded; guns were used against criminals one million times. Kleck concluded that victims who fight back stand a better chance of avoiding injury and crime completion than nonresisters. Self-protection has become a common trend in the American culture.

Discussion Questions

- Do you or your family own a gun? If so, why?
- Should a person have the right to shoot an intruder in his or her home without first finding out if the intruder is armed?

SOURCES: Gary Kleck, "Crime Control Through the Private Use of Armed Force," *Social Problems* 35(1988): 1–21; Douglas Smith and Craig Uchida, "The Social Organization of Self-Help: A Study of Defensive Weapon Ownership," *American Sociological Review* 53 (1988): 94–102; Catherine Whitaker, *Crime Prevention Measures* (Washington, D.C.: Bureau of Justice Statistics, 1986); James Wright, Peter Rossi, and Kathleen Daly, *Under the Gun: Weapons, Crime and Violence in America* (New York: Aldine, 1983).

thinkers, and so on. Criminologists use scientifically verified methods to pose research questions (**hypotheses**) and then test them empirically (through direct observation). They use numerous methods of established social science inquiry: analysis of existing records, experimental designs, surveys, historical analyses, and so on. It is the use of the scientific method that sets professional criminologists apart from laypeople interested in the study of crime.

CRIMINOLOGY: AN INTERDISCIPLINARY SCIENCE

Criminology is interdisciplinary. Relatively few academic centers grant graduate degrees in criminology. (The University of Maryland and Florida State University are among the few that do.) Therefore, most criminologists have been trained in diverse fields, most commonly sociology, but also political science, psychology, economics, and the natural sciences. In fact, **Cesare Lombroso,** often called the "father of criminology" was a medical doctor.[3]

For most of the twentieth century, criminology's primary orientation was sociological. However, it also has been influenced by the contributions of several other fields of study. For example, biologists and physicians have attempted to isolate particular traits and physical characteristics that seem to produce law-violating behavior. Similarly, psychologists and other members of the mental health professions have focused on the mental processes that are thought to produce antisocial behavior. Other contributions have been made by historians and political economists, who study the history of law and the evolving definition of crime.

The multidisciplinary nature of criminology has created some confusion over whether it should be considered an independent academic area or a subfield of a larger, more well-established discipline, such as sociology or even psychology. Vincent Webb and Dennis Hoffman suggest that a field becomes a discipline ". . . when it establishes that it has a body of knowledge that is distinct and autonomous."[4] Today, with its own professional organization (the **American Society of Criminology**) and a number of academic journals devoted to its study (*Criminology* and the *Journal of Criminal Law and Criminology*, for example), the study of criminology may be considered an indepen-

Cesare Lombroso is known as the "father of criminology."

dent area of scientific inquiry. According to two distinguished criminologists, Marvin Wolfgang and Franco Ferracuti, criminology is in fact a separate discipline that integrates knowledge from many fields because "it has accumulated its own set of organized data and theoretical conceptualizations that use the scientific method, approach to understanding, and attitude in research."[5]

Criminology can therefore be viewed as an integrated approach to the study of criminal behavior. Though it combines elements of other academic disciplines, its practitioners devote their primary interest to understanding the true nature of law, crime, and justice.

THE CRIMINOLOGICAL ENTERPRISE

Regardless of their background or training, criminologists are primarily interested in studying crime and criminal behavior. As Wolfgang and Ferracuti put it:

A criminologist is one whose professional training, occupational role, and pecuniary reward are primarily concentrated on a scientific approach to, and study and analysis of, the phenomenon of crime and criminal behavior.[6]

Within the broader arena of criminology are several subareas, which taken together make up the **criminological enterprise.** Criminologists may specialize in a subarea, in the same way that a psychologist might specialize in development, perception, personality, or psychopathology.

Criminal Statistics

The subarea of criminal statistics involves measuring the amount and trends of criminal activity. How much crime occurs annually? Who commits it? When and where does it occur? Which crimes are the most serious? (See Close-Up on "Crime Seriousness.") Criminologists interested in criminal statistics try to create valid and reliable measurements of criminal behavior. For example, they might review the records of police and court agencies. They survey large samples of citizens to determine the percentage of law violators who escape detection by the justice system. They also study the victims of crime to draw conclusions about the true number of criminal acts. The various measures of criminal behavior and their interpretation are reviewed in Chapters 3 and 4.

Sociology of Law

The sociology of law is a subarea of criminology concerned with the role of social forces in shaping criminal law and with the role of criminal law in shaping society. Criminologists study the history of legal thought in an effort to understand how particular laws developed. For example, criminal laws controlling theft, rape, and drug abuse evolved into their present state after years of change. How such modern crimes as racketeering, computer fraud, and price fixing developed are also of particular interest to criminologists. Similarly, the impact of law and its application to human behavior is an important area of criminological study. What effect does passing a tough new drunk-driving or gun-control law have on people's use of alcohol and guns? What effect does capital punishment have on the murder rate? The criminal law is discussed further in Chapter 2.

The Etiology of Crime

The etiology of crime focuses on the actual causes of criminal behavior. Certain questions have tormented criminologists from the first: Why do people engage in criminal acts? When they know their actions can bring harsh punishment and social disapproval, why do they steal, rape, and murder? In short, why do people behave the way they do? Does crime have a social or an individual basis? Is it a psychological, biological, social, political, or economic phenomenon?

Criminologists usually bring their personal beliefs and backgrounds to bear when they study these issues. Consequently, there are diverse theories of crime causation, each reflecting the orientation of its creator. Psychologically trained criminologists view crime as a function of personality, development, social learning, or intelligence. Biologically oriented criminologists study the biochemical, genetic, and neurological linkages to crime. Sociologically trained criminologists look at the social forces producing criminal behavior.

Despite important studies, understanding the cause of crime remains a difficult problem. Criminologists are still unsure why, given similar conditions, one person elects criminal solutions to his or her problems while another conforms to accepted social rules of behavior. Further, when attempts have been made to understand crime rates and trends, faulty data and unsound research methods have prevented criminologists from developing any firm conclusions. Understanding the nature and causes of crime is a goal that has so far eluded its seekers.

However, despite their ongoing disagreements over its cause, most criminologists agree that the factors which produce crime must be understood if society is to deal with crime effectively. The various theories of crime causation are discussed in Chapters 5 through 9.

Criminal Behavior Systems

The study of criminal behavior also involves research on the interrelationships between similar types of

CLOSE-UP

Crime Seriousness

How does the public view the seriousness of crime? The National Survey of Crime Severity measured public perceptions of the severity of 204 illegal events ranging from "playing hooky" to killing twenty people with a bomb. The survey results follow.

How Do People Rank the Severity of Crime?

Severity of score and offense

72.1. Planting a bomb in a public building. The bomb explodes and twenty people are killed.

52.8. A man forcibly rapes a woman. As a result of physical injuries, she dies.

43.2. Robbing a victim at gunpoint. The victim struggles and is shot to death.

39.2. A man stabs his wife. As a result, she dies.

35.7 Stabbing a victim to death.

35.6. Intentionally injuring a victim. As a result, the victim dies.

33.8. Running a narcotics ring.

27.9. A woman stabs her husband. As a result, he dies.

26.3. An armed person skyjacks an airplane and demands to be flown to another country.

25.9. A man forcibly rapes a woman. No other physical injury occurs.

24.9. Intentionally setting fire to a building causing $100,000 worth of damage.

22.9. A parent beats his young child with his fists. The child requires hospitalization.

21.2. Kidnapping a victim.

20.7. Selling heroin to others for resale.

19.5. Smuggling heroin into the country.

19.5. Killing a victim by recklessly driving an automobile.

17.9. Robbing a victim of $10 at gunpoint. The victim is wounded and requires hospitalization.

16.9. A man drags a woman into an alley, tears her clothes, but flees before she is physically harmed or sexually attacked.

16.4 Attempting to kill a victim with a gun. The gun misfires and the victim escapes unharmed.

15.9. A teenage boy beats his mother with his fists. The mother requires hospitalization.

15.5. Breaking into a bank at night and stealing $100,000.

14.1. A doctor cheats on claims he makes to a federal health insurance plan for patient services.

13.9. A legislator takes a bribe from a company to vote for a law favoring the company.

13.0. A factory knowingly gets rid of its waste in a way that pollutes the water supply of a city.

12.2. Paying a witness to give false testimony in a criminal trial.

12.0. A police officer takes a bribe not to interfere with an illegal gambling operation.

12.0. Intentionally injuring a victim. The victim is treated by a doctor and hospitalized.

11.8. A man beats a stranger with his fists. He requires hospitalization.

11.4. Knowingly lying under oath during a trial.

11.2. A company pays a bribe to a legislator to vote for a law favoring the company.

10.9. Stealing property worth $10,000 from outside a building.

10.5. Smuggling marijuana into the country for resale.

10.4. Intentionally hitting a victim with a lead pipe. The victim requires hospitalization.

10.3. Illegally selling barbiturates, such as prescription sleeping pills, to others for resale.

10.3. Operating a store that knowingly sells stolen property.

10.0. A government official intentionally hinders the investigation of a criminal offense.

9.7. Breaking into a school and stealing equipment worth $1,000.

9.7. Walking into a public museum and stealing a painting worth $1,000.

9.6. Breaking into a home and stealing $1,000.

9.6. A police officer knowingly makes a false arrest.

9.5. A public official takes $1,000 of public money for his own use.

9.4. Robbing a victim of $10 at gunpoint. No physical harm occurs.

9.3. Threatening to seriously injure a victim.

9.2. Several large companies illegally fix the retail prices of their products.

8.6. Performing an illegal abortion.

8.5. Selling marijuana to others for resale.

8.5. Intentionally injuring a victim. The victim is treated by a doctor but is not hospitalized.

8.2. Knowing that a shipment of cooking oil is bad, a store owner decides to sell it anyway. Only one bottle is sold and the purchaser is treated by a doctor but not hospitalized.

7.9. A teenage boy beats his father with his fists. The father requires hospitalization.

7.7. Knowing that a shipment of cooking oil is bad, a store owner decides to sell it anyway.

7.5. A person, armed with a lead pipe, robs a victim of $10. No physical harm occurs.

7.4. Illegally getting monthly welfare checks.

7.3. Threatening a victim with a weapon unless the victim gives money. The victim gives $10 and is not harmed.

7.3. Breaking into a department store and stealing merchandise worth $1,000.

7.2. Signing someone else's name to a check and cashing it.

6.9. Stealing property worth $1,000 from outside a building.

6.5. Using heroin.

6.5. An employer refuses to hire a qualified person because of that person's race.

6.4. Getting customers for a prostitute.

6.3. A person, free on bail for committing a serious crime, purposefully fails to appear in court on the day of the trial.

6.2. An employee embezzles $1,000 from an employer.

5.4. Possessing some heroin for personal use.

5.4. A real estate agent refuses to sell a house to a person because of that person's race.

5.4. Threatening to harm a victim unless the victim gives money. The victim gives $10 and is not harmed.

5.3. Loaning money at an illegally high interest rate.

5.1. A man runs his hands over the body of a female victim, then runs away.

5.1. A person, using force, robs a victim of $10. No physical harm occurs.

4.9. Snatching a handbag containing $10 from a victim on the street.

4.8. A man exposes himself in public.

4.6. Carrying a gun illegally.

4.5. Cheating on federal income tax return.

4.4. Picking a victim's pocket of $100.

4.2. Attempting to break into a home but running away when a police car approaches.

3.8. Turning in a false fire alarm.

3.7. A labor union official illegally threatens to organize a strike if an employer hires nonunion workers.

3.6. Knowingly passing a bad check.

3.6. Stealing property worth $100 from outside a building.

3.5. Running a place that permits gambling to occur illegally.

3.2. An employer illegally threatens to fire employees if they join a labor union.

2.4. Knowingly carrying an illegal knife.

2.2. Stealing $10 worth of merchandise from the counter of a department store.

2.1. A man is found firing a rifle for which he knows he has no permit.

2.1. A woman engages in prostitution.

1.9. Making an obscene phone call.

1.9. A store owner knowingly puts "large" eggs into containers marked "extra-large."

1.8. A youngster under 16 years old is drunk in public.

1.8. Knowingly being a customer in a place where gambling occurs illegally.

1.7. Stealing property worth $10 from outside a building.

1.6. Being a customer in a house of prostitution.

1.6. A male, over 16 years of age, has sexual relations with a willing female under 16.

1.5. Taking barbiturates, such as sleeping pills, without a legal prescription.

1.5. Intentionally shoving or pushing a victim. No medical treatment is required.

1.4. Smoking marijuana.

1.3. Two persons willingly engage in a homosexual act.

1.1. Disturbing the neighborhood with loud, noisy behavior.

1.1. Taking bets on the numbers.

1.1. A group continues to hang around a corner after being told to break up by a police officer.

0.9. A youngster under 16 years old runs away from home.

0.8. Being drunk in public.

0.7. A youngster under 16 years old breaks a curfew law by being out on the street after the hour permitted by law.

0.6. Trespassing in the backyard of a private home.

0.3. A person is a vagrant, that is, has no home and no visible means of support.

0.2. A youngster under 16 years old plays hooky from school.

In deciding severity, people seem to take into account such factors as—

- The victims' ability to protect themselves
- The extent of injury and loss
- For property crimes, the type of business or organization the property is stolen from
- The offender's relationship to the victim

Interestingly, white-collar crimes, such as consumer fraud, cheating on income taxes, pollution by factories, price fixing, and accepting bribes, are viewed at least as seriously as many conventional property and violent crimes.

Within particular categories of crime, severity assessments are affected by factors such as whether injury occurred and the extent of property loss. For example, all burglaries are not scored at the same severity level because of the differing characteristics of each event (even though all the events fit into the same crime category).

Discussion Questions

- How would you rate the seriousness of crimes?
- Should punishments be based on citizens' perceptions of crime seriousness?

SOURCE: "The Seriousness of Crime: Results of a National Survey," Center for Studies in Criminology and Criminal Law, University of Pennsylvania. In National Institute of Justice *Report to the Nation on Crime and Justice* (Washington, D.C.: 1983).

crime (such as crimes of interpersonal violence) or criminals (for example, mentally disordered offenders). These are known as **crime** or **criminal behavior typologies.** Criminologists try to determine whether there are some underlying patterns which can help explain why crimes occur and why certain individuals commit them.

There are many existing typologies, so no standard exists within the field. Some typologies focus on the criminal, suggesting the existence of offender groups such as professional criminals, psychotic criminals, and occasional criminals. Others focus on crimes, clustering them into categories such as property crimes or sex crimes.

In addition, it is also common for criminologists to focus their attention on a particular criminal behavior in order to fully understand its underlying nature. Prominent examples include Marvin Wolfgang's *Patterns in Criminal Homicide,* a landmark analysis of the nature of homicide and the relationship between victim and offender, and Edwin Sutherland's analysis of business-related offenses which helped coin a new phrase—**white-collar crime**—to describe the criminal activities of the upper classes.[7]

Chapters 10 through 13 discuss particular crime categories, including violent, economic, and public order crimes.

Penology

Penology focuses on efforts to correct and control known criminal offenders. One of the pioneers of modern criminology, Stephen Schafer, defined *penology* as follows:

> *Penology and correction . . . is the study of the consequences of crime; it analyzes how to change the lawbreaker to be a law-abiding member of society and how to repair the damage or harm caused to the victim of crime.[8]*

Thus, an important goal of criminology is to suggest theoretical strategies for crime control and then help to implement them as actual criminal justice system policy.

As is the case in most other areas of criminology, there is also disagreement over the direction penological efforts should take. Some criminologists view crime control as involving rehabilitation and treatment. Their efforts are directed at providing behavior alternatives for would-be criminals and treatment for individuals already convicted of law violations. They view the criminal as someone whom society has failed, who is under social, psychological, or economic stress, and who can be helped if society is willing to pay the price. Rehabilitation-oriented criminologists advocate such measures as improved educational opportunities, job training, counseling, and community corrections to reduce the crime rate.

In opposition to this view, more conservative criminologists argue that crime can only be prevented through a strict policy of social control, involving such measures as the threat of capital punishment, mandatory prison sentences, and an increased police presence.

Since penology is an important part of the criminological enterprise, the agencies and processes of justice are discussed in Chapters 14 through 17.

Victimology

The final segment of the criminological enterprise, **victimology,** focuses on the victims of crime. The popularity of victimology can be traced to the early work of Hans von Hentig and later work by Stephen Schafer.[9] These authors were among the first to suggest that victims play an important role in the criminal process, that their actions may actually precipitate crime, and that the study of crime is not complete unless the victim's role is considered.

In recent years criminologists have devoted ever-increasing attention to the victim's role in the criminal process. The areas of particular interest include: using victim surveys to measure the nature and extent of criminal behavior; calculating the actual costs of crime to victims; creating probabilities of victimization risk; studying victim culpability or precipitation of crime; and designing services for the victims of crime.

The study of victimology and our understanding of the victim's role in the crime process is undergoing rapid change. The materials throughout this book reflect victimology's influence on the criminological enterprise.

CRIMINOLOGY AND CRIMINAL JUSTICE

In the late 1960s, interest in the so-called crime problem gave rise to the development of academic programs devoted to studying the **criminal justice system.** Although the terms *criminology* and *criminal justice* may seem similar, there are major differences between them.

According to Marvin Zalman, *criminology* explains the etiology (origin), extent, and nature of crime in society, whereas *criminal justice* refers to the agencies of social control that deal with crime and delinquency. Zalman further suggests that while criminologists are mainly concerned with crime and its consequences, criminal justice scholars are engaged in describing, analyzing, and explaining the behavior of the agencies of justice—police departments, courts, and correctional facilities.[10]

Since both fields are crime-related, some overlap exists between them. Criminologists, especially those interested in penology, must be aware of how the agencies of justice operate and how they influence crime and criminals. Similarly, criminal justice experts cannot begin to design programs of crime prevention or rehabilitation without understanding something of the nature of crime. Hence, it is common for criminal justice programs to feature courses on criminology and for criminology courses to evaluate the agencies of justice.

The tremendous interest in criminal justice has led to the creation of more than a thousand justice-related academic programs; not surprisingly, these programs are often staffed by criminologists. Thus, it seems possible for the two fields not only to coexist but to help each other grow and develop.

CRIMINOLOGY AND DEVIANCE

Though criminology is often equated with the study of deviant behavior or the sociology of deviance, significant distinctions can be made between these two areas of scholarship.

Deviant behavior is behavior that departs from social norms.[11] Included within the broad spectrum of deviant acts are behaviors ranging from committing murder or rape to being a nudist or eating with one's fingers in public.

While crime and deviance are frequently associated, not all crimes are deviant and not all deviant acts are crimes. For example, smoking marijuana may be illegal, but is it deviant? Though most states' legal codes prohibit its use, a significant percentage of U.S. citizens have used or are using marijuana. Therefore, to argue that all crimes are behaviors that depart from the norms of society is probably erroneous.

Similarly, many deviant acts are not criminal. Suppose a passerby observes a person drowning and makes no effort to save that person. Though such callous behavior would violate prevailing social norms and therefore be considered as immoral or deviant, the action itself violates no law and the state could not take legal action (unless the observer was a lifeguard).

In sum, many criminal acts, but not all, fall within the concept of deviance. Similarly, some deviant acts, but not all, are considered crimes.

Two issues that involve deviance are of particular interest to criminologists: How do deviant behaviors become crimes, and when should crimes be considered only deviant behaviors and therefore not subject to state sanction?

The first issue involves the historical development of law. Many acts that are legally forbidden today were once considered merely unusual or deviant behavior. To understand the nature and purpose of law, criminologists study the process by which crimes are created from deviance. For example, the sale and possession of marijuana was legal in this country until 1937, when it became illegal under federal law (see Chapter 13). Marijuana use was banned because of an extensive lobbying effort by Harry Anslinger, head of the Federal Bureau of Narcotics, who used magazine articles, public appearances, and public testimony to sway public opinion against marijuana use.[12] In one famous article, which appeared in 1937, Anslinger told how "an entire family was murdered by a youthful [marijuana] addict in Florida [who] with an axe had killed his father, mother, two brothers, and a sister."[13] As a result of these efforts, a deviant behavior, marijuana use, became a criminal behavior and previously law-abiding citizens were now defined as criminal offenders.

Criminologists also consider whether outlawed behaviors have evolved into social norms and, if so, whether they should be **decriminalized**—either be legalized or have their penalties reduced. For example, there have been frequent debates over legalizing such acts as possession of firearms, marijuana use, abortion, gambling, and prostitution. If an illegal act becomes a norm, should society reevaluate its criminal status and let it become merely an unusual or deviant act? Conversely, if scientists show that a normative act such as smoking or drinking poses a serious health hazard, should it be made illegal? Many recent efforts have attempted to control morally questionable behavior and to restrict the rights of citizens.

In sum, criminologists are concerned with the concept of deviance and its relationship to criminality. The shifting definition of deviant behavior is closely associated with our concepts of crime.

——— CRIME AND CRIMINOLOGY ———

Professional criminologists usually align themselves with one of several schools of thought. Each school maintains its own view of what constitutes criminal behavior and what causes people to engage in criminality. This diversity of thought is not unique to criminology; biologists, psychologists, sociologists, historians, economists, and most natural and social science professionals disagree among themselves about critical issues in their fields. Considering the multidisciplinary nature of criminology, it is not surprising that conflicting views exist within it.

It is also common for criminologists to disagree on the nature and definition of crime itself. A criminologist's choice of orientation or perspective depends in part on his or her definition of crime. Thus, the beliefs and research orientations of most criminologists are related to their conceptualizations of crime.

This section discusses the three most common concepts of crime: the consensus view, which maintains that crime reflects traditional ethics and values; the conflict view, which suggests that crime reflects the needs of those holding social and political power; and the interactionist view, which sees crime as a function of prevailing moral views.

The Consensus View of Crime

The origin of the **consensus view** of crime can be traced to the functionalist school of sociology.[14] Func-

tionalism emphasizes the contributions each part of society makes to the whole. According to the functionalist model, the varied parts of a society are organized into an integrated structure, and change in one area of the institution exerts a powerful influence on other areas. In a perfectly integrated culture, social stability exists and societal members agree on norms, goals, rules, and values. In a maladapted society, upheaval and unrest are common and social goals confused and unclear. The functionalist model also suggests that society's members have a standard set of rules and values to guide their daily lives. The existing legal code reflects and codifies these generally agreed-upon conduct norms.

From the functionalist viewpoint, the criminal law reflects traditional values, beliefs, and opinions. Crimes are defined as violations of the criminal law and are believed to be behaviors repugnant to all elements of society. This view is referred to as the *consensus view of crime*, since it implies that there is general agreement among a majority of citizens on what behaviors should be governed by the criminal law and henceforth viewed as crimes.

Several attempts have been made to create a concise yet thorough consensus definition of crime. The eminent criminologists Edwin Sutherland and Donald Cressey have taken the popular stance of linking crime with the criminal law:

> *Criminal behavior is behavior in violation of the criminal law . . . [I]t is not a crime unless it is prohibited by the criminal law [which] is defined conventionally as a body of specific rules regarding human conduct which have been promulgated by political authority, which apply uniformly to all members of the classes to which the rules refer, and which are enforced by punishment administered by the state.*[15]

This approach to crime implies that its definition is a function of the beliefs, morality, and direction of the legitimate power structure. Note also Sutherland and Cressey's statement that the criminal law is applied "uniformly to all members of the classes to which the rules refer." This statement reveals the authors' faith in the concept of an ideal legal system that can deal adequately with all classes and types of people. According to the consensus view, crime is essentially a legal concept.

Crime and Criminal Law.   The consensus view, then, generally links the concept of crime to the substantive criminal law. That is, crimes are viewed as acts that violate the accepted legal code of the jurisdiction in which they occur.

Wayne LaFave and Austin Scott define the criminal law as "that law (1) [which] for the purpose of preventing harm to society (2) declares what conduct is criminal (3) prescribes the punishment to be imposed for such conduct."[16]

The three parts of this definition are worth noting: prevention of harm, criminal conduct, and punishment. The first part, prevention of harm, implies that the purpose of the criminal law is to protect society from acts that might otherwise hurt its members and institutions; damage and loss of property and physical injury are examples of harm associated with crime. From this perspective, the criminal law can be viewed as a collection of rules of conduct that, if obeyed, will produce an orderly and just society. Laws mediate the differences within society and allow social life to continue unimpeded. Crimes can be viewed as unconventional behavior in opposition to the will of the majority, behavior legally forbidden to all citizens. Thus, in the consensus model, criminal law serves a **social control** function.

The second part, criminal conduct, refers to the specific acts outlawed by the criminal code. Each act in the criminal code contains separate elements. For an individual's behavior to be considered criminal, it must loosely match the specific criteria contained in the criminal law. For example, if someone steals money by forcibly breaking into your house, the act may contain the elements of the crime of burglary; if instead the person threatens you with a gun and takes your wallet, the act most likely possesses the elements of the crime of robbery. The elements of crimes are described more explicitly in Chapter 2.

The final part, punishment, points out that the incentive people have to obey the rules of conduct contained in the criminal code is the knowledge that they will be punished, or **sanctioned,** if convicted of a law violation. There cannot be a crime without a corresponding punishment, nor can someone be punished without having been convicted of committing a crime. Moreover, society gives the right to punish law violators to the duly authorized government with legal control over the particular area.

The consensus model of crime is probably accepted by a majority of practicing criminologists and is the one most often used in criminology texts. Nonetheless, various issues confuse it, especially the relationship of crime to morality.

Crime and Morality.   Crime, as it is defined by the consensus model, seems closely intertwined with morality. Since both crime and immorality are considered violations of accepted societal principles of right or wrong, it seems logical to view crime as a type of immoral behavior. Consequently, law violators can be regarded as bad, evil, or wicked people. Similarly, if we view criminals as caring little for the rights of others, it is only fitting that society punish them harshly. Yet the link between crime and morality is often tenuous and confusing.

Many acts declared to be crimes by legal codes are behaviors that under some circumstances could be considered legal and moral. For example, most state criminal codes would find a friendly neighborhood poker game illegal, because it involves the crime of unlicensed gambling. Yet it is difficult for poker players to view gambling as immoral, especially since the same state's legal code may allow gambling at horse tracks or licensed casinos. Pornography is another area in which definitions of law and morality often seem confused. A state code may outlaw as obscene material that displays nude people engaging in sexual conduct, yet may allow the showing of nationally distributed films or the sale of magazines that seem to display just such conduct.

Confounding the issue further is the fact that a great deal of unethical, socially undesirable, or immoral behavior is not criminal. For example, students may consider racism, sexism, profiteering, lying, and personal selfishness more immoral than betting on football games or smoking marijuana; nonetheless, only the last two behaviors are usually considered illegal. Another example of this situation is state laws that hold that a passerby is not legally required to help an accident victim. Many might find such casual disregard for another's life and safety highly immoral.

Thus, it seems safe to conclude that not all law violations are immoral and not all immoral behaviors are law violators.

Why does such confusion arise? Probably because of the dualistic nature of consensus criminal law. Some illegal acts, referred to as violations of natural law or **mala in se crimes,** are rooted in the core values in-

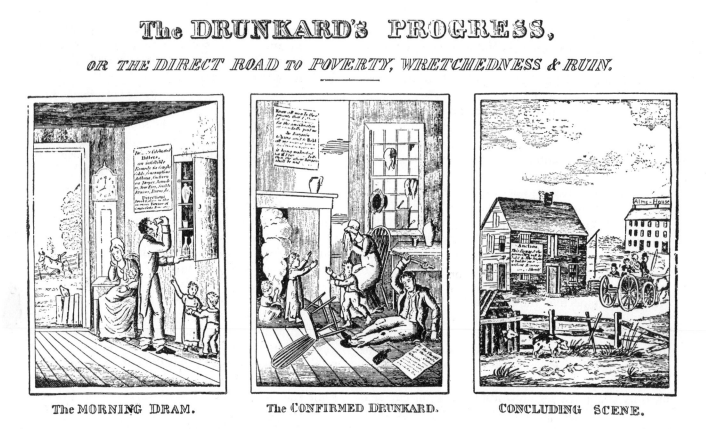

The DRUNKARD'S PROGRESS,
OR THE DIRECT ROAD TO POVERTY, WRETCHEDNESS & RUIN.

The MORNING DRAM.   The CONFIRMED DRUNKARD.   CONCLUDING SCENE.

Moral entrepreneurs believe it their duty to control the moral content of the law. This 1826 woodcut was designed to show the evils of selling alcohol to the public.

herent in Western civilization. **Natural laws** are designed to control such behaviors as inflicting physical harm on others (assault, rape, murder), taking possessions that rightfully belong to another (larceny, burglary, robbery), or harming another person's property (malicious damage, trespass).

Another type of crime, sometimes called **statutory** or **mala prohibitum crime,** involves laws passed by legislative bodies that reflect current mores, norms, and opinions of society. In essence, statutory crimes are believed to violate today's morality as expressed by the "right-thinking" members of society. These **moral entrepreneurs** (as the sociologist Howard Becker calls them) believe it is their duty to convince lawmakers that some particular behavior offends the conscience of the majority.[17] Hence, crimes are periodically created to control behaviors practiced by millions of otherwise law-abiding people. During our lifetime, controversy has swirled around laws legalizing (or

outlawing) abortion, guns, drug use, gambling, and prostitution. Often, acts are outlawed (or legitimized) because a relatively small group of powerful and vocal people convince lawmakers that they represent a far larger constituency than they actually do.

While it often may be easy to link natural laws to a basic concept of morality, it is much more difficult to do so in the case of statutory law. Crime, therefore, is a concept that constantly changes relative to a particular culture and often independently from any absolute moral code. Consequently, as is discussed later in this chapter, many criminologists charge that the consensus concept of crime does not really represent an accurate picture of public opinion.

Criminology and the Consensus View of Crime. Currently, two schools of criminology use the consensus definition of crime: **classical theorists** and **positivists.** Though they share a similar view of crime, these two schools of thought differ in many respects. The major assumptions of classical criminologists are: that people have free will to choose criminal or conventional means to get the goods and services they desire; that the threat of punishment will deter people from choosing criminal solutions; and that society can control criminal behavior by making the pain of punishment outweigh the pleasure of criminal gain. Classical criminologists believe that society can prevent crime by increasing the effectiveness of the criminal justice system, establishing stricter penalties for law violation, and incapacitating known criminals for extended periods of time. The classical perspective is discussed in greater detail in Chapter 5.

In contrast, positivist criminologists believe that behavior is determined by external forces over which people have little control. Positivists use the empirical scientific method, borrowed from the natural sciences, to investigate crime-promoting conditions or factors. Some positivist criminologists focus on the individual biological and psychological traits of offenders; their work is discussed in Chapter 6.[18] In contrast to this view, social positivists believe aspects of socialization and the social environment control human behavior choices; their work is discussed in Chapters 7 and 8.

Regardless of their differences, both classical and positivist criminologists view the criminal law as the means conventional society uses to define acceptable and unacceptable behavior. Those who violate legal rules and commit crimes, regardless of whether they want to or have to, are outlaws who put themselves in opposition to accepted rules of human behavior.

position, can control the behavior of others and gain a disproportionate share of what society has to offer.

Conflict criminologists often compare and contrast the severe penalties exacted on crimes of the lower classes (burglary, larceny) with the mild penalties for upper-class crimes (polluting the environment, securities violations). Moreover, they charge that while the poor go to prison for minor law violations, the wealthy are given lenient sentences for even the most serious breaches of law. Thus, the conflict perspective views the scope and definition of crime as being affected by the wealth, power, and position of those who control the political and law-making processes, and not by moral consensus or conventional values.[19] Theorist Richard Quinney has stated:

> Crime as a legal definition of human conduct is created by agents of the dominant class in a politically organized society . . . Definitions of crime are composed of behaviors that conflict with the interests of the dominant class.[20]

According to this definition, even prohibiting violent acts such as rape and murder may have political undertones: banning violent acts insures domestic tranquility and guarantees that the anger of the poor and disenfranchised classes will not be directed at the wealthy capitalists who exploit them.

The conflict view of crime is explored more fully in Chapter 9, which analyzes the writings of criminologists who view criminality as a sociopolitical behavior.

✛ The Conflict View of Crime

In opposition to the consensus view of crime, the **conflict view** depicts society as a collection of diverse groups—owners, workers, professionals, students, minority groups—who are in conflict with one another about a number of issues. Groups able to assert their political and economic power use the law and the criminal justice system to advance their own causes. Criminal laws, therefore, are viewed as acts created to maintain the existing power structure and the economic system under its control. According to conflict criminologists, the key to achieving success is power. Groups that attain power, usually through wealth and

✗ The Interactionist View of Crime

The **interactionist view** of crime traces its antecedents to the **symbolic interactionist** school of sociology, first popularized by George Herman Mead, Charles Horton Cooley, and W. I. Thomas.[21] This position holds that: people act according to their own interpretations of reality, according to the meaning things have for them; they learn the meaning of a thing from the way others react to it, either positively or negatively; and they reevaluate and interpret their own behavior according to the meaning and symbols they have learned from others.

With respect to crime, the interactionist view falls

According to conflict theory, groups use their political and economic power to influence the law and advance their own cause.

somewhere between the consensus and conflict perspectives. Unlike the consensus model, the interactionist view portrays crime and law as independent from the concept of an absolute moral code. According to this perspective, the definition of crime reflects the preferences of people who hold social power in a particular legal jurisdiction and who use their influence to impose their definition of right and wrong on the rest of the population. Criminals are individuals whom society chooses to label as outcasts or deviants because they have violated social rules. The classic statement on this matter has been supplied by sociologist Howard Becker, who claims that "the deviant is one to whom that label has successfully been applied; deviant behavior is behavior people so label."[22] Thus, the prevailing interactionist view is that crimes are outlawed behaviors simply because society defines them that way and not because they are inherently evil acts.

Even then, most serious mala in se crimes such as murder or theft may be viewed as violations of current social concerns and not as breaches of absolute human morality. For example, while U.S. culture labels the willful taking of another person's life as murder, it condones such action under certain circumstances—during wartime, in self-defense, when a law-enforcement agent believes a criminal fleeing from arrest is dangerous to her or himself or to others, or when a person is executed after conviction for a capital crime. Furthermore, in other cultures and at other times, acts we consider criminal have been viewed as conventional behavior, and people our society views as conventional have been considered deviant or criminal. For example, during the eighteenth century, a number of patent medicines were widely used in the United States and in England to relieve pain and cure every ailment from baldness to cancer. Some of these were Ayer's Cherry Pectoral, Mrs. Winslow's Soothing Syrup, McMunn's Elixer and Godfrey's Cordial. The secret of their popularity was their main ingredient: opium.[23]

The interactionist view of crime can also be compared with the conflict perspective. They are similar in that both suggest that behavior is outlawed when it offends the sensibilities of citizens who maintain the social, economic, and political power necessary to have the law conform to their interests or needs. However, unlike the conflict view, the interactionist perspective does not attribute capitalist economic and political motives to the process of defining crime. Instead, interactionists see the criminal law as conforming to the beliefs of moral entrepreneurs, who use their influence to shape the legal process in the way they see fit.[24] Laws against pornography, prostitution, and drugs are believed to be motivated more by moral crusades than by capitalist sensibilities. Consequently, interactionists are concerned with shifting moral and legal standards, or **social relativism.** As an example, it is now acceptable for cable TV stations to air R-rated films whereas twenty years ago such viewing would not have been tolerated.

Although the interactionist perspective provides a way of looking at crime, it is actually more concerned with the social consequences of law violation. As Becker comments:

> We are not so much interested in the person who commits a deviant act once as in the person who sustains a pattern of deviance over a long period of time, who makes of deviance a way of life, who organizes his identity around a pattern of deviant behavior.[25]

To the interactionist, crime has no meaning unless people react to it by labeling lawbreakers as deviant and setting them on a course of sustained criminal activity. The occasional criminal, if not caught or labeled, can forego further illicit activity with little permanent damage. The college student who tries marijuana does not view herself, nor do others view her, as a criminal or a drug addict. Only when prohibited acts are recognized and sanctioned do they become important life-transforming incidents. Consequently, interactionists believe that society should intervene as little as possible in the lives of law violators lest they be labeled and stigmatized.

The interactionist view of crime is examined in Chapter 8, when labeling theory is discussed in some detail.

⸽ Defining Crime

Each of the three models of crime provides important insight into its nature, structure, and intent. The consensus view concentrates on crime's social origins and its expression of existing moral values; the conflict view helps us understand the power relations working in criminal definitions; the interactionist perspective enables us to see the relativity and transience of crime.

Defining crime is important because criminologists' personal views of crime dominate their writing, research efforts, teaching, and all other professional activities. Because no single view of crime exists, criminologists have taken different directions in their quest for understanding crime and its control.

Considering these differences, it is possible to take elements from each school of thought to formulate an integrated definition of crime:

> Crime is a violation of societal rules of behavior as interpreted and expressed by a criminal code created by people holding social and political power. Individuals who violate these rules are subject to sanctions by state authority, social stigma, labeling, and loss of status.

This definition combines the consensus view's position that the criminal law defines crimes with the conflict perspective's emphasis on political power and control and the interactionist concept of stigma and labeling. Thus, crime as defined here is a political, social, and economic function of modern life.

⸜ ETHICAL ISSUES IN CRIMINOLOGY ⸝

A critical issue facing students of criminology involves recognizing the field's political and social consequences. All too often, criminologists forget the social responsibility they bear as experts in the area of crime and justice. When acted upon by government ager cies, their opinions become the basis for sweeping social policy; thus, the lives of millions of people are influenced by criminological research data. In recent years, these opinions and data have fueled debates over gun control, capital punishment, and mandatory sentencing. While some criminologists have successfully argued for massive social service programs to reduce the crime rate, others consider them a waste of time. By holding themselves up to be experts on law-violating behavior, criminologists place themselves in a position of power; the potential consequences of their actions are enormous. Therefore, they must be aware of the ethics of their profession and be prepared to defend their work in the light of public scrutiny. Major ethical issues include what is to be studied, who is to be studied, and how studies should be conducted.

Under ideal circumstances, when criminologists choose a subject for study they are guided by their own scholarly interests, pressing social needs, the availability of accurate data, and other similar concerns. Nonetheless, in recent years a great influx of government and institutional funding has influenced the direction of criminological inquiry. Major sources of monetary support include the Justice Department's National Institute of Justice (NIJ) and the Office of Juvenile Justice and Delinquency Prevention (OJJDP). Both the National Science Foundation (NSF) and the National Institute of Mental Health (NIMH) have been prominent sources of government funding. Private foundations, such as the Ford Foundation, also have played an important role in supporting criminological research.

The availability of research money has affected the directions research has taken. Since state and federal governments provide a significant percentage of available research monies, they also may dictate the areas that can be studied. A potential conflict of interest arises when the institution funding research is itself one of the principal subjects of the research project. There also may exist a not-so-subtle influence on the criminologist seeking research funding. If criminologists are too critical of the government's role in the crime process, they may be barred from receiving further financial help. This situation appears even more troublesome given the fact that criminologists typically work for universities or public agencies and are under pressure to bring in a steady flow of research funds or to maintain the continued viability of their

agency. Even when criminologists maintain discretion of choice, the direction of their efforts may not be truly objective. For example, if the federal government makes it a top priority to study the chronic offender, researchers wishing to gain funding may have to direct their energies in that particular direction and away from other important areas of interest.[26]

Austerity programs and budget cutbacks have severely limited the government's current role in funding social science research. It will be interesting to observe changes in the direction and objectivity of future criminological research efforts.

A second major ethical issue in criminology concerns who is to be the subject of inquiries and study. Too often, criminologists have focused their attention on the poor and minorities while ignoring the middle-class criminal, white-collar crime, organized crime, and government crime. Critics have charged that by "unmasking" the poor and desperate, criminologists have justified any harsh measures taken against them.[27] For example, a few social scientists have suggested that criminals have lower IQs than average citizens and that minority status is the single greatest predictor of criminality.[28] Though such research is often methodologically unsound and admittedly tentative, it can focus attention on the criminality of one element of the community while ignoring others. Also, subjects are often misled about the purpose of the research. When white and black youngsters are asked to participate in a survey of their behavior, they are rarely told in advance that the data they provide may later be used to prove the existence of significant racial differences in their self-reported crime rates. Should subjects be told what the true purpose of a survey is? Would such disclosures make meaningful research impossible?

Criminological research may also endanger the lives and privacy of its subjects. Laud Humphreys' well-known study, *Tea Room Trade*, involved his observance of gay sexual encounters in public restrooms.[29] Humphreys, who posed as a homosexual, recorded the license plate numbers of his subjects and later contacted them for interviews. When criminologists conduct such observations, should they identify themselves and state the purpose for their research? The homosexuals Humphreys observed were personally endangered, since their identities were recorded when they participated in an illegal act. Though Humphreys refused to cooperate with police authorities, the potential for harm was still there. By deceiving the men he observed, did Humphreys violate an unwritten ethical rule of social science? How far should criminologists go when collecting data? Is it ever permissible to deceive subjects in order to collect data?

CRIMINOLOGY TODAY

Criminology today can be characterized as a field marked by widely divergent opinions and political viewpoints. There is a powerful conservative wing in criminology which includes James Q. Wilson, Richard Herrnstein, and Ernest Van Den Haag. Among the conservative themes currently being explored is how to best use legal punishment to control or deter crime (see Chapter 5). Similarly, criminologists have identified a violence-prone career criminal type and suggest that such people be separated from the rest of society (see Chapter 4). Whereas liberals in the 1960s and 1970s sought to define the social factors that produce crime, conservatives are less concerned about what causes crime and more interested in determining what can be done to prevent it. Consequently, efforts are now being made to identify chronic offenders and develop a means of controlling them, rather than planning methods of treating offenders and providing alternatives to their criminality.

Criminology also contains significant numbers of liberal thinkers, including Francis Cullen, Samuel Walker, Barry Krisberg, Elliott Currie, and Jerome Miller, who still maintain that the forces producing crime lie outside of personal control. They contend that if crime rates are to be reduced, the answer lies not in punishing individual offenders, but in improving neighborhoods, upgrading schools, and strengthening families.

Criminology contains a radical wing which includes such social thinkers as Richard Quinney, Stephen Spitzer, Tony Platt, and Herman and Julia Schwendinger. They contend that the capitalist system must be examined in order to understand the crime-producing forces in society. Thus, there is much ideological polarization within criminology.

Beyond these splits, there is significant disagreement over the nature and extent of crime and its causes. Numerous competing theories abound, stressing such factors as learning, labeling, control, personality, genetics, and environment. It is not surprising that one of the most important recent trends in criminology is the combination of these competing models into complex integrated theories of crime.

There also has been an increased emphasis on the victim's role in crime. Victimization statistics have become a prominent method of identifying crime rates and trends. The relationship between the victim and criminal has become the focus of some studies. Increased attention has been given to the personal characteristics of victims and criminals, in order to assess the way crimes occur and society's reaction to them. For example, one prominent study has shown that when a murder case has a black criminal and a white victim, the criminal is more likely to receive the death penalty than if the offender and victim are both of the same race (see Chapter 5).

In step with the conservative leanings of the field has been an increased focus on nonsocial causes of criminal behavior. A liberal view would hold that we are all born equal but that social forces, such as poverty, racism, and lack of opportunity, propel some into a life of crime. Though among the earliest explanations of criminality, biological and psychological causes are once again being studied by some criminologists, who seek to explain the prevalence of violent and antisocial behavior patterns in our society (see Chapter 6). Concern for public safety has precipitated research studies designed to find the key to the personal factors that precipitate uncontrollable, violent behavior patterns. Since these crimes often seem random and unexplainable, some personal aberration is thought to account for them.

Finally, criminology seems to be maturing as an area of scientific study. Both the literature and the research of the field grow more scientifically advanced each year. Criminology has become as methodologically sophisticated as any other social science. Criminologists are feeling greater pressure to master the techniques of data analysis; thus, the body of knowledge about criminality and crime patterns continues to grow. And though some constants have been discovered, great controversy still exists over how data should be interpreted and what the findings actually mean.

These major issues should continue to be focal concerns for criminology through the 1990s. It is likely that there will be continued ideological in-fighting, the creation of more complex theoretical models, greater concern for the victims of crime, and ever more advanced statistical modeling. Criminology remains one of the most interesting and dynamic areas of academic study.

—————— SUMMARY ——————

Criminology is the scientific approach to the study of criminal behavior and society's reaction to it. It is essentially an interdisciplinary field; many of its practitioners were originally trained as sociologists, psychologists, economists, political scientists, historians, and natural scientists. In the late 1960s, criminal justice programs were created to examine and improve the U.S. system of justice. Today, many criminologists work in criminal justice educational programs, and the two fields are mutually dedicated to understanding the nature and control of criminal behavior.

Included among the various subareas that make up the criminological enterprise are criminal statistics, the sociology of law, the etiology of crime, criminal behavior systems, penology, and victimology.

In viewing crime, criminologists use one of three perspectives: the consensus view, the conflict view, and the interactionist view. The consensus view is that crime is illegal behavior defined by the existing criminal law, which reflects the values and morals of a majority of citizens. Crimes are behaviors prohibited so that society can operate in an orderly fashion. The conflict view is that crime is behavior defined so that economically powerful individuals can retain their control over society. The interactionist view portrays criminal behavior as a relativistic, constantly changing concept that reflects society's current thinking about deviant behavior. According to the interactionist view, criminal behavior is behavior so labeled; criminals are people society chooses to label as outsiders, or deviants.

Criminologists must critically examine the way they conduct research. Criminologists must be concerned with the ethics of their profession.

Criminology is undergoing great change in the late twentieth century. A swing in the direction from liberal and radical approaches to a more conservative outlook appears to be in motion.

—————— KEY TERMS ——————

criminology
criminologists
hypotheses
Cesare Lombroso
American Society
  of Criminology
criminological enterprise
crime typologies
criminal behavior
  typologies
white-collar crime
penology
victimology
criminal justice system
deviant behavior

decriminalized
consensus view
social control
sanctioned
mala in se crimes
natural laws
statutory crime
mala prohibitum crime
moral entrepreneurs
classical theorists
positivists
conflict view
interactionist view
symbolic interactionist
social relativism

—————— NOTES ——————

1. National Opinion Research Center data, reported in Katherine Jamieson and Timothy Flanagan, *Sourcebook of Criminal Justice Statistics* (Washington, D.C.: U.S. Government Printing Office, 1987), pp. 76, 109.
2. Edwin Sutherland and Donald Cressey, *Principles of Criminology*, 6th ed. (Philadelphia: J. B. Lippincott, 1960), p. 3.
3. See Marvin Wolfgang, "Cesare Lombroso," in *Pioneers in Criminology*, ed. Herman Mannheim (Montclair, N.J.: Patterson Smith, 1970), pp. 232–71.
4. Vincent Webb and Dennis Hoffman, "Criminal Justice as an Academic Discipline," *Journal of Criminal Justice* 6 (1978):349.
5. Marvin Wolfgang and Franco Ferracuti, *The Subculture of Violence* (London: Social Science Paperbacks, 1967), p. 20.
6. *Ibid.*, p. 27.
7. Edwin Sutherland, *White Collar Crime* (New York: Dryden Press, 1949); Marvin Wolfgang, *Patterns in Criminal Homicide* (Philadelphia: University of Pennsylvania Press, 1958).
8. Stephen Schafer, *Introduction to Criminology* (New York: McGraw-Hill, 1976), p. 3.
9. Hans von Hentig, *The Criminal and His Victim* (New Haven: Yale University Press, 1948); Stephen Schafer, *The Victim and His Criminal* (New York: Random House, 1968).
10. Marvin Zalman, *A Heuristic Model of Criminology and Criminal Justice* (Chicago: Joint Commission on Criminology Education and Standards, University of Illinois,

Chicago Circle, 1981), pp. 9–11.

11. Charles McCaghy, *Deviant Behavior* (New York: MacMillan, 1976), pp. 2–3.

12. Edward Brecher, *Licit and Illicit Drugs* (Boston: Little, Brown, 1972), pp. 413–16.

13. *Ibid.*, p. 414.

14. Jon Shephard, *Sociology* (St. Paul: West Publishing, 1981), p. 11.

15. Edwin Sutherland and Donald Cressey, *Criminology*, 8th ed. (Philadelphia: Lippincott, 1970), p. 8.

16. Wayne LaFave and Austin Scott, *Criminal Law* (St. Paul: West Publishing, 1972), p. 5.

17. Howard Becker, *Outsiders: Studies in the Sociology of Deviance* (New York: Free Press, 1963).

18. See Leonard Hippchen, *The Ecologic-Biochemical Approaches to Treatment of Delinquents and Criminals* (New York: Van Nostrand Reinhold, 1978).

19. Eugene Doleschal and Nora Klapmuts, "Toward a New Criminology," *Crime and Delinquency* 5 (1973):607.

20. Richard Quinney, *Criminology* (Boston: Little, Brown, 1975), pp. 37–41.

21. See Herbert Blumer, *Symbolic Interactionism* (Englewood Cliffs, N.J.: Prentice-Hall, 1969).

22. Becker, *Outsiders*, p. 21.

23. James Inciardi, *The War on Drugs, Heroin, Cocaine, Crime, and Public Policy* (Palo Alto, Cal.: Mayfield, 1986), pp. 2–3.

24. Becker, *Outsiders*, p. 9.

25. *Ibid.*

26. John Galliher and James McCartney, "The Influence of Funding Agencies on Delinquency Research," *Social Problems* 21 (1974):77–90.

27. See David Greenberg, *Crime and Capitalism* (Palo Alto, Calif.: Mayfield Press, 1981), pp. 1–15.

28. Michael Hindelang and Travis Hirschi, "Intelligence and Delinquency: A Revisionist Review," *American Sociological Review* 42 (1977):471–86.

29. Laud Humphreys, *Tea Room Trade* (Chicago: Aldine, 1975).

CHAPTER 2

THE CRIMINAL LAW AND ITS PROCESSES

INTRODUCTION

Despite the fact that criminologists hold different views about the concept of crime, most agree that it is the existing criminal law that defines crime in U.S. society. Each state government, as well as the federal government, has its own criminal code, developed over many generations and incorporating historical traditions, moral beliefs, social values, and political and economic developments and conditions. The criminal law is a living document, constantly evolving to keep pace with society. It governs the form and direction of almost all human interaction. Business practices, family life, education, property transfer, inheritance, and other common forms of social relations must conform to the rules set out by the legal code. Most importantly for our purposes, the law defines behavior society labels as criminal. As noted in Chapter 1, most criminologists have adopted the legal definition of crime in their research and writing. Consequently, it is important for students of criminology to have a basic understanding of the law and its relationship to crime and deviance.

This chapter reviews the nature and purpose of the law, charts its history, and discusses its elements.

HISTORICAL DEVELOPMENT OF LAW

The concept of law has been present throughout history. In primitive societies, customs and folkways were the equivalents of law. Each group had its own set of customs, which were usually created to deal with situations that arose in daily living. Often, these customs would be observed long after their origins were forgotten. Many customs had the force of law and eventually developed into formal or written law.[1]

Hammurabi's Code in Babylonia (2000 B.C.) and the Mosaic Code of the Israelites (1200 B.C.) are among the most famous of the early formal laws. The Mosaic Code, the law of the Jews, became a basis for the U.S. legal system. As Rene Wormser points out, "The law of the Jews became one of the chief root sources of both the law of the Continent of Europe and the English law upon which ours is directly based."[2] The Ten Commandments, part of the Mosaic Code, exemplify this point. The commandments proscribing killing, stealing, perjury, and adultery precede by several thousand years the same laws found in the U.S. legal system.

In addition to Mosaic law, early Greek law, Roman law, and the canon law of the early Catholic church have contributed greatly to the foundation of U.S. law. However, the major building block for the United States is English common law.

Origins of Common Law

Before the Norman Conquest in 1066, the legal system among the early English (Anglo-Saxons) was decentralized. Each country, or **shire**, was divided into units called **hundreds,** which were groups of one hundred families. The hundreds were further divided into groups of ten, called **tithings.** The tithings were responsible for maintaining order among themselves and dealing with disturbances, fires, wild animals, and so on. Legal disputes were tried by courts of the hundred group, the hundred-gemot. More serious and important cases could be appealed to assemblages of local landholders, the shire-gemot, or to the local noble, the hali-gemot. If the act concerned spiritual matters in any way, it could be judged by the clergy and church officials in courts known as holy-motes or ecclesiastics. The law varied in substance from county to county, hundred to hundred, and tithing to tithing. Except for the law of crimes, there was very little written law. Custom and law were one and the same to the Anglo-Saxons.

Crimes during this period were viewed as personal wrongs, and therefore compensation was often paid to the victims. If payment was not made, the victims' families would attempt to forcibly collect damages or seek revenge. The result could be a blood feud between two opposing families.

The recognized crimes were theft, violence, and disloyalty to a feudal lord. They included treason, homicide, rape, property theft, assault (putting another in fear), and battery (wounding another). For treasonous acts, the punishment was death. However, for many other acts, compensation could be paid to the victim. For example, a homicide could be settled by paying compensation to the deceased's family, unless the crime was carried out by poison or ambush—in that case it was punished by death. For killing in an open fight, a sum (*bot*) was paid; part of it (the *wer*)

This stele, dated 1800 B.C., was discovered in the ruins of Susa and depicts Hammurabi receiving the law from the sun god.

went to the king, and the remainder (the *wite*) went to the deceased's kin. A scale of compensation, called **wergild,** existed for lesser injuries, such as the loss of an arm or an eye. Important persons and clergy received a greater degree of restitution than the general population. Theft could result in slavery for the thieves and their families. If caught in the act of fleeing with the stolen goods, the thief could be killed. Thus, to a great degree, criminal law was designed to provide an equitable solution to what was considered a private dispute.

The Norman Conquest

After the Norman Conquest in 1066, William the Conqueror, the Norman leader, did not immediately change the substance of Anglo-Saxon law.[3] At the outset of William's reign, justice was administered as it had been in previous centuries. The church courts handled acts that might be considered sinful, and the

local hundred or manor courts, then referred to as the court-leet, dealt with most secular violations. However, to secure control of the countryside and to insure military supremacy over his newly won lands, William replaced the local tribunals with royal administrators who dealt with the most serious breaches of the peace. Since the royal administrators could not be continually present in each community, a system developed under which they traveled in a circuit throughout England, holding court in each county several times a year.

When court was in session, the royal administrator would summon a number of citizens who would relate the crimes and serious breaches of the peace that had occurred since the judge's last visit. The royal judge then decided what to do in each case, using local custom and rules of conduct as his guide. If, for example, a local freeholder was convicted of theft, he might be executed if those before him had been executed for similar offenses. However, if in previous cases the thief had been forced to make restitution to

☰ CLOSE-UP

Origin of the Jury Trial

In early medieval Europe and England, disputed criminal charges were often decided by an ordeal. In a trial by fire, the accused would grasp a rod of red-hot iron. If the accused's hand did not heal properly, it was considered proof of guilt. In a trial by combat, the defendant would challenge the accuser to a duel; accusers had the option of finding alternates to fight in their places.

Settling trials by ordeal fell out of favor when the Catholic Church, at the Fourth Lateran Council (1215), decreed that priests could no longer participate in them. Without the use of the ordeal in "disputed" criminal cases, courts both in England and in the rest of Europe were not sure how to proceed.

In England, the Church ban on ordeals meant a new method of deciding criminal trials needed to be developed. To fill the gap, British justices adapted a method which had long been used to determine real estate taxes.

Since the time of William the Conqueror, twelve knights in each district were called before an inquest of the king's justices to give local tax information. These "twelve free and lawful men of the neighborhood" would testify as to who last had peaceful possession of land so that an accurate tax accounting could be made. Since they were available when the king's justices were present on circuit, the *Writ of Novel Disseisin*, first established in 1166 under Henry II, also required them to settle "claim jumping" and other real estate title disputes.

By 1219, the group called to decide land cases also began to hear criminal cases. The term applied to them was *jury* (from the Latin term *jurati*, to be sworn). At first, jurors acted as if they were witnesses, telling the judge in court what they knew about the case; these courts were known as **assizes** (from the Latin *assideo*, to sit together). By the fourteenth century, jurors became the deciders of fact that we are familiar with today.

Over the centuries, the English jury came to be seen as a check on the government. The great case which established the principle of jury independence, *Bushell's Case* (1670), arose when a London jury acquitted William Penn, a leading Quaker and later the founder of Pennsylvania, of unlawful assembly in connection with his preaching in the street after a Quaker church was padlocked. The jurors were imprisoned by an angry royalist judge. They were freed when British Chief Judge Vaughn held that unless a jury was corrupt, it was free to reach a verdict based on the evidence.

Discussion Questions

1. Do you think that the common law development of a jury trial is relevant in today's world?
2. Should a jury of one's peers be replaced by professionals who are schooled in the law?

SOURCE: Carl Stephenson and F. G. Marcham, *Sources of English Constitutional History*, rev. ed. (New York: Harper and Row, 1972).

---

the victim, then that judgment would be rendered in the present case. This system was known as **stare decisis** (Latin for "to stand by decided cases"). Courts were bound to follow the law established in previously decided cases unless the law was overruled by a higher authority, such as the king or Pope.

The Common Law

The present system of English law came into existence during the reign of Henry II (1154–1189). Henry also used traveling judges, better known as **circuit judges.** These judges traveled a specific route, or circuit, and

heard the cases that previously had been under the jurisdiction of local courts. Juries, which began to develop about this time, were groups of local landholders called by the judges not only to decide the facts of the case, but also to investigate the crimes, accuse suspected offenders, and even give testimony at the trial (see Close-Up on the "Origin of the Jury Trial"). Gradually, royal prosecutors came into being. These representatives of the Crown submitted evidence and brought witnesses to testify before the jury. However, it was not until much later that the accused in a criminal action was allowed to bring forth witnesses to rebut charges; it was not until the eighteenth century that oath-taking by witnesses was required. Defense attorneys were not permitted in felonies until the nineteenth century. Few formal procedures existed, and both the judge and the prosecutor felt free to intimidate witnesses and jurors when they considered it necessary. The development of these routine judicial processes heralded the beginnings of the **common law.**

As it is used today, the term *common law* refers to a common law to all subjects of the land, without regard to geographic or social differences.[4] As best they could, Henry's judges began to apply a national law instead of the law that held sway in local jurisdictions. This attempt was somewhat confused at first, having to take into account both local custom and the Norman conquerors' feudal law. However, as new situations arose, judges took advantage of legal uncertainty by either inventing new solutions or borrowing from the laws of European countries. During formal and informal gatherings, the circuit judges shared these incidents, talked about unique cases, and discussed their decisions, thus developing an oral tradition of law. Later, as cases began to be written about, more concrete examples of common-law decisions began to emerge. Together, these cases and decisions filtered through the national court system and eventually produced a fixed body of legal rules and principles.

Thus, common law is judge-made law, or case law. It is the law found in previously decided cases. Crimes such as murder, burglary, arson, and rape are common-law crimes—they were initially defined and created by judges.

Common Law and Statutory Law

Common law was and still is the law of England. In most instances, the common law retains traditional Anglo-Saxon concepts. For example, the common law originally defined *murder* as the unlawful killing of another human being with malice aforethought.[5] By this definition, offenders found guilty of murder must have (1) planned the crime and (2) intentionally killed the victim out of spite or hatred. However, this broad, original definition proved inadequate to deal with the many situations in which one person took another's life. Over time, to bring the law closer to the realities of human behavior, English judges added other forms of murder: killing someone in the heat of passion;

killing someone out of negligence; and killing someone in the course of committing another crime, such as during a robbery. Each form of murder was given a different title (e.g., manslaughter, felony murder) and provided with a different degree of punishment. Thus, the common law was a constantly evolving legal code.

In some instances, the creation of a new common-law crime can be traced back to a particular case. For example, an unsuccessful attempt to commit an illegal act was not considered a crime under early common law. The modern doctrine that **criminal attempt** can be punished under law can be traced directly back to the case of *Rex v. Scofield* in 1784. Scofield was charged with having put a lit candle and combustible material in a house he was renting with the intention of burning it down; however, the house did not burn. He defended himself by arguing that an attempt to commit a misdemeanor was not actually a misdemeanor. In rejecting this argument, the court stated: "The intent may make an act, innocent in itself, criminal; nor is the completion of an act, criminal in itself, necessary to constitute criminality."[6] After *Scofield*, attempt became a common-law crime, and today most U.S. jurisdictions have enacted some form of criminal-attempt law.

When the situation required it, the English Parliament enacted legislation to supplement the judge-made common law. Violations of these laws are referred to as **statutory crimes.** For example, in 1723 the Waltham Black Act punished by death offenses against rural property, from the poaching of small game to arson, if the criminal was armed or disguised.[7] Moreover, the act eroded the rights of the accused; it allowed the death sentence to be carried out without a trial if the accused failed to surrender when ordered to do so. The underlying purpose of the act was the British Parliament's desire to control the behavior of peasants whose poverty forced them to poach on royal lands. In the Black Act, then, the British ruling class created a mechanism for protecting its property and social power.

Statutory laws usually reflect existing social conditions. They deal with issues of morality, such as gambling, sexual activity, and drug-related offenses. Sometimes they reflect changes in technology or social custom. For example, a whole series of statutory laws, such as those concerning embezzlement and fraud, were created to protect the well-being of British—and later American—business enterprise.[8] Chapter 11 discusses these crimes in greater detail.

Common Law in America

Before the American Revolution, the colonies were subject to the law handed down by English judges. After the colonies acquired their independence, they adapted and changed the English law to fit their needs. In many states, legislatures standardized such common-law crimes as murder, burglary, arson, and rape by putting them into statutory form. In other states, comprehensive penal codes were passed, thus abolishing the common-law crimes. An example of this process of modifying the common law can be found in the Massachusetts statute defining arson. The common-law definition of *arson* is "the malicious burning of the dwelling of another." Massachusetts expanded this definition by passing legislation defining *arson* as "the willful and malicious setting fire to, or burning of, *any building or contents* thereof *even if they were burned by the owner.*"[9]

As in England, whenever the common law proved inadequate to deal with changing social and moral issues, the colonists supplemented it with legislative statutes, creating new elements in the various state and federal legal codes. For example, early in the nation's history it was both legal and relatively easy to obtain narcotics such as heroin, opium, and cocaine.[10] Their use became habits of the middle class. However, public and governmental concern arose over the use of narcotics by immigrants, such as the Chinese, who had come to the United States to build railroads and work in mines. Changes in public sentiment eventually resulted in the 1914 passage of the Harrison Act, which outlawed trade in opium and its derivatives. Later, in 1937, pressure from federal law enforcement officials led to passage the Marijuana Tax Act, which outlawed the sale or possession of that substance.

The case of marijuana illustrates how the statutory law is subject to change. When marijuana use became widespread among the middle class in the 1960s, several states revised their laws and effectively decriminalized possession of marijuana. Thus, the statutory law began to reflect prevailing public opinion on the use of recreational drugs. In some states, marijuana possession is still punished by many years in prison; in others, by a small fine.

CRIMINAL LAW TODAY

The American system of criminal law is a direct descendant of the British common-law tradition. Much of English common law has become part of the criminal codes of the various state governments and the federal government. It has from time to time been supplemented by statutes that reflect current moral issues and public opinion. The following sections review the current nature of criminal law. They review the classification of criminal law, its function and purpose, and how it defines crime.

Classification of Law

Law can be divided into two broad categories—**criminal law** and **civil law.** Civil law is all law other than criminal law, such as tort law (the law of personal wrongs and damage), property law (the law governing transfer and ownership of property), and contract law (the law of personal agreements).

There are several differences between criminal law and civil law. First, the main purpose of criminal law is to give the state the power to protect the public from harm by punishing individuals whose actions threaten the social order. In civil law, the harm or injury is considered a private wrong, and the main concern is to compensate individuals for harm done to them by others. In a criminal action, the state initiates the legal proceedings by bringing charges and prosecuting the violator. If it is determined that the criminal law has been violated, the state can impose punishment, such as imprisonment, probation (community supervision by the court), or a fine payable to the state. In a civil action, however, the injured person must initiate proceedings. In a successful action, the plaintiff usually receives money to compensate for the harm done.

Another major difference is the **burden of proof** required to establish the defendant's liability. In criminal matters, the defendant's guilt must be proven **beyond a reasonable doubt.** This standard, while less than absolute certainty, means that the judges or jury, after considering the evidence presented to them, are entirely satisfied that the party is guilty as charged; if there is any doubt they must find for the defendant. In a civil case, the defendant is required to pay damages if, by a **preponderance of the evidence,** the judge or jury finds that he or she committed the wrong.

TABLE 2.1 A Comparison of Criminal and Tort Law

Similarities

Both criminal and tort law seek to control behavior.

Sanctions are imposed in both laws.

Similar areas of legal action exist; for example, personal assault and control of white-collar offenses such as environmental pollution.

Differences

Criminal Law	Tort Law
Crime is a public offense.	Tort is a civil or private wrong.
The sanction associated with criminal law is incarceration or death.	The sanction associated with a tort is monetary damages.
The right of enforcement is with the state.	The individual brings action.
The government ordinarily does not appeal.	Both parties can appeal.
Fines go to the state.	The individual receives damages as compensation for harm done.

According to this doctrine, while both parties may share some blame, the defendant is at fault if he or she contributed more than 50 percent to the cause of the dispute. Establishing guilt by a preponderance of the evidence is easier than establishing it beyond a reasonable doubt.[11]

Although major differences exist between criminal law and civil law, there are also many similarities, particularly in the area of tort law. A tort is a civil action in which an individual asks to be compensated for personal harm. The harm may be either physical or mental, and includes such acts as trespass, assault and battery, libel, and slander. Because some torts are similar to some criminal acts, a person can be held both criminally and civilly liable for one action. For example, if one man strikes another, it is possible for the assailant to be charged by the state with assault and battery and also sued by the victim in a tort action of assault. Perhaps the most important similarity is that criminal law and civil law have a common purpose. Both attempt to control people's behavior by setting limits on what acts are permissible; both accomplish this through state-imposed sanctions. Table 2.1 summarizes the similarities and differences between tort law and criminal law.

Felony and Misdemeanor

In addition to being distinguished from civil law, criminal laws can be further classified into either felonies or misdemeanors. The distinction is based on seriousness. A **felony** (from the term *felonia*, an act by which vassals forfeited their feudal rights) is a serious offense; a **misdemeanor** is a minor or petty crime. Crimes such as murder, rape, and burglary are felonies; crimes such as unarmed assault and battery, petty larceny, and disturbing the peace are misdemeanors.

Most states define a felony as a crime punishable by death or imprisonment in a state prison, and a misdemeanor as a crime punishable by fine or imprisonment in a local jail or house of correction. Some common felonies and misdemeanors are defined in the following Close-Up entitled "Common-Law Crimes."

FUNCTIONS OF THE CRIMINAL LAW

The **substantive criminal law** is a written code defining crimes and their punishments. In the United States, the state and federal governments have developed their own criminal codes. Though all the codes have their differences, most use comparable terms and the behaviors they are designed to control are often quite similar.

Regardless of which culture or jurisdiction created them, or when, criminal codes have several distinct

CLOSE-UP

Common-Law Crimes

The substantive law defines crimes and prescribes the punishments that can be imposed on people engaging in criminal activity. Though each state uses its own definitions, enough similarity exists among them to suggest a general formula for defining most common criminal activities. Below, some familiar illegal acts are set out and an example of each is given.

Crimes Against the Person

First-degree murder—unlawful killing of another human being with malice aforethought and with premeditation and deliberation.

Second-degree murder—unlawful killing of another human being with malice aforethought but without premeditation and deliberation.

Voluntary manslaughter—intentional killing committed under extenuating circumstances that mitigate the killing, such as killing in the heat of passion after being provoked.

Involuntary manslaughter—unintentional killing, without malice, that is neither excused nor justified, such as homicide resulting from criminal negligence.

Battery—unlawful touching of another with intent to cause injury.

Assault—intentional placing of another in fear of receiving an immediate battery.

Rape—unlawful sexual intercourse with a female by a male without her consent.

Sexual assault—forcible sexual relations with a person by another.

Statutory rape—sexual intercourse with a female who is under the age of consent.

Robbery—wrongful taking and carrying away of personal property from a person by violence or intimidation.

Examples

A person buys some poison and pours it into a cup of coffee another is drinking, intending to kill that person. The motive—to get the insurance benefits of the victim.

A person intending to greatly harm another after a disagreement in a bar hits that person in the head with a baseball bat and the victim dies as a result of the injury. Hitting someone hard with a bat is known to cause serious injury. Because the act was committed in spite of this fact, it is second-degree murder.

A husband coming home early from work finds his wife in bed with another man. The husband goes into a rage and shoots and kills both lovers with a gun he keeps by his bedside.

After becoming drunk, a woman drives a car at high speed down a crowded street and kills a pedestrian.

A person seeing someone sitting in his favorite seat in the cafeteria goes up to that person and pushes him out of the seat.

A person aims an unloaded gun at someone who believes the gun is loaded and says she is going to shoot.

After a party a man offers to drive a young female acquaintance home. He takes her to a wooded area and despite her protests forces her to have sexual relations with him.

An older man forces a young boy to have sexual relations with him.

A boy, aged eighteen, and his girlfriend, aged fifteen, have sexual relations. Though the victim voluntarily participates, her age makes her incapable of legally consenting to have sexual relations.

A man armed with a loaded gun approaches another man on a deserted street and demands his wallet.

Inchoate (Incomplete) Offenses

Attempt—an intentional act for the purpose of committing a crime that is more than mere preparation or planning of the crime. However, the crime is not completed.

Conspiracy—voluntary agreement between two or more persons to achieve an unlawful object or to achieve a lawful object using means forbidden by law.

Solicitation—efforts by one person to encourage another person to commit or attempt to commit a crime by means of advising, enticing, inciting, ordering, or otherwise.

Examples

A person intending to kill another places a bomb in the second person's car so that it will detonate when the ignition key is used. The bomb is discovered before the car is started. Attempted murder has been committed.

A drug company sells larger-than-normal quantities of drugs to a doctor, knowing that the doctor is distributing the drugs illegally. The drug company is guilty of conspiracy.

A person offers another a hundred dollars to set fire to a third person's house. The person requesting that the fire be set is guilty of solicitation, whether the fire is set or not.

Crimes Against Property

Burglary—breaking and entering of a dwelling house of another with the intent to commit a felony.

Arson—intentional burning of a dwelling of another.

Larceny—taking and carrying away the personal property of another with the intent to steal the property.

Embezzlement—fraudulent appropriation of another's property by one already in lawful possession.

Receiving stolen goods—receiving of stolen property with the knowledge that the property is stolen and with the intent to deprive the owner of the property.

Examples

Intending to steal some jewelry and silver, a person breaks a window and enters another's house at ten o'clock at night.

A person, angry that her boss did not give her a raise, goes to her boss's house and sets fire to it.

While a woman is shopping, she sees a diamond ring displayed at the jewelry counter. When no one is looking, the woman takes the ring and walks out of the store.

A bank teller receives a cash deposit from a customer and places it in the cash drawer with other deposits. A few minutes later, he takes the deposit out of the cash drawer and keeps it by placing it in his pocket.

A "fence" accepts some television sets from a thief with the intention of selling them, knowing that the sets have been stolen.

Discussion Questions

1. Do you know the definitions used for crimes such as burglary, murder, or rape in your jurisdiction?
2. Why is robbery considered a violent crime and not a property crime?
3. Should statutory rape be considered as serious as forcible rape?
4. What is the difference between *malice aforethought* and *premeditation*?

SOURCE: Developed by Therese J. Libby, J.D.

functions. The most important of these are described below.

✶ Social Control

The primary purpose of the criminal law is to control the behavior of people within its jurisdiction. The criminal law is a written statement of rules to which people's behavior must conform. Every society also maintains unwritten rules of conduct—ordinary customs and conventions referred to as **folkways,** and universally followed behavior norms and morals, called **mores.** However, it is the criminal law that formally prohibits behaviors believed by those in political power to threaten societal well-being, or to challenge their own authority. For example, in our society the criminal law incorporates centuries-old prohibitions against taking the possessions of another person, physically harming another person, damaging another person's property, and cheating another person out of his or her possessions. Similarly, the law prevents actions that challenge the legitimacy of the government, such as planning its overthrow or collaborating with its enemies. Whereas violations of folkways and mores may be informally punished by any person, control of the criminal law is given to those in political power.

Banishes Retribution

By delegating enforcement to others, the criminal law controls an individual's desire to seek **retribution,** or vengeance, against those who violate his or her rights. By punishing people who infringe on the rights, property, and freedom of others, the law shifts the burden of revenge from the individual to the state. As Oliver Wendell Holmes states, this prevents "the greater evil of private retribution."[12] Though state retaliation may offend the sensibilities of many citizens, it is greatly preferable to a system in which people would have to seek justice for themselves.

Public Opinion and Morality

The criminal law also reflects constantly changing public opinions and moral values. As noted in Chapter 1, mala in se crimes, such as murder and forcible rape, are almost universally prohibited. However, the prohibition of legislatively created mala prohibitum crimes, such as traffic law and gambling violations, changes according to shifting social conditions and attitudes. The criminal law is used to codify these changes. For example, if a state government decides to legalize certain previously outlawed behaviors, such as gambling or marijuana possession, it amends the state's criminal code. Thus, the criminal law defines the boundaries between current concepts of moral and immoral behavior and allows people to guide their activities accordingly.

The law's ability to reflect prevailing public opinion and morality is subject to much debate. The consensus view of crime is that the content of the criminal law reflects prevailing public opinion and norms. The interactionist view holds that the law's moral content is controlled by small but powerful interest groups. Similarly, a conflict theorist sees the law's moral content as reflecting the control of the "haves" over the "have-nots" in society. There is little question that an important goal of the criminal law is to express a moral viewpoint that defines the boundaries of socially acceptable behavior. However, it is the source of that viewpoint that is often the focus of controversy.

↘ Deterrence

The criminal law's social control function is realized through its ability to deter potential law violators. The threat of punishment associated with violating the law is intended to prevent crimes before they occur. During the Middle Ages, public executions were held to drive this point home. Today, the criminal law's impact is felt through news accounts of long prison sentences and an occasional execution. Does the law's deterrent power work as intended? This controversial question is explored in Chapter 5.

Punishment

The criminal law grants the government the ability to sanction offenders. Those violating mores and folkways are subject to social disapproval, whereas criminal law violators alone are subject to physical coercion

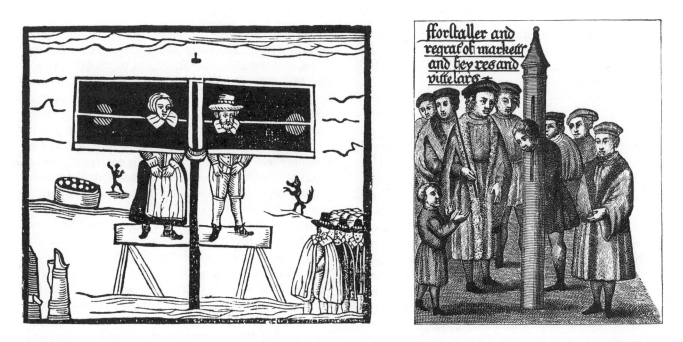

The law expresses public opinion and morality. In medieval times, exhibiting a convicted offender for public ridicule was a common punishment, even for the crimes of fortune-telling (left) and raising market prices (right).

and punishment under the jurisdiction of political agencies.

Legal punishment, as previously noted, is thought to deter would-be criminals. Criminals are punished in the belief that they will avoid the painful consequences of further law violation. Today, most felons are incarcerated. The most serious offenders are executed. Does punishment have its desired effect? This important question is reviewed in Chapter 5.

Socioeconomic Control

All legal systems are designed to support and maintain the boundaries of the socioeconomic system they serve. In medieval England, the law protected the feudal system by defining an orderly system of property transfer and ownership. At the other end of the legal spectrum, laws in socialist or communist nations protect the primacy of the state by strictly curtailing profiteering and individual enterprise. Our own capitalist system is also supported and sustained by the criminal law.

In a sense, the content of the criminal law is more a reflection of the needs of those who control the existing economic and political system than a representation of some idealized moral code. In U.S. society, by meting out punishment to those who damage or steal property, the law promotes the activities needed to sustain an economy based on the accumulation of wealth. It would be impossible to conduct business through the use of contracts, promissory notes, credit, and banking if the law did not protect private capital.

In fact, the criminal law has not always protected commercial enterprise. It was only in 1473, in the *Carrier's Case*, that an English court ruled that a merchant who held and transported merchandise for another was guilty of theft if he kept the goods for his own purposes.[13] Prior to the *Carrier's Case*, the law did not consider it a crime for people to keep something that was already in their possession. Breaking with legal precedent, the British court recognized that the new English mercantile trade system could not be sustained if property rights had to be individually enforced. To this day, the substantive criminal law prohibits such business-related acts as larceny, fraud, embezzlement, and commercial theft. Without the law to protect it, the free enterprise system could not exist.

The following Close-Up entitled "The Law of Vagrancy" analyzes the historical development of vagrancy law and illustrates the view that one of the purposes of the criminal law is to support the existing socioeconomic power structure.

THE LEGAL DEFINITION OF A CRIME

Newspapers often tell us about people who acknowledge at trial that they committed the act they are accused of, yet claim to be "not guilty" of the crime. Sometimes these explanations are bizarre and difficult to accept. For example, in the 1988 Chambers–Levin "Preppie Murder" case, defendant Robert Chambers admitted strangling Jennifer Levin but claimed that despite his advantage in strength and size, he was forced to kill her in self-defense against her "sexual advances"; Chambers later pleaded guilty to manslaughter. In most instances, a successful defense occurs because state or federal prosecutors cannot prove that the alleged behavior falls within the legal definition of a crime.

To fulfill the legal definition, all **elements of the crime** must be proven. For example, in Massachusetts the crime of burglary in the first degree is defined as:

> *Whoever breaks and enters a dwelling house in the nighttime, with intent to commit a felony, or whoever, after having entered with such intent, breaks into such dwelling house in the nighttime, any person being lawfully therein, and the offender being armed with a dangerous weapon at the time of such breaking or entry, or so arriving himself in such house or making an actual assault on a person lawfully therein, commits the crime of burglary.*[14]

Note that burglary has the following elements:

- It happens at night.
- It involves breaking or entering or both.
- It happens at a dwelling house.
- The accused is armed or arms himself or herself after entering the house or commits an actual assault on a person lawfully in the house.
- The accused intends to commit a felony.

In order for the state to prove that a crime occurred and the defendant committed it, the prosecutor must show that the accused engaged in the actus reus and had the mens rea to commit the act. The **actus reus** (guilty act) can be either an aggressive act such as taking money, burning a building, or shooting someone, or a failure to act when there is a legal duty to do so, such as a parent's neglecting to seek medical attention for a sick child. The **mens rea** (guilty mind) refers to the individual's state of mind at the time of the act or, more specifically, the person's intent to commit the crime.

For most cases, both the actus reus and the mens rea must be present for the act to be considered a crime. For example, if George decides to kill Bob and then takes a gun and shoots Bob, George can be convicted of the crime of murder, because both elements are present. George's shooting of Bob is the actus reus; his decision to kill Bob is the mens rea. However, if George only thinks about shooting Bob but does nothing about it, the element of actus reus is absent; and no crime has been committed. Thoughts of committing an act do not alone constitute a crime.

Actus Reus

As stated previously, the actus reus is the criminal act itself. For an act to be considered illegal, the action must be voluntary. For example, if one person shoots another, the shooting certainly could be considered a voluntary act. However, if the shooting occurs while the person holding the gun is having an epileptic seizure or a heart attack or while the person is sleepwalking, he or she will not be held criminally liable, because the act was not voluntary. On the other hand, if the individual knew of such a condition and did not take precautions to prevent the act from occurring, then the person could be held responsible for the criminal act. For instance, if Tom has an epileptic seizure while he is hunting and his gun goes off and kills Victor, Tom will not be held responsible for Victor's death. But if Tom knew of his condition and further knew that a seizure could occur at any time, he could be convicted of the crime if, although it was possible for him to foresee the danger of handling a gun, he nevertheless did nothing about it. Thus, the central issue concerning voluntariness is whether the individual has control

The Law of Vagrancy

According to *Black's Law Dictionary*, vagrancy is the common-law crime of "going about from place to place by a person without visible means of support, who is idle, and who, though able to work for his or her maintenance, refuses to do so, but lives without labor or on the charity of others." Vagrancy has long been considered an ideal vehicle to study the influence of changing social and economic conditions on the form and function of criminal law.

In 1964, Marxist criminologist William Chambliss published a well-known treatise linking the historical development of the law of vagrancy to the prevailing economic interests of the ruling class. He argued that the original vagrancy laws were formulated in the fourteenth century after the bubonic plague had killed significant numbers of English peasants, threatening the labor-intensive feudal economy. The first vagrancy laws were aimed at preventing workers from leaving their estates in order to secure higher wages elsewhere. They punished migration and permissionless travel, thereby mooring peasants to their manors.

According to Chambliss, vagrancy laws in their original form were aimed at maintaining the feudal system. However, as economic conditions changed, so did the content of the law. By the sixteenth century, the newly powerful merchant class had redirected vagrancy laws to control thieves who threatened their accumulated wealth; wandering peasants were ignored. By 1750, vagrancy laws had reached their final form, which was aimed at the social control of criminals who threatened the existing capitalist economic system. Chambliss stated that American vagrancy laws, brought over from England, also reflected the needs of the capitalist system to protect itself from social deviants and misfits.

Not all criminologists support Chambliss' view of legal development. Jeffery Adler finds that early English vagrancy laws were created with the purpose of controlling beggars and relieving the overburdened public relief and welfare systems; maintenance of the economic system was of little concern. Adler also finds that early American vagrancy laws provided town officials with a mechanism to repel the moral threat to the community posed by vagrants, "sabbath breakers," paupers, and the wandering poor. As the country matured, the purpose of vagrancy laws switched to distinguishing malingerers and able-bodied tramps from the deserving poor, those who actually needed public welfare. Focusing on vagrancy laws in St. Louis, Adler found that the factors that influenced their definition and intent were deeply rooted in the context of needs of the economic system. For example, after the Civil War, vagrancy laws changed to control disruptive elements of society because those in power feared modernization and wished to return to the mythical orderliness of the preindustrial world; economic demands had little to do with the content of the law.

The law of vagrancy illustrates the interrelationship between the socioeconomic system and criminal law. Even if Chambliss overstates the case for linking criminal law to the economic needs of capitalism, there is little doubt the law does not exist in a vacuum but reflects the socioeconomic conditions of the times.

Discussion Questions

1. What other crimes do you think have a largely economic basis?
2. Should human behavior which harms no one but the actor be punished by law?

SOURCES: William Chambliss, "A Sociological Analysis of the Law of Vagrancy," *Social Problems* 12 (1964):67–77; Jeffrey Adler, "William Chambliss and a Historical Analysis of the Law of Vagrancy," paper presented at the American Society of Criminology meeting, Montreal, Canada, 1987; Adler, "Vagging the Demons and Scoundrels: Vagrancy and the Growth of St. Louis, 1830–1861," *Journal of Urban History* 13 (1986):3–30.

over his or her actions.

A second type of actus reus is the failure to act when there is a legal duty to do so. A legal duty arises in three common situations:

1. *Relationship of parties based on status.* These relationships include parent/child and husband/wife. If a husband finds his wife unconscious because she took an overdose of sleeping pills, he has a duty to try to save her life by seeking medical aid. If he fails to do so and she dies, he can be held responsible for her death.

2. *Imposition by statute.* For example, some states have passed laws that require a person involved in an automobile accident to stop and help the other parties involved.

3. *Contractual relationship.* These relationships include lifeguard/swimmer, doctor/patient, and babysitter/child. Because lifeguards have been hired to insure the safety of swimmers, they have a legal duty to come to the aid of drowning persons. If a lifeguard knows a swimmer is in danger and does nothing about it and the swimmer drowns, the lifeguard can be held legally responsible for the swimmer's death.

In these three situations, the duty to act is a legal and not a moral one. The obligation arises from the relationship between the parties or from explicit legal requirements. For example, a private citizen who sees a person drowning is under no legal obligation to save that person. Although it may seem morally reprehensible, the private citizen could walk away and let the swimmer drown without facing legal sanctions.

In any discussion of the actus reus of a crime, it should be mentioned that in some circumstances words are considered acts. In the crime of sedition, the words of disloyalty constitute the actus reus. Further, if a person falsely yells "Fire!" in a crowded theater and people are injured in the rush to exit, that person can be held responsible for the injuries, because his or her word constitutes an illegal act.

Mens Rea

In most situations, for an act to constitute a crime it must be done with criminal intent—the mens rea. *Intent* in the legal sense can mean carrying out an act knowingly and willingly. However, the definition also encompasses situations in which recklessness or negligence establish the required criminal intent.

Some crimes require general intent and others require specific intent. The type of intent needed to establish criminal liability varies depending on how the crime is defined. Most crimes require a **general intent,** or an intent to commit the crime. Thus, when Ann picks Bill's pocket and takes his wallet, her intent is to steal. **Specific intent,** on the other hand, is an intent to accomplish a specific purpose as an element of the crime. For example, under common law, burglary in the first degree is the breaking and entering of a dwelling house in the nighttime with the intent to commit a felony. The breaking and entering aspect requires a general intent; the intent to commit a felony is a specific intent. Thus, if Dan breaks and enters Emily's house because he intends to steal Emily's jewelry, Dan is guilty of burglary. However, if Dan merely breaks and enters Emily's house but has no intent to commit a crime once inside, Dan cannot be convicted of burglary, because he lacked specific intent.

Criminal intent also exists if the results of an action, though originally unintended, are substantially certain to occur. For example, Kim, out for revenge against her former boyfriend John, poisons the punch bowl at John's party. Before he has a drink himself, several of John's guests die as a result of drinking the punch. Kim could be said to have intentionally killed the guests even though that was not the original intent of her action. The law would hold that Kim or any other person should be substantially certain that the others at the party would drink the punch and be poisoned along with John.

The concept of mens rea also encompasses the situation in which a person intends to commit a crime against one person but injures another party instead. For instance, if Sam, intending to kill Larry, shoots at Larry but misses and kills John, Sam is guilty of murdering John even though he did not intend to do so. Under the doctrine of **transferred intent,** the original criminal intent is transferred to the unintended victim.

Mens rea is also found in situations in which harm has resulted because a person has acted negligently or recklessly. Negligence involves a person's acting unreasonably under the circumstances. Criminal negligence is often found in situations involving drunken driving. If a drunken driver speeding and zigzagging from left to right hits and kills another person, criminal negligence exists. In the case of drunken driving, the law maintains that a reasonable person would not drive a car when drunk and thus unable to control the vehicle. The intent that underlies criminal liability for an unintentional act is known as **constructive intent.**

Exceptions to the Mens Rea Requirement.   In most cases, both the actus reus and the mens rea must be present before a person can be convicted of a crime. However, several crimes defined by statute do not require mens rea. The actor is guilty simply by doing what the statute prohibits; mental intent does not enter the picture. These offenses are known as **strict liability crimes,** or public welfare offenses. Health and safety regulations, traffic laws, and narcotic control laws are strict liability statutes.

The underlying purpose of these laws is to protect the public. For example, in the case of *United States v. Dotterweich,* the Supreme Court upheld the conviction of a drug company president for misbranding drugs, an act in violation of the federal Food, Drug, and Cosmetic Act. Dotterweich, as president, was in general charge of the business but had not personally mislabeled the drugs; his employees had done the labeling. The Court, finding Dotterweich liable for the illegal actions of his employees, maintained that strict liability legislation "dispenses with the conventional requirement for criminal and conduct awareness of some wrongdoing. In the interest of the larger good it puts the burden of acting at hazard upon a person otherwise innocent but standing in responsible relation to a public danger."[15] Dotterweich was fined $500 and given sixty days probation.

CRIMINAL DEFENSES

When persons defend themselves against criminal charges, they must refute one or more of the elements of the crime of which they have been accused. There are a number of different approaches to criminal defense. First, the defendant may deny the actus reas; for example, by arguing that he or she was falsely accused and the real culprit has not yet been identified.

Defendants may also claim that while they did engage in the criminal act they are accused of, they lacked the mens rea or intent needed to be found guilty of the crime. If persons whose mental states are impaired commit criminal acts, it is possible for them to **excuse** their law-violating actions by claiming they lacked the capacity to form sufficient intent to be held criminally responsible for their actions. Insanity, intoxication, necessity, and duress are types of excuse defenses.

Another type of defense is that of **justification.** Here, the individual usually admits committing the criminal act but maintains that the act was justified and that he or she therefore should not be held crim-

inally liable. Among the justification defenses are self-defense and entrapment.

Persons standing trial for criminal offenses may defend themselves by claiming either that their actions were justified under the circumstances or that their behavior can be excused by their lack of mens rea. If either the physical or mental elements of a crime cannot be proven, then the defendant cannot be convicted. It is common in rape cases, for example, for the defendant to admit to a sexual act with the victim but deny the element of force or intention to coerce the victim. If the claims are accepted by judge or jury, then the defendant cannot be held responsible for violating the law and will be found "not guilty as charged." In the next sections, some of these defenses and justifications are examined in greater detail.

χ *Ignorance or Mistake*

As a general rule, ignorance of the law is no excuse. However, courts have recognized that ignorance can be an excuse if the government fails to make enactment of a new law public, or if the offender relied on an official statement of the law that was later deemed incorrect.

Ignorance or mistake can be an excuse if it negates an element of a crime. For example, if Andrew purchases stolen merchandise from Eric but is unaware that the material was illegally obtained, he cannot be convicted of receiving stolen merchandise because he had no intent to do so. But if Rachel attempts to purchase marijuana from a drug dealer and mistakenly purchases hashish, she can be convicted of the more serious drug charge because she intended to purchase illegal goods; ignorance does not excuse evil intent.[16]

While ignorance or mistake does not excuse crime when there is evil intent, there is conflict when the evil was purely of moral and not legal consequence. For example, some cases of statutory rape (sexual relations with minor females) have been defended on the grounds that the perpetrator was ignorant of his victim's true age. This defense has been allowed in states where sex between consenting adults is legal, under the rationale that if a reasonable mistake had not been made, no crime would have occurred. Nonetheless, if the mistake seems unreasonable, for example, if the victim was a preteen, the original charge will stand.[17]

Insanity

Insanity is a defense against criminal prosecution in which the defendant's state of mind negates his or her criminal responsibility. A successful insanity defense results in a verdict of "not guilty by reason of insanity" (NGRI). Insanity is a legal category. As used in U.S. courts, it does not necessarily mean that persons using the defense are mentally ill or unbalanced, only that their state of mind at the time the crime was committed made it impossible for them to have the necessary intent to satisfy the legal definition of a crime. Thus, a person can be diagnosed a psychopath or psychotic but still be judged legally sane. However, it is usually left to psychiatric testimony in court to prove a defendant legally sane.

A person found to be legally insane at the time of trial is placed in the custody of state mental health authorities until diagnosed as sane. Sometimes, a person who was sane when he or she committed a crime becomes insane soon afterward. In that instance, the person receives psychiatric care until capable of standing trial and is then tried on the criminal charge, since the person actually had mens rea at the time the crime was committed. On rare occasions, persons who were legally insane at the time they committed a crime become rational soon afterward. In that instance, the state can neither try them for the criminal offense nor have them committed to a mental health facility. The test used to determine whether a person is legally insane varies between jurisdictions. U.S. courts have used one of four tests: (1) the M'Naghten Rule, (2) the Irresistible Impulse Test, (3) the Durham Rule, and (4) the Substantial Capacity Test.

The M'Naghten Rule.   In 1843, the English court established the M'Naghten Rule, also known as the right-wrong test. Daniel M'Naghten, believing Edward Drummond to be Sir Robert Peel, the Prime Minister of Great Britain, shot and killed Drummond (Peel's secretary). At his trial for murder, M'Naghten claimed that he could not be held responsible for the murder because his delusions had caused him to act. The jury agreed with M'Naghten and found him not guilty by reason of insanity. Because of the importance of the people involved in the case, the verdict was not well received. The British Parliament's House of Lords reviewed the decision and requested the court to clarify the law with respect to insane delusions. The

court's response became known as the M'Naghten Rule:

> *To establish a defense on the ground of insanity, it must be proved that at the time of the committing of the act the party accused was labouring under such a defect of reason from disease of the mind, as not to know the nature and quality of the act he was doing; or, if he did know, that he did not know he was doing what was wrong.*[18]

Essentially, the M'Naghten Rule maintains that an individual is insane if he or she is unable to tell the difference between right and wrong because of some mental disability.

The M'Naghten Rule is the test used for legal insanity in about 16 states. However, over the years much criticism has arisen concerning M'Naghten. First, great confusion has surfaced over such terms as *disease of the mind*, *known*, and the *nature and quality of the act*. These terms have never been properly clarified. Second, critiques, mainly from the mental health profession, have pointed out that the rule is unrealistic and narrow, in that it does not cover situations in which people know right from wrong but cannot control their actions.

The Irresistible Impulse Test.   Because of questions about M'Naghten, a number of state jurisdictions have supplemented the M'Naghten Rule with another test, known as the Irresistible Impulse Test.[19] This test allows the defense of insanity to be used for situations in which defendants were unable to control their behavior because of a mental disease. Thus, the defendants do not have to prove that they did not know the difference between right and wrong, only that they could not control themselves at the time of the crime.

The Durham Rule.   The Durham Rule, also known as the products test, originated in New Hampshire in 1871. In 1954, the U.S. Court of Appeals for the District of Columbia applied the products test in the case of *Durham v. United States*. The court held "that an accused is not criminally responsible if his unlawful act was the product of mental disease or defect."[20] The benefit of applying this test is that it allows psychiatrists, as expert witnesses, to have greater input about the defendant's mental condition. Critics of the

Durham Rule argue that because the term *product* is not defined, the jury has no standard for judging the evidence and must therefore rely on the psychiatrist's decision. Although the Durham Rule was once used in several states, it has since been abandoned in all states except New Hampshire.

The Substantial Capacity Test.   The most commonly used test for insanity is the Substantial Capacity Test, which was originally a section of the American Law Institute's *Model Penal Code*. It has, over the years, become increasingly popular with U.S. courts. The rule states:

> *A person is not responsible for criminal conduct if at the time of such conduct as a result of mental disease or defect he lacks substantial capacity either to appreciate the criminality [wrongfulness] of his conduct or to conform his conduct to the requirement of law.*[21]

The Substantial Capacity Test is essentially a combination of the M'Naghten Rule and the Irresistible Impulse Test. It is, however, broader in its interpretation of insanity. It requires only a lack of substantial capacity instead of complete impairment. This test also differs in that it uses the term *appreciate* instead of *know*. About half the states now use the Substantial Capacity Test.

The Insanity Controversy.   The purpose and appropriateness of the insanity defense has generated much discussion over the years. Many critics of the defense maintain that inquiry into a defendant's psychological makeup is inappropriate at the trial stage. These critics would prefer that the issue be raised at the sentencing stage, after guilt has been determined.

Opponents also charge that criminal responsibility is separate from mental illness and that the two should not be equated. It is a serious mistake, they argue, to consider criminal responsibility as a trait or quality that can be detected by a psychiatric evaluation.

Moreover, some criminals avoid punishment because they are erroneously judged by psychiatrists to have mental illnesses. Conversely, some people who are found not guilty by reason of insanity because they suffer from a mild personality disturbance are incarcerated as mental patients far longer than they would have been imprisoned if they had been convicted of a criminal offense.

Advocates of the insanity defense say that it serves a unique purpose. Most successful insanity verdicts result in the defendant's being committed to a mental institution until he or she has recovered. The general assumption, according to two legal authorities, Wayne LaFave and Austin Scott, is that the insanity defense makes it possible to single out for special treatment certain persons who would otherwise be subjected to further penal sanctions following conviction. LaFave and Scott further point out that an alternative view maintains that the "real function of the insanity defense is to authorize the state to hold those who must be found not to possess the guilty mind, even though the criminal law demands that no person be held criminally responsible if doubt is cast on any material element of the offense charged."[22]

The insanity plea was thrust into the spotlight when John Hinckley's unsuccessful attempt to kill President Ronald Reagan was captured by news cameras. Hinckley was found not guilty by reason of insanity. Public outcry against this seeming miscarriage of justice prompted some states to review their insanity statutes. Three states—Montana, Idaho, and Utah—have passed laws which abolished the insanity defense, but do consider psychiatric testimony. New Mexico, Georgia, Alaska, Delaware, Michigan, Illinois, and Indiana, among other states, created the defense plea of **guilty but insane,** in which the defendant is required to serve the first part of his or her sentence in a hospital, and once "cured," to be sent to prison. In 1984, the federal government revised its criminal code to restrict insanity as a defense solely to individuals who are unable to appreciate the nature and wrongfulness of their acts; a defendant's irresistible impulse will no longer be considered. There has been an important shift in the burden of proof from the prosecutor's need to prove sanity to the defendant's need to prove insanity.[23] More than 25 states have followed the federal government's lead and made this important change in their insanity defenses.

Although such backlash against the insanity plea is intended to close supposed legal loopholes allowing dangerous criminals to go free, the public's fear may be misplaced. It is estimated that fewer than 1 percent of all cases use the insanity plea. (See Close-Up entitled "How Much Insanity?") Moreover, evidence shows that relatively few insanity defense pleas are successful. Even if the defense is successful, the of-

CLOSE-UP

How Much Insanity?

In Massachusetts, fourteen-year-old Rod Matthews lures a young classmate, Shaun Ouillette, to a wooded area and kills him by repeatedly striking his head with a baseball bat. Afterwards he tells his friends that he did it because he always wanted to know what it felt like to kill someone. Matthews shows them the body, and they all go out for a pizza. Three weeks later, one of the boys finally sends an anonymous letter to the police telling them of Matthews' statements and giving directions on how to find the body. Tried as an adult, Matthews' lawyers claim he is mentally ill, that he has had a long history of mental instability, and that he was taking the mood-altering drug Ritalin at the time of the murder. The prosecution points to the calculated manner in which the victim was lured to his death as evidence that the crime was that of a rational mind driven by malice and not insanity. Despite his history of mental problems, the jury finds Matthews guilty of second-degree murder, a sentence that carries with it a minimum of fifteen years in prison.

The Matthews case illustrates the tremendous legal dilemmas caused by the insanity defense. Here a boy with obvious personality problems is found legally "sane," though his actions are obviously bizarre and abnormal. However, there are also cases when a seemingly dangerous, calculating offender is allowed to avoid a criminal conviction because he or she has made a successful insanity defense. Cases such as the John Hinckley trial bring renewed calls for the abolition of the insanity defense. Considering the controversy of the issue, how many people are actually found not guilty by reason of insanity?

In Massachusetts, where the Matthews case made headlines in 1988, the insanity defense is rarely successful. The state Department of Health studied all criminal cases during a three-year period and found that about one in 4,000 defendants is acquitted by reason of insanity; for the crime of murder the number rises to about two per 100 defendants (a total of eight in the three years studied).

According to Thomas Maeder, an authority on the subject, few defendants actually plead insanity and even fewer find that their defense is successful. According to Maeder, the only accurate tabulation of successful insanity defenses occurred in 1978, when of the more than 7 million people arrested, 1,625 defendants were found not guilty by reason of insanity. Moreover Maeder found that people pleading insanity were more often than not non-violent offenders. Even the insane killer does not really fit our preconception of the crazed maniac who beats the system due to psychiatric testimony. People who are found NGRI after committing a murder generally are abused wives who are driven to their crimes after years of physical and emotional abuse, or severely depressed persons who kill family members while in a disoriented mental state.

Of course, a successful insanity defense does not mean that defendants are free to enter society. Most people who are found NGRI spend years in mental institutions, often being incarcerated for a longer period than they would have been had they been convicted of a criminal offense. And there are a number of studies that show that NGRI patients have relatively low recidivism rates once they are returned to society.

Does the insanity plea allow hordes of dangerously mentally ill criminals back to prey upon society? The evidence does not support that contention.

Discussion Questions

1. Should the burden of proof be on the defendant to prove insanity or on the prosecutor to prove sanity?

2. Should legally insane murderers be required to spend the rest of their lives in mental hospitals, since sane murderers would have to spend theirs in prison?

SOURCES: Thomas Maeder, *Crime and Madness* (New York: Harper and Row, 1985); Richard Stewart, "Insanity Plea Not Very Effective in Massachusetts Courts, Study Says," *Boston Globe*, 8 March 1988, p. 22.

fender must be placed in a secure psychiatric hospital or the psychiatric ward of a state prison. Since many defendants who successfully plead insanity are non-violent offenders, it is certainly possible that their hospital stay will be longer than the prison term they would have received if convicted of the crimes they were originally accused of.[24]

Despite efforts to ban its use, the insanity plea is probably here to stay. Most crimes require mens rea, and unless we are willing to forego that standard of law, we will be forced to find not guilty those people whose mental states make it impossible for them to rationally control their behavior.

Intoxication

Intoxication, which includes the taking of alcohol or drugs, is generally not considered a defense. However, there are two exceptions to this rule. First, an individual who becomes intoxicated either by mistake, through force, or under duress can use involuntary intoxication as a defense.

Second, voluntary intoxication is a defense when specific intent is needed and the person could not have formed the intent because of his or her intoxicated condition. For example, if a person breaks and enters another's house but is so drunk that he or she cannot form the intent to commit a felony, the intoxication is a defense against burglary.

Duress

Duress is a defense against a crime when the defendant commits an illegal act because the defendant or a third person has been threatened by another with death or serious bodily harm if the act is not performed. For example, if Pete, holding a gun on Jerry, threatens to kill Jerry unless he breaks into and enters Ramon's house, Jerry has a defense of duress for the crime of breaking and entering.

This defense, however, does not cover situations in which defendants commit a serious crime such as murder to save themselves or others. The reason for this exception is that the defense is based on the social policy that, when faced with two evils (harm to oneself or violating the criminal law), it is better to commit the lesser evil in order to avoid the threatened harm. In the situation of murder versus threatened harm, however, the taking of another's life is considered the greater of the two evils.

Necessity

The defense of necessity is applied in situations in which a person must break the law in order to avoid a greater evil caused by natural physical forces (storms, earthquakes, illness). This defense is only available when committing the crime is the lesser of two evils. For example, a person lacking a driver's license is justified in driving a car to escape a fire.

However, as the famous English case *Regina v. Dudley and Stephens* indicates, necessity does not justify the intentional killing of another.[25] In that case, three sailors and a cabin boy had been shipwrecked and were floating on the open seas in a lifeboat. After nine days without food and seven without water, Dudley and Stephens killed the cabin boy and the three sailors ate his body. Four days later the sailors were rescued. The court acknowledged that the cabin boy most likely would have died naturally because he was in the weakest condition, and agreed that the killing was necessary to save the lives of the remaining crew. Nevertheless, the court judged the killing unjustified and sentenced the defendants to death; the defendants were later pardoned on the grounds that they had suffered enough.

Self-Defense

Self-defense involves a claim that the defendant's actions were a response to the provocative behavior of the victim. Self-defense can be used to protect one's person or one's property.

Defense of the Person.   At times, an individual is justified in using force against another to protect himself or herself. When that happens, the person claims to have acted in self-defense and is therefore not guilty of the harm done. If the defendant was justified in using force, self-defense excuses such crimes as murder, manslaughter, and assault and battery.

The law, however, has set limits as to what is reasonable and necessary self-defense. First, defendants must have a reasonable belief that they are in danger of death or great harm and that it is necessary for them to use force to prevent harm to themselves. For example, if Mary threatens to kill Jan but it is obvious that Mary is unarmed, Jan is not justified in pulling her gun and shooting Mary. However, if Mary, after threatening Jan, reaches into her pocket as if to get a gun, and Jan then pulls her gun and shoots Mary, Jan could claim self-defense, even if it is discovered that Mary was unarmed. In this situation, Jan had a reasonable belief that harm was imminent and that it was necessary to shoot first to avoid injury to herself.

Second, the amount of force used must be no greater than that necessary to prevent personal harm. For instance, if Steve punches Ben, Ben could not justifiably hit Steve with an iron rod. Ben could, however, punch Steve back if he believed Steve was going to continue punching.

Another issue arises concerning self-defense in situations in which deadly force may be necessary: Does a person have a duty to avoid using deadly force against an attacker by retreating if possible? U.S. courts are split on this issue. The majority of states maintain that the person attacked does not have to retreat, even if he or she can do so safely. This position is based on the policy that a person should not be forced to act in a humiliating or cowardly manner. However, many states do require that a person try to retreat, if it is possible to do so safely, before using deadly force. Even in most of these jurisdictions, however, people are not required to retreat if attacked in their homes or offices.

The rules concerning self-defense also apply to situations involving defense of a third person. Thus, if a person reasonably believes that another is in danger of unlawful bodily harm from an assailant, the person may use the force necessary to prevent the danger.

Defense of Property.   Using force to defend one's property from trespass or theft is allowable if the force is reasonable. This means that force should be a last resort, after requests to stop interfering with the property or legal action have failed. Also, the use of deadly force is not considered reasonable when only protection of property is concerned. This is based on the social policy that human life is more important than property, and on the legal view that property crimes cannot be punished by death.

Entrapment

Entrapment is another defense that excuses a defendant from criminal liability. The entrapment defense is raised when the defendant maintains that law-enforcement officers induced him or her to commit a crime. The defendant would not have committed the crime had it not been for trickery, persuasion, or fraud on the officers' part. In other words, if law-enforcement officers plan a crime, implant the criminal idea in a person's mind, and pressure that person into doing the act, the person may plead entrapment.

This situation is different from that in which an officer simply provides an opportunity for the crime to be committed, but the defendant is willing and ready to do the act. For example, if a plainclothes police officer poses as a potential customer and is approached by a prostitute, no entrapment has occurred. However, if the same officer approaches a woman and persuades her to commit an act of prostitution, the defense of entrapment is appropriate.

In the famous ABSCAM case, federal agents posing as Arab business associates recorded efforts by high-ranking government officials to solicit bribes as payment for using their influence in Congress. Though the federal agents were disguised and seemed to encourage the bribe attempts, courts ruled that their actions did not involve entrapment, since the agents were merely providing an opportunity for the bribe attempts to be made and not planting the criminal idea in the minds of the government officials.

However, in the equally famous DeLorean case, the jury believed millionaire car maker John DeLorean was entrapped by the FBI, since an informer acting on the FBI's behalf originally suggested the idea of importing cocaine. Though DeLorean was a willing participant in the $24 million deal, because the idea started with an agent of the government he was found not guilty.

—— REFORMING THE CRIMINAL LAW ——

In recent years, many states and the federal government have been examining their substantive criminal law. Since the law, in part, reflects public opinion regarding various forms of behavior, what was a crime forty years ago may not be considered so today. In some states, crimes such as possession of marijuana have been decriminalized—given reduced penalties. Such crimes may be punishable by a fine instead of a prison sentence. Other former criminal offenses, such as vagrancy, have been legalized—all criminal penalties have been removed. And, in some jurisdictions, penalties have been toughened, especially for violent crimes such as rape and assault. Still other states have changed their laws to reflect public awareness of social realities. For example, Nebraska has changed its law against rape to one banning sexual assault. Whereas the common-law crime of rape concerns a sexual assault of a female by a male, Nebraska's new law recognizes that sexual assaults can also take place between people of the same sex.

The most important criminal law reform has been the Federal Comprehensive Crime Control Act of 1984. The Act standardizes sentences, changes the concept of probation, revamps the insanity plea, and creates new substantive laws. For example, the Act prohibits convicted criminals from profiting from their misdeeds by selling their stories to the media. The revised code calls for profits from such sales to be given to a special fund to benefit the victims of crime. The code also imposes monetary penalties for federal crimes. Without question, this Act's most important provisions are in the sentencing area. Here, it eliminates indeterminate sentences, phases out parole, and makes sentences fairer and more certain. A sentencing commission was established to determine sentencing guidelines; it is hoped this will alleviate the problem of sentencing disparity by limiting judicial discretion.

In the future, the criminal law should continue to be a changing force, reflecting the times and the technology. Various state and federal criminal codes are likely to evolve to include new sections limiting computer tampering and illegal genetic engineering of life forms. As society changes, so must its laws.

SUMMARY

The substantive criminal law is a set of rules that specifies the behavior society has outlawed. The criminal law can be distinguished from the civil law in that the former involves powers given to the state to enforce social rules, while the latter controls interactions between private citizens. The criminal law serves important purposes: It represents public opinion and moral values, enforces social controls, deters criminal behavior and wrongdoing, and banishes private retribution.

The criminal law in the United States traces its origin to the English common law. Common law was formulated during the Middle Ages, when King Henry

II's judges began to use precedent set in one case to guide actions in another; this system is called *stare decisis*. In the U.S. legal system, common-law crimes have been codified by lawmakers into state and federal penal codes. Today, most crimes fall into the category of felony or misdemeanor. Felonies are serious crimes usually punished by a prison term, whereas misdemeanors are minor crimes that usually carry a fine or a light jail sentence. Common felonies include murder, rape, assault with a deadly weapon, and robbery; misdemeanors include larceny, simple assault, and possession of small amounts of drugs.

Every crime has specific elements. In most instances, these elements include the actus reus (guilty act), which is the actual physical part of the crime—for example, taking money or burning a building. Most crimes also contain a second element, the mens rea (guilty mind), which refers to the state of mind of the individual who commits a crime—more specifically, the person's intent to do the act.

At trial, a person can claim to have lacked mens rea and, therefore, not to be responsible for the criminal actions. One type of defense is excuse for mental reasons, such as insanity, intoxication, necessity, or duress. Another defense is justification, either by reason of self-defense or by entrapment.

Of all defenses, insanity is perhaps the most controversial. In most states, persons using an insanity defense claim that they did not know what they were doing when they committed a crime or that their mental state did not allow them to tell the difference between right and wrong (the M'Naghten Rule). Insanity defenses in the remaining jurisdictions include the claims that criminal actions were a product of mental illness, that the offender was motivated by an irresistible impulse, or that the offender lacked the substantial capacity to conform his or her conduct to the criminal law. Regardless of the insanity defense used, critics charge that mental illness is separate from legal responsibility and that the two should not be equated. Supporters counter with the argument that the insanity defense allows mentally ill people to avoid penal sanctions.

The criminal law is undergoing constant reform. Some acts are being decriminalized—having their penalties reduced—while other laws are being revised to make penalties for some acts more severe. One major revision effort is the modernization of the federal criminal code.

KEY TERMS

shire

hundreds

tithings

wergild

stare decisis

circuit judges

common law

assize

criminal attempt

statutory crimes

criminal law

civil law

burden of proof

beyond a reasonable doubt

preponderance of the
evidence

felony

misdemeanor

substantive criminal law

folkways

mores

retribution

elements of the crime

actus reus

mens rea

general intent

specific intent

transferred intent

constructive intent

strict liability crimes

excuse defense

justification defense

guilty but insane

NOTES

1. The criminal law concepts and terminology in this chapter are a synthesis of those contained in J. Grall Robinson, *Criminal Law Defenses* (St. Paul, Minn.: West Publishing, 1988); Wayne LaFave and Austin Scott, *Handbook on Criminal Law* (St. Paul: West Publishing, 1982); and Sanford Kadish and Monrad Paulsen, *Criminal Law and Its Processes* (Boston: Little, Brown, 1975).

2. Rene A. Wormser, *The Story of Law*, rev. ed. (New York: Simon and Schuster, 1962).

3. See, generally, Arthur Rossett and Donald Cressey, *Justice by Consent* (New York: J. B. Lippincott, 1976), pp. 48–50.

4. Wormser, *The Story of Law*.

5. LaFave and Scott, *Handbook on Criminal Law*, pp. 528–29.

6. Caldwell 397 (1984), cited in LaFave and Scott, *Handbook on Criminal Law*, p. 422.

7. George I, C. 22, 1723, cited in Douglas Hay, ''Crime and Justice in Eighteenth and Nineteenth Century England,'' in *Crime and Justice*, vol. 2, ed. Norval Norris and Michael Tonry (Chicago: University of Chicago Press, 1980), p. 51.

8. Jerome Hall, *Theft, Law and Society* (Indianapolis: Bobbs-Merrill, 1952). Chapter 1 is generally considered the best source for the history of common-law theft crimes.

9. Mass. Gen. Laws Ann. (West 1982) ch. 266, pp. 1–2.

10. See, generally, Alfred Lindesmith, *The Addict and the Law* (New York: Vintage Books, 1965), chap. 1.

11. For example, see *Brinegar v. United States*, 388 U.S. 160 (1949); *Speiser v. Randall*, 357 U.S. 513 (1958); *In re Winship*, 397 U.S. 358 (1970).

12. Oliver Wendell Holmes, *The Common Law*, ed. Mark De Wolf (Boston: Little, Brown, 1881), p.36.

13. *Carrier's Case*, Y.B. 13 Edw. 4, f. 9, pl. 5 (Star Chamber and Exchequer Chamber, 1473), discussed at length in Jerome Hall, *Theft, Law and Society* (Indianapolis: Bobbs-Merrill, 1952), chap. 1.

14. Mass. Gen. Laws Ann. (West 1983) ch. 266, p. 14.

15. 320 U.S. 277 (1943).

16. LaFave and Scott, *Handbook on Criminal Law*, p. 356.

17. *Ibid.*, p. 361.

18. 8 Eng. Rep. 718 (1843).

19. Kadish and Paulsen, *Criminal Law and Its Processes*, pp. 215–16.

20. 94 U.S. App. D.C. 228, 214 F. 2d 862 (1952.).

21. *Model Penal Code* 401 (1952).

22. LaFave and Scott, *Handbook on Criminal Law*, p. 516.

23. Comprehensive Crime Control Act of 1984—Pub. L. No. 98–473, 403.

24. Samuel Walker, *Sense and Nonsense About Crime* (Monterey, Cal.: Brooks Cole, 1985), p. 120.

25. *Regina v. Dudley and Stephens*, 14 Q.B. 273 (1884).

CHAPTER 3

MEASURING CRIMINAL BEHAVIOR

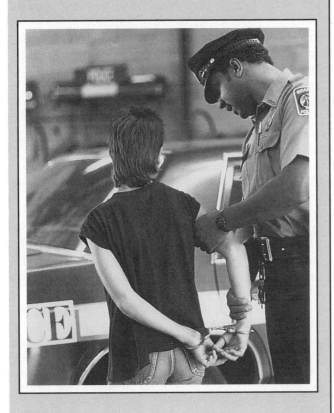

CHAPTER OUTLINE

INTRODUCTION

There are several reasons why the accurate measurement of criminal behavior is one of the most critical goals of the criminological enterprise. Measuring criminal behavior is essential if the root causes of crime are to be discovered. Criminologists have devoted a great deal of effort to the formulation of theories which can help explain the onset of criminal behavior (see Chapters 5 through 9). This task could not be undertaken unless accurate indicators of the crime rate could be produced and the personal characteristics—age, sex, race—of offenders determined. The answers to questions such as who commits crime, when do offenders begin their criminal careers, and where and how often do offenders commit crime have a great deal of bearing on efforts to determine *why* crime occurs.

Valid crime data is also necessary if criminologists are to effectively evaluate policy initiatives in the criminal justice system. For example, if a state legislature enacts a law banning the private possession of unlicensed handguns, it is important to evaluate what effect this legal measure has on the state's violent crime rate. Criminologists might be called on to study the issue. One possible approach might be to compare the state's violent crime rate before and after the gun control law took effect. If the number of violent crimes decreases soon after the law's passage, this may indicate that the handgun bill is a viable crime reduction technique. If, however, the handgun bill does not produce an appreciable change in the violent crime rate, rethinking the problem is in order. Perhaps the measure did not go far enough. Or perhaps legislation alone cannot influence the use of illegal handguns. Without accurate information, crime control policy cannot be effectively evaluated.

Measuring criminal behavior patterns is also important for everyday decision-making in the justice system. For example, policy chiefs need information on trends in illegal behavior if they are to make reasoned decisions on resource allocation, staffing, and patrol distribution. It would be foolish to put the largest contingent of police on the street at noon if most crimes occur at three o'clock in the morning. Similarly, surveys of inmates released from prison can help correctional authorities predict the likelihood that a particular type of offender will succeed in the outside world. This information can be used to select for early release programs those inmates who stand the best

chance for success.

Thus, in measuring criminal behavior, criminologists have three primary objectives: understanding the nature of crime and the criminal offender, evaluating the effectiveness of crime prevention programs, and aiding decision-making in the criminal justice system.

This chapter focuses on the measurement of crime. It contains a brief discussion of some of the methods used by criminologists to collect crime-related data, and an analysis of crime trends. In the following chapter, the major forms of crime information—surveys and aggregate data collections—are analyzed to reveal something about the nature of criminals and their victims.

ACQUIRING CRIME DATA

Criminologists have used a wide variety of research techniques to measure the nature and extent of criminal behavior. To understand and evaluate criminal behavior statistics, it is important to develop some knowledge of how these data are collected. It is also important to understand the methods used in criminology. This understanding provides insight into how professional criminologists approach various problems and questions in their field.

Survey Research

A great deal of crime measurement is based on analysis of **survey** data. Surveys include interviewing or questioning a group of subjects about research topics under consideration. This method is often used in **cross-sectional research,** which involves the simultaneous measurement of subjects who come from different backgrounds and groups (that is, a cross section of the community).

Most surveys involve **sampling**—selecting for study a limited number of subjects who are representative of entire groups sharing similar characteristics, called **populations.** For example, a criminologist might interview a sample of 3,000 prison inmates drawn from the population of 600,000 inmates in the United States; in this case, the sample represents the entire population of U.S. inmates. Or a sample of burglary incidents could be taken from the city of Miami; here, the sample would represent the population of Miami burglaries. It is assumed that the characteristics of people in a carefully selected sample will be quite similar to those of the population at large.

Survey research can be designed to measure the attitudes, beliefs, values, personality traits, and behavior of participants. **Self-report surveys** ask participants to describe in detail their recent and lifetime criminal activity; **victimization surveys** seek information from people who have been victims of crime; **attitude surveys** may measure the views of varied groups such as prostitutes, students, drug addicts, police officers, judges, juvenile delinquents, or the general public.

Surveys in Practice.   Survey research is one of the most widely used methods of criminological inquiry. Surveys are an excellent and cost-effective method of measuring the characteristics of large numbers of people. Because questions and methods are standardized for all subjects, uniformity is unaffected by the perceptions or biases of the person gathering the data. Moreover, statistical analysis of carefully drawn samples enables researchers to generalize their data from small groups to large populations. And since some criminologists maintain that crime is a consequence of relatively stable characteristics of people, measuring them at a single point in their life cycle can provide important information on the factors which influence their behavior.[1]

Despite their utility, surveys are not without their problems. One of their most serious drawbacks is that they often cannot show the true relationship between two acquired social traits or variables, because in a survey both are measured simultaneously. For example, surveys can examine the relationship between child abuse and delinquency by asking delinquent youths to describe their upbringing and discipline. While the survey may find that delinquents do in fact report greater amounts of abuse than nondelinquents, it is still impossible to determine whether a) delinquency is caused by physical punishment, b) antisocial youths eventually provoke their parents into using harsh physical punishment, or c) some other factor caused both the delinquency and child abuse to take place (such as growing up in a poverty area). While surveys can show an association between two variables, and can be used to support theoretical models,

they rarely can provide conclusive scientific proof.

In addition, surveys have been criticized because they rely on the assumption that an individual's response will be valid and accurate. Though efforts are usually made to insure the validity of questionnaire or interview items, it is difficult to guard against people who either deliberately lie and misrepresent information or who are unsure of answers and give mistaken responses. Moreover, surveys are limited when the area to be studied involves the way people interact with one another, or other topics an individual may not be able to judge personally. Despite these drawbacks, surveys continue to be an extremely popular method of gathering criminological data.

This chapter focuses on two types of crime measurement surveys; self-report surveys, in which criminal offenders are asked about their law-violating behaviors, and victimization surveys, in which the victims of crime provide information on their experiences.

Longitudinal Research

Longitudinal research involves the observation of a group of people who share a like characteristic over time.[2] This kind of group is called a **cohort.** For example, researchers might select all boys born in Albany, New York, in 1970, and then follow their behavior patterns for a twenty-year period. The research data might include their school and arrest records, hospitalization, and information about their family life (divorces, siblings, and so on). Using this data, it might be possible to uncover the factors associated with a criminogenic lifestyle. If the research were carefully conducted, it might be possible to determine which life experiences, such as growing up in an intact home or school failure, typically preceded the onset of crime and delinquency.

Since it is extremely difficult to follow a cohort over time, and since most of the sample do not become serious criminals, another approach is to take an intact group of known offenders and examine their early life experiences by back checking their records. This format is known as a **retrospective longitudinal study.**[3]

To carry out cohort studies, criminologists frequently use records of various social organizations. School records usually contain data on a student's academic performance, attendance record, IQ, disciplinary problems, and teacher ratings. Hospital records include incidents of drug use, suspicious wounds, and child abuse. Police files contain reports of criminal activity, arrest data, personal information on suspects, victim reports, and actions taken by police officers. Court records allow researchers to compare the personal characteristics of offenders with the outcomes of their court appearances—conviction rates and types of sentence. Prison records contain information on inmates' personal characteristics, adjustment problems, disciplinary records, rehabilitation efforts, and length of sentence served.

Aggregate Data Research

Criminologists also make use of large data bases gathered by government agencies and research foundations. U.S. Census Bureau data, Labor Department employment data, and reports of state correctional departments have all been used by criminologists in their research. The most important of these sources is the **Uniform Crime Report (UCR),** compiled by the Federal Bureau of Investigation.[4] The UCR is an annual report that reflects the number of crimes reported by citizens to local police departments and the number of arrests made by police agencies in a given year. The UCR is probably the most important source of official crime statistics. The significance of its findings are covered later in this chapter.

Aggregate data can be used to focus on the social forces which effect crime. For example, to study the relationship between crime and poverty, criminologists use data collected by the U.S. Census Bureau on income, number of people on welfare, and single-parent families in an area, and then cross-reference this information with official crime statistics from the same locality. Aggregate data can reveal the effect of overall social trends and patterns on the crime rate.

Experimental Research

To conduct experimental research, criminologists manipulate or intervene in the behavior of their subjects, in order to see the outcome or effect the intervention has. True experiments usually have three elements: random selection of subjects; a control or comparison group; and an experimental condition. For example,

experimental research might involve randomly selecting a sample of male college students, exposing them to a violent sex-related movie, and then comparing them with another group of randomly selected subjects who have viewed a Disney film. The criminologist would want to see if the experimentals would act more aggressively and hold more hostile attitudes toward women than the controls.

An intact-group or quasi-experiment is undertaken when it is impossible to randomly select subjects or manipulate experimental conditions. For example, if criminologists wished to study the effect of mandatory jail sentences for DWI on driving fatalities and drunk driving arrests, they might compare states in which strict mandatory sentences exist with similar states that do not have such legislation. While not a true experiment (since the states could not be randomly selected), this approach would give an indication of the effectiveness of mandatory sentences.

Criminological experiments are relatively rare. They are difficult and expensive to conduct, involve the manipulation of subjects' lives—which can cause ethical and legal roadblocks—and require long follow-up periods to verify results. Nonetheless, they have been an important source of criminological data.

Observational Research and First-Person Accounts

Another common criminological method is the first-hand observation of criminals in order to gain insight into their motives and activities. This may involve going into the field and participating in group activities, as in the case in William Whyte's famous study of a Boston gang, *Street Corner Society*.[5] Other observers conduct field studies but remain in the background, observing but not participating in the ongoing activity, as in the case of Herman and Julia Schwendinger's landmark study of gang delinquency.[6]

Still another type of observation involves bringing subjects into a structured laboratory setting and observing how they react to a predetermined condition or stimulus. This approach is common in studies testing the effect of observational learning on aggressive behavior.[7]

Still another criminological method involves examining the lifestyle of a single person (first-person

TABLE 3.1   UCR Crimes and Definitions

HOMICIDE Causing the death of another person without legal justification or excuse. Negligent manslaughter, suicide, and deaths due to accident are excluded.	**BURGLARY** Unlawful entry of any fixed structure, vehicle, or vessel used for regular residence, industry, or business, with or without force, with the intent to commit a felony or larceny.
RAPE Unlawful sexual intercourse with a female, by force or without legal or factual consent. Assaults or attempts to commit rape by force or threat of force are included; statutory rape without force and other sex offenses are excluded.	**LARCENY (THEFT)** Unlawful taking or attempted taking of property other than a motor vehicle from the possession of another, by stealth, without force and without deceit, with intent to permanently deprive the owner of the property. It includes pocket-picking, purse-snatching, theft from motor vehicles.
ROBBERY Unlawful taking or attempted taking of property that is in the immediate possession of another, by force or threat of force, or by putting the victim in fear.	**MOTOR VEHICLE THEFT** Unlawful taking or attempted taking of a motor vehicle owned by another, with the intent of depriving the owner of it permanently. It includes theft of cars, trucks, buses, motorcycles, and scooters.
ASSAULT Unlawful intentional inflicting, or attempted inflicting, of injury upon the person of another. *Aggravated assault* is the unlawful intentional inflicting of serious bodily injury or unlawful threat or attempt to inflict bodily injury or death by means of a deadly or dangerous weapon with or without actual infliction of injury. *Simple assault* is the unlawful intentional inflicting of less than serious bodily injury without a deadly or dangerous weapon or an attempt or threat to inflict bodily injury without a deadly or dangerous weapon.	**ARSON** Intentional damaging or destruction, or attempted damaging or destruction, by means of fire or explosion of the property without the consent of the owner, or of one's own property or that of another by fire or explosives with or without the intent to defraud.

SOURCE: Adapted from Federal Bureau of Investigation, *Uniform Crime Report, 1986.*

account), such as a professional thief, in order to gain insight into his or her behavior, motives, and associations. Both Carl Klockars and Darrell Steffensmeier have conducted this type of study with fences, professional purveyors of stolen goods (see Chapter 11).[8]

—— CRIME IN THE UNITED STATES ——

As you may recall, one of the principle roles of criminological research is to determine the nature and extent of crime in the United States. To reach this objective, criminologists have relied primarily on survey and aggregate data collection methods. In the following sections each of these data sources is explored.

✗ *Official Crime Statistics*

The term **official crime statistics** refers to the aggregate records of offenders and offenses processed by police, court, and correctional agencies. Criminologists use these records to study both crime rates and offenders' characteristics.

As indicated earlier, the FBI's Uniform Crime Report (UCR) is the best known and most widely cited source of criminal statistics.[9] The FBI receives and compiles reports from over 15,000 police departments serving a majority of the United States population. Its major unit of analysis involves **index crimes:** murder and nonnegligent manslaughter, forcible rape, robbery, aggravated assault, burglary, larceny, arson, and auto theft (see Table 3.1). The FBI annually tallies and publishes the number of reported offenses by city, county, standard metropolitan statistical area

(SMSA), and geographic divisions of the United States. In addition to these statistics, the UCR provides information on the number and characteristics of individuals who have been arrested and the number and location of assaults on police officers.

The methods used to compile the UCR are quite complex. Each month, law enforcement agencies report the number of index crimes known to them. A count of these crimes, which are also known as **Part I offenses,** is taken from records of all complaints of crime, either from victims, from officers who discovered the infractions, or from other sources.

Whenever complaints of crime are determined through investigation to be unfounded or false, they are eliminated from the actual count. The number of "actual offenses known" is reported to the FBI whether or not anyone is arrested for the crime, the stolen property is recovered, or prosecution is undertaken. In addition, each month law enforcement agencies report the total crimes that were cleared. Crimes are cleared in two ways: (1) when at least one person is arrested, charged, and turned over to the court for prosecution, or (2) by exceptional means, when some element beyond police control precludes the physical arrest of an offender (e.g., the offender flees the country). The number of clearances involving only the arrest of offenders under the age of eighteen, the value of property stolen and recovered in connection with Part I offenses, and detailed information pertaining to criminal homicide are also reported.

Arrest data, which include the age, sex, and race of persons arrested, are reported monthly by crime category for both Part I and Part II offenses. **Part II offenses,** while excluding traffic violations, include all other crimes except those classified as Part I.

The UCR employs three methods to express crime data. First, the number of crimes reported to the police and arrests made are expressed as raw figures (for example, 1,224,137 motor vehicle thefts occurred in 1986). In addition, the percent changes in the amount of crime between years is computed (for example, robbery increased 9 percent between 1985 and 1986). Finally, crime rates per 100,000 people are computed. That is, when the UCR indicates that the murder rate was 8.3 in 1987, it means that about 8 people in every 100,000 fell victim to murder between January 1 and December 31 of 1987. The equation used is:

$$\frac{Number\ of\ reported\ crimes}{Total\ U.S.\ population} \times 100,000 = Rate\ per\ 100,000$$

CRIME TRENDS IN THE UNITED STATES

Studies have indicated that a gradual increase in the crime rate, especially in the area of violent crime, occurred from 1830 to 1860. Following the Civil War, this rate increased significantly for about fifteen years. Then, from 1880 to the time of the first World War, with the possible exception of the years immediately preceding and following the war, the number of reported crimes decreased. After a period of readjustment, the crime rate steadily declined until the Depression, whereupon another general increase, or crime wave, was recorded.[10] Crime rates increased gradually through the 1930s until the 1960s, when the growth rate became much greater. The homicide rate, which had declined from the 1930s to the 1970s, also began a period of sharp increase.

As Table 3.2 indicates, the upswing in the crime rate continued through the 1970s until 1981, when more than 13.4 million index crimes were reported—a rate of 5,950 per 100,000 people.[11] However, from 1982 to 1984, the rate steadily declined, with overall drops of 7 percent in 1983 and in 1984, when slightly more than 11.1 million crimes were reported to police. Since then there has been a slow but steady increase in both the rate and amount of crime (up 5 percent in 1985, 6 percent in 1986, and 2 percent in 1987), so that the police are now once again recording more than 13 million crimes.[12]

How can the recent trends in the reported crime rate be explained? Most experts believe changes in the age distribution of the population have had the greatest influence on recent crime trends. The postwar "baby boom" generation reached its teenage years in the 1960s, just as the violent crime rate began a sharp increase. Since both the victims and perpetrators of violent crime tend to fall in the 18 to 25 year age category, the rise in crime reflects the age structure of society. With the "graying" of society in the 1980s, and a decline in the birth rate, it is not surprising that the crime rate has been more stable. However, the children of baby-boomers will be reaching "prime" crime age during the 1990s, and some forecasters pre-

TABLE 3.2   Index of Crime, United States, 1977–1987

Population[1]	Crime Index Total[2]	Violent Crime[3]	Property Crime[3]	Murder and Nonnegligent Manslaughter	Forcible Rape	Robbery	Aggravated Assault	Burglary	Larceny-Theft	Motor Vehicle Theft
Number of offenses:										
1978—218,059,000	11,209,000	1,085,550	10,123,400	19,560	67,610	426,930	571,460	3,128,300	5,991,000	1,004,100
1979—220,099,000	12,249,500	1,208,030	11,041,500	21,460	76,390	480,700	629,480	3,327,700	6,601,000	1,112,800
1980—225,349,264	13,408,300	1,344,520	12,063,700	23,040	82,990	565,840	672,650	3,795,200	7,136,900	1,131,700
1981—229,146,000	13,423,800	1,361,820	12,061,900	22,520	82,500	592,910	663,900	3,779,700	7,194,400	1,087,800
1982—231,534,000	12,974,400	1,322,390	11,652,000	21,010	78,770	553,130	669,480	3,447,100	7,142,500	1,062,400
1983—233,981,000	12,108,600	1,258,090	10,850,500	19,310	78,920	506,570	653,290	3,129,900	6,712,800	1,007,900
1984—236,158,000	11,881,800	1,273,280	10,608,500	18,690	84,230	485,010	685,350	2984,400	6591,900	1,032,200
1985—238,740,000	12,430,400	1,327,770	11,102,600	18,980	87,670	497,870	723,250	3,073,300	6,926,400	1,102,900
1986—241,077,000	13,210,800	1,488,140	11,722,700	20,610	90,430	542,780	834,320	3,241,400	7,257,200	1,224,100
1987—243,400,000	13,508,700	1,484,000	12,027,700	20,096	91,111	517,704	855,088	3,236,184	7,499,851	1,288,674
Percent change: number of offenses:										
1987/1986	+2.2	-.3	+2.6	-2.5	-.4	-4.6	+2.5	-.2	+3.3	+5.3
1986/1982	+1.8	+12.5	+.6	−1.9	+14.8	−1.9	+24.6	−6.0	+1.6	+15.2
1986/1977	+20.3	+44.5	+17.8	+7.8	+42.4	+31.5	+56.1	+5.5	+22.9	+25.2
Rate per 100,000 inhabitants:										
1978	5,140.3	497.8	4,642.5	9.0	31.0	195.8	262.1	1,434.6	2,747.4	460.5
1979	5,565.5	548.9	5,016.6	9.7	34.7	218.4	286.0	1,511.9	2,999.1	505.6
1980	5,950.0	596.6	5,353.3	10.2	36.8	251.1	298.5	1,684.1	3,167.0	502.2
1981	5,858.2	594.3	5,263.9	9.8	36.0	258.7	289.7	1,649.5	3,139.7	474.7
1982	5,603.6	571.1	5,032.5	9.1	34.0	238.9	289.2	1,488.8	3,084.8	458.8
1983	5,175.0	537.7	4,637.4	8.3	33.7	216.5	279.2	1,337.7	2,868.9	430.8
1984	5,031.3	539.2	4,492.1	7.9	35.7	205.4	290.2	1,263.7	2,791.3	437.1
1985	5,206.7	556.2	4,650.5	7.9	36.7	208.5	302.9	1,287.3	2,901.2	462.0
1986	5,479.9	617.3	4,862.6	8.6	37.5	225.1	346.1	1,344.6	3,010.3	507.8
1987	5,550.0	609.7	4,940.3	8.3	37.4	212.7	351.3	1,329.6	3,081.3	528.4
Percent change: rate per 100,000 inhabitants:										
1987/1986	+1.4	-1.3	+1.6	+3.5	-1.3	-5.5	+1.5	-1.1	+2.4	+4.3
1986/1982	−2.2	+8.1	−3.4	−5.5	+10.3	−5.8	+19.7	−9.7	−2.4	+10.7
1986/1977	+7.9	+29.7	+5.7	-2.3	+27.6	+18.0	+40.1	-5.3	+10.3	+12.4

[1]Populations are Bureau of the Census provisional estimates as of July 1, except April 1, 1980, preliminary census counts, and are subject to change.
[2]Because of rounding, the offenses may not add to totals.
[3]Violent crimes are offenses of murder, forcible rape, robbery, and aggravated assault. Property crimes are offenses of burglary, larceny-theft, and motor vehicle theft. Data are not included for the property crime of arson.
All rates were calculated on the offenses before rounding.

SOURCE: Federal Bureau of Investigation, *Crime in the United States, 1986*, p. 41, updated.

dict a corresponding rise in the crime rate.

A second explanation given for the decline in the crime rate in the early 1980s was the ''get-tough'' crime control policies favored by the Reagan administration. More than 600,000 people were locked in the nation's prisons. Tough sentencing policies, including mandatory prison terms for some crimes, coupled with the abolition of parole, helped account for a rapid increase in the prison population. Conservatives argued that this new hardline attitude toward criminal justice helped reduce the crime rate. They believed potential criminals are deterred through fear of pun-

TABLE 3.3   Crime Rate by Area, 1986 (Rate per 100,000 Inhabitants)

Offense	Total United States	Metropolitan Area	Other Cities	Rural Areas
Crime index total	5,479	6,236	4,793	1,853
Modified crime index total Violent crime	617	732	350	175
Property crime	4,862	5,503	4,443	1,678
Murder	8.6	9.6	5	5.3
Forcible rape	37.5	43	22	17
Robbery	225.1	286	48.8	14.9
Aggravated assault	346.1	393	274	137
Burglary	1,344.6	1,510	1,045	649
Larceny-theft	3,010.3	3,374	3,191	921
Motor vehicle theft	507.8	619	206	107.7

SOURCE: Federal Bureau of Investigation, *Uniform Crime Report, 1986*, p. 42.

ishment; convicted ones incapacitated in prison. Although it is often difficult to establish a direct link between crime rates and punishment levels, those favoring tough crime control policies consider deterrence to be an important moderating influence on crime.

The most recent increases in reported crime are more difficult to explain, considering that the teenage population continues to decline and the nation has not abandoned its "get-tough" law enforcement policies. One factor may be the relatively high unemployment, drug use, and school dropout rates among urban teenagers, which makes crime an attractive source of income and prestige for a group whose demographic characteristics make them especially prone to criminality. Another factor may be that more people are reporting crime to police, which by itself results in higher crime rates. For example, the reported crime increase of 5 percent between 1985 and 1986 may be explained in part by the fact that the percentage of victims reporting crime to the police increased about 3 percent during this period.[13]

In sum, after many years of rapid increase, the overall crime rate declined in the mid-1980s only to rise again towards the end of the decade. With an expected rise in the teenage population, the crime rate may eventually begin another rapid move upward.

THE NATURE OF CRIME

Perhaps the most important fact in criminology is that certain trends in the crime rate appear to be very stable. Because these are social trends, they are considered evidence that crime is a sociological phenomenon and thus must be analyzed through social research and analysis.

Season and Climate

Most reported crimes occur during the warm summer months of July and August. One possible explanation for this warm weather trend is that with school out, teenagers, whose crime rate is traditionally higher than all other age categories, have more free time and go relatively unsupervised. In addition, people spend more time outdoors during these months, making themselves easier targets. Similarly, homes are left vacant more often during the summer, making them more vulnerable to property crimes. Two exceptions to this trend are murders and robberies, which occur more frequently in December and January (though rates are also high during the summer).

Population Density

Table 3.3 shows the relationship between crime rate and population density. Areas with low per capita crime rates tend to be rural. Large urban areas have by far the highest crime rates. Exceptions to this trend are low-population resort areas with high transient or seasonal populations—such as Atlantic City, New Jersey, and Nantucket, Massachusetts.

It is interesting that the increase in crime in the

1980s was greater in rural and suburban areas than in larger cities. This trend might be a result of the youthful population in these areas.

Region

Definite differences are apparent in regional crime rates. In recent years, southern states have had a significantly higher crime rate than other regions of the country in almost all crime categories. Southern states have traditionally had the highest violence rate including murder, a factor which has given rise to the concept that there is a southern subculture of violence. (In Chapter 10, violence in southern areas is discussed further.)

Clearances

Crimes are cleared when perpetrators are arrested and turned over for prosecution. Traditionally, about 20 percent of all reported index crimes are cleared by arrest. Marked differences in clearance rates can be seen between property and violent crimes. As Table 3.4 indicates, violent crimes are much more likely to be solved than property crimes. This reflects both the greater resources police have available to solve the more serious violent crimes and the availability of witnesses to identify offenders. When Part II offenses are included, about 10 million people are arrested annually.

CRITICISMS OF THE UNIFORM CRIME REPORT

Despite its importance and wide use by criminologists, the accuracy of the UCR has been heavily criticized. The three greatest areas of concern—reporting practices, law enforcement practices, and methodological problems—are discussed below.

Reporting Problems

One major concern of criminologists is that many serious crimes are not reported by victims to police and

TABLE 3.4   Index Crimes Cleared by Arrest, 1986

Crime Type	Number Arrested	Percent Cleared*
Violent crimes		
Murder	19,190	70
Assault	351,770	59
Rape	37,140	52
Robbery	145,800	25
Total	553,900	46
Property crimes		
Burglary	450,000	14
Larceny	1,400,200	20
Motor vehicle theft	153,600	15
Arson	18,700	15
Total	2,023,200	18
Total arrests	2,577,100	21

*Rounded
SOURCE: Federal Bureau of Investigation, *Uniform Crime Report, 1986*, pp. 154–164.

therefore do not become part of the UCR. The reasons for not reporting vary. Some people do not have property insurance and therefore believe it is useless to report theft-related crimes. In other cases, the victim may fear reprisals from the offender's friends or family.

Several national surveys have attempted to discover why citizens decide not to report delinquent or criminal acts. In 1966, the President's Commission on Law Enforcement and the Administration of Justice sponsored one such effort. Using a nationally drawn sample of 10,000 citizens, the Commission found that the most common concerns were that the "police couldn't do anything about the matter," that "it was a private—not criminal—affair," that the person "was not sure if the real offenders would be caught," and that the "police wouldn't want to be bothered."[14]

The **National Crime Survey (NCS),** an annual survey of crime victimization, indicates that about half of all criminal incidents are not reported to the police primarily because the victims believed the incident was "a private matter," "nothing could be done," or the "victimization was not important enough."[15]

In an analysis of NCS data, Michael Hindelang and Michael Gottfredson found that for each category of crime, completed criminal acts were more often

Approximately 20 percent of all reported crimes are cleared by arrest.

reported than attempted victimizations.[16] Similarly, the seriousness of delinquent or criminal activity influenced reporting; for example, the use of a weapon in the crime increased the likelihood that police would be notified. As the value of monetary loss increased, so did the probability that the act would be reported.[17]

Hindelang and Gottfredson found that the personal characteristics of the victim also influenced reporting habits. As a general rule, the victim's age was strongly related to failure to report crimes—victims under thirty-five were much less likely to report crimes than those over thirty-five. Racial differences were found to be minor except among the youngest victims (those twelve to nineteen years old); whites were less likely to report crimes than blacks. Family income was found to be directly related to crime reporting—as income rose, so too did the probability that victims would contact police. Whether or not the criminal was an acquaintance of the victim did not seem to affect the likelihood of the crime's being reported.

Law Enforcement Practices

The way police departments record and report criminal and delinquent activity also affects the validity of UCR statistics. For example, in New York City for the period 1948 to 1952, burglaries rose from 2,726 to 42,491, and larcenies increased from 7,713 to 70,949.[18] These increases were found to be related to the change from a precinct to a centralized reporting system for crime statistics. A new central reporting system instituted in Philadelphia in 1952 resulted in a sharp rise in index crimes—from 16,773 in 1951 to 28,560 in 1953.[19] How police interpret the definitions of index crimes may also affect reporting practices.[20] For example, police in Boston were found to report only completed rapes to the FBI, while those in Los Angeles reported completed rapes, attempted rapes, and sexual assaults. Reporting practices helped account for the fact that the rape rate in Los Angeles is far higher than that in Boston.

A recent study by Lawrence Sherman and Barry Glick for the Police Foundation found that local police departments make systematic errors in UCR reporting.[21] All 196 departments they surveyed counted an arrest only after a formal booking procedure, although the UCR requires arrests to be counted if the suspect is released without a formal charge. Similarly, 29 percent of the departments surveyed did not include citations and 57 percent did not include summonses, though the UCR requires it. An audit of arrests found an error rate of about 10 percent in every Part I offense category.

Similarly, Patrick Jackson found that the FBI's newest crime category, arson, may be seriously underreported because many fire departments do not report to the UCR, and those that do exclude many fires which are probably set by arsonists.[22]

Of a more serious nature are allegations that police officials may deliberately alter reported crimes to put their departments in a more favorable light with the public. David Seidman and Michael Couzens suggest that police administrators, interested in lowering the crime rate and thus improving their departments' images, may falsify crime reporting by deliberately undervaluing the cost of stolen goods. For example, an index larceny will be relegated to a nonreportable offense category.[23] Thus, it is possible that political issues can help to raise or lower crime rates.

Finally, increased police efficiency and professionalism may actually help increase crime rates. As more sophisticated computer-aided technology is developed for police work, and as the education and training of police employees increases, so too might their ability to record and report crimes, thereby producing higher crime rates.

Methodological Problems

Methodological issues also add to the problems of the UCR's validity. Leonard Savitz has collected a list of twenty such issues, including:

1. No federal crimes are reported.
2. Reports are voluntary and vary in accuracy and completeness.
3. Not all police departments submit reports.
4. The FBI uses estimates in its total crime projections.
5. If multiple crimes are committed by an offender, only the most serious is recorded. Thus, if a narcotics addict rapes, robs, and murders a victim, only the murder is recorded as a crime.
6. For some crimes, each act is listed as a single offense. Thus, if a man robs six people in a bar, it's listed as one robbery; but if he assaults them, the crime would be listed as six separate assaults.
7. Uncompleted acts are lumped together with completed ones.
8. There are important differences between the FBI's definition of a crime and those used in a number of states.[24]

Future of the Uniform Crime Report

What does the future hold for the UCR? The FBI is preparing to implement some important changes in the Uniform Crime Reports. First, the definition of many crimes will undergo revision. For example, rape will be defined in sexually neutral terms:

> the carnal knowledge of a person, forcibly and/or against that person's will; or not forcibly or against the person's will where the victim is incapable of giving consent because of his/her temporary or permanent mental incapacity.

There will also be an attempt to provide more detailed information on individual criminal incidents. Instead of submitting statements of the kinds of crime that individual citizens reported to the police and summary statements of resulting arrests, it is planned that local police agencies will provide at least a brief account of each incident within the existing part I crime categories. In addition, agencies serving more than 100,000 people, and a sample of smaller departments, will provide detailed reports on 23 crime patterns, including incident, victim, and offender information. These expanded crime categories will include numerous additional crimes—such as blackmail embezzlement, drug offenses, and bribery—which will allow a national data base on the nature of crime, victims, and criminals to be developed. The third change will impose more stringent auditing techniques, to insure the accuracy and completeness of the material being submitted by the police.[25]

These changes are scheduled to be adopted in 1989. If implemented on schedule, the new UCR program may bring about greater uniformity in cross-jurisdictional reporting and improve the accuracy of official crime data.

SELF-REPORT STUDIES

The questionable validity of official data has been a serious problem for criminologists. If they base their work on inaccurate data, then all subsequent theory and policy decisions will be biased and misleading. Two sociologists, Roger Hood and Richard Sparks, have commented on the problem of uncertainty:

> In relying on this [official] data the theorist is faced with two problems. First, he must estimate to what extent those convicted differ from those who have committed identical acts but have not been caught or prosecuted. Secondly, he must try to disentangle those factors which explain criminal behavior from those which explain why a person has become officially processed as a delinquent or a criminal.[26]

The problems associated with official statistics have led many criminologists to seek alternative sources of information in assessing the true extent of crime patterns. In addition, official statistics do not say much about the personality, attitude, and behavior of individual criminals. Official statistics may illustrate broad concepts, such as trends in the relative frequency of crime, but they are an inadequate source of information about narrower theoretical issues, such as the relationship between the individual personality and criminal behavior. Thus, alternative sources of information about criminal behavior are needed to help determine its true extent, develop valid theories and test them, and make effective policy.

One frequently employed alternative to official statistics is the self-report survey. Self-report surveys are designed to allow participants to reveal information about their violations of the law. The surveys have many different formats. For example, the criminologist can approach people who have been arrested by police, or even prison inmates, and interview them about their illegal activities. Subjects also can be telephoned at home and then mailed a survey form. Most often, self-report surveys are administered to large groups through a mass distribution of questionnaires. The names of subjects can be requested, but more commonly they remain anonymous. (The accompanying Close-Up includes a sample self-report survey.)

The basic assumption of self-report studies is that anonymity and the promise of confidentiality backed by academic credentials will encourage people to describe their illegal activities accurately. Thus, self-reports are viewed as a mechanism to get at the dark figures of crime, the figures missed by official statistics either because victims chose not to report the crime to police, or because there were no real victims, for example, instances of drug possession and use.

Most self-report studies have focused on juvenile delinquency and youth crime, for two reasons.[27] First, it is more convenient to survey youths than adults. The school provides a setting in which literally thousands of subjects can be reached simultaneously. Second, since attendance is mandatory, a school-based self-report survey is usually considered a reliable estimate of the activities of all youths in a given community. Self-reports also have been used to examine the offense histories of prison inmates and to identify factors that can predict criminal behavior patterns.

Self-reports make it possible to assess both the number of people in the population who have committed illegal acts, and the frequency of their law violations. Since most self-report instruments also contain items measuring subjects' attitudes, values, personal characteristics, and behaviors, the data obtained from them can be used for various purposes, such as testing theories and measuring attitudes toward crime.

Self-report studies, then, allow criminologists to identify people who commit criminal acts but evade detection and thus do not figure in the official crime statistics. Self-reports provide a broader picture of the distribution of criminality, since they do not depend on the offender's being apprehended. Furthermore, since many criminologists believe that class bias exists in the criminal justice system, self-reports allow criminologists to evaluate the distribution of criminal behavior across class lines. One important goal of self-report studies is to determine whether differences exist in the law-violating behaviors of upper-, middle-, and lower-class individuals. This issue has major im-

CLOSE-UP

A Self-Report Instrument

Most self-report surveys are similar to the one illustrated below. Some ask subjects to check the appropriate spaces, while others allow them to write in the precise number of times they engaged in each criminal act. Note that this sample survey limits the reporting period to the past twelve months. Some surveys ask subjects to report their lifetime involvement in crime, while others use both techniques.

Surveys are also likely to contain items not directly related to criminal activity—for example, items requesting information on such diverse topics as subjects' self-image; intelligence; personality; attitudes toward family, friends, and school; and leisure activities. Self-report surveys also gather personal information on subjects' family background, social status, race, and sex.

SAMPLE SURVEY   Please indicate how often in the past twelve months you did each act. (Check the best answer.)

	Never did act	One time	2–5 times	6–9 times	10–13 times	14–17 times	18+ times
1. Stole something worth less than $50							
2. Stole something worth more than $50							
3. Snorted or sniffed heroin							
4. Injected heroin							
5. Used amphetamine pills (such as uppers, crystal meth, dex)							
6. Shot up amphetamines							
7. Got drunk on beer							
8. Got drunk on hard liquor							
9. Got drunk on wine							
10. Used marijuana (pot)							
11. Used downers (Valium, Librium, Darvon, Thorazine)							
12. Used psychedelics (LSD, mescaline)							
13. Used cocaine							
14. Been in a fistfight							
15. Carried a weapon such as a gun or knife							
16. Fought someone using a weapon							
17. Stole a car							
18. Used force to steal							
19. (For boys) Forced a girl to have sexual relations against her will							
20. Drove a car while drunk or high							
21. Damaged property worth more than $10							

Discussion Questions

1. Do you think subjects would answer these questions honestly if they were promised anonymity and confidentiality?

2. Have you participated in any of the acts listed in the sample survey?

SOURCE: Sample survey form from Larry Siegel and Spencer Rathus.

portance for the study of the causes of criminal behavior (see Chapters 7, 8, and 9).

Self-Report Data

As mentioned, most self-report instruments gather data from groups of high school students. In general, they indicate that the number of youths who break the law is far greater than had previously been believed. In fact, when truancy, alcohol consumption, petty theft, and soft drug use are included in self-report scales, almost everyone tested is found to have violated some law.[28] Furthermore, self-reports dispute the notion that criminals and delinquents specialize in one type of crime or another. Instead, offenders have been found to engage in a variety of crimes and deviance.[29]

Self-report studies indicate that the most common offenses are truancy, alcohol abuse, use of a false ID, shoplifting or larceny under $5, fighting, marijuana use and damage to the property of others. It has been estimated that almost 90 percent of all youths commit delinquent and criminal acts. In fact, several studies have suggested that there is actually little difference between the behavior of incarcerated youths and that of typical high-school students. It is not unusual for self-reports to indicate alcohol and drug abuse, theft, violence, and damage rates of more than 50 percent among suburban, rural, and urban high school youths. What is surprising is the consistency of these findings in samples taken from southern, eastern, midwestern, and western states.

When the results of recent self-report surveys are compared with various studies conducted over a twenty-year period, a uniform pattern emerges. The use of drugs and alcohol increased markedly in the 1970s and then leveled off in the 1980s; theft, violence, and damage-related crimes seem more stable. Although a self-reported crime wave has not occurred, neither has there been any visible reduction in teenage delinquency. For example, when Rosemary Sarri compared self-report data collected in the late 1960s with similar data form the late 1970s, she found that involvement in serious crimes by both males and females had remained stable, while involvement in such acts as alcohol abuse, marijuana use, and driving while intoxicated had increased.[30]

Self-report studies can provide much information about delinquent offenders who are not apprehended by the police. For example, a national study by Franklyn Dunford and Delbert Elliott found that only about 24 percent of all serious, chronic juvenile offenders were apprehended by police, and overall only 8 percent of all youths admitting delinquent acts were ever arrested.[31] So self-reports can provide a significant amount of information about youthful offenders that cannot be found in the official statistics.

Critique of Self-Report Studies

Though self-report studies had a profound effect on criminological theory in the 1960s and 1970s (see Chapter 7), their methodology has been criticized for various reasons. Critics of self-report studies frequently suggest that it is unreasonable to expect young people to candidly admit illegal acts. They have nothing to gain, and the ones taking the greatest risk are the ones with official records. On the other hand, some young people may exaggerate their delinquent acts, forget some of them, or be confused about what is being asked.

The validity of self-report studies cannot be determined because there is nothing reliable to measure them against. Correlation with official reports is expected to be low, because the inadequacies of such reports are largely responsible for researchers' asking youths themselves about their criminality in the first place.

Most self-reports have been used with youthful offenders who are not involved in adult criminality. Many contain an overabundance of trivial offenses—skipping school, running away, using a false ID—often lumped together with serious crimes to form a "total crime index."[32] Consequently, comparisons between groups can be highly misleading. Moreover, even if a large percentage of a school population voluntarily participates in a self-report, researchers can never be sure that the remaining few who refuse to participate or are absent that day do not engage in most of the serious crimes in the community.

Various techniques have been used to verify self-report data. The most common is to compare the answers youths give with their official police records.[33] A number of studies using this method have found a

There are more than 34 million victimizations in the U.S. each year. Here, a suspect is read his rights in the emergency room.

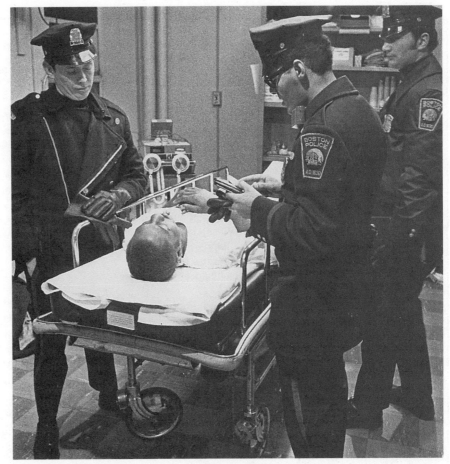

remarkable uniformity between self-reported answers and official records.

Other methods are also used to test the validity of self-reports.[34] The **known group method** compares incarcerated youths with "control" groups to see whether the former report more delinquency. Peer informants—friends who can verify the honesty of a subject's answers—are used. Subjects also can be tested twice to see if their answers remain the same. The questions are designed to reveal respondents who are lying on the exam—for example, an item might say: "I have never done anything wrong in my life." In general, these efforts have validated self-report studies.

In what is probably the most thorough analysis of self-report methodologies, Michael Hindelang, Travis Hirschi, and Joseph Weis closely reviewed the literature concerning the reliability and validity of self-

reports and conducted their own independent analysis using data gathered in Seattle, Washington, and other sites.[35] They concluded that the problems of accuracy in self-reports are "surmountable"; that self-reports are more accurate than most criminologists believe; and that self-reports and official statistics are quite compatible:

The method of self reports does not appear from these studies to be fundamentally flawed. Reliability measures are impressive and the majority of studies produce validity coefficients in the moderate to strong range.[36]

Thus, self-reports continue to be used as a standard method of delinquency research. Many of the studies discussed in Chapters 5 through 9 rely on self-reports for their data.

CLOSE-UP

Why Do Victims Fail to Report Crime?

Why are victims reluctant to report crimes to the police? According to the National Crime Survey, the most frequent reason is that the offense was not "serious enough to warrant police attention," followed by the belief that "nothing could be done about the crime."

Other factors certainly must play a role in the decision to report crime. After carefully reviewing the evidence, Robert Kidd and Ellen Chayet found that reporting decisions were based on three factors: victim fear and anxiety; feelings of powerlessness; and threat of further victimization from both the criminal and the authorities (who are insensitive to their condition). They concluded:

> Worrying about further victimization by the authorities may combine with the fear from the initial victimization experience. As a result of their original suffering, victims may become highly sensitive to the costs of reporting the crime. Not only are the police unlikely to capture the felon, but they also are unlikely to acknowledge the victim's plight. Furthermore, encounters in court would mean that the victim will have to recount the painful experience of being victimized.

Research by R. Barry Ruback, Martin Greenberg, and David Westcott found that victims also are influenced in their reporting decisions by the advice of friends and other people in four different ways:

1. *By cueing them to a particular option they have not yet considered.* For example, friends tell the victims to hire a lawyer and sue their assailants for damages.
2. *By providing informational influence.* A friend might encourage crime reporting by arguing that an insurance claim can be made only if the crime is reported to police.
3. *By giving them normative influences.* Their peers may tell the victim that calling the police is the "right thing." Conversely, they may reinforce the notion that "around here you never call the cops, no matter what."
4. *By providing emotional support.* Friends can give the victims support during their time of stress, encouraging them to take action. They also can blame them for their predicament, for example, suggesting to a rape victim that she "brought it on herself" by her lack of judgment.

In sum, the reasons victims decide to report crime to the police are complex, influenced in part by their perceptions of the incident, the likelihood of achieving a favorable outcome, and peer influence.

Discussion Questions

1. What factors would influence your reporting a crime to the police?
2. A friend of yours is assaulted in a bar for no apparent reason. Would you advise your friend to report the incident to police?

SOURCES: Robert Kidd and Ellen Chayet, "Why Do Victims Fail to Report? The Psychology of Criminal Victimization," *Journal of Social Issues* 40 (1984):39–50; R. Barry Ruback, Martin Greenberg, and David Westcott, "Social Influence and Crime-Victim Decision Making," *Journal of Social Issues* 40 (1984):51–76.

VICTIMIZATION STUDIES: THE NATIONAL CRIME SURVEY

The third component in the crime measurement triad is the victimization survey. Rather than depending on the agencies of justice or the criminals themselves for data, victim surveys measure the extent of criminal behavior by focusing on its target—the victims. Although there have been several significant victim surveys, the National Crime Survey is by far the most complex and far-reaching.[37] Consequently, this discussion focuses primarily on that survey.

The National Crime Survey (NCS) is collected by the U.S. Bureau of the Census, in cooperation with the Bureau of Justice Statistics of the U.S. Department of Justice. Samples of housing units are selected on the basis of a complex, multistage sampling technique.[38]

The total annual sample size for the national survey is about 60,000 households, containing about 136,000 individuals. The total sample is composed of

FIGURE 3.1
Percent Distribution of Victimizations
by Sector and Type of Crime

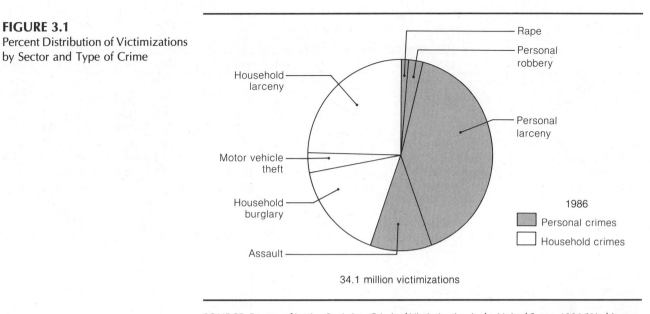

34.1 million victimizations

SOURCE: Bureau of Justice Statistics, *Criminal Victimization in the United States, 1986* (Washington, D.C. U.S. Government Printing Office, 1987), p. 3.

six independently selected subsamples, each with about 10,000 households, or 22,000 individuals. Each subsample is interviewed twice a year about victimization suffered in the preceding six months. For example, in January, individuals in 10,000 households are interviewed. In the following month—and in each of the four succeeding months—an independent probability sample of the same size is interviewed. In July, the original households are revisited and interviews are repeated. Likewise the original February sample units are revisited in August, and so on. Each time they are interviewed, respondents are asked about victimizations suffered during the six months preceding the month of interview.

The data reported represent estimates of crimes occurring in the United States, based on weighted sample data. It is possible to make these estimates because a probability sample of respondents also is surveyed. The interview completion rate in the national sample is about 95 percent of those elected to be interviewed in any given period; hence, population estimates should be relatively accurate.

The NCS data have been used to determine the nature and extent of crime in the United States. Survey data are subjected to elaborate statistical analysis to estimate the amount of crime occurring in the nation as a whole. This procedure presents a picture of the crime problem without the methodological problems that plague the Uniform Crime Report. NCS data indicate that only 45 percent of violent crimes, 24 percent of personal crimes of theft, and 38 percent of household crimes are brought to the attention of police. Many citizens report that, among other reasons, they failed to contact police because they "felt nothing could be done," or because they believed the criminal act "just wasn't important enough" to bother authorities.

Thus, NCS data account for many more criminal acts than those reported in the UCR. This is not to say that NCS data alone can be considered the "official" crime statistics. Victimization data are, of course, limited to crimes in which a victim exists. The data cannot be used to measure such victimless crimes as drug use and gambling. Nor can NCS data accurately account for crimes such as fraud, embezzlement, or tax violations. And, of course, the statistics remain estimates that may be subject to error and must be interpreted accordingly.

Selected Findings

The most recent data from the National Crime Survey indicate that about 34.1 million crimes, including both

TABLE 3.5   Victimization Rates for Personal and Household Crimes, 1973–1986

| | Victimization Rates per 1,000 Population Age 12 and Older or per 1,000 Households | | | | | | | | | | | | | |
	1973	1974	1975	1976	1977	1978	1979	1980	1981	1982	1983	1984	1985	1986
Personal crimes														
Crimes of violence	32.6	33.0	32.8	32.6	33.9	33.7	34.5	33.3	35.3	34.3	31.0	31.4	30.0	28.1
Rape	1.0	1.0	0.9	0.8	0.9	1.0	1.1	0.9	1.0	0.8	0.8	0.9	0.7	0.7
Robbery	6.7	7.2	6.8	6.5	6.2	5.9	6.3	6.6	7.4	7.1	6.0	5.7	5.1	5.1
Assault	24.9	24.8	25.2	25.3	26.8	26.9	27.2	25.8	27.0	26.4	24.1	24.7	24.2	22.3
Aggravated assault	10.1	10.4	9.6	9.9	10.0	9.7	9.9	9.3	9.6	9.3	8.0	9.0	8.3	7.9
Simple assault	14.8	14.4	15.6	15.4	16.8	17.2	17.3	16.5	17.3	17.1	16.2	15.7	15.9	14.4
Crimes of theft	91.1	95.1	96.0	96.1	97.3	96.8	91.9	83.0	85.1	82.5	76.9	71.8	69.4	67.5
Personal larceny with contact	3.1	3.1	3.1	2.9	2.7	3.1	2.9	3.0	3.3	3.1	3.0	2.8	2.7	2.7
Personal larcey without contact	88.0	92.0	92.9	93.2	94.6	93.6	89.0	80.0	81.9	79.5	74.0	69.1	66.7	64.7
Household crimes														
Household burglary	91.7	93.1	91.7	88.9	88.5	86.0	84.1	84.3	87.9	78.2	70.0	64.1	62.7	61.5
Household larceny	107.0	123.8	125.4	124.1	123.3	119.9	133.7	126.5	121.0	113.9	105.2	99.4	97.5	93.5
Motor vehicle theft	19.1	18.8	19.5	16.5	17.0	17.5	17.5	16.7	17.1	16.2	14.6	15.2	14.2	15.0

NOTE: Detail may not add to total shown because of rounding.

SOURCE: Bureau of Justice Statistics, *Criminal Victimization in the United States, 1986.*

completed acts and attempts, occurred in 1986 —approximately three times as many as reported by the UCR. Personal crimes, such as rape, personal robbery, and assault, made up slightly more than half the reported victimizations (about 18.7 million incidents). Household crimes, including larceny and burglary, accounted for slightly less than 50 percent of the total (about 15.3 million incidents). (See Figure 3.1.)

The NCS has recorded a long-term downward trend in reported victimizations. The total estimated number of victimizations peaked from 1979 to 1981, when more than 40 million crimes were reported annually (41.4 million in 1981). Since then, there has been a steady decline in both the number and rate of victimizations of all kinds. Table 3.5 illustrates the victimization rates per 1,000 people in the population 12 years and older in the United States, from 1973 to 1986. The overall victimization rate has declined since the early 1980s and is actually at its lowest level since 1973. This pattern holds for virtually every crime pattern. (The one exception, reported motor vehicle theft, increased slightly between 1985 and 1986.) The most dramatic long-term declines have been in the rates of household burglary, rape, personal larceny, and robbery, all of which declined 25 percent or more since 1973.

While there are significant discrepancies in frequency and rate, both the UCR and NCS show similar demographic patterns in the crime rate. Both indicate that larger cities have far higher violent and property crime rates than less densely populated areas. The differences are most dramatic with respect to violent crimes—metropolitan rape and robbery rates are three and four times as high as in rural areas (though the assault ratio is only about 1.5 to 1). Both UCR and NCS data also indicate that crime occurs more frequently in warmer summer months than during the winter.

TABLE 3.6   Comparison of UCR and NCS Rates for Selected Crimes

| | Rates per 1,000 Population | |
Crimes	UCR	NCS
Rape	.37	.70
Robbery	2.20	5.10
Assault	3.50	7.90
Larceny	30.10	67.50

SOURCES: *Criminal Victimization, 1986,* p. 3; *Crime in the United States, 1986,* pp. 13–29.

TABLE 3.7   Reporting Victimizations to the Police, 1973–1986

	Percent of Victimizations Reported to the Police													
	1973	1974	1975	1976	1977	1978	1979	1980	1981	1982	1983	1984	1985	1986
All crimes	32	33	35	35	34	33	33	36	35	36	35	35	36	37
Personal crimes														
Crimes of violence	46	47	47	49	46	44	45	47	47	48	47	47	48	50
Rape	49	52	56	53	58	49	51	41	56	53	47	56	61	48
Robbery	52	54	53	53	56	51	55	57	56	56	53	54	54	58
Assault	44	45	45	48	44	43	42	45	44	46	46	45	46	48
Aggravated assault	52	53	55	58	51	53	51	54	52	58	56	55	58	59
Simple assault	38	39	39	41	39	37	37	40	39	40	41	40	40	41
Crimes of theft	22	25	26	27	25	25	24	27	27	27	26	26	27	28
Personal larceny with contact	33	34	35	36	37	34	36	36	40	33	36	31	33	38
Personal larceny without contact	22	24	26	26	24	24	24	27	26	27	26	26	27	28
Household crimes	38	37	39	38	38	36	36	39	39	39	37	38	39	41
Household burglary	47	48	49	48	49	47	48	51	51	49	49	49	50	52
Household larceny	25	25	27	27	25	24	25	28	26	27	25	27	27	28
Motor vehicle theft	68	67	71	69	68	66	68	69	67	72	69	69	71	73

SOURCE: Bureau of Justice Statistics, *Criminal Victimization in the United States, 1986.*

Reported Crime Rates

Table 3.6 compares the rates reported by the FBI with those found by the NCS for selected crimes. The rate of criminal acts recorded by the NCS far exceeds those found in FBI data for comparable crimes. For example, whereas the FBI tallies two robberies per 1,000 population, the NCS records more than five; and while the FBI indicates that the assault rate is about 3.5, the NCS records it at about 8 per thousand.

How can these discrepancies be explained? One significant factor is that respondents to the NCS indicate that they report less than half of their victimizations to the police. As Table 3.7 shows, only about half of the serious crimes of rape, robbery, and burglary, and less than a third of the larcenies are reported to police. When victims are asked why they did not report crime, they usually respond that it was a private matter, they did not want to get involved, nothing could be done, or it was too trivial a matter. Despite such caution, the percentage of all crimes reported to police has been slowly increasing, indicating perhaps a greater confidence in the ability of law enforcement agencies. Close-Up entitled "Why Do Victims Fail to Report Crime?" describes research on victim reporting practices.

Critique of the National Crime Survey

Though the NCS eliminates the UCR's major methodological drawback—victims' failure to report crime—it, too, has problems that mitigate its value.[39] First, the NCS cannot measure crimes in which the victim may have participated, such as drug use, gambling, and fraud. Second, it is only an estimate of crime patterns that probably occurred. The NCS data should not be interpreted to mean that the crimes actually took place.

The NCS also may suffer from victims' underreporting or overreporting of crime. Victims may underreport because they have forgotten an incident or perhaps were not even aware of it—for example, a victim may have thought he misplaced his wallet when it actually was stolen. Victims may know the offender and mistakenly believe they will get the offender in trouble if they discuss the incident with interviewers. Some victims may be embarrassed by the crime and may not wish to discuss it with anyone.

Overreporting can result from victims' misinterpretation of noncriminal incidents. For example, an open front door may be viewed as evidence of attempted burglary, when it actually was the result of carelessness on the part of a family member. Victims may wish to show their cooperation by interpreting minor incidents—being jostled or pushed in the schoolyard, for example—as assaults or attacks.

It is also possible that bias, miscoding, or misinterpretation of fact, or interviewer error, affect the validity of NCS data. Some interviewers may believe they have to record crimes to justify their continued employment.

Though the NCS is not flawless, it represents a major criminological achievement. As you will see in the following chapters, its findings, together with self-reports and UCR data, can help criminologists better understand the nature of crime in the United States.

SUMMARY

Measuring crime is a major goal of criminology. Crime data are usually acquired from surveys of victims and criminals, from longitudinal studies of a cohort followed over time, from records of criminal justice agencies, and from experimental and observational studies.

Official crime statistics are composed of data from the records of police, court, and correctional agencies. The best known official data source is the Uniform Crime Report (UCR), compiled by the Federal Bureau of Investigation. The UCR compiles crimes reported to local police agencies, crimes cleared, and arrests made. The UCR indicates that large cities, warm weather months, and southern and western states have disproportionately high crime rates. In the past few years, about 13 million crimes have been reported annually in the UCR.

Self-report studies ask subjects to tell about their law-violating behavior. Self-reports indicate that the crime rate may be much higher than previously believed.

Victimization surveys ask the victims of crimes about their personal experiences. One study, the National Crime Survey, indicates that about 34 million crimes occur annually.

All three sources of crime statistics have methodological flaws that undermine their validity. The UCR has been criticized because of underreporting by victims, police mismanagement of criminal statistics, and methodological problems. Self-reports rely on the honesty of the respondents, who may or may not wish to reveal their behavior. They have also been criticized for containing trivial acts that are not "real crimes."

Victimization data may contain flaws derived from victims' misinterpretation of events, forgetfulness, and so on.

Nonetheless, all three sources—official crime statistics, self-report studies, and victimization surveys—agree that the crime rate declined between 1980 and 1984, and then increased once again between 1985 and 1987.

KEY TERMS

survey	cohort
cross-sectional research	Uniform Crime
sampling	Reports (UCR)
populations	official crime statistics
self-report surveys	index crimes
victimization surveys	Part I offenses
attitude surveys	Part II offenses
longitudinal research	National Crime
retrospective longitudinal	Survey (NCS)
study	known group method

NOTES

1. Michael Gottfredson and Travis Hirschi, "The Methodological Adequacy of Longitudinal Research on Crime," *Criminology* 25 (1987):581–614.
2. For a general review of the subject, see David Farrington, "Longitudinal Research on Crime and Delinquency," in *Crime and Justice*, vol. 1, ed. Norval Morris and Michael Tonry (Chicago: University of Chicago Press, 1979), pp. 288–348.
3. See, generally, David Farrington, Lloyd Ohlin, and James Q. Wilson, *Understanding and Controlling Crime* (New York: Springer-Verlag, 1986), pp. 11–18.
4. Federal Bureau of Investigation, *Crime in the United States, 1986* (Washington, D.C.: U.S. Government Printing Office, 1987). Herein cited as FBI, *Uniform Crime Report* in footnotes and referred to in text as Uniform Crime Report (UCR). Uniform Crime Report data are supplemented by data from the 1987 crime survey released by the FBI.
5. William F. Whyte, *Street Corner Society* (Chicago: University of Chicago Press, 1955).
6. Herman Schwendinger and Julia Schwendinger, *Adolescent Subcultures and Delinquency* (New York: Praeger, 1985).

7. For a review of these studies, see L. Rowell Huesmann and Neil Malamuth, eds., "Media Violence and Antisocial Behavior," *Journal of Social Issues* 42, no. 3, (1986).

8. Carl Klockars, *The Professional Fence* (New York: Free Press, 1976); Darrell Steffensmeier, *The Fence: In the Shadow of Two Worlds* (Totowa, N.J.: Rowman and Littlefield, 1986).

9. This section adapted from FBI *Uniform Crime Report, 1986*, pp. 1–5.

10. Clarence Schrag, *Crime and Justice: American Style* (Washington, D.C.: U.S. Government Printing Office, 1971).

11. FBI, *Uniform Crime Report, 1986*, p. 41.

12. FBI, *Uniform Crime Report, 1987*.

13. Marshall DeBerry and Catherine Whitaker, *Criminal Victimization, 1986* (Washington, D.C.: U.S. Department of Justice, 1987), p. 4.

14. Philip Ennes, *Criminal Victimization in the United States*, field survey 2 (Report on a National Survey by President's Commission on Law Enforcement and Criminal Justice, Washington, D.C., 1967).

15. Edmund McGarrell and Timothy Flanagan, *Sourcebook of Criminal Justice Statistics, 1984* (Washington, D.C.: U.S. Government Printing Office, 1985), table 3.6.

16. Michael Hindelang and Michael Gottfredson, "The Victim's Decision Not to Involve the Criminal Justice Process," in *Criminal Justice and the Victim*, ed. William F. McDonald (Beverly Hills, Cal.: Sage Publications, 1976), pp. 57–74.

17. Paul Tappan, *Crime, Justice and Corrections* (New York: McGraw-Hill, 1960).

18. Paul Tappan, *Crime, Justice and Corrections*.

19. Daniel Bell, *The End of Ideology* (New York: Free Press, 1967), p. 152.

20. Duncan Chappell, Gilbert Geis, Stephen Schafer, and Larry Siegel, "Forcible Rape: A Comparative Study of Offenses Known to the Police in Boston and Los Angeles," in *Studies in the Sociology of Sex*, ed. James Henslin (New York: Appleton Century Crofts, 1971), pp. 169–93.

21. Lawrence Sherman and Barry Glick, "The Quality of Arrest Statistics," *Police Foundation Reports* 2 (1984):1–8.

22. Patrick Jackson, "Assessing the Validity of Official Data on Arson," *Criminology* 26 (1988):181–95.

23. David Seidman and Michael Couzens, "Getting the Crime Rate Down: Political Pressure and Crime Reporting," *Law and Society Review* 8 (1974):457.

24. Leonard Savitz, "Official Statistics," in *Contemporary Criminology*, ed. Leonard Savitz and Norman Johnston (New York: John Wiley, 1982), pp. 3–15.

25. U.S. Department of Justice, *The Redesigned UCR Program* (Washington, D.C.: U.S. Department of Justice, n.d.).

26. Roger Hood and Richard Sparks, *Key Issues in Criminology* (New York: McGraw-Hill, 1970), p. 72.

27. A pioneering effort in self-report research is A. L. Porterfield, *Youth in Trouble* (Fort Worth, Tex.: Leo Potishman Foundation, 1946). For a review, see Robert Hardt and George Bodine, *Development of Self-Report Instruments in Delinquency Research: A Conference Report* (Syracuse, N.Y.: Syracuse University Youth Development Center, 1965). See also, Fred Murphy, Mary Shirley, and Helen Witner, "The Incidence of Hidden Delinquency," *American Journal of Orthopsychology* 16 (1946):686–96.

28. For example, the following studies have noted the great discrepancy between official statistics and self-report studies: Maynard Erickson and LaMar Empey, "Court Records, Undetected Delinquency and Decision-Making," *Journal of Criminal Law, Criminology and Police Science* 54 (1963):456–69; Martin Gold, "Undetected Delinquent Behavior," *Journal of Research in Crime and Delinquency* 3 (1966):27–46; James Short and F. Ivan Nye, "Extent of Undetected Delinquency, Tentative Conclusions," *Journal of Criminal Law, Criminology and Police Science* 49 (1958):296–302; David Farrington, "Self-Reports of Deviant Behavior: Predictive and Stable?" *Journal of Criminal Law and Criminology* 64 (1973):99–110; Michael Hindelang, "Causes of Delinquency: A Partial Replication and Extension," *Social Problems* 20 (1973):471–87.

29. D. Wayne Osgood, Lloyd Johnston, Patrick O'Malley, and Jerald Bachman, "The Generality of Deviance in Late Adolescence and Early Adulthood," *American Sociological Review* 53 (1988):81–93.

30. Rosemary Sarri, "Gender Issues in Juvenile Justice," *Crime and Delinquency* 29 (1983):381–97.

31. Franklyn Dunford and Delbert Elliott, "Identifying Career Criminals Using Self-Reported Data," *Journal of Research in Crime and Delinquency* 21 (1983):57–86.

32. See, generally, James Hackler and Melanie Lautt, "Systematic Bias in Measuring Self-Reported Delinquency," *Canadian Review of Sociology and Anthropology* 6 (1969):92–106.

33. See, for example: Harwin Voss, "Ethnic Differences in Delinquency in Honolulu," *Journal of Criminal Law, Criminology and Police Science* 54 (1963):322–327; Erickson and Empey, "Court Records"; H. B. Gibson, Sylvia Morrison, and D. J. West, "The Confession of Known Offenses in Response to a Self-Reported Delinquency Schedule," *British Journal of Criminology* 10 (1970):277–80; John Blackmore, "The Relationship Between Self-Reported Delinquency and Official Convictions Amongst Adolescent Boys," *British Journal of Criminology* 14 (1974):172–76.

34. See, for example: Spencer Rathus and Larry Siegel,

"Crime and Personality Revisited: Effects of MMPI Sets on Self-Report Studies," *Criminology* 18 (1980):245–51; John Clark and Larry Tifft, "Polygraph and Interview Validation of Self-Reported Deviant Behavior," *American Sociological Review* 31 (1966):516–23.

35. Michael Hindelang, Travis Hirschi, and Joseph Weis, *Measuring Delinquency* (Beverly Hills, Cal.: Sage Publications, 1981).

36. *Ibid.*, p. 196.

37. The data contained in the following sections were originally presented in National Crime Survey, *Criminal Victimization in the United States, 1986* (Washington, D.C.: U.S. Government Printing Office, 1987).

38. See, generally, James Levine, "The Potential for Crime Over-Reporting in Criminal Victimization Surveys," *Criminology* 14 (1976):307–30; Richard Sparks, "Surveys of Victimization–An Optimistic Assessment," in *Crime and Justice, An Annual Review of Research*, vol. 3, ed. Michael Tonry and Norval Morris (Chicago: University of Chicago Press, 1981), pp. 1–60.

39. See, generally, Levine, "The Potential for Crime Over-Reporting in Criminal Victimization Surveys."

☰ CHAPTER 4

PATTERNS OF CRIME AND VICTIMIZATION

INTRODUCTION

What do the various sources of criminological statistics tell us about crime in America? What is know about the nature of crime, criminals, and their victims? What sociological trends or patterns exist that can help us understand the causes of crime?

These questions are among the most important issues in the criminological literature. They focus attention on the root causes of crime and provide the raw material for criminological theory. Though each of the major sources of criminological research and crime statistics has its limitations, they share enough common ground to allow concrete inferences to be drawn about the nature of crime.

This chapter pulls together the various sources of crime statistics to analyze the social forces influencing crime trends: age, class, sex, and race. Then criminal statistics are used to analyze a major concept in criminological literature—the chronic offender or career criminal. It is alleged that in addition to dividing the population into criminals and noncriminals, the offending population itself can be further subdivided into one-time (or occasional) criminals and chronic offenders, a small group of people who are responsible for a disproportionate share of crime.

Finally, the victims of crime are the focus of analysis. Who are the victims? What factors increase victimization risk? What are the economic costs of crime to victims?

SOCIAL CLASS AND CRIME

A most important issue in the criminological literature is the relationship between **social class** and crime. Traditionally, crime has been thought to be a lower-class phenomenon. This belief is based on the idea that people at the bottom of the social structure have the greatest incentive to commit crimes. Those unable to obtain desired goods and services through conventional means may consequently resort to theft and other illegal activities—such as the sale of narcotics—to obtain them; these activities are referred to as **instrumental crimes.**

Those living in poverty areas are also believed to engage in disproportionate amounts of violent crime as a means of expressing their rage and frustration against society. These kinds of crimes, such as rape and assault, are known as **expressive crimes.** The rates for these crimes may also be higher in poverty areas because those engaging in violence can try to develop an alternative source of positive self-image by viewing themselves as tough or strong, or "bad." If this is so, the cause of crime would be related to a person's place in the social structure.

Official statistics indicate that crime rates in inner-city, high-poverty areas are generally higher than those in suburban or wealthier areas. Studies using aggregate police statistics (arrest records) have consistently shown that crime rates in lower-class areas are higher than in wealthier neighborhoods. Chapter 7 summarizes those theories which rely on the relationship between social class and crime. As a group, these theoretical models suggest that people who grow up in deteriorating neighborhoods, who attend substandard schools, and who desire middle-class luxuries but are incapable of achieving them are the ones most likely to commit criminal acts.[1] Backing up these views are research efforts which use aggregate police and census bureau statistics to show that crime rates are higher in lower-class neighborhoods.[2]

An alternate explanation for these findings is that the relationship between official crime and social class is a function of law enforcement practices and not actual criminal behavior patterns. Police may devote more resources to poverty areas and consequently apprehension rates may be higher there. Similarly, police may be more likely to formally arrest and prosecute lower-class citizens than those in the middle and upper classes.

Because of these factors, self-report data have been used extensively to test the class-crime relationship. If people in all social classes self-report similar crime patterns, but only those in the lower class are formally arrested, this would explain the higher crime rates in lower-class neighborhoods. However, if lower-class people report greater criminal activity than their middle- and upper-class peers, it would indicate that the official statistics are an accurate representation of the crime problem.

Surprisingly, the first self-report studies, specifically those conducted by James Short and F. Ivan Nye, did not find a direct relationship between social class and youth crime.[3] They found that socioeconomic class was related to official processing by police, court, and correctional agencies, but not to the actual commission of crimes. In other words, while lower-class and middle-class youths self-reported equal amounts of crime, the lower-class youths had a greater chance of being arrested, convicted, and incarcerated, and of becoming official delinquents. In addition, factors generally associated with lower-class membership, such as broken homes, were found to be related to institutionalization but not to admissions of delinquency. Other contemporary studies reached similar conclusions.[4]

For more than twenty years after the use of self-reports became widespread, a majority of self-report studies agreed that a class-crime relationship did not exist: if the poor possessed greater criminal records than the wealthy, it was because of differential law enforcement and not class-based behavior differences.[5] In what is considered to be the definitive work on this subject, Charles Tittle, Wayne Villemez, and Douglas Smith reviewed 35 studies containing 363 separate estimates concerning the relationship between class and crime.[6] They concluded that little if any support exists for the contention that crime is primarily a lower-class phenomenon. Consequently, Tittle and his associates argued that official statistics probably reflect class bias in the processing of the lower class.[7] The Tittle review is usually cited by criminologists as the strongest statement refuting the claim that the lower class is disproportionately criminal.

The Class/Crime Controversy

The self-report findings showing little or no relationship between class and crime have had a significant effect on criminological theory. If crime is not purely a function of social class, and if there are no significant distinctions in the crime rate across economic class lines, then it is evident that the causes of crime must be found in social experiences common to all people—poor family environment, peer pressure, school failure, stigma, and labeling. Consequently, sociological theories were developed that focus on *socialization* and not class membership as the primary cause of crime. (These theories are discussed in Chapter 8.)

However, not all criminologists agree with Tittle's findings. Critics usually point to the inclusion of trivial offenses—for example, using a false ID—in most self-report instruments. They contend that although

middle- and upper-class people may appear to be as criminal as those in the lower class, it is only because they frequently engage in trivial offenses such as petty larceny, using recreational drugs, and simple assault; conversely, if only serious Part I offenses are considered, a true class-crime relationship should emerge.

The most widely cited evidence that a class-crime relationship exists can be found in the work of Delbert Elliott and his colleagues Suzanne Ageton and David Huizinga. Using a carefully drawn national sample of 1,726 youths ages eleven to seventeen and a sophisticated self-report instrument, Elliott and Ageton found lower-class youths to be much more likely than middle-class youths to engage in serious delinquent acts such as burglary, assault, robbery, sexual assault, and vandalism.[8] Moreover, lower-class youths were much more likely than middle-class youths to have committed ''numerous'' serious personal and property crimes (more than 200). These findings forced Elliott and Ageton to conclude that self-report data give findings about class and crime that actually are similar to those of official data. Furthermore, the authors charge that studies showing middle- and lower-class youths to be equally delinquent rely on measures weighted toward minor crimes (for example, using a false ID or skipping school). When serious crimes like burglary and assault are used in the comparison, lower-class youths are significantly more delinquent.

In a follow-up study, Elliott and Huizinga again found that middle-class youths are much less likely to commit serious crime than lower-class youths. There were substantial class differences in both the prevalence and incidence of serious crime.[9]

The weight of recent evidence seems to point to the conclusion that serious crime is more prevalent among the lower classes. However, this is not the final word on the issue. In a landmark study, *Measuring Delinquency*, Michael Hindelang, Travis Hirschi, and Joseph Weis found that while self-reports and official statistics were comparable, the observable relationship between social class and crime was relatively weak in *both* self-report and official data. They concluded:

> There is no apparent systematic bias in either self-report or official measures of delinquency at the individual level associated with social class of sufficient magnitude to produce misleading results if one measure of delinquency rather than the other were used.[10]

TABLE 4.1   Arrests by Age
Distribution of the United States

Age	Percent of Population	Percent of Index Arrests	Percent of All Arrests
Under 10	15.0	0.7	0.4
10–12	4.0	2.7	1.4
13–14	3.0	7.3	5.5
15	1.5	5.5	4.8
16	1.5	5.8	5.1
17	1.5	5.4	4.5
18	1.5	4.8	4.2
19	1.6	4.3	4.2
20	1.7	4.0	4.1
21	1.7	3.8	4.3
22	1.7	3.8	4.4
23	1.7	3.7	4.4
24	1.8	3.5	4.2
25–29	9.0	15.4	18.0
30–34	8.0	10.7	12.2
35–39	7.0	6.7	7.6
40–44	6.0	3.8	4.2
45–64	18.0	6.8	5.9
Over 65	12.0	1.5	0.8

SOURCE: *Uniform Crime Reports, 1986* (1987); U.S. Dept. of Commerce, Census Data, 1986.

After careful analysis, these three eminent criminologists disputed a class-crime relationship in either self-report or official statistics.

Rethinking Class and Crime.   The class-crime relationship remains one of the most enduring criminological controversies. The confusion is likely to continue as long as different measures of crime and class are used. A number of researchers have found that the way these variables are interpreted and calculated influences the interrelationship between them. For example, David Brownfield found that some widely used measures of social class, such as parents' occupation and education, are only weakly related to self-reported crime, while others, such as being unemployed or a welfare recipient, were strong correlates of criminality.[11] Douglas Smith and Laura Davidson found that the comparability of self-reported crime measures varies across race and sex groups.[12] Similarly, Robert Sampson has shown that class-related variables have a different impact on the crime rate of people according to their age and race.[13]

These research efforts indicate that the class-crime relationship may vary according to the measures used and the people measured, a conclusion which highlights the need for more rigorous research efforts in the future.

AGE AND CRIME

There is general agreement that age is inversely related to criminality.[14] As criminologists Travis Hirschi and Michael Gottfredson state, "Age is everywhere correlated with crime. Its effects on crime do not depend on other demographic correlates of crime."[15] Regardless of economic or marital status, race, or sex, younger people commit crime more often than their older peers.

Official statistics tell us that young people are arrested at a disproportionate rate to their numbers in the population; victim surveys generate similar findings for crimes in which the age of the assailant can be determined. Table 4.1 provides arrest rates for people at various age levels compared to their percentage of the population. This data dramatically illustrates the age-crime relationship: while youths 15 to 18 collectively make up about 6 percent of the total U.S. population, they account for about 25 percent of the index crime arrests and 15 percent of the arrests for all crimes. As a general rule, the peak age for property crime is believed to be 16 and for violent crime 18. In contrast, adults 45 and over, who make up 30 percent of the population, account for only 6 percent of the index crime arrests. The elderly are particularly resistant to the temptations of crime: they make up 12 percent of the population and less than 1 percent of the arrests.[16] Elderly males 65 and over are predominantly arrested for alcohol-related matters (public drunkenness, drunk driving), and elderly females for larceny theft (shoplifting); the crime rate of both groups has remained stable for the past 20 years.[17]

It is also possible to derive some estimates of rates of offending by age for the violent personal crimes measured by the National Crime Survey (NCS), because the victims had the opportunity to view their attackers and estimate their age categories. Research by **John Laub** and his colleagues at the Hindelang Research Center in Albany, New York, shows that the estimated rates of offending for youths aged 18 to 20 is about three times greater than the estimated rate of adults 21 and over; youths 12 to 17 offended at a rate twice that of adults (see Figure 4.1). In addition, Laub found that for some specific crimes, such as robbery and personal larceny, the youthful offending rate is perceived to be almost six times the adult rate.[18]

The Age/Crime Controversy

The relationship between age and crime is of major theoretical importance because existing criminological theories fail to adequately explain why the crime rate drops with age; this drop is referred to as the **aging out** or **desistance phenomenon.** This theoretical failure has been the subject of considerable academic debate. One position, championed by criminologists **Travis Hirschi** and **Michael Gottfredson,** is that the relationship between age and crime is *constant*, and therefore, the age variable is actually irrelevant to the study of

crime.[19] Because all people, regardless of their demographic characteristics (race, gender, class, family structure, domicile, work status), commit less crime as they age, it is not important to consider age as a factor in explaining crime.[20] Even hard-core chronic offenders will commit less crime as they age.[21] Hirschi and Gottfredson find that differences in group offending rates (for example, between males and females or between the rich and poor) which exist at any point in the groups' life cycles will be maintained throughout their lives. In other words, if 15-year-old boys are four times as likely to commit crime as fifteen-year-old girls, then 50-year-old men will be four times as likely to commit crime as 50-year-old women (though the actual number of crimes committed by both males and females will constantly decline).

Hirschi and Gottfredson's view has biological overtones: as they age, people commit less crime because they lack strength, ambition, energy, mobility, and so on. This position has been supported by the research of Walter Gove, who finds that the "universality" of maturational changes in the crime rate suggests that it must be part of a biological "evolutionary process."[22]

Those who oppose the Hirschi/Gottfredson view of the age-crime relationship suggest that there are social factors directly associated with a person's age, such as lifestyle, economic situation, or peer relations, which explain the aging out process.[23] For example, David Farrington has shown that people begin to specialize in crime as they age, and that the frequency or type of an offender's criminal behavior is not constant. Farrington and his associates Alfred Blumstein and Jacqueline Cohen are the leading advocates of studying criminality as a career, which undergoes evolving patterns or cycles over a person's lifetime.[24]

The probability that a person will become a chronic or career criminal may be determined by the age at which that person begins his or her offending career.[25] Arnold Barnett, Alfred Blumstein, and David Farrington argue that the population may contain different sets of criminal offenders, one group whose criminality declines with age (as predicted by Hirschi and Gottfredson) and another whose criminal behavior remains constant as the group members mature.[26] This view is supported by research conducted by Darrell Steffensmeier and his associates, who found that while the rates of some crimes are associated with age, others do not peak as early or decline as fast.

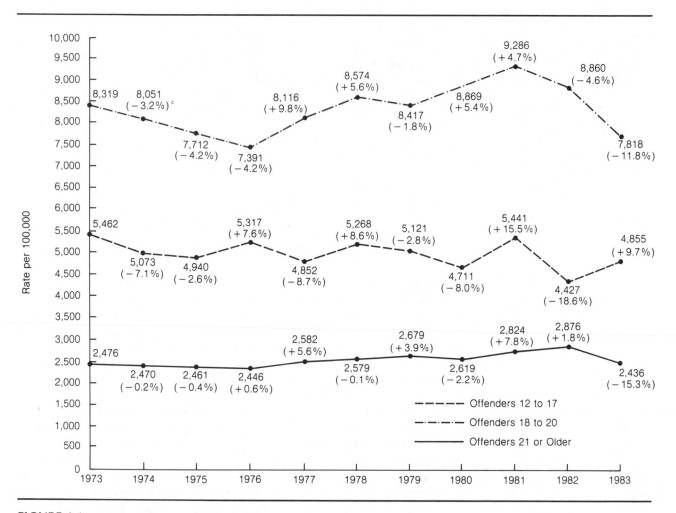

FIGURE 4.1   Estimated Rates of Offending in Total Personal Crimes, by Year and Perceived Age of Offender

SOURCE: Laub, et al., *Trends in Juvenile Crime (1987)*, p. 4.

Crimes which provide significant economic gain, such as gambling, embezzlement, and fraud, are less likely to decline with maturity than high-risk, low-profit offenses such as assault.[27] Steffensmeier's research also indicates that the age-crime pattern is changing: a greater proportion of criminal behavior is concentrated among youthful offenders than it was 40 years ago.

Other criminologists, most notably David Greenberg, have created theoretical models which directly link age to crime (see Chapter 9). Greenberg believes that age-related factors are important influences on criminality, and he, along with Farrington, maintains that the age when a person begins his or her criminal career is an important determinant of offending patterns.[28] A person who gets involved in criminality at a very early age and who gains an official record will be the most likely to become a career criminal: the age of onset of criminality is a key determinant of the probability of future law violations.[29]

In sum, some criminologists view the relationship between crime and age as constant, while others believe that it varies according to offense and offender. This difference has important implications for criminological research and theory. If age is a constant, then the criminality of any group can be accurately measured at any single point in time. If, on the other hand, the relationship between age and crime varies, it

There is general agreement that age is inversely related to criminality.

would be necessary to conduct longitudinal studies in order to fully understand how age influences offending patterns.[30] Crime then would be conceived of as a type of social event which takes on different meanings at different times in a person's life.[31] This critical issue has produced some of the most spirited debates in the recent criminological literature.[32]

Why Does Aging Out Occur?

Despite the debate raging over the relationship between age and crime, there is little question that the crime rate declines with age. Why does this phenomenon take place?

There are a number of explanations for the aging out or desistance phenomenon. Some recent research indicates that the desistance is caused by a cognitive change occurring in the late teens; at this point troubled youths are able to develop a long-term life view and resist the need for immediate gratification.[33] Gordon Trasler agrees with this view when he suggests that "much teenage crime is fun." Risky and exciting, youths view their petty crimes as a social activity which provide adventure in an otherwise boring and unsympathetic world. As they grow older, Trasler finds, their life patterns are inconsistent with criminality; delinquents literally grow out of crime.[34]

James Q. Wilson and Richard Herrnstein argue that the aging out process is a function of the natural history of the human life cycle.[35] Adolescent deviance is fueled by the need for conventionally unobtainable money and sex and reinforced by close relationships with peers who defy conventional morality. At the same time that teenagers are becoming independent from parents and other adults who enforce conventional standards, their new sense of energy and strength, combined with a lack of economic and social skills and relationships with peers who are similarly vigorous and frustrated, create the conditions needed for a rise in criminality.

Why does the crime rate then decline? Wilson and Herrnstein find that as a person matures, the small gains from petty crime lose their attraction. Legitimate sources of money, sex, alcohol, and status become available. Adulthood brings increasingly powerful ties to conventional society, not the least of which is the acquisition of a family. Adult peers further make crime an unattractive choice by expressing opinions in opposition to risk taking and law violation. Adults also develop the ability to delay gratification and forego the immediate gains that law violations bring.

Wilson and Herrnstein's explanation of the desistance phenomenon is closely linked to socialization. However, research conducted by Barry Glassner, Margaret Ksander, Bruce Berg, and Bruce Johnson finds that aging out of crime also might be linked to a very practical consideration: the fear of punishment.[36] According to Glassner and his associates, youths are well aware that once they reach their legal majority punishment takes a decidedly harsher turn. They are no longer protected by the kindly arms of the juvenile justice system. As one teenage boy told them:

> When you're a teenager you're rowdy. Nowadays you aren't rowdy. You know, you want to settle down because you can go to jail now. [When] you are a boy, you can be put into a detention home. But you can go to jail now. Jail ain't no place to go.[37]

Additionally, as Charles Tittle suggests, the likelihood of aging out of crime may be more a function of interpersonal relationships than the result of any physical or emotional process. Children who get in trouble with the law at an early age, who are labeled by teachers, police, parents, and neighbors as troublemakers, and who consequently may find their relationships to others weakened or broken, may have little choice but to remain committed to their criminal careers.[38] While most people desist, some may find a criminal career a reasonable alternative. Yet, even people who remain active in a criminal career will eventually slow down. Crime is too dangerous, physically taxing, and unrewarding, and punishments too harsh and long lasting, to become a long-term way of life for most people.

GENDER AND CRIME

The three major forms of criminal statistics generally agree that male crime rates are considerably higher than those of females. The National Crime Survey (NCS) indicates that the personal crime rate of male offenders 18 to 20 years old was an astounding 26,367 per 100,000, while the rate for females 18 to 20 years old was 2,088 per 100,000—about a tenth as much. In approximately 87 percent of all cases of violent personal crime, victims identified the offender as being male.[39]

The Uniform Crime Report (UCR) arrest statistics also indicate the predominance of male criminality. The overall male-female arrest ratio is usually about four male offenders to one female offender; for violent crimes the ratio is closer to nine males to one female. Recent self-report studies also show significant male-female differences. Rosemary Sarri found that while male-female ratios for minor offenses (truancy) were quite similar, there were major discrepancies for serious crimes, such as assault and burglary.[40] Delbert Elliott's National Youth Survey and the national survey by Jay Williams and Martin Gold also found that males commit more serious crimes. Hindelang, Hirschi, and Weis concluded that in general self-report results mirror official crime data—males commit much more serious crime than females.[41]

Early Views of Gender and Crime

Because of gender differences in the crime rate, the focus of criminology has been on male crime patterns. As a result, criticism has been leveled recently at the field's inattention to the role of women in the crime process.[42]

The early criminological literature paid scant attention to female criminals. Because of their relatively few numbers, some early writings portrayed female criminals as emotional, physical, or psychological aberrations. The most widely cited evidence was contained in Cesare Lombroso's 1895 book, *The Female Offender*.[43] Lombroso argued that whereas women generally were more passive and less criminal than men, there was a small group of female criminals who lacked "typical" female traits of "piety, maternity, underdeveloped intelligence, and weakness."[44] In physical appearance as well as in emotional makeup,

Freda Adler's research focused attention on the female offender.

delinquent females appeared closer to both criminal and noncriminal men than to other women. Lombroso's theory became known as the *masculinity hypothesis;* in essence, a few "masculine" females were responsible for the handful of crimes women actually commit.

Another early view of female crime focussed on the supposed dynamics of sexual relationships. Female criminals were in turn viewed as either sexually controlling or sexually naive; either manipulating men for profit or being manipulated by them. W. I. Thomas portrayed the female criminal as a member of the underclass, someone whose desire for excitement and wish fulfillment made her an easy prey for men who forced her into a life of crime and prostitution. Thirty years later, Otto Pollack described the female criminal as a "devious being," whose criminality was masked because criminal justice authorities were reluctant to take action against her.[45] Referred to as the **chivalry hypothesis,** this view holds that much of the criminality of women is masked because of the generally protective attitudes towards women in our culture.[46] In other words, police are less likely to arrest, juries less likely to convict, and judges less likely to incarcerate female offenders. Though most research efforts conclude that the differences in processing female and

male offenders has declined, some research efforts do show that the justice system is still more apt to severely punish males than females.[47] For example, Cassia Spohn and her associates found that prosecutors were more likely to dismiss charges made against female defendants and prosecute males to the fullest extent of the law.[48]

Recent Views of Female Criminality

By mid-century it was common for criminologists to portray gender differences in the crime rate as a function of socialization. Textbooks explained the relatively low female crime rate by citing the facts that in contrast to boys, girls were supervised more closely, taught to be "nice" and "ladylike" rather than rough and tough, protected from competition, and trained for a domestic life.[49] The few female criminals were described as troubled individuals, alienated at home, who pursued crime as a means of compensating for their disrupted personal lives.[50] The streets became a "second home" to girls whose physical and emotional adjustment was hampered by a strained home life, marked by such conditions as absent fathers and overly competitive mothers.

In the seventies, several influential works, most notably Freda Adler's *Sisters in Crime* and Rita James Simon's *The Contemporary Woman and Crime,* revolutionized thinking on the cause of gender differences in the crime rate.[51] Their research focused attention on the social and economic roles of women in society and their relationship to female crime rates. Both Adler and Simon believed that the traditionally lower crime rate for women could be explained by women's "second-class" economic and social position. They further contended that, as women's social roles changed and their lifestyles became more like those of males, their criminal activity also would become similar.

Criminologists, responding to this research, began to refer to the "new female criminal." The rapid increase in the female crime rate during the 1960s and 1970s, especially in areas that traditionally had been male dominated crimes (burglary, larceny) gave support to the model presented by Adler and Simon. In addition, self-report studies seemed to indicate that the pattern of female criminality, if not its frequency, was quite similar to that of male criminality.[52]

TABLE 4.2 Offense Patterns Differ for Males and Females

UCR Index Crimes	Percent of all arrests	
	Males	Females
Murder and non-negligent manslaughter	88	12
Rape	99	1
Robbery	92	8
Aggravated assault	87	14
Burglary	92	8
Larceny-theft	69	31
Motor vehicle theft	90	10
Arson	86	14

● Men are more likely than women to be arrested for the more serious crimes, such as murder, rape, robbery, or burglary.

● Arrest, jail, and prison data all suggest that a higher proportion of women than of men who commit crimes are involved in property crimes, such as larceny, forgery, fraud, and embezzlement, and in drug offenses.

SOURCE: FBI, *Crime in the United States, 1987.*

The "New" Female Criminal Reconsidered. Increases in the female crime rate were not sustained in the 1980s, causing some scholars to reassess the concept of the "new" female criminal.[53] Some criminologists conclude that the emancipation of women may have had relatively little influence on female crime rates.[54] As a group, they believe that any increase in the female arrest rate is not reflective of economic or social change brought about by the women's movement. For one thing, many female criminals come from the socioeconomic class least affected by the women's movement; their crimes seem more a function of economic inequality than feminine rights.[55] For another, the offense patterns of women are still quite different from those of men. Men still commit a disproportionate share of serious crimes, such as robbery, burglary, murder, and assault.[56] Another view reassessing the "new" female criminal maintains that female arrest rates rose in the 1960s and 1970s because police, angry over affirmative action programs, were willing to formally arrest and process female offenders. This view suggests that female liberation brought an end to the "chivalry hypothesis."[57]

In light of these findings, some criminologists are reconsidering their view of female criminality. Gender dissimilarities in the crime rate are once again being explained by differences in socialization and life experiences. Meda Chesney-Lind finds that a significant amount of female delinquency, which most often involves such acts as truancy, running away, and petty theft, can be traced to physical and sexual abuse in the home.[58] She writes, "Young women on the run from homes characterized by sexual abuse and parental neglect are forced, by the very statutes designed to protect them, into the life of an escaped convict."[59] Gregg Barak has shown that the criminal justice system's ability to reduce family violence directed against young girls remains inadequate.[60]

In their **power-control theory,** John Hagan and his associates have speculated that the onset of female criminality is influenced by economic conditions, social class position, and the structure of family life.[61] In lower-class, father-dominated or **paternalistic** families, the socialization process prepares girls for the "cult of domesticity," blunting both their freedom and the probability of their criminality. On the other hand, in middle-class **egalitarian** families—those, in which husband and wife share similar positions of power at home and in the workplace—and also in single-parent households, young girls gain a kind of freedom that reflects reduced parental control. These types of families produce daughters whose law-violating behavior resembles their brothers'.[62] By implication, middle-class girls are the most likely to violate the law because they are less closely controlled than their lower-class sisters.

As these views indicate, gender differences in the crime rate remain a hotly debated topic in the criminological community. However, there is general agreement that females are significantly less criminal than males, and that gender differences in criminality, once thought to be narrowing, have remained rather stable.

RACE AND CRIME

All three sources of criminal statistics provide evidence that minority group members are involved in a disproportionate share of criminal activity than the general population. The Uniform Crime Report (UCR) tells us that although black citizens make up about 12

TABLE 4.3   Race and Violent Crime: NCS and UCR
Percentages

Crime Category	UCR		NCS	
	White	Black	White	Black
Rape	50	48	67	33
Robbery	37	62	38	55
Aggravated assault	58	40	71	25

SOURCE: *Crime in the United States, 1986; Criminal Victimization in the United States, 1986.*

percent of the general population, they account for about 46 percent of the violent crime arrests and 30 percent of the property crime arrests, as well as a disproportionate number of Part II arrests (except for alcohol-related arrests, which are primarily of white offenders).[63] Since the UCR statistics represent arrest data, racial differences in the crime rate may be more a reflection of police practices than a true picture of criminal participation. Consequently, criminologists have sought to verify the UCR findings through analysis of NCS and self-report data.

The NCS supplies racial data on crimes in which victims were able to observe their attackers—rape, assault, and robbery. John Laub and his associates analyzed NCS data and found that the results were consistent with the official crime statistics.[64] As Table 4.3 shows, the proportion of victims who identified their assailant as black is comparable to the ratio of minorities in the arrest statistics.

Blacks are identified as committing a disproportionate share of personal violent crime. Nonetheless, the proportions are somewhat less than reported in the UCR arrest statistics, especially for the crime of rape. This could mean that police are more likely to arrest black suspects for that crime, or that women attacked by black offenders are more likely to report the crime to police. Also, rape tends to be an intraracial crime; black women are more likely to report rapes to police (67 percent) than white women (50 percent).

Explanations of Racial Differences

Racial differences in the crime rate is an extremely sensitive issue. Before victimization data were available, official crime (UCR) data were suspected of re-

flecting discriminatory arrest practices. In other words, racial differences could be explained by the reluctance of police to patrol and make arrests in primarily white areas, coupled with the concentration of resources in minority communities. However, today many criminologists recognize that recorded differences in the crime rate cannot be explained away solely by differential treatment within the criminal justice system.[65]

How, then, can racial disparities be explained? Most theories put forward to explain black-white crime differentials focus on elements of economic deprivation, social disorganization, subcultural adaptations, and the legacy of racism and discrimination on personality and behavior.[66]

One approach has been to trace the black experience in America. Some criminologists view black crime as a function of socialization in a society where the black family was torn apart and black culture destroyed in such a way that recovery has proven impossible. James P. Comer, in *American Violence and Public Policy*, argues that the early slave experiences left a wound that has been deepened by racism and lack of opportunity.[67] Children of the slave society were thrust into a system of forced dependency and negative self-feelings. Comer writes that it was a system that promoted powerful forces for identification with an aggressor (slave master and other whites) and ambivalence and antagonism toward one's self and group. After emancipation, blacks were shut out of the social and political mainstream. Frustrated, angry, they were isolated in segregated communities, turning within for support. Their entire American experience provided for negative self-images, anger, and rage. Comer states:

> In reaction to failure, the most vibrant and reactive often become disrupted and violent in and out of schools, both individually and in groups or gangs. Neighborhoods and communities of adequately functioning families are then overwhelmed by the reactive and most troubled individuals and families. Models of violence and other troublesome behavior for children abound in relatives, friends, and neighbors unsuccessful in previous generations.[68]

According to Comer, the intraracial nature of black violence is in reaction to an "inability to cope with the large society or to identify with black and white leaders and institutional achievements. Frustration and anger is taken out on people most like self."[69] Comer's view fits well with the criminological concept that a **subculture of violence,** which condones the use of physical force as a solution for everyday encounters, has developed in inner-city ghetto areas.[70]

In his influential book, *Criminal Violence, Criminal Justice,* Charles Silberman also views the problem as a function of the black experience in this country—"an experience that differs from that of other ethnic groups." Silberman's provocative argument is that black citizens have learned to be violent because of their treatment in U.S. society. First, they were violently uprooted from their African homeland. Then their slavery was maintained by violence. After emancipation, their lower-class position was enforced by violent means, such as intimidation by the Ku Klux Klan. To strike back meant harsh retaliation by the white-controlled law. Moving to northern cities, blacks suffered two burdens unknown to other migrants: their color and their heritage of slavery. After all, the color black in western culture connotes dirty or bad things, while white stands for goodness and purity. Consequently, to survive and to reach cultural and personal fulfillment, blacks have developed their own set of norms, values, and traditions. In the 1960s, many blacks began to adopt the image, first developed in southern folklore and myth, of being "bad" in their personal lives. After 350 years of fearing whites, Silberman writes, "Black Americans have discovered that the fear runs the other way, that whites are intimidated by their very presence; it would be hard to overestimate what an extraordinarily liberating force this discovery is . . . 350 years of festering hatred has come spilling out."[71]

Racial patterns in the crime rate also have been tied to trends in black political participation and educational attainment. Roy Austin found that the Black Power movement's emphasis on the self-concept of the black community, coupled with economic and social gains, was associated with a relative decrease in the ratio between white and black violence rates in the 1970s. Austin concludes that it may take a social movement as sweeping and powerful as Black Power to alter crime producing subcultural values and promote crime reducing social change, such as economic and political power in minority communities.[72]

The racial difference in the crime rate is a highly complex and emotional issue that still defies accurate interpretation. For example, even if arrest and victim data were interpreted as showing that minorities engage in a disproportionate amount of crime, we still would not be sure whether a larger proportion of the black population commits crime, or whether the percentage of white and black criminals is similar but a few black offenders commit crime more frequently or over a longer period of their lives.[73] The true nature of racial differences in the crime rate awaits further exploration.

THE CHRONIC OFFENDER: CAREER CRIMINALS

No issue in criminology has been more widely discussed than the "discovery" of the **chronic offender** or **career criminal.** Researchers, using survey and record data, have found that the offender population can be divided into a larger group of one-time or occasional criminals, and a small group of hard-core career offenders. This latter group commits a far greater share of the most serious and violent crimes, including armed robberies, burglaries, and assaults, than their numbers warrant. Chronic offenders become involved in crime at an extremely early age and are likely to persist as offenders as teenagers and into adulthood.[74]

The controversy surrounding the chronic offender concept involves its policy implications. If only a small group of people—the chronic offenders—commits enormous amounts of crime, it follows that if these people were incapacitated for long periods of time, their absence from society would have an appreciable effect on the crime rate. Criminal justice policy based on the chronic offender concept demands that career criminals be set apart from society based on their demonstrated threat to public safety and the high probability that they will engage in serious crime in the future.

The chronic offender concept is the result of research using both official and self-report data. Some important studies of the chronic offender are discussed in detail in the following sections.

Wolfgang's Delinquency in a Birth Cohort

The concept of the chronic or career offender is most closely associated with the research efforts of **Marvin**

Marvin Wolfgang (left) first identified the chronic offender. Robert Figlio (center) and Paul Tracy (right) also helped to conduct the birth cohort studies. These cohort studies are considered to be some of the most important studies of the twentieth century in this field.

Wolfgang and his associates at the University of Pennsylvania.[75] In 1972, Wolfgang, Robert Figlio, and Thorsten Sellin published a landmark study, *Delinquency in a Birth Cohort,* which has profoundly influenced the very concept of the criminal offender.

Wolfgang, Figlio, and Sellin used official records to follow the criminal careers of a cohort of 9,945 boys born in Philadelphia, Pennsylvania, in 1945, from the time of their birth until they reached 18 years of age in 1963. Official police records were used to identify delinquents. About one-third of the boys (3,475) had some police contact. The remaining two-thirds (6,470) had none. Each delinquent's actions were given a seriousness weight score for every delinquent act.[76] The weighting of delinquent acts allowed the researchers to differentiate, for example, between a simple assault requiring no medical attention for the victim and a serious assault in which the victim needed hospitalization.

Wolfgang and his colleagues obtained data from school records, including subject IQ scores and measures of academic performance and conduct. Socio-economic status was determined by locating the residence of each member of the cohort and assigning him the median family income for that area.

The most well-known discovery of Wolfgang and his associates was that of the so-called chronic offender. The cohort data indicated that 54 percent (1,862) of the sample's delinquent youths were repeat offenders, while the remaining 46 percent (1,613) were one-time offenders. However, the repeaters could be further categorized as nonchronic and **chronic recidivists.** The former consisted of 1,235 youths who had been arrested more than once but less than five times, and who made up 35.6 percent of all delinquents. The latter were a group of 627 boys arrested five times or more who accounted for 18 percent of the delinquents and 6 percent of the total sample of 9,945.[77]

It was the chronic offenders (known today as ''the chronic 6 percent'') who were involved in the most dramatic amounts of delinquent behavior; they were responsible for 5,305 offenses, or 51.9 percent of all offenses. Even more striking was the involvement of chronic offenders in serious criminal acts. Of the entire sample, they committed 71 percent of the homicides, 73 percent of the rapes, 82 percent of the robberies, and 69 percent of the aggravated assaults.

Wolfgang and his associates found that arrest and court experience did little to deter the chronic offenders. In fact, disposition was inversely related to chronic offending—the stricter the disposition chronic offenders received, the more likely they would be to engage in repeated criminal behavior. Strict dispositions also increased the probability that further court action would be taken. Two factors stood out as encouraging recidivism—the seriousness of the original offense and the severity of disposition.

Birth Cohort Follow-Up

In a second analysis, Wolfgang and his associates followed a 10 percent sample of the original cohort (974 subjects) through their adulthood to age 30. They divided the sample into three groups: those who had been juvenile offenders only, those who were adult offenders only, and persistent offenders (those who had offenses in both time periods). Those classified as chronic juvenile offenders in the original birth cohort made up 70 percent of the "persistent" group. They had an 80 percent change of becoming adult offenders and a 50 percent change of being arrested four or more times as adults. In comparison, subjects with no juvenile arrests had only an 18 percent chance of being arrested as an adult. The chronic offenders also continued to engage in the most serious crimes. Though they accounted for only 15 percent of the follow-up sample, the former chronic delinquents were involved in 74 percent of all arrests and 82 percent of all serious crimes, such as homicide, rape, and robbery. Clearly, chronic juvenile offenders continue their law-violating careers as adults.

Birth Cohort II

The subjects who made up Wolfgang's original birth cohort were born in 1945. How have behavior patterns changed in subsequent years? To answer this question, Wolfgang and his associates selected a new, larger birth cohort, born in Philadelphia in 1958, and followed them until their maturity. The 1958 cohort has 28,338 subjects—13,811 males and 14,527 females.

Although the proportion of delinquent youths is about the same as that in the 1945 cohort, those in the larger sample were involved in 20,089 delinquent arrests. Chronic offenders (five or more arrests for juveniles) made up 7.5 percent of the 1958 sample (compared with 6.3 percent in 1945) and 23 percent of all delinquent offenders (compared with 18 percent in 1945). Chronic female delinquency was relatively rare—only 1 percent of the females in the survey were chronic offenders.

Chronic male delinquents continued to commit more than their share of criminal behavior. They accounted for 61 percent of the total offenses and a disproportionate amount of the most serious crimes: 61 percent of the homicides, 76 percent of the rapes, 73 percent of the robberies, and 65 percent of the aggravated assaults. The chronic female offender was less likely to be involved in serious crimes.

It is interesting that the 1958 cohort, as a group, was involved in significantly more serious crime than the 1945 group. For example, their violent offense rate (149 per 1,000 in the sample) was three times higher than the rate for the 1945 cohort (which was 47 per 1,000 subjects).

The 1945 cohort study found that chronic offenders dominate the total crime rate and continue their law-violating careers as adults. The newer cohort study is showing that the chronic offender syndrome is being maintained in a group of subjects who were born 13 years later than the original cohort and, if anything, are more violent than their older brothers. Finally, the efforts of the justice system seem to have little deterrent effect on the behavior of chronic offenders: the more often a person was arrested, the more likely he or she was to be arrested again. For males, 26 percent of the entire group had one violent arrest; of that 26 percent, 34 percent went on to a second violent offense and 43 percent of the three-time offenders went on to a fourth arrest.

Policy Implications of the Chronic Offender Concept

Wolfgang's research has had a major effect on criminological thought. Subsequent efforts by researchers have in part duplicated Wolfgang's findings, both in the United States and abroad.[78] There has been a significant shift of both criminological attention and gov-

Most personal victimizations occur publicly in urban areas during the evening hours.

ernment funding toward the separate but interrelated concepts of "career criminals" and their "criminal careers."[79]

The chronic or career criminal has been an accepted element of criminological thought and criminal justice policy. The chronic offender is today a central focus of criminal justice system policy. Concern about repeat offenders has been translated into programs at various stages of the justice process. For example, police departments and district attorneys' offices around the nation have set up programs to focus their resources on capturing and prosecuting dangerous or repeat offenders. Susan Martin has described the encouraging results of the Repeat Offender Project of the Washington, D.C., police department, a 60-person unit designed to aggressively pursue suspected chronic offenders.[80]

Even more important has been the effect of the chronic offender on sentencing policy. Around the country, legal jurisdictions are developing sentencing policies designed to incapacitate serious offenders for long periods of time without hope of probation or parole. Among the programs spurred by the chronic offender concept is the use of mandatory sentences for violent or drug-related crimes in more than 30 state jurisdictions. The logic behind these policies is that since chronic offenders cannot be deterred, they must be incarcerated for as long as possible when found guilty of repeat offenses.

Since the nation's prison system is filled to capacity, any attempt to incarcerate large-numbers of dangerous offenders must be tempered by the limits of the penal system to house them. This dilemma has led senior Rand Corporation researcher Peter Greenwood to advocate a policy of **selective incapacitation** as a means of controlling career criminals.[81] According to Greenwood, career criminals usually share the following characteristics:

- Incarceration for more than half the two-year period preceding the most recent arrest
- A prior conviction for the crime that is being predicted
- Juvenile conviction prior to age 16
- Commitment to a state or federal juvenile facility
- Heroin or barbiturate use in the two-year period preceding the current arrest
- Heroin or barbiturate use as a juvenile
- Employment for less than half the two-year period preceding the current arrest

☰ CLOSE-UP

Criminals and Victims: Are They Really So Different?

The national victimization data show that the people most likely to become crime victims share many personal characteristics and traits, including gender, race, age, class, and environment, with those who are most likely to be arrested for criminal offenses. Is this relationship mere coincidence?

There are two explanations for this phenomenon which are currently popular among criminologists. One is that both groups live in close physical proximity to one another, and criminals tend to select victims who share similar backgrounds and circumstances. The second explanation is that the two groups are not really separate at all: crime victims will one day victimize other people; criminals were once victims themselves.

The proximity argument is based on the fact that both victims and criminals live in the same environment and engage in similar routine activities. People who live in high-crime areas, spend time in public places, and go out late at night are most likely to interact with lawbreakers who have similar lifestyles. In other words, crime is an inevitable consequence of having potential victims in close proximity to motivated offenders.

The second view, that victims and criminals share similar characteristics because they are not really separate groups, is supported by research which shows that crime victims report significant amounts of criminal behavior themselves. For example, Joan McDermott found that the young victims of school crime were likely to strike back at other students in order to regain lost possessions or recover their self-respect. In another study, Simon Singer employed data from the Philadelphia cohort and found that victims of violent assault are quite likely to become offenders themselves. And there are a number of studies which show that youths who are the victims of child abuse grow up to victimize their own children and families. Gary Jensen and David Brownfield conclude:

for personal victimizations, those most likely to be the victims of crime are those who have been most involved in crime; and the similarity of victims and offenders reflects that association.

The true nature of the victim-criminal association is far from certain. Some victims may commit criminal acts out of a sense of rage and frustration; some may have learned antisocial behavior as a consequence of their own experiences, as in the case of abused children; others may engage in law-violating behaviors as a means of revenge, self-defense, or social control. The relationship is a complex one. Certainly not all victims become criminals, nor have all criminals experienced victimization. Some recent research by Jeffrey Fagan and his associates shows that while a relationship between victimization and criminality exists, the social processes which produce both events are not identical. Further research is needed to fully understand this important interrelationship.

Discussion Questions

1. Have you ever been a victim of crime? Did you take your frustration out on others?
2. Should prior victimization ever be a defense against a criminal charge? What about battered wives who kill their husbands?

SOURCES: Gary Jensen and David Brownfield, "Gender, Lifestyles and Victimization: Beyond Routine Activities," Violence and Victims (1986):85–101; Joan McDermott, "Crime in the School and in the Community: Offenders, Victims and Fearful Youth," Crime and Delinquency 29 (1983):270–83; Simon Singer, "Homogeneous Victim-Offender Populations: A Review and Some Research Implications," Journal of Criminal Law and Criminology 72 (1981):779–99; Ross Vasta, "Physical Child Abuse: A Dual Component Analysis," Developmental Review 2 (1982):128–35; Jeffrey Fagan, Elizabeth Piper, and Yu-Teh Cheng, "Contributions of Victimization to Delinquency in Inner Cities," The Journal of Criminal Law and Criminology 78 (1987):586–613.

Greenwood believes that if judges used these characteristics in calculating prison sentences, both the prison population and the crime rate would be significantly reduced. For example, using California inmates, Greenwood estimates that selective incapacitation of offenders on the basis of these seven variables would result in a 15 percent decrease in the robbery rate and concomitant 5 percent drop in the number of inmates convicted of robbery. It would also put chronic offenders in prison and place nonchronic offenders on probation or in other forms of community treatment.

Greenwood's policy of selective incapacitation has become quite controversial. Two leading criminologists, Andrew von Hirsch and Don Gottfredson, suggest that if used it can lead to imprisonment of those falsely identified as high-risk offenders and result in release of dangerous criminals mistakenly identified as low-risk offenders.[82] This problem is quite critical since recent research indicates that minority group members stand the greatest risk of being inaccurately identified as potential chronic offenders.[83]

Von Hirsch and Gottfredson also argue that : (1) the self-report data Greenwood uses are unreliable; (2) Greenwood's study examines only incarcerated robbers and burglars; and (3) Greenwood does not acknowledge that many robberies and burglaries are committed in groups, and that incarcerating one participant will only cause the gang to find a new member.

In addition to these problems, Greenwood's formula relies on legally irrelevant personal information, such as prior employment record, which would be excluded at a sentencing hearing. Also, self-reports of drug use could not legally be obtained from offenders who were going to be sentenced to prison.[84]

The Chronic Offender in Review

While the chronic offender concept has had immense influence both on the field of criminology and on criminal justice system policy, it has not been embraced by all criminologists. As noted earlier in this chapter, criminologists Travis Hirschi and Michael Gottfredson have forcefully argued that the relationship between age and crime is constant and that all people commit less crime as they mature. Consequently, they eject the notion that persistent offenders begin their criminal careers at an early age and then continue to offend at the same or an increased rate throughout their lives.[85] This view is supported by research conducted in California by Robert Tillman, which indicates that the phenomenon of multiple arrests for serious crimes is not limited to a small group of offenders but is widely distributed among the population of young adults.[86] According to Tillman's research, more than 29,000 new "chronic offenders" must be absorbed by California's already overcrowded justice system each year; such numbers would make a strict incarceration policy impossible.[87]

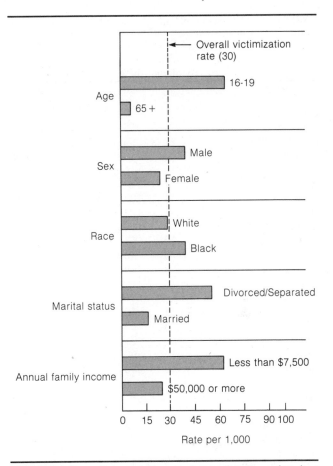

FIGURE 4.2   Selected Characteristics of Victims of Violent Crime, 1985

NOTE: *The differences between the rates within categories are statistically significant. Rate differences between categories may or may not be significant.*

SOURCE: Bureau of Justice Statistics, *Criminal Victimization in the United States, 1985.*

Those who question the importance of the chronic offender concept also argue that it unfairly equates the crime problem with the predatory crimes of urban males and ignores white-collar, organized, and other crime categories. In addition, the chronic offender concept seems to imply that some combination of personal characteristics produces persistent criminality and sets "real" criminals apart from the occasional offender. Such thinking draws attention away from the social, economic, and political conditions which produce crime. The focus on chronic offenders is a simple solution to a complex problem: locking up a few bad apples is significantly easier than reducing the

TABLE 4.4 Victimization Rates per 1,000 Persons Age 12 and Older

	Personal crimes of violence	theft		Personal crimes of violence	theft		Personal crimes of violence	theft
Total (U.S.)	30	69						
Sex			**Family income**			**Race, sex, and age summary**		
Male	39	75	Less than $7,500	52	68	White males		
Female	22	65	$7,500-$9,999	34	63	12-15	73	111
			$10,000-$14,999	32	65	16-19	92	134
			$15,000-$24,999	28	68	20-24	78	116
Age			$25,000-$29,999	29	69	25-34	44	87
12-15	54	108	$30,000-$49,999	22	76	35-49	23	66
16-19	67	122	$50,000 or more	25	90	50-64	11	42
20-24	60	108				65 and older	5	22
35-49	20	63	**Education**			White females		
50-64	10	40	0-4 years	13	23	12-15	39	116
65 and older	5	19	5-7 years	35	59	16-19	47	129
			8 years	34	57	20-24	42	103
Race and origin			9-11 years	39	71	25-34	28	78
White	29	70	High School graduate	27	60	35-49	15	62
Black	38	63	1-3 years of college	34	87	50-64	8	39
Other	25	73	College graduate	22	89	65 and older	3	17
Hispanic	30	60				Black males		
Non-Hispanic	30	70	**Employment status** (1984)			12-15	68	81
			Retired	5	20	16-19	69	74
Marital status by sex			Keeping house	14	35	20-24	67	103
Males			Unable to work	17	25	25-34	60	113
Never married	72	112	Employed	32	81	35-49	31	60
Divorced/separated	57	102	In school	45	110	50-64	27	48
Married	19	52	Unemployed	76	90	65 and older	*	21
Widowed	10	31				Black females		
Females			**Residence** (1984)			12-15	19	74
Never married	38	102	Central city	43	85	16-19	46	54
Divorced/separated	51	84	1,000,000 or more	45	80	20-24	58	70
Married	11	50	500,000-999,999	45	92	25-34	48	68
Widowed	7	21	250,000-499,999	37	88	35-49	20	54
			50,000-249,999	44	81	50-64	10	33
			Suburban	30	77	65 and older	*	12
			Rural	22	54			

SOURCE: Bureau of Justice Statistics, *Report to the Nation on Crime and Justice* (Washington D.C.: U.S. Government Printing Office, 1988).

crime producing conditions in the environment.

While such criticisms persist, there is no denying the impact the chronic offender concept has had and will continue to have on criminology. At this time the federal government has granted millions of dollars in support to fund longitudinal studies of the life cycle of chronic offenders, while state legislatures continue to base their policy initiatives on the control of habitual offenders.

CRIME VICTIMS

So far the personal characteristics of criminal offenders have been reviewed. The question remains: What are their victims like? National Crime Survey and other victimization data allow us to examine the criminal incident from the victim's perspective. Who has the greatest chance of becoming a crime victim? Under what circumstances is victimization most likely to take

TABLE 4.5 Percent of Households Touched by Crime, Selected Characteristics, 1987

	Annual family income							Region			
	Low	Medium		High							
Percent of households touched by:	Under $7,500	$7,500-$14,999	$15,000-$24,999	$25,000 or more	Place of residence			North-east	Mid-west	South	West
					Urban	Suburban	Rural				
Any NCS crime	23.9	22.7	24.0	26.9	28.6	24.2	18.5	19.2	24.7	24.3	29.4
Violent crime	6.3	5.2	4.3	4.1	5.8	4.1	3.7	3.7	5.0	4.3	5.6
Rape	.2	.1	.1	.1	.1	.1	.1	.1	.1	.1	.1
Robbery	1.6	1.1	.8	.7	1.6	.7	.5	1.0	1.1	.8	1.0
Assault	4.8	4.3	3.4	3.5	4.3	3.4	3.3	2.7	4.0	3.5	4.7
Aggravated	1.8	1.6	1.3	1.2	1.8	1.1	1.3	.8	1.3	1.5	1.9
Simple	3.4	3.0	2.4	2.5	2.9	2.6	2.3	2.0	3.0	2.3	3.3
Total theft	14.9	14.9	17.4	20.1	19.2	17.7	13.0	12.6	17.3	17.1	21.7
Personal theft	8.6	8.8	10.8	14.0	11.9	12.0	8.0	8.1	10.9	10.5	13.4
Household theft	8.2	7.8	8.3	8.2	9.9	7.4	6.2	5.2	7.8	8.1	10.5
Burglary	7.3	5.6	4.7	4.8	6.3	4.7	4.3	3.6	5.1	5.8	5.8
Motor vehicle theft	1.0	1.3	1.5	1.8	2.2	1.5	.6	1.7	1.5	1.3	1.7
Serious violent crime	3.5	2.7	2.2	2.0	3.5	1.8	1.8	1.9	2.3	2.3	2.9
Crimes of high concern	9.8	7.9	6.9	7.0	9.4	6.8	5.6	5.5	7.4	7.7	8.7

Note: Detail does not add to total because of overlap in households touched by various crimes
SOURCE: Michael Rand, *Households Touched by Crime, 1987* (Washington, D.C.: Bureau of Justice Statistics, 1988), p. 3.

place? What are the costs of crime? The NCS data have proven indispensable in understanding the nature of the criminal act.

Victim Characteristics

For over a decade, the victimization patterns measured by the NCS have been remarkably uniform.[88] Some of the most important differences in the social and economic characteristics of victims of violent personal crimes are presented in Figure 4.2. Victimization is most common among youths, males, divorcees, blacks, and the poor.

Table 4.4 points out some of the striking differences in victimization risk associated with race, sex, and age of crime victims. First, though many people believe that the elderly face the greatest risk of crime victimization, the nation's teenagers and young adults are actually most likely to become victims of violent and theft-related crimes. For example, the violent crime victimization rate of a black male teenager (68.9 per 1,000 population) is about 20 times greater than that of an elderly white female (3.4), and the risk of theft victimization is more than four times as great.

These data also show that crime victims and offenders share the same sociological characteristics.

Another important relationship uncovered by NCS data is the relationship between personal wealth and victimization. As Table 4.5 shows, as personal wealth increases, a person's chance of becoming a victim of violence and burglary decreases. But the chance of becoming a victim of personal thefts and larcenies increases as personal wealth increases. This may be interpreted to mean that criminals burglarize, use violence against, and steal from victims within their own environment, but selectively choose to economically victimize the wealthiest people within that environment.

Beyond these findings, the NCS data reveal that married and widowed people are less likely to be victimized than divorced and single people. Additionally, people over 25 with some college education are more likely than those with less schooling to be the victims of violent crime or personal larceny. Finally, people who live in large households (six or more members) and rent rather than own their dwellings have much higher victimization rates than those residing with fewer people and owning their own homes.

The picture that emerges of the crime victim, then,

☰ CLOSE-UP

Lifetime Likelihood of Victimization

Some disturbing information about the probability of becoming a victim of crime has been discovered in the National Crime Survey data. Recent analysis indicates that sometime during their lifetime about 80 percent of the 12-year-olds in the United States will become victims of completed or attempted violent crimes. 99 percent will experience theft, and 40 percent will be injured during the course of the crime (see Table A). Even more startling is the finding that 52 percent of the 12-year-olds will be the casualty of multiple acts of violence, and 95 percent will fall prey to multiple thefts.

As might be expected, personal characteristics influence one's lifetime chances of becoming a crime victim. For example, while the overall probability of someday being a victim of robbery is about 30 percent, about 50 percent of black youths will become victims as opposed to only 25 percent of white youths. Similarly, the lifetime chances of being the victim of rape are estimated to be one in 12 for white females and one in nine for black females. Males have a much higher probability of being the victim of violent crimes, and blacks in general can expect to be victimized more frequently than whites. It also appears that living in an urban environment significantly increases one's lifetime chance of victimization.

The lifetime prevalence rates mirror the annual rates supplied by the NCS. They indicate that crime is a basic social issue and most of us will feel its impact.

Discussion Questions

1. What can you do to limit victimization risk?
2. Why are there sex, age, and race differences in the victimization rate?

TABLE A   Lifetime Likelihood of Victimization, by Age

	Percent of Persons Who Will Be Victimized by Crime Starting at Various Ages			
	Total	Number of Victimizations		
	One or More Victimizations	One	Two	Three or More
Violent Crimes				
Current Age (in years)				
12	83	30	27	25
20	72	36	23	14
30	53	35	13	4
40	36	29	6	1
50	22	19	2	—
60	14	13	1	—
70	8	7	—	—
Robbery or Assault Resulting in Injury				
Current Age (in years)				
12	40	30	7	2
20	30	25	4	1
30	19	17	2	—
40	11	11	1	—
50	7	6	—	—
60	4	4	—	—
70	2	2	—	—
Personal Theft				
Current Age (in years)				
12	99	4	8	87
20	98	9	16	73
30	93	19	25	48
40	82	31	19	33
50	64	37	19	8
60	43	32	9	2
70	24	21	3	—

SOURCE: Herbert Koppel, *Lifetime Likelihood of Victimization* (Washington, D.C.: Bureau of Justice Statistics Technical Report, 1987).

is a young, poor, minority male, who is unemployed and living with a large family in a rental unit. From Chapter 3 data, we also know that the victim lives in a large city, probably in the south or west, and most likely will not bother to let police know about his or her victimization. (See Close-Up entitled Victims and Criminals: Are They Really So Different?".)

Crime Characteristics

The NCS data can be used to tell us something about the nature of the criminal offense itself. One important finding is that a significant amount of crime involves relatives and acquaintances. The UCR also has traditionally shown that a significant number of murder cases involve family and friends. For example, in 1986, only 13 percent of murders could be classified as involving strangers. Unfortunately, the UCR does not collect data on the victim-offender relationship for other crime categories. However, the NCS shows that only 60 percent of all other personal offenses involved strangers. This means that about 40 percent of rapes, robberies, and assaults were committed by someone the victim was acquainted with. This relationship is even more striking for divorced women, who report that they were acquainted with their attacker in 76 percent of rapes, 37 percent of robberies, and 73 percent of assaults. These data, however, must be interpreted with caution. The NCS respondents may be reluctant to report attacks by family or friends for fear of implicating them. Thus, it is possible that the number of crimes involving friends and family is even higher than that reported by the victim data.

The NCS also finds that most violent crimes occur at night, between 6:00 P.M. and 6:00 A.M. Though it is harder to establish the time of property crimes, most were distributed equally throughout the day and night—except for motor vehicle theft, which usually (65 percent) occurred at night.

Most violent crimes (about 40 percent) took place in an outdoor public area, such as a street or park. About 12 percent took place in public buildings and 9 percent in schools. Only 25 percent occurred in or near the victim's home. However, a substantial number of violent acts involving acquaintances occurred in or near the home, as compared to stranger-to-stranger offenses (40 percent versus 15 percent).

Most violent acts involved a single victim and offender (73 percent). Again, when victims were attacked by an acquaintance it was more likely to be a single-offender incident than when the incident involved a stranger.

In about one-third of all violent crimes, a weapon was used; in about three-fourths, the victims attempted to defend themselves. The NCS data indicate that those who used physical force to protect themselves were more likely to suffer serious injury than those who did absolutely nothing. However, victims who took nonviolent evasive action or tried to talk themselves out of their predicament were the least likely to suffer serious injury.

In summary, victimization risk is related to exposure to crimogenic conditions. People who place themselves in jeopardy by frequenting public places in the evening are more likely to become crime victims than those who stay home. Thus, the inner-city youth who goes to the park in the evening has a far greater victimization potential than the female senior citizen who goes home and locks her door in the evening. However, as the Close-Up on the "Lifetime Likelihood of Victimization" indicates, everyone has a good chance of experiencing crime firsthand.

SUMMARY

Official, victim, and self-report data provide information on the nature of crime and its victims. Among the issues of importance to criminologists, none is as important or confusing as the relationship between social class and crime. Although it seems logical that poor people commit crime, the data provide a rather confusing picture. Some studies indicate that lower-class citizens do in fact commit more crime than the upper classes, but others show that wealth and status are unrelated to criminality. If so, then other social forces aside from wealth must be influencing criminal behavior.

The data also show that young people, males, and minorities are more likely to commit crime than older people, females, and whites. Explanations for these differences usually focus on the socialization process. For example, women may be less violence-prone than men because their social role has stressed obedience and gentleness. Some criminologists believe that the women's movement has so altered women's role in society that their crime rates will eventually parallel those of male criminals.

Another phenomenon discovered in the crime data is that of chronic offenders. Several studies have shown that a small group of men commit a significant portion of all crimes. The most well-known research was conducted by Marvin Wolfgang, with a cohort of boys drawn from Philadelphia in 1945. Peter Greenwood of the Rand Corporation has suggested that these chronic offenders be incapacitated for long periods of time in order to reduce the overall crime rate.

Victim research helps us understand the nature of victimization in our society. Victims tend to have the same characteristics as criminals, that is, they are young, minorities, male, and poor. Studies show that victimization is related to the risks—such as going out at night to public places—victims take. It also has been found that the personal characteristics of victims and criminals are virtually identical, indicating that the choice of crime may not be random or haphazard.

——————— KEY TERMS ———————

social class
instrumental crimes
expressive crimes
John Laub
aging out
desistance phenomenon
chronic offender
career criminal
Marvin Wolfgang

masculinity hypothesis
chivalry hypothesis
power-control theory
paternalistic
egalitarian
subculture of violence
chronic recidivists
selective incapacitation

——————— NOTES ———————

1. See, generally, James Byrne and Robert Sampson, *The Social Ecology of Crime* (New York: Springer-Verlag, 1985).

2. Judith and Peter Blau, "The Cost of Inequality: Metropolitan Structure and Violent Crime," *American Sociological Review* 147 (1982):114–29; Richard Block, "Community Environment and Violent Crime," *Criminology* 17 (1979):46–57; Robert Sampson, "Structural Sources of Variation in Race-Age—Specific Rates of Offending Across Major U.S. Cities," *Criminology* 23 (1985):647–73.

3. James Short and F. Ivan Nye, "Reported Behavior as a Criterion of Deviant Behavior," *Social Problems* 5 (1958):207–13.

4. F. Ivan Nye, James Short, and Virgil Olson, "Socio-economic Status and Delinquent Behavior," *American Journal of Sociology* 63 (1958):381–89; Robert Dentler and Lawrence Monroe, "Social Correlates of Early Adolescent Theft," *American Sociological Review* 63 (1961):733–43. See, generally, John Clark and Eugene Wenninger, "Socio-economic Class and Area as Correlates of Illegal Behavior Among Juveniles," *American Sociological Review* 27 (1962):826–34; William Arnold, "Continuities in Research: Scaling Delinquent Behavior," *Social Problems* 13 (1965):59–66; LeMar Empey and Maynard Erickson, "Hidden Delinquency and Social Status," *Social Forces* 44 (1966):546–54; Jay

Williams and Martin Gold, "From Delinquent Behavior to Official Delinquency," *Social Problems* 20 (1972):209–29; Richard Johnson, "Social Class and Delinquency," *Criminology* 18 (1980):86–93.

5. Terence Thornberry and Margaret Farnsworth, "Social Correlates of Criminal Involvement: Further Evidence of the Relationship Between Social Status and Criminal Behavior," *American Sociological Review* 47 (1982):505–18.

6. Charles Tittle, Wayne Villemez, and Douglas Smith, "The Myth of Social Class and Criminality: An Empirical Assessment of the Empirical Evidence," *American Sociological Review* 43 (1978):643–56.

7. *Ibid.*

8. Delbert Elliott and Suzanne Ageton, "Reconciling Race and Class Differences in Self-Reported and Official Estimates of Delinquency," *American Sociological Review* 45 (1980):95–110.

9. Delbert Elliott and David Huizinga, "Social Class and Delinquent Behavior in a National Youth Panel: 1976–1980," *Criminology* 21 (1983):149–77.

10. Michael Hindelang, Travis Hirschi and Joseph Weis, *Measuring Delinquency* (Beverly Hills, Cal.: Sage, 1981), p. 196. For a similar view, see John Braithwaite, "The Myth of Social Class and Criminality Reconsidered," *American Sociological Review* 46 (1981):35–58.

11. David Brownfield, "Social Class and Violent Behavior," *Criminology* 24(1986):421–39.

12. Douglas Smith and Laura Davidson, "Interfacing Indicators and Constructs in Criminological Research: A Note on the Comparability of Self-Report Violence Data for Race and Sex Groups," *Criminology* 24(1986):473–88.

13. Sampson, "Structural Sources of Variation in Race-Age–Specific Rates," pp. 647–73.

14. Darrell Steffensmeier, Cathy Streifel, and Miles Harer, "Relative Cohort Size and Youth Crime in the United States, 1953–1984," *American Sociological Review* 52 (1987):702–10.

15. Travis Hirschi and Michael Gottfredson, "Age and Explanation of Crime," *American Journal of Sociology* 89 (1983):552–84, at 581.

16. For a comprehensive review of crime and the elderly, see Kyle Kercher, "Causes and Correlates of Crime Committed by the Elderly," in E. Borgatta and R. Montgomery, eds., *Critical Issues in Aging Policy* (Beverly Hills, Cal.: Sage, 1987), pp. 254–306.

17. Darrell Steffensmeier, "The Invention of the 'New' Senior Citizen Criminal," *Research on Aging* 9 (1987):281–311.

18. John Laub, David Clark, Leslie Siegel, and James Garofalo, *Trends in Juvenile Crime in the United States: 1973–1983* (Albany, N.Y.: Hindelang Criminal Justice Research Center, 1987). Preliminary draft.

19. Michael Gottfredson and Travis Hirschi, "Science, Public Policy, and the Career Paradigm," *Criminology* 26 (1988):37–57.

20. Travis Hirschi and Michael Gottfredson, "Age and the Explanation of Crime," *American Journal of Sociology* 89 (1983):552–84.

21. Michael Gottfredson and Travis Hirschi, "The True Value of Lambda Would Appear to Be Zero: An Essay on Career Criminals, Criminal Careers, Selective Incapacitation, Cohort Studies and Related Topics," *Criminology* 24 (1986):213–34. Further support for their position can be found in Lawrence Cohen and Kenneth Land, "Age Structure and Crime," *American Sociological Review* 52(1987):170–83.

22. Walter Gove, "The Effect of Age and Gender on Deviant Behavior: A Biopsychosocial Perspective," in A. Rossi, ed., *Gender and the Life Course* (Chicago: Aldine, 1985), p. 131.

23. Kyle Kercher, "Explaining the Relationship Between Age and Crime: The Biological vs. Sociological Model," Paper presented at the American Society of Criminology meeting, Montreal, Canada, November, 1987.

24. Alfred Blumstein, Jacqueline Cohen, and David Farrington, "Criminal Career Research: Its Value for Criminology," *Criminology* 26:(1988):1–37.

25. David Farrington, "Age and Crime," in Michael Tonry and David Farrington, *Crime and Justice* (Chicago: University of Chicago Press, 1986), pp. 236-237.

26. Arnold Barnett, Alfred Blumstein, and David Farrington, "Probabilistic Models of Youthful Criminal Careers," *Criminology* 25(1987):83–107.

27. Darrell Steffensmeier, Emilie Andersen Allan, Miles Harer, and Cathy Streifel, "Age and the Distribution of Crime: Variant or Invariant?" Paper presented at the American Society of Criminology meeting, Montreal, Canada, November, 1987.

28. David Greenberg, "Age, Crime and Social Explanation," *American Journal of Sociology* 91(1985):1–21.

29. Marvin Wolfgang, Robert Figlio, and Thorsten Sellin, *Delinquency in a Birth Cohort* (Chicago: University of Chicago Press, 1972); Lyle Shannon, *Assessing the Relationship of Adult Criminal Careers to Juvenile Careers: A Summary* (Washington, D.C.: U.S. Department of Justice, 1982); D. J. West and David P. Farrington, *The Delinquent Way of Life* (London: Heinemann, 1977); Donna Hamparian, Richard Schuster, Simon Dinitz, and John Conrad, *The Violent Few* (Lexington, Mass.: Lexington Books, 1978).

30. Peter Greenwood, "Difference in Criminal Behavior and Court Responses Among Juvenile and Young Adult Defendants," in Michael Tonry and Norval Morris, eds., *Crime and Justice, An Annual Review of Research* (Chicago: University of Chicago Press, 1986), pp. 151–89.

31. John Hagan and Alberto Palloni, "Crimes as Social Events in the Life Course: Reconceiving a Criminological Controversy," *Criminology* 26 (1988):87–101.

32. Travis Hirschi and Michael Gottfredson, "Age and Crime, Logic and Scholarship: Comment on Greenberg," *American Journal of Sociology* 91 (1985):22–27; Hirschi and Gottfredson, "All Wise After the Fact Learning Theory, Again: Reply to Baldwin," *American Journal of Sociology* 90 (1985):1330–33; John Baldwin, "Thrill and Adventure Seeking and the Age Distribution of Crime: Comment on Hirschi and Gottfredson," *American Journal of Sociology* 90 (1985):1326–29.

33. Edward Mulvey and John LaRosa, "Delinquency Cessation and Adolescent Development: Preliminary Data," *American Journal of Orthopsychiatry* 56 (1986):212–24.

34. Gordon Trasler, "Cautions for a Biological Approach to Crime," in Sarnoff Mednick, Terrie Moffitt, and Susan Stack, *The Causes of Crime, New Biological Approaches* (Cambridge, England: Cambridge University Press, 1987), pp. 7–25.

35. James Q. Wilson and Richard Herrnstein, *Crime and Human Nature* (New York: Simon and Schuster, 1985), pp. 126–47.

36. Barry Glassner, Margaret Ksander, Bruce Berg, and Bruce Johnson, "A Note on the Deterrent Effect of Juvenile vs. Adult Jurisdiction," *Social Problems* 31 (1983):219–21

37. *Ibid.*, p. 219.

38. Charles Tittle, "Two Empirical Regularities (Maybe) in Search of an Explanation: Commentary on the Age/Crime Debate," *Criminology* 26 (1988):75–85.

39. John Laub, *Juvenile Criminal Behavior in the United States: An Analysis of Offender and Victim Characteristics*, Working Paper 25, Michael J. Hindelang Criminal Justice Research Center (Albany, N.Y., 1983), p. 25; Bureau of Justice Statistics, *Criminal Victimization in the United States, 1985* (Washington, D.C.: National Institute of Justice, 1986), p. 47.

40. Rosemary Sarri, "Gender Issues in Juvenile Justice," *Crime and Delinquency* 29 (1983):381–97.

41. Elliott and Ageton, "Reconciling Race and Class Differences in Self-Reported and Official Estimates of Delinquency"; Williams and Gold, "From Delinquent Behavior to Official Delinquency"; Hindelang, Hirschi, and Weis, *Measuring Delinquency*.

42. Imogene Moyer, "Academic Criminology: A Need for Change," *American Journal of Criminal Justice* 9 (1985):197–212.

43. Cesare Lombroso, *The Female Offender* (New York:

Appleton Publishers, 1920).

44. *Ibid.*, p. 122.

45. Otto Pollack, *The Criminality of Women* (Philadelphia: University of Pennsylvania, 1950).

46. For a review of this issue, see Darrell Steffensmeier, "Assessing the Impact of the Women's Movement on Sex-Based Differences in the Handling of Adult Criminal Defendants," *Crime and Delinquency* 26 (1980):344–357.

47. *Ibid.*

48. Cassia Spohn, John Gruhl, and Susan Welch, "The Impact of the Ethnicity and Gender of Defendants on the Decision to Reject or Dismiss Felony Charges," *Criminology* 25 (1987):175–91.

49. Darrell Steffensmeier and Robert Clark, "Sociocultural vs. Biological/Sexist Explanations of Sex Differences in Crime: A Survey of American Criminology Textbooks, 1918–1965," *The American Sociologist* 15 (1980):246–55.

50. Gisela Konopka, *The Adolescent Girl in Conflict* (Englewood Cliffs, N.J.: Prentice-Hall, 1966); Clyde Vedder and Dora Somerville, *The Delinquent Girl* (Springfield, Ill.: Charles C. Thomas, 1970).

51. Freda Adler, *Sisters in Crime* (New York: McGraw-Hill, 1975); Rita James Simon, *The Contemporary Woman and Crime* (Washington, D.C.: U.S. Government Printing Office, 1975).

52. Michael Hindelang, "Age, Sex, and the Versatility of Delinquency Involvements," *Social Forces* 14 (1971):525–34; Martin Gold, *Delinquent Behavior in an American City* (Belmont, Cal.: Brooks/Cole, 1970); Gary Jensen and Raymond Eve, "Sex Differences in Delinquency: An Examination of Popular Sociological Explanations," *Criminology* 13 (1976):427–48.

53. Meda Chesney-Lind, "Female Offenders: Paternalism Reexamined," in Laura Crites and Winifred Hepperle, eds., *Women, the Courts and Equality* (Newberry Park, Cal.: Sage, 1987), pp. 114–39.

54. Darrel and Renee Hoffman Steffensmeier, "Trends in Female Delinquency," *Criminology* 18 (1980):62–85. See also, Steffensmeier and Steffensmeier, "Crime and the Contemporary Woman: An Analysis of Changing Levels of Female Property Crime, 1960–1975," *Social Forces* 57 (1978):566–84; Joseph Weis, "Liberation and Crime: The Invention of the New Female Criminal," *Crime and Social Justice* 1 (1976):17–27; Carol Smart, "The New Female Offender: Reality or Myth," *British Journal of Criminology* 19 (1979):50–59; Steven Box and Chris Hale, "Liberation/Emancipation, Economic Marginalization or Less Chivalry," *Criminology* 22 (1984):473–78.

55. Jane Chapman, *Economic Reality and the Female Offender* (Lexington, Mass.: Lexington Books, 1980).

56. Chesney-Lind, "Female Offenders: Paternalism Reexamined," p. 115.

57. Meda Chesney-Lind, "Women and Crime: The Female Offender," *Sigma: Journal of Women in Culture and Society* 12 (1986):78–96.

58. Meda Chesney-Line, "Girls' Crime and Women's Place: Toward a Feminist Model of Female Delinquency," Paper presented at the American Society of Criminology Meeting, Montreal, Canada, November, 1987.

59. *Ibid.*, p. 20.

60. Gregg Barak, "Feminist Connections and Movement Against Domestic Violence: Beyond Criminal Justice Reform," *Journal of Crime and Justice* 9 (1986):139–62.

61. John Hagan, A. R. Gillis, and John Simpson, "The Class Structure and Delinquency: Toward a Power-Control Theory of Common Delinquent Behavior," *American Journal of Sociology* 90 (1985):1151–78.

62. John Hagan, John Simpson, and A. R. Gillis, "Class in the Household: A Power-Control Theory of Gender and Delinquency," *American Journal of Sociology* 92 (1987):788–816.

63. FBI, *Uniform Crime Report, 1986*, p. 187.

64. Laub, Clark, Siegel, and Garofalo, *Trends in Juvenile Crime in the United States: 1973–1983.*

65. Daniel Georges-Abeyie, "Definitional Issues: Race, Ethnicity and Official Crime/Victimization Rates," in D. Georges-Abeyie, ed., *The Criminal Justice System and Blacks* (New York: Clark Boardman, 1984), p. 12; Robert Sampson, "Race and Criminal Violence: A Demographically Disaggregated Analysis of Urban Homicide," *Crime and Delinquency* 31 (1985):47–82.

66. Barry Sample and Michael Philip, "Perspectives on Race and Crime in Research and Planning," in Georges-Abeyie, ed., *The Criminal Justice System and Blacks*, pp. 21–36.

67. James Comer, "Black Violence and Public Policy," in Lynn Curtis, ed., *American Violence and Public Policy* (New Haven, Conn.: Yale University Press, 1985), pp. 63–86.

68. *Ibid.*, p. 80.

69. *Ibid.*, p. 81.

70. Marvin Wolfgang and Franco Ferracuti, *The Subculture of Violence* (London: Tavistock, 1967).

71. Charles Silberman, *Criminal Violence, Criminal Justice* (New York: Random House, 1979), pp. 153–65.

72. Roy Austin, "Progress Toward Racial Equality and Education of Black Criminal Violence," *Journal of Criminal Justice* 15 (1987):437–59.

73. Sheldon Messinger and Richard Berk, "Review Essay: Dangerous People," *Criminology* 25 (1987):767–81.

74. Rolf Loeber, "The Prevalence, Correlates, and Continuity of Serious Conduct Problems in Elementary School Children," *Criminology* 25 (1987):615–42.

75. Wolfgang, Figlio, and Sellin, *Delinquency in a Birth Cohort.*

76. See Thorsten Sellin and Marvin Wolfgang, *The Measurement of Delinquency* (New York: Wiley, 1964), p. 120.

77. Paul Tracy and Robert Figlio, "Chronic Recidivism in the 1958 Birth Cohort," Paper presented at the American Society of Criminology meeting, Toronto, Canada, October, 1982; Marvin Wolfgang, "Delinquency in Two Birth Cohorts," in Katherine Teilmann Van Dusen and Sarnoff Mednick, eds., *Perspective Studies of Crime and Delinquency,* (Boston: Kluwer-Nijhoff, 1983), pp. 7–17. The following sections rely heavily on these sources.

78. Lyle Shannon, *Assessing the Relationship of Adult Criminal Careers to Juvenile Careers: A Summary* (Washington, D.C.: U.S. Department of Justice, 1982); West and Farrington, *The Delinquent Way of Life*; Hamparian, Schuster, Dinitz, and Conrad, *The Violent Few*; Franklyn Dunford and Delbert Elliott, "Identifying Career Offenders Using Self-Reported Data," *Journal of Research in Crime and Delinquency* 21 (1984):57–86; Stephen VanDine, John Conrad, and Simon Dinitz, *Restraining the Wicked* (Lexington, Mass.: Lexington Books, 1979); Randall Shelden, "The Chronic Delinquent: Gender and Racial Differences," Paper presented at the American Society of Criminology meeting, Montreal, Canada, November, 1987.

79. Alfred Blumstein, Jacqueline Cohen, Jeffrey Roth, and Christy Visher, *Criminal Careers and "Career Criminals,"* vol. 1 (Washington, D.C.: National Academy Press, 1986).

80. Susan Martin, "Policing Career Criminals: An Examination of an Innovative Crime Control Program," *Journal of Criminal Law and Criminology* 77 (1986):1159–82.

81. Peter Greenwood, *Selective Incapacitation* (Santa Monica, Cal.: Rand Corporation, 1982).

82. Andrew von Hirsch and Don Gottfredson, "Selective Incapacitation: New Solution or Old Myth," *Criminal Justice Newsletter* (April 25, 1983):3–4.

83. Lawrence Rosen, Leonard Savitz, and Michael Lalli, "Issues in the Prediction of Adult Criminality," *International Journal of Sociology and Social Policy* (1988).

84. For an alternative form of selective incapacitation, see, Alfred Blumstein and Elizabeth Graddy, "Prevalence and Recidivism in Index Arrests: A Feedback Model," *Law and Society Review* 16 (1982):265–90; Jan Chaiken and Marsha Chaiken, *Varieties of Criminal Behavior* (Santa Monica, Cal.: Rand Corporation, 1982); Alfred Blumstein and Jacqueline Cohen, "Estimation of Individual Crime Rates from Arrest Records," *Journal of Criminal Law and Criminology* 70 (1979):561–81; Jacqueline Cohen, *Incapacitating Criminals: Recent Research Findings* (Washington, D.C.: National Institute of Justice, 1983).

85. Michael Gottfredson and Travis Hirschi, "The Methodological Adequacy of Longitudinal Research on Crime," *Criminology* 25 (1987):581–614.

86. Robert Tillman, "The Size of the 'Criminal Population': The Prevalence and Incidence of Adult Arrest," *Criminology* 25 (1987):561–79.

87. *Ibid.,* p. 577.

88. Data in this section come from Bureau of Justice Statistics, *Criminal Victimization in the United States, 1986.*

SECTION II

THEORIES OF CRIME CAUSATION

An important goal of the criminological enterprise is to create valid and accurate theories of crime causation. Social scientists have defined theory as:

Sets of statements that say why and how several concepts are related. For a set of statements to qualify as a theory, it must also be possible to deduce some conclusions from it that are subject to empirical verification; that is, theories must predict or prohibit certain observable events or conditions.*

Criminologists have sought to collect vital facts about crime and interpret them in a scientifically meaningful fashion. By developing empirically verifiable statements, or hypotheses, and organizing them into theories of crime causation, they hope to identify the root causes of crime. Since the late nineteenth century, criminological theory has pointed to various underlying causes of crime. The earliest theories generally attributed crime to a single underlying cause; atypical body build, genetic abnormality, insanity, physical anomalies, and poverty. Later theories attributed crime causation to multiple factors: poverty, peer influence, school problems, and family dysfunction.

In this section, theories of crime causation are grouped into five chapters. Chapters 5 and 6 focus on individual traits. They hold that crime is either a free-will choice made by an individual, or it is a function of personal psychological or biological maladaption, or both. Chapters 7 through 9 investigate theories based in sociology. These theories portray crime as a function of the structure, process, and conflicts of social living.

The goal of this section is to present the rich historical traditions and the current state of criminological theory. This section also describes the efforts being made by criminologists in various academic disciplines to uncover the true causes of crime and to suggest methods of eliminating it.

---

*Rodney Stark, *Sociology*, 2d edition (Belmont, Cal.: Wadsworth, 1987), p. 618.

≡ CHAPTER 5

CLASSICAL CRIMINOLOGY: CRIME AS CHOICE

CHAPTER OUTLINE

INTRODUCTION

To many criminologists, the decision to commit crime (stage a robbery, attack a rival, or submit a false tax return) is similar to deciding to undertake conventional actions, such as starting a new career or choosing a college. Motivation may stem from a number of different sources or needs, including greed, revenge, envy, anger, lust, thrill-seeking, or bravado. The central issue is that the offender's decision to commit crime is a matter of a rational choice, made after weighing the potential benefits and consequences of the actions. This view, that criminal behavior is a function of the human ability to choose an individual course of action, was originally referred to as **classical theory**. Modern variations on this basic theory include rational choice and routine activities theories.

This chapter reviews the philosophical underpinnings of the classical approach and briefly traces its history. It then discusses four concepts which have been closely associated with classical theory: general deterrence; special deterrence; incapacitation; and retribution. This chapter then focuses on two recent offshoots of classical theory: rational choice and routine activities theories. Finally, the chapter briefly reviews how classical theory has influenced policy-making in criminal justice.

CLASSICAL THEORY

Classical theory has several basic elements:

1. People in society have free will to choose criminal or conventional solutions to meet their needs or settle their problems.

2. Criminal solutions may be more attractive than conventional ones, because they usually require less work for a greater payoff.

3. A person's choice of criminal solutions may be controlled by fear of society's reaction to such acts.

4. The more *severe, certain,* and *swift* the reaction, the better it can control criminal behavior.

5. The most efficient crime prevention device is punishment sufficient to make crime an unattractive choice.

Thus, the basic premise of classical theory is that all men and women have the potential to be criminals if not kept in check by fear of punishment.

The classical view was one of the first formal criminological theories. Originally developed in the mid-eighteenth century, it provided the impetus for the penal reform movements of the nineteenth century.[1] Its roots can be traced to the philosophies of John Locke and Jean Jacques Rousseau, who recognized the rights of all people to be equal under the law, and who called for the state to protect people's natural rights to "life, liberty, and property."[2] Though these philosophers believed state-administered punishment was necessary to protect rights, they believed it should not be cruel, excessive, or capricious.

FOUNDATIONS OF CLASSICAL THEORY

When classical theory was being formulated, the existing systems of punishment, law, and justice were chaotic. Although there was general agreement as to what acts constituted crimes, the penalties for law violators were often arbitrary, discretionary, and cruel. In France, the Criminal Ordinance of 1670 was the first attempt to codify legal sanctions. It limited the arbitrary power of judges, but in several instances it did not specify a penalty, giving the magistrate discretion to increase or diminish punishments according to the circumstances of the case.[3]

Punishments included public flogging, branding, burning, beheading, and worse. By the sixteenth century, even simple wanderers and vagabonds had come to be viewed as dangerous and were subject to these extreme penalties. Well-known members of the clergy, such as Martin Luther, called for rulers to "pursue, beat, strangle, hang and torture" offenders. In England, by 1829, the number of crimes punished by the death penalty was in the hundreds.[4]

By the mid-eighteenth century, many social philosophers began to call for a rethinking of the prevailing concepts of law and justice. While a majority still advocated that the harshest possible penalties be meted out to law violators, others argued for a more rational approach to punishment. They stressed that the relationship between crimes and their punishment should be balanced and fair. Rather than public executions designed to frighten people into obedience, reformers called for a more moderate approach to penal sanctions.[5] Two of these reformers, **Cesare Beccaria** and **Jeremy Bentham,** are considered the founders of the classical approach.

Cesare Beccaria

Cesare Bonesana, Marquis of Beccaria, was born into an aristocratic family in Milan, Italy, in 1738. Beccaria was a firm advocate of the principle of **utility,** which maintains that people are basically rational creatures who choose their own courses of action. Humans, according to this view, want to achieve pleasure and avoid pain; crimes must therefore provide some pleasure to the criminal. It follows that to deter crime, pain must be administered in an appropriate amount to counterbalance the pleasure obtained from crime. In keeping with his utilitarian views, Beccaria stated: "The fundamental principle that should govern the creation and maintenance of laws is 'the greatest happiness to be shared by the greatest number of people.' "[6]

Like the French philosopher Jean Jacques Rousseau, Beccaria viewed law and justice as a social contract: a set of rules that guarantee life, liberty, and happiness to all people. Beccaria stated: "Weary of living in a continual state of war, and of enjoying a liberty rendered useless by the uncertainty of preserving it, [people] sacrificed a part so that they might enjoy the rest of it in peace and safety."[7] Yet, he did not suggest that people would obey laws freely, sacrificing a portion of their personal liberty merely to promote the common good. Since people are self-centered, they must be goaded by the fear of punishment, which provides a tangible motive for them to obey the law.

On Punishment. Beccaria believed that for a criminal penalty to achieve its purpose, the pain it inflicted had only to exceed the advantage that could be obtained from the crime it sought to control. In calculating the relationship between crime and punishment, he believed that the law should take into account the "certainty of punishment and loss of good the crime might have produced."[8] Certainty of punishment, rather than severity, was of the greatest import for deterrence.

Beccaria is credited with almost single-handedly causing the abolition of torture, which was used both to obtain confessions from the accused and to punish the convicted. He pointed out to world leaders how torture enabled the "robust scoundrel" who could resist it to go free, while condemning the innocent person who happened to be weak. Torture, Beccaria claimed, put the innocent in a position in which they could lose (if they confessed to a false accusation) and the guilty in a position in which they could gain (if they resisted torture and were absolved of a wrong).

Beccaria firmly believed that severe, brutal punishment was unnecessary. He suggested that people could adapt to even the most hideous punishment: "The severity of punishment of itself emboldens men to commit the very wrong it is supposed to prevent."[9] Moreover, he claimed that when punishment was very severe, criminals would commit additional crimes since they would have nothing more to lose. Beccaria was a staunch opponent of the indiscriminate use of capital punishment, believing it should be used only on rare occasions.

Crime and Punishment. Rather than increase the cruelty of punishment to control criminality, Beccaria believed it would be more effective to closely link crime with its consequences in the minds of would-be criminals. Of greatest importance to Beccaria was establishing the proper proportions between crimes and punishments.

There are several reasons for this approach. Most importantly, if two crimes that do not equally injure society are punished equally, then people will not be deterred from committing the greater of the two crimes. For example, if both bank robbery and murder are punished by death, a bank robber would have little reason to refrain from killing any witnesses to the robbery. To be effective, the punishment for a crime must be justified by the harm done.

Beccaria stated the following theorem:

In order for punishment not to be in every instance, an act of violence of one or many against a private citizen, it must be essentially public, prompt, necessary, the least possible in the given circumstances, proportionate to the crimes, dictated by the laws.[10]

Beccaria's principles of justice have continued to influence criminological thinking for two hundred years.

Jeremy Bentham, whose philosophy formed the foundations of utilitarianism.

Jeremy Bentham

The second major philosophical influence on the classical school was the British philosopher Jeremy Bentham. Born in 1748 to a well-to-do family, Bentham spent his life trying to develop a system of scientific jurisprudence and legislation. His writings made his thoughts famous at home and abroad. When he died in 1833, **Benthamism** continued as a philosophical system for more than fifty years. In addition, his philosophy had an important effect on British policy and governmental structure.

The Concept of Utility.   Bentham's thoughts on the nature of human behavior can be stated briefly:

> *Nature has placed mankind under the governance of two sovereign masters, pain and pleasure . . . they govern us in all we do, in all we say, in all we think: every effort we can make to throw off our subjection will serve but to demonstrate and confirm it.*[11]

Actions are evaluated by their tendency to produce advantages, pleasure, and happiness, and to avoid or prevent mischief, pain, evil, or unhappiness.

Bentham created a **moral calculus** for estimating the likelihood that any individual would engage in a particular act. It involves weighing the possibility that an act will cause current or future pleasure against the possibility that it will create current or future pain. Since human judgment is complex, Bentham provided hundreds of independent factors to be considered and evaluated. They included the pleasures wealth, skill, benevolence, and piety; the pains of desire and disappointment; and the senses, such as hunger or thirst.[12]

Law and Punishment.   Bentham believed that the purpose of all law was to produce and support the happiness of the community it served. Since punishment was in itself harmful, its existence was only justified if it promised to prevent greater evil than it created. Bentham stated that punishment, therefore, had four main objectives: (1) to prevent all criminal offenses; (2) when it cannot prevent a crime, to convince the offender to commit a less serious one; (3) to insure that a criminal uses no more force than is necessary; and (4) to prevent crime as cheaply as possible. He derived six rules to guide punishment:

1. The value of the punishment must not be less, in any case, than what is sufficient to outweigh that of the profit of the offense.
2. The greater the mischief of the offense, the greater is the expense which it may be worthwhile to be at, in the way of punishment.
3. Where two offenses come in competition, the punishment for the greater offense must be sufficient to induce a person to prefer the lesser.
4. The punishment should be adjusted in such a manner to each particular offense, that for every part of the mischief there may be a motive to restrain the offender from giving birth to it.
5. The punishment ought in no case to be more than what is necessary to bring it into conformity with the rules here given.
6. That the quantity actually inflicted on each individual offender may correspond to the quantity intended for similar offenders in general, the several circumstances influencing sensibility ought always to be taken into account.[13]

These rules are the theoretical concepts underlying what is known today as classical criminology.

——————— CLASSICAL JUSTICE ———————

Classical criminology as formulated by Beccaria and Bentham was a significant force in jurisprudence and legal policy for over 100 years. The belief that punishment should fit the crime and that people should be punished for what they did, and not to satisfy the whim of a capricious judge or ruler, was widely accepted throughout Europe and the United States. The most important example of how classical philosophy was embraced in Europe occurred in 1789, when France's post-revolutionary Constituent Assembly adopted this belief in the **Declaration of the Rights of Man:**

> The law has the right to prohibit only actions harmful to society . . . The law shall inflict only such punishments as are strictly and clearly necessary . . . no person shall be punished except by virtue of a law enacted and promulgated previous to the crime and applicable to its terms.[14]

Similarly, a prohibition against "cruel and unusual punishment" was incorporated in the Eighth Amendment to the U.S. Constitution. Thus, the use of torture and harsh punishment was largely abandoned in the nineteenth century. The practice of incarcerating criminals and structuring prison sentences to fit the severity of crime was a reflection of classical criminology.

The classical perspective had a significant influence on judicial and correctional philosophy throughout the nineteenth and early twentieth centuries. Fierce physical punishments and tortures gave way to prison sentences calibrated to fit the seriousness of the crime. Structured prison sentences became the punishment of choice in the United States and Europe. Capital punishment was still widely used, but slowly it began to be employed for only the most serious crimes. The byword was "let the punishment fit the crime."

The classical approach was not without its critics. Some criminologists, influenced by the emerging sciences of psychology and sociology, began to question its "free will" philosophy. Criminals, they argued, could not govern their behavior, since criminal behavior was a function of psychological, biological, or social abnormality. Factors such as personality, poverty, intelligence, and family life—not greed and immorality—were the true causes of criminality. It was therefore futile to use punishment as a means of controlling crime; treatment and rehabilitation were the keys to preventing crime.

This new **positivist** view of crime began to have an influence on justice policy. Positivists advocated treating the root cause of crime through rehabilitation programs, rather than deterring it through the fear of punishment. As early as 1866 in Massachusetts and 1877 in New York, the **indeterminate prison sentence** was legislated into being.[15] Under this model, prisoners were confined for at least a short stay; after the minimum sentence was up, they were kept in prison only until the authorities believed them rehabilitated sufficiently to be released. This sentencing philosophy became the most widespread in the United States, and indicated a preference for crime-control programs which stressed rehabilitation theory over the traditional reliance on the fear of legal punishment.

By the mid-twentieth century, positivist criminology became a dominant force in American jurisprudence. Though classical principles still controlled much of the legal process, and though some political candidates ran on 'law-and-order' planks, professional criminologists rejected the core concepts of classical criminology.[16]

The Rise of Modern Classicism

In the late 1970s and into the 1980s, three factors rekindled interest in classical criminology. First, there was disenchantment with the failure of positivist criminology to isolate specific crime-producing traits or factors. After 50 years of research, positivist criminologists were still unable to identify the "true" cause of criminality. Second, the rehabilitation of known criminals, considered a cornerstone of positivist policy, came under attack. A number of national surveys (the most well-known being Robert Martinson's *What Works?*) failed to uncover examples of rehabilitation programs that could prevent future criminal activity.[17] (See Close-Up entitled "Could Successful Rehabilitation Reduce the Crime Rate?" in this chapter.)

CLOSE-UP

Could Successful Rehabilitation Reduce the Crime Rate?

Ernest Van Den Haag is a well-known advocate of modern classical criminology. He has long championed the need for punishment to reduce crime rates and give criminals their just deserts. Conversely, he is skeptical about the worth of treatment-oriented programs in rehabilitating criminals.

In a widely read paper, Van Den Haag poses the question, "Could successful rehabilitation programs reduce the crime rate?" That is, if every known criminal could be successfully rehabilitated, would it appreciably influence the annual number of crimes taking place in the United States?

Van Den Haag thinks not. First, rehabilitation programs can only be used to control people who have already been caught. They are useless against both first offenders who have never been apprehended and habitual criminals who evade the net of justice.

But, even if recidivists (repeat offenders) committed almost all crimes and rehabilitation programs were uniformly successful in treating them, Van Den Haag still believed that rehabilitation cannot work. The number of persons engaged in any activity, legal or illegal, depends on the comparative net advantage they expect. For example, people become dentists because they expect profit, a respected social standing, and other benefits. Consequently, every dentist who retires, dies, or changes occupations is replaced by another because the need for dentistry remains constant. If many dentists were removed from the profession, a temporary disruption of services might result, but eventually the increased advantages of the field (since the patient-to-dentist ratio would now have increased) would draw recruits to the field.

By analogy, new car thieves, drug dealers, and burglars would be drawn to their respective "fields" if all current practitioners were "retired" through rehabilitation efforts. As long as there exists an advantage—in wealth, power, pleasure, and social gain—in committing crime, there will also exist a ready pool of recruits willing to take advantage of it.

Van Den Haag believes that crime can be controlled only through decreasing its advantages. When punishments are severe enough and the chance of apprehension great, only then will crime be reduced. Rehabilitation is doomed to failure. He concludes:

Our only hope for reducing the burgeoning crime rate lies in decreasing the expected net advantage of committing crimes (compared to lawful activities) by increasing the cost through increasing the expected severity of punishments and the probability of suffering them. The cost is low enough now to make crime pay for a rising number of persons, because of legal practices which were justified by the hope of rehabilitation and the mistaken idea that rehabilitation could reduce the crime rate. These legal practices, which have made the threats of the law less than daunting, must be abandoned if we are to reduce the crime rate. Probation must become exceptional. Parole and indeterminate sentences must be abolished, and so must judicial sentencing discretion and the numerous other programs meant to reduce the crime rate by rehabilitation. Punishment must become predictable. A higher apprehension and conviction rate is also needed, and could readily be produced by changes in counter-productive legal and judicial practices which make "the incarceration of even the most obviously guilty criminal . . . a task comparable to landing a barracuda with a trout-rod and a dry-fly." I believe we will move in that direction. Meanwhile, it may help if we stop relying on such dead-end streets as rehabilitation and the practices connected with it.

SOURCE: Ernest Van Den Haag, "Could Successful Rehabilitation Reduce the Crime Rate," *Journal of Criminal Law and Criminology* 73 (1985):1022–35.

Compounding the problems of positivist criminology, a significant increase in the reported crime rate, serious disturbances in the prison system, and the emergence of more conservative political views sparked the public demand for effective law enforcement and stricter criminal sanctions.[18] To many criminologists, reviving the classical concepts of deterrence, social control, and punishment made more sense than attempts to rehabilitate known criminals.[19]

In its modern form, classical theory embodies a

number of different concepts. It is possible for a criminologist to personally embrace only one or two of these concepts and still be considered a classicist. In the following sections, the most prominent concepts of classical theory are discussed. While each is an independent concept, the sum of these concepts is considered the heart of modern classical theory.

GENERAL DETERRENCE

General deterrence has been defined as "the inhibiting effect of sanctions on the criminal activity of people other than the sanctioned offender."[20] It refers to the anticipated inverse relationship between the probability a crime will occur and the severity, certainty, and celerity (speed) with which people who have committed that crime in the past have been punished. Put another way, if potential criminals believe there is a great deal of certainty that they will be apprehended by police, tried without delay, and punished severely, they will probably choose not to engage in law violations.

According to general deterrence theory, the factors of severity, certainty, and celerity are interrelated. For example, if a crime—say, robbery—has a severe penalty but few robbers are ever caught and punished, it is likely that the threat of punishment will not deter people from robbery. On the other hand, if the certainty of apprehension and conviction is increased through police efficiency, then even a mild punishment might be sufficient to deter the potential robber.

Another issue influencing the probability of deterrence is the level of crime prevention desired by lawmakers. In some cases, **partial deterrence** is desired; in these cases, the act is not eliminated but restricted or controlled in some way. For example, the sixty-five mile-per-hour speed limit might cause some offenders to violate the law by going only seventy miles-per-hour, when before they would have gone faster. Or, law banning the sale of alcohol on Sunday might restrict public intoxication to Monday through Saturday. Partial deterrence strategies define the boundaries of acceptable and unacceptable behavior.

In contrast, **absolute deterrence** is intended to totally eliminate a particular criminal act. For example, passage of a law requiring a mandatory life sentence for the sale of heroin would be construed as a measure seeking absolute deterrence of that act. The most powerful absolute deterrence measure is thought to be the death penalty. The effectiveness of the death penalty as a deterrent to murder is explored in some detail in the Close-Up entitled "Does the Death Penalty Deter Murder?".

Deterrence and Perceived Threat

The underlying assumption of the general deterrence model is that people are fully aware of the punishments associated with criminal acts and choose to forego law-violating behaviors because of those punishments. If people were unaware of the pains associated with criminal sanctions, then the force of punishment would have no effect on them.

Very little research has been done to determine if people really are aware of criminal penalties. One study found that among a general population sample, respondents could correctly answer only 25 to 30 percent of questions measuring knowledge of criminal penalties; when prisoners were asked the same questions, 57 percent were answered correctly.[21] These data seem to suggest that information on criminal penalties alone is not a deterrent.

Michael Geerken and Walter Gove have tried to place the perception issue into a theoretical framework.[22] They argue that the way perceptions of the certainty and severity of punishment are originally formed is a major contributing factor to the effectiveness of general deterrence. For example, they suggest that "the more members of the social system rely on the mass media for their information about criminal behavior, the greater the effects of the deterrence system."[23] Geerken and Gove believe that if people hear about crime and punishment from newspapers, television, and radio, they develop an exaggerated view of the effectiveness of law enforcement and the severity of punishment, because media sources tend to report on crimes that have been solved and offenders who have been punished. Furthermore, since the mass media report on individual cases, the deterrent effect is often graphic. In this case, deterrent measures should be effective.

However, Geerken and Gove also maintain that "the more members of a social system have detailed knowledge about crime, the more specific the deterrence message and the less efficient the deterrence

CLOSE-UP

Does the Death Penalty Deter Murder?

One of the cornerstones of the general deterrence concept is the view that death, the ultimate penalty, should deter murder, the ultimate crime. Considerable empirical research has been carried out on the effectiveness of capital punishment as a deterrent. Criminologists have tried to discover whether the death sentence serves as a more effective deterrent than life imprisonment for capital crimes such as homicide. In general, results have not supported a deterrent effect.

One of the first noteworthy studies was conducted in Philadelphia in 1935 by Robert Dann, who calculated the number of homicides in the 60-day period prior to and after five highly publicized executions. Dann found that more homicides occurred during the 60 days *following* an execution than prior to it, suggesting that the overall impact of executions might actually serve to increase the incidence of homicide rather than deter it. Dann's findings have been duplicated by other researchers, convincing some critics that the death penalty has a "brutalization effect," which encourages rather than deters lethal violence.

In another pioneering study, Karl Schuessler examined annual data for homicide rates and execution risks (the numbers of executions for murder per 1,000 homicides per year) in 11 states. He concluded that these variables were independent of each other. Extending this analysis to include European countries before and after the abolition of the death penalty, Schuessler found nothing in the data to suggest that homicide trends were influenced by capital punishment. More recent research by Dane Archer, Rosemary Gartner, and Marc Beittel, comparing homicide rates in 14 nations around the world, found that homicide rates declined after capital punishment was abolished, a direct contradiction to its supposed deterrent effect.

Another commonly used method of determining the deterrent effect of capital punishment is to compare the murder rates of states which maintain the death penalty with contiguous or similar jurisdictions which have abolished capital punishment. Two pioneering works, one by Thorsten Sellin and the other by Walter Reckless, found that states maintaining capital punishment had virtually identical homicide rates to those which had canceled its use. Recent updates of Sellin's work are consistent in showing that contiguous states with or without capital punishment have essentially the same homicide rates.

In one of the few research efforts showing capital punishment to have a deterrent effect, Isaac Ehrlich used econometric statistical techniques to uncover evidence that the likelihood of a person's committing a crime is influenced by his or her perception of execution risk. As a result of his analysis, Ehrlich concluded that each additional execution per year in the United States would save seven or eight people from murder.

Ehrlich's research has been widely cited by death penalty advocates as empirical proof of the deterrent effect of capital punishment. However, a subsequent analysis by William Bowers and Glenn Pierce, replicating Ehrlich's analysis but using a somewhat different statistical technique, showed that his approach merely confirms previous findings that capital punishment is no more effective a deterrent than life imprisonment.

In sum, studies that have attempted to show the actual impact of capital punishment on the murder rate indicate that the execution of convicted criminals is no more a deterrent than a long prison term. How can we explain this? The nature of the victim-criminal relationship in murder transactions is still the most likely reason. Most murders are the result of conflicts between friends, acquaintances, and family members, such as lovers' quarrels and domestic disputes. The passions involved in murder are so great that they may obstruct the deterrent power of the law. Similarly, many murders occur during felonies such as holdups and burglaries. An offender surprised in the act of committing a crime, perhaps under the influence of alcohol or drugs, may be far removed from the law's deterrent power.

---

system."[24] People in high-crime areas learn about the possibility of being punished for their criminal acts directly from active law violators. Therefore, they are more likely to be aware that the system of justice and punishment is less effective than the media make it out to be. Also, in high-crime jurisdictions, the strain on criminal justice resources is such that the probability of deterring a particular crime is lower than it would

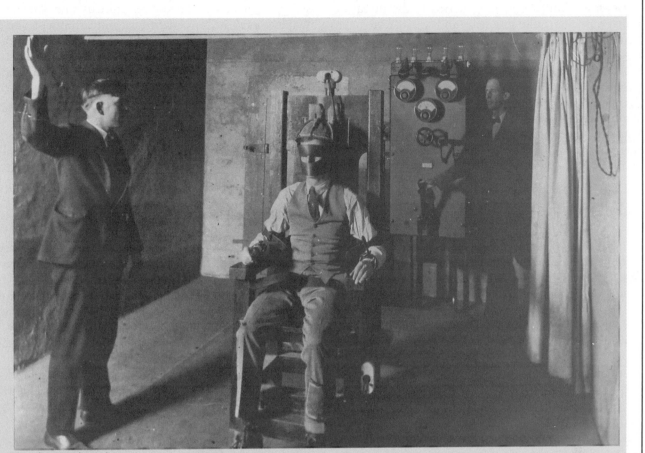

An electric chair demonstration, ca. 1928.

Discussion Questions

1. Do you think that the death penalty has a deterrent effect on murder?

2. If the death penalty does not deter murder, can its use be justified on other grounds?

SOURCES: Robert H. Dann, "The Deterrent Effect of Capital Punishment," *Friends Social Service Series* 29 (1935):1; David Phillips, "The Deterrent Effect of Capital Punishment," *American Journal of Sociology* 86 (1980):139–48; Karl F. Schuessler, "The Deterrent Influence of the Death Penalty," *Annals* 284 (1952):54; Dane Archer, Rosemary Gartner, and Marc Beittel, "Homicide and the Death Penalty: A Cross-National Test of a Deterrence Hypothesis," *The Journal of Criminal Law and Criminology* 74 (1983):991–1014; Thorsten Sellin, "Effect of Repeal and Reintroduction of the Death Penalty on Homicide Rates," in Thorsten Sellin, ed., *The Death Penalty* (Philadelphia: American Law Institute, 1959); Walter C. Reckless, "Use of the Death Penalty," *Crime and Delinquency* 15 (1969):43–53; Isaac Ehrlich, "The Deterrent Effect of Capital Punishment: A Question of Life or Death," *American Economic Review* 65 (1975):397; William J. Bowers and Glenn L. Pierce, "The Illusion of Deterrence in Isaac Ehrlich's Research on Capital Punishment," *Yale Law Journal* 85 (1975):187–208.

be in areas where the police and courts can devote more attention and resources to individual cases.

In a study of drug dealing, Sheldon Ekland-Olson, John Lieb, and Louis Zurcher found that the relationship between perceived threat and deterrence was complex.[25] If interpersonal relationships were unlikely to be affected by an arrest, the perceived severity of the arrest was low—"just a hassle." If, however, it was believed that an arrest would threaten a friendship circle or a criminal operating network, the threat of arrest was taken quite seriously, and arrests were to be avoided at all costs. Ekland-Olson and his associates also found that the fear of sanctions tends to increase solidarity among criminal groups.[26] To reduce the probability of arrest, a criminal will deal only with people of proven character. Such research suggests that those interested in deterrence must take into account the dynamics of criminal interaction when they attempt to understand the crime-prevention effect of punishment.

Research on Deterrence

A great deal of research has been devoted to determining whether deterrent measures, such as arrest and legal punishments, affect people's behavior. Some studies have made use of aggregate data sources, such as the Uniform Crime Report (UCR). Another approach has been to determine the effect of the perceived threat of punishment on potential offenders. Still another approach has been to conduct experiments which test the threat of punishment on behavior.

Aggregate Data Research. Criminologists who use aggregate data are interested in measuring the association between the risk of apprehension and punishment and the extent of crime. According to the general deterrence concept, those areas in which the probability of arrest and conviction is greatest and in which punishment is most severe also should have relatively low crime rates.

A number of studies have found that the frequency of arrest (arrest probability) does in fact significantly lower crime rates.[27] For example, Charles Tittle and Alan Rowe found that areas in which police officers achieved at least a 30 percent arrest rate experienced a deterrent effect on crime.[28] Similarly, Edwin Zedlewski discovered a relationship between the amount of police resources available and the rate of certain crimes such as burglary. In an analysis of National Crime Survey (NCS) victimization data, Zedlewski also found that every 1 percent increase in the arrest probability produced a corresponding 1.8 percent *decrease* in property crime victimizations.[29]

Not all research efforts have found that the de-

terrent effect of punishment reduces the crime rate. In an oft-cited study, Theodore Chiricos and Gordon Waldo developed a certainty of imprisonment variable, by computing the ratio between the number of prison admissions for one year and the average number of crimes known to the police.[30] They found an inconsistent relationship between the certainty and severity of punishment and the crime rate, including such serious offenses as homicide.

Nonetheless, the weight of the evidence is that the probability of arrest and punishment does have a measurable impact on the crime rate: some deterrent strategies may actually lower the crime rate. However, this conclusion must be accepted with some degree of caution. One problem is a possible displacement effect: severe and certain punishment may not permanently deter criminals but simply cause them to relocate to safer territory. Consequently, if every jurisdiction used the same crime-control mechanism, the crime rate would be unaffected. Similarly, as Daniel Nagin argues, a deterrent effect produced by increasing the probability of punishment may actually reflect the effects of incapacitation rather than the fear of legal sanctions. That is, deterrence strategies, such as increasing police effectiveness, conviction rates, and the length of prison sentences, will remove the most likely offenders from society and thereby reduce the crime rate. What appears to be a deterrent effect (fear of punishment frightening potential criminals) is actually an effect of incapacitation (crime is reduced because known criminals have a greater chance of being apprehended and locked up).[31]

Perceptual Research. Because of the problems inherent in using aggregate data, modern classical criminologists have turned to perceptual research to study deterrent effects. This approach uses self-report surveys to ask people whether they feel that they will be caught if they engage in some crime, and whether they actually engage in that crime. Deterrence theory is supported if people who feel they will be arrested or punished for an act also refrain from engaging in that act. Deterrence theory is contradicted if prior perceptions of punishment have little or no effect on subsequent behavior.

In recent years, several perceptual studies have been conducted to test deterrence. Unfortunately, because of methodological problems, results are rather inconclusive.[32] In one such study, Harold Grasnick and George Bryjak surveyed 400 people to determine whether perceived certainty and severity of punishment were related to criminality.[33] They found that the deterrence effect is most noticeable among people who believe they are: (1) certain to be arrested for a crime, and (2) certain to be punished if arrested. Put another way, people fear getting arrested if they also believe they are likely to be severely punished. In a similar research effort, Grasnick and his associate found that subjects who perceived the greatest certainty and severity of punishment also believed they would not engage in future criminal behavior.[34]

Other researchers have found the fear of legal sanctions is actually outweighed by nonlegal factors, such as personal values, fear of social disapproval, or loss of self-respect. For example, Dale Berger and John Snortum found that moral commitment against drinking and driving may outweigh perceptions of arrest risk as a deterrent to drunk driving.[35] Similarly, Charles Tittle found in a national survey of almost 2,000 subjects, that perception of **informal sanctions** was a more effective deterrent than perception of formal sanctions.[36] Tittle concluded that social control seems to be rooted almost entirely in how people perceive negative reactions from interpersonal acquaintances (family, friends), while formal sanctions (arrest, prison) are irrelevant in an immediate sense. Only experienced offenders seemed to fear societal punishment, causing Tittle to conclude that legal sanctions do no more than supplement informal control processes by influencing a small segment of "criminally inclined" persons.

Other studies support this finding. For example, Matthew Silberman found that commitment to "conventional morality" provided a general deterrent effect.[37] In a similar vein, Linda Anderson, Theodore Chiricos, and Gordon Waldo found that informal sanctions and peer disapproval were more important deterrents of drug use than fear of formal punishment.[38]

Panel Studies.   It is actually not surprising that people who have already committed criminal acts report that they do not feel threatened by legal sanctions. To show that the threat of legal punishment inhibits behavior, a researcher must prove that lawbreakers felt no threat before they engaged in criminal acts. A few studies have attempted to accomplish this goal by measuring an intact group, or *panel*, of subjects over time. The deterrence concept would be supported if:

(1) people's perceptions of sanctions could be shown to remain stable between measurements, and (2) those who at first feared the deterrent effect of the law later refrained from engaging in criminal behaviors.

Several studies have explored this issue. In one study, Donna Bishop surveyed 2,147 high-school students over a nine-month interval.[39] Although her data indicate that perceptions of deterrence are not stable, nevertheless there was a significant deterrent effect. Bishop concluded that current behavior choices influence subsequent criminal involvement. It seems that once criminal activity is successfully initiated, it tends to be followed by a reassessment of the likelihood of getting caught. If the perceptions of risk are lowered, this in turn promotes further criminality.

In contrast to Bishop's assessment, similar research by Raymond Paternoster and his associates, and by W. William Minor and Joseph Harry, found little evidence that perceptions of punishment actually deter crime.[40] All three studies agree, however, that perceptions of deterrence change over time, and that studies measuring deterrent effects must be longitudinal. Studies using a single measure of criminal behavior, and perceptions of deterrence such as those mentioned earlier, may be methodologically unsound.[41]

In sum, available research evidence so far has not shown that perceptions of punishment alone can deter crime. However, there are many conceptual and methodological issues still to be examined.[42] Further research is needed to identify the nonlegal factors, such as moral inhibition and fear of peer disapproval, which may play an important role in crime prevention.[43] As Raymond Paternoster points out, perceptual research is still in its infancy and has all too often employed nonrepresentative samples of college and high-school students, and trivial offense patterns such as smoking marijuana.[44]

Experimental Research.   One of the most significant drawbacks of existing deterrence research is that few true experiments have been run to test the effects of deterrence. Criminologists have rarely conducted research in which the subject's criminal behavior was observed, a deterrent factor was then introduced, and finally its effect was determined. The lack of experimental research is probably due to the difficulty of finding subjects whose criminal behavior can be subjected to a controlled deterrent. Most experimental

The underlying assumption of general deterrence is that people are aware of the punishments associated with criminal acts.

studies have dealt with deviant behaviors, such as cheating on tests, or motor vehicle offenses rather than with actual criminal behaviors.[45] The most well-known research of this sort is H. Laurence Ross's analysis of the deterrent effects of anti-drunk driving laws on motor vehicle violations. Ross found that when laws are toughened, there is a short-term deterrent effect. However, because the likelihood of getting caught is relatively low, the impact of deterrent measures on alcohol-impaired driving is negligible over the long term.[46]

One recent study by Gary Green has shown that for at least one crime—using an illegal unauthorized descrambler to obtain pay cable programs—deterrent strategies may work. Green first determined how many people out of a sample of 3,500 in a western town were using a descrambler and avoiding payments to the local cable company. Threatening letters, which conveyed the general message that illegal theft of cable signals would be criminally prosecuted, were sent to the 67 violators; the letters did not indicate that the subjects' personal violations had been discovered. Green found that about two-thirds of the 67 violators reacted to the threat by desisting and removing the

illegal devices; a six-month follow-up showed that the intervention effect had lasted.[47]

Though Green's research is restricted to an atypical crime pattern and a small sample, his positive results indicate the need for future experimental research in deterrence.

Analysis of the General Deterrence Concept. General deterrence is the heart of classical criminology. Modern classical theorists, like Ernest Van Den Haag, believe that the purpose of the law and justice system is to create a "threat system":

> Criminal laws prohibit some acts and try to deter from them by conditional threats which specify the punishments of persons who were not deterred. Sufficiently frequent imposition of these punishments by courts of law makes the threats credible. If the community feels that they are deserved, punishments also gratify its sense of justice, and help to legitimize the threat system of the criminal law by stigmatizing crime as morally odious.[48]

The legal threat of punishment should, on the face of it, deter lawbreakers through a generalized fear of punishment. How many people can claim that they never had an urge to commit crime that was deterred by fear of discovery and its consequences? Nonetheless, few studies show that perceptions of deterrence or deterrent measures actually reduce the propensity to commit crime or lower the crime rate. There is some indication that an increase in the arrest or conviction rate (or in the belief that an arrest or conviction will occur) is correlated with a decrease in crime, but the relationship seems far less substantial than classical theorists would like us to believe.

How can this discrepancy be explained? First, deterrence theory demands a rational weighing and shifting of costs and benefits by the potential offender. There is reason to believe that in many instances criminals are desperate people, either acting under the influence of drugs and alcohol, or suffering from personality disorders. Surveys of inmates show a significant proportion were under the influence of drugs at the time they committed the crimes they are being punished for. It is likely that general deterrence would have little influence on these offenders. Even Raymond Paternoster, one of the most methodologically sophisticated deterrence researchers, warns proponents of the deterrence doctrine to prepare themselves for possible bad news: the assumption that humans are rational, calculating creatures whose behavior is controlled by their fear of punishment may be a myth. After carefully reviewing more than a decade of deterrence research, Paternoster found little hard evidence that people who fear the law will also forego criminal behavior.[49]

Second, many offenders are members of what Ken Auletta calls the "under class"—people cut off from society, lacking the education, skills, and other traits they need to be in demand in the modern economy.[50] Can such desperate people be deterred by fear of punishment? What alternatives are open to them? It may be unreasonable to expect that people who have little chance of improving themselves through legitimate means will be deterred by an abstract fear of distant laws.

Third, as Beccaria's famous equation tells us, the threat of punishment involves not only its severity but its certainty and speed. Our legal system is not very effective. As noted in Chapter 3, only 10 percent of serious offenses are cleared by police. As apprehended offenders are processed through all the stages of the criminal justice system, the odds of their receiving serious punishment for committing an index crime approach 40 to one. As Geerken and Gove point out, these lessons are not lost on people involved in serious criminal behavior.

So, although general deterrence remains an intriguing concept—and is certainly responsible for some reduction in the crime rate—it seems an unlikely device for eliminating crime per se. Besides, would we want to live in a society whose laws were certain, swift, and severe enough to eliminate all law violations?

─────── SPECIAL DETERRENCE ───────

The term **special deterrence** refers to the inhibiting effect of punishment on the convicted criminal. The theory of special deterrence holds that if the memory of a punishment, such as a prison sentence, is so vivid that it exceeds the expected future benefits of crime, offenders will desist because they fear the consequences. The more intense and sure the punishment, the greater its potential as a special deterrent. The

belief that brutal punishment was an effective special deterrent was an important motivation for the use of physical chastisement, such as whipping, branding, and mutilation, in almost every Western society until the nineteenth century.

While the concept of special deterrence may seem to be valid, whether it works in practice is another matter. Many experts believe that our current system of punishing criminals, though often criticized for its severity, has relatively little effect on the recidivism (repeat offense) rate. Even the most severely punished offenders are likely to repeat their offenses; one recent study found that 72 percent of prison releases were rearrested within two years of their discharge.[51]

How can the alleged failure of special deterrence be explained? For one thing, our currently inconsistent forms of criminal punishment may embitter offenders, add to their sense of injustice, and increase rather than diminish their motivation to commit crime. Punishments which are actually severe enough to deter even the most motivated offender from further law violations may be so brutal that they shock the conscience, are offensive to most citizens, and violate constitutional prohibitions against "cruel and unusual punishment." In addition, punishing criminals so severely that they are afraid to commit crime seems to be in conflict with the social goal of rehabilitation and reform.

On a more practical level, punishment may have little effect on crime because the full weight of the law is seldom applied. Therefore, legal punishments have little influence on the offender's perception of the law's sanctioning power. In a recent study, George Bridges and James Stone found that offenders who had already experienced punishment had little fear of future penalties.[52] One reason may be that experienced criminals recognize that in our society even the most serious felons, such as convicted rapists, may receive probation or other lenient sentences.[53] A recent federal study of sentencing decisions in 28 jurisdictions found that about 8 percent of people convicted of homicide and 16 percent of those convicted of rape received a probation sentence only.[54]

Just and Painful

The use of special deterrence as a means of crime control has received support form Graeme Newman in his book *Just and Painful*.[55] Newman argues that society should return to the use of corporal punishment. He approves of using electric shocks because they are over with quickly, have no lasting effect, and can be adjusted to fit the severity of a crime. Newman's book puts forth some ideas, including:

- Acute corporal punishment should be introduced to fill the gap between the severe punishment of prison and the nonpunishment of probation.

- For the majority of property crimes, the preferred corporal punishment is that of electric shock, because it can be scientifically controlled and is relatively less violent in its application than other corporal punishments, such as whipping.

- For violent crimes in which the victim was terrified and humiliated, and for which a local community does not wish to incarcerate, a violent corporal punishment should be considered, such as whipping. In these cases, humiliation of the offender is seen as justifiably deserved.

- Every effort should be made to develop a split system of criminal justice: one system for the punishment of *crimes*, and one for the punishment of *criminals*. After an offender has committed a number of repeated offenses, or when the combined injury and damage of crimes reach a certain amount, that person will be treated as a criminal deserving incarceration.

In sum, Newman finds that special deterrence strategies can be useful if they are relatively inexpensive, of short duration, can be individualized, and leave no lasting disability.

----------- INCAPACITATION -----------

In our society, **incapacitation** is favored as a means of keeping dangerous criminals out of circulation and of protecting the victims of crime from further misdeeds. The best-known defense of incapacitation is the widely read book, *Thinking about Crime*, written by political scientist James Q. Wilson.[56]

Wilson asks the question, "What measures can be used to prevent crime without regard to the reasons why people engage in it in the first place?" In his opinion, punishment and incapacitation are the answers. He charges that a small number of people commit a great proportion of crimes, and that these individuals do not fear punishment even though they are frequently arrested. Wilson says the problem lies with the courts and correctional agencies, which, because of their desire to rehabilitate criminals, have neglected their job of protecting the public. Rehabilitation is not the answer because (1) treatment plans don't seem to work and (2) different people who commit the same crime often receive different sentences, thus violating the offenders' and the public's sense of justice.

Wilson therefore argues for abandoning rehabilitation and embracing classical theory:

Criminals may be willing to run greater risks (or they may have a weaker sense of morality) than the average citizen, but if the expected cost of crime goes up without a corresponding increase in the expected benefits then the would-be criminal—unless he or she is among that small fraction of criminals who are utterly irrational—engages in less crime.[57]

He suggests that the following policies be adopted to reduce crime:

- Devote the resources of the criminal courts to the issue of sentencing

- Create uniform sentencing practices

- Make every conviction for nontrivial offenses entail a penalty that involves "deprivation of liberty", or incarceration.

- Let deprivation of liberty make use of community-based programs that enable the inmate to work or receive treatment; however, the prospects for rehabilitation should not be allowed to govern the length of sentence.

- Make conviction for a subsequent offense invariably lead to an increased term of deprivation of liberty; penalties would be designed to fit the crime, with some discretion given to a judge to evaluate the circumstances of the case.

In conclusion, Wilson ways:

Some persons will shun crime even if we do nothing to deter them, while others will seek it out even if we do everything to reform them. Wicked people exist. Noth-

ing avails except to set them apart from innocent people. And many people, neither wicked nor innocent, but watchful, dissembling and calculating of their opportunities, ponder our reaction to wickedness as a cue to what they might profitably do.[58]

Research on Incapacitation

Research on the benefits of incapacitation has been at best inconclusive.[59] A few studies do show a crime prevention effect of incapacitation. For example, Shlomo Shinnar and Reuel Shinnar concluded that a policy of mandatory prison sentences of five years for violent crime and three for property offenses could reduce the reported crime rate by a factor of four or five.[60] Similarly, a study by Stephan Van Dine, Simon Dinitz, and John Conrad estimated that a mandatory prison sentence of five years for any felony offense could reduce the murder, rape, robbery, and serious assault rates by 17 percent. A similar sentence limited to repeat felons would reduce the rate of these crimes by 6 percent.[61]

This evidence is more than offset by research finding that an incapacitation policy can have little influence on the overall crime rate. David Greenberg employed prison and FBI index crime data to estimate the effect of imprisonment on crime rates.[62] He determined that if the prison population were cut in half, the crime rate would go up only 4 percent at most; if prisons were entirely eliminated, crime might increase 8 percent. Looking at this relationship from another perspective, if the average current prison sentence (two years) were increased 50 percent, the crime rate might be reduced only 4 percent. Greenberg says:

> *Prisons may be terribly unpleasant, psychologically destructive, and at times dangerous to life and limb, but there is no compelling evidence that imprisonment substantially increases (or decreases) the likelihood of subsequent criminal involvement.*[63]

Isaac Erlich obtained similar results in a study of prison rates and incapacitation; he estimated that a 50 percent reduction in average time served would result in only a 4.6 percent increase in property crime and a 2.5 percent increase in violent crime.[64] A recent study by Lee Bowker found that an increase in incarceration rates may actually lead to an increase in crime rate.[65]

In sum, as an recent review by Christy Visher indicates, while some studies do show that increasing incapacitation can reduce the crime rate, the weight of the evidence is that it has little practical effect.[66]

Does Incapacitation Work?

The incapacitation philosophy has had a powerful influence on criminological theory and policy. At the time of this writing, more than 600,000 people are incarcerated in the nation's prison system. Yet, incapacitation has not proven to be an effective crime control strategy.

First, incapacitating criminals is terribly expensive—prison costs today are over $13 billion annually.[67] Even if incarceration could reduce the crime rate, the costs would be enormous. As you may recall, some criminologists believe that if chronic offenders could be identified and incarcerated early in their offending careers, it stands to reason that the crime rate might be dramatically reduced. Though the policy of selectively incapacitating career criminals has piqued the interest of many criminologists, it so far has not been adopted, partly because of its potential costs for the prison system. The costs of implementing such a program are estimated at $60 to $75 billion for new prison construction and between $12 and $24 billion in annual maintenance fees.[68] At a time of deficits and austerity, it is doubtful that American taxpayers would be willing to spend billions on new prison construction and annual maintenance fees.

Second, there is little evidence that incapacitating criminals will deter them from future criminality, and even more reason to believe that the opposite will occur. A recent federal survey found that the more prior incarcerations inmates had, the more likely they were to recidivate within 12 months of their release.[69] Another study of parole violations found that parolees with one prior arrest had a 42 percent chance of being reincarcerated within six years of their release, while those with six priors had a 72 percent reincarceration rate.[70]

Whatever reasons a person had to commit crime before incarceration, there is little to suggest that a prison sentence will improve that person's lot. The criminal label precludes entry into many legitimate occupations and solidifies some offenders' attachment to criminal careers. Finally, as Charles Silberman suggests, the economics of crime is such that if money can be made from criminal activity, there will always be someone to take the place of the incarcerated offender.[71] New criminals will be recruited and trained, offsetting any benefit accrued by incarceration.

RETRIBUTION

Classical theory also holds that people should be punished solely because their law violations deserve either punishment or retribution. This view is based on the work of philosopher Immanuel Kant, who argued that rational people deserve punishment because the law promises to punish crime, and that offenders bring wrath on themselves when they violate social rules.[72] Criminals deserve the dignity of being treated as rational, intelligent people; they have a right to punishment. Moreover, punishment restores social equilibrium by taking away any unfair advantages criminals gained by violating the law.

Retribution remains a theme championed by many classical theorists. Those who hold this view maintain that people should be punished for what they have actually done, not for what they might do or what others might do. Retributionists propose a system of punishment that tries to square the gain a criminal makes from illegal activity with the loss suffered by the victim or by society as a whole. Since crime benefits one person at the expense of others, it is only fair to return the situation to its original state by penalizing the transgressor. They charge that wrongdoers deserve punishment for their misdeeds. If people were sanctioned before any other reason (for example, for deterrence or rehabilitation), then they would be little different from animals who are trained to meet the needs of their owners. Such a condition opens the way for a totalitarian state to undertake forcible "improvements" of its citizens without regard to whether their behavior has made them criminally or morally liable to social control.[73]

Retributionists maintain that the concept of deterrence is illogical and dangerous, because it is not absolutely necessary that the person punished even have committed the crime for deterrence to work. As C. S. Lewis has stated, rehabilitation-oriented treatment is equally dysfunctional:

To be taken without consent from my home and friends; to lose my liberty; to undergo all those assaults on my personality which modern psychotherapy knows how to deliver; to be remade after some pattern of "normality" hatched in a Viennese laboratory to which I never professed allegiance; to know that the process will never end until either my captors have succeeded or I grown wise enough to cheat them with apparent success—who cares whether this is called Punishment or not? That it includes most of the elements for which any punishment is feared—shame, exile, bondage and years eaten by the locust—is obvious.[74]

In an oft-cited statement of classical thought, J. D. Mabbott holds that retribution is the most logical basis for punishing criminals.[75] In his refutation of the concepts of deterrence and rehabilitation, Mabbott poses these questions: if it could be shown that a particular criminal had not been improved by punishment, and that no would-be criminals had been deterred by knowledge of the punishment, would that prove the punishment was unjust? Or suppose an innocent person went to prison and came out a much better, more successful person than before, and that many potential criminals were influenced by this fate; would the results justify punishing an innocent person? Mabbott concludes that punishing people for reasons other than that they deserve retribution is inherently unfair; it is essential that inflicting a punishment not be determined by some notion that it will do the criminal or society some "good."

K. G. Armstrong argues that retributive punishment is not revenge; revenge is personal and requires no authority to control its direction.[76] Retribution instead involves the lawful action of the state to protect society, reform the criminal, and recover for society—by force where necessary—what a "reluctant debtor" owes it.

Retributionists argue that punishments are fair and necessary in a just society. First, punishment assures law-abiding people that they are not assuming an unfair burden by their compliance with the conventional rules of society. Second, punishment assures compliance with rules that insure an orderly society and fair distribution of goods and services. Third, punishment is society's way of creating equilibrium among its members and institutions. If a person acquires an unfair advantage by disobeying the rules, then matters cannot be set straight until that advantage is erased. (See Close-Up on Bernhard Goetz.)

Just Desert

A more current version of retribution theory exists in the concept of **just desert.** Whereas the two positions seem almost identical, *desert* appears to be a less threatening term than *retribution*, which often has been closely linked with revenge. The just desert position has been most clearly spelled out by criminologist Andrew Von Hirsch in *Doing Justice*, the report of the Committee for the Study of Incarceration, a study group funded by several private foundations in the mid-1970s. In his report, Von Hirsch was generally critical of the rehabilitation/positivist criminology philosophy. He charges:

- The character or size of a penal institution has little to do with its effectiveness
- Probation (community supervision) does not seem more effective than prison
- More intensive supervision on the street does not seem to curb recidivism
- Vocational training has proven ineffective
- Small community-based programs are no more effective than traditional programs
- Social science has not proven that the best possible correctional treatment program is superior to no treatment at all.[77]

Von Hirsch therefore offers the concept of desert as a theoretical model to guide justice policy:

> To say someone "deserves" to be rewarded or punished is to refer to his past conduct and assert that its merit or demerit is reason for according him pleasant or unpleasant treatment.[78]

Just desert theory is based on a utilitarian view. It maintains that those who violate others' rights deserve to be punished. Just desert theory acknowledges that punishment makes those punished suffer, and that people should not deliberately add to human suffering. However, desert theorists are pragmatic; since punishment may prevent more misery than it inflicts, this conclusion reestablishes the need for desert-based punishment.[79] This utilitarian view is the key to the desert approach: punishment is needed to preserve the social equity disturbed by crime. However, severity of punishment should be commensurate with the seriousness of crime.

Desert theory is also concerned with the rights of the accused. It alleges that the rights of the person being punished should not be unduly sacrificed for the good of others (as they sometimes are with deterrence theory). The offender should not be treated as more (or less) **blameworthy,** or deserving of punishment, than is warranted by the character of his or her offense. (This means that if two crimes are equally serious, it is not fair to impose a harsher penalty for only one of the crimes, simply because severe penalties have been shown to have a deterrent effect for that crime. Conversely, it is not fair to impose a light sentence for a serious crime in order to aid the defendant's rehabilitation, because this would treat the offender as being less blameworthy than he or she is.

In sum, the just desert model suggests that retribution is justified because people deserve what they get for past misdeeds. On the other hand, punishment based on deterrence or incapacitation is wrong because it involves an offender's future actions, which cannot accurately be predicted.

Finally, just desert theory holds that punishment should be the same for all people who commit the same crime. Criminal sentences based on individual needs or characteristics are inherently unfair, since all people are equally blameworthy for their misdeeds.

RATIONAL CHOICE THEORY

To many modern criminologists, the basic principles of classical theory still hold today.[80] However there have been a number of efforts to refine the central view of classical theory—people choose to commit crime—by melding it with concepts such as the influence of lifestyle, the role of the victim, and the offender's use of information in his or her decision making. One of the most important of these recent constructs is **rational choice theory.**

Like classical theory, the rational choice approach assumes that offender's are rational beings who make decisions about crime, no matter how limited their mental ability, information, or time. However, ratio-

CLOSE-UP

Bernhard Goetz: Personal Retribution or Revenge?

The concept of retribution received national publicity when, on 22 December 1984, Bernhard Goetz shot four would-be robbers on a subway in New York. Despite some concern over the interracial nature of the incident (Goetz is white and his assailants black), public support seemed overwhelmingly on the side of Goetz's actions. At first, the New York grand jury failed to indict Goetz; later, when it was revealed that Goetz had made videotapes in which he admitted shooting his assailants after they were downed, public support swung the other way and Goetz was indicted.

The case was one of the most controversial of the past decade. The four youths admitted they were on their way to steal money from video games and had demanded money from Goetz in a threatening manner. However, the prosecution charged that Goetz was only approached by two of the youths who were "panhandling" and that Goetz not only overreacted to the instant provocation but used an illegal handgun to shoot the youths. The most powerful evidence for the prosecution was the taped interviews Goetz made after he had surrendered to police in Concord, New Hampshire. He said on the videotape, "I wanted to kill those guys. I wanted to maim those guys. I wanted to make them suffer in every way I could." On the tape, Goetz claimed to have approached one of the boys he shot and, leaning over him, said, "You look all right, here's another." The tapes were used by the prosecutor to show Goetz as an obsessed, paranoid person who lived by his own rules.

In his defense, Goetz argued that his videotaped statements should be discounted as the unreliable perceptions of a traumatized crime victim. He also brought in psychological testimony which indicated that the extreme fear he felt may have caused his body to go on "automatic pilot." The prosecution's case was not helped when two of the boys were convicted for violent offenses, including the rape of a pregnant woman, before the trial began. Nor was it helped by the fact that the jury foreman had been the victim of a subway robbery in 1981.

In the end, the case hinged on the judge's instructions to the jury that under New York law the use of force is justified if the defendant had a reasonable belief that he or she was under the treat of deadly force, or that he or she was to become the victim of a violent felony. The jury believed Goetz acted reasonably under the circumstances

Goetz arrives in New York City after turning himself in to authorities.

and acquitted him of all charges except the relatively minor one of possessing an illegal handgun.

Discussion Questions

1. Do you believe that the unarmed shooting of four would-be robbers is a legitimate exercise of retribution?

2. If Goetz were black and his victims white, would the outcome of the trial have been the same?

SOURCE: John Kennedy, "Goetz Acquitted of Major Charges in Subway Shooting," *Boston Globe*, June 17, 1987, p. 1.

nal choice theory adds to basic classical concepts the view that crime is both offense and offender specific.

That crime must be viewed as **offense specific** refers to the fact that offenders react selectively to the characteristics of particular offenses. Each criminal act has particular payoffs, carries certain risks, and requires unique skills. According to Ronald Clarke and Derek Cornish, theft involves such issues as the availability of suitable targets, skills such as safecracking or pickpocketing, likely cash yield, planning, resources such as a getaway car, timing, bravery, possible need for violence, probability of violence, difficulty of selling the stolen merchandise, and so on. The choice of a crime also might be influenced by offender perceptions of the probability of capture by police or the availability of legitimate alternatives.[81] The choice of a crime is made after at least a brief weighing and sorting of this offense specific data.

To say that crime is also **offender specific** refers to the fact that criminals are not simply driven people who for one reason or another engage in random acts of antisocial behavior. Before deciding to break the law, they briefly analyze the characteristics of the criminal situation, its opportunity, costs, benefits, and risks. They then consider their own motives and needs, such as lack of money or the need for sex or excitement. Criminal opportunities may be chosen only after legitimate means have been ruled out. Alternatives may be considered if the risk seems too great.

Offense and offender characteristics are interactive. Each offense has its own properties, including risk and payoff; each offender has a unique set of needs and skills. The interaction between the offender and offense provide a basis for selecting among alternative courses of action and therefore structure the offender's choice of behavior. This interaction is referred to as **choice structuring.** As Clarke and Cornish put it:

> It follows that the readiness with which the offender will be prepared to substitute one offense for another will depend upon the extent to which alternative offenses share characteristics which the offender considers salient to his or her goals or abilities.[82]

The rational choice approach is most closely associated with the work of criminologists Clarke, Cornish, Phillip Cook, and others.[83] They argue that

Ronald Clarke and others developed rational choice theory.

law-violating behavior takes place when an offender decides to take the chance of violating the law after considering his or her own personal situation (need for money, personal values, learning experiences and so on) and situational factors (how well the target is protected, whether people are at home, how wealthy the neighborhood is). Accordingly, entry into a criminal lifestyle and the decision to commit a specific type of crime is a personal matter based on weighing of available information.

Similarly, the decision to forego crime may be based on the criminal's perception that the economic benefits of crime are no longer there. For example, Neal Shover found that older criminals may turn from a life of crime when they develop a belief that the risk of crime is greater than its potential profit.[84] The solution to crime, therefore, may be the formulation of policies which will cause the potential criminal to choose conventional solutions over criminal.

Note the distinction made here between *crime* and *criminality.*[85] Crime is an event; criminality is a personal trait. While some people may have multiple traits associated with criminality (abnormal personality, residence in a poverty area, being a victim of child abuse), they may rarely if ever commit crimes. In contrast, under some circumstances, for example, in the face of significant need or provocation, any individual might violate the law. Criminality is not a sufficient condition for crime, nor is crime engaged in solely by criminals. Both concepts must be viewed and studied independently.

ROUTINE ACTIVITIES THEORY

Another variation on the rational choice model is the **routine activities theory.** This theory originated in the pioneering studies of victimization by Michael Hindelang, Michael Gottfredson, and James Garofalo, and has been subsequently refined by the research of criminologists Lawrence Cohen and Marcus Felson.[86]

According to this view, both the motivation to commit crime and the supply of willing offenders is constant.[87] That is, a certain percentage of the population will always have reason to violate the law for reasons of gain, need, greed, and so on. Consequently, the volume and distribution of **predatory crime** (violent crimes against the person and crimes in which an offender attempts to steal an object directly) are closely related not only to the behavior of criminals but to the routine daily activities of potential victims. Cohen and Felson clarify this view by linking crime rates to the interaction of three variables which reflect the routine activities found in everyday American life:

1. The availability of **suitable targets** (such as homes containing easily saleable goods)
2. The absence of **capable guardians** (such as homeowners and their neighbors, friends and relatives)
3. The presence of **motivated offenders** (such as unemployed teenagers).[88]

If all of these components are present, there is a greater likelihood that a predatory crime will take place.

Cohen and Felson have used the routine activities approach to explain the rise in the crime rate since 1960. They argue that the number of adult caretakers at home during the day (guardians) decreased because of increased female participation in the workforce; while both mothers and fathers are at work and children are in day-care, homes are left unguarded. Similarly, with the growth of suburbia and the decline of the traditional neighborhood, the number of such familiar guardians as family, neighbors, and friends has diminished. At the same time, the volume of easily transportable wealth has increased, creating a greater number of available targets. In one study, Cohen and his associates linked burglary rates to the purchase of one easily stolen and disposed of commodity: the television set.[89] Finally, with the baby boom generation coming of age between 1960 and 1980, there was an excess of motivated offenders and a not surprising increase in the crime rate.

The Lifestyles of Victims and Criminals

Routine activities theory portrays victimization as an everyday event influenced by lifestyle factors. The probability of victimization is increased by such personal behavior choices as going out on foot late at night or living in a densely populated area with a high unemployment rate.[90] For example, Marcus Felson has attributed the recent fluctuations in the crime rate to the availability of such lightweight consumer electronic gear such as videocassette recorders and compact disc players, which make a new and attractive form of "suitable targets."[91] Steven Messner and Kenneth Tardiff studied patterns of urban homicide and found that a person's lifestyle significantly influenced his or her victimization potential: people who tended to stay at home were the ones most likely to be killed by family or friends.[92] Michael Maxfield found that stay-at-homes were in greatest jeopardy in single-parent households, since the greatest risk of homicide is from present or former spouses.[93]

Routine activities also influence the behavior of offenders. People are more likely to commit crime if their lifestyles give them ample opportunity to come into contact with potential victims. Some recent research by James Garofalo and his associates shows that much of school crime is linked to routine interactions between pools of potential victims and offenders in the absence of capable guardians (teachers, security agents).[94] In another study, Marcus Felson and Michael Gottfredson show that the probability of families having meals together is inversely related to the tendency of youths to stay out late with their friends and presumably get in trouble.[95] Similarly, David Riley found that male teens who spend time at home are less likely to be delinquent than those who meet regularly with friends in public places like arcades and discos.[96]

In sum, if there are more plentiful and valuable items to steal and they are left unguarded, thefts will assuredly occur; if people put themselves in jeopardy, they will become victims of violent attacks.

POLICY IMPLICATIONS OF CLASSICAL THEORY

In recent years, classical criminology has had a great effect on policy making in the U.S. justice system. Modern classical concepts, such as deterrence, incapacitation, and just desert, have played an important role in criminal justice operations. This section briefly reviews how classical theory influences policy making.

Criminal Law

Classical theory has had an important influence on people's thoughts about the relationship between law, punishment, and crime. It is evident that policymakers accept the idea that punishment has a deterrent effect when they legislate tough criminal sentences in an effort to control crime. One striking example of this trend has been attempts by legislatures to control the criminal use of firearms by severely punishing criminals who use handguns in the commission of a crime. Michigan's Felony Firearms Statute adds a mandatory two years in prison to the sentence of any person convicted of a crime in which a gun was used.[97] Similarly, the Bartley-Fox gun law in Massachusetts provides a one-year mandatory prison term for merely carrying an unregistered firearm.[98] Research indicates that the Michigan law has reduced the use of handguns but promoted the use of other weapons in violent crimes.

Despite the lack of success of these efforts, it is evident that today's lawmakers still rely on the threat of penalties as a frontline crime deterrent. Increasing numbers of state jurisdictions are imposing longer mandatory sentences with the hope of deterring

crime. And some recent research efforts indicate that the public is in general agreement with the severity of punishments currently prescribed by law.[99] This issue is discussed further in Chapter 16.

Law Enforcement Practices

The very nature of police operations seems to embody classical principles. The mission of crime prevention is aided by the deterrent effect of police visibility on potential criminals. Easily recognizable uniforms and patrol cars serve as constant reminders that criminal violations can result in apprehension and serious punishments. In addition to deterring potential offenders, law enforcement agencies serve as an important cog in the social control and punishment of those already participating in criminal activity. For example, police departments have participated in efforts to crack down on chronic, career criminals by creating special units which target repeat offenders for arrest and prosecution.[100]

The police have undertaken several projects to determine whether they actually provide a deterrent to crime. The most famous study was conducted in Kansas City, Missouri.[101] To evaluate the effectiveness of police patrols, 15 independent police beats, or districts, were divided into three groups: the first retained normal police patrol; the second (*proactive*) was supplied with two to three times the normal amount of patrol forces; the third (*reactive*) eliminated its preventive patrol entirely, and police officers responded only when summoned by citizens to the scene of a crime.

Surprisingly, data from the Kansas City study indicated that these variations in patrol techniques had little effect on the crime patterns in the 15 locales. The presence or absence of patrols did not seem to affect residential or business burglaries, auto thefts, larcenies involving auto accessories, robberies, vandalism, or other criminal behavior. Variations in police patrol techniques also appeared to have little effect on citizens' attitudes toward the police, their satisfaction with police, or their fear of future criminal behavior.

Despite the questions raised by the Kansas City study, research conducted by Lawrence Sherman and Richard Berk has rekindled the belief that police actions may actually deter crime.[102] Sherman and Berk evaluated the program the Minneapolis Police Department created to control domestic (spousal) violence and abuse. In the program, police officers randomly assigned suspects to one of three response categories: (1) formal arrest; (2) "advice" such as counseling and mediation; and (3) an order that the suspect must leave the premises for eight hours. The results of the project were tracked for six months, using official data and victim reports. Sherman and Berk report that people subjected to the harshest response, arrest, were less likely to become involved in violence than those who were merely advised. The authors concluded that:

> . . . arrest and initial incarceration alone may produce a deterrent effect, regardless of how the courts treat such cases, and that arrest make an independent contribution to the deterrence potential of the criminal justice system.[103]

Punishment

Two hundred years after its inception, classical theory is still a primary influence on the makeup of criminal sanctions. Our system of criminal sentences still rests heavily on the concepts of just desert, general deterrence, and incapacitation. During the 1980s, our increasingly conservative society applauded efforts to control "the criminal element," even if it meant sentencing convicted offenders to death. There was an affirmative effort to lower the crime rate through the fear of tougher criminal penalties and the incapacitation of known criminals. For example, a number of states created mandatory sentencing laws, which require that convicted offenders serve time in prison for their acts and which concomitantly abolish early release from prison. In addition, a number of states, including California, Indiana, Illinois, and Maine, passed **presumptive sentencing** statutes.[104] These guarantee that most people sent to prison for a particular crime will get the same sentence and will serve the entire sentence without early release or parole (although there is usually a provision for time off for good behavior). Most presumptive sentencing statutes allow judges to add time to a sentence for a particularly serious crime or subtract time if the circumstances warrant it. However, the presumption is that offenders will get the sentence they deserve and that all similar offenders will serve the same number of years in prison.

Other state jurisdictions—including Michigan, Washington, and Minnesota—have implemented **sentencing guidelines** that instruct judges on the appropriate sentence for a particular crime. Sentencing guidelines follow the theory of just desert, because they are designed to uphold the principle that offenders who commit like crimes should receive like penalties (see Chapter 16). One result of these changes in the law is that the prison population is at an all-time high, approaching the 600,000 mark at the time of this writing.

Perhaps the most visible and dramatic influence classical theory has had on criminal justice policymaking is the employment of the **death penalty** as a punishment for murder. Capital punishment is the real-world embodiment of classical theory; its use can only be justified by the assumption that: (1) the decision to take a life is a rational choice; (2) this choice can be controlled by the fear of punishment; (3) those who already have taken a life are dangerous criminals who cannot be safely or effectively treated; and (4) such persons deserve to die at the hand of the state. In this regard, the death penalty contains aspects of general deterrence, special deterrence, desert, and incapacitation.

Corrections

Classical theory also has influenced the correctional process. Criminologist David Fogel's **justice model** of corrections has been adopted in several jurisdictions.[105] Fogel calls for the elimination of parole, or of any release based on an inmate's "rehabilitation" success. He instead advocates flat (determinate) sentences and prisons as places for punishment rather than treatment. Fogel believes that an inmate's sense of justice must be raised lest he or she feel victimized by the system. If everyone is treated equally and fairly, then even the severest punishment will be acceptable; but if inmates perceive that benefits and privileges are being unequally distributed, then their sense of injustice will outweigh any possible benefits of correctional rehabilitation efforts.

The justice model had an important influence on correctional policy in the 1980s. Most importantly, it has been used as a justification when state legislators wish to abolish parole or create more restrictive sentences (see Chapter 14).

SUMMARY

Classical theory assumes that each person has the free will to choose whether to commit criminal acts. However, people are influenced by their fear of the criminal penalties associated with being caught and convicted for law violations. The more severe, certain, and swift the punishment, the more likely it is to control crime.

The classical approach is rooted in the utilitarian philosophy of Cesare Beccaria and Jeremy Bentham. These eighteenth-century social philosophers argued that punishment should fit the crime. Though firmness was necessary, punishments should not exceed the actual cost of crime. Beccaria was particularly influential as a spokesperson against torture and the use of capital punishment.

Classical criminology influenced policy-making for almost a hundred years. Punishments were tailored to fit criminal acts. Use of the death penalty was limited. The growth of positivist criminology, which stressed external causes of crime and rehabilitation of known offenders, reduced the popularity of the classical approach in the twentieth century. However, classical criminology recently has become more popular with U.S. criminologists. Several classical concepts have been advocated as useful for the understanding of crime and its control.

Deterrence theory relates to the concept that an inverse relationship should exist between punishment and crime. However, a number of factors confound the relationship. For example, if people don't believe they will be caught, even harsh punishment may not deter crime. Deterrence theory has been criticized, on the grounds that it wrongfully assumes that criminals make a rational choice before committing crimes, ignores the intricacies of the criminal justice system, and does not take into account the social and psychological factors that may influence criminality. Research designed to test the validity of the deterrence concept has not indicated that deterrent measures actually reduce the crime rate.

Other classical concepts are incapacitation and special deterrence; their proponents hold that the crime rate can be reduced if dangerous people are locked up for extended periods and punished so severely that they never commit crimes again. The leading advocate of the incapacitation philosophy is the political scientist James Q. Wilson. Research efforts have not provided clear-cut proof that increasing the number of people in prison—and increasing prison sentences—will reduce crime rates.

An aspect of classical criminology that combines elements of deterrence and incapacitation is the increased use of the death penalty to prevent murder and other capital crimes. People in favor of capital punishment argue that it is the ultimate deterrent; however, empirical research has not proven that the death penalty reduces the murder rate.

The fourth branch of classical criminology includes the theories of retribution and just desert. Advocates of these theories suggest that the punishment should fit the crime. The justice system should be modified so that criminals serve their entire sentences behind bars. Desert-oriented criminologists advocate the abolition of parole and the widespread use of flat, or determinate, sentences.

In recent years, classical views have been incorporated into rational choice and routine activities theories, which hold that the criminal approaches crime as a decision-making process and that such issues as the availability of targets and the steps made to guard them can influence criminality.

Classical theory has been influential in shaping public policy. The criminal law is designed to deter potential criminals and fairly punish those who have been caught engaging in illegal acts. Police forces have operated to deter and prevent crime. Some courts have changed sentencing policies to adapt to classical principles, and the U.S. correctional system seems geared toward incapacitation and special deterrence. Recently, the Supreme Court has once again legalized the death penalty; its renewed use is a testimony to the importance of classical theory.

KEY TERMS

classical theory
Cesare Beccaria
utility
Jeremy Bentham
Benthamism
moral calculus
Declaration of the Rights
    of Man
positivist
indeterminate prison
    sentence

retribution
just desert
blameworthy
rational choice theory
offense specific and
    offender specific
choice structuring
routine activities theory
predatory crime
suitable targets
capable guardians

partial deterrence
absolute deterrence
informal sanctions
special deterrence
incapacitation

motivated offenders
presumptive sentencing
sentencing guidelines
death penalty
justice model

—————— NOTES ——————

1. Francis Edward Devine, "Cesare Beccaria and the Theoretical Foundations of Modern Penal Jurisprudence," *New England Journal on Prison Law* 7 (1982):8–21.
2. John Locke, *Two Treatises on Government*, 2d ed. (London: P. Lasslett, 1970), pp. 313–81.
3. Marcello Maestro, *Voltaire and Beccaria* (New York: Octagon, 1972), p. 2.
4. Ysabel Rennie, *The Search for Criminal Man* (Lexington, Mass.: Lexington Books, 1978), pp. 8–9.
5. James Health, *Eighteenth Century Penal Theory* (New York: Oxford University Press, 1963), p. 98.
6. Cesare Beccaria, *On Crimes and Punishments*, 6th ed., trans. Henry Paolucci (Indianapolis: Bobbs-Merrill, 1977).
7. *Ibid.*, p. 11.
8. *Ibid.*, p. 13.
9. *Ibid.*, p. 43.
10. *Ibid.*, p. 99.
11. Jeremy Bentham, *A Fragment on Government and An Introduction to the Principle of Morals and Legislation*, ed. Wilfred Harrison (Oxford: Basil Blackwell, 1967), p. 21.
12. *Ibid.*, p. 152.
13. Adapted from Rennie, *Search for Criminal Man*, p. 22.
14. *Ibid.*, p. 23.
15. Vincent Webb and Roy Roberg, *Issues in Corrections* (St. Paul, Minn.: West Publishing, 1981), p. 52.
16. *Ibid.*, p. 22.
17. Robert Martinson, "What Works?—Questions and Answers about Prison Reform," *Public Interest* 35 (1974):22–54.
18. Robert Langworthy and John Whitehead, "Liberalism and Fear as Explanations of Punitiveness," *Criminology* 24(1986):575–91.
19. Ronald Bayer, "Crime, Punishment and the Decline of Liberal Optimism," *Crime and Delinquency* 27 (1981):190.
20. Alfred Blumstein, Jacqueline Cohen, and Daniel Nagin, *Deterrence and Incapacitation: Estimating the Effects of Criminal Sanctions on Crime Rates* (Washington, D.C.: National Academy of Science, 1978), p. 3.
21. Carol Crowther, "Crimes, Penalties and Legislatures," *Annals of the American Academy of Political and Social Science* 381 (1969):147–58.
22. Michael Geerken and Walter Gove, "Deterrence: Some Theoretical Considerations," *Law and Society Review* 9 (1975):497–514.
23. *Ibid.*, p. 505.
24. *Ibid.*, p. 507.
25. Sheldon Ekland-Olson, John Lieb, and Louis Zurcher, "The Paradoxical Impact of Criminal Sanctions: Some Microstructural Findings," *Law and Society Review* 18 (1984):159–78.
26. *Ibid.*, p. 175.
27. Solomon Kobrin, E. W. Hansen, S. G. Lubeck, and R. Yeaman, *The Deterrent Effectiveness of Criminal Justice Sanction Strategies: Summary Report* (Washington, D.C.: U.S. Government Printing Office, 1972).
28. Charles Tittle and Alan Rowe, "Certainty of Arrest and Crime Rates: A Further Test of the Deterrence Hypothesis," *Social Forces* 52 (1974):455–62.
29. Edwin Zedlewski, "Deterrence Findings and Data Sources: A Comparison of the Uniform Crime Rates and the National Crime Surveys," *Journal of Research in Crime and Delinquency* 20 (1983):262–76.
30. Theodore Chiricos and Gordon Waldo, "Punishment and Crime: An Examination of Some Empirical Evidence," *Social Problems* 18 (1970):200–17.
31. Blumstein, Cohen, and Nagin, *Deterrence and Incapacitation*, p. 4.
32. David Demers and Richard Lundman, "Perceptual Deterrence Research: Some Additional Evidence for Designing Studies," *Journal of Quantitative Criminology* 3 (1987):185–94.
33. Harold Grasnick and George Bryjak, "The Deterrent Effect of Perceived Severity of Punishment," *Social Forces* 59 (1980):471–91.
34. Harold Grasnick and D. J. Green, "Legal Punishment, Social Disapproval and Internalization as Inhibitors of Illegal Behavior," *Journal of Criminal Law and Criminology* 71 (1980):325–35.
35. Dale Berger and John Snortum, "A Structural Model of Drinking and Driving: Alcohol Consumption, Social Norms, and Moral Commitments," *Criminology* 24 (1986):139–53.
36. Charles Tittle, *Sanctions and Social Deviance* (New York: Praeger, 1980).
37. Matthew Silberman, "Toward a Theory of Criminal Deterrence," *American Sociological Review* 41 (1976):442–61.
38. Linda Anderson, Theodore Chiricos, and Gordon Waldo, "Formal and Informal Sanctions: A Comparison of Deterrent Effects," *Social Problems* 25 (1977):103–14. See also, Maynard Erickson and Jack Gibbs, "Objective and Perceptual Properties of Legal Punishment and Deterrence Doctrine," *Social Problems* 25 (1978):253–64.

39. Donna Bishop, "Deterrence: A Panel Analysis," *Justice Quarterly* 1 (1984):311–28.

40. Raymond Paternoster, Linda Saltzman, Gordon Waldo, and Theodore Chiricos, "Estimating Perceptual Stability and Deterrent Effects: The Role and Perceived Legal Punishment in the Inhibition of Criminal Involvement," *Journal of Criminal Law and Criminology* 74 (1983):270–97; W. William Minor and Joseph Harry, "Deterrent and Experiential Effects in Perceptual Deterrence Research: A Replication and Extension," *Journal of Research in Crime and Delinquency* 19 (1982):190–203.

41. Raymond Paternoster, "The Use of Composite Scales in Perceptual Deterrence Research: A Cautionary Note," *Journal of Research in Crime and Delinquency* 23 (1986):128–68.

42. *Ibid.*

43. Johannes Andenaes, "The Moral of Educative Influence of Criminal Law," in June Trapp and Felice Levine, eds., *Law, Justice and the Individual in Society: Psychological and Legal Issues* (New York: Holt, Rinehart and Winston, 1977), pp. 120–38.

44. Raymond Paternoster, "The Deterrent Effect of Perceived Certainty and Severity of Punishment: A Review of the Evidence and Issues," *Justice Quarterly* 4(1987):214–15.

45. William Chambliss, "The Deterrent Effect of Punishment," *Crime and Delinquency* 12 (1966):70–75; Charles Tittle and Alan Rowe, "Moral Appeal, Sanction Threat, and Deviance: An Experimental Test," *Social Problems* 20 (1973):488–98.

46. H. Laurence Ross, "Implications of Drinking-and-Driving Law Studies for Deterrence Research," in Timothy Hartnagel and Robert Silverman, eds., *Critique and Explanation, Essays in Honor of Gwynne Nettler* (New Brunswick, N.J.: Transaction Books, 1986), pp. 159–71.

47. Gary Green, "General Deterrence and Television Cable Crime: A Field Experiment in Social Crime," *Criminology* 23 (1986):629–45.

48. Ernest Van Den Haag, "The Criminal Law as a Threat System," *Journal of Criminal Law and Criminology* 73 (1982):709–85.

49. Paternoster, "The Deterrent Effect of Perceived Certainty and Severity of Punishment," pp. 173–218.

50. Ken Auletta, *The Under Class* (New York: Random House, 1982).

51. Joan Petersilia, Susan Turner, James Kahan, and Joyce Peterson, *Prison versus Probation in California: Implications for Crime and Offender Recidivism* (Santa Monica, Cal.: Rand Corp., 1986).

52. George Bridges and James Stone, "Effects of Criminal Punishment on Perceived Threat of Punishment: Toward an Understanding of Specific Deterrence," *Journal of Research in Crime and Delinquency* 23 (1986):207–39.

53. Joan Petersilia, Susan Turner, James Kahan, and Joyce Peterson, *Granting Felons Probation: Public Risks and Alternatives* (Santa Monica, Cal.: Rand Corp., 1985).

54. *Felony Sentencing in 28 Local Jurisdictions* (Washington, D.C.: Bureau of Justice Statistics, 1988).

55. Graeme Newman, *Just and Painful* (New York: Macmillan, 1983), pp. 139–43.

56. James Q. Wilson, *Thinking about Crime* (New York: Basic Books, 1975).

57. *Ibid.*, p. 197.

58. *Ibid.*, p. 235.

59. Steven Clarke, "Getting 'Em Out of Circulation: Does Incarceration of Juvenile Offenders Reduce Crime?" *Journal of Criminal Law and Criminology* 65 (1974):528–35.

60. Reuel Shinnar and Shlomo Shinnar, "The Effects of the Criminal Justice System on the Control of Crime: A Quantitative Approach," *Law and Society Review* 9 (1975):581–611.

61. Stephan Van Dine, Simon Dinitz, and John Conrad, *Restraining the Wicked: The Dangerous Offender Project* (Lexington, Mass.: Lexington Books, 1979).

62. David Greenberg, "The Incapacitative Effects of Imprisonment: Some Estimates," *Law and Society Review* 9 (1975):541–80.

63. *Ibid.*, p. 558.

64. Isaac Erlich, "Participation in Illegitimate Activities: An Economic Analysis," *Journal of Political Economy* 81 (1973):521–67.

65. Lee Bowker, "Crime and the Use of Prisons in the United States: A Time Series Analysis," *Crime and Delinquency* 27 (1981):206–12.

66. Christy Visher, "Incapacitation and Crime Control: Does 'Lock 'Em Up' Strategy Reduce Crime?" *Justice Quarterly* 4 (1987):513–44.

67. Sue Lindgren, *Justice Expenditure and Employment, 1985* (Washington, D.C.: Bureau of Justice Statistics, 1987).

68. David Farrington, "Predicting Individual Crime Rates," in Don Gottfredson and Michael Tonry, eds., *Prediction and Classification, Criminal Justice Decision Making* (Chicago: University of Chicago Press, 1987), p. 94 (Vol. 9 of the *Crime and Justice* series); Samuel Walker, *Sense and Nonsense about Crime* (Monterey, Cal.: Brooks Cole, 1985), pp. 56–63.

69. John Wallerstedt, *Returning to Prison*, Bureau of Justice Statistics Special Report (Washington, D.C.: U.S. Department of Justice, 1984).

70. Allen Beck and Bernard Shipley, *Recidivism of Young Parolees* (Washington, D.C.: Bureau of Justice Statistics, 1987).

71. Charles Silberman, *Criminal Violence, Criminal Justice* (New York: Random House, 1978), p. 196.

72. For an analysis of Kant's work, see, Gray Cavender, "Justice, Sanctioning and the Justice Model," *Criminology* 22 (1984):203–13.

73. J. B. Hawkins, "Punishment and Moral Responsibility," *Modern Law Review* 7 (1944): 205–208.

74. C. S. Lewis, "The Humanitarian Theory of Punishment," *20th Century* 3 (1948–1949):4–16.

75. J. D. Mabbott, "Punishment," *Mind* 49 (1939):152–67.

76. K. G. Armstrong, "The Retributionist Hits Back," *Mind* 70 (1969):471–90.

77. Andrew Von Hirsch, *Doing Justice* (New York: Hill and Wang, 1976).

78. *Ibid.*, pp. 15–16.

79. *Ibid.*

80. Ernest Van Den Haag, "The Neoclassical Theory of Crime Control," in Robert Meier, *Theoretical Methods in Criminology* (Beverly Hills, Cal.: Sage, 1985), pp. 177–96.

81. Lloyd Phillips and Harold Votey, "The Influence of Police Interventions and Alternative Income Sources on the Dynamic Process of Choosing Crime as a Career," *Journal of Quantitative Criminology* 3 (1987):251–74.

82. Derek Cornish and Ronald V. Clarke, "Understanding Crime Displacement: An Application of Rational Choice Theory," *Criminology* 25 (1987):933–47, at 935.

83. Philip Cook, "The Demand and Supply of Criminal Opportunities," in Michael Tonry and Norval Morris, eds., *Crime and Justice*, Vol. 7 (Chicago: University of Chicago Press, 1986), pp. 1–28; Ronald Clarke and Derek Cornish, "Modeling Offenders' Decisions: A Framework for Research and Policy," in Michael Tonry and Norval Morris, eds., *Crime and Justice*, Vol. 6 (Chicago: University of Chicago Press, 1985), pp. 147–87; Morgan Reynolds, *Crime by Choice: An Economic Analysis* (Dallas: The Fisher Institute, 1985).

84. Neal Shover, *Aging Criminals* (Beverly Hills, Cal.: Sage, 1985).

85. Travis Hirschi and Michael Gottfredson, "The Distinction Between Crime and Criminality," in Hartnagel and Silverman, eds., *Critique and Explanation*, pp. 55–71.

86. Michael Hindelang, Michael Gottfredson, and James Garofalo, *Victims of Personal Crime: An Empirical Foundation for a Theory of Personal Victimization* (Cambridge, Mass.: Ballinger, 1978); Lawrence Cohen and Marcus Felson, "Social Change and Crime Rate Trends: A Routine Activities Approach," *American Sociological Review* 44 (1979):588–608; Lawrence Cohen, Marcus Felson, and Kenneth Land, "Property Crime Rates in the United States: A Macrodynamic Analysis, 1947–1977, with Ex-Ante Forecasts for the Mid-1980's," *American Journal of Sociology* 86 (1980):90–118.

87. For a review, see, James LeBeau and Thomas Castellano, *The Routine Activities Approach: An Inventory and Critique* (Carbondale, Ill.: Center for the Studies of Crime, Delinquency and Corrections, Southern Illinois University–Carbondale, unpublished, 1987).

88. Cohen and Felson, "Social Change and Crime Rate Trends," p. 589.

89. Cohen, Felson, and Land, "Property Crime Rates in the United States," pp. 90–118.

90. Robert Sampson and John Wooldredge, "Linking the Micro- and Macro-Level Dimensions of Lifestyle-Routine Activity and Opportunity Models of Predatory Victimization," *Journal of Quantitative Criminology* 3 (1987):371–93.

91. Marcus Felson, "Routine Activities and Crime Prevention in the Developing Metropolis," *Criminology* 25 (1987):911–31.

92. Steven Messner and Kenneth Tardiff, "The Social Ecology of Urban Homicide: An Application of the 'Routine Activities' Approach," *Criminology* 23 (1985):241–67.

93. Michael Maxfield, "Household Composition, Routine Activity, and Victimization: A Comparative Analysis," *Journal of Quantitative Criminology* 3 (1987):301–20.

94. James Garofalo, Leslie Siegel, and John Laub, "School-Related Victimizations Among Adolescents: An Analysis of National Crime Survey (NCS) Narratives," *Journal of Quantitative Criminology* 3 (1987):321–38.

95. Marcus Felson and Michael Gottfredson, "Adolescent Activities Near Peers and Parents," *Journal of Marriage and the Family* 46 (1984):709–14.

96. David Riley, "Time and Crime: The Link Between Teenager Lifestyle and Delinquency," *Journal of Quantitative Criminology* 3 (1987):339–54.

97. Colin Loftin and David McDowall, "One with a Gun Gets You Two: Mandatory Sentencing and Firearms Violence in Detroit," *Annals, AAPS* 455 (1981):158–68.

98. Glenn Pierce and William Bowers, "The Bartley-Fox Gun Law's Short-Term Impact on Crime in Boston," *Annals, AAPS* 455 (1981):128–37.

99. William Samuel and Elizabeth Moulds, "The Effect of Crime Severity on Perceptions of Fair Punishment: A California Case Study," *Journal of Criminal Law and Criminology* 77 (1986):931–48.

100. Susan Martin, "Policing Career Criminals: An Examination of an Innovative Crime Control Program," *Journal of Criminal Law and Criminology* 77 (1986):1159–82.

101. George Kelling, Tony Pate, Duane Dieckman, and Charles Brown, *The Kansas City Preventive Patrol Experiment: A Summary Report* (Washington, D.C.: Police Foundation, 1974).

102. Lawrence Sherman and Richard Berk, "The Specific Deterrent Effects of Arrest for Domestic Assault," *American Sociological Review* 49 (1984):261–72.

103. *Ibid.*, p. 271.
104. Stephen LaGoy, Fred Hussey, and John Kramer, "A Comparative Assessment of Determinate Sentencing in Four Pioneer States," *Crime and Delinquency* 24 (1980):385–400.
105. David Fogel, *We Are the Living Proof: The Justice Model for Corrections* (Cincinnati: Anderson, 1975).

≡ CHAPTER 6

PSYCHOLOGICAL AND BIOLOGICAL APPROACHES TO CRIME: TRAIT THEORY

INTRODUCTION

The preceding chapter reviewed theories which claim that criminals *choose* to violate the law after weighing the benefits and consequences of their actions. Not all criminologists, however, are convinced that this calculated thought process actually takes place. Since the middle of the nineteenth century, scientists have suggested that uncontrollable physical and environmental factors control human behavior. Biological, psychological, and social conditions have all been viewed as contributors. As a group, social scientists who believe behavior is determined by perceptible forces beyond an individual's control are referred to as *positivists*. This chapter concentrates on positivist theories which involve an individual's biological and psychological properties; the following two chapters focus on theories which involve societal factors.

Biocriminologists and psychocriminologists believe that criminality is a result of the behavioral influences of some underlying physical or mental condition. They are convinced that personal **traits**, or distinguishing characteristics, separate the criminal offender from the average law-abiding citizen. Both groups live under the same set of social conditions and are socialized in a similar fashion. For example, both criminals and noncriminals attend the same schools and churches and are exposed to comparable social values. Since their life experiences are so similar, individual differences must account for the reason why, when faced with the same life situations, one person acts in a conventional manner while another resorts to antisocial behavior. All people may be aware of and even fear the sanctioning power of the law, but some are unable to control their urges and passions. These people commit crimes of violence and destruction.

As a rule, no single biological or psychological concept is thought to be adequate as an explanation of all criminality. Rather, as common sense would suggest, each person possesses a singular set of physical and mental traits. Consequently, there is a unique explanation for each person's behavior. Violent behavior in one person may be explained by a brain lesion; another offender may be suffering from a genetic abnormality; a third may have a blood chemistry disorder. Modern positivists recognize many physical and social explanations for crime, since there are many differences among criminal offenders.[1]

This chapter first reviews the history and current status of biocriminology, a perspective which holds that criminals have in their physical makeup properties that make them prone to crime. The discussion then turns to psychological theories, which view crime as a product of personality, learning, and mental processes. Finally, James Q. Wilson and Richard Herrnstein's attempt to integrate classical theory with biological and psychological theory is discussed.

FOUNDATIONS OF BIOCRIMINOLOGY

Biological explanations of criminal behavior emerged during the eighteenth century. At that time, there was considerable ferment in the scientific community. A great deal of interest developed in **positivism**—the belief that scientific method and empirical analysis should be used to study behavior. While classical penologists such as Beccaria and Bentham were trying to explain people's behavior through armchair analysis and logic, others attempted to apply the scientific method to the study of criminal behavior. One natural avenue of inquiry was the association between biophysical makeup and crime.

The earliest biocriminologists were concerned with the shape of the head and body. **Physiognomists**, such as J. D. Lavater, studied the facial features of criminals to determine whether the shape and placement of the ears, nose, and eyes were associated with antisocial behavior. **Phrenologists**, such as Franz Joseph Gall and Johann K. Spurzheim, studied the shape of the skull and bumps on the head to determine whether these physical attributes were linked to criminal behavior. Phrenologists believed that external cranial characteristics dictate which areas of the brain control physical activity. Their primitive techniques and quasi-scientific methods have been discredited in this century.

CESARE LOMBROSO AND THE BORN CRIMINAL

With the publication of Charles Darwin's *Origin of Species* in 1859, the scientific quest to unlock the secrets of human origin and behavior received considerable momentum. In Italy, physician Cesare Lombroso,

(1835–1909), studied the physical characteristics of offenders convicted and executed for criminal offenses.[2] Lombroso, whose work led him to be known as the "father of criminology," concluded that serious offenders, those who engaged in repeated assault- or theft-related activities, were born to be criminals; they have inherited physical problems that impelled them into a life of crime.[3]

Lombroso claimed that *born criminals* suffer from **atavistic anomalies:** physically, they are throwbacks to more primitive times, when people were more savage. For example, criminals were believed to have the enormous jaws and strong canine teeth common to carnivores. In addition, Lombroso compared criminals' behavior to that of the mentally ill and of those suffering some forms of epilepsy.

According to Lombrosian theory, crimogenic traits could be acquired through heredity, from a "degenerate family with frequent cases of insanity, deafness, syphilis, epilepsy, and alcoholism among its members." In addition to heredity, environmental conditions, such as alcoholism, lack of education, temperature swings (hot temperatures were related to violent crime), and imitation of well-publicized crimes, could promote crime. Thus, while Lombroso believed that inherited biological factors were the primary cause of criminality, he also recognized that environment could affect antisocial behavior.[4]

Lombroso's work is regarded today as historical curiosity, not scientific fact. His research methodology has been discredited. He did not use control groups from the general population to compare his results. Many of the traits he assumed to be inherited are not really genetically determined. Moreover, many of the biological features he identified could be caused by deprivation in surrounding and diet. That is, even if certain biological traits were related to crime, they might be products of some environmental condition, such as poor nutrition or health care, rather than of heredity. Thus, it is conceivable that both criminal behavior and biological abnormality might be caused by the same unidentified environmental factor.

—— LOMBROSO'S CONTEMPORARIES ——

Lombroso's theories sparked great controversy and won him avid supporters as well as serious critics. One of his critics was Charles Goring (1870–1919). In a study of 3,000 English inmates, Goring found that criminal behavior bore a significant relationship to "defective intelligence."[5] He stated that this condition was inherited; therefore, it could best be controlled by regulating the reproduction of families exhibiting such traits as "feeblemindedness, epilepsy, insanity, and defective social instinct."[6]

A contemporary of Lombroso and Goring, Raffaele Garofalo (1852–1934), shared Lombroso's belief that certain physical characteristics indicated a criminal nature. For example, he stated that among criminals "a lower degree of sensibility to physical pain seems to be demonstrated by the readiness with which prisoners submit to the operation of tattooing."[7] Garofalo explained deviant behavior with his concept of **moral anomaly**—the criminal's lack of compassionate and altruistic feelings, a condition that has an organic root. The moral anomaly, said Garofalo, is a psychic force found more frequently in so-called inferior races and transmitted through heredity.

Enrico Ferri (1856–1929) is identified along with Lombroso and Garofalo as part of "the holy three of criminology." A student of Lombroso, Ferri believed that a number of biological, social, and organic factors caused delinquency and crime.[8]

As late as 1939, Ernest Hooton, a supporter of Lombroso, argued that the criminal was biologically and socially inferior. Hooton concluded:

> *In every population there are hereditary inferiors in mind and in body as well as physical and mental deficients . . . Our information definitely proves that it is from the physically inferior element of the population that native born criminals from native parentage are mainly derived.*[9]

The Inheritance School

Advocates of the **inheritance school** traced the activities of several generations of families believed to have an especially large number of criminal members. The most famous of these studies involved the Kallikaks and the Jukes. Henry Goddard studied the offspring of Martin Kallikak, and concluded that criminality was an inherited trait.[10] Richard Dugdale followed the offspring of Ada Jukes, whom he labeled as the "mother of criminals." Dugdale succeeded in locating over 1,000 of her descendants; he found that they included 280 paupers, 60 thieves, 7 murderers, 140 criminals, 40 persons with venereal disease, 50 prostitutes, and other assorted deviants. Arthur Estabrook later accumulated data on 2,000 family members and uncovered an additional 170 paupers, 118 criminals, 378 prostitutes, and still more assorted deviates.[11]

The inheritance school is no longer taken seriously today. Even if families with disproportionate numbers of deviant and/or criminal members could be located, this alone would not prove that they had crimogenic bloodlines. Considering the millions of families existing at any one time, it should not be surprising that a few contain a disproportionate number of criminals. If these families could be found, it would be difficult to determine if their behavior was a product of inherited or acquired traits. Since members of the same family share environmental and learning experiences, it is more likely that their lifestyle (and not their genetic makeup) influences their criminality.

Body Build Theories

Another early branch of biocriminology was the body build, or **somatotype,** school. Advocates of this approach argued that criminals manifest distinct physiques that make them susceptible to particular types of criminal behavior. The theory's most well-known proponent, William Sheldon, linked body type to delinquency.[12] In his analysis of youth, Sheldon discovered the existence of three basic body types. *Mesomorphs* have well-developed muscles and an athletic appearance. They are active, aggressive, sometimes violent, and are the most likely to become criminals. *Endomorphs* have heavy builds and are slow moving. They are known for lethargic behavior. *Ectomorphs* are tall and thin, less social, and more intellectual than the other types. Sheldon believed that most people maintained in their physical structure elements of all three body builds. He classified convicted offenders according to their body builds in a process he called *somatotyping*. Sheldon also believed there was a strong relationship between body build and psychiatric disorder.

Recent studies of the relationship of body build to delinquency were conducted by Sheldon and Eleanor

Glueck. The Gluecks used Sheldon's three body types and added a fourth, a "balanced type," that included boys with no discernible dominant body type. In a lengthy research effort involving large samples of delinquent and nondelinquent boys, the Gluecks found that mesomorphs were disproportionately represented among delinquent boys (60.1 percent versus 30.7 percent). Conversely, only 14.4 percent of the delinquents were ectomorphic; but 39.6 percent of the nondelinquents were ectomorphic.[13]

Body build theory was rejected by most criminologists after controlled research efforts found no significant relationship between body build and self-reported delinquency.[14] The work of Lombrosians and other biological determinists was viewed as methodologically unsound, racist, and generally invalid.

——— MODERN BIOCRIMINOLOGY ———

What seems no longer tenable at this juncture is any theory of human behavior which ignores biology and relies exclusively on socio-cultural learning . . . Most social scientists have been wrong in their dogmatic rejection and blissful ignorance of the biological parameters of our behavior.[15]

In the early 1970s, spurred by the publication of *Sociobiology* by **E. O. Wilson,** the biological basis for crime once again emerged into the limelight.[16]

Sociobiology differs from earlier theories of behavior in that it stresses that biological and genetic conditions affect the perception and learning of social behaviors, which in turn are linked to existing environmental structures. The gene is viewed as the ultimate unit of life which controls all human destiny. While the environment and experience do have an impact on behavior, most actions are controlled by a person's "biological machine."

Most important, people are controlled by the innate need to have their genetic material survive and dominate others. Consequently, they do everything in their power to ensure their own survival and that of others who share their gene pool. Even when they come to the aid of others, people are motivated by the belief that their actions will be reciprocated (reciprocal altruism) and that their gene survival capability will be

C. Ray Jeffrey is a leading proponent of modern biocriminology.

enhanced. According to sociobiology, crime can be viewed as a means of survival for people who perceive few other alternatives.[17]

Although sociobiology has been criticized as methodologically unsound and socially dangerous, it revived interest in finding a biological basis for crime and delinquency. If, as biocriminologists hold, a physical condition controls all human behavior, it follows that it should also be responsible for determining whether a person chooses law-violating or conventional behavior.

Modern biocriminologists, such as C. Ray Jeffrey, charge that mainstream criminologists ignore the recent advances made in the sciences of biology and experimental psychology. They contend that it is not enough to study reports of behavior, either through surveys or self-reports; they must observe the actual human behaviors they are allegedly concerned with.[18] Biocriminologists maintain that important genetic and reproductive patterns have been overlooked in the construction of modern criminological theory.[19]

These oversights seem especially ironic when the recent emphasis placed on the chronic offender is considered. Since the onset of chronic offending is believed to occur very early in childhood, it seems rea-

sonable to assume that a relatively rare pre-existing condition or trait may be responsible for repeat antisocial behavior. Biocriminologists find that some people acquire neurological and physical abnormalities as early as the fetal stage, which then control their subsequent behavior through their childhood and beyond.[20]

The following sections examine some of the more important issues in modern biocriminology.[21] First, the way in which biochemical factors are believed to affect the learning of proper behavior patterns is discussed. Then, the relationship of brain function and crime is reviewed. Finally, current ideas about genetic factors and crime are briefly considered.

It is important to keep in mind that biocriminology is a relatively new field. Many of the studies discussed here are case histories involving a few select subjects. Relatively few biocriminological studies involve rigorous scientific sampling, control group comparisons, and other validity checks. Therefore, rather than critiquing each study individually, it might be simpler to state that they represent conditional first attempts to study a complex phenomenon. If, indeed, there is a biosocial basis for crime, its undisputed proof will be for future research efforts to uncover.

Biochemical Factors

One area of biocriminological interest involves biochemical factors, such as those produced by diet, environmental conditions, and allergies. This view of crime received national attention when Dan White, the confessed killer of San Francisco mayor George Moscone and city council-member Harvey Milk, claimed his behavior was precipitated by an addiction to sugar-laden junk foods.[22] White's **Twinky defense** prompted a California jury to find him guilty of the lesser offense of diminished capacity manslaughter, rather than first-degree murder. (White committed suicide after serving his prison sentence.)

Chemical and Mineral Factors. Biocriminologists maintain that minimum levels of minerals and chemicals are needed for normal brain functioning and growth, especially in the early years of life. If people with normal needs do not receive the appropriate nutrition, they will suffer from **vitamin deficiency**. If people have genetic conditions that cause greater-than-normal needs for certain chemicals and minerals, they are said to suffer from **vitamin dependency.**

People with vitamin deficiency or dependency can manifest many physical, mental, and behavioral problems. For example, alcoholics often suffer from thiamine deficiency because of their poor diets; they are consequently susceptible to the serious, often fatal Wernicke-Korsakoff disease.[23] Research conducted over the past decade shows that the dietary inadequacy of certain chemicals and minerals, including sodium, potassium, calcium, amino acids, monoamines, and peptides, can lead to depression, mania, cognitive problems, memory loss, and abnormal sexual activity.[24]

Research studies examining the relationship between crime and vitamin deficiency/dependency have seemed to find a close link between antisocial behavior and insufficient quantities of some B vitamins—B_3 and B_6—and vitamin C. In addition, studies have purported to show that a major proportion of all schizophrenics and children with learning and behavior disorders are dependent on vitamin B_3 and B_6.[25]

Another suspected nutritional influence on behavior is a diet especially high in carbohydrates and sugar.[26] For example, recent research found that the way the brain processed glucose was related to scores on tests measuring reasoning power.[27] In addition, sugar intake levels have been associated with attention span deficiencies.[28]

Diets high in sugar and carbohydrates also have been linked to violence and aggression. For example, Stephen Schoenthaler conducted an experiment with 276 incarcerated youths to determine whether a change in the amount of processed sugar in their diet would have a corresponding influence on their behavior within the institutional setting.[29] In the experiment, several dietary changes were made: sweet drinks were replaced with fruit juices; table sugar was replaced with honey; breakfast cereals with high sugar content were eliminated; molasses was substituted for sugar in cooking. Schoenthaler found that these changes produced a significant reduction in disciplinary actions within the institution: the number of assaults, thefts, fights, and disobedience within the institution declined about 45 percent. These results were consistent when such factors as age, previous offense record, and race of the offender were considered.

These are but a few of the research efforts linking sugar intake to emotional, cognitive, and behavioral performance.[30] Nonetheless, it should be noted that a number of biologists have questioned this association, and some recent research efforts have failed to find a linkage between sugar consumption and violence.[31]

As a whole, these efforts seem to suggest that in every segment of society there are violent, aggressive, and amoral people and that improper food, vitamin, and mineral intake may be responsible for antisocial behavior. However, because of inadequate testing and nonscientific sampling techniques, there is little clear-cut proof that improper diet alone can be a cause of violence or other criminal behaviors.[32]

Hypoglycemia. **Hypoglycemia** occurs when glucose (sugar) in the blood falls below levels necessary for normal and efficient brain functioning. The brain is sensitive to the lack of blood sugar because it is the only organ that obtains its energy solely from the combustion of carbohydrates. Thus, when the brain is deprived of blood sugar, its metabolism slows down, impairing its function. Symptoms of hypoglycemia include irritability, anxiety, depression, crying spells, headaches, and confusion.

Research studies have linked hypoglycemia to outbursts of antisocial behavior and violence. As early as 1943, D. Hill and W. Sargent linked murder to hypoglycemia.[33] Several studies have related assaults and fatal sexual offenses to hypoglycemic reactions.[34] Hypoglycemia also has been connected with a syndrome characterized by aggressive and assaultive behavior, glucose disturbance, and brain dysfunction.

There have been some attempts to measure hypoglycemia, using subjects with a known history of criminal activity. Studies of jailed inmates and prison inmate populations have found a higher than normal level of hypoglycemia.[35] Similarly, Matti Virkkunen has found the presence of reactive hypoglycemia in groups of habitually violent and impulsive offenders.[36]

Hormonal Influences. There have been a number of research studies linking violence to abnormal hormone levels. One area of interest has been the principal male steroid hormone **testosterone,** which controls secondary sex characteristics such as facial hair and voice timbre. Evidence suggests that its production levels may be strongly related to criminal aggressiveness in human males. L. E. Kreuz and R. M. Rose found in a sample of inmates that testosterone levels were higher in men who committed violent crimes than in other prisoners, though results of comparisons with a noncriminal control group were insignificant.[37] Other studies, including those by Richard Rada, could not distinguish between violent and nonviolent offenders on the basis of testosterone levels.[38] A recent review of existing research by Robert Rubin also failed to find conclusive evidence of a consistent association between testosterone and violence.[39]

With regard to female offenders, there has long been the suspicion that the onset of the menstrual cycle triggered excessive amounts of estrogen and progesterone which effected antisocial aggressive behavior; this condition is commonly referred to as **Premenstrual Syndrome (PMS).** The link between PMS and delinquency was popularized by Katharina Dalton, whose studies of English women led her to conclude that females are more likely to commit suicide, be aggressive, and be otherwise antisocial before or during menstruation.[40] While the Dalton research is often cited as evidence of the link between PMS and crime, methodological problems make it impossible to accept her findings at face value. Criminologist Julie Horney impressively reviewed the literature on PMS and crime and found that existing evidence is inconclusive. Horney suggests there may be alternative explanations for a PMS-violence link. For example, it's possible that the psychological and physical stress of aggression produces early menstruation and not vice versa.[41]

Despite the uncertainty of evidence linking hormone levels to crime, drugs decreasing testosterone levels have been used to treat male sex offenders. Sarnoff Mednick and Jan Volavka warn that the long-term side effects of such treatment are still problematic.[42] Similarly, administration of the female hormone estrogen to sexually active men has led to a decrease in their sexual potency. Consequently, the female hormones estrogen and progesterone have been used to manage sex offenders.[43]

Allergies. Sociologists also are concerned with the effect of cerebral allergies and neuroallergies on criminal and otherwise deviant behavior. In general, allergies are defined as unusual or excessive reactions of the body to foreign substance.[44] For example, hay fever is an allergic reaction caused when pollen cells enter the body and are fought or neutral-

ized by the body's natural defenses. The results of the battle are itchy eyes, active sinuses, and swollen glands. **Cerebral allergies** cause an excessive reaction of the brain, whereas **neuroallergies** affect the nervous system.

Cerebral allergies and neuroallergies are believed to cause the allergic person to produce enzymes that attack wholesome foods as if they were dangerous to the body.[45] They also may cause swelling of the brain, which can produce mental, emotional, and behavioral problems including hyperemotionality, aggressiveness, and violent behavior. Cerebral allergy and neuroallergy problems also have been linked to hyperactivity in children, which may portend antisocial behavior and the labeling of children as potential delinquents.

The foods most commonly involved in producing such allergies are cow's milk, wheat, corn, soybeans, chocolate, citrus, and eggs; however, about 300 other foods have been identified as allergens. The potential seriousness of the problem has been raised by studies linking the average consumption of one suspected cerebral allergen—corn—to cross-national homicide rates.[46]

Environmental Contaminants. Recently, biocriminologists have begun to focus on the effects of environmental contaminants on behavior. Increasing amounts of lead, copper, cadmium, mercury, and inorganic gases such as chlorine and nitrogen dioxide have been found in the ecosystem. At high levels, these substances can cause severe illness or death; at more moderate levels, they have been linked to emotional and behavioral disorders.[47]

Some studies have linked food additives to crime. For example, C. Hawley and R. E. Buckley claim that food dyes and artificial colors and flavors can produce hostile, impulsive, and otherwise antisocial behavior in youths.[48]

Other research efforts have been directed at measuring the influence of lead on youths' behavior. For example, in one study of hyperactive children who manifested conduct problems and other antisocial behavior, Oliver David and his associates found that lead in the bloodstream may have had an important role in explaining the onset of the behavior.[49]

Lighting may be another important environmental influence on antisocial behavior. Research projects have suggested that radiation from artificial light sources, such as fluorescent tubes and television sets, may produce antisocial, aggressive behavior.[50]

Neurophysiological Factors

Another area of biocriminology involves **neurophysiology,** or the study of brain activity. This explanation of criminality has received a great deal of attention since August 1, 1966, when Charles Whitman, after killing his wife and his mother, barricaded himself in a tower at the University of Texas with a high-powered rifle and proceeded to kill 14 people and wound 24 others before he was killed by police. An autopsy revealed that Whitman suffered from a malignant infiltrating tumor. Whitman had previously experienced uncontrollable urges to kill and had actually gone to a psychiatrist seeking help for his problems. He kept careful notes documenting his feelings and his inability to control his homicidal urges. He also left instructions for his estate to be given to a mental health foundation so it could study mental problems such as his.[51]

This section discusses various brain function patterns that have been related to criminality.

Minimal Brain Dysfunction.   Minimal brain dysfunction (MBD) is related to an abnormality in cerebral structure. It has been defined as abruptly appearing, maladaptive behavior that interrupts the lifestyle of an individual. In its most serious form, MBD has been linked to serious antisocial acts, an imbalance in the urge-control mechanisms of the brain, and chemical abnormality. Included within the category of minimal brain dysfunction are several abnormal behavior patters: dyslexia, visual perception problems, hyperactivity, poor attention span, temper tantrums, and aggressiveness.

One type of minimal brain dysfunction that has been of great concern to biocriminologists manifests itself in periods of explosive rage. This form of the disorder is considered an important cause of such behavior as wife beating, child abuse, suicide, aggressiveness, and motiveless homicide. One perplexing feature of this syndrome is that people who are afflicted with it often maintain warm and pleasant personalities between episodes of violence.

Some studies have attempted to measure the presence of minimal brain dysfunction in offender populations. R. D. Robin and his associates found that 60 percent of a sample of suicidal adolescents exhibited brain dysfunction on psychological tests.[52] Lorne Yeudall studied 60 criminal patients and found that they were characterized by lateral brain dysfunction of the dominant hemisphere of the brain.[53] His data helped him predict with 95 percent accuracy the recidivism of violent criminals.[54]

Of interest to both educators and criminologists is the relationship between MBD and the so-called learning-disabled child. Research has shown that although learning-disabled (LD) children violate the law at the same rate as non-LD children, they are overrepresented in official arrest and juvenile court statistics.[55]

EEG Abnormality.   An **electroencephalogram (EEG)** records the electrical impulses given off by the brain.[56] The EEG represents a signal composed of various rhythms and transit electrical discharges, commonly called brain waves, which can be recorded by electrodes placed on the scalp. Brain wave frequencies are given in cycles per second, measured in hertz (Hz), and usually range from 0.5 to 30 Hz. Measurements of the EEG reflect the activity of neurons located in the cerebral cortex. The rhythmic nature of this brain activity is determined by mechanisms that involve subcortical structures, primarily the thalamus portion of the brain.

In what is considered the most significant investigation of EEG abnormality and crime, a randomly selected group of 335 violent delinquents was divided into those who were habitually violent and those who had committed a single violent act. While 65 percent of the habitually aggressive had abnormal EEG recordings, only 24 percent of the second group had recordings that deviated from the norm. When the records of individuals who had brain damage, were mentally retarded, or were epileptic were removed from the sample, the percentage of abnormality among boys who had committed a solitary violent crime was the same as that of the general population, about 12 percent. However, the habitually aggressive subjects still showed a 57 percent abnormality rate.[57]

Other research efforts have linked abnormal EEG recordings to antisocial behavior in children. Although about 5 to 15 percent of normal youths have abnormal EEG readings, about 50 to 60 percent of those with behavior disorders display abnormal recordings. In studies of problem children, more than half were found to have abnormal EEG activity.[58] Behaviors highly correlated with abnormal EEG included poor impulse control, inadequate social adaptation, hostility, temper tantrums, and destructiveness.[59]

Studies of adults have associated slow and bilateral brain waves with hostile, hypercritical, irritable, nonconforming, and impulsive behavior.[60] Psychiatric patients with EEG abnormalities have been reported to be highly combative and to suffer episodes of rage. Studies of murderers have shown that a disproportionate number manifest abnormal EEG rates.[61]

While there is some evidence that abnormal EEG readings are linked to violent behavior, a number of studies have found them to be weakly related because many nonviolent people also have atypical EEGs.[62] Despite such problems, researchers Diana Fishbein and Robert Thatcher have found that EEG analysis can detect a variety of organic problems linked to antisocial behavior, and that it therefore can be a valuable tool for detecting crime-producing physical conditions.[63]

Other Brain Dysfunctions. Other brain dysfunctions have been related to violent crime. Persistent criminality has been linked to dysfunction in the frontal and temporal regions of the brain. These regions are believed to play an important role in the regulation and inhibition of human behavior, including the formation of plans and intentions and the regulation of complex behaviors.[64] Researchers Lorne Yeudall and his associates found that brain lesions which occur in specific points in the neurological system, such as within the auditory system, can have permanent effects on behavior.[56] Clinical evaluation of depressed and aggressive psychopathic subjects showed a significant number (more than 75 percent had dysfunction of the temporal and frontal regions of the brain. Their conclusion:

> Evidence from our research over the past 13 years, as well as the findings of others, is consistent with the hypothesis of a high incidence of disturbed functioning of the central nervous system in the persistent offender.[65]

The presence of brain tumors also has been linked to a wide variety of psychological problems, including personality changes, hallucinations, and psychotic episodes.[67] There is evidence that people with tumors are prone to depression, irritability, temper outbursts, and even homicidal attacks. Clinical case studies of patients suffering from brain tumors indicate that they may undergo behavior changes so great that previously docile people attempt to seriously harm their families and friends; when the tumor is removed, behavior returns to normal.[68]

In addition to brain tumors, head injuries caused by accidents such as falls or auto crashes have been linked to personality reversals involving outbursts of antisocial and violent behavior.[69] A variety of central nervous system diseases, including cerebral arteriosclerosis, epilepsy, senile dementia, Korsakoff's syndrome, and Huntington's corea, also have been associated with memory deficiency, orientation loss, and affective (emotional) disturbances dominated by rage, anger, and increased irritability.[70]

Genetic Influences

Since its inception, biocriminology has been concerned with genetic influences on criminality. If some human behaviors are influenced by heredity, why not antisocial tendencies? Evidence exists that animals can be bred to have aggressive traits; pit bulldogs, fighting bulls, and fighting cocks have been selectively mated to produce superior predators. Of course, no similar data are available for people, but there is a growing body of research which focuses on the genetic factors associated with human behavior.[71] In the following sections, the role genetic makeup plays in human behavior is examined in some detail.

Chromosome Studies: The XYY Controversy. Chromosomes—microscopic structures contained in cell nuclei—carry the basic genetic material, genes. Human beings normally have 46 chromosomes, of which 44 determine the shape and structure of the body and two determine sex. The typical male chromosome contingent is recorded as 46, XY; the female as 46, XX.[72]

Sometimes individuals possess greater or fewer than the normal chromosome complement because of problems encountered soon after conception. Of concern are males who have an extra Y chromosome—the 47, XYY syndrome. Although males also can possess an extra X chromosome (47, XXY), this condition is of

Sarnoff Mednick has conducted important research on genetic factors in crime causation.

less importance to criminology.

Several early studies on the XYY phenomenon reported that XYY males tended to be very tall individuals with a disproportionate inclination to commit crimes of violence.[73] Surveys of tall men in institutions for the mentally ill and prisons suggested that the rate of institutionalized men with an extra Y chromosome was greater than the rate estimated for the population at large.[74] The XYY syndrome received a great deal of publicity when Richard Speck, the convicted killer of eight nurses in Chicago, was said to be an XYY. There was much public concern that all XYYs were potential killers and should be closely controlled. Civil libertarians expressed fear that all XYYs could be labeled dangerous and violent regardless of whether they had engaged in violent activities. Later research found that Speck did not have an extra Y chromosome.

Current research has cast doubt on the XYY hypothesis.[75] Biocriminologists have found that the proportion of XYYs in the prison population is not significantly higher than in the population at large (about 1 in 700 male births). However, some evidence shows that the number of XYY males in secure mental hospitals is higher than would be expected by chance alone.[76]

Twin Studies. If inherited traits cause criminal behaviors, it should be expected that twins should be quite similar in their antisocial activities. However, since twins are usually brought up in the same household and exposed to the same set of social conditions, it is difficult to determine whether their behavior is a result of biological, sociological, or psychological conditions. Biocriminologists have tried to overcome this dilemma by comparing identical, or monozygotic (MZ), twins with fraternal, or dizygotic (DZ), twins of the same sex.[77] MZ twins are genetically identical, while DZ twins have only half their genes in common. If heredity does determine criminal behavior, MZ twins should be much more similar in their antisocial activities than DZ twins.

The earliest studies conducted on the behavior of twins detected a significant relationship between the criminal activities of MZ twins and a much lower association between those of DZ twins. In a review of relevant studies conducted between 1929 and 1961, Sarnoff Mednick and Jan Volavka found that, overall, 60 percent of MZ twins shared criminal behavior patterns (if one twin was criminal, so was the other), while only 30 percent of DZ twins were similarly related.[78] These findings may be powerful evidence that a genetic basis for criminality exists.

More recent studies have supported these basic findings, though the level of association found between the behaviors of MZ twins is somewhat lower than previously thought. For example, Karl Christiansen studies 3,586 male twin pairs and found a 52 percent behavior concordance for MZ pairs and a 22 percent concordance for DZ pairs. His results suggest that the MZ twins may share a genetic characteristic that increases the risk of their engaging in criminality.[79] Similarly, David Rowe and D. Wayne Osgood analyzed the factors that influence self-reported delinquency in a sample of twin pairs. They concluded that genetic influences actually have greater explanatory power than other variables.[80]

While persuasive, this evidence is certainly not conclusive proof that crime is genetically predetermined. Not all research efforts have found that MZ twin pairs are more closely related in their criminal behavior than DZ twins or ordinary sibling pairs.[81] Even if MZ twins are more closely associated in their behavior than other siblings, there are alternate explanations for this phenomenon. Mednick and Volavka offer several interpretations for the MZ twins' higher criminality relationship. If a physical characteristic such as height were related to committing crimes, both MZ twins would be more likely to be tall than both DZ twins, since height is genetically transmitted. Or, if alcohol addiction increased the probability that someone would engage in antisocial behavior, it is possible that alcohol addiction is related to genetic factors more likely to be shared by MZ twins than by DZ twins. Put another way, a relationship between genetics and criminality might be accomplished through the influence of some undisclosed intervening variable. However, Mednick and Volavka concluded that:

> Despite the limitations of the twin method, the results of these studies are compatible with the hypothesis that genetic factors account for some of the variance associated with antisocial behavior.[82]

Adoption Studies. Another approach that has been used to determine whether heredity influences criminality has focused on the behavior of adopted children. If children's behavior is more similar to that of their biological parents than to that of their adoptive parents, then the idea of a genetic basis for criminality would be supported. If, on the other hand, adoptees are more similar to their adoptive parents than their biological parents, an environmental basis for crime would seem more valid.

Several studies indicate that some relationship may exist between the biological parents' behavior and the behavior of their children, even when their contact has been infrequent. In one major study, Barry Hutchings and Sarnoff Mednick analyzed 1,145 male adoptees born in Copenhagen, Denmark, between 1927 and 1941; of these, 185 had criminal records.[83] After following up on 143 of the criminal adoptees and matching them with a control group of 143 noncriminal adoptees, Hutchings and Mednick found that the criminality of the biological father was a strong predictor of the child's criminal behavior. Moreover, the researchers found that when *both* the biological and adoptive father were criminal, the probability that the youth would engage in criminal behavior greatly expanded. Of the boys whose adop-

tive and biological fathers were both criminals, 24.5 percent had been convicted of a criminal law violation, while only 13.5 percent of those whose biological and adoptive fathers were not criminals had similar conviction records.[84] Consequently, the authors concluded that both biological and environmental factors influence crime. These results were duplicated in studies by Sarnoff Mednick and his associates, using a sample of 14,427 adoptees born in Denmark between 1924 and 1947.[85]

Although the evidence is not conclusive, findings from twin and adoption studies have given preliminary support to the association of heredity, environment, and criminality.

Evaluation of the Biological Perspective

Biological perspectives on crime raise some challenging questions for criminology. However, critics suggest biological theory is racist and dysfunctional. The critics argue that if biology can explain the cause of street crimes (such as assault, murder, or rape) and if, as official crime statistics suggest, the poor and minority group members commit a disproportionate number of such acts, then by implication, biological theory says that member of these groups are biologically flawed or inferior. Biological theory is challenged because it downgrades or ignores the effect of a crime-producing social environment. It focuses on the violent crimes of the lower classes while it ignores the white-collar crime of the upper- and middle-classes. It gives short shrift to the geographic, social, and temporal patterns in the crime rate uncovered by the FBI and victimization data sources. Furthermore, biological theory seems to divide people into criminals and noncriminals on the basis of their physical makeup; it ignores the fact that almost everyone has engaged in some type of illegal activity at some time.

Modern biocriminologists counter that their views should not be confused with Lombrosian, deterministic biology. Rather than suggest that there are born criminals and noncriminals, they maintain that some people carry within them the potential to be violent or antisocial, and that environmental conditions sometimes can trigger antisocial responses.[86] This would explain why some otherwise law-abiding citizens engage in a single, seemingly unexplainable antisocial act and, conversely, why some people with long criminal careers often engage in conventional behavior. As Israel Naschson and Deborah Denno point out:

> As has been repeatedly pointed out, no biological factor, normal or abnormal, predetermines behavior, because behavior is a product of interacting biological and environmental events.[87]

Lee Ellis has proposed a "genetic-environmental-neurologically-medicated-interactionist" (GENMI) approach to understanding crime which incorporates these views into an integrated biosocial theory of crime.[88] According to Ellis: (1) the physical-chemical functioning of the brain is responsible for all human behavior; (2) brain function is controlled by genetic and environmental factors; and (3) environmental influences on brain function encompass both physical (drugs, chemicals, and injuries) and experiential (learning) factors. Ellis finds that all three components of modern biocriminology (biochemistry, genetics, and neurology) work in concert to control behavior.

Biological explanations may also account in part for cultural discrepancies in crime rates. The environment is viewed as a triggering mechanism; it is possible that people living in high-poverty, high-crime, inner-city areas are more likely to experience crime-producing stimuli than people living in more affluent neighborhoods. Moreover, wealthier citizens are better equipped to compensate for adverse biological conditions by diet, treatment, medication, and education. For example, in a wealthy school district, parents of a child who is suffering from a minimal brain dysfunction may avail themselves of special education and treatment programs unavailable in less affluent districts.

The major drawback to the biological perspective, as indicated earlier, is a lack of adequate empirical testing. In most research efforts, sample sizes are relatively small and poorly chosen. Even more serious is the fact that a great deal of biocriminological research is conducted with samples of adjudicated offenders who have been placed in clinical treatment settings. Thus, it is difficult to determine whether findings apply only to offenders who have been convicted of crimes and placed in treatment, or to the population of criminals as a whole. Consequently, the true relationship being measured could be that between biological treats and arrest or conviction, not between biological traits and criminality. A great deal more

research is needed if biological explanations of crime are to be considered truly valid.

PSYCHOLOGICAL THEORIES OF CRIME

Psychologists, psychiatrists, and other mental health professionals have long played an active role in formulating criminological theory. In their quest to understand and treat all varieties of abnormal mental conditions, psychologists have encountered clients whose behavior falls within categories society has labeled criminal, deviant, violent, and antisocial. Since psychologists view all human behavior as a function of some mental process, it is not surprising that they conclude that many criminal behaviors can be traced to personality disturbances. However, not even the staunchest supporter of psychological theory would suggest that all criminals are mentally ill or suffer an abnormal personality. Though some criminals are considered highly disturbed, they make up only a small percentage of the offender population. Psychologists do, however, trace the onset of criminality to mental processes. Therefore, they argue that criminologists will never understand the cause of criminality unless they determine the psychological processes that motivate it.

Early Psychological Theory

The very earliest psychological view was that criminals were possessed by evil spirits or demons. As the field of psychology developed, early theorists suggested that mental illness and insanity were inherited, and that deviants were mentally damaged because of their inferior genetic makeup.

An early pioneer of the concept of insanity was the English physician Henry Maudsley (1835–1918). Maudsley believed that insanity and criminal behavior were strongly linked: "Crime is a sort of outlet in which their unsound tendencies are discharged; they would go mad if they were not criminals, and they do not go mad because they are criminals.[89]

Maudsley was a firm believer that criminal-producing mental traits are inherited, leading to long lines of crime-prone **mental degenerates.** He stated that people who became criminals did not have the "aptitude of the higher industrial classes," and that they were "deficient in the power of attention . . . [had] bad memories and [made] slow progress in learning." Furthermore, Maudsley found criminals to be "inherently vicious," to "steal and lie with a skill hard to believe," to be "hopeless pupils," and to come from families in which insanity or some allied condition prevailed. In sum, Maudsley believed insanity was a hereditary condition that rendered the affected incapable of controlling their aggressive behavior.

Psychological Theory Today

When they study crime, psychocriminologists usually address basic issues of human behavior: why people engage in violence and aggression; whether there is such a thing as a criminal personality; and whether childhood experiences influence adult criminality. However, there is by no means unanimity among psychologists over the answers to these questions.[90] Some psychologists view antisocial behavior from a psychoanalytic perspective—their focus is on early childhood experiences and their effect on personality. Behaviorists stress social learning and behavior modeling as the keys to criminality. Psychobiologists are concerned with the links among biological processes, human personality, and criminality. The following sections review each of these perspectives independently. (See also the Close-Up entitled "The Cognitive Perspective" at the end of this chapter.)

Psychoanalytic Perspective

Psychoanalytic psychology is the creation of the Viennese doctor **Sigmund Freud** (1856–1939). **Psychoanalysis** has become the most well-known theory of human personality development.[91] Though many mental health professionals still use Freud's approach, there have been numerous efforts by his successors to expand, contradict, and reassess his pioneering concepts.

Structure of Mind and Personality. According to Freudian theory, the human mind performs three separate functions. The *conscious* mind is the aspect of the mind that people are most aware of—hunger, pain, thirst, desire. The *preconscious* mind contains elements of experiences that are out of awareness but can be brought back to consciousness at any time —memories, experiences. The *unconscious* part of the mind contains biological desires and urges that cannot readily be experienced as thoughts. Part of the unconscious contains feelings about sex and hostility, which people keep below the surface of consciousness by a process called **repression.**

Freud also postulated a three-part structure for the human personality. The *id*, the primitive part of people's mental makeup, is present at birth. It represents unconscious biological drives for sex, food, and other life-sustaining necessities. The id follows the pleasure principle—it requires instant gratification without concern for the rights of others.

The *ego* develops early in life, when an infant begins to learn that its wishes cannot be instantly gratified. The ego is that part of the personality that compensates for the demands of the id by helping people guide their actions to remain within the boundaries of social convention. The ego is guided by the reality principle—it takes into account what is practical and conventional by societal standards.

The *superego* develops when an individual assimilates the moral standards and values of parents and the community. It is the moral aspect of people's personalities; it passes judgment on their behavior.

All three parts of the personality operate to control behavior. An individual's id might demand pleasures, such as premarital sex; the superego makes the person feel guilty for these desires; the ego works out a compromise—the individual can engage in some sexual activities but must not go "too far" lest he or she "get in trouble."

Development. Freud postulated that the most basic human drive, or instinct, present at birth is *Eros*, the instinct to preserve and create life. Eros is expressed sexually. Consequently, humans experience sexuality very early in their development. Sexuality is expressed in seeking pleasure through various parts of the body. During the first year of life, a child attains pleasure by sucking and biting; Freud called this the *oral stage*. During the second and third years of life, the focus of sexual attention is on the elimination of bodily wastes—the *anal stage*. The *phallic stage* occurs during the third year of life; children now focus their attention

Movies such as ''Fatal Attraction'' often portray violent people as psychotics who display disturbances of thought, mood and behavior.

on their genitals. Males begin to have sexual feelings for their mother (the Oedipus complex) and girls for their fathers (the Electra complex). *Latency* begins at age six; during this period, feelings of sexuality are repressed until the *genital stage* begins at puberty; this marks the beginning of adult sexuality.

It conflicts are encountered during any of the psychosexual stage of development, a person can become **fixated** at that point. The person will as an adult exhibit behavior traits characteristic of those encountered during infantile sexual development. For example, an infant who does not receive enough oral gratification during the first year of life is likely as an adult to engage in such oral behavior as smoking, drinking, or drug abuse, or to be clinging and dependent in personal relationships.

Post-Freudian Psychoanalytic Theory.   Freud's view of the mind and personality has influenced several competing versions of psychoanalytic theory.[92] For example, **Carl Jung** (1875–1961), one of Freud's inner circle, developed *analytical psychology*. According to Jungian theory, an important aspect of the human psychic structure is the *collective unconscious*, which is a sort of racial memory of the past experience of the human species. Although these primitive images, or *archetypes*, remain unconscious, they influence human thought and emotion.

Alfred Adler (1870–1937) is credited with being the founder of *individual psychology*. Adler coined the term **inferiority complex.** Adler claimed most people have feelings of inferiority and compensate for them with a drive for superiority. Adler recognized that self-awareness plays an important part in personality, and that people have a *creative self*, exhibited by the desire to overcome obstacles and develop individual potential.

Erik Erikson's (1902–1984) theory of *psychosocial development* holds that humans go through eight stages of ego development. From birth to one year, the infants learn to trust their mothers and become acclimated to their surroundings. Later stages find individuals trying to master fundamental skills, learning careers, committing to love, being creative, and, finally, exhibiting wisdom and dignity. Erikson identified the **identity crisis**—a period of serious personal questioning people undertake in an effort to determine their own values and sense of direction.

Psychoanalysis and Criminal Behavior. Freud did not devote much time to crime theory. He did link criminality to an unconscious sense of guilt a person retains because of the childhood Oedipus complex. He stated:

> In many criminals, especially youthful ones, it is possible to detect a very powerful sense of guilt which existed before the crime, and is therefore not its result but its motive. It is as if it was a relief to be able to fasten the unconscious sense of guilt onto something real and immediate.[93]

Psychoanalysts have generally followed Freud in linking criminality to abnormal mental states produced by early childhood trauma.

Within classical Freudian theory, two mental conditions are thought to produce antisocial activity. A *neurosis* is a disorder characterized by extreme anxiety. It represents the feeling that repressed, unacceptable impulses may break through and take control. A more extreme form of mental disturbance is *psychosis*, abnormal behavior that impairs everyday functioning. Psychosis occurs when the primitive id functions take control of the personality.

Psychotics are people who manifest disturbances of thought, mood, and behavior. There are various specific psychotic disorders; of those, **schizophrenia** is perhaps most often linked to crime. Schizophrenics exhibit illogical and incoherent thought processes and a lack of insight into their behavior. They may experience delusions and hallucinate. For example, they may see themselves as agents of the devil, avenging

angels, or the recipients of messages from animals and plants. David Berkowitz, the "Son of Sam" or "44-caliber killer," exhibited these traits. Paranoid schizophrenics suffer complex behavior delusions involving wrong-doing or persecution—they think everyone is out to get them.

The psychoanalyst whose work is most closely associated with using Freudian concepts to explain criminality is **August Aichorn**.[94] After examining many delinquent youths, Aichorn concluded that societal stress, though damaging, could not alone result in a life of crime unless a predisposition existed that prepared youths psychologically for antisocial acts. He labeled this state *latent delinquency*. Latent delinquency is found in youngsters whose personality requires them to seek immediate gratification (to act impulsively), consider satisfaction of their personal needs more important than relating to others, and satisfy instinctive urges without consideration of right and wrong (that is, they lack guilt).

Psychoanalyst David Abrahamsen views the criminal as an id-dominated person who suffers from the inability to control impulsive, pleasure-seeking drives.[95] Perhaps because they suffered unhappy experiences in childhood, or had families who could not provide proper love and care, criminals suffer from weak or damaged egos that make them unable to cope with conventional society. In its most extreme form, criminality may be viewed as a form of psychosis that prevents offenders from empathizing with the feelings of their victims or controlling their own impulsive needs for gratification.

Some psychoanalysts view criminality as a manifestation of feelings of oppression and of the inability to do much about it. Criminality allows troubled people to survive by producing positive psychic results. It helps them to feel free and independent; gives them the possibility of excitement and the chance to use their skills and imagination; provides them with the promise of positive gain; allows them to blame others for their predicament (for example, the police); and gives them a chance to rationalize their sense of failure.[96]

The views of psychoanalysts are supported by research showing that many serious, violent offenders suffer from some sort of personality disturbance. James Sorrells' well-known study of juvenile murderers, "Kids Who Kill," found that many homicidal youths could be described in such terms as "overtly

CLOSE-UP

Crime and Mental Disorder

The psychoanalytic perspective links serious, violent criminal behavior to psychosis. According to this view, people suffering from schizophrenia, paranoia, and so on will be more likely to commit violent, aggressive crimes. Conversely, a disproportionate number of people who commit violent crimes are probably suffering from some type of severe personality disturbance. Just how accurate is this view? That is, are the mentally ill more likely to become involved in crime than the mentally sound?

To answer this question, psychologists John Monahan and Henry Steadman reviewed the existing body of literature on the relationship between mental disorder and crime. They found that the rate of mental disorder in a population must be thought of as either being the *true rate* (the percentage of the population mentally ill) or the *treated rate* (the percentage of the population under treatment for mental illness). Some of the findings are summarized below.

These are two kinds of studies of the true and treated rates of crime and mental disorder. The first kind looks at "pure" cases, in which rates of mental disorder are computed for groups of criminals or crime rates are computed for groups of the mentally disordered. That is, the study covers people who are "purely" in one category and inquires as to those who also fall into the other category.

The second kind of study considers "mixed" cases—persons who are being treated as both criminal and mentally disordered. These persons fall into various legal categories of "mentally disordered offenders."

Pure Cases of Criminal Behavior or Mental Disorder

Findings from the available research on the true and treated rates of mental disorder among criminals—and the true and treated rates of crime among the disorderrd—are summarized in Table A.

The scant research into mental disorder among persons who have been arrested ("true criminals") suggests that their rates of disorder are no higher than those of the general American population of comparable social class.

Several surveys have been made of the rates of mental disorder among persons in jails and prisons ("treated criminals"). These studies have reported rates of serious mental disorder ranging from 1 to 7 percent, whereas rates of less severe mental disorders range from 15 to 20 percent.

TABLE A Studies of Pure Cases of Criminal Behavior or Mental Disorder

Relationship at Issue	Amount of Evidence	Findings Compared with Matched Groups in the General Population
True disorder among true criminals	Little	No higher
True crime among truly disordered	None	—
True crime among treated disordered	Much	No higher
Treated disorder among true criminals	None	—
True disorder among treated criminals	Much	No higher
Treated crime among truly disordered	None	—
Treated disorder among treated criminals	Little	No comparison data
Treated crime among treated disordered	Little	Unclear

hostile," "explosive or volatile," "anxious," and "depressed."[97] Likewise, in a recent study of 45 males accused of murder, Richard Rosner and his associates found that 75 percent could be classified as having some mental illness, including schizophrenia.[98] However, as the Close-Up entitled "Crime and Mental

(Such questionable categories as sociopathy, alcoholism, and drug addiction are not included in these figures.) When comparing these rates with those found in surveys of the general population, it is necessary to recognize that jail and prison inmates are disproportionately persons of lower social class, and that such persons have disproportionately high rates of mental disorder. The conclusion that emerges: the rate of mental disorder among inmate populations does not exceed the rate of mental disorder among groups of comparable social class in the general community.

The following conclusions from the research appears justified:

- The arrest rate of mentally disordered offenders after their release from mental hospitals is very similar to the arrest rate of pure mental patients with a comparable prehospital arrest record.
- It is questionable how many persons legally adjudicated to be mentally disordered offenders are suffering from true mental disorder. The most frequent diagnosis given to mentally disordered sex offenders, for example, is "sexual deviation."
- The subsequent conviction rate of mentally disordered offenders (based on the little data that exist) is consistent with what one would predict from a knowledge of their criminal history and demographic characteristics.
- Likewise, the factors relating to the rehospitalization of pure mental patients (e.g., the number of times they have been hospitalized in the past) also seem to relate to the rehospitalization of mentally disordered offenders.

Mixed Cases of Criminal Behavior and Mental Disorder

Studies of cases of persons treated simultaneously for criminal behavior and mental disorder lead to the conclusion that rates of crime and mental disorder are about what one would expect from a knowledge of their demographic characteristics and their experience with the mental health and criminal justice systems.

Mentally disordered offenders is an umbrella term, covering four legal categories: (1) persons judged incompetent to stand trial, (2) persons found not guilty by reason of insanity, (3) mentally disordered sex offenders, and (4) persons transferred from prison to a mental hospital.

Implications

The correlates of crime among the mentally disordered appear to be the same as the correlates of crime among any other group: age, gender, race, social class, and prior criminality. Likewise, the correlates of mental disorder among criminal offenders appear to be the same as those in other populations: age, social class, and previous disorder. Populations characterized by the correlates of both crime and mental disorder (e.g., low social class) can be expected to show high rates of both, and they do.

It does appear from the data that, if one could excise approximately half the population of state mental hospitals (those with prior arrest records), then the remaining patients, on their release, would be no more criminal than the rest of us. However, the data do not reveal how this can be done without transferring many of these people to jails and prisons, and thereby aggravating the problems of those institutions.

In sum, Monahan and Steadman found little evidence that the mentally ill are any more criminal than the rest of society.

Discussion Questions

1. Does the finding that crime rates among the mentally ill are equivalent to those of the general population invalidate psychoanalytic theory?
2. Should a person who is evaluated as mentally ill by clinical personnel but legally sane under the law be responsible for their criminal actions?

SOURCE: Adapted from John Monahan and Henry Steadman, *Crime and Mental Disorder* (Washington, D.C.: National Institute of Justice Research in Brief, September 1984). Footnotes omitted.

Disorder" suggests, there is little evidence that most mentally ill people are generally violent or criminal. In sum, the psychoanalytic model of the criminal offender depicts an aggressive, frustrated person dominated by events that occurred early in childhood.

BEHAVIOR AND SOCIAL LEARNING THEORIES

Behavior theory maintains that human actions are developed through learning experiences. Rather than focusing on unconscious personality traits or cognitive development patterns produced early in childhood, behavior theorists are concerned with the actual behaviors people engage in during the course of their daily lives. The major premise of behavior theory is that people alter their behavior according to the reactions it receives from others. Consequently, behavior is constantly being shaped by life experiences. With respect to criminal activity, the behaviorist viewpoint is that crimes, especially violent acts, are learned responses to life situations and do not necessarily represent abnormal or morally immature responses.

Social Learning Theory

The **social learning** branch of behavior theory is the one most relevant to criminology, since it includes the acquisition of violent and aggressive behavior patterns.[99] Social learning theorists, most notably **Albert Bandura,** argue that people are not born with the ability to act violently but that they learn to be aggressive through their life experiences. These experiences include direct observation of others acting aggressively to achieve some goal, or watching others being rewarded for violent acts on television, in movies, and so on. Social learning theory maintains that children learn to act aggressively by modeling their behavior after the violent acts of adults. Later in life, these violent behavior patterns persist in social relationships.

In the social learning view, psychological or biological factors may predispose a person toward violence, but the activation of a person's violent tendencies is achieved by factors in the environment. Therefore, Bandura claims, the specific forms that aggressive behavior takes, the frequency with which it is expressed, the situations in which it is displayed, and the specific targets selected for attack are largely determined by social learning factors.

Social Learning and Violence.   Social learning theorists view violence as something learned through a process called **behavior modeling.** In modern society,

Albert Bandura is one of today's most persuasive social learning theorists.

aggressive acts are usually modeled after three principal sources. Most prominent is the behavior model reinforced by family members. According to Bandura, studies of family life show that children who use aggressive tactics have parents who use similar behaviors when dealing with others.

A second influence on the social learning of violence is provided by environmental experiences. People who reside in areas in which violence is a daily occurrence are more likely to act violently than those whose subcultural affiliations stress conventional behavior.

A third source of behavior modeling is provided by the mass media. It has been commonplace for films and television shows to graphically depict violence. Moreover, violence is often portrayed as an acceptable behavior, especially for heroes who never have to face legal consequences for their actions. For example, David Phillips found the homicide rate increases significantly immediately after a heavyweight championship prize fight.[100] (See Close-Up entitled "Television and Violence.")

What triggers violent acts? Various sources have been investigated by social learning theorists. One position is that a direct, pain-producing physical assault will usually trigger a violent response. Yet the relationship between painful attacks and aggressive responses has been found to be inconsistent; whether people counterattack in the face of physical attack depends in part on their skill in fighting and their perception of the strength of their attackers.

Verbal taunts and insults also have been linked to aggressive responses. People who are predisposed to aggression by their learning experience are likely to view insults from others as a challenge to their social status and to react with violence.

In sum, social learning theorists find that four factors help produce violence and aggression:

1. An event that heightens arousal—such as a physical assault or verbal abuse

2. Aggressive skills—learned aggressive responses picked up from observing others, either personally or through the media

3. Expected outcomes—the belief that aggression will somehow be rewarded; either through reducing tension or anger, gaining some financial reward, building self-esteem, or gaining the praise of others

4. Consistency of behavior with values—the belief that aggression is justified and appropriate given the circumstances of the current situation.

PSYCHOBIOLOGICAL PERSPECTIVES

Psychobiologists, or *physiological psychologists,* search for relationships among changes in brain cells, nervous system activity, and mental processes. They have used such research techniques as electrical stimulation of the brain to demonstrate that particular parts of the brain control a wide range of emotional and behavioral activity, ranging from sexuality to aggression.

Psychologists also have studied the effects of hormone and cell activity on behavior. Since these efforts are quite similar to those of biocriminologists, discussed early in this chapter, they need not be repeated here. However, two issues relating to biological psychology are of particular relevance to criminology: the psychopathic personality, and mental ability and crime.

The Psychopath

It has become commonplace for psychocriminologists to view morally indifferent people who have frequent brushes with the law as **sociopaths** or **psychopaths** (these terms are used interchangeably).[101] Clinicians view psychopaths as aggressive, dangerous, antisocial individuals who act in an unthinking and callous manner. They lack insight into their behavior and are likely to feel little remorse for their violent, aggressive, or criminal acts. Psychopaths neither learn from their mistakes nor are influenced by punishments. Though they may appear charming and have above-average intelligence, they lack emotional depth and are incapable of loving others. Psychopaths have been described as having an unstable, transient lifestyle without long-term commitments. Nonetheless, they do not display clinically significant intellectual or psychiatric symptoms. Perhaps their most important feature is a low level of anxiety, which contributes to their lack of remorse or guilt over their misdeeds.

Psychopaths are likely to be very dangerous. If a person has no feelings for others and acts on impulse, it follows that there will be little to bar him or her from expressing antisocial behavior. It is not surprising, therefore, that research studies show that people evaluated as psychopaths are significantly more criminal and violence-prone when compared to nonpsychopathic control groups. Moreover, as Robert Hare and Jeffrey Jutai report, psychopaths may continue their criminal careers long after other offenders "burn out" or "age out" of crime.[102] Psychopathy also has been linked to serious violent crimes such as mass murder or serial murder; this topic is discussed further in Chapter 10. Psychopaths are continually in trouble with the law, and therefore are likely to wind up in penal institutions. It has been estimated that up to 30 percent of all inmates can be classified as psychopaths or sociopaths, but a more realistic figure is probably 10 percent; not all psychopaths become criminals and, conversely, most criminals are not psychopathic.[103]

CLOSE-UP

Television and Violence

Does televised violence cause aggressive behavior in viewers? This question is of significant importance, considering the persistent theme of violence on television and the fact that systematic viewing of television begins at 2.5 years of age and continues at a high level during the preschool and early school years. It has been estimated that children ages two to five watch television 27.8 hours each week, children ages six to eleven watch 24.3 hours per week, and teens watch 23 hours per week.

There are several theories about the effects of television violence on behavior:

• Media violence can provide aggressive "scripts" that children store in memory. Repeated exposure to these scripts can increase their retention and lead to change in attitudes. Exposure to violent displays of any type could provide cues leading to the retrieval of these and other scripts and to aggressive behavior.

• Observational learning occurs when the violence seen on television is copied by the child viewer. Children learn to be violent from television in the same way that they learn cognitive and social skills from their parents and friends.

• Television violence increases the arousal levels of viewers and makes them more prone to act aggressively. Studies measuring the galvanic skin response of subjects—a physical indication of arousal based on the amount of electricity conducted across the palm of the hand—show that viewing violent television shows led to increased arousal levels in young children.

• Television violence promotes attitude changes, which can then result in behavior changes. Watching television violence promotes such negative attitudes as suspiciousness and the expectation that the viewer will become involved in violence. Attitudes of frequent television viewers toward aggression become positive when they see violence as a common and socially acceptable behavior.

• Television violence helps already aggressive youths justify their behavior. It is possible that, instead of *causing violence,* television helps violent youths rationalize their behavior as a socially acceptable and common activity.

• Television violence may disinhibit aggressive behavior, which is normally controlled by other learning processes. Disinhibition takes place when adults are viewed as being rewarded for violence, and when violence is seen as socially acceptable. This contradicts previous learning experiences in which violent behavior was viewed as wrong.

A number of recent research efforts indicate that watching violence on television leads to increased levels of violence in the laboratory as well as in natural settings. Such professional organizations as the American Psychological Association and the National Institute of Mental Health support the television-violence link.

However, a number of research efforts dispute a television-violent behavior link. For example, Steven Messner's recent research indicates that areas in which residents watch the highest levels of violent television also have the lowest rates of recorded violent crime. Similarly, Candace Kruttschnitt and her associates found that exposure to violent television shows is weakly related to subsequent violent behavior. However, the weight of the research evidence indicates that television violence can directly influence aggressive, antisocial behavior patterns.

Discussion Questions

1. Should the government limit the violent content of television shows?

2. How can the fact that millions of kids watch violent

Psychopathy and Physical Traits. There are several suspected causes of the psychopathic personality. Some psychologists believe that early development and nurturing contribute to the condition. Among the suspected causes are a sociopathic father, parental rejection and lack of love during childhood, loss of a parent during childhood, and inconsistent discipline.

The early relationship between mother and child is also quite significant. Children who lack the opportunity to form an attachment to a mother-figure in the first three years of life, who suffer sudden separation from the mother-figure, or who see changes in the mother-figure are most likely to develop psychopathic personalities.

Television often portrays violence as acceptable behavior, especially for heroes who never have to face legal consequences.

television and do not become violent themselves be explained?

SOURCE: L. Rowell Huesmann and Neil Malamuth, "Media Violence and Antisocial Behavior," *Journal of Social Issues*, 42 (1986):1–7; American Psychological Association, *Violence on TV: A Social Issue Release from the Board of Social and Ethical Responsibility for Psychology* (Washington, D.C.: APA, 1985); Steven Messner, "Television Violence and Violent Crime: An Aggregate Analysis," *Social Problems* 33 (1986):218–35;

Candace Kruttschnitt, Linda Heath, and David Ward, "Family Violence, Television Viewing Habits, and Other Adolescent Experiences Related to Violent Criminal Behavior," *Criminology* 243 (1986):235–67; Johnathon Freedman, "Television Violence and Aggression: A Rejoinder," *Psychological Bulletin* 100 (1986):372–78; Edward Donnerstein and Daniel Linz, "The Question of Pornography," *Psychology Today* 20 (1986):56–59; D. Pearl, L. Bouthilet, and D. Lazar, eds., *Television and Behavior*, vols. 1 and 2 (Washington, D.C.: U.S. Government Printing Office, 1982).

Although developmental factors are a suspected cause of psychopathy, physical traits also have been linked to the antisocial personality.[104] More than 20 years ago, Hans Eysenck proposed an **arousal theory** of psychopathy.[105] Eysenck found that some people have nervous systems which are insulated from the environment. These people are difficult to condition,

extremely tolerant of pain, and seekers of intense physical stimulation.

Psychopathy also has been linked autonomic nervous system (ANS) dysfunction. The ANS mediates physiological activities associated with emotions and is apparent in measurements such as heartbeat rate, blood pressure, respiration, muscle tension, pupillary size, and galvanic skin resistance (GSR), which is the electrical activity of the skin. Another view is that psychopathy is caused by a dysfunction of the limbic inhibitory system, a part of the brain that is concerned with emotion and motivation.[106] Both views suggest that the psychopath reacts less vigorously to stimuli that a normal person would find exciting, stressful, and frightening; psychopaths therefore seek out life experiences of great intensity and variety.

There is some research in support of the psychobiological view of psychopathy. Orestes and Shawn Fedora found evidence that psychopathy was related to dysfunction of the left hemisphere of the brain.[107] Research studies also have found that psychopaths have lower skin conductance levels and fewer spontaneous responses than normal subjects.[108] Though the existing data is inconsistent, there is some indication that psychopaths have lower levels of arousal to environmental stimulations such as noises and pain than do control subjects. Similarly, psychopaths have been found to be less likely to show physiological signs that they are apprehensive about threatened pain and punishment than normal subjects. Put simply, psychopaths seem to react differently to physical sensations than nonpsychopaths, and research has been undertaken to determine whether psychopaths are therefore unlikely to experience anxiety and to be deterred by punishment. In studies, clinically defined psychopaths who have had their levels of arousal increased through injections of the hormone adrenalin do in fact begin to respond as normal subjects do. It is possible that some psychopaths are thrillseekers who engage in high-risk activities to raise their general neurological level to a more optimal state.[109]

The IQ Controversy

A second biopsychological issue relating to crime is the controversy over the suspected relationship between intelligence and criminality. Some criminologists have maintained that many delinquents and criminals have a below-average intelligence quotient (IQ), and that low IQ is a cause of criminality.

Early criminologists believed that low intelligence was a major cause of crime and delinquency. Criminals were believed to be inherently substandard in intelligence and thus naturally inclined to commit more crimes than more intelligent persons. Further-

more, it was thought that if authorities could determine which individuals had low IQs, they might identify potential criminals before they committed socially harmful acts.

Since social scientists had a captive group of subjects in training schools and penal institutions, they began to measure the correlation between IQ and crime by testing adjudicated offenders. Thus, inmates of penal institutions were used as a test group around which numerous theories about intelligence were built, leading ultimately to the *nature versus nurture* controversy that is still going on today. These concepts are discussed in some detail in the following sections.

Nature Theory.   Nature theory argues that intelligence is largely determined genetically, and that low intelligence as demonstrated by low IQ is linked to behavior, including criminal behavior.

When the newly developed IQ tests were administered to inmates of prisons and juvenile training schools in the early 1900s, the nature position gained support. A very large proportion of the inmates scored low on the tests. During his studies in 1920, Henry Goddard found that many institutionalized persons were what he considered "feebleminded"; he concluded that at least half of all juvenile delinquents were mental defectives.[110] Goddard's results were challenged in 1931, when Edwin Sutherland evaluated IQ studies of criminals and delinquents and noted significant variations in the findings.[111] The discrepancies were believed to reflect refinements in testing methods and scoring, rather than differences in the mental ability of criminals.

In 1926, William Healy and Augusta Bronner tested a group of delinquent boys in Chicago and Boston and found that 37 percent were subnormal in intelligence. They concluded that delinquents were five to ten times more likely to be mentally deficient than "normal boys."[112]

These and other early studies were embraced as proof that low IQ scores could identify potentially delinquent children, and that a correlation existed between low intelligence and deviant behavior.[113] IQ tests were believed to measure the inborn genetic makeup of individuals, and many criminologists accepted the idea that individuals with substandard IQs were predisposed toward delinquency and adult criminality.

Nurture Theory.   The rise of culturally sensitive explanations of human behavior in the 1930s led to the nurture school of intelligence. This theory states that intelligence must be viewed as partly biological but primarily sociological. Nurture theorists discredited the notion that persons commit crimes because they have low IQs. Instead, they postulated that environmental stimulation from parents, relatives, social contacts, schools, peer groups, and innumerable other sources creates a child's IQ level; low IQs result from an environment that also encourages delinquent and criminal behavior. Thus, if low IQ scores are recorded among criminals, these scores may reflect the criminals' cultural background, not their mental ability.

Studies challenging the assumption that people automatically committed criminal acts because they had below-average IQs began to appear as early as the 1920s. John Slawson studied 1,543 delinquent boys in New York institutions and compared them with a control group of New York City boys in 1926.[114] Slawson found that although 80 percent of the delinquents achieved lower scores in abstract verbal intelligence, delinquents were about normal in mechanical aptitude and nonverbal intelligence. These results indicated the possibility of cultural bias in portions of the IQ tests. Slawson also found that there was no relationship between the number of arrests, the types of offenses, and IQ.

Kenneth Eels and his associates found that tests used in the 1950s systematically underestimated the abilities of children of the working class. They argued that traditional intelligence tests predict who will succeed in a school system that makes use of abstract ideas and experiences only middle-class children are likely to have: "There are reasoning abilities in the lower class that schooling could capitalize on if it were redesigned to be less verbal and culture-laden."[115] Robert Rosenthal and Lenore Jacobsen further debunked the notion that academic success and IQ scores were linked.[116]

Recent Trends.   There is still a great deal of controversy over the development of human intelligence. A few well-known scientists have come forward to claim that IQ is a function of genetic inheritance. The new heredity theorists, particularly Arthur Jensen and Richard Herrnstein, argue that genetic factors account for much of the variability in intelligence as measured by standard IQ scores, and that environmental factors account for little.[117] Jensen argues that race is the key to IQ differences; Herrnstein believes that social class is the determining factor. Both agree that the observable gap in intelligence between blacks and whites and lower- and middle-class groups will remain fixed as long as the environmental conditions with which heredity interacts do not change. Thus, although both men believe that intelligence has a genetic basis, they do not deny the influence of environmental factors.

Recently, however, social scientists have countered arguments based on heredity. In their study of black children adopted by white families, Sandra Scarr and Richard Weinberg found that social environment plays the dominant role in determining the average IQ level of the black children. Black adoptees scored as high on IQ tests as white adoptees in other studies. Scarr and Weinberg concluded: "The dramatic increase in the IQ mean and the additional finding that placement and adoptive family characteristics account for a major portion of the IQ differences . . . suggest that the IQ score of these children is malleable."[118]

Scarr and Weinberg are conducting a long-term study of adoptees in Minnesota.[119] Their sample includes both black and white children adopted into middle-class families. A longitudinal study of these youths confirms that racial difference do not account for a major portion of IQ performance, and that black and interracial children brought up in middle-class culture and schools perform as well as other adopted children in similar environments.[120] Thus, recent evidence seems to point to the influence of environment on IQ.

IQ and Criminality

While the alleged IQ-crime link was dismissed by mainstream criminologists during much of the 60s and 70s, it once again became an important area of study when respected criminologists Travis Hirschi and Michael Hindelang published a widely read paper linking the two variables.[121] After reexamining existing research data, Hirschi and Hindelang conclude that "the weight of evidence is that IQ is more important than race and social class" for predicting criminal and delinquent involvement. Rejecting the notion that IQ tests are race- and class-biased, they concluded that major differences exist between criminals and noncriminals within *similar* racial and socioeconomic

≡ CLOSE-UP

The Cognitive Perspective

One area of psychology which is having an increased impact on the study of human behavior is cognitive theory. Psychologists with a cognitive perspective focus on mental processes. They investigate the ways in which people perceive and mentally represent the world, how they go about solving problems, and how they dream and daydream. Cognitive psychologists, in short, attempt to study all those things referred to as "the mind."

Jean Piaget

One branch of cognitive theory is the developmental approach advanced by the Swiss biologist Jean Piaget, whose innovative study of the intellectual or cognitive development of children has inspired thousands of psychological research projects. The purpose of this research is to learn how children and adults mentally represent and reason about the world.

According to Piaget and his intellectual descendants, such as Lawrence Kohlberg, the conception of the world grows more sophisticated as people mature. Although experience is essential to children, their perception and understanding of the world unfolds as if guided by an inner clock. Piaget's views have been adapted in an effort to explain moral development and the acquisition of sex roles.

Information Processing

A more recent facet of the cognitive perspective is information processing. Many cognitive psychologists focus on how people process and store information, viewing the operation in the same way that computers function as information processors. This area of cognitive theory explores processes by which information is encoded (input), stored (kept in long-term memory), retrieved (placed in working memory), and manipulated in order to solve problems (output). Strategies for solving problems are sometimes referred to as "mental programs" or "software". In this realm of computer metaphor, the brain is translated into the "hardware" that "runs" mental programs. The brain becomes a very personal computer.

When psychologists who study information processing contemplate cognitive development, they are likely to talk in terms of the size of a child's working memory at a given age and the number of programs a child can run simultaneously. Research suggests that these can be useful ways of talking about child development and are expected to explain and predict behavior.

---

class categories. Their position is that low IQ increases the likelihood of criminal behavior through its effect on school performance. That is, youths with low IQs do poorly in school, and school failure and academic incompetence are highly related to delinquency, and later to adult criminality.

Hirschi and Hidelang's inferences have been supported by research conducted by both American and international scholars. For example, Robert Gordon's research on race, IQ, and crime has led him to the conclusion that IQ differences are a significant predictor of the lifetime prevalence of criminality and are the major source of racial differences in the crime rate.[122] Other researchers found a significant relationship between IQ and delinquency among samples of Danish youths. They concluded that children with a low IQ may be likely to engage in delinquent behavior because poor verbal ability is a handicap in the school environment.[123] In a study of repeat violent juvenile offenders, Deborah Denno discovered that chronically violent youths scored lower on verbal and general IQ tests than one time-offenders.[124] Further research found samples of delinquents possessed IQs about 20 points less than nondelinquent control groups on the Wechsler Adult Intelligence Scale (WAIS).[125] Other scientists have found that criminality is related to indicators of limited mental ability.[126]

The case for an IQ-delinquency link also is made by James Q. Wilson and Richard Herrnstein in their controversial book, *Crime and Human Nature*.[127] Wilson and Herrnstein, however, argue that the link is an indirect one: being in possession of a low IQ alone is

Aggression and Behavior

Cognitive psychologists assert that behavior is influenced by values, by the ways in which people interpret situations, and by choice. For example, some people who believe that aggression is necessary and justified, as in wartime, are likely to act aggressively. People who believe that a particular war or act of aggression is unjust, or who universally oppose aggression are less likely to behave aggressively.

Piaget and Kohlberg have focused on the ways in which processed information arrives at judgments of guilt or innocence during maturity. For instance, five-year-old children might consider an act of aggression wrong simply because they have been told that it is wrong. However, an eight-year-old child, while still believing aggression is wrong, would also be likely to consider the motives of the aggressor.

Cognitively-oriented psychologists also research ways in which thoughts and beliefs influence behavior. For example, some aggressive adolescents are frequently biased in their processing of social information: they perceive other people to be more aggressive than they actually are and/or assume that other people intend them ill when they do not. Therefore, adolescents are more likely to be vigilant, on-edge, or suspicious. When they attack victims, they may believe they are defending themselves even though they are simply misreading the situation. Similarly, some rapists, particularly date-rapists, tend to misread women's expressed wishes: they believe that when their dates say no to sexual advances that women are really "playing games" and actually want them to force sexual behavior.

Cognitively-oriented psychotherapists note that people are more likely to respond aggressively to a provocation when thoughts intensify the insult or otherwise stir feelings of anger. Thus, cognitive therapists attempt to teach explosive people to control aggressive impulses by viewing social provocations as problems demanding a solution, rather than as insults requiring retaliation. It is possible that cognitive thereapy may make a valuable contribution to the treatment of law-violating youths and adults.

Discussion Questions

1. Can some crimes be a matter of misreading social signals?
2. Explain the statement "an angry person sees the world as a hostile place."

SOURCE: D. Lipton, E. C. McDonel, and R. McFall, R. M. "Heterosocial Perception in Rapists," *Journal of Consulting and Clinical Psychology* 55 (1987): 17–21; J. E. Lochman, "Self and Peer Perceptions and Attributional Biases of Aggressive and Nonaggressive Boys in Dyadic Interactions," *Journal of Consulting and Clinical Psychology* 55 (1987): 404–410.

---

not enough to cause a person to engage in antisocial behavior. Rather they agree with Hirschi and Hindelang that the relationship is the product of a third intervening factor, poor school performance.[128] This conclusion is supported by research conducted by Deborah Denno, which found that school achievement is related to delinquency and that IQ level can be used to predict school achievement.[129]

IQ and Crime Reconsidered. While there is some evidence that IQ level has an indirect influence on crime, the issue is far from settled. There are a number of studies, such as that conducted by Scott Menard and Barbara Morse, which find that IQ level has a negligible influence on criminal behavior.[130] Deborah Denno, who had previously found evidence of an IQ-crime link, failed to substantiate any direct relationship between mental ability and delinquency among a sample of 800 black youths in Philadelphia.[131] In sum, no existing research has been able to show a direct causal relationship between intelligence and crime.

By their very nature, research efforts attempting to show a causal relationship between IQ and crime are beset by methodological difficulties. Aside from the well-documented criticisms of IQ tests, there is also the problem of sampling. Research using known criminals runs the risk of measuring the intelligence of only those people who have been apprehended, convicted, and sentenced. This group is unrepresentative of the criminal population, since it excludes offenders who escape detection. Even if it can be shown that known offenders have lower IQs than the general population, this relationship may be more a result of criminal justice system policy than of the propensity of people with low IQ to commit crime. Consequently, the true relationship between intelligence and crime is still uncertain.

CRIME AND PERSONALITY

Personality refers to the reasonably stable patterns of behavior, including thoughts, feelings, and emotions, that distinguish people from one another. Personality controls a person's way of adapting to life experiences and therefore separates people on the basis of their behavior.[132]

Each of the different psychological perspectives on crime—psychoanalytic, behavioral, and biological—has an independent view on the development of the human personality. All agree that human beings have the potential to develop abnormal, destructive personality characteristics, although they disagree on the process by which such development takes place. Keep in mind that psychoanalytic theory views personality conflict as a function of interpsychic conflict, where the ego is overwhelmed by the impulses of the id. Social-learning theorists counter that a disturbed personality is a product of a punitive upbringing in which good behavior gets very little reinforcement. Psychobiologists consider the personality as being the product of physical properties such as biochemical makeup.

A number of psychologists have linked criminality to disturbances of the personality. The relationship between criminality and the psychopathic personality structure has already been discussed. Another well-known but controversial view is that of psychiatrists Samuel Yochelson and Staton Samenow. Their studies of offenders in a hospital for the criminally insane led them to identify the existence of a criminal personality which maintains inherently abnormal thought patterns associated with antisocial behavior.[133]

In sum, psychocriminologists who link personality to crime believe that psychological makeup colors the way individuals perceive the world and controls their behavior choices. People who maintain an abnormal personality, whatever the cause, will be more likely to engage in antisocial behavior, because they view the world differently. They may be less troubled by conscience, less responsive to pain, and less caring about the future than people whose personalities fall within the "normal" range.

Personality Testing

Two types of standardized personality tests have been constructed to ease the measurement and analysis of personality traits. The first, projective techniques, require a subject to react to an ambiguous picture or shape by describing what it represents or by telling a story about it. The Rorschach Inkblot Test and the Thematic Apperception Test (TAT) are examples of two widely used projective tests. Such tests are given by clinicians trained to interpret responses and categorize them according to established behavioral patterns. While not used extensively, some early research found that delinquents and nondelinquents could be separated on the basis of their personality profiles.[134]

The second frequently used method of psychological testing is the personality inventory. These tests require subjects to agree or disagree with groups of questions in a self-administered survey. The most widely used psychological test is the Minnesota Multiphasic Personality Inventory, commonly called the MMPI. Developed by R. Starke Hathaway and J. Charnley McKinley, the MMPI has subscales that purport to measure many different personality traits, including psychopathic deviation (Pd scale), schizophrenia, and hypomania.[135]

Elio Monachesi and R. Starke Hathaway pioneered the use of the MMPI to predict criminal behavior. They concluded that scores on some of the MMPI scales, especially the Pd scale, predicted delinquency. In one major effort, they administered the MMPI to a sample of ninth-grade boys and girls in Minneapolis and found that Pd scores had a significant relationship to later delinquent involvement. Similar studies have been conducted by Hathaway, Monachesi, Lawrence Young, and William Kvaraceus and more recently, Michael Hindelang, Joseph Weis, Spencer Rathus, and Larry Siegel.[136] Another frequently-used personality test, the California Personality Inventory (CPI), also has been used to distinguish deviants from nondeviant groups.[137]

Despite the time and energy put into using MMPI and other scales to predict crime and delinquency, the

James Q. Wilson (left) and Richard Herrnstein (right) have attempted to combine trait and rational choice concepts into a single theoretical model.

results of personality scale studies have proved inconclusive. Three surveys of the literature of personality testing—one by Karl Schuessler and Donald Cressey (covering the pre-1950 period), another by Gordon Waldo and Simon Dinitz (covering 1950–1965), and a more recent survey by David Tennenbaum—found inconclusive evidence that personality traits could consistently predict criminal involvement.[138] While some law violators may suffer from an abnormal personality structure, there are also many more whose personalities are indistinguishable from the norm.

AN INTEGRATED APPROACH: CRIME AND HUMAN NATURE

James Q. Wilson and Richard Herrnstein's 1985 book, *Crime and Human Nature,* has become one of the most widely discussed works in the criminological literature.[139] Controversy has swirled around the fact that two prominent social scientists make a convincing argument that personal factors, such as genetic makeup, IQ, and body build, may outweigh the importance of social variables as predictors of the crime rate.

According to Wilson and Herrnstein, all human behavior, including criminality, is determined by its perceived consequences. A criminal incident occurs when an individual chooses criminal over conven-

tional behavior (referred to as **noncrime**) after weighing the potential gains and losses of each. According to Wilson and Herrnstein, "the larger the ratio of net rewards of crime to the net rewards of noncrime, the greater the tendency to commit the crime."[140]

The rewards for crime can include material gain, sexual gratification, revenge, and peer approval; the consequences can include pangs of conscience, revenge of the victim, disapproval of friends and associates, and the possibility of punishment.

In contrast, the rewards for choosing noncrime are gained in the future: maintaining one's self-image, reputation, happiness, and freedom. Of course, one can never be quite sure of the rewards of either crime or noncrime. The burglar may hope for the "big score" but instead experience arrest, conviction, and incarceration; the person who "plays it straight" may find that the sacrifice does not lead to the desired place in society.

The choice between crime and noncrime is quite often a difficult one. Criminal choices are reinforced by the desire to obtain basic rewards (food, clothing, or shelter), sex, or learned goals (wealth, power, or status) without having to work and save for them. Even if an individual has been socialized to choose noncrime, crime can be an attractive alternative, especially if any potential negative consequences are uncertain or delayed far into the future. By analogy, cigarette smoking is common because its potentially fatal consequences are distant and uncertain; taking cyanide or arsenic poison is rare because the effects are immediate and certain.

The Wilson-Herrnstein model closely resembles the rational choice approach. However, it becomes an integrated theory because they spend considerable attention cataloguing biological and psychological traits which influence the crime-noncrime choice. They find a close link exists between a person's decision to choose crime and such biosocial factors as low intelligence, mesomorphic body types, having a criminal father, impulsivity or extroversion, and possessing a nervous system that responds too quickly to stimuli. Having these traits will not by themselves guarantee that a person will become a criminal; however, all things being equal, those who experience them will be more likely to choose crime over noncrime in certain situations.

Wilson and Herrnstein do not ignore the influence of social factors on criminality. They believe that a turbulent family life, school failure, and membership in a deviant teenage subculture also have a powerful influence on criminality.

According to Wilson and Herrnstein, personal and social conditions working in concert can influence thought patterns and eventually individual behavior patterns. For example, one of their more controversial assertions is that the relationship between crime and intelligence is "robust and significant." There are a number of mechanisms through which IQ levels directly influence criminality, not the least of which is the role played by education:

A child who chronically loses standing in the competition of the classroom may feel justified in settling the score outside, by violence, theft, and other forms of defiant illegality. School failure enhances the rewards for crime by engendering feelings of unfairness. In addition, failure in school predicts, to a substantial degree, failure in the marketplace. For someone who stands to gain little from legitimate work, the rewards of noncrime are relatively weak. Failure in school therefore not only enhances the rewards for crime, but it predicts weak rewards for noncrime.[141]

Somewhat surprisingly, Wilson and Herrnstein do not view harsh punishment as the answer to the crime problem. They argue that the solution can be achieved by strengthening the besieged American family and helping it to orient children toward noncrime solutions. The family, regardless of its com-

position, can help a child cultivate character, conscience, and respect for the moral order. Similarly, schools can help by teaching the benefits of accepting personal responsibility and, within limits, helping students understand what constitutes "right conduct."[142]

Wilson and Herrnstein have assembled an impressive array of supportive research in *Crime and Human Nature*. Critics, however, have focused on the fact that much of the evidence suffers from methodological problems to which many bio- and psycho-criminological studies fall prey: sampling inadequacy, questionable measurement techniques, and observer bias. Such criticism aside, their work presents a dramatic attempt to integrate two of the most prominent theoretical movements in the study of criminality.

—— SOCIAL POLICY IMPLICATIONS ——

For most of the twentieth century, positivist views of criminality have had an important influence on crime control and prevention policy. Positivist views can be seen in **primary prevention** programs which seek to threat personal problems before they manifest themselves as crime. Thousands of family therapy organizations, substance abuse clinics, and mental health associations are operating around the United States. Referrals to these are made by teachers, employers, courts, welfare agencies, etc. It is assumed that if a person's problems can be treated before they become overwhelming, some future crimes will be prevented.

Secondary prevention programs provide treatment, such as psychological counseling, to youths and adults after they have violated the law. Attendance in such programs may be a mandatory requirement of a probation order, a diversionary sentence, or as aftercare, at the tail end of a prison sentence.

Biologically-oriented therapy is now being used in the criminal justice system. Programs have altered diet, changed lighting, compensated for learning disabilities, and treated allergies.[143] However, controversy has surrounded the use of mood-altering chemicals such as lithium, pemoline, imipramine, phenytoin, and benzodiazepines. Another practice which has raised concern is the use of brain surgery to control antisocial behavior; surgical procedures have been used extensively to alter the brain structure of convicted sex offenders in an effort to eliminate or control their sex drives. Results are still in the preliminary stages, but some critics have argued these procedures are without scientific merit.[144]

Some criminologists view biologically-oriented treatments as a key to solving the problem of the chronic offender. Sarnoff Mednick and his associates have suggested that the biological analysis of criminal traits could pave the way for the development of preventive measures, regardless of whether the trait is inherited or acquired.[145] They argue that a number of inherited physical traits which cause disease have been successfully treated with medication after their genetic code had been broken; why not then a genetic solution to crime?[146]

While bio-treatment is a relatively new phenomenon, since the 1920s it has become commonplace to offer psychological treatment to offenders before, during, and after a criminal conviction. For example, beginning in the 1970s, pretrial programs have sought to divert offenders into nonpunitive rehabilitative programs. Based on some type of counseling regime, diversion programs are commonly used with first offenders and nonviolent offenders.

At the trial stage, judges commonly order psychological profiles of convicted offenders for planning a treatment program. Should they be kept in the community? Do they need a more secure confinement to deal with their problems?

If correctional confinement is called for, inmates are commonly evaluated at a **correctional center** in order to measure their personality traits or disorders. Correctional facilities almost universally require inmates to take part in some form of psychological therapy: group therapy, individual analysis, or transactional analysis. Parole decisions may be influenced by the prison psychologist's evaluation of the offender's adjustment. Beyond these efforts, the law recognizes the psychological aspects of crime when it permits the insanity plea as an excuse for criminal liability or when it permits a trial delay because of mental incompetency.

SUMMARY

The earliest positivist criminologists were biologists. Led by Cesare Lombroso, early researchers believed some people manifested primitive traits that made them born criminals. Today, their research has been debunked because of poor methodology, testing, and logic.

Other pioneering biological research portrayed criminality as an inherited trait. Still another early direction of biocriminology focused on the body build of criminals. Criminals and delinquents were believed to have well-developed muscles and an athletic appearance, a body type known as mesomorphic.

Biological views fell out of favor in the early twentieth century. In the 1970s, spurred by the publication of E. O. Wilson's *Sociobiology*, some criminologists again turned to study of the biological basis of criminality. For the most part, the effort has focused on the cause of violent crime. Interest has centered on several areas: biochemical factors, such as diet, allergies, hormonal imbalances, and environmental contaminants; neurophysiological factors, such as brain disorders, EEG abnormalities, tumors, and head injuries; and genetic factors such as the XYY chromosome and inherited traits.

Psychological attempts to explain criminal behavior have their historical roots in the concept that criminals are insane or mentally damaged. This position is no longer accepted. Today, there are three main psychological perspectives. The psychoanalytic view, the creation of Sigmund Freud, links aggressive behavior to personality conflicts developed in childhood. According to some psychoanalysts, psychotics are aggressive, unstable people who easily can become involved in crime.

Learning theorists see criminality as a learned behavior. Children who are exposed to violence and see it rewarded may become violent as adults. Psychobiologists link psychological traits with biological factors. One important area of study has been the psychopath, a person who lacks emotion and concern for others. Another area of study has been the relationship of IQ to criminality. Cognitive theory is yet another emerging area of psychology.

Psychologists have developed standardized tests to measure personality traits. One avenue of research has been to determine whether criminals and noncriminals manifest any differences in their responses to test items. Major reviews of the literature have failed to find any direct link between criminality and personality.

One of the most controversial research efforts in

the past decade has been Wilson and Herrnstein's effort to integrate individual positivist views with classical theory. Wilson and Herrnstein hold that people choose to commit crime, based in part on physical and psychological traits.

---------------- KEY TERMS ----------------

traits	electroencephalogram
positivism	(EEG)
physiognomists	mental degenerates
phrenologists	psychoanalytic perspective
born criminals	Sigmund Freud
atavistic anomalies	psychoanalysis
moral anomaly	repression
inheritance school	fixated
somatotype	Carl Jung
E. O. Wilson	inferiority complex
sociobiology	identity crisis
Twinky defense	schizophrenia
vitamin deficiency	August Aichorn
vitamin dependency	social learning
hypoglycemia	Albert Bandura
testosterone	behavior modeling
Premenstrual Syndrome	psychobiologists
(PMS)	sociopaths
cerebral allergies	psychopaths
neuroallergies	arousal theory
neurophysiology	noncrime
minimal brain dysfunction	primary prevention
(MBD)	correctional center

---------------- NOTES ----------------

1. Deborah Denno, "Sociological and Human Developmental Explanations of Crime: Conflict or Consensus," *Criminology* 23 (1985):711–41.
2. Marvin Wolfgang, "Cesare Lombroso," in Hermann Mannheim, ed., *Pioneers in Criminology* (Montclaire, N.J.: Patterson Smith, 1970), pp. 232–71.
3. See, generally, Cesare Lombroso, *Crime, Its Causes and Remedies* (Montclair, N.J.: Patterson Smith, 1968).
4. Gina Lombroso-Ferrero, *Criminal Man According to the Classification of Cesare Lombroso* (Montclair, N.J.: Patterson Smith, 1972), p. 100.
5. Charles Goring, *The English Convict: A Statistical Study, 1913* (Montclair, N.J.: Patterson Smith, 1972).
6. Edwin Driver, "Charles Buckman Goring," in Hermann Mannheim, ed., *Pioneers in Criminology*, p. 440.
7. Raffaele Garofalo, *Criminology*, trans. Robert Miller (Boston: Little, Brown, 1914), p. 92.
8. Enrico Ferri, *Criminal Sociology* (New York: D. Appleton, 1909).
9. Ernest Hooton, *The American Criminal* (Cambridge, Mass.: Harvard University Press, 1939), p. 309.
10. Henry Herbert Goddard, *The Kallikak Family: A Study in the Heredity of Feeble-Mindedness* (New York: Macmillan, 1927).
11. Richard Dugdale, *The Jukes* (New York: Putnam, 1910); Arthur Estabrook, *The Jukes in 1915* (Washington, D.C.: The Carnegie Institute of Washington, 1916). The studies in this section are described in Stephen Schafer, *Introduction to Criminology* (Reston, Va.: Reston Publishing, 1976), pp. 60–61.
12. William Sheldon, *Varieties of Delinquent Youth* (New York: Harper & Bros., 1949).
13. Sheldon Glueck and Eleanor Glueck, *Of Delinquency and Crime* (Springfield, Ill.: Charles C. Thomas, 1974), p. 2.
14. B. R. McCandless, W. S. Pesons, and A. Roberts, "Perceived Opportunity, Delinquency, Race and Body Build Among Delinquent Youth," *Journal of Consulting and Clinical Psychology* 38 (1972):281.
15. Pierre van den Bergle, "Bringing the Beast Back In: Toward a Biosocial Theory of Aggression," *American Sociological Review* 39 (1974):779.
16. E. O. Wilson, *Sociobiology* (Cambridge, Mass.: Harvard University Press, 1975).
17. See, generally, R. Alexander, *Darwinism and Human Affairs* (Seattle: University of Washington Press, 1979).
18. C. Ray Jeffrey, "Criminology as an Interdisciplinary Behavioral Science," *Criminology* 16 (1978):161–62.
19. Lee Ellis, "Criminal Behavior and Selection: An Extension of Gene-Based Evolutionary Theory," *Deviant Behavior* 8 (1987):149–76.
20. See, for example, Sarnoff Mednick, Ricardo Machon, Matti Virkkunen and Douglas Bonett, "Adult Schizophrenia Following Prenatal Exposure to an Influenza Epidemic," *Archives of General Psychiatry* (1987):n.p.; C. A. Fogel, S. A. Mednick, and N. Michelson, "Hyperactive Behavior and Minor Physical Anomalies," *Acta Psychiatrica Scandinavia* 72 (1985):551–56.
21. Material in these sections relies heavily on Leonard Hippchen, "Some Possible Biochemical Aspects of Criminal Behavior," *Journal of Behavioral Ecology* 2 (1981):1–6; Sarnoff Mednick and Jan Volavka, "Biology and Crime," in Norval Morris and Michael Tonry, eds., *Crime and Justice* (Chicago: University of Chicago Press, 1980), pp. 85–159; Saleem Shah and Loren Roth, "Biological and Psychophysiological Factors in

Criminality," in Daniel Glazer, ed., *Handbook of Criminology* (Chicago: Rand McNally, 1974), pp. 125–40; Diana Fishbein and Susan Pease, *The Effects of Diet on Behavior: The Implications for Criminology and Corrections* (Santa Monica, Cal.: Rand Corporation, 1988).

22. *Time* 28 May 1979, p. 57.

23. Leonard Hippchen, ed., *Ecologic-Biochemical Approaches to Treatment of Delinquents and Criminals* (New York: Von Nostrand Reinhold, 1978), p. 14.

24. Michael Krassner, "Diet and Brain Function," *Nutrition Reviews* 44 (1986):12–15.

25. Hippchen, ed., *Ecologic-Biochemical Approaches*, p. 14.

26. J. Kershner and W. Hawke, "Megavitamins and Learning Disorders: A Controlled Double-Blind Experiment," *Journal of Nutrition* 109 (1979):819–26.

27. Richard Knox, "Test Shows Smart People's Brains Use Nutrients Better," *Boston Globe* 16 February 1988, p. 9.

28. Ronald Prinz and David Riddle, "Associations Between Nutrition and Behavior in Five-Year-Old Children," *Nutrition Reviews Supplement* 44 (1986):151–58.

29. Stephen Schoenthaler and Walter Doraz, "Types of Offenses Which Can Be Reduced in an Institutional Setting Using Nutritional Intervention," *International Journal of Biosocial Research* 4 (1983):74–84; Schoenthaler and Doraz, "Diet and Crime," *International Journal of Biosocial Research* 4 (1983):29–39; see also, A. G. Schauss, "Differential Outcomes among Probationers Comparing Orthomolecular Approaches to Conventional Casework Counseling," Paper presented at the Annual Meeting of the American Society of Criminology, Dallas, Texas, 9 November 1978; A. Schauss and C. Simonsen, "A Critical Analysis of the Diets of Chronic Juvenile Offenders, Part I," *Journal of Orthomolecular Psychiatry* 8 (1979):222–26; A. Hoffer, "Children with Learning and Behavioral Disorders," *Journal of Orthomolecular Psychiatry* 5 (1976):229.

30. Prinz and Riddle, "Associations Between Nutrition and Behavior in Five-Year-Old Children," pp. 151–58.

31. H. Bruce Ferguson, Clare Stoddart, and Jovan Simeon, "Double-Blind Challenge Studies of Behavioral and Cognitive Effects of Sucrose-Aspartame Ingestion in Normal Children," *Nutrition Reviews Supplement* 44 (1986):144–58.

32. Gregory Gray, "Diet, Crime and Delinquency: A Critique," *Nutrition Reviews* 44 (1986):89–94.

33. D. Hill and W. Sargent, "A Case of Matricide," *Lancet* 244 (1943):526–27.

34. E. Podolsky, "The Chemistry of Murder," *Pakistan Medical Journal* 15 (1964):9–14.

35. J. A. Yaryura-Tobias and F. Neziroglu, "Violent Behavior Brain Dysrhythmia and Glucose Dysfunction, A New Syndrome," *Journal of Orthopsychiatry* 4 (1975):182–88.

36. Matti Virkkunen, "Reactive Hypoglycemic Tendency among Habitually Violent Offenders," *Nutrition Reviews Supplement* 44 (1986):94–103.

37. L. E. Kreuz and R. M. Rose, "Assessment of Aggressive Behavior and Plasma Testosterone in a Young Criminal Population," *Psychosomatic Medicine* 34 (1972):321–32.

38. Richard Rada, "Plasma Androgens in Violent and Non-Violent Sex Offenders," *Bulletin of the American Academy of Psychiatry and the Law* 11 (1983):149–58; R. T. Rada, D. R. Laws, and R. Kellner, "Plasma Testosterone Levels in the Rapist," *Psychosomatic Medicine* 38 (1976):257–68.

39. Robert Rubin, "The Neuroendocrinology and Neurochemistry of Antisocial Behavior," in Sarnoff Mednick, Terrie Moffitt, and Susan Stack, eds., *The Causes of Crime, New Biological Approaches* (Cambridge, England: Cambridge University Press, 1987), pp. 239–62.

40. Katharina Dalton, *The Premenstrual Syndrome* (Springfield, Ill.: Charles C. Thomas, 1971). See also, D. H. Baucom, P. K. Besch, and S. Callahan, "Relationship between Testosterone Concentration, Sex Role Identity, and Personality Among Females," *Journal of Personality and Social Psychology* 48 (1985): 1218–26.

41. Julie Horney, "Menstrual Cycles and Criminal Responsibility," *Law and Human Nature* 2 (1978):25–36.

42. Sarnoff Mednick and Jan Volavka, "Biology and Crime."

43. J. Money, "Influence of Hormones on Psychosexual Differentiation," *Medical Aspects of Nutrition* 30 (1976):165.

44. H. E. Amos and J. J. P. Drake, "Problems Posed by Food Additives," *Journal of Human Nutrition* 30 (1976):165.

45. Ray Wunderlich, "Neuroallergy as a Contributing Factor to Social Misfits: Diagnosis and Treatment," in Hippchen, ed., *Ecological-Biochemical Approaches*, pp. 229–53.

46. A. R. Mawson and K. J. Jacobs, "Corn Consumption, Tryptothan, and Cross-National Homicide Rates," *Journal of Orthomolecular Psychiatry* 7 (1978):227–30.

47. A. Schauss, *Diet, Crime and Delinquency* (Berkeley, Cal.: Parker House, 1980).

48. C. Hawley and R. E. Buckley, "Food Dyes and Hyperkinetic Children," *Academy Therapy* 10 (1974):27–32.

49. Oliver David, et al., "Lead and Hyperactivity. Behavior Response to Chelation: A Pilot Study," *American Journal of Psychiatry* 133 1976):1155–58.

50. John Ott, "The Effects of Light and Radiation on Human Health and Behavior," in Hippchen, ed., *Ecologic-Biochemical Approaches*, pp. 105–83. See also, A. Kreuger and S. Sigel, "Ions in the Air," *Human Nature*, July (1978):46–47; Harry Wohlfarth, "The Effect of Color Psychodynamic Environmental Modification on Disci-

pline Incidents in Elementary Schools over One School Year: A Controlled Study," *International Journal of Biosocial Research* 6 (1984):44–53.

51. R. Johnson, *Aggression in Man and Animals* (Philadelphia: Saunders, 1972), p. 79.

52. R. D. Robin, et al., "Adolescents Who Attempt Suicide," *Journal of Pediatrics* 90 (1977):636–38.

53. L. T. Yeudall, *Childhood Experiences as Causes of Criminal Behavior* (Senate of Canada, Issue no. 1, Thirteenth Parliament, Ottawa, Canada, 1977).

54. *Ibid.*

55. C. Murray, *The Link Between Learning Disabilities and Juvenile Delinquency* (Washington, D.C.: U.S. Government Printing Office, 1976), p. 65. See also, B. Claire McCullough, Barbara Zaremba, and William Rich, "The Role of the Juvenile Justice System in the Link between Learning Disabilities and Delinquency," *State Court Journal* 3 (1979):45; Hill and Sargent, "A Case of Matricide."

56. Diana Fishbein and Robert Thatcher, "New Diagnostic Methods in Criminology: Assessing Organic Sources of Behavioral Disorders," *Journal of Research in Crime and Delinquency* 23 (1986):240–267.

57. D. Williams, "Neural Factors Related to Habitual Aggression—Consideration of Differences Between Habitual Aggressives and Others Who Have Committed Crimes of Violence," *Brain* 92 (1969):503–20.

58. Lorne Yeudall, "A Neuropsychosocial Perspective of Persistent Juvenile Delinquency and Criminal Behavior," Paper presented at the New York Academy of Sciences, 26 September 1979.

59. R. W. Aind and T. Yamamoto, "Behavior Disorders of Childhood," *Electroencephalography and Clinical Neurophysiology* 21 (1966):148–56.

60. See, generally, Jan Volavka, "Electroencephalogram among Criminals," in Mednick, Moffitt, and Stack, eds., *The Causes of Crime*, pp. 137–45.

61. Z. A. Zayed, S. A. Lewis, and R. P. Britain, "An Encephalographic and Psychiatric Study of 32 Insane Murderers," *British Journal of Psychiatry* 115 (1969):1115–24.

62. K. E. Moyer, *The Psychobiology of Aggression* (New York: Harper & Row, 1976).

63. Fishbein and Thatcher, "New Diagnostic Methods in Criminology," pp. 240–67.

64. Yeudall, "A Neuropsychosocial Perspective," p. 4; F. A. Elliott, "Neurological Aspects of Antisocial Behavior," in W. H. Reid, ed., *The Psychopath: A Comprehensive Study of Antisocial Disorders and Behaviors* (New York: Brunner/Mazel, 1978), pp. 146–89.

65. Lorne Yeudall, Orestes Fedora, and Delee Fromm, "A Neuropsychosocial Theory of Persistent Criminality: Implications for Assessment and Treatment," in Robert Rieber, ed., *Advances in Forensic Psychology and Psychiatry* (Norwood N.J.: Ablex Publishing, 1987), p. 177.

66. *Ibid.*, pp. 119–91.

67. *Ibid.*, pp. 24–25.

68. H. K. Kletschka, "Violent Behavior Associated with Brain Tumor," *Minnesota Medicine* 49 (1966):1853–55.

69. V. E. Krynicki, "Cerebral Dysfunction in Repetitively Assaultive Adolescents," *Journal of Nervous and Mental Disease* 166 (1978):59–67.

70. C. E. Lyght, ed., *The Merck Manual of Diagnosis and Therapy* (West Point, Fla.: Merck, 1966).

71. For a general view, see, Richard Lerner and Terryl Foch, *Biological-Psychosocial Interactions in Early Adolescence* (Hilldale, N.J.: Lawrence Erlbaum Associates, 1987).

72. This section relies heavily on Shah and Roth, "Biological and Psychophysiological Factors in Criminality," pp. 134–40; Lee Ellis, "Genetics and Criminal Behavior," *Criminology* 20 (1982):43–67.

73. A. A. Sandberg, G. F. Koeph, T. Ishiara, and T. S. Hauschka, "An XYY Human Male," *Lancet* 262 (1961):448–49.

74. Shah and Roth, "Biological and Psychophysiological Factors in Criminology," p. 135.

75. Mednick and Volavka, "Biology and Crime," p. 93.

76. Shah and Roth, "Biological and Psychophysiological Factors in Criminology," p. 137.

77. *Ibid.*, p. 94.

78. *Ibid.*, p. 95.

79. See, Sarnoff A. Mednick and Karl O. Christiansen, *Biological Bases in Criminal Behavior* (New York: Gardner Press, 1977).

80. David Rowe, "Genetic and Environmental Components of Antisocial Behavior: A Study of 265 Twin Pairs," *Criminology* 24 (1986):513–32; David Rowe and D. Wayne Osgood, "Heredity and Sociological Theories of Delinquency: A Reconsideration," *American Sociological Review* 49 (1984):526–40.

81. This pattern was found in subsequent research by David Rowe. See, David Rowe and Joseph Rodgers, "The Ohio Twin project and ADSEX Studies: Behavior Genetic Approaches to Understanding Antisocial Behavior," Paper presented at the American Society of Criminology meeting, Montreal, Canada, November, 1987.

82. Mednick and Volavka, "Biology and Crime," p. 97.

83. Barry Hutchings and Sarnoff A. Mednick, "Criminality in Adoptees and Their Adoptive and Biological Parents: A Pilot Study," in Mednick and Christiansen, eds., *Biological Bases in Criminal Behavior*.

84. Sarnoff Mednick, Terrie Moffit, William Gabrielli, and Barry Hutchings, "Genetic Factors in Criminal Behavior: A Review," in *Development of Antisocial and Prosocial*

Behavior 1986 (Academic Press, 1986), pp. 3–50.

85. Sarnoff Mednick, William Gabrielli, and Barry Hutchings, "Genetic Influences in Criminal Behavior: Evidence from an Adoption Cohort," in Katherine Teilmann, Van Dusen and Sarnoff Mednick, eds., *Perspective Studies of Crime and Delinquency*, (Boston: Kluver-Nijhoff, 1983), pp. 39–57; K. S. Van Dusen, S. Mednick, S. Gabrielli, and B. Hutchings, "Social Class and Crime in An Adoption Cohort," *Journal of Criminal Law and Criminology* (1983).

86. Jeffrey, "Criminology as an Interdisciplinary Behavioral Science."

87. Israel Nachson and Deborah Denno, "Violence and Cerebral Function," in Mednick, Moffitt, and Stack, eds., *The Causes of Crime*, pp. 185–217.

88. Lee Ellis, "Neurohormonal Bases of Varying Tendencies to Learn Delinquent and Criminal Behavior," in E. Morris and C. Braukmann, eds., *Behavioral Approaches to Crime and Delinquency* (New York: Plenum, 1988), pp. 499–518.

89. See, Peter Scott, "Henry Maudsley," in Hermann Mannheim, ed., *Pioneers in Criminology* (Montclair, N.J.: Prentice-Hall, 1981).

90. See, generally, Spencer Rathus, *Psychology* (New York: Holt, Rinehart and Winston, 1987).

91. See, generally, Donn Byrne and Kathryn Kelly, *An Introduction to Personality* (Englewood Cliffs, N.J.: Prentice-Hall, 1981).

92. This section adapted from Rathus, *Psychology*, pp. 412–20.

93. Sigmund Freud, "The Ego and the Id," in *Complete Psychological Works of Sigmund Freud*, vol. 19 (London: Hogarth, 1948), p. 52.

94. August Aichorn, *Wayward Youth* (New York: Viking Press, 1935).

95. David Abrahamsen, *Crime and the Human Mind* (New York: Columbia University Press, 1944), p. 137. See generally, Fritz Redl and Hans Toch, "The Psychoanalytic Perspective," in Hans Toch, ed., *Psychology of Crime and Criminal Justice* (New York: Holt, Rinehart and Winston, 1979), pp. 193–95.

96. Seymour Halleck, *Psychiatry and the Dilemmas of Crime* (Berkeley, Cal.: University of California Press, 1971).

97. James Sorrells, "Kids Who Kill," *Crime and Delinquency* 23 (1977):312–20.

98. Richard Rosner, "Adolescents Accused of Murder and Manslaughter: A Five Year Descriptive Study," *Bulletin of The American Academy of Psychiatry and The Law* 7 (1979):342–51.

99. This discussion is based on three works by Albert Bandura: *Aggression: A Social Learning Analysis* (Englewood Cliffs, N.J.: Prentice-Hall, 1973); *Social Learning Theory* (Englewood Cliffs, N.J.: Prentice-Hall, 1977); "The Social Learning Perspective: Mechanisms of Aggression," in Toch, ed., *Psychology of Crime and Criminal Justice*, pp. 198–236.

100. David Phillips, "The Impact of Mass Media Violence on U.S. Homicides," *American Sociological Review* 48 (1983):560–68.

101. See, generally, Albert Rabin, "The Antisocial Personality—Psychopathy and Sociopathy," in Toch, ed., *The Psychology of Crime and Criminal Justice*, pp. 236–51.

102. Robert Hare and Jeffrey Jutai, "Criminal History of the Male Psychopath: Some Preliminary Data," in Teilmann, Van Dusen, and Mednick, eds., *Perspective Studies of Crime and Delinquency*, pp. 225–36.

103. Halleck, *Psychiatry and the Dilemmas of Crime*, pp. 99–115.

104. See, generally, Mednick and Volavka, "Biology and Crime," pp. 105–23.

105. Hans Eysenck, *Crime and Personality* (London: Routledge and Kegan Paul, 1964).

106. D. M. Tucker, "Lateral Brain Function, Emotion and Conceptualization," *Psychological Bulletin* 89 (1981):19–46.

107. Orestes Fedora and Shawn Fedora, "Some Neuropsychological and Psychophysiological Aspects of Psychopathic and Nonpsychopathic Criminals," in P. Flor-Henry and J. Gruzelier, eds., *Laterality and Psychopathology*, Proceedings of Second International Conference, Banff, Canada, April, 1982.

108. Robert Hare, "Electrodermal and Cardiovascular Correlates of Psychopathy," in R. D. Hare and D. Schalling, eds., *Pschopathic Behavior: Approaches to Research* (New York: John Wiley, 1978), pp. 28–56.

109. Rathus, *Psychology*, p. 545.

110. Henry Goddard, *Efficiency and Levels of Intelligence* (Princeton, N.J.: Princeton University Press, 1920).

111. Edwin Sutherland, "Mental Deficiency and Crime," in Kimball Young, ed., *Social Attitudes* (New York: Henry Holt, 1931), p. 15.

112. William Healy and Augusta Bronner, *Delinquency and Criminals: Their Making and Unmaking* (New York: Macmillan, 1926).

113. See C. Burt, "The Inheritance of Mental Ability," *American Psychologist* 13 (1958):1–15.

114. John Slawson, *The Delinquent Boys* (Boston: Budget Press, 1926).

115. Kenneth Eels, et al., *Intelligence and Cultural Differences* (Chicago: University of Chicago Press, 1951), p. 181.

116. Robert Rosenthal and Lenore Jacobsen, *Pygmalion in the Classroom* (New York: Holt, 1968).

117. See, generally, Arthur Jensen, *Bias in Mental Testing* (New York: Free Press, 1979); see also Jensen, "How Much Can We Boost IQ and Scholastic Achievement?"

Harvard Educational Review 39 (1969):1–123.

118. Sandra Scarr and Richard Weinberg, "I.Q. Test Performance of Black Children Adopted by White Families," *American Psychologist* 31 (1976):726–39.

119. Sandra Scarr and Richard Weinberg, "The Minnesota Adoption Studies: Genetic Differences and Malleability," *Child Development* 54 (1983):260–67.

120. For an opposing view see, Joseph Horn, "The Texas Adoption Project: Adopted Children and Their Intellectual Resemblance to Biological and Adoptive Parents," *Child Development* 54 (1983):268–75.

121. Travis Hirschi and Michael Hindelang, "Intelligence and Delinquency: A Revisionist Review," *American Sociological Review* 42 (1977):471–586.

122. Robert Gordon, "IQ-Commensurability of Black-White Differences in Crime and Delinquency," Paper presented at the annual meeting of the American Psychological Association, Washington, D.C., August, 1986; Gordon, "Two Illustrations of the IQ-Surrogate Hypothesis: IQ Versus Parental Education and Occupational Status in the Race-IQ-Delinquency Model," Paper presented at the annual meeting of the American Society of Criminology, Montreal, Canada, November, 1987.

123. Terrie Moffit, William Gabrielli, Sarnoff Mednick, and Fini Schulsinger, "Socioeconomic Status, IQ, and Delinquency," *Journal of Abnormal Psychology* 90 (1981):152–56. For a similar finding, see L. Hubble and M. Groff, "Magnitude and Direction of WISC-R Verbal Performance IQ Discrepancies among Adjudicated Male Delinquents," *Journal of Youth and Adolescence* 10 (1981):179–83.

124. Deborah Denno, "Victim, Offender, and Situational Characteristics of Violent Crime," *The Journal of Criminal Law and Criminology* 77 (1986):1142–58.

125. Lorne Yeudall, Delee Fromm-Auch, and Priscilla Davies, "Neuropsychological Impairment of Persistent Delinquency," *The Journal of Nervous and Mental Disease* 170 (1982):257–65.

126. Christine Ward and Richard McFall, "Further Validation of the Problem Inventory for Adolescent Girls: Comparing Caucasian and Black Delinquents and Nondelinquents," *Journal of Consulting and Clinical Psychology* 54 (1986):732–33; Hubble and Groff, "Magnitude and Direction of WISC-R Verbal Performance," pp. 179–83.

127. James Q. Wilson and Richard Herrnstein, *Crime and Human Nature* (New York: Simon and Schuster, 1985), p. 148.

128. *Ibid.*, p. 171.

129. Deborah Denno, "Sociological and Human Developmental Explanations of Crime: Conflict or Consensus," *Criminology* 23 (1985):711–41.

130. Scott Menard and Barbara Morse, "A Structuralist Critique of the IQ-Delinquency Hypothesis: Theory and Evidence," *American Journal of Sociology* 89 (1984): 1347–78.

131. Denno, "Sociological and Human Developmental Explanations of Crime," pp. 711–41.

132. Spencer Rathus, *Psychology* (New York: Holt, Rinehart and Winston, 1987), p. 412.

133. Samuel Yochelson and Stanton Samenow, *The Criminal Personality* (New York: Jason Aronson, 1977).

134. Sheldon Glueck and Eleanor Glueck, *Delinquents and Nondelinquents in Perspective* (Cambridge, Mass.: Harvard University Press, 1968).

135. See, generally, R. Starke Hathaway and Elio Monachesi, *Analyzing and Predicting Juvenile Delinquency with the MMPI* (Minneapolis: University of Minnesota Press, 1953).

136. R. Starke Hathaway, Elio Monachesi, and Lawrence Young, "Delinquency Rates and Personality," *Journal of Criminal Law, Criminology and Police Science* 51 (1960):443–60; Michael Hindelang and Joseph Weis, "Personality and Self-Reported Delinquency: An Application of Cluster Analysis," *Criminology* 10 (1972):268; Spencer Rathus and Larry Siegel, "Crime and Personality Revisited," *Criminology* 18 (1980):245–51.

137. See, generally, Edward Megargee, *The California Psychological Inventory Handbook* (San Francisco: Josey Bass, 1972).

138. Karl Schuessler and Donald Cressey, "Personality Characteristics of Criminals," *American Journal of Sociology* 55 (1950):476–84; Gordon Waldo and Simon Dinitz, "Personality Attributes of the Criminal: An Analysis of Research Studies 1950–1965," *Journal of Research in Crime and Delinquency* 4 (1967):185–201; David Tennenbaum, "Research Studies of Personality and Criminality," *Journal of Criminal Justice* 5 (1977):1–19.

139. Wilson and Herrnstein, *Crime and Human Nature.*

140. *Ibid.*, p. 44.

141. *Ibid.*, p. 171.

142. *Ibid.*, p. 528.

143. Susan Pease and Craig T. Love, "Optimal Methods and Issues in Nutrition Research in the Correctional Setting," *Nutrition Reviews Supplement* 44 (1986):122–31.

144. Mark O'Callaghan and Douglas Carroll, "The Role of Psychosurgical Studies in the Control of Antisocial Behavior," in Mednick, Moffitt, and Stack, eds., *The Causes of Crime*, pp. 312–28.

145. Mednick, Moffitt, Gabrielli, and Hutchings, "Genetic Factors in Criminal Behavior," pp. 47–48.

146. *Ibid.*

≡ CHAPTER 7

SOCIOLOGICAL APPROACHES: SOCIAL STRUCTURE THEORIES

✗ INTRODUCTION

The preceding chapter reviewed positivist theories of crime causation, which focus on the individual. The next three chapters turn to sociological explanations of criminality. These explanations emphasize the role social institutions, structures, and processes play in shaping human behavior. This chapter reviews sociological theories that emphasize the relationship between people's social status and their criminal behavior. In the following chapter, the focus will shift to theories that analyze social processes and institutions and their influence on crime and deviance.

There are many reasons why sociology has been the predominant approach of U.S. criminologists during the twentieth century. First, it has long been evident that patterns of criminal behavior related to socioeconomic status, race, gender, and age exist within the social structure. Criminologists have attempted to discover why such patterns exist and how they can be explained. Theoretical models which ignore social factors cannot hope to provide a complete understanding of criminality. For example, if the cause off violent behavior were solely biological, it would be difficult to explain why some areas of the city experience more violence than others. If violence has a biological origin, shouldn't it be distributed more evenly throughout the social structure?

The sociological perspective is also relevant because it is concerned with social change and the dynamic aspects of human behavior. Sociologists seek to account for the way changing norms, values, institutions, and structures affect individual and group behavior. The shifting structure of modern post-industrial society seems to have had a tremendous effect on intergroup and interpersonal relationships.[1] For example, the influence of the extended family has been reduced and increased stress has been placed on individuality, independence, and isolation. It is not surprising that family disruption and conflict have been linked to the onset of criminality.[2]

Still another important social phenomenon has been the rapid increase in technology and its influence on the social system. One outcome has been the need for more service, technological, and white-collar workers and fewer blue-collar and agricultural workers. People who lack the requisite social and educational training, or who are the victims of racial prejudice and class bias, have found that the road to success through upward occupational mobility has become almost impassable. Lack of upward mobility, coupled with the failure of government-sponsored programs designed to alleviate poverty, may make crime an attractive solution to socially deprived but economically enterprising people.

Sociology's stress on intergroup and interpersonal transactions also promotes it as a source for criminological study. Criminologists believe that understanding the dynamics of personal interactions between individuals and their families, peers, schools, jobs, and the criminal justice agencies is important for understanding the cause of crime.[3] The relationship of one social class or group to another, or to the existing power structure that controls the nation's legal and economic system, also may be closely related to criminality. Sociology is concerned with the benefits of positive human interactions and the costs of negative ones. Crime is itself a human interaction; therefore it should not be studied without considering the behavior of all participants in a criminal act—the law violator, victim, law enforcers, lawmakers, and society in general. Individual-oriented explanations of crime neglect to consider these important factors. Factors such as the ecological distribution of crime, socialization, and the interactive nature of crime have made sociology the foundation of modern criminology.

FOUNDATIONS OF SOCIOLOGICAL CRIMINOLOGY

The foundations of sociological criminology can be traced to the works of L. A. J. Quetelet (1796–1874) and Emile Durkheim (1858–1917).

L. A. J. Quetelet

Quetelet was a Belgian mathematician who began (along with the French Andre-Michel Guerry) what is known as the **cartographic school** of criminology.[4] Quetelet was one of the first social scientists to use objective mathematical techniques to investigate the influence of social factors, such as season, climate, sex, and age, on the propensity to commit crime. Quetelet conducted his research using statistics developed in France in the early nineteenth century (the *comptes* *generaux de l'administration de la justice).*

Quetelet's most important finding was that social forces were strongly correlated with crime rates. In addition to finding a strong influence of age and sex on crime, Quetelet also uncovered evidence that season, climate, population composition, and poverty were related to criminality. More specifically, he found crime rates were greatest in the summer, in southern areas, among heterogeneous populations, among the poor and uneducated, and also were influenced by drinking habits.[5]

Quetelet was a pioneer of sociologically-oriented criminology. He identified many of the relationships between crime and social phenomena that serve as a basis for criminology today.

Emile Durkheim

Emile Durkheim was one of the founders of sociology and a significant contributor to criminology.[6] In fact, it is probable that his presentation of crime has been more influential on modern criminology than any other. Durkheim's most significant contribution was his conclusion that crime is a "normal" and necessary social behavior: since it has existed in every age, in both poverty and prosperity, crime seems part of human nature.[7]

According to Durkheim, the inevitability of crime is linked to the differences (heterogeneity) within society. Since people are so different from one another and employ such a variety of methods and forms of behavior to meet their needs, it is not surprising that some resort to criminality. Thus, as long as human differences exist, crime is inevitable and a fundamental condition of social life.

Some crimes, argued Durkheim, can also be a useful, and on occasion even healthy condition for a society to experience. The existence of crime implies that a way is open for social change, and that the social structure is not rigid or inflexible. Put another way, if crime did not exist, it would mean that everyone behaved the same way and agreed totally on what was right and wrong. Such universal conformity would stifle creativity and independent thinking.

To illustrate this concept, Durkheim offered the example of the Greek philosopher Socrates, who was considered a criminal and sentenced to death for corrupting the morals of youth. Durkheim distinguished this *altruistic criminal* type from the *common criminal* by analyzing the motivation behind the deviant behavior of each. The altruistic criminal is offended by the rules of society and seeks social change and an improved moral climate through his or her acts. The common criminal rejects all discipline, makes destruction or law violation an end in itself, and manifests little interest in moral conduct.

In addition, Durkheim argued that crime can have some benefits because it calls attention to social ills. A rising crime rate can signal the need for social change. It can promote a variety of programs designed to relieve the human suffering that may have caused the crime in the first place.

These early writings pointed the way for criminologists to examine the relationship between social variables and crime. The remainder of this chapter is devoted to one of the most important areas of sociological inquiry: social structure and its influence on behavior.

ECONOMIC STRUCTURE AND U.S. SOCIETY

People in the United States live in a **stratified** society. Social strata are created by the unequal distribution of wealth, power, and prestige. Social classes are segments of the population whose members have a relatively similar share of desirable things and who share attitudes, values, norms, and an identifiable lifestyle. In U.S. society, it is common to identify people as upper-, middle-, and lower-class citizens, with a broad range of economic variations existing within each group. The upper-upper class is reserved for a small number of exceptionally well-to-do families who maintain enormous financial and social resources.

The Internal Revenue Service estimates that more than 20,000 people have assets in excess of $5 million. While the richest 2.8 percent of U.S. families hold more than 28 percent of the nation's wealth, the poorest 20 percent have only 5 percent. The lower class contains the chronically poor, who are dependent on government supplements, such as welfare, to survive. Education, health, nutrition, occupational prestige, and social activities also are closely correlated with class membership.[8] A recent report, issued by the Physician Task Force on Hunger in America, found that many hard-working blue-collar workers are hungry and destitute. The report estimated that there are 20 million hungry people in America, and their plight is worsening.[9]

Members of the lower class also suffer in other ways. They are more prone to depression, less likely to have achievement motivation, and less likely to put off immediate gratification for future gain. Lower-class citizens are constantly bombarded with a flood of media advertisements linking material possessions to self-worth, but they are often unable to attain desired goods and services through conventional means. Thus, though they are members of a society that extols material success, they are unable to compete satisfactorily for such success with members of the upper classes.

Nowhere are the problems of the lower class more acute than those suffered by racial minorities. Black citizens, for example, have a median income level almost half that of whites, an unemployment rate almost twice as high, and a male high-school dropout rate 50 percent higher.[10] Racial minorities suffer from chronic underemployment and there is evidence that the economic gap between blacks and whites is growing.[11] Black citizens suffer from serious medical problems because of inadequate care in inner-city areas; the infant mortality rate of black infants is 65 percent higher than that of whites. In 1968, a Presidential Commission headed by Illinois Governor Otto Kerner looked into the cause of urban unrest and warned that the nation was being polarized into two groups: one white, one black; one rich, the other poor. Twenty years later the gap has not been closed.[12]

Underclass Culture

Lower-class slum areas are the scene of inadequate housing and health care, disrupted family lives, underemployment, and despair. More than half the families are fatherless and husbandless, headed by women who are the sole breadwinners and who often are assisted by welfare and ADC (Aid to Dependent Children). Today about 25 percent of all children under 18 years of age live in single-parent households, compared to 9 percent in 1960.[13] Though it is estimated that two-thirds to three-quarters of the urban poor are white, minorities are overrepresented within the poverty classes; children under 18 make up about 40 percent of the urban poor.[14]

Social scientists such as Oscar Lewis argue that the crushing lifestyle of slum areas produces a **culture of poverty** passed from one generation to the next.[15] The culture of poverty is marked by apathy, cynicism, helplessness, and mistrust of social institutions, such as schools, government agencies, and the police. This mistrust prevents those who live in slums from taking advantage of the meager opportunities available to them. In 1970, Gunnar Myrdal described a worldwide underclass, cut off from society, its members lacking the education and skills needed to be in demand in modern society; in 1983, Ken Auletta described an American **underclass** in much the same terms.[16] There is evidence that the underclass is growing. The Physician Task Force on Hunger found that the number of working poor whose earnings fell below the poverty line grew 36 percent between 1979 and 1987. The Task Force estimated that of the 13 million new jobs created in the 1980s, 8.2 million pay less than $7,000 annually.[17] Many of the new jobs politicians like to brag about are being created in high-tech industries located in the suburbs; steel, auto, and textile jobs, once the economic backbone of urban America, are being transferred overseas.

Despite our technological success, the fact that a significant percentage of U.S. citizens live in poverty and suffer its consequences remains an important social problem.

SOCIAL STRUCTURE THEORIES

Considering the deprivations suffered by the lower class, it is not surprising that a disadvantaged economic class position has been viewed by twentieth-century criminologists as a primary cause of crime. This view is referred to as **social structure theory.** As a group, social structure theories suggest that forces operating in lower-class areas of the environment push many of their residents into criminal behavior patterns. They consider the existence of unsupervised teenage gangs, high crime rates, and social disorder in slum areas as major social problems. Social structure theories are less concerned with why a particular individual commits crime, than with why crime rates are consistently higher in some areas and neighborhoods than in others. To social structure theorists, the answer lies in the conditions existing in lower-class slums.

Lower-class crime is often the violent, destructive product of youth gangs and marginally employed young adults. Although members of the middle and upper classes also engage in crime, social structure theorists view middle-class crime as being of relatively lower frequency, seriousness, and danger to the general public. Thus, social structure theory views the real crime problem as essentially a lower-class phenomenon, beginning in youth and continuing into young adulthood.

Most social structure theories focus on the law-violating behavior of youths. They suggest that the social forces that cause crime begin to have an effect on a person while he or she is relatively young, and then continue their influence throughout a person's life. Though not all youthful offenders become adult criminals, many begin their criminal training and learn criminal values while members of youth gangs and groups.

Social structure theorists dispute the notion that crime is solely an expression of psychological imbalance, biological traits, or personal insensitivity to social controls. If that were so, the crime rate would be consistent throughout the social structure, rather than skewed toward the lower classes. It is assumed that the social interaction of people living in similar social environments causes them to behave in a uniform, predictable fashion. If individuals acted independently, then it would be impossible that the mere fact of their social status could cause crime, or that lower-class life could influence their behavior.

Another assumption of social structure theories is that a tangible relationship exists between social position and crime. As noted in Chapter 4, official statistics almost uniformly support the contention that there is an inverse relationship between class and crime: the lower people are on the economic scale, the more likely they are to engage in serious criminal activities. Research using other measures of criminality—self-reports and victimization studies, for example—are less uniform but still seem to point in that direction. Moreover, it is alleged by social structure theorists that the most serious and violent crimes are, for the most part, committed by the lower classes.

✴ The Branches of Social Structure Theory

There are four overlapping branches within the social structure perspective: cultural deviance theory, strain theory, subcultural theory, and social ecology theory. While similar in perspective, each branch makes an independent contribution to social structure theory.

Cultural deviance theory, also referred to as **cultural transmission** or **culture conflict theory,** suggests that criminal behavior is an expression of conformity to lower-class cultural values and traditions. Obedience to the informal rules of behavior existing in slum areas causes inevitable conflict with the laws of conventional society. By adhering to the values of people with whom they are in close personal contact, lower-class citizens are often put in a position in which they must violate the law. Furthermore, nonconventional lower-class values are handed from one generation to the next; hence the term *cultural transmission.*

The second branch of social structure theory can be labeled **strain theory.** Strain theories are similar to cultural deviance theories in that they portray lower-class citizens as being more crime-prone than members of the middle and upper classes. Also, both strain and cultural deviance theories view crime as a collective response to culturally defined behavior demands.

The two perspectives differ in their treatment of the distribution of social norms, values, and goals. Whereas the cultural deviance school views the lower-class culture as maintaining its own unique set of values and goals, strain theorists argue that similar sets of goals and values are common to all economic strata; the overwhelming majority of people in the United States desire wealth, personal possessions, education, power, prestige, and other life comforts. Nonetheless, because of their economic and social disadvantages, lower-class citizens are unable to achieve these symbols of success through conventional means. Consequently, they feel anger, frustration, and resentment toward a society that placed them, by birth, within a disadvantaged economic category. Criminologists refer to these feelings of frustration as *strain.* As a consequence of perceived strain, lower-class citizens have some choices to make. They can accept their lot and live out their days as socially responsible, if unrewarded, citizens. Or they can choose an alternative means of achieving success. Gain through criminality is a popular choice.

The third branch of social structure theory is referred to as **subcultural theory.** This view, which combines elements of strain and cultural deviance, holds that lower-class youths enter a delinquent way of life because their alienation from conventional society causes them to seek alternative lifestyles or subcultures.

Finally, the **social ecology** view has emerged in recent years. While earlier social structure theories focused on cultural phenomena, such as reference group values and norms, social ecologists analyze macro-level aggregate data to identify the structural conditions within the urban environment which influence crime patterns. They believe that the interplay of several ecological and social variables creates the conditions in which crime is an inevitable result. In the accompanying Close-Up, one of those variables, the unemployment rate, is discussed in some detail.

✕CULTURAL DEVIANCE THEORY

Cultural deviance theory suggests that crime rates are highest in lower-class, inner-city areas because residents adhere to a unique, independent value system—a value system that places them in conflict with middle-class norms and rules. Lower-class values applaud such behaviors as being tough and "cool": never showing fear; being disrespectful to authority; living for today and letting tomorrow take care of itself; respecting "street smarts"; and disparaging formal education. More importantly, these distinct lower-class values are passed down from one generation to the next. Therefore, to understand crime, one must focus on the developing careers of young, teenage criminals as they mature into serious adult offenders.

The Chicago School

The Department of Sociology at the University of Chicago was the foundation of cultural deviance theory. Begun by Albion Woodbury Small in 1892, it was the home of such distinguished scholars as W. I. Thomas, Robert Ezra Park, and Ernest W. Burgess.

The Chicago School, as it is called, devoted a great deal of its attention to ecological studies of the city. In 1916, Robert Park called for anthropological methods of description and observation to be applied to urban life.[18] He was concerned about how neighborhood structure developed, how isolated pockets of poverty developed, and what social policies could be used to alleviate urban problems.

Over the next twenty years, Chicago School sociologists carried out an ambitious program of research and scholarship. Such works as Harvey Zorbaugh's *The Gold Coast and the Slum*, Frederick Thrasher's *The Gang*, and Louis Wirth's *The Ghetto* are classic examples of objective, highly descriptive accounts of urban life.[19]

The methods of the Chicago School were used by several of its resident scholars to study crime. Cultural deviance theory was popularized by the work of three Chicagoans: Henry McKay, Clifford R. Shaw, and Frederick Thrasher. They linked life in transitional slum areas to the inclination to commit crime. The following discussion examines their work more closely.

The Ecology of Crime. Clifford Shaw and Henry McKay began their pioneering work on crime in Chicago during the early 1920s.[20] This period in the city's history was typical of the transition taking place in many other urban areas. Chicago had experienced a mid-nineteenth century population expansion, fueled by a dramatic influx of foreign-born immigrants and, later, migrating southern black families. Congregating in the central city, the newcomers occupied the oldest housing and therefore faced numerous health and environmental hazards. Physically deteriorating sections of the city soon developed.

This condition prompted the city's wealthy, established citizens to become concerned about the moral fabric of Chicago society. There existed a widespread belief that foreign immigrants and blacks were crime-prone and morally dissolute. In fact, local groups were created with the very purpose of "saving" the children of poor families from moral decadence.[21] It was popular to view crime as the property of inferior racial and ethnic groups.

Based in Chicago, Shaw and McKay sought to explain crime and delinquency within the context of the changing urban environment. They rejected the racial and cultural explanations of criminality then popular, and instead viewed the ecological condition (physical environment) of the city itself as the real culprit in the creation of criminal behavior. They saw

CLOSE-UP

Crime and Unemployment

The social structure approach links crime to the economic deprivation experienced in ghetto areas. It follows that rates of unemployment are related to crime rates: if people don't hold jobs, they will be more likely to turn to crime as a means of support. Is this assumption valid? Is there a relationship between crime and unemployment?

Despite the logic of this proposition, little clear-cut evidence linking unemployment to high crime rates exists. For example, even during the economic prosperity of the 1960s, the crime rate rose dramatically.

Richard Freeman reviewed the literature on the subject and found that crime and unemployment are only weakly related. Though Freeman found evidence that criminals have poorer work records than noncriminals, there was little indication that changing market conditions would cause them to choose legitimate earning opportunities. Though crime rates in cities and states are slightly linked to labor market conditions, the sanctions and criminal penalties employed in these areas have a greater effect on the crime rate than market factors.

One possible reason for the weaker-than-expected relationship between crime and unemployment is that while joblessness increases the motivation to commit crime, it simultaneously decreases the opportunity to gain from criminal enterprise. During periods of economic hardship, potential victims will have fewer valuable items in their possession and will guard those valuables more closely. David Cantor and Kenneth Land explain that these two factors—supply and demand—cancel each other out, resulting in an insignificant relationship between crime and unemployment rates. Their findings jibe with the *routine activities* view that crime rates will vary not only with the presence of motivated offenders, but also with the presence of available, lightly protected targets.

While the link between crime and unemployment is thought to be weaker than expected, some recent research efforts raise doubt that the two variables are unrelated. For one thing, surveys of adult inmates show that many were unemployed and underemployed (about 40 percent) before their current incarceration; median income of both male and female inmates was below the poverty level. These data must be interpreted with caution, since they may reflect the relationship between economic status and criminal sentencing rather, than the one between crime

and workforce participation. Nonetheless, they are generally supportive of a crime-unemployment interrelationship.

In addition, research by Gary Kleck, Theodore Chiricos, and their associates indicates that the relationship between crime and unemployment is more complex than previously believed. Unemployment may have effects on the crime rate that are specific to offense, time period, sex, and age. In other words, unemployment may cause certain offenders to increase their likelihood of committing particular crimes at certain times. Unemployment seems to have the greatest influence on opportunistic property crimes, such as burglary, and the least on violent assaultive crimes.

This new research indicates that the relationship between crime and unemployment is not simply one in which limited income causes people to commit crime for the sake of economic gain. It is possible, Kleck and Chiricos conclude, that unemployment increases crime because it reduces people's stakes in conformity. By severing attachments to coworkers and reducing parents' ability to be breadwinners, unemployment reduces the attachment people have to conventional institutions and their ability to exert authority over their own children.

Discussion Questions

1. Should all people be guaranteed the right to work?
2. Would a job at the minimum wage be a realistic crime-reducing alternative to unemployment?

SOURCES: Theodore Chiricos, ''Rates of Crime and Unemployment: An Analysis of Aggregate Research Evidence,'' *Social Problems* 34 (1987):187–212; Gary Kleck, Theodore Chiricos, Michael Hayes, and Laura Myers, ''Unemployment, Crime, and Opportunity: A Target-Specific Crime Rate Analysis,'' Paper presented at the American Society of Criminology meeting, Montreal, Canada, November, 1987; David Cantor and Kenneth Land, ''Unemployment and Crime Rates in the Post-World War II United States: A Theoretical and Empirical Analysis,'' *American Sociological Review* 50 (1985):317–32; Richard Freeman, ''Crime and Unemployment,'' in James Q. Wilson, ed. *Crime and Public Policy* (San Francisco: Institute for Contemporary Studies, 1983), pp. 89–106.

Shaw and McKay viewed crime as a function of poor social and environmental conditions existing in turn-of-the-century urban slums.

that Chicago had developed into distinct neighborhoods, some marked by wealth and luxury and others by overcrowding, poor health and sanitary conditions, and extreme poverty. These slum areas were believed to be the spawning grounds of young criminals.

Shaw and McKay viewed crime as a product of the decaying **transitional neighborhood,** which manifested **social disorganization** and maintained conflicting values and social systems:

The successive changes in the composition of population, the disintegration of the alien cultures, the diffusion of divergent cultural standards, and the gradual industrialization of the area have resulted in a dissolution of the neighborhood culture and organization. The continuity of conventional neighborhood traditions and institutions is broken. Thus, the effectiveness of the neighborhood as a unit of control and as a medium for the transmission of the moral standards of society is greatly diminished. The boy who grows up in this area has little access to the cultural heritages of conventional society.

For the most part, the organization of his behavior takes place through his participation in the spontaneous play groups and organized gangs with which he had contact outside of the home . . . this area is an especially favorable habitat for the development of boys' gangs and organized criminal groups.[22]

Shaw and McKay identified the areas in Chicago where youthful delinquents were found. They noted that distinct ecological areas had developed in the city, comprising a series of five concentric circles, or zones, and that there were inter-zonal differences in the crime rate (see Figure 7.1). The zones with the highest crime rates were the transitional inner-city zones, where large numbers of foreign-born citizens had recently settled.[23] The zones farthest from the city's center were less prone to delinquency. Analysis of these data indicated a surprisingly stable pattern of delinquent activity in the five ecological zones over a 65-year period.

Shaw and McKay concluded that in the transitional neighborhoods deviant and conventional val-

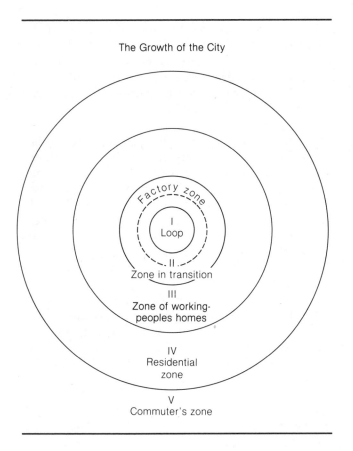

The Growth of the City

Factory zone

I
Loop

II
Zone in transition

III
Zone of working-
peoples homes

IV
Residential
zone

V
Commuter's zone

FIGURE 7.1   Shaw and McKay's Concentric Zone Model

ues compete side by side. Boys exposed to both value systems often are forced to choose between them. Thus, the development of teenage law-violating groups and gangs is an essential element of youthful misbehavior in slum areas.

Because of their deviant values, slum youths often come into conflict with existing middle-class norms, which demand strict obedience to the legal code. Consequently, a value conflict occurs that sets the delinquent boy and his peer group even farther apart from conventional society. The result is a fuller acceptance of deviant goals and behavior. Shut out of conventional society, neighborhood street gangs become fixed institutions, recruiting new members and passing on delinquent traditions from one generation to the next.

Shaw and McKay's statistical analysis confirmed their theoretical suspicions. They found that even though crime rates changed, the highest rates were always in zones I and II (central city and transitional area). Moreover, the areas with the highest crime rates retained high rates even when the ethnic composition of the zone changed from German and Irish to Italian and Polish.[24]

Most prominent among Shaw and McKay's many achievements was their finding that the ecology of the city influences criminal behavior. The Shaw-McKay model was an alternative to the view that criminals were either biological throwbacks, intellectually impaired individuals, or psychologically damaged people. Moreover, their research refuted the assumption that criminality is a property of any one minority or ethnic group.

Since the basis of their theory was that neighborhood disintegration and slum conditions are the primary causes of criminal behavior, Shaw and McKay paved the way for the many community action and treatment programs developed in the last half-century. Shaw himself was the founder of one very influential community-based treatment program, the *Chicago Area Project*, which is discussed later in this chapter.

Culture Conflict

There have been a number of other significant contributions to the cultural deviance school. Thorsten Sellin's famous work, *Culture Conflict and Crime*, is a theoretical attempt to link cultural adaptation to criminality.[25] Sellin's main premise is that criminal law is an expression of the rules of the dominant culture. The content of the law, therefore, may create a clash between conventional, middle-class rules and splinter groups such as ethnic and racial minorities, who maintain their own set of **conduct norms**—rules governing the day-to-day living conditions within these subcultures.

Law is also a constantly changing concept. Crimes of yesteryear may be legal conduct today, while what is a crime in one contemporary state may be legal conduct in another. Thus, to call persons deviant or criminal simply because they violate the rule of law is to neglect the diversity and heterogeneity that exists in society. To analyze crime, criminologists must be freed from dependence on law-oriented definitions.

Sellin instead focuses on conduct norms, which are the products of social life.[26] They reflect the restrictions social groups place on the activity of their members, restrictions aimed at protecting group norms. Violations of these norms might injure or harm the group. Each person belongs to social groups; and in a complex society, the number of groups they belong to—family, peer, occupation—is quite large. Sellin points out that the norms of these different groups may not mesh perfectly: "A conflict of norms is said to exist when more or less divergent rules of conduct govern the specific life situation in which a person may find himself."[27] Thus, obedience to the norms of one group, such as friends, may violate the norms of another, such as society. Conduct norms are universal; they are not the product of one group, culture, or political structure.

Sellin goes on to describe how culture conflict has produced crime and delinquency. He points to the growth of a technological society that creates both a confusion of norms and a vast extension of impersonal control agencies designed to enforce rules. For many people living in such a culture, certain life situations are governed by conflicting norms, so that no matter how they behave, they will be violating the rules of one group or another. Sellin argues that the Chicago area studies of Clifford Shaw are examples of the problems of culture conflict. He also finds that immigrants who adhere to the norms of their cultural origin may find themselves in conflict with the rules of the U.S. community. For example, Sellin cites the case of a Sicilian father in New Jersey who killed the 16-year-old seducer of his daughter and then expressed surprise at being arrested, because he had "merely defended his family honor in a traditional way."[28]

⅄ Focal Concerns and Crime

Walter Miller's theory of **lower-class culture conflict** is another important attempt to explain the criminal activity found in lower-class environments.[29] Instead of viewing crime as a psychological aberration or the product of a diseased personality, Miller, like Sellin, portrays criminal behavior as a normal reaction to the norms and values of a unique lower-class culture.

Miller views criminality as a product of the values and attitudes ingrained in all elements of lower-class culture.[30] According to Miller, a unique group of value- like *focal concerns* dominates life among the lower class. These concerns do not necessarily represent a rebellion against middle-class values; rather, they have evolved specifically to fit conditions in slum areas. The major focal concerns that Miller identified are set out in more detail below.[31]

Trouble.   Getting into and staying out of trouble is a major concern of lower-class citizens. Trouble includes such behavior as fighting, drinking, and sexual misconduct. In lower-class communities, people are evaluated by their actual or potential involvement in trouble-making activity. The attitude toward trouble is not always clear-cut. Sometimes it confers prestige —for example, when a man gets a reputation for being able to handle himself well in a fight. However, getting into trouble and having to pay the consequences can make a person look foolish and incompetent. In most instances, trouble-making escapades are undertaken with a goal in mind, such as stealing an automobile when the money to buy one is unobtainable. They are usually not merely unplanned, destructive behavior.

Toughness.   Lower-class males want local recognition of their physical and spiritual toughness. They refuse to be sentimental or soft; instead, they value physical strength, fighting ability, and athletic skill. Lower-class males who cannot meet these standards risk getting a reputation for being weak, inept, and effeminate.

Smartness.   Another critical concern of lower-class citizens is maintaining an image of streetwise savvy, which carries with it the ability to outfox and outcon the opponent. This, of course, does not mean that intellectual brilliance is admired; in fact, ivory-tower types are disdained. Smartness means knowing essential survival techniques, like gambling, conning, and outsmarting the law.

Excitement.   Another important feature of the lower-class lifestyle is the search for fun and excitement. The search for excitement may lead to drug use, gambling, fighting, getting drunk, seeking sex, and so on. Looking for excitement may eventually lead to another focal concern, trouble. Excitement is not sought all the time. In between, the lower-class citizen may simple "hang out" and "be cool."

According to Miller, some focal concerns of lower-class youth include autonomy, fate, toughness, and smartness.

Fate.   Lower-class citizens believe their lives are in the hands of strong spiritual force that guide their destinies. Getting lucky, finding good fortune, and hitting the jackpot are all daily dreams.

Autonomy.   A general concern exists in lower-class cultures about personal freedom and autonomy. Being in the control of authority figures such as the police, teachers, and parents is an unacceptable weakness, incompatible with toughness. Conflicts arise when the lower-class citizen is confronted with rigidly controlled environments like schools, hospitals, the military, courts, and prisons. The usual manner of dealing with these authoritarian regimes is to actively disdain them, a behavior response that frequently results in a continuing relationship with them. For example, such behavior in youths can result in their being held back in school.

Miller suggests that obedience to lower-class focal concerns will promote behavior that often runs afoul of the law. In this area, Miller's work is quite similar to Sellin's culture conflict approach. For example, proving one's toughness may demand that one never backs down from a fight. Displaying street smarts may lead to con games and other illegal schemes, while the

search for excitement may result in drinking, gambling, or drug abuse. Thus, it is obedience to existing cultural demands that precipitates lower-class crime, and not a sense of frustration or alienation from the greater society.

Miller maintains that lower-class culture is a stable condition in U.S. life which contains its own unique rules, values, and norms—all quite different from those of upper- and middle-class societies. Crime is a functional response to these values, rather than a violation of existing community rules.

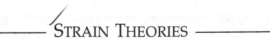

STRAIN THEORIES

Strain theories constitute the second branch of social structure theory. Collectively, they view crime and delinquency as a result of the frustration and anger people experience over their inability to achieve legitimate social and financial success. Strain theorists agree that most people originally share similar values and goals but that the ability to achieve them is stratified by socioeconomic class. In middle- and upper-class communities, strain does not exist, since education and prestigious occupations are readily

TABLE 7.1 Typology of Individual Modes of Adaptation

Modes of Adaptation	Cultural Goals	Institutionalized Means
I. Conformity	+	+
I. Innovation	+	-
II. Ritualism	-	+
V. Retreatism	-	-
V. Rebellion	±	±

SOURCE: Robert Merton, "Social Structure and Anomie," in *Social Theory and Social Structure* (Glencoe, Ill.: Free Press, 1957).

obtainable. In lower-class slum areas, strain occurs because legitimate avenues for success are all but closed. When no acceptable means for obtaining success exist, individuals may either use deviant methods to achieve their goals or reject socially accepted goals and substitute others for them.

This last point is quite important, because it distinguishes strain theory from cultural deviance theories. Strain theories hold that everyone desires middle-class goals but that the frustration of failing to achieve them causes lower-class people to substitute criminal behavior. Cultural deviance theories, on the other hand, maintain that many, if not all, lower-class people have a separate value system that places them in conflict with middle-class social control agents. The following sections examine the most significant strain theories in greater detail.

Merton's Theory of Anomie

The best-known strain theory is Robert Merton's **theory of anomie.**[32] Merton adapted Durkheim's concept of anomie to conditions in U.S. society. As initially developed by Durkheim, *anomie* was a condition of relative normlessness in a society or group. It referred to a property of the social structure, not to a property of the individual in relationship to society. Durkheim viewed an anomic condition as arising when the existing social structure could no longer establish and maintain control over individuals' wants and desires.

As originally conceived, anomie resulted from disruption in the social world. The disruption might come from natural or human-made catastrophes, such as economic depression, war, or famine. Durkheim also recognized an *anomie of prosperity*, which occurred

when sudden good fortune disrupted a person's concept of norms, rules, and behavior.

Merton adapted Durkheim's abstract concept to fit the conditions of American society. He believes that two elements of all modern cultures interact to produce potentially anomic conditions—culturally defined **goals**, and socially approved **means** for obtaining them. For example, U.S. society stresses the goals of acquiring wealth, success, and power. Socially permissible means include hard work, education, and thrift. Merton argues that every social system maintains a unique combination of goals and means.

Merton's position is that the legitimate means to acquire wealth are stratified across class and status lines. Those with little formal education and few economic resources soon find that they are denied the ability to legally acquire money and other symbols of success. When socially mandated goals are uniform throughout society and access to legitimate means is bound by class and status, the resulting strain produces an anomic condition among those who are locked out of the legitimate opportunity structure. Consequently, they may develop criminal or delinquent solutions to the problem of attaining goals.

Social Adaptations.   Merton argues that each person has his or her own concept of the goals of society and of the means available to attain them. U.S. society, as mentioned, stresses the success goal above all others. Whereas some people have inadequate means of attaining success, others, who do have the means, reject societal goals as being unsuited to them.

Table 7.1 shows Merton's diagram of the hypothetical relationship between social goals, the means for getting them, and the individual actor. The indi vidual can develop one of five adaptations to deal with the possibility of stress.

Conformity. Conformity occurs when individuals adopt social goals and also have the means at their disposal to attain them. In a balanced, stable society, this is the most common social adaptation. If a majority of its people did not practice conformity, the society would cease to exist.

Innovation. Innovation occurrs when an individual accepts the goals of society but rejects or is incapable of using legitimate means to attain them. For example, when people want luxuries but lack money, the resulting conflict sometimes forces them to adopt an innovative solution to the problem—they steal.

Of the five adaptations, innovation is most closely associated with criminal behavior. The demand to succeed that pervades U.S. culture places such an enormous burden on those lacking economic opportunity that deviant modes of adaptation are not a surprising result. This condition accounts for the high rate of crime in poverty areas, where access to legitimate means is severely limited. However, innovative adaptations can occur in any social class when members perceive a lack of appropriate means to gain social success. For example, witness the stock frauds and tax evasion schemes of the rich.

Successful innovation has long-term effects. A continued frequency of successful deviance tends to lessen, and possibly eliminate, the perceived legitimacy of conventional norms for others in the social system. Merton claims: "The process thus enlarges the extent of anomie within the system so that others, who did not respond in the form of deviant behavior to the relatively slight anomie which first obtained, come to do so as anomie is spread and is intensified."[33] Thus, anomie causes an interactive effect, in which people who observe the inability of society to control crime will resort to the law-violating means others have successfully used. This explains why crime is created and sustained in certain low-income ecological areas.

Ritualism. Ritualism results when goals are lowered in importance and means are at the same time rigidly adhered to. The maintenance of a strict set of manners and customs that serve no purpose is an example of ritualism. Such practices often exist in religious services, feudal societies, clubs, college fraternities, and other organizations. Ritualists gain pleasure from the practice of traditional ceremonies that have neither a real purpose nor a goal.

Retreatism. Retreatism entails a rejection of both the goals and the means of society. Merton suggests that people who adjust in this fashion are "in the society but not of it." Included in this category are "psychotics, psychoneurotics, chronic autists, pariahs, outcasts, vagrants, vagabonds, tramps, chronic drunkards, and drug addicts."[34] Often, this posture results when an individual accepts socially acceptable goals but is denied the means to attain them. Because such people are also morally or otherwise incapable of using illegitimate means, they attempt to escape their lack of success by withdrawing—either mentally or physically.

Rebellion. A rebellious adaptation involves the substitution of alternative sets of goals and means for the accepted ones of society. This adaptation is typical of revolutionary, who wish to promote radical change in the existing social structure and who call for alternative lifestyles, goals, and beliefs. For many years, revolutionaries groups have abounded in the United States, some espousing the violent overthrow of the existing social order, and others advocating the use of nonviolent, passive resistance to change society. The revolutionary orientation can be used as a reaction against a corrupt and hated regime or as an effort to create alternate opportunities and lifestyles within the existing system.

It is evident that behaviors associated with retreatism, rebellion, and innovation are relevant to the production of criminal behavior. Considering the apparent inequality in U.S. society, it is not surprising that large segments of the population react to the resulting anomic condition with innovations such as theft or extortion, with retreat into drugs or alcohol, or with rebellion exhibited by joining revolutionary or cultist groups.

Analysis of Anomie Theory

Since its publication, Merton's theoretical model has received praise for its scope and precision. It is more sophisticated than the earlier cultural deviance approach, since it raises the possibility of differing types or styles of both deviant and nondeviant behavior and offers explanations for the existence of each. Furthermore, by linking deviant behavior to the success goals that control social behavior, anomie theory attempts to pinpoint the cause of the conflict that produces personal frustration and consequent criminality.

Merton's theory does not actually concern itself with the reason why an individual becomes deviant. Instead, it attempts to explain crime rates that exist in society. By acknowledging that society unfairly distributes the legitimate means to achieving success, anomie theory helps explain the existence of high crime areas and the apparent predominance of delinquent and criminal behavior among particular social and ethnic groups. By suggesting that social conditions, not individual personalities, produce crime, Merton—together with Shaw and McKay, Miller, and other social theorists—has greatly influenced the directions taken to reduce and control criminality during the latter half of the twentieth century.

The concept of anomie also has been linked to individual criminality. Scales have been created to measure an individual's perceptions of anomie by asking questions such as: "I feel depressed much of the time."[35] Research studies have shown that self-reported delinquents and incarcerated offenders are more likely to report feelings of anomie than members of the general public.[36] Yet, such data must be regarded with caution, since it is difficult to determine whether the perceptions of anomie preceded criminal activity or developed as a consequence of the law violations.

A number of questions are left unanswered by anomie theory.[37] Merton does not explain why people differ in their choice of behavior. Why does one person become a mugger, another commits rape, while another chooses school and a job? Anomie may be used to explain differences in crime rates, but it cannot explain why a particular individual in an anomie-susceptible area becomes a criminal while another remains a conformist, or why one chooses rebellion and another innovation.

SUBCULTURAL THEORIES

Subcultures are groups of like-minded individuals who share similar ideas and values and who band together for support, defense, and mutual need. Subcultures are distinct elements within the larger culture; they share some of its features, but not all of them. Most importantly, members may engage in behaviors which confront the norms of conventional society.

Subcultural theories agree that lower-class people, especially youths, experience strain because they are alienated from conventional society. They lack the requisite education, family support, and social standing to achieve success as measured by middle-class standards. To compensate, they develop an alternative lifestyle, which provides them with the opportunity to feel important and successful. Unfortunately, this alternative lifestyle may include joining a group which condones violence and criminality as means of attaining status, wealth, and pride.

The subculture model seems similar to cultural deviance theories, but there is some distinction between the two approaches. Whereas the cultural deviance school suggests that people living in lower-class, high-crime areas develop their own set of values and norms, subcultural strain theories suggest most values and norms cut across class lines. In other words, there is little class distinction in the way people view common values, such as honesty, patriotism, friendship, and ambition. However, because lower-class citizens often find that their access to success is blocked or impeded, they are forced to turn from conventional values and enter into a deviant lifestyle. For example, while residents of both slums and suburbs may admire physicians and attorneys, only the latter can realistically expect to become a professional. Or, while a boy from the slums may want to join a college fraternity, he knows his most realistic option is the neighborhood gang.

The strain caused by holding upper-class goals while maintaining lower-class means eventually forces ghetto youths to seek alternate avenues to success and self-esteem. One method is to seek out like-minded peers who provide the support conventional society cannot provide. Members of this subculture engage in a mutual support system, in which teenage gangs form to prey upon victims; to provide members with a sense of belonging, camaraderie, and esteem; and to prepare members for a life of adult crime. Thus, subcultural strain theories focus on the development of teenage lower-class delinquents as they develop into career criminals.

Cohen's Theory of Delinquent Subcultures

Albert Cohen first articulated the theory of delinquent subculture in his 1955 book, Delinquent Boys.[38] Cohen's main purpose was to explain the disproportionate amount of officially recognized delinquent behavior found in lower-class slum neighborhoods. His central position was that the delinquent behavior of lower-class youths was a protest against the norms and values of middle-class U.S. culture. Because social conditions make them incapable of achieving success legitimately, lower-class youths experience a form of culture conflict that Cohen labeled **status frustration**.[39] As a result, many of them join together in teenage gangs and engage in behavior that is "nonutilitarian, malicious, and negativistic."[40] Cohen viewed delinquents as forming a separate subculture and possessing a value system directly in opposition to that of the larger society. He described the subculture as one that takes "its norms from the larger culture but turns them upside down. The delinquent's conduct is right by the standards of his subculture precisely because it is wrong by the norms of the larger cultures."[41]

Causes of Delinquency.   According to Cohen, the development of the delinquent subculture is a function of the social and familial conditions children experience as they mature in the ghetto or slum environment. Delinquency is not a product of inherent class inferiority. Rather, it is a result of the social and economic limitations suffered by members of the less fortunate groups in society. The numbing burden of poverty is the real villain in the creation of delinquent careers.

A critical element of lower-class life, one that directly influences later delinquent behavior, is the nature of the child's family structure. Cohen argues that the relative position of a child's family in the social structure determines the quality of experience and problems that the child will encounter later in life. By implication, Cohen suggests that lower-class families are incapable of teaching their offspring proper socialization techniques for entry into the dominant middle-class culture. Permanently cut off from the middle-class way of life, lower-class families produce children who lack the basic skills necessary to achieve social and economic success in a demanding society. Developmental handicaps produced by a lower-class upbringing include lack of educational training, poor speech and communication skills, and inability to delay gratification.

Middle-Class Measuring Rods.   One significant handicap that lower-class children face is the inability to positively impress authority figures, such as teachers, employers, or supervisors. In U.S. society, these positions tend to be held by members of the middle or upper class, who have difficulty relating to lower-class children. Cohen calls the standards set by these authority figures **middle-class measuring rods**. The conflict lower-class youths feel when they fail to meet these standards is a primary cause of delinquency.

In U.S. culture, people are constantly evaluated on their performance in institutional settings. Work, school, the military, and the justice system are all controlled by representatives of the middle class. Negative evaluations become part of a permanent file that follows an individual for the rest of his or her life. When the individual wants to improve, earlier failure to adjust to middle-class standards may be used to discourage advancement. For example, a school record may be reviewed by juvenile court authorities; a juvenile court record may be opened by the military; a military record can influence the securing of a job. Lower-class youths who have difficulty adjusting to the middle-class measuring rods of one institution may find themselves prejudged by others. As criminologist Clarence Schrag puts it:

> The ratings are reviewed, magnified, or deprecated by the periodic updating of records and by the informal exchanges of information that commonly occur among the leaders of institutions, who frequently are also the pillars and the decision-makers of the community. From this we may conclude that a person's status and esteem in the community are largely determined by the judgments of his elders, which judgments reflect the traditional values of American society and are therefore regarded as binding on the middle class and on "respectable members of the lower class as well.[42]

Reactions to Middle-Class Measuring Rods.   Cohen believes lower-class boys who suffer rejection by middle-class decision-makers become deeply affected by their lack of social recognition. They usually elect to adopt one of three alternative behaviors:

According to Cohen, the "corner boy" role is embraced by noncriminal youth for whom a middle-class lifestyle is not attainable.

the *corner boy* role, the *college boy* role, or the *delinquent boy* role.

The corner boy role is the most common response to middle-class rejection. The corner boy is not overly delinquent but behaves in a way that is sometimes defined as delinquent. For example, he is a truant. He hangs out in the neighborhood; engages in gambling, athletics, and other group activities; and eventually obtains a menial job. His main loyalty is to his peer group, on which he depends for support, motivation, and interest. His values, therefore, are those of the group with which he is in close personal contact. The corner boy, well aware of his failure to achieve the standards of the American dream, retreats into the comforting world of his lower-class peers and eventually becomes a stable member of his society.

The college boy embraces the cultural and social values of the middle class. Rather than scorning middle-class measuring rods, he actively strives to be successful by middle-class standards. Cohen views this type of youth as one who is embarking on an almost hopeless path, since he is ill-equipped academically, socially, and linguistically to achieve the rewards of middle-class life.

The delinquent boy adopts a set of norms and principles in direct opposition to middle-class society's. Cohen describes some general properties of the delinquent subculture. For one thing, its members often manifest **short-run hedonism.**[43] That is, they live for today and let tomorrow take care of itself. Although Cohen believes short-run hedonism

is a characteristic of lower-class culture as a whole, he finds it especially applicable to delinquent groups.

Members of the delinquent subculture are also careful to maintain **group autonomy.** They resist efforts by family, school, or other sources of authority to control their behavior. Although some individual delinquents may respond to direction from others, the gang itself is autonomous, the focus of "attraction, loyalty, and solidarity."[44]

Though members of the delinquent subculture often manifest negativistic and malicious behavior, Cohen believes they are still controlled to some degree by the norms and values of the generalized culture. They really want to be successful at school and jobs. To deal with the conflict inherent in this frustrating dilemma, the delinquent resorts to a process Cohen calls **reaction formation.** Symptoms of reaction formation include overly intense responses that seem disproportionate to the stimuli that trigger them. For the delinquent boy, this takes the form of "irrational, malicious, unaccountable hostility to the enemy within the gates as well as without—the norms of respectable middle-class society."[45] Reaction formation causes the delinquent boy to overreact to any perceived threat or slight. Consequently, the delinquent boy establishes himself as being quite distinct from middle-class society. Whereas the corner boy and college boy may be viewed as inferior to their middle-class counterparts, the delinquent's nonconformity to middle-class standards sets him, in his view, above the most exemplary college boy.

Analysis of Cohen's Theory of Delinquent Subcultures. Cohen carries the concept of cultural transmission a step further by explaining the factors that promote and sustain a delinquent subculture. By introducing the concepts of status frustration, failure to meet middle-class measuring rods, and family disability, Cohen makes a clear presentation of factors that cause lower-class delinquency. Furthermore, by introducing the corner boy–college boy–delinquent boy triad, he attempts to explain why some lower-class youths are able to avoid entry into the delinquent subculture.

Despite its merits, Cohen's work has been subject to significant criticisms. For one thing, he presents no rigorous empirical evidence to support his contentions; and, as indicated in Chapter 4, self-report studies have uncovered data indicating that delinquent behavior may be unrelated to social status or status frustration. Thus, although Cohen's theory seems plausible, he does not present enough evidence to unequivocally support its validity.

The internal consistency of Cohen's theory also has been brought into question. In a much-cited article, John Kitsuse and David Detrick note some ambiguities that run through Cohen's statements.[46] For example, at some points Cohen claims that delinquent boys value the opinion of middle-class persons; at others he says that they care little for middle-class opinions. Kitsuse and Detrick also question Cohen's concept of *reaction formation* and suggest that it is impossible to test the validity of this concept scientifically. Kitsuse and Detrick object to the categorization of delinquent behavior as nonutilitarian, malicious, and negativisitic. They point to evidence that delinquent behavior is often rational, calculated, and utilitarian. It is, they conclude, a serious mistake to categorize all delinquents as being similarly engaged in destructive and thoughtless behavior.

Responding to these and other criticisms, Cohen (in conjunction with James Short) presented a refined version of his original theory.[47] Cohen and Short acknowledged that the original formulation of the delinquent subculture may have been too simplistic and that a more complex model may be called for.

Results of studies specifically designed to test Cohen's theory have been inconclusive. Albert Reiss and Lewis Rhodes found little relationship between status deprivation and criminality.[48] Their findings were supported in a recent study by Marvin Krohn and his associates.[49] However, others have found that status perceptions were related to criminality.[50] Thus, although Cohen's view seems plausible enough, research conducted to test its validity has not yielded conclusive results.

Cloward and Ohlin's Theory of Differential Opportunity

In their well-known work *Delinquency and Opportunity*, Richard Cloward and Lloyd Ohlin add significantly to our knowledge of the development of criminal subcultures.[51]

Cloward and Ohlin propose that independent delinquent subcultures exist within society: "A delinquent subculture is one in which certain forms of delinquent activity are essential requirements for the performance of the dominant roles supported by the subculture."[52] Not all illegal acts are committed by youths who are part of this subculture; but the most serious, sustained, and costly ones are.

Delinquent subcultures spring up in areas where youths lack the opportunity to gain success through conventional means. True to strain theory principles, Cloward and Ohlin portray delinquents as individuals who want to conform to middle-class values but lack the means to do so: "Reaching out for socially approved goals under conditions that preclude their legitimate achievement may become a prelude to deviance."[53]

Differential Opportunities. The centerpiece of the Cloward and Ohlin theory is the concept of **differential opportunity.** The authors agree with Merton that people who perceive themselves as failures within conventional society will seek innovative ways to gain success; some will question the legitimacy of conventional codes of conduct as an appropriate guide for their own behavior and instead begin to use illegal means. The person who sees little hope for advancement by legitimate means may join with like-minded people to form a criminal subculture. Group support helps them handle the shame, fear, or guilt they may develop from engaging in illegal acts. Their participation in a delinquent subculture also gives them the opportunity to achieve personal success and satisfaction through the approval afforded them by their peers.

If the ecological area in which a person resides provides the opportunity for personal success through crime-related activities—theft, organized crime, and the like—then the person may make use of these illegitimate opportunities to achieve financial gain. For example, such a person may join a successful car-theft ring, become a member of organized crime, or get involved in gambling. However, not all lower-class areas are stable enough to provide even illegal opportunities.

Put another way, not only are conventional opportunities stratified unequally in the social structure, but so too are illegal opportunities. This is the basis of differential opportunity theory. Cloward and Ohlin propose the existence of three types of collective responses to blocked legitimate opportunities: *criminal gangs,* which seek monetary gain through crime; *conflict gangs,* which specialize in violence; and *retreatist gangs,* which are drug-related. The response taken depends on the means available.

Criminal Gangs.   Youths join criminal gangs as a training ground for adult criminal careers. The dominant feature of group membership involves learning the knowledge and skills needed for success in criminal activities. The gang member starts by learning to look up to older criminals, as a middle-class youth might admire athletes or rock stars. Delinquent experiences help the gang boy to learn the techniques and orientation of the criminal world and to "cooperate successfully with others in criminal enterprises."[54] The gang boy learns to regard the world with suspicion—everyone has a "racket." However, he must prove himself reliable in his contacts with his criminal associates and be a "right guy."

Youths can best pursue criminal careers by cultivating connections with successful older offenders who can help them "learn the ropes." Older offenders introduce aspiring delinquents to contacts in the crime business—drug dealers, fences, pawn shop operators—and also to legal connections—crooked police officers, lawyers, and politicians—who can insure their freedom of movement.

The criminal subculture is likely to arise in an area characterized by close connections among young, young adult, and adult offenders. It creates a new opportunity structure that provides "alternative avenues to success goals."[55] Furthermore, the subculture controls youths' behavior, limiting activities that would otherwise lessen the probability of their receiving illegal gain—for example, engaging in nonfunctional, irrational violence.

Conflict Gangs.   The stereotype of the conflict gang member is the young tough who swaggers with his gang, fights with weapons to win respect from rivals, and engages in unpredictable and destructive assaults on persons and property. The conflict gang member must be ready to fight to protect his own and his gang's integrity and honor. By doing so, he develops a reputation ("rep"), which provides him with a means for acquiring admiration from his peers and consequently helps him develop his own self-image. Conflict gangs "represent a way of securing access to the scarce resources for adolescent pleasure and opportunity in underprivileged areas."[56]

Conflict gangs develop in communities unable to provide either legitimate or illegitimate opportunities. These highly disorganized areas are marked by transient residents and physical deterioration. Crime in these areas is "individualistic, unorganized, petty, poorly paid and unprotected."[57] There are no successful adult criminal role models from whom youths can learn criminal skills. Thus, when severe limitations on both criminal and conventional opportunity intensify frustrations of the young, it is likely they will turn to violence as a means of gaining status.

Retreatist Gangs.   Members of the retreatist subculture are constantly in search of ways of getting high—alcohol, pot, heroin, unusual sexual experiences, music. They are always "cool," detached from relationships with the conventional world. To feed their habits, retreatists develop a "hustle"—pimping, conning, selling drugs, and committing other nonviolent crimes. Personal status derives from the respect retreatists get from the society of which they are members.

Many retreatists are double failures, unable to gain success through legitimate means and unwilling to do so through risky ones such as a robbery. Others have tried to use illegal or violent tactics but have failed to gain proficiency in them. Not all double failures become retreatists; some may choose to be the law-abiding corner boys previously identified by Albert Cohen.

Analysis of Differential Opportunity Theory

Cloward and Ohlin's theory has the distinct advantage of avoiding the pitfalls of previous theoretical models. It is neither so broad as to lack precision nor so narrow as to be unimportant. Their recognition of the existence of different types of delinquent gang cultures—criminal, conflict, retreatist—seems to be a more realistic reflection of the actual world of the delinquent than Cohen's original view of purely negativistic, destructive delinquent youths who oppose all social values. It is difficult to believe, as Cohen originally had it, that the majority of delinquent acts are purposeless and destructive, when statistics show that teenagers engage in many profit-related offenses, such as burglaries and robberies. Cloward and Ohlin's model seems to fit existing data more closely.

Cloward and Ohlin's tripartite model of urban delinquency also relates directly to the treatment and rehabilitation of delinquents. While other theorists, such as Cohen, Miller, Shaw, and McKay, see delinquent youths maintaining values and attitudes in opposition to middle-class culture, Cloward and Ohlin suggest that many delinquents share the goals and values of the general society but lack the means to obtain them. This position is an argument for rehabilitation programs, because it suggests that preventing delinquency does not involve changing basic attitudes and beliefs of delinquent youth. Rather, such programs have the somewhat simpler task of providing youths with the means for obtaining the success they truly desire. Later discussions will describe how Cloward and Ohlin's conceptualizations have influenced social policy and crime-prevention programs.

Several studies have been conducted to test Cloward and Ohlin's model. Judson Landis and Frank Scarpitti surveyed a group of incarcerated boys and a high-school control group and found that the delinquent youths perceived more limited opportunities than the nondelinquent youths.[58] These findings were supported by James Short, Ramon Rivera, and Ray Tennyson, who found in a study of gang delinquents that the perception of limited access to legitimate opportunity was more likely to be associated with delinquency than the perception of access to illegitimate opportunity.[59]

Despite this evidence, some research has produced results that conflict with opportunity theory. For example, when testing samples of lower- and middle-class delinquents, Leon Fannin and Marshall Clinard found that subjects differed in their attitudes and values:

> Lower-class boys felt themselves to be . . . tougher, more powerful, fierce, fearless, and dangerous than middle-class boys. Middle-class delinquents . . . conceived of themselves as being more loyal, clever, smart, smooth and bad . . . The lower class would like to be [ideal self] tougher, harder and more violent than the middle class, while the latter would like to be more loyal, lucky and firm.[60]

Fannin and Clinard's findings were supported by a similar study of peer associations conducted by Maynard Erickson and LaMar Empey.[61]

Some recent surveys of gang delinquency also have called into question Cloward and Ohlin's conclusions. They suggest that gangs are more pervasive than was previously expected, that more than one type of gang (conflict, criminal, retreatist) exists in a particular area, and that the commitment of gang boys to one another is less intense than opportunity theory would suggest. Moreover, gangs do not seem to specialize in any particular type of behavior. Thus, while some empirical evidence supports Cloward and Ohlin, an equal amount seems to contradict their approach. (For more discussion of gangs, see the accompanying Close-Up entitled "The Gang Today.")

SOCIAL ECOLOGY THEORY

Social ecology theory is the latest link in the theoretical chain which began with the demographic research of Quetelet, the area studies of Shaw and Mckay, and the value oriented research of Merton, Cohen and Cloward and Ohlin. However, today's social ecologists are little concerned with micro-level variables, such as the transmission of norms, culture conflict, or perceptions of blocked opportunities. Their domain of interest lies in the analysis of macro-level community variables, such as poverty rate, population shifts, housing conditions, social inequality and relative deprivation.[62] Their theoretical models are grounded on the sophisticated statistical analysis of large aggregate data bases, such as U.S. Census Bu-

≡ CLOSE-UP

The Gang Today

An important element of subcultural theory is the formation of teenage gangs and youth groups. Malcolm Klein has defined gangs as:

> Any denotable adolescent group of youngsters who (a) are generally perceived as a distinct aggregation by others in their neighborhood; (b) recognize themselves as a denotable group (almost invariably with a group name); and (c) have been involved in a sufficient number of delinquent incidents to call forth a consistent negative response from neighborhood residents and/or enforcement agencies.

While gangs first developed in the early nineteenth century, it was in the 1950s and early 1960s that the threat of gangs and gang violence swept the public consciousness. It was unusual for a week to go by without a major city newspaper featuring a story on the violent behavior of "bopping gangs" and their colorful leaders and names—the Egyptian Kings, the Young Lords, the Blackstone Rangers. These gangs fought for control of territory or "turf," and gang membership served as a substitute for success in conventional society. Social service and law enforcement agencies directed major efforts to either rehabilitate or destroy the gangs.

By the late 1960s, the gang menace seemed to have disappeared. Some experts attributed the decline of gang activity to successful gang-control programs; for example, in one program a social worker was attached directly to an individual gang to rechannel the energies of gang boys in useful directions (detached street worker). Others believe that gangs were eliminated because police gang-control units infiltrated gangs, arrested leaders, and constantly harassed members. Another explanation for the decline in gang activity was the increase in political awareness that developed during the 1960s. Many gang leaders were directed away from crime and into the social or political activities of groups such as the Black Panthers, civil rights groups, and anti-Vietnam War groups. In addition, many gang members were drafted. Still another explanation is that gang activity diminished because many gang members became active users of heroin and other drugs, which curtailed their group-related criminal activity.

Gang activity began anew in the early 1970s. Walter Miller comments on the New York scene:

> All was quiet on the gang front for almost 10 years. Then, suddenly and without advance warning, the gangs reappeared. Bearing such names as Savage Skulls and Black Assassins, they began to form in the South Bronx in the spring of 1971, quickly spread to other parts of the city, and by 1975 comprised 275 police-verified gangs with 11,000 members. These new and mysteriously merging gangs were far more lethal than their predecessors—heavily armed, incited and directed by violence-hardened older men, and directing their lethal activities far more to the victimization of ordinary citizens than to one another.

---

reau, National Crime Survey, and Uniform Crime Report data.

The beginning of this tradition can be traced to the 1950s and 1960s, when studies conducted by Bernard Lander in Baltimore, David Bordua in Detroit, and Roland Chilton in Indianapolis generally showed that such ecological conditions as substandard housing, low income, and transient households predicted a high incidence of criminality.[63] By implication, this research showed that the structure and quality of a community's social institutions determined its crime rate.

Social ecologists have expanded on these pioneering efforts. They have labored to identify the effects ecological and social conditions have on crime patterns.[64] Some studies have focused directly on the social disorganization variables first articulated by Shaw and Mckay, while others, continuing the strain perspective, are concerned with the effect of disparate economic conditions.

Relative Deprivation

One trend in social ecology theory, reflecting the strain tradition, is that the **relative deprivation** experienced

The Savage Skulls are one of the most violent gangs in the South Bronx.

Gang activity also reemerged in other major cities, especially Philadelphia, Los Angeles, and Chicago.

Today the number of gang youths appears, at least in these major cities, to be at an all-time high. In Los Angeles, well-organized, heavily armed youth gangs seem to be taking over the narcotics trade from traditional organized crime families. Gang control of cocaine and crack distribution has produced both large profits and a corresponding escalation in the level of gang violence. Police in Los Angeles estimate that the increase in gang activity has resulted in the deaths of over 300 people and in 5,000 other violent acts per year. The two largest gangs, the Crips and the Bloods, have a total of 15,000 members, armed with AK-47 assault rifles and other automatic weapons.

Today's gangs seem to be following the path of what Cloward and Ohlin referred to as the criminal subculture. Their goal is profit. With unprocessed cocaine selling for about $20,000 a kilo, 14-year-old gang boys are known to have made $300,000 a year selling on the street. The turf wars of the 50s have given way to commercial conflicts in the 1980s.

Discussion Questions

1. Why should a youth forego the lure of gang profits to work in a menial job?
2. Are teen gangs a substitute for the family, or the beginnings of a new type of organized crime?

SOURCES: Walter Miller, *Violence by Youth Gangs and Youth Groups as a Crime Problem in Major American Cities* (Washington, D.C.: U.S. Government Printing Office, 1975); Malcolm Klein, *Street Gangs and Street Workers* (Englewood Cliffs, N.J.: Prentice-Hall, 1971), p. 13; George Hackett and Michael Lerner, "L.A. Law: Gangs and Crack," *Newsweek* 27 April 1987, pp. 35–36.

---

by some members of society is a direct cause of their criminal behavior. This view is most closely associated with sociologists Judith and Peter Blau. They maintain that a sense of social injustice leads to a state of disorganization and anger, which in turn leads to expressions of hostility and criminal behavior. This sense of injustice is directly related to income inequality in communities in which the poor and wealthy live in close proximity to one another. According to the Blaus' theoretical model, persons residing in an inner-city poverty area, such as those common to New York, Chicago, and Los Angeles, will experience crime-generating status frustration because their neighborhoods are located near some of the most well-to-do areas in the United States. While deprived teenagers can witness wealth and luxury firsthand, they cannot partake of it through conventional means. This condition is felt most acutely by black youths, since black citizens consistently suffer racial and economic deprivations which put them in a lower status with respect to the rest of society.[65]

Research supportive of the relative deprivation model has been conducted by a number of criminologists. Richard Block found that the variable best able to predict Chicago crime rates was the proximity in which poor and wealthy people lived to one another.[66]

Wesley Skogan has linked crime rates to the proximity of middle-class suburbs and lower-class central city areas, a pattern also found by John Farley.[67] Similar findings were obtained by Robert Sampson in a study of crime rates across the United States; however, Sampson found that juveniles may be more immune to economic conditions than adults, and that some forms of antisocial behavior may be motivated by noneconomic factors such as peer pressure.[68]

The relative deprivation view also has been supported by Richard Rosenfeld, whose analysis of national crime patterns suggested that crime rates were high in lower-class areas whose residents had high aspirations (such as obtaining a good education) but lacked the means of achieving them.[69] And, using international data, Harvey Krahn and his associates found that economic inequality has a significant effect on murder rates in democratic nations.[70]

Taken in sum, these studies indicate that people who live in deteriorated areas of the city but are in close proximity to more affluent areas may experience the status frustration which results in crimes such as homicide, robbery, and aggravated assault.[71]

Urbanism

Some social ecologists have questioned whether perceptions of inequality alone can explain crime rates.[72] Alternative views of the relationship between social ecology and the crime rate are currently being formulated.[73] There is a growing body of important research studies which indicates that it is the influence of living in an urban environment, or **urbanism,** which produces crimogenic conditions.[74] Factors related to urbanism, such as social disorder, levels of alienation and disassociation, and fear of crime, may alone be able to explain crime rates.[75] For example, research conducted by such authorities as Steven Messner and Kenneth Tardiff shows that while measures of relative economic inequality are only weakly related to murder rates, the percentage of the population living in poverty and the percent of broken homes are strongly related to area homicide rates.[76]

In a similar vein, Richard McGahey's analysis of delinquency-producing economic conditions in urban areas found evidence that neighborhoods with little employment opportunities for youths and adults were the most vulnerable to predatory crime.[77] Unemploy-

ment helps destabilize households. Unstable families are the ones most vulnerable to producing children who put a premium on violence and aggressiveness as a means of dealing with limited opportunity; for example, physical prowess is a way of providing a social identity. A lack of employment opportunities also reduces the number of older people on the street, resulting in a domination of street life by youth gangs. According to McGahey, these community patterns lead to the fear of crime and increased opportunities for predatory crime. Although even the most deteriorated neighborhoods have a surprising degree of kinship strength, the consistent pattern of crime and neighborhood disorganization can soon overcome them.

Can people living in high risk urban areas alter their lifestyle and routine activities to reduce the risk of victimization? Robert Sampson argues that the probability of victimization is greater in impersonalized urban environments. High-density population increases the chance of contact with predatory strangers and decreases the ability to guard against victimization.[78] Living in a high-risk urban area may also increase the probability of victimization, regardless of defensive measures such as walking in pairs, avoiding bars, buying a burglar alarm, or staying home at night.[79]

If crime and urbanism are closely associated, can change in the urban structure effect crime rates? Leo Scheurman and Solomon Kobrin found that communities go through cycles, in which neighborhood deterioration precedes increasing rates of crime and delinquency.[80] Communities which may experience a rapid increase in antisocial behavior are likely to be middle-aged rather than old, are experiencing rapid increases in the number of single parent families and unrelated people living together, have undergone changes in land use from owner-occupied to renter-occupied units, and have an economic base that has witnessed a loss of semi-skilled and unskilled jobs (indicating a growing residue of discouraged workers who are no longer seeking employment).[81]

Looking at this relationship from another perspective, Janet Heitgerd and Robert Bursik have found that areas which are adjoined to neighborhoods undergoing racial change will experience corresponding increases in their crime rates.[82] The authors speculate that this phenomenon may reflect community reaction to perceived racial conflict. Adults may support law-violating behavior of youths which is directed at keeping racial minorities out of the neighborhood and maintaining the traditional way of life. This research reflects another aspect of community strain on delinquent behavior.

The association between crime and urbanism holds that social disorganization and neighborhood deterioration are directly related to criminality. And although recent research efforts have not found the same pattern of stable community disorganization originally projected by Shaw and McKay, many of the relationships formulated by the early cultural deviance theorists between crime and community structure seem relevant today.[83]

EVALUATION OF SOCIAL STRUCTURE THEORIES

The social structure approach has had a significant influence on both criminological theory and crime-prevention strategy. Its core hypothesis seem valid, considering the high crime rate of inner-city slum areas. Most people's image of the slum includes roaming bands of violent teenage gangs, drug users, prostitutes, muggers, and similar frightening examples of criminality.

Despite such associations, it is still not certain whether a causal relationship exists between crime rates and environmental factors. First, a number of recent research studies have failed to find a significant relationship between community variables, such as poverty rate and housing values, and individual crime rates.[84] Secondly, criminologists criticize the social structure approach because it fails to account for the crimes found among the middle and upper classes, ranging from the drug use of suburban high schoolers to the white-collar crimes committed by their parents. Certainly these offenses cannot be explained away by such concepts as strain, cultural deviance, or relative deprivation. Because of this omission, the social structure tradition can be criticized. Its reliance on official statistics which only report the crimes of the lower classes appears to leave social structure theory too narrow in its focus.

Another question left unanswered by social structure theory is whether the various social classes are truly independent and culturally distinct. There are

several reasons to doubt the cultural diversity hypothesized by social structure theory. Public opinion polls show that a majority of lower-class citizens maintain middle-class values. For example, a national survey found that people earning under $3,000 were more likely to advocate more spending to stop crime than citizens who earned more than $15,000 a year. Similarly, about the same percentage of citizens earning less than $10,000 rated police as being honest and ethical as those earning more than $50,000 a year.[85] These opinions seem similar to conventional middle-class values, rather than representative of an independent, deviant subculture. In addition, several researchers have found that gang boys and other delinquent youths seem to value middle-class concepts such as sharing, earning money, respecting the law, and receiving an education as highly as middle-class youths.[86]

Social structure theorists counter these dissenting views by reminding critics that their purpose is to explain why *crime rates* are higher in some areas than in others. Any explanation of criminality which focuses solely on individual differences, traits, or characteristics fails to address this issue. Even if a particular individual trait, such as IQ, personality, or body build, were found to be associated with criminality, it still would not explain why people who have those traits are more likely to commit crime if they live in one area of the environment rather than in another.

The development of social ecological models has reawakened interest in social structure theory. There is growing concern for the role of the community in the production and distribution of crime rates. Intriguing questions have been posed about the ecology of crime that still require informative answers. For example, Rodney Stark argues that some neighborhoods draw crime-prone people to them because of lax law enforcement. Already stigmatized neighborhoods become "the 'soft spot' for drugs, prostitution and the like."[87] As James Q. Wilson and Richard Herrnstein suggest, "A neighborhood may have much crime because conditions there cause it or because certain kinds of neighborhoods attract persons predisposed to criminality."[88] Are some neighborhoods crime magnets, drawing criminogenic people to them? Or do people get involved in crime because their surroundings give them no other choice? Questions such as this will be the continuing focus of social structure theorists. An overview of social struc-

TABLE 7.2 Social Structure Theories

Theory	Major Premise	Strengths	Unanswered Questions and Other Weaknesses
Cultural Deviance Theories			
Shaw and McKay's Ecological Theory	Crime is a product of transitional neighborhoods that manifest social disorganization and value conflict.	Identifies why crime rates are highest in slum areas. Points out the factors that produce crime. Suggests programs to help reduce crime.	Why does middle-class crime occur? Why are some youths insulated from a delinquent career? What causes gang members to forego criminality as adults? How accurate are official statistics?
Sellin's Culture Conflict Theory	Obedience to the norms of their lower-class culture puts people in conflict with the norms of the dominant culture.	Identifies the aspects of lower-class life that produce street crime. Adds to Shaw and McKay's analysis. Creates the concept of culture conflict.	Ignores middle-class crime. Does not provide an adequate means of testing theoretical premises. Uses vague terms (e.g., *conduct norms*).
Miller's Lower-Class Culture Conflict Theory	Citizens who obey the street rules of lower-class life (focal concerns) find themselves in conflict with the dominant culture.	Identifies more coherently the elements of lower-class culture that push people into committing street crimes.	Does not provide empirical support for the existence of a lower-class culture. Does not account for middle-class influence. Does not explain upper-class crime.
Strain Theories			
Merton's Theory of Anomie	People who adopt the goals of society but lack the means to attain them seek alternatives such as crime.	Points out how success goal creates conflict and crime. Suggests that social conditions and not personality can account for crime. Can explain middle- and upper-class crime.	Does not explain why people choose the crime patterns they do. Does not account for violent and senseless acts.
Subcultural Theories			
Cohen's Theory of Delinquent Subcultures	Status frustration of lower-class boys, created by their failure to achieve middle-class success, causes them to join gangs.	Shows how the conditions of lower-class life produce crime. Explains violence and destructive acts. Identifies conflict of lower class with middle class.	Does not account for middle-class crime. Has not been empirically tested. Research efforts have been inconclusive. Ignores delinquency that is rational and profitable.
Cloward and Ohlin's Theory of Differential Opportunity	Blockage of conventional opportunities causes lower-class youths to join criminal, conflict, or retreatist gangs.	Shows that even illegal opportunities are structured in society. Indicates why people become involved in a particular type of criminal activity. Presents a way of preventing crime.	Does not account for middle-class crime. Assumes that lower-class citizens have the same values as the middle class. Gang surveys indicate that delinquent gang boys do not specialize in one type of crime.
Social Ecology Theories			
Relative Deprivation	Crime occurs when the wealthy and poor live in close proximity to one another.	Explains high crime rates in deteriorated inner-city areas.	Does not account for noncriminals in poor areas. Is limited to explaining urban crime rates.
Urbanism	The conflicts and problems of urban social life and communities control the crime rate.	Accounts for urban crime rates and trends.	Is limited to urban crime rates. Does not account for individual differences.

SOURCES: Faith Lamb Parker, Chaya Piorkowski, and Lenore Peay, "Head Start as Social Support for Mothers: The Psychological Benefits of Involvement," *American Journal of Orthopsychiatry* 57 (1987):220–33; Seymour Sarason and Michael Klaber, "The School As A Social Situation," *Annual Review of Psychology* 36 (1985):115–40; Spencer Rathus, *Psychology*, 3d ed. (New York: Holt, Rinehart and Winston, 1987), p. 308.

CLOSE-UP

Head Start

One of the most well-known efforts to help lower-class youths achieve proper socialization and in so doing reduce their potential for future criminality, is the Head Start program. Head Start programs were instituted in the 1960s as part of the Johnson Administration's War on Poverty. Today there are over 9,400 centers around the nation servicing 500,000 children and their families, on a budget of over $1 billion annually. They are government-funded efforts to provide underprivileged preschoolers with an enriched educational environment to develop their learning and cognitive skills. Children in these programs are given the opportunity to use pegs and pegboards, puzzles, toy animals, dolls, letters and numbers, and other materials that middle-class youths take for granted and which give them a leg up in the educational process.

There has been considerable controversy surrounding the success of the Head Start program. In 1970, the Westinghouse Learning Corporation issued a definitive evaluation of the Head Start effort and concluded that there was no evidence of lasting cognitive gains on the part of the participating children. Initial gains seemed to evaporate during the elementary school years, and by the third grade the performance of the Head Start children was no different than their peers. However, more recent research has produced dramatically different results. One report found that by age five, children who experienced enriched day care averaged 30 points higher on their IQ scores than their peers who did not utilize the program. Other research that carefully compared Head Start children to similar youths who did not attend the program found that the former made significant intellectual gains: Head Start children were less likely to have been left back or placed in classes for slow learners; they outperformed peers on achievement tests; and, they were more likely to graduate from high school. In addition, research by Faith Lamb Parker shows that the Head Start program can have important psychological benefits for the mothers of participants, such as decreasing depression and anxiety and increasing feelings of life satisfaction.

If, as many experts believe, there is a close link between school performance, family life, and crime programs such as Head Start can help some potentially criminal youths avoid problems with the law. By implication, their success indicates that programs which help socialize youngsters can be used to combat urban criminality.

ture, subculture and social ecology theories is given in Table 7.2.

SOCIAL STRUCTURE THEORY AND SOCIAL POLICY

Social structure theory has profoundly affected social policy. If the cause of criminality is viewed as a function of living in an area marked by poverty and social disorganization, it seems logical that alternatives to criminal behavior can be provided by giving the disadvantaged residents of these areas opportunities to share in the goals and benefits of society.

Crime-prevention efforts based on social structure precepts can be traced back to the Chicago Area Project, supervised by Clifford R. Shaw. This program attempted to organize existing community structures in slum areas, in order to develop social stability. The project sponsored recreation programs for children in the neighborhood, including summer camping. It campaigned for community improvement in such areas as education, sanitation, traffic safety, physical conservation, and law enforcement. Project members also worked with police and court agencies to supervise and treat gang youth and adult offenders. In a 25-year assessment of the project, Solomon Kobrin found that it was successful in demonstrating the feasibility of creating youth welfare organizations in high-delinquency areas.[89] Kobrin also discovered that the project made a distinct contribution to channeling urban males back into the mainstream of society.

Social structure concepts, especially the views of Cloward and Ohlin, were a critical ingredient in the Kennedy and Johnson Administrations' War on Poverty, begun in the early 1960s. Rather than organizing existing community structures, as Shaw's Chicago Area Project had done, this later effort called for an all-out attack on the crime-producing structures of slum areas.

The cornerstone of the War on Poverty's crime-prevention effort was called Mobilization for Youth (MFY). This New York City–based program was funded for over $12 million. It was designed to serve multiple purposes: it provided teacher training and education to help educators deal with problem youth; created work opportunities through a youth job center; organized neighborhood councils and associations; provided street workers to deal with teen gangs; and set up counseling services and assistance for neighborhood families. Subsequent War on Poverty programs included the Job Corps; VISTA (the urban Peace Corps); Head Start (see accompanying Close-Up) and Upward Bound (educational enrichment programs); Neighborhood Legal Services; and the largest community organizing effort, the Community Action Program (CAP).[90]

War on Poverty programs such as Mobilization for Youth were sweeping efforts to change the social structure of the slum area. They sought to reduce crime by developing a sense of community pride and solidarity and by providing educational and job opportunities. Unfortunately, the programs failed. Federal and state funding often fell into the hands of middle-class managers and community developers, rather than to the people it was designed to help. Managers were accused of graft and corruption. Some community organizers engineered rent strikes, lawsuits, and protests, which angered government officials and convinced them that financial backing of such programs should be ended. Rather than appeal to the political power structure, program administrators alienated them. Still later, the mood of the country began to change. The more conservative political climate under the Nixon, Ford, Carter, and Reagan Administrations did not favor federal sponsorship of radical change in U.S. cities. Instead of a total community approach to solving the crime problem, a more selective crime prevention policy was adopted (see Chapters 5 and 8). Some War on Poverty programs—Head Start, Neighborhood Legal Services, and the Community Action Program—have continued to give people aid. Nonetheless, as an attempt to change the very structure of society, it must be judged for now a noble failure.

SUMMARY

Sociological theory links crime to social institutions and processes. There are three main areas of sociological criminology: social structure theory, social process theory, and social conflict theory. Sociology has been the main orientation of criminologists because they know that crime rates vary among elements of the social structure, that society goes through changes that affect crime, and that social interaction relates to criminality.

Social structure theories suggest that people's places in the socioeconomic structure of society influence their chances of becoming criminal. Poor people are more likely to commit crimes because they are unable to achieve monetary or social success in any other way.

Social structure theory has four main schools of thought: cultural deviance theory, strain theory, subcultural theory, and social ecology theory. Cultural deviance theory suggests that residents of poverty areas violate the law because they adhere to a unique value system existing within their environment. Lower-class values approve of behaviors such as being tough, never showing fear, and defying authority. The origin of cultural deviance theory is traced to the Chicago School. Clifford R. Shaw and Henry D. McKay's ecological maps of Chicago showed the concentration of delinquents in the most decayed and poverty-stricken inner-city areas; they concluded that disorganized areas marked by divergent values and transitional populations produced criminality. Thorstein Sellin's culture conflict theory suggests that conduct norms that reflect the rules of small social groups are the key to crime causation. When persons adhere to the conduct norms of one group, they may find themselves in conflict with the rules of conventional society. Similarly, Walter Miller's theory of lower-class culture conflict suggests that lower-class citizens maintain a unique group of focal concerns that result in their committing law violations.

Strain theories comprise the second branch of the social structure approach. They view crime as a result of the anger people experience over their inability to achieve legitimate social and economic success. Strain theories hold that most people share common values and beliefs but that the ability to achieve them is differentiated throughout the social structure. The best-known strain theory is Robert Merton's theory of anomie, which describes what happens when the means people have at their disposal are not adequate to satisfy their goals.

The third branch of social structure theory, subcultural strain theories, are an extension of Merton's work. They suggest that people perceiving strain will bond together in their own groups or subcultures for support and recognition. Albert Cohen links the formation of subcultures to the failure of lower-class citizens to achieve recognition from middle-class decision-makers, or live up to middle-class measuring rods. Similarly, Richard Cloward and Lloyd Ohlin have argued that crime results from lower-class people's perception that their opportunity for success is limited. Consequently, youths in low-income areas may join criminal, conflict, or retreatist gangs.

The most recent form of social structure theory involves analysis of aggregate data comparing community structure and crime rates. The social ecological approach holds that residence in a deteriorated inner-city area, where relative deprivation may be apparent, can have a negative influence on crime rates.

However, empirical research on social structure theory has not provided clear-cut evidence that it is a valid explanation of the cause of crime. Some studies show that crime is prevalent in the middle and upper classes as well as in lower-class culture; this may be interpreted as being in opposition to the social structure approach. On the other hand, recent studies have differentiated between lower- and middle-class crime. Research has also indicated that, though gangs do exist in lower-class areas, they may not take the forms predicted by social structure theorists.

Social structure theories have been influential in shaping social policy. In the 1960s, community action and delinquency prevention programs were based on concepts of Cloward and Ohlin's differential opportunity theory.

KEY TERMS

cartographic school
stratified
culture of poverty
underclass
social structure theory
cultural deviance theory
cultural transmission theory
culture conflict theory
strain theory
subcultural theory
social ecology
transitional neighborhood
social disorganization
conduct norms

Walter Miller
lower-class culture conflict
theory of anomie
goals
means
subcultures
status frustration
middle-class measuring rods
short-run hedonism
group autonomy
reaction formation
differential opportunity
relative deprivation
urbanism

NOTES

1. Daniel Bell, *The Coming of Post-Industrial Society* (New York: Basic Books, 1973).
2. Rolf Loeber and Magda Stouthamer-Loeber, "Models and Meta-Analysis of the Relationship between Family Variables and Juvenile Conduct Problems and Delinquency," In Norval Morris and Michael Tonry, eds., *Crime and Justice: An Annual Review of Research*, vol. 7 (Chicago: University of Chicago Press, 1986).
3. Edwin Lemert, *Human Deviance, Social Problems and Social Control* (Englewood Cliffs, N.J.: Prentice-Hall, 1967).
4. L. A. J. Quetelet, *A Treatise on Man and the Development of His Faculties* (Gainesville, Fla.: Scholars' Facsimiles and Reprints, 1969), pp. 82–96.
5. *Ibid.*, p. 95.
6. Robert Nisbet, *The Sociology of Emile Durkheim* (New York: Oxford University Press, 1974), p. 209.
7. Emile Durkheim, *Rules of the Sociological Method*, trans. S. A. Solvay and J. H. Mueller, ed. G. Catlin (New York: Free Press, 1966), pp. 65–73.
8. "Twenty-Eight Percent of Wealth Held by 2.8 Percent of Population," *Omaha World Herald*, 8 March 1985, p. 48.
9. Physician Task Force on Hunger in America, *Hunger Reaches Blue-Collar America: An Unbalanced Recovery in a Service Economy* (Cambridge, Mass.: Harvard University, 1987).
10. Jon Shepherd, *Sociology* (St. Paul, Minn.: West Publishing, 1981), p. 202.
11. Daniel Lichter, "Racial Differences in Underemployment in American Cities," *American Journal of Sociology*

93 (1988):771–92.

12. Alex Kotlowitz, "Blacks' Hopes Raised by '68 Kerner Report, Are Mainly Unfulfilled," *Wall Street Journal* 26 February 1988, p. 1.

13. UPI, "U.S.: One in Four Children Had Single Parent," *Boston Globe*, 21 January 1988, p. 21.

14. "One in Five Children Live in Poverty," *Omaha World Herald*, 1 March 1984, p. 17A.

15. Oscar Lewis, "The Culture of Poverty," *Scientific American* 215 (1966):19–25.

16. Gunnar Myrdal, *The Challenge of World Poverty* (New York: Vintage Books, 1970); Ken Auletta, *The Under Class* (New York: Random House, 1982).

17. Physician Task Force on Hunger, *Hunger Reaches Blue-Collar America*, pp. 11–12.

18. Robert E. Park, "The City: Suggestions for the Investigation of Human Behavior in the Urban Environment," in Robert E. Park, ed., *Human Communities* (New York: Free Press, 1952), pp. 13–51.

19. Harvey Zorbaugh, *The Gold Coast and the Slum* (Chicago: University of Chicago Press, 1929); Frederick Thrasher, *The Gang* (Chicago: University of Chicago Press, 1927); Louis Wirth, *The Ghetto* (Chicago: University of Chicago Press, 1928).

20. Clifford R. Shaw and Henry D. McKay, *Juvenile Delinquency and Urban Areas*, rev. ed. (Chicago: University of Chicago Press, 1972).

21. Anthony Platt, *The Child Savers: The Invention of Delinquency* (Chicago: University of Chicago Press, 1968).

22. Clifford Shaw, *The Natural History of a Delinquent Career* (Philadelphia: Albert Saifer, 1951), p. 15.

23. Shaw and McKay, *Juvenile Delinquency and Urban Areas*, p. 52.

24. *Ibid.*, p. 171.

25. Thorsten Sellin, *Culture Conflict and Crime*, bulletin no. 41 (New York: Social Science Research Council, 1938).

26. *Ibid.*, p. 22.

27. *Ibid.*, p. 29.

28. *Ibid.*, p. 68.

29. Walter Miller, "Lower-Class Culture as a Generating Milieu of Gang Delinquency," *Journal of Social Issues* 14 (1958):5–19.

30. *Ibid.*, p. 13.

31. *Ibid.*, p. 14–17.

32. Robert Merton, *Social Theory and Social Structure*, enlarged ed. (New York: Free Press, 1968).

33. *Ibid.*, p. 234.

34. *Ibid.*, p. 236.

35. Leo Srole, "Social Integration and Certain Corollaries," *American Sociological Review* 21 (1956):709–16.

36. For a general review, see, M. Rosenberg, *Society and the Adolescent Self-Image* (Princeton, N.J.: Princeton University Press, 1965).

37. Albert Cohen, "The Sociology of the Deviant Act: Anomie Theory and Beyond," *American Sociological Review* 30 (1965):5–14.

38. Albert Cohen, *Delinquent Boys* (New York: Free Press, 1955).

39. *Ibid.*, p. 25.

40. *Ibid.*, p. 28.

41. *Ibid.*

42. Clarence Schrag, *Crime and Justice American Style* (Washington, D.C.: U.S. Government Printing Office, 1971), p. 74.

43. Cohen, *Delinquent Boys*, p. 30.

44. *Ibid.*, p. 31.

45. *Ibid.*, p. 133.

46. John Kitsuse and David Detrick, "Delinquent Boys: A Critique," *American Sociological Review* 24 (1958):20.

47. Albert Cohen and James Short, "Research on Delinquent Subcultures," *Journal of Social Issues* 14 (1958):20.

48. Albert Reiss and H. Lewis Rhodes, "The Distribution of Delinquency in the Social Class Structure," *American Sociological Review* 26 (1961):720–32.

49. M. Krohn, R. Akers, M. Radosovich, and L. Lanza-Kaduce, "Social Stratus and Deviance," *Criminology* 18 (1980):303–17.

50. J. Johnstone, "Social Class, Social Areas, and Delinquency," *Sociology and Social Research* 63 (1978):49–72; Joseph Harry, "Social Class and Delinquency: One More Time," *Sociological Quarterly* 15 (1974):294–301.

51. Richard Cloward and Lloyd Ohlin, *Delinquency and Opportunity* (New York: Free Press, 1960).

52. *Ibid.*, p. 7.

53. *Ibid.*, p. 85.

54. *Ibid.*, p. 23.

55. *Ibid.*, p. 171.

56. *Ibid.*, p. 24.

57. *Ibid.*, p. 73.

58. Judson Landis and Frank Scarpitti, "Perceptions Regarding Value Orientation and Legitimate Opportunity: Delinquents and Non-Delinquents," *Social Forces* 84 (1965):57–61.

59. James Short, Ramon Rivera, and Ray Tennyson, "Perceived Opportunities, Gang Membership and Delinquency," *American Sociological Review* 30 (1965):56–57.

60. Leon Fannin and Marshall Clinard, "Differences in the Conception of Self as a Male among Lower- and Middle-Class Delinquents," *Social Problems* 13 (1965):205–15.

61. LaMar Empey and Maynard Erickson, "Class Position, Peers, and Delinquency," *Sociology and Social Research* 49 (1965):268–82.

62. Peter Blau, *Inequality and Heterogeneity: A Primitive Theory of Social Structure* (New York: Free Press, 1977).

63. Bernard Lander, *Towards an Understanding of Juvenile*

Delinquency (New York: Columbia University Press, 1954); David Bordua, "Juvenile Delinquency and 'Anomie': An Attempt at Replication," *Social Problems* 6 (1958):230–38; Roland Chilton, "Continuities in Delinquency Area Research: A Comparison of Studies in Baltimore, Detroit, and Indianapolis," *American Sociological Review* 29 (1964):71–73.

64. For a general review, see, James Byrne and Robert Sampson, *The Social Ecology of Crime* (New York: Springer-Verlag, 1985); Albert Reiss and Michael Tonry, *Communities and Crime* (Chicago: University of Chicago Press, 1986).

65. Judith Blau and Peter Blau, "The Cost of Inequality: Metropolitan Structure and Violent Crime," *American Sociological Review* 147 (1982):114–29.

66. Richard Block, "Community Environment and Violent Crime," *Criminology* 17 (1979):46–57.

67. Wesley Skogan, "The Changing Distribution of Big-City Crime: A Multi-City Time Series Analysis," *Urban Affairs Quarterly* 13 (1977):33–48; John Farley, "Suburbanization and Central City Crime Rates: New Evidence and a Reinterpretation," *American Journal of Sociology* 93 (1987):688–700.

68. Robert Sampson, "Structural Sources of Variation in Race-Age-Specific Rates of Offending Across Major U.S. Cities," *Criminology* 23 (1985):647–73.

69. Richard Rosenfeld, "Urban Crime Rates: Effects of Inequality, Welfare Dependency, Region and Race," in Byrne and Sampson, *The Social Ecology of Crime*, pp. 116–30.

70. Harvey Krahn, Timothy Hartnagel, and John Gartrell, "Income Inequality and Homicide Rates: Cross-National Data and Criminological Theories," *Criminology* 24 (1986):269–95.

71. See also, Peter Blau and Reid Golden, "Metropolitan Structure and Criminal Violence," *Sociological Quarterly* 27 (1986):15–26.

72. Reid Golden and Steven Messner, "Dimensions of Racial Inequality and Rates of Violent Crime," *Criminology* 25 (1987):525–41.

73. Leo Carroll and Pamela Irving Jackson, "Inequality, Opportunity, and Crime Rates in Central Cities," *Criminology* 21 (1983):178–94.

74. John Laub, "Urbanism, Race, and Crime," *Journal of Research in Crime and Delinquency* 20 (1983):183–98.

75. Ora Simcha-Fagan and Joseph Schwartz, "Neighborhood and Delinquency: An Assessment of Contextual Effects," *Criminology* 24 (1986):667–703.

76. Steven Messner and Kenneth Tardiff, "Economic Inequality and Levels of Homicide: An Analysis of Urban Neighborhoods," *Criminology* 24 (1986):297–317.

77. Richard McGahey, "Economic Conditions, Organization, and Urban Crime," in Reiss and Tonry, eds., *Communities and Crime*, pp. 231–70.

78. Robert Sampson, "Personal Violence by Strangers: An Extension and Test of the Opportunity Model of Predatory Victimization," *Journal of Criminal Law and Criminology* 78 (1987):327–56.

79. *Ibid.*, p. 355.

80. Leo Scheurman and Solomon Kobrin, "Community Careers in Crime," in Reiss and Tonry, eds., *Communities and Crime*, pp. 67–100.

81. *Ibid.*, p. 96.

82. Janet Heitgerd and Robert Bursik, Jr., "Extracommunity Dynamics and the Ecology of Delinquency," *American Journal of Sociology* 92 (1987):775–87.

83. Douglas Smith and G. Roger Jarjoura, "Social Structure and Criminal Victimization," *Journal of Research in Crime and Delinquency* 25 (1988):27–52.

84. Denise Gottfredson, Rich McNeil, and Gary Gottfredson, "Community Influences on Individual Delinquency," Paper presented at the American Society of Criminology meeting, Montreal, Canada, November, 1987; Ora Simcha-Fagan and Joseph Schwartz, "Neighborhood and Delinquency: An Assessment of Contextural Effects," *Criminology* 24 (1986):667–703.

85. Katherine Jamieson and Timothy Flanagan, *Sourcebook of Criminal Justice Statistics—1986* (Washington, D.C.: U.S. Government Printing Office, 1987), p. 188.

86. Kenneth Polk and F. Lynn Richmond, "Those Who Fail," in Kenneth Polk and Walter Schafer, eds., *Schools and Delinquency* (Englewood Cliffs, N.J.: Prentice-Hall, 1974), p. 67.

87. Rodney Stark, "Deviant Places: A Theory of the Ecology of Crime," *Criminology* 25 (1987): 903.

88. James Q. Wilson and Richard Herrnstein, *Crime and Human Nature* (New York: Simon and Schuster, 1985), p. 291.

89. Solomon Kobrin, "The Chicago Area Project–25-Year Assessment," *Annals of the American Academy of Political and Social Science* 322 (1959):20–29.

90. See, Barry Krisberg and James Austin, *Children of Ishmael* (Palo Alto, Cal.: Mayfield Publishing, 1978), p. 37.

≡ CHAPTER 8

SOCIOLOGICAL
APPROACHES:
SOCIAL
PROCESS
THEORIES

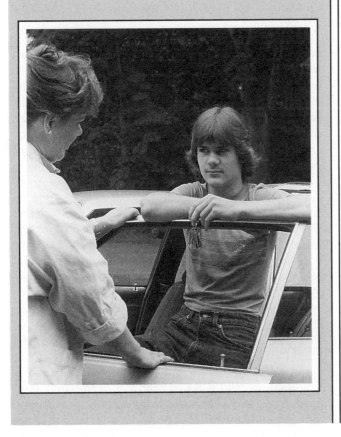

CHAPTER OUTLINE

Introduction

Social Processes and Crime

Social Process Theories

Social Learning Theories
Differential Association Theory
Differential Reinforcement Theory
Neutralization Theory

Control Theories
Hirschi's Control Theory
Analysis of Control Theory

Labeling Theory
Crime and Labeling Theory
Differential Enforcement
Becoming Labeled
Consequences of Labeling
Research on Labeling Theory
Analysis of Labeling Theory

Integrated Theories
Social Development Theory
Elliott's Integrated Theory
Interactional Theory

An Evaluation of Social Process Theory

Social Process Theory and Social Policy

INTRODUCTION

Not all criminologists believe that a person's place in the social structure controls his or her criminal behavior patterns. After all, many people who reside in the most deteriorated areas of the country are law-abiding citizens who compensate for their financial problems by hard work, frugal living, and an eye to the future. Conversely, many members of the privileged classes engage in theft, drug use, and other crimes. To explain these theoretical discrepancies, some criminologists focus their attention on **social processes** lying outside the economic sphere.

Social process theories hold that criminality is a function of individual **socialization** and the sociopsychological interactions people have with the various organizations, institutions, and processes of society. For example, people may be influenced toward criminal behavior by poor familial relationships, peer group pressure, lack of educational success, or negative reactions by agents of the justice system. They may have differences of opinion, but all social process theorists share one basic concept: *people in all walks of life have the potential to become delinquents or criminals.* Although lower-class citizens may have the added burden of poverty, racism, and low status, even middle- or upper-class citizens may turn to crime if their life experiences are intolerable or destructive. Consequently, social process theorists focus their attention on the socialization of youths and attempt to identify the developmental factors—family relationships, peer influences, educational difficulties, self-image development—which lead them first into delinquent behavior and then to adult criminality.

The social process view reached its zenith in the 1960s and 1970s, because other criminological theories seemed inadequate as an explanation of existing crime patterns. Self-report studies made it clear that many youths from middle-class backgrounds engaged in frequent and serious criminal behavior. Even college students seemed to be engaging in widespread drug use. Because so many middle-class people began to reject conventional goals and values, the forces associated with crime and deviance seemed to be operating at all levels of the social structure. Social process theories became dominant because they avoided the narrow focus of the prevailing social structure approaches.

SOCIAL PROCESSES AND CRIME

Criminologists have long studied the critical elements of socialization to determine how they contribute to the development of a criminal career. Prominent among these elements are the family, peer group, school, and agents of the criminal justice system.

The family has long been considered a major determinant of criminal or conventional behavior.[1] It is alleged that youths who grow up in a household characterized by conflict and tension, where parents are absent or separated, or where there is a lack of familial love and support, will be susceptible to the crime-promoting forces in the environment.[2] Conversely, some criminologists maintain that even those children living in so-called high-crime areas will be better able to resist the temptations of the streets if they receive fair discipline, care, and support from parents who provide them with strong, positive role models.[3] The relationship between family structure and crime is critical when the high divorce and single-parent rate is considered: in 1960, there were 35 divorced people for every 1,000 in an intact marriage; today there are 131 per 1,000.[4]

Numerous studies have suggested a relationship between experiences in the family and crime. At one time growing up in a **broken home** was considered a primary cause of criminal behavior; the prevailing view tends to discount the association between family structure and the onset of delinquency.[5] However, some recent research indicates that family disruption may be significantly associated with particular crime patterns.[6]

Family factors now considered to have the greatest predictive value for criminal behavior include inconsistent discipline, poor supervision, and lack of a warm, loving, supportive parent-child relationship. Intrafamily conflict and parental deviance also have been linked to a child's criminal behavior. Of recent interest has been the link between child abuse, neglect, or sexual abuse and crime.[7] A growing number of studies are finding that people who were abused as children are likely to engage in violent crime when they mature into adulthood.[8] (See the Close-Up entitled "Socialization and Crime.")

A person's relationship with school and the educational process also has been linked to criminality. Studies show that children who do poorly in school, lack educational motivation, and feel alienated are

A person's relationship with school and the educational process is linked to his or her subsequent criminality.

the most likely to engage in criminal acts.[9] Schools help contribute to criminality when they set problem youths apart from conventional society, by creating track systems that identify some students as college-bound and others as academic underachievers or potential drop-outs.[10] School failure also has been closely linked to criminal career formation. Recent research by Terence Thornberry, Melanie Moore, and R. L. Christenson indicates that school drop-outs face a significant chance of entering a criminal career.[11] It is not surprising that U.S. school systems have been the subject of recent criticism concerning its methods, goals, and objectives.[12] Most importantly, surveys indicate an extraordinary amount of serious criminal behavior occurs within the schools themselves.[13]

Peer group and peer relations also have been the focus of significant criminological inquiry. It is believed that much adolescent criminal activity begins as a group process, and that the delinquent gang is the spawning ground of adult criminals. Surveys indicate that possibly over a million youths belong to delinquent gangs and law-violating youth groups.[14] Delinquent peers exert tremendous influence on a person's behavior, attitudes, and beliefs. In every element of the social structure, those youths who fall in with a "bad crowd" become more susceptible to delinquent,

and later criminal, behavior patterns.

Finally, some criminologists believe that youths labeled by the agents of society as outsiders, delinquents, criminals, or deviants will internalize these labels and accept them as fitting portrayals of their character. For example, the person whom teachers consider unmanageable or in need of special education will perceive these views as accurate, since they come from those in power.[15] After the label is bestowed, such students may feel conventional modes of success are closed to them and subsequently seek illegal modes of gaining respect or achievement; this is referred to as a **self-fulfilling prophecy.**

⟩SOCIAL PROCESS THEORIES

To many criminologists, socialization experiences are the chief determinants of criminal behavior. They claim that people living in even the most deteriorated urban areas can successfully survive inducements to crime if they have the support of their parents, peers, and neighbors. They point to studies showing an absence of a clear-cut relationship between social class and crime rates (see Chapter 4) as proof that forces other than economic ones influence criminal behavior.

☰ CLOSE-UP

Socialization and Crime

Social process theory holds that a turbulent home life, poor school relations, lack of family ties, and other personal problems are at the root of the crime problem. It therefore follows that people who have been involved in crime should manifest a significant amount of these problems. In order to test this assumption, the federal government sponsored a survey of the nation's prison inmates. Some of the survey findings are reprinted below.

Relationship of an Offender's Background to Crime Debatable

There is no agreement over the relationship between crime and various social and economic factors. Some researchers believe that crime results from deprived backgrounds, while others see criminal behavior as another symptom of maladjustment. Whatever the relationship might be, we can measure certain characteristics of offenders and compare them to the population as a whole to give a profile of the offending population. This profile does not indicate which came first, the social and economic characteristic or the criminal behavior. It also does not explain why some people with similar characteristics do commit crimes and others do not.

Single-Parent Homes

About 48 percent of jail and prison inmates grew up primarily with one parent or other relatives. In 1980, 20 percent of the children under age 18 in the United States were living with one parent. Moreover about 15 percent of the jail inmates and 16 percent of the prison inmates grew up with neither parent, whereas 4 percent of all children under age 18 in the United States in 1980 were living with neither parent. Some studies suggest that the relationship between family background and delinquency is particularly strong for females.

Childhood Abuse Victims

A study of inmates at the California Institution for Men at San Quentin found that many had been abused extensively as children. Although data are limited, some studies suggest that adolescents subjected to extreme abuse and violence at home may develop psychotic symptoms, neurological abnormalities, and violent behavior.

Relatives Who Served Time

About 40 percent of the prison inmates in 1979 and 34 percent of the jail inmates in 1983 had an immediate family member (father, mother, brother, sister, spouse, or child) who had been incarcerated in the past. Baunach found that 53 percent of the 180 inmates who were mothers had other family members with criminal records. These family members were primarily siblings (59 percent) and husbands, ex-husbands, or lovers (28 percent).

Unmarried

Among jail and prison inmates—

• About half had never been married and another 24 percent were divorced or separated (vs. 54 percent unmarried and 4 percent divorced or separated among all U.S. males age 20-29).

• 22 percent of the prison and 21 percent of the jail population were married (vs. 47 percent of the comparable U.S. population).

The proportion of divorced and separated whites was much higher in jails and prisons than in the U.S. population; the marital status of black inmates was closer to that of blacks in the U.S. population.

Most Have Dependent Children

Women offenders are more likely than men to have dependent children. In 1979, 74 percent of women prison inmates and 54 percent of the men had dependent children. In jails in 1983, 71 percent of the women and 54 percent of the men had dependent children. Of those inmates who had children, about 67 percent of those in jail and 71 percent of those in prison had 1 or 2 children.

Level of Education

• About 40 percent of all jail and 28 percent of all prison inmates had completed high school as compared to 85 percent of males age 20-29 in the U.S. population.

• About 45 percent of all prison and 41 percent of all jail inmates as compared with 11 percent of the U.S. population of males age 20-29 began but did not complete high school.

• As compared with the U.S. population of males age 20-29, there were few college graduates in jail or prison.

Educational Level and Type of Offense

| Offense | Percent of inmates who completed high school | |
	Jail	Prison
Drug	34	29
Violent	27	21
Property	27	19
Public order	31	18

Unemployment

The highest incarceration rate among U.S. males age 16-64 was among those who were unemployed prior to arrest.

| | Inmates per 100,000 U.S. population | |
	Jail	Prison
In labor force	330	396
Employed	220	356
Unemployed	1,792	933
Not in labor force	323	442
Total	329	405

About 45 percent of all males in jail in 1983 were unemployed at the time they entered jail. Among the 55 percent who were working, 22 percent were working only part-time. In the U.S. male population age 16-64, 84 percent are employed and of these 3 percent work part-time.

High Proportion Lack Steady Employment

Adult felons were more likely than the general population never to have worked at all or to have held a wide variety of short-term jobs. Of the prisoners in a RAND Corporation study, 20 percent had never worked and another 20 percent held a variety of short-term jobs. On average, felons in these groups committed more crimes, particularly more property crimes, than the 60 percent who had had a more stable employment history.

High Proportion of Blue-Collar Workers

Occupation	Prison population	U.S. population age 16-64
White-collar	15	51
Blue-collar	68	33
Farm	2	3
Service	14	13

SOURCES: BJS Survey of Inmates of State Correctional Facilities, 1979, unpublished data. *The current population survey 1972-81: A Data Book,* volume I, Bureau of Labor Statistics Bulletin, September 1982.

Few Work in Their Customary Occupation

Before their arrest, 30 percent of all jail inmates in 1983 who were working were employed outside what they considered to be their customary occupation. Earlier surveys of prison inmates had similar findings. In addition to an inability to find work in their chosen field, this suggests some degree of underemployment.

Poverty Level before Entering Jail

In 1983 about half the males in jail who had been out of jail or prison for at least a year had annual incomes under $5,600, a median income of about half that of men in the general population ($11,848) in 1981. Female jail inmates reported a median income of about $4,000 during the year before arrest, slightly more than half of that for women in the general population ($7,370). The median income for both male and female jail inmates in 1983 did not exceed the poverty level as defined by the U.S. Government.

Income from Nontraditional Sources before Entering Jail

Among jail inmates—

- 22 percent depended on welfare, Social Security, or unemployment benefits
- 7 percent said that their main source of income was illegal
- 60 percent said that their main source of income had been a wage or a salary.

A larger proportion of female than male inmates—

- depended on welfare, unemployment benefits, or Social Security (38 percent vs. 22 percent)
- depended on family or friends for their subsistence (31 percent vs. 23 percent)
- admitted that their main income was from illegal activities (11 percent vs. 7 percent).

Discussion Questions

1. Do these findings support the crime-socialization link?
2. What policy implications can be derived from these findings?

SOURCE: Bureau of Justice Statistics, *Report to The Nation on Crime and Justice,* 2d ed. (Washington, D.C.: U.S. Government Printing Office, 1988), pp. 48-49.

FIGURE 8.1
Social Process Theories

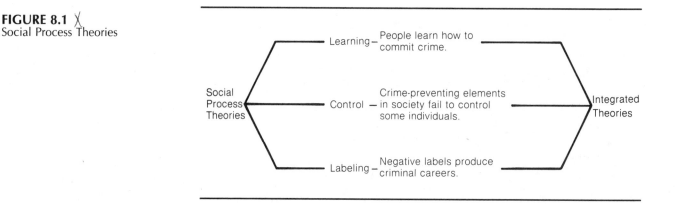

Even if it can be shown that crime rates are actually higher in lower-class areas, the presence of significant amounts of middle- and upper-class crime indicates that the crime problem cannot be explained solely by one's position in the social class structure.

Criminologists who hold these views have produced theoretical models dependent on socio-psychological, social development, and social interaction variables; as a group, these models are referred to as **social process theories.**

Like social structure theories, the social process approach has several independent branches (see Figure 8.1). The first branch, **social learning theory,** suggests that people learn the techniques of crime from intimate relationships with criminal peers. The second, **control theory,** maintains that everyone has the potential to become a criminal but that most people are controlled by their bond to society. The third branch, **labeling theory,** says people become criminals when significant members of society label them as such and they accept those labels. Finally, **integrated theory** attempts to interweave elements of socialization with cultural factors in order to achieve greater explanatory power.

SOCIAL LEARNING THEORIES

Social learning theory holds that crime is a product of learning the norms, values, and behaviors associated with criminal activity. Social learning can involve the actual techniques of crime—how to hotwire a car or roll a joint—as well as the psychological aspects of criminality—how to rationalize or neutralize the guilt or shame associated with illegal activities.

The origins of the social learning perspective can be traced to the late nineteenth century and Gabriel Tarde's *theory of imitation.*[16] Tarde proposed three laws of imitation to describe why people engage in crime. First, individuals in close and intimate contact with one another imitate each other's behavior. Second, imitation spreads from the top down; consequently, youngsters imitate older individuals, the poor imitate the rich, peasants imitate royalty. Crime among young, poor, or low-status people is really their effort to imitate wealthy, older, high-status people.

Tarde's third law is the law of *insertion.* New acts and behaviors are superimposed on old ones and subsequently act either to reinforce or to discourage previous customs. For example, drug-taking may be popular among college students who previously used alcohol. However, students may find that a combination of both substances provides even greater stimulation, causing the use of both drugs and alcohol to increase. Or, a new criminal custom can develop that eliminates an older one—for example, train robbery has been replaced by truck hijacking.

This section briefly reviews the three prominent forms of social learning theory—differential association theory, differential reinforcement theory, and neutralization theory—that are the descendants of Tarde's laws of imitation.

Differential Association Theory

Edwin H. Sutherland, often considered the preeminent U.S. criminologist, first put forth the theory of differential association in 1939, in his text *Principles of*

Criminology.[17] The final form of the theory appeared in 1947. When Sutherland died in 1950, his work was continued by his long-time associate **Donald Cressey.** Cressey was so successful in explaining and popularizing his mentor's efforts that differential association remains one of the most enduring explanations of criminal behavior.

Sutherland's research on white-collar crime, professional theft, and intelligence led him to dispute the notion that crime was a function of the inadequacy of people in the lower classes.[18] To Sutherland, criminality stemmed neither from individual traits nor socioeconomic position; instead, he believed it to be a function of a learning process which could affect any individual in any culture.

A couple of ideas are basic to the theory of differential association.[19] First, crime is a politically defined construct. It is defined by government authorities who are in control of a particular jurisdiction. In societies characterized by culture conflict, the definition of crime may be inconsistent and consequently rejected by some groups of people. Put another way, people may vary in their relative attachments to criminal and noncriminal definitions. Second, the acquisition of behavior is a social learning process, not a political-legal process. Skills and motives conducive to crime are learned as a result of contacts with pro-crime values, attitudes, and definitions, and other patterns of criminal behavior.

Principles of Differential Association. The first principle of differential association is that *criminal behavior is learned.*[20] This statement differentiates Sutherland's theory from prior attempts to classify criminal behavior as an inherent characteristic of born criminals. By suggesting that delinquent, deviant and criminal behavior is actually learned, Sutherland implied that it can be classified in the same manner as any other learned behavior, such as writing, painting, or reading.

In addition, *criminal behavior is learned in interaction with other persons in a process of communication.* Sutherland believed that illegal behavior is learned actively. An individual does not become a law violator simply by living in a crimogenic environment or by manifesting personal characteristics—such as low IQ or family problems—associated with criminality. People actively participate in the process with other individuals who serve as teachers and guides to crime.

Thus, criminality cannot occur without the aid of others.

The third principle of differential association theory is that *the principal part of the learning of criminal behavior occurs within intimate personal groups.* People's contacts with their most intimate social companions—family, friends, peers—have the greatest influence on their learning of deviant behavior and attitudes. Relationships with these individuals color and control the interpretation of everyday events. For example, research shows that children who grow up in homes where parents abuse alcohol are more likely to view drinking as being socially and physically beneficial.[21] Social support for deviance helps people to overcome social controls so that they can embrace criminal values and behaviors. The intimacy of these associations far outweighs the importance of any other form of communication—for example, movies or television. Even on those rare occasions when violent motion pictures seem to provoke mass criminal episodes, these outbreaks can be more readily explained as a reaction to peer group pressure than as a reaction to the films themselves.

Next, *learning criminal behavior includes: (1) learning the techniques of committing the crime, which are sometimes very complicated; and (2) learning the specific direction of motives, drives, rationalizations, and attitudes.* Since criminal behavior is similar to other learned behavior, it follows that the actual techniques of criminality must be acquired. For example, young delinquents learn from their associates the proper way to pick a lock, shoplift, and obtain and use narcotics. In addition, novice criminals must learn to use the proper terminology for their acts and then acquire the proper personal reactions to them. For example, getting high on marijuana and learning the proper way to "smoke a joint" are behavior patterns usually acquired from more experienced companions. Moreover, criminals must learn how to react properly to their illegal acts—when to defend them, rationalize them, or show remorse for them.

Fourth, *the specific direction of motives and drives is learned from perceptions of various aspects of the legal code as being favorable or unfavorable.* Since the reaction to social rules and laws is not uniform across society, people constantly come into contact with others who maintain different views on the utility of obeying the legal code. When definitions of right and wrong are extremely varied, people experience what Sutherland called *culture conflict*. The attitudes toward criminal behavior of significant others in an individual's life influence the attitudes that individual develops. The conflict of social attitudes is the basis for the concept of differential association.

Another principle of differential association theory is that *a person becomes delinquent when he or she perceives more favorable than unfavorable consequences to violating the law*. According to Sutherland's theory, individuals become law violators when they are in contact with persons, groups, or events that produce an excess of definitions favorable toward criminality and are isolated from counteracting forces. A definition favorable toward criminality occurs, for example, when friends talk about sneaking into a theater to avoid paying for a ticket or talk about the virtues of getting high. A definition unfavorable toward crime occurs when friends or parents demonstrate their disapproval of crime. Of course, neutral behavior exists, such as reading a book. It is neither positive or negative with respect to law violation. Cressey argues that this behavior is important, "especially as an occupier of the time of a child so that he is not in contact with criminal behaviors during the time he is so engaged in the neutral behavior."[22]

A sixth principle is that *differential associations may vary in frequency, duration, priority, and intensity*. Whether a person learns to obey the law or to disregard it is influenced by the quality of social interactions. Those of lasting duration have the greatest influence. Similarly, frequent contacts have greater effect than rare and haphazard contacts. Sutherland did not specify what he meant by priority, but Cressey and others have interpreted the term to mean the age of children when they first encounter definitions of criminality. Contacts made early in life probably have a greater and more far-reaching influence than those developed later on. Finally, intensity is generally interpreted to mean the importance and prestige attributed to the individual or groups from whom the definitions are learned. For example, the influence of a father, mother, or trusted friend far outweighs the effect of more socially distant figures.

Differential association theory also holds that *the process of learning criminal behavior by association with criminal and anticriminal patterns involves all of the mechanisms that are involved in any other learning*. This suggests that the learning of criminal behavior patterns is not a matter of mere imitation.

Finally, *while criminal behavior is an expression of general needs and values, it is not excused by those general needs and values*. This principle suggests that the motives for criminal behavior cannot logically be the same as those for conventional behavior. Sutherland rules out such motives as desire to accumulate money or social status, personal frustration, or low self-concept as causes of crime, since they are just as likely to produce noncriminal behavior, such as getting a better education or working harder on a job. It is only the learning of deviant norms through contact with an excess of definitions favorable to criminality that produces illegal behavior.

Empirical Research on Differential Association. Despite the importance of differential association theory, research devoted to testing its assumptions has been less than adequate. It is difficult to conceptualize the principles of the theory in a way that lends itself to empirical measurement. For example, social scientists find it hard to evaluate such vague concepts as "definition toward criminality." However, several notable research efforts have been undertaken to test the validity of Sutherland's approach.

Among the most oft-cited studies is James Short's finding that a consistent relationship existed between criminal behavior and prior associations with delinquent youths in a sample of institutionalized youths.[23] Similarly, Albert Reiss and A. Lewis Rhodes found an association between delinquent friendship patterns and the probability that a youth would commit a criminal act.[24] More recently, Charles Tittle surveyed almost 2,000 adults in New Jersey, Oregon, and Iowa and found that a scale measuring differential associations correlated significantly with such criminal activity as income tax cheating, theft, gambling, and assault.[25] Ross Matsueda and Karen Heimer's analysis of a multiracial sample of youths showed that variables measuring the learning of delinquent values were a strong predictor of criminality.[26]

Existing research in support of differential association concepts must be interpreted with caution, since it is associational and not experimental. Since people are asked about their perception of differential associations and their criminal behaviors at the same time, it is impossible to determine whether the former preceded or caused the onset of criminality. In other words, it is also possible that criminals seek out like-minded peers *after* they engage in antisocial acts, and that the internalization of deviant attitudes *follows* rather than *precedes* criminality.[27]

Analysis of Differential Association. The principles of differential association as formulated by Sutherland and interpreted by Cressey are a significant contribution to our understanding of the onset of criminal behavior. Nonetheless, the theory's intent and purpose have often been misunderstood by critics. For example, some have maintained that differential association erroneously depicts law-violating behavior as being learned only through contact with delinquents and criminals. As Cressey explains, even though differential association theory stresses the importance of an excess of definitions favorable toward criminality, it does not specify that they must come solely from criminal sources.[28] For example, seemingly law-abiding parents can encourage delinquent behavior by telling their children that it is acceptable to cheat on a test if that's the only way to get ahead.

A more telling criticism is that the theory fails to account for the origin of criminal definitions. How did the first "teacher" learn criminal techniques and definitions? Similarly, Sutherland ignores spontaneous and wanton acts of violence and damage that appear to have little utility or purpose, such as acts of teenage vandalism. But perhaps the most serious criticism of differential association theory concerns its use of abstract and vague terminology. For example, what exactly constitutes an "excess of definitions toward criminality"? How can we determine whether an individual actually has a pro-criminal imbalance of these definitions? It is simplistic to assume that, by definition, all criminals have experienced a majority of definitions favorable toward criminality, and all noncriminals a minority of them. Unless the terms employed in the theory can be defined more precisely, its validity remains a matter of guesswork.

Despite these criticisms, differential association theory maintains an important place in the study of delinquent and criminal behavior. Unlike social structure theories, it is not limited to the explanation of a single facet of antisocial activity—for example, lower-class gang activity. The theory also may be used to explain criminality across class structures. Even corporate executives may be exposed to a variety of pro-criminal definitions from such sources as overly opportunistic colleagues and friends. Thus, differential association theory has greater application than the

Ronald Akers formulated and tested differential reinforcement theory.

subcultural strain theory discussed earlier.

✗ Differential Reinforcement Theory

Differential reinforcement theory is another attempt to explain crime as a type of learned behavior. It is a revision of Sutherland's work that incorporates elements of the learning theory popularized by B. F. Skinner and applied to criminology by Albert Bandura (see Chapter 6).[29] The description of the theory is summarized in **Ronald Akers'** 1977 work, *Deviant Behavior: A Social Learning Approach.*[30]

According to Akers, people learn social behavior by **operant conditioning,** behavior controlled by stimuli that follow the behavior. Social behavior is acquired through direct conditioning and modeling of others' behavior. Behavior is reinforced when positive rewards are gained or punishment is avoided (negative reinforcement). It is weakened by negative stimuli (punishment) and loss of reward (negative punishment). Whether deviant or criminal behavior is begun or persists depends on the degree to which it has been rewarded or punished and the rewards or punishments attached to its alternatives. This is the theory of **differential reinforcement.**

According to Akers, people learn to evaluate their own behavior through interaction with significant others in their lives. This process makes use of such devices as norms, attitudes, and orientations. The more individuals learn to define their behavior as good or at least as justified, rather than as undesirable, the more likely they are to engage in it.

Akers' theory posits that the principal influence on behavior comes from "those groups which control individuals' major sources of reinforcement and punishment and expose them to behavioral models and normative definitions."[31] The important groups are the ones with which a person is in **differential association**—peer and friendship groups, schools, churches, and similar institutions. Behavior results when an individual perceives an excess of reinforcements over punishments for certain acts or their alternatives. Definitions conducive to deviant behavior occur when positive or neutralizing definitions of that behavior offset negative definitions of it. Subsequently, "deviant behavior can be expected to the extent that it has been differentially reinforced over alternative behavior . . . and is defined as desirable or justified."[32]

Once people are initiated into crime-related activities, their behavior is influenced by a variety of factors: social reinforcement; exposure to deviant behavior models; association with deviant peers; and lack of negative sanctions from parents, peers, and so on. The deviant behavior, originated by imitation, is sustained by social support.

Research on Differential Reinforcement Theory. In a test of his theory, Akers and his associates surveyed 3,065 male and female adolescents on drug- and alcohol-related activities and their perception of variables related to social learning and differential reinforcement. Items in the scale included the respondents' perception of the attitudes toward drug and alcohol use of the adults and peers they admired; the number of people they admired who actually used controlled substances; and whether people they ad-

mired would reward or punish them for substance abuse. Akers found a strong association between drug and alcohol abuse and the social learning variables, with particular emphasis on differential association.[33] Other research efforts have supported Akers' work. For example, a recent study by Marvin Krohn and his associates found that social learning principles were effective for predicting the maintenance (or cessation) of a particular deviant behavior, cigarette smoking, in a sample of junior and senior high-school boys measured over a three-year period.[34] Krohn found that reinforcement of smoking by parents and friends contributed to adolescent misbehavior and that differential associations by themselves were insufficient to predict deviance.

In addition to these efforts, there is a growing body of research which provides indirect support for Akers' model by showing that delinquents model their behavior after peers whom they are in close and intimate contact with.[35] For example, a number of studies, including those by Helene Raskin White and Randy LaGrange, have shown that delinquent behavior is directly influenced by peer group relations.[36] Similarly, Peggy Giordano and her associates have shown that delinquents have closer ties to their peers than conventional youths.[37] These research efforts support the learning theory hypothesis that antisocial behavior is related to the tendency of youths to associate with, be influenced by, and model their behavior after other youths who engage in delinquent activities.

Akers' work has emerged as an important view of the cause of criminal activity. It is one of the few prominent theoretical models that successfully links sociological and psychological variables. Moreover, it relates classical criminology (discussed in Chapter 5) to sociological theory by suggesting that punishment for criminal acts should reinforce conventional behaviors.[38]

Neutralization Theory

Neutralization theory is identified with the writings of **David Matza** and his associate, **Gresham Sykes.**[39] Sykes and Matza also view the process of becoming a criminal as a learning experience. However, while other learning theorists such as Sutherland and Akers dwell on the learning of techniques, values, and attitudes necessary for performing criminal acts, Sykes and Matza maintain that most delinquents and criminals hold conventional values and attitudes but master techniques that enable them to neutralize these values and drift back and forth between illegitimate and conventional behavior.

Matza argues that even the most committed criminals and delinquents are not involved in criminality all the time; they also attend schools, family functions, and so on. Therefore, human behavior can be pictured as falling along a continuum between total freedom and total restraint. Matza identifies a process, which he calls **drift,** whereby an individual moves from one extreme of behavior to another, behaving sometimes in an unconventional, free, or deviant manner, and at other times with constraint and sobriety.[40] Learning **techniques of neutralization** allows a person to temporarily drift away from conventional behavior and get involved in deviance.[41]

Techniques of Neutralization. Sykes and Matza suggest that juveniles develop a distinct set of justifications for their behavior when it violates accepted social norms. These neutralization techniques allow youths to temporarily drift away from the rules of the normative society and participate in subterranean behaviors. Sykes and Matza base their theoretical model on several observations.[42]

First, delinquents sometimes voice a sense of guilt over their illegal acts. If a stable delinquent value system existed in opposition to generally held values and rules, it would be unlikely that delinquents would exhibit any remorse for their acts other than regret at being apprehended.

Second, juvenile offenders frequently respect and admire honest, law-abiding persons. Really honest persons are often revered; if for some reason such persons are accused of misbehavior, the delinquent is quick to defend their integrity. Those admired may include sports figures, members of the clergy, parents, teachers, and neighbors.

Third, delinquents draw a line between those whom they can victimize and those whom they cannot. Members of similar ethnic groups, churches, or neighborhoods are often off limits. This practice implies that delinquents are aware of the wrongfulness of their acts.

Finally, delinquents are not immune to the demands of conformity. Most delinquents frequently participate in many of the same social functions as law-abiding youths—for example, in school, church, and family activities.

Sykes and Matza argue that such evidence substantiates the idea that delinquents operate as part of the normative culture and adhere to its values and standards. They suggest that delinquency is a result of the neutralization of accepted social values through the employment of a standard set of rationalizations for illegal behavior. Thus, most youths generally adhere to the rules of society but learn techniques to temporarily release themselves from these moral constraints. These techniques include:[43]

• *Denial of responsibility.* Young offenders sometimes claim their unlawful acts were simply not their fault; they resulted from forces beyond their control or were accidents.

• *Denial of injury.* By denying the wrongfulness of an act, criminals are able to rationalize their illegal behavior. Society often agrees with delinquents, labeling illegal behavior as "pranks" and thereby reaffirming the delinquents' view that crime can be socially acceptable.

• *Denial of victim.* Juveniles sometimes rationalize their behavior by maintaining that the victim of a crime "had it coming." Thus, vandalism may be directed against a disliked teacher or neighbor; or homosexuals may be beaten up by a gang because their behavior is considered offensive. Denying the victim may also take the form of ignoring the rights of an absent or unknown victim, such as the unseen owner of a department store. It becomes morally acceptable for delinquents to commit crimes such as vandalism when the victims, because of their absence, cannot be sympathized with or respected.

• *Condemnation of the condemners.* The youthful offender views the world as a corrupt place with a dog-eat-dog code. Since police and judges are on the take, teachers show favoritism, and parents take out their frustrations on their kids, it is ironic and unfair for these authorities to condemn youthful misconduct. By shifting the blame to others, delinquents are able to repress the feeling that their own acts are wrong.

• *Appeal to higher loyalties.* Novice criminals often argue that they are caught in the dilemma of being loyal to their own peer group while at the same time attempting to abide by the rules of the larger society.

The needs of the group take precedence over the rules of society because the demands of the former are immediate and localized.

In sum, the theory of neutralization presupposes a condition in which such slogans as "I didn't mean to do it," "I didn't really hurt anybody," "They had it coming to them," "Everybody's picking on me," and "I didn't do it for myself" are used by youths to rationalize unconventional norms and values so they can drift into delinquent modes of behavior.

Empirical Research on Neutralization Theory. Several attempts have been made to empirically verify the assumptions of neutralization theory. Robert Ball's study of institutionalized youths showed that they accepted excuses for deviant behavior to a significantly greater degree than control subjects.[44] Similar findings were achieved by Robert Regoli and Eric Poole.[45]

In contrast to these views, Michael Hindelang's self-report study found that delinquents and nondelinquents had different moral values, a finding that contradicts basic principles of the neutralization approach.[46]

Even studies that support Matza's approach have failed to show that the neutralization of moral restraints precedes the onset of criminality. A valid test of neutralization theory would have to be able to show that a person first neutralized his or her moral beliefs and then drifted into delinquency. Otherwise, any data that showed an association between crime and neutralization could be interpreted as suggesting that people who commit crime later make attempt to rationalize their behavior. The validity of Matza's model depends on showing that the neutralizations come first, causing the criminal behavior to follow; so far such data are unavailable.

CONTROL THEORIES

The second major branch of the social process perspective, control theory, maintains that all people have the potential to violate the law and that modern society presents many opportunities for illegal activity. The question control theorists pose is: "Why, then, do people obey the rules of society?" To a classical theorist, the answer would be "fear of punishment, the most basic element of social control." In contrast, control theorists such as Scott Briar and Irving Piliavin view fear of punishment as only one element of the social ties that bind people to society. People may refrain from committing crime because they have a **commitment to conformity**—a real, present, and logical reason to obey the rules of society. For example, they may believe that getting caught at criminal activity will hurt a dearly loved parent or jeopardize their chances for a college scholarship, or they may feel that their jobs will soon allow them to save enough to obtain what they want without resorting to illegitimate means.[47]

In another early version of control theory, **Walter Reckless** and his associates argued that youths growing up in even the most criminogenic areas can insulate themselves from crime through **containments,** such as "a positive self-image, ego strength, high frustration tolerance, goal orientation, a sense of belongingness, consistent moral front, reinforcement of norms, goals, and values, effective supervision, discipline, and meaningful social role."[48]

In sum, control theory maintains that elements of interpersonal interaction counteract crime-producing forces in the environment. All people perceive inducements to crime; some are better able to deal with them than others. Travis Hirschi's control theory, currently the most widely cited version of this criminological perspective, is reviewed in detail in the following sections.

Hirschi's Control Theory

Travis Hirschi's version of control theory, articulated in his famous book, *Causes of Delinquency*, replaced Reckless's containment theory as the dominant version of social control theory.[49]

Hirschi links the onset of criminality to the weakening, in a person's youth, of the ties that bind him or her to society. Hirschi assumes that all individuals are potential law violators. They are kept under control by their fear that illegal behavior may lead to irreparable harm in their relationships with friends, parents, neighbors, and important social institutions such as schools, jobs, and the like. Without social bonds, and

According to control theory, attachment to parents helps control delinquent behavior.

in the absence of sensitivity to and interest in others, a person is free to commit criminal acts.

Like most social process theorists, Hirschi does not believe that different elements of society maintain separate and unique value systems that reject conventional norms and behaviors. Rather, he suggests that in all elements of society there exist variations in the way people respond to social rules and values. Thus, even in the middle and upper classes, a person whose bond to society is weak may fall prey to criminogenic behavior patterns.

Elements of the Social Bond.   Hirschi argues that the social bond a person maintains with society is divided into four main elements: attachment, commitment, involvement, and belief.

Attachment.   Attachment refers to a person's sensitivity to and interest in others.[50] Psychologists believe that without a sense of attachment, a person becomes a psychopath and loses the ability to relate coherently to the world. The acceptance of social norms and the development of a social conscience depend on attachment to other human beings.

Hirschi views parents, peers, and schools as the important social institutions with which a person should maintain ties. Attachment to parents is the most important. Even if a family is shattered by divorce and separation, a child must retain a strong attachment to one or both parents. Without attachment to family, it is unlikely that feelings of respect for others in authority will develop.

Commitment.   Commitment involves the time, energy, and effort expended in conventional lines of action. It embraces such activities as getting an education and saving money for the future. Social bond theory holds that if people build up a strong involvement in life, property, and reputation, they will be less likely to engage in acts that will jeopardize their positions. Conversely, lack of commitment to conventional values may foreshadow a condition in which risk-taking behavior, such as crime, becomes a reasonable behavior alternative.

Involvement.   Heavy involvement in conventional activities leaves little time for illegal behavior. Hirschi believes that involvement insulates a person from the potential lure of criminal behavior, while idleness enhances it.

Belief.   People who live in the same social setting often share common moral beliefs; they may adhere to such values as sharing, sensitivity to the rights of others, and admiration for the legal code. If these beliefs are absent or weakened, individuals are more likely to participate in antisocial acts.

Hirschi further suggests that the interrelationship of elements of the social bond influences whether an individual pursues illegal or conventional activities. For example, people who feel kinship and sensitivity to parents and friends should be more likely to adopt and work toward legitimate goals. On the other hand, a person who rejects social relationships probably lacks commitment to conventional goals. Similarly, people who are highly committed to conventional acts and beliefs are more likely to be involved in conventional activities.

Empirical Research on Control Theory.   One of Hirschi's most significant contributions was his attempt to test the principal hypotheses of control theory. He administered a detailed self-report survey to a sample of over 4,000 junior and senior high-school students in Contra Costa County, California.[51] In a detailed analysis of the data, Hirschi found considerable evidence to support the control theory model.

Among Hirschi's more important findings were the following:

• Youths who were strongly attached to their parents were less likely to commit criminal acts.

• Commitment to conventional values, such as striving to get a good education and refusing to drink and "cruise around," was also related to conventional behavior.

• Youths involved in conventional activity, such as homework, were less likely to engage in criminal behavior; youths involved in unconventional behavior, such as smoking and drinking, were more delinquency-prone.

• Delinquent youths maintained weak and distant relationships with people; nondelinquents were attached to their peers.

• Delinquents and nondelinquents shared similar beliefs about society.

Hirschi's data lent important support to the validity of control theory. Even when the statistical significance of his findings was less than he expected, the direction of his research data were extremely consistent. Only in very rare instances did his findings contradict the theory's most critical assumptions.

There have been other attempts to corroborate Hirschi's findings, most notably by Michael Hindelang. Using subjects in the sixth through twelfth grades in a rural New York State school system, Hindelang replicated several of Hirschi's most important results. With few exceptions, Hindelang's evidence supported Hirschi's control theory principles. The major discrepancy found by Hindelang was in the area of attachment to peers. Hindelang found that close identification with peers was directly related to delinquent activity, while Hirschi's research produced the opposite result.[52]

Hindelang's research reflects one of the more questioned aspects of Hirschi's work. Hirschi claimed that any kind of attachment was beneficial, even if those admired by delinquents were deviants themselves. In addition to Hindelang's research, there are a number of other efforts which show that delinquents are not lone wolves whose only personal relationships are exploitative. Peggy Giordano and her associates found that delinquents' friendship patterns are quite close to those of conventional youth.[53] Gary Jensen and David Brownfield (agreeing with Hindelang) found that Hirschi may have been overly optimistic about the positive effects of attachment. Their research data indicates that youths attached to parents who use drugs are more likely to become drug users themselves.[54]

Opposing Views.   While there has been significant empirical support for Hirschi's work, there are also those who question some or all of its elements. For example, one issue has been whether the theory can explain all modes of criminality (as Hirschi maintains) or is restricted to particular groups or forms of criminality. This problem was addressed by a research effort conducted by Marvin Krohn and James Massey.[55] Using a sample of 3,065 junior and senior high-school students, Krohn and Massey found that the element of commitment was a more powerful predictor of delinquency than attachment or belief. They also found that control theory was better able to explain female delinquency than male delinquency, and

Travis Hirschi not only expanded social control theory, but also carried out research to test its principles.

minor delinquency (such as alcohol and marijuana abuse) than more serious criminal acts. Krohn and Massey concluded that Hirschi's model was useful to explain the onset of delinquent behavior, a period when youthful offenders begin to question their commitment and attachment to social institutions.

Another research effort, by Randy LaGrange and Helene Raskin White, addressed another important issue left unanswered by Hirschi and his supporters: do elements of the social bond change over time?[56] Using samples of 12-, 15- and 18-year-old boys, LaGrange and White found that there was indeed age differences in the perceptions of the social bond. Mid-teens were more likely to be influenced by their parents and teachers; boys in the other two age groups were more deeply influenced by their deviant peers. LaGrange and White attributed this finding to the problems of mid-adolescence, when there is a great need to develop "psychological anchors" to conformity.

While research efforts have been generally supportive of the basic elements of control theory, sociologist Robert Agnew has raised some significant questions about its general theoretical utility.[57] Using a sample of subjects measured over time, Agnew found that the importance of Hirschi's theory has been exaggerated, because the theory miscalculates the direction of the relationship between criminality and a weakened social bond. In other words, while Hirschi's theory projects that a weak bond causes delinquency, Agnew suggests that the reverse is true: delinquency may in fact weaken a youth's bond to parents, schools, and society. Other studies also have found that criminal behavior weakens social bonds and not vice versa.[58]

In sum, while some research has given unqualified support to social control theory, other efforts have questioned some or all of its explanatory power. Nonetheless, the weight of the existing empirical evidence is supportive of control theory. It has emerged as one of the preeminent theories in the criminological literature.[59]

Analysis of Control Theory

Since it has cross-cultural applications, Hirschi's control theory model avoids the narrow focus of sociocultural theories. For example, in lower-class areas, control may be weakened because of limited access to conventional means for success, lack of attachment to the school, unattainable social goals, and strained parental relationships. Middle- and upper-class youths may find that relationships to upwardly mobile parents are tenuous, that their academic abilities fall short of expectations, or that their lives lack purpose or commitment. Consequently, it can easily be adapted as a basis for crime prevention programs.

Another strength of control theory is its adaptability to empirical measurement. Many of the theoretical models discussed previously rely heavily on ambiguous concepts, such as anomie, definitions toward crime, and drift. Control theorists define elements of the bond in simple, straightforward terms. For example, a person's involvement can be measured by actual participation in cultural activities, community programs, and religious services. Attachment to and belief in conventional goals, values, and institutions can be operationalized by research using standard attitude and personality measures.

Despite its merits, control theory fails to explain some important issues. How are social bonds formed and why do they weaken? Are all the elements of the bond equally important? Does weakening of one element of the bond precipitate criminality, or must all

202 THEORIES OF CRIME CAUSATION

the elements be affected in concert? How does control theory explain the aging out process: that is, once weakened can a social bond be strengthened?

⟩LABELING THEORY

Labeling theory reached prominence in the mid-seventies as an **interactionist** explanation of criminal careerism. Using the interactionist concept of crime and deviance discussed in Chapter 1, labeling theorists attempt to show how crime is a product of social interactions and encounters. People are portrayed as becoming deviant and criminal when significant others—teachers, police, neighbors, parents, friends—label them as such. Labeling theory seems to place the blame for criminal career formation on the agencies of social control operating in society. Often mistrustful of institutions such as schools, mental hospitals, police, court, and correctional agencies, labeling advocates find it logical to say that these institutions can produce stigma harmful to the very people they are trying to treat or correct.

Members of the labeling school view negative labels, such as "dummy," "poor reader," "mentally unstable person," "criminal," and "delinquent," as causing permanent harm to the people on whom they are bestowed.

The way labels are applied, and the nature of the labels themselves, is likely to have important future consequences for the offender. For example, the degree to which a person is perceived a criminal may affect his or her treatment at home, at work, at school, and in other social situations. Young offenders may find that their parents consider them a negative influence on younger brothers and sisters. School officials may limit them to classes reserved for people with behavior problems. Adults who have been given official labels, such as "criminal," "ex-con," "mental patient," or "addict," may find their eligibility for employment severely restricted. And, of course, if the label is bestowed as the result of conviction for a criminal offense, the labeled person may be subject to official sanctions ranging from a mild reprimand to incarceration.

Beyond these immediate results, labeling advocates maintain that, depending on the visibility of the label and the manner and severity with which it is applied, a person will have an increasing commitment to a deviant career: "Thereafter he may be watched; he may be suspect . . . he may be excluded more and more from legitimate opportunities."[60] Consequently, labeled persons may find themselves turning to other similarly labeled persons for support. At the conclusion of the labeling process, stigmatized persons may find themselves isolated from conventional society and locked into deviant careers. Thereafter, they may identify themselves as members of an outcast group.

Though the labeling perspective has been used to describe a variety of deviant identities—homosexual, mental patient, alcoholic—this discussion limits its application to crime and delinquency.

Crime and Labeling Theory

Labeling theorists use an interactionist definition of crime. Sociologist Kai Erickson argues "Deviance is not a property inherent in certain forms of behavior, it is a property conferred upon those forms by the audience which directly or indirectly witnesses them."[61] This definition has been amplified by Edwin Schur:

> Human behavior is deviant to the extent that it comes to be viewed as involving a personally discreditable departure from a group's normative expectation, and it elicits interpersonal and collective reactions that serve to "isolate," "treat," "correct" or "punish" individuals engaged in such behavior.[62]

Crime and deviance, therefore, are defined by the social audience's reaction to people and their behavior and the subsequent effects of that reaction; they are not defined by the moral content of the illegal act itself. In its purest form, labeling theory argues that crimes such as murder, rape, and assault are only bad or evil because people label them as such. After all, the difference between an excusable act and a criminal one is often a matter of legal definition, which can change from place to place and from year to year. Labeling theorists would argue that acts such as abortion, use of marijuana, possession of a handgun, and gambling have been legal at some points and places in history and illegal at others. Howard Becker refers to people who create rules as *moral entrepreneurs*. He sums up their effect as follows:

> Social groups create deviance by making rules whose infractions constitute deviance, and by applying those rules to particular people and labeling them as outsiders. From this point of view, deviance is not a quality of the act a person commits, but rather a consequence of the application by others of rules and sanctions to an "offender." The deviant is one to whom the label has successfully been applied; deviant behavior is behavior that people so label.[63]

Differential Enforcement

An important principle of labeling theory is that the law is differentially applied, benefiting those who hold economic and social power, and penalizing the powerless. In this respect, labeling theory is similar to the social conflict theories discussed in Chapter 9.

Labeling theorists argue that the probability of being brought under the control of legal authority is a function of a person's race, wealth, sex, and social standing. They point to studies indicating that police officers are more likely to formally arrest males, minority group members, and those in the lower class, and to use their discretionary powers to give beneficial treatment to more favored groups.[64] Similarly, labeling advocates cite evidence that minorities and the poor are more likely to be prosecuted for criminal offenses and receive harsher punishments when convicted.[65] This evidence supports the labeling concept that personal characteristics and social interactions are actually more important variables in the criminal career formation process than the mere violation of the criminal law.

Labeling theorists also argue that the content of the law reflects power relationships in society. They point to the evidence that white-collar crimes are most often punished by a relatively small fine and rarely result in prison sentences, and contrast this treatment with the long prison sentences given to those convicted of "street crimes," such as burglary or car theft.[66]

In sum, a major premise of labeling theory is that the law is differentially constructed and applied. It favors the powerful members of society who direct its content and penalizes people whose actions represent a threat to those in control.[67]

Becoming Labeled

Labeling theorists are not especially concerned with explaining why people originally engage in acts that result in their being labeled. Walter Gove has listed some reasons why persons may participate in outlawed behavior: (1) they may belong to minority groups or subcultures whose values and expected behaviors may lead to violations of the rules of the dominant group; (2) they may have conflicting personal responsibilities, so that adequately performing one task produces violations in a second role; (3) their desire for personal gain, coupled with their belief that they will not be caught, may lead them into law violations; and (4) they may simply be unaware of the rules and may violate them unintentionally.[68] Gove concludes that the forces that initiate participation in deviant acts may be traced to inconsistencies in the social structure, to hedonistic variables (the desire for wealth and luxury), or to ignorance.[69] Labeling theorists would not dispute any of the previously discussed theories of the onset of criminality. Their concern is with criminal career formation and not the origin of criminal acts.

It is consistent with the labeling approach to suggest that social factors influence the likelihood of a person's engaging in label-producing acts. An individual's place in the social structure may influence both the probability that he or she will engage in disapproved behavior and the chance that he or she will be sanctioned for those actions. For example, the poor or minority-group teenager may run a greater chance of being officially processed for delinquent acts by police, court, and correctional agencies than the wealthy white youth. In the labeling view, a person is labeled deviant primarily as a consequence of societal characteristics—most specifically, the power and resources of the individual, the social distance between the labeler and the person labeled, the tolerance level in the community, and the visibility of the individual's deviant behavior.

Of course, not all labeled people have chosen to engage in label-producing activities such as crime. Some labels are bestowed on people for behaviors over which they have little control. Negative labels of this sort include "homosexual," "mentally ill," "alien," and "mentally deficient" persons. In these categories, too, the probability of being labeled may depend on the visibility of the person in the community, the tol-

Labels produce stigma and tend to re-define the whole person. "Label" the people in this photo. Then, consider that they are at a Rock Against Racism rally and see if your "labels" stay the same.

erance of the community for unusual behavior, and the person's own power to combat labels.

Consequences of Labeling

Criminologists are more concerned with two effects of labeling: the creation of stigma and the effect on self-image. Labels are believed to produce **stigma.** The labeled deviant becomes a social outcast who may be prevented from enjoying higher education, well-paying jobs, and other social benefits. Labeling theorists consider public condemnation an important part of the label-producing process. It may be accomplished in such "ceremonies" as a hearing in which a person is found to be mentally ill, or a trial in which an individual is convicted of crime. Public record of the deviant acts causes the denounced person to be ritu-

ally separated from a place in the legitimate order and placed outside the world occupied by citizens of good standing. Harold Garfinkle has called transactions that produce irreversible, permanent labels *successful degradation ceremonies.*[70]

Beyond these immediate results, the label tends to redefine the whole person. For example, the label "ex-con" may create in people's imaginations a whole series of behavior descriptions—tough, mean, dangerous, aggressive, untrustworthy, sneaky—that a person who has been in prison may or may not possess. People begin to react to the content of the label and what the label signifies, and not to the actual behavior of the person who bears it. This is referred to as **retrospective reading,** a process in which the past of the labeled person is reviewed and reevaluated to fit his or her current outcast status. For example, boyhood friends of an assassin or killer are interviewed by the media and report that the suspect was withdrawn, suspicious, and negativistic as a youth. Such reports are taken to explain what prompted his current behavior; the label must certainly be accurate.[71]

The second important consequence of being labeled is the acceptance of the label as a personal identity. As the negative feedback of law enforcement agencies, parents, friends, teachers, and other figures amplifies the force of the original label, stigmatized offenders may begin to reevaluate their own identities. They may begin to believe that they really are evil or bad. Frank Tannenbaum referred to this process as the **dramatization of evil.** With respect to the consequences of labeling delinquent behavior, Tannenbaum states:

> The process of making the criminal, therefore, is a process of tagging, defining, identifying, making conscious and self-conscious; it becomes a way of stimulating, suggesting and evoking the very traits that are complained of. If the theory of relation of response to stimulus has any meaning, the entire process of dealing with the young delinquent is mischievous insofar as it identifies him to himself or to the environment as a delinquent person. The person becomes the thing he is described as being.[72]

Primary and Secondary Deviance. One of the more well-known views on the consequences of becoming labeled is Edwin Lemert's concept of **primary** and **secondary deviance.**[73] According to Lemert, primary deviations are initial acts of norm violations or crimes that have very little influence on the actor and can be quickly forgotten; for example, a college student taking a "five-finger discount" at the campus bookstore.

In contrast, secondary deviance occurs when the actor reorganizes his or her personality around the consequences of the deviant act. The drug experimenter becomes an addict; the recreational drinker an alcoholic; the joy-rider a car thief. Secondary deviance occurs when society begins to recognize and sanction these roles, and a **deviance amplification** effect occurs. The offenders feel isolated from the mainstream of society and become firmly locked within their deviant roles. They may seek out others similarly labeled in order to form deviant subcultures or groups. Secondary deviance is a product of resocialization, in which the deviant role becomes the central fact of existence and the person is transformed into one who

"employs his behavior or a role based upon it as a means of defense, attack, or adjustment to the overt and covert problems created by the consequent social reaction to him."[74]

Lemert's concept of secondary deviance expresses the core of labeling theory: deviance is a process in which one's identity is transformed. Efforts to control offenders, whether by treatment or punishment, simply help lock them in their deviant role.

Research on Labeling Theory

Research on labeling theory falls into two distinct categories. The first focuses on the characteristics of offenders who are chosen for labels. Labeling theory maintains that these offenders should be relatively powerless people who are unable to defend themselves against the negative labeling. The second type of research attempts to discover the effects of being labeled. Labeling theorists predict that people who are labeled should view themselves as deviant and commit increasing amounts of criminal behavior.

With regard to the first category, research results seem inconclusive. Some studies (such as those mentioned earlier in the chapter) do in fact show that poor and powerless people are victimized by the justice system, and that labels are not equally distributed across class and racial lines. However, other research indicates that the justice system operates more fairly than labeling theorists would have us believe. That is, such procedures as arrest, prosecution, and sentencing may actually be based on behaviors, past and present, rather than personal characteristics. Nonetheless, enough evidence of class and racial bias exists to convince labeling theorists that the probability of receiving labels is unequally distributed. For example, the National Minority Advisory Council on Criminal Justice states:

> Although substantive and procedural laws govern almost every aspect of the American criminal justice system, discretionary decision making controls its operation at every level. From the police officer's decision on whom to arrest; to the prosecutor's decisions on whom to charge and for how many and what kind of charges; to the court's decision on whom to release or on whom to pyramid bail; to the Grand Jury decision on indictment; to the judge's decision on how long to sentence,

discretion that works to the detriment of minority people is a source of concern to black, Hispanic, Asian-American and Indian-American peoples.[75]

Conditions such as these would help explain racial and class differences in the crime rate.

With regard to the second category, support has been inconsistent for the proposition that becoming labeled actually has a dramatic and negative influence on the self-image of offenders. Research studies indicate that the effects of stigma-generating encounters have a relatively minor effect.[76]

In an in-depth analysis of research on the crime-producing effects of labels, Charles Tittle found little evidence that stigma produces crime. He states that "studies of recidivism do not confirm labeling expectations that more than half will be recidivists, and case materials provide many exceptions to labeling predictions.[77] Tittle also claimed that case materials challenge labeling hypotheses by showing that many criminal careers occur without labeling, that labeling often comes after rather than before adoption of a criminal career, and that criminal careers may not follow even when labeling takes place.

Despite the negative evidence, a few research studies have indicated that processing by agencies of the justice system does influence self-perception and through it criminal behavior. Melvin Ray and William Downs found that male drug use was significantly though indirectly influenced by formal labeling. They found that labeling by social control agencies produced deviant self-labels, which in turn accelerated criminal behavior; labeling did not seem to have an influence on female drug use.[78] Other efforts also have found evidence of a link between official labels, self-labels, and criminality.[79]

The weight of the empirical evidence has not supported the basic principles of labeling theory. While there is considerable evidence that people who are labeled by the criminal justice system through arrest, trial, and conviction stand a good chance of continuing in their deviant careers, the question remains whether the mere fact of being labeled accounts for criminal career formation or whether it can be better explained by other personal and social factors. For example, those who believe in the deterrence model dispute the effects of labeling and counter that the significant relationship between official labels and future deviance results from the le-

Edwin Lemert originated the concepts of primary and secondary deviance.

niency of sanctions rather than their severity. Attention has shifted from concern over the effect of negative labels to concern over how labels and sanctions can be efficiently and uniformly applied.

Analysis of Labeling Theory

Labeling theory has been the subject of significant academic debate. Those who criticize it point to its inability to specify the conditions that must exist before an act or individual is labeled deviant; that is, why some people are labeled while others remain "secret deviants."[80] Critics also charge that labeling theory fails to explain differences in crime rates; if crime is a function of stigma and labels, why are crime rates higher in some parts of the country, or at particular times of the year?[81] Labeling theory also ignores the onset of deviant behavior (that is, fails to ask why people commit the initial deviant act), and does not deal with the reasons delinquents and criminals decide to forego a deviant career.[82]

One sociologist, Charles Wellford, questions the validity of several premises essential to the labeling approach. He takes particular issue with the labeling

FIGURE 8.2 Social Development: An Integration of Control and Cultural Deviance Theories

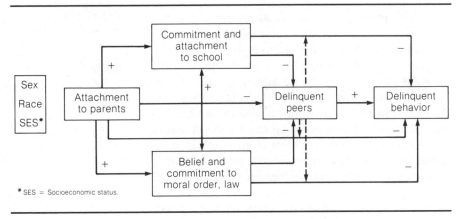

SOURCE: Joseph Weis and John Sederstrom. *Reports of the National Juvenile Justice Assessment Centers, The Prevention of Serious Delinquency: What to Do* (Washington, D.C.: U.S. Department of Justice, 1981), p. 35.

assumption that no act is intrinsically criminal. Wellford points to the fact that some crimes, such as rape and homicide, are almost universally sanctioned. He says: "Serious violations of the law are universally understood and are, therefore, in that sense, intrinsically criminal."[83] Furthermore, he suggests, the labeling theory proposition that almost all law enforcement is biased against the poor and minorities is equally spurious: "I contend that the overwhelming evidence is in the direction of minimal differential law enforcement, determination of guilt and application of sanction."[84]

According to Wellford, this means that law enforcement officials most often base their arrest decisions on such factors as the seriousness of the offense, and pay less attention to such issues as the race, class, and demeanor of the offender—factors that labeling theorists often link to the labeling decision.

Finally, Wellford questions the concept of self-labeling. Though labeling may indeed affect offenders' attitudes about themselves, there is little evidence that attitude changes are related to actual behavior changes. Wellford believes instead that criminal behavior is situationally motivated and depends on ecological and personal conditions.[85]

Because of these criticisms, a number of criminologists who once valued its premise now reject labeling theory. Some charge that it all too often focuses on "nuts, sluts, and perverts" and ignores the root causes of crime.[86] Nonetheless, labeling concepts can make

an important contribution to the understanding of criminal behavior if its original purpose, to explain deviance amplification and secondary deviance, is kept in mind. This orientation may be of special value as a possible explanation of the criminal career patterns of the chronic offender. It is ironic that, until quite recently, scant attention has been paid to the fact that criminal careers may be a function of negative labeling and the onset of secondary deviance; this despite the fact that a chronic offender is defined as someone who has been labeled criminal or delinquent multiple times.[87] Theorists who are studying chronic offenders, and policy-makers who are trying to decide what is to be done with them, should pay careful attention to what labeling theory has to say about the effects of negative sanctions and labels, becoming an outsider, and the building of a long-term deviant identity.

INTEGRATED THEORIES

One of the more important recent criminological developments has been the attempt to integrate aspects of various theories into a comprehensive model of crime and delinquency. Advocates of this approach argue that each component can add explanatory power. For example, James Q. Wilson and Richard Herrnstein's attempt to integrate biological and classical theory was reviewed in Chapter 6.[88] Though some critics charge that adding additional elements to an already valid theory is of dubious value, the movement towards theory integration is in full swing.[89]

Actually, the attempt to integrate criminological theory is not new. Over a decade ago, Daniel Glazer combined elements of differential association with classical criminology and control theory in his **differential anticipation theory.**[90] Glazer's version asserts: "A person's crime or restraint from crime is determined by the consequences he anticipates from it."[91] According to Glazer, people commit crimes whenever and wherever the expectations of gain from them exceed expectations of losses (rationale choice). This decision is tempered by the quality of an individual's social bonds and his or her relationships with others (control theory), as well as by prior learning experiences (learning theory).[92]

Since Glazer's pioneering efforts, significant attempts have been made to integrate social process concepts such as learning, labeling, and control with structural and other variables.[93] A few prominent examples of integrated theory are briefly discussed below.

Social Development Theory

Joseph Weis and his associates have attempted to integrate the social control approach with the social structure models discussed earlier.[94] Weis recognizes that factors related to a person's place in the social structure—sex, race, and economic status—do in fact exert powerful forces on that person's behavioral choices. At the same time, socialization also contributes to the likelihood that an individual will engage in criminal or conventional behavior.

Weis, working with J. David Hawkins and John Sederstrom, developed the model of criminality illustrated in Figure 8.2. The model uses elements of both control and social structure theories. In a low-income, disorganized community, the influences of front-line socializing institutions are weak. Families are under great stress; educational facilities are inadequate; there are fewer material goods; respect for the law is weak. Because existing crime rates are high, there are greater opportunities for law violation, putting even greater strain on the agencies of social control.

Within this context of weak social control and

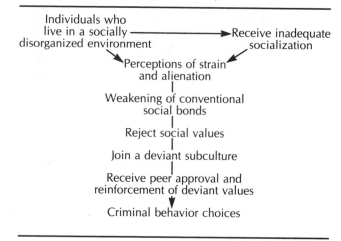

TABLE 8.1   Elliott's Integrated Theory

community disorganization, legitimate social institutions are incapable of combatting the lure of criminal groups and gangs. The family remains the front-line defense against a criminal career. Positive familial relationships are related to developing a commitment and attachment to school and the educational process. Concomitantly, youths whose educational experience is meaningful, marked by academic success and commitment to educational achievement, will be more likely to develop conventional beliefs and values, become committed to conventional activities, and seek out and be influenced by noncriminal peers. If a person does not find participation in school and family activities rewarding, he or she will likely seek associations with youths who are equally disillusioned and consequently engage in deviant activities that hold the promise of alternative rewards.

Weis's model can account for both the high crime rates found in lower-class areas as well as the influence of critical agents of the social order on criminal behavior.

Elliott's Integrated Theory

Another attempt at theory integration has been proposed by **Delbert Elliott** and his colleagues David Huizinga and Suzanne Ageton.[95] Their view combines the features of strain (Chapter 7), social learning, and control theories into a single theoretical model.

According to the Elliott view, perceptions of strain (the condition which occurs when a person begins to believe he or she cannot achieve success through conventional means), inadequate socialization, and living in a socially disorganized area lead youths to develop weak bonds with conventional groups, activities, and norms. Weak conventional bonds and continued high levels of perceived strain lead some youths to seek out and become bonded to like-minded peer groups. From these delinquent associations come positive reinforcements for delinquent behaviors; delinquent peers help provide role models for antisocial behavior. Bonding to delinquent groups, when combined with alienation from conventional groups and norms, leads to a high probability of involvement in delinquent behavior.

Elliott and his colleagues tested their theoretical model with data taken from a national youth survey of approximately 1,800 youths, who were interviewed annually over a three-year period. With only a few minor exceptions, the results supported their integrated theory. One difference was that some subjects reported developing strong bonds to delinquent peers even if they did not reject the values of conventional society. Elliott and colleagues interpret this finding as suggesting that youths living in disorganized areas may have little choice but to join with law-violating youth groups, since conventional groups simply do not exist.[96] Elliott also found that initial experimentation with drugs and delinquency predicted both joining a teenage law-violating peer group and becoming involved with additional delinquency.

The picture Elliott draws of the teenage delinquent is not dissimilar to Weis's social development model. Living in a disorganized neighborhood, feeling hopeless and unable to get ahead, and becoming involved in petty crimes eventually lead to a condition where conventional social values become weak and attenuated. Concern for education, family relations, and respect for the social order are weakened. A deviant peer group becomes an acceptable substitute, and consequently the attitudes and skills which support delinquent tendencies are amplified.

Interactional Theory

A recent addition to theory integration is **Terence Thornberry**'s interactional theory.[97] Thornberry agrees with both Weis and Elliott that the onset of crime can be traced to a deterioration of the social bond during adolescence. This deterioration is marked by a weakened attachment to parents, school, and a belief in conventional values. Thornberry also recognizes the influence of social class position and other structural variables. Youths growing up in areas characterized by underclass status and social disorganization will also be the ones who stand the greatest risk of a weakened social bond and subsequent delinquency. The onset of a criminal career is supported by residence in a social setting in which deviant values and attitudes can be learned and reinforced by delinquent peers.

Thornberry's most important theoretical contribution is his theory's incorporation of elements similar to those of the **cognitive perspective** in psychology. This view, pioneered by Jean Piaget (1896–1980), holds that as people mature they enter into separate stages of reasoning and sophistication.[98] Thornberry applies this concept when he suggests that criminality is a developmental process which takes on different meaning and form as a person matures. As he puts it, "The causal process is a dynamic one that develops over a person's life."[99] During early adolescence, the family is the single most important determinant of whether a youth will adjust to conventional society and be shielded from delinquency. As the youth matures to mid-adolescence, the influence of the family is replaced by the "world of friends, school and youth culture."[100] Finally, in adulthood, a person's behavioral choices are shaped by his or her place in conventional society, the nuclear family, and so on.

Thornberry's model is in its early stages of development and is currently being tested with a panel of Rochester, New York, youths, who will be followed through their offending careers.[101]

AN EVALUATION OF SOCIAL PROCESS THEORY

The three original branches of social process theory—social learning, control, and labeling—are compatible: they all suggest that criminal behavior is an ongoing social psychological process in which actors are influenced by the people and institutions sur-

☰ CLOSE-UP

Crime Prevention through Family Training

In the reading below, criminologist Rolf Loeber discusses the role of the family in crime prevention strategies.

Increasingly, investigators, clinicians, and child-rearing experts are focusing their attention on early rather than later child problem behavior. A primary reason is that most children learn deviant and approved behavior in the family home long before they are exposed to deviant peers. If the conditions that predispose some children to become delinquents can be ameliorated or prevented, there is hope that later conduct problems can be reduced. Another reason for concentrating on early childhood is that the learning of deviant behavior is importantly shaped by the quality and quantity of parent-child interactions. Many forms of delinquency and serious misbehavior are more common among children raised in broken homes, or in conditions of poverty and material deprivation, than in families that do not suffer from these disadvantages. Nonetheless, for any specific category of family, the behavior problems are more pronounced in families characterized by poor parenting skills.

One feature of youngsters' antisocial development is that they often direct antisocial behavior—particularly aggression and lying—against their parents. As a consequence, parents become less able to exercise their parental authority and may, in effect, especially with older children, abdicate their parental responsibilities.

Clinicians and researchers have long argued that parents' inadequate child-rearing practices can be improved, regardless of whether the skills were inadequate to begin with or were undermined by youngsters' antisocial behavior. The basic idea is that improvements in child-rearing practices can lead to improvements in the youngsters' problem behavior.

What Is the Evidence for Parent Training?

Systematic evaluation of parent training began only a few decades ago. Since them, a number of studies have shown that well-planned training sessions can help parents improve their child-rearing practices, which in turn can achieve improvements in children's behavior. Although parent training programs vary, most include the following features:

- Parents are taught to identify their children's problem behavior.
- Parents are taught to apply more appropriate consequences to misbehavior. They are encouraged to use less "nagging" and to increase the use of nonphysical punishment such as loss of privileges. At the same time, constructive behavior is rewarded.
- Parents are taught to negotiate the resolution of problems, especially with their older children.
- Parents are taught to supervise their children more closely and to monitor their comings and goings, their activities, and their choice of friends.

rounding them. Though the three branches disagree about the relative importance of those influences and the form the influences take, there seems to be little question that social process theories involve perception of outside influences that shape and control the beliefs, values, and self-image of the offender. Persons who have been negatively influenced—either by learning deviant social values, finding themselves detached from conventional others, or being negatively labeled by them—will be the most likely to fall prey to the attractions of criminal behavior. These negative influences can influence people in all walks of life, beginning in their youth and continuing through

their adulthood.

Integrated social process theories expand on earlier works by accounting for the effects of social, structural, psychological and other theoretical variables, as well as by incorporating a variety of social process elements and concepts. If these factors can be effectively combined, then it is likely that integrated models can achieve a more comprehensive view of criminality than any singular theory can provide. However, simply adding variables does not necessarily guarantee greater explanatory power, since the added concepts may be correlated with the existing ones. Another danger of integrated theories

So far, these programs have been especially successful in dealing with aggression in children. Careful observations in family homes before, during, and after parent training have shown that the frequency of children's aggression was significantly reduced in the majority of the studies. This was confirmed by parental reports.

Most of the training programs that work with the natural parents have focused on preadolescent rather than on adolescent youngsters. It is likely that parent training is more effective when children are young; by middle adolescence behavior may be so entrenched or so subject to peer influences that changes can be made only with extraordinary efforts.

Another line of parent training has focused on foster parents who, for a period of time, work with problem youngsters whose own parents are unable to carry out their parental duties. These programs are often called "specialized child care," because the host parents are specifically trained for this task. Many of the principles listed above are used in their training; in addition, the parents are educated to develop positive relationships with the youngsters and, through the use of individualized written contracts between foster parent and child, to teach the children to become responsible individuals.

Parents in training programs are often assisted in their difficult tasks by a support network of other parents and supervisory staff. Both efforts—the training of natural parents and of specialized foster parents—appear to be more viable and humane approaches for dealing with problem children than institutionalization, which may be the only other option for some children.

Although training of natural parents has been among the most promising approaches for dealing with the conduct of problem youngsters, a number of issues remain. For instance, we do not know enough about the effect of parent training on youngsters' concealment of their antisocial acts. And few studies have demonstrated that parent training prevents or reduces existing delinquency or drug use.

Although parent training programs show promise as an approach for dealing with conduct problems, especially in very young children, important issues must be resolved before we can say that parent training can play a major role in preventing delinquency. For example, existing programs are quite expensive. Many parents do not have insurance, cannot afford the cost of participating in these programs, and cannot afford to pay for their children's participation. It may not be realistic to expect that parent training can reach a significant fraction of parents of problem children. Moreover, it is not clear how long the beneficial effects of training last.

Discussion Questions

1. What rationales justify use of parent training as a tool to reduce delinquency?
2. Which forms of family malfunctioning are most susceptible to improvement as a result of parent training?
3. How can parents be helped to prevent delinquency in their offspring?

SOURCE: Rolf Loeber, *Families and Crime* (Washington, D.C.: National Institute of Justice, 1988).

is that they may become so complex and unwieldy that they are impossible to test and difficult to understand.

SOCIAL PROCESS THEORY AND SOCIAL POLICY

Social process theories have had a great influence on social policy making from the 1950s through the 1980s. However, because of the divergent viewpoints existing within the perspective, policies influenced by social process theories often seem to oppose one another.

Learning theories have greatly influenced concepts of treatment of the criminal offender. Their effect has mainly been felt by young offenders, who are viewed as being more salvageable than "hardened" criminals. Advocates of the social learning approach argue that if people become criminal by learning definitions and attitudes toward criminality, they can "unlearn" them by being exposed to definitions toward conventional behavior.

This philosophy was used in numerous treatment facilities throughout the United States, the most fa-

TABLE 8.2 Overview of Social Process Theories

Theory	Major Premise	Strengths	Unanswered Questions and Other Weaknesses
Social Learning Theories			
Differential Association Theory	People learn to commit crime from exposure to antisocial definitions.	Explains onset of criminality. Explains the presence of crime in all elements of social structure. Explains why some people in high-crime areas refrain from criminality. Can apply to adults and juveniles.	Where do antisocial definitions originate? How can we measure antisocial definitions or prove that someone has been exposed to an excess of them? Fails to explain illogical acts of violence and destruction. Fails to discuss how to test theory adequately.
Differential Reinforcement Theory	Criminal behavior depends on the person's experiences with rewards for conventional behaviors and punishments for deviant ones. Being rewarded for deviance leads to crime.	Adds learning theory principles to differential association. Links sociological and psychological principles.	Fails to explain why those rewarded for conventional behavior, such as middle-class youths, commit crimes. Fails to explain why some delinquent youths do not become adult criminals despite their having been rewarded for crime.
Neutralization Theory	Youths learn ways of neutralizing moral restraints and periodically drift in and out of criminal behavior patterns.	Explains why many delinquents do not become adult criminals. Explains why youthful law violators can participate in conventional behavior.	Fails to show whether neutralizations occur before or after law violations. Does not explain why some youths drift and others do not. Cannot explain self-destructive acts such as heroin addiction.
Control Theories			
Social Bond Theory	A person's bond to society prevents him or her from violating social rules. If the bond weakens, the person is free to commit crime.	Explains onset of crime; can apply to both middle- and lower-class crime. Explains its theoretical constructs adequately so they can be measured. Has been empirically tested.	Fails to explain differences in crime rates. Fails to show whether a weakened bond can be strengthened. Does not distinguish the importance of different elements of the social bond—for example, is attachment more important than commitment?

mous being the Highfields Project in New Jersey and the Silverlake Program in Los Angeles. These residential treatment programs for young male offenders used group interaction sessions to attack the criminal behavior orientations held by residents (being tough, using alcohol and drugs, believing that school was for "sissies"), while promoting conventional lines of behavior (going straight, saving money, giving up drugs). Nonresidential programs offering a similar treatment orientation were experimented with in

TABLE 8.2 Overview of Social Process Theories—cont'd

Theories	Major Premise	Strengths	Unanswered Questions and Other Weaknesses
Theory of Commitment to Conformity	Short-term stimuli influence behavior. Their influence is controlled by a person's commitment to conventional society. Commitment helps people resist temptations.	Can explain middle- and lower-class crime. Shows how control is manifested over middle-class youths.	Fails to explain variations in crime rates. Fails to explain why some children develop commitments and others do not. Fails to explain variations in crime rates.
Containment Theory	Society produces pushes and pulls toward crime. In some people, they are counteracted by internal and external containments such as a good self-concept and group cohesiveness.	Brings together psychological and sociological principles. Can explain why some people are able to resist the strongest social pressures to commit crime.	The methodology used to support the theory has been heavily criticized. Does low self-concept cause delinquency, or are delinquent youths subject to social conditions and destroy their self-images?
Differential Anticipation Theory	People commit crimes whenever and wherever expectations of gain from crime exceed expectations of losses with respect to social bonds. Expectations determine conduct.	Combines principles of social bond, differential association, and classical theories.	Has not been subject to extensive empirical testing. Does not explain why expectations vary. Does not explain crime rate variations.
Labeling Theories	People enter into law-violating careers when they are labeled for their acts and organize their personalities around the labels.	Explains the role of society in creating deviance. Explains why some juvenile offenders do not become adult criminals. Develops concepts of criminal careers.	Does not explain the original reason why a person commits a crime. Places too much emphasis on society's role in the labeling process. Empirical verification is inconsistent.
Integrated Theories Social Development Theory	Weak social controls produce crime. A person's place in the social structure influences his or her bond to society.	Combines elements of social structural and social process theories. Accounts for variations in the crime rate.	Has not been subject to rigorous empirical testing.
Elliott's Integrated Theory	Strained and weak social bonds lead youths to associate and learn from deviant peers.	Combines elements of learning, strain, and control theories.	Assumes youths have close peer ties. Since deviance is amplified by learning, does not account for aging out process.
Interactional Theory	Delinquents go through lifestyle changes during their offending career.	Combines sociological and psychological theories.	Has not yet been empirically tested.

Provo, Utah, and Essex County, New Jersey, and more recently in Boston and in Boulder, Colorado. Though small in scale, these programs have been promoted by their originators as significant contributions to rehabilitation strategies.

Control theories also have indirectly influenced criminal justice and other social policy-making. Programs have been developed to improve people's commitments to conventional lines of action. A number of programs have been implemented to train parents to better deal with problem youth (see Close-Up called "Crime Prevention through Family Training"). Examples of this approach within the criminal justice system are the career, work furlough, and educational opportunity programs being developed in the nation's prisons. These programs are designed to help inmates maintain a stake in society, so they will be less willing to resort to criminal activity on their release. Lack of funding and the generally overcrowded condition of the prison system has seriously impeded these efforts (see Chapter 17).

The educational system has been the scene of numerous programs designed to improve basic skills and create an atmosphere in which youths will develop a bond to their schools. At the same time, the nation's social service agencies have made a concerted effort to help people adjust to middle-class society's rules and values.

Labeling theorists have suggested that an opposite tack be taken. Rather than ask social agencies to attempt to rehabilitate people who may be manifesting problems with the law, they argue that less is better. Put another way, the more institutions try to "help" people, the more these people will be stigmatized and labeled. For example, a special education program designed to help problem readers may cause them to be labeled by themselves and others as slow or stupid; a mental health rehabilitation program created with the best intentions may cause clients to be labeled crazy or dangerous.

The influence of labeling theory can be viewed in the development of diversion and restitution programs. *Diversion* programs are designed to remove both juvenile and adult offenders from the normal channels of the criminal justice process by placing them in programs designed for rehabilitation. For example, a college student whose careless drunken driving causes injury to a pedestrian may, before a trial takes place, be placed for six months in an alcohol treatment program. If the student successfully completes the program, charges will be dismissed and the stigma of a criminal label will be avoided. Such programs are common throughout the nation. Often, they offer counseling; vocational, educational, and family services; and medical advice.

Another label-avoiding innovation that has gained popularity is *restitution*. Rather than face the stigma of a formal trial, an offender is asked to either pay back the victim of the crime for any loss incurred or do some useful work in the community in lieu of receiving a court-ordered sentence.

Despite their good intentions, stigma-reducing programs have not met with great success. Critics charge that they substitute one kind of stigma for another—for instance, attending a mental health program in lieu of a criminal trial. In addition, diversion and restitution programs usually screen out violent and repeat offenders. Finally, there is little hard evidence that the recidivism rate of people who have attended alternative programs represents an improvement over the rate shown by people who have been involved in the traditional criminal justice process.

SUMMARY

Social process theories view criminality as a function of people's interaction with various organizations, institutions, and processes in society. People in all walks of life have the potential to become criminals if they maintain destructive social relationships. Social process theory has three main branches: social learning theory stresses that people learn how to commit crimes; social control theory analyzes the failure of society to control the criminal tendencies of certain people; and labeling theory maintains that negative labels produce criminal careers.

The social learning branch of social process theory suggests that people learn criminal behavior much as they learn conventional behavior. Differential association theory, formulated by Edwin Sutherland, holds that criminality is a result of a person's perceiving an excess of definitions in favor of crime over definitions that uphold conventional values. Ronald Akers has reformulated Sutherland's work using psychological learning theory. His approach is called differential reinforcement theory. David Matza's theory of neutralization stresses youths' learning of behavior rationalizations that enable them to overcome societal values and norms and engage in illegal behavior.

Control theory is the second branch of the social process approach. Control theories maintain that all people have the potential to become criminals but that their bonds to conventional society prevent them from violating the law. Travis Hirschi describes the social bond as containing elements of belief, commitment, attachment, and involvement. Briar and Piliavin describe a person's commitment to conformity and how situational inducements can overcome it. Walter Reckless's containment theory suggests that a person's self-concept aids his or her commitment to conventional action. Daniel Glazer has also formulated a control theory, called differential anticipation theory.

Labeling theory argues that a person's criminality is promoted by his or her being negatively labeled by significant others. Labels, such as "criminal," "ex-con," and "junkie," serve to isolate people from society and lock them into lives of crime. Labels create expectations that the labeled person will act in a certain way; so labeled people are always watched and suspected. Eventually, these people begin to accept their labels as personal identities, locking them further into lives of crime and deviance. Edwin Lemert has said that people who accept labels are involved in secondary deviance. Unfortunately, research on labeling has not supported its major premises. Consequently, critics have charged that it lacks credibility as a description of crime causation. Integrated theories attempt to combine elements of social process with other models such as social structure, trait, and rational choice theories.

Social process theories have had a great influence on social policy. They have controlled treatment orientations as well as community action policies.

KEY TERMS

social processes	techniques of neutralization
socialization	commitment to conformity
broken home	Walter Reckless
self-fulfilling prophecy	containments
social learning theory	Travis Hirschi
control theory	interactionist
labeling theory	stigma
integrated theory	retrospective reading
Edwin H. Sutherland	dramatization of evil
Donald Cressey	primary deviance
Ronald Akers	secondary deviance
operant conditioning	deviance amplification
differential reinforcement	differential anticipation
differential association	theory
David Matza	Delbert Elliott
Gresham Sykes	Terence Thornberry
drift	cognitive perspective

NOTES

1. Sheldon Glueck and Eleanor Glueck, *Unraveling Juvenile Delinquency* (Cambridge, Mass.: Harvard University Press, 1950); Ashley Weeks, "Predicting Juvenile Delinquency," *American Sociological Review* 8 (1943):40–46.

2. For general reviews of the relationship between families and delinquency, see, Alan Jay Lincoln and Murray Straus, *Crime and The Family* (Springfield, Ill.: Charles C. Thomas, 1985); Rolf Loeber and Magda Stouthamer-Loeber, "Family Factors as Correlates and Predictors of Juvenile Conduct Problems and Delinquency," in Michael Tonry and Norval Morris, eds. *Crime and Justice, An Annual Review of Research,* vol. 7 (Chicago: University of Chicago Press, 1986), pp. 29–151.

3. Joseph Weis, Katherine Worsley, and Carol Zeiss, "The Family and Delinquency: Organizing the Conceptual Chaos" (Monograph, Center for Law and Justice, University of Washington, 1982).

4. UPI, "U.S.: One in Four Children had Single Parent," *Boston Globe,* 21 January 1988, p. 11.

5. Lawrence Rosen and Kathleen Neilson, "Broken Homes," in Leonard Savitz and Norman Johnston, eds., *Contemporary Criminology* (New York: Wiley, 1982), pp. 126–35.

6. Robert Sampson, "Urban Black Violence: The Effect of Male Joblessness and Family Disruption," *American Journal of Sociology* 93 (1987):348–82.

7. Richard Smith and James Walters, "Delinquent and Non-delinquent Males' Perceptions of Their Fathers," *Adolescence* 13 (1978):21–28; Paul Robinson, "Parents of 'Beyond Control' Adolescents," *Adolescence* 13 (1978):116–19.

8. Ruth Inglis, *Sins of Fathers: A Study of the Physical and Emotional Abuse of Children* (New York: St. Martin's Press, 1978).

9. Delos Kelly and William Pink, "School Crime and Individual Responsibility: The Perpetuation of a Myth," *The Urban Review* 14 (1982):47–63.

10. Jeannie Oakes, *Keeping Track, How Schools Structure Inequality* (New Haven, Conn.: Yale University Press, 1985).

11. Terence Thornberry, Melanie Moore, and R. L. Christenson, "The Effect of Dropping Out of High School on Subsequent Criminal Behavior," *Criminology* 23 (1985):3–18.

12. National Commission on Excellence in Education, *A Nation at Risk* (Washington, D.C.: U.S. Government Printing Office, 1982).

13. U.S. Department of Justice, *Disorder in Our Public*

Schools (Washington, D.C.: U.S. Government Printing Office, 1984).

14. Walter Miller, *Violence by Youth Gangs and Youth Groups as a Crime Problem in Major American Cities* (Washington, D.C.: U.S. Government Printing Office, 1975).

15. Delos Kelly, *Creating School Failure, Youth Crime, and Deviance* (Los Angeles: Trident Shop, 1982); Delos Kelly and W. Grove, "Teachers' Nominations and the Production of Academic Misfits," *Education* 101 (1981):246–63.

16. Gabriel Tarde, *The Laws of Imitation* (1903; reprint ed. Gloucester, Mass.: Peter Smith, 1962). For an analysis of Tarde's work, see, Piers Beirne, "Between Classicism and Positivism: Crime and Penality in the Writings of Gabriel Tarde," *Criminology* 25 (1987):785–819.

17. Edwin Sutherland, *Principles of Criminology* (Philadelphia: Lippincott, 1939).

18. See, for example, Edwin Sutherland, "White-Collar Criminality," *American Sociological Review* 5 (1940):2–10.

19. This section is adapted from Clarence Schrag, *Crime and Justice: American Style* (Washington, D.C.: U.S. Government Printing Office, 1971), p. 46.

20. See, Edwin Sutherland and Donald Cressey, *Criminology*, 8th ed. (Philadelphia: Lippincott, 1970), pp. 77–79.

21. Sandra Brown, Vicki Creamer, and Barbara Stetson, "Adolescent Alcohol Expectancies in Relation to Personal and Parental Drinking Patterns," *Journal of Abnormal Psychology* 96(1987):117–21.

22. *Ibid.*

23. James Short, "Differential Association as a Hypothesis: Problems of Empirical Testing," *Social Problems* 8 (1960):14–25.

24. Albert Reiss and A. Lewis Rhodes, "The Distribution of Delinquency in the Social Class Structure," *American Sociological Review* 26 (1961):732.

25. Charles Tittle, *Sanctions and Social Deviance* (New York: Praeger, 1980).

26. Ross Matsueda and Karen Heimer, "Race, Family Structure and Delinquency: A Test of Differential Association and Social Control Theories," *American Sociological Review* 52 (1987):826–40.

27. Robert Burgess and Ronald Akers, "A Differential Association—Reinforcement Theory of Criminal Behavior," *Social Problems* 14 (1966):128–47.

28. Donald Cressey, "Epidemiologies and Individual Conduct: A Case from Criminology," *Pacific Sociological Review* 3 (1960):128–47.

29. See, for example, Albert Bandura, *Social Learning and Personality Development* (New York: Holt, Rinehart and Winston, 1963).

30. Ronald Akers, *Deviant Behavior: A Social Learning Approach*, 2d ed. (Belmont, Mass.: Wadsworth, 1977).

31. Ronald Akers, Marvin Krohn, Lonn Lonza-Kaduce,

and Marcia Radosevich, "Social Learning and Deviant Behavior: A Specific Test of a General Theory," *American Sociological Review* 44 (1979):638.

32. *Ibid.*

33. *Ibid.*, pp. 636–55.

34. Marvin Krohn, William Skinner, James Massey, and Ronald Akers, "Social Learning Theory and Adolescent Cigarette Smoking: A Longitudinal Study," *Social Problems* 32 (1985):455–71.

35. Anastasios Marcos, Stephen Bahr, and Richard Johnson, "Test of a Bonding/Association Theory of Adolescent Drug Use," *Social Forces* 65 (1986):135–61.

36. Helene Raskin White and Randy LaGrange, "An Assessment of Gender Effects in Self Report Delinquency," *Sociological Focus* 20 (1987):195–214.

37. Peggy Giordano, Stephen Cernkovich, and M. D. Pugh, "Friendship and Delinquency," *American Journal of Sociology* 91 (1986):1170–1202.

38. For an opposing view, see, C. Ray Jeffrey, "Criminal Law and Learning Theory," *Journal of Criminal Law, Criminology, and Police Science* 56 (1965):300.

39. Gresham Sykes and David Matza, "Techniques of Neutralization: A Theory of Delinquency," *American Sociological Review* 22 (1957):664–70; David Matza, *Delinquency and Drift* (New York: John Wiley, 1964).

40. Matza, *Delinquency and Drift*, p. 51.

41. Sykes and Matza, "Techniques of Neutralization," pp. 664–70; see also, David Matza, "Subterranean Traditions of Youths," *Annals of the American Academy of Political and Social Science* 378 (1961):116.

42. Sykes and Matza, "Techniques of Neutralization," pp. 664–70.

43. *Ibid.*

44. Robert Ball, "An Empirical Exploration of Neutralization Theory," *Criminologica* 4 (1966):22–32. For a similar view, see, M. William Minor, "The Neutralization of Criminal Offense," *Criminology* 18 (1980):103–20.

45. Robert Regoli and Eric Poole, "The Commitment of Delinquents to Their Misdeeds: A Reexamination," *Journal of Criminal Justice* 6 (1978):261–69.

46. Michael Hindelang, "The Commitment of Delinquents to Their Misdeeds: Do Delinquents Drift?" *Social Problems* 17 (1970):509.

47. Scott Briar and Irving Piliavin, "Delinquency, Situational Inducements and Commitment to Conformity," *Social Problems* 13 (1965–1966):35–45.

48. The description of inner and outer containments is from Schrag, *Crime and Justice: American Style*, p. 85; see generally, Walter Reckless, *The Crime Problem* (New York: Appleton Century Crofts, 1967). Among the many research reports by Walter Reckless and his colleagues are: W. Reckless, Simon Dinitz, and Ellen Murray, "Self-Concept as an Insulator Against Delin-

quency," *American Sociological Review* 21 (1956):744–46; Reckless, Dinitz, and Murray, "The Good Boy in a High Delinquency Area," *Journal of Criminal Law, Criminology, and Police Science* 48 (1957):1826; Walter Reckless, Simon Dinitz, and Barbara Kay, "The Self-Component in Potential Delinquency and Potential Non-delinquency," *American Sociological Review* 22 (1957):566–70; Walter Reckless and Simon Dinitz, "Pioneering with Self-Concept as a Vulnerability Factor in Delinquency," *Journal of Criminal Law, Criminology, and Police Science* 58 (1967):515-23.

49. Hirschi, *Causes of Delinquency.*

50. *Ibid.*, p. 231.

51. *Ibid.*, p. 66–74.

52. Michael Hindelang, "Causes of Delinquency: A Partial Replication and Extension," *Social Problems* 21 (1973):471–87.

53. Giordano, Cernkovich, and Pugh, "Friendships and Delinquency," pp. 1170–1202.

54. Gary Jensen and David Brownfield, "Parents and Drugs," *Criminology* 21 (1983):543–54. See also, M. Wiatrowski, D. Griswold, and M. Roberts, "Social Control Theory and Delinquency," *American Sociological Review* 46 (1981):525–41.

55. Marvin Krohn and James Massey, "Social Control and Delinquent Behavior: An Examination of the Elements of the Social Bond," *Sociological Quarterly* 21 (1980):529–43.

56. Randy LaGrange and Helene Raskin White, "Age Differences in Delinquency: A Test of Theory," *Criminology* 23 (1985):19–45.

57. Robert Agnew, "Social Control Theory and Delinquency: A Longitudinal Test," *Criminology* 23 (1985):47–61.

58. Alan E. Liska and M. D. Reed, "Ties to Conventional Institutions and Delinquency: Estimating Reciprocal Effects," *American Sociological Review* 50 (1985):547–60.

59. Terence Thornberry, "Toward an Interactional Theory of Delinquency," *Criminology* 25 (1987):863–91; Michael Wiatrowski, David Griswold, and Mary K. Roberts, "Social Control Theory and Delinquency," *American Sociological Review* 46 (1981):525–41.

60. President's Commission on Law Enforcement and the Administration of Youth Crime, *Task Force Report: Juvenile Delinquency and Youth* (Washington, D.C.: U.S. Government Printing Office, 1967), p. 43.

61. Kai Erickson, "Notes on the Sociology of Deviance," *Social Problems* 9 (1962):397–414.

62. Edwin Schur, *Labeling Deviant Behavior* (New York: Harper & Row, 1972), p. 21.

63. Howard Becker, *Outsiders, Studies in the Sociology of Deviance* (New York: Macmillan, 1963), p. 9.

64. Christy Visher, "Gender, Police Arrest Decision, and Notions of Chivalry," *Criminology* 21 (1983):5–28.

65. Marjorie Zatz, "Race, Ethnicity and Determinate Sentencing," *Criminology* 22 (1984):147–71.

66. Roland Chilton and Jim Galvin, "Race, Crime and Criminal Justice," *Crime and Delinquency* 31 (1985):3–14.

67. Joan Petersilia, "Racial Disparities in the Criminal Justice System: A Summary," *Crime and Delinquency* 31 (1985):15–34.

68. Walter Gove, ed., *The Labeling of Deviance: Evaluating a Perspective* (New York: John Wiley, 1975), p. 5.

69. *Ibid.*, p. 9.

70. Harold Garfinkle, "Conditions of Successful Degradation Ceremonies," *American Journal of Sociology* 61 (1956):420–24.

71. John Lofland, *Deviance and Identity* (Englewood Cliffs, N.J.: Prentice-Hall, 1969).

72. Frank Tannenbaum, *Crime and the Community* (New York: Columbia University Press, 1938), pp. 19–20.

73. Edwin Lemert, *Social Pathology* (New York: McGraw-Hill, 1951).

74. *Ibid.*, p. 211.

75. National Minority Council on Criminal Justice, *The Inequality of Justice* (Washington, D.C.: National Minority Advisory Council on Criminal Justice, 1981), p. 200.

76. Paul Lipsett, "The Juvenile Offender's Perception," *Crime and Delinquency* 14 (1968):49; Jack Foster, Simon Dinitz, and Walter Reckless, "Perception of Stigma Following Public Intervention for Delinquent Behavior," *Social Problems* 20 (1972):202.

77. Charles Tittle, "Labeling and Crime: An Empirical Evaluation," in Gove, ed., *The Labeling of Deviance*, pp. 157–79.

78. Melvin Ray and William Downs, "An Empirical Test of Labeling Theory Using Longitudinal Data," *Journal of Research in Crime and Delinquency* 23 (1986):169–94.

79. Susan Ageton and Delbert Elliott, "The Effect of Legal Processing on Self-Concept," (Boulder, Colo.: Institute of Behavioral Science, 1973).

80. Jack Gibbs, "Conceptions of Deviant Behavior: The Old and the New," *Pacific Sociological Review* 9 (1966):11–13.

81. Schur, *Labeling Deviant Behavior*, p. 14.

82. Ronald Akers, "Problems in the Sociology of Deviance," *Social Problems* 46 (1968):463.

83. Charles Wellford, "Labeling Theory and Criminology: An Assessment," *Social Problems* 22 (1975):335.

84. *Ibid.*

85. *Ibid.*, p. 107.

86. Alexander Liazos, "The Poverty of the Sociology of Deviance: Nuts, Sluts, and Perverts," *Social Problems* 20 (1971):103–120.

87. Charles Tittle, "Two Empirical Regularities (Maybe) in Search of an Explanation: Commentary on the Age/Crime Debate," *Criminology* 26 (1988):75–85.

88. James Q. Wilson and Richard Herrnstein, *Crime and Human Nature* (New York: Simon and Schuster, 1985).

89. Travis Hirschi, "Exploring Alternatives to Integrated Theory," Conference paper, Theoretical Integration in the Study of Deviance and Crime: Problems and Prospects, State University of New York at Albany, May, 1987.

90. Daniel Glazer, *Crime in Our Changing Society* (New York: Holt, Rinehart and Winston, 1978).

91. *Ibid.*, p. 125.

92. *Ibid.*

93. Richard Johnson, Anatasios Marcos, and Stephen Bahr, "The Role of Peers in the Complex Etiology of Adolescent Drug Use," *Criminology* 25 (1987):323–39.

94. Joseph Weis and J. David Hawkins, *Reports of the National Juvenile Assessment Centers, Preventing Delinquency* (Washington, D.C.: U.S. Department of Justice, 1981); Joseph Weis and John Sederstrom, *Reports of the National Juvenile Justice Assessment Centers, The Prevention of Serious Delinquency: What to Do* (Washington, D.C.: U.S. Department of Justice, 1981).

95. Delbert Elliott, David Huizinga and Suzanne Ageton, *Explaining Delinquency and Drug Use* (Beverly Hills, Cal.: Sage, 1985).

96. *Ibid.*, p. 147.

97. Thornberry, "Toward an Interactional Theory of Delinquency," pp. 863–91.

98. See, for example, Jean Piaget, *The Grasp of Consciousness* (Cambridge, Mass.: Harvard University Press, 1976).

99. Thornberry, "Toward an Interactional Theory of Delinquency," p. 885.

100. *Ibid.*, p. 886.

101. This research is known as the Rochester Youth Development Study. Thornberry's colleagues include Alan Lizotte, Margaret Farnsworth, and Susan Stern.

CHAPTER 9

SOCIOLOGICAL APPROACHES: SOCIAL CONFLICT THEORY

INTRODUCTION

It would be unusual to pick up the morning paper without seeing headlines loudly proclaiming renewed strife between the United States and her overseas adversaries, between union negotiators and management attorneys, between citizens and police authorities, or between Republicans and Democrats (or between Democrats and Democrats). The world is filled with conflict. Conflict can be destructive when it leads to war, violence, and death; it can be functional when it results in positive social change.

This chapter reviews criminological theories that allege that crime is a function of the conflict existing in almost every society. Theorists who hold a conflict orientation see the criminal law as an expression of the beliefs and values of the ruling class, and they see the criminal justice system as its social control mechanism. In contrast to the consensus-positivist position, the conflict position views crime as a reaction to the unfair distribution of wealth and power existing in society.

Conflict theorists are concerned with such issues as the role the government plays in creating a crimogenic environment; the relationship between personal or group power and the controlling and shaping of the criminal law; the role of bias in the operations of the justice system; and the relationship between a capitalist free-enterprise economy and crime rates.

Conflict theorists view crime as the outcome of class struggle. Conflict works to promote crime by creating a social atmosphere in which the law is a mechanism for controlling dissatisfied, "have-not" members of society while maintaining the position of the powerful. That is why crimes which are the province of the wealthy, such as illegal corporate activities, are punished much more leniently than those such as burglary, which are considered lower-class activities.

Social conflict theory has several independent branches. The first branch, generally referred to as **conflict theory,** assumes that crime is caused by the intergroup rivalry which exists in every society. The second branch is based more closely on the writings of Karl Marx and focuses on the crime-producing traits of capitalist society; the terms used to describe this approach are **critical, radical,** or **Marxist criminology.** While related, these two theoretical viewpoints are different enough to warrant independent analysis.

MARXIST THOUGHT

The foundation of conflict theory can be traced to the political and economic philosophy of **Karl Marx** (1818–1883) and his colleague Friedrich Engels (1820–1895).[1] Marx believed that the character of every civilization is determined by its mode of production —the way its people develop and produce material goods (**materialism**). Production has two components: (1) **productive forces,** which include such things as technology, energy sources, and material resources; and (2) **productive relations,** which are the relationships that exist among the people producing goods and services. The most important relationship in industrial culture is between the owners of the means of production, the **capitalist bourgeoisie,** and the people who do the actual labor, the **proletariat.** Throughout history, society has been organized along the same lines: master–slave, lord–serf, and now capitalist–proletarian.

According to Marx and Engels, capitalist society is subject to the development of a rigid **class** structure. At the top is the capitalist bourgeoisie. Next comes the working proletariat, which actually produces goods and services. At the bottom of society are the fringe members, who produce nothing and live off the work of others: the **lumpen proletariat.**

In Marxist theory, the term *class* does not refer to an attribute or characteristic of a person or a group; rather, it denotes position in relation to others. Thus, it is not necessary to have a particular amount of wealth or prestige to be a member of the capitalist class; it is more important to have the power to exploit others economically, legally, and socially.

The political and economic philosophy of the dominant class influences all aspects of life. Consciously or unconsciously, artists, writers, and teachers bend their work to the whims of the capitalist system. Thus, the economic system controls all facets of human life; and consequently, people's lives revolve around the means of production. As Marx says in *Grundrisse:*

> *In all forms of society there is one specific kind of production which predominates over the rest, whose relations thus assign rank and influence to the others. It is a general illumination which bathes all the other colours and modifies their particularity. It is a particular ether which determines the specific gravity of every being which has materialized within it.[2]*

Karl Marx was so impoverished while writing *Das Kapital* that one of his children died of malnutrition.

Marx believed that societies and their structures were not stable but could change through slow evolution or sudden violence. Historically, such change occurs because of contradictions present in a society. These contradictions are antagonisms, or conflicts, between elements in the existing social arrangement that in the long run are incompatible with one another. If these social conflicts are not resolved, they tend to destabilize society, leading to social change.

How could social change occur in capitalist society? Marx held that the laboring class produces goods that exceed wages in value. This theory is called **surplus value.** The surplus value goes into the hands of the capitalists as profit, and it is used to acquire an ever-expanding capitalist base that relies on advanced technology for efficiency. Since capitalists are in constant competition with each other, they must find ways of producing goods more efficiently and cheaply. One way is to pay workers the lowest possible wages

or to replace them with labor-saving machinery. Soon the supply of efficiently made goods outstrips the ability of the laboring classes to purchase them, a condition that precipitates an economic crisis. During this period, weaker enterprises go under. They are consequently incorporated into ever-expanding, monopolistic mega-corporations strong enough to further exploit the workers. Marx believed that in the ebb and flow of the business cycle, the capitalist system contained the seeds of its own destruction, and that from its ashes would grow a socialist state in which the workers themselves would own the means of production.

In his analysis, Marx used the **dialectic** method, based on the analysis developed by the philosopher Georg Hegel (1770–1831). Hegel argued that for every idea, or *thesis*, there exists an opposing argument, or *antithesis*. Since neither position can ever be truly accepted, the result is a merger of the two ideas, a *syn-*

thesis. Marx adapted this analytic method for his study of class struggle. History, argued Marx, is replete with examples of two opposing forces whose conflict promotes social change. When conditions are bad enough, the oppressed will rise up against the owners and eventually replace them. Thus, in the end, the capitalist system will destroy itself.

Marx on Crime

Marx did not write a great deal on the subject of crime. His collaborator Fredrich Engels did spend some time on the subject, in his work *The Condition of the Working Class in England in 1844.*[3] He portrayed crime as a function of social demoralization: a collapse of people's humanity reflecting a decline in society. Workers, demoralized by capitalist society, are caught up in a process that leads to crime and violence.

Marx's most famous statement on crime seems almost tongue-in-cheek:

> *A philosopher produces ideas, a poet poems, a clergyman sermons, a professor compendia and so on. A criminal produces crime. If we look a little closer at the connection between this latter branch of production and society as a whole, we shall rid ourselves of many prejudices. The criminal produces not only crimes but also criminal law, and with this also the professor who gives lectures on criminal law and in addition to this the inevitable compendium in which this same professor throws his lectures onto the general market as "commodities" . . .*

> *The criminal moreover produces the whole of the police and of criminal justice, constables, judges, hangmen, juries, etc.; and all these different lines of business, which form equally many categories of the social division of labour, develop different capacities of the human spirit, create new needs and new ways of satisfying them. Torture alone has given rise to the most ingenious mechanical inventions, and employed many honorable craftsmen in the production of instruments.*[4]

Marx seems to imply that there are benefits to crime and its role in producing social institutions —police, courts, law, and law professors. Criminologists Ian Taylor, Paul Walton, and Jock Young interpret Marx's passage as emphasizing the criminal nature of the capitalist system.[5] They argue that Marx

is suggesting the possibility of a crime-free society by showing that capitalist economic and social relationships produce crime. Moreover, these authors believe Marx is ridiculing the consensus-functionalist theorists, who maintain that all behavior serves a function or reflects a consensus of societal viewpoints. So long as capitalism exists, it is foolish to think that people obey the law because it is "right"; they do so because the law represents the will of those who hold power.

Marxist thought provides a point of departure from which crime and deviance can be understood. It points out the relationship between economic conditions and the decision to violate the law. Theorists who use Marxian analysis reject the notions that law is designed to maintain a tranquil and fair society, and that criminals are malevolent people who wish to trample the rights of others. By focusing on the capitalist state's role in producing a crimogenic society, Marxist thought serves as the basis for all conflict theory.

CONFLICT THEORY

Conflict theory rose to criminological prominence during the 1960s and 1970s, when a number of developments expanded its influence among criminologists. One was the proliferation of research using self-report scales. These studies yielded data suggesting that crime and delinquency were much more evenly distributed through the social structure than had been indicated by the official statistics.[6] If this were true, then middle-class participation in crime was going unrecorded, while the lower class was the subject of discriminatory law enforcement practices by the criminal justice system. Criminologists began to view the justice system as a mechanism to control the lower class and maintain the status quo, rather than as the means of dispensing fair and even-handed justice.[7]

The popularity of the labeling perspective in the late 1960s and early 1970s also contributed to the development of the conflict model. Labeling theorists, such as Howard Becker, rejected the notion that crime is morally wrong and called for the analysis of the interaction among crime, criminal, victim, and labeling authorities.

Yet some criminologists charged that labeling theory did not go far enough in analyzing the important relationships in society: it simply dwelled on "nuts, sluts and perverts."[8] Consequently, a group of criminologists led by Richard Quinney, Austin Turk, William Chambliss, Herman and Julia Schwendinger, Tony Platt, and Paul Takagi began to produce scholarship and research directed at (1) identifying "real" crimes in U.S. society, such as profiteering, sexism, and racism; (2) evaluating how the criminal law is used as a mechanism of social control; and (3) turning the attention of citizens to the inequities in U.S. society.[9] Their efforts were guided by the writings of two prominent social theoreticians, Ralf Dahrendorf and George Vold, whose thoughts are set out in the accompanying Close-Up. One sociologist, David Greenberg, comments on the scholarship that was produced:

> The theme that dominated much of the work in this area was the contention that criminal legislation was determined not by moral consensus or the common interests of the entire society, but by the relative power of groups determined to use the criminal law to advance their own special interests or to impose their moral preferences on others.[10]

Adding impetus to this movement was the general and widespread social and political upheaval of the late sixties and early seventies. These forces included Vietnam War protests, counterculture movements, and various forms of political protest. Conflict theory flourished within this framework, since it provided a systematic basis for challenging the legitimacy of the government's creation and application of law. The crackdown on political dissidents by agents of the federal government, the prosecution of draft resistors, and similar events seemed designed to maintain control in the hands of political power brokers.

——— CONFLICT CRIMINOLOGY ———

In the early 1970s, conflict theory began to have a significant influence on criminological study. Several influential scholars, inspired by the writings of social philosophers such as Ralf Dahrendorf and George Vold, abandoned the criminological mainstream and adapted a conflict orientation. For example, William Chambliss and Robert Seidman wrote the well-respected treatise *Law, Order and Power*, which documents how the justice system operates to protect the rich and powerful. After closely observing its operations, Chambliss and Seidman drew this conclusion:

> In America it is frequently argued that to have "freedom" is to have a system which allows one group to make a profit over another. To maintain the existing legal system requires a choice. On this argument that choice is between maintaining a legal system that serves to support the existing economic system with its power structure and developing an equitable legal system accompanied by the loss of "personal freedom." But the old question comes back to plague us: Freedom for whom? Is the black man who provides such a ready source of cases for the welfare workers, the mental hospitals, and the prisons "free"? Are the slum dwellers who are arrested night after night for "loitering," "drunkenness," or being "suspicious" free? The freedom protected by the system of law is the freedom of those who can afford it. The law serves their interests, but they are not "society"; they are one element of society. They may in some complex societies even be a majority (though this is very rare), but the myth that the law serves the interests of "society" misrepresents the facts.[11]

Chambliss and Seidman's writing displays some of the common objectives of conflict criminology: to describe how the control of the political and economic system affects the administration of criminal justice; to show how the definitions of crime favor those who control the justice system; and to analyze the role of conflict in contemporary society. Their scholarship also reflects another major objective of conflict theory: to show how justice is American society is skewed so that those who deserve to be punished the most (wealthy white-collar criminals whose crimes cost society millions of dollars) are actually punished the least, while those whose crime are relatively minor and committed out of economic necessity (petty underclass thieves) receive the stricter sanctions.[12]

Power Relations

A principle motive of conflict theory is to describe the crimogenic influence of social and economic **power**—the ability of persons and groups to determine and control the behavior of others.[13] The unequal distribution of power produces conflict; conflict

CLOSE-UP

Ralf Dahrendorf and George Vold: The Roots of Conflict Criminology

In formulating their views of society's influence on crime, modern conflict theorists rely heavily on the writings of pioneering social thinkers **Ralf Dahrendorf** and **George Vold.** Below their views of the nature of crime and conflict and crime are highlighted.

Ralf Dahrendorf is considered one of the major contributors to the modern conflict perspective. He believed that the consensus-functionalist model of society is utopian, without basis in the real world. Instead, society should be seen as organized into *imperatively coordinated associations.* These relationships comprise two groups: those who dominate (possess authority) and those who are subject to authority. However, since dominating one section of society (such as industry) does not mean dominating another (such as government) society is a plurality of competing interest groups.

In his classic work, *Class and Class Conflict in Industrial Society,* Dahrendorf attempted to show how society has changed since Marx formulated his concepts of class, state, and conflict. Dahrendorf argues that Marx did not foresee the changes that have occurred in the laboring classes: "The working class of today, far from being a homogeneous group of equally unskilled and impoverished people, is in fact a stratum differentiated by numerous subtle and not so subtle distinctions." Workers are divided into the unskilled, semi-skilled, and skilled; the interests of one group may not match the needs of the others. Consequently, Marx's concept of a cohesive proletarian class has proved inaccurate. Consequently, Dahrendorf embraces a "pure" conflict rather than Marxist orientation.

Dahrendorf proposes a unified conflict theory of human behavior, which can be summarized in the following statements:

• Every society is at every point subject to processes of change; social change is everywhere.

• Every society displays at every point dissent and conflict; social conflict is everywhere.

• Every element in a society renders a contribution to its disintegration and change.

• Every society is based on the coercion of some of its members by others.

Dahrendorf does not speak directly to the issue of crime, but his model of conflict serves as a pillar of modern conflict criminology.

Though Dahrendorf contributed its theoretical underpinnings, conflict theory was actually adapted to criminology by George Vold. Vold argued that crime also can be explained by social conflict. Laws are created by politically oriented groups who seek the assistance of the government to help them defend their rights and protect their interests. If a group can marshal enough support, a law will be created to hamper and curb the interests of some opposition group. As Vold says, "The whole political process of law making, law breaking and law enforcement becomes a direct reflection of deep-seated and fundamental conflicts between interest groups and their more general struggles for the control of the police power of the state." Every stage of the process—from the passage of the law, to the prosecution of the case, to the relationships between inmate and guard and parole agent and parolee—is marked by conflict.

Vold finds that criminal acts are a consequence of direct contact between forces struggling to control society. Though their criminal content may mask their political meaning, closer examination of even the most basic violent acts often reveals political undertones.

Vold's model cannot be used to explain all types of crime. It is limited to situations in which rival group loyalties collide. It cannot explain impulsive, irrational acts unrelated to any group's interest. Despite this limitation, Vold finds that a great deal of criminal activity results from intergroup clashes.

Discussion Questions

1. Are criminal acts the result of social conflict?

2. How would a conflict theorist such as Vold account for violent personal crimes such as rape or robbery?

SOURCES: Ralf Dahrendorf, *Class and Class Conflict in Industrial Society* (Stanford, Conn.: Stanford University Press, 1959); George Vold, *Theoretical Criminology* (New York: Oxford University Press, 1958).

According to Chambliss and Seidman, "it is frequently argued that to have 'freedom' is to have a system which allows one group to make a profit over another."

is rooted in the competition for power. Power is the means by which people shape public opinion to meet their personal interests. According to the conflict view, crime is defined by those in power; laws are culturally relative and not bound by any absolute standard of right and wrong.[14]

Richard Quinney, before he became an instrumental Marxist (see below), was one of the most influential conflict theorists. He integrated his beliefs about power, society, and criminality into a theory he referred to as the **social reality of crime.** The theory's six propositions are contained in Table 9.1.[15]

According to Quinney, criminal definitions (law) represent the interests of those who hold power in society. Where there is conflict between social groups —for example, the wealthy and the poor—those who hold power will create laws to benefit themselves and hold rivals in check. The rather harsh punishments for property crime in the United States are designed to help those who already have wealth keep it in their possession; in contrast, the lenient sanctions attached to corporate crimes are designed to give the

already powerful a free hand at economic exploitation. Quinney wrote that the formulation of criminal definitions is based on such factors as (1) changing social conditions; (2) emerging interests; (3) increasing demands that political, economic, and religious interests be protected; and (4) changing conceptions of public interest. In the sixth statement, Quinney pulls together the ideas he developed in the preceding five: concepts of crime are controlled by the powerful, and the criminal justice system works to secure the needs of the powerful. When people develop behavior patterns that conflict with these needs, the agents of the rich—the justice system—define them as criminals.

Because of their reliance on power relations, criminal definitions are a constantly changing set of concepts that mirror the political organization of society. Law is not an abstract body of rules that represents an absolute moral code. Law is an integral part of society, a force that represents a way of life and a method of doing things. Crime is a function of power relations and an inevitable result of social con-

TABLE 9.1   The Social Reality of Crime

1. *Definition of Crime:* Crime is a definition of human conduct that is created by authorized agents in a politically organized society.

2. *Formulation of Criminal Definitions:* Criminal definitions describe behaviors that conflict with the interests of the segments of society that have the power of shape public policy.

3. *Application of Criminal Definitions:* Criminal definitions are applied by the segments of society that have the power to shape the enforcement and administration of criminal law.

4. *Development of Behavior Patterns in Relation to Criminal Definitions:* Behavior patterns are structured in segmentally organized society in relation to criminal definitions, and within this context persons engage in actions that have relative probabilities of being defined as criminal.

5. *Construction of Criminal Conceptions:* Conceptions of crime are constructed and diffused in the segments of society by various means of communication.

6. *The Social Reality of Crime:* The social reality of crime is constructed by the formulation and application of criminal definitions, the development of behavior patterns to criminal definitions, and the construction of criminal conceptions.

SOURCE: Richard Quinney, *The Social Reality of Crime* (Boston, Mass.: Little, Brown, 1970), pp. 15–23.

flict. Criminals are not simply social misfits, but people who have come up short in the struggle for success and are seeking alternative means of achieving wealth, status, or even survival.[16] Consequently, law violations can be viewed as political or even quasi-revolutionary acts.[17]

Research on Conflict Theory

Research efforts designed to test conflict theory seem quite different from those that evaluate consensus models. Similar methodologies are often used, but conflict-centered research places less emphasis on testing hypotheses of a particular theory and instead attempts to show that conflict principles hold up under empirical scrutiny. Topics of interest include such issues as comparing the crime rates of members of powerless groups with those of members of the elite classes. Conflict researchers examine the operation of

the justice system to uncover bias and discrimination. They also attempt to chart the historical development of criminal law and to identify laws created with the intent of preserving the power of the elite classes at the expense of the poor.

Conflict theorists maintain that social inequality creates the need for people to commit some crimes—such as burglary and larceny—as a means of social and economic survival, and to commit others—such as assault, homicide, and drug use—as a means of expressing rage and frustration. Conflict theorists point to data showing that crime rates vary according to indicators of poverty and need. For example, David McDowall compared homicide rates in Detroit, Baltimore, Cleveland, and Memphis with infant mortality rates over a 50-year period (since the latter variable is an efficient measure of poverty), and found that they were significantly interrelated.[18] Other data collected by ecologists (see Chapter 6) show that crime is strongly related to measures of social inequality, such as income level, deteriorated living conditions, and relative economic deprivation.[19]

Another area of conflict-oriented research involves the operations of the criminal justice system. Does it operate as an instrument of class oppression or as a fair and even-handed social control agency? Some conflict researchers have found evidence of class bias. For example, criminologists David Jacobs and David Britt found that state jurisdictions with significant levels of economic disparity were also the most likely to have the largest number of police shooting fatalities. Their data suggests that police act more forcefully in areas where class conflicts create the perception that extreme forms of social control are needed to maintain order.[20] Similarly, Alan Lizotte examined 816 criminal cases processed by the Chicago criminal courts during a one-year period and found that members of powerless, disenfranchised groups are the most likely to receive prejudicial sentences in criminal courts.[21] Other research efforts have shown that both white and black offenders are more likely to receive stricter sentences in criminal courts if their personal characteristics (single, young, urban, male) give them the appearance of being a member of the "dangerous classes."[22] Conflict theorists also point to studies which show that the criminal justice system is quick to take action when the victim of crime is wealthy, white, and male, but are disinterested when the victim is poor, black, and fe-

Conflict theorists view crime as the outcome of a never-ending class struggle. Here, police break up a peaceful demonstration by strikers at a steel plant in Chicago, 1937.

male, as evidence of the how power positions affect justice.[23]

Analysis of Conflict Theory

Conflict theory attempts to identify the power relations in society and draw attention to their role in promoting criminal behavior. Conflict criminologists adopt the labeling-interactionist approach but push it beyond the study of deviant groups. Their aims are more global. They wish to describe how class differentials produce an ecology of human behavior that favors the wealthy and powerful over the poor and weak. Conflict criminologists reject the consensus view that law is designed to create a just society and that criminals are predators who violate the rights of others.

This view is not without its critics. Some criminologists claim that the conflict view is naive, sug-

gesting instead that crime is a matter of rational choice and may be motivated more by greed and selfishness than poverty and hopelessness.[24] Critics point to data indicating a weak relationship between unemployment and crime rates; they conclude that crime is less likely to be a function of poverty and class conflict than it is a product of personal needs, socialization, or some other related factor.[25]

Similarly, studies of the criminal justice system often fail to prove conclusively that it is used only to support the status quo. Studies in the area of police discretion, criminal court sentencing, and correctional policy have drawn mixed conclusions. While some studies show discrimination against the poor and minority group members, others indicate that the system is relatively unbiased.[26] For example, Theodore Chiricos and Gordon Waldo found little support for conflict theory after examining the prison sentences of 10,488 inmates in three southeastern states.[27] They concluded:

CLOSE-UP

Willem Bonger: The Roots of Marxist Criminology

Marxist criminologists are influenced by numerous historically important sources. Of course, the writings of Marx and Engels have had the greatest influence on their thinking. Another significant influence is George Rusche and Otto Kircheimer's *Punishment and Social Structure*, which traces the influence of capitalism on concepts of law and justice. However, the most important historical influence probably is the writing of **Willem Bonger.** Born in 1876 in Holland, Bonger committed suicide in 1940 rather than submit to Nazi rule. He is famous for his Marxist socialist concepts of crime causation.

According to Bonger's criminological theory, the abnormal element of crime is of social and not biological origin. With the exception of a few special cases, crime lies within the boundaries of normal human behavior. The response to crime is punishment—the application of penalties considered more severe than spontaneous moral condemnation. It is administered by those in political control—that is, by the state.

Another element of Bonger's theory is that no act is naturally immoral or criminal. Crimes are antisocial acts that reflect current morality. Since the social structure is changing continually, ideas of what is moral and what is not change continually. The tension between rapidly changing morality, which is common in modern society, and a comparatively static, predominately bourgeois criminal law can become very great.

Similarly, crimes are antisocial acts harmful to those who have the power at their command to control society. Society is divided into have and have-not groups, not on the basis of people's innate ability, but because of the system of production that is in force. In every society divided into a ruling class and an inferior class, penal law serves the will of the former. Even though criminal laws may appear to protect members of both classes, hardly any act is punished that does not injure the interests of the dominant class.

The capitalist system, characterized by extreme competition, is held together by force rather than consensus. Attempts to control law violations through force are a sign of a weak society. The social order is maintained for the benefit of the capitalists at the expense of the population as a whole.

Bonger states that the desire for pleasure is innate in everyone. Unfortunately, in capitalist society people can enjoy luxuries and advantages only if they possess large amounts of capital. Nonetheless, the present society exhorts all people to obtain pleasure in general and money in particular. People are encouraged by capitalist society to be egotistical, caring only for their own lives and pleasures and ignoring the plight of the disadvantaged. As a

What the data suggest, rather conclusively, is that the socioeconomic status of convicted criminal offenders is unrelated to the severity of the state's official sanction, as reflected in the length of prison terms assigned by the courts. Such a conclusion, which strongly contradicts common folklore and the general expectations of conflict criminology, is given added credence by the fact that it is true for a total of seventeen different criminal offenses and for three separate states. Furthermore, that conclusion is sustained (for Florida) regardless of the age, race, number of prior arrests, felony convictions or juvenile commitments.[28]

While conflict definitions seem to have validity, considering the social and economic bias that exists in the United States today, some criminologists continue to challenge the principles underlying the conflict view.

MARXIST CRIMINOLOGY

Above all, Marxism is a critique of capitalism.[29]

The second branch of social conflict theory is known as Marxist, radical, or critical criminology.[30] As you may recall, radical criminologists view crime as a function of the capitalist mode of production: capitalism produces haves and have-nots, each engaging in a particular type of criminality. Unlike conflict theorists, radicals do not view crime as being subjective; crimes consequence of the present environment, Bonger claims, people have become more capable of crime than if the environment had developed under a socialist philosophy. *Though the environment makes both the proletariat and the bourgeoisie crime-prone, only the former are likely to become officially recognized criminals. The key to this problem is that the legal system discriminates against the poor by legalizing the egoistic actions of the wealthy. However, upper-class individuals, the bourgeoisie, will commit crime if (1) they have an opportunity to gain an illegal advantage; and (2) their lack of moral sense enables them to violate social rules. It is the drive toward success at any price that pushes wealthier individuals toward criminality.*

Bonger maintains that crime is a function of poverty. The relationship can be direct, as when a person steals to survive, or indirect, as when poverty kills the social sentiments in each person and destroys the sentiments between people. It is not the absolute amount of wealth that affects crime, but its distribution. If wealth is distributed unequally through the social structure and people are taught to equate economic advantage with superiority, then those who are poor and therefore inferior will be crime-prone. In other words, the economic system will intensify any personal disadvantage people have—for example, psychological problems—and increase their propensity to commit crime.

Finally, Bonger's theory states that almost all crime will disappear if society progresses from competitive capitalism, to monopoly capitalism, to having the means of production held in common, to the ultimate stage of society: the redistribution of property according to the maxim "each according to his needs." If this state of society cannot be reached, a residue of crime will always occur. If socialism can be achieved, then remaining crimes will be of the irrational psychopathic type caused by individual mental problems.

Bonger's writing continues to be one of the most oft-cited sources of Marxist thought.

Discussion Questions

1. Would a pure Marxist economic system remove the need to commit crime?
2. Is greed a natural human trait?

SOURCES: Willem Bonger, *Criminality and Economic Conditions*, abridged ed. (Bloomington, Ind.: Indiana University Press, 1969); George Rusche and Otto Kircheimer, *Punishment and Social Structure* (New York: Columbia University Press, 1939).

are considered socially harmful acts whose consequences are objectively dangerous and undesirable.[31]

In a capitalist society, those in political power also control the definition of crime and the emphasis of the criminal justice system. Consequently, the proletariat commit heavily punished street crimes—rape, murder, mugging—since those are the only crimes available to them. Members of the middle class or petit bourgeoisie cheat on their taxes and engage in petty corporate crime (employee theft), acts which generate social disapproval but are rarely punished severely. The wealthy bourgeoisie are involved in acts that should be described as crimes but are not—racism, sexism, profiteering. Though there are regulatory laws which control business activities, these are rarely enforced and lightly punished. Laws regulating corporate crime are really "window dressing," designed to impress the working class with how fair the justice system is. In reality, the justice system is the equivalent of an army which defends the owners of property in their ongoing struggle against the workers.[32]

Marxist criminology has many historical roots. One of the most important sources is the writing of Dutch social philosopher Willem Bonger; his thoughts are set out in the accompanying Close-Up.

Origins of Marxist Criminology

The emergence of modern Marxist criminology can be traced to the publication in 1973 of *The New Criminol-*

ogy, by Ian Taylor, Paul Walston, and Jock Young.[33] This brilliant work was a far-reaching critique of existing concepts in criminology and a call for development of new criminological methods. However, the work had an antecedent in the National Deviancy Conference (NDC), formed in 1968 by a group of British sociologists. Numbering about 300, this organization sponsored several national symposiums and dialogues. Members of the group came from all walks of life, but at its core was a group of academics who were critical of the positivist criminology being taught in English and American universities. More specifically, they rejected the conservative stance of criminologists and their close financial relationship with government funding agencies.

Originally, the NDC was not a Marxist-oriented group, but rather investigated the concept of deviance from a labeling perspective. They called attention to ways in which social control might actually be a cause of deviance rather than a response to it. However, by 1973 many conference members became concerned about the political nature of social control. A schism developed within the NDC, with one group clinging to the now-conservative interactionist-labeling perspective while the second embraced Marxist thought.

While these events were transpiring in Britain, a small group of scholars in the United States began to follow a new radical approach to criminology. The locus of the radical school was the criminology program at the University of California at Berkeley. The most noted Marxist scholars at that institution were Anthony Platt, Paul Takagi, and Herman and Julia Schwendinger. Marxist scholars at other U.S. academic institutions included Richard Quinney, William Chambliss, and Barry Krisberg. The U.S. radicals were influenced by the widespread social ferment occurring during the late 1960s and early 1970s. The war in Vietnam, prison struggles, and the civil rights and feminist movements produced a climate in which criticism of the ruling class seemed a natural by-product. Mainstream, positivist criminology was criticized as being overtly conservative, pro-government, and antihuman. Critical criminologists scoffed when their fellow scholars used statistical analysis of computerized data to describe criminal and delinquent behavior. As Barry Krisberg has written:

> *Many of our scientific heroes of the past, upon rereading, turned out to be racists or, more generally, apol-*

ogists for social injustice. In response to the widespread protests on campuses and throughout society, many of the contemporary giants of social science emerged as defenders of the status quo and vocally dismissed the claims of the oppressed for social justice.[34]

Many of the new Marxist criminologists had enjoyed distinguished careers as positivist criminologists. Some, such as William Chambliss and Richard Quinney, were moved by career interests from positivism to social conflict theory to a radical-Marxist approach to crime. Marxists did not meet widespread approval at major universities. Rumors of purges were common during the 1970s, and the criminology school at Berkeley was eventually closed for what many believe were political reasons. Even today there exists conflict between critical thinkers and mainstream academics. Prestigious Harvard Law School, as well as other law centers, have been the scene of conflict and charges of purges and tenure denials because some professors have held critical views of law and society.

Fundamentals of Marxist Criminology

As a general rule, Marxist criminologists ignore formal theory construction with its heavy emphasis on empirical testing. They scoff at the objective "value free" stance of mainstream criminologists and instead argue that there should be a political or ideological basis for criminological scholarship.[35] Marxists consider it essential to **demystify** law and justice, that is, to unmask its true purpose. They charge that conventional criminology is devoted to identifying the social conditions which cause crime. Such studies which focus upon the crime-producing effects of family structure, intelligence, peer relations, and school performance serve to keep the lower classes servile by showing why they are more criminal, less intelligent, and more prone to school failure and family problems than the middle class. Demystification involves the identification of the destructive intent of capitalist inspired and funded criminology, rather than adding to its literature.

While no single view defines Marxist criminology today, its general theme is the relationship between crime and the ownership and control of private property in a capitalist society.[36] According to sociologist Gregg Barak, ownership and control of productive private property is the principal basis of power in U.S.

society.[37] Social conflict is fundamentally related to the historical and social distribution of productive private property. Destructive social conflicts inherent within the capitalist system cannot be resolved unless that system is itself destroyed or ended.

Instrumental Marxism.   One group of Marxists is referred to as **instrumentalists.**[38] They view the criminal law and criminal justice system solely as an instrument for controlling the poor, have-not members of society. According to the instrumental view, capitalist justice serves the powerful and rich and enables them to impose their morality and standards of behavior on the entire society. Under capitalism, economic power enables its holders to extend their self-serving definition of illegal or criminal behavior to encompass those who might threaten the status quo or interfere with their quest for ever-increasing profits.[39] For example, David Jacobs' research shows how the concentration of monetary assets in the nation's largest firms is translated into the political power needed to control the tax laws and limit the firms' tax liabilities.[40]

The poor, according to this branch of Marxist theory, may or may not commit more crimes than the rich; but they certainly are arrested and punished more often. Under the capitalist system, the poor are driven to crime because a natural frustration exists in a society in which affluence is well publicized but unattainable. Because of class conflict, a deep-rooted hostility is generated among members of the lower class toward a social order they are not allowed to shape or participate in.[41]

Richard Quinney is one of the most influential instrumental Marxists. He argues that the goal of criminology should be to explicate the rule of law in capitalist society, and show how it works to preserve ruling class power. Quinney's Marxist theory can be summarized in the following statements:

- American society is based on an advanced capitalist economy, and the state is organized to serve the interests of the dominant economic class, the capitalist ruling class.

- Criminal law is an instrument of the state and ruling class to maintain and perpetuate the existing social and economic order.

- Crime control in capitalist society is accomplished through a variety of institutions and agencies estab-

lished and administered by a governmental elite, representing ruling class interests for the purpose of establishing domestic order.

- The contradictions of advanced capitalism—the disjunction between existence and essence—require that the subordinate classes remain oppressed by whatever means necessary, especially through the coercion and violence of the legal system.

- Only with the collapse of capitalist society and the creation of a new society, based on socialist principles, will there be a solution to the crime problem.[42]

The writings of a number of other influential Marxist theorists have helped shape this field of inquiry. Among the most prominent are **Herman Schwendinger** and **Julia Siegel Schwendinger.** According to their view, legal relations in the United States secure an economic infrastructure that centers around a capitalist mode of production. The legal system is designed to guard the position of the owners (bourgeoisie) at the expense of the workers (proletariat). Legal relations maintain the family and school structure so as to secure the labor force. Even common-law crimes, such as murder and rape, are implemented to protect capitalism.

According to the Schwendingers, the basic laws of the land (such as constitutional laws) are based on the conditions that reproduce the class system as a whole. Laws are aimed at securing the domination of the capitalist system. Though the system may at times secure the interests of the working class—for example, when laws are created which protect collective bargaining—due to the inherent antagonisms built into the capitalist system, all laws generally contradict their stated purpose of producing justice. Legal relations maintain patterns of individualism and selfishness, and in so doing perpetuate a class system characterized by anarchy, oppression, and crime.[43]

Barry Krisberg has linked crime to the differentials in privilege that exist in capitalist society. According to Krisberg, crime is a function of **privilege.** Crimes are created by the powerful to further their domination. Crimes serve to deflect attention from the violence and social injustice the rich inflict upon the masses to keep them subordinate and oppressed.

Krisberg is concerned with how privilege influences criminality. He defines *privilege* as the possession of that which is valued by a particular social group in a given historical period. Privilege includes rights, such as life, liberty, and happiness; traits, such as intelligence, sensitivity, and humanity; and material goods, such as monetary wealth, luxuries, and land. The privilege system is also concerned with the distribution and preservation of privilege. Krisberg argues that force—the effective use of violence and coercion—is the major factor in determining which social group ascends to the position of defining and holding privilege.[44]

Other Marxist scholars have called for a review of the role of the professional criminologist. For example, Anthony Platt has charged that criminologists have helped support state repression with their focus on poor and minority criminals:

> We are just beginning to realize that criminology has serviced domestic repression in the same way that economics, political science, and anthropology have greased the wheels and even manufactured some of the important parts of modern imperialism. Given the ways in which this system has been used to repress and maintain the powerlessness of poor people, people of color, and young people, it is not too far-fetched to characterize many criminologists as domestic war criminals.[45]

Platt goes on to suggest that criminology must redefine its goals and definitions:

> In the past we have been constrained by a legal definition of crime which restricts us to studying and ultimately helping to control only legally defined "criminals." We need a more humanistic definition of crime, one which reflects the reality of a legal system based on power and privilege. To accept the legal definition of crime is to accept the fiction of neutral law. A human rights definition of crime frees us to examine imperialism, racism, sexism, capitalism, exploitation and other political or economic systems which contribute to human misery and deprive people of their potentialities.[46]

Structural Marxism.   Structural Marxists disagree with the view that the relationship between law and capitalism is undimensional, always working for the rich and against the poor. Law is not the exclusive domain of the rich; it works to maintain the long-term interests of the capitalist system. If law and justice were purely instruments of the capitalist class, why would anti-trust and other white-collar crime be cre-

ated? To a structuralist, the law is designed to keep the system operating in an efficient manner, and anyone—capitalist or proletarian—who rocks the boat is sanctioned. For example, anti-trust legislation is designed to prevent any single capitalist from dominating the system and preventing others from "playing the game." One person cannot get too powerful at the expense of the economic system as a whole.

Despite such misapprehension over the role of traditional science, there have been some efforts to create somewhat "formal" theories within the framework of Marxist criminology. One of the most highly regarded is **Stephen Spitzer**'s Marxian theory of deviance.[47] He finds that law in the capitalist system defines as deviant (or criminal) any person who disturbs, hinders, or calls into question any of the following:

- Capitalist modes of appropriating the product of human labor (for example, when the poor "steal" from the rich)
- The social conditions under which capitalist production takes place (for example, when some persons refuse or are unable to perform wage labor)
- Patterns of distribution and consumption in capitalist society (for example, when persons use drugs for escape and transcendence rather than sociability and adjustment)
- The process of socialization for productive and nonproductive roles (for example, when youths refuse to be schooled or deny the validity of "family life")
- The ideology that supports the functioning of capitalist society (for example, when people become proponents of alternative forms of social organization).

Among the many important points Spitzer makes is that capitalist societies have special ways of dealing with troublesome numbers of deviants. One mechanism is to *normalize* formerly deviant or illegal acts by absorbing them into the mainstream of society—for example, through legalization of small amounts of marijuana. *Conversion* involves co-opting deviants by making them part of the system—for example, a gang leader may be recruited to work with younger delinquents. *Containment* involves segregation of deviants into isolated geographic areas so that they can easily be controlled—for example, by creating a ghetto. Fi-

Marxists view the justice system as the equivalent of an army which defends the owners of property against the poor and powerless.

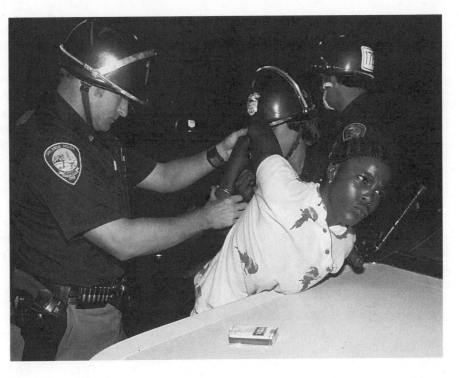

nally, Spitzer believes that capitalist society actively supports some criminal enterprises, such as organized crime, so that such enterprises can provide a means of support for groups who might otherwise become a burden on the state.

Integrated Marxist Theory

One recent trend in critical criminology has been to integrate some of the basic principles of Marxist theory with concepts derived from traditional theories, such as cultural deviance, social control, and labeling. Some Marxists recognize that these mainstream approaches are compatible with their own views of society.[48] For example, strain theory describes the outcome of economic inequality which Marxists believe is inevitable in capitalist society. Similarly, social control theory rests on the deviant's detachment from significant others and groups, a condition which is not incompatible with the view that capitalism destroys social cohesion. As W. Byron Groves and Robert Sampson put it:

> . . . traditional criminologists had hit on several crucial ideas, and had translated those ideas into empirical

conclusions that were compatible with a radical explanation of lower-class criminality.[49]

With this recognition of the contribution of mainstream criminology in mind, Marxists have begun to create integrated views of criminality. Below, three of the most important integrated theories are briefly discussed.

Power-Control Theory.   John Hagan and his associates have created a theoretical model which combines social control and Marxist theory concepts to explain gender differences in the onset of juvenile delinquency. Hagan's view is that crime and delinquency rates are a function of two factors: (1) class position and (2) family functions.[50] The link between these two variables is that parents reproduce within the family the power relationships they hold within the workplace.

The class position and work experiences of parents influence the criminality of children. A position of dominance at work is equated with control in the household. In families which are *paternalistic*, fathers assume the traditional role of breadwinners, while mothers have menial jobs or remain at home to supervise domestic matters. Within the paternalistic home, mothers are expected to control the behavior of their daughters while granting greater freedom to sons. In such a home, the parent-daughter relationship can be viewed as a preparation for the "cult of domesticity." This makes girls' involvement in delinquency unlikely, while boys are freer to deviate because they are not subject to maternal control. Consequently, males exhibit a higher degree of delinquent behavior than their sisters.

On the other hand, in *egalitarian* families—those in which husband and wife share similar positions of power at home and in the workplace—daughters gain a kind of freedom that reflects reduced parental control. These families produce daughters whose law-violating behavior mirrors their brothers. Ironically, these kind of relationships also occur in female-headed households with absent fathers. Similarly, Hagan and his associates found that when both father and mother hold equally valued managerial positions, the similarity between the rates of their daughters' and sons' delinquency is greatest. By implication, middle-class girls are the most likely to violate the law because they are less closely controlled than their lower-class sisters. And in homes in which both parents hold positions of power, girls are more likely to have the same expectations of career success as their brothers. Consequently, siblings of both sexes will be socialized to take risks and engage in other behavior related to delinquency.

While its basic premises have not yet been thoroughly tested, and some recent research evidence contradicts its core assumptions,[51] power-control theory is important because it encourages a new approach to the study of criminality, one that includes gender differences, class position, and the structure of the family. It is likely to have a major influence on conflict theory concepts.

Instrumental Theory.   Another attempt to integrate conflict concepts with mainstream sociological theory is **instrumental theory,** developed by Herman and Julia Schwendinger.[52] The Schwendingers' work seeks to explain, in theoretical terms, the paradox caused by the seeming lack of relationship between social class and crime. As noted in Chapter 4, many self-report surveys find that middle-class youths commit as many delinquent acts as lower-class youths, despite the common sense view that poor,

underprivileged children commit more crime. Although official record surveys, such as Wolfgang's cohort study, support a lower-class status-delinquency relationship, this has not been the case for most self-report studies.

The Schwendingers believe that this puzzling relationship can be explained by the nature of the onset of a criminal career. They find that delinquency is overwhelmingly concentrated within stratified adolescent formations that are relatively independent of social class; they refer to these as "stradom formations."

Stradom formations are adolescent social networks whose members have distinct dress, grooming, and linguistic behavior. Many of us remember these groups from our high-school experience, and recall referring to someone as a "greaser," "hood," "preppie," "socialite," or "jock," based on that person's friendship patterns, dress, attitudes, and concerns (in fact, we ourselves may have been part of such a group).

According to instrumental theory, economically diverse communities produce three distinct adolescent groupings that emerge as early as the sixth to eighth grades. Using the Schwendingers' terms, the "socialites" (sometimes called "soshes," "frats," "elites," or "colleges") are predominantly middle-class youths who band together in cliques that remain intact throughout high school. These youths are the children of less affluent but still middle-class parents, who wish to imitate the lifestyle of the more affluent.[53]

At the other end of the economic spectrum, the Schwendingers found street-corner groups known as "greasers," "homeboys," "hodad," or "hoods." Falling between these two extremes are groups characterized by an independent lifestyle or intermediate status, for example, "surfers," "hot rodders," or "gremmies." Some intermediate groups may have mixed identifies, such as "sosh-surfers." Each of the three stradom formations is marked by a relatively high delinquency rate.

Not all youths become members of a stradom group. Some are involved in organized, adult-controlled activities, such as science clubs, church groups, or the 4-H club. Others, because of school achievements, are known as "brains" or "intellectuals"; still others are "turkeys," "clods," or "nerds." In general, nonstradom youths have lower delinquency rates.

Stradom groups may display a class bias and contain members of predominately one class, but this does not prevent crossovers. For example, some (hoods and greasers) may come from middle-class backgrounds, while lower-class youths can become members of the socialite stradom; intermediary groups can be even more economically heterogeneous.

Criminal modalities. According to the Schwendingers' theory, there is a natural history, or life cycle, of criminal participation. As the stradoms undergo change, as their members mature, so do the varieties of their conduct. Early in adolescence, there occurs the *generalized modality,* marked by indifference to the needs of others and a cynical attitude toward outsiders in general. During this period, group members engage in petty thievery, vandalism, truancy, fighting, and other less serious delinquent acts.

By the end of junior high school, *ethnocentric delinquency* emerges. This modality is characterized by stradom rivalries. It may include such behaviors as group fights and vandalism motivated by group rivalries, and the placing of graffiti that proclaims the superiority of one's stradom over another. Conflict may be intra-stradom or inter-stradom.

In later adolescence, delinquency enters the *informal economic stage.* Now, for the first time, delinquent acts are instrumental—designed to bring economic reward to the offender. Criminal acts now involve burglary, larceny, robbery, and drug sales. Violence and other acting-out behaviors are supported by this modality. Generally, development of the informal economic stage is dependent on the financial status of individuals and communities. Economically deprived youths are much more likely to be thrust into economic delinquency than middle-class stradom members. However, members of all groups help sustain delinquency because they are consumers of illegally gained materials, ranging from stolen auto parts to illegal drugs.

In sum, stradom members are more likely to become delinquent than nonstradom youths, and lower-class street-corner groups are more likely to contain conventional delinquents than socialite and intermediate groups. However, since middle-class stradom members are initially as or more delinquent than nonstradom lower-class youths, the relationship between class and delinquency is confounded. In other words, group-affiliated youths are more likely to engage in deviant behavior than unaffiliated youths, regardless of their social class. This explains the apparent failure of self-report studies to detect an economic bias in delinquency.

The Schwendingers' work combines elements of conflict and subcultural theory. It shows that subcultural norms initially influence antisocial behavior choices, but that eventually social class affiliation eventually controls crime rates. According to the Schwendingers, criminality is a product of market relations and demands, societal relationships, and the changing lifestyles of adolescents.

Integrated-Structural Marxist Theory. Mark Colvin and John Pauly have created an integrated conflict theory of crime which they label *integrated structural theory.*[54]

According to Colvin and Pauly, crime is a result of socialization within the family. However, family relations are actually controlled by the marketplace. The quality of one's work experience has been shaped by the historical interaction between competition among capitalists and the level of class struggle.[55] Wage earners who occupy a inferior position in the economic hierarchy will experience coercive relationships with their supervisors and employers. Negative experiences in the workplace create strain and alienation within the family setting, which in turn relates to inconsistent and overly punitive discipline at home. Juveniles who live in such an environment will become alienated from their parents, and at the same time experience conflict with social institutions, especially the school. For example, youths growing up in a family headed by parents who are at the bottom of workplace control structures are also the ones most likely to go to poorly funded schools, do poorly on standardized tests, and be placed in slow learning tracks; each of these factors has been correlated with delinquent behavior.

The subsequent feelings of alienation are reinforced by associations with groups of similarly alienated peers. In some cases, the peer group will be oriented toward patterns of violent behavior, while in other instances, the group will enable its members to benefit economically from criminal behavior.

According to integrated structural theory, it is naive to believe that a crime control policy can be formulated without regard for its basic root causes. Coercive punishments or misguided treatments cannot be effective unless the core relationships with regard to material production are changed. Those who produce goods must be given a greater opportunity to control the forms of production and, in so doing, must be given the power to shape their lives and the lives of their families.

RESEARCH ON MARXIST CRIMINOLOGY

Marxist criminologists rarely use standard social science methodologies to test their views, because many believe traditional approaches to measuring research subjects are antihuman and insensitive.[56] Marxists believe that the research conducted by mainstream liberal-positivist criminologists is designed to unmask the weak and powerless members of society so they can be better dealt with by the legal system—a process called **correctionalism**. They are particularly offended by purely empirical studies, such as those showing that minority group members have lower IQs than the white majority or that the inner city is the site of the most serious crime while middle-class areas are relatively crime-free.

These caveats not withstanding, empirical research is not considered incompatible with Marxist criminology, and there have been some important efforts to quantitatively test its fundamental assumptions.[57] For example, Alan Lizotte and his associates have shown that the property crime rate reflects change in the level of surplus value; the capitalist system's emphasis on excessive profits accounts for the need of the working class to commit property crime.[58]

Despite a few exceptions, Marxist research tends to be historical and analytical, and not quantitative and empirical. Social trends are interpreted in order to understand how capitalism has affected human interaction. Marxists investigate both macro-level issues, such as how the accumulation of wealth affects crime rates, and micro-level issues, such as the effect of criminal interactions on the lives of individuals living in a capitalist society. Of particular importance to Marxist critical thinkers is analysis of the historical development of capitalist social control institutions, such as criminal law, police agencies, courts, and prison systems.

Crime, the Individual, and the State

Marxists devote considerable attention to the study of the relationships between crime, victims, the criminal, and the state.[59] Two common themes emerge: (1) crime and its control are a function of capitalism; and (2) the justice system is biased against the working class and favors upper-class interests. Marxian analysis of the criminal justice system is designed to identify the often hidden processes that exert control over people's lives. It seeks an understanding of how conditions, processes, and structures became as they are today.

For example, William Chambliss analyzed the process by which deviant behavior is defined as criminal or delinquent in U.S. society.[60] In a similar vein, Timothy Carter and Donald Clelland used a Marxist approach to show that dispositions in a juvenile court were a function of social class.[61] David Greenberg also studied the association between social class and sentencing and later, with Drew Humphries, evaluated how power relationships help undermine any benefit the lower class gets from sentencing reforms.[62] In general, Marxist research efforts have yielded evidence linking operations of the justice system to class bias.[63]

In addition to conducting studies showing the relationship between crime and the state, some critical researchers have attempted to show how capitalism intervenes throughout the entire spectrum of crime-related phenomena. Research by Herman and Julia Schwendinger attempts to show how capitalist social expectations affect women in the aftermath of a rape experience. Described in the accompanying Close-Up, the Schwendingers' effort is a good example of Marxist analytical research.[64]

Critical research of this sort is designed to reinterpret commonly held beliefs about society within the framework of Marxist social and economic ideas. The goal is not to prove statistically that capitalist causes crime, but rather to show that it creates an environment in which crime is inevitable. Marxist research is humanistic, situational, descriptive, and analytical, rather than statistical, rigid, and methodological.

CLOSE-UP

How Capitalism Influences Rape

Herman and Julia Schwendinger's study of rape provides an excellent example of Marxian critical analysis.

The Schwendingers' goal is to find out why women who are raped often feel guilty about their role in the rape experience. The Schwendingers believe that a rape victim frequently experiences guilt because she has been raised in a sexist society and has internalized discriminatory norms.

Women have traditionally been viewed as the weaker sex, dependent on persons in authority such as parents or husbands. The Schwendingers postulate that dependency originates historically in socioeconomic conditions that are often directly related to family life in capitalist society. During the early stages of capitalism, families underwent strain when industry demanded a labor force of men, only infrequently supplemented by single women. The role of father was strained as men were separated from their households. Woman's role became more narrowly defined as childbearer and child raiser. The limited economic role of women helped to define them as dependents. Married women, especially, were viewed as nonproductive, since they did not participate in commodity markets, where people earn money.

In reality, women's household productivity must be viewed as an essential contribution to working-class life; yet, theirs is an unpaid contribution that often goes unappreciated by husbands and the rest of society. Since the housewife only produces for family use, her labor is necessarily unpayable; and while her needs are partly supported by the husband's wage, she is totally dependent on that wage for access to the commodities necessary for the family's existence.

Because she has been socialized into dependency by the capitalist system, a woman's sense of self-worth may be more responsive to the evaluations of other persons. Furthermore, negative evaluations, such as those created by a rape experience, are likely to be turned inward by the woman herself, creating unwarranted self-recrimination and remorse.

The family is not the only culprit in this transaction. Schools and mass media further reinforce dependency by teaching boys and girls in school to "look down on women." Textbooks stereotype the woman's role; girls are depicted as helpless and frightened. Vocational tests provide fewer opportunities for girls. In media presentations, women are usually depicted as housewives and mothers. When women are portrayed on television commercials, they seem "concerned mainly with clean floors and clean hair—housework and their personal appearance."

Though women have made strides in the job market, their labor is often in low-paid, low-mobility occupations such as secretary or piece worker. Consequently, their appearance in the labor force often does little to improve their economic dependency.

It is for these reasons that women often blame themselves for being raped. The Schwendingers imply that women feel they have "let down" the people they depend on when they are trapped in a rape encounter. A woman's own sense of inadequacy leads to self-blame for the attack and prevents her from focusing on the true culprits: the rapist and the capitalist system whose economic structure results in a rape-producing climate.

The Schwendingers' research approach illustrates the Marxian stress on analysis and interpretation of social process and their disdain for quantitative statistical evidence.

Discussion Questions

1. What can society do to help women who are the victims of rape?
2. Does the Schwendingers' portrayal of a rape victim seem accurate?

SOURCE: Herman and Julia Schwendinger, "Rape Victims and the False Sense of Guilt," *Crime and Social Justice* 13 (1980):4–17.

Historical Analyses

A second type of Marxist research focuses on the historical background of commonly held institutional beliefs and practices. One aim is to show how changes in the criminal law corresponded to the development of capitalist economy. For example, Michael Rustigan analyzed historical records to show that law reform in nineteenth-century England was largely a response to pressure from the business community to make the

CLOSE-UP

A Marxist Analysis of Police

Sidney Harring has attempted to show how police forces developed as an instrument of the capitalist state. In one study, Harring sets out to prove that police played an important role in eighteenth- and nineteenth-century capitalism by working repeatedly to break working-class resistance to corporate power, to socialize new immigrants to the demands of monopoly capitalism, to provide protection to strike-bound companies and those threatened with strikes, to control rebellious segments of the working-class population, and to gather intelligence in working-class communities.

Harring takes the nontraditional position that during the 1880s the police were transformed into a far more efficient, better organized, and better disciplined system than ever before. For example, Buffalo, New York's police force went from 200 to 900 men in the space of 20 years. The strikes and labor movements of the 1870s and 1880s brought demands for increased police power to control workers. Larger, more efficient police departments meant that long-term antistrike campaigns could be carried out. Increased size was matched by improved technology—patrol wagons and signal alarm systems were placed throughout larger cities; police used them to get information and to request help. "Reputable" citizens were given access to the call boxes so that they would have greater access to police services. Harring attributes the use of these measures directly to the police establishment's role in controlling strikes and labor unrest.

During this period, police departments became more stable and efficient. At the same time, control of police departments fell into the hands of industrialists, who began to see the value of police officers as strike breakers. The police aided industrialists like Cyrus McCormick when their plants were closed by strikes.

Officers suspected of prolabor sentiments were disciplined or removed. (During a 1913 strike, 33 Indianapolis police officers were suspended for refusing to ride on subway cars driven by "scabs," or workers hired to replace strikers.) Though police work was not financially rewarding, it provided secure work at pay somewhat higher than a laborer's, creating a class distinction between the police and the laboring classes.

Harring concludes that police agencies in the late nineteenth and early twentieth centuries were violently antilabor. He states that though labor activists were sometimes violent, "since police and scabs provided considerable violence, police repression must be seen as more than simple defense."

Discussion Questions

1. How does Harring's view that police were agents of the capitalist system jibe with the low pay and poor working conditions of turn-of-the-century police officers?
2. Are police "agents of the capitalist state" today?

SOURCES: Sidney Harring, "Policing a Class Society: The Expansion of the Urban Police in the Late Nineteenth and Early Twentieth Century," in David Greenberg, ed., Crime and Capitalism (Palo Alto, Cal.: Mayfield Publishing, 1981), pp. 292–313.

punishment for property law violations more acceptable.[65]

In a similar vein, Rosalind Petchesky has explained how the relationship between prison industries and capitalism evolved during the nineteenth century, while Paul Takagi has described the rise of state prisons as an element of centralized state control over deviants.[66] Another topic of importance to Marxist critical thinkers is the development of modern police agencies. Since police often play an active role in putting down labor disputes and controlling the activities of political dissidents, their interrelationship with capitalist economics is of particular importance to Marxists. Prominent examples of research in this area include Stephen Spitzer and A. T. Scull's discussion of the history of private police, and Dennis Hoffman's historical analysis of police excesses in the repression of an early union, the International Workers of the World (popularly known as the Wobblies).[67] Sidney Harring has provided one of the more important analyses of the development of modern policing; his work is described in the Close-Up entitled "A Marxist Analysis of Police," to provide an example of Marxist historical research.[68]

CRITIQUE OF MARXIST CRIMINOLOGY

Marxist criminology has met with a great deal of criticism from some members of the criminological mainstream, who charge that its contribution has "been hot air, heat but no real light."[69] In turn, Marxists have accused mainstream criminologists of being culprits in the development of state control over individual lives and of "selling out" their ideals for the chance to receive government funding. In so doing, these theorists have caused disturbance in the halls of academia. Rumors of purges of Marxist theorists have cropped up; lawsuits involving the denial of academic tenure to Marxists have not been uncommon. It was a sad but not surprising commentary on American education when Herman and Julia Schwendinger, two of the most well-respected radical criminologists in the United States, wrote in the *Criminologist* of their career-long difficulties in obtaining and sustaining academic employment, of vendettas against radicals for using disapproved books, and of the closing of the criminology school at the University of California-Berkeley because of the political beliefs of the professors.

Mainstream criminologists also have attacked the substance of Marxist thought. For example, Jackson Toby argues that Marxist theory is a simple rehash of the old tradition of helping the underdog. He likens the ideas behind Marxist criminology to the ideas in such traditional and literary works as *Robin Hood* and Victor Hugo's *Les Miserables*, in which the poor stole from the rich to survive.[70] In reality, Toby claims, most theft is for luxury, not survival. Moreover, he disputes the idea that the crimes of the rich are more reprehensible and less understandable than those of the poor. Criminality and immoral behavior occur at every social level, but Toby believes that the relatively disadvantaged contribute disproportionately to crime and delinquency rates.

Richard Spark's thorough critique of Marxist criminology leads him to conclude that the quality of research efforts made to test its assumptions are faulty.[71] He believes it unlikely that Marxist criminology will ever have a great effect on criminological thought.

The most stunning and controversial critique of Marxist criminology has been rendered by a sociologist, Carl Klockars.[72] Klockars finds that the core issue for Marxist criminologists is class. Marxists assume that class conflict, created by the unequal distribution of wealth, is the cause of most of society's evils: war, racism, sexism, poverty, and crime. Klockars debates this point. He claims that class differences may actually have a beneficial effect on society. During periods of great artistic and cultural achievements, class differences serve to protect innovators from the power of the state and the jealousy and envy of the masses. Historically, class differences performed the important function of creating, maintaining, and perpetuating a set of standards that carried authority and inspired the rest of society. Further, in today's American culture, the poorer classes enjoy more luxuries and benefits than ever before, so the concept of poverty has lost much of its meaning.

Klockars further asserts that Marxists mistakenly equate ownership of production with control of production. The former is open to anyone who is willing to buy a share of stock or participate in a job-related pension fund. But owners do not necessarily control the means of production. This is left to managers and bureaucrats, who may or may not own the institutions and agencies they control (a conclusion similar to those of Ralf Dahrendorf, discussed earlier).

Klockars also focuses on Marxist criminologists' concern for **class interest** as a dominant factor in U.S. life. He charges that Marxists ignore all the varied prestige and interest groups that exist in a pluralistic society and focus almost unilaterally on class differentials. Moreover, their claim that capitalism is the root of all evil is untestable by research. Klockars scoffs, for example, at critical thinkers who charge that legal reforms are really disguised means of placating the masses. Is it logical to believe that giving people more rights is a trick to allow greater control to be exerted over them? Klockars states:

> People are more powerful with the right to a jury than without it . . . The rights of free speech, free press, free association, public trial, habeas corpus and governmental petition extended substantial power to colonials . . . who had previously been denied them.[73]

Klockars lists several problems of Marxist theory. First, Marxist criminology as a social movement is untrustworthy. Marxists refuse to confront the problems and conflicts of socialist countries, such as the Gulags and purges of Stalinist Russia. Second, Marxist criminology is predictable. Capitalism is blamed for every human vice:

> *After class explains everything, after the whole legal order is critiqued, after all predatory and personal crime is attributed to the conditions and reproduction of capitalism, there is nothing more to say—except more of the same.*[74]

Klockars also states that Marxist theory does little to explain the criminality existing in states that have abolished the private ownership of the means of production, such as Cuba, China, and Russia. Furthermore, Marxists ignore objective reality. For example, they overlook empirical evidence of distinctions that exist between people in different classes. Such tactics will eventually destroy the foundation for a new postrevolutionary social science, should one be needed.

Another criticism Klockars levels is that Marxists attempt to explicate issues which, for most people, need no explanation. The revelation that politicians are corrupt and businesspeople greedy comes as a shock to no one. On the other hand, the evil that Marxists consistently discover and dramatize is seen from a moral ground set so high that it loses meaning and perspective. Every aspect of capitalist society is suspect, including practices and freedoms most people cherish as the cornerstones of democracy (right to trial, free press, religion, and so on).

Finally, Klockars charges that by presenting itself as a mystical, religion-like entity, Marxist criminology is relieved of the responsibility for the exploitation, corruption, crime, and human abuse that has been and continues to be perpetrated in socialist countries.

Klockars' criticism of Marxist theory is fairly specific. In general, those who criticize the radical view question both its methodological rigor and political naivete.

Marxists have responded to these criticisms in a number of different ways. The development of integrated theories signals an end to the scholarly insulation which separated most radicals from the criminological mainstream. Other radicals, such as Tony Platt, have written of the need for the left to respond to the increasing power of the emerging right and

address problems such as street crime and violence. Platt has called for a coalition of liberals, radicals, and progressives to fight the right wing and identified five areas of importance that need to be addressed by radical scholars.[75]

SUMMARY

Social conflict theorists view crime as a function of the conflict that exists in society. It has its theoretical basis in the works of Karl Marx.

Pure conflict theorists suggest that crime in any society is caused by class conflict. Laws are created by those in power to protect their rights and interests. All criminal acts have political undertones. Richard Quinney has called this concept the "social reality of crime." Unfortunately, research efforts to validate the conflict approach have not produced significant findings. One of conflict theory's most important premises is that the justice system is biased and designed to protect the wealthy. Research has not been unanimous in supporting this point.

The second division of social conflict theory is Marxist criminology. Marxists view the competitive nature of the capitalist system as a major cause of crime. The poor commit crimes because of their frustration, anger, and need. The wealthy engage in illegal acts because they are used to competition and also because they must do so to keep their positions in society. Marxist scholars, such as Richard Quinney, Anthony Platt, and Barry Krisberg, have attempted to show that the law is designed to protect the wealthy and powerful and to control the poor, have-not members of society.

Research on Marxist theory focuses on how the system of justice was designed and how it currently operates to further class interests. Quite often, it uses historical analysis to show how the capitalist classes have exerted their control over police, court, and correctional agencies.

Both Marxist and conflict criminology have been heavily criticized by consensus criminologists. Richard Sparks finds the research of Marxists faulty. Jackson Toby sees Marxists as being sentimental and unwilling to face reality. Carl Klockars' criticism suggests Marxists make fundamental errors in their concepts of ownership and class interest. Finally, Tony Platt suggests that Marxists must reorient their thinking in the future.

KEY TERMS

conflict theory
critical criminology
radical criminology
Marxist criminology
Karl Marx
materialism
productive forces
productive relations
capitalist bourgeoisie
proletariat
class
lumpen proletariat
surplus value
dialectic
Ralf Dahrendorf

George Vold
power
Richard Quinney
social reality of crime
Willem Bonger
demystify
instrumentalists
Herman Schwendinger
Julia Siegel Schwendinger
privilege
Stephen Spitzer
instrumental theory
stradom formations
correctionalism
class interest

NOTES

1. Karl Marx and Friedrich Engels, *Capital: A Critique of Political Economy*, trans. E. Aveling (Chicago: Charles Kern, 1906); Karl Marx, *Selected Writings in Sociology and Social Philosophy*, trans. P. B. Bottomore (New York: McGraw-Hill, 1956). For a general discussion of Marxist thought, see, Michael Lynch and W. Byron Groves, *A Primer in Radical Criminology* (New York: Harrow and Heston, 1986), pp. 6–26.
2. Karl Marx, *Grundrisse: Introduction to the Critique of Political Economy*, trans. Martin Nicolaus (New York: Vintage, 1973), pp. 106–107.
3. Friedrich Engels, *The Condition of the Working Class in England in 1844* (London: Allen and Unwin, 1950).
4. Karl Marx, *Theories of Surplus Value*, vol. 1 (London: Lawrence and Wishart, 1969), pp. 387–88.
5. Ian Taylor, Paul Walton, and Jock Young, *The New Criminology: For a Social Theory of Deviance* (London: Routledge and Kegan Paul, 1973), p. 212.
6. Charles Tittle, Wayne Villemez, and Douglas Smith, "The Myth of Social Class and Criminality: An Empirical Assessment of the Empirical Evidence," *American Sociological Review* 43 (1978):643–56.
7. For a general view, see, David Friedrichs, "Crime, Deviance and Criminal Justice: In Search of a Radical Humanistic Perspective," *Humanity and Society* 6 (1982):200–26.
8. Alexander Liazos, "The Poverty of the Sociology of Deviance: Nuts, Sluts and Perverts," *Social Problems* 20 (1972):103–20.
9. See generally, Robert Meier, "The New Criminology: Continuity in Criminological Theory," *Journal of Criminal Law and Criminology* 67 (1977):461–69.
10. David Greenberg, ed., *Crime and Capitalism* (Palo Alto, Cal.: Mayfield Publishing, 1981), p. 3.
11. William Chambliss and Robert Seidman, *Law, Order and Power* (Reading, Mass.: Addison-Wesley, 1971), p. 503.
12. John Braithwaite, "Retributivism, Punishment and Privilege," in W. Byron Groves and Graeme Newman, eds., *Punishment and Privilege* (Albany, N.Y.: Harrow and Heston, 1986), pp. 55–66.
13. See generally, Gerhard Lenski, *Power and Privilege* (New York: McGraw-Hill, 1966).
14. Austin Turk, "Class, Conflict and Criminology," *Sociological Focus* 10 (1977):209–20.
15. Richard Quinney, *The Social Reality of Crime* (Boston: Little, Brown, 1970).
16. Austin Turk, *Criminality and Legal Order* (Chicago: Rand McNally, 1969), p. 58.
17. Lynch and Groves, *A Primer in Radical Criminology*, p. 38.
18. David McDowall, "Poverty and Homicide in Detroit, 1926–1978," *Victims and Violence* 1 (1986):23–34; David McDowall and Sandra Norris, "Poverty and Homicide in Baltimore, Cleveland, and Memphis, 1937–1980," Paper presented at the American Society of Criminology meeting, Montreal, Canada, November, 1987.
19. Judith Blau and Peter Blau, "The Cost of Inequality: Metropolitan Structure and Violent Crime," *American Sociological Review* 147 (1982):114–29; Richard Block, "Community Environment and Violent Crime," *Criminology* 17 (1979):46–57; Robert Sampson, "Structural Sources of Variation in Race-Age-Specific Rates of Offending across Major U.S. Cities," *Criminology* 23 (1985):647–73.
20. David Jacobs and David Britt, "Inequality and Police Use of Deadly Force: An Empirical Assessment of a Conflict Hypothesis," *Social Problems* 26 (1979):403–12.
21. Alan Lizotte, "Extra-Legal Factors in Chicago's Criminal Courts: Testing the Conflict Model of Criminal Justice," *Social Problems* 25 (1978):564–80.
22. Terance Miethe and Charles Moore, "Radical Differences in Criminal Processing: The Consequences of Model Selection on Conclusions about Differential Treatment," *The Sociological Quarterly* 27 (1987):217–37.
23. Douglas Smith, Christy Visher, and Laura Davidson, "Equity and Discretionary Justice: The Influence of Race on Police Arrest Decisions," *Journal of Criminal*

Law and Criminology 75 (1984):234–49.

24. Jackson Toby, "The New Criminology is the Old Sentimentality," *Criminology* 16 (1979):513–26.

25. Kenneth Land and Marcus Felson, "A General Framework for Building Dynamic Macro Social Indicator Models: An Analysis of Changes in Crime Rates and Police Expenditures," *American Journal of Sociology* 82 (1976):565–604.

26. Charles Wellford, "Labeling Theory and Criminology: An Assessment," *Social Problems* 22 (1975):332–45.

27. Theodore Chiricos and Gordon Waldo, "Socioeconomic Status and Criminal Sentencing: An Empirical Assessment of a Conflict Proposition," *American Sociological Review* 40 (1975):753–72.

28. *Ibid.*, p. 767.

29. Lynch and Groves, *A Primer in Radical Criminology*, p. 6.

30. This section borrows heavily from Richard Sparks, "A Critique of Marxist Criminology," in Norval Morris and Michael Tonry, eds., *Crime and Justice*, vol. 2 (Chicago: University of Chicago Press, 1980), pp. 159–208.

31. Jeffrey Reiman, *The Rich Get Richer and the Poor Get Prison* (New York: Wiley, 1984), pp. 43–44.

32. For a general review of Marxist criminology, see, Lynch and Groves, *A Primer in Radical Criminology*.

33. Taylor, Walton, and Young, *The New Criminology*.

34. Barry Krisberg, *Crime and Privilege: Toward a New Criminology* (Englewood Cliffs, N.J.: Prentice-Hall, 1975), p. 167.

35. R. M. Bohm, "Radical Criminology: An Explication," *Criminology* 19 (1982):565–89.

36. W. Byron Groves and Robert Sampson, "Critical Theory and Criminology," *Social Problems* 33 (1986):58–80.

37. Gregg Barak, " 'Crimes of the Homeless' or the 'Crime of Homelessness': A Self-Reflexive, New-Marxist Analysis of Crime and Social Control," Paper presented at the annual meeting of the American Society of Criminology, Montreal, Canada, November, 1987.

38. The dichotomy between instrumental and structural Marxism is expressed in Lynch and Groves, *A Primer in Radical Criminology*.

39. Gresham Sykes, "The Rise of Critical Criminology," *Journal of Criminal Law and Criminology* 65 (1974):211.

40. David Jacobs, "Corporate Economic Power and the State: A Longitudinal Assessment of Two Explanations," *American Journal of Sociology* 93 (1988):852–81.

41. *Ibid.*

42. Richard Quinney, "Crime Control in Capitalist Society," in Taylor, Walton and Young, eds., *Critical Criminology*, p.199.

43. Herman Schwendinger and Julia Schwendinger, "Delinquency and Social Reform: A Radical Perspective,"

in Lamar Empey, ed., *Juvenile Justice* (Charlottesville: University of Virginia Press, 1979), pp. 246–90.

44. Krisberg, *Crime and Privilege*.

45. Elliott Currie, "A Dialogue with Anthony M. Platt," *Issues in Criminology* 8 (1973):28.

46. *Ibid.*, p. 29.

47. Stephen Spitzer, "Toward a Marxian Theory of Deviance," *Social Problems* 22 (1975):638–51.

48. W. Byron Groves and Robert Sampson, "Traditional Contributions to Radical Criminology," *Journal of Research in Crime and Delinquency* 24 (1987):181–88.

49. W. Byron Groves and Robert Sampson, "Removing Radical Blinders on the Study of Crime Causation: Reply to Bohm and Barak," *Journal of Research in Crime and Delinquency* 24 (1987):336–40.

50. John Hagan, A. R. Gillis, and John Simpson, "The Class Structure and Delinquency: Toward A Power-Control Theory of Common Delinquent Behavior," *American Journal of Sociology* 90 (1985):1151–78; John Hagan, John Simpson, and A. R. Gillis, "Class in the Household: A Power-Control Theory of Gender and Delinquency," *American Journal of Sociology* 92:788–816 (1987).

51. Simon Singer and Murray Levine, "Re-Examining Class in the Household and a Power-Control Theory of Gender and Delinquency," Paper presented at the American Society of Criminology annual meeting, Montreal, Canada, November, 1987.

52. Herman Schwendinger and Julia Schwendinger, *Adolescent Subcultures and Delinquency* (New York: Praeger, 1985). See also, Schwendinger and Schwendinger, "The Paradigmatic Crisis in Delinquency Theory," *Crime and Social Justice* 18 (1982):70–78; "The Collective Varieties of Youth," *Crime and Social Justice* 5 (1976):7–25; and "Marginal Youth and Social Policy," *Social Problems* 24 (1976):184–91.

53. Schwendinger and Schwendinger, *Adolescent Subcultures and Delinquency*, p. 55.

54. Mark Colvin and John Pauly, "A Critique of Criminology: Toward an Integrated Structural-Marxist Theory of Delinquency Production," *American Journal of Sociology* 89 (1983):513–51.

55. *Ibid.*, p. 542.

56. Roy Bhaskar, "Empiricism," in T. Bottomore, ed., *A Dictionary of Marxist Thought* (Cambridge, Mass.: Harvard University Press, 1983), p. 149–50.

57. Byron Groves, "Marxism and Positivism," *Crime and Social Justice* 23 (1985):129–50; Michael Lynch, "Quantitative Analysis and Marxist Criminology: Some Old Answers to a Dilemma in Marxist Criminology," *Crime and Social Justice* 29 (1987):110–112.

58. Alan Lizotte, James Mercy, and Eric Monkkonen, "Crime and Police Strength in an Urban Setting:

Chicago 1947–1970," in John Hagan, ed., *Quantitative Criminology* (Beverly Hills, Cal.: Sage Publications, 1982), pp. 129–48.

59. See, for example, Tony Platt, "U.S. Criminal Justice in the Reagan Era: An Assessment," *Crime and Social Justice* 29 (1988):58–69.

60. William Chambliss, "The State, the Law and the Definition of Behavior as Criminal or Delinquent," in D. Glazer, ed., *Handbook of Criminology* (Chicago: Rand McNally, 1974), pp. 7–44.

61. Timothy Carter and Donald Clelland, "A Neo-Marxian Critique, Formulation and Test of Juvenile Dispositions as a Function of Social Class," *Social Problems* 27 (1979):96–108.

62. David Greenberg, "Socio-Economic Status and Criminal Sentences: Is There an Association?" *American Sociological Review* 42 (1977):174–75; David Greenberg and Drew Humphries, "The Co-optation of Fixed Sentencing Reform," *Crime and Delinquency* 26 (1980):206–25.

63. Steven Box, *Power, Crime and Mystification* (London: Tavistock, 1984); Gregg Barak, *In Defense of Whom? A Critique of Criminal Justice Reform* (Cincinnati: Anderson Publishing Co., 1980). For an opposing view, see, Franklin Williams, "Conflict Theory and Differential Processing: An Analysis of the Research Literature," in J. Inciardi, ed., *Radical Criminology: The Coming Crisis* (Beverly Hills, Cal.: Sage Publications, 1980), pp. 213–31.

64. Herman Schwendinger and Julia Schwendinger, "Rape Victims and the False Sense of Guilt," *Crime and Social Justice* 13 (1980):4–17.

65. Michael Rustigan, "A Reinterpretation of Criminal Law Reform in Nineteenth Century England," in D. Greenberg, ed., *Crime and Capitalism* (Palo Alto, Cal.: Mayfield Publishing, 1981), pp. 255–78.

66. Rosalind Petchesky, "At Hard Labor: Penal Confinement and Production in Nineteenth Century America," in D. Greenberg, ed., *Crime and Capitalism*, pp. 341–57; Paul Takagi, "The Walnut Street Jail: A Penal Reform to Centralize the Powers of the State," *Federal Probation* 49 (1975):18–26.

67. S. Spitzer and A. T. Scull, "Privatization and Capitalist Development: The Case of the Private Police," *Social Problems* 25 (1977):18–29; Dennis Hoffman, "Cops and Wobblies" (Ph.D. diss., Portland State University, 1977).

68. Sidney Harring, "Policing a Class Society: The Expansion of the Urban Police in the Late Nineteenth and Early Twentieth Centuries," in D. Greenberg, ed., *Crime and Capitalism*, pp. 292–313.

69. Jack Gibbs, cited in *The Criminologist* 12 (1987):2–3.

70. Toby, "The New Criminology is the Old Sentimentality."

71. Sparks, "A Critique of Marxist Criminology," pp. 198–99.

72. Carl Klockars, "The Contemporary Crises of Marxist Criminology," in J. Inciardi, ed., *Radical Criminology: The Coming Crisis*, pp. 92–123.

73. *Ibid.*, pp. 112–14.

74. *Ibid.*

75. Tony Platt, "Criminology in the 1980's: Progressive Alternatives to 'Law and Order,'" *Crime and Social Justice* 21-22 (1985):191–99.

SECTION III

CRIME TYPOLOGIES

Regardless of why people commit crime in the first place, their actions are defined by law as falling into particular crime categories, or *typologies*. Criminologists often seek to link individual criminal offenders or behaviors together so they may be more easily studied and understood. These are referred to as crime or offender typologies.

In this section, crime patterns are clustered into four typologies: violent crime (Chapter 10); economic crimes involving common theft offenses (Chapter 11); economic crimes involving criminal organizations (Chapter 12); and public-order crimes, such as prostitution and drug abuse (Chapter 13). This format groups criminal behaviors by their focuses and consequences: bringing physical harm to others; misappropriating other people's property; and violating laws designed to protect public morals.

Typologies can be useful in classifying large numbers of criminal offenses or offenders into easily understood categories. This text has grouped offenses and offenders on the basis of their (1) legal definitions and (2) collective goals, objectives, and consequences.

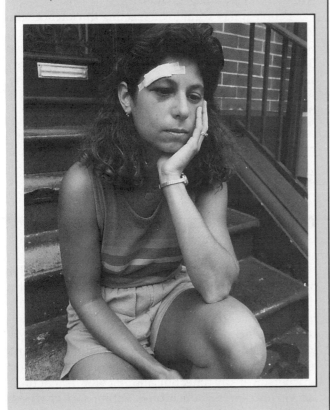

CHAPTER 10

VIOLENT CRIME

---------------- INTRODUCTION ----------------

U.S. society has at various times been called violent, sick, and diseased. Violence has been described as being as "American as cherry pie."[1] People's daily lives have been influenced by fear of violent crime. More than 80 percent of high-school seniors answered affirmatively when asked in a national survey if they worried about crime and violence; about one-half of all Americans report limiting or changing activities in the past few years because of crime.[2]

Many people have personally experienced violence or have a friend who has been victimized; most everyone has heard about someone's being robbed, beaten, or killed; riots and mass disturbances have ravaged urban areas; racial attacks plague schools and college campuses; assassination has claimed the lives of political, religious, and social leaders all over the world. One commentator notes:

> During the crises that follow assassinations and riots, the speculation about violence reaches feverish proportions. Violence becomes the monomania of the press, the core substance of politics, the mainstay of the cocktail party, and the obsession of the public. Violence is promiscuously viewed, and it is seen everywhere. Historically, it becomes the theme of evolution; psychologically, the corollary of human nature; educationally, the enemy of learning; socially, the wrong road to change.[3]

Public attitudes towards violence are often influenced by a few bizarre cases of extreme violence. For example, the nation was shocked in 1988 when Robert Chambers, a former prep school student, admitted strangling Jennifer Levin after a night of "rough sex" in New York's Central Park. Over six feet tall and 200 pounds, Chambers claimed he was acting in "self-defense" against the sexual advances of the 5'3" Levin. He eventually pleaded guilty, and was given a very lenient five-year sentence for manslaughter in what became known as the "preppie murder case." Afterward, a videotape was made public in which a carefree Chambers could be viewed making light of his crime. In another widely publicized case, Lawrence Singleton made national headlines when he was paroled after serving eight years in prison for raping a 15-year-old girl and cutting her arms off with an axe. Angry residents of Richmond, California, the town in which Singleton took up residence, threat-

ened to kill him; correctional authorities eventually found a temporary home for Singleton on prison grounds; his parole ended and he was released in April 1988.[4]

Such bizarre crimes, though relatively infrequent, renew demands from both the public and professional community for the death penalty and long, mandatory prison sentences. Even professionals are not immune: at a recent national convention, one criminologist advocated using laser-induced lobotomies on homicidal recidivists.[5] Some recent trends in violent crime are illustrated in Table 10.1.

Ironically, while the threat of interpersonal violence is disturbing, there is relatively little public outrage when the state uses it as a social control mechanism. Public opinion polls indicate that about 70 percent of Americans favor the use of capital punishment for persons convicted of murder.[6] Sometimes such harsh measures have unexpected consequences: research has shown that states which allow corporal punishment in their schools are also the ones with juveniles on death row. This raises the question of whether violence begets violence?[7]

People today seem to be reacting to violence with violent measures of their own and applauding others who take the initiative in violent encounters. When Bernhard Goetz shot four assailants on a New York subway in 1984, many in the city cheered his efforts. A rock group wrote a song in his honor, which said in part:

> I'm not going to give you my pay
> Try and take it away
> Come on make my day
> They call him the vigilante.

T-shirts went on sale with a "Thug Buster" logo.[8] Goetz was later acquitted on all charges save possession of a handgun.

Despite all this attention and concern, the causes of violence remain uncertain. Some experts suggest that the problem is created by a small number of inherently violence-prone individuals, who are themselves the victims of physical or psychological abnormalities. Other social scientists consider violence and aggression inherently human traits which can effect any person at any time. Still another view is that there are violence-prone **subcultures** within society whose members value force, routinely carry weapons, and

TABLE 10.1   Trends in Violent Crime

Each year, about four in every 10 violent crime victimizations by strangers involved an armed offender.

Since 1976, the percentage of violent crimes by strangers in which the offender was armed with a gun was between 13 and 14 percent, except for 1983, when it was 11 percent.

About one-fourth of all victims of violent crime by strangers were injured each year.

The percentage of victims of violent crime by strangers who were injured seriously or who required some medical care for their injuries changed little since 1973.

During the 1980s, robbery victims who took no self-protective measures were somewhat less likely to be injured than similar robbery victims during the 1970s.

The victimization rate for men has decreased more than that for women since 1981.

The victimization rate for blacks increased from 1973 to 1981 but has fallen since then. The rate for whites showed little year-to-year change but has fallen since 1982.

People living in cities experienced greater decreases in violent crime rates since 1981 than did people living in suburban or rural areas, although urban areas still had the highest violent crime rates.

While the violent crime rate rose during the 1970s for persons under age 35, persons 35 and older had rates that remained stable or fell.

Among violent crimes, robbery was most likely to be committed by a stranger; homicide, least likely.

Most violent crimes by strangers (70 percent) were committed against males; most crimes by relatives (77 percent) were committed against females.

Spouses or ex-spouses committed over half of all crimes by relatives and about two-thirds of all crimes by relatives against women.

Crimes by strangers were more often committed by two or more offenders than were crimes by nonstrangers.

Stranger-to-stranger crimes more often involved a weapon but less often resulted in an attack than nonstranger crimes. Crimes by relatives involved an attack and injury more often than crimes by either strangers or acquaintances.

Of those injured, victims of stranger crimes and victims of crimes by acquaintances were more likely to require medical attention than victims of crimes committed by relatives.

SOURCES: Adapted from Michael Rand, *Violent Crime Trends* (Washington, D.C.: Bureau of Justice Statistics, 1987), p. 1; Anita Timrots and Michael Rand, *Violent Crime by Strangers and Nonstrangers* (Washington, D.C.: Bureau of Justice Statistics, 1987), p. 1.

consider violence to have an acceptable place in social interaction.[9]

This chapter surveys the nature and extent of violent crime. First, it briefly reviews some of the patterns and causes of violence. Then it turns to specific types of interpersonal violence: rape, assault, homicide, robbery, and domestic violence. Then it examines violence against the state, or terrorism.

THE ROOTS OF VIOLENCE

What causes people to behave violently? There are a number of competing explanations for violent behavior. A few of the most prominent—physical and psychological traits, human instinct, and sociocultural factors—are discussed below.

Physical and Psychological Traits

As you may recall, Chapter 6 reviewed the growing body of literature linking criminal behavior to particular biological or psychological traits. It has been suggested that such characteristics as abnormal or sub-par intelligence, brain structure, diet, genetic makeup, personality, and physical anomalies are associated with aggression, violence, and other antisocial activities.[10] Research indicates that habitually aggressive behavior is learned in homes in which children are frustrated and victimized and parents serve as aggressive role models; learned violence then persists into adulthood.[11] In one important study, Dorothy Lewis and her associates examined the childhood characteristics of nine convicted murderers. The study found that the subjects could be characterized as: having had a childhood marked by severe physical abuse; having committed serious violent acts during childhood; having showed signs of major neurological impairment (such as abnormal EEG, multiple psychomotor impairment, and severe seizures); having a psychotic close relative; and having experienced psychotic symptoms such as paranoia, illogical thinking, and hallucinations.[12]

Despite such claims, there is by no means conclusive evidence that biological or psychological abnormality alone can be the cause of a violent lifestyle. For example, while some experts associate antisocial behavior with personality disorder and mental illness,[13] others have found little evidence that the mentally ill are any more violence-prone than the rest of society.[14] While it is true that some mentally ill people may become violent, there are many others whose emotional problems manifest themselves in nonviolent behavior, such as passivity, delusion, and depression.

Few criminologists today would argue that all violent people share a particular trait, such as substandard intelligence, and that possession of that single trait is sufficient to cause them to become violent.[15] Even the most ardent bio- and psychocriminologists maintain that individual traits interact with environmental and social conditions to produce antisocial behavior. At best, they maintain that physical and mental conditions predispose (rather than cause) some people to react violently to certain social and behavioral stimuli.

Instinct

Another view is that violent responses and emotions are actually ingrained within all humans, needing the right spark to trigger them. For example, among the concepts introduced by Sigmund Freud was the belief that human aggression and violence were produced by **instinctual drives**.[16] Freud maintained that humans possess two opposing instinctual drives whose interrelationship controls behavior: **eros,** the life instinct, which drives people to self-fulfillment and enjoyment; and **thanatos,** the death instinct, which operates to produce self-destruction. Thanatos can be expressed externally (as violence and sadism) or internally (as suicide, alcoholism, or other self-destructive habits). Because aggression was instinctual, Freud saw little hope in treating it.

A few biologists also have speculated that instinc-

tual violence-promoting traits may be common to the human species as a whole. One view is that aggression and violence are results of instincts in all animals, including human beings. A leading proponent of this view, Konrad Lorenz, developed this theory in his famous book, *On Aggression.*[17] Lorenz argues that aggressive energy is produced by instincts that are independent of environmental forces. In the animal kingdom, aggression usually serves a productive purpose—for example, it leads members of grazing species to spread out over available territory to insure an ample food supply and the survival of the fittest.

Lorenz believes that humans possess some of the same aggressive instincts as animals, but without the inhibitions against fatal violence that members of lower species usually maintain. That is, among lower species, aggression is rarely fatal; when a conflict occurs, the winner is determined through a test of skill or endurance. This inhibition against killing members of their own species protects animals from self-extinction. Humans, lacking this inhibition against fatal violence, are thoroughly capable of killing their own kind; as technology develops and more lethal weapons are produced, the extinction of the human species becomes a significant possibility.

In a similar vein, Robert Ardrey, an anthropologist, has argued that humans' evolution and development are due to their innate aggressiveness, their ability to kill, and their love of weapons—from the crude weapons of early people to the guns of modern criminals.[18]

The works of Lorenz and Ardrey have been disputed on two significant points. First, they neglect to determine whether the varied ecological and environmental conditions under which humans exist today influence their behavior. Second, they disregard the human capacity to learn from mistakes and the effect of this capacity on the development of aggression inhibitors. According to another anthropologist, Ashley Montagu—one of Lorenz's staunchest critics—people's ability to adapt and control their environment actually makes the human species better equipped to survive than lower species.[19]

Sociocultural Factors

Explanations of the cause of violent behavior that focus on the individual offender fail to account for the

Konrad Lorenz argues that aggression and violence are instincts, perhaps explaining the popularity of fictional characters such as *Rambo*.

patterns of violence in the United States. The various sources of crime statistics tell us that interpersonal violence is more common in certain areas (large, urban communities), at certain times of year (July, August), and among certain groups (young males). Though most personal violence occurs between strangers, an alarming number (about 40 percent) involves friends and family members, including former wives and husbands.[20] Because such predictable patterns exist, it seems evident that social forces must be operating when people engage in violent behavior.

The sociological theories of crime discussed in Chapters 7 through 9 described how various social conditions and interactions produce a climate in which violence seems inevitable—or at least predictable. A number of social factors have been linked to violence, including family disruption, relative deprivation, learning from deviant peers, school failure, and weakened bonds to conventional groups and norms.

To explain the existence of areas and groups within the social structure with disproportionately high violence rates, Marvin Wolfgang and Franco Ferracuti have suggested that a **subculture of violence** exists.[21] The subculture's norms are separate from the central, dominant value system. In this subculture, a potent theme of violence influences lifestyles, the socialization process, and interpersonal relationships. Even though the subculture's members share some of the values of the dominant culture, they expect that violence will be used to solve social conflicts and dilemmas. In fact, members who act nonviolently will be rejected by their peer group.

According to Wolfgang and Ferracuti, violence can become part of one's daily lifestyle, the theme for solving difficult problems and problem situations. Within the subculture, violent individuals will not be burdened by guilt. After all, they will be attacking people of similar age, race, and economic status, who also share their cultural values. Even law-abiding citizens within the subculture of violence do not view violence as menacing or immoral. In some communities, violence is tolerated because it fits with community values and standards which approve of the forceful maintenance of personal "honor."[22] Violence is legitimized by custom and norms; it is "appropriate" behavior within culturally defined situations.

The subculture of violence thesis is supported by the distribution of violent crime and victimization in American society.[23] There is also empirical evidence showing that regional and other related factors are strongly associated with violence rates.[24] While some studies have questioned whether the noncriminal residents of the subculture actually condone violence themselves, there seems to be little question that the demographic distribution of violent crime supports Wolfgang and Ferracuti's model.[25]

So far, a few of the various factors which are the suspected causes of violent crime have been reviewed. The remainder of this chapter focuses on the individual acts which comprise violent crime in our society.

FORCIBLE RAPE

Rape—defined by the common law as "the carnal knowledge of a female forcibly and against her will"—is one of the most loathed, misunderstood, and frightening of crimes. Under traditional common-law definitions, rape involved nonconsensual sexual intercourse performed by a male against a female he was neither married to nor cohabitating with. Excluded from the crime of rape are sexual acts which, though illegal, are usually included in other crime categories; for example:

- Forced participation in fellatio, cunnilingus, and, in many states, anal intercourse
- Coerced participation of a male in intercourse or other sexual activity by a female or by another male, or of a female by another female
- Coerced sexual intercourse or other sexual abuse within marriage or between cohabitants
- Coerced sexual intercourse induced by the threat of social, economic, or vocational harm rather than of physical injury.[26]

Within this framework, rape can take many different forms: stranger-to-stranger rapes; "acquaintance rapes" involving friends and family members; rapes involving alcohol or drug abuse; and marital rapes. Some rapists are one-time offenders; others engage in serial rapes. Some attack their victims without warning ("blitz rapes"); others try to "capture" their victims by striking up a conversation or offering them a ride; while still others use personal relationships to gain access to their prey.[27]

Because of its content, rape was often viewed as a sexual offense in the traditional criminological literature. In recent times, the violent, coercive nature of rape has become fully appreciated. It is today considered an expression of anger and aggression against women, rather than a forceful manifestation of sexuality. Women's groups have mounted a national campaign designed to alert the public about the seriousness of rape, to initiate help for victims, and to change legal definitions to facilitate prosecution of rape offenders. Such efforts have been only marginally effective in reducing rape rates, but there has been significant change in liberalizing rape laws and a vast social service network to aid victims has been developed.

History of Rape

Rape has been known throughout history. It has been the subject of art, literature, film, and theater. Paintings, such as the *Rape of the Sabine Women*, novels such as *Clarissa* by Samuel Richardson, poems such as "The Rape of Lucrece" by William Shakespeare, and films such as *Anatomy of a Murder* and *Roshomon* have as their central themes sexual violence.

In early civilization, rape was a common occurrence. Men staked a claim of ownership of a woman by forcibly abducting and raping her. This practice, claims Susan Brownmiller, led to males' solidification of power and their historical domination of women.[28] In fact, in her widely read book, *Against Our Will*, Brownmiller charges that the criminalization of rape occurred only after the development of a monetary economy. Thereafter, the violation of a virgin caused an economic hardship on her family, which expected a significant dowry for her hand. According to Brownmiller, further proof of the sexist basis of rape law can be seen in Babylonian and Hebraic law. These ancient peoples considered a married rape victim and her attacker as being of equal blame and sentenced the victim to death for adultery.

During the Middle Ages, Brownmiller says, forcible sex was first outlawed only if the victim was highborn, and later for all classes of females; married women were not considered rape victims until the fourteenth century. The Christian condemnation of sex during this period was also a denunciation of women as evil, with lust in their hearts, redeemable only by motherhood. A woman who was raped was almost automatically suspected of contributing to her attack.

Throughout recorded history, rape also has been associated with warfare. Soldiers of conquering armies have considered sexual possession of enemy women as one of the spoils of war. Among the ancient Greeks, rape was socially acceptable and well within the rules of warfare. During the Crusades, even knights and pilgrims, ostensibly bound by vows of chivalry and Christian piety, committed rape as they marched toward Constantinople. The belief that women are part of the spoils of war has continued through the ages, from the Crusades to the war in Vietnam.

Incidence of Rape

Most of what we know today about the scope of the rape problem comes from two national statistical sources: the Uniform Crime Report and the National Crime Survey (see Chapter 3).

The Uniform Crime Report is an indicator of rape offenses known to the police.[29] However, this data must be interpreted with caution. First, rape has frequently been underreported by victims, so trends in the rape rate may reflect reporting practices rather than crime trends. Second, the UCR employs a common-law definition of rape (the carnal knowledge of a female forcibly and against her will) which may not jibe with current state definitions. Also, the UCR includes in its computations assaults or attempts to commit rape; the interpretation of these incidents may differ widely from state to state. Finally, the acts committed by serial rapists make the relationship between number of crimes and number of offenders problematic.[30]

Keeping this in mind, what does the UCR tell us about rape in the United States? The 1987 data show that 91,111 rapes or attempted rapes were reported to police, or about 73 per 100,000 females; in 1987 reported rapes dropped about .4 percent. The number of forcible rapes reported to the police has risen dramatically: up 15 percent since 1982 and 42 percent since 1977.

Geographical and ecological conditions influenced the probability that a woman would be raped. Though most rapes occurred in the south (36 percent) and the least in the northeast (16 percent), the western states had the highest rape rate (83 per 100,000 females). Population density also influenced the rape rate; metropolitan areas had a rate of 84 per 100,000; smaller cities, 43; rural areas, 35.

The police cleared 53 percent of all reported rape offenses by arrest. Of those arrested, 45 percent were under 25 years of age, and 29 percent were aged 18 to 24. Whites comprised 50 percent of those arrested, while 48 percent were black; the racial pattern of rape arrests has been fairly consistent for some time. Finally, rape is a warm-weather crime—most occur during July and August, with the lowest rates occurring during December, January, and February.

Victim Accounts.   The National Crime Survey also has been used to reveal information about rapists and their victims. Preliminary data for 1986 indicates that about 130,000 rapes and attempted rapes occurred; about 1 woman in every 1,000 women over 12 years old was a rape victim.[31] Other recent findings about rape victimization include:

- Victims of rape tend to be in the 16- to 24-year-old age bracket
- Males report a 0.1 percent rate of attempted and completed rapes
- Black women are three times as likely to be the victims of rape than white women
- Married women and widows have a significantly lower risk of being the victim of rape than single or divorced women
- A woman was more likely to be attacked by a stranger (57 percent) than by someone she knew (43 percent). About 25 percent of all rapes occurred in the victim's home, 20 percent in a friend or relative's home, and the remainder in public places such as a street or parking lot; an estimated 4.4 percent occurred on school property

A rape victim of Lawrence Singleton at age 15, Mary Vincent tells the media how he chopped off her arms with an axe.

(a) *About 20 percent of the incidents involved an armed offender; the victim fought back in about 75 percent of the rape incidents*

(b) *The victimization rate for women reporting incomes under $7,500 was five times greater than that of women whose household income was more than $50,000. About 10 percent of the incidents involved more than one assailant.*[32]

The NCS also tells us something about the rape offender. Victims who were able to describe their attacker's described them as usually being over 21 years of age. Rapes were described as being intraracial—blacks raped blacks, whites raped whites. However, the chance of a black offender raping a white victim was greater than that of a black victim being raped by a white offender. Rapes tended to occur in the evening hours, were committed by a single offender, and in-volved a single victim.

The NCS indicates that about 60 percent of all victims reported their crimes to police; those not reporting claimed it was a "private matter" or that "nothing could be done."

Finally, most rape victims tried to protect themselves from their attackers. Those who did tended to be more seriously injured than those who complied with the attack; however, resisters were also more likely to fight off the attack completely.

The picture of the rape victim that emerges from the data is of a younger, single, lower-class woman who frequents public places during the evening hours and is raped by an assailant who is generally of the same age and racial group. In contrast, older women, married or widowed, who stayed home, especially during the evening and summer months, were more likely to avoid sexual attacks.

Date Rape

Though crime data indicate that most rapists and victims were strangers to one another, there is a disturbing trend of rapes that involve people who knew each other beforehand. For example, the date rape is believed to occur frequently on college campuses. It has been estimated that 20 percent of all college women are victims of rape or attempted rape; one survey conducted on a midwestern campus found that 100 percent of all self-reported rapists knew their victim beforehand.[33] Well-publicized gang rapes have occurred at the University of New Hampshire, Duke, Florida State, and Pennsylvania State universities, and at Bentley College in Massachusetts.[34] The Alpha Tau Omega Fraternity at Penn State was suspended after a 1983 gang rape. Despite their prevalence, less than one in ten date rapes may be reported to police. Some victims do not even view their experiences as a real rape, which they believe involves a strange man jumping out of the bushes. Coercive sexual encounters have become a disturbingly common occurrence in our culture.

Reporting Rape

One significant problem confounding the study and control of rape is that only half of all rapes are reported to police. Women who do not report rape usually believe that nothing can be done about the crime, that it is a private matter; or perhaps they are embarrassed about having friends and relatives hear about the attack. The well-publicized rape that occurred in Big Dan's Bar in New Bedford, Massachusetts, illustrates the potential embarrassment caused by a rape trial. In that incident, a woman reported being raped by six attackers on the bar's pool table. At first the news media reported to a shocked nation that a large group of bar patrons actually cheered the proceedings. But later, during a televised trial, what actually took place seemed markedly different: only a few people were in the bar during the attack, and some witnesses had attempted to call police.[35] Though the rapists were convicted at trial, the sensationalism and publicity generated by the case are believed to have inhibited some women from reporting similar attacks.[36]

Despite these problems, NCS data indicates that more women are reporting rape to the police. Increased rape reporting may be a function of greater sensitivity on the part of police and the public or the recent changes in state legal codes designed to protect the victim during trial.[37]

Criminologist Alan Lizotte used NCS data to identify the crime-specific factors which prompt women to report rapes to the police. Lizotte found that the major reporting factors were seriousness of the crime and the probability that the offender would eventually be convicted if brought to trial.[38] For example, if a rapist robs or assaults his victim in addition to raping her, the victim will be more likely to report the rape to police because the crime seems more serious.

The familiarity of the offender to the victim is another important predictor of rape reporting. If the offender had the right to be present when the attack occurred, such as during a date rape, women are less likely to call the police. They may fear their stories will not be believed if their attacker is a personal friend or relative. However, a married woman is more likely to report rapes, since her marital status implies that the actions against her were forced and unwarranted.

Although Lizotte's findings show that crime seriousness and convictability were related to reporting rapes, there were some exceptions. For example, interracial rapes and rapes involving multiple victims, the use of a weapon by the offender, or victims who were highly educated were less likely to be reported. With regard to the last factor, Lizotte believes it pos-

sible that college-educated women, knowing the limitations of the criminal justice system, refrain from reporting their sexual assaults to the police.

✗ Causes of Rape

What factors predispose some men to commit rape? The answers formulated by criminologists to this question are almost as varied as the varieties of the crime of rape itself. However, most explanations can be grouped into a few consistent categories.

Biological Factors.   One explanation focuses on the biological aspects of the male sexual drive. It is suggested that rape may be an instinctual male drive, developed over the ages as a means of perpetuating the species. In more primitive times, forcible sexual contact may have served the purpose of spreading the gene pool and maximizing offspring. Some believe that these primitive drives remain in modern man. Biologist Donald Symons suggests that males still have a built-in sexual drive that encourages them to have intimate relations with as many women as possible.[39] Symons upholds the sociobiological view that the sexual urge is correlated with the need to preserve the species. He argues that rape is bound up with sexuality as well as violence.

Male Socialization.   In contrast to the biological view, some researchers argue that rape is a function of male socialization in modern society. In her book *The Politics of Rape*, Diana Russell suggests that rape is actually not a deviant act but one conforming to the qualities regarded as masculine in U.S. society.[40] From an early age, boys are taught to be aggressive, forceful, tough, and domineering. Men are taught to dominate at the same time that they are led to believe that women want to be dominated. Russell's view conforms to Susan Brownmiller's portrait of the male as a predatory animal and the female as the victim of his sexual aggression. Russell describes the **virility mystique**—the belief that males learn to separate their sexual feelings from needs for love, respect, and affection. She believes that men are socialized to be aggressors and expect to be sexually active with many women; male virginity and sexual inexperience are marks of shame. Similarly, sexually aggressive women frighten some men and cause them to doubt their own

≡ CLOSE-UP

Rape and the Macho Male

If rape is an expression of male anger and devaluation of women, and not an act motivated by sexual desire, it follows that men who hold so-called "macho" attitudes will be more likely to engage in sexual violence than men who scorn hypermasculinity. To test the association between masculine attitudes and violent sexual behavior, psychologists Donald Mosher and Ronald Anderson surveyed 175 male college sophomores on their sexual attitudes and their history of sexual aggression. They found that males who held callous sexual attitudes, for example agreeing with the statement "Get a woman drunk, high or hot, and she'll let you do whatever you want," were also the ones most likely to use sexually coercive behavior. Mosher and Anderson found that their subjects frequently used aggressive tactics: 75 percent admitted using drugs or alcohol to have sex with a date; 69 percent used verbal manipulation; 40 percent anger; 13 percent threatened force; 20 percent actually used force.

Mosher and Anderson also had subjects listen to a taped account of a man describing the rape of a woman he had encountered on a country road. After asking the subjects to imagine themselves as the rapist, the researchers found that macho-oriented men experienced less intense negative emotions than non-macho men, and that subjects with a history of sexual aggressiveness reported more sexual arousal from the event. These findings led Mosher and Anderson to conclude:

. . . the socialization of the macho man, if it does not directly produce a rapist, appears to produce callous sex attitudes toward women and rape and proclivities toward forceful exploitative tactics to gain sexual access to reluctant women.

Discussion Questions

1. Should a rape victim's sexual behavior be considered during trial?
2. What can women do to protect themselves from the macho male?

SOURCE: Donald Mosher and Ronald Anderson,"Macho Personality, Sexual Aggression and Reactions to Guided Imagery of Realistic Rape," *Journal of Research in Personality* 20 (1987):77–94.

masculinity. Sexual insecurity may lead some men to commit rape in order to bolster their self-image and masculine identity. Rape, argues Russell, helps keep women in their place. (See Close-Up entitled "Rape and the Macho Male.")

Subculture of Violence. The subculture of violence concept holds that men who reside in a highly violent environment, and whose peers hold similar views, will be the most likely to use violence to obtain sex. In these areas, traditional sex roles stress that males are expected to seduce and females to be seduced.[41] The more strongly some men are socialized into traditional sex role stereotypes, the more likely they are to be sexually aggressive. In fact, the sexually aggressive male may view the female as a legitimate victim of sexual violence. Women, they believe, may want to be knocked around or dominated. Or victims may be perceived as teasers, who deserve what's coming to them. Sexual aggression may help increase the of-fender's status among peers, proving that he is a "man's man." Christine Adler's self-report study of sexual aggression among prison inmates found that perceptions of peers' sexual aggression was the most significant predictor of personal aggression.[42] Thus, the socialization view holds that all men are brought up in an environment that supports rape, whereas the subculture of violence theory suggests that environmental and peer pressure will increase the likelihood of violent sexual relations.

Psychological Views. Another view is that rapists are suffering from some type of personality disorder or mental illness. Paul Gebhard and his associates concluded that a significant percentage of incarcerated rapists exhibits psychotic tendencies, while many others have hostile and sadistic feelings toward women.[43] Similarly, Richard Rada found that many rapists were psychotics, others could be classified as sociopaths, and a large group suffered from a masculine identity crisis that made them oblivious to the sufferings of their victims.[44]

One of the best-known attempts to classify the personality of rapists was made by psychologist A. Nicholas Groth. According to Dr. Groth, every rape encounter contains three elements: anger, power, and sadism. Consequently, rapists can be classified according to one of these dimensions. Groth's views on rape are presented in the Close-Up entitled "Who Is the Rapist?"

Another viewpoint is that men learn to commit rapes much as they learn any other behavior. This view conforms to the learning theory models discussed in Chapter 6. For example, Groth found that 40 percent of the rapists he studied were sexually victimized themselves as adolescents.[45] A growing body of literature links personal sexual trauma with the desire to inflict sexual trauma on others.

In a similar vein, evidence is mounting that some men are influenced by observing films and books with both violent and sexual content.[46] In other words, watching violent or pornographic films featuring women who are beaten, raped, or tortured has been linked to sexually aggressive behavior in men.[47] In one startling case, a 12-year-old Providence, Rhode Island, boy sexually assaulted a 10-year-old girl on a pool table after watching trial coverage of the Big Dan's rape case on television.[48]

In sum, while criminologists are still at odds over the precise cause of rape, there is evidence that it is the product of a number of social, cultural, and psychological forces.[49] Though some experts view rape as a normal response to an abnormal environment, others view rape as the product of a disturbed mind and deviant life experiences.

Rape and the Law

Of all violent crimes, none has created such conflict in the legal system as rape. Women who are sexually assaulted are reluctant to report the crime to the police because of the discriminatory provisions built into rape laws; the sexist treatment given women by police, prosecutors, and court personnel; and the legal technicalities that authorize invasion of women's privacy when a rape case is tried in court. Some state laws continue to make rape so difficult to prove that women believe that the slim chance their attacker will be con-

victed is not sufficient to warrant their participation in the prosecutorial process.

There are a number of reasons why rape represents a major legal challenge to the criminal justice system.[50] One issue involves the concept of **consent.** In most jurisdictions, it is essential to prove that the attack was forced and that the victim did not give voluntary consent to her attacker. In a sense, the burden of proof is on the victim to prove that her character is beyond question and that she in no way encouraged, enticed, or misled the accused rapist. Evidence of the victim's character and behavior can be introduced by the defense in order to create a reasonable doubt about the woman's credibility. Unfortunately, it may be relatively easy for a defense attorney to create in the minds of a jury suspicion that the woman may have consented to the sexual act and later regretted her decision. Conversely, it is difficult for a prosecuting attorney to establish that a woman's character is so impeccable that the absence of consent is a certainty. Such distinctions are important in rape cases, because male jurors may be sympathetic to the accused if the victim is portrayed as unchaste. Simply referring to the woman as "sexually liberated" may be enough to result in exoneration of the accused, even if violence and brutality were used in the attack.

In addition to requiring evidence that consent was not given, some states still require **corroboration** that the crime of rape actually took place. This involves evidence that the accused is actually the person who committed the crime, that sexual penetration took place, and that force was present and consent absent. A few states require a third-party eyewitness to corroborate that a rape occurred. Often this testimony can come from a third party, such as a police officer, to whom the rape was reported shortly after it occurred. Even when corroboration by others is not required, it is essential that the victim establish her intimate and detailed knowledge of the act in order for her testimony to be believed in court. This may include searching questions about her assailant's appearance, the location in which the crime took place, and the nature of the physical assault itself. Embarrassing questions of this sort are partially responsible for the low number of rapes reported to police.

Proving a rape case often also involves convincing a jury that penetration of the woman's sex organs actually took place. This usually involves the medical evidence supplied by the doctors who examined the

≡ CLOSE-UP ────────────────────

Who Is the Rapist?

People have varied visions of the rapist—the psychopath who can't control his sexual urges, the college boy who gets drunk and forces his will on a young classmate, the gang member who participates in a rape to prove his manhood.

A leading expert on the personality and behavior of rapists, Dr. A. Nicholas Groth, has disputed the idea that rapists are oversexed people or, indeed, that rape is a sexual act. Dr. Groth maintains that rape is always a symptom of some psychological dysfunction, either temporary and transient or chronic and repetitive. Furthermore, it is usually a desperate act that results when an emotionally weak and insecure individual is unable to handle the stresses and demands of his life.

After observing 500 convicted rapists in his role as director of the sex offenders program for Connecticut's department of corrections, Groth found that in every act of rape, both aggression and sexuality were involved, but that sexuality became the means of expressing the aggressive needs and feelings that underlay the assault.

Groth identifies three patterns, or typologies, of rape offenders; these typologies help explain the hostility, control, and dominance associated with the act.

The *anger rape* occurs when sexuality becomes a means of expressing and discharging pent-up anger and rage. The rapist uses far more brutality than would have been necessary if his real objective had been simply to have sexual relations with his victim. His aim is to hurt his victim as much as possible; the sexual aspect of rape may have been an afterthought. Often the anger rapist acts on the spur of the moment after an upsetting incident has caused him conflict, irritation, or aggravation. Surprisingly, anger rapes are less psychologically traumatic for the victim than might be expected. Since a woman is usually physically beaten, she is more likely to receive sympathy from her peers, relatives, and the justice system and consequently be immune from any suggestion that she complied with the attack.

The *power rape* involves an attacker who does not want to harm his victim as much as he wants to possess her sexually. His goal is sexual conquest, and he uses only the amount of force necessary to achieve his objective. The power rapist wants to be in control, to be able to dominate women and have them at his mercy. Yet it is not sexual gratification that drives the power rapist; in fact, he often has consenting relationships with his wife or girlfriend. Rape is instead a way of putting personal insecurities to rest, of asserting heterosexuality and preserving a sense of manhood. The power rape's victim usually is a woman equal in age to or younger than the rapist. The lack of physical violence may reduce the support given the victim by family and friends. Therefore, the victim's personal guilt over her rape experience is increased—perhaps, she thinks, she could have done something to get away.

In some rape cases, both sexuality and aggression are fused into a single psychological trait that Groth calls *sadism*. The *sadistic rapist* is bound up in ritual—he may torment his victim, bind her, torture her. Victims are usually related in the rapist's view by a personal characteristic that he wants to harm or destroy. The rape experience is intensely exciting to the sadist; he gets satisfaction from abusing, degrading, or humiliating his captive. This type of rape is particularly traumatic for the victim; Groth found that victims of such crimes need psychiatric care long after their physical wounds have healed.

In his treatment of rape offenders, Groth found that about 55 percent were of the power type; about 40 percent, the anger type; and about 5 percent, the sadistic type. Groth's major contribution has been his recognition that rape is generally a crime of violence and not a sexual act.

Discussion Questions

1. Can rape be motivated by sexual drive or by aggression?
2. What do you think is an appropriate penalty for rape?

SOURCE: A. Nicholas Groth and Jean Birnbaum, *Men Who Rape* (New York: Plenum Press, 1979).

victim, the condition of the woman's clothing and effects when she reported the crime, whether semen or blood was found on the victim or the accused rapist, the woman's testimony backed by the absence of any motive to falsify evidence, and so on. Though medical evidence is often critical, proving the case hinges on the information given to police soon after the act occurs. One of the greatest traumas associated with the rape experience involves the often embarrassing questions police ask the victim. The reluctance of women to discuss the humiliating details of a rape soon after it has occurred is yet another reason why many rape cases are not reported to the criminal justice system.

The need for stringent proof has been justified in rape cases, for several reasons. First, some male psychiatrists and therapists still maintain that women fantasize rape and therefore may falsely accuse their alleged attackers. Some judges also fear that women may charge men with rape because of jealousy, false proposals of marriage, or pregnancy.

Second, the stigma associated with a conviction for rape and the severity of the criminal penalties that accompany it make it imperative that the defendant be given every opportunity to prove his innocence. Third, it is assumed that the jury will have a natural sympathy toward the victim, who has been so severely hurt; therefore, the law makes proof of rape especially rigorous. Fourth, the sexism that exists in U.S. society has resulted in a cultural suspiciousness toward women, who are often seen as provocateurs in any sexual encounter with men. Consequently, the burden is shifted to the woman to prove she has not provoked or condoned the rape. Although the law does not recognize it, jurors are sometimes swayed by the insinuation that the rape was victim-precipitated; thus, the blame is shifted from rapist to victim. To get a conviction, it becomes essential for prosecutors to establish that the act was forced and violent and that no question of voluntary compliance exists. Thus, the legal consequences of rape often reflect archaic legal traditions along with inherent male prejudices and suspicions.

The debate over the level of evidence required for proving rape surfaced in March of 1985, when Cathleen Webb, alleged rape victim, stepped forward and claimed that Gary Dotson, convicted of raping her in Illinois six years earlier, had actually been falsely accused.[51] Webb stated before a national audience that her fear of a teenage pregnancy led her to accuse Dotson of a crime that never actually occurred. The news that an innocent man had spent six years in prison shocked the nation's conscience. Ironically, despite Webb's recantation, the judge who originally presided in the case returned Dotson to prison, letting stand his earlier conviction. Dotson's case was then brought before the governor of Illinois, who ordered his release.

Changes in Rape Laws. The law of rape has been changing around the country. All 50 states and the federal government have developed **shield laws,** which protect women from being questioned about their sexual history unless it is judged to have a direct bearing on the case. In some instances, these laws are quite restrictive; in others, the laws grant the trial judge considerable discretion to admit prior sexual conduct in evidence if it is deemed relevant for the defense.[52]

In addition, the **marital exemption** has been under attack. Traditionally, a legally married husband could not be charged with raping his own wife. However, about ten state courts, including those in New York, have convicted husbands of marital rapes, making forced sex a crime even among married couples.[53]

Some state jurisdictions have abolished the legal category of rape and have substituted the sexually neutral concept of sexual assault.[54] Sexual assault laws outlaw any type of forcible sex, including homosexual rape. Martin Schwartz and Todd Clear go one step further by suggesting that rape laws be blended with existing assault statutes.[55] The creation of a special status for assaulted women, they argue, is one of the barriers that prevents them from being the political equals of men.

Several states, among them Nebraska and Michigan, have already substituted sexual assault statutes for traditional rape laws in an effort to remove the barriers from rape convictions. Have these changes proved effective? A recent study by Susan Caringella-MacDonald compared the processing of sexual assault cases with nonsexual assault cases in Michigan. There was some similarity, but the credibility of sexual assault victims was more likely to be challenged in court; concomitantly, offenders were more likely to receive significant sentence reductions when they plea bargained. Caringella-MacDonald concludes that "the historic difficulties in adjudicating sexual assault offenses cannot be erased by the stroke of a pen."[56]

Similar reforms have been tried in other states. For example, California's new rape law prevents defense attorneys from using a victim's prior sexual history in proving consent.[57] The law also created mandatory prison terms of up to eight years for more serious rape cases. If the offender was sent to prison in the absence of mitigating circumstances, the mandatory sentence would be six years. Although rape reform in California has not significantly increased the number of crimes reported to the police, the probability of arrest, or the percentage of convictions, it has substantially increased the probability of a convicted offender's receiving a prison sentence—from 58 percent in 1975 to 81 percent in 1982.[58]

In addition to these reforms, feminist groups have lobbied hard for reform of rape laws. Changes advocated by the antirape movement and legislated in some jurisdictions include:

- Eliminating corroboration requirements that necessitate evidence—in addition to the victim's testimony—that the alleged offense did, in fact, occur
- Strictly enforcing the limits on the defense attorney's ability to make the victim's past sexual conduct an issue at trial
- Repealing provisions requiring corroborating evidence of resistance on the part of the victim
- Eliminating "spousal immunity" to the charge of rape
- Making rape a "sex-neutral" offense, thereby providing for prosecution as rape of cases in which the victims are males or the offenders are females
- Broadening the legal definition of forcible rape to include coerced sexual acts in addition to intercourse
- Broadening the concept of "coercion" to include psychological, economic, and vocational coercion.[59]

Rape and the Community Today

In the past few years, a greater sensitivity to the plight of rape victims has developed. An antirape philosophy has been incorporated in feminine consciousness. Rape crisis centers have been opened around the country; these centers typically feature 24-hour-a-day emergency phone lines and information on police, medical, and court procedures. Some provide volunteers to assist the victim as her case is processed through the justice system. The growth of these services—which began with the Washington, D.C., Rape Crisis Center's phone line in 1972—has been so explosive that services are available in almost all major cities and college communities. Today there are over a thousand rape-related programs in the United States.[60]

Most rape programs provide two types of services.[61] *Direct services* involve interaction between center staff and clients. They provide: emergency assistance, including information, referral, and some support, usually provided over the telephone, and available 24 hours a day; face-to-face crisis intervention, or accompaniment, usually provided in the hospital, police station, courts, or other public location, also available 24 hours a day; and counseling, either one-on-one or in groups, a varying number of sessions, often provided at the center, usually scheduled, and limited to business hours and evenings.[62]

In addition, *indirect services* involve prevention and community education efforts, which usually involve four relatively distinct components: (1) public education, usually to lay audiences, most frequently to business and professional groups, schools, women's groups, civic associations, and other community organizations; (2) organization, training, and monitoring of other professional agencies, including medical, law enforcement, criminal justice agencies, and—less often—mental health professionals; (3) lobbying, usually at the state level, for legislative changes relevant to rape and other forms of violence against women; and (4) political action work, including sponsoring or supporting demonstrations, rallies, marches, protests, boycotts, and other types of actions aimed at bringing about change, either in the activities of individuals or agencies or general changes in the attitudes or awareness of the community.[63]

MURDER

Murder is defined in the common law as "the unlawful killing of a human being with malice aforethought."[64] In most state jurisdictions, in order for a person to be legally responsible for killing another, that person must intentionally and with malice have desired the death of the person killed. Two types of malice are recognized in law. **Express malice** is the state of mind assumed to exist when someone kills another person in the absence of any apparent provocation. **Implied malice** is considered to exist when a death results from negligent or unthinking behavior, even though the intention to kill was absent—for example, when a drunk driver kills a pedestrian or when a bystander is killed during the course of a robbery. Even though the perpetrator did not wish to kill the victim, the killing was the result of an inherently dangerous act and therefore is considered murder.

There are gradations of homicide. **Murder in the first degree,** usually punishable by death or imprisonment for life, occurs when a person kills another after premeditation and deliberation. **Premeditation** means that the killing was considered beforehand and suggests that it was motivated by more than a simple desire to engage in an act of violence. **Deliberation** means the killing was planned and decided on after careful thought, rather than carried out on impulse: "To constitute a deliberate and premeditated killing, the slayer must weigh and consider the question of killing and the reasons for and against such a choice; having in mind the consequences, he decides to and does kill."[65] The planning implied by this definition need not involve a long, drawn-out process but rather may involve an almost instantaneous decision to take another's life. Also, a killing accompanying a felony such as robbery or rape usually constitutes first-degree murder.

In contrast, second-degree murder requires the actor to have malice aforethought but not premeditation or deliberation. A second-degree murder occurs when a person's wanton or disregard for the victim's life and his or her desire to inflict serious bodily harm on the victim results in the loss of human life.

An unlawful homicide without malice is called manslaughter and is usually punished by anywhere between one and 15 years in prison. **Voluntary manslaughter** refers to a killing committed in the heat of passion or during a sudden quarrel considered to have provided sufficient provocation to produce violence; while intent may be present, malice is not. **Involuntary manslaughter** refers to a killing that occurs due to an individual's negligent behavior, such as when a drunk driver causes the death of a pedestrian.

These definitions are illustrated in the following examples: If, during a bar fight, one person punched another and the blow caused the victim's death, the act would probably be considered manslaughter, since the violent act was intentional but the death could not be foreseen and was not intended. If, in the heat of the fight, one person pulled out a knife and subsequently killed another, it might be construed a second-degree murder, since the act was performed with malice but the actual killing probably was not planned or thought out. On the other hand, if, after the fight, one of the combatants went home, got a gun and loaded it, re-turned to the bar an hour later, and killed his opponent, he would probably be charged with first-degree murder, since after he had had a chance to cool off, he planned and carried out the death of another.

A homicide can also be **justifiable homicide** and therefore go unpunished if it is performed in self-defense or is allowed by law, such as when a police officer shoots a dangerous felon. To qualify as self-defense, the offense must be proven unavoidable and justifiable in light of the perceived threat. For example, if an attacker uses only fists, it would not be justifiable homicide to shoot him or her in self-defense. Table 10.2 outlines state laws which allow a citizen to use deadly force.

Excusable homicide results from an unintentional killing, or accident. For a killing to be ruled an accident, it must be proven in court that the behavior that led to the death was not the product of negligence and that the accused acted as any reasonable and prudent person would have under the same set of circumstances.

Incidence of Murder

The murder rate began declining in 1980, after it had reached a peak of 10.2 murders per 100,000 persons (a total of 23,000). In 1984 the rate hit 8 per 100,000 (18,690); it slowly increased to about 8.6 in 1986 (20,610), and then dropped 2.5 percent in 1987 (20,096).

According to official crime statistics, murder victims tend to be male (74 percent), over 18 years of age (90 percent), and white (53 percent), though a disproportionate number of victims are black (45 percent). Murder, like rape, tends to be an intraracial crime; about 90 percent of victims are slain by members of their own race. Similarly, people arrested for murder are generally male (87 percent), black (52 percent), and young (44 percent under 25). In an important analysis of homicide, Marc Reidel and Margaret Zahn found that these patterns were quite consistent over a 10-year period.[66]

The environmental pattern of murder also is similar to that of rape. Murder rates are highest in large cities, in the South, and during the summer months and holiday seasons. In contrast, rural counties and the midwestern states have relatively low murder rates.

TABLE 10.2   State Laws Defining Circumstances Where Citizens May Use Deadly Force

| State | Even if life is not threatened, deadly force may be justified to protect: | | Specific crime |
	Dwelling	Property	
Alabama	Yes	No	Arson, burglary, rape, kidnaping, or robbery in "any degree"
Alaska	Yes	No	Actual commission of felony
Arizona	Yes	No	Arson, burglary, kidnaping, aggravated assaults
Arkansas	Yes	No	Felonies as defined by statute
California	Yes	No	Unlawful or forcible entry
Colorado	Yes	No	Felonies, including assault, robbery, rape, arson, kidnaping
Connecticut	Yes	No	Any violent crime
Delaware	Yes	No	Felonious activity
D.C.	Yes	No	Felony
Florida	Yes	No	Forcible felony
Georgia	Yes	Yes	Actual commission of a forcible felony
Hawaii	Yes	Yes	Felonious property damage, burglary, robbery, etc.
Idaho	Yes	Yes	Felonious breaking and entering
Illinois	Yes	Yes	Forcible felony
Indiana	Yes	No	Unlawful entry
Iowa	Yes	Yes	Breaking and entering
Kansas	Yes	No	Breaking and entering including attempts
Kentucky	No	No	—
Louisiana	Yes	No	Unlawful entry including attemps
Maine	Yes	No	Criminal trespass, kidnaping, rape, arson
Maryland	No	No	—
Massachusetts	No	No	—
Michigan	Yes	No	Circumstances on a case by case basis
Minnesota	Yes	No	Felony
Mississippi	Yes	—	Felony including attempts
Missouri	No	No	—
Montana	Yes	Yes	Any forcible felony
Nebraska	Yes	No	Unlawful entry, kidnaping, and rape
Nevada	Yes	—	Actual commission of felony
New Hampshire	Yes	—	Felony
New Jersey	Yes	No	Burglary, arson, and robbery
New Mexico	Yes	Yes	Any felony
New York	Yes	No	Burglary, arson, kidnaping, and robbery including attempts
North Carolina	Yes	No	Intending to commit a felony
North Dakota	Yes	No	Any violent felony
Ohio	—	—	
Oklahoma	Yes	No	Felony within a dwelling
Oregon	Yes	—	Burglary in a dwelling including attempts
Pennsylvania	Yes	—	Burglary or criminal trespass
Rhode Island	Yes	—	Breaking or entering
South Carolina	No	No	—
South Dakota	Yes	—	Burglary including attempts
Tennessee	Yes	No	Felony
Texas	Yes	No	Burglary, robbery, or theft during the night
Utah	Yes	—	Felony
Vermont	Yes	—	Forcible felony
Virginia	No	No	—
Washington	No	No	—
West Virginia	Yes	No	Any felony
Wisconsin	No	No	—
Wyoming	No	No	—

—No specific reference indicated in the statute.
SOURCE: Bureau of Justice Statistics, *Report to the Nation on Crime and Justice,* 2d ed., 1988, p. 31.

The UCR also collects information on the circumstances of murder. A number of important patterns stand out. Where it could be determined, most victims knew or were acquainted with their assailant; strangers committed only 13 percent of murders. The most common offenders were acquaintances (30 percent), friends (5 percent), or wives (4.8 percent).

Another trend was that most murders involved firearms (59 percent); about 20 percent involved knives or cutting instruments. Some well-known weapons, such as poison (0.1 percent), narcotics (0.1 percent) and strangulation (1.8 percent) are actually quite rare; there were only 14 known poisonings in 1986. Of the known murder circumstances, about 19 percent occurred during commission of a felony; 37 percent followed an argument and another 19 percent were related to drug and alcohol use.

Today, few would deny that some relationship exists between social and ecological factors and murder. The following section explores some of the more important issues related to these factors.

Murderous Relations

One factor that has received a great deal of attention from criminologists is the relationship that allegedly exists between the murderer and the victim. Unlike most other criminals, murderers usually know their victims and have had some sort of personal relationship with them.[67] For example, in 1986, in murders in which the police were able to determine the relationship between criminal and victim, only 13 percent of the actors were classified as strangers to one another.[68] In most instances, the victim and criminal were either related (husband, wife, brother, son, or the like) or acquainted (friend, boyfriend, girlfriend, neighbor, and so on).

This relationship pattern underscores one of the most important concepts in criminology, the view that murder can be **victim-precipitated.** This refers to the view that murder often involves an interaction between victim and offender in which the victim's behavior contributed to the violent incident which brought about his or her death. This position is most closely associated with Marvin Wolfgang, the criminologist who first used the term in his study of criminal homicide patterns.[69] He defined the term as follows:

The term "victim-precipitated" is applied to those criminal homicides in which the victim is a direct, positive precipitator in the crime. The role of the victim is characterized by his having been the first in the homicide drama to use physical force against his subsequent slayer. The victim-precipitated cases are those in which the victim was the first to show and use a deadly weapon, to strike a blow in an altercation—in short, the first to commence the interplay or resort to physical violence.[70]

Examples of a victim-precipitated homicide include the death of an aggressor in a barroom brawl, or a wife who kills her husband after he attacks and threatens to kill her. Wolfgang found that 150, or 26 percent, of the 588 homicides in his sample could be classified as victim-precipitated.

Since Wolfgang's work was published, the concept of victim precipitation has remained somewhat controversial. For example, Menachim Amir's suggestion that rape is victim-precipitated has been viewed as a sexist concept implying that some women desire to be raped.[71]

Stranger Homicides. Not all murders involve friends, family, and acquaintances. Though the actual number is open to debate, Marc Reidel reports that somewhere between 14 and 29 percent of homicides are committed by strangers, and in some areas the percentage of stranger murders is increasing.[72] In contrast, recent research by John Hewitt shows that the rate of stranger homicides during the past two decades has remained relatively stable, while the rate of homicides among acquaintances has increased significantly.[73]

Under what circumstances do stranger homicides occur? In a study of homicide in nine U.S. cities, Margaret Zahn and Philip Sagi found that while 72 percent involved family or acquaintances, 28 percent were stranger homicides. This latter group involved mostly **felony murders,** (16 percent) which occur during crimes such as rapes, robberies, and burglaries. In addition, about 12 percent consisted of random acts of urban violence: a homeowner tells a motorist to move his car because it is blocking the driveway, an argument ensues, and the homeowner gets a pistol and kills the motorist; a young boy kills a store manager because "something came into my head to hurt the lady."[74] Zahn and Sagi found important patterns in the stranger, nonfelony cases. For example, white victims were significantly older than their attackers, while there was little age differential between black and Hispanic victims and criminals. Zahn and Sagi attribute this difference to the fact that urban homicides occur in central city areas. While white families with young children have left for suburbia, older whites have remained and become vulnerable to predatory crime.[75]

Murder Transactions

At one time it was popular to view murderers as mentally unstable persons who killed because they were driven by psychotic personalities or were so deeply disturbed that they did not know what they were doing. Although it is true that some convicted murderers suffer from mental illnesses, such as schizophrenia or paranoia, it also is probably true that the incidence of psychosis among murderers is no greater than the incidence of psychosis in the total population.

Today, criminologists have revised their concepts of murder. Attempts have been made to classify criminal homicide by its cause and the relationship between the actors involved in it. For example, James Boudouris classifies murder interaction as follows: Domestic relations (husband-wife); lovers' affairs; relations between friends and acquaintances; business relations (landlord-tenant, doctor-patient, employer-employee); criminal transactions (holdup-store owner, drug user-pusher); noncriminal homicide (police officer-holdup); cultural recreation–causal (bar fight, quarrel over car accident); subcultural recreation–causal (two gamblers fight over card game); psychiatric (murder by a mentally disturbed person); suicide-murder (the killer immediately kills himself or herself); incidental (a peacemaker in a fight is accidentally killed); unknown cause. In a study of homicides occurring in Detroit between 1926 and 1968, Boudouris found that an overwhelming number were related to domestic and family quarrels and that relatively few murders were caused by psychiatrically disturbed persons.[76]

David Luckenbill studied murder transactions to determine whether particular patterns of behavior are common to the transaction between killer and victim.[77] Luckenbill found that many homicides take a sequential form: the victim makes what the offender considers an offensive move; the offender typically

retaliates in a verbal or physical manner; an agreement to end things violently is forged with the victim's response; the battle ensues, leaving the victim dead or dying; the offender's escape is shaped by his or her relationship to the victim or the reaction of the audience, if any.

Thus, whereas some murders may be the result of wanton violence by a stranger, the typical homicide seems to involve a social interaction between two or more people who know each other and whose destructive social interaction leads to the death of one party.[78] If anything, recent research seems to support Wolfgang's victim precipitation model.

Geographic Issues

One issue debated by criminologists is whether the southern part of the United States is significantly more homicide-prone than other parts of the country. In a well-known paper, Raymond Gastil found that a significant relationship existed between murder rates and residence in the South; that these differences predated the Civil War; and that in states outside the South, homicide rates increased when southerners had moved into the state.[79] Gastil attributed high homicide rates to the culture of the South, which stresses a "frontier" mentality, mob violence, night riders, the acceptance of personal vengeance by the legal system, and the widespread availability of firearms.

In a follow-up study, Colin Loftin and Robert Hill introduced economic variables into the study of southern homicide rates and concluded that any argument pointing to a southern culture of lethal violence and murder was fallacious.[80] The Loftin-Hill study did not put this debate to rest, however. Further analyses, using different data, by Howard Erlanger and later by William Doerner, also disputed the idea that southerners are more violence-prone than others.[81] However, the debate over this issue still rages; and Gastil himself replied to his critics by stating that they missed his real view—that southern culture promotes legal violence, not just the approval of violence.[82]

Serial Murder

Donald Harvey is described as being neat, pleasant, outgoing, and remarkably normal by those who know him best. However, his coworkers in a Cincinnati area hospital where he worked as a nurses' aide referred to Harvey as the "angel of death" because so many patients died in his ward. Their fears convinced a local television station to conduct an investigation which resulted in Harvey's arrest and conviction on multiple murder charges. Harvey plead guilty to killing at least 21 patients and three other people, and he claims to have killed 28 others, though he cannot remember details of their deaths. Harvey claims that he was a mercy killer who "gained relief for the patients"; prosecutors described him as a thrill seeker whose behavior was triggered by his sexual ambivalence.[83] He was sentenced to life in prison with possibility of parole in 95 years. When all his activities come to light, Harvey may become known as the most prolific killer in U.S. history.

Donald Harvey's murderous actions fall within a frightening pattern referred to as **serial murder.** Some serial murderers, such as Theodore Bundy and the Australian race-car driver and photographer Christopher Wilder, roam the country killing at random.[84] Others terrorize a city, such as the Los Angeles-based Night Stalker; the Green River Killer, who at the time of this writing is believed to have slain more than 27 young women in Seattle; and the Hillside Strangler(s), Kenneth Bianchi and Angelo Buono, who tortured and killed 10 women in the Los Angeles area.[85] A third type of serial murderer, such as Donald Harvey, kills so cunningly, that many victims are dispatched before the authorities even realize the deaths can be attributed to a single perpetrator.[86]

Serial killers operate over a long period of time and can be distinguished from mass murderers, who kill many victims in a single violent outburst. For example, James Huberty killed more than 20 people in a McDonald's in San Ysidro, California. Mass and serial murders have even occurred in usually nonviolent Great Britain.[87] For example, on August 20, 1987, 25-year-old gun enthusiast Michael Ryan killed 14 people in a random shooting spree.[88]

There is no distinct type of serial killer. Some seem to be monsters—such as Edmund Kemper who, in addition to killing six young female hitchhikers, killed his mother, cut off her head, and used it as a dartboard. Others—like Bianchi, Wilder, and Bundy—were suave lady's men whose murderous actions surprised even close friends. Consequently,

the cause of serial murder eludes criminologists. Such widely disparate factors as mental illness, sexual frustration, neurological damage, child abuse and neglect, smothering relationships with mother (David Berkowitz, the Son of Sam, slept in his parents' bed until he was 10), and childhood anxiety have been suggested as possible causes. However, most experts view serial killers as sociopaths who from early childhood demonstrated bizarre behavior, such as torturing animals, who enjoy killing, are immune to their victims' suffering, and who, when caught, bask in the media limelight. Wayne Henley, Jr., who along with Dean Corril killed 27 boys in Houston, offered to help prosecutors find the bodies of additional victims so he could break Chicago killer Wayne Gacy's record of 33 murders.[89] However, Philip Jenkin's study of serial murder in England identified one group of offenders who had no apparent personality problems until late in their lives, were married, respectable, and even had careers in the armed services and police.[90]

Serial killers come from diverse backgrounds. They have been described by Ann Rule, an expert on **mass murder,** as follows:

Most of them are very intelligent; if they're not intelligent, they are very conniving and clever. The dumb ones are caught early on; they can't run up a string of 35 murders. Now the street-smarts may make up for a lack of IQ, but most of them are very bright.

A lot of them are handsome. I think women particularly expect a serial killer to look like Frankenstein, but he doesn't. Most of them have relationships with women, pretty women who love them. That's not why they're killing.

Most of these serial killers have tremendous egos, and when they're caught and they're backed into a corner, they like to brag about what they've done.

A lot of them are very attracted to law enforcement. They're either police groupies, where they hang around the cops, or they serve as reserve officers, or they may use police uniforms as disguise. Kenneth Bianchi, the Hillside Strangler, wore a police uniform, and when he was finally caught in Washington he was working for a security service, and was just about ready to be appointed a reserve deputy sheriff.

They travel continually. Where we might put 10,000 to 20,000 miles a year on our cars, a serial killer will put on 100,000 miles a year. They're always trolling for victims. They will pick certain types of victims—like Ted (Bundy) chose college girls with long dark hair parted in the middle. Historically victims of serial killers are young women, prostitutes, homosexuals, children, vagrants and old people, people who are very vulnerable. I have yet to find a serial killer that has gone after body-builders.

They usually will stick within their victim pattern, they usually kill within their own race. Therefore a white serial killer kills whites. Actually you rarely find a black serial killer. Often they lead such double lives that when they're arrested finally, they're utterly shocked.[91]

So far law enforcement officials have been at a loss to control random killers who leave few clues, constantly change their whereabouts, and have little connection to their victims. Catching serial killers is often a matter of luck. To help local law enforcement officials, the FBI has developed a profiling system to identify potential suspects. In addition, the Justice Department's Violent Criminal Apprehension Program (VI-CAP) is a computerized information service that gathers information and matches offense characteristics on violent crimes around the country.[92] This way crimes can be linked to determine if they are the product of a single culprit. The Close-Up entitled "Mass Murder" further discusses this issue.

SERIOUS ASSAULT

The FBI defines serious assault, or **aggravated assault,** as "an unlawful attack by one person upon another for the purpose of inflicting severe or aggravated bodily injury"; this definition is similar to the one used in most state jurisdictions.[93] The pattern of criminal assault is quite similar to that of homicide—one could say that the only difference between the two is that the victim survived. In 1987, the FBI recorded 855,080 assaults, a rate of 351 per 100,000; in 1987 aggravated assaults rose 2 percent. The assault rate has risen significantly in the past few years, up 20 percent since 1982 levels.

The pattern of assault is quite similar to that of both rape and murder. People arrested for assault and those identified by victims seem to be young, male, and white, though a disproportionate number of arrestees are minority group members (30 percent). Similarly, assault rates were highest in urban areas, during the summer months, and in southern regions. The most common weapons used in assaults were blunt instruments (32 percent), firearms (21 percent), and knives (22 percent).

Assault in the Home

One of the most frightening aspects of assaultive behavior today is the incidence of violent attacks in the home. Criminologists are now aware that intrafamily violence is an enduring social problem in the United States.

One arena of intrafamily violence that has received a great deal of media attention is **child abuse.** This term describes any physical or emotional trauma to a child for which no reasonable explanation, such as an accident or ordinary disciplinary practices, can be found.[94] Child abuse can result from actual physical beatings being administered to a child by hands, feet, weapons, belts, sticks, or burnings. Another form of abuse results from **neglect**—not providing a child with the care and shelter to which it is entitled. Another aspect of the abuse syndrome is **sexual abuse**—the exploitation of children through rape, incest, and molestation by parents and guardians.

It is difficult to estimate the actual number of child abuse cases, since so many incidents are never reported to the police. Nonetheless, child abuse and neglect appear to have reached epidemic proportions in recent years.[95] A national survey conducted in 1975 by two sociologists, Richard Gelles and Murray Straus, first focused attention on the child abuse problem. Gelles and Straus found that between 1.4 and 1.9 million children in the United States are subject in a given year to physical abuse from their parents; a 10-year follow-up found that the rate of severe abuse had declined.[96] However, Gelles and Straus's data still indicates that more than one million instances of severe child abuse occur each year, and their more recent survey did not include single-parent households. Moreover, physical abuse was rarely found to be a one-time event: the average number of assaults per

CLOSE-UP

Mass Murder

In a recent book, sociologists Jack Levin and James Fox analyze one of the most frightening aspects of modern violence—mass murder.

According to Levin and Fox, about 35 mass murderers are active across the United States today. They include serial killers, who wander the country killing at random. Other serial killers stay in their hometown and lure victims to their death. Theodore Bundy, convicted killer of three girls and suspected killer of many others, roamed the country killing as he went, while Wayne Gacy killed over 30 young boys without leaving Chicago. Mass murder also can be part of a single, uncontrollable outburst called simultaneous killing. Examples of simultaneous mass murderers include Charles Whitman, who killed 14 people and wounded 30 others from atop the 307-foot tower on the University of Texas campus on August 1, 1966; and James Huberty, who killed 21 people in a McDonald's in San Ysidro, California on July 18, 1984.

Levin and Fox dispute the notion that all mass murderers have some form of biological or psychological problems, such as genetic anomalies or schizophrenia. They contend that mass murderers are actually ordinary citizens driven to extreme acts. They reached this conclusion by intensively studying 156 cases of mass murder involving 675 victims.

Levin and Fox found that even the most sadistic mass murderers are more "evil than crazy." Few are mentally ill and driven by delusions or hallucinations. Instead, they typically exhibit a sociopathic personality that deprives them of feelings of conscience or guilt to guide their behavior. They maintain the need to control and dominate their victims without concern about the victims' feelings.

Mass murderers are often motivated by profit and expediency: to get rid of witnesses, to stifle troubling family members, to eliminate snitches. There is usually a reason for the attack; rarely are total strangers victimized. Even serial killers look for particular physical or emotional features in their victims. They usually prey on people vulnerable to attack—prostitutes, hitchhikers, runaways. However, some sadistic types kill because they enjoy their victim's sufferings or get sexual gratification from them.

No one can predict who will turn out to be a mass murderer. Many are the "boy next door," whose neighbors are astonished to find out about their murderous rampages. Some are motivated by overwhelming personal problems that trigger an emotional bombshell. Others, like San Francisco's Zebra killers who executed 14 people in 1973 and 1974, may be part of a cult or group that espouses murder.

So far police have been successful in capturing simultaneous killers whose outburst is directed at family members or friends. The serial killer has proven a more elusive target. Today the U.S. Justice Department is coordinating efforts to gather information on unsolved murders in different jurisdictions in order to find patterns linking the crimes. Unfortunately, when a serial murderer is caught, it is often the work of luck—or a snitch—and not investigative skill.

Discussion Questions

1. Can a mass murderer be legally sane?
2. Should there be a mandatory death sentence for all serial killers?

SOURCE: Jack Levin and James Alan Fox, *Mass Murder* (New York: Plenum Press, 1985), p. 47.

year was 10.5; the median, 4.5. Children of all ages suffer abuse. In general, boys are more frequently abused than girls until age 12. Among teenagers, girls are more frequently the object of abuse. Finally, the American Humane Society, which collects national data on child abuse, estimates that two million cases are now reported each year.[97]

Though it is difficult to estimate incidence of sexual abuse, Diana Russell's survey of women in the San Francisco area found that 38 percent had experienced intra- or extrafamilial sexual abuse by the time they reached 18.[98]

Child Abuse

Why do parents physically assault their children? Such maltreatment is a highly complex problem with neither a single cause nor a readily available solution. It cuts across ethnic, religious, and socioeconomic backgrounds. Abusive parents cannot be categorized by sex, age, or educational level; they are persons from all walks of life. Some general factors do seem to be present with some frequency in families in which abuse and neglect take place. One factor is familial stress. Abusive parents are unable to cope with life crises—divorce, financial problems, alcohol and drug abuse, poor housing conditions. This inability leads them to maltreat their children.

Statistics also show that a high rate of assault on children occurs among the lower economic classes. This has led to the misconception that lower-class parents are more abusive than those in the upper classes. However, two conditions may account for this discrepancy. First, low-income people are often subject to greater levels of environmental stress and have fewer resources available to deal with such stress. Second, cases of abuse among poor families are more likely to be dealt with by public agencies and therefore are more frequently counted in official statistics.[99]

Two other factors have a direct correlation with abuse and neglect. First, parents who themselves suffered abuse as children tend to abuse their own children. Second, isolated and alienated families tend to become abusive. A cyclical pattern of family violence seems to be perpetuated from one generation to another within families. Evidence indicates that a large number of abused and neglected children grow into adolescence and adulthood with a tendency to engage in violent behavior. The behavior of abusive parents often can be traced to negative experiences in their own childhood—physical abuse, lack of love, emotional neglect, and incest. These parents become unable to separate their own childhood traumas from their relationships with their children. They also often have unrealistic perceptions of the appropriate stages of childhood development. Thus, when their children are unable to act "appropriately"—when they cry, throw food, or strike their parents—the parents may react in an abusive manner. For parents such as these, "the axiom about not being able to love when you have not known love yourself is painfully borne out in their case histories . . . They spend their days going around the house, ticking away like unexploded bombs. A fussy baby can be the lighted match."[100]

Parents also become abusive if they are isolated from friends, neighbors, or relatives who can provide a lifeline in times of crisis:

Potentially or actually abusing parents are those who live in states of alienation from society, couples who have carried the concept of the shrinking nuclear family to its most extreme form, cut off as they are from ties of kinship and contact with other people in the neighborhood.[101]

Many of the abusive and neglectful parents describe themselves as highly alienated from their families and lacking close relationships with persons who could provide help and support in stressful situations.

It would be misleading to pinpoint any one factor as a definitive explanation of why abuse and neglect occur. It does seem, however, that a combination of the following elements is likely to result in parental maltreatment of children:

- The parents have a history of having been abused, neglected, or deprived as children
- The parents are isolated, with no lifeline for help in a crisis
- The parents perceive their child as disappointing in some way
- A crisis precipitates the abuse[102]

Child Protection.   Parents who assault their children are subject to prosecution in criminal courts under the traditional statutes against assault and battery. Though special abuse laws exist in each state, they are generally more concerned with the care and protection of children than the punishment of parents.

Abuse cases are referred to family or juvenile courts. Children are represented by a court-appointed attorney called a **guardian ad litem.** If parents are found to be abusive, the child can be removed from the home while treatment is provided. In severe cases, the court has the right to terminate the rights of parents over their children and place battered children in permanent foster care. This is actually a rare occurrence, since courts are reluctant to separate family members.

Although an increased awareness of the child abuse syndrome has led to the development of programs designed to treat assaultive parents, the fact that most abuse occurs behind closed doors makes it difficult to eliminate this social problem. The reporting of child abuse by doctors, social workers, and other such persons is mandated by law. Nonetheless, it is difficult to isolate child abuse from accidents or other unintentional physical harm. (See Close-Up on "Reporting Sexual Abuse.")

Spouse Abuse

Spouse abuse, which usually involves the physical assault of a wife by a husband (though husband abuse is not unknown), has occurred throughout recorded history. During the Roman era, men had the legal right to beat their wives for minor acts, such as attending public games without permission, drinking wine, or walking outdoors with their faces uncovered.[103] More serious transgressions, such as adultery, were punishable by death. During the later stages of the Roman Empire, the practice of wife-beating abated; and by the fourth century A.D., excessive violence on the part of husband or wife could be used as sufficient grounds for divorce.[104]

During the early Middle Ages, there was a clear distinction between love and marriage.[105] The feminine ideal was protected and cherished. Marriages usually were arranged by family ties. Wives were guarded jealously and could be punished severely for violations of duty. Husbands were expected to beat their wives for "misbehaviors" and might be punished by neighbors if they failed to do so.[106] Through the later Middle Ages and into modern times—that is, from 1400 to 1900—there was little objection within the community to a man's using force against his wife as long as the assaults did not exceed certain limits, usually construed as death or disfigurement. By the mid-nineteenth century, severe wife-beating fell into disfavor; and accused wife-beaters were subject to public ridicule. Nonetheless, limited chastisement was still the rule.

By the close of the nineteenth century, laws had been passed in England and the United States outlawing wife beating. Yet the long history of husbands' domination of their wives' lives made physical coercion hard to control. Until recent times, the typically subordinate position of women in the family was believed to give husbands the legal and moral obligation to manage their wives' behavior. These ideas form the foundation of men's traditional physical control of women and have led to severe cases of spousal assault.

The Nature and Extent of Spouse Abuse. It is difficult to estimate the extent of spouse abuse today; however, some statistics give indications of the extent of the problem. In their national survey of family violence, Gelles and Straus found that 16 percent of surveyed families had experienced husband-wife assaults. In police departments around the country, 60 to 70 percent of evening calls involve domestic disputes. Nor is violence restricted to the postmarital stage of domestic relations. In a national survey of college students, James Makepeace found that more than 20 percent of the females had experienced violence during their dating and courtship relationships.[107]

What are the characteristics of the wife assaulter? After a careful analysis of the factors correlated with spouse abuse, criminologist Graeme Newman has identified the following traits:

- *Presence of alcohol:* excessive alcohol use may turn otherwise docile husbands into wife assaulters
- *Hostility dependency:* some husbands who appear docile and passive may resent their dependency on their wives and react with rage and violence; this factor has been linked to sexual inadequacy
- *Excessive brooding:* obsession with a wife's behavior, however trivial, can result in violent assaults
- *Social approval:* some husbands believe that society approves of wife assault and use these beliefs to justify their violent behavior
- *Socioeconomic factors:* men who fail as providers and are under economic stress may take their frustrations out on their wives
- *Flash of anger:* a significant amount of family violence results from a sudden burst of anger after a verbal dispute
- *Military service:* spouse abuse among men who have seen military service is extremely high; similarly, those currently serving in the military are more likely to assault their wives than civilian husbands; the reasons for this phenomenon may be (1) the violence promoted by military training and (2) the

CLOSE-UP

Reporting Sexual Abuse

While child sexual abuse is a significant social problem, it is difficult to control because many cases are not reported to the authorities. Albert Cardarelli studied the case histories of 156 sexually-abused children who were treated at the Family Crisis Program, Tuft's New England Medical Center, Boston, in order to determine why cases are not reported to the police. Some of his findings are described here.

The Findings

In this study, 96 families, or 62 percent of the total chose not to report the abuse to the police. As with most activities involving interpersonal violence, the reasons for not reporting were varied.

Most victims are obviously either too young or too frightened and intimidated to take such action against their parents or other adults in authoritative roles. A small number of cases are reported by the victim's friends or neighbors, or by hospital personnel and social workers who have come in contact with the victim. The findings indicate either that few families seek medical help, or if they do, hospital and mental health professionals are unwilling to involve police with the family. An increasing percentage of cases are reported as one moves from offenders who are family members and relatives to those who are friends,

acquaintances, or strangers.

These results provide further evidence that sexual abuse or incest between family members is unlikely to come to the attention of law enforcement authorities. Many children do not reveal the incest for a long period of time, either because of a sense of guilt, or from fear of the consequences if such behavior becomes known. Studies have also shown that even when a mother is aware of incestuous activity between her daughter and a parent figure, she may decide not to intervene in order to avoid retaliatory violence to herself.

Overall, once a complaint against an offender is begun, the child may have to repeat the details of the incident to many law enforcement officials, ranging from the police to the prosecutor. The constant repetition of these details in a public forum can cause serious emotional stress and tension for both the victim and the family. Furthermore, the court process may keep alive memories of the sexual experience at a time when the child would do better to repress it.

Characteristics of Abuse Reporting

Although most research indicates that females are sexually victimized much more often than males during childhood, recent studies have shown that sexual abuse of males is higher than it was once believed to be and that the fate of reporting is lower for males than for females. In this study,

---

close proximity of military families to one another
- *Having been battered children:* husbands who assault their wives often were battered as children[108]

Similar research by Glenda Kaufman and Murray Straus finds the typical wife-beater to be a blue-collar worker, who approves of violence and who has a drinking problem.[109]

A growing amount of support is being given to battered women. Shelters for assaulted wives are springing up around the country, and laws are being passed to protect a wife's interests. It is essential that this problem be brought to public light and controlled.

ROBBERY

The common-law definition of robbery, and the one used by the FBI, is "the taking or attempting to take anything of value from the care, custody or control of a person or persons by force or threat of force or violence and/or by putting the victim in fear."[110] A robbery is a crime of violence because it involves the use of force to obtain money or goods. Robbery is punished severely because the victim's life is put in jeopardy; the value of the items taken has nothing to do with the punishment meted out.

In 1987, 517,704 robberies were reported in the UCR, a rate of 212 per 100,000 population; however,

no difference was found in the percent of cases reported to the police based on the sex of the victim.

Prior to the research, it was hypothesized that there would be a greater sense of outrage, and therefore a greater willingness to report a case of sexual abuse, the younger the age of the victim, especially when the offender was not a family member. Children between 3 months and 3 years of age are most vulnerable to abuse, while being least capable of communicating the abuse to those who might take some corrective action. While a slightly higher percent of cases were reported covering children 3 years old or less, the differences between the age groups are not significant. In this study, as in many studies of child sexual abuse, the majority of victims were 7 years and older, with 35 percent of the victims between 13 and 18 years of age.

Almost half the families whose child was victimized through sexual intercourse reported the abuse to the police, in contrast to only 30 percent of the families where the abuse involved fondling or mutual masturbation. These results not only point to the vast under-reporting of certain forms of child sexual abuse, but to the continued need for researchers and policymakers to establish incidence projections based on the *variations of sexual abuse* by which the children are victimized.

There is considerable discussion about the role that social class and race play in child abuse and neglect situations. Variations in the philosophies and practices of child rearing among social and ethnic groups are often reflected in the incidence rates of abuse found among these groups. The findings showed a significant difference between the percentage of white and nonwhite families reporting the abuse to the police. Only 10 percent of the cases of sexual abuse among nonwhite victims were reported, in contrast to almost 45 percent among white victims. The results suggest that the level of abuse among minority families may be much greater than what official data and studies have shown in the past.

The findings also showed that "blue-collar" families reported a greater proportion of incidents. However, there were no significant differences in the willingness of the families in all four strata (business/professional, skilled, semiskilled, and nonskilled) to report the abuse. Those in the business/professional strata had the lowest percentage of reporting, and this may reflect their greater access to private resources for resolution compared to families within the "blue-collar" strata.

Discussion Questions

- Is the statement of a small child enough to begin a child sexual abuse complaint?
- Should nonabusing parents be held criminally responsible if they fail to report a case of child sexual abuse?

SOURCE: Albert Cardarelli, "Child Sexual Abuse: Factors in Family Reporting," *National Institute of Justice Reports*, June 1988, pp. 10-11.

---

in 1987 reported robberies declined 5 percent.

The ecologic pattern for robbery is similar to that of other violent crimes, with two major discrepancies. First, northeastern states have by far the highest robbery rate (284 per 100,000) while the South, which has high rates for other violent crimes, reported 192 robberies per 100,000 population. Second, minorities accounted for a significant portion of all persons arrested for robbery (63 percent).

National Crime Survey data indicate that robbery is more of a problem than the FBI data show; according to the NCS, about 1 million robberies are committed each year. However, victim data indicates that the overall robbery rate has been declining, at a rate of 24 percent between 1973 and 1986. The two data sources agree, however, on the age, race, and sexual makeup of the offenders—they are disproportionately young, male, and minority.

The Nature of Robbery

Robbery is most often a street crime—that is, fewer robberies occur in the home than in public places such as parks, streets, and alleys. For example, 25 percent of rapes reported by victims to NCS researchers occurred in the home, but only 13 percent of reported robberies. About 50 percent of robberies occurred in

TABLE 10.3   Robbery Victims

On average, 1,223,400 persons were robbed annually, a rate of almost seven robberies for every 1,000 persons 12 years of age and older in the United States.	Over half of all robbery victims were attacked. Female robbery victims were more likely to be attacked than were male victims; victims 65 and older were more likely to be attacked than victims under 65.
About one in 12 robbery victims experienced serious injuries such as rape, knife or gunshot wounds, broken bones, or being knocked unconscious.	Victims who were attacked were more likely to be injured if they were female, if the incident occurred at night, if there was more than one offender, or if a weapon was present.
About half of all completed robberies involved losses of $82 or less; 10 percent involved losses of $800 or more. Most theft losses were never recovered.	Robbery rates declined by 15 percent from 1973, largely because of a decline in attempted robberies.
Offenders displayed weapons in almost half of all robberies; they had guns in about one in five. Offenders with weapons were more likely to threaten than attack their victims.	Robbery victims were more likely than rape or assault victims to encounter multiple offenders, strangers, or offenders with weapons.
In almost nine out of 10 robbery victimizations, robbers were male; in about half, they were black or worked in groups of two or more.	Blacks experienced robberies at two and a half times the rate for whites; the rate for male victims was twice the rate for female victims.

SOURCE: Adapted from Caroline Wolf Harlow, *Robbery Victims* (Washington, D.C.: Bureau of Justice Statistics, 1987), p. 1.

streets or parking lots.[111]

The Bureau of Justice Statistics analyzed over 14 million robbery victimizations between 1973 and 1984, in order to provide a more complete picture of the nature and extent of robbery. They found that about two-thirds of victims had property stolen, a third were injured, and a fourth suffered both personal injury and property loss.[112] Other important findings are included in Table 10.3.

The public nature of robbery has had a great influence on people's behavior. Most people believe that large cities suffer the most serious instances of violent crimes such as robbery; and, not surprisingly, many people have moved out of inner-city areas into suburban communities.

Robber Typologies

Attempts have been made to classify and explain the nature and dynamics of robbery. One study found that robbery follows one of five patterns:

1. *Robbery of persons who, as part of their employment, are in charge of money or goods.* This category includes robberies in jewelry stores, banks, offices, and other places in which money changes hands. In

recent years, the rate of this category of robbery has dramatically increased. For example, robberies of convenience and grocery stores increased 47 percent between 1976 and 1980, while bank robbery was up 71 percent, commercial house robbery up 20 percent, and gas station robbery up 5 percent.

2. *Robbery in an open area.* These robberies include street offenses, muggings, purse snatchings, and other attacks. In urban areas, this type of robbery constitutes about 60 percent of reported totals. Street robbery is most closely associated with *mugging* or *yoking*—grabbing victims from behind and threatening them with a weapon.

3. *Robbery on private premises.* This type of robbery involves robbing people after breaking into homes. FBI records indicate that this type of robbery accounts for about 10 percent of offenses.

4. *Robbery after preliminary association of short duration.* This type of robbery comes in the aftermath of a chance encounter—in a bar, at a party, or after a sexual encounter.

5. *Robbery after previous association of some duration.* Incidents in patterns 4 and 5 are substantially less common than stranger-to-stranger robberies, which account for more than 75 percent of the total.[113]

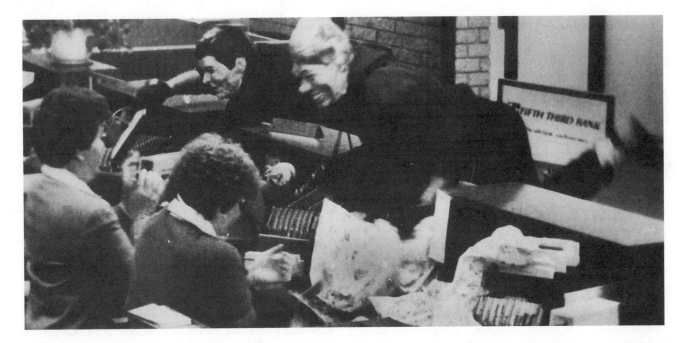

The trademarks of the professional robber are planning and skill. The bank job filmed above was the fifth success for this pair of robbers.

Another well-known robber typology has been created by John Conklin. Instead of focusing on the nature of robbery incidents, Conklin categorizes robber types into the following various specialties.[114]

Professional Robber. Professionals are those who "manifest a long-term commitment to crime as a source of livelihood, who plan and organize their crimes prior to committing them, and who seek money to support a particular lifestyle that may be called hedonistic." Some professionals are exclusively robbers, while others may engage in other types of crimes. Professionals are committed to robbing because it is direct, fast, and very profitable. They hold no other steady job and plan three or four "big scores" a year to support themselves. Planning and skill are the trademark of the professional robber. Operating in groups in which assigned roles are the rule, professionals usually steal large amounts from commercial establishments. After a score, they may take a few weeks off until "things cool off."

Opportunist Robber. Opportunists steal to obtain small amounts of money when an accessible and vulnerable target presents itself. They are not committed to robbery but will steal from cab drivers, drunks, the elderly, and other such persons if they need some extra spending money for clothes or other elements of their lifestyle. Opportunists are usually young minority group members who do not plan their crimes. Although they operate within the milieu of the juvenile gang, they are seldom organized and spend little time discussing weapon use, getaway plans, or other strategies.

Addict Robber. Addict robbers steal to support their drug habits. They have a low commitment to robbery because of its danger, but a high commitment to theft because it supplies needed funds. The addict is less likely to plan crime or use weapons than the professional robber but is more cautious than the opportunist. Addicts choose targets that present a minimum of risk; however, when desperate for funds, they are sometimes careless in selecting the victim and executing the crime. They rarely think in terms of the big score; they only want enough money to get their next fix.

Alcoholic Robber.   Many robbers steal for reasons related to their excessive consumption of alcohol. Alcoholic robbers steal (1) when, in a disoriented state, they attempt to get some money to buy liquor or (2) when their condition makes them unemployable and they need funds. Alcoholic robbers have no real commitment to robbery as a way of life. They plan their crimes randomly and give little thought to victim, circumstance, or escape; for that reason, they are the most likely to be caught.

CONTROLLING INTERPERSONAL VIOLENCE

Interpersonal violence continues to provoke fear in the American public. How can it be controlled? The typical strategy is to deter crime through fear of legal punishments. Consequently, most jurisdictions maintain long prison sentences and in some instances the death penalty as punishments for violent crimes. Nonetheless, efforts to control violent crimes through deterrence strategies alone have not met with success. One reason for this failure is the nature of violent crime itself. For example, violent episodes are the result of emotion-laden interpersonal experiences which are quite difficult to deter. Many murderers know their victims beforehand, and murder has been described as a behavioral transaction often precipitated by the victim's conduct. Other criminologists attribute violence-proneness to a disturbed personality such as psychopathy, which by definition is immune to the threat of punishment.

What alternatives have been suggested, then, to reduce violence? Certainly one approach is to reduce the root causes of crime—poverty, social inequality, racism, and so on. Yet to be effective, such measures must be carried out on a scale that heretofore has seemed unachievable.

A more conservative approach has been to encourage community cooperation with police, improve police effectiveness, create longer prison sentences for repeat or violent offenders, discourage plea bargaining, and use the death penalty. This approach is designed not so much to prevent violence before it occurs, but to lower violence rates through a policy of incapacitation. Though it is in vogue today, this policy has had the unfortunate side effect of creating an overcrowded prison system whose size is increasing at a far higher pace than the crime rate. Furthermore, studies measuring recidivism rates give little support to a policy of crime control through incarceration since once released former inmates have a significant chance of returning to the institution. It is unlikely that whatever drove a person to be violent in the first place will be eliminated by a prison stay.

The physical environment also has been the focus of violence-control efforts. In the 1970s, Oscar Newman formulated the concept of **defensible space.** Newman argued that "targets" could be hardened or protected, street lighting improved, surveillance made easier, and people given a sense of belonging, or territoriality.[115] However, attempts to put Newman's ideas into operation did not meet with any clear-cut success.[116] Nonetheless, the emergence of rational choice theory (Chapter 5) and the realization that a thinking criminal may avoid difficult targets has renewed interest in crime prevention through target hardening, defensible space, and effective guardianship. There are indications that the environment can be altered to reduce the threat of violence. For example, neighborhood watch programs have been hailed for their crime-reducing potential. This jibes with the findings of R. Lance Shotland and Lynne Goodstein that the presence of bystanders will significantly reduce the probability that a crime will occur.[117]

Gun Control

One method long advocated for controlling interpersonal violence has been handgun control. The FBI has found that about half of all murders and a third of all rapes and robberies are committed with a handgun. Handguns were the cause of death for two-thirds of all police killed in the line of duty. Considering the estimated 30 to 50 million illegal handguns in the United States today, these findings certainly should not be surprising.[118]

Efforts to control handguns have many different sources. Each state and many local jurisdictions have laws banning or restricting sales or possession of guns. Others regulate dealers who sell guns. For example, the Federal Gun Control Act of 1968 prohibits dealers from selling guns to minors, ex-felons, drug users, and so on. In addition, each dealer must keep detailed records of who purchases guns. Unfortunately, the resources available to enforce this law are meager.[119]

Do strict gun-control laws make a difference in the violent crime rate? The jury is still out on this issue. The most famous attempt to regulate handguns is the Massachusetts Bartley-Fox Law, which provides a mandatory one-year prison term for possession of a handgun (outside the home) without a permit. A detailed analysis of violent crime in Boston in the years after the law's passage found that the use of handguns in robberies and murders did decline substantially (robbery 35 percent, and murder 55 percent in a two-year period). However, these optimistic results must be tempered by two facts: rates for similar crimes dropped significantly in comparable cities that did not have gun-control laws; and the use of other weapons, such as knives, increased.[120]

Another gun-control method is to add an extra punishment for any crime involving a handgun. A well-known example is Michigan's Felony Firearm Statute, which requires that anyone convicted of a crime in which a handgun was used receive an additional two years tacked on to the sentence. An analysis by Colin Loftin and his associates found that the Michigan law had little effect on the sentence given to convicted offenders, and little effect on violent crime in Detroit.[121] Similarly, in a study evaluating the handgun laws of all fifty states, David Lester found little evidence that strict handgun laws influence homicide rates.[122]

The use of handguns in political crimes, such as the Robert Kennedy assassination, has spurred a majority of Americans to advocate control of the sale and manufacture of handguns, and a ban on cheap "Saturday Night Specials." Some states, like Maryland, have already banned "Saturday Night Specials." Some conversatives view gun control as a threat to personal liberty and call instead for severe punishment of criminals rather than control of handguns. In either event, gun-control efforts may have little effect on violence.[123] There are so many guns in the United States that banning their manufacture would have a relatively small effect for years to come. And if they are made more valuable by banning their manufacture or sale, illegal overseas importation of guns might increase, as it has for another controlled substance—narcotics. Increasing penalties for gun-related crimes has also met with limited success, since judges may be reluctant to alter their sentencing policies to accommodate legislators. Regulating dealers is difficult and would only encourage private sales and bartering. Nonetheless, some combination of control and penalty may prove useful, and efforts should be made to discover, if at all possible, whether handgun control could indeed reduce violent crime rates.

X
POLITICAL VIOLENCE

While interpersonal violence and street crime have been on most people's minds, many people also are very concerned about violence against the state, or political violence. Every day seems to bring news of terrorist plots, bombings, and assassinations. Yet these activities represent only a small aspect of the entire range of activity engaged in by political criminals.

Political crime has existed throughout history. Stephen Schafer maintains that it is virtually impossible to find a history book of any society that does not record the existence of political criminals, "those craftsmen of dreams who possess a gigantic reservoir of creative energy as well as destructive force."[124]

Political crime can be defined in various ways. Barton Ingraham suggests that it can be divided into two broad categories: (1) acts that are seen as involving betrayal of allegiance to principles or persons that bind the political order; and (2) acts that are viewed as involving a challenge to or hindrance of political authority.[125] Ernest Van Den Haag views political crimes as law violations used to acquire power, exercise power, challenge authority, and enforce authority.[126]

It is often difficult to separate violent political crimes from interpersonal crimes of violence. For example, if a group robs a bank in order to obtain funds for its revolutionary struggles, should the act be treated as a political crime or a common bank robbery? In this instance, the definition of a crime as political depends on the kind of legal response the act evokes from those in power. To be a political crime, an act must carry with it the intent to disrupt and change the government and must not merely be a common-law crime committed for reasons of greed or egotism. Schafer refers to those who violate the law because they believe their actions will ultimately benefit society as **convictional criminals.** They are

Terrorism for political purposes has a long history but only recently has it become an international event. The TWA hijacking at Beirut by Shiite Moslems (1985) set a precedent since no country would allow the plane to land.

constantly caught in the dilemma of knowing their actions may be wrong and harmful but also believing these actions are necessary to create the changes they fervently desire. Schafer argues, "A member of the Second World War Resistance may have condemned violence, yet his own conviction overshadowed any sense of repugnance and induced him to engage in violent crimes in an effort to expel the invader from his Fatherland."[127]

Terrorism

One aspect of political violence that is of great concern to criminologists is **terrorism**.[128] Terrorism has been defined by the National Advisory Commission on Criminal Justice as "a tactic or technique by means of which a violent act or the threat thereof is used for the prime purpose of creating overwhelming fear for coercive purposes."[129] Terrorism is a type of political crime that emphasizes violence as a mechanism to promote change. Other political criminals may engage in acts such as demonstrating, counterfeiting, selling secrets, and spying. Terrorists make systematic use of murder and destruction or the threat of such violence to terrorize individuals, groups, communities, or governments into conceding to their political demands.[130]

The term *terrorist* is often used interchangeably

with the term *guerrilla*. The latter term, meaning "little war," developed out of the rebellion directed against French troops by Spanish rebels after Napoleon's invasion of the Iberian peninsula in 1808.[131] Daniel Georges-Abeyie distinguishes between the two terms by suggesting that terrorists have an urban focus; that the objects of their attacks include the property and persons of civilians; and that they operate in small bands, or cadres, of three to five members.[132] Guerrillas, on the other hand, are located in rural areas; the objects of their attacks include the military, the police, and government officials; and their organization can grow quite large and eventually take the form of a conventional military force. However, guerrillas can infiltrate urban areas in small bands, while terrorists can make forays into the countryside; consequently, the terms have come to be used interchangeably.[133]

Today, terrorism is used to promote political goals. Terrorists use violence as a tool to invoke fear in those in power and in those who support authority. Terrorist actions—kidnapping, assassination, bombing—are used to draw repressive responses from governments trying to defend themselves. These responses help revolutionaries to expose, through the skilled use of media coverage, the governments' antihuman nature. The original reason for the governments' harsh response may be lost as the effects of counterterrorist activities are felt by uninvolved people.

Historical Perspective

Acts of terrorism have been known throughout history. The assassination of Julius Caesar on 15 March, 44 B.C. can be considered an act of terrorism. Terrorism became widespread at the end of the Middle Ages, when political leaders were subject to assassination by their enemies. The word *assassin* was derived from an Arabic term meaning "hashish-eater"; it referred to members of a drug-using Moslem terrorist organization that carried out plots against prominent Christians and other religious enemies.[134] At a time when rulers were absolute despots, terrorist acts were viewed as one of the only means of gaining political rights. At times, European states encouraged terrorist acts against their enemies. For example, Queen Elizabeth I empowered her "sea-dogs," John Hawkins and Francis Drake, to carry out attacks against the Spanish fleet. These privateers would have been considered pirates had they not operated with government approval. American privateers operated against the British during the American Revolution and the War of 1812. History can turn terrorists into heroes, depending on whose side wins.

The term *terrorist* became popular during the French Revolution. From the fall of the Bastille on 14 July, 1789, until July 1794, thousands suspected of counterrevolutionary activity went to their deaths on the guillotine. Here, again, the relative nature of political crime is documented: while most victims of the French Terror were revolutionaries who had been denounced by rival factions, thousands of members of the hated nobility lived their lives in relative tranquillity. The end of the Terror was signaled by the death of its prime mover, Maximilien Robespierre, on 28 July, 1794, as the result of a successful plot to end his rule; he was executed on the same guillotine to which he sent almost 20,000 people to their deaths.

In the hundred years after the French Revolution, terrorism continued around the world. The Hur Brotherhood in India was made up of religious fanatics who carried out terrorist acts.[135] In Eastern Europe, the Internal Macedonian Revolutionary Organization (IMRO) campaigned against the Turkish government, which controlled its homeland (Macedonia is now part of Yugoslavia). Similarly, the protest of the Union of Death Society, or Black Hand, against the Austro-Hungarian empire's control of Serbia led to the group's assassination of Archduke Franz Ferdinand, an act that signaled the beginning of World War I. The Irish Republican Army (IRA) developed around 1916 and kept up a steady battle with British forces from 1919 to 1923, culminating in the southern part of Ireland's gaining independence.

Between the world wars, right-wing terrorism existed in Germany, Spain, and Italy, while Russia was the scene of left-wing revolutionary activity leading to the death of the czar and the rise of the Marxist state. During World War II, resistance to the Germans was common throughout Europe; these terrorists are now, of course, considered heroes. In Palestine, Jewish terrorist groups—the Haganah, Irgun, and Stern Gang, whose leaders included Menachim Begin—waged war against the British to force them to allow Jewish survivors of the Holocaust to settle in their traditional homeland.

U.S. Terrorist Groups

It is difficult to provide an up-to-date assessment of terrorist activity in modern times, since the national and international scene has been changing so rapidly. However, some general observations can be made about the nature and extent of terrorist activity today.

In the United States, terrorist activities have been carried out by several groups. The Armed Forces of National Liberation for Puerto Rico (FALN) has supported the goal of independence for Puerto Rico and the Puerto Rican Socialist Party. It has claimed responsibility for more than a hundred bomb attacks in New York, Washington, and Chicago. Other Puerto Rican groups include the Organization of Volunteers for the Puerto Rican Independence (OVRP), Ejercito Popular Boricua (ERB)-Macheteros, and Armed Forces of Popular Resistance (FARP).

During the 1960s and early 1970s, terrorist groups grew up around the dual themes of racial conflict and anti-imperialism. On the West Coast, the New World Liberation Front (NWLF), a Marxist-Leninist group that advocated the overthrow of the U.S. government and corporate interests, claimed to be responsible for more than 40 bombings, including one that caused $1 million worth of damage at the Hearst Castle at San Simeon, California. The NWLF was closely associated with other groups, including the Friends and Neighbors of the Poor (FNP), the People's Light Brigade (PLB), and the Jonathon Jackson Brigade; these groups have claimed responsibility for bombings of stores, government offices, and power stations on the West Coast.[136]

Fueled by antiwar sentiment, the Revolutionary Action Movement (RAM), the Black Liberation Army (BLA), and the Weather Underground were quite active. After the riots at the 1968 Democratic convention in Chicago, commonly called the "Days of Rage," many of these groups went underground—that is, they withdrew from public view. Years later, one clique of the Weather Underground, the best-known radical group, split off from the main organization and formed the above-ground Prairie Fire Organizing Committee in order to better recruit new members. The organization's leaders were arrested in 1977 on the charge of recruiting members for an underground organization whose primary objective was the assassination of public figures and bombing of public buildings. These arrests caused the demise of Prairie Fire.[137] However, other members of the Weather Underground, led by Bernadine Dohrn, continued their antigovernment activities. When Dohrn surrendered to authorities after 10 years as a fugitive, the Weather Underground appeared defunct. Then, in October 1981, a series of robberies and killings in New York linked the Weather Underground with elements of the Black Liberation Army, the Black Panthers, and several European groups, including the Irish Republican Army (IRA). Kathy Boudin, another Weather Underground leader who had been a fugitive for 11 years, was arrested in connection with a robbery and killing of two police officers. By December 1981, the FBI was able to state: "The Weather Underground is not a viable organization. There is no evidence that such an organization is functioning."[138] However, other groups such as the Sam Melville-Jonathon Jackson unit may still be active despite arrests of their leaders. There have been few left-wing terrorist acts in recent years and the FBI classifies these groups now as dormant.

Right-Wing Terrorism. Whereas the above-mentioned groups have a left-wing orientation, there is growing awareness of political violence associated with ultra-conservative right-wing groups. The Anti-Defamation League estimated that there are 71 such groups currently active in the United States.[139] These groups tend to be heavily armed and organized around such themes as white supremacy, Nazism,

militant tax resistance, and religious revisionism. Identified groups include the closely aligned Aryan Nations, the Order, the Brotherhood, Posse Comitatus, Silent Brotherhood, and the White American Bastion, as well as the traditional Ku Klux Klan organizations. Some of these groups have formed their own churches; for example, the Church of Jesus Christ Christian claims that Jesus was born an Aryan rather than a Jew and that white Anglo-Saxons are the true "chosen people."[140]

Right-wing political violence first became national news in 1983, when Posse Comitatus member Gordon Kahl murdered two federal marshals in North Dakota and was later slain in a gun battle with federal agents in Arkansas. On 9 December, 1984, Robert Matthews, leader of the Order, was killed in a shootout on Whidby Island off Seattle, Washington. The government's interest in right-wing groups is heightened, since some have declared war on the United States and made officials and federal agents top enemies.[141]

The accompanying Close-Up describes a few of the most active terrorist groups in the United States.

International Terrorism.   On the international scene, terrorism for political purposes has been much more extensive and much more deadly than in the United States.[142] For example, in 1985 an Air India jet was blown up with 329 people aboard, and on 23 April, 1988, a car bomb in Tripoli, Lebanon killed 54 and wounded 125.[143]

In many instances, Marxist terrorist groups have been pitted against capitalist governments. In Germany, the Red Army Faction (RAF) has been active in the name of "anti-imperialism." In France, the Action Direct (AD) is divided into two groups: one is opposed to international imperialism, the U.S., and NATO (the North Atlantic Treaty Organization), while the nationalist branch directs its energies on French targets.

In Italy, the Red Brigade (BR), which had succeeded in kidnapping and executing a former Italian president, Albert Moro, is still active despite the arrest and 1986 conviction of its leaders, Barbara Balzarani and Giovanni Senzani.

When the Red Brigade kidnapped James Dozier, a U.S. general, in Italy during December 1981, it issued a communique that sums up the Marxist group's goals for Europe: to wage war against the Western powers; to prevent a buildup of nuclear arms by NATO in

CLOSE-UP

U.S. Terrorist Groups

The following are descriptions of terrorist groups operating in the United States today.

Armed Forces of Popular Resistance

The Armed Forces of Popular Resistance (FARP) is a Puerto Rican pro-independence terrorist group which describes itself as a military-political organization. The FARP first came to light in January of 1978, but is suspected of having been involved in several robberies prior to that time. Since 1978, the FARP has been involved in terrorist incidents, including the ambush of a U.S. Navy personnel bus on December 3, 1979, in Sabana Seca, Puerto Rico, which was jointly claimed by the FARP, the EPB-Macheteros and the FARP.

Ejercito Popular Boricua (EPB)-Macheteros

The Ejercito Popular Boricua (EPB)-Macheteros claimed total or joint responsibility for eight terrorist incidents in 1986, including seven terrorist incidents on October 28, 1986, which were jointly claimed by members of the OVRP and the FARP.

The EPB-Macheteros emerged in 1978, and is a self-described, pro-independence clandestine terrorist group which operates both alone and jointly with other terrorist organizations in Puerto Rico. The announced goal of this group is to obtain the independence of Puerto Rico through the use of violence. This group, which is more commonly known as the Macheteros, has claimed responsibility for terrorist acts through communiques or has otherwise been linked to some of the most violent terrorist activities in Puerto Rico. Since this group's emergence in 1978, the Macheteros have been linked to at least 18 incidents, including the December 3, 1979, ambush of U.S. service members in Sabana Seca, Puerto Rico, which took two lives and injured nine others.

Aryan Nations (AN)

The AN, also known as the Church of Jesus Christ Christian, was founded by Richard Butler at Hayden Lake, Idaho, in the late 1970s. The AN is described as the action arm of the church. Butler and his group profess white supremacy and they advocate the elimination of blacks and Jews from society.

The AN is headquartered on a fenced 20-acre com-pound which is located 10 miles north of Hayden Lake, Idaho. The AN uses this location to print and distribute hate literature, as well as to provide recordings of Butler's sermons, which preach white supremacy and denounce blacks, Jews, and other nonwhites throughout the country. In addition, these messages have been distributed to white prison gangs, such as the Aryan Brotherhood and the Aryan Special Forces. The AN acts as a disbursal and clearing house for the money obtained by the prison gangs through illegal activities in both federal and state penal institutions. These prison groups have been known to participate in loan sharking, extortion, and gambling, as well as being suspects in the murders of other convicts and prison guards.

Organization of Volunteers for the Puerto Rican Revolution (OVRP)

The OVRP claimed total or joint responsibility for nine terrorist incidents in 1986. Seven of these terrorist incidents were claimed jointly with the Ejercito Popular Boricua (EPB)-Macheteros and the Armed Forces of Popular Resistance (FARP).

The OVRP is a self-described political-military group in Puerto Rico, whose objective is to gain independence for Puerto Rico through armed revolution. The OVRP emerged in 1978, when it claimed joint credit with the EPB-Macheteros for an explosives theft from a public works warehouse in Manati, Puerto Rico. Since its inception, the OVRP has had close ties with other Puerto Rican terrorist groups with which it has claimed responsibility for terrorist acts. The most serious of these terrorist acts was the December 3, 1979, ambush of a U.S. Navy bus at Sabana Seca, Puerto Rico. This attack was claimed jointly with the EPB-Macheteros and the FARP. The ambush claimed the lives of two Navy personnel and left nine others wounded. During October, 1979, the OVRP bombed numerous government facilities. Due to its extensive use of violence for a number of years, the OVRP is considered to be one of the most dangerous terrorist organizations in Puerto Rico.

Discussion Questions

1. Should terrorists be treated as ordinary criminals?
2. Are terrorists "freedom fighters" for a cause we aren't involved with?

SOURCE: Adapted from FBI Analysis of Terrorist Incidents in the United States, 1986 (Washington, D.C.: Federal Bureau of Investigation, 1988).

Europe; and to cause dissension in chief NATO countries such as Italy, Germany, and Spain.[144] The recapture of General Dozier by Italian police temporarily interrupted the power of terrorists in Italy and has restricted BR activity since.

It has become common to link left-wing terrorism abroad with the Libyan government's efforts to sponsor terrorist groups. The "Libyan Connection" has been linked to numerous Middle East and European organizations. The 5 April, 1986, bombing of a West Berlin nightclub resulted in a retaliatory bombing raid by U.S. aircraft against Libyan targets. Such reaction is in step with that of another target of Libyan-sponsored terrorism—Israel—whose "Iron Fist" policy demands retribution in blood for any terrorist act.[145]

Not all terrorist activity abroad is left-oriented. Many nationalist groups, such as the IRA, the Palestine Liberation Organization (PLO), and Sikh radicals use violence for the purpose of recovering what they believe to be lost homelands. In fact, some experts believe the true focus of terrorism is not radical or extreme change, but the conservative goal of creating a nationalistic identity for an oppressed people.[146] Of course their actions are no less deadly: Sikh militants were responsible for Indian leader Indira Gandhi's assassination on 6 November, 1984, in retaliation for the government's storming of their Golden Temple religious shrine (and revolutionary base) in June 1984; in 1985 they were responsible for the Air India jet bombing and death of the 329 persons aboard.[147]

The Extent of Terrorism

It is difficult to estimate the extent of violent terrorism around the world. In the United States, the government estimates that more than 10,000 terrorists (including the Klan) are operating. During the past decade, between seven and 51 terrorist acts have taken place in the United States, though the per year incident rate has generally declined.[148]

In contrast, international terrorism is growing by leaps and bounds. As Figure 10.1 indicates, international terrorism increased from less than 500 acts in 1982 to about 774 in 1986. In 1968, 20 people were killed in terrorist acts; by 1986, the casualty list had grown to 576 killed.[149] As Figure 10.2 indicates, about

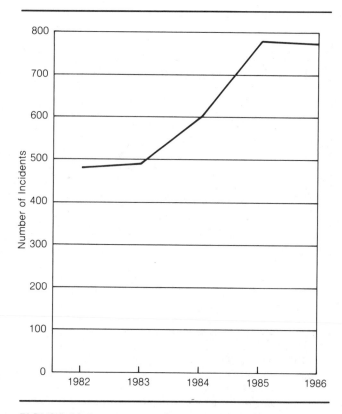

FIGURE 10.1 International Terrorist Incidents

SOURCE: United States Department of State, *Patterns of Global Terrorism 1986* (Washington, D.C.: U.S. Government Printing Office, 1988), p. 3.

half of all international terrorism takes place in the Middle East, 20 percent in Western Europe, and 20 percent in Latin America. Asia, Africa, and North America are relatively terrorist-free.

Who Is the Terrorist?

Terrorists engage in criminal activities, such as bombings, shootings, and kidnappings. What motivates these individuals to risk their lives and those of the innocent people who may fall victim to their activities? M. Cherif Bassiouni describes the steps by which ideological terrorists become enmeshed in their activities as follows:

• Heightened perception of oppressive conditions —whether real or imaginary

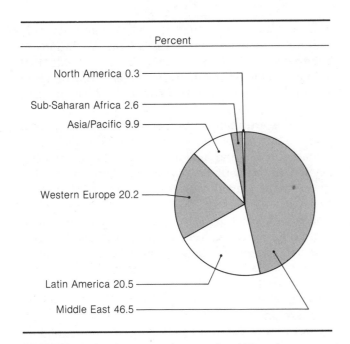

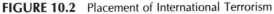

Percent

North America 0.3

Sub-Saharan Africa 2.6

Asia/Pacific 9.9

Western Europe 20.2

Latin America 20.5

Middle East 46.5

FIGURE 10.2   Placement of International Terrorism

SOURCE: United States Department of State, *Patterns of Global Terrorism 1986* (Washington, D.C.: U.S. Government Printing Office, 1988), p. 3.

- Recognition that such conditions are not the immutable order of things, but are amenable to active reform
- Recognition that action designed to promote change is not forthcoming
- Recognition that one must at last resort to violence
- Recognition that such action need not be successful, but only contribute to setting in motion a series of events enlisting others and leading to change (a realization that dissemination of the cause is more important than success of the action)
- Recognition that the individual's self-sacrifice outweighs the guilt borne by committing a violent act (thus, violence without guilt)
- Recognition that the cause transcends the need to rationalize the act of violence (the self-gratification merges with the higher purpose)[150]

According to Austin Turk, terrorists tend to come from upper- rather than lower-class backgrounds.[151] This may be because the upper classes can produce people who are more politically sensitive, articulate, and focused in their resentments. Since their position in the class structure gives them the feeling that they can influence or change society, upper-class citizens are more likely to seek confrontations with the authorities.

Class differences are also manifested in different approaches to political violence. The violence of the lower class is more often associated with spontaneous expressions of dissatisfaction, manifested in collective riots and rampages and politically inconsequential acts. Upper-class violence tends to be more calculated and organized and uses elaborate strategies of resistance. Revolutionary cells, campaigns of terror and assassination, logically complex and expensive assaults, and writing and disseminating formal critiques, manifestos, and theories are typically acts of the socially elite.

Responses to Terrorism

Governments have attempted numerous responses to terrorism. Law enforcement agencies have infiltrated terrorist groups and turned members over to police.[152] Rewards have been given for information leading to the arrest of terrorists. "Democratic" elections have been held to discredit terrorists' complaints that the state is oppressive. Counterterrorism laws have been passed to increase penalties and decrease political rights. For example, Israel has passed the Administrative Detention Law, which allows searches and detention of suspected terrorists. The West German Contract Ban Law, passed in 1977, deals with terrorists as follows:

1. Permits complete isolation of a terrorist inmate who is suspected of involvement in outside terrorist activities. This applies especially to his or her attorney.
2. Provides for acceleration of court proceedings.
3. Tightens the law on illegal possession of weapons.
4. Introduces regulations for theft-proof license plates, plate numbers, and automobile papers.

In the United States, antiterrorist legislation and activities have not been closely coordinated. While the threat of skyjacking has been reduced by better airport security, other efforts have not been as successful.

The U.S. federal government entered into counterterrorist activities in 1972, when President Nixon formed the cabinet-level Committee to Combat Terrorism. However, no federal law has been passed to unify efforts against terrorists; and strict behavior codes have limited the activities of the FBI and the Central Intelligence Agency (CIA) in infiltrating terrorist groups.

The United Nations has passed numerous resolutions condemning terrorism but has refrained from taking an active antiterrorist stance. Cooperation among countries has tended to be on an individual basis. For example, the United States and Cuba signed an anti-hijacking agreement on 15 February, 1973.

Although the United States has stated a policy prohibiting violence or assassination attempts against suspected terrorists, both federal law enforcement agencies and the U.S. military have specially trained antiterrorist squads. The military, for example, has created the renowned Delta Force, made up of members from the four service areas.[153] Delta Force activities are generally secret, but it is known that the force saw action in Iran (1980), Honduras (1982), Sudan (1983), and during the Grenada invasion (1983), and was prepared to take action against the hijacking of the ship the Achille Lauro (1985).

Despite the U.S. government's efforts to control terrorism, any attempts to meet force with force are fraught with danger. If the government's response is retaliation in kind, it could provoke increased terrorist activity—for revenge or to gain the release of captured comrades. Of course, a weak response may be interpreted as a license for terrorists to operate with impunity. The alternative is a prevention model. For example, the U.S. Congress is now considering such measures as putting U.S. Sky Marshalls on overseas flights and monitoring security at overseas airports. Nonetheless, preventing terrorism is a task that so far has stymied the governments of most of the world's nations.

SUMMARY

People in the United States live in an extremely violent society. Among the various explanations for violent crimes, one postulate is the existence of a subculture of violence that stresses violent solutions to interpersonal problems. Another view holds that humans may be instinctively violent. Still another claims that violence is related to economic inequality.

There are many types of interpersonal violent crime. Rape is defined as the carnal knowledge of a female forcibly and against her will. Rape has been known throughout history; at one time, it was believed that a woman was as guilty as her attacker for her rape. At present, 80,000 rapes are reported to police each year; but the true number is probably much higher. Rape is an extremely difficult charge to prove in court. The victim's lack of consent must be proven; therefore, it almost seems that the victim is on trial. Consequently, rape crisis centers to aid victims have been developed and changes in rape law and procedure are ongoing.

Murder is the unlawful killing of a human being with malice aforethought. There are different degrees of murder, and punishments vary accordingly. The murder rate has declined in the past few years to about eight per 100,000 people. One important characteristic of murder is that the victim and criminal often know each other. This has caused some criminologists to believe that murder is a victim-precipitated crime. Murder victims and offenders tend to be young, black, and male. There is also a tendency for the South to have a higher murder rate than other parts of the country.

Assault is another serious interpersonal violent crime. One important type of assault is that occurring in the home, including child abuse and spouse abuse. It has been estimated that almost 2 million children are abused by their parents each year, and that 16 percent of families report husband-wife violence. It even appears there is a trend toward violence between dating couples on college campuses.

Robbery involves theft by force, usually in a public place. Types of offenders include professional, opportunist, addict, and alcoholic robbers.

Political violence is another serious problem. Many terrorist groups exist, both at the national and international level. Hundreds of terrorist acts are reported each year in the United States alone. Terrorists may be motivated by criminal gain, psychosis, grievance against the state, or ideology.

KEY TERMS

subcultures

instinctual drives

eros

thanatos

subculture of violence

virility mystique

consent

corroboration

shield laws

marital exemption

express malice

implied malice

murder in the first degree

premeditation

deliberation

voluntary manslaughter

involuntary manslaughter

justifiable homicide

excusable homicide

victim-precipitated

felony murder

serial murder

mass murder

aggravated assault

child abuse

neglect

sexual abuse

guardian ad litem

defensible space

convictional criminals

terrorism

NOTES

1. Graeme Newman, *Understanding Violence* (New York: Lippincott, 1979), p. 89.

2. Lloyd Johnston, Jerald Bachman, and Patrick O'Malley, *Monitoring the Future, 1986* (Ann Arbor, Mich.: Institute for Social Research, 1987), p. 174; Michael Hindelang, Michael Gottfredson, and Timothy Flanagan, *Sourcebook of Criminal Justice Statistics, 1980* (Washington, D.C.: U.S. Government Printing Office, 1981), p. 171.

3. Hans Toch, *Violent Men* (Chicago: Aldine, 1969), p. 1.

4. "Not in My Town," *Time* (1 June 1987), p. 31.

5. John Vollman, "Neutering Homicidal Recidivists in Jurisdictions without Capital Punishment," Paper presented at the American Society of Criminology Meeting, Montreal, Canada, November, 1987.

6. Katherine Jamieson and Timothy Flanagan, *Sourcebook of Criminal Justice Statistics* (Washington, D.C.: U.S. Government Printing Office, 1987), pp. 100–101 (data from the Gallup Poll, 1986).

7. Harriet Frazier, "Spare the Rod: Corporal Punishment and the Death Penalty for Juveniles," Paper presented at the American Society of Criminology Meeting, Montreal, Canada, November, 1987.

8. John Leo, "Low Profile for a Legend," *Time* (21 January 1985).

9. Robert Nash Parker and Catherine Colony, "Relationships, Homicides and Weapons: A Detailed Analysis," Paper presented at the American Society of Criminology Meeting, Montreal, Canada, November, 1987.

10. See, for example, C. A. Fogel, S. A. Mednick, and N. Michelsen, "Hyperactive Behavior and Minor Physical Anomalies," *Acta Psychiatrica Scandinavia* 72 (1985):551–56.

11. L. R. Huesmann and L. D. Eron, "Cognitive Processes and the Persistence of Aggressive Behavior," *Aggressive Behavior* 10 (1984):243–51; Lee Ellis, "Evolution and the Nonlegal Equivalent of Aggressive Criminal Behavior," *Aggressive Behavior* 12 (1985):57–71.

12. Dorothy Otnow Lewis, Ernest Moy, Lori Jackson, Robert Aaronson, Nicholas Restifo, Susan Serra, and Alexander Simos, "Biopsychosocial Characteristics of Children Who Later Murder," *American Journal of Psychiatry* 142 (1985):1161–67.

13. See, for example, James Q. Wilson and Richard Herrnstein, *Crime and Human Nature* (New York: Simon and Schuster, 1985), pp. 173–212.

14. John Monahan and Henry Steadman, *Crime and Mental Disorder* (Washington, D.C.: National Institute of Justice, 1984).

15. Travis Hirschi and Michael Hindelang, "Intelligence and Delinquency: A Revisionist Review," *American Sociological Review* 42 (1977):471–586; Terrie Moffit, William Gabrielli, Sarnoff Mednick, and Fini Schulsinger, "Socioeconomic Status, IQ, and Delinquency," *Journal of Abnormal Psychology* 90 (1981):152–56. For an opposing view see, Scott Menard and Barbara Morse, "A Structuralist Critique of the IQ-Delinquency Hypothesis: Theory and Evidence," *American Journal of Sociology* 89 (1984):1347–78.

16. Sigmund Freud, *Beyond the Pleasure Principle* (London: Inter-Psychoanalytic Press, 1922).

17. Konrad Lorenz, *On Aggression* (New York: Harcourt, Brace, Jovanovich, 1966).

18. Robert Ardrey, *African Genesis* (New York: Atheneum, 1963).

19. Ashley Montagu, *Man and Aggression* (New York: Oxford University Press, 1968).

20. Anita Timrots and Michael Rand, *Violent Crime by Strangers and Nonstrangers* (Washington, D.C.: Bureau of Justice Statistics, 1987), p. 1.

21. Marvin Wolfgang and Franco Ferracuti, *The Subculture of Violence* (London: Tavistock, 1967).

22. Ruth Horowitz, "Community Tolerance of Gang Violence," *Social Problems* 34 (1987):437–50.

23. Neil Alan Weiner and Marvin Wolfgang, "The Extent and Character of Violent Crime in America, 1969–1982," in Lynn Curtis, ed., *American Violence and Public Policy* (New Haven, Conn.: Yale University Press, 1985), pp. 17–39.

24. Steven Messner, "Regional and Racial Effects on the Urban Homicide Rate: The Subculture of Violence Revisited," *American Journal of Sociology* 88

(1983):997–1007.

25. For a contrasting view, see, Donald Shoemaker and J. Sherwood Williams, "The Subculture of Violence and Ethnicity," *Journal of Criminal Justice* 15 (1987):461–72.

26. Susan Randall and Vicki McNickle Rose, "Forcible Rape," in Robert Meyer, ed., *Major Forms of Crime* (Beverly Hills, Cal.: Sage Publications, 1984), p. 47.

27. James LeBeau, "Patterns of Stranger and Serial Rape Offending: Factors Distinguishing Apprehended and At Large Offenders," *The Journal of Criminal Law and Delinquency* 78 (1987):309–26.

28. Susan Brownmiller, *Against Our Will: Men, Women and Rape* (New York: Simon & Schuster, 1975).

29. Federal Bureau of Investigation, *Crime in the United States, 1987* (Washington, D.C.: U.S. Government Printing Office, 1988), pp. 13–15.

30. James LeBeau, "Some Problems with Measuring and Describing Rape Presented by the Serial Offender," *Justice Quarterly* 2 (1985):385–98.

31. Marshall DeBerry and Catherine Whitaker, *Criminal Victimization 1986* (Washington, D.C.: Bureau of Justice Statistics, 1987), p. 2.

32. Anita Timrots and Marshall DeBerry, *Criminal Victimization in the United States, 1986* (Washington, D.C.: U.S. Government Printing Office, 1987).

33. Thomas Meyer, "Date Rape: A Serious Campus Problem that Few Talk About," *Chronicle of Higher Education* 29 (5 December 1984):15.

34. *Ibid.*

35. Larry Siegel, "Rape Case May Have Been Distorted by Rush to Judgment," *Omaha World Herald* (25 March 1984), p. 18A.

36. UPI, "Officials Say Women Alarmed by Questions," *Omaha World Herald* (19 March 1984), p. 8; "The Crime That Tarnished a Town," *Time* (5 March 1984), p. 19.

37. James LeBeau, "The Methods and Measures of Centrography and the Spatial Dynamics of Rape," *Journal of Quantitative Criminology* 3 (1987):125–41.

38. Alan Lizotte, "The Uniqueness of Rape: Reporting Assaultive Violence to Police," *Crime and Delinquency* 31 (1985):169–91.

39. Donald Symons, *The Evolution of Human Sexuality* (London: Oxford University Press, 1979).

40. Diana Russell, *The Politics of Rape* (New York: Stein and Day, 1975).

41. Charles McCaghy, *Deviant Behavior Crime, Conflict and Interest Groups* (New York: Macmillan, 1976).

42. Christine Adler, "An Exploration of Self-Reported Aggressive Behavior," *Crime and Delinquency* 31 (1985):306–31.

43. Paul Gebhard, John Gagnon, Wardell Pomeroy, and Cornelia Christenson, *Sex Offenders: An Analysis of Types* (New York: Harper & Row, 1965), pp. 198–205.

44. Richard Rada, ed., *Clinical Aspects of the Rapist* (New York: Grune & Stratton, 1978), pp. 122–30.

45. A. Nicholas Groth and Jean Birnbaum, *Men Who Rape* (New York: Plenum, 1979), p. 101.

46. See, generally, Edward Donnerstein, Daniel Linz and Steven Penrod, *The Question of Pornography* (New York: Free Press, 1987); Diana Russell, *Sexual Exploitation* (Beverly Hills, Cal.: Sage Publications, 1985), pp. 115–16.

47. Neil Malamuth and John Briere, "Sexual Violence in the Media: Indirect Effects on Aggression Against Women," *Journal of Social Issues* 42 (1986):75–92.

48. Associated Press, "Trial of TV May Have Influenced Boy Facing Sexual-Assault Count," *Omaha World Herald* (18 April 1984), p. 50.

49. Larry Baron and Murray Straus, "Four Theories of Rape: A Macrosociological Analysis," *Social Problems* 34 (1987):467–89.

50. Gerald Robin, "Forcible Rape: Institutionalized Sexism in the Criminal Justice System," *Crime and Delinquency* 23 (1977):136–53.

51. "Woman Urges Dotson's Release," *Omaha World Herald* (25 April 1985), p. 3.

52. Comment, "The Rape Shield Paradox: Complainant Protection Amidst Oscillating Trends of State Judicial Interpretation," *The Journal of Criminal Law and Criminology* 78 (1987):644–98.

53. Associated Press, "New York Judge Rules Husbands May Be Convicted of Rape," *Omaha World Herald* (21 December 1984), p. 28.

54. See, for example, Mich. Comp. Laws Annotated, Sec. 750.5200-(1); Florida Statutes Annotated, Sec. 794.011. See, generally, Gary LaFree, "Official Reactions to Rape," *American Sociological Review* 45 (1980):842–54.

55. Martin Schwartz and Todd Clear, "Toward a New Law on Rape," *Crime and Delinquency* 26 (1980):129–51.

56. Susan Caringella-MacDonald, "The Comparability in Sexual and Nonsexual Assault Case Treatment: Did Statute Change Meet the Objective," *Crime and Delinquency* 31 (1985):206–23.

57. West's Ann. Cal. Penal Code Sec. 261, 1978.

58. Kenneth Polk, "Rape Reform and Criminal Justice Processing," *Crime and Delinquency* 31 (1985):191–206.

59. Randall and McNickel Rose, "Forcible Rape," p. 48.

60. Vicki McNickel Rose, "Rape as a Social Problem: A By-product of the Feminist Movement," *Social Problems* 25 (1977):75–89.

61. Janet Gornick, Martha Burt, and Karen Pittman, "Structure and Activities of Rape Crises Centers in the Early 1980s," *Crime and Delinquency* 31 (1985):247–68.

62. *Ibid.*, p. 258.

63. *Ibid.*

64. Donald Lunde, *Murder and Madness* (San Francisco: San

Francisco Book Co., 1977), p. 3.

65. *Ibid.*

66. Marc Reidel and Margaret Zahn, *The Nature and Pattern of American Homicide* (Washington, D.C.: U.S. Government Printing Office, 1985).

67. See, generally, Reidel and Zahn, *The Nature and Pattern of American Homicide.*

68. FBI, *Crime in the United States, 1987*, p. 12.

69. Marvin Wolfgang, *Patterns in Criminal Homicide* (New York: John Wiley, 1966), p. 253.

70. *Ibid.*, p. 252.

71. Menachim Amir, *Patterns in Forcible Rape* (Chicago: University of Chicago Press, 1971).

72. Marc Riedel, "Stranger Violence: Perspectives, Issues, and Problems," *The Journal of Criminal Law and Criminology* 78 (1987):223–58 at 229.

73. John Hewitt, "The Victim-Offender Relationship In Convicted Homicide Cases: 1960-1984," *Journal of Criminal Justice* 16 (1988):25–33.

74. Margaret Zahn and Philip Sagi, "Stranger Homicides in Nine American Cities," *The Journal of Criminal Law and Criminology* 78 (1987):377–97.

75. *Ibid.*, p. 396.

76. James Boudouris, "A Classification of Homicide," *Criminology* 11 (1974):525–40.

77. David Luckenbill, "Criminal Homicide as a Situational Transaction," *Social Problems* 25 (1977):176–86.

78. Michael Hazlett and Thomas Tomlinson, "Females Involved in Homicides: Victims and Offenders in Two Southern States," Paper presented at the American Society of Criminology Meeting, Montreal, Canada, November, 1987; revised version, 1988.

79. Raymond Gastil, "Homicide and the Regional Culture of Violence," *American Sociological Review* 36 (1971):412–27.

80. Colin Loftin and Robert Hill, "Regional Subculture of Violence: An Examination of the Gastril-Hackney Thesis," *American Sociological Review* 39 (1974):714–24.

81. Howard Erlanger, "Is There a Subculture of Violence in the South," *Journal of Criminal Law and Criminology* 66 (1976):483–90.

82. Raymond Gastil, "Comments," *Criminology* 16 (1975):60–64.

83. Thomas Palmer, "A Doctor Smelled Arsenic, Leading to Arrest of Serial Killer," *Boston Globe* (August 20, 1987), p. 3.

84. "Police Suspect 'Something Snapped' to Ignite Wilder's Crime Spree," *Omaha World Herald* (15 April 1984), p. 21A.

85. Mark Starr, "The Random Killers," *Newsweek* (26 November 1984), pp. 100–106.

86. Thomas Palmer, "Ex-Hospital Aide Admits Killing 24 in Cincinnati," *Boston Globe* (19 August 1987), p. 3.

87. Philip Jenkins, "Serial Murder in England 1940–1985," *Journal of Criminal Justice* 16 (1988):1–15.

88. Associated Press, "Briton Kills 14 in Rampage," *Boston Globe* (20 August 1987), p. 3.

89. *Ibid.*, p. 6.

90. Jenkins, "Serial Murder in England 1940–1985," p. 9.

91. Jennifer Browdy, "Interview with Ann Rule," *Law Enforcement News* (21 May 1984), p. 12.

92. Jennifer Browdy, "VI-CAP System to be Operational This Summer," *Law Enforcement News* (21 May 1984), p. 1.

93. *Uniform Crime Reports, 1986*, p. 21.

94. See, generally, Ruth S. Kempe and C. Henry Kempe, *Child Abuse* (Cambridge, Mass.: Harvard University Press, 1978).

95. Douglas J. Besharov, "The Legal Aspects of Reporting Known and Suspected Child Abuse and Neglect," *Villanova Law Review* 23 (1978):458.

96. Richard Gelles and Murray Straus, "Violence in the American Family," *Journal of Social Issues* 35 (1979):15–39; Richard Gelles and Murray Staurs, *Is Violence Toward Children Increasing? A Comparison of 1975 and 1985 National Survey Rates* (Durham, N.H.: Family Violence Research Program, 1985).

97. The American Humane Society, *Highlights of Official Child Neglect and Abuse Reporting* (Denver: 1987).

98. Diana Russell, "The Incidence and Prevalence of Intrafamilial and Extrafamilial Sexual Abuse of Female Children," *Child Abuse and Neglect* 7 (1983):133–46; see also, David Finkelhor, *Sexually Victimized Children* (New York: Free Press, 1979), p. 88.

99. Brandt Steele, "Violence Within the Family," in R. Helfer and C. H. Kempe, eds., *Child Abuse and Neglect: The Family and the Community* (Cambridge, Mass.: Ballinger Publishing, 1976), p. 12.

100. Ruth Inglis, *Sins of the Fathers: A Study of the Physical and Emotional Abuse of Children* (New York: St. Martin's Press, 1978), p. 68.

101. *Ibid.*, p. 53.

102. Kempe and Kempe, *Child Abuse*, p. 24.

103. R. Emerson Dobash and Russel Dobash, *Violence against Wives* (New York: Free Press, 1979).

104. Julia O'Faolain and Laura Martines, eds., *Not in God's Image: Women in History* (Glasgow, Scotland: Fontana/Collins, 1974).

105. Laurence Stone, "The Rise of the Nuclear Family in Modern England: The Patriarchal Stage," in Charles Rosenberg, ed., *The Family in History* (Philadelphia: University of Pennsylvania Press, 1975), p. 53.

106. Dobash and Dobash, *Violence against Wives*, p. 46.

107. James Makepeace, "Social Factor and Victim-Offender Differences in Courtship Violence," *Family Relations* 33 (1987):87–91.

108. Newman, *Understanding Violence*, pp. 145–46.

109. Glenda Kaufman Kantor and Murray Straus, "The 'Drunken Bum' Theory of Wife Beating," *Social Problems* 34 (1987):213–30.

110. FBI, *Crime in the United States, 1987*, p. 16.

111. *Criminal Victimization, 1985*, p. 50.

112. Caroline Wolf Harlow, *Robbery Victims* (Washington, D.C.: Bureau of Justice Statistics, 1987).

113. F. H. McClintock and Evelyn Gibson, *Robbery in London* (London: Macmillan, 1961), p. 15.

114. John Conklin, *Robbery and the Criminal Justice System* (New York: Lippincott, 1972), pp. 1–80.

115. Oscar Newman, *Defensible Space: Crime Prevention through Urban Design* (New York: Macmillan, 1972).

116. Charles Murray, "The Physical Environment and Community Control of Crime," in James Q. Wilson, ed., *Crime and Public Policy* (San Francisco: ICS Press, 1983), pp. 107–25.

117. R. Lance Shotland and Lynne Goodstein, "The Role of Bystanders in Crime Control," *Journal of Social Issues* 40 (1984):9–26.

118. Samuel Walker, *Sense and Nonsense about Crime* (Monterey, Cal.: Brooks/Cole, 1985), p. 152.

119. Franklin Zimring, "Firearms and Federal Law: The Gun Control Act of 1968," *Journal of Legal Studies* 4 (1975):133–98.

120. Glenn Pierce and William Bowers, "The Bartley-Fox Gun Law's Short-Term Impact on Crime," *The Annals* 455 (1981):120–37; Walker, *Sense and Nonsense*, pp. 70–71.

121. Colin Loftin, Milton Heumann, and David McDowall, "Mandatory Sentencing and Firearms Violence: Evaluating an Alternative to Gun Control," *Law and Society Review* 17 (1983):287–319.

122. David Lester, *Gun Control* (Springfield, Ill.: Charles Thomas, 1984).

123. See, generally, James Wright, Peter Rossi, and Kathleen Daly, *Under the Gun: Weapons, Crime and Violence in America* (New York: Aldine, 1983).

124. Stephen Schafer, *The Political Criminal* (New York: Free Press, 1974), p. 1.

125. Barton Ingraham, *Political Crime in Europe* (Berkeley: University of California Press, 1979), pp. vi–viii.

126. Ernest Van Den Haag, *Political Violence and Civil Disobedience* (New York: Harper & Row, 1972).

127. Schafer, *The Political Criminal*, p. 150.

128. Robert Friedlander, *Terrorism* (Dobbs Ferry, N.Y.: Oceana Publishers, 1979).

129. National Advisory Commission on Criminal Justice Standards and Goals, *Report of the Task Force on Disorders and Terrorism* (Washington, D.C.: U.S. Government Printing Office, 1976), p. 3.

130. Paul Wilkinson, *Terrorism and the Liberal State* (New York: John Wiley, 1977), p. 49.

131. Friedlander, *Terrorism*, p. 14.

132. Daniel Georges-Abeyie, "Political Crime and Terrorism," in Graeme Newman, ed., *Crime and Deviance: A Comparative Perspective* (Beverly Hills, Cal.: Sage Publications, 1980), pp. 313–33.

133. *Ibid.*, p. 319.

134. This section relies heavily on Friedlander, *Terrorism*, pp. 8–20.

135. See, Friedlander, *Terrorism*, p. 16.

136. See, generally, John Wolf, "Domestic Terrorist Movements," in Yonah Alexander and Robert Kilmark, eds., *Political Terrorism and Business* (New York: Praeger, 1979), pp. 12–33.

137. "Five Held in Plot to Bomb California Aide's Office," *New York Times* (21 November 1977), p. 6.

138. "FBI: Gang May Be Tied to the IRA," *Omaha World Herald* (25 October 1981), p. 18A; "FBI Chief: Terrorism Up, No U.S. Political Focus Seen," *Omaha World Herald* (30 December 1981), p. 15.

139. UPI, "Attacks on Blacks, Jews Reportedly Rose," *Boston Globe* (11 February 1988), p. 16.

140. Robert Zint, "Dreams of a Bigots Revolution," *Time* (18 February 1985), p. 42.

141. *Ibid.*

142. M. Cherif Bassiouni, "Terrorism, Law Enforcement, and Mass Media: Perspectives, Problems and Proposals," *Journal of Criminal Law and Criminology* 72 (1981):1–51.

143. Rodeina Kennan, "Bomb Kills 54, Injures 125 in Lebanon," *Boston Globe* (24 April 1988), p. 1.

144. Claire Sterling, "Gen. Dozier and the International Terror Network," *Wall Street Journal* (29 December 1981), p. 12.

145. "Grave Doubts," *Time* (30 April 1984), p. 38.

146. Richard Rubenstien, *Alchemists of Revolution, Terrorism in the Modern World* (New York: Basic Books, 1987).

147. William Smith, "Libya's Ministry of Fear," *Time* (30 April 1984), pp. 36–38.

148. Target Research and Analytical Center Terrorism Section, *FBI Analysis of Terrorist Incidents in the United States, 1986* (Washington, D.C.: FBI, 1987).

149. U.S. Department of State, *Patterns of Global Terrorism: 1986* (Washington, D.C.: U.S. Government Printing Office, 1988), pp. 1–3. See also, *Public Report of the Vice President's Task Force on Combatting Terrorism* (Washington, D.C: U.S. Government Printing Office, 1986), pp. 1–7.

150. Bassiouni, "Terrorism, Law Enforcement, and Mass Media," p. 10.

151. Austin Turk, "Political Crime," in R. Meier, ed., *Major*

Forms of Crime, pp. 119–35.

152. C. Allen Graves, "The U.S. Government's Response to Terrorism," in Alexander and Kilmark, eds., *Political*

Terrorism and Business, pp. 175–83.

153. Ignatius, "U.S. Readies Anti-Terrorism Policy," *Wall Street Journal* (12 March 1984), p. 30.

CHAPTER 11

ECONOMIC CRIMES: STREET CRIMES

INTRODUCTION

As a group, **economic crimes** can be defined as acts in violation of the criminal law designed to bring financial reward to an offender. In U.S. society, the range and scope of criminal activity motivated by financial gain is tremendous: self-report studies show that property crime among the young of every social class is widespread; national surveys of criminal behavior indicate that more than 30 million personal and household thefts occur annually; corporate and other white-collar crimes are accepted as commonplace; political scandals, such as the Pentagon procurement scandal, indicate that bribery and corruption reach even the highest levels of government.

Though average citizens may be puzzled and enraged by violent crimes, believing them to be both senseless and cruel, the same citizens often view economic crimes with a great deal more ambivalence. While it is true that society generally disapproves of crimes involving theft and corruption, the public seems quite tolerant of the "gentleman bandit." Such characters appear in popular myths and legends —Robin Hood, Jesse James, Bonnie and Clyde, D. B. Cooper. They are the heroic subjects of books and films such as *Burglar* and *48 Hours*.

How can such ambivalence be explained? For one thing, national tolerance toward economic criminals may be prompted by the fact that, if self-report studies are to be believed, almost every U.S. citizen has at some time been involved in economic crime. Many who would never consider themselves criminals may have at one time engaged in petty theft, cheated on their income taxes, stolen a textbook from a college bookstore, or pilfered from their place of employment. Consequently, it may be difficult for society to condemn economic criminals without feeling somewhat hypocritical. (See Close-Up on the "Causes of Economic Crime.")

People also may be somewhat more tolerant of economic crimes because they never seem to seriously hurt anyone. Banks are insured; large businesses pass along losses to consumers; stolen cars can be easily replaced. The true pain of economic crime often goes unappreciated. It is not uncommon for convicted offenders, especially businesspeople who commit white-collar crimes involving millions of dollars, to be punished rather lightly.

This chapter is the first of two that review the nature and extent of economic crime in the United States. It is divided into two principal sections. The first deals with the concept of **professional crime** and focuses on two types of professional criminals—the **fence** (a buyer and seller of stolen merchandise), and **commercial thieves** who steal from business establishments. Then this chapter turns to a discussion of common theft-related offenses, often referred to by criminologists as **street crimes.** These crimes include the major forms of common theft: larceny, embezzlement, and theft by false pretenses. Included within these general offense categories are such common crimes as auto theft, shoplifting, and credit card fraud. The chapter next discusses a more serious form of theft—burglary—which involves forcible entry into a person's home or place of work for the purpose of theft. Finally, the crime of arson is discussed briefly. In the following chapter, attention is given to economic crimes that involve organizations devoted to criminal enterprise.

PROFESSIONAL AND AMATEUR

As you may recall, millions of property and theft-related crimes occur each year. Many are committed by **occasional criminals,** who do not define themselves by a criminal role or view themselves as committed career criminals; other theft-offenders are in fact skilled, professional criminals. The following sections review these two orientations toward property crime.

Occasional Criminals

Though criminologists are not certain, they suspect that the great majority of economic crimes are the work of amateur criminals, whose decision to steal is spontaneous and whose acts are unskilled, unplanned, and haphazard. As noted in Chapter 3, millions of theft-related crimes occur each year, and most are not reported to police agencies. Many of these theft offenses are committed by school-age youths who are unlikely to enter into a criminal career, and whose behavior has been described as drifting between conventional and criminal behavior. Added to the pool of amateur thieves are the millions of adults—

▤ CLOSE-UP

Causes of Economic Crime

Each of the major criminological perspectives maintains its own position on the root causes and possible solutions to theft-related offenses. Some of these positions are presented below.

Perspective	Cause	Solution
Classical	Economic crime is caused by greed, lack of fear of possible punishments, ineffectiveness of criminal justice system to deter crime.	Increase criminal penalties; increase efficiency of justice system; incapacitate known criminals.
Routine Activities	Available, unguarded targets are incentives to commit crime.	Harden targets; increase visible, effective guardians.
Individual		
Biological	Unique physical characteristics make some people unable to control their behavior. Possible factors include low IQ, psychopathy, blood-chemistry disorders, brain dysfunction. Under certain environmental conditions, these factors promote illegal behavior solutions.	Physically evaluate offenders; treat individual physical problems; improve environmental conditions.
Psychological Behaviorist	Offenders learn that theft is appropriate under certain circumstances. They receive rewards for illegal acts.	Change learning patterns; reward conventional behavior; provide proper role models.
Psychoanalytic	Offenders' behavior is an impulsive manifestation of their early childhood frustrations. Weak ego development causes frustration and aggression.	Provide psychiatric evaluation and treatment of offenders to help them uncover the root causes of their behavior and effectively control it.
Sociological		
Social Structure	Individuals' positions in the social structure determine their behavior. Those in the lower economic classes lack the opportunity and skill to earn money through conventional means. Consequently, they seek criminal solutions to their financial problems. Poverty causes crime.	Provide economic opportunities for lower-class citizens; create job, education, welfare, and child-care programs.
Social Process	Individuals' relationships with social institutions determine their behavior. Some people learn to steal in interaction with others. Some feel alienated from society and therefore feel free to violate its rules.	Provide counseling and outreach for potential criminals; make them feel part of conventional society; help them establish bonds, strengthen family ties.
Social Conflict	Economic crime is a function of the conflict between the haves and have-nots. For the poor, theft is a means of survival. For the wealthy, it is a means of maintaining or increasing social position. In capitalist societies, the wealthy use their positions to "steal" through legal means such as profiteering, stock market manipulation, price-fixing, monopolies.	Marxists would restructure society; end the capitalist system; create a world in which people are concerned with each others' welfare. Pure conflict theorists would limit the economic gulf between rich and poor; enforce laws against the economic crimes of the wealthy.

Discussion Questions

1. Which of the criminological perspectives provides the most reasonable explanation of economic crime?

2. If each position has some merit, what does this mean for crime control?

shoplifters, pilferers, tax cheats—whose main source of income comes from conventional means and whose self-identity is noncriminal. Added together, their behaviors form the bulk of theft crimes.

According to John Hepburn, occasional property crime occurs when there is an opportunity or **situational inducement** to commit crime.[1] Opportunities are available to members of all classes, but members of the upper class have the opportunity to engage in the more lucrative business-related crimes, such as price-fixing, bribery, and embezzlement. Situational inducements are short-run influences on a person's behavior that increase risk-taking. These include psychological factors, such as financial problems, and social factors, such as peer pressure.

According to Hepburn, opportunity and situational inducements are not the cause of crime; rather, they are the *occasion* for crime; hence the term occasional criminal. It seems evident that opportunity and inducements are not randomly situated. Consequently, the frequency of occasional property crime varies according to age, class, and sex.

Occasional offenders are not professional criminals, nor do they make crime their occupation. They do not rely on skills or knowledge to commit their crimes, they do not organize their daily activities around crime, and they are not committed to crime as a way of life.

Occasional criminals have little group support for their acts. Unlike professionals, they do not receive informal, peer group support for their crimes. In fact, they deny any connection to a criminal lifestyle and instead view their transgressions as being "out of character." They may see their crimes as being motivated by necessity. For example, they were only "borrowing" the car the police caught them with; they were going to pay back the store they stole merchandise from. Because of the lack of commitment, occasional offenders may be the most likely to respond to the general deterrent effect of the law.

Professional Criminals

In contrast to amateurs, **professional criminals** make a significant portion of their income from crime. Professionals do not delude themselves with the belief that their acts are impulsive, one-time efforts, nor do they employ elaborate rationalizations to excuse the

While shoplifting is considered an amateur crime, it can be done quite professionally, as this store manager shows. This "booster box" allows a shoplifter to stuff merchandise through the trap door, while appearing to be a gift-wrapped package.

harmfulness of their action ("shoplifting doesn't really hurt anyone"). Consequently, professionals pursue their craft with vigor, attempting to learn from older, experienced criminals the techniques that will earn them the most money with the least risk. Though their numbers are relatively small, professionals engage in crimes that produce the greater losses to society and perhaps cause the more significant social harm.

Professional theft traditionally refers to nonviolent forms of criminal behavior that are undertaken with a high degree of skill for monetary gain. Professional thieves tend to maximize financial opportunities and minimize the possibilities of apprehension. The most typical forms of theft include pocket picking, burglary, shoplifting, forgery and counterfeiting, extortion, sneak theft, and confidence swindling.[2]

Relatively little is known about the career patterns of professional thieves and criminals. From the literature on crime and delinquency, three patterns emerge: youths come under the influence of older, experienced criminals who teach them the trade; juvenile gang members continue their illegal activities at a time when most of their peers have dropped out to marry, raise families, and take conventional jobs; youths sent to prison for minor offenses learn the techniques of crime from more experienced thieves. Harry King, a professional thief, relates this story about his entry into crime after being placed in a shelter-care home by his recently divorced mother:

> *It was while I was at this parental school that I learned that some of the kids had been committed there by the court for stealing bikes. They taught me how to steal and where to steal them and where to sell them. Incidentally, some of the "nicer people" were the ones who bought bikes from the kids. They would dismantle the bike and use the parts: the wheels, chains, handle bars and so forth.*[3]

There is some debate in the criminological literature over who may be defined as a professional criminal. Some criminologists, such as Edwin Sutherland, use the term to refer only to thieves who do not use force or physical violence in their crimes and live solely by their wits and skill.[4] However, other criminologists use the term to refer to any criminal who identifies with a criminal subculture, who makes the bulk of his or her living from crime, and who possesses a degree of skill in his or her chosen trade.[5] Thus, one can become a professional safecracker, burglar, car thief, or fence. However, drug addicts who steal to support their habit would not be considered professionals; they lack skill and therefore are amateur opportunists rather than professional technicians. (The criminal activities of drug addicts are discussed in Chapter 13.)

Sutherland's Professional Criminal

Knowledge about the lives of professional criminals has come through journals, diaries, and autobiographies, or through the first-person accounts they have given to criminologists. The best-known account of

professional theft is Edwin Sutherland's recording of the life of a professional thief or con man, Chic Conwell, in his classic book, *The Professional Thief.*[6]

Conwell and Sutherland's concept of professional theft has two critical dimensions. First, professional thieves engage in limited types of crime. They can be described by the following labels:

- Pickpocket ("cannon")
- Sneak thief from stores, banks, and offices ("heel")
- Shoplifter ("booster")
- Jewel thief who substitutes fake gems for real ones ("pennyweighter")
- Thief who steals from hotel rooms ("hotel prowl")
- Confidence game artist
- Thief in rackets related to confidence games
- Forger
- Extortionist from those engaging in illegal acts ("shakedown artist")[7]

Professionals depend solely on their wit and skill. Thieves who use force or commit crimes that require little expertise are not considered worthy of the title "professional." Amateur areas of activity include such "heavy rackets" as bank robbery, car theft, burglary, and safecracking. Conwell and Sutherland's criteria for professionalism are weighted heavily toward con games and trickery and give little attention to common street crimes.

The second requirement to establish professionalism as a thief is the exclusive use of wit, "front" (a believable demeanor), and talking ability. Manual dexterity and physical force are of little importance. Moreover, professional thieves must acquire status in their profession. Status is based on technical skill, financial standing, connections, power, dress, manners, and wide knowledge. In their world, "thief" is a title worn with pride.

Conwell and Sutherland also argue that professional thieves share feelings, sentiments, and behaviors. Of these, none is more important than the code of honor of the underworld; even under threat of the most severe punishment, a professional thief must never inform (squeal) on his or her fellows.

Sutherland and Conwell view professional theft as an occupation with much the same internal organization as that characterizing such legitimate professions as advertising, teaching, or police work. They conclude:

> A person can be a professional thief only if he is recognized and received as such by other professional thieves. Professional theft is a group way of life. One can get into the group and remain in it only by the consent of those previously in the group. Recognition as a professional thief by other professional thieves is the absolutely necessary, universal and definitive characteristic of the professional thief.[8]

Professional Crime: Stooping and Fencing

Some experts have argued that Sutherland's view of the professional thief may be outdated, because modern thieves often work alone, are not part of a criminal subculture, and were not tutored early in their careers by other criminals.[9] However, some recent research efforts show that the principles set down by Sutherland still have value for understanding the behavior of modern professional criminals.

Stooping. John Rosecrance found that one type of modern professional criminal, **stoopers,** organized their behavior according to the principles set down by Sutherland.[10] Stoopers are people who hang out at race tracks and recover winning tickets accidently discarded by patrons; this behavior is a violation of state criminal law (pandering). Through in-depth interviews, Rosecrance found that modern day stoopers employed specialized skills, derived personal status and satisfaction from their professionalism while being contemptuous of amateurs, were informally organized, helped tutor novices in the field, and developed an informal code of acceptable group behavior. These traits make them a group of professional criminals who continue to behave in the "Sutherland manner."[11]

Fencing. Nowhere is the concept of professional theft better illustrated than in the crime of buying and reselling stolen merchandise, or *fencing*.

Professional fences play an important role in the thief's working world. They act as agents who purchase stolen merchandise—ranging from diamonds to auto hubcaps—and then resell them to merchants who market them to legitimate customers. The fence's crit-

ical role in criminal transactions has long been appreciated. As early as 1795, Patrick Colquhoun stated in his book, *A Treatise on the Police of the Metropolis:*

> In contemplating the characters of all these different classes of delinquents (that is Thieves, Robbers, Cheats and Swindlers), there can be little hesitation in pronouncing the Receivers to be the most mischievous of the whole: inasmuch as without the aid they afford, in purchasing and concealing every species of property stolen or fraudulently obtained, Thieves, Robbers and Swindlers . . . must quit the trade, as unproductive and hazardous in the extreme.

> Nothing therefore can be more just than the old observation, "that if there were no Receivers there would be no Thieves."—Deprive a thief of a safe and ready market for his goods and he is undone.[12]

Much of what is known about fencing comes from two in-depth studies of individual fences, Carl Klockars' work, *The Professional Fence,* and Darrell Steffensmeier's *The Fence.*[13]

Klockars examined the life and times of one successful fence, who used the alias "Vincent Swaggi." Through 400 hours of listening to and observing Swaggi, Klockars found that this highly professional criminal had developed techniques that made him almost immune to prosecution. Consequently, during the course of a long and profitable career in crime, Swaggi spent only four months in prison. He stayed in business in part because of his sophisticated knowledge of the law of stolen property: to convict someone of receiving stolen goods, the prosecution must prove that the accused was in possession of the goods and knew that they had been stolen. Swaggi had the skills to make sure that these elements could never be proven.

Also helping Swaggi stay out of the law's grasp were the close working associations he maintained with society's upper classes, including influential members of the justice system. Swaggi helped them purchase items at below-cost, bargain prices. He also helped authorities recover stolen goods and therefore remained in their good graces. Klockars' work strongly suggests that fences customarily cheat their thief-clients and at the same time cooperate with the law.

Sam Goodman, the fence studied by Darrell Steffensmeier, lived in a world similar to that of

Vincent Swaggi. He also purchased stolen goods from a wide variety of thieves and suppliers, including burglars, drug addicts, shoplifters, dockworkers, and truck drivers. According to Goodman, to be successful, a fence must meet the following conditions:

1. *Upfront cash*—All deals are cash transactions, so an adequate supply of ready cash must always be on hand.
2. *Knowledge of dealing: learning the ropes*—The fence must be schooled in the trade: developing a "larceny sense"; learning to "buy right" at acceptable prices; being able to "cover one's back" and not get caught; finding out how to make the right contacts; knowing how to "wheel and deal" and create opportunities for profit.
3. *Connections with suppliers of stolen goods*—The successful fence is able to engage in long-term relationships with suppliers of high-value stolen goods who are relatively free of police interference. The warehouse worker who pilfers is a better supplier than the narcotics addict, who is more likely to be apprehended and talk to the police.
4. *Connections with buyers*—The successful fence must have continuing access to buyers of stolen merchandise which are closed to the common thief.
5. *Complicity with law enforcers*—The fence must work out a relationship with law enforcement officials, who invariably find out about their operations.

Steffensmeier found that to stay in business the fence must either bribe officials with good deals on merchandise and cash payments or act as an informer who helps police recover particularly important merchandise and arrest thieves. This latter role of informer differentiates Steffensmeier's description of the fence's role from that of Klockars.[14]

Fencing seems to contain many of the elements of professional theft as described by Sutherland. Fences live by their wits; never engage in violence; depend on their skill in negotiating; maintain community standing based on connections and power; and share the sentiments and behaviors of their fellows. The only divergence between Sutherland's thief and the fence is the code of honor. It seems likely that the fence is much more willing to cooperate with authorities than most other professional criminals.

In the accompanying Close-Up, another type of professional criminal—the commercial thief—is examined in some detail.

HISTORY OF THEFT OFFENSES

Theft offenses are frequent occurrence. Millions of auto thefts, shoplifting incidents, embezzlements, burglaries, and larcenies are recorded each year. National surveys indicate that almost 15 percent of the U.S. population are victims of theft offenses each year.

The theft of personal property has been known throughout recorded history. The Crusades of the eleventh century inspired peasants and downtrodden nobles to leave the shelter of their estates to prey upon passing pilgrims.[15] Not surprisingly, Crusaders felt it within their rights to appropriate the possessions of any non-Roman Catholics they happened to encounter during their travels. By the thirteenth century, returning pilgrims—not content to live as serfs on feudal estates—gathered in the forests of England and the Continent to poach game that was the rightful property of their lord or king and to steal from passing strangers. By the fourteenth century, many such highway robbers and poachers were full-time livestock thieves, stealing great numbers of cattle and sheep.[16]

The fifteenth and sixteenth centuries brought the onset of hostilities between England and France in what has come to be known as the Hundred Years' War. Foreign mercenary troops fighting for both sides roamed the countryside; loot and pillage were viewed as a rightful part of their pay.

Theft became more professional with the rise of the city and the establishment of a permanent class of propertyless urban poor.[17] By the eighteenth century, three separate groups of property criminals were active. In the larger cities, such as London and Paris, groups of skilled thieves, pickpockets, forgers, and counterfeiters operated freely. They congregated in **flash houses**—public meeting places, often taverns, that served as headquarters for gangs. Here, deals were made, crimes plotted, and the sale of stolen goods negotiated.[18]

The second group of thieves were the **smugglers,** who moved freely in sparsely populated areas and

CLOSE-UP

Life in the Fast Lane: Commercial Thieves

Another type of professional criminal is the commercial thief. Two researchers, John Gibbs and Peggy Shelly, have found that professional commercial thieves can be further classified into two categories: (1) commercial burglars and (2) hijackers.

Burglars' main goal is to acquire cash. They specialize in victimizing establishments that primarily do a cash rather than credit business: supermarkets, bars, restaurants. Between two to six men form the burglary team. Each may specialize in a different skill: opening safes, using torches, handling explosives, bypassing alarms.

When possible, the commercial burglar will carefully choose a site, waiting for a day when the maximum amount of money will be on hand. The vulnerability of the site has an important influence on the decision to steal. For example, a freestanding building is more dangerous than a shopping center because the center cannot be easily surrounded by police. As one subject said:

> . . . it's a lot more difficult for them to surround a shopping center than it would be to surround one single building . . . I just go out the back. There's no way he can get around that building fast enough. If the car pulls in around the back, I go out the front. You know, so the chances are good that I'll get away, especially with the doors locked. They're not positive that somebody's in there yet because they haven't seen anybody, you know, so usually they'll check the doors and call the

manager, and they wait until the manager comes, and then they go inside the building. By that time, I'm long gone.

Commercial burglars differ in their approach from household thieves. They have more information about the content of their target, whereas the household burglar usually chooses a target at random. More skill is required in commercial theft since few houses have protective security devices.

The second broad occupational classification of commercial theft is *hijackers*, who steal goods in transit from trucks. These targets are selected because (1) they contain large quantities of goods, (2) the goods are ready for transport, and (3) the merchandise is less well protected than it would be in a warehouse.

The most common method of theft is to just take trucks away when left unattended. As one pro remarked:

> There were certain areas, right, certain days of the week, you know, certain areas that would get deliveries, we'd go in that area, we'd walk up and down the street and we'd spot a truck, mostly we'd spot a truck as it pulls up; like standing on the corner or sitting on the stoop and watch them take off what they're going to deliver and watch them go into the building or apartment . . . By the time they go in the building I usually jump in the truck. It don't take more than 3 or 4 seconds, more like 10 seconds . . . You use what you call a pulley, some people call it a slap hammer, it's a rod about so long, you got a screw at the end, and you got like a weight in the middle that you slide up and

transported goods without bothering to pay tax or duty. The third group were the **poachers,** who lived in the country and supplemented their diet and income with game that belonged to a landlord.

By the eighteenth century, professional thieves in the larger cities had banded together into gangs to protect themselves, to increase the scope of their activities, and to help dispose of stolen goods. Jack Wild, perhaps London's most famous thief, perfected the process of buying and selling stolen goods and gave himself the title of "Thief-Taker General of Great Britain and Ireland." Before he was hanged, Wild controlled numerous gangs and dealt harshly with any

thief who violated his strict code of conduct.[19]

During this period, individual theft-related crimes began to be defined by the common law. The most important of these categories are still in use today.

LARCENY/THEFT

Larceny/theft was one of the earliest common-law crimes. It was created by English judges to define acts in which one person took for his or her own use the property of another.[20] In common law, larceny was

down, slide it up and down the bar, screw that into the ignition and you just hit it and it comes up and you can stick anything in there and it starts.

Some thieves work in collusion with the truck driver, while others stop trucks and kidnap drivers before making off with the merchandise.

The secret to successful hijacking is to be able to distribute stolen goods. This is almost always done through a fence. Later in their careers, many thieves make a career move up to the less risky work of a fence.

Careers of Commercial Thieves

Gibbs and Shelly found that most commercial thieves did not specialize in one type of crime their whole lives. Though they may have preferred one type of theft, when opportunities arose in other areas of crime the thieves would not be reluctant to take advantage of them.

Why did these men enter into professional crime? Some saw themselves as "born criminals," others attributed their life to a disorganized environment, a few blamed economic problems and the need to make a "fast buck." Most, however, considered that they learned to become seasoned professional thieves after an early jail experience:

Well, you might say, everything I've learned, I've learned in jail. That's where it comes from really. I didn't learn it on the street. Most of my thing was when I was in county jail, I think on my first bit, let me see, I went to the county jail when I was 16. In jail, in the county

jail a lot of guys meet there and you have bull sessions and they explain how to do it, "This is how you rob a safe, how you do this," and you go by things that they told you. And you did it yourself, tried it out, and it worked. You know what to look for, how to break an alarm system, how to wire, everything, and people would explain, this is right down the line, everything would be explained.

Most thieves felt that their illegal gains gave them the opportunity to live in the "fast lane." They spent their ill-gotten gains as fast as they earned them on luxuries: alcohol, clothes, and cars. The excitement of making deals, of meeting and wooing fences and other professionals all added to the glamour of being a professional criminal. Though most made in excess of $75,000 a year, few thought of saving for the future. Being realists, professional thieves assumed they would eventually get caught; so why live for tomorrow, when tomorrow you might be in Joliet or Attica?

Discussion Questions

1. What legitimate professions are similar to that of commercial thief?
2. What theoretical models are supported by the lifestyle of professional thieves?

SOURCE: John Gibbs and Peggy Shelly, "Life in the Fast Lane: A Retrospective View by Commercial Thieves," *Journal of Research in Crime and Delinquency* 19 (1982):229–330. Quotes from pp. 309, 314, 321.

---

defined as "the trespassory taking and carrying away of the personal property of another with intent to steal."[21] Most state jurisdictions have incorporated the common-law crime of larceny in their legal codes. Today, definitions of larceny often include such familiar acts as shoplifting, auto theft, passing bad checks, and other theft offenses that do not involve using force or threats on the victim or forcibly breaking into a person's home or place of work. (The former is robbery; the latter, burglary.)

As originally construed, larceny involved only taking property that was in the possession of the rightful owners. For example, it would have been considered

larceny for someone to go secretly into a farmer's field and steal a cow. Thus, the original common-law definition required a "trespass in the taking"; this meant that for an act to be considered larceny, goods must have been taken from the physical possession of the rightful owner.

In creating this definition of larceny, English judges were more concerned with disturbance of the peace than they were with theft. They reasoned that if someone tried to steal property from another's possession, the act could eventually lead to a physical confrontation and possibly the death of one party or the other. Consequently, the original definition of larceny did not include crimes in which the thief had come into the possession of the stolen property by trickery or deceit. For example, if someone entrusted with another person's property decided to keep it, it was not considered larceny.

The growth of manufacturing and the development of the free-enterprise system required that greater protection be given private property. The pursuit of commercial enterprise often required that one person's legal property be entrusted to a second party; therefore, larceny evolved to include the theft of goods that had come into the thief's possession through legitimate means.

To get around the element of "trespass in the taking," English judges created the concept of **constructive possession.** This legal fiction applied to situations in which persons voluntarily and temporarily gave up custody of their property but still believed that the property was legally theirs. For example, if a person gave a jeweler her watch for repair, she would still believe she owned the watch, although she had handed it over to the jeweler. Similarly, when a person misplaces his wallet and someone else finds it and keeps it—although identification of the owner can be plainly seen—the concept of constructive possession makes the person who has kept the wallet guilty of larceny.

Larceny Today

Most state jurisdictions have incorporated larceny in their criminal codes. Larceny is usually separated by state statute into *petit* (or petty) *larceny* and *grand larceny.* The former involves small amounts of money or property; it is punished as a misdemeanor. Grand larceny, involving merchandise of greater value, is considered a felony and is punished by a sentence in the state prison.

This distinction often presents a serious problem for the justice system. Car thefts and other larcenies involving high-priced merchandise are easily classified, but it is often difficult to decide whether a particular theft should be considered petty or grand larceny. For example, if a 10-year-old watch that originally cost $500 is stolen, should its value be based on its original cost, on its current worth of $50, or on its replacement cost of $1,000? As most statutes are worded, the current market value of the property gov-

erns its worth. Thus, the theft of the watch would be considered petty larceny, since its worth today is only $50. However, if a painting originally bought for $25 has a current market value of $500, its theft would be considered grand larceny.

Larceny/theft is probably the most common criminal offense. Self-report studies, discussed in Chapter 3, indicate that a significant number of youths have engaged in theft-related activities. The FBI recorded about 7.5 million acts of larceny in 1987, a rate of 3,081 per 100,000 persons; in 1987 the larceny rate rose about 3 percent.[22]

False Pretenses/Fraud

False pretenses, or **fraud,** involves misrepresenting a fact to cause a victim to willingly give his or her property to the wrongdoer, who keeps it.[23]

The definition of false pretenses was created by the English Parliament in 1757, to cover an area of law left untouched by larceny statutes. The first false pretenses law punished people who "knowingly and designedly by false pretense or pretenses, [obtained] from any person or persons, money, goods, wares or merchandise with intent to cheat or defraud any person or persons of the same."[24] False pretenses differs from traditional larceny because the victims willingly give their possessions to the offender; unlike larceny, it does not involve a "trespass in the taking."

An example of false pretenses would be if an unscrupulous merchant sold someone a chair, claiming it was an antique but knowing that it actually was a cheap copy. Another example would be if a phony healer sold a victim a bottle of colored sugar water and called it an "elixir" that would cure a disease.

Some states retain the crime of false pretenses in their criminal code; others have combined it with larceny into a general theft category.

Embezzlement

The crime of embezzlement was created by the English Parliament during the sixteenth century to fill a gap in the law of larceny.[25] Until then, to be guilty of theft, a person had to take goods from the physical possession of another ("trespass in the taking"). However, this definition did not cover instances in which one person trusted another and willfully gave that person temporary custody of his or her property. For example, in everyday commerce, store clerks, bank tellers, brokers, and merchants gain lawful possession but not legal ownership of other people's money. Embezzlement occurs when someone who is so trusted with property fraudulently converts it—that is, keeps it for his or her own use or the use of others.

Most U.S. courts require that a serious breach of trust have occurred before a person can be convicted of embezzlement. The mere act of moving property without the owner's consent, or damaging it, or using it, is not considered embezzlement. However, using it up, selling it, pledging it, giving it away, or holding it against the owner's will is considered embezzlement.[26]

Although it is impossible to know how many embezzlement incidents occur annually, the FBI recorded 12,700 arrests for embezzlement in 1987—probably an extremely small percentage of all embezzlers (see the section in Chapter 12 on white-collar crime for more on embezzlement).

MODERN THEFT CATEGORIES

Many state jurisdictions have found it necessary to create additional theft-related offenses to meet the conditions created by changing social mores. This section reviews some representative examples of modern theft offenses.

Bad Checks

Most state jurisdictions have passed laws making it a criminal act to obtain money or property in exchange for a check that is knowingly and intentionally drawn on a nonexistent or underfunded back account. In general, for a person to be guilty of passing a bad check, the bank the check is drawn on must refuse payment and the check casher must fail to make the check good within 10 days after finding out the check was not honored.

The best-known study of check forgers was conducted by Edwin Lemert.[27] Lemert found that the majority of check forgers—he calls them **naive check forgers**—are amateurs who don't believe their actions

will hurt anyone. Most naive check forgers come from middle-class backgrounds and have little identification with a criminal subculture. They cash bad checks because of a financial crisis that demands an immediate resolution—perhaps they have lost money at the horse track and have some pressing bills to pay. Lemert refers to this condition as **closure.** Naive check forgers often are socially isolated people who have been unsuccessful in their personal relationships. They are risk-prone when faced with a situation that is unusually stressful to them. The willingness of stores and other commercial establishments to cash checks with a minimum of fuss in order to promote business encourages the check forger to risk committing a criminal act.

Not all check forgers are amateurs. Lemert found that a few professionals—whom he calls **systematic forgers**—make a substantial living by passing bad checks. However, professionals constitute a relatively small segment of the total population of check forgers.

It is difficult to estimate the number of check forgeries committed each year, or the amounts involved. Stores and banks may choose not to press charges, since the effort to collect the money due them is often not worth their while. It is also difficult to separate the true check forger from the neglectful shopper. However, FBI figures indicate that annually about 350,000 people in the United States are arrested on fraud charges and 94,000 for forgery and counterfeiting.[28]

Confidence Games

Many state jurisdictions have created criminal laws to protect people from swindlers whose goal is to separate a victim (or "sucker") from his or her hard-earned money. "Con games" usually involve getting a "mark" interested in some get-rich-quick scheme, which may have illegal overtones. The criminal's hope is that when victims lose their money they will be either too embarrassed or too afraid to call the police.

There are hundreds of varieties of con games. The most common is called the **pigeon drop.**[29] A package or wallet containing money is "found" by a con artist. A passing victim is stopped and asked for advice about what to do, since no identification can be found. Another "stranger," who is part of the con, approaches and enters the discussion. The three decide to split the money; but first, to make sure everything is legal, one of the swindlers goes off to consult a lawyer. Upon returning, he or she says that the lawyer claims the money can be split up; first, however, each party must prove he or she has the means to reimburse the original owner, should one ever show up. The victim then is asked to give some good-faith money for the lawyer to hold. When the victim goes to the lawyer's office to pick up a share of the loot, he or she finds the address is bogus and the money gone.

It is difficult to estimate the extent of con games, since many victims will not report their involvement to the authorities. However, as shown in Chapter 12, swindles involving business-related crimes can run into the billions of dollars.

Credit Card Theft

The use of stolen credit cards has become a major problem in U.S. society. It has been estimated that a billion-dollar loss through fraud has been experienced by credit card companies. In New York City, police officials estimate that 5,000 credit cards are stolen each month.[30]

Most credit card abuse is the work of amateurs, who acquire stolen cards through theft or mugging and then use them for two or three days. However, professional credit card rings may be getting into the act. For example, in Los Angeles, members of a credit card gang got jobs as clerks in several stores, where they collected the names and credit card numbers of customers. Gang members bought plain plastic cards and had the names and numbers of the customers embossed on them. The gang created a fictitious wholesale jewelry company and applied for and received authorization to accept credit cards from the "customers." The thieves then used the phony cards to run up charges for nonexistent jewelry purchases on the accounts of the people whose names and card numbers they had collected. The banks that issued the original cards honored over $200,000 in payments before the thieves withdrew the money from their business account and left town.[31]

To combat losses from credit card theft, Congress passed a law in 1971 limiting a person's liability to $50 per stolen card. Similarly, some states, such as California, have passed specific statutes making it a misdemeanor to obtain property or services by means of stolen, forged, canceled, or revoked credit cards, or cards whose use is for any reason unauthorized.[32]

Shoplifting

Shoplifting is a common form of larceny involving the theft of goods from retail stores. Usually shoplifters try to snatch goods—jewelry, clothes, records, appliances—when store personnel are otherwise occupied and hide the goods on their person. The "five-finger discount" is an extremely common form of crime; losses from shoplifting are measured in the billions of dollars each year.[33] Retail security measures add to the already high cost of this crime, all of which is passed on to the consumer.

Shoplifting incidents have increased dramatically in the past 20 years, and retailers now expect an annual increase of from 10 to 15 percent. Some studies estimate that about one in every nine shoppers steals from department stores. Moreover, popular discount stores, such as K-Mart, Target, and Walmart, have a minimum of sales help and depend on highly visible merchandise displays to attract purchasers, all of which makes them particularly vulnerable to shoplifters.

The classic study of shoplifting was conducted by Mary Owen Cameron.[34] In her pioneering effort, Cameron found that about 10 percent of all shoplifters were professionals who derived the majority of their income from shoplifting. Sometimes called **boosters** or **heels,** professional shoplifters intend to resell stolen merchandise to pawnshops or fences, usually at half the original price.[35]

According to Cameron's study, most shoplifters are pilferers, called **snitches** in thieves' argot. Snitches usually are respectable persons who don't conceive of themselves as thieves. Nonetheless, they are systematic shoplifters who steal merchandise for their own use. They are not simply taken by an uncontrollable urge to take something that attracts them; they come equipped to steal. Usually, snitches who are arrested are first offenders who have never been apprehended before. For the most part, they are people who lack the kinds of criminal experience that suggests extensive association with a criminal subculture.

Controlling Shoplifting.   One major problem associated with combatting shoplifting is that many customers who observe pilferage are reluctant to report it

About 1 million auto thefts occur annually, accounting for a total loss of $5 billion.

to security agents. Store employees themselves are often reluctant to get involved in apprehending a shoplifter. For example, in a controlled experiment, Donald Hartmann and his associates found that customers observed only 28 percent of staged shoplifting incidents that had been designed to get their attention.[36] Furthermore, only 28 percent of people who said they had observed an incident reported it to store employees.

In another controlled experiment using staged shoplifting incidents, Erhard Blankenburg found that less than 10 percent of shoplifting was detected by store employees and that customers appeared unwilling to report even serious cases.[37] Even in stores with an announced policy of full reporting and prosecution, only 70 percent of the shoplifting detected by employees was actually reported to managers; and only 5 percent was prosecuted. According to Blankenburg, foreigners, adults, and blue-collar workers were disproportionately represented among those officially punished.

In a study that reached a different conclusion, Michael Hindelang found that the decision of store owners to refer shoplifters to the police was more closely related to the value of the goods stolen, the nature of the goods stolen, and the manner of the theft, than to the race, sex, or age of the offender.[38] For example, shoplifters who had used an apparatus, such as a bag pinned to the inside of their clothing, were more apt to be prosecuted than those who had impulsively put merchandise into their pockets.

In general, criminologists view shoplifters as people who are likely to reform if apprehended. Mary Owen Cameron reasons that snitches are not part of a criminal subculture and do not think of themselves as criminals. Consequently, being arrested has a traumatic effect on them, and they will not risk a second offense.[39] Findings of a similar nature were uncovered in a study by Laurence Cohen and Rodney Stark.[40] However, in a recent study of juvenile shoplifters, Lloyd Klemke found that youths who had been apprehended previously for shoplifting reported more current shoplifting activity than unapprehended youths, and that apprehended youths who had been processed by police authorities were more likely to recidivate than those handled by store personnel alone.[41] Though Klemke's work contradicts that of Cameron and of Cohen and Starke, his sample consisted solely of juvenile offenders, who may react quite differently to apprehension than middle-aged, middle-class adults.

As stated earlier, shoplifting continues to be a

TABLE 11.1   Motor Vehicle Theft

The number of motor vehicles stolen declined 33 percent during the 1973 to 1985 period, from nine to six per 1,000 registered vehicles.

Motor vehicle thefts, whether completed or attempted, most often took place at night; vehicles were most often parked near the victim's home, in noncommercial parking lots, or on the street.

A household member was present in about 9 percent of all motor vehicle theft incidents, and in 3 percent the offender either threatened or physically attacked the victim.

Attempted thefts were more likely than completed thefts to occur at night, have a household member present, result in property damage, and be reported to police by someone outside the household.

Stolen motor vehicles were recovered in 62 percent of the incidents.

In half of all completed motor vehicle thefts, property worth $2,455 or more was stolen; in more than 1 in 4 thefts, property worth at least $5,000 was stolen; and in 1 in 10, the loss was $10,000 or more.

Losses from completed motor vehicle thefts after recoveries and reimbursements by insurance companies amounted to $16.1 billion, or $1.2 billion annually.

Blacks, Hispanics, households headed by persons under age 25, people living in multiple-dwelling units, residents of central cities, and low-income households were among those most likely to be victimized by motor vehicle theft.

Those least likely to experience a motor vehicle theft included those 55 and older, people who owned their own homes, and those living in rural areas.

Almost 9 in 10 completed motor vehicle thefts were reported to police. The percentage of thefts reported increased as the value of the stolen property increased.

SOURCE: Caroline Wolf Harlow, *Motor Vehicle Theft* (Washington, D.C.: Bureau of Justice Statistics, 1988), p. 1.

serious problem. FBI data indicate that shoplifting comprises about 15 percent of all larceny cases—about one million cases in 1986.[42] Many stores have installed elaborate security devices to combat shoplifting, but the growth of this type of larceny has continued.

Auto Theft

Motor vehicle theft is another common larceny offense. The FBI estimates that over a 1.3 million auto thefts occurred in 1987, accounting for a total loss of over $6 billion.[43]

Auto theft is usually considered the pastime of relatively affluent, white, middle-class teenagers looking for excitement through **joyriding**. Currently, about 40 percent of the people arrested for auto theft are under 18, and 58 percent are 21 or younger. Moreover, of the people arrested for auto theft, 60 percent are white and 91 percent are male.[44]

The patterns of auto theft recorded in the National Crime Survey (900,000 thefts annually) is quite similar to UCR data. The similarity of data between these sources is a result of insurance regulations. Since almost every state jurisdiction requires owners to insure their vehicles, auto theft is one of the most highly

reported of all major crimes (90 percent of completed auto thefts are reported to police). A summary of findings on motor vehicle theft, compiled by Caroline Wolf Harlow of the Bureau of Justice Statistics and using data from the NCS, is contained in Table 11.1.[45]

The Nature of Auto Theft.   In an effort to shed some light on the true nature of auto theft, Charles McCaghy and his associates examined data from police and court files in several state jurisdictions.[46] The researchers uncovered five categories of auto theft transactions:

1. *Joyriding*—Many car thefts are motivated by teenagers' desire to acquire the power, prestige, sexual potency, and recognition associated with an automobile. Joyriders do not steal cars for profit or gain but to experience, even briefly, the benefits associated with owning an automobile.
2. *Short-term transportation*—Auto theft for short-term transportation is similar to joyriding. It involves the theft of a car simply to go from one place to another. In more serious cases, the thief may drive to another city or state and then steal another car to continue the journey.
3. *Long-term transportation*—Thieves who steal cars for long-term transportation intend to keep the

cars for their personal use. Usually older than joyriders and from a lower-class background, these auto thieves may repaint and otherwise disguise cars to avoid detection.

4. *Profit*—Auto theft for profit is, of course, motivated by hope for monetary gain. At one extreme are highly organized professionals who resell expensive cars after altering their identification numbers and falsifying their registration papers. At the other end of the scale are amateur auto strippers who steal batteries, tires, and wheel covers in order to sell them or reequip their own cars.

5. *Commission of another crime*—A small portion of auto thieves steal cars so they can be used in other crimes, such as robberies and thefts. This type of auto thief desires both mobility and anonymity.[47]

BURGLARY

The common-law definition of **burglary** is "the breaking and entering of a dwelling house of another in the nighttime with the intent to commit a felony within."[48] Burglary is considered a much more serious crime than larceny/theft, since it involves entering another's home, a situation in which the threat of harm to occupants is great. Even though at the time of the burglary the home may be unoccupied, the potential for harm to the family is so significant that most state jurisdictions punish burglary as a felony.

The legal definition of burglary has undergone considerable change since its common-law origins. When first created by English judges during the late Middle Ages, laws against burglary were designed to protect a family whose home might be set upon by wandering criminals. Including the phrase "breaking and entering" in the definition protected people from unwarranted intrusions; if an invited guest stole something, it would not be considered a burglary. Similarly, the requirement that the crime be committed at nighttime was added because evening was considered the time when honest people might fall prey to criminals.[49]

In more recent times, state jurisdictions have changed the legal requirements of burglary; most have discarded the necessity of forced entry. Many now protect all structures, and not just dwelling houses. A majority of states have removed the nighttime element from burglary definitions as well.

It is quite common for states to enact laws creating different degrees of burglary. In this instance, the more serious and heavily punished crimes involve a nighttime forced entry into the home; the least serious involve a daytime entry into a non-residence by an unarmed offender. Several gradations of the offense may be found between these extremes.

Careers in Burglary

Great variety exists among the ranks of burglars. Many are crude thieves who, with little finesse, will smash a window and enter a vacant home or structure with minimal preparation. However, because it involves planning, risk, and skill, burglary has been a crime long associated with professional thieves.

To become a skilled practitioner of burglary, the would-be burglar must learn the craft from an experienced burglar. For example, Francis Hoheimer, an experienced professional burglar, has described his education in the craft of burglary by Oklahoma Smith, when the two were serving time in Illinois State Penitentiary. Among Smith's recommendations:

Never wear deodorant or shaving lotion, the strange scent might wake someone up. The more people there are in a house, the safer you are. If someone hears you moving around, they will think it's someone else . . . If they call answer in a muffled sleepy voice . . . Never be afraid of dogs, they can sense fear. Most dogs are friendly, snap your fingers, they come right to you . . .[50]

When he was released from prison, Hoheimer formed a criminal gang that specialized in burglary. Hoheimer and his associates would check into a motel near the home of their intended victim. Registering under assumed names and giving false addresses, they would correctly describe their cars but mix up license plate numbers. Checking out of the motel before the burglary, they would enter the victim's home between two o'clock and five o'clock in the morning. If the owners were present, they would be tied, hand and foot, with surgical tape. Hoheimer and his gang concentrated on taking jewelery, furs, and money. The victims would be asked for the location of wall

CLOSE-UP

The Professional Burglar

This excerpt, from Marilyn Walsh's study of fencing, describes the methods and operations of a professional burglar.

Greg is a jewelry and fur specialist who has taken a gemology course in order to evaluate and learn about the property he steals. He has jewelers' tools and removes stones from their settings to weigh and safely secure them. His main targets are the homes of wealthy persons who, he takes pains to discover, have such property in their homes rather than in a bank vault. Greg spends considerable time, before contemplating a theft, researching possible victims to build a profile of them. He searches the social register, the social and financial pages of the newspapers, the city directory, and the directories of corporate officials. He visits the neighborhoods of the wealthy at different times and days to get a feel for their living patterns. When satisfied that an individual not only is likely to possess property he might be interested in, but also maintains a lifestyle that includes substantial periods away from home, Greg will add him to a list of *possible* targets. This list includes the name, address, and phone number of that individual as well as a notation about any item that he may have heard about or seen worn by one of the occupants (in a news photo, for example) that particularly interests him.

When he is ready to pull a job, he has a group of three or four other burglars with whom he works. They begin by calling individuals on Greg's list until they find a home with no one answering. Next they proceed toward the target, stopping at a phone booth to try the residence again. If still no one answers, the drama begins.

They are equipped with two police radios and a walkie-talkie. One of them is designated as the driver, and he lets the others out of the car somewhere near the preferred approach to the house. The driver then proceeds to a phone booth and, giving his cohorts approximately 10 minutes, he calls the home once more. If no one or someone unfamiliar answers, he proceeds immediately to a predetermined pick-up point. If his friends answer, he gives them his number and begins waiting at the booth, monitoring police calls and phoning them intermittently to be advised of their progress.

In the house the thieves again divide the labors. One of them waits for the phone call and mans the walkie-talkie if it becomes necessary for them to be separated on different floors of the house. The first step is to find the luggage owned by the occupants, for they will be using this to transport the property from the house. This done, they proceed to steal what they will, opening a safe if that is necessary or merely lifting what is around of value. Their ease of operation will depend on what they have calculated to be the maximum time they will have to operate inside. Thus, if they know the occupants to be at a social function, they will use the luxury of several hours to do a thorough job. If, however, they have determined that their victims are out dining, they may allow themselves less time to complete the job and execute their exit.

When they have finished, they notify their driver, with whom they have been in intermittent contact, and proceed to the arranged pick-up point, leaving as they came, through a side door or a back window with suitcases in hand. Anything they decide is of little value, for example costume jewelry picked up by mistake, is put back in the suitcases and, bag and baggage, is taken to another predetermined safe place and disposed of. (Their preference was a desolated wharf area, where they would drop the merchandise they didn't want into a swift-flowing channel.)

Discussion Questions

1. How do Greg's preparations compare with those of other professionals, such as a lawyer preparing a case or a surgeon preparing for an operation?
2. Can thieves like Greg be deterred?

SOURCE: Marilyn E. Walsh, "The Decreasing Utility of the Fence Game," in *The Fence, A New Look at the World of Property Theft* (Contributions in Sociology, No. 21, Greenwood Press, Inc., Westport, CT, 1977), pp. 164–66. Copyright 1977 by Marilyn E. Walsh. Reprinted with permission.

safes and valuables. While on the job, Hoheimer carried a handgun as well as an attache case containing such items as ski masks, work gloves, pen-type flashlights, propane tank with torch head, pry bar, screwdriver, lock pliers, wirecutters, glass cutter, and six rolls of surgical tape. Despite his elaborate preparations, Hoheimer spent many years confined for his acts.

The Good Burglar

Neal Shover has studied the careers of professional burglars and uncovered the existence of a particularly successful type—the **good burglar**.[51] This characterization is applied by professional burglars to colleagues who have distinguished themselves as burglars. Characteristics of the good burglar include: (1) technical competence; (2) maintenance of personal integrity; (3) specialization in burglary; (4) financial success at crime; and (5) ability to avoid prison sentences.

Shover found that to receive recognition as good burglars, novices must learn to overcome four problems of the trade. First, they must learn the many skills needed to commit lucrative burglaries. This process may include learning such techniques as how to gain entry into homes and apartment houses, how to select targets with high potential payoffs, how to choose items with a high resale value, how to properly open safes without damaging their contents, and how to use the proper equipment—including cutting torches, electric saws, explosives, and metal bars.

Second, the good burglar must be able to team up to form a criminal gang. Choosing trustworthy companions is essential if the obstacles to completing a successful job—police, alarms, secure safes—are to be overcome.

Third, the good burglar must have inside information. Without knowledge of what awaits them inside, burglars can spend a tremendous amount of time and effort on empty safes and jewelery boxes.

Finally, the good burglar must cultivate fences or buyers for stolen wares. Once the burglar gains access to people who buy and sell stolen goods, he or she also must learn how to successfully sell these goods for a reasonable profit.

Shover finds that the process of becoming a professional burglar is similar to the process Sutherland described in his theory of differential association (described in Chapter 8). According to Shover, a person becomes a good burglar through learning the techniques of the trade from older, more experienced burglars. During this process, the older burglar teaches the novice such tricks of the trade as dealing with defense attorneys, bail bonding companies, and other agents of the justice system. Consequently, the opportunity to become a good burglar is not open to everyone. Apprentices must be known to have the appropriate character before they are taken under the wing of the "old pro." Usually the opportunity to learn burglary comes as a reward for being a highly respected juvenile gang member; from knowing someone in the neighborhood who has made a living at burglary; or, more often, from having built a reputation for being trustworthy and dependable while serving time in prison.

Other attempts have been made to analyze and classify the characteristics of burglars. H. A. Scarr distinguishes between professional burglars and high-school-age, drug abusing, "casual" burglars.[52] Thomas Repetto investigated burglary in the Boston area and found that the typical burglar was a young, nonwhite male who was not skilled at his trade (not a professional, or good burglar).[53] Using a complex statistical analysis of burglary incidents in California, Carl Pope found there was no relationship between the racial or criminal backgrounds of offenders and the patterns of their burglary offenses. Pope concluded: "Unlike violent crimes . . . burglary, and other property crimes as well, may reflect more opportunity than choice."[54] (See Close-Up entitled "The Professional Burglar.")

The Extent of Burglary

The FBI's definition of burglary is not restricted to burglary from a person's home; it includes any unlawful entry of a structure to commit theft or felony. Burglary is further categorized into three subclasses: forcible entry, unlawful entry where no force is used, and attempted forcible entry.[55]

According to the UCR, 3,236,184 burglaries occurred in 1987, a decrease of about .2 percent from the preceding year. Most burglaries (66 percent) were of private residences; the remainder were business-related. Victims suffered a loss of $3.1 billion due to burglary.

The Bureau of Justice Statistics has analyzed NCS data in order to provide a picture of burglary victimization. Some highlights of the survey include:

- About 40 percent of all burglaries were committed by family or acquaintances of the victim.

≡ CLOSE-UP

The Professional Torch

The following selection describes the activities of "torches"—professional criminals who make their living from setting fires.

In arson-for-profit, individuals hired to start fires, "torches," range from amateurs to professionals. Torches are the most familiar criminal specialists, but they are often the most difficult to apprehend. One reason for this difficulty is that many torches are recruited from the ranks of burglars and other petty thieves who know how to case a neighborhood and building, and how to enter and exit at night without being noticed. Another reason is that the "technology" required to set incendiary fires is very basic, and the use of gasoline or other available accelerants leaves few traces that automatically point to a particular torch. A third reason is that the requirements of proof under most arson statutes involve a showing of exclusive opportunity to set the fire, and when the owner-insured has contracted out the arson to a torch (amateur or professional), the question of who had exclusive opportunity to set the fire becomes very difficult to answer.

Torches often specialize in the types of structures they burn. This seems to be largely a function of their familiarity with a certain section of a city or with certain types of housing or commercial establishments. A further distinction can be drawn among amateur, semi-professional, and professional torches based on their use of timing devices, accelerants, or explosives.

The professional torch is knowledgeable in the sophisticated use of timing devices, chemicals that do not leave an easily traceable accelerant pattern (as does gasoline), and explosives used in burning commercial structures. The semiprofessional torch is adept in the proper and relatively safe use of gasoline and paint thinner as accelerants, probably with the use of trailers. He has some basic knowledge as to the necessity of proper ventilation if a building is to burn successfully. The amateur torch can be a one-time or occasionally an experienced torch, who simply uses a relatively small quantity of gasoline and immediate ignition devices, such as matches or railroad flares. The amateur lacks knowledge as to the true burning characteristics of fire, ignition devices, chemicals, and explosives; the amateur is also unsophisticated in terms of the evidence left behind and the relative dangers in immediate ignition of an incendiary fire. It is not uncommon for amateurs to kill or burn themselves in the act.

While most torches are known to boast about their professional expertise, the handiwork of those who are more amateur than professional can be seen in cases where adjacent buildings were badly damaged or fire fighters were injured or killed. Very often, the use of extraordinary quantities of accelerant, seriously endangering fire fighters and occupants, is a sign of an amateur. One hallmark of a true professional is the total engagement of the target premises (and no damage to another) by the time the fire service arrives. What may be deceiving is the first try of a torch experienced at setting multifamily residential fires, who tries his or her hand at an industrial facility and comes wide of the mark, either through the use of too much gasoline or through explosives improperly placed.

As torches progress in their criminal careers, many graduate into planning and supervisory roles. These individuals may be termed "master torches." Usually they act as prime contractors for the owner or fire broker and procure others to commit the actual incendiarism. Because their experience builds over the years, proficient master torches generally know just how much accelerant to use and whether an explosive device may be needed. Because they act as prime contractors, they frequently serve as agents between the actual torches who set the fires and fire brokers or owners. It also is not uncommon to find a fire broker whose fascination with incendiary crime leads him or her to assume the additional role of master torch. In so doing, the fire broker brings increased specialization to the task without the added cost of a separate specialist. However, that person also increases his or her vulnerability because of additional interactions with torches, owners, and others who are involved to discuss specific plans for the fire. If a master torch is at all active in a jurisdiction, his or her role in a conspiracy probably will be central enough to implicate the others.

Torches are usually paid a flat fee, rather than a percentage of the insurance, for their services. Professional torches, especially the very good ones, normally command between $1,000 and $5,000 per arson fire. The fee for semiprofessional torches normally ranges from $500 to $1,000, and amateurs usually receive between $100 and $500. In contrast to the fortunes that other fraud schemers make in arson frauds, the torch, certainly a specialist, may seem in comparison to be underpaid. This phenomenon has several explanations. First, the torch is usually paid in cash, with a "good faith" down payment prior to the fire, and the remainder afterwards. Second, the amount paid to

More than 30 people died when an arsonist set fire to the Dupont Plaza Hotel in San Juan, Puerto Rico, in 1986.

a torch is controlled by the simple law of supply and demand. In any jurisdiction there are enough freelance torches so that the availability of this essentially cheap, semiskilled labor has the effect of driving down the price any one torch can command. If the price for a commercial business is $1,000, and a torch who is asked to set that fire refuses, demanding $2,000, the owner merely says, ''Ridiculous—too high,'' and proceeds to find one of the many other equally competent and trustworthy torches who will set the fire for the prevailing wage. Third, torches are basically freelance underworld fringe figures, handling perhaps a burglary here, a fire there. While many of them do not exactly live hand-to-mouth, the irregular and often unpredictable demand for their services makes almost any arson offer attractive, especially because it carries the promise of quick payment.

There have been instances of a torch reportedly being paid upwards of $5,000 for a fire, or possibly 10 percent of the insurance settlement. Such apparent exceptions to the rule can be explained. Basically, the deal that a torch strikes alone with an owner is a bargain between the two of them. When there is no organized market for the services of a torch, or when the owner is naive and does not check prevailing torch fees, negotiations often turn to the advantage of the torch. One reason for the attractiveness of pigeons and fire brokers to owners is that these specialists, who market the commodity of information, help the owner understand what he or she will have to do to execute an arson fraud, and how much he or she can expect to pay for ''quality.'' Just as in the world of legitimate business, the owner pays the broker or pigeon a consideration for access to this valuable, highly technical information on prices and quality.

Torches come from many underworld quarters, but they are mainly fringe figures in crime who perform a variety of usually dirty, manual tasks. Many double as either drug user-dealers or burglars, or got their start earlier in burglary or other petty thieving. Others became torchers because they were seasonally unemployed as lower-level fringe figures in white-collar or organized crime or in a legitimate business (such as contracting), where they rubbed shoulders with financial schemers looking for torches. There are reports that many torches have a violent streak that causes them to enjoy the damage done by incendiary fires. Those who describe such torches also point to their frequent eagerness to serve as underworld enforcers, suggesting that they especially enjoy such tasks as threatening or beating loan shark clients who are in default. Altogether, too few torches have been caught to permit an objective study of their psychological motivation. Clearly, their economic motivation, of which more is known, goes a considerable length in explaining this criminal behavior.

Discussion Questions

1. Which are the most serious criminals—the torches or the businesspersons who hire them?

2. Should arson for profit be punished more severely than crimes such as robbery, rape, or burglary?

SOURCE: Leigh Edward Somers, *Economic Crimes* (New York: Clark Boardman, 1984), pp. 158–68.

- Black homes were victimized much more frequently than white homes.
- Families with the lowest (under $7,500) and highest (over $25,000) incomes experienced the most burglaries.
- Homeowners and single-family residences had lower burglary rates than renters and multiple-family dwellings.
- Urban areas had significantly higher burglary rates than rural areas.
- Burglary occurs more often in warm summer months.
- During a 10-year period, 2.8 million acts of violence were committed during an act of burglary.[56]

ARSON

Arson is the willful and malicious burning of a home, public building, vehicle, or commercial building of another. The FBI found that 102,410 arsons were set in 1987—about 50 per 100,000; in 1987 the number of arsons declined 5 percent.[57]

Arson is a young person's crime. Of the 18,000 people arrested in 1987, about 63 percent were under 25, 41 percent were 18 and under, and 25 percent were 15 and under. The percentage of young teens arrested for the crime of arson was higher than it was for any other Part I crime and for most Part II crimes (except vandalism, runaways, and curfew violations). Also, arson is primarily a white (73 percent) and male (87 percent) crime.

There are several motives for arson. Some arsons stem from personal psychological problems; others are the work of a deranged person bent on revenge; still others are simply the result of teenagers out to vandalize property. However, a growing phenomenon is **arson for profit,** or **arson fraud,** which involves a business owner burning his or her property, or hiring someone to do it, to escape from financial problems.[58] Over the years, investigators have found that businesspeople are willing to become involved in arson for a number of reasons. The primary reason is to collect fire insurance. However, some of the other reasons include:

- To obtain money during a period of financial crisis

- To get rid of outdated or slow-moving inventory, or to destroy outmoded machines and technology
- To pay off legal and illegal debts
- To relocate or remodel a business; for example, when a "theme" restaurant has not been accepted by customers
- To take advantage of government funds available for redevelopment; for example, owners might apply for government building money, pocket it without making repairs, and then claim that fire destroyed the "rehabilitated" building
- To plan bankruptcies to eliminate debts from creditors; the merchandise supposedly destroyed is secretly sold before the fire
- To eliminate business competition by burning out rivals
- To employ extortion schemes that demand pay-up or the rest of the victim's holdings will be burned
- To solve labor-management problems; arson may be committed by a disgruntled employee
- To conceal another crime, for example, embezzlement.

The Close-Up entitled "The Professional Torch" describes the activities of an important participant in the crime of arson for profit, the **torch.**

SUMMARY

Economic crimes are designed to bring financial reward to the offender. The majority of economic crimes are committed by opportunistic amateurs. However, economic crime also has attracted professional criminals. Professionals earn the bulk of their income from crime, view themselves as criminals, and possess skills that aid them in their law breaking.

Edwin Sutherland's classic book, *The Professional Thief,* is perhaps the most famous portrayal of professional crime. According to Sutherland and his informant Chic Conwell, professionals live by their wits and never resort to violence. A good example of the professional criminal is the fence who buys and sells stolen merchandise.

Common theft offenses include larceny, embezzlement, fraud, and burglary. These are common-law crimes, created by English judges to meet existing social needs. Larceny involves taking the legal possessions of another. Petty larceny is theft of amounts under $100; grand larceny, of amounts usually over $100. The crime of false pretenses, or fraud, is similar to larceny because it involves the theft of goods or money; but it differs from larceny because the criminal tricks victims into voluntarily giving up their possessions. Embezzlement is another theft crime. It involves taking something that was only temporarily entrusted, such as bank tellers' taking money out of the cash drawer and keeping it for themselves. Most states have codified these common-law crimes in their state codes. New larceny crimes also have been defined to keep abreast of changing social conditions: passing bad checks, stealing or illegally using credit cards, shoplifting, stealing autos.

Burglary, a more serious theft offense, was defined in the common law as the "breaking and entering of a dwelling house of another in the nighttime with the intent to commit a felony within." Today, most states have modified their definitions of burglary to include theft from any structure at any time of day. Because burglary involves planning and risk, it attracts professional thieves. The most competent are known as good burglars. Good burglars have technical competence and personal integrity, specialize in burglary, are financially successful, and avoid prison sentences.

Arson is another serious property crime. Though most arsonists are teenage vandals, there are professional arsonists who specialize in burning commercial buildings for profit.

KEY TERMS

economic crimes	fraud
professional crime	naive check forgers
fence	closure
commercial thieves	systematic forgers
street crimes	pigeon drop
occasional criminals	boosters
situational inducement	heels
professional criminals	snitches
stoopers	joyriding
flash houses	burglary
smugglers	good burglar

poachers	arson for profit
constructive possession	arson fraud
false pretenses	torch

NOTES

1. John Hepburn, "Occasional Criminals," in Robert Meier, ed., *Major Forms of Crime* (Beverly Hills, Cal.: Sage Publications, 1984), pp. 73–94.
2. James Inciardi, "Professional Crime," in Meier, *Major Forms of Crime*, p. 223.
3. Harry King and William Chambliss, *Box Man: A Professional Thief's Journal* (New York: Harper & Row, 1972), p. 24.
4. Edwin Sutherland, "White-Collar Criminality," *American Sociological Review* 5 (1940):2–10.
5. Gilbert Geis, "Avocational Crime," in D. Glazer, ed., *Handbook of Criminology*, (Chicago: Rand McNally, 1974), p. 284.
6. Edwin Sutherland and Chic Conwell, *The Professional Thief* (Chicago: University of Chicago Press, 1937).
7. *Ibid.*, pp. 197–98.
8. *Ibid.*, p. 212.
9. See, for example, Edwin Lemert, "The Behavior of the Systematic Check Forger," *Social Problems* 6 (1958):141–48.
10. John Rosencrance, "The Stooper: A Professional Thief in The Sutherland Manner," *Criminology* 24 (1986):29–40.
11. *Ibid.*, p. 39.
12. Cited in Marilyn Walsh, *The Fence* (Westport, Conn.: Greenwood Press, 1977), p. 1.
13. Carl Klockars, *The Professional Fence* (New York: Free Press, 1976); Darrell Steffensmeir, *The Fence: In the Shadow of Two Worlds* (Totowa, N.J.: Rowman and Littlefield, 1986).
14. In her study of fencing, Marilyn Walsh draws this picture of the professional fence: he is a white male in his middle to late forties, owns and operates a legitimate retail establishment, probably never has been arrested, and looks very much like a totally legitimate manager or business administrator; Walsh, *The Fence.*
15. Andrew McCall, *The Medieval Underworld* (London: Hamish Hamilton, 1979), p. 86.
16. *Ibid.*, p. 104.
17. J. J. Tobias, *Crime and Police in England 1700–1900* (London: Gill and Macmillan, 1979).
18. *Ibid.*, p. 9.
19. Walsh, *The Fence*, pp. 18–25.
20. This section depends heavily on a classic book, Wayne La Fave and Austin Scott, *Handbook on Criminal Law* (St.

Paul, Minn.: West Publishing Company, 1972).

21. *Ibid.*, p. 622.

22. FBI, *Crime in the United States, 1987* (Washington, D.C.: U.S. Government Printing Office, 1988), p. 28, updated.

23. La Fave and Scott, *Handbook on Criminal Law,* p. 655.

24. 30 Geo. III, C. 24 (1975).

25. La Fave and Scott, *Handbook on Criminal Law,* p. 644.

26. *Ibid.*, p. 649.

27. Edwin Lemert, "An Isolation and Closure Theory of Naive Check Forgery," *Journal of Criminal Law, Criminology and Police Science* 44 (1953):297–98.

28. FBI, *Crime in the United States, 1987,* p. 170.

29. As described in Charles McCaghy, *Deviant Behavior* (New York: Macmillan, 1976), pp. 230–31.

30. "Credit Card Fraud Toll One Billion," *Omaha World Herald* (16 March 1986), p. 16.

31. *Ibid.*

32. La Fave and Scott, *Handbook on Criminal Law,* p. 672.

33. D. Hartmann, D. Gelfand, B. Page, and P. Walder, "Rates of Bystander Observation and Reporting of Contrived Shoplifting Incidents," *Criminology* 10 (1972):248.

34. Mary Owen Cameron, *The Booster and the Snitch* (New York: Free Press, 1964).

35. *Ibid.*, p. 57.

36. Hartmann, et al., "Rates of Bystander Observation and Reporting," p. 267.

37. Erhard Blankenburg, "The Selectivity of Legal Sanctions: An Empirical Investigation of Shoplifting," *Law and Society Review* 11 (1976):109–29.

38. Michael Hindelang, "Decisions of Shoplifting Victims to Invoke the Criminal Justice Process," *Social Problems* 21 (1974):580–95.

39. Cameron, *The Booster and the Snitch,* p. 63.

40. Laurence Cohen and Rodney Stark, "Discriminatory Labeling and the Five-Finger Discount: An Empirical Analysis of Differential Shoplifting Dispositions," *Journal of Research on Crime and Delinquency* 11 (1974):25–35.

41. Lloyd Klemke, "Does Apprehension for Shoplifting Amplify or Terminate Shoplifting Activity?" *Law and Society Review* 12 (1978):390–403.

42. *Crime in the United States, 1986,* pp. 29–31.

43. *Ibid.*, p. 34.

44. *Ibid.*

45. Caroline Wolf Harlow, *Motor Vehicle Theft* (Washington, D.C.: Bureau of Justice Statistics, 1987), p. 1.

46. Charles McCaghy, Peggy Giordano, and Trudy Knicely Henson, "Auto Theft," *Criminology* 15 (1977):367–81.

47. *Ibid.*, pp. 370–80.

48. La Fave and Scott, *Handbook on Criminal Law,* p. 708.

49. E. Blackstone, *Commentaries on the Laws of England* (London: 1769), p. 224.

50. Frank Hoheimer, *The Home Invaders: Confessions of a Cat Burglar* (Chicago: Chicago Review, 1975), cited in J. Macdonald, *Burglary and Theft* (Springfield, Ill.: Charles C. Thomas, 1980), p. 21.

51. See, generally, Neal Shover, "Structures and Careers in Burglary," *Journal of Criminal Law, Criminology and Police Science* 63 (1972):540–49.

52. H. A. Scarr, *Patterns of Burglary* (Washington, D.C.: U.S. Government Printing Office, 1973).

53. Thomas Repetto, *Residential Crime* (Cambridge, Mass.: Ballinger, 1974).

54. Carl Pope, "Patterns in Burglary: An Empirical Examination of Offense and Offender Characteristics," *Journal of Criminal Justice* 8 (1980):39–51.

55. See, generally, *Crime in the United States, 1987,* pp. 24–26.

56. Bureau of Justice Statistics, *Household Burglary* (Washington, D.C.: National Institute of Justice, 1985).

57. *Uniform Crime Reports, 1986,* pp. 37–41.

58. Leigh Edward Somers, *Economic Crimes* (New York: Clark Boardman, 1984), pp. 158–68.

CHAPTER 12

ECONOMIC CRIMES: ORGANIZATIONAL CRIMINALITY

CHAPTER OUTLINE

INTRODUCTION

The second component of economic crime involves illegal business activity. In this chapter, these crimes of illicit **entrepreneurship** are divided into two distinct categories: **white-collar crime** and **organized crime.** The former involves the illegal activities of people and institutions whose acknowledged purpose is profit and gain through *legitimate* business transactions. The second category, organized crime, involves the illegal activity of people and organizations whose acknowledged purpose is profit and gain through *illegitimate* business enterprise.

Organized crime and white-collar crime are linked together here because, as criminologist Dwight Smith argues, **enterprise** and not crime is the governing characteristic of both phenomena:

> *White-collar crime is not simply a dysfunctional aberration. Organized crime is not something ominously alien to the American economic system. Both are made criminal by laws declaring that certain ways of doing business, or certain products of business, are illegal. In other words, criminality is not an inherent characteristic either of certain persons or of certain business activities but rather, an externally imposed evaluation of alternative modes of behavior and action.[1]*

According to Smith, business enterprise can be viewed as flowing through a spectrum of acts ranging from the most saintly to the most sinful.[2] Though "sinful" organizational practices may be desirable to many consumers (e.g., sale of narcotics) or an efficient way of doing business (e.g., dumping of hazardous wastes), society has seen fit to regulate or outlaw these behaviors. Consequently, organized crime and the crimes of business are the results of a process by which "political, value-based constraints are based on economic activity."[3] In fact, some criminologists view the motive for white-collar crime and organized crime to be identical: the profit motive inherent in the capitalist system. According to William Chambliss, organized crime is a product of the legitimate economy, and its connection to legitimate business and political systems makes its growth unavoidable.[4]

Organizational crimes can be regarded as the "dark side" of the free market system; they involve all phases of illegal entrepreneurial activity. White-collar crimes involve the use of illegal business practices (embezzlement, price-fixing, bribery) to merchandise what are ordinarily legitimate commercial products. Those commonly known as "organized crime" involve individuals or groups whose marketing techniques (threat, extortion, smuggling) and product lines (drugs, sex, gambling, loan sharking) have been outlawed. Both crime patterns involve exploitive commercial practices and attempts by society to control their abuse.

WHITE-COLLAR CRIME

In the late 1930s, distinguished criminologist Edwin Sutherland first used the phrase "white-collar crime" to describe the criminal activities of the rich and powerful. He defined white-collar crime as "a crime committed by a person of respectability and high social status in the course of his occupation."[5] As Sutherland saw it, white-collar crime involved conspiracies by members of the wealthy classes to use their position in commerce and industry for personal gain without regard to the law. All too often these actions were handled by civil courts, since injured parties were more concerned with getting back their losses than with seeing the offenders punished. Consequently, Sutherland believed that the great majority of white-collar criminals did not become the subject of criminological study. Yet their crimes were very costly:

> *The financial cost of white-collar crime is probably several times as great as the financial cost of all the crimes which are customarily regarded as the "crime problem." The financial loss from white-collar crime, great as it is, is less important than the damage to social relations. White-collar crimes violate trust and therefore create distrust, which lowers social morale and produces disorganization on a large scale. Other crimes produce relatively little effect on social institutions or social organization.[6]*

Though Sutherland's work is considered a milestone in criminological history, his focus was on corporate criminality. Today, there exists some disagreement over the precise definition of white-collar crime. Sutherland's major concern was the crimes of the rich and powerful. Modern criminologists have broadened their definition of white-collar crime so that it now includes a wide variety, of situations.[7] For example, today's definition of white-collar criminals can include people acting as individuals who use the marketplace for the purpose of their criminal activity. This category of crime includes such acts as income tax evasion, credit card fraud, and bankruptcy fraud. Other white-collar criminals use their positions of trust in business or government to commit crimes. Their activities might include pilfering, soliciting bribes or kickbacks, and embezzlement. Some white-collar criminals set up business for the sole purpose of victimizing the general public. They engage in land swindles (such as representing swamps as choice building sites), securities thefts, medical or health frauds, and so on.

In addition to acting as individuals, some white-collar criminals become involved in criminal conspiracies designed to improve the market share or profitability of their corporations. This type of white-collar crime, which includes antitrust violations, price-fixing, and false advertising, is also known as **corporate crime.**

It is evident that Sutherland's original concept of the upper-class, white-collar criminal has been expanded by these later formulations. Today, as a general rule, criminologists use the term white-collar crime to refer to almost any occupationally oriented law violation. "White-collar crimes can be committed by persons in all social classes," claims one sociologist, Gilbert Geis. His perspective has been accepted by most mainstream criminologists.[8]

THE WHITE-COLLAR CRIME PROBLEM

It is difficult to estimate the extent and influence of white-collar crime. Some experts place its total monetary value in the hundreds of billions of dollars, far outstripping the expense of any other type of crime. Beyond the monetary cost, white-collar crimes often involve damage to property and loss of human life. Violations of safety standards, pollution of the environment, and industrial accidents due to negligence can be classified as corporate violence. Laura Schrager and James Short suggest that corporate crime annually results in 20 million serious injuries, including 110,000 people who become permanently disabled and 30,000 deaths.[9] They state that "The potential impact ranges

from acute environmental catastrophes such as the collapse of a dam to the chronic effects of diseases resulting from industrial pollution."[10]

In a similar vein, sociologist Gilbert Geis charges that white-collar crime is actually much more serious than street crime:

It destroys confidence, saps the integrity of commercial life and has the potential for devastating destruction. Think of the possible results if nuclear regulatory rules are flouted or if toxic wastes are dumped into a community's drinking water supply.[11]

The public has begun to recognize the seriousness of white-collar crimes and demand that they be controlled. A national survey of crime seriousness found that people saw white-collar crimes—such as a county judge taking a bribe to give a light sentence, a doctor cheating on Medicare forms, and a factory knowingly getting rid of waste in a way that pollutes the water supply—as being more serious than a person stabbing another with a knife or stealing property worth $10,000 from outside a building.[12] In addition, the 1988 national scandal generated by the closing of beaches along the east coast because of the illegal dumping of medical wastes helped focus attention on environmental crimes.

Public concern has been matched by the government's recent zeal in prosecuting white-collar criminals, a development which is discussed later in this chapter. Nonetheless, monetary fines and short-term prison sentences in country-club like facilities are the usual choice of judges and prosecutors, who are loath to incarcerate offenders who do not fit the image of "common criminals."

The leniency afforded white-collar criminals is illustrated by two incidents involving big business which received widespread national attention.[13] In one case, the brokerage firm E. F. Hutton pleaded guilty to 2,000 counts of fraud arising from a multi-billion-dollar bad check scheme. More than 20 Hutton executives defrauded 400 banks out of millions of dollars in interest. The penalty: a fine of $2.75 million and an order to repay the banks. In the second case, General Electric was found guilty of defrauding the Air Force of $800,000 on a nuclear warhead contract. Their penalty: $1.84 million. To multi-billion-dollar companies, these penalties are a slap on the wrist. No company officers went to prison, nor were they personally penalized. A senate investigating committee looking into these cases made note of a concurrent incident in which a woman who shoplifted four sweaters received a 30-day jail sentence; society still punishes nonviolent street crimes more severely than multimillion-dollar white-collar crimes.

COMPONENTS OF WHITE-COLLAR CRIME

As noted, white-collar crimes today represent a range of behaviors involving individuals acting alone and also within the context of a business structure. The victims of white-collar crime can be the general public, the organization that employs the offender, or another competing organization.

Numerous attempts have been made to create subcategories, or typologies, of white-collar criminality. One of the most well-known was presented by Marshall Clinard and Richard Quinney, who divide white-collar crime into occupational and corporate categories. The former involves offenses committed by individuals in the course of their occupation and the crimes of employees against their employers. The second category, corporate crime, involves "the offenses committed by corporate officials for the corporation and the offenses of the corporation itself."[14] While this definition recognizes the dual nature of white-collar crime, it fails to take into account all of its many facets, for example, a public official selling undeserved privileges to the public.

Several more recent efforts have attempted to account for this diversity. For example, Herbert Edelhertz divides white-collar criminality into four distinct categories:

1. *Ad hoc violations*—Committed for personal profit on an episodic basis; for example, welfare fraud, tax cheating.

2. *Abuses of trust*—Committed by a person in a place of trust in an organization against the organization; for example, embezzlement, bribery, or taking kickbacks.

3. *Collateral business crimes*—Committed by organizations to further their business interests; for example, antitrust violations, use of false weights

and measures, concealment of environmental crimes.

4. *Con games*—Committed for the sole purpose of cheating clients; for example, fraudulent land sales, sales of bogus securities, sales of questionable tax shelters.[15]

Edelhertz's typology captures the diverse nature of white-collar criminality and illustrates how both individuals and institutions and be victims and offenders of a white-collar crime.

In the present text, a typology created by criminologist **Mark Moore** is adapted to organize the analysis of white-collar crime.[16] Moore's typology contains seven elements, ranging from an individual using a business enterprise to commit theft-related crimes, to an individual using his or her place within a business enterprise for illegal gain, to business enterprises themselves collectively engaging in illegitimate activity. While no single typology may be sufficient to encompass the complex array of acts which the term usually denotes, the analysis of white-collar crime here is meant to be as so broad and inclusive that it contains the areas commonly considered important for criminological study.[17]

Stings and Swindles

The first category of white-collar crime involves stealing through deception by individuals who have no continuing institutional or business position, and whose entire purpose is to bilk people out of their money. Offenses in this category range from frauds involving the door-to-door sale of faulty merchandise to the passing of millions of dollars in counterfeit stock certificates to an established brokerage firm. If caught, white-collar swindlers are usually charged with common-law crimes such as embezzlement or fraud.

Swindles can run into millions of dollars. In one well-known case, Gary Lewellyn misappropriated almost $18 million, most of it from an Iowa bank his father managed. He used the money to manipulate and drive up the price of stock he purchased in Safeguard Scientific, Inc. When his scheme was uncovered, the stock's price plummeted, wiping Lewellyn out. As a final gesture, he withdrew $500,000 of embezzled money and flew to Las Vegas, where he played blackjack 16 hours a day to try to recoup his losses; he lost $300,000 more. After his father's bank went bankrupt, Lewellyn received a 20-year prison sentence.[18]

The extent of Lewellyn's actions are staggering, but they pale in comparison with the case of the Equity Funding Corporation of America, whose officers bilked the public out of an estimated $2 billion in 1973. The directors of this firm, a life insurance company, claimed to have 90,000 policy holders. However, more than 60,000 of them existed as fictitious entries in the company's computer banks. Equity sold ownership and management of these bogus policies to reinsurance companies, and corporate officers pocketed the profit. The $2 billion loss probably is the greatest all-time loss from a white-collar crime.[19]

Although scams such as these have received widespread publicity, the public seems quite willing to continue to be fleeced by business-related cons. For example, a task force in securities fraud, formed in the state of Utah, estimated that 12,000 investors lost at least $215 million in phony stock deals in a five-year period ending in 1985.[20]

Chiseling

Chiseling, the second category of white-collar crime, involves cheating consumers on a regular basis. This can involve charging for bogus auto repairs, cheating customers on home repairs, or short-weighing in supermarkets of dairies. The offenders may be individuals looking to make quick profits in their own businesses, or employees of large organizations who decide to cheat on obligations to customers or clients by doing something contrary to company policy.[21] Even large companies can engage in chiseling. Chrysler Motor executives used company cars, rolled back odometers and sold them as new. In 1988, Hertz Corporation acknowledged that it cheated customers by overcharging them on repair bills. Helping the chiselers are the facts that few government agencies keep reliable statistics and that each program uses different requirements and terminology.

Some people view chiseling as a lower-class phenomenon, but it is not uncommon for professionals to use their positions to commit this type of crime. Pharmacists have been known to alter prescriptions or substitute low-cost generic drugs for more expensive name brands. In a study of prescription violations,

Richard Quinney found that the professional orientation of individual pharmacists had a significant influence on their law-violating behavior.[22] Pharmacists who were business-oriented—and therefore stressed merchandising, inventory turnover, and sales rather than servicing the public—were more inclined to chisel customers. Quinney attributed their fraudulent acts to the pursuit of profit at the expense of professional ethics.

The legal profession also has come under fire because of the unscrupulous behavior of some of its members. The Watergate hearings, which revealed the unethical behavior of high-ranking government attorneys, prompted the American Bar association to require that all law students take a course in legal ethics.

Another common chiseling crime involves **churning** of a client's account by an unscrupulous stockbroker. Churning refers to repeated, excessive, and unnecessary buying and selling of stock. In one case, a broker for Drexel, Burnham, Lambert pleaded guilty to bilking elderly clients out of $570,000 in fees.[23] The broker covered up the crime by diverting the clients' brokerage statements to a post office box and mailing out false statements.

Individual Exploitation of Institutional Position

The third type of white-collar crime involves individuals' exploiting their power or position in organizations to take advantage of other individuals who have an interest in how that power is used. For example, a fire inspector who demands that the owner of a restaurant pay him or her in order to be granted an operating license is abusing his or her institutional position. In most cases, this type of offense occurs when the victim has a clear right to expect a service and the offender uses his or her power to ask for an additional payment or bribe.

Exploitation in Government. U.S. political and governmental figures have long been accused of using their positions to profit from bribes and kickbacks.[24] As early as the 1830s, New York's political leaders used their position to control and profit from the city's police force. In the early nineteenth century, New York City's police chief, George Matsell, was the subject of numerous charges of bribe taking and profiteering. Though no evidence of his wrongdoing was ever proven in court, it was revealed five years after he retired in 1851 that Matsell had "saved" enough on his modest salary to build a 20-room mansion on a 3,000-acre estate.

During the Civil War, corruption increased proportionately with the amount of money being spent on the war effort. After the war, the nation's largest cities were controlled by political machines that used their offices to buy and sell political favors. The most notorious of these corrupt politicians was William Marcy "Boss" Tweed, who ruled New York City's Democratic party (Tammany Hall) from 1857 to 1871. During Tweed's reign, every company doing business with the city had to give kickbacks. Crime flourished under the protection of Tweed's Tammany Hall political allies. Within three miles of city hall, 400 brothels employing 4,000 prostitutes survived by paying protection money directly to city officials.[25] Time and anticorruption campaigns eventually caught up with Tweed, and he died in jail.[26]

The use of political office for economic gain has not subsided. It is common for scandals to emerge naming liquor license board members, food inspectors, and fire inspectors as bribe takers. It is not unusual for building inspectors to expect a payoff in return for approving a construction project. One survey of New York City workers who had contact with the building and construction trade found that all who responded to the survey either had been personally involved with corruption or had heard of its existence.[27] One of the most pervasive examples of exploitation was uncovered in 1988, when senior officials at the Pentagon were found to have received hundred of thousands in bribes in order to secure contracts for military manufacturers. The corruption is thought to be so pervasive that the military is currently finding it hard to locate sufficient replacement manufacturers who are not involved in the scandal.[28]

Exploitation in Business.   Exploitation also occurs in private industry. It is common for purchasing agents in large industries to demand a piece of the action for awarding contracts to suppliers and distributors. Marshall Clinard and Peter Yeager report on many cases, such as the one involving a J. C. Penney's employee who received $1.4 million from a contractor. The contractor eventually did $23 million of business with the firm.[29] In another case, a purchasing agent for

Former White House political director Lyn Nofziger following his conviction for illegal lobbying.

the American Chiclets division of Warner-Lambert received a $300,000 kickback from the makers of the wire racks used to display the gum products in supermarkets.

In sum, exploitation in the business world involves using one's position to secure illegal payments and profits. For many Americans, this has become an accepted way of life.

Illegal lobbying.   One type of exploitation which bridges the gap between government and business is illegal **lobbying** efforts by former government officials to secure favored treatment for their clients. In 1988, two prominent Reagan administration officials, Lyn Nofziger and Michael Deaver, were both found guilty of using their former positions to illegally lobby government officials; Nofziger received a 90-day prison sentence under federal laws making it a crime for former executive branch officials to lobby their former colleagues within a year of leaving office. Congress, whose former members presently are exempt from control, is considering laws restricting the lobbying of former lawmakers.[30]

Illegal lobbying efforts are attractive because they can produce billions in federal subsidies for clients, and fees run in the hundreds of thousands. For example, in 1988 a congressional investigation began on the activities of the International Medical Centers (IMC), formerly the nation's largest health maintenance organization (HMO). The IMC is believed to have hired numerous former federal officials in an effort to subvert normal government procedures designed to regulate Medicare beneficiaries; IMC officials are accused of defrauding the government of millions for poor or nonexistent medical care.[31]

Embezzlement and Employee Fraud

The fourth type of white-collar crime involves individuals' use of their positions to embezzle company funds or appropriate company property for themselves. Here, the company or organization that employs the criminal, rather than an outsider, is the victim of white-collar crime.

Employee theft can reach all levels of the organizational structure. One significant problem has been widespread theft of company property or profits by employees, commonly called **pilferage.** It is difficult to determine the value of goods taken by employees, but it has been estimated that pilferage accounts for 30 to 75 percent of all shrinkage and amounts to losses of $5 to $10 billion annually.[32]

The techniques of employee theft are quite varied. Charles McCaghy reported numerous methods used to steal from employers; including:

• Piece workers zip completed garments into their clothing and take them home.

• Cashiers ring up lower prices on single-item purchases and pocket the difference. Some work with an accomplice and ring up lower prices as the accomplice goes through the line.

• Clerks do not tag sale merchandise and then sell the merchandise at its original cost, pocketing the difference.

• Receiving clerks obtain duplicate keys to storage facilities and then return after-hours to steal.

• Truck drivers make fictitious purchases of fuel and repairs and then split the gains with truck stop owners. Truckers also have been known to cooperate with the receiving staff of department stores to cheat employers. In one instance, truckers would keep 20 cases of goods out of every 100 delivered. The store receiving staff would sign a bill of lading for all 100, and the two groups would split the profits after the stolen goods were sold to a fence.

• Some employees simply hide items in garbage pails, incinerators, or under trash heaps until they can be retrieved later.[33]

In their study of workplace theft, John Clark and Richard Hollinger found that about 35 percent of employees reported involvement in pilferage.[34] Clark and Hollinger's data indicate that employee theft is most accurately explained by factors relevant to the work setting, such as job dissatisfaction and the workers' feeling that they were being exploited by employers or supervisors. In contrast, economic problems played a relatively small role in the decision to pilfer. Even though economic and community variables can help explain street crime, they have relatively little effect on employee crime.

Management Fraud.   Blue-collar workers are not the only employees who commit corporate theft. Management-level fraud is also quite common. Such acts include: (1) converting company assets for personal benefit; (2) fraudulently receiving increases in compensation (such as raises or bonuses); (3) fraudulently increasing personal holdings of company stock; (4) retaining one's present position within the company by manipulating accounts; and (5) concealing unacceptable performance from stockholders.[35]

A well-publicized example of corporate theft by management involved the Bronx-based defense contractor, the Wedtech Corporation. Wedtech officials used fraudulent accounting methods to list contracts in their financial reports which the company did not receive, and they counted profits for work before they were actually accrued. Their efforts helped the company sell $160 million in bonds and stocks to unsuspecting investors. A government investigation in 1987 resulted in guilty pleas by company officials to fraud and bribery charges.[36] Further investigations implicated prominent government officials including Mario Biaggi, congressman from New York, who was convicted of soliciting bribes in order to obtain special government support for Wedtech.[37]

Computer Crime.   Computer-related thefts are a new trend in employee theft and embezzlement. The widespread use of computers to records business transactions has encouraged some people to use them for illegal purposes. Computer crimes generally fall into one of four categories: (1) theft of services, in which the criminal uses the computer for unauthorized purposes or an unauthorized user penetrates the computer system; (2) use of data in a computer system for personal gain; (3) unauthorized use of computers employed for various types of financial processing to obtain assets; and (4) theft of property by computer for personal use or conversion to profit.[38] In addition, it has become commonplace to insert **"virus" programs** into computer systems. These are programs which actually attack and destroy existing software. The "virus" may be installed as a purely malicious act or as part of an extortion scheme, in which a company is threatened with a "virus" unless it pays off the rogue programmer.

Several common techniques are used by computer criminals. In fact, computer theft has become so common that experts have created their own jargon to describe theft styles and methods:

- *The trojan horse*—One computer is used to reprogram another for illicit purposes. In one incident, two high-school-age computer users reprogrammed the computer at DePaul University, preventing that institution from using its own processing facilities. The youths were convicted of a misdemeanor.

- *The salami slice*—An employee sets up a dummy account in the company's computerized records. A small amount—even a few pennies—is subtracted from customers' accounts and added to the account of the thief. Even if they detect the loss, the customers don't complain, since a few cents is an insignificant amount to them. The pennies picked up here and there eventually amount to thousands of dollars in losses.

- *Super-zapping*—Most computer programs used in business have built-in antitheft safeguards. However, employees can use a repair or maintenance program to supersede the antitheft program. Some tinkering with the program is required, but the

"super-zapper" is soon able to order the system to issue checks to his or her private account.

- *The logic bomb*—A program is secretly attached to the company's computer system. The new program monitors the company's work and waits for a sign of error to appear, some illogic that was designed for the computer to follow. Illogic causes the logic bomb to kick into action and exploit the weakness. The way the thief exploits the situation depends on his or her original intent—theft of money, theft of defense secrets, sabotage, and so on.

- *Impersonation*—An unauthorized person uses the identity of an authorized computer user.

- *Data leakage*—A person illegally obtains data from a computer system by leaking it out in small amounts.

Several well-publicized cases have involved computer theft. A federal grand jury indicted a boxing promoter and two bank officials on charges of embezzling more than $21 million by computer from the Wells Fargo Bank. The bank officials knew how to submit false credits and debits to the computer in time to prevent the bank's internal security system from detecting the fraud. In a similar case, Jerry Schneider, an employee of Pacific Telephone and Telegraph, gained access to the company's computers and authorized them to make daily deliveries of equipment to a warehouse he rented.[39] After he had stolen $1 million worth of telephone parts, his crimes were detected; Schneider was sentenced to 60 days in jail. Upon his release, he was hired as a computer security consultant.

An accurate accounting of computer crime will probably never be made, since so many offenses go unreported. One computer consultant, Robert H. Courtney, claims that the likelihood of prosecution is inversely proportional to the amount of money involved: "The bigger the theft, the greater the embarrassment to the company." Though one of Courtney's clients, an insurance company, lost $38.1 million to a senior officer, management refused to report the crime to police lest they display their managerial incompetence to stockholders and competitors.[40]

It is likely that computer-related crime will blossom as business becomes more computer-dependent. For example, such recent advances as automatic bank teller machines have been a source of illegal gain. Bank employees have used returned or unused bank cards to make withdrawals after electronically transferring funds to nonexistent accounts. Similarly, computer culprits have benefited from the increased use of computerized phone networks like Sprint and MCI; in California, "hackers" made $60,000 worth of illegal charges on the Sprint account of a man whose access number they obtained.[41] Thus, as computer applications become more varied, so too will the use of computers for illegal purposes.

The growth of computer-related crimes prompted Congress to enact the Counterfeit Active Device and Computer Fraud and Abuse Act in 1984. This statute makes it a felony for a person to use illegal entry to a computer to make a gain of $5,000, or cause another to incur a loss of $5,000, or to access data affecting the national interest. Violation of this act can bring up to 10 years in prison and a $10,000 fine. Repeat offenders can receive 20-year prison sentences and $100,000 fines.[42]

Client Frauds

The fifth component of white-collar crime is theft by an economic client from an organization that advances credit to its clients. Included in this category are insurance fraud, credit card fraud, fraud related to welfare and Medicare programs, and tax evasion. These offenses are linked together because they involve theft from organizations that have many individual clients, who may take advantage of their positions of trust to steal from the organizations.

For example, some physicians have been caught cheating the federal government out of Medicare or Medicaid payments. Abusive practices include such techniques as "ping-ponging" (referring patients to other physicians in the same office), "gang visits" (billing for multiple services), and "steering" (directing patients to particular pharmacies). Doctors who abuse their Medicaid/Medicare patients in this way are liable to civil suit.[43]

Of a more serious nature are fraudulent acts designed to cheat both the government and the consumer. Such Medicaid frauds generally involve billing for services not actually rendered, billing in excessive amounts, setting up kickback schemes, and providing false identification on reimbursement forms. Doctors involved in these schemes are liable to criminal prosecution under federal and state law.[44] It has been

estimated that between 10 and 25 percent of the $100 billion spent on federal health care is lost to fraudulent practices.[45]

Despite the magnitude of this abuse, the state and federal governments have been reluctant to prosecute Medicaid fraud. A year long study of enforcement practices in 18 states uncovered no convictions for Medicaid abuse, and the national average over a seven-year period was found to be 1.5 convictions per state per year. One trend has been to establish Medicaid fraud investigation units. The 30 states that have employed such measures have already disallowed $86.5 million in faulty Medicaid bills.[46]

Tax Evasion.   An important aspect of client fraud is tax evasion. This is a particularly challenging area for criminological study, since (1) so many U.S. citizens regularly underreport their income, and (2) it is often difficult to separate honest error from deliberate tax evasion.

The basic law on tax evasion is contained in the Federal Internal Revenue Code, section 7201, which states:

Any person who willfully attempts in any manner to evade or defeat any tax imposed by this title or the payment thereof shall, in addition to other penalties provided by law, be guilty of a felony and, upon conviction thereof, shall be fined not more than $10,000 or imprisoned not more than five years, or both, together with the costs of prosecution.

To prove tax fraud, the government must find that the taxpayer either underreported his or her income or did not report taxable income. No minimum dollar amount of fraud must exist before the government takes action. Theoretically, a person can be prosecuted for underreporting even one dollar. In practice, the government usually takes legal action when there is a "substantial underpayment of tax" and when the evader either deposits unreported money in a bank or spends it.

A second element of tax fraud is "willfulness" on the part of the tax evader. In the major case on this issue, willfulness was defined as a "voluntary, intentional violation of a known legal duty and not the careless disregard for the truth."[47]

Finally, to prove tax fraud, the government must show that the taxpayer has purposely attempted to evade or defeat a tax payment. If the offender is guilty of *passive neglect*, the offense is a misdemeanor. Passive neglect simply means not paying taxes, not reporting income, or not paying taxes when due. On the other hand, affirmative tax evasion, such as keeping double books, making false entries, destroying books or records, concealing assets, or covering up sources of income, constitutes a felony.

Tax evasion is a difficult crime to prosecute. Since legal tax avoidance is a favorite U.S. pastime, it is often difficult to prove the difference between the careless, unintentional nonreporting of income and fraud. The line between legal and fraudulent behavior is often so fine that many people are willing to step over it. In fact, it has been estimated that the "underground economy" may amount to about 33 percent of the nation's production; working under the table and off the books ranges from moonlighting construction workers to "gypsy" cabdrivers (there are an estimated 21,000 gypsy cabs in New York City alone, twice the number of legal ones).[48] The Internal Revenue Service estimates that more than $100 billion in taxes goes uncollected each year because individuals failed to report all their income; nearly a third of that amount was from self-employed workers, including professionals, laborers, and door-to-door salespeople.[49]

The IRS may be losing its battle against tax cheats. The number of audits it conducts is actually declining. In 1960 it audited 5 percent of all returns; today the number is less than 2 percent.[50] Nonetheless, as Steven Klepper and Daniel Nagin have found, those people who do report their income are relatively accurate in their estimations and are deterred by the fear of IRS sanctions, even if the chance of detection is relatively insignificant.[51]

Influence Peddling and Bribery

The sixth component of white-collar crime involves the situation in which an individual with an important institutional position sells power, influence, and information to outsiders who have an interest in reinfluencing or predicting the activities of the institution. Offenses within this category include government employees taking kickbacks from contractors in return for awarding them contracts they could not have won on merit; or outsiders bribing government officials, such as those in the Securities and Exchange Commission, who might sell information about future government activities.

One major difference distinguishes influence peddling from the previously discussed exploitation of an institutional position. Exploitation involves forcing victims to pay for services to which they have a clear right. In contrast, influence peddlers and bribe takers use their institutional positions to grant favors and sell information which their co-conspirators are not entitled to. Thus, in crimes of institutional exploitation, the victim is the person forced to pay, whereas the victim of influence peddling is the organization compromised by its own employees for their personal interests.

Influence Peddling in Government. The seriousness of bribery was dramatically brought home to U.S. citizens by the ABSCAM case. Here, FBI agents, working with a convicted swindler, Melvin Weinberg, posed as wealthy Arabs looking for favorable treatment from high-ranking politicians. The agents said they wished to obtain U.S. citizenship and receive favorable treatment in business ventures. Several office holders were indicted, including U.S. Senator Harrison Williams from New Jersey.[52] Senator Williams was convicted of accepting an interest in an Arab-backed mining venture in return for promising to use his influence to obtain government contracts. The senator also promised to use his influence to help the "Arab sheik" enter and stay in the United States. At Williams's trail, the prosecution played tapes showing Williams meeting with federal undercover agents, boasting of his influence in the government, and saying he could "with great pleasure talk to the President of the United States" about the business venture; a later tape showed the senator promising to seek immigration help for the bogus sheik and agreeing to take part in the mining operation.

It also has been common for police officers to be accused of using their positions of power to coerce citizens into making payoffs. The best-known instance of police corruption was brought to light when a former New York mayor, John Lindsay, appointed a commission under the direction of Judge Whitman Knapp to investigate allegations of police corruption. The **Knapp Commission** found that police corruption was widespread, ranging from patrol officers' accepting small gratuities from local business people to senior officers' receiving payoffs in the thousands from gamblers and narcotics violators.[53]

The Commission found that construction firms made payoffs to have police ignore violations of city ordinances such as double parking, obstruction of sidewalks, and noise pollution. Bar owners paid police to allow them to operate after hours or to give free reign to the prostitutes, drug pushers, and gamblers operating on their premises. Drug dealers allowed police to keep money and narcotics confiscated during raids in return for their freedom. Police also gave confiscated narcotics to informers for their own use or sale to others. Gamblers made regular payoffs to keep their operations going. The average individual share was $400 to $1,500 per month.

The Knapp Commission Report and other public scandals have not deterred incidents of government agents' exploiting their positions for gain. More recently, federal prosecutors mounted **Operation Greylord** to expose corruption in the Cook County (Illinois) court system. They uncovered examples of judges selling favors to corrupt attorneys for up to $50,000 in under-the-table payments; one culprit received a 15-year sentence.[54]

In 1988, another case of government influence peddling made national headlines. Senior Pentagon officials were accused of receiving bribes from defense consultants and manufacturers in return for providing classified documents. The documents contained information on competitive bids, designs, and other items which would give suppliers an edge in securing government contracts. Contracts worth more than one billion dollars were suspended until the legitimacy of their award could be determined. The scandal, which is still under investigation, involves some of the largest defense contractors in the United States, including Raytheon, Unysis, and Lockheed.[55]

In addition to personal gain, influence peddling can also involve securing a favored position for one's political party or interest group. In one recent incident, New York Senate Democratic leader Manfred Ohrenstein and State Senator Howard Babush were indicted on grounds of misappropriating $500,000 of state funds in order to rig state elections and allow the Democratic party to control the state Senate. According to the charges filed against them, the two used public money to hire political workers who campaigned for democratic candidates and covered their tracks with false filings and documents.[56]

Influence Peddling in Business.   Politicians are not the only ones accused of bribery; business has had its share of scandals. In the 1970s, revelations were made that multinational corporations regularly made payoffs to foreign officials and businesspeople in order to secure business contracts. Gulf Oil executives admitted paying $4 million to the South Korean ruling party; Burroughs Corporation admitted paying $1.5 million to foreign officials; Lockheed Aircraft admitted paying $202 million. In a more recent case, McDonnell-Douglas Aircraft Corporation was indicted for paying $1 million in bribes to officials of Pakistani International Airlines in order to secure orders.[57] In 1984 the Justice Department began an investigation of the Bechtel Corporation's alleged bribing of South Korean officials.[58]

To counter such incidents, Congress in 1977 passed the Foreign Corrupt Practices Act (FCPA), which makes it a criminal offense to pay bribes to foreign officials or make other questionable overseas payments. Violations of the FCPA draw strict penalties for both the defendant company and its officers.[59] Moreover, all fines imposed on corporate officers are paid by them and not absorbed by the company. For example, for violation of the antibribery provisions of the FCPA, a domestic corporation can be fined up to $1 million. Moreover, company officers, employees, or stockholders who are convicted of bribery may have to serve a prison sentence of up to five years and pay a $10,000 fine. Congressional dissatisfaction with the harshness and ambiguity of the bill has caused numerous revisions to be considered; these revisions are currently being reviewed by Congress.

Despite the penalties imposed by the FCPA, corporations that deal in foreign trade have continued to give bribes to secure favorable trade agreements.[60] They have come up with a variety of schemes to defeat the federal law. One way is to join with a foreign company that is not controlled by U.S. law and let it negotiate the contracts.

The typical bribery case involves a large project in an industry made up of highly competitive companies whose products differ little from one another. The large amounts of money involved allow the parties to hide the payoffs in the price without drawing the attention of auditors. The likelihood of bribery is also usually affected by the number of competitors—the greater the competition, the more likely bribery will occur. These conditions are most likely to be found in the sale of telecommunications equipment, aircraft, and large-scale construction work. For example, it has been reported that leading European electric companies paid as much as $140 million in payoffs and kickbacks to win shares of the construction of a $10 billion dam built jointly by Brazil and Paraguay.[61]

Not surprisingly, U.S. businesses have complained that stiff penalties for bribery give foreign competitors the edge over domestic corporations. In European countries such as Italy and France, giving bribes to secure contracts is perfectly legal; and in West Germany, bribes are actually tax-deductible Consequently, it is possible that any future changes in the FCPA will decriminalize some forms of bribery.[62]

Securities fraud.   Another twist on the exploitation of a business position involves using deceptive practices to buy and sell shares in publicly traded companies. The federal securities laws which control trading in public companies can be found in a number of different statutes, but the two primary sources are the **Securities Act of 1933** and the **Securities and Exchange Act of 1934.**[63] These acts prohibit the use of manipulative or deceptive devices, such as mail and wire fraud, making false statements in order to increase market share, conspiracy, and similar acts of unfair market practices. The federal watchdog agency, the **Securities and Exchange Commission (SEC),** has within its code Rule 10b-5, which articulates general antifraud provisions for security trading:

> It shall be unlawful for any person directly or indirectly, by the use of any means or instrumentality of interstate commerce, or of the mails or of any facility of any national securities exchange,
>
> (a) To employ any device, scheme, or artifice to defraud,
>
> (b) To make any untrue statement of a material fact or to omit to state a material fact necessary in order to make the statements made, in light of the circumstances under which they were made, not misleading, or
>
> (c) To engage in any act, practice, or course of business which operates or would operate as a fraud or deceit upon any person, in connection with the purchase of sale of any security.[64]

One type of security fraud which has received recent national attention is **insider trading.** Traditionally, this crime occurs when a corporate employee with direct knowledge of market-sensitive information uses that information for his or her own benefit.[65] In recent years, the definition of insider trading has been expanded by federal courts to include employees of financial institutions, such as law or banking firms, who misappropriate confidential information on pending corporate actions to purchase stock, or who give the information to a third party so he or she may buy shares in the company. Courts have ruled that such actions are deceptive and in violation of security trading codes.[66]

Interpretations of what constitutes insider trading vary widely. To many, the "hot tip" is the bread and butter of stock market speculators, and the point when a tip becomes a criminal act is often fuzzy. For example, in one celebrated case, R. Foster Winans, the writer of the *Wall Street Journal's* influential "Heard on the Street" column, was convicted on misappropriation of information charges after he wrote favorably about stocks purchased previously by a co-conspirator and then sold for profits in which the writer shared.[67] In a landmark decision, the U.S. Supreme Court upheld the conviction of Winans and his co-conspirators on the grounds that their actions fraudulently deprived Winan's employer (the *Wall Street Journal*) of its "property," the information contained in his column; their actions also amounted to a "scheme to defraud" under the Securities and Exchange Act.[68] The *Winans* case is important because it signifies that insider trading can occur even if the offender is neither an employee nor has a fiduciary interest (such as the companies' outside accountants would have) in a company whose stock is traded; the Court also found that there need not be a "victim" who loses tangible property for the crime to take place.

The events described in the accompanying Close-Up involve the most famous insider trading case so far, the Boesky case.

Corporate Crime

The final component of white-collar crime involves situations in which powerful institutions or their representatives wilfully violate the laws that restrain these institutions from doing social harm or require them to

CLOSE-UP

Insider Trading

When government investigators received information that Dennis Levine, a 34-year-old managing director of the prestigious Wall Street firm Drexel, Burnham, Lambert, had been using confidential information on pending mergers to secretly buy stock and profit in the millions, they may not have realized how deep into the backrooms of Wall Street their investigation would take them However, under the pressure of indictment, Levine implicated others in his security fraud schemes—including Ivan Boesky one of the most prominent **arbitrage** experts in the United States. Arbitragers speculate on the stock of companies which are rumored to be takeover targets by other firms; they hope to make a profit on the difference between current stock prices and the price the acquiring company is willing to pay.

Levine fed Boesky inside information on such deals as the merger negotiations between International Telephone and Telegraph and Sperry Corp., Coastal Corp.'s takeover of American Natural Resources, and the leveraged buyout of McGraw Edison. Possession of this information allowed Boesky to profit in the millions. Levine's guilty plea earned him a two-year prison sentence and $362,000 fine. He also settled a civil suit with the SEC for $11.6 million.

Aware of the information provided by Levine, and facing a long jail sentence, Boesky implicated others who had provided him with inside information. In return for his cooperation, Boesky received a three-year prison sentence.

One of the saddest falls from grace was that of Martin Siegel, a prominent investment banker who had begun to provide Boesky with inside information for cash payments when he was with the investment firm of Kidder, Peabody. For example, in 1984 he told Boesky that Carnation Corp. most likely would be sold; Boesky made $28.3 million on that deal alone. Among other penalties, Siegel's guilty plea to security law violation cost him a $9 million fine and loss of salary and bonuses of $11 million. Others questioned in the Boesky investigation were Robert Freeman, head of Goldman, Sachs and Co.'s arbitrage trading unit; Richard Wigton of Kidder, Peabody; and Timothy Tabor of Kidder, Peabody, and of Merrill Lynch.

The Levine-Boesky investigation rocked Wall Street. Political leaders such as William Proxmire, chairman of the Senate Banking Committee, began a congressional investigation into Wall Street practices with the aim of drafting

Martin Siegel pled guilty to insider trading in the Boesky investigation.

legislation to slow the pace of takeovers, curtail manipulative and deceptive practices, and regulate arbitrators. State legislators began passing rule changes which barred takeovers of critical state industries by outsiders. There seems to be little question that the insider trading scandal may help control illegal trading practices on Wall Street.

Discussion Questions

1. Would long prison sentences help to deter this type of economic crime?

2. Are stock market manipulators "real criminals" or people who have learned to play the "success game" better than their rivals?

SOURCES: James Stewart and Daniel Hertzberg, "The Wall Street Career of Martin Siegel Was a Dream Gone Wrong," *Wall Street Journal* (17 February 1987), p. 1; Tim Metz and Michael Miller, "Boesky's Rise and Fall Illustrate a Compulsion to Profit by Getting Inside Track on Market," *Wall Street Journal* (17 November 1986), p. 28.

do social good. This is also known as **corporate** or **organizational crime.**

Corporate crime is probably what Sutherland had in mind when he coined the term *white-collar crime.* These illegal acts are committed by the wealthy and powerful to further their business interests. They include such acts as price-fixing and illegal restraint of trade, false advertising, and the use of company practices that violate environmental protection statutes. The variety of crimes contained within this category is great, and the damage they cause vast. The following subsections examine some of the most important offenses.

Illegal Restraint of Trade and Price-Fixing. A restraint of trade involves a contract or conspiracy designed to stifle competition, create a monopoly, artificially maintain prices, or otherwise interfere with free-market competition.

The control of restraint of trade violations has its legal basis in the **Sherman Antitrust Act.** For violations of its provisions, this federal law created criminal penalties of up to three years imprisonment and up to $100,000 in fines for individuals and $1 million in fines for corporations.[69]

The Sherman Antitrust Act outlaws conspiracies between corporations designed to control the marketplace. In most instances, the act leaves to the presiding court's judgment the determination of whether corporations have conspired to "unreasonably restrain competition." However, four types of market conditions are considered so inherently anticompetitive that federal courts, through the Sherman Antitrust Act, have defined them as illegal per se, without regard to the facts or circumstances of the case. The first is *division of markets;* here, firms divide a region into territories, and each firm agrees not to compete in the others' territories.[70] The second is the *tying arrangement,* in which a corporation requires customers of one of its services to use other services it offers. For example, in the case of *Northern Pacific Railway Co. vs. United States,* a federal court ruled that the railroad's requirement that all tenants of its land use the railroad to ship all goods produced on the land was an illegal restraint of trade.[71]

A third type of absolute Sherman Act violation is the *group boycott,* in which an organization or company boycotts retail stores that do not comply with its rules or desires.

Finally, *price-fixing*—a conspiracy to set and control the price of a necessary commodity—is considered an absolute violation of the act. Of all criminal violations associated with restraint of trade, none, perhaps, is as important as price-fixing.

Michael Maltz and Stephen Pollack have described the four forms that price-fixing usually takes.[72] The first is *predation,* in which large firms agree among themselves to bid below market prices to drive out weaker firms. The goal is to reduce competition and permit the remaining firms to raise their prices with relative impunity.

A second price-fixing scheme is *identical bidding.* Here, all competitors agree to submit identical bids for each contract, although they may vary bids from contract to contract. The price is well above what would have been expected if collusion had not occurred. Purchasing agents use their discretion to choose among bidders. However, identical bidding usually assures all vendors of getting a share of the marketplace without losing any profitability.

Geographical market sharing (when price-fixing) involves dividing the potential market into territories within which only one member of the conspiring group is permitted a low bid. The remaining conspirators either refrain from bidding or give artificially high bids.

Rotational bidding involves a price-fixing conspiracy in which the opportunity to submit a winning bid for a government or business contract is rotated among the institutional bidders. The conspirators meet in advance and determine who will give the low bid. The winning bid is, of course, higher than it should be, since the losers have all submitted abnormally high bids. Close coordination among the bidders is essential; therefore, these schemes usually involve only a few large firms.

Despite enforcement efforts, restraint-of-trade conspiracies are quite common. The best-known case involved some of the largest members of the electrical equipment industry.[73] In 1961, 21 corporations, including industry leaders Westinghouse and General Electric, were successfully prosecuted; 45 executives were found guilty of criminal violations of the Sherman Antitrust Act. Company executives met secretly—they referred to their meetings as "choir practice"—and arranged the setting of prices on sales of equipment, the allocation of markets and territories, and the rigging of bids. At the sentencing, fines amounting to $1,924,500 were levied against the defendants, including fines of $437,500 against General Electric and $372,500 against Westinghouse. Although these fines meant little to the giant corporations, subsequent civil suits cost General Electric $160 million. Even more significant was that seven defendants, all high-ranking executives, were sentenced to jail terms.

In subsequent cases, American Cyanamid, Charles Pfizer, and Bristol Myers, all pharmaceutical companies, were convicted of price-fixing and monopolistic practices. In the case of one drug produced by the firms, tetracycline, the government found that the conspirators had guaranteed themselves a markup of 3,350 percent. In another case, American Standard and 14 other firms were found guilty of conspiring to set artificially high prices in the billion-dollar-a-year plumbing fixture market.[74] And, in California, the state brought action against seven major oil firms—including Mobil, Arco, and Shell—to recover $256 million they underpaid the government for crude oil taken from public lands.[75]

It is common for even the largest American corporations to use *deceptive pricing* schemes when they respond to contract solicitations. Deceptive pricing occurs when contractors provide the government or other corporations with incomplete or misleading information on how much it will actually cost to fulfill the contract they are bidding on, or when companies mischarge once the contracts are signed.[76] For example, defense contractors have been prosecuted for charging the government for costs actually incurred on work they are doing for private firms or shifting the costs on fixed-price contracts to ones in which the government reimburses the contractor for all expenses ("cost-plus" contracts).

One well-known example of deceptive pricing occurred when the Lockheed Corp. withheld information that its wage costs would be lower than expected on the C-5 cargo plane. The resulting overcharges were an estimated $150 million. Though the government was able to negotiate a cheaper price for future C-5 orders, it did not demand repayment on the earlier contract.

The government prosecutes approximately 100 cases of deceptive pricing in defense work each year involving 59 percent of the nation's largest contractors.[77]

False Claims and Advertising.   Executives in even the largest corporations are sometimes caught in the position in which stockholders' expectations of ever-increasing company profits seem to demand that sales be increased at any cost. At times, executives respond to this challenge by making claims about their product that cannot be justified by its actual performance. However, the line between clever, aggressive sales techniques and fraudulent claims is a fine one. It is traditional to show a product in its best light, even if that involves resorting to fantasy. Thus, it is not fraudulent to show a crown suddenly appearing on the head of a person eating a certain brand of margarine, nor is it fraudulent to imply that taking one sip of iced tea will make people feel they have just jumped into a swimming pool. However, it is illegal to knowingly and purposely advertise a product as possessing qualities that the manufacturer realizes it does not have.

Charges stemming from false and misleading claims have been common in several U.S. industries. For example, the Federal Trade Commission reviewed and disallowed advertising by the three major U.S. car companies; the advertising alleged that new cars got higher gas mileage than buyers actually could expect.

In the pharmaceutical industry, false advertising has a long history. It has been common for medicines to be advertised as cure-alls for previously incurable diseases. Such medicines include alleged cures for cancer and arthritis and drugs advertised to give energy and sexual potency. The Warner-Lambert Drug Company was prohibited from claiming that Listerine mouthwash could prevent or cure colds. Sterling Drug was prohibited from claiming that Lysol disinfectant killed germs associated with colds and flu. An administrative judge ruled that the American Home Products Company falsely advertised Anacin as a tension reliever. The list seems to go on endlessly.[78]

How can we explain the frequency of false advertising by drug manufacturers? Often the problem arises because several competing companies market similar products, and the key to successful sales is believed to be convincing the public that one of these products is far superior to the rest. Sometimes the intense drive for profits leads to falsification of data and unethical and illegal sales promotions. For example, when the Richardson-Merrill pharmaceutical company launched a highly aggressive campaign for an anticholesterol drug, Mer-29, it downplayed efforts to warn the public about the drug's harmful side effects, such as sexual dysfunction, loss of hair, and development of eye cataracts.[79] Even after the company learned of these problems, it issued a memorandum to its salespeople warning them to avoid mentioning the problems. When warnings were finally issued, their purpose was to protect the company against damage suits rather than to aid customers. Eventually, permission to market the drug was withdrawn by the Food and Drug Administration. Though no criminal charges were filed, one commentator has stated: "Here we see a company in a highly competitive and highly profitable industry resorting to unethical and probably illegal tactics to sell its products."[80]

The Merrill-Richardson case is certainly not the end of such matters. In 1984 the Smith Kline Beckman Corp. pleaded guilty to failing to make timely reports on a drug, Selacryn, which was linked to 25 deaths before being removed from the market. Despite the legal action in U.S. courts, the drug continues to be sold in France.[81]

It has been difficult for authorities to police such violations of the public trust. Often, the most serious consequence to the corporation is an order that it refrain from using the advertising or withdraw the advertising claims. Criminal penalties for false claims are rarely given. However, the offending parties can be sued civilly by their competitors for loss of revenue. In one case, U-Haul received a $40 million judgment against Jartran, a rival truck rental outfit, when the latter company's ad campaign photographically reduced a larger U-Haul truck so it looked the same size as a smaller Jartran truck.[82]

Environmental Crimes. Much attention has been called to the intentional or negligent environmental pollution caused by many large corporations. The numerous allegations in this area involve almost every aspect of U.S. business. This type of crime was brought to the forefront of public concern during the summer of 1988 when large amounts of medical wastes — syringes, blood samples, used bandages — which had been illegally dumped in the ocean washed up on beaches from Cape Cod to North Carolina.

There are many different types of environmental crimes. Some corporations have endangered the lives of their own workers by maintaining unsafe conditions in their plants and mines. It has been estimated that 21 million workers have been exposed to hazard-

ous materials while on the job. The National Institute of Occupational Safety and Health estimated that it would cost about $40 million just to alert these workers to the danger of their exposure to hazardous waste, and $54 billion to watch them and keep track of whether they developed occupationally related diseases.[83]

Some industries have been particularly hard-hit by complaints and allegations. The asbestos industry was the target of a flood of lawsuits after environmental scientists found a close association between exposure to asbestos and development of cancer. Over 250,000 people have filed 12,000 lawsuits against 260 asbestos manufacturers. In all, some insurance company officials estimate, asbestos-related lawsuits could amount to $120 to $150 billion. Similarly, some 100,000 cotton mill workers suffer from some form of respiratory disease linked to prolonged exposure to cotton dust. About one-third of the workers are seriously disabled by brown lung disease, an illness similar to emphysema.[84]

The control of workers' safety has been the province of the Occupational Safety and Health Administration (OSHA). OSHA provides industry standards for the proper use of such chemicals as benzene, arsenic, lead, and coke. Intentional violation of OSHA standards can eventually involve criminal penalties.

Environmental Pollution. A second type of environmental crime committed by large corporations is the illegal pollution of the environment. Sometimes pollution involves individual acts caused by negligence on the part of the polluter. For example, in 1981 a leak of the chemical hexane into the sewers of Louisville, Kentucky, caused three miles of that city's streets, sidewalks, and sewers to explode. The company responsible for the leak, Ralston-Purina, promptly paid the $62,000 fine for environmental pollution; however, the company still faced millions in damage charges.[85]

The most striking pollution case so far, albeit one that has not been decided by the courts, involves the leaking of methyl isocyanate from a Union Carbide plant in Bhopal, India, on December 3, 1984. Estimates of the death toll range from 1,400 to 10,000 people; another 60,000 were injured. Union Carbide later reported that the plant had not been operating safely and should have been closed. They blamed the negligence, however, on local officials who were running the plant in India. The Bhopal incident may prove to be one of the largest settlements in U.S. legal history.[86]

Equally serious is the prolonged, intentional pollution of the environment. A case in point is the illegal dumping of the substance polychlorinated biphenyl (PCB).[87] This compound has been used since 1929 in power transformers, electric typewriters, and electrical capacitators. However, scientists have linked PCB to cancer and birth defects in laboratory animals. In Japan, people who ate rice oil contaminated with PCB suffered a variety of health problems. Chemical companies have been ordered not to use PCB; however, a serious problem exists with regard to disposing of the chemical. The Environmental Protection Agency (EPA) estimates that 20 million pounds await disposal and that 750 million pounds must eventually be destroyed. Some chemical companies have dumped their PCB stocks along public highways and in remote, illegal dumpsites. In some areas, illegally dumped PCB has proven extremely hazardous. When it has been carelessly dropped in landfills, pits, and lagoons, PCB has contaminated waters, fish, and wildlife. Because of PCB contamination, fishing has been restricted in rivers in New York, Connecticut, Michigan, and other states.

The EPA has estimated that the cost of cleaning up the 1,500 to 2,500 hazardous waste dumpsites scattered around the United States ranges from $7.6 billion to $22.7 billion; their best overall estimate is $11.7 billion. Although the cleanup is expected to be supported by taxes on petrochemicals, which go into a "superfund," some experts believe that it is unrealistic to believe that private industry will pay for even half the costs.[88]

Controlling Environmental Pollution.   The nature and scope of environmental crimes have prompted the federal government to pass a series of control measures designed to outlaw the worst abuses. These measures are described below.

Clean Air Act (CAA).   The CAA provides sanctions for companies that do not comply with the air quality standards established by the EPA.[89] The CAA can impose penalties on any person or institution that, for example, knowingly violates EPA plan requirements or emission standards, tampers with EPA monitoring devices, or makes false statements to EPA officials.

Clean Water Act (CWA).   The CWA punishes the knowing or negligent discharge of a pollutant into navigable waters.[90] According to the CWA, a *pollutant* is any "man-made or man-induced alteration of the chemical, physical, biological, and radiological integrity of the water."

Rivers and Harbors Act of 1899 (Refuse Act).   The Refuse Act punishes any discharge of waste materials that damages natural water quality.[91]

Resource Conservation and Recovery Act of 1976 (RCRA).   The RCRA provides criminal penalties for four acts involving illegal treatment of solid wastes: (1) the knowing transportation of any hazardous waste to a facility that does not have a legal permit for solid waste disposal; (2) the knowing treatment, storage, or disposal of any hazardous waste without a government permit or in violation of the provision of the permit; (3) the deliberate making of any false statement or representation in a report filed in compliance with the RCRA; and (4) the destruction or alteration of records required to be maintained by the RCRA.[92]

Toxic Substance Control Act (TSCA).   The TSCA prohibits the following: manufacturing, processing, or distributing chemical mixtures or substances in a manner not in accordance with established testing or manufacturing requirements; commercial use of a chemical substance or mixture that the commercial user knew was manufactured, processed, or distributed in violation of TSCA requirements; and noncompliance with the reporting and inspection requirements of the TSCA.[93]

Considering the uncertainties of federal budget allocations, there is some question whether these acts can effectively deter environmental crime.

———— WHY DO THEY DO IT? ————

When Ivan Boesky plead guilty to one count of security fraud, he agreed to pay a civil fine of $100 million, the largest in SEC history. The fine wiped out his $50 million profit from insider trading and most of the rest of his fortune. How, people asked, could a person with so much disposable wealth get involved in a risky scheme to produce even more?

There probably are as many explanations for white-collar crime as there are white-collar crimes themselves. Herbert Edelhertz, an expert on the white-collar crime phenomenon, suggests that many offenders feel free to engage in business crime because they can easily rationalize its effects. Some convince themselves that their actions are not really crimes, because the acts involved do not resemble street crimes. For example, a banker who uses his position of trust to lend his institution's assets to a company he secretly controls may see himself as a shrewd businessman, not as a criminal. Or a pharmacist who chisels customers on prescription drugs may rationalize by telling herself her behavior doesn't really hurt anyone.

Further, some businesspeople feel justified in committing white-collar crimes because they believe that government regulators do not really understand the business world or the problems of competing in the free-enterprise system. Even when caught, many white-collar criminals cannot see the error of their ways. For example, one offender who was convicted in the electrical industry price-fixing conspiracy discussed earlier categorically denied the illegality of his actions. "We did not fix prices," he said, "I am telling you that all we did was recover costs."[94]

Some white-collar criminals believe that everyone violates business laws and that it therefore is not so bad if they do so themselves. The "everyone is doing it" rationale operates in such crimes as income tax evasion and bribe-taking by government employees. White-collar crimes are viewed as morally neutral.

Need also plays an important role in all levels of white-collar crime. Executives may tamper with company books because they feel the need to keep or improve their jobs, satisfy their egos, or support their children. Blue-collar workers may pilfer because they feel the need to keep pace with inflation or buy a new car. Even someone in the upper echelon of the financial world may carry scars from an earlier needy period which can only be healed by accumulating greater amounts of money. As one of Boesky's associates put it:

> I don't know what his devils were. Maybe he's greedy beyond the wildest imaginings of mere mortals like you and me. And maybe part of what drives the guy is an inherent insecurity that was operative here even after he had arrived. Maybe he never arrived.[95]

A well-known study of embezzlers, by Donald Cressey, illustrates the important role need plays in white-collar crime.[96] According to Cressey, embezzlement is caused by what he calls a "nonshareable financial problem." This condition may be the result of offenders' living beyond their means, perhaps piling up gambling debts; offenders feel they can't let anyone know about such financial problems without ruining their reputations. Cressey claims that the door to solving personal financial problems through criminal means is opened by the rationalizations society has developed for white-collar crime: "Some of our most respectable citizens get their start in life by using other people's money temporarily." In the real estate business, there is nothing wrong about using deposits before the deal is closed: "All people steal when they get in a tight spot."[97] Offenders make use of these and other rationalizations to resolve the conflict they experience over engaging in illegal behavior. Rationalizations allow offenders' financial needs to be met without compromising their values. In many ways, Cressey's concepts are similar to the techniques of neutralization discussed in Chapter 8.

Beyond personal need and greed, the structure of business organizations itself promotes white-collar criminality. Some managers, feeling the pressure of stockholders' demands, cut corners simply to keep their positions. Ronald Kramer argues that explanations of organizational or corporate crime involve three structural factors:

1. Business organizations as institutions committed to goal attainment will engage in criminal behavior if they encounter serious difficulties in attaining their goals, especially profits. In addition, product-goals play a role in the decision to violate rules, for example, when a car company tries to design a low-cost competitive model and sacrifices safety features.

2. The internal structure of an organization can also influence decisions to violate the law. Structure can have a significant influence on corporate goals. For example it can translate the overall quest for profit into subgoals, such as cost reductions, which foster criminality. In some organiza-

tions law-breaking and corner-cutting become norms which are passed on to employees: "This is the way things are done here; don't worry about it."

3. Organizational environment influences criminality. The economic, political, cultural, legal, technological, and interorganizational factors influence corporate behavior. For example, if market conditions are weak, competition intense, law enforcement lax, and the existing social norms stress success at any cost, the conditions for corporate crime are maximized.[98]

These explanations suggest that the underlying causes of large-scale white-collar crime may be subject to analysis using the traditional concepts of criminological theory. Such efforts are still being developed. The Close-Up entitled "Toward a Theory of White-Collar Crime" analyzes recent attempts to create a general theory of corporate criminal behavior.

X
——————— CONTROLLING ———————
WHITE-COLLAR CRIME

Conflict theorists are quick to point out that, unlike lower-class street criminals, white-collar criminals are rarely prosecuted; when convicted, they receive relatively light sentences. This claim is supported by studies of white-collar criminality that show it is rare for a corporate or white-collar criminal to receive a serious criminal penalty.[99] Paul Jesilow, Henry Pontell and Gilbert Geis found that physicians who engage in Medicaid fraud are rarely prosecuted and judges are reluctant to severely punish them. As one official told them, "When we convicted a guy I wanted to see him do hard time. But what the hell, seeing what's going on in prisons these days and things like that, I think to put one of these guys in prison for hard time doesn't make any sense . . . "[100]

Marshall Clinard and Peter Yeager's analysis of 477 corporations found that only one in 10 serious corporate violations and one in 20 moderate violations resulted in sanctions.[101] In a subsequent analysis, Yeager found that when white-collar statutes are enforced there is a tendency to penalize small, powerless businesses while treating the market leaders

more leniently.[102] There are a number of reasons for the leniency afforded white-collar criminals. Though white-collar criminals may produce millions of dollars of losses and endanger human life, some judges believe they are not "real criminals"—just business people trying to make a living.[103] As Clinard and Yeager report, businesspeople often seek legal advice and are well aware of the loopholes in the law. If caught, they can always claim that they had sought legal advice and believed they were in compliance with the law.[104]

White-collar criminals often are considered nondangerous offenders, usually respectable older citizens who have families to support. These "pillars of the community" are not seen in the same light as a teenager who breaks into a drugstore to steal a few dollars. Their public humiliation at being caught is usually deemed punishment enough; a prison sentence seems unnecessarily cruel. Judges and prosecutors may identify with the white-collar criminal based on shared background and world views; they may even have engaged in similar types of illegal behavior themselves.[105]

Still another factor complicating white-collar crime enforcement is that many legal business acts seem as morally tinged as those made illegal by government regulation. Consider **greenmail,** a common event in the 1980s. Here a speculator buys up stock in a company, threatening to take it over and replace management. To save their jobs, company executives eventually give in and repurchase the stock with company funds. Of course, the repurchase price is considerably higher than the speculator paid originally. One greenmail expert, T. Boone Picksen of Mesa Petroleum, made $900 million for his partners and himself between 1982 and 1985 using takeover tactics and threats.[106]

Despite its questionable ethics, greenmail is not a crime, but rather a clever business ploy that can have the potential for huge legitimate profits. Yet when it is compared to other business practices made illegal by government regulation, such as price-fixing, the distinctions are hard to see. It may seem unfair to prosecutors and judges to penalize some businessperson for actions not too dissimilar from those applauded in the *Wall Street Journal*. In the wake of the Boesky insider trading scandal, the *Journal* published an article in which experts, including at least one business school dean, expressed the belief that insider trading

CLOSE-UP

Toward a Theory of White-Collar Crime

Criminologists are beginning to evaluate white-collar criminality as they would any other crime pattern. A new integrated theory of white-collar crime, developed by Australian sociologist John Braithwaite, makes an important addition to this literature. In the tradition of social structure theory (Chapter 7), Braithwaite views white-collar crime as a product of the *corporate culture*.

According to Braithwaite's model, businesspeople in any society may find themselves in a situation where their organization's stated goals cannot be achieved through conventional business practices; in a sense, the upper-class executive perceives "blocked opportunities." In a capitalist society, the up-and-coming young executive may find that profit ratios are considered below par; in a socialist society, the young commissar may panic when production levels fall short of the five-year plan.

Perceiving "strain" the entrepreneur may find that illegitimate opportunities are the only solution to the problem; the career must be saved at all costs. When a government official is willing to take a bribe in order to overlook costly safety violations, the bribe is gratefully offered. Or when insider trading can increase profits, the investment banker leaps at the chance.

But how can traditionally law-abiding people overcome the ties of conventional law and morality? Braithwaite believes that organizational crime is a function of the existing corporate climate. Organizational crime flourishes in corporations which contain an ongoing employee subculture which resists government regulation and socializes new workers in the skills and attitudes necessary to violate the law. For example, junior executives may learn from their seniors how to meet clandestinely with their competitors in order to fix prices and how to rationalize this as good, necessary, or inevitable.

The existence of law-violating subcultures is enhanced when a hostile relationship exists between the organizations and the governmental bodies which regulate them. When the government is viewed as uncooperative, untrustworthy, and resistant to change, corporations will be more likely to develop clandestine law-violating subcultures. A positive working relationship with government regulators will reduce the need for a secret law-violating infrastructure.

Illegal corporate behavior can only exist in secrecy; public scrutiny brings the shame of a criminal label to people whose social life and community standing rests upon their good name and character. The shame of discovery has an important moderating influence on corporate crime. Its source may be external: the general com-

---

was a legitimate exercise of the free-market system and that the government should leave its regulation to corporations.[107]

Finally, some corporate practices which result in death or disfigurement are treated as civil actions in which victims receive monetary damages. The most well-known case involves the A. H. Robins Company. The company's Dalkon Shield IUD caused hundreds of thousands of women to undergo massive trauma including pelvic disease, infertility, and septic abortions, and is suspected in 20 deaths. The outcome of the case: the company underwent a bankruptcy proceeding and set up a multibillion dollar trust for the survivors.[108] A case such as the Dalkon Shield involves much more serious injury than insider trading but was not considered a criminal matter.

WHITE-COLLAR LAW ENFORCEMENT

White-collar crime activity is controlled by law enforcement agencies such as the FBI or regulatory agencies such as the Federal Communications Commission (FCC). In general, there are two types of enforcement strategies—**compliance** and **deterrence**—available to control organizational deviance.[109] Compliance aims for law conformity without the necessity of detecting, processing, or penalizing violators. Compliance systems attempt to create conformity by providing economic incentives, or by using administrative efforts to prevent unwanted conditions before they occur. The core violation in a compliance system is often referred to as a **technical violation.** For example, the Securities and Exchange Commission has a host of regulations, munity; professional or industry peers; government regulatory agencies. The source of shame and disapproval also can be internal. Many corporations have stated policies which firmly admonish employees to obey the law. For example, it is common for corporations to encourage whistle-blowing from coworkers and sanction workers who violate the law and cause embarrassment. These organizations are "full of antennas" to pick up irregularities and make it widely known that certain individuals or subunits are responsible for law violations. In a sense, corporations which maintain an excess of definitions unfavorable to violating the law will be less likely to contain deviant subcultures and concomitantly less likely to violate business regulations. In contrast, corporate crime thrives in organizations which isolate people within spheres of responsibility, where lines of communication are blocked or stretched thin, and in which deviant subcultures are allowed to develop.

Not all criminologists agree with the basic premises of Braithwaite's theory. Travis Hirschi and Michael Gottfredson take exception to the hypothesis that white-collar crime is a product of the corporate culture. If that were true, they argue, there would be much more white-collar crime than actually exists, and white-collar criminals would not be embarrassed by their misdeeds as most of them prove to be. Instead, Hirschi and Gottfredson maintain that the motives which produce white-collar crimes are based on rational choice: "the desire for relatively quick, relatively certain benefit, with minimal effort."

These two views represent the extremes of criminological thinking about white-collar crime, and for that matter about crime in general. Braithwaite's view portrays white-collar crime as a function of norms and values developed within a corporate subcultural environment. Hirschi and Gottfredson's view portrays white-collar crime as an act motivated by the rational choice of an offender who believes it will hold some particular advantage for him or her.

Discussion Questions

1. Do you think that most people would bend the rules to make some quick profits if everyone else at their workplace were doing so?
2. Are criminals, including the white-collar variety, motivated by greed or need?

SOURCES: John Braithwaite, "Toward a Theory of Organizational Crime," Paper presented at the American Society of Criminology Annual Meeting, Montreal, Canada, November, 1987; Travis Hirschi and Michael Gottfredson, "Causes of White-Collar Crime," *Criminology* 25 (1987):949–74.

relating to bookkeeping and reporting of stock transactions, in which failure to report is a technical violation. There the incentive is to abide by the rules in order to remain in the good graces of the industry's licensing agency and forego any chance of criminal prosecution.

In contrast, deterrence strategies secure law conformity by detecting violations of the law, determining who is responsible, and penalizing them to deter future violations.[110] Punishment serves as a warning to potential violators. Deterrence systems are oriented toward apprehending violators and punishing them, rather than creating conditions that induce conformity. The core violation in a deterrence system is the immediately harmful behavior, rather than the long-term behaviors that compliance systems seek to control.

Many organizations that pursue white-collar crime use a mix of strategies, depending on the circumstance. Compliance is generally used when the concern is with the *violation* and not the *violator*. Rather than punishing individuals for their specific crimes, as in the case of deterrence, compliance is concerned with insuring that laws are obeyed and in obtaining future conformity once they are broken. Deterrence systems seek to penalize persons or organizations for the harms they have caused; compliance systems seek to avoid harms and their consequences.

Another example of the compliance approach to controlling white-collar crime can be found in the area of environmental crimes, such as pollution. Compliance (also referred to as **economism**) involves controlling wrongdoing through economic incentives, such as levying heavy taxes on the quantity and qual-

The film *Wall Street* depicted a stock market manipulator, reminiscent of Ivan Boesky, in a role played by Michael Douglas. Charlie Sheen portrayed his protegee, forced to testify about insider trading schemes or face a prison sentence. As in this film, could jail terms deter white-collar crime?

ity of pollution released into the environment.[111] A number of states, including New Jersey, Arkansas, California, and Ohio, have passed stringent laws making firms liable for cleaning toxic sites; some prohibit the sale of companies or their assets unless environmental safety conditions have been met.[112] In another form of economism, the federal government has instituted a policy of barring people and businesses from receiving future government contracts if they are found to have engaged in fraudulent practices, such as bribing public officials.[113]

In sum, compliance strategies attempt to create a marketplace incentive to obey the law—for example, the more a company pollutes, the more costly and unprofitable that pollution becomes. Compliance or economism has become the favored method of enforcement, since criminal sanctions against corporations are often difficult to achieve.

Compliance systems are not applauded by all criminologists. Some experts point out that economic sanctions have limited value in controlling white-collar crime because economic penalties are imposed only after crimes have occurred, require careful governmental regulation, and often amount to only a slap on the wrist.[114] Furthermore, as Raymond Michalowski and Ronald Kramer point out, corporations can get around economic sanctions by moving their rule-violating activities overseas, where legal controls over injurious corporate activities are lax or nonexistent.[115] In contrast, more punitive deterrent strategies should—and have—worked, since white-collar crime by its nature is a rational act whose perpetrators are extremely sensitive to the threat of criminal sanctions. Gilbert Geis cites numerous instances in which prison sentences for corporate crimes have produced a significant decline in white-collar activity.[116] However, the favored method of controlling white-collar crimes remains economic. For example, in April 1985 the Pentagon decided to withhold all payments to General Dynamics Corporation until $124 million in contract overruns were repaid. Though this amount seems large, it would take only a few days for the company to recoup, since General Dynamics regularly bills the government $700 million a month.[117] Similary, in 1988, Hertz agreed to repay customers $13.5 million and received a fine of $6.8 million for overcharging on car repairs.

Law Enforcement Systems

On the federal level, detection of white-collar crime is primarily in the hands of administrative departments and agencies.[118] Any evidence of criminal activity is then sent to the Department of Justice or the FBI for investigation. Some other federal agencies, such as the Securities and Exchange Commission and Postal Service, have their own investigative arms. Usually enforcement is reactive (generated by complaints) rather than proactive (involving ongoing investigations or the monitoring of activities).

Investigations are carried out by the various federal agencies and the FBI. The FBI has established enforcement of white-collar laws as one of its three top priorities (along with foreign counterintelligence and organized crime).

If criminal prosecution is called for, a case will be handled by attorneys from the Criminal, Tax, Antitrust, and Civil Rights divisions of he Justice Department. If insufficient evidence is available to warrant a criminal prosecution, a case will be handled civilly or administratively by some other federal agency. For example, the Federal Trade Commission can issue a cease and desist order in antitrust or merchandising fraud cases.

On the state and local level, enforcement of white-collar laws is often disorganized and inefficient. Confusion may exist over the jurisdiction of the state attorney general and local prosecutors. The technical expertise of the federal government is often lacking on the state level. One area the states have made progress in is the control of consumer fraud. Similarly, there is a clear movement toward state-funded technical assistance offices to help local prosecutors; more than 40 states offer such services.

White-collar crime law enforcement is often left to business organizations themselves. Corporations spend hundreds of millions of dollars each year on internal audits that help unearth white-collar offenses. Local chambers of commerce, the insurance industry, and other elements of the business community have mounted campaigns against white-collar crime.

Aiding the investigation of white-collar offenses is a movement toward protecting employees who blow the whistle on their firm's violations. At least five states (Michigan, Connecticut, Maine, California, and New York) have passed laws protecting workers from being fired if they testify about violations.[119] Without such help, the hands of justice are tied.

PUNISHING WHITE-COLLAR CRIMINALS: IS THE SYSTEM CHANGING?

Despite the prevalence of economism, dramatic deterrence strategies have been used by federal and state justice systems to prevent white-collar crime. It is not extraordinary today to hear of corporate officers receiving long prison sentences in conjunction with corporate crimes. For example, Gilbert Schulman, a former top executive in the defunct government securities firm, Bevill, Bresler and Schulman, received an eight-year sentence for acts ranging from tax evasion to misuse of customers' securities.[120] Are such stiff penalties the norm? Corporate executives have even been charged with murder because of the actions of their companies (see Close-Up entitled "Can Corporations Commit Murder?").[121]

Two recent surveys conducted by the federal government's Bureau of Justice Statistics shed some light on this issue.[122] The first, a review of enforcement practices in nine states found that: (1) white-collar crimes account for about 6 percent of all arrest dispositions; (2) 88 percent of all those arrested for white-collar crimes were prosecuted; and (3) 74 percent were subsequently convicted in criminal court. The survey also showed that while 60 percent of white-collar criminals convicted in state court were incarcerated (a number comparable to the punishment given most other offenders), relatively few white-collar offenders (18 percent) received a prison term of more than a year.

The second survey followed white-collar cases prosecuted by the U.S. government between 1980 and

CLOSE-UP

Can Corporations Commit Murder?

One of the most controversial issues involving the punishment of white-collar criminals involves the prosecution of corporate executives who work for companies which manufacturer products believed to have caused the deaths of workers or consumers. Are the executives guilty of manslaughter or even murder?

The most famous case took place in 1978, when a local prosecutor attempted to indict Ford executives on charges of homicide in an accident case involving the Pinto compact care. The Pinto uses a thinly-protected gas tank which bursts into flame when involved in a low velocity rear-end collision. Though the design defect could have been corrected for about $20 per car, the company knew of the defect and still failed to take prompt action. When three teenage girls were killed in such a rear-end collision, an Indiana prosecutor brought murder charges against Ford executives. The executives were acquitted because the jury did not find sufficient evidence that they intended the deaths to occur. Subsequent Pinto accident trials in other states have won large restitutions from Ford for other deaths, but no indictments.

The issue of whether corporate executives could be successfully prosecuted for murder was answered on 16 June 1985, when an Illinois judge found three officials of the Film Recovery Systems corporation guilty of murder in the death of a worker. The employee died after inhaling cyanide poison under "totally unsafe" work conditions.

During the trial, evidence was presented showing that employees were not warned that they were working with dangerous substances, that company officials ignored complaints of illness, and that safety precautions had been deliberately ignored.

While the Film Recovery case may be unique, there is little question that corporate liability may be increasing. As Nancy Frank points out, a number of states have adopted the concept of unintended murder in their legal codes. This means that persons can be charged and convicted of murder if their acts, though essentially unintended, are imminently dangerous to another or have a strong probability of causing death or great bodily harm. This legal theory would include corporate executives who knew about the dangers of their products beforehand but chose to do nothing, either because their correction would lower profits or they simply did not care about consumers or workers.

Discussion Questions

1. If the Ford executives knew they had a dangerous car, should they have been found guilty of murder, even though the deaths were caused by the actions of a third party?

2. Is it fair to blame a single executive for the activities of a company which has thousands of employees?

SOURCES: Nancy Frank, "Unintended Murder and Corporate Risk-Taking: Defining the Concept of Justifiability," *Journal of*

1985. Consistent with its recent get-tough policy on white-collar crime, convictions rose 18 percent between 1980 and 1985, and the conviction rate for white-collar offenders (85 percent) was higher than that for all other federal crimes (78 percent). However, as was found in state courts, federal white-collar criminals received more lenient sentences than other offenders. For example, of those white-collar offenders sentenced to prison (about 40 percent of all those convicted), the average period of incarceration was 29 months, while all other federal offenders (54 percent were incarcerated) averaged 50 months.

These data make it clear that when white-collar criminals are apprehended they are as likely to be brought to justice as other offenders; nonetheless, they also show that their punishment is rarely severe. Of equal importance is the finding that almost all white-collar cases included in the two surveys involved individual common law crimes—forgery, fraud, embezzlement, and counterfeiting—and relatively few corporate or regulatory crimes. Of the more than 10,000 federal court convictions for white-collar crimes in 1985, only 491 were for regulatory crimes. While as a group white-collar convictions increased 18 percent between 1980 and 1985, convictions for regulatory crimes decreased 19 percent (from 609 to 491).

These findings must be viewed in the context of

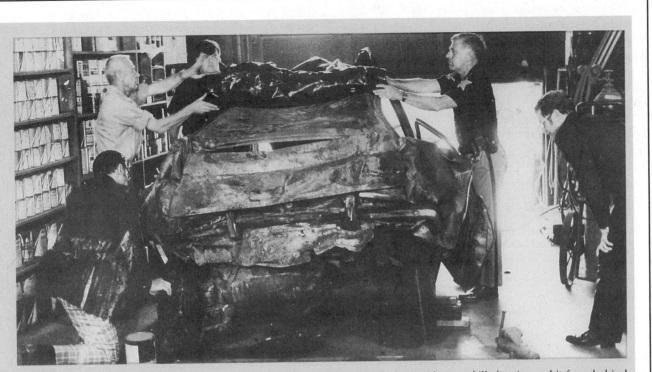

Indiana police and Ford Motor Co. officials view the 1973 Pinto in which three girls were killed as it was hit from behind by another vehicle at low velocity (1978).

Criminal Justice 16 (1988):17–24; Francis Cullen, William Maakestad, and Gray Cavender, ''The Ford Pinto Case and Beyond: Corporate Crime, Moral Boundaries and the Criminal Sanc-

tion,'' in Ellen Hochstedler, ed., *Corporations as Criminals* (Beverly Hills, Cal.: Sage Publications, 1984), pp. 107–30.

the times. While white-collar offenders are still treated with relative lenience, the federal and state governments have made the control of white-collar crime a top priority. Punishments are today more severe than in past decades. Some sociologists, including Stanton Wheeler and his associates, view this as part of a post-Watergate syndrome of cracking down on corporate and governmental law violators.[123] However, some criminologists question whether upper-class violators are in any more jeopardy then in years past; for example, Michael Benson and Esteban Walker found that high-status white-collar offenders are no more likely to be punished today than their low-status peers.[124]

Organized Crime

The second branch of organizational criminality involves ongoing criminal enterprise groups whose ultimate purpose is economic gain through illegitimate means: **organized crime.** Here a structured enterprise system is set up to supply consumers on a continuing basis with merchandise and services banned by the existing criminal law but for which a ready market exists: prostitution, pornography, gambling, narcotics. The system may resemble a legitimate business run by an ambitious chief executive officer, assistants, staff attorneys, and accountants, and a highly thorough and efficient accounts receivable and compliant department.[125]

Because of its secrecy, power and fabulous wealth, a great mystique has grown up about organized crime. Its legendary leaders—Al Capone, Meyer Lansky, Lucky Luciano—are the subject of books and films. The famous *Godfather* series popularized and humanized organized crime figures. Most citizens believe that organized criminals are capable of taking over legitimate business enterprises if the opportunity presents itself. Almost everyone is familiar with terms like the *mob, underworld, Mafia,* *"wiseguys", syndicate,* or *La Cosa Nostra* to refer to organized crime. Though most people have neither met or seen members of organized crime, they most certainly fear them. This section briefly defines organized crime, reviews its history, and discusses its economic effect and control.

CHARACTERISTICS OF ORGANIZED CRIME

A precise description of the characteristics of organized crime is difficult to formulate, but some of its general traits are included here.[126]

Organized crime is a conspiratorial activity, involving the coordination of numerous persons in the planning and execution of illegal acts or in the pursuit of a legitimate objective by unlawful means (for example, threatening businesses in order to get a stake in a legitimate corporation). Organized crime involves continuous commitment by primary members, although individuals with specialized skills may be brought in when the need arises. Organized crime organizations are usually structured along hierarchical lines—a chieftain supported by close advisers, lower subordinates, and so on.

Organized crime has economic gain as its primary goal, through achievement of power or status may also be a motivating factor. Economic gain is achieved through maintenance of a near monopoly on illegal goods and services, including drugs, gambling, pornography, and prostitution. However, organized crime activities are not limited to providing illicit services. They include such sophisticated activities as laundering illegal money through legitimate businesses, land fraud, and computer crimes.

Organized crime employs predatory tactics such as intimidation, violence, and corruption. It appeals to greed to accomplish its objectives and preserve its gains. By experience, custom, and practice, organized crime's conspiratorial groups are usually very quick and effective in controlling and disciplining their members, associates, and victims. The individuals involved know that any deviation from the rules of the organization will evoke a prompt response from the other participants. This response may range from a reduction in rank and responsibility to a death sentence.

Organized crime is not synonymous with the Mafia (or La Cosa Nostra—"Our Thing"), the most experienced, most diversified, and possibly best-disciplined of these groups. The **Mafia** is actually a common stereotype of organized crime. Although several families in the organization called **La Cosa Nostra** are important components of organized crime activities, they do not hold a monopoly on underworld activities. Many other ethnic and racial groups have become important components of organized crime.

Organized crime does not include terrorists dedicated to political change. Although violent acts are a major tactic of organized crime, the use of violence does not mean that a group is part of a confederacy of organized criminals.

ACTIVITIES OF ORGANIZED CRIME

The traditional sources of income for organized crime are derived from providing illicit materials and using force to enter into and maximize profits in legitimate businesses.[127] Annual gross income from criminal activity is at least $50 billion, more than 1 percent of the GNP; some estimates put gross earnings as high as $90 billion, outranking most major industries in the United States.[128]

Most organized crime income comes from narcotics distribution (over $30 billion annually), loan sharking, or lending money at illegal rates ($7 billion), and prostitution ($3 billion). However, additional billions come from gambling, theft rings, and other illegal enterprises. For example, The Attorney Generals' Commission on Pornography concluded that organized crime figures exert substantial influence and control over the obscenity industry.[129] Organized

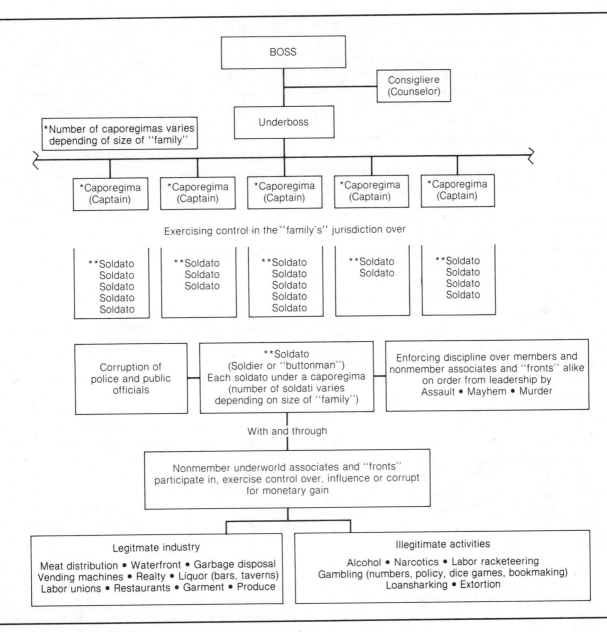

FIGURE 12.1   Traditional Organization of the Mafia "Family"

SOURCE: U.S. Senate, Permanent Subcommittee on Investigations, Committee on Governmental Affairs, *Hearings on Organized Crime and Use of Violence*, 96th Cong., 2d Sess., April 1980, p. 117.

criminals have infiltrated labor unions, taking control of their pension funds and dues; control of unions gives organized crime groups the clout to gain entry into legitimate business through the treat of strikes, work stoppages, and so on. Alan Block has described mob control of the New York waterfront and its influence on the use of union funds to buy insurance, health care, and other benefits from mob-controlled companies.[130] Hijacking of shipments and cargo theft are other sources of income. One study found that the annual losses due to theft of air cargo amount to $400 million, rail cargo $600 million, trucking $1.2 billion, and maritime shipment $300 million.[131] Underworld figures engage in fencing high-value items and maintain international sales territories. In recent years they have branched into computer crime and other white-collar activities.

Organized Crime and Legitimate Enterprise

In addition to criminal enterprises, additional billions are earned by organized crime figures who force or buy their way into legitimate businesses and use them both for profit and a means of siphoning off ("laundering") otherwise unaccountable profits. Merry Morash claims that mob control of legitimate enterprise today is influenced by market conditions. Businesses most likely to be affected are low-technology (such as garbage collection), have uniform products, and operate in rigid markets where increases in price will not result in reduced demand. In addition, industries most affected by labor pressure are highly susceptible to takeovers, because a mob-controlled work stoppage would destroy a product or delay meeting deadlines. Morash lists five ways that organized criminals become involved in legitimate enterprise today:

1. Business activity that supports illegal enterprises —for example, providing a front

2. Predatory or parasitic exploitation—for example, demanding protection money

3. Organization of monopolies or cartels to limit competition

4. Unfair advantages gained by practices such as manipulation of labor unions and corruption of public officials

5. Illegal manipulation of legal vehicles, particularly stocks and bonds[132]

These traits show how organized crime is more like a business enterprise than a confederation of criminals seeking to merely enhance their power. No where has this relationship been more visible than in the 1985 scandal that rocked the prestigious First National Bank of Boston. Federal prosecutors charged that the bank made unreported cash shipments of $1.2 million. They received $529,000 in small bills and sent

$690,000 in bills of $100 or more. The bank was fined $500,000 for violating a law which requires that banks report any cash transaction of $10,000 or more. The bank's transactions came under scrutiny during an FBI investigation of the Angiulo crime family, which bought more than $41.7 million in cashier's checks from the bank.[133]

The First National scandal illustrates that organized crime today involves a cooperative relationship between big business, politicians, and racketeers. The relationship is an expensive one: it has been estimated that organized crime activities stifle competition, resulting in the loss of 400,000 jobs and $18 billion in productivity. Since organized crime profits go unreported, the rest of the population pays an extra $6.5 billion in taxes.[134]

THE CONCEPT OF ORGANIZED CRIME

The term *organized crime* conjures up images of strong men in dark suits, machine-gun–toting bodyguards, rituals of allegiance to secret organizations, professional "gangland" killings, and meetings of "family" leaders who chart the course of crime much like the board members at General Motors decide on the country's transportation needs. These images have become part of what criminologists refer to as the **alien conspiracy theory** concept of organized crime. This is the belief, adhered to by the federal government and many respected criminologists, that organized crime is a direct offshoot of a criminal society—the Mafia—that first originated in Italy and Sicily and now controls racketeering in major American cities. A major premise of the alien conspiracy theory is that the Mafia is centrally coordinated by a national committee which settles disputes, dictates policy, and assigns territory.[135]

Not all criminologists believe in this narrow concept of organized crime and view the alien conspiracy theory as a figment of the media's imagination.[136] Their view depicts organized crime as a group of ethnically diverse gangs or groups who compete for profit in the sale of illegal goods and services, or who use force and violence to extort money from legitimate enterprises. These groups are not bound by a central national organi-

FIGURE 12.2

Sites of La Cosa Nostra Headquarter Cities

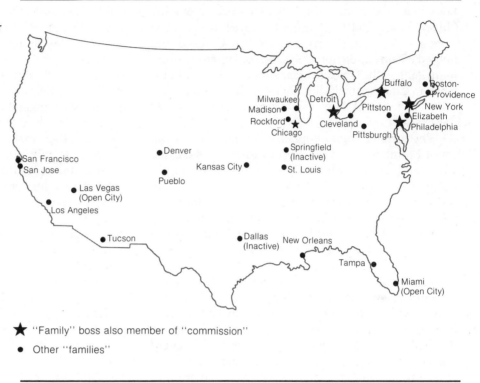

★ "Family" boss also member of "commission"

● Other "families"

SOURCE: U.S. Senate, Permanent Subcommittee on Investigations, Committee on Governmental Affairs, *Hearings on Organized Crime and Use of Violence,* 96th Cong., 2d Sess., April 1980, p. 116.

zation but act independently on their own turf. Each of these two perspectives is examined in some detail in the following sections.

Alien Conspiracy Theory: La Cosa Nostra

According to the alien conspiracy theory, organized crime is really comprised of a national syndicate of 25 or so Italian-dominated crime families who call themselves La Cosa Nostra. The major families have a total membership of about 1,700 "made men," and another 17,000 "associates" who are criminally involved with syndicate members.[137] The families control crime in distinct geographic areas (see Figure 12.1). New York City, the most important organized crime area, alone contains five families—Gambino, Columbo, Lucchese, Bonnano, and Genovese—named after their founding "godfathers"; in contrast, Chicago contains a single mob organization called the "outfit" which also influences racketeering in cities such as Milwaukee,

Kansas City, and Phoenix. The families are believed to be ruled by a "Commission," made up of the heads of the five New York families and bosses from Detroit, Buffalo, Chicago, and Philadelphia, which settles personal problems and jurisdictional conflicts, and enforces rules that allow members to gain huge profits through manufacture and sale of illegal goods and services (see Figure 12.2).[138]

Development of a National "Syndicate." How did this concept of a national crime cartel develop? Actually the first "organized" gangs were comprised of Irish immigrants who made their home in the slum districts of New York City.[139] The "Forty Thieves," considered the first New York gang with a definite acknowledged leadership, were muggers, thieves, and pickpockets on the Lower East Side of Manhattan from the 1820s to just before the Civil War.

Around 1890, Italian immigrants began forming gangs modeled after the Sicilian crime organization known as the Mafia; these gangs were called the "Black Hand." In 1900, Johnny Torrio, a leader of New York's "Five Points" gang, moved to Chicago and helped his uncle, Big Jim Colosimo, organize the dominant gang in the Chicago area. Other gangs also flourished in Chicago, including those of Hymie Weiss and "Bugs" Moran. A later leader was the infamous Al "Scarface" Capone.

The turning point of organized crime was the onset of Prohibition and the Volstead Act. This created a multimillion-dollar bootlegging industry overnight. Gangs vied for a share of the business, and bloody wars for control of rackets and profits became common. However, the problems of supplying liquor to thousands of illegal drinking establishments (speakeasies) required organization and an end to open warfare.

In the late 1920s, several events helped create the structure of organized crime. First, Johnny Torrio became leader of the Unione Siciliano, and ethnic self-help group that had begun as a legitimate enterprise but had been taken over by racketeers. This event helped bring together the Chicago and New York crime groups; since Torrio was Italian, it also brought the beginnings of detente between Italians and Sicilians, who heretofore had been at odds with one another. Also during the 1920s, more than 500 members of the Sicilian Mafia fled to the United States to avoid prosecution; these new arrivals included future gang leaders Carlo Gambino, Joseph Profaci, Stefano Maggadino, and Joseph Bonnano.[140]

In December 1925, gang leaders from across the nation met in Cleveland to discuss strategies for mediating their differences in a nonviolent manner and for maximizing profits. A similar meeting, which took place in Atlantic City in 1929, was attended by 20 gang leaders, including Lucky Luciano, Al Capone, and "Dutch" Schultz.

Despite such efforts, however, gang wars continued into the 1930s. In 1934, according to some accounts, another meeting in New York, called by Johnny Torrio and Lucky Luciano, led to the formation of a national crime commission and acknowledged the territorial claims of 24 crime families around the country. This was considered the beginning of La Cosa Nostra.

Under the leadership of the national crime commission, organized crime began to expand in a more orderly fashion. Bugsy Siegel was dispatched to California to oversee West Coast operations. The end of Prohibition required a new source of profits, and narcotic sales became the mainstay of gangland business. Al Polizzi, a Cleveland crime boss, formed a news service that provided information on horse racing, thereby helping create a national network of gang-dominated bookmakers.

After World War II, organized crime families began using their vast profits from liquor, gambling, and narcotics to buy into legitimate businesses, such as entertainment, legal gambling in Cuba and Las Vegas, hotel chains, jukebox concerns, restaurants, and taverns. By paying off politicians, police, and judges, and by using blackmail and coercion, organized criminals became almost immune to prosecution. The machine-gun-toting gangster had given way to the business-man-racketeer.

In the 1950s, cooperation among gangland figures reached its zenith. Gang control over unions became widespread, and many legitimate businesses made payoffs to promote labor peace. New gang organizations arose in Los Angeles, Kansas City, and Dallas.

The Mob in the Fifties. In 1950, the Senate Special Committee to Investigate Organized Crime in Interstate Commerce, better known as the **Kefauver Committee** (after its chairman), was formed to look into organized crime. It reported the existence of a national crime cartel, whose members cooperated to make a profit and engaged in joint ventures to eliminate enemies. The Kefauver Committee also made public the syndicate's enforcement arm, Murder Inc., which, under the leadership of Albert Anastasia, disposed of enemies for a price.

The Kefauver Committee also found that corruption and bribery of local political officials was widespread. This theme was revived by the Senate Subcommittee on Investigations, better known as the **McClellan Committee,** in its investigation of the role organized crime played in labor racketeering. The committee and its chief counsel, Robert Kennedy, uncovered a close relationship between gang activity and the Teamsters Union, then led by Jimmy Hoffa. Hoffa's eventual death has been linked to his gangland connections.

Later investigations by the committee produced the testimony of Joseph Valachi, former underworld "soldier" who detailed the inner workings of La Cosa Nostra. The leaders of the national crime cartel at this time were Frank Costello, Vito Genovese, Carlo Gambino, Joe Bonnano, and Joe Profaci, all of New York; Sam Giancana of Chicago; and Angelo Bruno of Philadelphia.

During the next 15 years, gang activity expanded further into legitimate businesses. Nonetheless, gangland jealousy, competition, and questions of succession produced an occasional flare-up of violence. The most well-publicized conflict occurred between the Gallo brothers of Brooklyn—Albert, Larry, and Crazy Joe—and the Profaci crime family. The feud continued through the 1960s, uninterrupted by the death of Joe Profaci and the new leadership of his group by Joe Colombo. Eventually Colombo was severely injured by a Gallo hired assassin, and in return Joey Gallo was killed in a New York restaurant, Umberto's Clam House. Gallo's death once again brought peace in the underworld. Emerging as the most powerful syndicate boss was Carlo Gambino, who held this position until his death by natural causes in 1976.

In recent years, La Cosa Nostra is said to be undergoing some major changes. First, a number of the reigning family heads are quite old, in their seventies and eighties, indicating that a younger generation will soon step in to take control of the families. In addition, active government enforcement policies has halved what the estimated membership was 20 years ago; a number of the highest ranking leaders have been imprisoned. Additional pressure comes from newly emerging ethnic gangs which want to muscle in on traditional syndicate activities such as drug sales and gambling.

Despite such stresses, alien conspiracy theorists view La Cosa Nostra as having the ability to survive and continue its dominant position in the organized crime world.

The Mafia Myth

Some scholars charge that this version of organized crime is fanciful. They argue that the alien conspiracy theory is too heavily influenced by media accounts and by the testimony of a single person, mobster Joseph Valachi, before a U.S. Senate investigation committee headed by Senator John McClellan. Valachi's description of the Cosa Nostra was relied upon by conspiracy theorists as an accurate portrayal of mob activities. Yet critics question its authenticity

and direction. For example, criminologist Jay Albanese compared Valachi's statements to those of another mob informer, Jimmy Frantianno, and found major discrepancies with respect to the location and size of organized criminal activity.[141]

The challenges to the alien conspiracy theory have produced alternative views of organized crime. For example, Philip Jenkins and Gary Potter studied organized crime in Philadelphia and found little evidence that this supposed "Mafia stronghold" was controlled by an Italian-dominated crime family.[142]

Sociologist Alan Block has argued that organized crime is both a loosely constructed social system and a social world that reflects the existing American system, and not a tightly organized national criminal syndicate. The system is composed of "relationships binding professional criminals, politicians, law enforcers, and various entrepreneurs."[143] In contrast, the social world of organized crime is often chaotic because of the constant power struggle between competing groups. Block rejects the view that an all-powerful organized crime commission exists. He instead views the world of professional criminals as one shaped by the political economy. He finds that independent crime organizations can be characterized as either **enterprise syndicates** or **power syndicates.** The former are involved in providing services and include madams, drug distributors, and bookmakers. These individuals are "workers in the world of illegal enterprise." They have set positions in an illegal enterprise system, with special tasks to perform if the enterprise is to function.

In contrast, power syndicates perform no set task except to extort or terrorize. Their leaders can operate against legitimate business or against fellow criminals who operate enterprise syndicates. Through coercion, buy-outs, and other similar means, power syndicates graft themselves onto enterprise systems, legal business, and trade unions.

Block's view of organized crime is revisionist, since it portrays mob activity as a quasi-economic enterprise system swayed by social forces, and not a tightly knit, unified cartel dominated by ethnic minorities carrying out European traditions. His world of organized crime is dominated by business leaders, politicians, and union leaders who work hand-in-hand with criminals. Moreover, the violent, chaotic social world of power syndicates does not lend itself to a tightly controlled syndicate.

ORGANIZED CRIME GROUPS

Even devoted alien conspiracy advocates such as theU.S. Justice Department now concede that organized crime is a loose confederation of ethnic and regional crime groups, bound together by a commonality of economic and political objectives.[144] Some of these groups are located in fixed geographical areas. For example, the so-called Dixie Mafia operates in the South. Chicano crime families are found in areas with significant Hispanic populations, such as California and Arizona. Irish and Jewish crime organizations are found across the nation, while some of the Italian and Cuban groups operate internationally. Some have preserved their past identity, while others are constantly changing organizations.

One important recent change in organized crime is the interweaving of ethnic groups into the traditional structure. Blacks, Puerto Rican, Cuban, Chinese, and other emerging ethnic groups now compete with Italian, Irish, and Jewish racketeers. In black or Hispanic areas these new ethnics oversee the distribution of drugs, prostitution, and gambling in a symbiotic relationship with old-line racketeers. As the traditional organized crime families drift into legitimate businesses, the distribution of contraband on the street is handled by newcomers, characterized by Francis Ianni as "urban social bandits."[145] However, as Robert Kelly and Rufus Schatzberg point out, minority gangs have not yet been able to crack the network of organized corruption which involves bribing city officials and control of union funds.[146]

As law enforcement pressure on traditional organized crime figures has increased, other groups have filled the vacuum. For example, the Hell's Angels motorcycle club is now believed to be one of the leading distributors of narcotics in the United States. Similarly, Chinese criminal gangs have taken over the dominant role in New York City's heroin supply market from the traditional Italian-run syndicates.[147]

It is still difficult to assess the accuracy of any view of organized crime. Nonetheless, to speak about organized crime as a national syndicate that controls all illegitimate rackets in an orderly fashion seems to ignore the variety of gangs and groups, their membership and their relationship to the outside world.[148] Mafia-type groups may play a major role in organized crime, but they are by no means the only ones that can be considered organized criminals.[149]

CONTROLLING ORGANIZED CRIME

George Vold has argued that the development of organized crime parallels early capitalist enterprises. Organized crime employs ruthless and monopolistic tactics to maximize profits; it also is secretive, protective of its operations, and defensive against any outside intrusion.[150] Consequently, efforts to control its activities are extremely difficult.

Until fairly recently, the federal and state governments actually did little to combat organized crime. One of the first direct anti-organized crime measures was the Interstate and Foreign Travel or Transportation in Aid of Racketeering Enterprises Act (Travel Act).[151] The Travel Act prohibits interstate commerce and the use of interstate facilities with the intent to promote, manage, establish, carry on, or facilitate an unlawful activity; it also prohibits the actual or attempted engagement in these activities.

In 1970, Congress passed the Organized Crime Control Act. Highlights include:

- The establishment of special grand juries in localities where there are major organized crime operations. These grand juries have expanded power to control the duration of their terms and the right to appeal any arbitrary termination. They also may issue reports recommending removal of any public officer or employee for noncriminal misconduct involving organized criminal activity and reports concerning organized crime conditions generally in their districts.

- A general federal immunity statute under which witnesses can be ordered by a court to testify in return for immunity from prosecution, and can be jailed for up to 18 months if they refuse to do so. Witnesses are given "use immunity," rather than the "transactional immunity" provided for in legislation that the 1970 act supersedes. Use immunity forbids the use of information derived from witnesses while they are under court order to testify but does not protect them from prosecution for those acts about which they testified, if evidence is developed entirely independently.

≡ CLOSE-UP

Forfeiture

Forfeiture is government seizure of property derived from or used in criminal activity. Its use as a sanction aims to strip racketeers and drug traffickers of their economic power because the traditional sanctions of imprisonment and fines have been found inadequate to deter or punish enormously profitable crimes. Seizure of assets aims not only to reduce the profitability of illegal activity but to curtail the financial ability of criminal organizations to continue illegal operations.

Two Types of Forfeiture: Civil and Criminal

Civil forfeiture is a proceeding against property used in criminal activity. Property subject to civil forfeiture often includes vehicles used to transport contraband, equipment used to manufacture illegal drugs, cash used in illegal transactions, and property purchased with the proceeds of the crime. No finding of criminal guilt is required in such proceedings. The government is required to post notice of the proceedings so that any party who has an interest in the property may contest the forfeiture.

The types of property that may be forfeited have been expanded since the 1970s to include assets, cash, securities, negotiable instruments, property including houses or other real estate, and proceeds traceable directly or indirectly to violations of certain laws. Common provisions permit seizure of conveyances such as airplanes, boats, or cars; raw materials, products, and equipment used in manufacturing, trafficking, or cultivation of illegal drugs; and drug paraphernalia.

Criminal forfeiture is a part of the criminal action taken against a defendant accused of racketeering or drug trafficking. The forfeiture is a sanction imposed on conviction that requires the defendant to forfeit various property rights and interests related to the violation. In 1970 Congress revived this sanction that had been dormant in American law since the Revolution.

Use of Forfeiture Varies among Jurisdictions

The Federal Government originally provided for criminal forfeiture in the Racketeer Influenced and Corrupt Organization (RICO) statute and the Comprehensive Drug Prevention and Control Act, both enacted in 1970. Before that time civil forfeiture had been provided in federal laws on some narcotics, customs, and revenue infractions. More recently, language on forfeiture has been included in the Comprehensive Crime Control Act of 1984, the Money Laundering Act of 1986, and the Anti-Drug Abuse Act of 1986.

Most state forfeiture procedures appear in controlled substances or RICO laws. A few states provide for forfeiture of property connected with the commission of any felony. Most state forfeiture provisions allow for civil rather than criminal forfeiture. A recent survey responded to by 44 states and territories found that under the controlled substances laws most states provided only for civil forfeiture. Eight States (Arizona, Kentucky, Nevada, New Mexico, North Carolina, Utah, Vermont, and West Virginia), however, have criminal forfeiture provisions. Of the 19 states with RICO statutes, all but 8 include the criminal forfeiture sanction.

What Happens to Forfeited Property?

In 1984 the federal government established the Department of Justice Assets Forfeiture Fund to collect proceeds from forfeitures and defray the costs of forfeitures under the Comprehensive Drug Abuse Prevention and Control Act and the Customs Forfeiture Fund for forfeitures under customs laws. These acts also require that the property and proceeds of forfeiture be shared equitably with state and local law enforcement commensurate with their participation in the investigations leading to forfeiture.

Discussion Questions

1. Should a person's car be seized if police find a small amount of narcotics in the back seat?

2. Should all convicted criminals be stripped of their assets?

SOURCE: Bureau of Justice Statistics, *Report to the Nation on Crime and Justice*, 2d ed. (Washington, D.C.: National Institute of Justice, 1988), p. 93.

- Protection for witnesses in organized crime cases and for members of their families. Federal officials are authorized to provide secure housing and otherwise insure the safety of witnesses.

- Perjury prosecution when a witness knowingly makes a false statement under oath or makes two sworn statements that are completely contradictory. The law eliminates previous requirements of two witnesses and direct evidence for proof of perjury.

- The taking and use of pretrial depositions "whenever due to exceptional circumstances it is in the interest of justice."

- Expansion of federal jurisdiction over illegal gambling operation because it "involves widespread use of, and has an effect upon, interstate commerce . . ."

- Prohibits persons who engage in a "pattern of racketeering activity" from using their illegal profits for the purpose of penetrating and taking over legitimate businesses and unions.

- Extends sentences for persons convicted of participation in continuing illegal businesses, or who are habitual criminals, chief participants in conspiracies, or repeat offenders.

Title IX of the act, and probably its most effective measure, has been the **Racketeer Influenced and Corrupt Organization Act (RICO)**.[152] RICO did not create new categories of crimes, but it did create new categories of offenses in racketeering activity, which it defined as involvement in two or more acts prohibited by 24 existing federal statutes and eight state statutes.[153] The offenses listed in RICO include state-defined crimes such as murder, kidnapping, gambling, arson, robbery, bribery, extortion, and narcotics violations, and federally defined crimes such as bribery, counterfeiting, transmission of gambling information, prostitution, and mail fraud.

RICO is designed to limit patterns of organized criminal activity by defining racketeering as an act intended to:

- Derive income from racketeering or the unlawful collection of debts and to use or invest such income

- Acquire through racketeering an interest in or control over any enterprise engaged in interstate or foreign commerce

- Conduct business enterprises through a pattern of racketeering.

- Conspire to use racketeering as a means of making income, collecting loans, or conducting business.

An individual convicted under RICO is subject to 20 years in prison and a $25,000 fine. Additionally, the accused must forfeit to the U.S. government any interest in a business violation of RICO. These penalties are much more potent than simple conviction and imprisonment (see Close-Up on Forfeiture).

To enforce these policy initiatives, the federal government created the Strike Force Program. This program, operating in 18 cities, brings together various state and federal law enforcement officers and prosecutors to work as a team against racketeering. Several states, including New York, Illinois, New Jersey, and New Mexico, have created their own special investigative teams devoted to organized criminal activity.

These efforts began to pay off in 1984, when 3,118 RICO indictments were issued and 2,194 convictions resulted. In April 1985, a New York–based strike force was successful in indicting and later convicting members of the Lucchese, Genovese, and Bonnano families.[154] The investigation also uncovered evidence to support the national crime cartel concept. Similar sweeps were conducted in Boston, Chicago, and Miami.

While these actions are considered a major blow to Italian-dominated organized crime cartels, they are unlikely to stifle criminal entrepreneurship. As long as vast profits can be made from selling narcotics, producing pornography, or taking illegal bets, many groups stand ready to fill the gaps and reap the profits of providing illegal goods and services.

SUMMARY

White-collar and organized criminals are similar because they both use ongoing illegal business enterprise to make personal profits. They are various types of white-collar crime. Stings and swindles involve the use of deception to bilk people out of their money. Chiseling customers, businesses, or the government on a regular basis is a second common type of white-collar crime. Surprisingly, many professionals engage in chiseling offenses.

Other white-collar criminals use their positions in business and the marketplace to commit economic crimes. Their crimes include exploitation of position in a company or the government to secure illegal payments; embezzlement and employee pilferage and fraud; client fraud; and influence peddling and bribery. Further, corporate officers sometimes violate the law to improve the position and profitability of their businesses. Their crimes include price fixing, false advertising, and environmental crimes.

So far, little has been done to combat white-collar crimes. Most offenders do not view themselves as criminals and therefore do not seem to be deterred by criminal statutes. Though thousands of white-collar criminals are prosecuted each year, their numbers are insignificant compared with the magnitude of the problem.

The government has used various law enforcement strategies to combat white-collar crime. Some involve deterrence, which uses punishment to frighten potential abusers. Others involve economism or compliance strategies, which create economic incentives to obey the law.

The demand for illegal goods and services has produced a symbiotic relationship between the public and an organized criminal network. Though criminal gangs have existed since the early nineteenth century, their power and size were spurred by the Volstead Act and Prohibition in the 1920s. Organized crime supplies alcohol, gambling, drugs, prostitutes, and pornography to the public. It is immune from prosecution because of public apathy and because of its own strong political connections. Though organized criminals used to be white ethnics—Jews, Italians, and Irish—today blacks, Hispanics, and other groups have become involved in organized crime activities. The old-line "families" are more likely to use their criminal wealth and power to buy into legitimate businesses.

There is debate over the control of organized crime. Some experts believe there is a national crime cartel that controls all activities. Others view organized crime as a group of disorganized, competing gangs dedicated to extortion or to providing illegal goods and services.

Efforts to control organized crime have been stepped up. The federal government has used anti-racketeering statutes to arrest syndicate leaders. But as long as there are vast profits to be made, illegal enterprise will continue to flourish.

KEY TERMS

entrepreneurship
white-collar crime
organized crime
enterprise
corporate crime
Mark Moore
churning
lobbying
pilferage
"virus" programs
Knapp Commission
Operation Greylord
Securities Act of 1933
Securities and Exchange Act of 1934
Securities and Exchange Commission (SEC)
insider trading
arbitrage

corporate crime
organizational crime
Sherman Antitrust Act
greenmail
compliance
deterrence
technical violation
economism
organized crime
Mafia
La Cosa Nostra
alien conspiracy theory
Kefauver Committee
McClellan Committee
enterprise syndicates
power syndicates
Racketeer Influenced and Corrupt Organization Act (RICO)

NOTES

1. Dwight Smith, "White-Collar Crime, Organized Crime and the Business Establishment: Resolving a Crisis in Criminological Theory," in P. Wickman and T. Dailey, eds., *White Collar and Economic Crime: A Multidisciplinary and Crossnational Perspective* (Lexington, Mass.: Lexington Books, 1982), p. 53.
2. See, generally, Dwight Smith, Jr., "Organized Crime and Entrepreneurship," *International Journal of Criminology and Penology* 6 (1978):161–77; Dwight C. Smith, Jr., "Paragons, Pariahs, and Pirates: A Spectrum-Based Theory of Enterprise," *Crime and Delinquency* 26 (1980):358–86: Dwight C. Smith, Jr. and Richard S. Alba, "Organized Crime and American Life," *Society* 16 (1979):32–38.
3. Smith, "White-Collar Crime, Organized Crime and the Business Establishment," p. 33.
4. William Chambliss, *On the Take: From Petty Crook to Presidents* (Bloomington, Ind.: Indiana University Press, 1978).
5. Edwin Sutherland, *White Collar Crime: The Uncut Version* (New Haven, Conn.: Yale University Press, 1983), p. 7.
6. Edwin Sutherland, "White-Collar Criminality," *American Sociological Review* 5 (1940):2–10.
7. See, generally, Herbert Edelhertz, *The Nature, Impact and Prosecution of White-Collar Crime* (Washington, D.C.:

U.S. Government Printing Office, 1970), pp. 73–75.

8. Gilbert Geis, "Avocational Crime," in Daniel Glazer, ed., *Handbook of Criminology* (Chicago: Rand McNally, 1974), p. 284.

9. Laura Schrager and James Short, "Toward a Sociology of Organization Crime," *Social Problems* 25 (1978):415–25.

10. *Ibid.*, p. 415.

11. Gilbert Geis, "White-Collar and Corporate Crime," in ed., Robert Meier, *Major Forms of Crime* (Beverly Hills, Cal.: Sage Publications, 1984), p. 145.

12. Bureau of Justice Statistics, *The Severity of Crime* (Washington, D.C.: U.S. Government Printing Office, 1984).

13. Knight-Rider, Inc., Washington Bureau, "Senators Say GE, Hutton Cases Follow Dual Standard," *Omaha World Herald* (16 May 1985), p. 14.

14. Marshall Clinard and Richard Quinney, *Criminal Behavior Systems: A Typology* (New York: Holt Rinehart and Winston, 1973), p. 117.

15. Edelhertz, *The Nature, Impact and Prosecution of White-Collar Crime*, pp. 73–75.

16. Mark Moore, "Notes Toward a National Strategy to Deal with White Collar Crime," in Herbert Edelhertz and Charles Rogovin, ed., *A National Strategy for Containing White Collar Crime* (Lexington, Mass.: Lexington Books, 1980), pp. 32–44.

17. For a general review, see, John Braithwaite, "White Collar Crime," *Annual Review of Sociology* 11 (1985):1–25.

18. "Catch Me If You Can," *Time* (26 April 1982), p. 55.

19. Scott Paltrow, "Goldblum Now in Consulting and on Parole," *Wall Street Journal* (22 March 1982), p. 25.

20. Bruce Ingersoll, "Utah Investors Said to Lose $215 Million in Securities Scam," *Wall Street Journal* (6 December 1984), p. 36.

21. "Report: Fraud Costs Billions for Taxpayers," *Omaha World Herald* (17 May 1982), p. 9.

22. Richard Quinney, "Occupational Structure and Criminal Behavior: Prescription Violation of Retail Pharmacists," *Social Problems* 11 (1963):179–85. See also, John Braithwaite, *Corporate Crime in the Pharmaceutical Industry* (London: Routledge and Kegan Paul, 1984).

23. "Former Broker to Plead Guilty to Defrauding $570,000 from Clients," *Wall Street Journal* (8 October 1984), p. 35.

24. This section depends heavily on Frank Browning and John Gerassi, *The American Way of Crime* (New York: Putnam, 1980), p. 151.

25. *Ibid.*, p. 293.

26. *Ibid.*

27. Edward Ranzal, "City Report Finds Building Industry Infested by Graft," *New York Times* (8 November 1974), p. 1.

28. Edward Pound, "Honored Employee is a Key in Huge Fraud in Defense Purchasing," *Wall Street Journal* (2 March 1988), p. 1.

29. Marshall Clinard and Peter Yeager, *Corporate Crime* (New York: Free Press, 1980), pp. 166–67.

30. David Goeller, "Bill Curbing Ex-Lawmakers Clears Senate," *Boston Globe* (20 April 1988), p. 3.

31. Murray Waas, "Report Tells of 'Scheme' by HMO to Cheat U.S.," *Boston Globe* (19 April 1988), p. 9.

32. Charles McCaghy, *Deviant Behavior* (New York: Macmillan, 1976), p. 178.

33. *Ibid.*, p. 168.

34. John Clark and Richard Hollinger, *Theft by Employees in Work Organizations* (Washington, D.C.: U.S. Government Printing Office, 1983), pp. 2–3.

35. J. Sorenson, H. Grove, and T. Sorenson, "Detecting Management Fraud: The Role of the Independent Auditor," in G. Geis and E. Stotland, eds., *White-Collar Crime, Theory and Research* (Beverly Hills, Cal.: Sage Publications, 1980), pp. 221–51.

36. Lee Berton, "Wedtech Used Gimmickry, False Invoices to Thrive," *Wall Street Journal* (23 February 1987), p. 6.

37. William Power, "New York Rep. Biaggi, Six Others Indicted as Wedtech Scandal Greatly Expands," *Wall Street Journal* (4 June 1987), p. 7.

38. M. Swanson and J. Terriot, "Computer Crime: Dimensions, Types, Causes and Investigations," *Journal of Political Science and Administration* 8 (1980):305–306. See also, Donn Parker, "Computer Related White Collar Crime," in G. Geis and E. Stotland, eds., *White Collar Crime, Theory and Research*, pp. 199–220.

39. Tom Nugent, "Security Experts Say Thefts Exceed $100 Million a Year," *Omaha World Herald* (13 May 1982), p. 35.

40. Erik Larson, "Computers Turn Out to Be Valuable Aid in Employee Crime," *Wall Street Journal* (14 January 1985), p. 1.

41. "Computer Hackers Charge $60,000 to Sprint Number," *Omaha World Herald* (6 February 1985), p. 1.

42. Comprehensive Crime Control Act of 1984, Pub. L. No. 98-473, Sec. 2101-03, 98 Stat. 1837, Sec. 2190 (1984), adding 18 USC Sec. 1030 (1984).

43. This subsection and the following ones rely heavily on "White-Collar Crime: Second Annual Survey of Laws," *American Criminal Law Review* 19 (1986):173–520.

44. Medicare and Medicaid Anti-Fraud and Abuse Amendment of 1977, Title XVIII, Pub. Law No. 95-142, 91 Stat. 1175.

45. Jesilow, Pontell, and Geis, "Physician Immunity From Prosecution and Punishment for Medical Program Fraud," p. 19.

46. Robert Pear, "Panel Says Most States Fail on Policing

Medicaid Fraud," *New York Times* (27 March 1982), p. 7.

47. U.S. v. Bishop, 412 U.S. 346 (1973).

48. Carl Hartman, "Study Says Underground Economy May Represent 33% of Production," *Boston Globe* (16 February 1988), p. 38.

49. Alan Murray, "IRS in Losing Battle Against Tax Evaders Despite Its New Gear," *Wall Street Journal* (10 April 1984), p. 1.

50. *Ibid.*

51. Steven Klepper and Daniel Nagin, "The Anatomy of Tax Evasion," Paper presented at the Annual Meeting of the American Society of Criminology, Montreal, Canada, November, 1987.

52. "Now Williams—Last, Not Least of ABSCAM Trials," *New York Times* (5 April 1982), p. E-7.

53. *The Knapp Commission Report on Police Corruption* (New York: George Braziller, 1973), pp. 1–3, 170–82.

54. "Greylord Term for Ex-Judge is Harshest Yet," *Omaha World Herald* (19 December 1984), p. 8; "Police Official Sentenced to 18 Years for Extortion," *Wall Street Journal* (25 September 1984), p. 6.

55. Richard Stevenson, "The High Cost of an Arms Scandal," *New York Times* (10 July 1988), section 3, p. 1.

56. United Press International, "Minority Leader in N.Y. Senate is Charged," *Boston Globe* (17 September 1987), p. 20.

57. Cited in Hugh Barlow, *Introduction to Criminology*, 2d ed. (Boston: Little, Brown, 1984).

58. Robert Taylor, "Bechtel Is Said to Be Linked to Bid-Rigging, Bribes in Getting Contracts in South Korea," *Wall Street Journal* (25 April 1984), p. 2.

59. Pub. Law No. 95-213, 101-104, 91 Stat. 1494.

60. Christopher Bryon, "Big Profits in Big Bribery," *Time* (16 March 1981), pp. 58–67.

61. *Ibid.*, p. 59.

62. *Ibid.*, p. 67.

63. Securities Act of 1933, 15 U.S.C. Sec. 77a to 77aa (1982); Securities Exchange Act of 1934 15 U.S.C. sec. 78a to 78kk (1982).

64. 17 C.F.R. 240. 10b-5 (1987).

65. James Stewart, "Death of a Theory? Supreme Court May Revamp Insider-Trading Law," *Wall Street Journal* (30 September 1987), p. 39.

66. United States v. Newman 664 F.2d 12 (2d cir. 1981).

67. John Boland, "The SEC Trims the First Amendment," *Wall Street Journal* (4 December 1984), p. 28; "Winans Testifies He Didn't Tamper with Stock Column," *Wall Street Journal* (20 March 1985), p. 10.

68. Carpenter, Felis and Winans v. U.S., 56 LW 4007 (1987).

69. 15 U.S.C. 1-7 (1976).

70. See U.S. v. Sealy, Inc., 383 U.S. 350.

71. Northern Pacific Railways v. U.S., 356 U.S. 1 (1958).

72. M. Maltz and S. Pollack, "Suspected Collusion Among Bidders," in G. Geis and E. Stotland, eds., *White Collar Crime, Theory and Research*, pp. 174–98.

73. Gilbert Geis, "White Collar Crime: The Heavy Electrical Equipment Antitrust Cases of 1961," in M. Erdmann and R. Lundman, eds., *Corporate and Governmental Deviance* (New York: Oxford University Press, 1978), pp. 58–79.

74. Cited in Clinard and Yeager, *Corporate Crime.*

75. Brooks Jackson, "ARCO Will Pay $22.5 Million to Settle Its Part of Lawsuit Against Oil Firms," in M. Erdmann and R. Lundman, eds., *Corporate and Governmental Deviance*, pp. 58–79.

76. Tim Carrington, "Federal Probes of Contractors Rise for Year," *Wall Street Journal* (23 February 1987), p. 50.

77. *Ibid.*

78. Clinard and Yeager, *Corporate Crime.*

79. John Conklin, *Illegal but Not Criminal* (Englewood Cliffs, N.J.: Prentice-Hall, 1972), pp. 45–46.

80. *Ibid.*

81. Richard Koenig, "Smith/Kline Pleads Guilty to U.S. Charges It Was Slow to Report Drug's Side Effects," *Wall Street Journal* (14 December 1984), p. 15.

82. "U-Haul Is Awarded $40 Million in Civil Suit Against Hall's Jartran," *Wall Street Journal* (30 November 1984), p. 56.

83. "Econotes," *Environmental Action* 13 (October 1981):7.

84. "Econotes," *Environmental Action* 13 (September 1981):5.

85. "Econotes," *Environmental Action* 13 (February 1982):7.

86. "Union Carbide Says Bhopal Plant Should Have Been Closed," *Wall Street Journal* (21 March 1985), p. 18.

87. See, generally, Paul Sweeney, "This Town's Not for Burning," *Environmental Action* 13 (February 1982):9.

88. Robert Taylor, "EPA Says Cleanup of Sites Will Cost $11.7 Billion More," *Wall Street Journal* (14 December 1984), p. 21.

89. 42 USC 7413 (C) (Supp. II, 1979).

90. 33 USC 1342 (1976); 33 USC 1362 (19).

91. 33 USC 401-407 (1976).

92. 42 USC 6901-87 (1976, Supp. III and Supp. IV, 1980).

93. 15 USC 2601-29 (1976).

94. Herbert Edelhertz and Charles Rogovin, eds., *A National Strategy for Containing White Collar Crime* (Lexington, Mass.: Lexington Books, 1980), Appendix A, pp. 122–23.

95. Quoted in Tim Metz and Michael Miller, "Boesky's Rise and Fall Illustrate a Compulsion to Profit by Getting Inside Track on Markets," *Wall Street Journal* (17 November 1986), p. 28.

96. Donald Cressey, *Other People's Money: A Study of the Social Psychology of Embezzlement* (Glencoe, Ill.: Free Press, 1973).

97. *Ibid.*, p. 96.
98. Ronald Kramer, "Corporate Crime: An Organizational Perspective," in Wickman and Dailey, eds., *White Collar and Economic Crime*, pp. 75–94.
99. David Simon and D. Stanley Eitzen, *Elite Deviance* (Boston: Allyn and Bacon, 1982), p. 28.
100. Jesilow, Pontell, and Geis, "Physician Immunity from Prosecution and Punishment for Medical Program Fraud," p. 19.
101. Clinard and Yeager, *Corporate Crime*, p. 124.
102. Peter Yeager, "Structural Bias in Regulatory Law Enforcement: The Case of the U.S. Environmental Protection Agency," *Social Problems* 34 (1987):330–44.
103. Geis, "Avocational Crime," p. 390.
104. Clinard and Yeager, *Corporate Crime*, p. 288.
105. *Ibid.*
106. *Time* (4 March 1985), p. 55.
107. Paul Blustein, "Disputes Arise Over Value of Laws on Insider Trading," *Wall Street Journal* (17 November 1986), p. 28.
108. Paul Barrett, "For Many Dalkon Shield Claimants Settlement Won't End the Trauma," *Wall Street Journal* (9 March 1988), p. 29.
109. This section relies heavily on Albert Reiss, Jr., "Selecting Strategies of Social Control over Organizational Life," in Keith Hawkins and John M. Thomas, eds., *Enforcing Regulation* (Boston: Klowver Publications, 1984), pp. 25–37.
110. *Ibid.*
111. John Braithwaite, "The Limits of Economism in Controlling Harmful Corporate Conduct," *Law and Society Review* 16 (1981–1982):481–504.
112. "Making Firms Liable For Cleaning Toxic Sites," *Wall Street Journal* (9 March 1988), p. 29.
113. Pound, "Honored Employee is a Key in Huge Fraud in Defense Purchasing," p. 1.
114. John Braithwaite and Gilbert Geis, "On Theory and Action for Corporate Crime Control," *Crime and Delinquency* 28 (1982):292–314.
115. Raymond Michalowski and Ronald Kramer, "The Space Between Laws: The Problem of Corporate Crime in a Transnational Context," *Social Problems* 34 (1987):34–53.
116. Geis, "White Collar and Corporate Crime," p. 154.
117. Tom Carrington, "Pay for General Dynamics Corporation to Be Withheld," *Wall Street Journal* (8 April 1985), p. 2.
118. This section relies heavily on Daniel Skoler, "White Collar Crime and the Criminal Justice System: Problems and Challenges," in Edelhertz and Rogovin, eds., *A National Strategy for Containing White Collar Crime*, pp. 57–76.
119. Alan Otten, "States Begin to Protect Employees Who Blow Whistle on Their Firms," *Wall Street Journal* (31 December 1984), p. 11.
120. William Power, "Belvill Ex-Aides are Sentenced to Prison Terms," *Wall Street Journal* (10 September 1987), p. 8.
121. Bill Richards and Alex Kotlowitz, "Judge Finds Three Corporate Officials Guilty of Murder in Cyanide Death of Worker," *Wall Street Journal* (17 June 1985), p. 2.
122. Donald Manson, *Tracking Offenders: White-Collar Crime* (Washington, D.C.: Bureau of Justice Statistics, 1986); Kenneth Carlson and Jan Chaiken, *White Collar Crime* (Washington, D.C.: Bureau of Justice Statistics, 1987).
123. Stanton Wheeler, David Weisburd, and Nancy Bode, "Sentencing the White-Collar Offender: Rhetoric and Reality," *American Sociological Review* 47 (1982):641–59.
124. Michael Benson and Esteban Walker, "Sentencing the White Collar Offender," *American Sociological Review* 53 (1988):294–302. See also, John Hagan and Alberto Palloni, " 'Club Fed' and the Sentencing of White-Collar Offenders Before and After Watergate," *Criminology* 24 (1986):603–22; Gary Marx, "Restoring Realism and Logic to Convert Facilitation Debate," *Journal of Social Issues* 43 (1987):43–55.
125. See, generally, President's Commission on Organized Crime, Report to the President and the Attorney General, *The Impact: Organized Crime Today* (Washington, D.C.: U.S. Government Printing Office, 1986). (Hereafter cited as Organized Crime Commission.)
126. This section was adapted from Task Force on Organized Crime, *Organized Crime* (Washington, D.C.: U.S. Government Printing Office, 1976), pp. 7–8.
127. Alan Block and William Chambliss, *Organizing Crime* (New York: Elsevier, 1981).
128. Organized Crime Commission, p. 462.
129. Attorney General's Commission on Pornography, *Final Report* (Washington, D.C.: U.S. Government Printing Office 1986), p. 1053.
130. Alan Block, *East Side/West Side* (New Brunswick, N.J.: Transaction Books, 1983), pp. vii, 10–11.
131. G. R. Blakey and M. Goldsmith, "Criminal Redistribution of Stolen Property: The Need for Law Reform," *Michigan Law Review* 81 (August 1976):45–46.
132. Merry Morash, "Organized Crime," in Robert Meier, ed., *Major Forms of Crime* (Beverly Hills, Cal.: Sage, 1986), pp. 198.
133. Stephen Koepp, "Dirty Cash and Tarnished Vaults," *Time* (25 February 1985), p. 65.
134. Roy Rowan, "The 50 Biggest Mafia Bosses," *Fortune* (10 November 1986), p. 24.
135. Donald Cressey, *Theft of the Nation* (New York: Harper and Row, 1969).
136. Dwight Smith, *The Mafia Mystique* (New York: Basic Books, 1975).

137. Organized Crime Commission, p. 489.

138. Robert Rhodes, *Organized Crime, Crime Control vs. Civil Liberties* (New York: Random House, 1984).

139. This section borrows heavily from James Inciardi, *Reflections on Crime* (New York: Holt, Rinehart, and Winston, 1978), pp. 34–53; F. Browning and J. Gerassi, *The American Way of Crime* (New York: Putnam, 1980), pp. 288–472; August Bequai, *Organized Crime* (Lexington, Mass.: Lexington Books, 1979).

140. Organized Crime Commission, p. 52.

141. Jay Albanese, "God and the Mafia Revisited: From Valachi to Frantianno," Paper presented at the Annual Meeting of the American Society of Criminology, Toronto, Canada, 1982.

142. Philip Jenkins and Gary Potter, "The Politics and Mythology of Organized Crime: A Philadelphia Case Study," *Journal of Criminal Justice* 15 (1987):473–84.

143. Block, *East Side/West Side.*

144. This model is recognized by the Organized Crime Commission.

145. Francis Ianni, *Black Mafia: Ethnic Succession in Organized Crime* (New York: Pocket Books, 1975).

146. Robert Kelly and Rufus Schatzberg, "Types of Minority Organized Crime: Some Considerations," Paper presented at the American Society of Criminology Meeting, Montreal, Canada, November, 1987.

147. Peter Kerr, "Chinese Now Dominate New York Heroin Trade," *The New York Times* (9 August 1987), p. 1.

148. Jenkins and Potter, "The Politics and Mythology of Organized Crime," pp. 473–84.

149. William Chambliss, *On the Take* (Bloomington, Ind.: Indiana University Press, 1978).

150. George Vold, *Theoretical Criminology,* 2d ed., rev. by Thomas Bernard (New York: Oxford University Press, 1979).

151. 18 USC 1952 (1976).

152. Pub. L. No. 91-452, Title IX, 84 Stat. 922 (1970) (codified at 18 USC 1961-68, 1976).

153. This section was adapted from "White-Collar Crime: Second Annual Review of Law," *American Criminal Law Review* 19 (1986):351.

154. Ed Magnuson, "Hard Days for the Mafia," *Time* (4 March 1985).

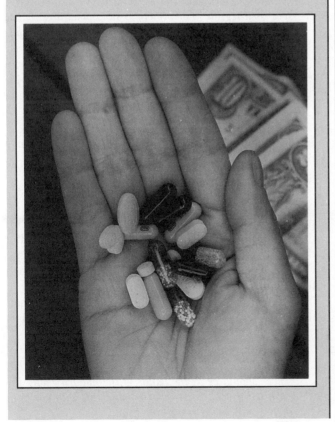

☰ CHAPTER 13

PUBLIC
ORDER
CRIME

INTRODUCTION

The preceding three chapters discussed crimes of theft and violence. There is usually little question that, as a group, these acts are essentially harmful to their victims and should be eliminated from society. They are *mala in se* crimes—evil unto themselves. In this chapter, **public order crimes** are the focus of attention. They are often referred to as **victimless crimes,** though that title can be misleading.[1] Public order crimes involve acts that interfere with the operations of society and the ability of people to function efficiently. As a group, such crimes are **mala prohibitum**—outlawed because they conflict with social policy, prevailing moral rules, and current public opinion.

Statutes designed to uphold public order usually prohibit the distribution of morally questionable goods and services—erotic material, commercial sex, gambling, drugs. They are controversial in part because millions of otherwise law-abiding citizens—students, workers, professionals—often partake of these outlawed activities and consequently become involved in criminal activity. There is also controversy because they represent the selective prohibition of desired goods and services; in other words, they outlaw what some people consider "sin" and "vice".

This chapter is divided into three main sections. The first briefly discusses the relationship of law and morality. The second deals with public order crimes of a sexual nature: homosexual acts, prostitution, and pornography. The third section focuses on substance abuse: drugs and alcohol.

LAW AND MORALITY

Legislation of moral issues always has been debated. It is generally agreed that the law should protect society and reduce social harm, but the question arises of whether harm is really done by public order crimes or by any other acts made illegal because they violate prevailing moral standards.

When a store is robbed or a child assaulted, it is relatively easy to understand and condemn the social harm done the victim. However, it is more difficult to sympathize with or even identify the victim in a crime such as prostitution or pornography. Is the victim the prostitute? While some women who engage in sex for profit may be considered victims, others are willing and successful entrepreneurs earning $75,000 or more a year. Is the victim the client? Hardly, since he has made a voluntary and determined effort to procure her services. If public order crimes do not harm their participants, then perhaps society as a whole should be considered the "victim" of crime.

Some scholars argue that acts such as prostitution, pornography, and drug use erode the moral fabric of society and therefore should be punished by law. They are crimes, this argument goes, because "it is one of the functions of the criminal law to give expression to the collective feeling of revulsion toward certain acts, even when they are not very dangerous."[2]

In his classic statement on the function of morality in the law, Sir Patrick Devlin states:

> *Without shared ideas on politics, morals, and ethics no society can exist . . . If men and women try to create a society in which there is no fundamental agreement about good and evil they will fail; if having based it on common agreement, the agreement goes, the society will disintegrate. For society is not something that is kept together physically; it is held by the invisible bonds of common thought. If the bonds were too far relaxed the members would drift apart. A common morality is part of the bondage. The bondage is part of the price of society; and mankind, which needs society, must pay its price.*[3]

In sum, society outlaws so-called victimless crimes because one of the functions of criminal law is to express public morality.[4]

However, opponents of this view reach a very different conclusion. Basing criminal definitions on moral beliefs, they argue, has always been a difficult decision: Who defines *deviance?* Are we not punishing differences rather than social harm? As Justice William O. Douglas so succinctly put it, "What may be trash to me may be prized by others."[5]

Some influential legal scholars have questioned the propriety of legislating morals. H. L. A. Hart states:

> *It is fatally easy to confuse the democratic principle that power should be in the hands of the majority with the utterly different claim that the majority, with power in their hands, need respect no limits.*

Certainly there is a special risk in a democracy that the majority may dictate how all should live.[6]

Joseph Gussfield argues that the purpose of outlawing acts because they are immoral is to show the moral superiority of those who condemn the act over those who partake of them. The legislation of morality "enhances the social status of groups carrying the affirmed culture and degrades groups carrying that which is condemned as deviant."[7] In other words, banning deviance has no intrinsic moral or social purpose.

Violations of conventional morality can also serve a useful social function. For example, there is some evidence that watching pornographic films can provide excitement and release tension which might otherwise be satisfied in more harmful and violent acts. Deviant behaviors also may be endured because they enhance legitimate enterprises to which they are connected: illegal gambling draws people to the neighborhood bar; people attend legal bingo games which also allow them to engage in illegal betting; people go to legitimate massage parlors whose employees engage in sex for profit on the side.[8]

Howard Becker has labeled those who wish to control such immorality as **moral entrepreneurs.** These rule creators, argues Becker, go on **moral crusades** to rid the world of evil. They operate with an absolute certainty that their way is right and that any means are justified to get their way: "The crusader is fervent and righteous, often self-righteous."[9]

The prevailing view of "proper" moral behavior is constantly changing, and laws created to govern its direction are accordingly subject to a great variety of personal interpretation. Consequently, public order laws are unevenly enforced, vary in content from jurisdiction to jurisdiction, and carry a wide range of sanctions. For example, in some states possession of marijuana is punished by years in prison; in others by a small fine. The decriminalization of public order crimes is always a matter for public debate.

Enforcement of morally tinged statutes is also a significant problem for law enforcement agencies. If police agencies enforce laws governing morality too vigorously, they are branded as reactionaries who waste time on petty issues. Why arrest prostitutes when murderers go free? If, on the other hand, police agencies ignore public order crimes, they are accused of being too lazy to do anything about immorality and

social degeneracy. It has become fashionable for Hollywood producers to portray the lone vigilante who gets rid of pushers and pimps when the police won't take action (for example, *Death Wish, The Equalizer,* etc.).

In the following sections some of the most familiar public order crimes are explored.

ILLEGAL SEXUALITY

One type of public order crime relates to what conventional society considers to be deviant sexual practices. Among these outlawed practices are included: homosexual acts, prostitution, and pornography. Laws controlling these behaviors have been the focus of much debate.

Homosexuality

Homosexuality—the word derives from the Greek **homos,** meaning "same"—refers to erotic interest in members of one's own sex. However, to engage in homosexual behavior does not necessarily mean one is a homosexual. People may engage in homosexuality because heterosexual partners are unavailable (for example, in the armed services). Some may have sex forced on them by aggressive homosexual partners, a condition common to prison inmates. Some adolescents may experiment with partners of the same sex, though their sexual affiliation is heterosexual. Albert Reiss has described the behavior of delinquent youths, who engage in homosexual behavior for money but still regard themselves as heterosexuals, and who discontinue all homosexual activities as adults.[10] Finally, it is possible to be a homosexual and not engage in sexual conduct with members of the same sex. To avoid this confusion, it might be helpful to adopt the definition of a homosexual as one who is "motivated in adult life by a definite preferential erotic attraction to members of the same sex and who usually (but not necessarily) engages in overt sexual relations with them."[11]

Homosexual behavior has existed in most societies. Records of its presence can be found in prehistoric art and hieroglyphics. In their view of the literature on 76 preliterate societies, C. S. Ford and F. A. Beach found that male homosexuality was viewed as normal in 49, female homosexuality in 17. Even when homosexuality was banned or sanctioned, it still persisted.[12] The incidence of male homosexuality in the United States has been estimated at anywhere between 3 and 16 percent of the male population and between 2 and 6 percent of the female population, though many more individuals may have had homosexual experiences sometime in their lives.[13]

Attitudes Toward Homosexuality. Throughout Western history, homosexuals have been subject to discrimination, sanction, and violence. The Bible expressly forbids homosexuality—Leviticus in the Old Testament, Paul's Epistles Romans and Corinthians in the New Testament—and the prohibition has been the basis for repressing homosexual behavior.[14] Homosexuals were brutalized and killed by the ancient Hebrews, a practice continued by the Christians who ruled Western Europe. Laws providing the death penalty for homosexuals existed until 1791 in France, until 1861 in England, and until 1889 in Scotland. Up until the Revolution, some American colonies punished homosexuality with death. In Hitler's Germany, 50,000 homosexuals were put in concentration camps; up to 400,000 more from occupied countries were killed.

Today there are many reasons given for an extremely negative overreaction to homosexuals, referred to as **homophobia.** As already mentioned, some religious people believe that the Bible condemns same-sex relations and that this behavior is therefore a sin. Others develop a deep-rooted hatred of gays because they are insecure about their own sexual identity. Some are ignorant about the lifestyle of gays and fear that homosexuality is a disease that can be caught or that homosexuals will seduce their children.[15]

Are antigay attitudes changing? There is evidence that negative attitudes toward gays persist in our society. During the 1960s, 67 percent of people surveyed believed that homosexuality was obscene and vulgar. Fewer than 20 percent believed that laws banning homosexuality should be lifted.[16] Studies conducted since 1970 indicate that a majority of people still view gays as sick, sinful, or dangerous.[17]

Even today there is some question about whether homosexuality is a disease, a mental illness, or an acceptable lifestyle. It took until 1973 for the American Psychiatric Association (APA) to remove homosexuality from its list of mental illnesses. However, a subsequent survey of 2,500 members of the APA found that 69 percent held the belief that homosexuality was an abnormal way of satisfying sexual need, 60 percent saw homosexuals as less capable than heterosexuals of mature relationships, and 70 percent thought that homosexuals' problems were more likely to stem from inner conflicts than from prejudice.[18] These attitudes are reflected in the legal penalties suffered by gays.

Fears about the disease AIDS have added to these tensions and further restricted the acceptance of homosexual behavior by mainstream America. A survey by the National Gay and Lesbian Task Force found that the number of attacks against gay men and women has increased significantly in recent years. Their 1987 survey uncovered more than 7,008 incidents in 32 states; a 1986 survey uncovered 4,946 attacks in 27 states. AIDS was a factor in about 15 percent of the attacks against gays. The relative increase "gay bashing" incidents gives weight to the charge that the country is becoming increasingly "homophobic".[19]

Homosexuality and the Law. Homosexuality, considered a legal and moral crime throughout most of Western history, is no longer a crime in the United States. In the case of *Robinson v. California*, the U.S. Supreme Court determined that people could not be criminally prosecuted because of their status (for example, drug addict or homosexual).[20]

However, in most states the lifestyle and activities of homosexuals are considered illegal. The United States actually has some of the harshest laws against homosexuality. For example, all forms of nongenital heterosexual intercourse are illegal in about half the states under statutes prohibiting **sodomy,** deviant sexuality, or buggery. Maximum penalties range from three years to life imprisonment, with 10 years being the most common sentence.[21]

In 1986, the Supreme Court in *Bowers v. Hardwick* upheld a Georgia statute making it a crime to engage in consensual sodomy, even within the confines of one's own home.[22] The Court disregarded the *Bowers* claim that homosexuals have a "fundamental right" to engage in sexual activity and that consensual, voluntary sex between adults in the home was a private matter which should not be controlled by the law. If all sex within the home were a private matter, Justice White argued for the majority, then such crimes as incest and adultery could not be prosecuted. Citing the historical legal prohibitions against homosexual sodomy, the Court distinguished between the right of gay couples to engage in the sexual behavior of their choice and the sexual privacy the law affords married heterosexual couples. Ironically, the Georgia statute, which carries a 20-year prison sentence, is not directed solely towards homosexuals but refers to "a person . . ." in its prohibition of sodomy.[23]

Prestigious legal bodies, such as the American Law Institute (ALI), have called for the abolition of statutes prohibiting nonheterosexual sex, unless force or coercion is used.[24] A number of states, including Illinois, Connecticut, and Nebraska, have adopted the ALI's Model Penal Code policy of legalizing any consensual sexual behavior between adults as long as it is conducted in private and is not forced; in all, about 20 states have decriminalized private, consensual sodomy between adult homosexuals.[25]

Homosexuals still suffer other legal restrictions. Although 40 states have laws banning sexual discrimination, Miami repealed its gay rights ordinance in 1977, and in 1985 Houston voters rejected by a 4 to 1 margin a proposal to eliminate sexual preference in hiring, firing, and promoting city employees.[26] Though the federal government's Civil Service Commission found in 1975 that homosexuals could not be barred from federal employment, gays are still considered security risks and are not allowed to work in the CIA or FBI; they are also barred from military service. In the case of *Dronenburg v. Zech*, a U.S. Circuit Court of Appeals ruled that the Navy's policy of mandatory discharge for homosexuals does not violate their constitutional rights.[27]

Homosexuals may still be evicted from private housing at the landlord's discretion. Gays are prohibited from living together in public housing projects. In most areas, private employers may also discriminate against gay men and women. For example, a federal court upheld the right of an airline to fire a pilot who underwent a sex change operation.[28]

In sum, though it is not a crime to be a homosexual, homosexual acts are still illegal in most states. However, most police agencies enforce laws banning homosexual practices only if they are forced to do so, if the acts occur in public places, of if the acts are done for financial consideration.[29]

Prostitution

Prostitution, derived from the Latin *prostituere*, which means "to cause to stand in front of," has been known for thousands of years. It is the so-called "oldest profession." By implication, the prostitute is viewed as publicly offering her body for sale. The earliest record of prostitution appears in ancient Mesopotamia, where priests engaged in sex to promote fertility in the community. All women were required to put in some time at temple duty, and passing strangers were expected to make donations to the temple after enjoying its services.[30]

Modern commercial sex appears to have its roots in ancient Greece, where Solon established licensed brothels in 550 B.C. The earnings of Greek prostitutes helped pay for the temple of Aphrodite. Famous men openly went to prostitutes to enjoy intellectual, aesthetic, and sexual stimulation.[31]

Today there are many variations of prostitution, but in general the term can be defined as the granting of nonmarital sexual access, established by mutual agreement of the prostitutes, their clients, and their employers, for remuneration. This definition is sexually neutral, since prostitutes can, of course, be straight or gay, male or female.[32] Prostitutes also come from all age groups, and there is growing concern for youthful runaways who sell themselves for survival; in 1986 police reported arresting 247 children under age 15 for prostitution.[33] At the other extreme is the case of 77-year-old Helen Kehoe, who on 22 April 1988 became one of the oldest women ever jailed for prostitution (she actually ran a brothel); in all, 457 people over 65 were arrested for prostitution in 1986.[34]

A recent analysis has amplified the definition of prostitution by describing the conditions usually present in a commercial sexual transaction:

• *Activity that has sexual significance for the customer*—this includes the entire range of sexual behavior, from sexual intercourse to exhibitionism, sadism/masochism, and oral sex.

• *Economic transaction*—something of economic value, not necessarily money, is exchanged for the activity

• *Emotional indifference*—the sexual exchange is simply for economic consideration; though the participants may know one another, their interaction has nothing to do with affection for one another.[35]

The following sections focus primarily on the nature and extent of heterosexual prostitution.

Incidence of Prostitution.   It is difficult to assess the number of prostitutes operating in the United States. One estimate is one-quarter to one-half million full- or part-time prostitutes—one in 200 to 500 women.[36]

Kinsey's study of male sexuality found that nearly 50 percent of white males had visited a prostitute at least once. However, commercial sex was linked to social and educational standing. By age 25, about two-thirds of non–college-educated men, but only about one-fourth of college-educated men, had visited a prostitute. Moreover, Kinsey found that about 20 percent of college men had been sexually initiated by prostitutes.[37]

It is likely that the number of men who hire prostitutes is declining. Hunt's 1974 study found that only 10 percent of college-educated men had been sexually initiated by prostitutes, half the number found by Kinsey in 1948. He states:

> *A century ago, and even a generation ago, a considerable number of young males went to prostitutes for their sexual initiation, and some males—especially those in the lower social and educational levels—resorted to them often and regularly prior to marriage. The current wave of sexual liberation has made prostitution far more open and visible than ever before, as witness the burgeoning of "massage" and "body rub" establishments, commercially sponsored sex clubs, so-called dating bureaus, street-corner solicitation . . . and hooker traffic in singles bars. Yet our data show that, despite all this, there have been distinct decreases in the past generation in the percentage of American males who are sexually initiated by prostitutes, and in the average frequency with which they have such experiences.[38]*

How can these changes be accounted for? One possibility is changing sexual mores brought about by the so-called sexual revolution. Men are less likely to engage prostitutes because legitimate alternatives for sexuality are more open to them. In recent years, the fear of AIDS has changed sexual attitudes to the point where many men may avoid visiting prostitutes for fear of irreversible health hazards.

Despite such supposed changes in sexual morality, arrests for prostitution have increased dramatically in the past decade. The Uniform Crime Reports indicate that such arrests increased 25 percent between 1978 and 1987 (from 76,000 to 95,000); males accounted for about 32,000 of these arrests.[39] More alarming is the fact that about 1,300 arrests were of women under 18. In 1987, about 500 recorded arrests were of children 15 and under; 11 of those arrested *were under 10 years old*. The argument that the law should not interfere with sexual transactions because no one is harmed is undermined by these disturbing statistics.

Types of Prostitution.   Several different types of prostitutes operate in the United States.

Streetwalkers.   Working the streets in plain sight of police, citizens, and customers are streetwalkers. They are considered the least attractive, lowest paid, most vulnerable women in the profession.

Streetwalkers wear bright clothing, makeup, and jewelery to attract customers; they take their customers to hotels. However, the term *hooker* is not derived from the ability of streetwalkers to hook clients with their charms. The term actually stems from the popular name given women who followed Union General "Fighting Joe" Hooker's army during the Civil War.[40]

Because streetwalkers must openly display their occupation, they are very likely to be involved with the police. Studies indicate they are most likely to be members of ethnic or racial minorities who live in poverty. Of all prostitutes, streetwalkers have the highest incidence of drug abuse and larceny arrests.[41]

Bar girls.   B-girls (bar girls) spend their time in bars, drinking and waiting to be picked up by customers. Though alcoholism may be problem, B-girls usually work out an arrangement with the bartender so they are served diluted drinks or water colored with dye or tea, for which the customer is charged an exorbitant price. In some bars, the B-girl is given a credit for each drink she gets the customer to buy. It is common to find B-girls in towns with military bases and large transient populations, such as Boston and San Diego.[42]

Brothels.   Also called bordellos, cathouses, sporting houses, and houses of ill repute, **brothels** flourished in the nineteenth and early twentieth centuries. They were large establishments, usually run by **madams,** that housed several prostitutes. The madam, often a retired prostitute, was the senior administrator and owner. She made arrangements for opening the place, attracted prostitutes and customers, worked out understandings with police authorities, and pacified neighbors.[43] The madam was part psychologist, part parent-figure, part business entrepreneur.

Some brothels and their madams have received national notoriety. Polly Adler wrote a highly publicized autobiography called *A House is Not a Home*. Sally Stanford maintained a succession of luxuriously furnished brothels in San Francisco. Stanford never made a secret of her profession; she actually listed her phone number in the city directory. In 1962 and 1970 she ran for the San Francisco City Council. Madam Xaviera Hollander made national headlines with the publication of her book *The Happy Hooker*.

Brothels declined in importance following World War II. The closing of the last brothel in Texas is chronicled in the play and movie *The Best Little Whorehouse in Texas*. Today, the most well-known brothels exist in Nevada, where prostitution is legal outside large population centers. Such houses as "Mustang Ranch," "Miss Kitty's," and "Pink Pussycat" service customers who are willing to drive out of Reno and Las Vegas to partake of their services.

In 1984, brothels made national news when socialite Sydney Biddle Barrows was arrested by New York police for operating a $1 million per year prostitution ring out of a bordello on West 74th Street.[44] From a socially prominent family who traced their descendants to the *Mayflower*, Barrows ranked her 20 girls on looks and personality from As ($125 per hour) to Cs ($400 per hour) and kept 60 percent of their take. Her "black book" of clients was described by police as a mini *Who's Who*.

Call girls. The aristocrats of prostitution are **call girls.** They charge customers up to $1,000 per night and may net up to $100,000 per year.

Many call girls come from middle-class backgrounds and service upper-class customers. Attempting to dispel the notion that their service is simply sex for money, they concentrate on making their clients feel important and attractive.

Working exclusively via telephone "dates," call girls get their clients by word of mouth or by making arrangements with local bellhops, cab drivers, and so on. They either entertain clients in their own apartments or do "outcalls" to clients' hotels and apartments. Upon retiring from "the life," a call girl can sell her datebook listing client names and sexual preferences for thousands of dollars. Despite the lucrative nature of their business, call girls suffer considerable risk by being alone and unprotected with strangers. It is common for them to request the business cards of their clients to make sure they are dealing with "upstanding citizens."

Circuit travelers. Prostitutes known as circuit travelers travel in groups of two or three to lumber camps and labor camps. They will ask the foremen for permission to ply their trade, service the whole crew in an evening, and then move on.

Rap booths. A new phenomenon in commercial sex, rap booths are located in the adult entertainment zones of New York, Boston, and San Francisco.[45] The prostitute and her customer occupy separate booths, screened off by a glass wall. They talk via telephone for as long as the customer is willing to pay. The more money he spends, the more she engages in sexual banter and disrobing. There is no actual touching, and sex is through masturbation, with the prostitute serving as a masturbation aid similar in function to a pornographic magazine.

Other varieties. Some "working girls" are based in **massage parlors.** Though it is unusual for a masseuse to offer all the services of prostitution, oral sex and manual stimulation are common. Most localities have attempted to limit commercial sex in massage parlors by passing ordinances specifying that the masseuse keep certain parts of her body covered and limiting the areas of the body that can be massaged.

Photography studios and model and escort services sometimes serve as covers for commercial sex. Some photo studies will allow customers to use body paint on models before the photo sessions start. Stag party girls will service all-male parties and groups by putting on shows and having sex with participants.

In years past, many hotels had live-in prostitutes. Today's hotel prostitute makes a deal with the bell captain or manager to refer customers to her for a fee; some second-rate hotels still have resident prostitutes.

Becoming a Prostitute. Why does a woman turn to prostitution? Prostitutes often come from troubled homes marked by extreme conflict and hostility and from poor urban areas or rural communities. Hostility toward the father is common, as is incest and child molesting. Many prostitutes were initiated into sex by family members as early as 10 to 12 years of age. Lower-class girls who get into "the life" report conflict with school authorities, poor grades, and an overly regimented school experience.[46]

In a similar vein, Charles Winick and Paul Kinsie provide this portrait of the girl who becomes a prostitute: she grew up in a slum neighborhood or broken home; was born out of wedlock; was a school dropout; is a minority group member; fantasizes about money and success; is a member of a "loose crowd"; had seen prostitutes in the neighborhood; father was absent, or abusive; had unfortunate experiences with husband or boyfriend; has trouble keeping a job.[47]

However, there is no actual evidence that girls become prostitutes because of psychological problems or personality disturbances. In a study of white female prostitutes, Paul Gebhard found that very few (about 4 percent) were forced into the life; most reported entering prostitution voluntarily because they disliked the discipline of conventional work.[48] Also, Gebhard's study dispels the notion that prostitutes were seduced and abandoned as young girls, have insatiable sexual desires, or are drug addicts.

Jennifer James claims that the primary cause of women's becoming prostitutes is the supply and demand equation operating in society.[49] She contends that male clients are socialized to view sex as a commodity that can be purchased. The quantity of sex, rather than its quality, has the higher value for U.S. males. Women who are socialized to view themselves as sex objects may easily step over the line of propriety and accept money for their favors. These women view their bodies as saleable commodities, and most prostitution does in fact pay better than other occupations available for women with limited education. Helping push the woman to take the final step into prostitution are the troubled personal circumstances described previously. James backs up her view with a research study that found that only 8 percent of prostitutes claim to have started because of dire economic necessity, while 57 percent were motivated by a desire for money and luxuries.

Pimps.   A pimp derives part or all of his livelihood from the earnings of a prostitute. The pimp helps steer customers to the prostitute, stays on the alert for and

deals with police, posts bail, and protects his girls from unruly customers.[50] To the prostitute, the pimp is a surrogate father, husband, and lover figure. She may sell her body to customers, but the prostitute reserves care and affection for her pimp.

Pimps can pick up established "working girls" or they can "turn out" young girls who have never been in "the life." Occasionally, but not as often as the media would like us to believe, they pick up young runaways, buy them clothes and jewelery, and turn them into **baby pros.**

What attracts men to the life of the pimp? One view is that many pimps originally worked on the fringes of prostitution as bellhops, elevator operators, or barmen and subsequently drifted into the profession. An opposing view is that pimps began as young men seduced by older prostitutes, who taught them how to succeed in "the life," how to behave, and how to control women.[51]

In the 1920s and 1930s, most pimps were white ethnics. Today they are predominantly black, and the few whites who enter the profession adopt a black lifestyle. However, the decline of the brothel, the development of independent prostitutes, and the control of prostitution by organized crime has decreased the number of full-time pimps. In the last 20 years, the terms *popcorn pimps, chili pimps,* and *coffee and cake pimps* have increasingly been used to describe the low esteem pimps are held in and their reduced importance to prostitutes.[52]

Prostitution and the Law.   Although prostitution could not exist without a great deal of public support, it is currently illegal in all states except Nevada. The federal government's Mann Act (1925) prohibits bringing women into the country or transporting them across state lines for the purposes of prostitution. Often called the **white slave act,** it carries with it a $5,000 fine, five years in prison, or both.

Typically, prostitution is considered a misdemeanor, punishable by a fine or a short jail sentence. Consequently, even if arrested, most "working girls" are bailed out and are soon back on the street. Many streetwalkers have been arrested 30 or 40 times. Of course, the longer their police record, the less likely they will be to quickly re-enter conventional society.

Though police administrators may find the enforcement of solicitation laws a nuisance, they are often prodded into action by complaints of citizens and the news media. It is common for legitimate restaurant, theater, an store owners to pressure police officials to control streetwalkers, massage parlors, and B-girls who are disturbing customers in their areas. Prostitution is also associated with other criminal acts and environments that demand police attention: drug use, larceny, the spread of venereal disease, and organized crime.

The classic confrontation between police and prostitutes occurs over the method of control. To prove solicitation, the police must be able to testify in court that they were approached and asked for payment for sexual services. Obviously, plainclothes officers are needed for this work. Most big-city police departments maintain vice squads whose members pose as customers and arrest prostitutes who solicit them. The line between legitimate police control and illegal entrapment of prostitutes is a fine one. Many cases get thrown out of court because police were too zealous in their jobs.[53]

To mitigate the conflict, some cities have set up areas where detente exists between prostitutes and law enforcement. In San Francisco it is the Tenderloin area, in New York it is 8th Avenue, and in Boston it is the Combat Zone. As long as pimps, streetwalkers, and B-girls stay in these areas, they are allowed to ply their trade with impunity. The concept of an adult entertainment zone is designed to limit the public's moral outrage, provide access to commercial sex for those adults who desire it, and reduce the costs to the criminal justice system of processing prostitutes.

Another legal ploy used to control prostitution is active enforcement of laws making it a crime to solicit prostitutes. Though clients are rarely arrested, some jurisdictions publish their names or license plate numbers in newspapers.

It is unlikely that the law will ever control prostitution. If the "oldest profession" is to end, it probably will be due to changing sexual morality, fear of disease, and increased economic opportunities for women.

Pornography

Pornography is another moral-legal issue for criminological study. The term derives from the Greek *porne*, meaning "prostitute," and *graphein*, meaning "to

write." In the heart of many major cities are stores devoted to the display and sale of books, magazines, and films that depict explicit sex acts. The purpose of this material is to provide sexual titillation and excitement for paying customers.

Through material depicting nudity and sex is legal, most criminal codes contain provisions prohibiting the production, display, and sale of obscene material. *Obscenity*, the word derived form the Latin term *caenum* ("filth"), is currently defined by Webster's dictionary as "deeply offensive to morality or decency . . . designed to incite to lust or depravity."[54]

The problem of controlling pornography centers on this definition of obscenity. Police and law enforcement officials can legally seize only material that is judged obscene. "But who," critics ask, "is to judge what is truly obscene?" At one time, such novels as *Tropic of Cancer* by Henry Miller, *Ulysses* by James Joyce, and *Lady Chatterly's Lover* by D. H. Lawrence were prohibited because they were considered obscene. Today they are considered works of great literary value. Thus, what is obscene today may be considered a work of art, or at least socially acceptable, at a future time. *Playboy* and *Penthouse* magazines, sold openly on most college campuses, display nude men and women in all kinds of sexually explicit poses. Moreover, the First Amendment of the U.S. Constitution guarantees freedom of speech and expression. Allowing individual judgments on what is obscene makes the Constitution's guarantee of free speech unworkable. For example, what happens if a judge rules that books on communism are obscene? Could not anti-obscenity statutes also be used to control political and social dissent?

Opponents of pornography argue that it degrades the men and women who are featured in "dirty pictures," customers, and members of the public who are sometimes forced to see obscene material. Pornographers also exploit women and children. The **Attorney General's Commission on Pornography,** set up by the Reagan Administration to review the sale and distribution of sexually explicit material, concluded that many performers and models are the victims of physical and psychological coercion.[55] The so-called **kiddy porn** industry is estimated to amount to over $1 billion of a total $2.5 billion spent on pornography. In Houston, police uncovered a warehouse filled with 15,000 color slides of children, as well as

Skyrocketing real estate values, and not law enforcement vigilance, may speed the end of adult theaters and bookstores.

thousands of pornographic magazines and reels of film. Each year, over a million children are used in pornography or prostitution, many of them runaways whose plight is exploited by adults. In New York City, Convenant House, a shelter care home for children, annually aids about 5,000 runaways. Of these 2,000 have been involved in pornography and 1,000 are under 12 years of age.[56]

Ann Wolbert Burgess studied 55 child pornography rings and found that the typical one contained between three and 11 children, predominantly males, some of nursery school age. The adults who controlled the ring used a position of trust to recruit the children and then continued to exploit them through a combination of material and psychological rewards. Burgess found that different types of child pornography rings exist. *Transition rings* are impromptu groups set up to sell and trade photos and sex. *Syndicated rings* have well-structured organizations that recruit chil-

dren and create extensive networks of customers who desire sexual services.[57]

Critics of pornography also charge that it denigrates and exploits women. Laura Lederer cites the case of *Bondage* magazine, which regularly shows women being tied up and having scissors, hot irons, torches, and knives held to their breasts and vaginas.[58] Another magazine, *Brutal Trio*, in one issue shows three men kidnapping a young woman, a 12-year-old girl, and a grandmother and beating them senseless, kicking them until they pass out, then raping them and beating them again. Even nationally distributed magazines such as *Playboy* are taken to task for their destructive view of women:

By socializing the view of women as unreal sex objects, Playboy and the magazines that have followed its lead have contributed to the increasing antagonism and subsequent violence between males and females, methodi-

cally helping break down the ability and need to care which . . . human beings are born with and which, as social animals, we need in order to survive.[59]

Does Pornography Cause Violence?   An issue critical to the debate over pornography is whether viewing it produces sexual violence or assaultive behavior against women.

There is some evidence that viewing sexually explicit material actually has little effect on behavior. In 1970, the **National Commission on Obscenity and Pornography** reviewed all available material on the effects of pornography and authorized independent research projects. The Commission found no clear relationship between pornography and violence, and it recommended that federal, state, and local legislation should not interfere with the rights of adults who wish to read, obtain, or view explicit sexual materials.[60] Almost 20 years later, the highly controversial Attorney General's Commission on Pornography, sponsored by a conservative Reagan Administration, called for legal attacks on hard-core pornography and condemnation of all sexually-related material; it also found little evidence that obscenity was a per se cause of antisocial behavior.[61]

How might we account for this surprisingly insignificant association? Some explanation may be found in Danish sociologist Berl Kutchinsky's widely cited research, showing that the rate of sex offenses actually declined shortly after pornography was decriminalized in Denmark in 1967.[62] He attributed this trend to the fact that viewing erotic material may act as a safety valve for those whose impulses might otherwise lead them to violence. In a similar vein, Michael Goldstein found that convicted rapists and sex offenders report less exposure to pornography than a control group of nonoffenders.[63] It is possible that viewing prurient material may have the unintended side-effect of satisfying erotic impulses which otherwise might have resulted in more sexually aggressive behavior.

However, this issue is far from settled. There are a number of criminologists who believe that the positive relationship between pornography consumption and rape rates in various countries, including the United States, is evidence that obscenity may indeed have a powerful influence on criminality.[64] Nonetheless, the weight of the evidence shows little relationship between violence and pornography per se.

Violent Pornography and Violent Crime.   While there is little documentation of a correlation between pornography and violent crime, there is stronger evidence that people exposed to erotic literature that portrays violence and sadism and which indicates that women enjoy being raped and degraded are likely to be sexually aggressive towards female victims.[65] In 1986 the Attorney General's Commission on Pornography concluded that a causal link could be drawn between exposure to sexually explicit material with violent themes and sexual violence.[66] After reviewing the literature on the subject, the Commission found that while the behavioral effects of nonviolent, nonsexually degrading pornography was insignificant, exposure to sexually violent and degrading materials:

1. Leads to a greater acceptance of rape myths and violence against women

2. Has more pronounced effects when the victim is shown enjoying the use of force or violence

3. Is arousing for rapists and for some males in the general population

4. Has resulted in sexual aggression against women in controlled laboratory settings[67]

Experimental laboratory studies by Edward Donnerstein and Seymour Fishbach and by Neal Malamuth have found that men exposed to violence in pornography are more likely to act aggressively toward women.[68]

The evidence suggests that violence and sexual aggression are not linked to erotic or pornographic films per se, but that erotic films depicting violence, rape, brutality, and aggression may evoke similar feelings in viewers. This finding is especially distressing because it is common for adults only books and films to have sexually violent themes such as rape, bondage, and mutilation.[69]

Pornography and the Law.   The First Amendment of the Constitution protects free speech and prohibits police agencies from limiting the public's right of free expression. However, the U.S. Supreme Court held in the twin cases of *Roth v. United States* and *Alberts v. California* that obscenity was not covered by the First Amendment.[70] In deciding these cases, the Court stated that the First Amendment protects all "ideas

CLOSE-UP

Obscenity

Under current legal philosophy local communities must define standard for what material is considered obscene. The standard created for Council Bluffs, Iowa, is typical of local obscenity statues:

43.101 Sale of obscene material to minors. It is unlawful to sell or display to minors with or without monetary consideration certain printed matter, photographs, motion picture film, and other similar visual representations depicting sexual conduct, nudity, or sado-masochistic abuse which is harmful to minors, or to exhibit, give, or sell admission tickets to premises wherein there are exhibited motion pictures depicting the same. (Chap 3897 1 (part), 1970).

43.020 Definitions. For the purposes of this chapter the following terms and phrases shall have the following meanings:

1. "Minor" means any person under the age of 18 years;

2. "Nudity" means the showing of the human male or female genitals, pubic area, or buttocks with less than a full opaque covering, or the showing of the female breast with less than a fully opaque covering of any portion thereof below the top of the nipple, or the depiction of covered male genitals in a discernible turgid state;

3. "Sexual conduct" means acts of masturbation, homosexuality, sexual intercourse, or physical contact with a person's clothed or unclothed genitals, public area, buttocks, or, if the person be a female, breast;

4. "Sexual excitement" means the condition of human male or female genitals when in a state of sexual stimulation or arousal;

5. "Sado-mascochistic abuse" means flagellation or torture by or upon a person clad in undergarments, a mask, or bizarre costume, or the condition of being fettered, bound, or otherwise physically restrained on the part of those clothed;

6. "Harmful to minors" means that quality of any description or representation, in whatever form, of nudity, sexual conduct, sexual excitement, or sado-masochistic abuse, when it:

   (a) predominantly appeals to the prurient, shameful, or morbid interest of minors, and

   (b) is patently offensive to prevailing standards in the adult community as a whole with respect to what is suitable material for minors.

Discussion Questions

1. Does the legal definition of obscenity accurately and adequately define the term?

2. Do you agree with the legal definition of obscenity?

SOURCE: *Local Ordinances, Council Bluffs, Iowa*, Chap. 8, 43, Section 010, 020.

---

with even the slightest redeeming social importance—unorthodox ideas, controversial ideas, even ideas hateful to the prevailing climate of opinion . . . but implicit in the history of the First Amendment is the rejection of obscenity as *utterly without redeeming social importance.*" In the 1966 case *Memoirs v. Massachusetts*, the Supreme Court again required that in order for a work to be considered obscene it must be shown to be "utterly without redeeming social value."[71]

These decisions left unclear how obscenity is defined. A spate of sexually explicit movies after the decision were alleged to be educational or to tell a moral tale, so they could not be said to lack redeeming social importance. Many state obscenity cases were appealed to federal courts so judges could decide whether the films totally lacked redeeming social importance (see Close-Up entitled "Obscenity").

To rectify the situation, the Supreme Court redefined its concept of obscenity in the case of *Miller v. California*:

The basic guidelines for the trier of fact must be (a) whether the average person applying contemporary community standards would find that the work taken as a whole appeals to the prurient interest; (b) whether the work depicts or describes, in a patently offensive way, sexual conduct specifically defined by the applicable state law, and (c) whether the work, taken as a whole, lacks serious literary, artistic, political or scientific value.[72]

To convict a person of obscenity under the *Miller* doctrine, the state or local jurisdiction must specifically define obscene conduct in its statute, and the pornographer must engage in that behavior. The Court gave some examples of what is considered obscene: "patently offensive representations or descriptions of masturbation, excretory functions and lewd exhibition of the genitals." In subsequent cases the court overruled convictions for "offensive" or "immoral" behavior; these are not considered obscene.

The *Miller* doctrine has been criticized for not spelling out how community standards are to be determined.[73] Obviously, a plebiscite cannot be held to determine the community's attitude for every trial concerning the sale of pornography. Works which are considered obscene in Omaha might be considered routine in New York. To remedy this dilemma, the Supreme Court articulated in *Pope v. Illinois* a **reasonableness doctrine**: a work is obscene if a reasonable person applying objective (national) standards, would find the material lacking in any social value.[74] While *Pope* should help clarify the legal definition of obscenity, the issue is far from settled. Justice Stevens in his dissent offered one interesting alternative: the First Amendment protects material "if *some reasonable persons* could [find] serious literary[,] artistic, political or scientific value" in it.[75] Stevens believes that if *anyone* finds merit in work it should be protected.

Controlling the Sex for Profit Industry

Sex for profit predates Western civilization. Considering its longevity, there seems to be little evidence that it can be controlled or eliminated by criminal justice agencies alone. The Attorney General's Commission on Pornography suggested a strict law enforcement policy to control obscenity, advocating that "the prosecution of obscene materials that portray sexual violence be treated as a matter of special urgency."[76] However, such efforts may not necessarily have the desired outcomes. A get-tough policy could make sex-related goods and services a scarce commodity, driving up prices and making their sale even more desirable and profitable.

An alternative approach has been to control or restrict the sale of pornography and prostitution within acceptable boundaries and areas. For example, municipal governments have tolerated or even established restricted **adult entertainment zones** in which obscene material can be openly sold. In the case of *Young v. American Mini Theaters*, the Supreme Court permitted a zoning ordinance that restricted theaters showing erotic movies to one area of the city, even though it did not find that any of the movies shown were obscene.[77] The state therefore has the right to regulate adult films as long as the public has the right to view them.

Restricting the sale of sexually related material to a particular area can have unforeseen consequences. Skyrocketing downtown real estate prices in areas such as Boston and New York have made the running of sex clubs and stores relatively unprofitable. Land which was used for adult movie houses has been converted into high priced condos and office buildings. For example, the number of strip tease clubs in Boston's Combat Zone shrank from 22 in 1977 to five in 1987 as the area underwent redevelopment.[78]

The threat of governmental regulation may also convince some members of the sex for profit industry to police themselves. While local law enforcement agencies will tolerate some forms of sexually explicit material and activities, others will bring about prompt legal control. For example, child pornography usually prompts otherwise complacent governmental agencies to take swift action. Efforts to control this problem have been supported by the courts. The landmark *New York v. Ferber* case indicates the Supreme Court's willingness to allow the state to control child pornography.[79] In this case, Paul Ferber, a Manhattan bookstore owner, was sentenced to 45 days in jail for violating a New York statute banning material that portrays children in sexually explicit, though not necessarily obscene, conduct. He challenged the law as a violation of free speech. By unanimously upholding Ferber's conviction, the Supreme Court found that kiddy porn is damaging to the children it exploits and therefore can be legally banned. In his opinion, Justice Byron White said, "It has been found that sexually exploited children are unable to develop healthy affectionate relationships in later life, have sexual dysfunction and have a tendency to become sexual abusers as adults." The Court also found that the films were an invasion of the child's privacy that the child could not control.

Fear of governmental control may have already had an influence on the content of nationally distributed adult magazines. Criminologists have uncovered a correlation between rape rates and the circulation rates of national adult magazines.[80] The federal government has consequently asked the states to toughen their laws governing the distribution of sex-related material. Some mainstream sex magazines may have altered their content rather than risk provoking official action. Evidence of this subtle change can be found in Joseph Scott and Steven Cuvelier's analysis of the content of *Playboy* magazine over a 30-year period. Scott and Cuvelier found that cartoons and pictorials which were judged to have a violent theme were actually decreasing. Scott and Cuvelier also found that violent cartoons and pictures were actually quite rare in *Playboy*, amounting to about 3.5 pages in every 1,000.[81]

Technology also has caused change in the sex for profit industry. Adult movie theaters are closing all over the nation as suburbanites are able to buy or rent prerecorded films in their local video store and play them in the privacy of their homes. About 25 percent of the adult movie houses in Boston closed in the three-year period form 1984 to 1987.[82]

A final modification may be brought about by the fear of AIDS and other sex-related diseases. There has been a notable decrease in the number of local prostitutes and streetwalkers in downtown areas.

Do these changes mean the end of criminal sex for profit in the United States? Hardly. The adult movie market has shifted its locale from downtown theaters to suburban video stores. And while inner-city streetwalkers may be declining in number, their place may be taken by suburban prostitution rings which operate under the guise of escort services or massage parlors. For example, in 1985 police in Weston, Massachusetts, arrested a women who was conducting a $5,000 a day prostitution ring out of her home; Weston is one of the most exclusive towns in Massachusetts, with a per capita income of over $35,000.[83]

——————— SUBSTANCE ABUSE ———————

The use of chemical substances to alter reality and provide stimulation, relief, or relaxation has gone on for thousands of years. Mesopotamian writings indicate that opium was used 4,000 years ago—it was known as the "plant of joy."[84] The ancient Greeks knew and understood the problems of drug use. At the time of the Crusades, the Arabs were using marijuana. In the Americas, natives of Mexico and South America chewed coca leaves and used "magic mushrooms" in their religious ceremonies.[85]

Today, in the United States, the control of drug and alcohol abuse has become a top national priority and a national political campaign issue. There is significant concern about the use of drugs by the young and about the relationship between drugs and crime. Recent gang activity on both coasts has focused public attention on the widespread cocaine and crack use by inner-city youths and the tremendous profits even young teenagers can make in the drug trade. Similarly, films such as *Bright Lights/Big City* and *Less than Zero* have addressed the problem of drug abuse by the middle class, preppies who use cocaine and other substances to ease the burden of being upwardly mobile. The government's action against major international drug dealers, such as Carlos Lehder, recently convicted in federal court, and General Manual Noriega of Panama, show how universal the drug trade is and how profits can run into the billions of dollars.

Despite widespread public concern, there is still debate over the course the government should take to control drugs and alcohol. Some argue that their use is a private matter and that making it illegal is a matter of government intrusion into a person's private life; drug abuse is considered to be a victimless crime. Furthermore, legalization could reduce the profit of selling illegal substances and drive suppliers out of the market.[86] Others see drugs as dangerous, believing that the criminal activity of users makes the term *victimless* nonsensical. Still another position is that the possession and use of all drugs and alcohol should be legalized, but that the sale and distribution of drugs should be heavily penalized. This would punish those profiting from drugs and would enable users to be helped without fear of criminal punishment.

In sum, the manufacture, sale, and use of illegal drugs and alcohol is considered to be one of the nation's most significant social problems and an important topic for criminological inquiry. This section discusses the nature of illegal drugs, analyzes the nature and extent of drug abuse, and briefly discusses drug enforcement efforts.

Commonly Abused Drugs

A wide variety of drugs are sold and used by drug abusers. Some are addicting, others not. Some provide hallucinations; other cause a depressing, relaxing stupor; a few give an immediate exhilarating uplift. This section discusses some of the most widely used illegal drugs.[87]

Anesthetics.   Anesthetic drugs are used as nervous system depressants. Local anesthetics block nervous system transmissions; general anesthetics act on the brain to produce a generalized loss of sensation, stupor, or unconsciousness (called **narcosis**).

The most widely abused anesthetic drug is phencyclidine (PCP), known on the street as "angel dust." PCP can be sprayed on marijuana or other plant leaves and smoked, drunk, or injected; the last two methods are extremely hazardous. Originally developed as an animal tranquilizer, PCP causes hallucinations and a spaced-out feeling. The effects of PCP can last up to two days; the danger of overdose is extremely high.

Narcotics.   Narcotic drugs have the ability to produce insensibility to pain (analgesia) and to free the mind of anxiety and emotion (sedation). Users experience a rush of euphoria, relief from fear and apprehension, release of tension, and elevation of spirits. After experiencing this uplifting mood for a short period, the user becomes apathetic and drowsy and nods off. Narcotics can be injected under the skin or in a muscle (skin pop). Experienced users inject the drugs directly into the bloodstream (mainlining), which provides an immediate "fix."

The most common narcotics are derivatives of opium, a drug produced from the opium poppy flower. The Chinese popularized the habit of smoking or chewing opium extract to produce euphoric feelings. Morphine, a derivative of opium, is about 10 times as strong and is used legally by physicians to relieve pain.

Heroin, the most commonly used narcotic in the United States, is produced from morphine but has an effect 25 times more powerful. Consequently, dealers cut it with neutral substances such as sugar (lactose). Street heroin is often only 1 to 4 percent pure. The danger of heroin is that users can rapidly build a tolerance for it. They constantly need more drugs to feel an effect and also will change the method of ingestion to get the desired "kick." At first heroin is usually sniffed or snorted; as tolerance builds, it is skin-popped and then finally mainlined. Through the process the user becomes an **addict**—a person with an overpowering physical and psychological need to continue taking a particular substance or drug by any means possible. If addicts can't get a supply of heroin sufficient to meet their habit, they will suffer withdrawal symptoms. These include irritability, emotional depression, extreme nervousness, pain in the abdomen, and nausea. Heroin addiction is discussed in subsequent sections.

Other opium derivatives used by drug abusers include codeine, dilaudid, percodan, and prinadol. It is also possible to create synthetic narcotics in the laboratory. Synthetics include demerol, methadone, nalline, and darvon. It is less likely that a user will become addicted to synthetic narcotics, but it is still possible, and withdrawal symptoms are similar to those experienced by users of natural narcotics.

Volatile Liquids.   Volatile liquids are liquids that are easily vaporized. Some substance abusers inhale vapors from lighter fluid, paint thinner, cleaning fluid, and model airplane glue to reach a drowsy, dizzy state sometimes accompanied by hallucinations. The psychological effect produced by inhaling these substances is a short-term sense of excitement and euphoria followed by a period of disorientation, slurred speech, and drowsiness. Amyl nitrate ("poppers") is a commonly used volatile liquid that is sold in capsules that are broken and inhaled. Poppers allegedly increase sensation and are sometimes used during sexual activity to prolong and intensify the experience.

Barbiturates.   The hypnotic-sedative drug—barbiturates—are able to depress the central nervous system into a sleeplike condition. On the illegal market, barbiturates are called goffballs or downers or are known by the color of the capsules—reds (seconal), blue dragons (amytal), and "rainbows" (tulinal).

Barbiturates can be prescribed by doctors as sleeping pills. In the illegal market they are used to create relaxed, sociable, and good-humored feelings. However, if dosages get too high, users become irritable and obnoxious, and finally they slump off into sleep. Barbiturate overdoses are probably the major source of drug overdose deaths.

Not all people agree with laws banning "victimless" crimes. These protesters are calling for the legalization of marijuana in California.

Tranquilizers.   Tranquilizers have the ability to relieve uncomfortable emotional feelings by reducing levels of anxiety. They relieve tension and promote a state of relaxation.

The major tranquilizers are used to control the behavior of the mentally ill who are suffering from psychoses, aggressiveness, and agitation. They are known by their brand names—Ampazine, Thorazine, Pacatal, Sparine.

The minor tranquilizers are used by the average citizen to combat anxiety, tension, fast heart rate, and headaches. The most common are valium, librium, miltown, and equanil. These mild tranquilizers are easily obtained by prescription. However, increased dosages can lead to addiction, and withdrawal can be painful and hazardous.

Cannabis (Marijuana).   Commonly called "pot," "grass," "ganja," "maryjane," "dope," and a variety of other names, marijuana is produced from the leaves of *Cannabis sativa*, a plant grown throughout the world. Hashish (hash) is a concentrated form of cannabis made from unadulterated resin from the female plant.

Smoking large amounts of pot or hash can cause drastic distortion in auditory and visual perception, even producing hallucinatory effects. Small doses produce an early excitement ("high") that gives way to a sedated effect and drowsiness. Pot use is also related to decreased physical activity, overestimation in time and space, and increased food consumption ("the munchies"). When the user is alone, marijuana produces a quiet, dreamy state. In a group, it is common for users to become giddy and lose perspective. Though marijuana is nonaddicting, its long-term effects have been the subject of much debate.

Hallucinogens.   Hallucinogens are drugs, either natural or synthetic, that produce vivid distortions of the senses without greatly disturbing the viewer's consciousness. Some produce hallucinations, and others cause psychotic behavior in otherwise normal people.

One common hallucinogen is mescaline, named after the Mescalero Apaches, who first used it. Mescaline occurs naturally in the peyote, a small cactus that grows in Mexico and the southwestern United States. After initial discomfort, mescaline produces vivid hallucinations in all ranges of colors and geometric patterns, a feeling of depersonalization, and out-of-body sensations. A synthetic and highly dangerous form of mescaline used for a brief period in the 1960s was called STP. However, the danger of this drug made its use short-lived.

A second group of hallucinogens are alkaloid compounds. Alkaloids occur in nature or can be made in the laboratory. They include such familiar hallucinogens as DMT, morning-glory seeds, and psilocybin.

These compounds can be transformed into a D-lysergic acid diethylamide-25, commonly called LSD. This powerful substance (800 times more potent than mescaline) stimulates cerebral sensory centers to produce visual hallucinations in all ranges of colors, to intensify hearing, and to increase sensitivity. Users often report a scrambling of sensations; they may "hear colors" and "smell music." Users also report feeling euphoric and mentally superior, though to an observer they appear disoriented and confused. Unfortunately, anxiety and panic (a "bad trip") may occur during the LSD experience, and overdoses can produce psychotic episodes, flashbacks, and even death.

Cocaine.   Cocaine is a alkaloid derivative of the coca leaf first isolated in 1860 by Albert Niemann of Gottingen, Germany. When originally discovered it was considered a medicinal breakthrough which could relieve fatigue, depression, and various other symptoms. Its discovery was embraced by no less a luminary than Sigmund Freud, who used it himself and prescribed it for his friends, patients, and relatives. It quickly became a staple of popular patent medicines. When its addictive qualities and dangerous side effects became apparent, its use was controlled by the Pure Food and Drug Act of 1906. Until the 1970s, cocaine remained an underground drug—the property of artists, jazz musicians, beatniks, and sometimes even "jetsetters."

Cocaine is the most powerful natural stimulant. Its use produces ephoria, laughter, restlessness, and excitement. Overdoses can cause delirium, increased reflexes, violent manic behavior, and possible respiratory failure.

Cocaine can be sniffed, or "snorted," into the nostrils or injected. The immediate feeling of euphoria ("rush") is short-lived, and heavy users may snort coke as often as every 10 minutes. Mixing cocaine and heroin is called "speedballing"; it is a practice that is highly dangerous and is alleged to have killed comedian John Belushi.

Amphetamines.   Amphetamines ("uppers," "beans," "pep pills") are synthetic drugs that stimulate action in the central nervous system. They produce an intense physical reaction: increased blood pressure, breathing rate, bodily activity, and elevation of mood. Amphetamines also produce psychological effects such as increased confidence, euphoria, fearlessness, talkativeness, impulsive behavior, and loss of appetite.

The commonly used amphetamines are Benzedrine ("bennies"), Dexedrine ("dex"), Dexamyl, Bephetamine ("whites"), and Methedrine ("meth," "speed," "crystal meth").

Methedrine is probably the most widely used and most dangerous amphetamine. Some people swallow it; heavy users inject it for a quick rush. Long-term heavy use can result in exhaustion, anxiety, prolonged depression, and hallucinations.

Drug Use in the United States

In the early years of the United States, opium and its derivatives were easily obtained. Opium-based drugs were adopted for use in various patent medicine cure-alls. Morphine was used extensively to relieve the pain of wounded soldiers in the Civil War. By the turn of the century an estimated 1 million Americans were opiate users.[88]

Several factors precipitated the stringent drug laws that are in force today. Domestic issues included:

- The rural creeds of the nineteenth century—for example, Methodist, Presbyterian, Baptist—emphasized individual human toil and self-sufficiency while designating the use of intoxicating substances as an unwholesome surrender to the evils of urban morality.
- Religious leaders were thoroughly opposed to the use and sale of narcotics.
- The medical literature of the late 1800s began to arbitrarily designate the use of morphine and opium as a vice, a habit, an appetite, and a disease.
- Nineteenth and early twentieth century police literature described drug users as habitual criminals.
- Moral crusaders in the nineteenth century defined drug use as evil and directed the actions of local and national rule creators to outlaw their sale and possession.
- Some well-publicized research efforts categorized drug use as highly dangerous.[89]

Another important factor leading to the control of drugs was their association with foreign immigrants.

Immigrant groups recruited to work in factories and mines brought with them their national drug habits; for example, Mexicans brought marijuana and Chinese brought opium. Though narcotics were still widely used by many middle-class Americans, they came to be associated with these foreign groups. Consequently, early antidrug legislation appears tied to prejudice against ethnic minorities.[90]

After the Spanish-American War of 1898, the United States inherited Spain's opium monopoly in the Philippines. Concern over this international situation, plus the domestic issues outlined above, led the U.S. government to participate in the First International Drug Conference, held in Shanghai in 1908, and a second one at the Hague in 1912. Participants in these two conferences were asked to strongly oppose free trade in drugs. The international pressure, coupled with a growing national concern, led to the passage of the antidrug laws discussed here.

The Nature of Drug Addiction

Drug abusers in the United States can be seen as two distinct types: those involved in narcotics use, typically heroin, which leads to dependency and addiction; recreational users who engage in the occasional use of nonaddictive drugs.

Heroin Use. It is estimated that there are about 500,000 practicing heroin addicts, and an additional two and three million people who have tried heroin at least once in their lives.[91]

Heroin abuse is generally considered a lower-class phenomenon, though a fair number of middle- and upper-class users exist. Even physicians are known to have serious narcotics abuse problems.[92] None the less, it is common to associate heroin addiction with minority youths in lower-class inner-city neighborhoods.

The disproportionate number of heroin abusers found among black and Hispanic citizens has been tied to such factors as racial prejudice, "devalued identities" and low self-esteem, poor socioeconomic status, and the stress of living in the harsh urban environment.[93] The relationship of drug addiction, race, and poverty has been attributed to the high level of mistrust, negativism, and defiance found in lower socioeconomic areas.[94]

Residing in a deteriorated inner-city slum area is often correlated with entrance into a drug subculture. Youths living in depressed area, where feelings of alienation and hopelessness run high, often come in contact with established drug users who teach them that narcotics provide an answer to their feelings of personal inadequacy and stress.[95] Perhaps the youths will join with peers to learn the techniques of drug use and receive social support for their habit. Shared feelings and a sense of intimacy lead the youths to become fully enmeshed in what has been described as the "drug use subculture."[96]

But not all ghetto residents become drug addicts. Cloward and Ohlin have explained this as a function of some slum residents having access to illegitimate sources of income or prestige. Those who cannot function as fighters or thieves may seek to lose themselves in the drug world.

Another explanation is that drug users come from the most unstable elements of the ghetto. An often encountered personal characteristic of lower-class heroin abusers is a poor family life and troubled adolescence. One study concluded that the majority of addicts led an unhappy childhood, which included harsh physical punishment and parental neglect and rejection.[97] It is also common to associate addiction with large families and parents who are divorced, separated, or absent.[98]

Personality disturbance is also associated with drug abuse. Research on the psychological characteristics of narcotics addicts reveals the presence of a significant degree of pathology. Personality testing of known users suggests that a significant percentage suffer from psychotic disorders, including various levels of schizophrenia. Studies have found that addicts suffer personality disorders characterized by a weak ego, low frustration tolerance, anxiety, and fantasies of omnipotence. Still another view is that addicts exhibit psychopathic or sociopathic behavior characteristics, forming what they call an "addiction-prone personality."[99]

In sum, there are many different views of why people take heroin. No one theory has proven to be an adequate explanation of all forms of addiction. As James Inciardi points out:

In all likelihood, there are as many reasons for using drugs as there are individuals who use drugs. For some it may be a function of family disorganization, or cul-

CLOSE-UP

Addict Career Structure

Do most heroin abusers maintain consistent lifestyles, or does their behavior undergo change during their careers as addicts? To investigate this question, Charles Faupel and Carl Klockars interviewed 32 hard-core heroin addicts and recorded their life histories. They found that heroin addicts can be classified on the basis of their ability to obtain narcotics and the quality of their lifestyle.

As Table A indicates there may be four stages of heroin addiction.

TABLE A   The Career Pattern of Heroin Users

	Life Structure	
Heroin Availability	**High**	**Low**
High	Stabilized	Free-Wheeling
Low	Occasional User	Street Junkie

Faupel and Klockars found that *occasional users* are people just beginning their addiction. They use small amounts of narcotics, and their habit can be supported by income from conventional jobs; narcotics has relatively little influence on their lifestyles. In contrast, *stabilized junkies* have learned the skills needed to purchase and process larger amounts of heroin. Their addiction enables them to maintain their normal lifestyle, though they may turn to drug dealing to create contacts with drug suppliers. If stable users make a "big score," perhaps through a successful drug deal, they may significantly increase their drug use and become *free-wheelers*. Their increased narcotics consumption then destabilizes their lifestyle, destroying family and career ties. When their finances dry up, free-wheelers may return to stabilized use or turn to the life of the *street junkie*, whose habit cannot be satisfied through conventional means. After the destruction of their traditional lifestyle, street addicts turn to petty crime to maintain an adequate supply of drugs:

> Cut off from a stable source of quality heroin, not knowing from where his or her next "fix" or the money to pay for it will come, looking for any opportunity to make a buck, getting "sick" or "jonesing," being pathetically unkempt and unable to maintain even the most primitive routines of health or hygiene, the street junkie lives a very difficult, hand-to-mouth (or more precisely arm-to-arm) existence.

Because they are unreliable and likely to turn police informants, street junkies pay the highest prices for the poorest quality heroin; lack of availability increases their need to commit habit-supporting crimes.

Faupel and Klockars conclude that addiction is not a undimensional process. There are various stages in the career of a hard drug user, and criminal activity may vary according to one's drug lifestyle. Their view is that crime is a "drug facilitator," enabling addicts to increase their heroin consumption according to the success of their criminal careers. To devise successful enforcement and rehabilitation strategies to counteract heroin addiction, the life history of addicts must be the focus of continued research efforts.

Discussion Questions

1. How can drug users maintain stable lifestyles?
2. Should addiction be considered a disease or a criminal activity?
3. Do you think that drugs cause crime or that crime causes drugs?

SOURCE: Charles Faupel and Carl Klockars, "Drugs/Crime Connections: Elaborations from the Life Histories of Hard-Core Heroin Addicts," *Social Problems* 34 (1987):54–68.

---

tural learning, or maladjusted personality, or an "addiction-prone" personality . . . For others heroin use may be no more than a normal response to the world in which they live.[100]

Some major changes seem to be occurring in the heroin subculture. It appears that heroin is now being "cut" with fillers much more significantly than in the past. Consequently, "true" addiction is less likely to occur than in the past. Also, studies seem to indicate that addicts can control their compulsion for drugs and can actually decrease or terminate drug usage for long time periods (see Close-Up entitled "Addict Career Structure"). Often, control is exerted before critical events such as committing a crime, and intensive usage is resumed at a more appropriate time.[101]

Recreational Drug Use

In the 1960s, a drug subculture or counterculture arose on U.S. campuses. Marijuana, hashish, and cocaine use, which had been the province of jazz musicians and lower-class slums, became a middle-class youth phenomenon. The counterculture developed a separate set of rules and values and created its own language. Phrases such as "getting stoned after a couple of hits on a joint" became common in campus discussions.

Though nonaddicting drug use has become a stable element of U.S. culture, possession and sale of marijuana, cocaine, and hallucinogens are still illegal. Those who favor outlawing these drugs claim they are dangerous and addictive and may lead to heavy drug abuse. Recreational drug users argue that few ever go on to use hard drugs like crack and heroin, and that the use of recreational drugs is more akin to alcohol consumption. A number of states, such as Oregon and Vermont, have decriminalized marijuana possession, making it—like a parking offense—subject to a small fine. However, a majority of states still restrict possession and sale of recreational drugs and attach serious penalties for violation.

The Cocaine Controversy.   Of all recreational drugs, none is considered as important or dangerous as cocaine. While not addicting in a physical sense, as is heroin, heavy cocaine use can lead to a psychological addiction, so that cessation of use brings on a severe depression which can only be relieved through resumption of the habit. Cocaine has become the drug of choice for large segments of the user population, ranging from inner-city gang kids to Wall Street executives. Coke is considered a recreational drug because most users are experimenters who might use it at a party or rock concert simply because it makes them feel good. Others, however, become so involved with cocaine that they base their entire lives around obtaining and using the drug. Some "coke heads" spend thousands of dollars a day on their habit.

A great deal of public attention has been focused on the popularity of new, more potent forms of cocaine, such as **freebase, basuco,** and the nationally publicized menace, **crack.**[102] Freebase, for example, is a new chemical produced from street cocaine. To create freebase, the user treats the street cocaine with a liquid to remove the hydrochloric acid with which pure cocaine is bonded during manufacture. The free cocaine, or cocaine base (hence, freebase), is then dissolved in a solvent, usually ether, which crystallizes the purified cocaine. The resulting crystals are crushed and used in a special glass pipe. When smoked, freebase provides a high more immediate and powerful than snorting street strength coke. Unfortunately for the user, freebase is dangerous to make. It involves highly flammable products such as ether (freebasing was the alleged cause of the accident that seriously injured comedian Richard Pryor), it is expensive, and it is highly addictive.

Basuco is the paste left behind as a residue in the manufacture of cocaine. It is popular throughout Latin America because of its considerable potency; it can have a cocaine concentration ranging from 40 percent to 90 percent. In the United States, basuco is referred to as "bubblegum," since it sounds like the name of a popular brand of chewing gum, "Bazooka." Basuco is extremely dangerous. It contains significant amounts of the chemicals used in cocaine manufacture, including kerosene, sulfuric acid, and leaded gasoline.

Despite the publicity, crack is not a new substance and has been on the street for more than 15 years. Crack, like freebase, is processed street cocaine. Its manufacture involves using ammonia or baking soda to remove the hydrochlorides and create a crystalline form of cocaine base which can then be smoked. However, unlike freebase, crack is not a pure form of the cocaine; it contains remnants of hydrochloride along with additional residue from the baking soda (sodium bicarbonate). In fact, crack gets its name from the fact that the sodium bicarbonate often emits a crackling sound when the substance is smoked.

Also referred to as "rock", "gravel", and "roxanne", crack seems to have been introduced and have gained popularity on both coasts simultaneously. It is relatively inexpensive and can provide a powerful high. In 1986, during the furor over crack use and its suspected contingent problems, an even more powerful form of the drug was introduced, *spacebase*—crack laced with LSD, heroin, or PCP.

TABLE 13.1   Trends in Lifetime Use of 16 Types of Drugs

High School Students	Percent Ever Used													
	Class of 1975	Class of 1976	Class of 1977	Class of 1978	Class of 1979	Class of 1980	Class of 1981	Class of 1982	Class of 1983	Class of 1984	Class of 1985	Class of 1986	Class of 1987	'86–'87 change
Approx. N =	(9400)	(15400)	(17100)	(17800)	(15500)	(15900)	(17500)	(17700)	(16300)	(15900)	(16000)	(15200)	(16300)	
Marijuana/Hashish	47.3	52.8	56.4	59.2	60.4	60.3	59.5	58.7	57.0	54.9	54.2	50.9	50.2	-0.7
Inhalants	NA	10.3	11.1	12.0	12.7	11.9	12.3	12.8	13.6	14.4	15.4	15.9	17.0	+1.1
Inhalants Adjusted	*NA*	*NA*	*NA*	*NA*	*18.2*	*17.3*	*17.2*	*17.7*	*18.2*	*18.0*	*18.1*	*20.1*	*18.6*	*-1.5*
Amyl & Butyl Nitrites	NA	NA	NA	NA	11.1	11.1	10.1	9.8	8.4	8.1	7.9	8.6	4.7	-3.9sss
Hallucinogens	16.3	15.1	13.9	14.3	14.1	13.3	13.3	12.5	11.9	10.7	10.3	9.7	10.3	+0.6
Hallucinogens Adjusted	*NA*	*NA*	*NA*	*NA*	*17.7*	*15.6*	*15.3*	*14.3*	*13.6*	*12.3*	*12.1*	*11.9*	*10.6*	*-1.3s*
LSD	11.3	11.0	9.8	9.7	9.5	9.3	9.8	9.6	8.9	8.0	7.5	7.2	8.4	+1.2s
PCP	NA	NA	NA	NA	12.8	9.6	7.8	6.0	5.6	5.0	4.9	4.8	3.0	-1.8ss
Cocaine	9.0	9.7	10.8	12.9	15.4	15.7	16.5	16.0	16.2	16.1	17.3	16.9	15.2	-1.7s
"Crack"	NA	NA	NA	NA	NA	NA	NA	NA	NA	NA	NA	NA	5.6	NA
Other cocaine	NA	NA	NA	NA	NA	NA	NA	NA	NA	NA	NA	NA	14.0	NA
Heroin	2.2	1.8	1.8	1.6	1.1	1.1	1.1	1.2	1.2	1.3	1.2	1.1	1.2	+0.1
Other opiates	9.0	9.6	10.3	9.9	10.1	9.8	10.1	9.6	9.4	9.7	10.2	9.0	9.2	+0.2
Stimulants	22.3	22.6	23.0	22.9	24.2	26.4	32.2	35.6	35.4	NA	NA	NA	NA	NA
Stimulants Adjusted (Revised Question)	*NA*	*NA*	*NA*	*NA*	*NA*	*NA*	*NA*	*27.9*	*26.9*	*27.9*	*26.2*	*23.4*	*21.6*	*-1.8s*
Sedatives	18.2	17.7	17.4	16.0	14.6	14.9	16.0	15.2	14.4	13.3	11.8	10.4	8.7	-1.7ss
Barbiturates	16.9	16.2	15.6	13.7	11.8	11.0	11.3	10.3	9.9	9.9	9.2	8.4	7.4	-1.0
Methaqualone	8.1	7.8	8.5	7.9	8.3	9.5	10.6	10.7	10.1	8.3	6.7	5.2	4.0	-1.2ss
Tranquilizers	17.0	16.8	18.0	17.0	16.3	15.2	14.7	14.0	13.3	12.4	11.9	10.9	10.9	0.0
Alcohol	90.4	91.9	92.5	93.1	93.0	93.2	92.6	92.8	92.6	92.6	92.2	91.3	92.2	+0.9
Cigarettes	73.6	75.4	75.7	75.3	74.0	71.0	71.0	70.1	70.6	69.7	68.8	67.6	67.2	-0.4

SOURCE: Institute for Social Research (Ann Arbor, Michigan: 1988).

How widespread is the use of crack? The annual Institute of Social Research (ISR) at the University of Michigan national survey of drug use shows that about 6 percent of high-school seniors have tried crack. While this number does not indicate that it is a growing national menace, its use among lower-class youths is disturbing. In one study of drug using delinquents in Miami, James Inciardi found that about 90 percent had used crack during their lifetime and about 30 percent report being daily users. Importantly, control of the crack trade in Los Angeles and other cities has encouraged the redevelopment of youth gangs, who contend for control of the cocaine trade. So while crack may not be the national epidemic some thought it would turn into, its use can be added to the current list of drug problems.

The Extent of Drug Abuse

How much substance abuse occurs in the United States? One indication is the annual self-report survey of drug abuse among high-school seniors, conducted by the Institute of Social Research at the University of Michigan.[103] The most recent survey available indicates that while drug use is still frequent, it has either leveled off and/or declined in the past few years. Table 13.1 shows the prevalence rate among the almost 17,000 students who responded to the annual nationwide survey. The lifetime use of all drugs has declined from the highpoint in the late 70s and early 80s. Even cocaine use, which has increased markedly in the past few years, declined. These same trends were evident in surveys of about 1,200 youths who were followed

TABLE 13.2   Comparison of Urine Tests Results for Arrestees in 1984 and 1986

Tested Positive for:	Percentage of Arrestees in 1984 (N = 4,847)	Percentage of Arrestees Sept. and Oct. 1986 (N = 414)	Percentage of Arrestees in Nov. 1986 (N = 201)
Cocaine	42	83	68
Opiates	21	22	20
Methadone	8	8	10
PCP	12	4	3
Any of above	56	85	73
2 + of above	23	30	23

SOURCE: Eric Wish, *Drug Use Forecasting: New York, 1984 to 1986* (Washington, D.C.: National Institute of Justice, 1987).

one to four years beyond high school. Not surprisingly, the percentage of youths who consider drugs harmful and who disapproved of taking drugs has simultaneously increased.

While these data indicate that drug use has at least stabilized, they must be interpreted with caution. First, self-report evidence is subject to error. Second, the survey involves only students who remain in high school until their senior year, and not drop-outs who may in fact be the most frequent users of dangerous drugs. Third, while drug use has declined, it still remains a serious problem: half of all students have tried marijuana, 15 percent cocaine, and about 6 percent crack. Finally, while drug use among the general population may be in a decline, its prevalence among individuals involved in street crime and violence seems to be widespread. At a time when the middle class may be turning away from drug abuse, the consumption of narcotics by the urban poor remains a significant national social problem.

Drugs and Crime

One of the main reasons for the criminalization of particular substances is the significant association believed to exist between drug abuse and crime. Research suggests that many criminal offenders have extensive experience with drug use, and drug users do in fact commit an enormous amount of crime. However, it is still uncertain whether there is a causal connection between drug use and crime, since many users had a prior history of criminal activity before the onset of their drug usage.[104] However, it is safe to conclude that even if drug use does not cause otherwise law-abiding citizens to become criminals, it certainly magnifies their preexisting criminality.[105] Moreover, as addiction level increases, so too does the frequency and seriousness of criminality. It is not surprising, therefore, that a recent federal survey found that 35 percent of state prison inmates claimed to be under the influence of drugs when they committed the crime for which they were imprisoned, and 43 percent were daily users of drugs in the month before they were convicted.[106]

The fact that many law violators are experienced drug users is supported by research conducted by Eric Wish in New York City.[107] After three years of testing arrestees in Manhattan's Central Booking facility, Wish found that a significant number were active drug users. As Table 13.2 indicates, cocaine was the most widely used drug, and its use has substantially increased in the past few years; the use of other drugs has remained more stable. Wish also found that offenders preferred smoking or snorting cocaine over using crack, since the latter was considered "too dangerous." (About 7 percent were active crack users and 25 percent had at least tried crack.) In a more recent federal study of 2,000 men arrested for serious offenses in 12 large cities, 70 percent tested positive for recent drug use; nearly two-thirds of the arrestees in New York and half of those in Washington, D.C., and Detroit tested positively for cocaine.[108]

Similarly, James Inciardi studied 356 addicts in Miami and found that they committed 118,134 criminal offenses during a 12-month period; of these, 27,464 were index crimes.[109]

Evidence of the vast criminal activity of narcotics

TABLE 13.3 Common Roles and Functions at Various Levels of the Drug Distribution Business

Approximate Role Equivalents in Legal Markets	Roles by "Common Names" at Various Stages of the Drug Distribution Business	Major Functions Accomplished at This Level
Grower/Producer	Coca Farmer, Opium Farmer, Marijuana Grower	Grow coca, opium, marijuana; the raw materials
Manufacturer	Collector, Transporter, Elaborator, Chemist, Drug Lord	All stages for preparation of heroin, cocaine, marijuana as commonly sold
Traffickers		
Importer	Multi-Kilo Importer, Mule, Airplane Pilot, Smuggler, Trafficker, Money Launderer	Smuggling of large quantities of substances into United States
Wholesale Distributor	Major Distributor, Kilo Connection	Transportation and redistribution of multi- and single-kilograms
Dealers		
Regional Distributor	Pound and Ounce Men, Weight Dealers	Adulteration and sale of moderately expensive product
Retail Store Owner	House Connections, Suppliers, Crack House Supplier	Adulteration and production of retail level dosage units ("bags," "vials," "grams") in very large numbers
Assistant Manager, Security Chief, Accountant	Lieutenant, Muscle Men, Transporter, Crew Boss, Crack House Manager/Proprietor	Supervises three or more sellers, enforces informal contracts, collects money, distributes multiple dosage units to actual sellers
Sellers		
Store Clerk, Salesperson (Door-to-Door and Phone)	Street Drug Seller, Runner, Juggler, Private Seller	Makes actual direct sales to consumer; responsible for both money and drugs
Low Level Distributors		
Advertiser, Security Guards, Leaflet Distributor	Steerer, Tout, Cop Man, Lookout, Holder, Runner, Help Friend, Guard, Go-Between	Assists in making sales, advertises, protects seller from police and criminals, solicits customers; handles drugs or money but not both
Servant, Temporary Employee	Run Shooting Gallery, Injector (of drugs), Freebaser, Taster, Apartment Cleaner, Drug Bagger, Fence, Money Launderer	Provides short-term services to drug users or sellers for money or drugs; not responsible for money or drugs

SOURCE: Bruce Johnson, Ansley Hamid, Edmundo Morales, and Harry Sanabria, "Dimensions of Crack Distribution," Paper presented at the Annual Meeting of the American Society of Criminology, Montreal, Canada, November, 1987. Reprinted with permission.

users has been used to support the vision of drug user as super criminal. In sum, research shows a very strong association between drug use and crime. Even if the crime rate of narcotics addicts were actually 50 percent of that reported in the research literature, such as the Inciardi study, the current 500,000 addicts would be responsible for a significant portion of the total criminal activity in the United States.

Drugs and the Law

The federal government first initiated legal action to curtail the use of some drugs early in the twentieth century.[110] In 1906 the Pure Food and Drug Act required manufacturers to list the amounts of habit-forming drugs in products on the labels but did not restrict their use. However, the act prohibited the importation and sale of opiates except for medicinal purposes.

In 1914 the Harrison Narcotics Act restricted the importation, manufacture, sale, and dispensing of narcotics. It defined *narcotics* as any drug that produces sleep and relieves pain, such as heroin, morphine, and opium. The act was revised in 1922 to allow the importation of opium and coca (cocaine) leaves for qualified medical practitioners.

The Marijuana Tax Act of 1937 required registration and payment of a tax by all persons who imported, sold, or manufactured marijuana. Since marijuana was classified as a narcotic, those registering also would be subject to criminal penalty.

In later years, other federal laws were passed to clarify existing drug statutes or revise penalties. For example, the Boggs Act of 1951 provided mandatory sentences for violating federal drug laws. The Durham-Humphrey Act of 1951 made it illegal to dispense barbiturates and amphetamines without a prescription. The Narcotic Control Act of 1956 increased penalties for drug offenders.

In 1965 the Drug Abuse Control amendment set up stringent guidelines for the legal use and sale of mood-modifying drugs, such as barbiturates, amphetamines, LSD, and any other "dangerous drugs" except narcotics prescribed by doctors and pharmacists. Illegal possession was punished as a misdemeanor and manufacture or sale as a felony.

Then, in 1970, the Comprehensive Drug Abuse Prevention and Control Act set up unified categories of illegal drugs and the penalties associated with their sale, manufacture, or possession. The law gives the U.S. Attorney General discretion to decide in which category to place any new drug. Since 1970 there have been additional modifications in federal law, such as the Anti-Drug Abuse Act of 1986 which toughened penalties and provided for the forfeiture of property.

For the most part, state laws mirror federal statutes. Some, such as New York's, apply extremely heavy penalties for sale of distribution of dangerous drugs, involving long mandatory prison sentences.

Controlling the Drug Problem

Can illegal drug use be eliminated or controlled? A number of strategies have been tried, including eliminating the source of drugs, treating addicts, punishing dealers, and educating potential users.

One important approach to drug control has been a massive and concerted effort to control the flow of illegal substances into the United States. The effort involves federal enforcement agencies, the military, Coast Guard, and others. Some foreign governments have cooperated by arresting drug smugglers and destroying supplies. A recent survey prepared for the U.S. Customs Bureau found that state, local, and federal law enforcement agencies spend $6.2 billion annually on controlling the drug trade. State and local government agencies spend an additional $4.9 billion, or 18 percent of their operating budgets, on drug enforcement efforts.[111]

Adding to the deterrent effect of the law is the policy of **forfeiture:** any car, house, boat, or airplane found to contain illegal drugs is forfeited and put on auction. The Coast Guard has even used a **zero tolerance** approach: any trace of narcotics, even a tenth of an ounce found aboard a million-dollar yacht, could result in forfeiture. While such measures may be an effective deterrent, they also invite charges of over-enforcement and invasion of privacy.

Despite massive law enforcement efforts, the fight against drugs has not proved successful. The overwhelming problem associated with drug control is the enormous profits involved in the drug trade: 500 kilos of coca leaves worth $4,000 to a grower yield about eight kilos of street cocaine valued at $500,000. A drug dealer who can move 100 pounds of coke into the United States can make $1.5 million in one shipment. An estimated 60 tons of cocaine are imported into the country each year, with a street value of $17 billion.[112] Government crackdowns simply serve to drive up the price of drugs and encourage more illegal entrepreneurs to enter the market. For example, the Hell's Angels motorcycle club has become one of the primary distributors of cocaine and amphetamines in the United States.[113] Movies like *Scarface*, which depicted the rise and fall of a cocaine dealer, may be viewed as a warning to potential drug dealers, but they also indicate the lavish lifestyles and unlimited cash supplies associated with life in the drug trade. The immense profit associated with the drug trade can even drive respectable businesspeople, like John DeLorean, to get involved in drug trading as a quick cash fix for their ailing businesses. DeLorean was eventually acquitted, based on the defense of entrapment.)

Adding to the allure of drug profits is the fact that

the relatively few drug dealers who are caught are treated with comparative lenience. Surveys of state court jurisdictions indicate that only 54 percent of people arrested on drug offenses are eventually convicted (compared to a 62 percent conviction rate for other felonies). And despite the heavily publicized crusade against drug dealers, only 10 percent of those convicted are sentenced to more than a year in prison (in comparison, about 20 percent of burglars receive more than a year in prison); about one-third of convicted drug offenders are given a probation sentence. In addition, those drug offenders sentenced to lengthy prison terms rarely serve their entire sentences; for example, people convicted on drug trafficking charges serve an average of only 38 percent of their sentence behind bars.[114] While it is difficult to know how far such information filters down to drug importers and distributors, the fact that long prison sentences are uncommon does not add to the law's deterrent power.

To remedy this situation, the federal government has begun to stress the arrest and conviction of drug traffickers. A recent survey found that between 1980 and 1986, the number of drug related convictions in federal courts more than doubled (from 5,244 in 1980 to 12,285 in 1986). This 134 percent increase was significantly higher than the 27 percent increase in convictions for other federal crimes. In addition, the percentage of convictees receiving a prison sentence increased from 71 percent to 77 percent, and the average sentence increased from four years to five years.[115]

These data indicated that despite a spate of "get tough" rhetoric by politicians at the state and national levels, narcotics dealers are treated relatively leniently. Though it is often difficult to gain convictions in narcotics cases, many defendants receive probation or a short term prison sentence. Nonetheless, federal data seems to indicate a trend toward toughening criminal justice sentencing policy in an effort to limit the drug trade by incapacitating known suppliers and deterring potential ones.

Getting the cooperation of governments whose countries supply drugs is also difficult. Though some South American and Asian governments have entered the fight against the drug trade, attempting to cut off the drug supply at its source, underdeveloped nations actually have an economic incentive to allow this lucrative cash crop to flourish. If drug crops are destroyed, their national economies will lose millions of

General Manuel Noriega, international drug smuggler, was on the CIA payroll for years. He answered a U.S. indictment with a coup which made him military commander of Panama in 1988.

dollars in foreign currency, and their governments will face the displeasure of unemployed farmers. If the U.S. helps compensate for losses, other nations will be encouraged to get into the drug-producing business to cash in on American aid. The political scandal involving General Manuel Noriega of Panama, a national figure indicted for drug smuggling, highlights the problem.

Another suggested approach to drug control has been to legalize or decriminalize controlled substances and thereby remove them as a law enforcement issue. This policy has been attempted in England, where private physicians and later government-run clinics have the power to legally prescribe heroin. While some criminologists view the English approach as a viable solution to the heroin problem in the United States, Inciardi proclaims it a failure because the addiction rate has risen in Great Britain while actually declining in the United States.[116]

Identifying and treating drug users also has been tried as a control technique. Identification has been facilitated by mandatory drug testing programs in gov-

CLOSE-UP

Drug Trafficking Approaches

In the following passages, criminologist Mark Moore of Harvard University discusses the benefits and drawbacks of the various strategies which have been used to stop or control the drug trade.

Choices between approaches for dealing with drug trafficking will depend on which aspects of the trafficking problem are deemed most important and on the costs and efficacy of particular policies.

Legalization

The most radical approach to dealing with drug trafficking is to legalize the drugs. At one extreme, it can mean complete elimination of any legal restrictions on the production, distribution, possession, or use of any drug. At the other extreme, it can mean allowing some limited uses of some particular drugs, producing the drugs only under government auspices, distributing them through tightly regulated distribution systems, and punishing with severe criminal penalties any production or use outside the authorized system.

The goal of legalizing drugs is to bring them under effective legal control. If it were legal to produce and distribute drugs, legitimate businessmen would enter the business. There would be less need for violence and corruption since the industry would have access to the courts. And, instead of absorbing tax dollars as targets of expensive enforcement efforts, the drug sellers might begin to pay taxes.

An alternative is to choose a system more restrictive than outright legalization but one that still leaves room for legitimate uses of some drugs. Arguably, such a policy would produce some of the potential benefits of legalization without accelerating growth in the level of drug use. The difficulty is that wherever the boundary between the legitimate and illicit use of drugs is drawn, an illicit market will develop just outside the boundary. Indeed, the more restrictive the boundary, the larger and more controlled by "organized crime" the resulting black market.

That there are some legal uses of these drugs has not eliminated illicit trafficking. For marijuana, heroin, and cocaine, the restrictions are so sharp relative to the current demand for the drugs that virtually the entire distribution system remains illicit and depends on drug trafficking. For amphetamines, barbiturates, and

tranquilizers, the restrictions are fewer, so a larger portion of the demand is met from legitimate illicit distribution. Distribution of these drugs takes the form of diversion from legitimate channels rather than wholly illicit production and distribution.

Source Country Crop Control

A second approach to dealing with drug trafficking is to try to eliminate the raw materials that are used to produce the drugs. For heroin, cocaine, and marijuana, this means controlling opium, coca leaf, and marijuana crops in countries such as Turkey, Afghanistan, Thailand, Bolivia, Colombia, Peru, Mexico, and Jamaica. For marijuana, illicit domestic production is also important.

In general, these efforts suffer from two major difficulties. First, there seems to be no shortage of locations where the crops may be grown. If Turkey stops growing opium poppies, Mexico, Afghanistan, and Southeast Asia can eventually take up the slack. If Colombia stops growing coca, Peru can replace it. If Mexico eliminated marijuana production, the hills of California would be even more densely filled with marijuana plants than they now are.

The second problem is that foreign governments cannot always be relied on to pursue crop control policies vigorously. Sometimes the difficulty is that the crops lie in parts of the country that are not under effective governmental control. Other times the problem is inefficiency or corruption in the agencies that are managing the programs. In the worst cases, the crops are sufficiently important to the domestic economy (or the personal well-being of high government officials) that the government prefers not to act at all.

Interdiction

Interdiction efforts aimed at stopping illicit drugs at the border are appealing. First the imagery is compelling. If we cannot rely on foreign countries to help us with our drug problem, we will do it ourselves by establishing defenses at the border.

Second, government agencies have special powers to search at the border, which should make it easier to find illicit drugs. Forces of the U.S. Customs Agency and the U.S. Immigration and Naturalization Service inspect people and goods passing through official "ports of entry," and they patrol between "ports of entry," to ensure that no one can cross the border without facing inspection. The Coast

Guard, the military, and civilian aviation authorities all have capabilities that allow the government to detect who is crossing the border and to prevent illegal crossings.

There are, however, two problems with interdiction. One is the sheer size of the inspection task. More than 12,000 miles of international boundary must be patrolled. Over 420 billion tons of goods, and more than 270 million people, cross these boundaries each year, yet the quantities of drugs are small—a few hundred tons of marijuana and less than 20 tons of heroin or cocaine. Moreover, the heroin and cocaine arrive in lots of less than a hundred pounds.

That the volume of heroin and cocaine imported is much less than the volume of marijuana points to the second problem with interdiction. It is a strategy that is more successful with marijuana than with heroin or cocaine. Marijuana's bulkiness makes it more vulnerable to interdiction efforts.

High-Level Enforcement

A fourth attack on illicit trafficking is directed at the organizations responsible for producing, importing, and distributing drugs. The basic aim is to immobilize or destroy the trafficking networks.

In the past, enforcement agencies have tended to view this problem as "getting to Mr. Big"—the individual kingpin who, it was assumed, controlled an organization's capacity to distribute drugs. If that person could be arrested, prosecuted, and imprisoned, the network would fall apart.

More recently, the law enforcement community has become less certain that this strategy can succeed. Even when "Mr. Big" is in prison, he can continue to manage the distribution of drugs. Moreover, the organizations seem less dependent on single individuals than enforcement officials once assumed. Finally, the whole drug distribution system is less centralized than was once assumed. Relatively small and impermanent organizations—freelance entrepreneurs—supply a large proportion of illicit drugs.

Street-Level Enforcement

Another line of attack is to go after street-level dealing through the use of physical surveillance or "buy and bust" operations. In the recent past, this approach has been deemphasized. It seemed to have no impact on the overall supply because dealers who were arrested were jailed only intermittently and when they were, they were easily replaced. At best, drug dealing was driven off the street temporarily, or to a different street. Many hours were spent to produce small, transient results, and these operations seemed to invite abuses of authority and corruption. As a result, many police were removed from street-level enforcement.

Recently, police have renewed street-level enforcement efforts, but they have altered their objectives. To the extent that street-level enforcement increases the "hassle" associated with using drugs, it can make a contribution to the objective of reducing drug use. If drugs, already expensive, can be made inconvenient to purchase, some nonaddicted users may be persuaded to abandon drugs. More experienced users can benefit if treatment programs are available. Ultimately, street-level enforcement can contribute to the quality of life in neighborhoods by returning the streets to community control.

Discussion Questions

1. Why should drug use be prohibited? Is it to reduce crime or to achieve a social welfare objective?

2. Are the drug laws an appropriate use of the criminal sanction?

SOURCE: Mark Moore, *Drug Trafficking* (Washington, D.C.: National Institute of Justice, 1988).

ernment and industry. About 25 percent of the country's largest companies, including IBM and ATT, test job applicants for drugs. A number of different treatment strategies have been employed. In the United States, *methadone maintenance* has been used to treat drug addicts. Methadone is a drug similar to heroin, and addicts can be treated at clinics where they receive methadone under controlled conditions. However, methadone programs have been undermined because some users sell their methadone in the black market, while others supplement their dosages with illegally obtained heroin.

In the United States and elsewhere, the drug user is viewed more as a victim than a culprit of the drug trade. In Holland, for example, heroin users are allowed to enter methadone treatment programs though they still openly use heroin. The government assumes that a certain percentage of the population will always be addicts; it tries to accommodate and treat them, rather than inflict criminal penalties. In fact, the city of Amsterdam is considering a program to give heroin to addicts in order to lessen their dependence on illegal supplies.[117]

What may be the most realistic drug control technique is the massive educational programs currently being undertaken in the nation's schools. Sponsored by local groups and school districts, sometimes with the backing of the federal government, educational programs teach about the harm caused by narcotics and other illegal drugs and teach kids how to successfully resist peer pressure to get involved with substance abuse. Many of these programs are still in the early stages of development, but recent declines in the overall use of drugs by high-school seniors may be an indication of their success.

Drug use will only disappear if demand dries up and the profits are taken out of the drug trade. While enforcement measures are helpful, the most promising solution to the drug problem is to reduce the number of users, reducing demand and making drug manufacture and distribution less profitable. To reach this state, the potential users, school-age children, must be taught about the consequences of drug use and at the same time be given conventional alternatives which are more attractive. At the same time, foreign governments must continue to be pressured to control the manufacture and export of drugs and threatened with economic sanctions for noncompliance. And finally, the already extensive drug control and border search

efforts must be continued and expanded. The Close-Up entitled "Drug Trafficking Approaches" discusses various approaches to control of drug use.

ALCOHOL ABUSE

Though the purchase and sale of alcohol is legal today in most U.S. jurisdictions, alcohol abuse is a major criminological issue. There are two factors behind the crime-alcohol association. First, most jurisdictions maintain criminal laws prohibiting drunk driving, public intoxication, and the sale and use of liquor by minors. Second, there is a strong association between the use of alcohol and criminal activity.

The history of alcohol and the law in the United States has been controversial and dramatic. At the turn of the century, a drive was mustered to prohibit the sale of alcohol. The temperance movement was fueled by the belief that the purity of the U.S. agrarian culture was being destroyed by the growth of the city. Urbanism was viewed as a threat to the lifestyle of the majority of the nation's population, then living on farms and in villages.

The forces behind the temperance movement were lobbying groups, such as the Anti-Saloon League, the Women's Temperance Union, and the Protestant clergy of the Baptist, Methodist, and Congregationalist faiths.[118] They viewed the growing city, filled with newly arriving Irish, Italian, and Eastern European immigrants, as centers of degradation and wickedness. The ethnics' propensity to drink heavily was viewed as the main force behind their "degenerate" lifestyles. The eventual prohibition of the sale of alcoholic beverages, brought about by ratification of the Eighteenth Amendment in 1919, was viewed as a triumph of the morality of middle- and upper-class Protestants over the threat posed to their culture by the "new Americans."[119]

Prohibition turned out to be a failure. It was enforced by the Volstead Act, which defined intoxicating beverages as those containing at least one-half of 1 percent alcohol.[120] What doomed Prohibition? One factor was the use of organized crime to supply illicit liquor. Also, the law made it illegal only to sell alcohol, not to purchase it; this factor cut into the law's deterrent capability. Finally, despite the work of Elliot Ness and his "Untouchables," law enforcement agencies

TABLE 13.4 Drunk Driving Trends

Between 1970 and 1986 arrests for DUI increased nearly 223 percent, while the number of licensed drivers increased by 42 percent.

Arrest rates for DUI were highest among 21-year-olds and reached their peak in 1983 with a rate of 1 arrest for every 39 licensed drivers of that age.

Since 1983 most States have phased in new laws raising the minimum age for the purchase or sale of alcoholic beverages to 21. Per capita arrest rates for DUI for those age 18 to 20 have decreased by 14 percent since then—more than twice the rate of decrease for those age 21 to 24.

Prior to their arrest for DWI, convicted offenders had consumed a median of 6 ounces of pure alcohol (about equal to the alcoholic content of 12 bottles of beer or 8 mixed drinks) in a median of 4 hours. About 26 percent consumed at least 10 ounces of pure alcohol (equivalent to 20 beers or 13 mixed drinks).

About 54 percent reported drinking only beer, about 2 percent only wine, 23 percent liquor only, and 21 percent had been drinking two or more different beverages. This last group consumed the most alcohol prior to arrest, about three times more than those who drank only beer.

For DWI offenders sentenced to jail, the median term imposed was 5 months; those with prior DWI sentences received sentences that were about twice as long as first-timers.

About 7 percent of all persons confined in local jails in June 30, 1983, were charged with or convicted of DWI; nearly 13 percent of jail inmates had a current charge or prior conviction for DWI.

Those in jail for DWI were 95 percent male, had a median age of 32, and reflected a racial distribution similar to the adult general population. Nearly 80 percent were not living with a spouse at the time of arrest, and they were more likely to be unemployed than adults in the civilian labor force.

Nearly half of those in jail for DWI had previously been sentenced to probation, jail, or prison for DWI, and three-quarters had a prior sentence for any crime (including DWI).

Nearly half of all inmates in jail for DWI had previously been involved in an alcohol abuse treatment program—about 1 in 11 were in treatment at the time of the arrest for DWI.

SOURCE: Lawrence Greenfield, *Drunk Driving* (Washington, D.C.: Bureau of Justice Statistics, 1988), pp. 1-2.

were inadequate, and officials were more than likely to be corrupted by wealthy bootleggers.[121] Eventually, in 1933, the Twenty-First Amendment to the Constitution repealed Prohibition, signaling the end of the "noble experiment."

Alcohol and the Law

Alcohol-related activities provide a serious problem for the criminal justice system. In 1986, the FBI reported that 1,793,300 people were arrested for driving under the influence of alcohol; another 933,000 for public drunkenness; and 600,000 for various liquor violations.[122] Furthermore, there is an alarming rate of alcohol abuse among young people. In the ISR survey of substance abuse, 37 percent said they had five or more drinks in a row during the last two weeks, and 5 percent said they drank every day.[123]

One of the more serious problems of widespread drinking is the alarming number of highway fatalities linked to drunk driving. In an average week, nearly 500 people die in alcohol-related accidents, and 20,000 are injured. On a yearly basis, that amounts to 25,000 deaths, or about half of all auto fatalities. Table 13.4 discusses trends in drunk driving since 1970.

Spurred by groups like Mothers Against Drunk Drivers (MADD), state legislatures are beginning to create more stringent penalties for drunk driving. For example, Florida has enacted legislation creating a minimum fine of $250, 50 hours community service, and six months' loss of license for a first offense; a second offense brings a $500 fine and 10 days in jail. In Quincy, Massachusetts, judges have agreed to put every drunk-driving offender in jail for three days.[124]

In California, a drunk driver faces a maximum of six months in jail, a $500 fine, suspension of operator's license for six months, and impoundment of the vehicle. As a minimum penalty, the first offender could

TABLE 13.5 Comparison of licensed drivers and estimated arrests for driving under the influence, by age, 1975 and 1986

Age	1975			1986			Percent change in rate, 1975-86
	Percent of		Arrests per 100,000 drivers	Percent of		Arrests per 100,000 drivers	
	Drivers	Arrests		Drivers	Arrests		
Total	100	100	729	100	100	1,130	+55
16-17 years old	3.7	1.8	352	2.6	1.5	647	+84
18-24	18.9	25.3	979	15.7	28.8	2,075	+112
25-29	12.9	15.0	847	13.0	22.0	1,909	+125
30-34	10.3	12.2	867	12.2	15.8	1,471	+70
35-39	8.5	10.6	909	10.9	11.1	1,158	+27
40-44	7.9	9.8	904	8.5	7.2	968	+7
45-49	8.0	8.9	812	6.9	4.9	805	-1
50-54	7.9	7.3	675	6.3	3.4	609	-10
55-59	6.8	4.6	490	6.3	2.4	434	-11
60-64	5.7	2.7	347	5.9	1.6	299	-14
65 and older	9.5	1.8	141	11.9	1.2	118	-16

SOURCE: Lawrence Greenfield, *Drunk Driving* (Washington, D.C.: Bureau of Justice Statistics, 1988), pp. 1-2.

get four days in jail, a $375 fine, and loss of license for six months, or three years' probation, a $375 fine, and either two days in jail or restricted driving privileges for 90 days.[125]

In New York, persons arrested for drunk driving now risk having their automobiles seized by the government under the state's new Civil Forfeiture Law. Originally designed to combat drug trafficking and racketeering, the new law will allow state prosecutors to confiscate cars involved in felony drunk driving cases, sell them at auction, and give the proceeds to the victims of crime; Texas enacted a similar law in 1984.[126]

More than 40 states have now passed laws providing severe penalties for drunk drivers, including mandatory jail sentences. A study conducted by the federal government's National Institute of Justice in such cities as Seattle, Minneapolis, and Cincinnati found that such measures significantly reduced traffic fatalities in the target areas studies.[127] However, there is a price to pay for get-tough policies. In California, arrest rates and court workload increased dramatically; plea bargaining, while at first decreasing, eventually went up and reduced the impact of legal reform.[128] Similarly, corrections departments have become overloaded, prompting the building of expensive new facilities exclusively to house drunk-

driving offenders. The federal survey concluded that a feasible approach to paying for these programs is to require convicted offenders to reimburse the government for their confinement or treatment in alcohol abuse programs. Aid is certainly needed, for as Table 13.5 indicates, the number of arrests for drunk driving per 100,000 drivers has increased 55 percent since 1975.

Alcoholics are a serious problem, because treatment efforts to help chronic sufferers have not proved successful.[129] A recent study of sanctions on drunk drivers indicates that severe punishments have little effect on their future behavior.[130] In addition, chronic alcoholics are arrested over and over again for public drunkenness and are therefore a burden on the justice system. To remedy this situation, a federal court in 1966 ruled that chronic alcoholism may be used as a defense to crime.[131] However, in a subsequent case, *Powell v. Texas*, the Supreme Court ruled that a chronic alcoholic could be convicted under state public drunkenness laws.[132] Nonetheless, the narrowness of the decision, 5–4, allowed those states desiring to excuse chronic alcoholics from criminal responsibility to do so. Thus, the trend has been to place arrested alcoholics in detoxification centers under a civil order, rather than to treat them as part of the justice system.

SUMMARY

Public order crimes are acts considered illegal because they conflict with social policy, accepted moral rules, and public opinion.

There is usually great debate over public order crimes. Some charge that they are not really crimes at all and that it is foolish to legislate morality. Others view such morally tinged acts as prostitution, gambling, and drug abuse as harmful and therefore subject to public control.

Many public order crimes are sex-related. Though homosexuality is not a crime per se, homosexual acts are subject to legal control. Some states still follow the archaic custom of long prison terms for consensual homosexual sex.

Prostitution is another sex-related public order crime. Though prostitution has been practiced for thousands of years and is legal in some areas, most states outlaw commercial sex. There are a variety of prostitutes, including streetwalkers, B-girls, and call girls. Studies indicate that prostitutes came from poor, troubled families and have abusive parents. However, there is little evidence that prostitutes are emotionally disturbed, addicted to drugs, or sexually abnormal. Though prostitution is illegal, some cities have set up adult entertainment areas where commercial sex is tolerated by law enforcement agents.

Pornography involves the sale of sexually explicit material intended to sexually excite paying customers. The depiction of sex and nudity is not illegal, but it does violate the law when it is judged obscene. *Obscene material* is a legal term that today is defined as material offensive to community standards. Thus, each local jurisdiction must decide what pornographic material is obscene. A growing problem is in the exploitation of children in obscenity—kiddy porn. Recently, the Supreme Court has ruled that local communities can pass statutes outlawing this practice. There is no hard evidence that pornography is related to crime or aggression, but data suggest that sexual material with a violent theme is related to sexual violence by those who view it.

Substance abuse is another type of public order crime. There is great debate over the legalization of drugs, usually centering around nonaddictive drugs such as marijuana and cocaine. However, most states and the federal government outlaw a wide variety of drugs they consider harmful, including narcotics, amphetamines, barbiturates, cocaine, hallucinogens, and marijuana. One of the main reasons for the continued ban on drugs is their relationship to crime. Numerous studies have found that drug addicts commit enormous amounts of property crime.

Alcohol is another commonly abused substance. Although it is legal to possess alcohol, it too has been linked to crime. Drunk driving and highway deaths caused by drunk drivers are a growing national problem.

KEY TERMS

public order crime
victimless crime
mala prohibitum
moral entrepreneurs
moral crusades
homosexuality
homophobia
sodomy
prostitution
brothels
madams
call girls
massage parlors
baby pros
white slave act
pornography

Attorney General's Commission on Pornography
kiddy porn
National Commission on Obscenity and Pornography
reasonableness doctrine
adult entertainment zones
narcosis
addict
freebase
basuco
crack
forfeiture
zero tolerance

NOTES

1. Edwin Schur, *Crimes Without Victims* (Englewood Cliffs, N.J.: Prentice-Hall, 1965).
2. Morris Cohen, "Moral Aspects of the Criminal Law," *Yale Law Journal* 49 (1940):1017.
3. Sir Patrick Devlin, *The Enforcement of Morals* (New York: Oxford University Press, 1959), p. 20.
4. See, Joel Feinberg, *Social Philosophy* (Englewood Cliffs, N.J.: Prentice-Hall, 1973), Chapters 2 and 3.
5. United States v. 12 200-ft Reels of Super 8mm. Film, 413 U.S. 123 (1973) at 137.
6. H. L. A. Hart, "Immorality and Treason," *Listener* 62 (1959):163.
7. Joseph Gussfield, "On Legislating Morals: The Symbolic Process of Designating Deviancy," *California Law Review* 56 (1968):58–59.

8. Henry Lesieur and Joseph Sheley, "Illegal Appended Enterprises: Selling the Lines," *Social Problems* 34 (1987):249–60.

9. Howard Becker, *Outsiders* (New York: Macmillan, 1963), pp. 13–14.

10. Albert Reiss, "The Social Integration of Queers and Peers," *Social Problems* 9 (1961):102–20.

11. Judd Marmor, "The Multiple Roots of Homosexual Behavior," in J. Marmor, ed., *Homosexual Behavior* (New York: Basic Books, 1980), p.5.

12. C. S. Ford and F. A. Beach, *Patterns of Sexual Behavior* (New York: Harper & Bros., 1951).

13. A. Kinsey, W. Pomeroy, and C. Martin, *Sexual Behavior in the Human Male* (Philadelphia: W. B. Saunders, 1948); A. Kinsey, et al., *Sexual Behavior in the Human Female* (Philadelphia: W. B. Saunders, 1953); Morton Hunt, *Sexual Behavior in the 1970's* (New York: Dell Books, 1974), p. 317.

14. J. McNeil, *The Church and the Homosexual* (Kansas City, Mo.: Sheed, Andrews, and McNeel, 1976).

15. Marmor, "The Multiple Roots of Homosexual Behavior," pp. 18–19.

16. M. Weinberg and C. J. Williams, *Male Homosexuals: Problems and Adaptations* (New York: Oxford University Press, 1974).

17. Spencer Rathus, *Human Sexuality* (New York: Holt, Rinehart and Winston, 1983), p. 395.

18. *Ibid.*, p. 409.

19. Kim Painter, "Report: Attacks on Gays on the Rise," *USA Today* (8 June 1988), p. 3.

20. 376 U.S. 660; 82 S. Ct. 1417; 8 L. Ed. 2d 758 (1962).

21. F. Inbau, J. Thompson, and J. Zagel, *Criminal Law and Its Administration* (Mineola, N.Y.: Foundation Press, 1974), p. 287.

22. Bowers v. Hardwick, 106 S. Ct. 2841 (1986); reh. den. 107 S. Ct. 29 (1986).

23. Georgia Code Ann., Sec. 16-6-2 (1984).

24. American Law Institute, Model Penal Code, Section 207.5.

25. Gary Caplan, "Fourteenth Amendment—The Supreme Court Limits the Right to Privacy," *The Journal of Criminal Law and Criminology* 77 (1986):894–930.

26. Associated Press, "Voters in Houston Defeat 'Sexual Orientations' Issues," *Omaha World Herald*, (20 January 1985), p. 1.

27. 741 F. 2d 1388 (1984).

28. Associated Press, "Court Rules Against Transsexual Pilot," *Omaha World Herald* (31 August 1984), p. 3.

29. For the classic study of homosexual encounters, see, Laud Humphreys, *Tearoom Trade: Impersonal Sex in Public Places* (Chicago: Aldine, 1970).

30. See, generally, V. Bullogh, *Sexual Variance in Society and History* (Chicago: University of Chicago Press, 1980).

31. Rathus, *Human Sexuality*, p. 463.

32. Loosely adapted from Charles Winick and Paul Kinsie, *The Lively Commerce* (Chicago: Quadrangle Books, 1971), p. 3.

33. *Uniform Crime Reports, 1986*, p. 174.

34. UPI, "77-Year-Old Jailed on Prostitution," *Manchester Union Leader* (24 April 1988), p. 1B.

35. Charles McCaghy, *Deviant Behavior* (New York: Macmillan, 1976), pp. 348–49.

36. Rathus, *Human Sexuality*, p. 463.

37. *Ibid.*

38. Hunt, *Sexual Behavior in the 1970's*, pp. 143–44.

39. Federal Bureau of Investigation, *Crime in the United States, 1988* (Washington, D.C.: U.S. Government Printing Office, 1981), p. 194.

40. Charles Winick and Paul Kinsie, *The Lively Commerce* (Chicago: Quadrangle Books, 1971), p. 58.

41. Jennifer James, "Prostitutes and Prostitution," in E. Sagarin and F. Montanino, eds., *Deviants: Voluntary Action in a Hostile World* (Glenview, Ill.: Scott, Foresman, 1977), p. 384.

42. Wincik and Kinsie, *The Live Commerce*, pp. 172–73.

43. *Ibid.*, p. 97.

44. Alessandra Stanley, "Case of the Classy Madam," *Time* (29 October 1984), p. 39.

45. Described in Rathus, *Human Sexuality*, p. 468.

46. N. Jackman, Richard O'Toole, and Gilbert Geis, "The Self-Image of the Prostitute," in J. Gagnon and W. Simon, eds., *Sexual Deviance* (New York: Harper and Row, 1967), pp. 152–53.

47. Winick and Kinsie, *The Lively Commerce*, p. 51.

48. Paul Gebhard, "Misconceptions About Female Prostitutes," *Medical Aspects of Human Sexuality* 3 (July 1969):28–30.

49. James, "Prostitutes and Prostitution," pp. 388–89.

50. Winick and Kinsie, *The Lively Commerce*, p. 109.

51. James, "Prostitutes and Prostitution," p. 419.

52. Winick and Kinsie, *The Lively Commerce*, p. 120.

53. Susan Hall, *Ladies of the Night* (New York: Trident Press, 1973).

54. *The Merriam-Webster Dictionary* (New York: Pocket Books, 1974), p. 484.

55. Final Report, *Attorney General's Commission Report on Pornography* (Washington, D.C.: U.S. Government Printing Office, 1986), pp. 837–902. Hereafter cited as Pornography Commission.

56. John Hurst, "Children—A Big Profit Item for the Smut Peddlers," *Los Angeles Times* (26 May 1977), cited in Laura Lederer, ed., *Take Back the Night* (New York: William Morrow, 1980), pp. 77–78.

57. Ann Wolbert Burgess, *Child Pornography and Sex Rings* (Lexington, Mass.: Lexington Books, 1984).

58. Lederer, "Introduction," in Lederer, *Take Back the Night*, p. 18.
59. Lederer, "Playboy Isn't Playing: An Interview with Judith Bat-Ada," in Lederer, *Take Back the Night*, p. 124.
60. *The Report of the Commission on Obscenity and Pornography* (Washington, D.C.: Government Printing Office, 1970).
61. Pornography Commission, p. 2158.
62. Berl Kutchinsky, "The Effect of Easy Availability of Pornography on the Incidence of Sex Crimes," *Journal of Social Issues* 29 (1973):95–112.
63. Michael Goldstein, "Exposure to Erotic Stimuli and Sexual Deviance," *Journal of Social Issues* 29 (1973):197–219.
64. John Court, "Sex and Violence: A Ripple Effect," in Neal Malamuth and Edward Donnerstein, eds., *Pornography and Aggression* (Orlando, Fl.: Academic Press, 1984).
65. See, Edward Donnerstein, Daniel Linz, and Steven Penrod, *The Question of Pornography* (New York: Free Press, 1987).
66. Pornography Commission, pp. 901–1037.
67. Pornography Commission, p. 1005.
68. Edward Donnerstein, "Pornography and Violence Against Women," *Annals of the New York Academy of Science* 347 (1980):277–88; E. Donnerstein and J. Hallam, "Facilitating Effects of Erotica on Aggression Against Women," *Journal of Personality and Social Psychology* 36 (1977):1270–77; Seymour Fishbach and Neal Malamuth, "Sex and Aggression: Proving the Link," *Psychology Today* 12 (1978):111–22.
69. Don Smith, "Sexual Aggression in American Pornography: The Stereotype of Rape," Paper presented at the Annual Meeting of the American Sociological Association, 1976, cited in Lederer, *Take Back the Night*, p. 213.
70. 354 U.S. 476; 77 S. Ct. 1304 (1957).
71. 383 U.S. 413 (1966).
72. 413 U.S. 15 (1973).
73. R. George Wright, "Defining Obscenity: The Criterion of Value," *New England Law Review* 22 (1987):315–41.
74. Pope v. Illinois, 107 S. Ct. 1918 (1987).
75. Id. at 1927 (Stevens, J. dissenting).
76. Pornography Commission; pp. 376–77.
77. 427 U.S. 50 (1976).
78. Kevin Cullen, "The Bad Old Days are Over," *Boston Globe* (23 December 1987), p. 33.
79. New York v. Ferber, 50 L.W. 5077 (1982).
80. Joseph Scott, "Violence and Erotic Material—The Relationship Between Adult Entertainment and Rape," Paper presented at the Annual Meeting of the American Association for the Advancement of Science, Los Angeles, California, 1985.
81. Joseph Scott and Steven Cuvelier, "Violence in *Playboy* Magazine: A Longitudinal Analysis," *Archives of Sexual Behavior* 16 (1987):279–88.
82. *Ibid.*
83. Andrew Dabilis, "Is It Shifting Toward Suburbia?" *Boston Globe* (23 December 1987), pp. 33–35.
84. James Inciardi, *The War on Drugs* (Palo Alto, Cal.: Mayfield, 1986), p. 2.
85. See, generally, David Pittman, "Drug Addiction and Crime," in D. Glazer, ed., *Handbook of Criminology* (Chicago: Rand McNally, 1974), pp. 209–32; Board of Directors, National Council on Crime and Delinquency, "Drug Addiction: A Medical, Not a Law Enforcement, Problem," *Crime and Delinquency* 20 (1974):4–9.
86. Arnold Trebach, *The Heroin Solution* (New Haven, Conn.: Yale University Press, 1982).
87. This section relies heavily on the descriptions provided by Kenneth Jones, Louis Shainberg, and Curtin Byer, *Drugs and Alcohol* (New York: Harper & Row, 1979), pp. 57–114.
88. See, Edwin Brecher, *Licit and Illicit Drugs* (Boston: Little, Brown, 1972).
89. James Inciardi, *Reflections on Crime* (New York: Holt, Rinehart and Winston, 1978), p. 15.
90. William Bates and Betty Crowther, "Drug Abuse," in Sagarin and Montanino, eds., *Deviants: Voluntary Actors in a Hostile World*, p. 269.
91. These numbers are open to debate. See, Inciardi, *The War on Drugs*, pp. 70–71; Jerome Platt and Christina Platt, *Heroin Addiction* (New York: Wiley, 1976), p. 324.
92. Charles Winick, "Physician Narcotics Addicts," *Social Problems* 9 (1961):174–86.
93. G. E. Vallant, "Parent-Child Disparity and Drug Addiction," *Journal of Nervous and Mental Disease* 142 (1966):534–39.
94. Charles Winick, "Epidemiology of Narcotics Use," in D. Wilner and G. Kassenbaum, ed., *Narcotics* (New York: McGraw-Hill, 1965), pp. 3–18.
95. C. Bowden, "Determinants of Initial Use of Opioids," *Comprehensive Psychiatry* 12 (1971):136–40.
96. R. Cloward and L. Ohlin, *Delinquency and Opportunity: A Theory of Delinquent Gangs* (Glencoe, Ill.: Free Press, 1960).
97. D. Baer and J. Corrado, "Heroin Addict Relationships with Parents During Childhood and Early Adolescent Years," *Journal of Genetic Psychology* 124 (1974):99–103.
98. See, S. F. Bucky, "The Relationship between Background and Extent of Heroin Use," *American Journal of Psychiatry* 130 (1973):709–10; I. Chien, D. L. Gerard, R. Lee, and E. Rosenfield, *The Road to H: Narcotics Delinquency and Social Policy* (New York: Basic Books, 1964).
99. Platt and Platt, *Heroin Addiction*, p. 127.
100. Inciardi, *The War Against Drugs*, p. 60.

101. B. Johnson, E.Wish, and D. Huizinga, "The Concentration of Delinquent Offending: The Contribution of Serious Drug Involvement to High Rate of Delinquency," Paper presented at the American Society of Criminology, Denver, 1983, cited in Paul Gropper, "Probing the Links Between Drugs and Crime," *NIJ Reports* (November 1984):5–8.

102. This section is derived from James Inciardi, "Beyond Cocaine: Basuco, Crack and Other Coca Products," Paper presented at the Academy of Criminal Justice Sciences, St. Louis, Missouri, 1987.

103. University of Michigan News Release, January 12, 1988. The annual survey is conducted by Lloyd Johnston, Jerald Bachman, and Patrick O'Malley.

104. George Speckart and M. Douglas Anglin, "Narcotics Use and Crime: An Overview of Recent Research Advances," *Contemporary Drug Problems* 13 (1986):741–69; Charles Faupel and Carl Klockars, "Drugs-Crime Connections: Elaborations from the Life Histories of Hard-Core Heroin Addicts," *Social Problems* 34 (1987):54–68.

105. M. Douglas Anglin, Elizabeth Piper Deschenes, and George Speckart, "The Effect of Legal Supervision on Narcotic Addiction and Criminal Behavior," Paper presented at the American Society of Criminology Meeting, Montreal, Canada, November, 1987, p. 2.

106. Christopher Innes, *Drug Use and Crime* (Washington, D.C.: Bureau of Justice Statistics, 1988).

107. Eric Wish, *Drug Use Forecasting: New York 1984 to 1986* (Washington, D.C.: National Institute of Justice, 1987).

108. "Of 2,000 Arrestees Nationwide, 70% Tested Positive for Drugs," *Criminal Justice Newsletter* (1 February 1988), p. 4.

109. James Inciardi, "Heroin Use and Street Crime," *Crime and Delinquency* 25 (1979):335–46. See also, W. McGlothlin, M. Anglin, and B. Wilson, "Narcotic Addiction and Crime," *Criminology* 16 (1978):293–311.

110. See Jones, Shainberg, and Byer, *Drugs and Alcohol*, pp. 137–46.

111. "Drug War Cost Put at $6.2b in 1986," *Boston Globe* (19 October 1987), p. 4.

112. Robert Taylor and Gary Cohen, "War Against Narcotics by U.S. Government Isn't Slowing Influx," *Wall Street Journal* (27 November 1984), p. 1.

113. Walter Shapiro, "Going After the Hell's Angels," *Newsweek* (13 May 1985), p. 41.

114. This information comes from Stephanie Minor-Harper and Christopher Innes, *Time Served in Prison and on Parole, 1984* (Washington, D.C.: Bureau of Justice Statistics, 1987); Edward Lisefski and Donald Manson, *Tracking Offenders, 1984* (Washington, D.C.: Bureau of Justice Statistics, 1988); Mark Cuniff, *Sentencing Outcomes in 28 Felony Courts* (Washington, D.C.: Bureau of Justice Statistics, 1987).

115. Jan Chaiken and Douglas McDonald, *Federal Drug Law Violators* (Washington, D.C.: Bureau of Justice Statistics, 1988).

116. Inciardi, *The War on Drugs*, pp. 155–56. For an opposing view, see, Harold Pepinsky and Paul Jesilow, *Myths that Cause Crime* (Cabin John Md.: Seven Locks Press, 1984), and Arnold Trebach, *The Heroin Solution;* Mary Graham, *Controlling Drug Abuse and Crime: A Research Update* (Washington, D.C.: U.S. Department of Justice, 1987), p. 6.

117. L. Erik Calonius, "Controversy Surrounds the Way the Dutch Treat Heroin Addicts," *Wall Street Journal* (December 1984), p. 1.

118. James Inciardi, *Reflections on Crime* (New York: Holt, Rinehart and Winston, 1978), pp. 8–10. See also, A. Greeley, William McCready, and Gary Theisen, *Ethnic Drinking Subcultures* (New York: Praeger, 1980).

119. Joseph Gusfield, *Symbolic Crusade* (Urbana, Ill.: University of Illinois Press, 1963), Chap. 3.

120. McCaghy, *Deviant Behavior*, p. 280.

121. *Ibid.*

122. *Uniform Crime Reports, 1986*, p. 164.

123. Johnston, Bachman, and O'Malley, University of Michigan press release, Jan. 12, 1988.

124. Bennett Beach, "Is the Party Finally Over?" *Time* (26 April 1982), p. 58.

125. "New Drunken Driver Law Shows Results in California," *Omaha World Herald* (26 May 1982), p. 34.

126. Faye Silas, "Gimme the Keys," *ABA Journal* 71 (1985):36.

127. Fred Heinzelmann, *Jailing Drunk Drivers* (Washington, D.C.: National Institute of Justice, 1984).

128. Rodney Kingsworth and Michael Jungsten, "Driving Under the Influence: The Impact of Legislative Reform on Court Sentencing Practices," *Crime and Delinquency* 34 (1988):3–28.

129. Jones, Shainberg, and Byer, *Drugs and Alcohol*, pp. 190–93.

130. Gerald Wheeler and Rodney Hissong, "Effects of Criminal Sanctions on Drunk Drivers: Beyond Incarceration," *Crime and Delinquency* 34 (1988):29–42.

131. Easter v. District of Columbia, 361 F. 2d 50 (D.C. Cir. 1966).

132. 392 U.S. 514 (1968).

SECTION IV

THE
CRIMINAL
JUSTICE
SYSTEM

The text's final section reviews the agencies and the process of justice designed to exert social control over criminal offenders. Chapter 14 provides an overview of the justice system and describes its major institutions and processes; Chapter 15 looks at the police; Chapter 16 and 17 analyze the court and correctional systems.

This vast array of people and institutions is beset by conflicting goals and values. Some view it as a mammoth agency of social control; others see it as a great social service dispensing therapy to those who cannot fit within the boundaries of society.

Consequently, a major goal of justice system policy makers is to formulate and disseminate effective models of crime prevention and control. Efforts are now being undertaken at all levels of the justice system to improve information flow, experiment with new program concepts, and evaluate current operating procedures.

There are many important links within the system, so the agencies of justice can be studied on a cross-national level. For example, all agencies must obey the rule of law, and most use a common framework of operations in such everyday events as arrest, detention, bail, and trial. However, the system fails to communicate effectively in getting out information on what works, what doesn't, and why.

These chapters provide a good foundation for studying the justice system and its links to criminological thought.

CHAPTER 14

OVERVIEW OF THE CRIMINAL JUSTICE SYSTEM

INTRODUCTION

On December 20, 1986, a gang of white youths attacked three black men in the Howard Beach section of Queens. Two of the men were beaten, and one, Michael Griffith, was killed when struck by a car while trying to escape from the mob. The case polarized New York and made front-page headlines around the country. On December 22, 1987, three of the youths involved in the beatings were convicted of manslaughter and sent to Attica prison. The verdict was criticized by some as being too lenient considering the facts of the case; to others, the youths were the scapegoats of a criminal justice system trying to make amends for long years of racial injustice.[1]

The Howard Beach incident points up the dilemmas faced by the American system of criminal justice. On the one hand, its component agencies—police, courts, and corrections—are charged by law with meeting fair and equal justice. On the other hand, the justice system must face the overwhelming reality of its task: maintaining the rule of law in a society beset by racial and social injustice and conflict.

How far should the justice system go in maintaining order? If the police carry out their task too vigorously, if courts meet out lengthy sentences, if prison administrators are tough disciplinarians, then the justice system is criticized for its police-state mentality. If the system seems too concerned with the rights and treatment of criminal offenders and ignores both the victim's and society's desire for revenge, its executives are accused of being wishy-washy and endangering the public welfare by coddling dangerous criminals.

Criminal justice refers to both the formal process and the component agencies that have been established to apprehend, adjudicate, sanction and treat criminal offenders. In recent yeas it has become popular to refer to the components of justice as "the criminal justice system." This term implies that the major segments of justice—the various police, court, and correctional agencies—operate as a unified whole. Change in one area of the system should automatically produce a corresponding change in the others. In addition, the systems approach to criminal justice suggests that the planning and coordination of justice-related agencies would best be served by creating unified rules, policies, and procedures which would be uniformly beneficial to the agencies within the justice network and to the people who come into contact with them.

Unfortunately, there is little actual "system" to justice in the United States. The various elements of the criminal justice system—police, courts, and corrections—are all related, but they are influenced by each other's policies and practices only to a degree. They have not yet become so well coordinated that they can be described as operating in unison. *Fragmented*, *divided*, and *splintered* continue to be the adjectives most commonly used to describe the U.S. system of criminal justice.[2] Critics have referred to the justice process as the **criminal justice nonsystem**.[3]

In this chapter, the various components and processes of criminal justice are reviewed. Then the legal constraints on criminal justice agencies are discussed. Some of the philosophical concepts that dominate the system are mentioned, and the role of the government in aiding the victims of crime also is discussed.

COMPONENTS OF CRIMINAL JUSTICE

The basic components of the criminal justice system are the various police, court, and correctional agencies organized on the local, state, and federal levels of government. Together they encompass a large and diverse collection of approximately 55,000 separate agencies engaging in justice-related activities.[4] The overwhelming majority (81 percent) are part of local government structures, and the remainder are funded by state and federal jurisdictions; there also is a separate juvenile justice system (see Close-Up).

Police

Approximately 20,000 law enforcement agencies are operating in the United States. Most are municipal, general-purpose police forces, numbering about 13,600 in all. In addition, local jurisdictions maintain over 1,000 special police units, including park rangers, harbor police, transit police, and campus security agencies at local universities. At the county level of government, there are approximately 3,000 **sheriff's departments** which, depending on the jurisdiction, provide police protection in the unincorporated areas of the county, perform judicial functions such as serving subpoenas, and maintain the county jail and detention facilities. Almost every state maintains either a highway patrol or other police organization. The federal government has its own law enforcement agencies, including the FBI and the Secret Service. All told, there are approximately 700,000 federal, state, county, and local law enforcement officers and more than 150,000 civilian employees working in police agencies.[5]

Since their origin in early nineteenth-century Britain, law enforcement agencies have been charged with peacekeeping, deterring potential criminals, and apprehending law violators.[6] The traditional police role also involved "order maintenance" through patrolling public streets and highways, responding to calls for assistance, investigating crimes, and identifying criminal suspects. The police role gradually has expanded to include a variety of human service functions, which include: preventing youth crime and diverting juvenile offenders from the criminal justice system; resolving family conflicts; facilitating the movement of people and vehicles; preserving civil order during emergencies; providing emergency medical care; and improving police-community relations.[7]

By the nature of their functions and roles, police are the most visible agents of the justice process. Their reactions to victims and offenders are carefully scrutinized in the news media. On numerous occasions the police have been criticized for being too harsh or too lenient, too violent or too passive. Police control of such groups as youthful offenders, political dissidents, protestors, and union workers has been the topic of serious public debate. Compounding the problem is the tremendous **discretion** afforded police officers. The officer has the power to determine when a domestic dispute becomes disorderly conduct or criminal assault, whether it is appropriate to arrest a juvenile or refer her or him to a social agency, and when to assume that probable cause exists to arrest a suspect for a crime.[8] At the same time, police agencies have themselves been questioned for using poor judgment in such areas as internal corruption, inefficiency, lack of effectiveness, brutality, and discriminatory hiring.[9] Consequently, at all levels of government the police traditionally have been defensive toward and suspicious of the public, resistant to change and secretive in their activities.

Courts

There are approximately 25,000 court-related agencies in the United States. These include more than 16,000 criminal courts, of which about 13,000 try misdemeanor cases, 3,235 are felony courts, and 207 are appellate courts. In addition, there also are slightly more than 8,000 federal, state, and local prosecutors' offices, which represent the government in criminal and civil trials and appeals. Over half of these offices are municipal, about one-third are county, and the remainder are state and federally affiliated. In addition, some 1,000 public defender offices, which dispense free legal aid to indigent defendants, are in operation around the country.

The **criminal court** is considered by many to be the core element in the administration of criminal justice. In the purest sense of justice, the court is responsible for determining the criminal liability of criminal defendants. Ideally, it is expected to convict and sentence those found guilty of crimes, while insuring that the innocent are freed without any consequence or burden. The courts are formally required to seek the truth, to obtain justice, and to maintain the integrity of the government's rule of law.

Once the truth has been determined, and in the event the defendant is found guilty, the criminal court is responsible for sentencing the offender. Whatever sentence is ordered by the court may serve not only to rehabilitate the offender but also to deter others from crime. Once sentencing is accomplished, the corrections component of criminal justice begins to function.

Hypothetically, the entire criminal court process is undertaken with the recognition that the rights of the individual should be protected at all times. These rights, determined by federal and state constitutional mandates, statutes, and case law, form the foundation for protection of the accused. They include such basic concepts as the right to an attorney, the right to a jury trial, and the right to a speedy trial. Under the Fifth and Fourteenth Amendments of the U.S. Constitution, the defendant also has the right to due process, or the right to be treated with **fundamental fairness.** Under the protective umbrella of due process are included the rights to be present at trial, to be notified of the charges, to have an opportunity to confront hostile witnesses, and to have favorable witnesses appear. Such practices are an integral part of a process that seeks to balance the interests of the in-

CLOSE-UP

Juvenile Justice

Independent of but interrelated with the adult criminal justice system, the juvenile justice system is primarily responsible for dealing with juveniles who commit crimes (*delinquents*), and those who are incorrigible, truants, runaways, or unmanageable (*status offenders*).

The notion that juveniles who commit criminal acts should be treated separately from adults is a relatively new one. Until the late nineteenth century, youthful criminals were tried in adult courts and punished in adult institutions. However, in the 1890s, reformers, today known as "child savers," lobbied to separate young offenders from serious adult criminals. Their efforts were rewarded when the first separate juvenile court was set up in Chicago, Illinois, in 1899. Over the next 20 years, most other states created separate juvenile court and correctional systems.

At first the juvenile system was based on the philosophy of parens *patriae*. This meant that the state was acting in the best interests of children in trouble who could not care for themselves. Under the parens patriae doctrine, delinquents and status offenders (sometimes called "wayward minors" or "children in need of supervision") were adjudicated in an informal juvenile court hearing without the benefit of counsel or other procedural rights. The juvenile correctional system, designed for treatment rather than punishment, was usually located in small institutions referred to as schools or camps. (The first juvenile reform school was opened in 1847 in Massachusetts.) However, after the separate juvenile justice system was developed, almost all incarcerated youths were maintained in separate juvenile institutions that stressed individualized treatment, education, and counseling.

In the 1960s the Supreme Court revolutionized the juvenile justice system when, in a series of cases—most importantly *In Re Gault*—it granted procedural and due process rights, such as the right to legal counsel, to juveniles at trial. The Court recognized that many youths were receiving long sentences without the benefit of counsel and other Fifth and Sixth Amendment rights and that many institutions did not carry out their treatment role. Consequently, the juvenile justice process became similar to the adult process.

In the 1970s the diversion movement once again changed juvenile justice. Every effort was made to remove youths from the official justice process and place them in

TABLE A   Similarities Between Juvenile and Adult Justice Systems

- Police officers, judges, and correctional personnel use discretion in decision-making in both adult and juvenile systems.
- The right to receive *Miranda* warnings applies to juveniles as well as to adults.
- Procedural safeguards similar to those of adults protect juveniles when they admit guilt.
- Prosecutors and defense attorneys play an equally critical role in juvenile and adult advocacy.
- Juveniles and adults have the right to counsel at most crucial stages of the court process.
- Pretrial motions are available in juvenile and criminal court proceedings.
- Negotiations and plea-bargaining exist for juvenile and adult offenders.
- Both juveniles and adults have a right to a hearing and an appeal.
- The standard of evidence in juvenile delinquency adjudications, as in adult criminal trials, is proof beyond a reasonable doubt.
- Both juveniles and adults can be kept in preventive pretrial detention without bail if they are considered dangerous or a risk to themselves or society.
- Juveniles and adults can be placed on probation by the court, or placed in community treatment programs.

alternative, community-based treatment programs. One state, Massachusetts, went so far as to close its secure correctional facilities and place all youths, no matter how serious their crimes, in community programs.

Today, concern over juvenile violence has caused some critics to question the juvenile justice system's treatment philosophy. Some states, such as New York, have liberalized their procedures for trying serious juvenile offenders in the adult system, consequently making them eligible for incarceration in adult prisons. The general trend has been to remove as many nonviolent and status offenders as possible from secure placements in juvenile institutions and at the same time to lengthen the sentences of

serious offenders or to move such offenders to the adult system.

Some of the similarities between the adult and juvenile justice systems are listed in Table A. Some of the differences are listed in Table B.

Discussion Questions

1. Should serious juvenile offenders be treated like adults and tried in adult courts?

2. Should incorrigible and truant youths be given the same treatment as delinquents (criminal youths)?

TABLE B Differences Between Juvenile and Adult Justice Systems

- The primary purpose of juvenile procedures is protection and treatment; with adults, the aim is punishment of the guilty.
- Age determines the jurisdiction of the juvenile court; in the adult system, jurisdiction is determined by the nature of the offense.
- Juveniles can be apprehended for acts that would not be criminal if they were committed by an adult (status offenses), such as truancy or running away from home.
- Juvenile proceedings are not considered criminal; adult proceedings are.
- Juvenile court procedures are generally informal and private; those of adult courts are more formal and are open to the public.
- Courts cannot release identifying information concerning a juvenile to the press, but must release information about an adult.
- Parents are highly involved in the juvenile process but not in the adult process.
- The standard of arrest is more stringent for adults than for juveniles.
- Juveniles are released into parental custody while adults are generally given the opportunity for bail.
- Juveniles have no constitutional right to a jury trial; adults have this right.
- Juveniles have the right to treatment under the Fourteenth Amendment; adult offenders have no such recognized right.
- A juvenile's record is sealed when the age of majority is reached; an adult's record is permanent.
- Underage children cannot be given the death penalty.
- A juvenile court cannot sentence juveniles to county jails or state prisons, which are reserved for adults.
- Juveniles can be searched under circumstances in which adults would be immune. For example, teachers can search students without probable cause that a crime has been committed.

SOURCE: Tables A and B are from Larry Siegel and Joseph Senna, *Juvenile Delinquency*, 3d ed. (St. Paul, Minn.: West Publishing, 1987), p. 340.

dividual and the state.

Unfortunately, the ideal conditions of objectivity, fairness, and equal rights under which the nation's courts should operate are rarely matched by actual practice or procedure. While some well-publicized defendants, such as John Hinckley and Michael Deaver, receive their full share of rights and privileges, a significant number of defendants are herded through the court system with a minimum of interest or care. Court dockets are too crowded, and funds are insufficient to grant each defendant the full share of justice. Consequently, a system known as **plea bargaining** has developed; in it, defendants are asked to plead guilty as charged in return for consideration of leniency or mercy.[10] "Bargain justice" is estimated to occur in more than 90 percent of all criminal cases. Although the criminal court system is founded on the concept of equality before the law, there are unquestionably differences in the treatment that poor and wealthy citizens receive when they are accused of crimes. These concerns are discussed more fully in Chapter 16.

Corrections

There are 9,000 agencies devoted to the correction and treatment of convicted offenders. Approximately 3,500 are adult and juvenile probation and parole agencies supervising offenders in the community. There also are about 5,700 residential correctional facilities, divided into 3,500 jails, 800 prisons, and 1,100 juvenile institutions. About three million Americans under some form of correction.

Following a criminal trial that results in conviction and sentencing, the offender enters the **correctional system.** Corrections agencies are charged with administering the post-conviction care given to offenders. Depending on the seriousness of the crime and the individual needs of offenders, this care can range from casual community monitoring to solitary confinement in a maximum-security prison.

The most common correctional treatment, **probation,** is a legal disposition that allows the convicted offender to remain in the community, subject to conditions imposed by court order under the supervision of a probation officer. It allows the offender to continue working and providing for the family and to avoid the debilitating effects of incarceration. Today more than two million adults and about 400,000 youths

An inmate is searched before entering the cell blocks of Stateville Prison near Joliet, Illinois, a maximum security institution for serious felons.

are on probation, and more than 25 percent of felony offenders receive a probation sentence.

A person given a sentence involving incarceration ordinarily is confined to a correctional institution for a specified period of time. Different types of institutions are used to hold offenders. Jails or houses of correction hold offenders convicted of misdemeanors and those awaiting trial or involved in other proceedings, such as grand jury deliberations, arraignments, or preliminary hearings. Many of these short-term institutions are administered by local county governments and, consequently, little is done in the way of inmate treatment, principally because the personnel and institutions lack the qualifications, services, and resources.

State and federally operated facilities that receive felony offenders sentenced by the criminal courts are called prisons or **penitentiaries.** They are often divided into minimum-, medium-, and maximum-security institutions. Prison facilities vary throughout the country. Some have high walls, cells, and large, heterogeneous inmate populations; others offer much freedom, good correctional programs, and small, homogeneous populations.

Most new inmates are first sent to a reception and **classification center,** where they are given diagnostic evaluations and are assigned to institutions that meet individual needs as much as possible within the system's resources. The diagnostic process in the reception center may range from a physical examination and a single interview to an extensive series of psychiatric tests, orientation sessions, and numerous personal interviews. Classification is a way of evaluating inmates and assigning them to appropriate placements and activities within the state institutional system.

The gap between what correctional programs promise to deliver and their actual performance is often significant. Many jurisdictions have therefore instituted a fourth type of confinement—**community-based correctional facilities.** These programs emphasize the use of small neighborhood residential centers, halfway houses, prerelease centers, and work-release and home-furlough programs. This movement results from the experts' belief that only a small percentage of prison inmates require maximum security and that most can be more effectively rehabilitated in community-based facilities. Such programs offer the opportunity to maintain normal family and social relationships while giving access to rehabilitative services and resources at lower cost to taxpayers. Despite such efforts, the prison population is at an all-time high of about 600,000 people.

The last segment of the corrections system, **parole** is a process whereby an inmate is selected for early release and serves the remainder of the sentence in the community under the supervision of a parole officer. The main purpose of parole is to help the ex-inmate bridge the gap between institutional confinement and a positive adjustment within the community. All parolees must adhere to a set of rules of behavior while they are "on the outside." If these rules are violated, the parole privilege can be terminated (revoked), and the parolee will be sent back to the institution to serve the remainder of the sentence.

Other ways an offender may be released from an institution include mandatory release upon completion of the sentence, and the pardon, a form of executive clemency.

COSTS OF JUSTICE

This complex array of agencies handles upward of two million offenders a year and employs more than 1.4 million people: about 700,000 in law enforcement agencies, 300,000 in the courts, and 400,000 in correctional agencies.[11]

The costs of maintaining this system are vast. It costs about $25,000 annually to keep one juvenile in an institution; a prison cell costs about $100,000 to construct. The monetary burden on each American for the justice system is $191 annually, almost as much as the per capita costs for transportation ($240) and hospital and health care ($267).[12] The estimated cost of operating the system is more than $50 billion annually. (See Close-Up on the costs of crime and justice.)

THE JUSTICE PROCESS

In addition to viewing the criminal justice system as a collection of agencies, it is also possible to see it as a series of decision points through which offenders flow. This process begins with an initial contact with police and ends with the offender's reentry into society. At any point in the process, the accused may no longer be considered an offender and may be allowed back into society without further penalty. This can happen for such reasons as:

1. The case is considered unimportant or trivial.
2. Legally admissible evidence is unavailable.
3. The accused is considered not to need further treatment, punishment, or attention.
4. Those in power decide not to take further action in the case for personal reasons (discretion).

Herbert Packer has described this process as follows:

The image that comes to mind is an assembly line conveyor belt down which moves an endless stream of cases, never stopping, carrying them to workers who stand at fixed stations and who perform on each case as it comes by the same small but essential operation that brings it one step closer to being a finished product, or to exchange the metaphor for the reality, a closed file. The

CLOSE-UP

The Costs of Crime and Justice

The costs of crime and criminal justice are not insignificant. While it is difficult to pinpoint economic losses due to crime, the total is in the multi-billions. For example, the FBI estimates that about $12 billion in goods and currency are stolen annually and about $4 billion recovered. National Crime Survey data indicate that each year more than three million crimes occur which involve losses of more than $500 each; more than 98 percent of all crimes involve the loss of goods or money.

White-collar offenses, such as illegal stock market manipulation, illegal waste dumping, tax evasion, and pilferage, involve losses in the hundreds of billions annually. Similarly, the "underground economy" of prostitution, gambling, drug sales, and pornography may run an additional $400 billion. Of course, there are also the incidental costs of lost tax revenues, days lost from work, medical care for victims, higher insurance rates, and higher production costs.

Beyond these immediate costs are the vast sums spent on the criminal justice system for police, court, and correctional agencies. The most recent figures, shown in Table A, show that more than $45 billion were spent by all levels of government on criminal justice system operations. This amount represents an increase of 132 percent in a 10-year period (1976 to 1985). Figuring on a modest inflation rate, today's costs are most likely over $50 billion.

On average, each U.S. taxpayer pays about $200 each year for criminal justice protection. However, there is considerable disparity between state jurisdictions. While each Alaskan pays out $592 per year to state and local governments, each New Yorker pays $293, and residents of West Virginia and Mississippi average $82 for criminal justice annually.

TABLE A Justice System Expenditures, by Level of Government (In Thousands of Dollars)

Expenditure Type by Level of Government	Total	Police Protection	Judicial and Legal Services				Corrections	Other Justice Activities
			Trial System Total	Courts Only	Prosecution and Legal Services	Public Defense		
All Expenditures	$45,607,142	$22,013,594	$10,070,399	$5,780,163	$3,235,732	$1,054,504	$13,034,221	$488,928
Federal	5,819,476	2,767,514	1,998,904	852,095	803,548	343,261	778,581	274,477
Direct	5,683,841	2,767,514	1,998,904	852,095	803,548	343,261	706,653	210,770
Intergovernmental	135,635	0	0	0	0	0	71,928	63,707
State	16,013,455	3,511,035	3,360,030	2,262,380	800,095	297,555	8,883,654	258,736
Direct	14,663,715	3,227,814	3,172,303	2,122,148	771,693	278,462	8,080,703	182,895
Intergovernmental	1,349,740	283,221	187,727	140,232	28,402	19,093	802,951	75,841
Total local	25,372,747	16,025,853	4,934,711	2,840,787	1,660,856	433,068	4,316,481	95,702
Direct	25,259,586	16,018,266	4,899,192	2,805,920	1,660,491	432,781	4,246,865	95,263
Intergovernmental	113,161	7,587	35,519	34,867	365	287	69,616	439
County	10,563,171	3,688,740	3,558,054	2,202,504	1,004,947	350,603	3,252,103	64,274
Direct	10,465,369	3,677,977	3,526,243	2,172,353	1,004,222	349,668	3,197,603	63,546
Intergovernmental	97,802	10,763	31,811	30,151	725	935	54,500	728
Municipal	15,064,352	12,512,804	1,401,212	655,733	659,697	85,782	1,118,504	31,832
Direct	14,794,217	12,340,289	1,372,949	633,567	656,269	83,113	1,049,262	31,717
Intergovernmental	270,135	172,515	28,263	22,166	3,428	2,669	69,242	115

NOTE: Intergovernmental expenditure consists of payments from one government to another. Such expenditure eventually will show up as a direct expenditure of a recipient government. Duplicative transactions between levels of governments are excluded from the totals for all governments and local governments.

Discussion Questions

1. Does spending $50 billion on the justice system represent failure of the American system?

2. Should convicted offenders forfeit personal possessions to pay back the costs of crime?

SOURCES: FBI, *Crime in the United States, 1986* (Washington, D.C.: U.S. Government Printing Office, 1987); Anita Timrots and Marshall DeBerry, *Criminal Victimization in the United States, 1985* (Washington, D.C.: U.S. Government Printing Office, 1987); Sue Lindren, *Justice Expenditures and Employment, 1985* (Washington, D.C.: Bureau of Justice Statistics, 1987).

criminal process is seen as a screening process in which each successive stage—pre-arrest investigation, arrest, post-arrest investigation, preparation for trial, trial or entry of plea, conviction, disposition—involves a series of routinized operations whose success is gauged primarily by their tendency to pass the case along to a successful conclusion.[13]

A recent federal survey of over 500,000 cases in 11 states gives one indication of how this process works.[14] As Figure 14.1 shows, about 84 percent of all persons arrested for felonies are eventually prosecuted, and 62 percent are convicted; 36 percent were sentenced to incarceration, and 13 percent were imprisoned for more than a year. As might be expected, violent offenders (murder, rape, and robbery) have the greatest chance of being sentenced for more than a year. However, even for those people convicted of a *violent felony*, 36 percent received a nonincarceration sentence, 31 percent received a prison sentence of one year or less, and only 34 percent received more than a year in prison. These figures illustrate the tremendous disparity in criminal justice system processing: some offenders have their cases dismissed while others are prosecuted and convicted; some who are convicted for serious felonies receive nonincarceration sentences while others are sent to state prison.

Processing Offenders

Though each jurisdiction is somewhat different, a comprehensive view of the processing of a felony offender would probably contain the following decision points.

Initial Contact. The initial contact an offender has with the justice system is usually with police. Police officers may observe a criminal act during their patrol of city streets, parks, or highways. They also may find out about a crime through a citizen or victim complaint. Similarly, an informer can alert them about criminal activity in return for financial or other consideration. Sometimes political officials, such as the mayor or city council, will ask police to look into an ongoing criminal activity—such as gambling—and during their subsequent investigations, police officers will encounter an illegal act.

Investigation. Regardless of whether the police observe, hear of, or receive a complaint about a crime, they may choose to conduct an investigation. The purpose of this procedure is to gather sufficient facts, or **evidence,** to identify the perpetrator, justify an arrest, and bring the offender to trial. An investigation may take a few minutes, as when police officers see a burglary in progress and apprehend the burglar at the scene of the crime. It may take months and involve hundreds of investigators, as was the case with the Atlanta murders investigation, which lasted from 1980 through 1981.

Arrest. An arrest occurs when the police take a person into custody and deprive that person of freedom for allegedly committing a criminal act. An arrest is legal when all of the following conditions exist:

1. The police officer believes there is sufficient evidence (probable cause) that a crime is being or has been committed and intends to restrain the suspect.
2. The police officer deprives the individual of freedom.
3. The suspect believes that he or she is in the custody of a police officer and cannot voluntarily leave.

The police officer is not required to use the word *arrest* or any similar word to initiate an arrest; nor does the officer first have to bring the suspect to the police station. For all practical purposes, a person who has been deprived of liberty is under arrest. Arrests can be made at the scene of a crime or upon a warrant being issued by a magistrate.

Custody. After arrest, the suspect remains in police custody. The person may be taken to the police station to be fingerprinted and photographed and to have personal information recorded—a procedure popularly referred to as **booking.** Witnesses may be brought in to view the suspect (in a **lineup**), and further evidence may be gathered on the case. Suspects may be interrogated by police officers to get their side of the story, they may be asked to sign a **confession** of guilt, or they may be asked to identify others involved in the crime. The law allows suspects to have their lawyers

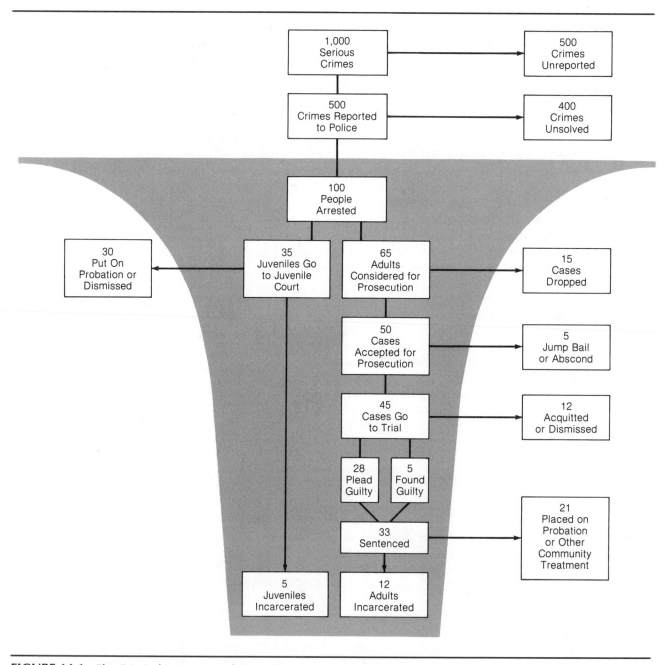

FIGURE 14.1   The Criminal Justice Funnel

SOURCE: Edward Lisefski and Donald Manson, *Tracking Offenders, 1984* (Washington, D.C.: Bureau of Justice Statistics, 1988).

present when police conduct in-custody interrogations.

Complaint.   After police turn evidence on a case over to the prosecutor, who is entrusted with representing the state at any criminal proceedings, a decision will be made whether to file a **complaint, information,** or **bill of indictment** with the court having jurisdiction over the case. Complaints are used in misdemeanors; information and indictment are employed in felonies. Each is a charging document asking the court to bring a case forward to be tried. The decision of whether to charge an offender with a criminal offense is a complex one that is discussed further in Chapter 16.

Grand Jury and Preliminary Hearing.   Since it is a tremendous personal and financial burden to stand trial for a serious felony crime, the U.S. Constitution provides that the state must first prove to an impartial hearing board that there is **probable cause** that the accused committed the crime and, therefore, that there is sufficient reason to try the person as charged. In about half the states and in the federal system, the decision on whether to bring a suspect to trial (indictment) is made by a group of citizens brought together to form a **grand jury.** The grand jury considers the case in a closed hearing, in which only the prosecutor presents evidence.

In the remaining states, an information is filed before a lower-court judge, who decides whether the case should go forward. This is known as a **preliminary hearing** or probable cause hearing. The defendant may appear at a preliminary hearing and dispute the prosecutor's charges. During either procedure, if the prosecution's evidence is accepted as factual and sufficient, the suspect will be called to stand trial for the crime. These procedures are not used for misdemeanors.

Arraignment.   An **arraignment** brings the accused before the court that will actually try the case. During an arraignment, defendants are apprised of the formal charges, informed of their constitutional rights (such as the right to legal counsel), have their bail considered, and have the trial date set.

Bail or Detention.   If the bail decision has not been considered previously, it will be evaluated at arraignment. Bail is a money bond, the amount of which is set by judicial authority; it is intended to insure the presence of suspects at trial while allowing them their freedom until that time. Suspects who do not show up for trial forfeit their bail. Suspects who cannot afford bail or whose cases are so serious that a judge refuses them bail (usually restricted to capital cases) must remain in detention until trial. In most instances, this means an extended stay in the county jail. In many

jurisdictions, programs have been developed to allow defendants awaiting trial to be released on their own recognizance, without bail, if they are stable members of the community.

Plea Bargaining.   After arraignment, it is common for the prosecutor to meet with the defendant and his or her attorney to discuss a possible guilty plea arrangement. If a bargain can be struck, the accused will plead guilty as charged, thus ending the criminal trial process. In return for the plea, the prosecutor may reduce charges, request a lenient sentence, or grant the defendant some other consideration.

Adjudication.   If a plea bargain cannot be arranged, a criminal trial will take place. This involves a full-scale inquiry into the facts of the case before a judge, a jury, or both. The defendant can be found guilty or not guilty, or the jury can fail to reach a decision (hung jury), thereby leaving the case unresolved and open for a possible retrial.

Disposition.   After a criminal trial, a defendant who is found guilty as charged will be sentenced by the presiding judge. Disposition usually involves either a fine, a term of community supervision (probation), a period of incarceration in a penal institution, or some combination of the above. In the most serious capital cases, it is possible to sentence the offender to death. Dispositions are usually made after a presentencing investigation is conducted by the court's probation staff. After disposition, the defendant may appeal the conviction to a higher court.

Correctional Treatment.   Offenders who are found guilty and are formally sentenced come under the jurisdiction of correctional authorities. They may serve a term of community supervision under control of the county probation department, they may have a term in a community correctional center, or they may be incarcerated in a large penal institution.

Release.   At the end of the correctional sentence, the offender is released into the community. Many incarcerated offenders are granted parole before the expiration of the maximum term given them by the court, and therefore finish their prison sentences in the community under supervision of the parole department. Offenders sentenced to community supervision, if

FIGURE 14.2
The Criminal Justice "Wedding Cake"

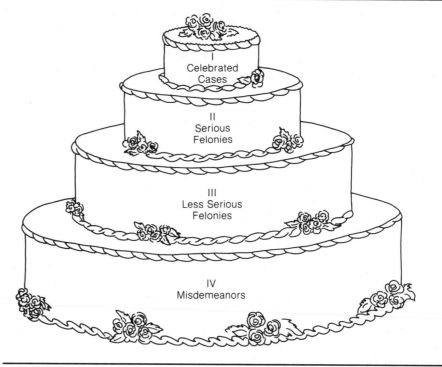

Based on Samuel Walker, *Sense and Nonsense about Crime* (Belmont, Cal.: Wadsworth Publishers, 1985).

successful, simply finish their terms and resume their lives unsupervised by court authorities.

The "Wedding Cake" Model

The traditional model of the criminal justice process described above depicts it as a uniform series of decision points through which cases flow, each characterized by uniform procedures and rights. Yet many experts view this model as fanciful; they argue that the justice system is a political entity which actually works in a much more subjective fashion. While some cases receive the full attention of the law, the great majority are settled with a minimum of legal and procedural due process.

Samuel Walker, a justice historian, suggests that the criminal justice process is best conceived as a four-layer cake, as depicted in Figure 14.2.[15] The relatively small first layer of Walker's model is made up of the celebrated cases involving the wealthy and powerful, such as John DeLorean, Claus von Bulow, and Ivan

Boesky, or the not-so-powerful who victimize a famous person—for example, Mark Chapman (John Lennon's killer) or John Hinkley (Ronald Reagan's would-be assassin). Also included within this category are unknown criminals whose cases become celebrated, either because they are brought before the Supreme Court because of some procedural irregularity (for example, Ernesto Miranda or Clarence Gideon), or because the involve a media event (such as the Robert Chambers or Bernhard Goetz cases). People in the first layer of the criminal justice cake receive a great deal of public attention. Their cases usually involve the full panoply of criminal justice procedures, including famous defense attorneys, jury trials, and elaborate appeals. Because the public hears so much about these cases, it believes them to be a norm; in reality they do not represent how the system really operates.

The second and third layers of the cake are made up of the bulk of serious felonies encountered daily in urban jurisdictions around the U.S., such as robberies, burglaries, rapes, and homocides. Those which fall in the second layer do so by virtue of their seriousness, the prior record of the defendant, and the defendant's relationship to the victim. For example, a million-dollar burglary is treated quite differently than a simple break-in which netted the criminal a stereo. Similarly, a rape involving a stranger is perceived by criminal justice decision-makers as being more serious than one which occurs between people who knew each other previously, such as a date rape. The more serious second-level crimes are likely to receive a jury trial and the full attention of the criminal justice process. If convicted, offenders will receive lengthy prison sentences.

In contrast, felonies relegated to the third layer, often involving acquaintances or less serious felonies, will usually be dealt with outright dismissal, a plea bargain, reduction in charges, and a probationary sentence. A typical third level case might involve the sale of a small amount of narcotics or an auto theft. While technically serious felonies, thousands of these cases are heard by courts each year. Consequently, they are usually not taken seriously by prosecution or defense. The goal is to get them over with as quickly and cheaply as possible.

The fourth layer of the cake is made up of the millions of misdemeanors, such as disorderly conduct, shoplifting, public drunkenness, and minor assault. These are handled by the lower criminal courts in assembly line fashion. Few defendants insist on exercising their constitutional rights because it would delay matters, costing them valuable time and money. Since the typical penalty is a small fine, everyone wants to get the case over with and move on to other matters. Malcolm Feeley's study of the lower court in New Haven, Connecticut, found that, in a sense, the experience of going to court is the real punishment in a misdemeanor case; few (4.9 percent) of the cases involved any jail time.[16]

The wedding cake model is an intriguing alternative to the traditional criminal justice flowchart. According to Walker's view, criminal justice officials handle different kinds of cases quite differently. Within each layer there is a high degree of consistency, no matter where the jurisdiction. The model is useful because it helps point out that public opinion about criminal justice is all too often formed on the basis of what happens in a few celebrated cases. In fact, it has become common for criminal justice experts to view the process as being dominated by judges, prosecu-

tors, and defense counsels who work in concert to "get the job done" in most cases processed through the system. The tired assistant DA, irritable judge, and overworked public defender who get together to settle cases involving lower-class victims and offenders are now common characters in television shows, films, and books. In contrast are the relatively few celebrated cases, such as the Jeffery MacDonald or Joe Hunt murder trials, which have become the subject of television miniseries (*Fatal Vision, Billionaire Boys Club*). Such "important" cases may occur only once in a prosecutor's or judge's career, followed by a return to the routine of the criminal justice assembly line.

CRIMINAL JUSTICE AND THE RULE OF LAW

For many years, U.S. courts exercised little control over the operations of criminal justice agencies, believing that their actions were not an area of judicial concern. This policy is referred to as the **hands-off doctrine.** However, in the 1960s, under the guidance of Chief Justice Earl Warren, the U.S. Supreme Court became more active in the affairs of the justice system, thereby lifting the hands-off doctrine. Today, each component of the justice system is closely supervised by state and federal courts. In this section, the influence of the rule of law on criminal justice agencies and how it affects daily operations and decision-making are reviewed.

Procedural Law

The law of criminal procedure guarantees citizens certain rights and privileges when they are accused of crime. Procedural laws control the action of the agencies of justice and define the rights of criminal defendants. They first come into play when people are suspected of committing crimes and the police wish to investigate them. Here the law answers such questions as: "Can the police search my home if I don't want them to?" and "Do I have to answer their questions even if I don't want to?" If a formal charge is filed, procedural laws guide pretrial and trail activities. For example, they determine when and if people can obtain state-financed attorneys or when they can be released on bail. If, after a trial, a person is found guilty of committing a criminal offense, procedural laws guide the posttrial and correctional process. For example, they determine when a conviction can be appealed.

Procedural laws have several different sources. Most important are the first ten amendments of the U.S. Constitution, ratified in 1791 and generally called the Bill of Rights. The original Constitution, ratified in 1788, set up the structure of government and set out the rights and duties of its executive, legislative, and judicial branches. However, aware of the abuses people had been subjected to by royal decree in England and its colonies, the framers of the Constitution wanted to insure that the national government could not usurp the personal rights of citizens. Therefore, the Bill of Rights guaranteed, among other things, the rights of the people to practice the religion of their choice, have freedom of speech and press, be secure in their homes from unwarranted intrusion by government agents, and be protected against cruel punishments, such as torture.

The guarantees of freedom contained in the Bill of Rights initially applied only to the federal government and did not affect individual states. Then, in 1868, the Fourteenth Amendment made the first ten amendments to the Constitution binding on state governments. However, it has remained the duty of state and federal court systems to interpret constitutional law and develop a body of case law that spells out the exact procedural rights a person is entitled to. For example, the Sixth Amendment states that a person has the right to be represented by legal counsel at a criminal trial. This right once had little meaning, because many criminal defendants were indigent and could not afford to pay for their legal defense. Then, in 1963, the U.S. Supreme Court interpreted the Sixth Amendment to mean that all people accused of felonies had the right to counsel; if they could not afford an attorney, the state had to provide the funds to hire one for them. Thus, it is the U.S. Supreme Court that interprets the Constitution and sets out the procedural laws that must be followed by the lower federal and state courts. If the Supreme Court has not ruled on a procedural issue, then the lower courts are free to interpret the Constitution as they see fit.

Court Decision-Making.   Until the passage of the Fourteenth Amendment, the rights and privileges

made binding on the federal government by the first ten amendments did not apply to the states. However, ratification of the Fourteenth Amendment did not mean that the granting of rights and liberties was an automatic process. Instead, each right was decided upon when cases dealing with the particular issue came before the Supreme Court. Determining how to incorporate the rights into state criminal procedures became a topic of some debate. In the late 1930s, the Supreme Court developed the concept of fundamental fairness and used it to guide its own decision-making. Under this concept, if the Supreme Court decides that a particular guarantee in the Bill of Rights is fundamental to and implicit in the U.S. system of justice, it would hold that guarantee applicable to the states.

With this formula, the provisions of the Bill of Rights were incorporated by the states, case by case. In 1953, Earl Warren became the Chief Justice of the U.S. Supreme Court; under his leadership, the due process movement reached its peak. Numerous landmark cases focusing on the rights of the accused were decided, and a revolution in the area of constitutional criminal procedure resulted. The Warren Court granted many new rights to those accused of crimes and went so far as to impose specific guidelines on the policies of police, courts, and correctional services to insure that due process of law would be maintained. However, the more conservative Chief Justices Warren Burger and William Rehnquist have moved somewhat more cautiously in granting additional rights; in some areas, such as prisoners' rights, the Burger and Rehnquist Courts have reversed the trend toward liberalism established by the Warren Court.

COURTS AND CRIMINAL JUSTICE POLICY

Court decision-making has had the effect of dictating policy within the criminal justice system. Most states and the federal government have codified the judge-made procedural laws. In essence, state codes of criminal procedure contain the holdings of Supreme Court judgments plus additional rules of law covering issues the Supreme Court has so far ignored. For example, the New York State Code of Criminal Procedure lists the following restrictions on the police power to arrest;

During the adjudication stage, a full-scale inquiry is held on the facts of the case. Here, jurors listen as the defending attorney questions a witness at a murder trial in Orange County, California.

a peace officer may, without a warrant, arrest a person,

1. *For an offense, committed or attempted in his presence, or where a police officer . . . has reasonable grounds for believing that an offense is being committed in his presence;*

2. *When the person arrested has committed a felony, although not in his presence;*

3. *When a felony has in fact been committed, and he has reasonable cause for believing the person to be arrested to have committed it;*

4. *When he has reasonable cause for believing that a felony has been committed, and that the person arrested has committed it, though it should afterward appear that no felony has been committed, or, if committed, that the person arrested did not commit it.*[17]

Because the makeup of the Supreme Court can change, procedural laws are subject to different interpretations and can change at any time. The Constitution and Bill of Rights are fairly abstract documents; hence, there is much leeway as to the direction and content of procedural laws—what is law today may not be tomorrow.

The role courts play, especially the U.S. Supreme Court, in influencing the operations of the criminal justice system is quite controversial. When **Earl Warren** was Chief Justice of the Supreme court, the court's rulings revolutionized criminal justice by liberating and enlarging the rights of people accused of crime. Under Chief Justice **Warren Burger,** the Court steered a more conservative course, and consequently the rights of criminal defendants have narrowed. Warren's court was accused by conservatives such as Richard Nixon and Gerald Ford of coddling criminals and eroding the rights of victims. In contrast, the Burger Court was castigated by liberals for threatening civil rights and opening the door to a "police state." With the appointment of **William Rehnquist** as Chief Justice and Sandra Day O'Conner, Antonin Scalia, and Anthony Kennedy as Associate Justices, the Reagan Administration has assured that the Court will continue its conservative leanings.

Of the criminal justice issues the courts deal with, few are as important and have as much influence on the justice system as the concepts of due process and the exclusionary rule. Therefore, these legal issues are reviewed here in some detail.

Due Process

The concept of **due process** is mentioned in the Fifth (where it is applied to the federal government) and Fourteenth Amendments (where it is applied to the states) of the U.S. Constitution. It is usually divided into both substantive an procedural areas. The substantive aspects are generally used to determine whether a statute is fair, reasonable, and an appropriate use of the legal power of the legislature. The concept of substantive due process was used extensively in the 1930s and 1940s to invalidate minimum-wage standards, price-fixing, and employment restriction statutes. Today it is used more sparingly; for example, it may be employed to hold that criminal statutes dealing with disorderly conduct, capital punishment, or a ban on pornography may be unconstitutional because they are arbitrary or unreasonable.

Much more important today are the procedural aspects of due process. In seeking to define the term, most legal experts indicate that it refers to the essential elements of fairness under law. An elaborate and complex definition of *due process* is found in *Black's Law Dictionary:*

> *Due process of law in each particular case means such an exercise of the powers of government as the settled maxims of law permit and sanction, and under such safeguards for the protection of individual rights as those maxims prescribe for the class of cases to which the one in question belongs.*[18]

This definition refers to the need for rules and procedures in the legal system to protect individual rights. The objectives of due process help define the term even more explicitly. Due process seeks to insure that no person will be deprived of life, liberty, or property without notice of charges, assistance from legal counsel, a hearing and an opportunity to confront accusers. Basically, due process is intended to guarantee that functional fairness exists in each individual case.

Abstract definitions are only one aspect of due process. Much more significant are the procedures that give meaning to due process in the everyday practices of the criminal justice system. In this regard, due process provides numerous procedural safeguards for the offender, including:

- Notice of charges
- A formal hearing
- The right to counsel or some other representation
- The opportunity to respond to charges
- The opportunity to confront and cross-examine witnesses and accusers
- The privilege to be free from self-incrimination
- The opportunity to present one's own witnesses
- A decision made on the basis of substantial evidence and facts produced at the hearing
- A written statement of the reasons for the decision
- An appellate review procedure

Exactly what constitutes due process in a specific case depends on the facts of the case, the federal and state constitutional and statutory provisions, previous court decisions, and the ideas and principles that society considers important at a given time and in a given place.[19] Justice Felix Frankfurter emphasized this point in *Rochin v. California* (1952), when he wrote:

> *Due process of law requires an evaluation based on a disinterested inquiry, pursued in the spirit of science on a balanced order of facts, exactly and clearly stated, on the detached consideration of conflicting claims . . . on a judgment not ad hoc and episodic but duly mindful of reconciling the needs both of continuity and of change in a progressive society.*[20]

Both the elements and the definition of due process seem to be flexible and constantly changing. For example, due process at one time did not require a formal hearing for parole revocation, but today it does. Before 1968, juvenile offenders did not have the right to an attorney at their adjudication; counsel is now required in the juvenile court system. Thus, the interpretations of due process of law reflect what society deems fair and just at a particular time and in a particular place. The degree of loss suffered by the individual (victim or offender) balanced against the state's interest also determines which and how many due process requirements are ordinarily applied. When the accused person's freedom is at stake in the criminal justice system, all applicable due process rights are usually granted; in other cases, due process may be modified.

Changing Concepts of Due Process. In recent years, the concept of due process as applied by the courts seems to be changing. The balance of fairness is shifting away from the criminal; emphasis instead is being placed more squarely on the needs of the states to protect their citizens. The rights of both those accused of crime and those convicted of crime have been curtailed. For example, police have been given a freer hand in questioning suspects, searching for evidence, and obtaining search warrants. Courts have resumed using the death penalty with fewer judicial restraints. Prison administrators have been given a freer hand to deal with inmates as they see fit. There seems little question that the Supreme Court has set the stage for a reevaluation of the due process concept.

Nonetheless, the concept of due process is securely held to in our legal system. Freedom from self-incrimination, the right to legal representation at all stages of the justice system, a fair hearing and trial, and sentencing review are rights that seem immutable. And while courts continue to redefine rights, they do so in the spirit of granting fairness to the criminal defendant without sacrificing the public interest.

In this context, focus has turned to the exclusionary rule, considered by some to be a cornerstone of individual freedom and by others to be a serious impediment to public safety. Discussion will now turn to this important aspect of fairness and liberty.

The Exclusionary Rule

The foundation of the **exclusionary rule** is contained in the Fourth Amendment of the Constitution, which states that:

> *The right of the people to be secure in their persons, houses, papers, and effects, against unreasonable searches and seizures, shall not be violated and no warrant shall issue, but upon probable cause, supported by oath or affirmation, and particularly describing the place to be searched, and the persons or things to be seized.*

The primary function of the Fourth Amendment is to protect the individual against an illegal arrest and prevent illegal searches and seizures of a person's possessions. This means that police must follow certain guidelines in searching for and seizing evidence. As a general rule of thumb, they must have a properly drawn up search warrant. The warrant must be obtained from a court officer after evidence is presented that a crime has occurred and that there is probable cause to believe that the person or place to be searched is involved in it; the police cannot act arbitrarily. Over the years, the Court has articulated exceptions to the search warrant rule. In other words, there are times, such as when a suspect volunteers to be searched, that a warrant need not be obtained. The standard as stated in the Fourth Amendment is that of reasonableness, and the Supreme Court has gone to great lengths to explain and interpret what this means. In doing so, the Court has balanced the individual's right to privacy with the right of the public to be protected against crime. Consequently, there exists a large body of case law describing how searches are to be conducted, when police can seize evidence, when search warrants are needed, and so on.

The Fourth Amendment clearly states that an individual's right against unreasonable searches and seizures is to be protected. However, for many years, evidence obtained in violation of the Fourth Amendment was admitted in criminal trials even though it should have been considered illegal. In 1914 the Supreme Court rectified this injustice in the case of *Weeks v. United States*.[21] The defendant, Weeks, was accused of the federal violation of using the mails for illegal purposes. The evidence on which he was convicted was acquired through a search of his room without a valid search warrant. The Supreme Court ruled that, in a federal criminal trial, evidence acquired through an unreasonable search and seizure must be excluded. Thus the exclusionary rule was established.

However, the ruling in *Weeks* applied only to the federal government. The states were still free to admit evidence obtained by unreasonable searches and seizures. It was not until 1969, in the case of *Mapp v. Ohio*, that the Supreme Court made the exclusionary rule applicable to the states.[22] Thus, for the first time, the Supreme Court required that state law enforcement employees follow federal constitutional standards (see Close-Up).

In sum, the exclusionary rule means that evidence judged to be improperly obtained by police through illegal interrogation of suspects or searches of their person and property cannot be used (or even mentioned) against them in a court of law. It is as if it did not exist.

CLOSE-UP

Mapp v. Ohio

Facts

On 23 May 1957, three police officers arrived at Dolree Mapp's residence pursuant to information that "a person (was) hiding out in the home, who was wanted for questioning in connection with a recent bombing, and that there was a large amount of police paraphernalia being hidden in the home." Mapp and her daughter by a former marriage lived on the top floor of the two-family dwelling. Upon their arrival at the house, the officers knocked on the door and demanded entrance but Mapp, after telephoning her attorney, refused to admit them without a search warrant.

The officers again sought entrance three hours later when four or more additional officers arrived on the scene. When Mapp did not immediately come to the door, the police forcibly opened one of the doors to the house and gained admittance. Meanwhile, Mapp's attorney arrived, but the officers would not permit him to see Mapp or to enter the house. Mapp was halfway down the stairs from the upper floor to the front door when the officers broke into the hall. She demanded to see the search warrant. A paper, claimed to be a search warrant, was held up by one of the officers. (It was later discovered that the warrant was not valid.) She grabbed the "warrant" and placed it in her bosom. A struggle ensued in which the officers recovered the piece of paper and handcuffed Mapp because she had ostensibly been belligerent.

Mapp was then forcibly taken upstairs to her bedroom, where the officials searched a dresser, a chest of drawers, a closet, and some suitcases. They also looked into a photo album and through personal papers belonging to her. The search spread to the rest of the second floor, including the child's bedroom, the living room, the kitchen, and the dinette. In the course of the search, the police officers found pornographic literature. Mapp was arrested and subsequently convicted in a Ohio court of possessing obscene materials.

Decision

The question in the *Mapp* case was whether the illegally seized evidence was in violation of the search and seizure provisions of the Fourth Amendment and therefore inadmissible in the state trial, which resulted in an obscenity conviction. The Supreme Court of Ohio found the conviction valid. However, the U.S. Supreme Court overturned it, stating that the Fourth Amendment's prohibition against unreasonable searches and seizures, enforcible against the states through the due process clause, had been violated by the police. Justice Thomas Clark, in delivering the majority opinion of the Court, made clear the importance of this constitutional right in the administration of criminal justice when he stated:

> There are those who say, as did Justice (then Judge) Cardozo, that under our constitutional exclusionary doctrine "the criminal is to go free because the constable has blundered." In some cases this will undoubt-

The exclusionary rule has been one of the most controversial aspects of justice system legal control. Its opponents argue that it permits the guilty to go free if the police err in the handling of a case. Thus, the rights of individual citizens and society as a whole are threatened because of arbitrary court rulings. Moreover, it weakens the power of the justice system to deter crime because victims and witnesses are reluctant to come forward, for fear that an obviously guilty defendant will be released on a technicality.

In contrast, those in favor of the exclusionary rule find that it is one of the cornerstones of freedom and that it protects citizens from becoming a police state,

in which law enforcement agents may use any means at their disposal to investigate crime. Without the exclusionary rule, houses could be broken into, phones tapped, people searched, and cars stopped—with impunity. The exclusionary rule separates U.S. society from totalitarian regimes:

> If constitutional rights are to be anything more than pious pronouncements, then some measurable consequence must be attached to their violation. It would be intolerable if the guarantee against unreasonable search and seizure could be violated without practical consequences.[23]

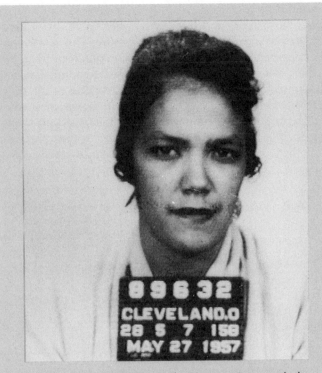

The appeal of Dolree Mapp to the Supreme Court made the exclusionary rule binding on the states.

edly be the result. But . . . there is another consideration—the imperative of judicial integrity . . . The criminal goes free, if he must, but it is the law that sets him free. Nothing can destroy a government more quickly than its failure to observe its own laws, or worse, its disregard of the charter of its own existence.

Significance of the Case

In previous decisions, the U.S. Supreme Court had refused to exclude evidence in state court proceedings based upon Fourth Amendment violations of search and seizure. The *Mapp* case overruled such decisions, including that of *Wolf v. Colorado*, and held that evidence gathered in violation of the Fourth Amendment would be inadmissible in a state prosecution. For the first time, the Court imposed federal constitutional standards on state law enforcement personnel. In addition, the Court reemphasized the point that a relationship exists between the Fourth and Fifth Amendments which forms a constitutional basis requiring the use of the exclusionary rule.

Discussion Questions

1. If police operating in violation of the Fourth Amendment uncover important evidence, should it be excluded from the trial even if a guilty person will then go free?

2. What remedies other than the exclusionary rule can be used to control police violations of the Fourth Amendment?

SOURCE: Mapp v. Ohio, 367 U.S. 643 (1969).

The Future of the Exclusionary Rule. The exclusionary rule is under legal attack. For example, in *Illinois v. Gates* the Supreme Court allowed the use of a search warrant which had been obtained upon consideration of information contained in an anonymous letter to police; prior to *Gates*, warrants had to be based on verifiable information.[24] And in *California v. Ciraolo* the Court held that a warrantless surveillance of a person's backyard from an airplane in order to confirm a tip about growing marijuana did not violate that person's right to privacy.[25]

In two cases, *U.S. v. Leon* and *Massachusetts v. Shepperd*, the U.S. Supreme Court spelled out what is known as the *good faith exception* to the rule.[26] The Court said that if police officers acted in what they believed to be a proper manner in obtaining evidence, and it was discovered later that they or a magistrate had made an unintentional legal or administrative error invalidating the search warrant, the evidence might still be admitted in a court of law.

Critics believe that these and similar cases foretell a new era of a weakened exclusionary rule.[27] There seems little doubt that the nation's courts are now granting the police and other agencies of justice greater leeway in conducting their business, even if it means restricting the rights of criminal suspects. But how much will these measures actually affect the justice system? Studies conducted by the federal government's National Institute of Justice, as well as by private researchers, all indicate that exclusionary rule violations occur rather infrequently.[28] In most of the jurisdictions studied, about 1 to 2 percent of all criminal cases were rejected because police made a technical legal error resulting in the invocation of the exclusionary rule. For violent crimes, the number was generally less than 1 percent. Of all crime types, only in narcotics-related offenses were a significant number of cases terminated because of exclusionary rule violations; again, the percentages were smaller than might be expected—under 3 percent in the jurisdictions surveyed. Police appear more apt to illegally seize evidence in narcotics cases because there is usually no victim or complaining party to help them obtain proper search warrants.

Though abolishing or severely limiting the exclusionary rule might have relatively little effect on the justice system, the rule itself is of great symbolic value. It stands for the primacy of the individual over the state, and the right to privacy. Even if relatively few cases are thrown out of court on exclusionary rule violations, knowing of its existence places law enforcement agents on notice: obey constitutional limitations, respect the individual's right to privacy, or pay the consequences in court. The exclusionary rule must be evaluated not by those few cases that see the light of public scrutiny, but by the millions of others in which police power is limited by the rule's influence.

In the following chapters, the effect of the law on the individual components of the justice system are reviewed in greater detail. Table 14.1 summarizes some of the more important constitutional cases that define procedural law.

CONCEPTS OF JUSTICE

Many justice system operations are controlled by the rule of law, but they also are influenced by the various philosophies or viewpoints held by its practitioners and policymakers. These in turn have been influenced by criminological theory and research. Knowledge about crime, its causes, and its control has significantly affected perceptions of how criminal justice should be managed.

Not surprisingly, many competing views of justice exist simultaneously in our culture. Those in favor of one position or another try to win public opinion to their side, hoping to influence legislative, judicial, or administrative decision-making. Over the years, different philosophical viewpoints tend to predominate, only to fall into disfavor as programs based on their principles fail to prove effective. The most important of these concepts of criminal justice are briefly discussed below.

Crime Control Model

Those embracing the crime control model believe that the overriding purpose of the justice system is protection of the public, deterrence of criminal behavior, and incapacitation of known criminals. Those who espouse its principles view the justice system as a barrier between destructive criminal elements and conventional society. Speedy and efficient justice, unencumbered by legal red tape and followed by punishment designed to fit the crime, is the goal of crime control. The means to achieve this goal must be available, including increasing the size of police forces, maximizing the use of discretion, building more prisons, using the death penalty, and reducing legal controls on the justice system such as the exclusionary rule.

The crime control model has its roots in classical theory. Fear of criminal sanctions is viewed as the primary deterrent to crime. Since criminals are rational and choose to commit crime, it stands to reason that their activities can be controlled if the costs of crime become too high. Swift, sure, and efficient justice are considered essential elements of an orderly society.

The crime control philosophy emphasizes the protection of society and the compensation of victims. The criminal is someone who is responsible for his or her actions and who has broken faith with society and chosen to violate the law for such reasons as anger, greed, or revenge. Therefore, money spent should be directed not at making criminals more comfortable, but at increasing the efficiency of police

Crime control advocates believe the justice system's purpose is protection of the public, deterrence of criminal behavior, and apprehension and punishment of known offenders. This Denver SWAT team enters the scene of a shootout, only to find a suicide victim.

to apprehend them and the courts to effectively try them.

The crime control philosophy has become a dominant force in American justice. Fear of crime in the 1960s and 1970s was coupled with a growing skepticism about the effectiveness of rehabilitation efforts. A number of important reviews claimed that treatment and rehabilitation efforts directed at known criminals did not work.[29] Only recently, criminologists Steven Lab and John Whitehead reviewed 55 different treatment programs which made more than 85 comparisons between treatment and control groups. They concluded: ". . . at least half of the studies reported negative or no impact on recidivism and many of the positive findings were based on dubious, subjective evaluations."[30]

The lack of clear-cut evidence that criminals can be successfully "treated" has produced a climate in which conservative, hard-line solutions to the crime problem are being sought. The results of this swing can be seen in such phenomena as the resumption of the death penalty, erosion of the exclusionary rule, prison overcrowding, and limiting the insanity defense.

Rehabilitation Model

The rehabilitation model embraces the notion that, given the proper care and treatment, criminals can be changed into productive, law-abiding citizens. Influenced by positivist criminology, the rehabilitation school suggests that people commit crimes through no fault of their own. Instead, criminals themselves are the victims of social injustice, poverty, and racism; their acts are a response to a society that has betrayed them. Because of their disturbed and impoverished upbringing, they may be suffering psychological problems and personality disturbances that further enhance their crime-committing capabilities.

To deal effectively with crime, its root causes must be attacked. First, funds must be devoted to equalize access to conventional means of success. This means supporting such programs as Aid to Dependent Children, educational opportunity, and job training. If individuals run afoul of the law, efforts should be made to treat and not punish them. This means emphasizing counseling and psychological care in community-based treatment programs. Whenever

TABLE 14.1   Some Leading Constitutional Cases and Their Findings

The Police Process

Miranda v. Arizona, 384 U.S. 436 (1966)	The police have a duty to warn a suspect in custody of the basic Fifth Amendment right against self-incrimination. If the warning is not given, any statement made by the defendant must be excluded from the evidence.
Katz v. United States, 389 U.S. 347 (1967)	The Fourth Amendment protects a person's right to privacy at all times and is not limited to certain places or property. A search occurs whenever police activity violates a person's privacy.
Bumper v. North Carolina, 391 U.S. 543 (1968)	In order for a consent search to be effective, the consent must be voluntary; threat or compulsion will invalidate the search.
Terry v. Ohio, 392 U.S. 1 (1968)	Even though there is no probable cause to arrest, the police have the power to stop an individual and conduct a pat-down search of outer clothing for weapons, if an officer has reasonable belief that a threat to safety exists.
Chimel v. California, 395 U.S. 752 (1969)	In a search incident to an arrest, the police are allowed to search only the defendant and the surroundings that are under the defendant's immediate control.
Mapp v. Ohio, 367 U.S. 643 (1969)	When evidence is obtained in violation of the Fourth Amendment's right against unreasonable searches and seizures, it is not admissible in a state trial. This case made the exclusionary rule applicable to the states through the due process clause of the Fourteenth Amendment.
Steagald v. United States, 451 U.S. 204 (1981)	The Fourth Amendment privacy principle applies not only when searching a home for property but also when searching a home for a person.
New York v. Belton, 453 U.S. 454 (1981)	The passenger compartment of a car is within the scope of a search when an arrest takes place after the car is stopped for a speeding violation.
United States v. Ross, 72 L. Ed. 2d 572 (1982)	Opening and searching without a warrant the closed opaque containers found in a car is legal if the officers have probable cause to believe that contraband is concealed somewhere in the car.
Illinois v. Gates, 103 S. Ct. 2317 (1983)	A judge may issue a search warrant based on the "totality of the circumstances" of the case.
New York v. Quarles, 104 S. Ct. 2626 (1984)	A suspect's statements made without benefit of the Miranda warning are admissible if "public safety" is at risk.
Nix v. Williams, 104 S. Ct. 2501 (1984)	Evidence can be seized without a warrant if it would have been "inevitably discovered by police officers."
U.S. v. Leon, 104 S. Ct. 3405 (1984)	Evidence may be admitted to trial even if a search warrant was faulty but the police officers acted on "good faith."
Morcan v. Burbine, 106 S. Ct. 1135 (1986)	Police need not tell suspects in custody about a call from their attorney.
Colorado v. Connelly, 107 S. Ct. SIS (1986)	Mentally impaired defendant's can waive their Miranda rights.
Arizona v. Hicks, 107 S. Ct. 1149 (1987)	Probable cause is required to invoke the plain view doctrine.
Colorado v. Spring, 107 S. Ct. 851 (1987)	A suspect need not be aware of all the topics of questioning in order for the Miranda waiver to be valid.

TABLE 14.1   (Cont.)

The Trial Stage

Powell v. Alabama, 287 U.S. 45 (1932)	The state must provide counsel to an indigent defendant who is prosecuted for a capital offense.
Gideon v. Wainwright, 372 U.S. 335 (1963)	An indigent defendant subjected to a felony prosecution must have counsel provided by the state. This Sixth Amendment right was made applicable to the states through the due process clause of the Fourteenth Amendment.
Klopfer v. North Carolina, 387 U.S. 213 (1967)	The Sixth Amendment right to a speedy trial is applicable to the states through the due process clause of the Fourteenth Amendment.
Duncan v. Louisiana, 391 U.S. 145 (1968)	The Sixth Amendment right to a jury trial when the defendant is accused of a serious offense is applicable to the states through the due process clause of the Fourteenth Amendment.
North Carolina v. Pearce, 395 U.S. 711 (1969)	A judge who imposes a more severe sentence upon reconviction must state the reasons for the more severe sentence on the record.
Benton v. Maryland, 395 U. S. 784 (1969)	The Fifth Amendment protection against double jeopardy is applicable to the states through the due process clause of the Fourteenth Amendment.
Baldwin v. New York, 399 U.S. 66 (1970)	A defendant has a constitutional right to a jury trial under the Sixth and Fourteenth Amendments when the penalty is imprisonment for six months or more.
Williams v. Florida, 399 U.S. 78 (1970)	A six-person jury fulfills a defendant's Sixth Amendment right to a jury trial.
Argersinger v. Hamlin, 407 U.S. 25 (1972)	The state must provide an indigent defendant with counsel in any case in which the sentence results in imprisonment, regardless of whether the crime is classified as a misdemeanor or a felony.
Apodica v. Oregon, 406 U.S. 404 (1972)	A criminal conviction by less than a unanimous jury verdict in a non–first-degree murder case is constitutional under the Sixth and Fourteenth Amendments when a 12-person jury is used.
Barker v. Wingo, 407 U.S. 514 (1972)	Four factors must be considered when determining whether a defendant's right to a speedy trial has been violated: (1) length of the delay; (2) reason for the delay; (3) defendant's assertion of the right; and (4) prejudice to the defendant.
Strunk v. United States, 412 U.S. 434 (1973)	When a person's right to a speedy trial is violated, the charges against the person must be dismissed.
Richmond Newspapers v. Virginia, 448 U.S. 555 (1980)	The press has the right to attend and report on trials.
Strickland v. Washington, 104 S. Ct. 2052 (1984)	Defendants have a right to effective, competent counsel in criminal cases.
United States v. Salerno, 107 S. Ct. 2095 (1987)	A dangerous person may be held in pretrial detention without bail.

Sentencing and Corrections

Gagnon v. Scarpelli, 411 U.S. 778 (1973)	Probationers and parolees are entitled to limited representation of counsel at revocation hearings.
Wolff v. McDonnell, 418 U.S. 539 (1974)	Prisoners who may face sanctions because of disciplinary problems are entitled to a hearing to defend their behavior.
Gregg v. Georgia, 482 U.S. 153 (1976)	The death penalty may be applied when aggravating circumstances exist in a murder case, such as murder for profit.
Estelle v. Gamble, 429 U.S. 97 (1976)	An inmate is entitled to proper medical care.
Rhodes v. Chapman, 452 U.S. 337 (1981)	Prisoners may be forced to share a cell if prison overcrowding exists.
McCleskey v. Kemp, 107 S. Ct. 1756 (1987)	The death penalty is not unconstitutional, even if it can be shown that black offenders in general have a greater chance of receiving it in a particular jurisdiction.

possible, offenders should be placed on probation in halfway houses or in other rehabilitation-oriented programs.

This view of the justice system portrays it as a method for dispensing "treatment" to needy "patients." Also known as the "medical model," it portrays offenders as people who, because they have failed to exercise self-control, need the aid of the state. The medical model rejects the crime control philosophy on the ground that it ignores the needs of offenders, who are actually people whom society has failed to help. In a significant review, Marvin Zalman shows how the popularity of the medical model reached its zenith on the 1960s, when the Johnson Administration's **President's Commission on Law Enforcement and Criminal Justice** embraced it as the best means to control crime in America; enthusiasm for it waned in the 1970s and 1980s when research failed to support the benefits of rehabilitation while the crime rate soared.[31]

Rehabilitation still retains its enthusiasts. In contradistinction to literature reviews that find that treatment has little or no effect on known offenders, there have been competing analyses which find that a number of programs can have an important influence on offenders.[32] Paul Gendreau and Robert Ross have impressively reviewed evidence from 1981 to 1987 and conclude: ". . . it is downright ridiculous to say 'Nothing works' . . . offender rehabilitation has been, can be and will be achieved."[33]

Due Process Model

In *The Limits of the Criminal Sanction,* Herbert Packer contrasted the crime control model with an opposing view that he referred to as the *due process model.*[34] According to Packer, the due process model combines elements of liberal-positivist criminology with the legal concept of procedural fairness for the accused. Those who adhere to due process principles believe in individualized justice, treatment, and rehabilitation of the offender. If discretion exists in the criminal justice system, it should be used to evaluate the treatment needs of the offender. Most importantly, the civil rights of the accused should be protected at all possible costs. This means practices such as strict scrutiny of police search and interrogation procedures, review of sentencing poli-

cies, and development of prisoners' rights.

Advocates of due process have influenced the trial stage of the criminal process by demanding defense counsel, jury trials, and other procedural safeguards. Furthermore, this model tends to restrict the legal definition of criminal behavior by removing certain offenses, such as victimless crimes, juvenile delinquency, traffic offenses, and certain drug violations, from the criminal statutes. It has resulted in the elimination of a variety of vague laws, such as overly broad juvenile delinquency, vagrancy, and disorderly conduct statutes. Beyond this, the due process model has resulted in the establishment of various procedures to cover the ways that criminal justice agencies operate, particularly with regard to their discretionary power.

For obvious reasons, proponents of the due process philosophy are usually members of the legal profession who see themselves as protectors of civil rights. They view overzealous police as violators of basic constitutional rights. Similarly, they are skeptical about the intentions of social workers, whose "treatment" often entails greater confinement and penalties than punishment ever did. Due process is there to protect citizens—both from those who wish to punish them and those who wish to treat them without regard for legal and civil rights.

Nonintervention Model

The fourth approach to justice was influenced by the popularity of the labeling theory in the late 1960s and 1970s. Both the rehabilitation ideal and the due process movement where viewed suspiciously by experts concerned with the stigmatization of offenders. Regardless of the purpose, the more the government intervenes in the lives of people, the greater the harm done to their future behavior patterns.

Noninterventionist philosophy was influenced by Edwin Lemert's call for **judicious nonintervention,** and Edwin Schur's 1971 book, *Radical Nonintervention.*[35] These called for limitations on government intrusion into the lives of people, especially minors, who run afoul of the law. They advocated **deinstitutionalization** of nonserious offenders, **diversion** from formal court processes into informal treatment programs, and **decriminalization** of nonserious offenses such as the possession of small amounts of marijuana. Under this concept, the justice system should have as little interaction as possible with offenders. Police, courts, and correctional agencies would concentrate their efforts on diverting law violators out of the formal justice system, thereby helping them avoid the stigma of formal labels such as "delinquent" or "excon." Programs instituted under this model include diversion and community-based corrections.

The popularity of the noninterventionist philosophy has cooled in the 1980s. There has been little evidence that alternative programs actually reduce recidivism rates. Similarly, critics charge that alternative programs result in "widening the net."[36] This refers to the process by which efforts to remove people from the justice system actually enmesh them further within it. For example, programs have been created around the United States to divert first-time petty offenders from the trial process into treatment-oriented counseling centers. However, many offenders spend more time in the alternative programs than they would have in the formal justice system. Whereas a fine or warning would have been the typical response in the past, the nonintervention approach now produces greater interaction with the justice system than does the formal legal process.

Despite such criticism, the nonintervention philosophy is alive and well. For example, the juvenile justice system has made a major effort to remove youths from adult jails and reduce the use of pretrial detention. In the adult system, pretrial release programs (alternatives to bail) are now the norm instead of an experimental innovation. And, though the prison population is rising, probation remains the model correctional treatment in the United States.

Radical Model

There is also a radical-conflict view of the justice system. Radicals reject the due process–crime control dichotomy. Instead they view the justice system as a "state-initiated and state-supported effort to rationalize mechanisms of social control."[37] The criminologist's role is to expose the aspects of the justice system that are designed to specifically control or exploit the laboring classes. Conflict criminologists call this **praxis,** the bringing about through writing, discussion, or social action of a transformation of the current arrangements and relationships in society. There is no

question that in modern American society, long accustomed to abuse of the political process through revelations such as the Pentagon purchasing scandal, Iran-Contra arms deal, and Wall Street insider trading, there is greater sensitivity than ever before to conflict issues.

Justice Model

One of he newer models of criminal justice is known as the justice model.[38] First articulated by correctional expert David Fogel, the justice model contains elements of both liberal and conservative philosophies. Put another way, it is an essentially conservative view that is palatable to liberals because of its emphasis on fairness and due process.

Essentially, the justice model holds that it is futile to rehabilitate criminals because treatment programs are ineffective. Moreover, the needs of the rehabilitation models, which include individualized treatment and discretion, are basically an unfair violation of the constitutional right to equal protection. If two people commit the same crime but receive different sentences because one is receptive to treatment and the other not, the consequences are a sense of injustice in the criminal justice system and inmate anger at those who placed them in an institution. Beyond these problems, justice advocates find fault with both crime control and rehabilitation because they depend on predicting what an offender will do in the future when deciding what to do with them in the present.

As an alternative, the justice model calls for fairness in criminal procedure. This means **flat or determinate sentencing** models, in which all offenders in a particular crime category would receive the same prison sentence. Furthermore, prisons would be viewed as places of just and evenhanded punishment and not rehabilitation. Parole would be abolished to avoid the discretionary unfairness associated with that mechanism of early release.

The justice model has had an important influence on criminal justice policymaking. Some states have adopted flat sentencing statutes and have limited the use of parole. There is a trend toward giving prison sentences because people deserve punishment rather than because the sentence will deter or rehabilitate them.

CRIMINAL JUSTICE TODAY

The various philosophies of justice compete today for dominance in the criminal justice system. Each has supporters who lobby diligently for their positions. At the time of this writing, it seems that the crime control and justice models have captured the support of legislators and the general public. There is a growing emphasis on protection of the public, supplemented by attempts to create fair and equal punishments.

This is not to say that the other views of justice have been abandoned. Police, courts, and correctional agencies still supply a wide range of treatment alternatives to criminal offenders at all stages of the justice system. Whenever possible, especially in the juvenile system, offenders are given the least restrictive alternative, and offshoot of the noninterventionist view.

Similarly, the radical viewpoint has helped shift public focus to corrupt practices and unfair procedures in the justice system. Are police too harsh in dealing with the underprivileged? Is there a disproportionate number of minorities in prison and on death row? Has the justice system been zealous enough in prosecuting white-collar offenders? These views also fit well with due process advocates, who are also determined to root out injustice in the justice system.

Another theme that has begun to dominate justice policy is the need to create and emphasize nontraditional methods of punishment and correction. As the cost of justice skyrockets and the correctional system becomes increasingly overcrowded, alternatives such as house arrest, electronic monitoring, intensive probation supervision, and other cost-effective programs (see Chapter 17) have come to the forefront. There has been a demand for punitive treatment for serious, chronic offenders while necessity has opened the door for greater reliance on treatment and limited intervention for nonviolent, nonchronic offenders. Consequently, rehabilitation and noninterventionist programs may actually increase in the years ahead.

CRIMINAL JUSTICE AND VICTIMS

One of the most significant criminal justice issues to surface in recent years is the concern for the victims of crime.[39] Within the last decade, criminal justice experts and legal commentators have pointed out that the crime victim often suffers as a result of the criminal action. Such harm generally revolves around financial problems, mental stress, and physical hardship. Assisting the victim in dealing with these problems has become the responsibility of society and, specifically, the criminal justice system. Law enforcement agencies, courts, and correctional systems have come to realize that due process and human rights exist both for the defendant and for the victim of criminal behavior.

During the mid-1960s, the Department of Justice produced crime victim surveys which found that victims of crime had negative attitudes as a result of insensitive treatment received from the criminal justice process.[40] Consequently, the Justice Department provided research funds for victim-witness programs, which identified the needs of victims and witnesses who were involved in a criminal incident. The plight of the victim has thus been identified and has today become an even greater concern of the public and the justice system.

Because of concern over the effect of violent personal crime, a Federal Task Force on Victims of Crime was created in 1982.[41] This group undertook an extensive study on crime victimization in America and determine how victims of crime could be given assistance. It found that crime victims had been transformed into a group of citizens burdened by a justice system that had been designed to protect them. Their participation both as victims and as witnesses was often overlooked, and concern for the defendant was given greater emphasis. The task force suggested hat a balance be achieved between recognizing the rights of the victim and providing due process for the defendant. Its most significant recommendation was that the Sixth Amendment to the Constitution be augmented by a statement that says: "In every criminal prosecution, the victim shall have the right to be present and to be heard at all critical stages of the judicial proceedings."[42] Other recommendation involving victims and witnesses of crime included providing for protection of witnesses and victims from intimidation, requiring restitution in criminal cases, developing guidelines for fair treatment of crime victims and witnesses, and expanding programs of victim compensation.[43] More than 35 states have adopted legislation implementing these suggested policies. For example, California has legislatively created a Victims'

TABLE 14.2 Compensation Programs to Help Victims of Violent Crime in 44 States

State	Victim compensation board location[a]	Financial award	To qualify, victim must—		
			show financial need	report to police within	file claim within
Alabama	Alabama Crime Victim Compensation Commission	$0-10,000	No	3 days	12 mos.
Alaska	Department of Public Safety	$0-40,000	Yes	5	24
Arizona	Arizona Criminal Justice Commission	**	Yes	3	**
California	State Board of Control	$100-46,000	Yes	*	12
Colorado	Judicial district boards	$25-10,000	No	3	6
Connecticut	Criminal Injuries Compensation Board	$100-10,000	No	5	24
Delaware	Violent Crimes Board	$25-20,000	No	*	12
D.C.	Office of Crime Victim Compensation	$100-25,000	Yes	7	6
Florida	Department of Labor and Employment Security, Workmen's Compensation Division	$0-10,000	Yes	3	12
Hawaii	Department of Corrections	$0-10,000	No	*	18
Idaho	Industrial Commission	$0-25,000	No	3	12
Illinois	Court of Claims	$0-25,000	No	3	12
Indiana	Industrial Board	$100-10,000	No	2	24
Iowa	Department of Public Safety	$0-20,000	No	1	6
Kansas	Executive Department	$100-10,000	Yes	-3	12
Kentucky	Victim Compensation Board	$0-25,000	Yes	2	12
Louisiana	Commission on Law Enforcement	$100-10,000	No	3	12
Maryland	Criminal Injuries Compensation Board	$0-45,000	Yes	2	6
Massachusetts	District court system	$0-25,000	No	2	12
Michigan	Department of Management and Budget	$200-15,000	Yes	2	12
Minnesota	Crime Victims Reparation Board	$100-50,000	No	5	12
Missouri	Division of Workmen's Compensation	$200-10,000	No	2	12
Montana	Crime Control Division	$0-25,000	No	3	12
Nebraska	Commission on Law Enforcement and Criminal Justice	$0-10,000	Yes	3	24
Nevada	Board of Examiners and Department of Administration	$0-15,000	Yes	5	12
New Jersey	Executive Branch	$0-25,000	No	90	24
New Mexico	Executive Branch	$0-12,500	No	30	12
New York	Executive Department	$0-30,000+	Yes	7	12
North Carolina[b]	Department of Crime Control and Public Safety	$100-20,000		3	24
North Dakota	Workmen's Compensation Bureau	$0-25,000	No	3	12
Ohio	Court of Claims Commissioners	$0-25,000	No	3	12
Oklahoma	Crime Victims Board	$0-10,000	No	3	12
Oregon	Department of Justice/Workmen's Compensation Board	$250-23,000	No	3	6
Pennsylvania	Crime Victims Board	$0-35,000	No	3	12
Rhode Island	Superior court system	$0-25,000	No	10	24
South Carolina	Crime Victims Advisory Board	$100-3,000	No	2	6
Tennessee	Court of Claims Commission	$0-5,000	No	2	12
Texas	Industrial Accident Board	$0-25,000	No	3	6
Utah	Department of Administrative Services	$0-25,000	**	7	12
Virgin Islands	Department of Social Welfare	Up to $25,000	No	1	24
Virginia	Industrial Commission	$0-15,000	No	5	24
Washington	Department of Labor and Industries	$0-15,000+	No	3	12
West Virginia	Court of Claims Commissioner	$0-35,000	No	3	24
Wisconsin	Department of Justice	$0-40,000	No	5	12

[a]if location of the board is not indicated in the State statute the board itself is noted.
[b]North Carolina's program is administratively established but not funded.
*Must report but no time limit specified.
**No reference in statute.
+Plus unlimited medical expenses.
SOURCE: *Report to the Nation on Crime and Justice*, 2d ed. (Washington, D.C.: Bureau of Justice Statistics, 1988), p. 37.

Bill of Rights, which includes provisions allowing victims to attend all sentencing hearings and to present their views and experiences.[44]

One primary concern of victim advocates has been crime victim compensation programs. In recent years, more than 40 states and the federal government have enacted crime victim compensation programs (see Table 14.2). As a result of such legislation, the victim ordinarily receives compensation from the state to pay for damages associated with the crime. Rarely are two compensation schemes alike, however, and many state programs suffer from lack of adequate funding and proper organization within the criminal justice system. However, the victim assistance projects that have been developed do seek to help the victim learn about victim compensation services and related programs.[45]

In addition to victim compensation and victim service programs, some criminal justice practitioners suggest that, under the Constitution, victims also have designated rights that are not being provided them. Frank Carrington suggests that the crime victim has rights that should insure basic services within the criminal justice system.[46] According to Carrington, just as the offender has the right to counsel and a fair trial, so society also has the obligation to ensure basic rights for law-abiding citizens. These rights range from adequate violent crime protection under the law to victim compensation and assistance from the criminal justice system.

In addition to relying on the justice system for aid and compensation, it has become common for victims to take matters into their own hands by bringing civil actions against those who victimized them. For example, the widow of the aspiring actor killed by Jack Henry Abbot, author of *In the Belly of the Beast*, sued to collect proceeds of his book sales under a New York law that prevents felons from cashing in on their crimes through book and movie sales (known as the "Son of Sam law," it was created to prevent the mass murderer from collecting on his fame).[47] In a more recent incident, a Boston jury ordered a doctor to pay $4 million in civil damages to a woman he had raped.[48] Though most offenders do not have the financial ability to pay judgments, some victims simply want to feel they did their part to seek retribution and justice. Others will go after third parties indirectly responsible for the incident, such as a building security company that was negligent in its duties.

In sum, both government programs and individ-

ual initiatives have increased the protection and services given victims of crime.

SUMMARY

Criminal justice refers to the formal processes and institutions that have been established to apprehend, try, punish, and treat law violators. The major components of the criminal justice system are the police, courts, and correctional agencies. Police maintain public order, deter crime, and apprehend law violators. The courts are charged with determining the criminal liability of accused offenders brought before them and with dispensing fair and effective sanctions to those found guilty of crime. Corrections agencies provide postadjudicatory care to offenders who are sentenced by the courts to confinement or community supervision. Dissatisfaction with traditional forms of corrections has spurred the development of community-based facilities and work-release and work-furlough programs. There are about 55,000 justice-related agencies in the United States. About 20,000 of them are police-related and 25,000 are court-related; 10,000 are correctional agencies. They employ about 1.4 million people and cost taxpayers about $50 billion per year.

Justice also can be conceived of as a process. The justice process begins with an initial contact by a police agency and proceeds through investigation and police custody, early trial and trial stages, and correctional system processing. At any stage of the process, the offender can be excused because a lack of evidence exists, the case is trivial, or a decision-maker simply decides to discontinue interest in the case.

Procedures, policies, and practices employed within the criminal justice system are scrutinized by the courts to make sure they do not violate the guidelines set down by the first ten amendments to the Constitution. If a violation occurs, the defendant can appeal the case and seek to overturn the conviction. Among the rights that must be honored are freedom from illegal searches and seizures and treatment with overall fairness and due process.

Several different philosophies or perspectives dominate the justice process. One is the crime control model, which asserts that the goals of justice are protection of the public and incapacitation of known offenders. In contrast, the due process model empha sizes liberal principles such as legal rights and procedural fairness for the offender. Another approach is the rehabilitation model, which views the justice system as a wise and caring parent. The interactionist perspective calls for a minimum of interference in offenders' lives. The radical approach tries to expose the capitalist tendencies of the justice system. Finally, the justice model calls for fair, equal treatment for all offenders.

KEY TERMS

criminal justice
criminal justice nonsystem
sheriff's departments
discretion
criminal court
fundamental fairness
plea bargaining
correctional system
probation
penitentiaries
classification center
community-based
　correctional facilities
parole
evidence
booking
lineup
confession
complaint
information
bill of indictment

probable cause
preliminary hearing
arraignment
hands-off doctrine
Earl Warren
Warren Burger
William Rehnquist
due process
exclusionary rule
President's Commission on
　Law
Enforcement and Criminal
　Justice
judicious nonintervention
deinstitutionalization
diversion
decriminalization
praxis
flat or determinate
　sentencing

NOTES

1. See, for example, Karen Polk, "New Yorkers Split by Race on Verdict in Howard Beach," *Boston Globe* (23 December 1987), p. 3; Elliott Lee, "To C. Vernon Mason Justice in New York Is Guilty of Racism," *Wall Street Journal* (23 December 1987), pp. 1, 8.
2. National Advisory Commission on Criminal Justice Standards and Goals, *A National Strategy to Reduce Crime* (Washington, D.C.: U.S. Government Printing Office, 1973), p. 41.
3. Daniel Skoler, "Antidote for the Non-System: State Criminal Justice Superagencies," *State Government* 46 (1976):2.

4. This section is adapted from Department of Justice, *Justice Agencies in the United States* (Washington, D.C.: U.S. Government Printing Office, 1981), pp. vii–21.
5. Federal Bureau of Investigation, *Crime in the United States, 1986* (Washington, D.C.: U.S. Government Printing Office, 1987), p. 242.
6. See, Albert Reiss, *Police and the Public* (New Haven, Conn.: Yale University Press, 1972).
7. American Bar Association, *Standards Relating to the Urban Police Function* (New York: Institute of Judicial Administration, 1973), Standard 2.2, p. 9.
8. Kenneth L. David, *Police Discretion* (St. Paul, Minn.: West Publishing, 1975).
9. See, Peter Manning and John Van Mannen, eds., *Policing: A View from the Streets* (Santa Monica, Cal.: Goodyear Publishing, 1978).
10. See, Donald Newman, *Conviction: The Determination of Guilt or Innocence? Without Trial* (Boston: Little, Brown, 1966).
11. Sue Lindgren, *Justice Expenditure and Employment, 1985* (Washington, D.C.: Bureau of Justice Statistics, 1987).
12. *Ibid.* p. 4.
13. Herbert L. Packer, *The Limits of the Criminal Sanction* (Stanford, Cal.: Stanford University Press, 1968), p. 159.
14. Edward Lisefski and Donald Manson, *Tracking Offenders, 1984* (Washington, D.C.: Bureau of Justice Statistics, 1988).
15. Samuel Walker, *Sense and Nonsense about Crime*, (Belmont, Cal.: Wadsworth Publishers, 1985).
16. Malcolm Feeley, *The Process Is the Punishment* (New York: Russell Stage Foundation, 1979).
17. New York Criminal Code, Section 177, "Arrest by an Officer, Without a Warrant."
18. *Black's Law Dictionary*, 4th ed. rev. (St. Paul, Minn.: West Publishing, 1957), p. 590.
19. See, Joseph J. Senna, "Changes in Due Process of Law," *Social Work* 19 (1974):319.
20. 342 U.S. 165 (1952).
21. 323 U.S. 383 (1914).
22. 367 U.S. 643 (1969).
23. D. H. Oaks, "Studying the Exclusionary Rule in Search and Seizure," *University of Chicago Law Review* 37 (Summer 1970):756.
24. Illinois v. Gates, 462 U.S. 213 (1983).
25. California v. Ciraolo 106 S. Ct. 1809 (1986).
26. 104 S. Ct. 3405 (1984); 104 S. Ct. 2424 (1984).
27. Robert Misner, "Limiting Leon: A Mistake of Law Analogy," *Journal of Criminal Law and Criminology* 77 (1986):507–45.
28. U.S. Department of Justice, *The Efforts of the Exclusionary Rule: A Study in California* (Washington, D.C.: U.S. Government Printing Office, 1982); Sheldon Krantz,

Bernard Gilman, Charles Benda, Carol Rogoff Halst, and Gail Nadworny, *Police Policymaking* (Lexington, Mass.: Lexington Books, 1979); Brian Forst, Judith Lucianovic, and Sarah Cox, *What Happens After Arrest* (Washington, D.C.: Inslaw, 1977).

29. The most oft-cited of these is Douglas Lipton, Robert Martinson, and Judith Wilks, *The Effectiveness of Correctional Treatment: A Survey of Treatment Evaluation Studies* (New York: Praeger, 1975).

30. Steven Lab and John Whitehead, "An Analysis of Juvenile Correctional Treatment," *Crime and Delinquency* 34 (1988):60–83.

31. Marvin Zalman, "Sentencing in a Free Society: The Failure of the President's Crime Commission to Influence Sentencing Policy," *Justice Quarterly* 4 (1987):545–70.

32. For example, see, Carol Garret, "Effects of Residential Treatment on Adjudicated Delinquents: A Meta-Analysis," *Journal of Research in Crime and Delinquency* 22 (1985):287–308.

33. Paul Gendreau and Robert Ross, "Revivification of Rehabilitation: Evidence from the 1980's," *Justice Quarterly* 4 (1987):349–407.

34. Packer, *Limits of the Criminal Sanction.*

35. Edwin M. Lemert, "The Juvenile Court—Quest and Realities," in President's Commission on Law Enforcement and the Administration of Justice, *Task Force Report: Juvenile Delinquency and Youth Crime* (Washington, D.C.: U.S. Government Printing Office, 1967); Edwin Schur, *Radical Nonintervention* (Englewood Cliffs, N.J.: Prentice-Hall, 1973).

36. James Austin and Barry Krisberg, "The Unmet Promise of Alternatives to Incarceration," *Crime and Delinquency* 28 (1982):3–19. For an alternative view, see, Arnold Binder and Gilbert Geis, "Ad Populum Argumentation in Criminology: Juvenile Diversion as Rhetoric," *Criminology* 30 (1984):309–33.

37. Ian Taylor, Paul Walton, and Jack Young, *Critical Criminology* (London: Routledge and Kegan Paul, 1975), p. 24.

38. David Fogel, . . . *We Are the Living Proof* (Cincinnati, Ohio: Anderson, 1975). See also, Fogel, *Justice as Fairness* (Cincinnati: Anderson, 1980).

39. See generally, William F. McDonald, ed., *Criminal Justice and the Victim: An Introduction* (Beverly Hills, Cal.: Sage Publications, 1976); American Bar Association, *Reducing Victim-Witness Compensation* (Chicago: American Bar Association, 1979).

40. Peter Finn and Beverly Lee, *Serving Two Masters: The Issue for Victim Assistance* (Cambridge, Mass.: Abt Associates, 1981).

41. U.S. Department of Justice, *Report of the President's Task Force on Victims of Crime* (Washington, D.C.: U.S. Government Printing Office, 1983).

42. *Ibid.*, p. 115.

43. *Ibid.*, pp. 2–10; "Review on Victims—Witnesses of Crime," *Massachusetts Lawyers Weekly* (25 April 1983), p. 26.

44. Edwin Villamore and Virginia Neto, *Victim Appearances at Sentencing Under California's Victims' Bill of Rights,* (Washington, D.C.: National Institute of Justice, 1987).

45. Randall Schmidt, "Crime Victim Compensation Legislation: A Comparative Study," *Victimology* 5 (1980):428–37.

46. See, Frank Carrington, "Victim's Rights Litigation: A Wave of the Future," in Burt Galaway and Joe Hudson, eds., *Perspectives on Crime Victims* (St. Louis: C. V. Mosby Co., 1981).

47. Bennett Beach, "Getting Status and Getting Even," *Time* (7 February 1983), p. 40.

48. United Press International, "Doctor Is Told to Pay $4 Million in Rape Case," *Omaha World Herald* (17 February 1985), p. 17A.

CHAPTER 15

THE POLICE

INTRODUCTION

The police are the **gatekeepers** of the criminal justice process. They initiate contact with law violators and decide whether to formally arrest them and begin their journey through the criminal justice system. The police may also settle the issue in a nonformal way (such as by issuing a warning), or simply use their discretion and take no action at all. The strategic position of law enforcement officers, their visibility and contact with the public, and their use of weapons and arrest power have kept them in the forefront of public thought for most of the twentieth century.

In the late 1960s and early 1970s, great issue was taken with the existing political and social role of the police. Critics viewed police agencies as biased organizations that harassed minority citizens, controlled political dissidents, and generally seemed out of touch with the changing times. The major issue of the day appeared to be controlling the abuse of police power and making police agencies more responsible to public control.

During this period, major efforts were undertaken in the nation's largest cities to curb police power. Chapter 12 discussed the work of the Knapp Commission, which investigated police corruption in New York. Police review boards designed to allow members of the community to oversee police policies and operations and to investigate citizen complaints, were set up in such cities as Philadelphia, New York, and Detroit.

Since the mid-1970s, change has occurred in the overt relationship between police and the public. Police departments have become more sensitive about their public image. Programs have been created to improve relations between police and community, to help police officers on the beat to be more sensitive to the needs of the public, and to help police cope more effectively with the stress of their jobs.

Nonetheless, major city police departments continue to be the subject of public scrutiny. There is continuing concern over the police use of force and police treatment of citizens. At the same time, people are more concerned than ever with increasing police effectiveness: the public wants its police agencies to control the law-violating members of society. Consequently, questions are being asked about what should be the proper role of police in society. Are they strictly crime fighters or multi-faceted social service agents who include law enforcement in the broad repertoire of their activities?

This chapter reviews the function and role of police in U.S. society. First, the history of police is briefly discussed. Then, the role and structure of police agencies is covered. Finally, some of the critical issues facing the police in society are analyzed.

HISTORY OF THE POLICE

Like the criminal law, the origin of U.S. police agencies can be traced back to early English society.[1] Before the Norman Conquest, there was no regular English police force. Villagers scattered throughout the countryside were responsible for aiding their neighbors and protecting the settlement from thieves and marauders. This was known as the **pledge system.** As noted in Chapter 2, families were grouped into collectives of ten families called a *tithing* and entrusted with policing their own minor problems. Ten collectives, or tithings, were grouped into a *hundred*, whose affairs were supervised by a **constable** appointed by the local noble. The constable, who might be considered the first real police officer, dealt with more serious breaches of the law.[2]

Later, the hundreds were grouped into *shires* resembling the counties of today. The **shire reeve** was appointed by the crown to supervise a certain territory and assure the local noble that order would be kept. The shire reeve, forerunner of today's *sheriff,* soon began to pursue and apprehend law violators.

In the thirteenth century, during the reign of King Edward I, the **watch system** was created to help protect property in England's larger cities and towns. The watch patrolled at night and helped protect against robberies, fires, and disturbances. The watch reported to the area constable, who became the primary metropolitan law enforcement agent. In larger cities such as London, the watch was organized within church parishes; those applying for the job were usually members of the parish they protected.

In 1326, the office of **justice of the peace** was created to assist the shire reeve in controlling the county. Eventually, the justices took on judicial functions in addition to their primary duty as peacekeeper. A system developed in which the local constable became the operational assistant to the justice of the peace, supervising the night watch, investigating offenses, serving summons, executing warrants, and securing prisoners. This working format helped delineate the relationship between police and the judiciary that has existed intact for 500 years.

At first, the position of constable was an honorary one, given to a respected person in the village or parish for a one-year period. Often, constables were wealthy merchants who had little time for their duties. It was common for them to hire assistants to help them fulfill their obligations, thereby creating another element of a paid police force. Thus, by the seventeenth century, the justice of the peace, the constable, the constable's assistants, and the night watch formed the nucleus of the local metropolitan justice system. (The sheriff's duties lay outside the cities and towns.)

Eighteenth-Century Developments

At the end of the eighteenth century, the industrial revolution lured thousands from the English countryside to work in the larger factory towns. The swelling population of urban poor, whose low wages could hardly sustain them, heightened the need for police protection. In response to pressure from established citizens, the government passed statutes creating new police offices in London. These offices employed three justices of the peace, who were each authorized to employ six paid constables. Law enforcement began to be more centralized and professional. However, many parishes still maintained their own foot patrols, horse patrols, and private investigators.

In 1829, **Sir Robert Peel,** England's Home Secretary, guided through Parliament an "Act for Improving the Police In and Near the Metropolis." The act established the first organized police force in London. Composed of over a thousand men, the London police force was structured along military lines. Its members wore a distinctive uniform and were led by two magistrates, who were later given the title of commissioner. However, the ultimate responsibility for the police fell to the Home Secretary and consequently the Parliament.

The London experiment proved so successful that the metropolitan police soon began sending aid to outlying areas that requested assistance in law enforcement matters. Another act of Parliament allowed justices of the peace to establish local police forces; by 1856, every borough and county in England was required to form its own police force.

The American Colonial Experience

Law enforcement in colonial America paralleled the British model. In the colonies, the county sheriff became the most important law enforcement agent.[3] In addition to peacekeeping and crime fighting, sheriffs collected taxes, supervised elections, and handled a great deal of other legal business.

Colonial sheriffs did not patrol or seek out crime. Instead, they reacted to citizens' complaints and investigated crimes that had already occurred. Their salaries were related to their effectiveness. Sheriffs were paid by the fee system. They were given a fixed amount for every arrest made, subpoena served, or court appearance made. Unfortunately, their tax collecting chores were more lucrative than crime fighting; so law enforcement was not one of their primary concerns.

In the cities, law enforcement was the province of the town marshal, who was aided—often unwillingly—by a variety of constables, night watchmen, police justices, and city council members. However, local governments had little power of administration, and enforcement of the criminal law was largely an individual or community responsibility. Individual initiate was encouraged by the practice of offering rewards for the capture of felons.[4] If trouble arose, citizens might be called on to form a posse to chase offenders or break up an angry mob.

As the size of cities grew, it became exceedingly difficult for local leaders to step in and organize citizens' groups. Moreover, the early nineteenth century was an era of widespread urban unrest and mob violence. Local leaders began to realize that a more structured police force was needed to control demonstrators and keep peace.

Early Police Agencies

The modern police department was born out of urban mob violence, which wracked the nation's cities in the nineteenth century. Boston created the first formal U.S. police department in 1838. New York formed its police department in 1844; Philadelphia, in 1854. The new police departments replaced the night watch system and relegated constables and sheriffs to serving court orders and running jails.

At first, the urban police departments inherited the functions of the older institutions they replaced. For example, Boston police were charged with maintaining public health until 1853; in New York, the police were responsible for street sweeping until 1881.

Politics dominated the departments and determined the recruitment of new officers and promotion of supervisors. An individual with the right connections could be hired despite a lack of qualifications. Writes one justice historian, Samuel Walker:

> In addition to the pervasive brutality and corruption, the police did little to effectively prevent crime or provide public services . . . Officers were primarily tools of local politicians; they were not impartial and professional public servants.[5]

At mid-nineteenth century, the detective bureau was set up as part of the Boston police. Until then, "thief-taking" had been the province of amateur bounty hunters, who hired themselves out to victims for a price. When professional police departments replaced bounty hunters, the close working relationships that developed between police detectives and their underworld informants produced many scandals and consequently high personnel turnover.

Police during the nineteenth century were generally incompetent, corrupt, and disliked by the people they served. The police role was only minimally directed at law enforcement. Its primary function was serving as the enforcement arm of the reigning political power, protecting private property, and keeping control of the ever-rising numbers of foreign immigrants.

Reform Movements

Police agencies evolved slowly through the latter half of the nineteenth century. Uniforms were introduced in New York in 1853. Technological innovations, such as linking precincts to central headquarters by telegraph, appeared in the late 1850s. Somewhat later, call boxes allowed police patrols on the beat to commu-

nicate with their commanders. Nonpolice functions, such as care of the streets, began to be abandoned after the Civil War.

Despite any impetus toward improvement, big-city police were neither respected by the public, nor successful in their role as crime stoppers, nor involved in progressive activities. The control of police departments by local politicians impeded effective law enforcement and fostered an atmosphere of graft and corruption.

In an effort to control police corruption, civil leaders in some jurisdictions created police administrative boards to reduce the control over police exercised by local officials. These tribunals were given the responsibilities of appointing police administrators and of controlling police affairs. In many instances, these measures failed because the private citizens appointed to the review boards lacked expertise in the intricacies of police work.

Another reform movement was the takeover of some big-city police agencies by state legislators. Though police budgets were paid through local taxes, control of police was usurped by rural politicians in the state capitals. It was not until the first decades of the twentieth century that cities regained control of their police forces.

The Boston police strike of 1914 heightened interest in police reform. The strike was brought about by dissatisfaction with the status police officers held in society. While other professions were unionized and increasing their standards of living, police salaries lagged behind. The Boston police officers' organization, the Boston Social Club, voted to become a union affiliated with the American Federation of Labor (AFL). The officers struck on 9 September 1914. Rioting and looting broke out, resulting in Governor Calvin Coolidge's mobilization of the state militia to take over the city. Public support turned against the police, and the strike was broken. Eventually, all the striking officers were fired and replaced by new recruits. The Boston police strike ended police unionism for decades and solidified power in the hands of reactionary, autocratic police administration.

In the aftermath of the strike, crime commissions on the local, state, and national level began to investigate the extent of crime and the ability of the justice system to effectively deal with it. The **Wickersham Commission** was created by President Herbert Hoover to study police issues on a national scale. In its 1931

Today, police often conduct drug awareness programs in schools to advocate community outreach.

report, the Commission found that the average police supervisor's term of office was too short and that the responsibility to political officials made the position insecure. The Commission also disclosed a lack of effective, efficient, and honest patrols. It said that no intensive effort was being made to educate, train, and discipline prospective officers or to eliminate those who were incompetent.

The Wickersham Commission also found that, with few exceptions, police forces in cities with populations above 300,000 had neither adequate communications systems nor the equipment necessary to enforce the law effectively. The police task, according to the Commission, was made much more difficult by the excessively rapid growth of U.S. cities in the past half-century and by the tendency of ethnic groups to retain their languages and customs in large cities.

Finally, the Commission said too many duties were cast upon each officer and patrolman.[6] The Missouri Crime Commission reported that in a typical U.S. city, the police were expected to be familiar with and enforce 30,000 federal, state, and local enactments.[7] However, with the onset of the Great Depression, justice reform became a less important issue than economic revival; for many years, there was little change in the nature of policing.

The Advent of Professionalism

The onset of police professionalism can be traced to the 1920s and the influence of **August Vollmer**.[8] While serving as police chief of Berkeley, California, Vollmer instituted university training as an important part of his development of young officers. He also helped develop the School of Criminology at the University of California at Berkeley, which became the model of justice-related programs around the country.

Vollmer's disciples included O. W. Wilson, who pioneered the use of advanced training for officers when he took over and reformed the Wichita, Kansas, police department in 1923. Wilson also was instrumental in applying modern management and administrative techniques to policing. His text, *Police Administration*, became the single most influential work on the subject. Wilson eventually took over as dean of the Criminology School at Berkeley and ended his career in Chicago when Mayor Richard J. Daley asked him to take over and reform the Chicago police department in 1960.

One important aspect of professionalism was the technological breakthroughs which significantly increased and expanded the scope of police operations. The first technological breakthroughs in police operations came in the area of communications. In 1867 the first telegraph police boxes were installed; an officer could turn a key in a box and the location and number would automatically register at headquarters.

Additional technological advances were made in the area of transportation. The Detroit police department outfitted some of its patrol officers with bicycles in 1897. By 1913, the motorcycle was being employed by departments in the eastern part of the country. The first police car used in Akron, Ohio, in 1910; the police wagon became popular in Cincinnati, Ohio, in 1912.

In recent years, the use of technology in police work has markedly increased, prompted in part by World War II scientific breakthroughs and by the infusion of federal support for research in the law enforcement field. In no area have these changes been more apparent than in electronic data processing. In 1967, for example, only one city, St. Louis, had a police computer system; by 1968, 10 states and 50 cities had state-level criminal justice information systems.

Through the 1960s, police professionalism was interpreted as a tough, highly trained, rule-oriented law enforcement department organized along militaristic lines. The most respected department was in Los Angeles, under the leadership of its no-nonsense chief, William Parker. Two of the most popular police television shows of the period, "Dragnet" and "Adam-12," stressed the high motivation, competence, and integrity of Los Angeles police officers.

The urban unrest of the late 1960s changed the course of police department development. Efforts were made to promote understanding between police and community, to reduce police brutality, and to recognize the stresses of police work. Efforts also were made—usually under court order—to add members of minority groups and women to police departments. The federal government's Law Enforcement Education Program (LEEP) encouraged officers to get college training. Rank-and-file patrol officers became dissatisfied with administration from the top down; consequently, local police unions were formed.

Also as a result of increasing professionalism, the ideal police officer came to be viewed as a product of the computer age, skilled in using the most advanced techniques to fight crime. A significant majority of funds went toward developing police hardware; in some quarters, technological advances were seen as the answer to the crime problem.[9]

Despite technological and professional achievements, the effectiveness of the police is still ques-

tioned. Their ability to control crime is still considered problematic. Critics argue that plans to increase police professionalism place too much emphasis on hardware and not enough on police-citizen cooperation.

LAW ENFORCEMENT AGENCIES

Law enforcement duties are distributed across local, county, state, and federal jurisdictions. In addition, public law enforcement is being supplemented by private security agencies (see Close-Up on private security). This section discusses the role of federal, state and county agencies. The remainder of the chapter focuses more directly on local police.

Federal Law Enforcement

The federal government maintains about 50 organizations that are involved in law enforcement duties. Some of the most important of these are discussed below.

The Federal Bureau of Investigation. In 1870, the U.S. Department of Justice became involved in actual policing when the Attorney General hired investigators to enforce the Mann Act (which prohibited white slavery). In 1908, this group of investigators was formally made a distinct branch of the government, the Bureau of Investigation; in the 1930s, the agency was reorganized into the Federal Bureau of Investigation (FBI) under the direction of J. Edgar Hoover.

Today's FBI is not a police agency but an investigative agency, with jurisdiction over all matters in which the United States is, or may be, an interested party. It limits its jurisdiction to federal laws, including all federal statutes not specifically assigned to other agencies.[10] These include statutes dealing with espionage, sabotage, treason, civil rights violations, the murder and assault of federal officers, mail fraud, robbery and burglary of federally insured (FDIC) banks, kidnapping, and interstate transportation of stolen vehicles and property.

The FBI offers important services to local law enforcement agencies. Its identification division, established in 1924, collects and maintains a vast fingerprint file that can be used for identification purposes by local

☰ CLOSE-UP

Private Security

The first private security officer, Allan Pinkerton, had a tremendous impact on private security through his work with the railroads and through his establishment of the first private security firm. Owing to the lack of a federal law enforcement agency, Pinkerton's security agency was hired by the federal government in 1861. More recently there has been increased need for private security, particularly to protect defense secrets and defense supplies provided by the private sector. More recent growth in private security is in response to growth of crime and security needs in businesses.

Protecting Private Concerns Against Losses

This for-profit industry provides—

- personnel, such as guards, investigators, couriers, body-guards.
- equipment, including safes, locks, lighting, fencing, alarm systems, closed circuit television, smoke detectors, fire extinguishers, and automatic sprinkler systems.
- services, including alarm monitoring; employee background checks and drug testing; evacuation planning; computer security planning; and polygraph testing.

    Private security is provided either by direct hiring (proprietary security) or by hiring specific services or equipment (contract security). Over 1 million people are employed in private security. The industry continues to grow and has outnumbered public police since the 1950s.

Authority of Private Security Varies

Many states give private security personnel authority to make felony arrests when there is "reasonable cause" to believe a crime has been committed. Unlike sworn police officers, private personnel are not obligated to tell arrestees of their rights. Private security usually cannot detain suspects or conduct searches without the suspect's consent. Some state laws give private security authority to act as "special police" within a specific jurisdiction such as a plant, a store, or university campus.

Many Are Licensed or Regulated

In some jurisdictions both state and local requirements must be met to obtain a license to provide private security. At the state level—

- 35 states license guard and patrol firms.
- 22 states and the District of Columbia require the registration of guards.
- 37 states license private investigators.
- Alarm companies must obtain a license in 25 states and are regulated in 10 states.
- 8 states license armored car companies and 6 states license couriers.
- In fewer than 12 states, the same agency or board regulates alarm companies and armored car firms, as well as guard, patrol, and investigative firms.
- 3 states have independent regulatory boards; 6 states have such boards in state agencies.
- Private security is regulated by the department of public safety or state police in 15 states, the department of commerce or occupational licensing agency in 7 states, and the department of state in 5 states.

Public Police Are Often Employed

Some police officers "moonlight" as private security officers in their off-duty hours. According to the Hallcrest survey, 81 percent of the surveyed police departments permit moonlighting, but most estimated that 20 percent or less of their officers are working as private security personnel. Acting like a contract security firm, some police departments provide personnel to private concerns and use the revenue for the department.

Discussion Questions

1. Does the growth of private security reflect the failure of police agencies to control crime?
2. Should private security officers be allowed to carry and use firearms?

SOURCE: *Report to the Nation on Crime and Justice*, 2d ed. (Washington, D.C.: Bureau of Justice Statistics, 1988), p. 66.

police agencies. Its sophisticated crime laboratory, established in 1932, aids local police in testing and identifying evidence such as hairs, fibers, blood, tire tracks, and drugs.

The Uniform Crime Report is another service of the FBI. As discussed in Chapter 3, the UCR is an annual compilation of data on crimes reported to local police agencies, arrests, police killed or wounded in action, and so on. Finally, the FBI's National Crime Information Center is a computerized network linked to local police departments. Information on stolen vehicles, wanted persons, and stolen guns is made available to local law enforcement agencies.

For many years, the FBI was considered to be the elite U.S. law enforcement agency. Its agents were considered incorruptible, highly trained, and professional. FBI agents always were successful whether the quarry was a gangster of the 1930s such as John Dillinger, a Nazi saboteur during World War II, or a Russian secret agent during the Cold War. However, during the era of political suspicion that followed the Watergate break-ins, information came to light that tarnished the agency's image. J. Edgar Hoover was portrayed as placing undue emphasis on controlling radical groups and harassing black civil rights leaders. One infamous incident was the bugging of Martin Luther King, Jr.'s hotel rooms. The FBI's COINTELPRO (counterintelligence program) used wiretaps, opened mail, and burglarized the offices of radical political groups.[11] After a period of turmoil and internal unrest, the FBI seems to have successfully restricted its activities and is now directed toward more vigorously pursuing organized crime figures, enforcing white-collar crime statutes, and pursuing U.S. terrorist groups.

Other Federal Agencies.   The U.S. government's interest in drug trafficking can be traced back to 1914, when the Harrison Act established federal jurisdiction over the supply and use of narcotics. Several drug enforcement units, including the Bureau of Narcotics and Dangerous Drugs, were originally charged with enforcing drug laws. However, in 1973 these agencies were combined to form the Drug Enforcement Administration (DEA). Agents of the DEA assist local and state authorities in their investigation of illegal drug use and carry out independent surveillance and enforcement activities to control the importation of narcotics.

Federal law enforcement agencies under the direction of the Justice Department include the U.S. marshals, the Immigration and Naturalization Service, and the Organized Crime and Racketeering Unit. The U.S. marshals are court officers who help implement federal court rulings, transport prisoners, and enforce court orders. The Immigration and Naturalization Service is responsible for administration and deportation of illegal aliens and naturalization of aliens lawfully present in the United States. This service also maintains border patrols to prevent illegal aliens from entering the United States. The Organized Crime and Racketeering Unit, under the direction of the U.S. Attorney General, has coordinated federal efforts to curtail organized crime and to contain members of the alleged national criminal syndicate.

The Treasury Department maintains the Alcohol, Tobacco, and Firearms Bureau, which has jurisdiction over sales and distribution of illegal firearms, explosives, liquor, and untaxed cigarettes.

The Internal Revenue Service, established in 1862, enforces violations of income, excise, stamp, and other tax laws. Its Intelligence Division actively pursues gamblers, narcotics dealers, and other violators who do not report their illegal financial gains as taxable income.

The Customs Bureau guards points of entry into the United States and prevents smuggling of contraband into (or out of) the country.

The Secret Service, an arm of the Treasury Department, was originally charged with enforcing laws against counterfeiting. Today the Secret Service also is accountable for the protection of the president and vice-president and their families, of presidential candidates, and of former presidents.

County Law Enforcement

The county police department is an independent agency whose senior officer, the **sheriff,** is usually an elected political official. The county sheriff's role has evolved from that of the early English shire reeve, whose main duty was to assist the royal judges in trying prisoners and enforcing the law outside of cities. From the time of U.S. westward expansion until municipal departments were developed, the sheriff often acted as the sole legal authority over vast territories.

The duties of a county sheriff's department vary according to the size and degree of development of the county where it is located. Officials within the department may serve as coroners, tax assessors, tax collectors, overseers of highways and bridges, custodians of the county treasury, keepers of the county jail, court attendants, and executors of criminal and civil processes; in years past, sheriffs' offices also conducted executions. Many of the sheriff's law enforcement functions today are carried out only in incorporated areas within a county or in response to city departments' requests for aid in such matters as patrol or investigation.

Probably the most extensive sheriff's department is located in Los Angeles County. This department provides services to over three million people and has service contracts with 32 cities.[12] It maintains a modern communications system and a police laboratory, in addition to performing standard enforcement functions.

State Police

The Texas Rangers, organized in 1835, are considered the first state police force. However, the Rangers were more a quasi-military force that supported the Texas state militia than a true law enforcement body. The first true state police forces emerged at the turn of the twentieth century, with Pennsylvania's force leading the way.

The impetus for creating state police agencies can be traced both to the public's low regard for the crime fighting ability of local police agencies and to the increasingly greater mobility of law violators. Using automobiles, thieves could strike at will and be out of the jurisdiction of local police before an investigation could be mounted. Therefore, a law enforcement agency with statewide jurisdiction was needed. Also, state police gave governors a powerful enforcement arm that was under their personal control and not that of city politicans.

Today the major role of state police is controlling traffic on the highway system, helping trace stolen automobiles, and aiding in disturbances and crowd control. In states with large and powerful county sheriff's departments, the state police function is usually restricted to highway patrol. In others, where the county sheriff's law enforcement role is limited, state police usually maintain a more active investigative and enforcement role.

Local Police

Metropolitan police agencies make up the vast majority of the law enforcement community's members. They range in size from New York's, which employs around 34,000 people, including 27,000 sworn officers, to several rural departments which maintain only a single police officer.[13]

Most larger urban departments are independent agencies operating without specific administrative control from any higher governmental authority. They are organized at the executive level of government. It is therefore common for the city mayor (or the equivalent) to control the hiring and firing of the police chief and consequently determine departmental policies.

Most municipal departments are organized in a military way; they often use military terms to designate seniority (sergeant, lieutenant, captain).

The organization of a typical metropolitan police department is illustrated in Figure 15.1. This complex structure is a function of the multiplicity of roles that police are entrusted with. Among the daily activities of police agencies are included:

- Identifying criminal suspects
- Investigating crimes
- Apprehending offenders and participating in their trials
- Deterring crime through patrol
- Aiding individuals in danger or in need of assistance; providing emergency services
- Resolving conflict and keeping the peace
- Maintaining a sense of community security
- Keeping automobile traffic and pedestrian movement efficient
- Promoting civil order
- Operating and administering the police department

The remainder of this chapter is devoted to the nature of local policing.

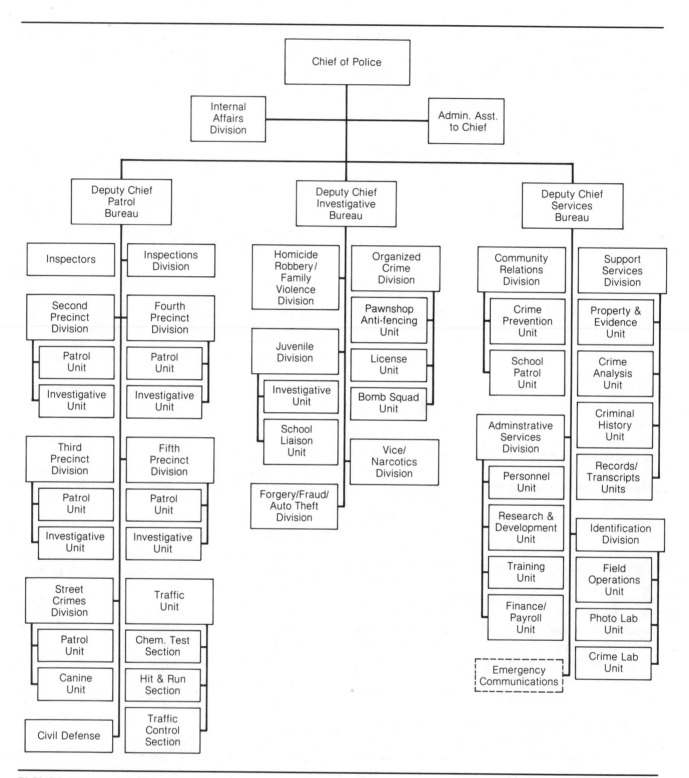

FIGURE 15.1   Police Department Structure—Organizational Chart of the Minneapolis Police Department
SOURCE: Joel Samaha, *Criminal Justice* (St. Paul, Minn.: West Publishing, 1988), p. 157.

POLICE ROLE

If you watch television and movies, it is easy to see why many people believe that the major police role is law enforcement. However, research indicates that very little of a police officer's time is spent on "crime-fighting duties."[14] Instead, the great bulk of effort is devoted to what has been described as *order maintenance*, or peacekeeping.[15] James Q. Wilson's pioneering work, *Varieties of Police Behavior*, viewed the major police role to be "handling the situation."[16] Wilson found that police encounter many troubling incidents that need some sort of "fixing up." Enforcing the law might be one tool a police officer uses; threat, coercion, sympathy, understanding, and apathy might be others. Most important is "keeping things under control so that there are no complaints that he is doing nothing or that he is doing too much."

The peacekeeping role of the police has been documented by several different studies, which find that the police function primarily as order-keeping, dispute-settling agents of public health and safety.[17] Just being there to handle the situation is the officers' main task; the better they are at it, the less likely they are to resort to violence. Unfortunately, police have a tendency to dominate actions and sometimes disregard the feelings of those who need their aid.

The police officer's role is recognized as being multidimensional. Police officers are required to be keepers of the peace, investigators of crime, emergency medical technicians, traffic controllers, and symbols of public morality and stability. The burdens of police work have helped set law enforcement officers outside the mainstream of society and have encouraged the development of a police subculture marked by insulation from the outside world and code of secrecy.[18]

Community Policing

In a highly regarded article, James Q. Wilson and George Kelling call for a return to a nineteenth-century style of policing, in which police maintain a presence in the community, walk beats, get to know citizens, and inspired feelings of public safety.[19] Wilson and Kelling ask police administrators to get their officers out of depersonalized patrol cars. Instead of deploying police on the basis of crime rates or in areas where citizens make the most calls for help, police administrators should station their personnel where they can do the most to promote public confidence and elicit citizen cooperation. Community preservation, public safety, and order maintenance—not crime fighting—should become the primary focus of police:

> *Just as physicians now recognize the importance of fostering health rather than simply treating illness, so the police—and the rest of us—ought to recognize the importance of maintaining intact communities without broken windows.*[20]

Of course, not all police experts agree that a return to the police officer of yesteryear—more a watch than a crime fighter—is the panacea it is thought to be by Wilson and Kelling. For example, Samuel Walker disputes Wilson and Kelling's analysis on the grounds that they misread police history.[21] First, though the use of patrol cars may have produced some depersonalization of the police since the 1930s, this has been counteracted by the modern communication devices that have helped bring police and the community closer together. For example, use of the telephone allows the police to more easily "enter" people's residences and become involved in their personal problems such as family disputes and/or substance abuse. Second, the crime control orientation of the police has been exaggerated. In reality, police have acted as peacekeepers during most of the twentieth century. Third, there is little evidence that, in the "good old days," police enjoyed political legitimacy among the masses. Actually, they rarely enjoyed political acceptance during the nineteenth and early twentieth centuries. Finally, the watch style proposed by Wilson and Kelling is essentially ineffective and does not serve neighborhood needs. Walker concludes that the police are actually incapable of improving the community's perceptions of public safety.

Despite such criticism, police concern for community needs seems to be increasing. Some jurisdictions have implemented the **problem-oriented policing** concept, in which police work with the community to identify problem areas, analyze what can be done to correct them, work with citizens and the community to respond to the problem and then assess the impact of their efforts (see Close-Up on problem-oriented policing).[22]

CLOSE-UP

Problem-Oriented Policing

The reading below discusses a common criminal incident and how police used problem-oriented police techniques to resolve the situation.

At 1:32 A.M. a man we will call Fred Snyder dials 911 from a downtown corner phone booth. The dispatcher notes his location and calls the nearest patrol unit. Officer Knox arrives four minutes later.

Snyder says he was beaten and robbed 20 minutes before but didn't see the robber. Under persistent questioning Snyder admits he was with a prostitute, picked up in a bar. Later, in a hotel room, he discovered the prostitute was actually a man, who then beat Snyder and took his wallet.

Snyder wants to let the whole matter drop. He refuses medical treatment for his injuries. Knox finishes his report and lets Snyder go home. Later that day Knox's report reaches Detective Alexander's desk. She knows from experience the case will go nowhere, but she calls Snyder at work.

Snyder confirms the report but refuses to cooperate further. Knox and Alexander go on to other cases. Months later, reviewing crime statistics, the city council deplores the difficulty of attracting businesses or people downtown.

The Problem-Oriented Approach

Midnight-watch patrol officers are tired of taking calls like Snyder's. They and their sergeant, James Hogan, decide to reduce prostitution-related robberies, and Officer James Boswell volunteers to lead the effort.

First, Boswell interviews the 28 prostitutes who work the downtown area to learn how they solicit, what happens when they get caught, and why they are not deterred.

They work downtown bars, they tell him, because customers are easy to find and police patrols don't spot them soliciting. Arrests, the prostitutes tell Boswell, are just an inconvenience: judges routinely sentence them to probation, and probation conditions are not enforced.

Based on what he has learned form the interviews and his previous experience, Boswell devises a response. He works with the Alcoholic Beverage Control Board and local barowners to move the prostitutes into the street. At police request, the Commonwealth's Attorney agrees to ask the judges to put stiffer conditions on probation: convicted prostitutes would be given a map of the city and told to stay out of the downtown area or go to jail for three months.

Boswell then works with the vice unit to make sure that downtown prostitutes are arrested and convicted, and that patrol officers know which prostitutes are on probation. Probation violators are sent to jail, and within weeks all but a few of the prostitutes have left downtown.

Then Boswell talks to the prostitutes' customers, most of whom don't know that almost half the prostitutes working the street are actually men, posing as women. He intervenes in street transactions, formally introducing the customers to their male dates. The Navy sets up talks for him with incoming sailors to tell them about the male prostitutes and the associated safety and health risks.

In three months, the number of prostitutes working downtown drops from 28 to six, and robbery rates are cut in half. After 18 months neither robbery nor prostitution show signs of returning to their earlier levels.

Discussion Questions

1. Should police deal with problems or crimes?
2. Considering the "new" police role, what sort of training or education should officers receive?

SOURCE: William Spelman and John Eck. *Problem-Oriented Policing* (Washington, D.C.: National Institute of Justice, 1987).

The "broken windows" argument highlights the dilemma facing American police agencies today. While in the past there was a great deal of mistrust of the police, public opinion has shifted toward a more sympathetic view of policing. A recent Gallup Poll found that the public rated the honesty and ethical standards of police over those of bankers, lawyers, journalists, and senators (college professors were rated higher); only 10 percent of those surveyed rated police poorly.[23] The public seems to want a return of the incorruptible, tough "supercop"; people, even presidents, cheer when Clint Eastwood's Lt. Harry

Callahan tells the bad guy, "Make my day." Yet, police experts realize the limited capability police have to affect the crime rate. They are simply more effective at peacekeeping and maintaining order than at crime control.

So, to meet the public's need for safety and control, police agencies have turned to programs featuring greater visibility and citizen contact, such as foot patrols, school outreach programs, and neighborhood mini-precincts. Even if the police cannot actually make the public safer, they can try to make them feel safer.

——— POLICE FUNCTIONS ———

What do local police actually do? What are their major functions and how well do they perform them? This section discusses a few of the most critical police functions.

Patrol

Patrol entails police officers' visible presence on the streets and in public places of their jurisdiction. The purpose of patrol is to deter crime, maintain order, enforce laws, and aid in service functions, such as emergency medical care. There are a large variety of patrol techniques. In early police forces, foot patrol was almost exclusively used. Each officer had a particular area, or *beat*, to walk; the police officer was the symbol of state authority in that area. The beat officer dispensed "street justice," and some became infamous for their use of clubs or nightsticks.

When the old-style beat officers needed assistance, they would pound the pavement with their sticks to summon colleagues from nearby areas. Later, call boxes were introduced so officers could communicate more easily with headquarters. Today, the introduction of patrol cars as well as motorcycles, helicopters, and other types of mechanized transportation has all but ended **walking the beat.** Though the patrol car allows the police to supervise more territory with fewer officers, it has removed and isolated patrol officers from the communities they serve. Some experts argue that this impersonal style of enforcement has worsened relations between police and community. In some communities, **aggressive preventive patrol,** de-

signed to suppress crime before it occurs, has heighted tensions between the police and the minority community.

Considerable tension is involved in patrolling, especially in high-crime areas, where police feel they are open targets. The patrol officer must learn to work the street, taking whatever action is necessary to control the situation and no more.

When patrol officers take inappropriate action, or when their behavior results in violence or death, they are subject to intense scrutiny by public agencies and may be subject to disciplinary measures from the police department's **internal affairs division.** Thus, patrol officers are expected to make mature and reasoned decisions while facing a constant flow of people in emotional crisis.

A patrol officer's job is extremely demanding; at the same time, it is often unrewarding and unappreciated. It is not surprising that the attitudes of police officers toward the public have been characterized by ambivalence, cynicism, and tension.[24]

How Effective is Patrol?   In most police departments, the majority of officers are assigned to patrol work; the patrol officer is the backbone of policing. Yet the question remains: "Do police patrols deter crime?" Put another way, should police spend so much time and resources keeping a visible presence on the street if their efforts have little effect on crime control?

The most comprehensive effort to evaluate the patrol function, the **Kansas City Study,** was conducted in Kansas City, Missouri, under sponsorship of the Police Foundation. To evaluate the effectiveness of patrol, 15 independent police beats or districts were divided into three groups; one group retained normal police patrol; the second (proactive) set of districts was supplied with two to three times the normal amount of patrol forces; and the third (reactive) group had its preventive patrol entirely eliminated, and police officers responded only when summoned by citizens to the scene of a particular crime.

Surprisingly, data from the Kansas City Study indicated that these variations in patrol techniques had little effect on the crime patterns in the 15 locales. The presence or absence of patrol did not seem to affect residential or business burglaries, auto theft, larcenies involving auto accessories, robberies, vandalism, or other criminal behavior.[25]

Moreover, variations in police patrol techniques

Television shows like *Hill St. Blues* have helped to convince the public that the major police role is law enforcement and that police officers are effective crime fighters.

appeared to have little effect on citizens' attitudes toward the police, their satisfaction with police, or their fear of being victimized by criminal behavior.[26]

Other studies have indicated that patrol officers rarely invoke the criminal law. Albert Reiss found that the typical tour of duty does not involve a single arrest.[27] Egon Bittner concluded that patrol officers average about 10 arrests per month and only three index crime arrests per year.[28] Although arrests alone cannot be equated with effectiveness, they do give some indication of the relative value of patrol work.

Patrol Innovations.   Police departments have responded to the challenge of patrol ineffectiveness by attempting to implement innovations in patrol techniques. One approach has been to allocate staff on the basis of computer analysis of previous offense patterns. Another approach has been to use hidden cameras in areas where numerous crimes have occurred.

Another innovative approach that gained popularity in the 1970s was **team policing.**[29] In its most

basic form, this concept brought together groups of junior officers and a supervisor, who were given jurisdiction over a designated neighborhood area on a 24-hour-a-day basis. The supervisor had complete responsibility for the team area, and the team could patrol the area in the manner it believed would be the most effective. The team determined its own deployment, working hours, assignments, and methods within broad policy guidelines established by the department. The purpose of the team was to create strong ties between the police officers and the community they served, and to involve the neighborhood in police operation. Team police models have not received widespread acceptance; where adopted, they have met with only intermittent success. Yet, they illustrate the efforts made by police agencies to improve patrol effectiveness.[30]

Foot patrol.   Still another approach to improving patrol effectiveness has been to reintroduce walking the beat, or **foot patrols,** in over 100 jurisdictions. Returning to the early twentieth-century practice of patrol in today's age of technology is believed to improve police-citizen cooperation and to increase perceptions of public safety. The Police Foundation evaluated several of these programs in New Jersey and found that foot patrol had little effect on the crime rate, but it did help to improve citizen attitudes toward the police.[31]

Those in favor of foot patrol argue that it helps police monitor community concerns and control low-level drug selling, vandalism, and other misdemeanors associated with community decline. Officers on foot are more easily approachable and offer a comforting presence to citizens. With today's mobile communication gear, foot patrol officers are not isolated on the street. In many cities they carry the same communications gear that is used in patrol cars.

The foot patrol concept is growing. Begun in Flint, Michigan, in 1978, foot patrol is seen as an effective means of improving police-community relations in larger departments such as New York's. About 15 percent of San Francisco's police force is now devoted to foot patrol.

Not all supervisors agree that foot patrol is an ideal solution. Some do not want their officers to mingle in neighborhood problems, turning themselves into impromptu social workers. Similarly, they argue that it is difficult to manage foot patrol officers and monitor their whereabouts. Advocates counter that foot patrol can be a flexible supplement to motor patrol, producing increased community support and improved departmental morale.

Investigation

The second prominent police role is investigation and crime detection. The **detective** has been a figure of great romantic appeal since the first independent bureau was established by the London Metropolitan Police in 1841. The detective has been portrayed as the elite of the police force in such films and television shows as *Dirty Harry, Sudden Impact*, and "Miami Vice," to name but a few.

Detective branches are organized on the individual precinct level or out of a central headquarters, and perform various functions. Some jurisdictions maintain morals squads or vice squads, which are usually staffed by plainclothes officers or detectives specializing in victimless crimes, such as prostitution or gambling. Vice squad officers may set themselves up as customers for illicit activities in order to make arrests. For example, undercover detectives may frequent public men's rooms and make themselves available to loitering men; those who make advances toward them are arrested for homosexual soliciting. In other instances, female police officers may pose as prostitutes. These covert police activities have often been criticized as violating the personal rights of citizens, and their appropriateness and fairness have been questioned.

Investigators often must enter a case after it has been reported to police and attempt to accumulate enough evidence to identify the perpetrator.[32] Detectives use various techniques in their investigatory function. Sometimes they obtain fingerprints from the scene of a crime and match them with those on file. Other cases demand the aid of informers to help identify perpetrators. In some instances, victims or witnesses are asked to identify offenders by viewing their pictures, or mug shots, or by pulling them out of lineups. It is also possible for detectives to solve a crime by being familiar with the working methods of particular offenders—their modus operandi, or MO. The detective identifies the criminal by matching the facts of the crime with the criminal's peculiar habits or actions. In some cases, stolen property is located and then the case is cleared. Either the suspect is arrested on another matter and subsequently found to be in possession of stolen merchandise, or during routine questioning a person confesses to criminal acts the police did not suspect him or her of in the first place.

Finally, detectives can use their own initiative to take special action in solving a case. For example, the **sting** type of operation has received widespread publicity.[33] Here, detectives pose as fences and conduct property transactions with thieves interested in selling stolen merchandise. Transactions are videotaped to provide prosecutors with extremely strong cases. A study of sting operations conducted in 40 jurisdictions over a seven-year period found that 9,970 criminals were arrested and $300 million in stolen property recovered at a cost of $30 million.[34]

Sting-type undercover operations are controversial, since they involve a police officer's becoming involved in illegal activity and encouraging offenders to break the law.[35] The ethics of these operations have been questioned, especially when the police actively recruit criminals, as they did in the DeLorean case. Nonetheless, the sting operation seems to have found a permanent place in the law enforcement repertoire.

Are Investigations Effective?   Although detectives in the movies and on television always capture the villain, research evidence indicates that real detectives are much less successful. The Rand Corporation, in a 1975 study of 153 detective bureaus, found that a great deal of detectives' time was spent in nonproductive work and that investigative expertise did little to help them solve cases.[36] In more than half of the cases cleared, simple routine actions solved the case; there was little need for scientific, highly trained investigators. The Rand researchers estimated that half of all detectives could be removed without negatively influencing crime clearance rates.

The Rand findings have been replicated by Mark Willman and John Snortum, who tracked 5,336 reported crimes and spent thousands of hours monitoring detective work in a suburban U.S. police department.[37] They found that when a suspect was identified, it usually occurred *before* the case was assigned to a detective. Initial identification usually took place at the scene of the crime or through routine follow-up procedures. Similarly, the Police Executive Research Forum found that a great majority of solved cases involved data gathered at the crime scene by patrol officers; detectives dropped 75 percent of cases after one day and spent an average of four hours on each case.[38]

Efforts have been made to revamp investigation procedures. One practice has been for patrol officers to be given greater responsibilities in conducting preliminary investigations at the scene of the crime. In addition, the precinct detective is being replaced by specialized units, such as homicide or burglary squads, which operate over larger areas and can bring specific expertise to bear on a particular case.

Another trend has been the development of regional squads of local, state, and federal officers (regional strike forces) who concentrate on major crimes, such as narcotics offenses and organized crime, and use their wider jurisdiction and expertise to provide services beyond the capability of a metropolitan police department. Another common operation is to focus efforts on the investigation and arrest of hard-core career criminals.[39]

Other Police Functions

Another important public-contact police task is traffic control. It involves such activities as directing traffic intersection control, traffic law enforcement, radar operations, parking law enforcement, and accident investigations.[40]

Traffic control is a complex daily task involving thousands, even millions, of motor vehicles within a single police jurisdiction. Consequently, police departments use **selective enforcement** in maintaining traffic laws. Police departments neither expect nor wish to punish all traffic violators. A department may set up traffic control units only at particular intersections, although its traffic coordinators know that many other areas of the city are experiencing violations. Personnel may be allocated to the traffic division based on prediction of accident or violation expectancy rates, determined by statistical analysis of previous patterns and incidents.

As the model of the typical police department in Figure 15.1 indicates, various other roles are carried out by police agencies. For example, most departments take responsibility for the administration and control of their departmental budgets. This task involves purchasing equipment and services, planning for future expenditures, and managing the department's resources.

Many departments maintain separate units that keep records on offenders. Modern data management systems have been used to provide easy access to records for case investigations. Similarly, most larger departments have sophisticated communications networks, which process citizen complaints and police calls for assistance and dispatch vehicles to respond to them as efficiently as possible.

To promote citizen cooperation, many police departments maintain specialized community relations officers. Community relations teams perform such tasks as working with citizen groups, lecturing high-school students on traffic safety, and creating neighborhood programs to prevent crime.

Some police agencies maintain (or have access to) forensic laboratories, which enable them to identify substances to be used as evidence, classify fingerprints, and augment investigations in other ways.

Another function often found in larger departments is planning and research. The planning and research division designs new programs to increase police efficiency and develops strategies to test programs' effectiveness. Police planners monitor recent technological developments and institute programs to adapt them to ongoing police services.

POLICE AND THE RULE OF LAW

Like other areas of criminal justice, police behavior is carefully controlled by court action. On the one hand, police want a free hand to enforce the law as they see fit. On the other hand, the courts must balance the needs of efficient law enforcement with the rights of citizens under the U.S. Constitution. Some important legal issues have emerged from this conflict, the most critical being citizen rights during a police interrogation and the right to be free from illegal searches and seizures by police officers.

Custodial Interrogation

The Fifth Amendment guarantees people the right to be free from self-incrimination. This has been interpreted as meaning that law enforcement agents cannot use physical or psychological coercion while interrogating suspects under their control, in order to get them to confess or give information.

The federal government has long held that a confession must be made voluntarily if it is to be admissible as evidence in a criminal trial. Confessions obtained from defendants through coercion, force, trickery, or promises of leniency are inadmissible because their trustworthiness is questionable. The rule of voluntariness applies to confessions obtained at any time, whether the defendant was in police custody or not. In the past, one of the major drawbacks to determining the voluntariness of confessions was that the decisions was made case by case, and was subjective in nature.

In 1966 the Supreme Court, in the case of *Miranda v. Arizona*, created objective standards for questioning by police after a defendant has been taken into custody.[41] Custody occurs when a person is not free to walk away, as when a person is arrested. The Court maintained that before the police can question a person who has been arrested or is in custody, they must inform the individual of the Fifth Amendment right to be free from self-incrimination. This is accomplished by the police issuing what is known as the **Miranda warning.** The warning informs the suspect that:

1. He or she has the right to remain silent.
2. If he or she makes a statement, it can be used against him or her in court.
3. He or she has the right to consult an attorney and to have the attorney present at the time of the interrogation.
4. If he or she cannot afford an attorney, one will be appointed by the state.

If the defendant is not given the Miranda warning prior to the investigation, the evidence obtained from the interrogation cannot be admitted at the trial. Finally, the accused can waive Miranda rights at any time and talk freely to police officers. However, in order for the waiver to be effective, the state must first show that the defendant was aware of all the Miranda rights and must then prove that the waiver was made with the full knowledge of constitutional rights.

The Miranda Rule Today.   Since its inception, the Supreme Court has used case law to define the boundaries of the Miranda warning. Important Supreme Court rulings on Miranda have created the following guidelines.

1. Evidence obtained in violation of the Miranda warning can be used by the government to impeach a defendant's testimony during trial.[42]
2. At trial, the testimony of a witness is permissible even if the witness's identity was revealed by the defendant in violation of the Miranda rule.[43]
3. It is permissible to renew questioning of a suspect who had previously invoked the Miranda right to remain silent if the warning is restated by police.
4. The Miranda warning applies only to attorneys and not to priests, probation officers, or any other officials.[44]
5. Information provided by a suspect in violation of their Fifth Amendment rights which leads to the seizure of incriminating evidence is permissible, if the evidence would have been obtained anyway by other means or sources. This is now referred to as the **inevitable discovery rule.**[45]

Attorney John J. Flynn (left) and Ernesto Miranda in 1967. Miranda's successful appeal against a rape-kidnap conviction prompted the Supreme Court to establish the ''Miranda warning,'' requiring that criminal suspects be told of their rights when taken into custody.

6. A suspect can be questioned in the field without a Miranda warning if the information the police seek is needed to protect public safety; for example, in an emergency the suspect can be asked where he or she hid a weapon.[46]

7. Initial errors by police in getting statements do not make subsequent statements inadmissible; a subsequent properly given Miranda warning can ''cure the condition'' that made the initial statements inadmissible.[47]

8. A suspect need not be aware of all the possible outcomes of waiving their rights in order for the Miranda warning to be deemed properly given.[48]

9. The admissions of a mentally impaired defendant can be admitted in evidence, as long as the police acted properly and there is a ''preponderance of the evidence'' that the defendant understood the meaning of Miranda.[49]

10. An attorney's request to see the defendant does not affect the validity of the defendant's waiver of the right to counsel; police misinformation to an attorney does not affect waiver of Miranda rights.[50]

In sum, though the Miranda warning controls police procedures in obtaining confessions, recent case law has narrowed its scope and given police greater leeway in their actions.[51]

Search and Seizure

A second critical area involving police procedures and the rule of law is the issue of Fourth Amendment rights and the exclusionary rule. As reviewed in Chapter 13, if police officers violate the privacy of a citizen when obtaining evidence, it is possible to have that evidence excluded form trial by a court order. Thus, even if a suspect is caught with damaging contraband, such as narcotics, a police error in obtaining the evidence can make the suspect immune from prosecution. It is not surprising that most police officers view the exclusionary rule as a serious infringement on their effectiveness. The following sections review the legal restraints placed on police investigations by the courts.

Search Warrant. As stated previously, the Fourth Amendment protects the individual against unreasonable searches and seizures. This means that, with some exceptions, police officers must have a **search warrant** issued by a magistrate in order to search a person and his or her possessions.

When the police try to obtain search warrants, they most often rely on the word of informers. For many years, the courts required that before the police could obtain a search warrant based on an informer's information they had to prove that (1) the informer was reliable and (2) the informer had firsthand knowledge of the crime (known as the **two-pronged test**). In a dramatic move, the court abandoned this standard in the case of *Illinois v. Gates.*[52] In that case, police received the following anonymous letter and used it to get a warrant to search the Gates home:

> *This letter is to inform you that you have a couple in your town who strictly make their living on selling drugs. They are Sue and Lance Gates, they live on Greenway, off Bloomingdale Rd. in the condominiums. Most of their buys are done in Florida. Sue his wife drives their car to Florida, where she leaves it to be loaded with drugs, then Lance flies down and drives it back. Sue flies back after she drops the car off in Florida. May 3 she is driving down there again and Lance will be flying down in a few days to drive it back. At the time Lance drives the car back he has the trunk loaded with over $100,000.00 in drugs. Presently they have over $100,000.00 worth of drugs in their basement.*
>
> *They brag about the fact that they never have to work, and make their entire living on pushers.*
>
> *I guarantee if you watch them carefully you will make a big catch. They are friends with some big drug dealers, who visit their house often:*
> *Lance & Susan Gates*
> *Greenway*
> *in condominiums*

Though the letter was anonymous and therefore the reliability of the informant could not be determined, the Court ruled that the evidence police obtained was admissible because the letter showed in-depth knowledge of the Gates's activities. The Court changed the standard of obtaining a warrant to what is known as the **totality of the circumstances** test. Loosely interpreted, if judges are presented with sufficient, knowledgeable evidence for issuing a warrant, they may do so even if the source of the information is unknown. The *Gates* doctrine makes it significantly easier for police to obtain legally valid search warrants.

Warrantless Search. Under certain circumstances, a valid search may be conducted by police officers without a search warrant. There are seven major exceptions to the search warrant rule.

1. *Search Incident to an Arrest*—A warrantless search is valid if it is made incident to a lawful arrest. The reason for this exception is that the arresting officer must have the power to disarm the accused, protect her or himself, preserve the evidence of the crime, and prevent the accused's escape from custody. Since the search is lawful, the officer retains what is found if it is connected with a crime. The officer is permitted to search only the defendant's person and the areas in the defendant's immediate physical surroundings that are under his or her control.[53]

2. *Threshold Inquiry (Stop and Frisk)*—Threshold inquiry deals with the situation in which, although the officer does not have probable cause to arrest, his or her suspicions are raised concerning the behavior of an individual. In such a case, the officer has a right to stop and question the individual; if the officer has reason to believe that the person is carrying a concealed weapon, he or she may frisk the suspect. Unlike searching, frisking is a limited procedure; it is a patdown of the outer clothing for the purpose of finding a concealed weapon. If no weapon is found, the search must stop. However, if an illegal weapon is found, then an arrest can be made and a search incident to the arrest can be performed.[54] In a threshold inquiry situation, a police officer is permitted to conduct a limited search—that is, one confined to determining whether a suspect is armed.

3. *Automobile Search*—An automobile may be searched without a warrant if there is probable

cause to believe that the car was involved in a crime.[55] The rationale for allowing a search of an automobile involves mobility—there is a significant chance that the evidence will be lost if the search is not conducted immediately—and the fact that people should not expect as much privacy in their cars as in their homes.[56] Police officers who have legitimately stopped an automobile and who have probable cause to believe that contraband is concealed somewhere within it may conduct a warrantless search of the vehicle that is as thorough as a magistrate could authorize by warrant.

4. *Consent Search*—In a consent search, individuals waive their constitutional rights; therefore, neither a warrant nor probable cause need exist. However, for the search to be effective, the consent must be given voluntarily; threat or compulsion invalidates the search.[57] Although it has been held that a voluntary consent is required, it also has been maintained that the police are under no obligation to inform individuals of their right to refuse the search.

5. *Plain View*—Even when an object is in a house or in other areas involving an expectation of privacy, the object can be freely inspected if it can be seen by the general public. For example, if a police officer looks through a fence and sees marijuana growing in the suspect's fields, then no search warrant is needed in order for the property to be seized. The articles are considered to be in plain view, and therefore a search warrant need not be obtained to seize them.[58]

6. *Seizure of Nonphysical Evidence*—Police can seize nonphysical evidence, such as a conversation, if the suspects had no reason to expect privacy; for example, police may overhear and record a conversation in which two people conspire to kill a third party. In *Katz v. United States*, the Supreme Court addressed the issue that the Fourth Amendment protects people and not property.[59] In *Katz*, the FBI attached an electronic listening and recording device to a public telephone booth for the purpose of obtaining evidence that the defendant was transmitting wagering information in violation of a federal statute. The Court held that such action constituted an unreasonable search and seizure. The Court maintained that a search occurs whenever police activity violates a person's privacy. In this case, it was reasonable for the defendant to expect that he would have privacy in a phone booth.

7. *Hot Pursuit*—Police officers pursuing a known felon may enter and search premises or structures without a warrant if they have cause to believe the fugitive has used them for refuge.

In recent years the Court has given police greater latitude to search and seize evidence. It has allowed extended on-the-spot detention of a suspect for preliminary questioning and investigation;[60] detention by mobile teams to take fingerprints from suspects on the street;[61] search of a mobile home without a warrant;[62] administrative searches in a public school with less than probable cause;[63] and a search of sealed packages in a car three days after the car was seized.[64] The Court's policy has reflected the legal orientation of its more conservative members. And, concomitantly, it has provided the police with the leeway to conduct their operations in a less restrictive environment. The exclusionary rule (Chapter 14), once a powerful control on police evidence gathering procedures, has been substantially weakened.

ISSUES IN POLICING

A number of important issues face police departments today. Though an all-encompassing discussion of each is beyond the scope of this text, a few of the more important aspects of policing are discussed below.

Police Personality and Subculture

It has become commonplace to argue that a majority of U.S. police officers maintain a unique set of personality traits that place them apart from the average citizen. The typical police personality is thought to include authoritanianism, suspicion, racism, hostility, insecurity, conservatism, and **cynicism**.[65] Maintenance of these negative values and attitudes is believed to cause police officers to be secretive and isolated from the rest of society, producing what has been described by William Westly as the **blue curtain** subculture.[66]

There are two opposing viewpoints on the cause

of this phenomenon: one position holds that police departments attract recruits who are by nature cynical, authoritarian, secretive, and so on; other experts maintain that socialization and experience on the police force cause these character traits to develop in police officers.[67] Since research evidence supportive of both viewpoints has been produced, neither position dominates the issue of how the police personality develops; it is not even certain that one actually exists.

Research studies have attempted to describe the development of the police personality. One of the most influential authorities in this area is social psychologist Milton Rokeach.[68] In comparing the values of police officers in Lansing, Michigan, with those of a national sample of private citizens, Rokeach and his associates found some significant differences: police officers seemed more oriented toward self-control and obedience than the average citizen; in addition, police were more interested in personal goals, such as "an exciting life," and less interested in social goals, such as "a world at peace." When comparing the values of veteran officers with those of recruits, Rokeach and his associates found evidence that police officers' on-the-job experience had not significantly influenced their personalities and that most police officers probably had had a unique value orientation and personality when they first embarked upon their careers in the police force.

Probably the best-known study of police personality is Arthur Niederhoffer's *Behind the Shield*.[69] Niederhoffer examined the assumption first popularized by William Westly that most police officers develop into cynics because of their daily duties.[70] Westly had maintained that police officers learn to mistrust the citizens they protect because they are constantly faced with keeping people in line; they come to believe that most people are out to break the law or to harm a police officer. Niederhoffer tested Westly's assumption by distributing a survey measuring attitudes and values of 220 New York City police officers. Among his most important findings were that cynicism did increase with length of service, that patrol officers with college educations became quite cynical if they were denied promotion, and that military-like police academy training caused new recruits to quickly become cynical about themselves, the department, and the community. For example, Niederhoffer found that nearly 80 percent of first-day recruits believed that the police department

was an "efficient, smoothly operating organization"; two months later, less than a third professed that belief. Similarly, half the new recruits believed that a police superior was "very interested in the welfare of his subordinates"; two months later, that number declined to 13 percent.[71]

It has been charged that the unique police personality causes most officers to band together in a police subculture characterized by clannishness, secrecy, and insulation from others in society. Police officers tend to socialize with each other and believe their occupation cuts them off from relationships with civilians. Joining the police subculture means having to support fellow officers against outsiders; to maintain a tough exterior personality; and to mistrust the motives and behavior of outsiders.[72] The most serious consequences of the police subculture are police officers' resistance to change and mistrust of the public they serve. Opening the police to change will be a prime task of police officials who seek professionalism and progress in their department.

Developing the Police Personality. The police personality seems to develop through the ongoing process of doing police work. At first, police recruits become socialized into their roles in the police academy. Their field training officer (FTO) teaches them the ins and outs of police work, helping them through the rites de passage of becoming a "real cop."[73] The folklore, tales, myths, and legends surrounding the department are communicated to recruits. Soon, they begin to understand the rules of police work. John Van Maanen suggests that "The adjustment of a newcomer in police departments is one which follows the line of least resistance."[74] By becoming similar in sentiments and behavior to their peers, recruits avoid censure by their department, their supervisor, and, most importantly, their colleagues. Thus, young officers adapt their personality to that of the "ideal cop."

George Kirkham, a professor who also served as a police officer, has described how the explosive and violent situations he faced as a police officer changed his own personality:

> As someone who had always regarded policemen as a "paranoid" lot, I discovered in the daily round of violence which became part of my life that chronic suspiciousness is something that a good cop cultivates in the interest of going home to his family each evening.[75]

Egon Bittner concludes that an esprit de corps develops in police work because of the dangerous and unpleasant tasks police officers are required to do. Police solidarity and a "one for all, and all for one" attitude are two of the most cherished aspects of the police occupation.[76]

While most experts agree that police develop an insulated subculture, there also is evidence showing that police roles and job views vary considerably within each department. Some officers are service-oriented while others take a much more active law enforcement role; while some are more concerned about their advancement through the ranks, others enjoy the action of the streets (see Close-Up on "Police Officer's Style"). Research indicates that even at the chief level there is variation in police personality and attitude; for example, one study found cynicism inversely related to prior education and size of the department administered.[78]

While there is disagreement over the exact nature and definition of police working personality, research by William Walsh has shown that police officers who define themselves as "active" are much more likely to make arrests than their peers who are looking merely to retire and who already hold outside jobs.[79] Consequently, understanding the nature and direction of the police personality and its effect on role definition and job performance is an essential task of police administrators and reformers.

Discretion

In one of the most important papers on a justice-related issue, Joseph Goldstein argued in 1960 that the law enforcement function of police is not merely a matter of enforcing the rule of law, but also involves an enormous amount of personal **discretion** as to whether to invoke the power of arrest.[80] Since then, police discretion has been recognized as a crucial force in all law enforcement decision making.

Richard Donnelly describes police discretion in these terms:

The policeman's lot is indeed a difficult one. He is charged with applying or enforcing a multitude of laws or ordinances in a degree or proportion and in a manner that maintains a delicate degree of social protection. His task requires a sensitive and wise discretion in deciding whether or not to invoke the criminal process. He must not only know whether certain behavior violates the law but also whether there is probable cause to believe that the law has been violated. He must enforce the law, yet he must determine whether a particular violation should be handled by warning or arrest . . . He is not expected to arrest every violator. Some laws were never intended by the enactors to be enforced, and others condemn behavior that is not contrary to significant moral values. If he arrested all violators, the courts would find it impossible to do their work, and he would be in court so frequently that he could not perform his other professional duties. Consequently, the policeman must judge and informally settle more cases than he takes to court.[81]

Thus, police discretion involves the selective enforcement of the law by duly authorized police agents. However, unlike members of almost every other criminal justice agency, police officers are neither regulated in their daily procedures by administrative scrutiny nor subjected to judicial review (except when their behavior clearly violates an offender's constitutional rights). As a result, the exercise of discretion may sometimes deteriorate into discrimination, violence, and other abusive practices on the part of police.[82]

Various factors have been associated with the exercise of police discretion. Some relate to the officers' working environment, the size of the department, and the officers' view of their professional worth.[83] Community attitudes and beliefs certainly influence the enforcement or nonenforcement of certain laws (for example, obscenity statutes), as do policies, practices, and customs of the local police department. An individual supervisor, such as a sergeant or lieutenant, can influence subordinates' decisions by making well known his or her personal preferences and attitudes.

Peer pressure from fellow officers also influences decision-making. Fellow police officers dictate acceptable responses to street-level problems by displaying or withholding approval in office discussions. The officer who takes the job seriously and desires the respect and friendship of others will take their advice, abide by their norms, and seek out the most experienced and most influential patrol officers on the force to follow their behavior models.

A final environmental factor affecting the police officer's performance is his or her perception of community alternatives to police intervention or processing. A police officer may exercise discretion and arrest

CLOSE-UP

Police Officers' Style

One important factor influencing police officers' use of discretion is their personal style, or approach to police work. Numerous attempts have been made in recent years to identify typologies of police behavior and describe "ideal cop" types. In a recent paper, Ellen Hochstedler has tried to synthesize these various attempts into four distinct types that describe the bulk of working police officers. According to Hochstedler, the following types of police merge from the literature.

Supercop

Supercops take their role as law enforcers quite seriously. They do not refrain from using force when they have to and sometimes use it too quickly and excessively. Their view of the police task tends to be narrow, emphasizing fighting "real crimes," such as rape and robbery, and ignoring service functions. They view themselves as part of the "thin blue line" that protects society from the forces of evil. In using discretion, the supercop probably ignores minor law violations and domestic squabbles, considering them not police business. Supercops are interested only in arresting serious street criminals.

Professional

Professionals have a broad, inclusive definition of their task and a balanced perception of their professional identity. They are not crusaders on a mission but skilled workers performing a difficult and complex task. They are the officers best able to separate the individual from the job and to avoid feeling personally harmed when the police role is attacked. These police officers are able to see both sides of many issues and can therefore think coolly and rationally in many situations. Their use of discretion is professional, reasoned, and competent.

Service Oriented

Service-oriented officers are not interested in crime fighting but are totally committed to helping people. They rely heavily on persuasion and talk. Their approach is that of a change agent and their stance is that of a social worker. They regard their clients with respect and hope to have a positive effect on anyone they come into contact with. Service-oriented officers are dedicated to their jobs but also experience some frustration because they want to effect lasting change but are unable to do so. These officers try to use the treatment resources of the community rather than their arrest powers, if at all possible.

Avoider

The avoider is characterized as a shirker. These officers do as little as possible, either by design or because they are inept or inefficient. They are not necessarily lazy but may be confused, frightened, or burned out. The avoider probably takes as little action as possible in any situation.

In a research study using officers in the Dallas Police Department, Hochstedler tried to empirically test the existence of these ideal types. Her results proved inconclusive. Though further research is necessary, the existence of ideal types of police officers who share similar attitudes and operating styles, and who use their discretion accordingly, may be more a matter of police folklore than a true picture of reality. Hochstedler's views challenge the traditional beliefs of many well-known police authorities.

Discussion Questions

1. Do you think that supercops, who abound in TV programs and movies, really exist?
2. Can you create typologies for other professions—for example, college professors?

SOURCES: Ellen Hochstedler, "Testing Types, a Review and Test of Police Types," *Journal of Criminal Justice* 9 (1981):451–66. For more information on police types, see J. Broderick, *Police in a Time of Change* (Morristown, N.J.: General Leasing Press, 1977); M. Brown, *Working the Street* (New York: Russel Sage Foundation, 1981); W. Muir, *Police: Streetcorner Politicians* (Chicago: University of Chicago Press, 1977); M. O'Neill, "The Role of the Police—Normative Role Expectations in a Metropolitan Police Department (Ph.D. diss., State University of New York at Albany, 1974); J. Q. Wilson, *Varieties of Police Behavior* (Cambridge, Mass.: Harvard University Press, 1968).

an individual in a particular circumstance if it seems that nothing else can be done, even if the officer does not believe that an arrest is the best possible example of good police work. In an environment in which a proliferation of social agencies exist—detoxification units, drug control centers, and child-care services, for example—a police officer obviously has more alternatives from which to choose in the decision-making process. In fact, referring cases to these alternative agencies saves the officer both time and effort—no records need be made out and court appearances can be avoided. Thus, social agencies provide for greater latitude in police decision-making.

Another discretionary influence is the way that a crime or situation is encountered. If, for example, a police officer stumbles on an altercation or a break-in, the discretionary response may be quite different than if the officer had been summoned by police radio. If official police recognition has been given to an act, action must be taken or an explanation must be made as to why it was not taken. If a matter is brought to an officer's attention by a citizen observer, the officer can ignore the request and risk a complaint, or take discretionary action. When an officer chooses to become involved in a situation without benefit of a summons or complaint, maximum discretion can be used. Even in this circumstance, however, the presence of a crowd or of witnesses may contribute to the officer's decision. Finally, of course, the officer who acts alone is affected by personal matters—physical condition, mental state, and whether there are other duties to perform.

The race, age, and sex of the offender also may be considered when police officers decide to invoke their arrest powers. This issue is open to some debate, but empirical studies indicate that police discretion works against the young, the poor, and members of minority groups; discretion may favor the wealthy, the politically well connected, and members of the majority group.[84] (This issue is discussed in greater detail below.)

Numerous efforts have been made to limit police discretion. The courts have placed controls on what police can do during investigations and interrogations. Police administrators have attempted to establish guidelines for police officers' operating behavior.[85] Some have established special units to oversee patrol activities; others have created boundaries of police efficiency and suggested that any be-

havior in excess of these limits would not be tolerated in the department.[86] However, despite some success, limiting police discretion has proven to be a difficult task. It has proven harder to control police officers' behavior when they refuse to take action than when they invoke their police powers.

With but a few exceptions, no clear answer to the management of police discretion exists.[87] Advocates of specialized units, policy statements, legal mandates, and other approaches can only assume that the officer in the field will comply with the intent and spirit of the administrator's desires. Little information is currently available concerning what the specific influence of any particular legal or administrative measure on police discretion will be, whether it will affect all officers equally, or why some officers will respond in one way and others in an other way. It is not known what police officers are really like, how they differ from or resemble one another, or how they react to pressures from above.

Do Social Factors Influence Discretion?   One important issue in the study of police discretion is whether police discriminate on the basis of sex, race, ethnic origin, or class. Early studies indicated that police discretion worked against the poor, minorities, and women.[88] However, efforts to improve police sensitivity to minority rights may have helped reduce racial and sex discrimination. For example, Marvin Krohn and his associates examined almost 20,000 cases in a north-central American city in order to identify whether sex bias exists in the disposition of police contacts.[89] Though sex bias existed during the entire period of their examination, they also discovered that a consistent pattern of diminishing differences occurred over time. And even during the years of greatest disparity, the disposition of males and females were closer than the authors expected. They concluded that sex bias was a long-term problem but not one of great magnitude. In another study of police arrest decision-making, Douglas Smith and Jodie Klein also failed to discover racial bias in the police use of discretion, though they did find that sex and socioeconomic variables were taken into account when police made decisions: police tended to disregard nonviolent disputes involving female complainants in lower-class neighborhoods.[90]

Similarly, Richard Hollinger studied the use of police discretion in arresting drunk drivers in

Georgia.[91] He found that police "bias" was a function of the socioeconomic status of the culprit and not of racial background. If blacks were overrepresented in the arrested group, it was because of their overrepresentation in the lower economic classes.

One possible area of police arrest discrimination overlooked by most research is the influence of the victim of crime on the arrest decision. (Most studies focus on the offender.) In one study, Douglas Smith and his associates uncovered little evidence of racial bias in police decision-making.[92] However, police are more likely to take action if whites rather than blacks were the victims of crime. Thus, the sexual and racial background of the victims of crime may be a more important determinant of arrest decision-making than the race and sex of the suspect.

While there is little conclusive evidence of widespread personal bias in police decision-making, organizational behavior may play an important role in the way police deal with different groups in society. Police departments may routinely patrol particular areas of the city while leaving others relatively unattended. Consequently, residents in certain areas have a greater chance of experiencing detection and arrest. Though racial bias in arrest decisions violates constitutional rights, courts have upheld the use of race as a personal identifying factor that helps narrow police searches for suspect. Police manuals also suggest that officers be aware of race when on the lookout for suspicious characters (for example, questioning those who do not "belong" on their beat). Similarly, courts have upheld the government's use of race as a condition of determining probable case in searches for illegal aliens and in drug courier profiles.[93]

In sum, research indicates that the effect of offenders' class, race, and sexual characteristics may be diminishing in magnitude, but it continues to influence police discretion.

Higher Education and Police Effectiveness

In recent years, police departments have stressed the advantages of college education for their recruits. Though the great majority of U.S. police departments still do not require a college degree of recruits, many give credit for education when considering candidates for promotion or special assignments.

There has been some debate over the value of a college education for police officers. Some people suggest that a college education can do little to help the average police officer perform daily activities.[94] The diversity of the police role, the need for split-second decision-making, and the often boring and mundane tasks police officers are required to do are all considered reasons why formal education for police officers may be a waste of time.[95] Moreover, as Solomon Gross has argued, a college education may simply frustrate officers who must perform many routine jobs. Consequently, there may be a higher dropout rate among college-trained officers.[96]

However, a growing body of literature suggests that education benefits the officer's performance and job satisfaction. Studies conducted by R. P. Witte, Wayne Cascio, Merlyn Moore, James Finnegen, B. E. Sanderson, and others have found that higher education correlates favorably with such factors as training academy performance, citizens' attitudes toward police, low absentee rates, and promotion.[97]

Another important question involves what type of education police officers should receive. One approach favors hands-on training programs; another suggests an academically oriented general liberal arts or criminal justice approach. This important issue has been addressed in a report by the National Advisory Commission on Higher Education for Police Officers (commonly called the **Sherman Report**).[98] The Sherman Report examined the findings of a national study of existing college curriculums and educational delivery systems for police education in the United States. Generally critical of existing police education techniques, the Sherman Report recommended that several basic changes be made. It called for a halt to programs with narrow curriculums and unqualified faculty. The report was especially critical of police educational programs with limited, academic orientations. The Sherman Report instead advocated a limit to the number of criminal justice courses that could be allowed in any in-service or preservice student program. It also called for discontinuing the practice of granting academic credit for in-service training programs, such as those conducted by various state police academies. Finally, the report stressed that courses and course material should emphasize ethical considerations and moral values in law enforcement, not the "nuts and bolts" of police procedures.

Despite the controversy surrounding higher education for police, it is evident that today's officer

Two female police officers arrest a suspect for possession of rock cocaine during a 1988 task force crackdown on the ''Wet Town'' gang in Los Angeles.

realizes that the road to advancement in the police field necessitates receiving proper academic credentials. Higher education for police officers is here to stay.[99]

Women and Minority Police Officers

For the past decade, U.S. police departments have made a concerted effort to attract women and minority police officers. The latter group includes blacks, Orientals, Hispanics, Native Americans, and members of other racial minorities. The reasons for recruiting minority and female officers are varied. Viewed in its most positive light, such recruitment reflects police departments' desire to field a more balanced force that truly represents the community it serves. A heterogeneous police force can be instrumental in gaining the public's confidence by helping to dispel the view that police departments are generally bigoted or biased organizations. Furthermore, women and minority police officers possess special qualities that can improve police performance.

Another important reason for recruiting women and minority police officers is the need to comply with various federal guidelines on hiring.[100] A series of legal actions brought by minority representatives have resulted in local, state, and federal courts' ordering police departments to either create hiring quotas to increase minority representation or rewrite entrance exams and requirements to encourage the employment of women and minorities. In one of the most important recent cases, *U.S. v. Paradise*, the U.S. Supreme Court upheld the use of racial quotas as a measure to counter the effects of past discrimination. The decision upheld a lower court ruling which ordered the Alabama Department of Public Safety to promote one black trooper for every white candidate elevated in rank as long as qualified black candidates were available, until 25 percent of each rank was filled by minorities; this would represent the actual racial makeup of the labor market.[101] Several lawsuits have resulted in either court-ordered hiring judgments or voluntary compliance. Consequently, the numbers of women and minorities in police departments have increased dramatically.

Ellen Hochstedler and her associates studied recruitment of women and minorities in 20 large U.S. police departments.[102] They found impressive increases in representation between 1967 and 1981, the mean being a 330 percent increase in the number of minority and female officers hired during this period. However, women only made up about 6 percent of the officers in the sample, and consequently progress in recruiting females was judged inadequate.

Even if legally possible, many jurisdictions would probably not wish to end quota hiring, which is viewed as a means of protecting the interests of women and minority group members, and consequently of maintaining the support of the minority community for police. Even without federal government pressure, there should be an increasing number of female officers on the nation's police forces in the years to come.

Black Police Officers.   Blacks have served on police forces since the mid-nineteenth century. A Republican mayor appointed the first black police officer in Chicago in 1872; by 1894, there were 23 black officers serving in that city.[103] Nonetheless, even today, blacks are underrepresented on the police forces of the nation's larger cities; as mentioned previously, legal and social pressure has been mounted to increase their numbers. The reduction in local operating funds experienced in recent years has not helped alleviate this problem.

The life of the black officer can be difficult. As Nicholas Alex points out, black police officers suffer "double marginality."[104] On the one hand, the black officers must deal with the expectation that they will give members of their own race a break. On the other hand, black officers often experience overt racism from police colleagues.

Alex found that black officers' treatment of other blacks ranges from denying that blacks should be treated differently from whites to treating black offenders more harshly than white offenders to prove lack of bias. Alex offers various reasons why some black police officers are tougher on black offenders: they desire acceptance from their white colleagues; they are particularly sensitive to any disrespect given them by black teenagers; they view themselves as the protectors of the black community.[105]

The problems of black officers also can be exacerbated by the cool reception they are given by their white colleagues, who see them as potential competitors for promotions and special assignments. As James Jacobs and Jay Cohen point out, white police officers view affirmative action hiring and promotion

program as a threat to their job security.[106] They note that in Chicago, white officers intervened on the side of the city when a black police officers' organization filed suit to change criteria for promotion.[107]

As a greater number of minorities join U.S. police forces, it is likely that they will experience the same problems encountered by white officers. For example, fifteen years after the Alex research Stephen Leinen interviewed black police officers in New York City and found that their attitudes toward policing were similar to those of white police officers.[108] They were dissatisfied that people in the black community still expressed mistrust and contempt for police, even though an increasing number of black officers had been assigned to these areas. They believed that black cops would be better able to deal with problems in minority communities than whites. Nonetheless, their job perception seemed to mirror the cynicism and apathy that have plagued white police officers.

Female Police Officers.   The first female police officers were appointed in New York as early as 1845; but they were designated as "matrons," and their duties were restricted to handling females in jail custody.[109] In 1893, Chicago hired women police but again restricted their activities to making court visitations and assisting male detectives with cases involving women and children. However, it was not until the passage of the final version of Title VII of the Civil Rights Act in 1972 that police departments around the nation began to hire females and assign them to regular patrol duties.

In general, evaluations of female officers show them to be equal or superior to male officers in some areas of police work. In the most highly regarded study, Catherine Milton found that female officers in Washington, D.C., responded to similar types of calls as their male colleagues and that the arrests they made were as likely to result in conviction.[110] Women were more likely to receive support from the community and less likely to be charged with police misconduct. On the negative side, women made fewer felony and misdemeanor arrests and received lower supervisory ratings than male officers. The generally favorable results obtained by Milton have also been found in other studies assessing women's police performance.[111]

Despite their relative proficiency, female police officers have not received general support form their colleagues or the public. One study found that male officers perceive the public to be less cooperative toward them if females are on patrol and report that they receive more insults and threats when patrolling with female partners.[112] Consequently, surveys have shown a relatively low acceptance rate for females in police functions, especially those involving hazardous duties.[113] Some jurisdictions still assign women officers to secretarial and clerical posts; and in some cities, when budget cutbacks require layoffs, women officers are released in disproportionate numbers.[114]

In a study of women entering police training in Florida, Sally Gross found that though subjects had a high degree of self-confidence and idealism on entry, their self-perceptions diminished significantly after eight weeks of academy life.[115] Sex-role conflicts produced disillusionment with police work, accompanied by denial, self-doubt, repressed anger, and confusion.

The Police and Violence

Police officers are empowered to use force and violence in pursuit of their daily task. Some scholars argued that this is the core of the police role:

> The role of the police is best understood as a mechanism for the distribution of non-negotiably coercive force employed in accordance with the dictates of an intuitive group of situational exigencies.[116]

Police violence first became a major topic for discussion in the 1940s, when rioting provoked serious police backlash. Thurgood Marshall, then of the NAACP, referred to the Detroit police as a "gestapo" after a 1943 race riot left 34 people dead.[117] Twenty-five years later, excessive police force was again an issue when television cameras captured police violence against protestors at the 1968 Democratic National Convention in Chicago.

However, general day-to-day police brutality against individual citizens seems to be diminishing. In 1967, a presidentially-appointed task force concluded:

> The Commission [on Law Enforcement and the Administration of Justice] believes that physical abuse is not as serious a problem as it was in the past. The few statistics which do exist suggest small numbers of cases involving excessive use of force. Although the relatively small number of reported complaints cannot be considered an

accurate measurement of the total problem, most persons, including civil rights leaders, believe that verbal abuse and harassment, not excessive use of force, is the major police-community relations problem today.[118]

Similarly, a study by Albert Reiss found that police abuse was verbal and coercive rather than physically violent. Reiss found little difference in the way police treated blacks and whites; when force was used, it was used more selectively, against those who showed disrespect or disregard for police authority once they had been arrested.[119] Thus, while not perfect, police officers do seem to have improved their relationships with citizens of all races.

A more recent area of concern has been the use of deadly force in apprehending fleeing or violent offenders. As commonly used, **deadly force** refers to the actions of a police officer who shoots and kills a suspect who is either fleeing from arrest, assaulting a victim, or attacking the police officer.

The justification for the use of deadly force can be traced to English common law, in which almost every criminal offense merited a felony status and subsequent death penalty. Thus, execution effected during the arrest of a felon was considered expedient, saving the state from the burden of trial.[120]

Research studies indicate that the following factors have been related to police use of force:[121]

- *Exposure to threat and stress*—Areas with an unusually high incidence of violent crime are likely to experience shootings by police
- *Police workload*—Violence corresponds with the number of police officers on the street, the number of calls for service, the number and nature of police dispatches, and the number of arrests made in a given jurisdiction
- *Firearm availability*—Cities that experience a large number of crimes committed with firearms are also likely to have high police violence rates; Houston, which ranks first in firearms availability, had 21.5 police shootings per 1,000 arrests for violent crimes, while San Francisco, which ranks tenth, hand only 1.5 shootings per 1,000 such arrests
- *Population type and density*—Jurisdictions swollen by large numbers and varied types of transients and nonresidents also experience a disproportionate amount of police shootings; research findings sug-

gest that many individuals shot by police are non-residents caught at or near the scenes of robberies or burglaries of commercial establishments

- *Racial variations*—It is alleged that blacks and other racial minorities are killed at a significantly higher rate than whites. Catherine Milton and her associates found that 70 percent of those shot by police in the seven cities they studied were black (blacks made up 39 percent of the population of the cities). In a similar study, Betty Jenkins and Adrienne Faison found that 52 percent of those killed by police in a three year period were black, and 21 percent, Hispanic. It is common to focus on the racial factor as the primary predictive factor in police violence.[122]

Despite the evidence indicating that police shootings are motivated by racial bias, research conducted by James Fyfe reveals some contradictory results. In a study of New York City shootings occurring over a five-year period (1971 to 1975), Fyfe found that police officers were most likely to shoot suspects when they attacked police officers, that many shootings stemmed from incidents in which police officers themselves were injured or killed, and that minorities were more likely to be involved in weapon assaults on police officers than whites (37 percent of events involving white citizens were gun incidents, while the rates for blacks and Hispanics were 58 and 56 percent).[123]

Fyfe's data revealed that minority police officers in New York were responsible for a disproportionate number of police shootings. Fyfe found that minority officers were often assigned to inner-city ghetto areas in which violence against police was common; it is therefore not surprising that minority officers' use of violence was relatively more frequent. However, in a subsequent analysis of police shootings in the city of Memphis, Tennessee, Fyfe found that police were more likely to shoot black citizens than white and that "police there did differentiate racially with their trigger fingers, by shooting blacks in circumstances less threatening than those in which they shot whites."[124] Thus, the charge that police "have one trigger finger for whites and another for blacks" may have more validity in some areas than in others.

Not all research suggests that personal factors account for police shooting. Some points to the nature of the criminal interaction itself. Peter Scharf and Arnold Binder found that police shootings are influenced by the nature of the opponent the officer faced; whether they were on duty or off duty; the number of officers present; and the nature of the physical environment.[125] Rather than being purely spontaneous, Binder and Scharf found that shootings actually can be described as following a five-step model involving anticipation, confrontation, dialogue, shooting, and aftermath stages. Their research led them to suggest that police departments develop policies stressing containment of armed offenders while specially trained backup teams are sent to take charge of the situation. Similarly, training might emphasize the choices available in situations involving violence and conflict.

Controlling Deadly Force. In 1985, the Supreme Court moved to restrict police use of deadly force when, in *Tennessee v. Garner*, it banned the shooting of unarmed or nondangerous fleeing felons.[126] The Court based it s decision on the premise that shooting an unarmed nondangerous suspect was an illegal seizure of his or her body under the Fourth Amendment. According to the ruling, police could not justifiably use force unless it was "necessary to prevent the escape, and the officer has probable cause to believe that the suspect poses a significant threat of death or serious physical injury to the officers or others"; for example, if the suspect threatens the officer or the officer has probable cause to believe that he has committed a crime involving serious physical harm. Before *Garner*, the policy of shooting unarmed fleeing felons was still in use in 17 states.

Another method of controlling police shootings is through internal review and policymaking by police departments themselves. For example, in New York City, the police department established a new firearms policy based on the American Law Institute's Model Penal Code. The new policy stated:

a. *In all cases, only the minimum amount of force will be used which is consistent with the accomplishment of a mission. Every other reasonable means will be utilized for arresting, preventing or terminating a felony or for the defense of oneself or another before a police officer resorts to the use of his firearms.*

b. *A firearm shall not be discharged under circumstances where lives of innocent persons may be endangered.*

c. *The firing of a warning shot is prohibited.*

d. *The discharging of a firearm to summon assistance is prohibited, except where the police officer's safety is endangered.*

e. *Discharging a firearm at or from a moving vehicle is prohibited unless the occupants of the other vehicle are using deadly force against the officer or another, by means other than the vehicle.*[127]

The New York Police department also created the Firearm Discharge Review Board to evaluate shooting incidents. In an examination of the effects of this policy, James Fyfe found that a considerable reduction in the frequency of police shootings followed the policy change.[128]

Change in law and policy may not always work in changing police behavior. William Waegel studied police shootings in Philadelphia before (1970 to 1972) and after (1974 to 1978) the "fleeing felon" rule was voluntarily abandoned. He found that after the state had restricted the police use of deadly force, about 20 percent of all shootings violated the new shooting code. In the five-year period after the rule change, police continued to violate shooting rules, and few officers were punished for their transgressions. Waegel found that shooting restrictions clash with the informal rules of the police culture. Unless police departments actively counteract informal pro-violence attitudes, changes in law and police may be ineffective.[129]

While the police use of force continues to be an important issue, there is little question that control measures seem to be working. Lawrence Sherman found that the number of civilians killed by police had dropped from a high of 353 in 1971 to 172 in 1984.[130] Similarly, the number of law enforcement officers killed on duty also has declined, from 104 in 1980 to 72 in 1987 (including 42 city police).[131]

IMPROVING POLICE EFFECTIVENESS

What can police agencies do to become more effective crime fighters and peacekeepers? Over the past 25 years, a number of approaches have been tried and the results have been mixed.

One approach has been to increase the number of sworn officers, on the theory that more police will provide greater public protection and deter crime. Research has not shown this to be the case. In one study, David Greenberg and his associates examined the relationship between police employment levels and crime in over 500 jurisdictions.[132] They concluded that although cities responded to violent crime rate increases by hiring more police, there is little evidence that police employment levels are related to crime rate reductions. Similarly, Craig Uchida and Robert Goldberg found in a study of 88 American cities that jurisdictions with the highest crime rates were also ones which spent the most on police services; between 1960 and 1980, cities with the highest crime rates tripled their expenditures on police services.[133]

Another approach has been to improve police response time through improved communications (911 systems). This approach has potential only if it encourages citizens to report crime frequently and promptly. Research shows that there is significant relationship between the time it takes to report a crime and the probability of making an arrest. The Police Executive Research Forum (PERF) found that if a crime is reported while in progress there is a 33 percent chance of making an arrest; the arrest probability declines to 10 percent if the crime is reported one minute later and to about 5 percent if 15 minutes have elapsed.[134]

While the Kansas City study cast doubt on the ability of police presence to deter potential law violators, there is a growing body of evidence that when police take aggressive formal action they may be able to prevent future crime, regardless of the action taken by the courts or correctional systems. In one important study, Larry Sherman and Richard Berk evaluated the effect of arrests on domestic dispute cases in Minneapolis. They found that the more formal the response of police (arrest versus warning), the less likely the perpetrators were to repeat their actions. The deterrent effect of arrest was present regardless of what later happened to the offender in court.[135]

Similarly, using data from drunken driving arrests in Sweden from 1976 to 1979, Perry Shapiro and Harold Votey found that an arrest experience reduces the probability that a person will drive while drunk.[136] An arrest increases a person's perceived probability of being rearrested and also the perceptions of the unpleasantness of arrest, which lead to a reduced chance of drunk driving. Shapiro and Votey also found that violators could be classified into two groups: easily

CLOSE-UP

Self-Help

Concern about crime has prompted many Americans to play a more active role in law enforcement in order to supplement or aid local police departments. One method is simply to arm themselves and train to resist attacks. Robert Young, David McDowall, and Colin Loftin found that using firearms for protection was often a function of loss of confidence in police and the courts.

While an armed citizenry may not be the only means to supplement the police, there are some indications that it can be effective. David Bordua and Gary Kleck found that a well-publicized program which gave firearms training to 6,000 women in Orlando, Florida, corresponded to a dramatic decline in the local rape rate, as well as reductions in other crime patterns such as burglary. However, Gary Green has reevaluated the Orlando experience and, among other criticisms, finds that gun ownership for self-protection may not deter crime but displace it to unarmed victims. That is, arming citizens causes criminals to seek out unarmed targets to prey upon. In addition Green finds that firearm ownership brings with it many other social problems, including accidental deaths and the use of stolen guns in other crimes. According to Green, the use of violent self-protection methods may have some benefits which are counter-balanced by their drawbacks.

Another approach to self-help has been the **Crime Stoppers** programs, in which actors recreate recent crimes on local TV stations and ask viewers to call in if they have any information. It is common to offer an monetary award put up by corporate or civic sponsors. A national evaluation of Crime Stoppers found it to be a reasonably effective addition to police investigations, helping to solve almost 100,000 felonies and recover more than $500 million in property and contraband.

Other methods of self-help include citizen patrol, neighborhood watch, and similar programs. Some are organized as auxiliaries of local police agencies, while others act as independent forces. The most famous of the latter type is the **Guardian Angels,** the red-bereted band of youthful peacekeepers, founded in 1979 by Curtis Sliwa, who patrol streets in more than 50 American cities. A national assessment of the Angels' activity in more than 20 American cities found that they do become involved in crime-related incidents and that, at least in some areas, their patrols may reduce the rate of property crimes; they seem to have less an impact on violent crime. In addition, the Angels do assist citizens in need and have helped police during crime incidents. The Angels' greatest benefit appears to be in fear reduction. Most citizens report feeling safer if the Guardian Angels are on patrol. And though private citizens held higher opinions about the Angels than did the local police, most police administrators and city government representatives agreed that the patrols are beneficial and should be continued in their jurisdiction.

These are but a few of the many ways private citizens have aided professional law enforcement agents. It is likely that these efforts will continue to flourish in the near future.

Discussion Questions

1. Should handguns be more easily obtainable for self-protection?

2. Should a victim be punished for shooting an unarmed criminal?

3. Should groups like the Guardian Angels be encouraged?

SOURCES: Robert Young, David McDowall, and Colin Loftin, "Collective Security and Ownership of Firearms for Protection," *Criminology* 25 (1987):47–62; Gary Kleck and David Bordua, "The Factual Foundation for Certain Key Assumptions of Gun Control," *Law and Policy Quarterly* 5 (1983):271–98; Gary Green, "Citizen Gun Ownership and Criminal Deterrence: Theory, Research and Policy," *Criminology* 25 (1987):63–81; Susan Pennell, Christine Curtis, Joel Henderson, *Guardian Angels: An Assessment of Citizen Response to Crime* (Washington, D.C.: U.S. Department of Justice, 1986); Dennis Rosenbaum, Arthur Lurigio, and Paul Lavrakas, *Crime Stoppers—A National Evaluation* (Washington, D.C.: National Institute of Justice, 1986).

deterrable offenders and those immune to the deterrent effect of an arrest. The authors say that the former group is capable of learning from its mistakes, while the latter "persists in ignoring the law and the extent of penalties." These studies seem to suggest that although police patrol cannot reduce crime per se, aggressive formal actions by police can certainly have an effect on reducing repeat offenses.

There have been many other efforts to improve police performance through such devices as training, education, and technological advances. However, the greatest effort today seems to be in involving the public in law enforcement, either by conducting educational programs in the school and community, involving citizens in Crime Stoppers, citizen watch and patrol programs, or by bringing police into closer contact with the neighborhood through foot patrol or other such programs. (see Close-Up entitled "Self-Help".)

SUMMARY

Police officers are the gatekeepers of the criminal justice process. They use their power to arrest to initiate the justice process.

U.S. police agencies are modeled after their British counterparts. Early in British history, law enforcement was a personal matter. Later, constables were appointed to keep peace among groups of a hundred families. From this rudimentary beginning came the seed of today's police departments. In 1838, the first true U.S. police department was developed in Boston.

The first U.S. departments were created because of the need to control mob violence, which was common during the nineteenth century. The police were viewed as being dominated by political bosses who controlled their hiring practices and polices.

Reform movements begun during the 1920s culminated in the concept of professionalism in the 1950s and 1960s. Police professionalism was interpreted to mean tough, rule-oriented police work featuring advanced technology and hardware. However, the view that these measures would quickly reduce crime proved incorrect.

There are several major law enforcement agencies. On the federal level, the FBI is the premier law enforcement organization. Other agencies include the Drug Enforcement Administration, the U.S. marshals, and the Secret Service. County-level law enforcement is provided by sheriff's departments, and most states maintain state police agencies. However, the great bulk of law enforcement activities are carried out by local police agencies.

The police role is multilevel. Police officers fight crime, keep the peace, and provide community services. The conflicts and burdens involved in their work insulate them from the community and create great stress. Police officers suffer from high alcoholism, divorce, and suicide rates.

In carrying out their roles, police departments provide various services. The patrol function is designed to deter crime, keep the peace, and provide services. There is some question whether police patrol is actually effective. One important study conducted in Kansas City found that the extent of patrol had little effect on the crime rate or on citizens' satisfaction. Police departments have responded by creating innovative patrol mechanisms such as computer-dictated beats, hidden cameras, and team policing.

The second prominent police role is investigation. Detectives collect evidence in order to identify perpetrators. Although detectives use various techniques, including the successful sting operations, studies have shown that detective work is generally ineffective.

Other police functions include traffic control, departmental administration and maintenance, and improvement of relations between police and community.

In recent years, many police operations have been controlled by court decisions. Most importantly, the courts have set limits on the extent of police interrogations and search and seizure of evidence.

Police departments face crucial issues today. One involves understanding the police personality and its effect on performance. Another involves police officers' use of discretion and how it can be controlled. Debate also continues over whether police officers should receive a higher education and what that education should include. Women and minority officers probably will become more prevalent on police departments, and their worth must be more fully appreciated by rank-and-file patrols. Police violence has received much attention. There is some debate whether police officers kill members of minorities more frequently than white citizens. Recent evidence indicates that may be the case in some cities.

KEY TERMS

gatekeepers	team policing
pledge system	foot patrols
constable	detective
shire reeve	sting
watch system	selective enforcement

justice of the peace
Sir Robert Peel
Wickersham Commission
August Vollmer
sheriff
problem-oriented policing
patrol
walking the beat
aggressive preventive
  patrol
internal affairs division
Kansas City Study

Miranda warning
inevitable discovery rule
search warrant
two-pronged test
totality of the circumstances
cynicism
blue curtain
discretion
Sherman Report
deadly force
Crime Stoppers
Guardian Angels

―――――――――― NOTES ――――――――――

1. This section relies heavily on Daniel Devlin, *Police Procedure, Administration and Organization* (London: Butterworth, 1966); Robert Fogelson, *Big City Police* (Cambridge, Mass.: Harvard University Press, 1977); Roger Lane, *Policing the City, Boston 1822–1855* (Cambridge, Mass.: Harvard University Press, 1967); Roger Lane, "Urban Police and Crime in Nineteenth Century America," in N. Morris and M. Torrey, eds., *Crime and Justice*, vol. 2, (Chicago: University of Chicago Press, 1980), pp. 1–45; J. J. Tobias, *Crime and Industrial Society in the Nineteenth Century* (New York: Schoken Books, 1967); Samuel Walker, *A Critical History of Police Reform: The Emergence of Professionalism* (Lexington, Mass.: Lexington Books, 1977); Samuel Walker, *Popular Justice* (New York: Oxford University Press, 1980); President's Commission on Law Enforcement and the Administration of Justice, *Task Force Report: The Police* (Washington, D.C.: U.S. Government Printing Office, 1967), pp. 1–9.
2. Devlin, *Police Procedure, Administration and Organization*, p. 3.
3. Walker, *Popular Justice*, p. 18.
4. Lane, "Urban Police and Crime in Nineteenth Century America," p. 5.
5. Walker, *Popular Justice*, p. 61.
6. National Commission on Law Observance and Enforcement, *Report on the Police* (Washington, D.C.: U.S. Government Printing Office, 1931), pp. 5–7.
7. Preston William Slossom, *A History of American Life*, 12 vols., ed. 35; Arthur M. Schlesinger and Dixon Ryan Fox, vol. 12, *The Great Crusade and After, 1914–1929* (New York: Macmillan, 1931), p. 102.
8. See, generally, Walker, *A Critical History of Police Reform*.
9. This section was adapted from Law Enforcement Assistance Administration, *Two Hundred Years of American Criminal Justice* (Washington, D.C.: U.S. Government Printing Office, 1976).
10. Thomas Adams, *Law Enforcement* (Englewood Cliffs, N.J.: Prentice-Hall, 1968), p. 99.
11. Walker, *Popular Justice*, p. 238.
12. John Sullivan, *Introduction to Police Science* (New York: McGraw-Hill, 1968), p. 24.
13. The personnel distribution of local police agencies is listed in Federal Bureau of Investigation, *Crime in the United States, 1986* (Washington, D.C.: U.S. Government Printing Office, 1987).
14. See, Clarence Schrag, *Crime and Justice: American Style* (Washington, D.C.: U.S. Government Printing Office, 1970), p. 47.
15. Egon Bittner, *The Functions of Police in Modern Society* (Cambridge, Mass.: Delgeschlager, Gunn and Hain, 1980), p. 149.
16. James Q. Wilson, *Varieties of Police Behavior: The Management of Law and Order in Eight Communities* (Cambridge, Mass.: Harvard University Press, 1968).
17. Richard Sykes and Edward Brent, *Policing: A Social Behaviorist Perspective* (New Brunswick, N.J.: Rutgers University Press, 1983).
18. Bittner, *The Functions of Police in Modern Society*, pp. 63–72.
19. James Q. Wilson and George Kelling, "Broken Windows: The Police and Neighborhood Safety," *Atlantic Monthly* (March 1982), pp. 29–38.
20. Ibid., p. 37.
21. Samuel Walker, "Broken Windows and Fractured History: The Use and Misuse of History in Recent Police Patrol Analysis," *Justice Quarterly* 1 (1984):75–90.
22. William Spelman and John Eck, *Problem-Oriented Policing* (Washington, D.C.: National Institute of Justice, 1987).
23. George Gallup, Jr., *The Gallup Poll* (Princeton, New Jersey, 1985), p. 2.
24. See, Harlan Hahn, "A Profile of Urban Police," in A. Niederhoffer and A. Blumberg, eds., *The Ambivalent Force* (Hinsdale, Ill.: Dryden Press, 1967), p. 59.
25. George Kelling, Tony Pate, Duane Dieckman, and Charles Brown, *The Kansas City Preventive Patrol Experiment: A Summary Report* (Washington, D.C.: Police Foundation, 1974).
26. Ibid., pp. 3–4.
27. Albert J. Reiss, *The Police and the Public* (New Haven, Conn.: Yale University Press, 1971), p. 19.
28. Bittner, *The Functions of Police in Modern Society*, p. 127.
29. See, generally, Lawrence Sherman, et al., *Team Policing—Seven Case Studies* (Washington, D.C.: Police Foundation, 1973).
30. John Angell, "The Democratic Model Needs a Fair

Trial: Angell's Response," *Criminology* 12 (1975):379–84.

31. "Many Cities Experimenting with Foot Patrol," *Criminal Justice Newsletter* 16 (15 May 1985):1–2.

32. See, generally, P. Greenwood and J. Petersilia, *The Criminal Investigation Process, Volume I: Summary and Policy Implications* (Santa Monica, Cal.: Rand Corporation, 1975); P. Greenwood, J. Chaiken, J. Petersilia, and L. Prusoff, *The Criminal Investigation Process, Volume III: Observations and Analysis* (Santa Monica, Cal.: Rand Corporation, 1975).

33. C. Cotter and J. Burrows, *Property Crime Program, A Special Report: Overview of the STING Program and Project Summaries* (Washington, D.C.: Criminal Conspiracies Division, Office of Criminal Justice Programs, Law Enforcement Assistance Administration, U.S. Department of Justice, 1981).

34. *Ibid.*, p. 8.

35. Robert Langworthy, "Stings: A Crime Control Tool," Paper presented at the American Society of Criminology, Atlanta, Georgia, November, 1986.

36. Greenwood and Petersilia, *The Criminal Investigation Process, Volume 1.*

37. Mark T. Willman and John R. Snortum, "Detective Work: The Criminal Investigation Process in a Medium-Size Police Department," *Criminal Justice Review* 9 (1984):33–39.

38. John Eck, *Solving Crimes: The Investigation of Burglary and Robbery* (Washington, D.C.: Police Executive Research Forum, 1984).

39. See, for example, Susan Martin, "Policing Career Criminals: An Examination of an Innovative Crime Control Program," *The Journal of Criminal Law and Criminology* 77 (1986):1159–82.

40. See, generally, Robert Sheehan and Gary Cordner, *Introduction to Police Administration* (Reading, Mass.: Addison-Wesley, 1979).

41. Miranda v. Arizona, 384 U.S. 436 (1966).

42. Harris v. New York, 401 U.S. 222 (1971).

43. Michigan v. Tucker, 417 U.S. 433 (1974).

44. Moran v. Burbine, 106 S.Ct. 1135 (1986); Michigan v. Mosely, 423 U.S. 96 (1975); Fare v. Michael C. 442 U.S. 23 (1979).

45. Nix v. Williams, 104 S.Ct. 2501 (1984).

46. New York v. Quarles, 104 S.Ct. 2626 (1984).

47. Oregon v. Elstad, 105 S.Ct. 1285 (1985).

48. Colorado v. Spring, 107 S.Ct. 851 (1987).

49. Colorado v. Connelly, 107 S.Ct. 515 (1986).

50. Moran v. Burbine, 106 S.Ct. 1135 (1986).

51. See, generally, Donald Dripps, "Against Police Interrogation—And the Privilege Against Self-Incrimination," *The Journal of Criminal Law and Criminology* 78 (1988):699–734.

52. Illinois v. Gates, 104 S.Ct. 2626 (1984).

53. Chimel v. California, 395 U.S. 752 (1969).

54. Terry v. Ohio, 392 U.S. 1 (1968).

55. Carroll v. United States, 267 U.S. 132 (1925).

56. United States v. Ross, 102 S.Ct. 2147 (1982).

57. Bumper v. North Carolina, 391 U.S. 543 (1960).

58. Limitations on the plain view doctrine have recently been defined in Arizona v. Hicks, 107 S.Ct. 1149 (1984). The recording of serial numbers from stereo components in a suspect's apartment could not be justified as being in plain view.

59. Katz v. United States, 389 U.S. 347 (1967).

60. United States v. Sharpe, 389 U.S. 347 (1967).

61. Hayes v. Florida, No. 83–6766 (1985).

62. California v. Carney, No. 83–859 (1985).

63. New Jersey v. TLO, No. 83–712 (1985).

64. United States v. Johns, No. 83–1625 (1985).

65. Richard Lundman, *Police and Policing* (New York: Holt, Rinehart and Winston, 1980). See also, Jerome Skolnick, *Justice Without Trial* (New York: Wiley, 1966).

66. Cited in Authur Neiderhoffer, *Behind the Shield: The Police in Urban Society* (Garden City, N.Y.: Doubleday, 1967), p. 65.

67. See, for example, Richard Bennett and Theodore Greenstein, "The Police Personality: A Test of the Predispositional Model," *Journal of Police Science and Administration* 3 (1975):439–45.

68. Milton Rokeach, Martin Miller, and John Snyder, "The Value Gap between Police and Policed," *Journal of Social Issues* 27 (1971): 155–71. For a similar view, see, James Teevan and Bernard Dolnick, "The Values of the Police: A Reconsideration and Interpretation," *Journal of Police Science and Administration* 1 (1973):366–69.

69. Niederhoffer, *Behind the Shield.*

70. William Westly, *Violence and the Police: A Sociological Study of Law, Custom and Morality* (Cambridge, Mass: MIT Press, 1970); W. Westly, "Violence and the Police," *American Journal of Sociology* 49 (1953):34–41.

71. Niederhoffer, *Behind the Shield,* pp. 216–20.

72. See, for example, Richard Harris, *The Police Academy: An Inside View* (New York: Wiley, 1973); John Van Maanen, "Observations on the Making of Policemen," *Human Organization* 32 (1973):407–18; Jonathan Rubenstein, *City Police* (New York: Ballantine, 1973); John Broderick, *Police in a Time of Change* (Morristown, N.J.: General Learning Press, 1977).

73. John Van Maanen, "Observations on the Making of Policemen," in R. Culbertson and M. Tezak, eds., *Order Under Law* (Prospect Heights, Ill.: Waveland Press, 1981), p. 59.

74. *Ibid.*, p. 66.

75. George Kirkham, "A Professor's 'Street Lessons,' " in Culbertson and Tezak, eds., *Order Under Law*, p. 81.

76. Bittner, *The Function of Police in Modern Society*, p. 63.

77. Michael Brown, *Working the Street: Police Discretion and the Dilemmas of Reform* (New York: Russell Sage Foundation, 1981); William Muir, *Police: Streetcorner Politicians* (Chicago: University of Chicago Press, 1977).

78. John Crank, Robert Regoli, Eric Poole, and Robert Culbertson, "Cynicism Among Police Chiefs," *Justice Quarterly* 3 (1986):342–52.

79. William Walsh, "Patrol Officer Arrest Rates: A Study of the Social Organization of Police Work," *Justice Quarterly* 2 (1986):271–90.

80. Joseph Goldstein, "Police Discretion Not to Invoke the Criminal Process," *Yale Law Journal* 69 (1960):543–94.

81. Richard C. Donnelly, "Police Authority and Practices," *Annals of the American Academy of Political and Social Science* 339 (January 1962): 91–92.

82. See, generally, Kenneth C. Davis, *Discretionary Justice—A Preliminary Inquiry* (Baton Rouge: Louisiana State University Press, 1969).

83. Stephen Mastrofski, R. Richard Ritti, and Debra Hoffmaster, "Organizational Determinants of Police Discretion: The Case of Drinking and Driving," *Journal of Criminal Justice* 15 (1987):387–402.

84. See, for example, Nathan Goldman, *The Differential Selection of Juvenile Offenders for Court Appearance* (New York: National Council on Crime and Delinquency, 1963); Aaron Cicourel, *The Social Organization of Juvenile Justice* (New York: Wiley, 1968); Irving Piliavin and Scott Briar, "Police Encounters with Juveniles," *American Journal of Sociology* 70 (1964):206.

85. Jerome Skolnick and J. Richard Woodworth, "Bureaucracy, Information and Social Control: A Study of a Morals Detail," in David Bordua, ed., *The Police, Six Sociological Essays* (New York: Wiley, 1960).

86. John Gardiner, *Traffic and the Police: Variations in Law Enforcement Policy* (Cambridge, Mass.: Harvard University Press, 1969).

87. One notable exception is control of deadly force, which is discussed later in this chapter.

88. Donnelly, "Police Authority and Practices," pp. 91–92.

89. Marvin Krohn, James Curry, and Shirley Nelson-Kilger, "Is Chivalry Dead? An Analysis of Changes in Police Dispositions of Males and Females," *Criminology* 21 (1983):417–37.

90. Douglas Smith and Jody Klein, "Police Control of Interpersonal Disputes," *Social Problems* 31 (1984):468–81.

91. Richard C. Hollinger, "Race, Occupational Status and Pro-Active Police Arrest for Drinking and Driving," *Journal of Criminal Justice* 12 (1984):173–83.

92. Douglas A. Smith, Christy A. Visher, and Laura A. Davidson, "Equity and Discretionary Justice: The Influence of Race on Police Arrest Decisions," *Journal of Criminal Law and Criminology* 75 (1984):234–49.

93. Sherri Lynn Johnson, "Race and the Decision to Detain a Suspect," *Yale Law Journal* 93 (1983):214–58.

94. See, for example, James Erickson and Mathew Neary, "Criminal Justice Education: Is It Criminal?" *Police Chief* 42 (1975):38–40.

95. See, Lawrence Sherman and Warren Bennis, "Higher Education for Police Officers: The Central Issues," *Police Chief* 42 (1975):38–40.

96. Solomon Gross, "Higher Education and Police: Is There a Need for a Closer Look," *Journal of Police Science and Administration* 1 (1973):336–44.

97. See, for example, B. E. Sanderson, "Police Officers: The Relationship of a College Education to Job Performance," *Police Chief* 44 (1977):62; James Finnegan, "A Study of Relationships between College Education and Police Performance in Baltimore, Maryland," *Police Chief* 43 (1976):50; Robert Trojanowicz and Tomas Nicholson, "A Comparison of Behavioral Styles of College Graduate Police Officers v. Non–College-Going Police Officers," *Police Chief* 43 (1967):57; R. P. Witte, "The Dumb Cop," *Police Chief* 36 (1969):38; Wayne Cascio, "Formal Education and Police Officer Performance," *Journal of Police Science and Administration* 5 (1977):89; Merlyn Moore, "The Field and Academia—A Message," *Police Chief* 42 (1975):66–69.

98. Lawrence Sherman, et al., *The Quality of Police Education* (San Francisco: Jossey-Bass, 1978).

99. Robert Fischer, "Is Education Really an Alternative? The End of a Long Controversy," *Journal of Police Science and Administration* 9 (1981):313–16.

100. Most important is the Equal Employment Opportunity Act of 1972, amending Title VII of the Civil Rights Act of 1964.

101. U.S. v. Paradise, 55 LW 4211 (1987).

102. Ellen Hochstedler, Robert M. Regoli, and Eric D. Poole, "Changing the Guard in American Cities: A Current Empirical Assessment of Integration in Twenty Municipal Police Departments," *Criminal Justice Review* 9 (1984):8–14.

103. Walker, *Popular Justice*, p. 61.

104. Nicholas Alex, *Black in Blue: A Study of the Negro Policeman* (New York: Appleton Century Crofts, 1969).

105. *Ibid.*, p. 154.

106. James Jacobs and Jay Cohen, "The Impact of Racial Integration on the Police," *Journal of Police Science and Administration* 6 (1978):182.

107. See, Afro-American Patrolmen's League v. Duck, 366 F. Supp. 1095 (1973); 503 F. 2d 294 (6th Cir., 1974); 538 F. 2d 328 (6th Cir., 1976).

108. Stephen Leinen, *Black Police, White Society* (New York: New York University Press, 1984).

109. See, generally, David J. Bell, "Policewomen: Myths and Reality," *Journal of Police Science and Administration*

10 (1982):122–20.

110. Catherine Milton, *Women in Policing* (Washington, D.C.: Police Foundation, 1972).

111. See, generally, A. Bouza, "Women in Policing," *FBI Law Enforcement Bulletin* 44 (1975):2–7; Joyce Sichel, Lucy Friedman, Janet Quint, and Micall Smith, *Women on Patrol: A Pilot Study of Police Performance in New York City* (Washington, D.C.: National Criminal Justice Reference Service, 1978); William Weldy, "Women in Policing: A Positive Step toward Increased Police Enthusiasm," *Police Chief* 43 (1976):47.

112. Patricia Marshall, "Policewomen on Patrol," *Manpower* 5 (1973):14–20.

113. R. Hindman, "A Survey Related to Use of Female Law Enforcment Officers," *Police Chief* 42 (1975):58–60.

114. Bell, "Policewomen: Myths and Realities," p.114.

115. Sally Gross, "Women Becoming Cops: Developmental Issues and Solutions," *Police Chief* 51 (1984):32–35.

116. Bittner, *The Functions of Police in Modern Society*, p. 46.

117. Walker, *Popular Justice*, p. 197.

118. President's Commission on Law Enforcement and the Administration of Justice, *Task Force Report: The Police* (Washington, D.C.: U.S. Government Printing Office, 1967), pp. 181–82.

119. Albert Reiss, *The Police and the Public*.

120. Kenneth Mattulla, *A Balance of Forces* (Washington, D.C.: U.S. Government Printing Office, 1982), p. 17.

121. This discussion is adapted from James Fyfe, "Toward a Typology of Police Shootings," Paper presented at the Annual Meeting of the Academy of Criminal Justice Sciences, Oklahoma City (March 1980) to be included in James Fyfe, ed., *Contemporary Issues in Law Enforcement* (Beverly Hills, Cal.: Sage Publications, forthcoming).

122. Milton, et al., *Use of Deadly Force*; Betty Jenkins and Adrienne Faison, *An Analysis of 248 Persons Killed by New York City Policemen* (New York: Metropolitan Applied Research Center, 1974).

123. James Fyfe, "Race and Extreme Police-Citizen Violence," in *Race, Crime and Criminal Justice*, R. L. McNeely and Carl Pope, eds. (Beverly Hills, Cal.: Sage Publications, 1981).

124. James Fyfe, "Blind Justice? Police Shooting in Memphis," Paper prepared for the Annual Meeting of the Academy of Criminal Justice Science, Philadelphia (March 1981), p. 18.

125. Peter Scharf and Arnold Binder, *The Badge and the Bullet: Police Use of Deadly Force* (New York: Praeger, 1983).

126. *Tennessee v. Garner*, 105 S. Ct. 1694 (1985).

127. New York City Police Department, *Temporary Operating Procedure 237*, p. 1.

128. James Fyfe, "Administrative Interventions on Police Shooting Discretion: An Empirical Examination," *Journal of Criminal Justice* 7 (1979):309–23.

129. William Waegel, "The Use of Lethal Force by Police: The Effect of Statutory Change," *Crime and Delinquency* 30 (1984):121–40.

130. "Study Shows Drop in Killings by Policemen," *Boston Globe* (October 20, 1986), p. 4.

131. "146 Officers Killed On-Duty in 1987, an Increase Over '86," *Criminal Justice Newsletter* (2 May 1988):5.

132. David Greenberg, Ronald Kessler, and Colin Loftin, "The Effect of Police Employment on Crime," *Criminology* 21 (1983):375–94.

133. Craig Uchida and Robert Goldberg, *Police Employment and Expenditure Trends* (Washington, D.C.: Bureau of Justice Statistics, 1986); see also, Colin Loftin and David McDowall, "The Police, Crime, and Economic Theory: An Assessment," *American Sociological Review* 47 (1982):393–401.

134. *Calling the Police: Citizen Reporting of Serious Crime* (Washington, D.C.: Police Executive Research Forum, 1981).

135. Laurence Sherman and Richard Berk, "The Specific Deterrent Effects of Arrest for Domestic Assault," *American Sociological Review* 49 (1984):261–72.

136. Perry Shapiro and Harold Votey, "Deterrence and Subjective Probabilities of Arrest: Modeling Individual Decisions to Drink and Drive in Sweden," *Law and Society Review* 18 (1984):111–49.

≣ CHAPTER 16

THE JUDICATORY PROCESS

INTRODUCTION

The judicatory process is designed to provide an open and impartial forum for deciding the justice of a conflict between two or more parties. The conflict may be between criminal and victim, law enforcement agents and violators of the law, parent and child, federal government and violators of governmental regulations. Regardless of the parties or issues involved, their presence in a courtroom should guarantee them a hearing conducted under regulated rules of procedure, that the outcome of the hearing will be clear, and that the hearing will take place in an atmosphere of fair play and objectivity. If the defendant believes that the ground rules have been violated, he or she may take the case to a higher court, where the procedures of the original trial will be examined. If, upon reexamination, it is found that a violation of legal rights has occurred, the appellate court may deem the findings of the original trial improper and either order a new hearing or hold that some other measure must be carried out—for example, the court may dismiss the charge outright.

The court is a complex social agency with many independent but interrelated subsystems—police, prosecutor, defense attorney, judge, and probation department—each having a role in the court's operation. It is also the scene of many important elements of criminal justice decision-making—detention, jury selection, trial, and sentencing.

Ideally, the judicatory process operates under a cloak of absolute fairness and equality. The entire process—from the filing of the initial complaint to final sentencing of the defendant—is governed by precise rules of law designed to insure that fairness exists. No defendant being tried before a U.S. court should suffer, or benefit, because of his or her personal characteristics, beliefs, or affiliations.

However, U.S. criminal justice can be a very selective process. Decision-makers' discretion follows defendants through every step of the process of justice, determining what will happen to them and how their cases will finally be resolved. Sometimes the direction justice takes is difficult to understand. For example, while some convicted of homicide receive the death penalty, about 9 percent receive a probationary sentence; similarly, about 13 percent of convicted rapists are awarded probation although their offenses may at first seem indistinguishable from the offenses of those who are imprisoned.[1] For every hundred adults convicted on violent felony charges, about 25 percent get probation only, while, in contrast, 34 percent get more than a year in prison.[2] Although the judicatory process should be impartial and fair, very often it is marked by the same informal, low-visibility decision-making that characterizes the law enforcement process.[3]

This chapter reviews some of the institutions and processes involved in adjudication and trial. First, the chapter briefly describes the court structure. Then, a discussion of the actors in the process—prosecution, defense, judges, and juries—is undertaken. The pretrial stage of the justice process is the next focus of attention. Issues such as bail and plea bargaining are described. The criminal trial is then discussed in some detail; and finally, sentencing formats are explained.

COURT STRUCTURE

The criminal adjudication process is played out within the confines of the court system. As mentioned in Chapter 14, there are over 16,000 courts operating in the United States. They are organized on the municipal, county, state, and federal levels of jurisdiction.

State Courts

The typical state court structure is illustrated in Figure 16.1. Most states employ a three- or four-tiered court structure. Lower courts try misdemeanors and also conduct the preliminary processing of felony offenses. Superior trial courts have jurisdiction over the actual trying of felony cases. Appellate courts review the criminal procedures of trial courts to determine whether the offenders were treated fairly. Superior appellate courts or state supreme courts, used in about half the states, review lower appellate court decisions.

Federal Courts

The federal court system maintains a three-tiered model of court jurisdiction, as shown in Figure 16.2.

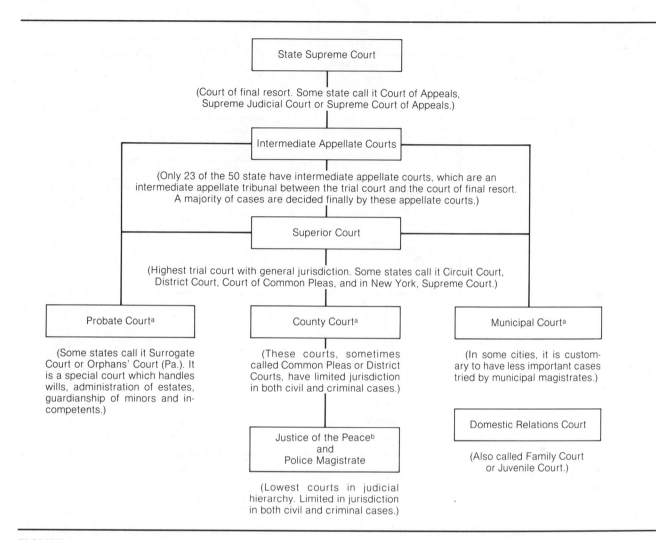

FIGURE 16.1 State Judicial System

[a]Courts of special jurisdiction, such as Probate, Family, or Juvenile, and the so-called inferior courts, such as Common Pleas or Municipal courts, may be separate courts or may be part of the trial court of general jurisdiction.

[b]Justices of the Peace do not exist in all states. Their jurisdictions vary greatly from state to state when they do exist.

SOURCE: American Bar Association, *Law and the Courts* (Chicago: American Bar Association, 1974), p. 20.

The **United States District Courts** are the trial courts of the system; they maintain jurisdiction over cases involving violations of federal law, such as interstate transportation of stolen vehicle and RICO prosecution.

Appeals from the district court are heard in one of the intermediate **Federal Courts of Appeal.** However, the highest federal appeals court is the **U.S. Supreme Court.**

The U.S. Supreme Court, as the nation's highest appellate body, is the court of last resort for all cases tried in the various federal and state courts. In certain rare instances, however, the Supreme Court can actually sit as a trial court—for example, in cases involving ambassadors or in suits between states.

The Supreme Court is composed of nine members, appointed for lifetime terms by the President

FIGURE 16.2
Federal Judicial System

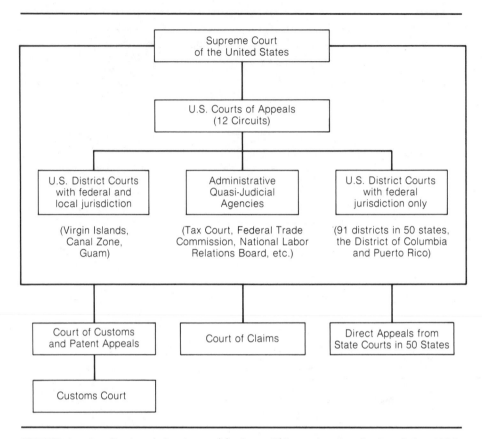

SOURCE: American Bar Association, *Law and the Courts* (Chicago: American Bar Association, 1974), p. 21.

with the approval of Congress. In general, the Court has discretion as to which cases it will consider and may choose to hear only those it deems important, appropriate, and worthy of its attention. When the Court decides to hear a case it usually grants a **writ of certiorari,** requesting a transcript of the proceedings of the case for review.

The Supreme Court must accept jurisdiction in all cases in which:

• A federal court holds an act of Congress to be unconstitutional

• A U.S. Court of Appeals finds a state statute unconstitutional

• A state's highest court holds a federal law to be invalid

• An individual's challenge to a state statute on con-

stitutional grounds is upheld by a state supreme court

When the Supreme Court chooses to, it can word a decision so that it becomes a precedent that must be honored by all lower courts. For example, if the Court grants a particular litigant the right to counsel at a police lineup, then all people in similar situations must be given the same right. This type of ruling is usually referred to as a **landmark decision.** The use of precedent in the legal system gives the Supreme Court power to influence and mold the everyday operating procedures of police agencies, trial courts, and corrections institutions. In the past, this influence was not nearly as pronounced as it has been during the tenure of three of the most recent chief justices, Earl Warren, Warren Burger and William Rehnquist. Warren and Burger greatly amplified and extended the power of the Court to affect criminal justice policies. Chief Justice Rehnquist seems to follow a similar, although more conservative, path.

Court Caseloads

The American court system is a vast enterprise. Each year an estimated 80 million new cases of all kinds and 200,000 appeals are brought before the courts of the 50 states and the District of Columbia.[4] In addition, federal courts try about 35,000 criminal cases and hear 5,000 appeals.

These statistics can be misleading, since about 60 to 70 percent of all cases are traffic violations handled by municipal or traffic court. Nonetheless, about 12 million cases involving criminal actions are handled by the courts each year, including approximately 1.5 million felony cases.[5]

The trend toward a rapidly expanding criminal court caseload may be ending due to the more stable crime rate. Nonetheless, if currently popular get-tough policies persist, the percentage of apprehended offenders brought to trial may increase, helping to maintain the court system's overwhelming criminal caseload.

——— ACTORS IN THE ———
JUDICATORY PROCESS

This section describes the major actors in the pretrial, trial, and sentencing process—the prosecutor, the defense attorney, and the judge.

Prosecutor

The major role of the **prosecution** is to represent the state in criminal matters that come before the court system. Prosecutors at all levels have many of the same major duties, some of which are listed here.

- *Conduct investigations of law violations.* Prosecutors are empowered to conduct their own investigations into alleged violations of the law. In some jurisdictions, they maintain their own staff of detectives and investigators; in others they rely on local or state police. In jurisdictions with grand jury systems, the prosecutor can convene the grand jury to act as a fact-finding body. A grand jury collects information and interviews witnesses for the purpose of accumulating enough evidence to indict suspects in criminal conspiracies.

- *Cooperate with police.* The prosecutor's office usually maintains a close working relationship with police agencies. Police prepare the investigation report of a crime according to the format desired by the prosecutor's office. Prosecutors also advise police agents about the legal issues in a given case. For example, prosecutors supervise the drawing up of requests, or **affidavits,** for search warrants; they then make sure that the police understand the limitations presented by the warrant. Some prosecutor's offices help train police officers, making them aware of the legal issues involved in securing a warrant or a legal arrest, interrogating a suspect, and so on.

- *Determine charges.* It is the prosecutor who makes the final determination of the charges to be brought against a suspect. The charge on which persons are brought to trial may have little resemblance to the original reason for which they were arrested. For example, a suspect picked up for disorderly conduct may later be identified at a police lineup as the perpetrator of a string of liquor store robberies. The disorderly conduct charge may then be dropped in favor of prosecution on the more serious robbery charges.

- *Represent the government in pretrial hearings and motions.* The prosecutor is charged with bringing the case to trial. Prosecutors make contact with witnesses and prepare them to testify; secure physical evidence; and discuss the victim's testimony. If the defendant attempts to have evidence suppressed at a pretrial hearing (for example, because of violations of the exclusionary rule), the prosecutor represents the state's position on the matter.

- *Plea bargaining.* The prosecutor is empowered to negotiate a guilty plea with the defendant, thereby ending the formal trial process.

- *Try the case.* The prosecutor acts as the state's attorney at criminal trials. Consequently, another name for the prosecutor is *people's attorney.*

- *Sentencing.* The prosecutor recommends dispositions at the completion of the trial. Usually, the type of sentence recommended is influenced by plea bargaining cooperation, public opinion, the seriousness of the crime, the offender's prior record, and other factors related to the case.

• *Represent the government at appeals.* If the defendant is found guilty as charged, he or she may appeal the conviction before a higher court. It is part of the prosecutor's overall duties to represent the government at these hearings.

• *Conduct special investigations.* Some jurisdictions empower special prosecutors to seek indictments for serious crimes considered of importance to public interest. This practice became well known during the Watergate investigation, when first Archibald Cox and then Leon Jaworski were appointed special prosecutors to investigate the break-ins and subsequent cover-up.

Types of Prosecutors. In the federal system, the chief prosecutor officer is the U.S. Attorney General; other prosecutors are known as U.S. Attorneys and are appointed by the President. They are responsible for representing the government in federal district courts. The chief prosecutor is usually an administrator, while assistants normally handle the actual preparation and trial work. Federal prosecutors are professional civil service employees.

At the state level, the chief prosecuting officer is the attorney general; at the county level, the district attorney. Both are elected officials. Again, the bulk of criminal prosecution and staff work is performed by scores of full-time and part-time attorneys, police investigators, and clerical personnel. Most attorneys who work for prosecutors at state and county levels are political appointees who earn low salaries; handle many cases; and in some jurisdictions, maintain private law practices. Many young lawyers serve in this capacity to gain trial experience, and leave when they obtain better-paying positions. In some state, county, and municipal jurisdictions, however, the office of the prosecutor can be described as meeting the highest standards of professional skill, personal integrity, and working conditions.

In urban settings, the structure of the district attorney's office is often specialized, with separate divisions for felonies, misdemeanors, and trial and appeal assignments. In rural offices, chief prosecutors handle many of the criminal cases themselves. Where assistant prosecutors are employed, they often work part-time, have limited professional opportunities, and depend on the political patronage of chief prosecutors for their positions.

Prosecutorial Discretion. Prosecutors maintain broad **discretion** in the exercise of their duties. In fact, full enforcement of the law is so rare that it is assumed that prosecutors will pick and choose the cases they decide to bring to court. Over 40 years ago, Newman Baker discussed the problems of prosecutorial decision-making:

> *"To prosecute or not to prosecute?" is a question which comes to the mind of this official scores of times each day. A law has been contravened and the statute says he [or she] is bound to commence proceedings. His [or her] legal duty is clear. But, what will be the result? Will it be a waste of time? Will it be expensive to the state? Will it be unfair to the defendant (the prosecutor applying own ideas of justice)? Will it serve any good purpose to society in general? Will it have good publicity value? Will it cause a political squabble? Will it prevent the prosecutor from carrying the offender's home precinct when the prosecutor runs for Congress after a term as prosecutor? Was the law violated a foolish piece of legislation? If the offender is a friend, is it the square thing to do to reward friendship by initiating criminal proceedings? These and many similar considerations are bound to come to the mind of the person responsible for setting the wheels of criminal justice in motion.*[6]

Prosecutors exercise their discretion in a variety of circumstances. One major decision involves the choice of either acting on the information brought by police or deciding not to file for an indictment. The prosecutor can also attempt to prosecute and then decide to take official action to drop the case; this is known as a **nolle prosequi.**

Figure 16.3 shows the pattern of prosecutor decision-making found by Barbara Boland in three large urban jurisdictions: New Orleans, Washington, D.C., and the Manhattan Borough court in New York. As Figure 16.3 indicates, the number of felony cases screened out before trial varies widely between jurisdictions. Nolle prosequi cases ranged from 8 percent to 32 percent. Prosecutorial discretion resulted in the dismissal of between 40 and 55 percent of the felony cases filed in the three jurisdictions.[7] In a more recent

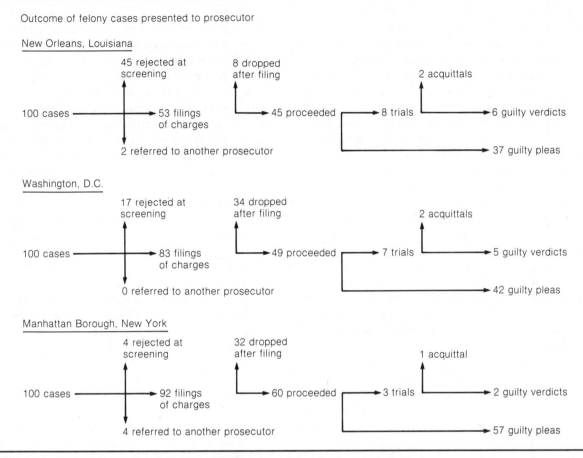

Outcome of felony cases presented to prosecutor

FIGURE 16.3   Differences in How Prosecutors Handle Felony Cases in Three Jurisdictions
SOURCE: B. Boland, *The Prosecution of Felony Arrests* (Washington, D.C.: INSLAW, Inc., 1983).

study, the federal government tracked more than 500,000 felony arrests in 11 states and found that about 84 percent eventually were prosecuted and about 62 percent convicted, a somewhat higher total than found in the Boland research.[8]

In making their decisions, prosecutors have a significant effect on the criminal justice process. If they attempted to formally handle all suspects arrested by police, they would clog the courts with many petty crimes and would prosecute cases in which there was little chance for conviction. By effectively screening out cases in which conviction could not reasonably be expected, cases inappropriate for criminal action (such as minor thefts by first offenders), and cases involving offenders with special needs (such as the emotionally disturbed or mentally retarded), the prosecutor can concentrate on bringing to trial those who commit more serious criminal offenses.

Factors Influencing Decision-Making.   What factors influence prosecutorial discretion? Numerous attempts have been made to examine the charging decision. Best-known is the classic work *Prosecution: The Decision to Charge a Subject*, by Frank Miller.[9] In his incisive analysis, Miller pinpoints factors influencing prosecutorial discretion, including: (1) the attitude of the victim; (2) the cost of prosecution to the criminal justice system; (3) the possibility of undue harm to the suspect; (4) the availability of alternative procedures; (5) the availability of civil sanctions; and (6) the willingness of the suspect to cooperate with law enforcement authorities.

In another classic work, Wayne LaFave also identified factors related to the decision to invoke prosecutorial discretion.[10] According to LaFave, when acts have been **overcriminalized**—for example, when laws provide stiff sentences for neighborhood poker games—they are not prosecuted. Further, limited resources force the prosecutor to select only the most serious cases. Finally, alternatives to prosecution are used whenever possible to spare the offenders the stigma of a criminal conviction.

In some instances, LaFave found that the prosecutor may decide to take no action; this occurs when the victim expresses the desire not to prosecute, when the cost would be excessive, when the harm of prosecution outweighs the benefits, or when the harm done by the offender can be corrected without a criminal trial. LaFave also points out that prosecutors have tools at their disposal to invoke obscure statutes to punish non-repenting offenders or to refuse leniency to defendants who will not cooperate with them. Thus, to LaFave, prosecutorial discretion is a two-edged sword.

In addition, the following have been identified as influencing prosecutorial discretion:

- *Evidence problems*—A failure to find sufficient physical evidence that links the defendant to the offense
- *Witness problems*—For example, when a witness fails to appear, gives unclear or inconsistent statements, is reluctant to testify, or is unsure of the identity of the offender
- *Office policy*—A decision not to prosecute certain types of offenses, particularly those that violate the letter but not the spirit of the law (for example, offenses involving insignificant amounts of property damage)
- *Due process problems*—Violations of the constitutional requirements for seizing evidence and for questioning the accused
- *Combination with other cases*—For example, when the accused is charged in several cases and the prosecutor prosecutes all of the charges in a single case
- *Pretrial diversion*—The prosecutor and the court agree to drop charges when the accused successfully meets the conditions for diversion, such as completion of a treatment program[11]

One other factor, **case pressure,** has long been thought to influence prosecutorial discretion. While some criminologists dispute whether prosecutorial decision-making is based on work schedule, others view the prosecutor deluged by serious cases as the one most likely to nolle prosequi or offer a plea bargain. A recent government survey indicates prosecutors in large counties (over 600,000 population) are less likely to bring felons to trial (28 percent) than those in smaller, less crime-ridden counties (38 percent). While these data are not conclusive proof of the effect of case pressure (an alternative explanation is that police are sloppier in urban areas, forcing prosecutors to drop cases), they show that jurisdictions where prosecutors are forced to deal with the more serious and violent felonies are also the ones in which the most selectivity is used in deciding to which cases limited resources should be devoted.[12]

Is prosecutorial discretion inherently harmful? Not according to most experts, who view it as a necessary component of efficiency in the criminal justice system. For example, Judge Charles Breitel has stated:

> *If every policeman, every prosecutor, every court, and every postsentence agency performed his or its responsibility in strict accordance with rules of law, precisely and narrowly laid down, the criminal law would be ordered but intolerable. Living would be a sterile compliance with soul-killing rules and taboos. By comparison, a primitive tribal society would seem free, indeed.*[13]

Although eliminating prosecutorial discretion may not always be desirable, efforts have been made to control its content and direction. For example, national commissions have established guidelines for the exercise of appropriate prosecutorial actions.[14] Other methods of controlling prosecutorial decision making include: (1) identification of the reasons for charging decision; (2) publication of prosecution office policies; (3) reviews by nonprosecutorial groups; (4) charging conferences; and (5) evaluation of charging policies and decisions and development of screening, diversion, and plea negotiation procedures.[15]

Defense Attorney

The **defense** counsel performs many functions while representing the accused in the criminal process.

These functions include, but are not limited to, the following:

- Investigating the incident
- Interviewing the client, police officers, and other witnesses
- Discussing the matter with the prosecutor
- Representing the defendant at the various prejudicial procedures, such as arrest, interrogation, lineup, and arraignment
- Entering into plea negotiations
- Preparing the case for trial, including developing the tactics and strategy to be used
- Filing and arguing legal motions with the court
- Representing the defendant at trial
- Providing assistance at sentencing
- Determining the appropriate basis for appeal

Despite the numerous prominent criminal defense lawyers in the United States, the majority of criminal defendants are indigents who cannot afford legal counsel. The Supreme Court has interpreted the Sixth Amendment of the Constitution to mean that people facing trial for offenses that can be punished by incarceration have the right to legal counsel.[16] If they cannot afford counsel, the state must provide an attorney free of charge. Consequently, three systems have been developed to provide legal counsel to the indigent:

1. Assigning private attorneys to represent indigent clients on a case-by-case basis (sometimes referred to as an attorney list system), with the state paying their fees.
2. Contracting with a law firm or group of private attorneys to regularly provide defense services to indigents.
3. Creating a publicly funded defender's office.

These three systems can be used independently or in combination. In general, the **attorney list/assigned counsel** system is used in less populated areas, where case flow is minimal and a full-time public defender not needed. **Public defenders** are usually found in larger urban areas with high case-flow rates. So, while a proportionately larger area of the country is served by the assigned counsel system, a significant propor-

tion of criminal defendants receive public defenders. Public defenders can be part of a statewide agency (25 percent), county government (38 percent), or the judiciary (23 percent); or they can be set up as an independent nonprofit organization or other institution (14 percent).

A government survey found that of the 3,082 counties served by indigent defendant services, 1,833 (60 percent) had assigned counsel systems, 1,048 (34 percent) had public defenders, and 201 (6 percent) had contract attorneys.[17] However, public defenders were found in the most populous counties, containing 68 percent of the U.S. population. Since crime rates are also higher in larger metropolitan areas, public defenders serve a majority of all criminal defendants. The survey also found that indigent defense systems handle about 3 million cases annually and cost taxpayers around $600 million.

Conflicts of Defense.   Because of the way the U.S. system of justice operates today, criminal defense attorneys face many role conflicts. They are viewed as prime movers in what is essentially an **adversarial process:** the prosecution and the defense engage in conflict over the facts of the case at hand, with the prosecutor arguing the case for the state and the defense counsel using all the means at his or her disposal to aid the client.

However, as members of the legal profession, defense counsels must be aware of their role as officers of the court. As an attorney, the defense counsel is obligated to uphold the integrity of the legal profession and to observe the requirements of the Code of Professional Responsibility of the American Bar Association in the defense of a client. The code makes the following statement regarding the duties of the lawyer in the adversary system of justice:

Our legal system provides for the adjudication of disputes governed by the rules of substantive, evidentiary, and procedural law. An adversary presentation counters the natural human tendency to judge too swiftly in terms of the familiar that which is not yet fully known; the advocate, by his zealous preparation of facts and law, enables the tribunal to come to the hearing with an open and neutral mind and to render impartial judgments. The duty of a lawyer to his client and his duty to the legal system are the same: To present his client zealously within the boundaries of the law.[18]

In this dual capacity of being both a defensive advocate and an officer of the court, the attorney is often confronted with conflicting obligations to client and profession. Monroe Freedman identifies three of the most difficult problems involving the professional responsibility of the criminal defense lawyer:

1. Is it proper to cross-examine for the purpose of discrediting the reliability or credibility of an adverse witness whom you know to be telling the truth?
2. Is it proper to put a witness on the stand when you know he or she will commit perjury?
3. Is it proper to give your client legal advice when you have reason to believe that the knowledge you give will tempt him or her to commit perjury?[19]

These questions and others reveal serious difficulties with respect to a lawyer's ethical responsibilities. These issues are often so complex that even the Supreme Court has had difficulty in setting standards of proper behavior. However, in *Nix v. Whiteside* the Court went as far as sustaining an attorney's right to refuse to represent a client whom he or she suspected would commit perjury. The Court also ruled that an attorney's threat to withdraw from the case and tell the court of the perjury did not violate the client's right to competent assistance of counsel.[20]

There are other, equally important issues. Suppose, for example, that a client confides that she is planning to commit a crime. What are the defense attorney's ethical responsibilities in this case? Obviously, the lawyer must counsel the client to obey the law; if he assisted the client in engaging in illegal behavior, he would be subject to charges of unprofessional conduct and even criminal liability. In another area, what is the duty of the defense attorney who is well aware that her client committed the act of which he is accused, but is also aware that the police made a procedural error in the case and that the client could be let off on a technicality? The criminal lawyer must be aware of these troublesome situations in order to properly balance the duties of being an attorney with those of being an officer of the court.

Another problem defense lawyers face is a reputation for underhanded methods and unscrupulous conduct, which may or may not be deserved:

The criminal lawyer is identified unjustifiably in the public eye with the client he [or she] represents. Indeed, some criminal lawyers are in fact house counsel for criminal groups engaged in gambling, prostitution, and narcotics. The reprehensible conduct of the few sometimes leads the public to see honest, competent practitioners as "mouthpieces" also. Furthermore, in nearly every large city a private defense bar of low legal and dubious ethical quality can be found. Few in number, these lawyers typically carry large caseloads and in many cities dominate the practice in routine cases. They frequent courthouse corridors, bondsmen's offices, and police stations for clients, and rely not on legal knowledge but on their capacity to manipulate the system. Their low repute often accurately reflects the quality of the services they render. The public image of the criminal lawyer is a serious obstacle to the attraction of able young lawyers, and reputable and seasoned practitioners as well, to the criminal law.[21]

Beyond their ethical problems, criminal defense attorneys often find themselves at the bottom of the legal profession's financial hierarchy. In prestigious New York law firms, attorneys begin at about $71,000, average $140,000 by their seventh year, and between $250,000 and $600,000 when they become partners.[22] In contrast, a public defender averages between $25,000 and $30,000.[23] Consequently, talented criminal attorneys feel pressure to leave the field and enter more lucrative areas of the law.

Judge

The third major participant in the criminal trial is the **judge**—the senior officer in a court of criminal law. Judges' duties are quite varied and are far more extensive than the average citizen might suspect. During trials, the judge rules on the appropriateness of conduct, settles questions of evidence and procedure, and guides the questioning of witnesses. When a jury trial occurs, the judge must instruct jury members on which evidence is proper to examine and which should be ignored. The judge also formally **charges the jury** by instructing its members on what points of law and evidence they must consider before reaching a decision of guilty or innocent. When a jury trial is waived, the judge must decide whether to hold for the complainant or the defendant. Finally,

Members of the Supreme Court, 1988. From left front: Thurgood Marshall, William Brennan, Chief Justice William Rehnquist, Byron White, and Harry Blackmun. From left rear: Antonin Scalia, John Paul Stevens, Sandra Day O'Connor, and Anthony M. Kennedy.

in the event that a defendant is found guilty, the judge has the authority to decide on the sentence (in some cases, the sentence is legislatively determined). This duty includes choosing the type of sentence, its length, and—in the case of probation—the conditions under which it may be revoked. Obviously, this decision has a significant effect on an offender's future.[24]

Beyond these stated duties, the trial judge has extensive control and influence over the other service agencies of the court: probation agencies, court clerks, police agencies, and the district attorney's office. Probation and the clerk may be under the judge's explicit control. In some courts, the operations, philosophy, and procedures of these agencies are within the magistrate's administrative domain. In other courts—for example, where a state agency controls the probation department—the attitudes of the county or district court judge still have a great deal of influence on how a probation department is run and how its decisions are made.[25]

The magistrate also has considerable influence on the operations of the local police and prosecutor's offices. For example, if a judge usually chooses a minimal sentence—such as a fine—for a particular offense, then police may be reluctant to arrest offenders for that crime, knowing that the outcome of the criminal justice procedure for that offense will not justify the time spent. Similarly, if a judge is known to have a liberal attitude toward police discretion, then the local department may be more inclined to engage in practices that border on entrapment; or they may become involved in cases requiring the use of easily obtained wiretaps. The district attorney's office may also be sensitive to judicial attitudes. The district attorney might forgo indictments for offenses the presiding magistrate expressly considers trivial or quasi-criminal and for which he or she has been known to take only token action, such as the prosecution of pornographers.

Finally, the judge considers requests by police and prosecutors for leniency (or severity) in sentencing.

The judge's reaction to these requests is important if police officers or the district attorney are to honor the bargains they have made with defendants to secure information, cooperation, or guilty pleas. For example, when police officers tell informers that they will try to convince the judge to be lenient with them in exchange for required information, they have to be sure that their requests will later be honored, or at least considered, by the presiding magistrate.

Judicial Selection.   Several methods are used to select state court judges.[26] In some jurisdictions, the governor simply appoints judges. In others, judicial recommendations must be confirmed by either (1) the state senate, (2) the governor's council, (3) a special confirmation committee, (4) an executive council elected by the state assembly, or (5) an elected review board. Some states employ screening bodies that submit names to the governor for approval.

Another form of judicial selection is through popular election, either partisan or nonpartisan. This practice is used in a majority of states.

About 11 states have adopted what is known as the **Missouri Plan** to select judges. This three-part approach consists of: (1) a judicial nominating commission to nominate candidates for the bench; (2) an elected official (usually from the executive branch) to make appointments from the list submitted by the commission; and (3) subsequent nonpartisan and noncompetitive elections in which incumbent judges run on their records.

There has been great concern about the qualifications of judges. In most states, people appointed to the bench have had little or no training in the role of judge. Others may have held administrative posts and may not have appeared before a court in years. In fact, if local justices of the peace are included, the majority of U.S. judges have not graduated from law school or even from college.

Several agencies have been created to improve the quality of the judiciary. The National Conference of State Court Judges and the National College of Juvenile Justice both operate judicial training seminars and publish manuals and guides on state-of-the-art judicial techniques. Their ongoing efforts are designed to improve the quality of the nation's judges.

Now that the actors in the adjudicatory process have been introduced and the structure within which they work defined, the discussion will turn to the three main stages of the process itself: pretrial procedures, the trial, and sentencing.

PRETRIAL PROCEDURES

After arrest, or if an arrest warrant has been served, a criminal charge is drawn up by the appropriate prosecutor's office. The charge is a formal written document identifying the criminal activity, the facts of the case, and the circumstances of the arrest. If the crime is a felony, the charge is called a **bill of indictment** if it is to be considered by a grand jury, or an **information** if that particular jurisdiction uses the preliminary hearing system; misdemeanants are charged with a **complaint.**

After an indictment or information in a felony offense is filed, the accused is brought before the trial court for arraignment, at which time the judge informs the defendant of the charge, insures that the accused is properly represented by counsel, and determines whether the person should be released on bail or some alternative plan pending a hearing or trial.

The defendant who is arraigned on an indictment or information can ordinarily plead guilty, not guilty, or **nolo contendere,** which is equivalent to a guilty plea. When a guilty plea is entered, the defendant admits to all the elements of the crime and the court begins to review the person's background for sentencing purposes. A plea of not guilty sets the stage for a trial on the merits of the case or for negotiations between the prosecutor and defense attorneys with the aim of reaching a guilty plea arrangement.

This section reviews in more detail three important issues related to pretrial procedures: bail, plea bargaining, and noncriminal alternatives to prosecution.

Bail

Bail represents money or some other security provided to the court to insure the appearance of the defendant at trial. The amount of bail is set by a magistrate, who reviews the facts of the case and the history of the defendant. Defendants who cannot afford or are denied bail are kept in secure detention, usually in a county jail or lockup until their trial date. Table

TABLE 16.1   Bail Release Mechanisms

Field Citation Release. Under this form of release, an arresting officer releases the arrestee on a written promise to appear in court, at or near the actual time and location of the arrest. This procedure is commonly used for misdemeanor charges and is similar to issuing a traffic ticket. The criteria used by the arresting officer are those established by the local police department in conformity with the provisions of state statutes. At a minimum, these criteria require that the arrestee be properly identified and have no outstanding warrants. A field citation release is the least formal nonfinancial technique available to assure court appearance of an arrestee.

Station-house Citation Release. Under this form of release, the determination of an arrestee's eligibility and suitability for release and the actual release of the arrestee are deferred until after he or she has been removed from the scene of an arrest and brought to the department's station-house or headquarters. Station-house release allows the police officer or pretrial services officer to verify the information provided by the arrestee prior to the issuance of a citation and permits the release of an arrestee without booking. Station-house release may save traveling time in that it eliminates transporting the arrestee to jail where final booking takes place.

Jail Citation Release. Under this form of release, the determination of an arrestee's eligibility and suitability for citation release and the actual release of the arrestee is deferred until after he or she has been delivered by the arresting department to a jail or other pretrial detention facility for screening, booking, and/or admission. This form of release is used extensively in California. In some counties in California, the booking sergeant or watch commander in the jail is assisted in the selection of persons for citation release by pretrial program staff.

Direct Release Authority by Pretrial Program. To streamline release processes and reduce length of stay, courts may authorize pretrial programs to release defendants without direct judicial involvement. Where court rule delegates such authority, the practice is generally limited to misdemeanor charges, but felony release authority has been granted in some jurisdictions.

Bail Schedule. Under this form of release, an arrestee can post bail at the station-house or jail according to amounts specified in a bail schedule. The schedule is a list of all bailable charges and a corresponding dollar amount for each. Schedules may vary widely from jurisdiction to jurisdiction. An arrestee may effect release by posting the full amount of bail required or by engaging a bondsman who will post the bail amount for a fee (usually 10 percent of the total bail).

Judicial Release. Arrestees who have not been released either by the police or jailer and who have not posted bail appear at the hearing before a judge, magistrate, or bail commissioner within a set period of time. In jurisdictions with pretrial release programs, program staff often interview arrestees detained at the jail prior to the first hearing, verify the background information, and present recommendations to the court at arraignment. At the arraignment hearing, the judicial officer can authorize a variety of nonfinancial and financial release options. There are two types of nonfinancial release options: release on recognizance and conditional release.

SOURCE: Andy Hall, *Pretrial Release Program Options* (Washington, D.C.: National Institute of Justice, 1984), pp. 30-31.

16.1 illustrates the stages of the criminal justice system in which bail may be granted.

The bail system goes back to Great Britain and the English common law. At one time, the legal relationship existing in the contract law of bailment even permitted the trying and sentencing of the bailor (the person who posted bail) if the bailee did not appear for trial.[27]

Under the U.S. system of justice, the right to bail comes from the Eighth Amendment of the Constitution. However, the Eighth Amendment does not guarantee bail; rather, it states that people can expect to be released on reasonable bail in all but capital cases. Thus, in most cases, accused persons have the right to be released on reasonable bail in order to prepare their defense and continue their life in the community.

The Problems of Bail.   Bail is quite controversial because it penalizes the indigent offender who does not have the means to make bail. Of concern is the fact that detention centers are dreary dangerous places and those who are held in them can be victims of the justice system though they are innocent of all charges. Caleb

Foote, one of the nation's leading experts on bail, has said:

> *The basic problem—poor people and those being locked up before trial—remains. I still think pretrial detention is the most pervasive denial of equal protection and equal rights in American law.*[28]

The bail system is also costly, since it causes the state to pay for the detention of offenders who are unable to raise bail and who might otherwise remain in the community. The significance of bail is further amplified because both the amount of bail ordered and length of stay in pretrial detention for those who cannot raise bail are associated with a greater likelihood of conviction and a longer prison sentence after conviction.[29]

Another problem of the bail system is the institution of the professional bail **bondsman.** Normally, bail bondsmen put up 90 percent of a bond fee and the defendant the remaining 10 percent. When the defendant appears at trial, the bail is returned and the bondsman keeps the entire amount, the defendant's 10 percent serving as the bondsman's commission. If the defendant does not show up for trial, the bondsman must pay the entire bail. Usually, bondsmen expect defendants, their friends, or their relatives to put up further collateral (such as the deed to their house) to cover the risk. If collateral is unavailable or the bondsman believes the offender presents too great a risk, the bondsman will refuse bond, relegating the defendant to a jail stay until the trial date.

Bail bondsmen often have been accused of unscrupulous practices, such as bribing police and court personnel to secure referrals. Some judges have been accused of refusing to collect forfeited bail owed from professional bondsmen.[30] Abuses of the system have prompted bail reform movements and a number of jurisdictions, including Wisconsin, Nebraska, Kentucky, Oregon and Illinois, have set up systems to replace bondsmen.

Bail Reform. The bail reform movement was started in 1961 to help alleviate the problems presented by the bail process. In New York, the **Vera Foundation,** set up by the philanthropist Louis Schweitzer and later supported by the Ford Foundation, pioneered the concept of **release on recognizance** (ROR).[31] This project found that if the court had sufficient background information about the defendant, it could make a reasonably good judgment about whether the accused would return to court. The project found that most defendants, selected on the basis of such information as the nature of the offense, family ties, employment record, and other factors, returned to court without the need for money bail. The findings suggested that releasing a person on the basis of verified information more effectively guaranteed appearance in court than did money bail.

The Vera Project employed college students to evaluate potential candidates on four criteria:

1. *Residence*—Whether defendants lived in the area, as well as their record of domicile (for example, how often they moved).
2. *Community ties*—Whether defendants had family ties and contacts in the area.
3. *Employment record*—Present job and history of employment.
4. *Character*—Referees' assessments of defendant's character.

The project proved to be a great success. A significant majority of clients returned for trial when released on their own recognizance. The success of ROR in New York prompted its adoption in many other large cities around the country. The **Federal Bail Reform Act of 1984** has made release on recognizance an assumption in cases unless the need for greater control can be shown in court.

Bail reform has been considered one of the great successes in criminal justice reform, but some research efforts indicate great disparity in the way judges handle bail decisions. They also show that racial and socioeconomic disparity might be a factor in decision-making.[32] If this is so, then the original purposes of creating bail reform would be negated by bias in the justice system. One approach to limit disparity is **bail guidelines** which set standard bail amounts based on such factors as criminal history and current charge.[33]

In sum, bail reform movements have encouraged the use of pretrial release. Studies show that most defendants do return for trial and that most bailees do not commit more crime while in the community.

TABLE 16.2   Legislative Provisions to Assure Community Safety

Type of provision	States that have enacted the provision
Exclusion of certain crimes from automatic bail eligibility	Colorado, District of Columbia, Florida, Georgia, Michigan, Nebraska, Wisconsin
Definition of the purpose of bail to ensure appearance and safety	Alaska, Arizona, California, Delaware, District of Columbia, Florida, Hawaii, Minnesota, South Carolina, South Dakota, Vermont, Virginia, Wisconsin
Inclusion of crime control factors in the release decision	Alabama, California, Florida, Georgia, Minnesota, South Dakota, Wisconsin
Inclusion of release conditions related to crime control	Alaska, Arkansas, Colorado, Delaware, District of Columbia, Florida, Hawaii, Illinois, Iowa, Minnesota, New Mexico, North Carolina, South Carolina, South Dakota, Vermont, Virginia, Washington, Wisconsin
Limitations on the right to bail for those previously convicted	Colorado, District of Columbia, Florida, Georgia, Hawaii, Indiana, Michigan, New Mexico, Texas, Utah, Wisconsin
Revocation of pretrial release when there is evidence that the accused committed a new crime	Arizona, Arkansas, Colorado, District of Columbia, Georgia, Hawaii, Illinois, Indiana, Maryland, Massachusetts, Michigan, Nevada, New Mexico, New York, Rhode Island, Texas, Utah, Vermont, Wisconsin
Limitations on the right to bail for crimes alleged to have been committed while on release	Arizona, Arkansas, Colorado, District of Columbia, Florida, Georgia, Illinois, Indiana, Maryland, Massachusetts, Michigan, Minnesota, Nevada, New Mexico, New York, Rhode Island, Tennessee, Texas, Utah, Vermont, Wisconsin
Provisions for pretrial detention to ensure safety	Arizona, Arkansas, California, Colorado, District of Columbia, Florida, Georgia, Hawaii, Illinois, Indiana, Maryland, Massachusetts, Michigan, Nebraska, Nevada, New Mexico, New York, Rhode Island, South Dakota, Texas, Utah, Vermont, Virginia, Washington, Wisconsin

SOURCES: Elizabeth Gaynes, *Typology of State Laws which Permit Consideration of Danger in the Pretrial Release Decision* (Washington: Pretrial Services Resource Center, 1982) and updated from Barbara Gottlieb, *Public Danger as a Factor in Pretrial Release: A Comparative Analysis of State Laws* (National Institute of Justice, July 1985); *Report to the Nation on Crime and Justice,* 2d ed. (Washington, D.C.: Bureau of Justice Statistics, 1988), p. 77.

Preventive Detention

Research studies indicate that the great majority of criminal defendants released on bail return for their trial.[34] Nonetheless, there is still concern over the criminal behavior of bailees awaiting trial. One study of eight state jurisdictions found that about 15 percent of defendants released by local courts were rearrested before trial, while another found that about 10 percent of defendants released by federal district courts were rearrested before trial.[35] Those rearrested tended to (1) be on bail longer (nine months or more); (2) have a serious prior record; (3) be drug abusers; (4) have a poor work record; and (5) be disproportionately young, male, and nonwhite. The federal courts study

also found that people detained before trial get significantly longer sentences than those granted pretrial release.

While only 10 to 15 percent of bailees commit crime before trial, the threat they present to the public is disturbing. After all, if about 1.5 million felony defendants receive bail each year, that means that more than 200,000 crimes are committed by bailees.

Because of the concern over defendant misconduct while on bail, about 30 states have made provisions to limit bail for certain offenses and offenders, such as those who previously absconded, recidivists, or offenders with violent histories (see Table 16.2). Similarly, the Bail Reform Act of 1984 provides that federal offenders may be detained without bail if "no condition or combination·of conditions [of bail] will reasonably assure . . . the safety of any other person and the community."[36]

The issue of preventive detention is particularly vexing, since it means that persons who have not been convicted of any crime may be incarcerated for extended periods of time without the chance to participate in their own defense. Those supporting preventive detention argue that it will help control witness intimidation and reduce avoidable criminal acts.

In a landmark decision, *United States v. Salerno*, the Supreme Court upheld the Bail Reform Act's preventive detention provision on the grounds that its purpose was public safety, that it was not excessive for its stated purpose, and that it contained no punitive intent but was designed to regulate the behavior of accused criminals in a legally permissible way.[37] In a similar fashion, the case of *Schall v. Martin* upheld a New York law providing for the preventive detention of a juvenile offender if the judicial authority believes the offender will be a danger to community safety.[38]

A recent analysis of the federal Bail Reform Act shows that it did increase the number of people being held before trial. Before the Act took effect, about 24 percent of all defendants were detained or did not make bail; after the Act took effect the number went up to 29 percent; 19 percent of the detainees did not qualify for bail consideration under the new guidelines.[39] Most of those held without bail were involved in the use of firearms, were drug offenders, or had violated immigration laws.

Plea Bargaining

The majority of defendants in criminal trials are convicted by their own pleas of guilty. A leading authority, Donald Newman, estimates that about 90 percent of all those charged with serious crimes plead guilty; if minor crimes are included, the percentage jumps to 98 percent.[40]

The plea bargaining process usually occurs between arraignment (or initial appearance, in the case of a misdemeanor) and the onset of trial. Normally, there are four ways a bargain can be made between the prosecutor and the defense attorney: (1) the initial charges may be reduced to those of a lesser offense, thus automatically reducing the sentence imposed; (2) in cases in which many counts are charged, the pros-

ecutor may reduce the number of counts; (3) the prosecutor may promise to recommend a lenient sentence, such as probation; and (4) when the charge imposed has a negative label attached (for example, child molester), the prosecutor may alter the charge to a more socially acceptable one (for example, assault) in exchange for a plea of guilty. In a jurisdiction in which it is common knowledge that sentencing disparity between judges exists, the prosecutor may even agree to arrange that the defendant appear before a lenient judge to insure the court's agreement to the bargain.

There are a number of different motivations for plea bargaining. Defendants, well aware of the evidence against them, plea bargain for obvious reasons. They wish to minimize their sentence and avoid negative labels and the harmful publicity of a conviction for a serious crime. Occasionally, people accept a bargain to protect accomplices or confederates by "taking the rap" themselves.[41] It is also possible that defendants who actually are innocent will accept a plea to a reduced charge because they fear the consequences of a trial on a more serious charge.

The defense attorney may seek a bargain to limit his or her own involvement in the case. In some instances, counsel for the defense may wish to increase his or her operating profits by minimizing the effort put forth for an obviously guilty client.[42] In other instances, counsel may simply wish to adapt the bureaucratic structure favorable to plea bargaining that exists in most U.S. criminal courts.[43] In some cases, defense attorneys may wish to secure noncriminal dispositions for their clients, such as placement in a treatment program, and may advise them to plead guilty in exchange for this consideration.

The prosecution also may seek to plea bargain, for various reasons. For one thing, the prosecutor's case may be weaker than hoped for; and it may therefore be safer to accept a plea to a lesser charge than to risk an acquittal. Or perhaps the prosecutor believes police officers have made a serious error in securing evidence, and is therefore afraid to bring the case to trial. When a defendant pleads guilty, it voids all prior constitutional errors made in that case. Of course, no matter how strong the state's case, there is always the chance that a jury will render an unfavorable decision. Prosecutors also bargain to gain the cooperation of informers and codefendants.

Some prosecutors may be reluctant to press charges against some offenders whose conviction

CLOSE-UP

Is It Really a Bargain?

Many Americans disapprove of plea bargains because they believe that they enable criminals to "get away with murder." How accurate is this perception? Do many criminals "beat the rap"?

To answer this question, the federal government sponsored a survey of felony plea negotiations in 14 jurisdictions. The survey found wide disparity in the use of pleas; some jurisdictions averaged four pleas per trial, while others conducted more than 20; overall, pleas were used in 80 percent of felony cases. The survey found that, surprisingly, 60 percent of the pleas were to the top charge filed. This implies that most plea negotiations are directed at achieving a reduced sentence, or at dropping lesser included charges that could add to the sentence (such as possession of a firearm), rather than at lowering the most serious charge filed against the defendant. Even in jurisdictions where prosecutors are reluctant to reduce charges or engage in bargaining, a majority of defendants still enter a guilty plea.

These findings are supported by Douglas Smith's analysis of 3,397 felony cases in six separate legal jurisdictions. Smith found that the probability of receiving an incarcer-

ation sentence was roughly equal for those who pleaded guilty and those who actually went to trial. Surprisingly, defendants who benefited the most from bargains committed the least serious offenses and had the best prior records.

Smith's findings coincide with the "wedding cake" model of criminal justice because they indicate that minor cases committed by offenders perceived to be nondangerous are disposed of as quickly as possible. Those criminal acts perceived by courtroom decision-makers to be serious or committed by chronic offenders are dealt with more formally and harshly, regardless of whether a plea or trial takes place.

Discussion Questions

1. Should felony plea negotiations be eliminated or strictly controlled?

2. How could plea negotiations convince an "innocent" person to plead guilty?

SOURCES: Douglas Smith, "The Plea Bargaining Controversy," *Journal of Criminal Law and Criminology* 77 (1986):949–67; Bureau of Justice Statistics, *The Prevalence of Guilty Pleas* (Washington, D.C.: U.S. Department of Justice, 1984).

could result in their receiving long sentences without chance of parole. For example, some states have passed drug laws that provide mandatory sentences for convicted offenders. However, when the legislature passed these statutes, its intent was to control serious, professional drug dealers. Therefore, the amateur "campus pusher" who falls into police hands may be charged with a lesser offense.

Plea Bargaining Issues. Those who favor plea bargaining argue that it actually benefits both the state and the defendant in the following ways: (1) the overall financial costs of criminal prosecution are reduced; (2) the administrative efficiency of the courts is greatly improved; (3) the prosecution is able to devote more time to cases of greater seriousness and importance; and (4) the defendant avoids possible detention and extended trial and may receive a reduced sentence.[44] Thus, those who favor plea bargaining believe it is

appropriate to enter into plea discussions where the interests of effective administration of justice will be served.

It has been argued, however, that plea bargaining is basically objectionable because it encourages a defendant to waive the constitutional right to a trial. In addition, some experts suggest that sentences tend to be less severe in guilty plea situations than in actual trials and that plea bargains result in even greater sentencing disparity. Particularly in the eyes of the general public, this allows the defendant to beat the system and further tarnishes the criminal justice process. Plea bargaining also raises the danger that an innocent person will be convicted of a crime if convinced that the lighter treatment resulting from a guilty plea is preferable to the possible risk of a harsher sentence following a formal trial. Richard Kuh argues that plea bargaining allows dangerous offenders to get off lightly and therefore weakens the deterrent effect of the criminal law.[45] Albert Alschuler, a legal scholar, has forcibly argued that whereas plea bargains may have an internal, administrative logic, the general public views their outcome as illogical (see Close-Up entitled "Is It Really a Bargain?").[46]

Control of Plea Bargaining.   It is unlikely that plea negotiations will be eliminated or severely curtailed in the near future. Those who support their total abolition are in the minority. As a result of abuses, however, efforts are being made to improve plea bargaining operations. Such reforms include the development of uniform plea practices, the presence of counsel during plea negotiations, and the establishment of time limits on plea negotiations.[47]

In recent years, some efforts have been made to convert the practice of plea bargaining into a more visible, understandable, and fair dispositional process. On the one hand, safeguards and guidelines have been developed in many jurisdictions to prevent violations of due process and to insure that innocent defendants do not plead guilty under coercion. Such safeguards include the following: (1) the judge questions the defendant about the facts of the guilty plea before accepting the plea; (2) the defense counsel is present and able to advise the defendant of his or her rights; (3) open discussions about the plea occur between prosecutor and defense attorney; (4) full and frank information regarding the offender and offense is made available at this stage of the process. In addition, judicial supervision is an effective mechanism to insure that plea bargaining is undertaken fairly.

Another method of reform has involved the development of specific guidelines by the office of the chief prosecutor. Also, some jurisdictions have adopted the use of prepleading investigations, which are summaries of the case prepared before a plea is made rather than after the plea is given to the court. The use of the prepleading report helps provide information to all the participants in the negotiations.

The pretrial settlement conference is another method used to improve the visibility and fairness of plea bargaining. In such a conference, the participants include the judge, victim, defendant, and police, as well as the prosecutor and defense attorney. Generally, the defendant's guilt is assumed by the parties, and efforts are made to contribute to a settlement of the case. If a settlement is reached and approved by the judge, the defendant enters a plea in open court.

The most extreme method of reforming plea bargaining has been to abolish it completely. A ban on plea bargaining has been tried in numerous jurisdictions throughout the country. In 1975, the state of Alaska eliminated the practice. In Honolulu, Hawaii, efforts were made to abolish plea bargaining. Jurisdictions in other states, including Iowa, Arizona, and Delaware, and in the District of Columbia, also have sought to limit the use of plea bargaining.[48] These jurisdictions give no consideration or concessions to the defendant in exchange for a guilty plea.

Efforts to control plea bargaining have met with mixed results. Evaluation of the Alaska experiment found that the number of pleas did not change significantly after plea bargaining was eliminated, nor did it increase the prison sentences given to the most serious offenders.[49] This and other similar efforts indicate that attempts to eliminate plea bargaining will most likely move prosecutorial discretion further up in the system. For example, eliminating felony plea bargaining may cause prosecutors to automatically charge offenders with a misdemeanor, so they can retain the option of offering them a "deal" in exchange for their cooperation before trial.

Legal Issues in Plea Bargaining.   The U.S. Supreme Court has reviewed the propriety of plea bargaining in several court decisions, particularly in regard to the voluntariness of guilty pleas. In *Boykin v. Alabama*, the court held that an effort must be made in open court to question the defendant on the voluntariness of the admission of guilt before a trial judge may accept a guilty plea.[50] This is essential, since a guilty plea constitutes a waiver of the defendant's Fifth Amendment right to avoid self-incrimination and Sixth Amendment right to a jury trial. After the *Boykin* case, the court ruled in the case of *Brady v. United States* that a guilty plea is not invalid merely because it is entered to avoid the possibility of the death penalty.[51] And in *Santobello v. New York*, which involved a guilty plea made after plea bargaining, the Court held that the promise of the prosecutor must be kept and that the breaking of a plea bargaining agreement by the prosecutor required a reversal for the defendant.[52] The Court ruled in the 1978 case of *Brodenkircher v. Hayes* that a defendant's due process rights are not violated when a prosecutor threatens to reindict the accused on more serious charges if he or she does not plead guilty to the original offense.[53]

The problem of controlling plea bargaining remains. Despite calls for its abolishment, it flourishes in U.S. trial practice. As Donald Newman states:

> There are at present, no good answers to all of the unresolved bargaining issues. One thing, however, is abundantly clear; plea bargaining is with us and is probably here to stay in most jurisdictions throughout the country.[54]

Alternatives to Prosecution: Diversion

In the past 20 years, great effort has been made to remove as many people as possible from the formal criminal justice process and to deal with them in an informal, treatment-oriented fashion.

Several reasons underlie this movement. On the one hand, advocates of the labeling perspective forcefully argue that the stigma of criminal conviction serves only to reinvolve the offender in crime. Thus, noncriminal alternatives can, in the long run, help reduce criminal activity.

From another viewpoint, it is alleged that pretrial alternatives to prosecution are usually cheaper than full trials, and more importantly, that they free the justice system to concentrate on more serious offenders. Alternatives to prosecution can reduce the need for plea bargaining by reducing caseload pressure to settle cases.

In most instances, pretrial programs are designed to treat offenders rather than punish them. Some pretrial programs are organized around a particular type of rehabilitation effort. For example, a judge may allow a case to continue indefinitely without a hearing if the offender voluntarily enrolls in a residential alcohol or drug treatment program.

More common today are formalized **diversion** programs operating out of the local police, prosecutor's, or probation department. Involvement with a diversion program usually begins after the arrest and arraignment of the individual but before the trial. Selected individuals are released on a continuance to the diversion program—that is, the trial is postponed—if the relevant court personnel (judge,

probation officer, assistant district attorney, defense lawyer, arresting officer) and the program representative agree on the potential suitability of the accused for the program.

Services rendered by most adult pretrial diversion programs can be classified into three complementary areas:

1. Counseling is undertaken by an advocate, who conducts individual and group sessions with clients throughout the initial period.
2. Employment services are offered by a career developer, who evaluates and implements career goals in a team effort with the client and the advocate.
3. Human services are provided, including health care, educational programs, emergency housing, and a variety of testing to assess needs and capabilities.[55]

The diversion movement was originally supported by federal government money funneled to local jurisdictions. However, many programs begun with federal funds are now being underwritten by local money.

Despite the prevalence of diversion, critics have claimed that the practice is no more successful than the formal justice system. In some cases it entangles the offender in the social service area more intensely than if he or she had gone to trial; this effect is known as **widening the net.**

THE CRIMINAL TRIAL

Although the jury trial is a relatively rare occurrence, it is still one of the cornerstones of the criminal justice process. Although most criminal prosecutions result in a plea bargain and do not involve the adversary determination of guilty or innocence, the trial process remains a matter of vital importance to the criminal justice system (see Close-Up on adversary justice). The opportunity to go to trial provides a valuable safeguard against abuse of informal processing and a basis for encouraging faith in the criminal justice system.[56] Because of its importance, jury trial stages, critical issues, and associated legal rights are discussed below.

CLOSE-UP

Adversary Justice v. the Courtroom Work Group

The hard fought criminal trial is a popular topic for literature and the media. Every defendant has a fair chance if he or she can retain Perry Mason, Matlock, or the "L.A. Law" firm of MacKenzie and Brackman. Films such as the *Jagged Edge* hinge on glib lawyers convincing the jury of their clients' innocence. But does it really work that way? Of course not.

On television and in the movies, defendants are typically attractive and wealthy. While this type of defendant actually exists, most typically defendants are urban, lower-class teenagers who are heavy users of drugs or alcohol when they are arrested. If they could have afforded a Perry Mason or Michael Kuzak, they probably would not have committed the crime in the first place.

Most criminal defendants retain public defenders. Because of their career conflicts, case pressure, and ambivalent feelings toward their clients, public defenders and other attorneys for the indigent have been accused of caring more about their reputation in court and their relationship with prosecutors and judges than about their clients. Private attorneys who are criminal court regulars are seen as businesspeople, for whom profit and not justice is the major motivating force.

Beyond these issues, the overwhelming number of cases in the criminal dockets, many of them involving acquaintances and family members, has created a situation in which "settling the matter" and cutting legal corners has supplanted the adversary system of justice. Rather than opposing each other in court, the prosecution and defense, sometimes aided by the magistrate, form a relationship which has been described as a **courtroom work group.** This group functions to streamline the process of justice through the extensive use of plea bargaining and other alternatives, rather than to provide a spirited defense or prosecution. In most criminal cases, cooperation rather than conflict between prosecution and defense appears to be the norm. It is only in the widely publicized "heavy" criminal cases involving rape or murder (the top layer of the criminal justice "wedding cake") that the adversarial process is called into play. Consequently, upward of 80 percent of all felony cases and over 90 percent of misdemeanors are settled without trial.

What has developed is a system in which criminal court experiences can be viewed as a training ground for young attorneys. Newly established lawyers may see the criminal court as an opportunity to receive government compensation for cases taken to get their practice going; established firms may see it as an arena in which they can place their new associates for seasoning before assigning them to paying clients. Prosecutors may be looking forward to a political career or to joining a high-paid firm.

While the courtroom work group limits the constitutional rights of defendants, it may be essential for keeping our overburdened justice system afloat. Moreover, while informal justice exists, it is not absolutely certain that it is inherently unfair to both victim and offender. The research evidence shows that the defendants who benefit the most from informal court procedures commit the least serious crimes; the more chronic offender gains relatively little.

Discussion Questions

1. Which kind of cases do you think are most likely to be handled informally?

2. Does the courtroom work group ethic erode faith in the fairness of the law and legal system?

SOURCES: James Eisenstein and Herbert Jacob, *Felony Justice* (Boston, Mass.: Little, Brown, 1977); Peter Nardulli, *The Courtroom Elite* (Cambridge, Mass.: Ballinger, 1978); Paul Wice, *Chaos in the Courthouse* (New York: Praeger, 1985); Marcia Lipetz, *Routine Justice: Processing Cases in Women's Court* (New Brunswick, N.J.: Transaction Books, 1983); Douglas Smith, "The Plea Bargaining Controversy," *The Journal of Criminal Law and Criminology* 77 (1986):949–67.

Jury Selection

The first stage of the trial process involves jury selection. Jurors are selected randomly in both civil and criminal cases from tax assessment or voter registration lists within each court's jurisdiction. The initial list of persons chosen, which is called a **venire,** or jury array, provides the state with a group of potentially capable citizens able to serve on a jury. Many states, by rule of law, review the venire to eliminate unqualified persons and to exempt those who by reason of their professions are not allowed to be jurors; this latter group may include (but is not limited to) physicians, the clergy, and government officials. The actual jury selection process begins with those remaining on the list.

The court clerk, who handles the administrative affairs of the trial—including the processing of the complaint, the evidence, and other documents—randomly selects enough names (sometimes from a box) to fill the required number of places on the jury. In most cases, the jury in a criminal trial consists of 12 persons, with two alternate jurors standing by to serve should one of the regular jurors be unable to complete the trial.

Once the prospective jurors have been chosen, the process of **voir dire** is begun; all persons selected are questioned by both the prosecutor and the defense to determine their appropriateness to sit on the jury. They are examined under oath by the government, the defense, and sometimes the judge about their backgrounds, occupations, residences, and possible knowledge or interest in the case. A juror who acknowledges any bias for or prejudice against the defendant—a juror who is a friend or relative of the defendant, for example, or who has already formed an opinion about the case—is removed for *cause* and replaced with another. Thus, any prospective juror who reveals an inability to be impartial and render a verdict solely on the basis of the evidence to be presented at the trial may be removed by attorneys for either the prosecution or defense. Because no limit is normally placed on the number of challenges for cause that can be offered, it often takes considerable time to select a jury for controversial and highly publicized criminal cases.

In addition to challenges for cause, both the prosecution and the defense are allowed **peremptory challenges,** which allow the attorneys to excuse jurors for no particular reason or for reasons that remain undisclosed. For example, a prosecutor might not want a bartender as a juror in a drunken driving case, believing that a person in that occupation might be sympathetic to the accused. Or a defense attorney might excuse a male prospective juror because the attorney prefers to have a predominantly female jury for the client. The number of peremptory challenges permitted is limited by state statute and often varies by case and jurisdiction.

The peremptory challenge has long been criticized by legal experts, who question the fairness and pro-priety with which it has been employed.[57] In a significant case, *Batson v. Kentucky*, the Supreme Court ruled that the use of peremptory challenge to dismiss all black jurors was a violation of the defendant's right to equal protection of the law.[58]

The Sixth Amendment to the U.S. Constitution provides for the right to a speedy and public trial by an impartial jury. The Supreme Court has sought to insure compliance with this constitutional mandate of impartiality through recent decisions eliminating racial discrimination in jury selection. For instance, in *Ham v. South Carolina*, the Court held that the defense counsel of a black civil rights leader was entitled to question each juror on the issue of racial prejudice.[59] In *Turner v. Murray*, the Court ruled that black defendants accused of murdering whites are entitled to have jurors questioned about their racial bias.[60] In *Taylor v. Louisiana*, the Court overturned the conviction of a man by a all-male jury because a Louisiana statute allowed women but not men to exempt themselves from jury duty.[61] These and other similar decisions have had the effect of providing safeguards against jury bias. Nevertheless, there are many areas still left undecided. For example, *Ham* applied to a case involving a civil rights worker and *Turner* is limited to capital cases; it is still unclear whether the racial bias of jurors is an issue in other cases, or how prejudices can be accurately determined.[62] Similarly, evidence shows that juries have trouble understanding the intricacies of the legal process and often misinterpret the instructions given them by the judge.

Trial Process

The trial of a criminal case is a formal process conducted in a specific and orderly fashion in accordance with rules of criminal law, procedure, and evidence. Unlike trials in popular television programs, where witnesses are often asked leading and prejudicial questions and where judges go far beyond their supervisory role, the modern criminal trial is a complicated and often time-consuming technical affair. It is a structured adversary proceeding in which both the prosecution and the defense follow specific procedures and argue the merits of their cases before the judge and jury.

Each side seeks to present its case in the most favorable light. Where possible, the prosecutor and

A criminal trial is a formal process involving criminal law, rules of procedure, and presentation of evidence. During Big Dan's barroom rape trial, the defense attorney (right) and client (left) describe the scene to the jury by using a model. The woman at center is a bilingual interpreter.

the defense attorney object to evidence they consider damaging to their individual points of view. The prosecutor uses direct testimony, physical evidence, and a confession, if available, to convince the jury that the accused is guilty beyond a reasonable doubt. The defense attorney rebuts the government's case with his or her own evidence, makes certain that the rights of the criminal defendant under the federal and state constitutions are considered during all phases of the trial, and determines whether an appeal is appropriate if the client is found guilty. From the beginning of the process to its completion, the judge promotes an orderly and fair administration of the criminal trial.

Although each administration in the United States differs in its trial procedures, all conduct criminal trials in a generally similar fashion. The basic steps of the criminal trial proceed in the following established order.

Opening Statements.   As the trial begins, both prosecution and defense address the jury and present their cases. They alert the jury to what they will attempt to prove and what the major facts of the case are. They introduce the witnesses, prepare the jury for their testimony, and tell them what information to be sure to listen for. The defense begins to emphasize that any doubts about the guilt of the accused must be trans-

lated into an acquittal; the prosecution dwells on civic duty and responsibility.

The Prosecution's Case.   Following the opening statement, the government begins its case by presenting evidence to the court through its witnesses. Those called as witnesses—such as police officers, victims, or expert witnesses—provide testimony via *direct examination*, during which the prosecutor questions the witness to reveal the facts believed pertinent to the government case. Testimony involves what the witness actually saw, heard, or touched, and does not include opinions. However, a witness's opinion can be given in certain situations, such as in describing the motion of a vehicle or indicating whether a defendant appeared to act intoxicated or insane. Witnesses also may qualify to give their opinions because of their professions as experts on a particular subject relevant to the case; for example, a psychiatrist may testify as to a defendant's mental capacity at the time of the crime.

After the prosecutor finishes questioning a witness, the defense cross-examines the same witness by asking questions in an attempt to clarify the defendant's role in the crime. If desired, the prosecutor may seek a *redirect examination* after the defense attorney has completed cross-examination; this allows the prosecutor to ask additional questions about information brought out during cross-examination. Finally, the defense attorney may question or cross-examine the witness once again. All witnesses for the trial are sworn in and questioned in the same basic manner.

The Defense's Case.   At the close of the prosecution's case, the defense may ask the presiding judge to rule on a *motion for a directed verdict*. If this motion is sustained, the judge will direct the jury to acquit the defendant, thereby ending the trial. A directed verdict means that the prosecution did not present enough evidence to prove all the elements of the alleged crime. If the judge fails to sustain the motion, the defense will present its case. Witnesses are called to testify in the same manner used by the prosecution.

After the defense concludes its case, the government may present *rebuttal evidence*. This normally involves bringing evidence forward that was not used when the prosecution initially presented its case. The defense may examine the rebuttal witnesses and introduce new witnesses in a process called *surrebuttal*. After all the evidence has been presented to the court, the defense attorney may again submit a motion for a directed verdict. If the motion is denied, both the prosecution and the defense prepare to make closing arguments; and the case on the evidence is ready for consideration by the jury.

Closing Arguments.   Closing arguments are used by the attorneys to review the facts and evidence of the case in a manner favorable to their positions. At this stage of the trial, both prosecution and defense are permitted to draw reasonable inferences and show how the facts prove or refute the defendant's guilt. Often, both attorneys have a free hand in arguing about facts, issues, and evidence, including the applicable law. They cannot comment on matters not in evidence, however; nor, where applicable, can they comment on the defendant's failure to testify. Normally, the defense attorney makes a closing statement first, followed by the prosecutor. Either party can elect to forgo the right to make a final summation to the jury.

Instructions to the Jury.   In a criminal trial, the judge instructs, or charges, the jury on the principles of law that ought to guide and control the decision on the defendant's innocence or guilt. Included in the charge are information about the elements of the alleged offense, the type of evidence needed to prove each element, and the burden of proof required to obtain a guilty verdict. Although the judge commonly provides the instructions, he or she may ask the prosecutor and the defense attorney to submit instructions for consideration; the judge then uses discretion in determining whether to use any of their instructions. The instructions that cover the law applicable to the case are extremely important, since they may serve as the basis for a subsequent criminal appeal.

One important aspect of instructing the jury is explaining the level of proof needed to find the person guilty of a crime. The U.S. system of justice requires guilt to be proven *beyond a reasonable doubt*. The judge must inform the jurors that if they have a reasonable suspicion that the defendant is not guilty, then they cannot find for the prosecution. Also, the judge must explain how, in criminal cases, the burden of proof is on the prosecution to prove the defendant guilty; the accused does not have to prove his or her innocence.

Verdict, Sentence, and Appeal.   Once the charge has been given to the jury, the jurors retire to deliberate on a verdict. The verdict in a criminal case—regardless of whether the trial involves a six-person or a 12-person jury—is usually required to be unanimous. A review of the case by the jury may take hours or even days. The jurors are always sequestered during their deliberations; and in some lengthy, highly publicized cases, they are kept overnight in a hotel until the verdict is reached. In less sensational cases, the jurors may be allowed to go home but are often cautioned not to discuss the case with anyone. If a verdict cannot be reached, the trial may result in a hung jury; in this case, the prosecutor has to bring the defendant to trial again if the prosecution desires a conviction. If found not guilty, the defendant is released from the criminal process.

If the defendant is convicted, the judge normally orders a presentence investigation by the probation department preparatory to imposing a sentence. Prior to sentencing, the defense attorney often submits a motion for a new trial, alleging that legal errors occurred in the trial proceedings. The judge may deny the motion and impose a sentence immediately, a practice quite familiar in most misdemeanor offenses. In felony cases, however, the judge sets a date for sentencing and the defendant is either placed on bail or held in custody until that time.

Sentencing usually occurs a short time after trial. In most jurisdictions, the typical criminal penalties include fines, community supervision, incarceration, and the death penalty.

After sentencing, defendants have the right to appeal the case, charging either that the law under which they were tried was unconstitutional (for example, discriminatory or vague) or that the procedures used by agents of the justice system violated their constitutional rights (for example, police did not give them a proper Miranda warning or improperly obtained evidence was used at trial). If the appeal is granted, a new trial may be ordered. If the appeal is not sustained, the convicted offender will begin serving the sentence imposed, thus marking the end of the judicatory process.

Trials and the Rule of Law

Every trial has its constitutional issues, complex legal procedures, rules of court, and interpretations of statutes, all designed to insure that the accused will have a fair trial. This section discusses the most important constitutional rights of the accused at the trial stage of the criminal justice system and reviews the legal nature of the trial process.

Right to a Speedy and Public Trial.   The Sixth Amendment guarantees a defendant the right to a speedy trial. This means that an accused is entitled to be tried within a reasonable period of time. If a person's right to a speedy trial is violated, then a complete dismissal of the charges against him or her is required, according to *Strunk v. United States*.[63] The right to a speedy trial was made applicable to state courts through the Due Process Clause of the Fourteenth Amendment in the case of *Klopfer v. North Carolina*.[64] It should be noted, however, that a defendant can waive the right to a speedy trial. A waiver of the right is implied when defendants cause the delay or when they do not assert their right even though the trial takes too long to get under way.

In determining whether a violation of a defendant's right to speedy trial has occurred, several factors are taken into consideration; length of the delay alone is not enough to constitute a violation. The Supreme Court, in the case of *Barker v. Wingo*, enumerated the factors that should be considered in determining whether the speedy trial requirement has been complied with: (1) the length of the delay, (2) the reason for the delay, (3) the timeliness of the defendant's assertion of right to a speedy trial, and (4) the prejudice to the defendant.[65]

How speedy does a speedy trial have to be? There is no set standard, but the Federal Speedy Trial Act of 1974 mandates 30 days from arrest to indictment and 70 days from indictment to trial. However, the states vary widely in their definitions of a speedy trial. For example, in Louisiana the limit is 730 days (two years) in a noncapital case and 1,095 days in capital cases; in New York, the time limit is 180 days.[66]

Right to a Jury Trial.   Because a jury trial is considered a fundamental right, the Supreme Court, in the case of *Duncan v. Louisiana*, made the guarantee applicable to the states through the Fourteenth Amendment.[67] However, the question arises as to whether this right extends to all defendants—those charged with misdemeanors as well as felonies. The Supreme Court addressed this issue in the case of *Baldwin v. New York*, in which it decided that an accused facing the possibility of a prison sentence of more than six months is entitled to a jury trial.[68]

Although most people think of a jury as having 12 members (historically most juries have had 12 members), the Sixth Amendment does not specify that a 12-person jury is required. In fact, in the case of *Williams v. Florida*, the Supreme Court held that a six-person jury fulfilled a defendant's right to a trial by jury.[69] However, a unanimous verdict is required when a six-person jury is used. When a 12-person jury is used, the Supreme Court has maintained that the Sixth Amendment does not require a unanimous verdict, except in first-degree murder cases. In *Apodaca v. Oregon*, the Court found constitutional an Oregon statute that required a finding of guilty by 10 out of 12 jurors in cases dealing with assault with a deadly weapon, burglary, and larceny.[70] However, it should be noted that the majority of states and the federal courts still require a unanimous verdict.

Right to Be Free from Double Jeopardy.   The Fifth Amendment provides that no person shall "be subject for the same offense to be twice put in jeopardy of life or limb." This means that a defendant cannot be prosecuted by a jurisdiction more than once for a single offense. For example, if a defendant is tried and con-

Powell v. Alabama, known as the "Scottsboro Boys" case, involved seven young men falsely accused of rape. They are shown here in 1935 with defense attorney Samuel Liebowitz (second from left). Since they had originally been denied counsel, the Supreme Court ruled that an attorney was essential in capital cases where the defendant's life was at stake.

victed of murder in the state of Texas, he or she cannot be tried again for the same murder in Texas. The right to be protected from double jeopardy was made applicable to the states through the Fourteenth Amendment in the case of *Benton v. Maryland.*[71] However, a person tried in federal court can be tried in state court, and vice versa.[72] And in 1986 the Court ruled in *Heath v. Alabama* that if a single act violates the laws of two states, the offender may be punished for each offense under the **dual sovereignty doctrine**: legal jurisdictions have the right to enforce their own laws and a single act can violate the laws of two separate jurisdictions.[73]

Right to Legal Counsel. Regardless of the legal rights citizens command at trial, without legal counsel to aid them they would be rendered defenseless before the law. Consequently, the Sixth Amendment provides the right to be represented by an attorney in criminal trials. However, the vast majority of criminal defendants are indigents who cannot afford private legal services. In a series of cases beginning in the 1930s, the U.S. Supreme Court established the defendant's right to be represented by an attorney and, in the event the defendant cannot pay for representation, to have the state provide free legal services. First, in *Powell v. Alabama,* the court held that an attorney was essential in capital cases where the defendant's life was at stake.[74] Then, in the critically important case of *Gideon v. Wainwright,* the court granted the absolute right to counsel in all felony cases.[75] Finally, in *Argersinger v. Hamlin,* the defendant's right to counsel in misdemeanor cases was established.[76] Today, most defendants are represented by attorneys from the time they are in police custody until their final sentencing and appeal.

Right to Competent Legal Representation.   In the 1984 case of *Strickland v. Washington*, the Supreme Court found that defendants also have the right to *reasonably effective assistance* of counsel. The court enumerated the qualities characterizing competent representation:

> *Representation of a criminal defendant entails certain basic duties. Counsel's function is to assist the defendant, and hence counsel owes the client a duty of loyalty, a duty to avoid conflicts of interest. From counsel's function as assistant to the defendant derive the overreaching duty to advocate the defendant's cause and the more particular duties to consult with the defendant on important decisions and to keep the defendant informed of important developments in the course of the prosecution. Counsel also has a duty to bring to bear such skill and knowledge as will render the trial a reliable adversarial testing process.[77]*

If convicted, defendants can have their sentence overturned if they can prove that (1) counsel's performance was so deficient that they were not functioning as the counsel guaranteed by the Sixth Amendment, and (2) the deficient performance prejudiced the case and deprived the defendant of a fair trial.

SENTENCING

After a defendant has been found guilty of a criminal offense or has entered a plea of guilty, he or she is brought before the court for imposition of a criminal penalty—sentencing.

Historically, a full range of punishments has been meted out to criminal offenders: corporal punishments, such as whipping or mutilation; fines; banishment; incarceration; death. The evolution of punishment as a means of correction is discussed in Chapter 17.

In U.S. society, incarceration in a federal, state, or local institution is generally the most serious penalty meted out to offenders. In addition the death penalty remains on the statute books of most jurisdictions, and has been used at an increasing rate in recent years.

Purposes of Sentencing

There are many purposes behind the imposition of a criminal sentence.[78] It is safe to say no single philosophy of justice holds sway when a sentencing decision is made. Each jurisdiction employs its own sentencing philosophies, and each individual decision-maker views the purpose of sentencing differently. Thus, a 23-year-old college student arrested for selling cocaine might be seen as essentially harmless by one judge and therefore given a light sentence. Another judge might see the young drug dealer as a dangerous destroyer of the moral fabric of society, deserving the harshest punishment possible. Thus, one of the great flaws of the U.S. system of justice has been the extraordinary amount of *disparity* in the way criminal punishment has been meted out.[79]

In general, four goals—deterrence, incapacitation, rehabilitation, and desert or retribution—are associated with imposition of a sentence.[80]

1. *Deterrence*—By imposing a sentence on the convicted criminal, the court hopes to deter others from committing similar crimes. The validity of deterrence rests on the premise that punishing the offender will have a future payoff in a reduced crime rate.

2. *Incapacitation*—Incapacitation is used because, at least for the period during which offenders are under control, they will not repeat their criminal behavior. In some instances, incapacitation involves keeping offenders under supervision while they remain in the community. In others, it calls for their confinement in an institution. Incapacitation involves prediction of behavior patterns: offenders are confined not for what they have done but for what it is feared they might do in the future.

3. *Rehabilitation*—Correctional treatment is another goal of sentencing. Its purpose is to lessen the probability that the offender will commit additional criminal acts by administering some type of rehabilitory therapy under supervision of correctional agents. Rehabilitation may help offenders

deal emotionally with the stresses of modern life, enroll them in vocational training, or provide them with an education. Again, the concept complies that current actions by the justice system can help change future behaviors.

4. *Desert or Retribution*—The final goal of sentencing is to exact punishment on offenders for what they have already done. Whereas the goals of deterrence, incapacitation, and rehabilitation are based on what might happen or what the offender might do, desert focuses on the event that led to conviction. Desert or retribution is grounded in equity: criminals benefited from their acts; they must now pay society back to make things even. For example, it is only fair that criminals who have committed the worst crime, murder, receive most severe penalty, death.

Each of these goals is in operation when a person is sentenced. Sometimes, one policy or goal becomes popular in public opinion and for a while dominates sentencing considerations. In the 1960s and 1970s, rehabilitation became the prime goal of sentencing; and innovative treatment methods were stressed. Today, the supposed failure of rehabilitation and a generally conservative outlook make desert, deterrence, and incapacitation the primary sentencing goals.

Sentencing Dispositions

Generally, five kinds of sentences or dispositions are available to the court: (1) a fine; (2) a suspended sentence; (3) probation; (4) incarceration; and (5) capital punishment.

A fine is usually exacted for a minor crime and may also be combined with other sentencing alternatives, such as probation or confinement.[81] A **suspended sentence** represents an effort by the court to refrain from enforcing a sentence, instead allowing the offender to remain in the community, often without supervision, in order to obtain nonpunitive treatment or rehabilitation services. The most common sentence is community supervision, or probation, by which the offender is permitted to live in the community subject to compliance with legally imposed conditions. The sentence of total confinement, or incarceration, is imposed when it has been decided that

the general public needs to be protected from further criminal activity by the defendant. Capital punishment, or the death penalty, is reserved for people who commit first-degree murder under aggravated circumstances, such as with extreme cruelty, violence, or torture.

Imposing the Sentence. The sentence itself is generally imposed by the judge, and sentencing is one of the most crucial functions of judgeship. Sentencing authority also may be exercised by the jury, an administrative body, or a group of judges, or may be mandated by statute. As previously mentioned, the length of the sentence is determined by the limits of the statute defining the particular offense. In most felony cases, save for where the law provides for *mandatory prison terms*, sentencing is usually based on a **presentence investigation** report by the probation department. This report, which is a social and personal history as well as an evaluation of the defendant, is used by the judge in making a sentencing decision.[82] Some judges heavily weigh the presentence investigation report; others may dismiss it completely or rely only on certain portions of it. However, such criteria as the nature of the offense and the previous record of the defendant are of prime importance to most judges in determining the type and length of sentence to be imposed. Thus, in most jurisdictions, the judge has the choice of treating offenders in the community or giving them prison terms.

When an accused is convicted of more than one charge, he or she must be sentenced on each charge. If the sentences are **concurrent,** they begin the same day and sentence is completed after the longest term has been served. For example, if a defendant is sentenced to three years imprisonment on a charge of assault and 10 years for burglary, and the sentences are to be served concurrently, the sentences would be completed after ten years. Conversely, a **consecutive sentence** means that upon completion of one sentence the other term of incarceration begins. For example, if a defendant is sentenced to three years imprisonment on a charge of assault and 10 years for burglary, and the sentences are to be served consecutively, after three years are served on the assault charge, the offender begins serving the burglary sentence. Therefore, the total term on the two charges would be thirteen years. In most instances, sentences are given concurrently.

Sentencing Structures

When a convicted offender is sentenced to prison, the statutes of the jurisdiction in which the crime was committed determine the penalties that may be imposed by the court. Over the years a variety of sentencing structures have been used in the United States. They include determinate sentences, indeterminate sentences, mandatory sentences, and presumptive sentences.

Determinate Sentences. Determinate sentences were the first kind used in the United States; they are still employed today in many jurisdictions. A determinate sentence is a fixed term of years, set by the legislature, to be served by the offender sentenced to prison for a particular crime. For example, in one type of determinate sentencing structure, the legislature may set a term of 10 years for all people convicted of robbery who are not eligible for community supervision. If the judge decides to impose a prison sentence, it must be 10 years and it must be served in its entirety without parole. This approach is known as *flat* or *fixed,* sentencing. Maine is a state that imposes flat sentences.

Another variation of the determinate sentence is to have the legislature create the maximum sentence a person can serve for a crime, but to allow the judge discretion within that limit. For example, the maximum sentence for robbery may be 10 years, but judges may be given the opportunity to reduce the sentence at their discretion (for example, to seven years, to three years, or even to grant probation).

Though determinate sentences provide a single term of years to be served, the actual time spent in prison can be reduced by several methods. Inmates can accrue *good time*—time off for good behavior—at a rate ranging from 10 to 15 days per month. In some states, like California, half of a determinate sentence can be erased by accumulating good time. In addition, some correctional authorities grant sentence reductions to inmates who participate in treatment programs, such as educational and vocational training. In some jurisdictions, there is also a parole board which can release prisoners after a percentage of their determinate sentence has been served.

Indeterminate Sentences. In the 1870s, prison reformers such as Enoch Wines and Zebulon Brockway

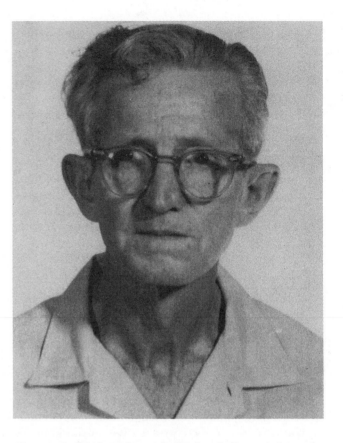

Clarence Earl Gideon's appeal of his burglary conviction to the Supreme Court in 1963 established an indigent defendant's right to counsel in felony cases.

called for creation of indeterminate sentences. They believed that prison sentences should be tailored to fit individual needs and that offenders should only be placed in confinement until they were rehabilitated. Indeterminate sentencing was influenced by positivist criminology and the belief that criminals were "sick" people who could be treated in prison. The wisdom of putting an offender away for a fixed period of time was disputed. Rather than the "punishment fitting the crime," reformers believed the "treatment should fit the offender." The indeterminate sentence became the most widely used type of sentence in the United States.[83]

This concept, still used in the majority of states, gives convicted offenders who are not eligible for community supervision a light minimum sentence that must be served and a lengthy maximum sentence that is the outer boundary of the time that can be served.

For example, the legislature might set a sentence of a minimum of five years and a maximum of 20 years for burglary.

Under this scheme, the actual length of time served by the inmate is controlled by the correction agency. The inmate can be paroled from confinement after serving the minimum sentence whenever the institution and parole personnel believe that he or she is ready to live in the community. The basic purpose underlying the indeterminate sentencing approach, particularly during the middle of the twentieth century, was to individualize each sentence in the interests of rehabilitating the offender. This type of sentencing allows for flexibility, not only in the type of sentence to be imposed but also in the length of time to be served. Indeterminate sentences also are subject to reduction for good time. Following are some variations on the indeterminate sentence:

1. The legislature determines minimum and maximum sentence and the judge cannot change either. For example, each offender sent to prison for burglary receives a sentence of one to twenty years.

2. Maximum sentence is set by legislature and cannot be changed; minimum is determined by judge. For example, offender A receives one to 20 years for burglary; offender B, 16 to 20 ; offender C, 10 to 20.

3. Judge sets both maximum and minimum sentence within guidelines set up by legislature. For example, minimum and maximum sentence for burglary is one to 20 years. Offender A gets one to 20; offender B, four to 10; offender C, three to six. The maximum the judge uses cannot exceed 20 years; the minimum cannot be less than one.

4. Maximum set by judge within upper limit, minimum determined by legislature. For example, all sentenced burglars do at least one year in prison but no more than 20. Offender A receives one to 10; offender B, one to 20; offender C, one to five.

The indeterminate sentence has come under attack in recent years for various reasons. One group of critics charges that it produces great disparity in the way people are treated in the correctional system. For example, one offender may serve one year and another may serve 20 for the same crime. Further, the indeterminate sentence is believed to take control of sentencing out of the hands of the judiciary and place it within the framework of corrections. The protections of due process that a person maintains in the courtrooms are absent in the correctional setting.

Finally, conservatives charge that serious criminals are given the opportunity to serve little or no time in prison, thereby weakening the power of the criminal law to deter crime.

In response to these charges, new sentencing structures have been developed. Two of the more important ones are described below.

Mandatory Sentences. One effort to limit judicial discretion has been the development of the mandatory sentence. Some states, for example, prohibit people convicted of certain offenses, such as violent crimes, or multiple offenders (recidivists) from being placed on probation; still others bar certain offenders from being considered for parole. Mandatory sentencing legislation may impose minimum and maximum terms or fixed prison sentences. Crimes that often call for mandatory prison sentences include murder and multiple convictions for crimes such as rape, drug violations, and robbery. Mandatory sentencing generally limits the judge's discretionary power to impose any disposition but that authorized by the legislature; as a result, it limits the idea of the individualized sentence and restricts sentencing disparity. Mandatory sentencing provides equal treatment for all offenders who commit the same crime, regardless of age, sex, or other individual characteristics.

One illustration of a mandatory sentence is the Massachusetts Gun Control Law, which requires a sentence of imprisonment for not less than one year nor more than two and one-half years for illegally carrying a firearm.[84] The unique feature of this statute is that the punishment is a mandatory sentence of at least one year in prison, which cannot be suspended by the court. Neither can the offender be considered for probation, parole, or other forms of early release until completion of the one-year sentence.

Another type of mandatory sentence is designed for chronic, multiple, or career criminals. Habitual offender statutes can be found in the criminal codes of most states. They are employed at the discretion of the prosecutor when an offender is found to have been convicted for previous felony offenses. If found guilty when charged as a habitual felon, the defendant is given a long prison sentence, sometimes life in prison without hope of parole. Habitual offender statutes are aimed at career criminals and represent the dominance of the conservative incapacitation philosophy in the nation's sentencing policies.

More than 35 states have already replaced discretionary sentencing with fixed-term mandatory sentences for such crimes as the sale of hard drugs, kidnapping, gun possession, and arson. The primary purpose behind such laws is to impose swift and certain punishment on the offender. It is difficult to say if depriving the judiciary of discretion and placing all sentencing power in the hands of the legislature will have a deterrent effect on the commission of these offenses. Only time and further research will provide the answer.

Presumptive Sentences. Presumptive sentencing plans create a statutorily determined sentence that convicted offenders should presume they will receive if sent to prison. Offenders convicted under this scheme are given this specific sentence unless mitigating or aggravating circumstances are found in the commission of the offense or in the offender's personal background. In other words, a judge is permitted to sentence below or above the maximum but is required to write an opinion justifying such action. For example, the legislature might set a penalty of six years for armed robbery with a mitigation factor of plus or minus two years. Thus, the "ordinary" robber should be given six years in prison. A first offender who has a good prior record might have the sentence reduced to four years; the multiple offender who uses excess brutality could receive up to eight years. However, the range of possible sentence length is reduced and thus sentencing disparity should be limited.

In addition, most presumptive sentencing statutes abolish early release via parole, though maintaining the use of good-time credit. Forms of this method have already been adopted in states such as California, Illinois, and Indiana.

Critics maintain that presumptive sentences will help increase the size of prison populations to a dangerous level.[85] On the other hand, supporters of presumptive sentencing believe that it creates fairness in the justice process, helps eliminate sentencing disparity, and increases the deterrent effect of punishment.[86]

THE DEATH PENALTY

Though the execution of convicted criminals has been common throughout human history, it is a topic that has long perplexed social thinkers. Today the death penalty for murder is used in 37 states, with the approval of about 75 percent of the population (see Table 16.3). Capital punishment has become a fairly commonplace event in American culture: about 1,900 people are on death row and more than 70 people have been executed since 1976.[87] This section reviews the arguments for and against capital punishment and briefly discusses its legal status.

Death Penalty Debate

The death penalty has long been one of the most controversial aspects of the justice system. There is little reason to suspect that it will not continue to be a source of significant debate.

Arguments for the Death Penalty. Various arguments have been offered in support of the death penalty by modern classical thinkers. One is that executions have always been used, that it is inherent in human nature to punish the wicked. The Bible describes methods of executing criminals. Many moral philosophers and religious leaders, such as Thomas More, John Locke, and Immanuel Kant, did not oppose the death penalty; neither did the framers of the U.S. Constitution.

The death penalty also seems to be in keeping with the current mode of dispensing punishment. The criminal law exacts proportionately harsher penalties for crimes based on their seriousness; logic says that this practice is testimony to a retributionist philosophy. Therefore, the harshest penalty for the most severe crime represents a logical step in the process.

Modern classical thinkers also argue that the death penalty is sometimes the only real threat available to deter crime. For example, prison inmates serving life sentences can be controlled only if they are aware that further transgressions can lead to death. A person committing a crime that carries with it a long prison sentence might be less likely to kill witnesses if deterred by the threat of death.

Death is the ultimate incapacitation. Some offend-

TABLE 16.3 Methods of Execution

Lethal injection	Electrocution	Lethal gas	Hanging	Firing squad
Arkansas	Alabama	Arizona	Delaware	Idaho
Idaho	Arkansas	California	Montana	Utah
Illinois	Connecticut	Colorado	New Hampshire	
Mississippi*	Florida	Maryland	Washington	
Montana	Georgia	Mississippi*		
Nevada	Indiana	Missouri		
New Jersey	Kentucky	North Carolina		
New Mexico	Louisiana	Wyoming		
North Carolina	Nebraska			
Oklahoma**	Ohio			
Oregon	Pennsylvania			
South Dakota	South Carolina			
Texas	Tennessee			
Utah	Vermont			
Washington	Virginia			
Wyoming				

*Mississippi authorizes lethal injection for persons convicted after 7/1/84; executions of persons convicted before that date are to be carried out with lethal gas.
**Should lethal injection be found to be unconstitutional, Oklahoma authorizes use of electrocution or firing squad.

SOURCE: *Report to the Nation on Crime and Justice*, 2d ed. (Washington, D.C.: Bureau of Justice Statistics, 1988), p. 99.

ers are so dangerous that they can never be safely let out in society. The death penalty is a sure way of preventing these people from ever harming others; it simply may be the only alternative available.

Finally, the death penalty is believed to be cost effective. Considering the crowded state of the nation's prison system and the expense of keeping an inmate locked up for many years, an execution may make financial sense.

In summary, supporters view capital punishment as the ultimate deterrent to crime. They believe that so serious a sanction prevents many potential criminals from taking the lives of innocent victims. The justification for the death penalty, therefore, relies on the premise that sacrificing the lives of a few evil people is a cost-effective way to save the lives of many innocent ones.

Arguments against the Death Penalty. Opponents of the death penalty argue that "social vengeance by death is a primitive way of revenge which stands in the way of moral progress."[88] Its inherent brutality places it in violation of the Eighth Amendment of the U.S. Constitution, which prohibits "cruel and unusual punishment."

Opponents also object to the finality of the death penalty. It is quite possible for an innocent person to be convicted of crime; once the person is executed, the mistake can never be rectified.[89] "It is better that a thousand guilty go free than one innocent man be executed" is a statement death penalty abolitionists often make.

The discretionary nature of the death penalty also draws criticism from opponents. Legal scholar Charles Black argues that "arbitrary discretion pervades every road to the chair."[90] The prosecutor has the unreviewable power to decide what to charge the defendant with and later makes the decision whether to allow the accused to plead guilty to a lighter sentence. The jury, before it finds a person guilty, must deal with such thorny legal issues as premeditation and insanity, issues legal scholars have not precisely understood nor defined. In murder cases, the jury is almost always told it can find the defendant guilty of a "lesser included offense" (for example, second-degree rather than first-degree murder), and their de-

CLOSE-UP

Race and the Death Penalty

An important criticism of the death penalty is that it has traditionally been given to a disproportionate number of minority citizens. This issue is still with us today.

Some research indicates that the death penalty is not used in a discriminatory fashion, but an important study conducted by Raymond Paternoster in South Carolina found that race does play a role in death penalty sentences. However, Paternoster's research focuses attention on the race of the victim as well as the criminal. Table A was constructed with data from Paternoster's study. It indicates that blacks who kill whites have over a 4.5 times greater risk of having the prosecutor seek the death penalty than do blacks who kill blacks. Paternoster found that the overall probability of a death sentence being requested for killers of blacks is 0.163, while for killers of whites it is 0.438, or 2.5 times greater. When the race of the victim is ignored, the chance of blacks and whites receiving the death penalty is almost equal. Thus, it is race of the victim and not of the offender that is most likely to bring about the death penalty. Similarly, Paternoster found that prosecutors in rural counties were more likely to ask for the death penalty than those in urban areas. In sum, extralegal factors seem to play a major role in the decision to seek the death penalty.

TABLE A Probability of Prosecutor Seeking Death Penalty by Race of Offender and Victim

Offender/Victim Combination	Probability of Death Requests	
	All Homicides	Capital Murders*
Black kills white	.365	.486
White kills white	.079	.389
Black kills black	.009	.105
White kills black	.130	.438

*Capital cases are aggravated murders; they are the only cases in which death can be sought.

Discussion Questions

1. How can the effect of a victim's race be minimized in capital punishment decision-making?

2. Does discrimination in the sentencing of the death penalty make the death penalty inherently cruel and unusual punishment?

SOURCE: Raymond Paternoster, "Race of the Victim and Location of Crime: The Decision to Seek the Death Penalty in South Carolina," *Journal of Criminal Law and Criminology* 74 (1983):754–85. Table A adapted from p. 767.

cision is not reviewable by higher authority. Clemency by executive pardon, the final stage in the process, is entirely discretionary. Concludes Black, "The net result is that no one knows why 500 or so people on death row have really been picked for this agony, in a country where a homicide occurs every twenty-six minutes."[91] As Hugo Bedeau puts it, outlawing the death penalty enables society to avoid "the unsolvable problem of picking and choosing among the bad to find the worst, in order to execute them."[92]

Opponents of the death penalty also charge that it has been employed in a discriminatory fashion. Between 1930 and 1967, 3,859 alleged criminals were executed in the United States. Of those executed, 53.5 percent were black and 45.4 percent white. This trend has not changed; in 1987 about half of all prisoners on death row were black, Hispanic, or Native American.[93]

Research indicates that white defendants convicted of murder actually have a greater probability of receiving the death penalty than black defendants.[94] One reason is that it seems to be the victim's race which controls death penalty decision-making, and not the offender's. People who kill whites are significantly more likely to be sentenced to death than people who kill blacks.[95] Since murder is essentially intraracial, whites are more likely to receive capital sentence. Nonetheless, the likelihood of receiving the death penalty is greatest in the relatively infrequent instance where a black criminal kills a white victim.[96] (See Close-Up entitled "Race and the Death Penalty.")

Abolitionists claim that capital punishment has

never proven to be a deterrent any more than has life in prison. There is little hard evidence that the threat of capital punishment is related to murder rates (Chapter 5). In fact, capital punishment may encourage murder, since it sets an example of violence and brutality.[97]

The Legality of the Death Penalty

For most of this country's history, capital punishment was used in a discretionary, haphazard manner without strict legal controls. As a result, its application was marked by extreme racial disparity; more than half the executions conducted in America involved blacks. Then, in 1972, the U.S. Supreme Court ruled in *Furman v. Georgia* that the discretionary imposition of the death penalty was cruel and unusual punishment under the Eighth and Fourteenth Amendments of the Constitution.[98] The Court did not rule out the use of capital punishment as a penalty; rather, it objected to the arbitrary and capricious manner in which it was imposed. After *Furman*, many states changed statutes that had previously allowed juries discretion in imposing the death penalty. In some states, this was accomplished by enacting statutory guidelines for jury decisions spelling out specific condition of aggravation which must be met for the death penalty to be considered.

Despite these changes in statutory law, no further executions were carried out while the Supreme Court pondered additional cases concerning the death penalty. In July 1976, the Supreme Court ruled on the constitutionality of five states' death penalty statutes. In the first case, *Gregg v. Georgia*, the Court found valid the Georgia statute that held that a jury must find at least one "aggravating circumstance" out of 10 before the death penalty can be imposed in murder cases.[99] In *Gregg*, for example, the jury imposed the death penalty after establishing beyond a reasonable doubt the presence of two aggravating circumstances:

1. The murder was committed while the offender was engaged in the commission of two other capital felonies.
2. The offender committed the murder for the purpose of receiving money and other financial gains (an automobile).

The Court also upheld the constitutionality of a Texas statute on capital punishment in *Jurek v. Texas* and of a Florida statute in *Proffitt v. Florida*.[100] These statutes are similar to Georgia's in that they limit sentencing discretion not only by specifying the crimes for which capital punishment can be handed down, but also by stipulating criteria concerning the circumstances surrounding the crimes. However, the Supreme Court declared that mandatory death sentences were unconstitutional.

In the late 1970s and early 1980s, a more conservative Supreme Court has eased the way for executions by lifting some of the legal roadblocks to capital punishment, such as allowing the removal of jurors who are opposed to the death penalty.[101] In what may be the most important capital punishment case of the 1980s, *McLesky v. Kemp*, the Supreme Court upheld the conviction of a black man in Georgia despite social science evidence that black criminals who kill whites have a much greater chance of receiving the death penalty than white criminals who kill blacks.[102] Many observers feel that this case was the last legal obstacle the death penalty had to overcome in order to be a standard mode of punishment in the American justice system.

SENTENCING DISPARITY AND CONTROL

Sentencing disparity has long been a problem in the justice system. Simply put, it is common for people to be convicted of similar criminal acts but to receive widely different sentences. For example, one person convicted of burglary may receive a three-year prison sentence while another may be granted probation. Such differences seem a violation of the constitutional rights to due process and equal protection. (See Close-Up entitled "Sentencing and Time Served in Prison.")

State sentencing codes usually include various factors which can legitimately influence the length of prison sentences, including: how severe the offense is; the offender's prior criminal record; whether the offender used violence; whether the offender used weapons; and whether the crime was committed for money.

☰ CLOSE-UP

Sentencing and Time Served in Prison

What is the "typical" sentence given to convicted felons, and how much time do they actually do in prison? Data collected in two federal surveys can help answer this question.

The first survey analyzed sentencing practices in 28 jurisdictions. In Table A, sentencing outcomes for seven felony offenses are illustrated. First, despite the seriousness of these charges, only 45 percent received prison sentences; in contrast, 26 percent were granted probation. Even a conviction for rape, robbery, or homicide did not guarantee a prison stay.

The second study looked at sentence length and actual time served in prison in 33 jurisdictions. Table B shows the sentence length, time served in prison and jail, and the percent of sentence served in confinement for people being released from prison for the first time on their current sentence (this excludes people released who had been returned to prison for parole or conditional release violations). As Table B shows, the average sentence was about 65 months, while the amount of time served was 23 months, or 45 percent of the sentence. As might be expected, those committing rape (four years) or murder (seven years) served the most time. Of interest is the fact that of all offenders, those involved in drug-related offenses served the smallest percentage of their sentence (38 percent). While the average sentence for drug traffickers was almost five years, most actually served 16 months.

Findings such as these raise questions of the "is the cup half empty or half full" variety. Are we sending too many people to prison for too long, or too few for too little? Is an average of seven years in prison for murder and four for rape too strict or too lenient a sentence to serve the purposes of justice? Are too many felons being granted probation, or should incarceration be mandatory for violent criminals? These studies show that the criminal sentencing process is the subject of great discretion and corresponding disparity.

TABLE A Type of Sentence Imposed by Crime Type, 1985

Conviction Offense	Type of Sentence Imposed					
	Prison	Jail Only	Jail and Probation	Probation Only	Other	Total
Total	45%	7%	22%	26%	1%	100%
Homicide	84	1	7	8	—	100
Rape	65	1	17	16	—	100
Robbery	67	7	13	13	—	100
Aggravated assault	42	7	26	24	1	100
Burglary	49	7	20	25	—	100
Larceny	32	10	19	38	1	100
Drug trafficking	27	6	34	32	1	100

NOTE: Percentages may not total to 100 percent because of rounding.
— indicates less than 0.5 percent.

Research studies do in fact show a strong correlation between these legal variables and the type and length of sentence received. Of greater significance is the charge that race, sex, and economic status influence sentencing outcomes. These extralegal factors appear to influence sentencing because the inmate population is disproportionately male, black, and lower-class. Although this phenomenon may be a result of disparity and discrimination, it also could be simply a function of existing crime patterns—males, minorities, and members of the lower class commit the crimes that are most likely to result in a prison sen-

TABLE B First Releases from State Prisons, 1984

Most Serious Offense	Sentence Length		Time Served in:				Percent of Sentence Served in Confinement
			Prison Only		Jail and Prison		
	Median	Mean	Median	Mean	Median	Mean	
All offenses (months)	36	64.7	13	19.6	17	23.4	45.4%
Violent offenses	60	92.2	23	31.0	28	35.7	50.5
Murder	180	244.8	65	76.0	78	85.3	42.2
Manslaughter	60	95.4	24	29.3	32	35.2	50.2
Kidnapping	60	106.5	25	34.4	31	38.4	51.8
Rape	72	113.1	37	44.2	44	49.2	50.7
Other sexual assault	60	86.5	19	25.5	26	31.3	43.6
Robbery	60	96.3	25	31.4	30	35.4	52.4
Assault	36	59.8	15	20.7	22	26.2	51.4
Other violent	36	65.7	12	15.1	16	19.6	46.7
Property Offenses	36	53.2	11	15.2	15	18.5	44.0
Burglary	36	60.5	13	17.3	17	20.6	44.2
Larceny/theft	24	46.8	9	13.1	12	16.1	43.4
Motor vehicle theft	24	36.5	10	12.8	14	16.4	55.3
Arson	60	80.0	14	19.5	19	23.1	39.7
Fraud	36	46.2	9	13.3	13	16.3	42.5
Stolen property	36	45.1	10	13.6	13	16.9	41.5
Other property	36	46.2	9	13.0	12	16.6	46.8
Drug Offenses	36	55.2	10	13.5	14	16.7	38.8
Possession	24	44.2	8	11.3	12	13.9	39.2
Trafficking	36	54.4	11	14.1	16	17.9	38.7
Other drug	36	63.0	11	14.1	13	16.6	38.7
Public-Order Offenses	24	35.4	6	10.4	9	13.2	39.5
Weapons	36	47.3	11	14.6	15	18.0	48.9
Other public-order	18	31.4	6	9.5	7	11.5	35.7
Other Offenses	24	51.4	10	13.8	15	17.8	50.6
Number of releases	68,868		89,545		64,973		64,089

Discussion Questions

1. Do you feel the average time served in prison is adequate for most crimes?

2. Should a convicted rapist or murderer be given probation under any circumstances?

3. Should there be mandatory minimum sentences for violent felonies or drug trafficking?

SOURCES: Stephanie Minor-Harper and Christopher Innes, *Time Served in Prison and on Parole, 1984* (Washington, D.C.: Bureau of Justice Statistics, 1987); Mark Cuniff, *Sentencing Outcomes in 28 Felony Courts, 1985* (Washington, D.C.: Bureau of Justice Statistics, 1987).

tence (homicide, rape, armed robbery).

Numerous research studies have been conducted to determine the cause of sentencing disparity in the United States.[103] Some studies have found a pattern of racial discrimination in sentencing, while others indicate that class bias exists.[104] There also is considerable evidence being assembled that the race and class of the victim and not the offender may be the most important factor in sentencing decisions. Crimes involving a white victim seem to be more heavily punished than those in which a minority group member is the target.[105]

Determining Sentencing Bias

While considerable effort has been expended to gather evidence of race and class bias in criminal sentencing, the actual impact of extralegal factors is often hard to determine.[106] There is competing evidence that the effect of legal factors, such as crime seriousness, prior record, and whether a weapon was used, are far more important factors in sentencing than race, sex, or class.[107] However, the true effects of extralegal factors on sentencing may be hard to detect. For example, studies of sentencing disparity are usually conducted on a statewide basis. As George Bridges and his associates encountered in Washington state, discrimination may vary considerably between court jurisdictions within a single state, masking the overall sentencing patterns.[108] Bridges found that officials in highly urbanized counties with large minority populations were likely to practice racial discrimination because they developed stereotyped attitudes towards minorities and perceived them as a threat to community order; officials in less populated areas were less likely to hold such attitudes. Terance Miethe and Charles Moore also have found evidence that racial bias in sentencing may be hard to detect because of within-group and between-group differences.[109] Their research found that black defendants who are considered low risks (married, high-school grads, nonviolent offenders) actually receive *shorter* sentences than white defendants with similar backgrounds; in contrast, black defendants characterized as high risks (single, high-school dropouts, unemployed, prior felony record) received *longer sentences* than whites. Similar findings were obtained by James Unnever and Larry Hebroff, who found little racial or ethnic differences in sentencing of the most and least serious cases of drug offenders in Miami; in average cases, in which discretion could most easily be used, blacks and Hispanics had a significantly higher incarceration rate than whites.[110]

Other criminologists argue that even where there is little direct evidence of race or class bias, it is likely that sentencing outcome is influenced indirectly by discriminatory practices in the criminal justice system. For example, Joan Petersilia's study of racial disparity found that, all things considered, blacks did receive longer sentences than whites.[111] However, racial differences could be explained by the white defendants' use of plea bargains and the favorable descriptions of white defendants by probation officers in court-ordered presentence reports; judicial discrimination was not a significant factor. Other studies show that defendants who can afford bail receive more lenient sentences than those who remain in pretrial detention.[112] There also is evidence that sentencing outcome is indirectly affected by the defendant's ability to afford a private attorney, though research does not always support this contention.[113] And while consideration of prior record may be legitimate in forming sentencing decisions, there is evidence that blacks and poor whites are more likely to have prior records because of organizational and individual bias on the part of police.[114]

In sum, the evidence seems to show that whereas racial and class discrimination may have been an important factor in the past, the *direct* influence of discrimination on sentencing may be decreasing today.[115] However, other correlates of racial and class bias within the criminal justice system may indirectly influence sentencing outcome. Defendants who cannot afford to make bail, obtain proper legal representation, or take advantage of plea bargaining, or whose background fails to impress the probation department, are the ones who will receive the most severe criminal sentences; all too often these are the poor and minority group members.

Because of the lingering problem of racial and class bias in the sentencing process, one primary goal of the criminal justice system during the 1980s was to reduce disparity by creating new forms of criminal sentences which would limit judicial discretion and be aimed at uniformity and fairness.

Restricting Sentencing Discretion

One approach to sentencing disparity has been to legislate flat, mandatory, or presumptive sentences that are designed to reduce discretion in sentencing decision-making. These sentencing models originally were developed to promote fairness and reduce disparity in the criminal sentencing process. However, these measures can be bypassed by judges and prosecutors who wish to maintain their independence by shifting discretion further up the justice system. For example, if a mandatory one-year sentence exists for firearm possession, a prosecutor can arrange a plea bargain to a lesser charge in order to retain discretion.

FIGURE 16.4 Minnesota Sentencing Guidelines Grid

SEVERITY LEVELS OF CONVICTION OFFENSE		CRIMINAL HISTORY (# OF PRIOR OFFENSES) (presumptive sentence lengths in months)						
		0	**1**	**2**	**3**	**4**	**5**	**6 or more**
Unauthorized use of motor vehicle Possession of marijuana	I	12*	12*	12*	15	18	21 24 23-25	
Theft related crimes ($150-$2500) Sale of marijuana	II	12*	12*	14	17	20	23	27 25-29
Theft crimes ($150-$2500)	III	12*	13	16	19	22 21-23	27 25-29	32 30-34
Burglary-Felony intent Receiving stolen goods ($150-$2500)	IV	12*	15	18	21	25 24-26	32 30-34	41 37-45
Simple robbery	V	18	23	27	30 29-31	38 36-40	46 43-49	54 50-58
Assault, 2nd degree	VI	21	26	30	34 33-35	44 42-46	54 50-58	65 60-70
Aggravated robbery	VII	24 23-25	32 30-34	41 38-44	49 42-53	65 60-70	81 75-87	97 90-104
Assault, 1st degree Criminal sexual conduct, 1st degree	VIII	43 41-45	54 50-58	65 60-70	76 71-81	95 89-101	113 106-120	132 124-140
Murder, 3rd degree	IX	97 94-100	119 116-122	127 124-130	149 143-155	176 168-184	205 192-215	230 218-242
Murder, 2nd degree	X	116 111-121	140 133-147	162 153-171	203 192-214	243 231-255	284 270-298	324 309-339

Italicized numbers within the grid denote the range within which a judge may sentence without the sentence being deemed a departure.
1st degree murder is excluded from the guidelines by law and continues to have a mandatory life sentence.
Cells below heavy line receive a presumptive prison sentence.
Cells above line receive a presumptive non-prison sentence.
The numbers in these cells refer to duration of confinement if probation is revoked.
*One year and one day.
SOURCE: Minnesota Sentencing Guidelines Commission, 1981.

Another approach to reducing disparity has been to create judicial **sentencing councils.** Sentencing councils are meetings of the judges who sit regularly in a particular court. During a sentencing council, the judges discuss appropriate dispositions of defendants awaiting sentencing. The sentencing judge retains the ultimate responsibility for selecting and imposing the sentence, while the other judges act in an advisory capacity. Normally, the judges meet in groups of three to consider the sentencing alternatives in pending cases. The sentencing council has the following advantages: (1) it reveals to judges their differences in sentencing philosophies; (2) it provides an opportunity for judges to debate their differences; and (3) it provides a forum for periodic evaluation of a court's sentencing practice. Such councils have been implemented in federal courts as well as in state court systems.

Another approach is the **sentencing guidelines** model, pioneered by Leslie Wilkins and currently used by federal government and various state jurisdictions. Guidelines classify offenders based on personal factors, such as age, prior offense history, and current criminal behavior (for example, narcotics violations, robbery, or theft). For example, the typical sentence given to young, first-offense narcotics violators or robbers can be computed. A sentencing judge knows whether his or her decision in the case at hand differs significantly from decisions made by colleagues in similar cases. Guidelines can be used to control disparity, but judges still make their own decisions in each case.[116] The use of guidelines has been adapted in Michigan, Minnesota, and other states. (The guidelines used in Minnesota are illustrated in Figure 16.4.)

The federal government's **Crime Control Act of 1984** created the **U.S. Sentencing Commission,** an independent body in the judicial branch of the government which has been charged with establishing sentencing policy for the federal government. The nine-person Commission has produced a set of guidelines which took effect on November 1, 1987. The guidelines contain elements of both individualized and determinate justice.[117] Among the major changes suggested by the Commission is a significant decline in the number of "straight" probation sentences (which require no time being served in an institution) and the concomitant growth of "split sentences" (which require as a condition of probation a short period of confinement). In addition, the guidelines increase the average time served for some offenses while decreasing the time for others. For example, if the guidelines are followed, the average time served for violent crime should increase by about two years; the time served for property and immigration law violations should decrease slightly. (At the time of this writing, the federal guidelines are under considerable legal attack. The Supreme Court has been asked to rule whether they represent a violation of the separation of powers doctrine.)

The jury is still out on the effectiveness of guidelines. An evaluation of the Minnesota experiment found mixed results.[118] Minnesota's judges strictly adhered to guidelines recommendations the first year

they were in effect (1980), but began to deviate from them after two years. Some racial disparity was indicated the first year after the guidelines were adapted, but it diminished over time. The most important result of applying the guidelines was a 73 percent increase in incarceration for serious offenders and a 72 percent reduction for nonserious offenders.

Among the questions that still remain about the use of guidelines are (1) the compliance rate of judges; (2) the effect on the already overcrowded prison system; (3) whether they produce unanticipated and undesired sentencing disparity; and (4) the effect on plea negotiations.[119] With respect to the latter issue, it is possible that strict guidelines will encourage greater reliance on pleas because offenders believe that the hope of a probationary sentence is open to them. While this is possible, Terance Miethe found that the Minnesota guidelines neither had a dramatic effect on the plea bargaining process nor did they increase racial or cultural bias in plea outcome.[120]

Sentencing Today

Sentencing reform has been influenced by the belief that a crime control orientation can help to deter crime and incapacitate dangerous offenders. The rehabilitation-treatment goal of sentencing has been subordinated to the goals of social control and protecting public safety. Jurisdictions that previously had employed indeterminate sentences, which allow early release from prison after correctional authorities deem the inmate rehabilitated, have been replacing them with determinate and mandatory sentences, which insure that convicted persons will be separated from society for a predictable number of years. Consequently, the number of people behind bars has risen at a significant pace.

Sentencing practices today reflect the view that criminals are rational decision-makers who consider the consequences of their behavior before they take action. While some critics argue that sentencing practices today ignore the potential of offender rehabilitation, advocates counter with the view that modern sentences are more fair, eliminate disparity, and increase the inmate's sense of justice. Regardless of the merits of either argument, attempts to remove or restrict the uncertainty in sentences will probably continue.

SUMMARY

The judicatory process is designed to provide an important forum for deciding the justice of a conflict between two or more parties. Unfortunately, discretion and personal decision-making interfere with the equality that should be built into the law.

The judicatory process is played out in the nation's court system. State courts usually involve a three- or four-tiered system—lower trial courts; superior trial courts; appellate courts; supreme court. The federal system is similar; it contains trial courts, appellate courts, and the Supreme Court. The U.S. Supreme Court is the final court of appeals for all cases on both state and federal levels.

There are three main actors in the judicatory process. The prosecutor brings charges against the offender and represents the state in all criminal matters. The defense attorney represents the accused at all stages of the adjudicatory process. Some defense attorneys offer private counsel, but the majority are appointed and paid for by the state. The judge controls the trial, rules on issues of evidence, charges the jury, and in some cases can choose the type and length of sentence.

The pretrial stage of the justice process involves such issues as bail, plea bargaining, and alternatives to prosecution. Bail is a money bond the defendant puts up to secure freedom before trial. It is controversial, since those who cannot make bail must spend their time in detention. Critics charge that bail discriminates against the poor, who can neither afford bond nor borrow it from bondsmen. Consequently, reform programs such as release on recognizance have been started.

Plea bargaining involves the prosecutor's allowing people to plead guilty as charged in return for some consideration—for example, a reduced sentence or dropped charges. Plea bargaining has been criticized, since it represents the unchecked use of discretion by prosecutors. Often, serious criminals can receive light sentences by bargaining, while some people may be coerced into pleading guilty because they fear a harsh sentence if they go to trial. An effort has been made to control plea bargains, but they are still frequently used.

One way of influencing plea bargains is through noncriminal alternatives to prosecution. These include diversion and other types of treatment-oriented programs.

The second stage of the judicatory process is the criminal trial. The trial has a number of distinct stages, including: jury selection; opening statements; presentation of evidence by prosecution and defense; closing arguments; instructions to the jury; and verdict, sentence, and appeal. The rule of law also affects criminal trials. The Supreme Court has required that trials be speedy, public, and fair, and has ruled that people have a right to be free from double jeopardy and to be represented by competent counsel.

After a conviction, sentencing occurs. Each state and the federal government have their own type of sentences and punishments. In all, fines, suspended sentences, community supervision, and prison are the most common forms of punishment. Prison sentences are divided into determinate, indeterminate, mandatory, and presumptive. Efforts to control sentencing disparity include the use of sentencing councils and sentencing guidelines, as well as determinate, mandatory, and presumptive sentences.

KEY TERMS

United States District Courts
Federal Courts of Appeal
U.S. Supreme Court
writ of certiorari
landmark decision
prosecution
affidavits
discretion
nolle prosequi
overcriminalized
case pressure
defense
attorney list/assigned counsel
public defenders
adversarial process
judge
charging the jury
Missouri Plan
bill of indictment
complaint
nolo contendere
bail
bondsman

Vera Foundation
release on recognizance (ROR)
Federal Bail Reform Act of 1984
bail guidelines
diversion
widening the net
courtroom workgroup
venire
voir dire
peremptory challenge
dual sovereignty doctrine
suspended sentence
presentence investigation
concurrent sentence
consecutive sentence
sentencing disparity
sentencing councils
sentencing guidelines
Crime Control Act of 1984
U.S. Sentencing Commission

——————————— Notes ———————————

1. Edward Lisefski and Donald Manson, *Tracking Offenders, 1984* (Washington, D.C.: Bureau of Justice Statistics, 1988).

2. *Ibid.*

3. See, generally, Jerome Skolnick, *Justice Without Trial* (New York: Wiley, 1966).

4. Patrick Langan, *State Felony Courts and Felony Laws* (Washington, D.C.: Bureau of Justice Statistics, 1987); Bureau of Justice Statistics, *Case Filings in State Courts, State Court Caseload Statistics* (Washington, D.C.: U.S. Department of Justice, 1984).

5. Patrick Langan, *State Felony Courts and Felony Laws* (Washington, D.C.: Bureau of Justice Statistics, 1987).

6. Adapted from, Newman Baker, "The Prosecutor Initiation of Prosecution," *Journal of Criminal Law, Criminology and Police Science* 23 (1933):770–71.

7. Cited in Bureau of Justice Statistics, *Report to the Nation on Crime and Justice* (Washington, D.C.: U.S. Department of Justice, 1983), p. 55. Subsequent references cited as *Report to the Nation.*

8. Edward Lisefski and Donald Manson, *Tracking Offenders, 1984* (Washington, D.C.: Bureau of Justice Statistics, 1988), p. 1.

9. Frank W. Miller, *Prosecution: The Decision to Charge a Suspect with a Crime* (Boston: Little, Brown, 1970).

10. Wayne LaFave, "The Prosecutor's Discretion in the United States," *American Journal of Comparative Law* 18 (1970):532–48.

11. *Report to the Nation,* p. 56.

12. Langan, *State Felony Courts and Felony Laws,* pp. 1–3.

13. Charles Breitel, "Controls in Criminal Law Enforcement," *University of Chicago Law Review* 27 (1960):427–35.

14. See, generally, "A Symposium on Prosecutorial Discretion," *American Criminal Law Review* (1976):379–99.

15. George Cole, "The Decision to Prosecute," *Law and Society Review* 4 (1970):331–43.

16. Gideon v. Wainwright, 372 U.S. 335 (1963); Argersinger v. Hamlin, 407 U.S. 25 (1972).

17. Bureau of Justice Statistics, *Criminal Defense Systems* (Washington, D.C.: U.S. Department of Justice, 1984).

18. See, American Bar Association, Special Committee on Evaluation of Ethical Standards, *Code of Professional Responsibility* (Chicago: American Bar Association, 1982), p. 81.

19. Monroe H. Freedman, "Professional Responsibility of the Criminal Defense Lawyer: The Three Hardest Questions," *Michigan Law Review* 64 (1966):1468.

20. Nix v. Whiteside, 106 S.Ct. 988 (1986).

21. President's Commission on Law Enforcement and the Administration of Justice, *The Challenge of Crime in a Free Society* (Washington, D.C.: U.S. Government Printing Office, 1967), p. 152.

22. Associated Press, "Big NYC Law Firms Pay $71,000 to Start," *The Boston Globe* (18 April 1988), p. 27.

23. See, generally, Malcom Feeley, *The Process is the Punishment* (New York: Russell Sage Foundation, 1979); James Eisenstein and Jacob Herbert, *Felony Justice* (Boston: Little, Brown, 1977).

24. William Lineberry, ed., *Justice in America: Law, Order and the Courts* (New York: H. W. Wilson Co., 1972).

25. John MacKenzie, *The Appearance of Justice* (New York: Charles Scribner's Sons, 1974).

26. Sari Escovitz with Fred Kurland and Nan Gold, *Judicial Selection and Tenure* (Chicago: American Judicature Society, 1974), pp. 3–16.

27. M. Ozanne, R. Wilson, and D. Gedney, Jr., "Toward a Theory of Bail Risk," *Criminology* 18 (1980):149.

28. Cited in Gettinger, "Bail Reform," p. 83.

29. John Goldkamp, *Two Classes of Accused* (Cambridge, Mass.: Ballinger, 1979); William Rhodes, *Pretrial Release and Misconduct* (Washington, D.C.: Bureau of Justice Statistics, 1985).

30. See, generally, Gettinger, "Bail Reform."

31. Vera Institute of Justice, *Programs in Criminal Justice* (New York: Vera Institute, 1972).

32. Malcolm Feeley, *Court Reform on Trial* (New York: Basic Books, 1983); John Goldkamp, "Judicial Reform of Bail Practices: The Philadelphia Experiment," *Court Management Journal* (1983):16–20.

33. John Goldkamp and Michael Gottfredson, *Judicial Decision Guidelines for Bail: The Philadelphia Experiment* (Washington, D.C.: National Institute of Justice, 1983).

34. Mary Toborg, *Pretrial Release: A National Evaluation of Practices and Outcomes* (Washington, D.C.: U.S. Government Printing Office, 1981); Donald Pryor and Walter Smith, "Significant Research Findings Concerning Pre-Trial Release," *Pretrial Issues* (Washington, D.C.: Pretrial Services Resource Center, 1982).

35. Toborg, *Pretrial Release;* William Rhodes, *Pretrial Release and Misconduct* (Washington, D.C.: U.S. Department of Justice, 1985).

36. 18 U.S.C. Sec. 3142(e)(1985).

37. United States v. Salerno, 107 S.Ct. 2095 (1987).

38. Schall v. Martin, 104 S.Ct. 2403 (1984).

39. Stephen Kennedy and Kenneth Carlson, *Pretrial Release and Detention: The Bail Reform Act of 1984* (Washington, D.C.: Bureau of Justice Statistics, 1988).

40. Donald Newman, "Making a Deal," in N. Johnston and L. Savitz, eds., *Legal Process and Corrections* (New York: Wiley, 1982), p. 93.

41. *Ibid.,* pp. 96–97.

42. These sentiments are similar to those expressed by Abraham Blumberg in "The Practice of Law as a Con-

fidence Game: Organizational Co-Optation of a Profession," *Law and Society Review* 1 (1967):15–39.

43. Again, these thoughts are similar to Blumberg's views as expressed in "Law as a Confidence Game."

44. National Advisory Commission on Criminal Justice Standards and Goals, *Courts* (Washington, D.C.: U.S. Government Printing Office, 1976).

45. Richard Kuh, "Plea Copping," *Bar Bulletin* 24 (1966–1967):160–68.

46. Alan Alschuler, "The Defense Counsel's Role in Plea Bargaining," *Yale Law Journal* 84 (1975):1179–92).

47. See, generally, Milton Heuman, "A Note on Plea Bargaining and Case Pressure," *Law and Society Review* 9 (1975):515–30.

48. National Institute of Law Enforcement and Criminal Justice, *Plea Bargaining in the United States* (Washington, D.C.: Georgetown University, 1978), p. 8.

49. Michael Rubenstein, Stevens Clarke, and Teresa White, *Alaska Bans Plea Bargaining* (Washington, D.C.: U.S. Department of Justice, 1980).

50. Boykin v. Alabama, 395 U.S. 238, 89 S.Ct. 1709, 23 L.Ed. 2d 274 (1969).

51. Brady v. United States, 297 U.S. 742, 90 S.Ct. 1463, 25 L.Ed. 2d 747 (1970).

52. Santobello v. New York, 404 U.S. 257, 92 S.Ct. 495, 30 L.Ed. 2d 427 (1971).

53. Brodenkircher v. Hayes, 434 U.S. 357 (1978).

54. Newman, "Making a Deal," p. 102.

55. National Pretrial Intervention Service Center, American Bar Association, *Portfolio of Descriptive Profiles on Selected Pretrial Criminal Justice Intervention Programs* (Chicago: American Bar Association, 1974); A.B.T. Associates, *Pretrial Intervention Program of the Manpower Administration* (Washington, D.C.: Department of Labor, 1971–1972).

56. National Advisory Commission on Criminal Justice Standards and Goals, *Courts*, p. 66.

57. See, for example, "Limiting the Peremptory Challenge: Representation of Groups on Petit Juries," *Yale Law Journal* 86 (1977):1715.

58. Batson v. Kentucky 54 L.W. 4425 (1986).

59. Ham v. South Carolina, 409 U.S. 524, 93 S.Ct. 848, 35 L.Ed. 2d 46 (1973).

60. Turner v. Murray, 106 S.Ct. 1683 (1986).

61. Taylor v. Louisiana, 419 U.S. 522, 42 L.Ed. 2d 690, 95 S.Ct. 692 (1975).

62. In Ristaino v. Ross, the Court said questioning the jury on racial issues was not automatic in all interracial crimes (424 U.S. 589 [1976]).

63. Strunk v. United States, 412 U.S. 434 (1973).

64. Klopfer v. North Carolina, 38 U.S. 213 (1967).

65. Barker v. Wingo, 404 U.S. 307 (1971).

66. *Report to the Nation*, p. 66.

67. Duncan v. Louisiana, 391 U.S. 145 (1968).

68. Baldwin v. New York, 399 U.S. 66 (1970).

69. Williams v. Florida, 399 U.S. 78 (1970).

70. Apodaca v. Oregon, 406 U.S. 404 (1972).

71. Benton v. Maryland, 395 U.S. 784 (1969).

72. United States v. Lanza, 260 U.S. 377 (1922); Bartkus v. Illinois, 359 U.S. 121 (1959); Abbate v. United States, 359 U.S. 187 (1959).

73. Heath v. Alabama, 106 S.Ct. 433 (1985).

74. Powell v. Alabama, 287 U.S. 45 (1932).

75. Gideon v. Wainwright, 372 U.S. 335 (1963).

76. Argersinger v. Hamlin, 407 U.S. 25 (1972).

77. Strickland v. Washington, 104 S.Ct. 2052 (1984).

78. See, Marvin E. Frankel, *Criminal Sentences—Law Without Order* (New York: Hill & Wang, 1973).

79. See, generally, Norval Morris, *Equal Justice under the Law* (Washington, D.C.: U.S. Government Printing Office, 1977).

80. See, V. O'Leary, M. Gottfredson, and A. Gelman, "Contemporary Sentencing Proposals," *Criminal Law Bulletin* 11 (1975):558–60.

81. Sally Hillsman, Barry Mahoney, George Cole, and Bernard Auchter, *Fines as Criminal Sanctions* (Washington, D.C.: National Institute of Justice, 1987).

82. Kriss Drass and J. William Spencer, "Accounting for Pre-Sentencing Recommendations: Typologies and Probation Officers' Theory of Office," *Social Problems* 34 (1987):277–93.

83. Marvin Zalman, "The Rise and Fall of the Indeterminate Sentence," *Wayne Law Review* 24 (1978):857.

84. See, Massachusetts General Laws, Chap. 369:10, Chap. 649, Acts of 1974.

85. Todd R. Clear, Robert D. Hewitt, and Robert M. Regoli, "Discretion and the Determinate Sentence: Its Distribution, Control and Effect on Time Served," *Crime and Delinquency* 20 (1974):428–45.

86. See, David Fogel, *Justice as Fairness* (Cincinnati: W. H. Anderson, 1981).

87. Lawrence Greenfield, *Capital Punishment, 1986* (Washington, D.C.: Bureau of Justice Statistics, 1987).

88. See, for example, Ernest Van Den Haag, *Punishing Criminals: Concerning a Very Old and Painful Question* (New York: Basic Books, 1975), pp. 209–11; Walter Berns, "Defending the Death Penalty," *Crime and Delinquency* 26 (1980):503–11.

89. Kilman Shin, *Death Penalty and Crime* (Fairfax, Va.: George Mason University, 1978), p. 1.

90. Charles Black, "Objections to S. 1382, a Bill to Establish Rational Criteria for the Imposition of Capital Punishment," *Crime and Delinquency* 26 (1980):441–53.

91. Hugo Adam Bedeau, *Death Is Different* (Boston: Northeastern University Press, 1987), p. 442.

92. Bedeau, *Death Is Different*, p. 245.

93. *Capital Punishment, 1986* (Washington, D.C.: National Institute of Justice, 1987), p. 5.

94. Lawrence Greenfield and David Hinners, *Capital Punishment, 1984* (Washington, D.C.: Bureau of Justice Statistics, 1985).

95. David Baldus, C. Pulaski, and G. Woodworth, "Comparative Review of Death Sentences: An Empirical Study of the Georgia Experience," *Journal of Criminal Law and Criminology* 74 (1983):661–85.

96. D. Dwayne Smith, "Patterns of Discrimination in Assessments of the Death Penalty: The Case of Louisiana," *Journal of Criminal Justice* 15 (1987):279–86; S. Gross and R. Mauro, "Patterns of Death: An Analysis of Racial Disparities in Capital Sentencing and Homicide Victimization," *Stanford Law Review* 37 (1984):27–153.

97. William Bowers and Glenn Pierce, "Deterrence or Brutalization: What is the Effect of Executions," *Crime and Delinquency* 26 (1980):453–84.

98. 408 U.S. 238, 92 S.Ct. 2726, 33 L.Ed. 2d 346 (1972).

99. 428 U.S. 153, 96 S.Ct. 2909, 49 L.Ed. 2d 859 (1976).

100. 428 U.S. 262, 96 S.Ct. 2950, 49 L.Ed. 2d 929 (1976); 428 U.S. 325, 96 S.Ct. 3001, 49 L.Ed. 2d 944 (1976).

101. Witherspoon v. Illinois, 391 U.S. 510 (1968); Wainwright v. Witt, 469 U.S. 412 (1985).

102. McLesky v. Kemp, 106 S. Ct. 1331 (1986).

103. For a general review of this issue, see, Florence Ferguson, "Sentencing Guidelines: Are [Black] Offenders Given Just Treatment?" Paper presented at the American Society of Criminology Meeting, Montreal, Canada, November, 1987.

104. *Ibid.*

105. Raymond Paternoster, "Race of the Victim and Location of the Crime: The Decision to See the Death Penalty in South Carolina," *Journal of Criminal Law and Criminology* 74 (1983):754–85.

106. Cassia Spohn and Susan Welch, "The Effect of Prior Record in Sentencing Research: An Examination of the Assumption that Any Measure Is Adequate," *Justice Quarterly* 4 (1987):286–302.

107. Alan Lizotte, "Extra-Legal Factors in Chicago's Criminal Courts: Testing the Conflict Model of Criminal Justice," *Social Problems* 25 (1978):564–80; P. Burke and A. Turk, "Factors Affecting Post-Arrest Dispositions: A Model for Analysis," *Social Problems* 22 (1975):313–32; Terrence Thornberry, "Race, Socioeconomic Status and Sentencing in the Juvenile Justice System," *Journal of Criminal Law and Criminology* 64 (1973):90–98.

108. George Bridges, Robert Crutchfield, and Edith Simpson, "Crime, Social Structure and Criminal Punishment: White and Nonwhite Rates of Imprisonment," *Social Problems* 34 (1987):345–61.

109. Terance Miethe and Charles Moore, "Racial Differences in Criminal Processing: The Consequences of Model Selection on Conclusions About Differential Treatment," *The Sociological Quarterly* 27 (1987):217–37.

110. James Unnever and Larry Hembroff, "The Prediction of Racial/Ethic Sentencing Disparities," *Journal of Research in Crime and Delinquency* 25 (1988):53–82.

111. Joan Petersilia, *Racial Disparities in the Criminal Justice System* (Santa Monica, Cal.: Rand Corporation, 1983).

112. William Rhodes, *Pretrial Release and Misconduct* (Washington, D.C.: U.S. Government Printing Office, 1985).

113. David Willison, "The Effects of Counsel on the Severity of Criminal Sentences: A Statistical Assessment," *Justice System Journal* 9 (1984):87–101.

114. Dale Dannefer and Russell Schutt, "Race and Juvenile Justice Processing in Court and Police Agencies," *American Journal of Sociology* 87 (1982):1113–32; Douglas Smith and Christy Visher, "Street-Level Justice: Situational Determinants of Police Arrest Decisions," *Social Problems* 29 (1981):267–77.

115. Charles R. Pruitt and James Q. Wilson, "A Longitudinal Study of the Effect of Race on Sentencing," *Law and Society Review* 17 (1983):613–35; Candace Kruttschnitt, "Sex and Criminal Court Dispositions," *Journal of Research in Crime and Delinquency* 21 (1984):213–32; Cynthia Kempinen, "Changes in the Sentencing Patterns of Male and Female Defendants," *Prison Journal* 63 (1983):3–11.

116. See, Leslie Wilkins, *The Principle of Guidelines for Sentencing* (Washington, D.C.: U.S. Government Printing Office, 1981).

117. Michael Block and William Rhodes, "The Impact of Federal Sentencing Guidelines," in National Institute of Justice, *NIJ Reports* 205 (Sept./Oct. 1987): 2–7.

118. Minnesota Sentencing Guidelines Commission, *The Impact of the Minnesota Sentencing Guidelines: Three-Year Evaluation* (St. Paul, Minn.: 1984), p. 162.

119. David Griswold, "Deviation from Sentencing Guidelines: The Issue of Unwarranted Disparity," *Journal of Criminal Justice* 15 (1987):317–29.

120. Terance Miethe, "Charging and Plea Bargaining Practices Under Determinate Sentencing: An Investigation of the Hydraulic Displacement of Discretion," *Journal of Criminal Law and Criminology* 78 (1986):155–76.

≡ CHAPTER 17

CORRECTIONS

INTRODUCTION

When a person is convicted for a criminal offense, society exercises the right to punish or *correct* his or her behavior. Equating crime and punishment is certainly not a new practice. Criminal offenders have been subjected to punishment by governmental authority throughout recorded history. Over the centuries, there has been significant debate as to why people should be punished and what type of punishment is most appropriate to correct, treat, or deter criminal offender. The style and purpose of criminal corrections has gone through many evolutionary stages and has featured a variety of penal sanctions (see Close-Up).

In U.S. society, correctional jurisdiction is divided among the federal, state, and local levels of government. If they are not eligible for some sort of community supervision program because of the seriousness of their crimes, felons usually are incarcerated in state of federal **prisons**. Misdemeanants are housed in county **jails** or reformatories. In addition, there exists a wide variety of **community-based correctional institutions** and **halfway houses.**

The entire correctional system has been a source of great controversy. Prisons have been viewed as warehouses that—far from helping rehabilitate inmates—are places of violence and degradation. Jails have been the scene of suicides and rapes. Some critics call for the tearing down of prisons, while others argue that new ones should be built and sentences lengthened.[1] Well-publicized riots and conflicts have made the prison the subject of much public attention.

This chapter reviews some of the basic elements of correctional treatment in U.S. society. First, a history of corrections is undertaken to show how our current system evolved over time and the social trends which influenced its development. Then, modern correctional institutions are explored. Such issues are penal institutions, the prisoner's social world, correctional treatment, and prisoners' rights are discussed.

HISTORY OF PUNISHMENT AND CORRECTIONS

Throughout history punishment, in its severest physical forms, has been present in all major institutions.[2]

The **punishment** of criminals has undergone many noteworthy changes, reflecting custom, economic conditions, and religious and political ideals.[3]

In ancient times, the most common state-administered punishment was banishment or exile. Only slaves were commonly subject to harsh physical punishment for their misdeeds. In Rome, for example, the only crime for which capital punishment could be administered was *furtum manifestum*—a thief caught in the act was executed on the spot. More common were economic sanctions and fines, levied for such crimes as assault on a slave, arson, or housebreaking.

In both ancient Greece and ancient Rome, interpersonal violence, even when it resulted in death, was viewed as a private matter. Neither Greek nor Roman (until quite late in their histories) state laws provided for the punishment of a violent crime. Execution of an offender was looked upon as the prerogative of the deceased's family.

The Middle Ages

As noted in Chapter 2, little law or governmental control existed during the early Middle Ages (fifth century to eleventh century A.D.). Offenses were settled by blood feuds carried out by the families of the injured parties. When possible, the Roman custom of settling disputes by fine or an exchange of property was adopted as a means of resolving interpersonal conflicts with a minimum of bloodshed.

After the eleventh century, during the feudal period, forfeiture of land and property was common punishment for persons who violated law and customs or who failed in the feudal obligations to their lord. The word *felony* actually comes from the twelfth century, when the term *felonia* referred to a breach of faith with one's fuedal lord.

During this period in history, the main emphasis on criminal law and punishment lay in maintaining public order.[4] If, in the heat of passion or in a state of intoxication, one person severely injured or killed another, freemen in the area would gather to pronounce a judgment and make the culprit do penance or pay a fine called *wergild* (see Chapter 2). The purpose of the fine was to pacify the injured party and to insure that the conflict would not develop into a blood feud and anarchy. The inability of the lower-class offender to pay a fine led to the development of corporal pun-

CLOSE-UP

Perspectives on Corrections

The major criminological perspectives maintain differing views on the functions and purpose of corrections.

Criminological Perspective	Correctional Viewpoint
Classical Perspective	Correctional institutions are designed to incapacitate known criminals and make them so fearful of punishment that they will not risk repeating their criminal behavior. The threat of punishment also should deter potential criminals. Punishment should be fair and should fit the crime. Crime causes the need for correction.
Positivist Perspective (Individual)	Corrections should be used to treat the offender. Correctional institutions should be turned into "therapeutic communities." Psychologists and psychiatrists should help formulate prison policy and plan treatment routines. Inmates should be released when they are rehabilitated. Treatment should fit the inmate. Social pathology causes the need for correction.
Positivist Perspective (Sociological)	Corrections should help the inmate readjust to society. Vocational and educational training should be stressed. If inmates can learn to adjust to prison, then they will be better able to adjust to society when released. Maintaining social order causes the need for correction.
Interactionist Perspective	Prisons stigmative inmates. Every effort should be made to keep offenders in the community. Use of community-based corrections should be emphasized. Correction causes crime.
Social Conflict Perspective (Conflict)	The "have-nots" go to prison while the "haves" go free. Prison should not be used to punish the lower class while the wealthy are treated leniently. Criminals of all classes should be treated equally. Social power struggles produce the need for correctional institutions.
Social Conflict Perspective (Marxist)	Prisons are an element of class struggle used to punish people who rebel against class-created laws. Corrections should be used to treat the "true capitalist criminals." Capitalism creates the need for correction. In a Marxist society, corrections would not be needed.

Discussion Questions

1. Which perspective on corrections do you agree with?   2. Can a society exist without corrections institutions?

ishment, such as whipping or branding, as a substitute penalty.

By the fifteenth century, changing social conditions influenced the relationship between crime and punishment. First the population of England and Europe began to increase, after a century of being decimated by constant warfare and plagues. At the same time, the developing commercial system caused large tracts of agricultural fields to be converted to grazing lands. Soon, unemployed peasants and land less nobles began flocking to newly developing urban centers, such as London and Paris, or taking to the roads as highway robbers, beggars, or vagabonds.

The later Middle Ages also saw the rise of strong monarchs, such as Henry VIII and Elizabeth I of England, who were determined to keep a powerful grip on their realm. The administration of the "King's Peace" under the shire reeve and constable became stronger.

These developments led to the increased use of **capital** and **corporal punishment** to control the criminal poor. While the wealthy could buy their way out of punishment and into exile, the poor were executed and mutilated at ever-increasing rates. It is estimated that 72,000 thieves were hung during the reign of Henry VIII alone.[5] Execution, banishment, mutilation, branding, and flogging were used on a wide range of offenders, from murderers and robbers to vagrants and gypsies. Punishments became unmatched in their cruelty, featuring a gruesome variety of physical tortures. Also during this period, punishment became a public spectacle, presumably so the sadistic sanctions would act as a deterrent. But the variety and imagination of the tortures inflicted on even minor criminals before their death suggests that sadism and spectacle were more important than any presumed deterrent effect.

Punishment in the Seventeenth and Eighteenth Centuries

By the end of the sixteenth century, the rise of the city and overseas colonization provided tremendous markets for manufactured goods. In England and France, population growth was checked by constant warfare and internal disturbances. Labor was scarce in many manufacturing areas of England, Germany, and Holland. The Thirty Years' War in Germany and the constant warfare among England, France, and Spain helped drain the population.

The punishment of criminals changed to meet the demands created by these social conditions. Instead of the wholesale use of capital and corporal punishment, many offenders were made to do forced labor for their crimes. **Poor Laws,** developed in the early seventeenth century, required that the poor, vagrants, and vagabonds be put to work in public or private enterprise. Houses of correction were developed to make it

convenient for petty law violators to be assigned to work details. Many convicted offenders were pressed into sea duty as galley slaves, a fate considered so loathsome that many convicts practiced self-mutilation rather submit to it.

The constant shortage of labor in the colonies also prompted the authorities to transport convicts overseas. In England, *The Vagrancy Act of 1597* legalized deportation for the first time. *An Order in Council of 1617* granted a reprieve and stay of execution to people convicted of robbery and other felonies who were strong enough to be employed overseas. Similar measures were employed in France and Italy to recruit galley slaves and workers.

Transportation to the colonies became popular; it supplied labor, cost little, and was actually profitable for the government, since manufacturers and plantation owners paid for convicts' services. The Old Bailey Court in London supplied at least 10,000 convicts between 1717 and 1775.[6] Convicts would serve a period as workers and then become free again.

Transportation to the colonies waned as a method of punishment with the increase in colonial population, the further development of the land, and the increasing impact of slavery in the Americas. The American Revolution ended transportation of felons to North America; the remaining areas used were Australia and New Zealand.

Corrections in the Late Eighteenth and Nineteenth Centuries

Between the American Revolution in 1776 and the first decades of the nineteenth century, the population of Europe and America increased rapidly. The gulf between poor workers and wealthy landowners and merchants widened. The crime rate rose significantly, prompting a return to physical punishment and the increased use of the death penalty. During the last part of the eighteenth century, 350 types of crime in England were punishable by death.[7] Although many people sentenced to death for trivial offenses were spared the gallows, there is little question that the use of capital punishment rose significantly between 1750 and 1800.[8] Prompted by these excesses, legal philosophers, such as Jeremy Bentham and Cesare Beccaria (see Chapter 5), argued that physical punishment should be replaced

English inmates enroute to the penal colony in Botany Bay, Australia (19th century).

by periods of confinement and incapacitation in prison.

It was in the United States that correctional reform was first instituted. The U.S. correctional system originated in Pennsylvania under the leadership of William Penn.[9] At the end of the seventeenth century, Penn revised Pennsylvania's criminal code to forbid torture and the capricious use of mutilation and physical punishment. These devices were replaced by the penalties of imprisonment at hard labor, moderate flogging, fines, and forfeiture of property. All lands and goods belonging to felons were to be used to make restitution to the victims of crimes, with restitution being limited to twice the value of the damages. Felons who owned no property were required by law to labor in the prison workhouse until the victim was compensated.

Penn ordered that a new type of institution be built to replace the widely used public forms of punishment—stocks, pillories, the gallows, and the branding iron. Each county was instructed to build a house of corrections similar to today's jails. These measures remained in effect until Penn's death in 1718, when the criminal penal code reverted to its earlier format of open public punishment and harsh brutality.

In 1776, postrevolutionary Pennsylvania again adopted William Penn's code, and in 1787 a group of Quakers led by Dr. Benjamin Rush formed the Philadelphia **Society for Alleviating the Miseries of Public Prisons.** The aim of the society was to bring some degree of humane and orderly treatment to the growing penal system. The Quakers' influence on the legislature resulted in limiting the use of the death penalty to cases involving treason, murder, rape, and arson. Their next step was to reform the existing institutional system so that the prison could serve as a suitable alternative to physical punishment.

The only models of custodial institutions at that time were the local county jails that Penn had established. These facilities were designed to detain offenders, to securely incarcerate convicts awaiting other punishment, or to hold offenders who were working off their crimes. The Pennsylvania jails placed men, women, and children of all ages indiscriminately in one room. Liquor was often freely sold. Under pressure from the Quakers to improve these conditions, the Pennsylvania State Legislature in 1790 called for the renovation of the prison system. The ultimate result was the creation of Philadelphia's **Walnut Street Prison.** At this institution, most prisoners were placed in solitary cells, where they remained in isolation and did not have the right to work.[10] Quarters that contained the solitary or separate cells were called the *penitentiary house,* as was already the custom in England.

The new Pennsylvania prison system took credit for a rapid decrease in the crime rate—from 131 convictions in 1789 to 45 in 1793.[11] The prison became known as a school for reform and a place for public labor. The Walnut Street Prison's equitable conditions were credited with reducing escapes to none in the first four years of its existence (except for 14 on opening day).

However, the Walnut Street Prison was not a total success. Overcrowding undermined the goal of solitary confinement of serious offenders, and soon more than one inmate was placed in each cell. Despite these difficulties, similar institutions were erected in New York (Newgate in 1791), New Jersey (Trenton in 1798), Virginia (1800), and Kentucky (1800).

The Auburn System

In the early 1800s, both the Pennsylvania and the New York prison systems were experiencing difficulties maintaining the ever-increasing numbers of convicted criminals. Initially, administrators dealt with the problem by increasing the use of pardons, relaxing prison discipline, and limiting supervision.

In 1816, the state of New York built a new prison at Auburn, hoping to alleviate some of the overcrowding at Newgate. The Auburn Prison design became known as the *tier system,* because cells were built vertically on five floors of the structure. It was sometimes also referred to as the *congregate system,* since most prisoners ate and worked in groups. Later, in 1819, construction was started on a wing of solitary cells to house unruly prisoners. Three classes of prisoners were then created: one group remained continually in

solitary confinement as a result of breaches of prison discipline; the second group was allowed labor as an occasional form of recreation; and the third and largest class worked and ate together during the days and only went into seclusion at night.

The philosophy of the **Auburn System** was crime prevention through fear of punishment and silent confinement. The worst felons were to be cut off from all contact with other prisoners; and although they were treated and fed relatively well, they had no hope of pardon to relieve their isolation. For a time, some of the worst convicts were forced to remain totally alone and silent during the entire day; this practice caused many prisoners to have mental breakdowns, resulting in many suicides and self-mutilations. This practice was abolished in 1823.[12]

The combination of silence and solitude as a method of punishment was not abandoned easily. Prison officials sought to overcome the side effects of total isolation while maintaining the penitentiary system. The solution Auburn adopted was to keep convicts in separate cells at night but allow them to work together during the days under enforced silence. Hard work and silence became the foundation of the Auburn system wherever it was adopted. Silence was the key to prison discipline; it prohibited the formulation of escape plans, it averted plots and riots, and it allowed prisoners to contemplate their infractions.

Early Application of the Auburn System. The practice in early prisons of using harsh discipline and control to "retrain" the heart and soul of offenders is the subject of an important book on penal philosophy, *Discipline and Punish,* by the French sociologist Michel Foucault.[13] Foucault's thesis is that as societies evolve and become more complex, they create increasingly more elaborate mechanisms to discipline their recalcitrant members and make them "docile" enough to obey social rules.[14] In the seventeenth and eighteenth centuries, discipline was directed toward the human body itself, through torture. In the development of the nineteenth-century prison, the object was to discipline the offender psychologically: "The expiation that once rained down upon the body must be replaced by a punishment that acts in the depths of the heart."[15] We can still see remnants of that philosophy in today's prisons.

According to one historian, David Rothman, regimentation became the standard mode of prison life.

Convicts did not simply walk from place to place; rather, they went in close order and single file, each looking over the shoulder of the preceding person, faces inclined to the right, feet moving in unison. The lockstep prison shuffle was developed at Auburn and is still employed in some institutions today.[16]

When discipline was breached in the Auburn system, punishment was applied in the form of a rawhide whip on the inmate's back. Immediate and effective, Auburn discipline was so successful that when a hundred inmates were chosen to build the famous Sing-Sing prison in 1825, not one dared escape, although they were housed in an open field with only minimal supervision.[17]

The New Pennsylvania System

In 1818, the state of Pennsylvania took the radical step of establishing a prison that placed each inmate in a single cell and did not provide them with any work to do. Classifications were abolished, because each cell was intended as a miniature prison that would prevent the inmates from contaminating one another.

The new Pennsylvania state prison, called the Western Penitentiary, had an unusual architectural design. It was built in a semicircle, with the cells positioned along its circumference. Built back-to-back, some cells faced the boundary wall while others faced the internal area of the circle. Its inmates were kept in solitary confinement almost constantly, being allowed about an hour a day for exercise. In 1820, a second, similar penitentiary using the isolate system was built in Philadelphia and called the Eastern Penitentiary.

The supporters of the Pennsylvania system believed that the penitentiary was truly a place to do penance. By advocating totally removing the sinner from society and allowing the prisoner a period of isolation in which to reflect alone upon the evils of crime, the supporters of the Pennsylvania system reflected the influence of religion and religious philosophy on corrections. In fact, its advocates believed that solitary confinement (with in-cell labor as a recreation) would eventually make working so attractive that upon release the inmate would be well-suited to resume a productive existence in society. The Pennsylvania system obviated the need for large numbers of guards or disciplinary measures. Isolated from each other, inmates could not plan escapes or collec-

tively break rules. When discipline was a problem, however, the whip and the iron gag were used.

Many fiery debates occurred between advocates of the Pennsylvania system and the Auburn system. Those supporting the latter position boasted of its supposed advantages; their system was the cheapest and most productive way to reform prisoners. They criticized the Pennsylvania system as cruel and inhumane, suggesting that solitary confinement was both physically and mentally damaging. The Pennsylvania system's devotees, on the other hand, argued that their system was quiet, efficient, humane, well-ordered, and provided the ultimate correctional facility.[18] They chided the Auburn system for tempting inmates to talk by putting them together for meals and work and then punishing them when they did talk. Finally, the Auburn system was accused of becoming a breeding place for criminal associations by allowing inmates to get to know one another.

The Auburn system eventually prevailed and spread throughout the United States; many of its features are still used today. Its innovations include congregate working conditions, the use of solitary confinement to punish unruly inmates, military regimentation, and discipline. In Auburn-like institutions, prisoners were marched from place to place; their time was regulated by bells telling them to wake up, sleep, and work. The system was so like the military that many of its early administrators were recruited from the armed services.

Although the prison was viewed as an improvement over capital and corporal punishment, it quickly became the scene of depressed conditions; inmates were treated harshly, and routinely whipped and tortured. As one historian, Samuel Walker, notes:

> *Prison brutality flourished. It was ironic that the prison had been devised as a more human alternative to corporal and capital punishment. Instead, it simply moved corporal punishment indoors where, hidden from public view, it became even more savage.*[19]

Post-Civil War Developments

The prison of the late nineteenth century was remarkably similar to that of today. The congregate system was adapted in all states except Pennsylvania. Prisons experienced overcrowding, and the single-cell principle was often ignored. The prison, like the police department, became the scene of political intrigue and efforts by political administrators to control the hiring of personnel and dispensing of patronage.

Prison industry developed and became the predominant theme around which institutions were organized. Some prisons used the *contract system*, in which officials sold the labor of inmates to private businesses. Sometimes, the contractor supervised the inmates inside the prison itself. Under the *convict-lease system*, the state leased its prisoners to a business for a fixed annual fee and gave up supervision and control. Finally, the *state account system* had prisoners produce goods in prison for state use.[20]

The development of prison industry quickly led to abuse of inmates, who were forced to work for almost no wages, and to profiteering by dishonest administrators and businesspeople. During the Civil War era, prisons were major manufacturers of clothes, shoes, boots, furniture, and the like. During the 1880s, opposition by trade unions sparked restrictions on interstate commerce in prison goods and ended their profitability.

There were also reforms in prison operations. **Z. R. Brockway,** warden at the Elmira Reformatory in New York, advocated individualized treatment, the indeterminate sentence, and parole. The reformatory program initiated by Brockway included elementary education for illiterates, designated library hours, lectures by faculty members of the local Elmira College, and a group of vocational training shops. The cost to the state of the institution's operations was to be held to a minimum. Although Brockway proclaimed Elmira to be an ideal reformatory, his actual achievements were limited. The greatest significance of his contribution was the injection of a degree of humanitarianism into the industrial prisons of that day. However, although many institutions were constructed across the country and labeled reformatories as a result of the Elmira model, most of them continued to be industrially oriented.[21]

The Progressive Era and Beyond

The early twentieth century was a time of contrasts in the prison system of the United States.[22] At one extreme were those who advocated reform, such as the Mutual Welfare League, led by Thomas Mott Osborne.

Prison reform groups proposed better treatment for inmates, an end to harsh corporal punishment, and the creation of meaningful prison industries and educational programs. Reformers argued that prisoners should not be isolated from society, but that the best elements of society—education, religion, meaningful work, self-governance—should be brought to the prison. Osborne went so far as to spend one week in New York's notorious Sing-Sing Prison to learn about its conditions firsthand.

Opposed to the reformers were conservative prison administrators and state officials, who believed that stern disciplinary measures were needed to control dangerous prison inmates. They continued the time-honored system of regimentation and discipline. Although the whip and the lash were eventually abolished, solitary confinement in dark, bare cells became a common penal practice.

In time, some of the more rigid prison rules gave way to reform. By the mid-1930s, few prisons required inmates to wear the red-and-white-striped convict suit and substituted nondescript gray uniforms. The code of silence ended, as did the lockstep shuffle. Prisoners were allowed "the freedom of the yard" to mingle and exercise an hour or two each day.[23] Movies and radio appeared in the 1930s. Visiting policies and mail privileges were liberalized.

A more important trend was the development of specialized prisons designed to treat particular types of offenders. For example, in New York the prisons at Clinton and Auburn were viewed as industrial facilities for hard-core inmates, Great Meadow as an agricultural center to house nondangerous offenders, and Dannemora as a facility for the criminally insane. In California, San Quentin housed inmates considered salvageable by correctional authorities, while Folsom was reserved for the hard-core offender.[24]

Prison industry also evolved. Opposition by organized labor helped put an end to the convict-lease system and forced inmate labor. Although some vestiges of private prison industry existed into the 1920s, most convict labor was devoted to state-use items, such as license plates and laundry.

Despite these changes and reforms, the prison in the mid-twentieth century remained a destructive total institution. Although some aspects of inmate life improved, severe discipline, harsh rules, and solitary confinement were the way of life in prison.

The Modern Era

In the modern era we have witnessed a period of change and turmoil in the nation's correctional system. Three trends stand out. First, a great deal of litigation has been brought by inmates seeking greater rights and privileges. Since the 1960s, state and federal courts have ruled in numerous cases concerning an inmate's rights to freedom of religion and speech, medical care, due process, and proper living conditions. In many areas inmates have won rights unheard of in earlier nineteenth- and twentieth-century prisons.

Second, violence within the correctional system has become a national scandal. Well-publicized riots at New York's Attica Prison and the New Mexico State Penitentiary have drawn attention to the potential for death and destruction that lurks in every prison. One reaction has been to improve conditions and provide innovative programs that give inmates a voice in running the institution. Another has been to tighten discipline and call for the building of new maximum-security prisons to control dangerous offenders.

Third, the alleged failure of correctional rehabilitation has prompted many **penologists** (criminologists who deal with prison management and the treatment of offenders) to reconsider the purpose of incapacitating criminals. Today it is more common to view the correctional system as a mechanism for control and punishment than as a device for rehabilitation and reform.

The alleged failure of correctional treatment has prompted the development of alternatives to incarceration: diversion, restitution, and community-based corrections. As the 1990s begin, the nation's correctional policy seems to be to keep as many nonthreatening offenders out of the correctional system as possible by means of community-based programs, and conversely to incarcerate dangerous, violent offenders for long periods of time.[25] Unfortunately, despite the development of alternatives to incarceration, the number of people under lock and key has skyrocketed.

Corrections Today

Correctional treatment can be divided into four main components: community-based corrections, jail, prisons, and parole. Community-based corrections programs include probation—community supervision under the control of the sentencing court—and an array of institutional facilities located in the community, usually called halfway houses or community correctional centers. Treatment in the community is viewed as a viable alternative to traditional correctional practices.[26] First, it is significantly less expensive to supervise inmates in the community than to house them in secure institutional facilities. Second, community-based corrections are necessary if the prison system is not to be overwhelmed by an influx of offenders. Third, community-based treatment is viewed as a charitable gesture given to less serious offenders so they can avoid the stigma and pains of imprisonment.

The second element of corrections involves secure confinement. The jail houses misdemeanants (and some felons) serving their sentences, as well as felons and misdemeanants awaiting trial who have not been released on bail. State and federal **prisons** are used to incarcerate felons for extended periods of time. Finally, **parole** and aftercare agencies supervise prisoners who have been given early release from their sentences.

COMMUNITY-BASED CORRECTIONS

The major forms of community-based corrections, probation and community-based facilities, are discussed below.

Probation

Probation usually involves the suspension of the offender's sentence, in return for the promise of good behavior in the community, under the supervision of the probation department. Probation replaces a term in an institution, although minors can simply be placed on probation without the threat of detention. In about one-fourth of the states, the offender is first sentenced to a prison term, and then the sentence is suspended and the defendant placed on probation. In another one-fourth of the states, the imposition of a prison sentence is delayed while the offender is put on probation. In the rest, courts may use either mechanism.[27]

As practiced in all 50 states and by the federal government, probation implies a contract between the court and the offender in which the former promises to hold a prison term in abeyance while the latter promises to adhere to a set of rules or conditions required by the court. If the rules are violated, and especially if the probationer commits another criminal offense, probation may be *revoked*; this means that the contract is terminated and the original sentence enforced. If an offender on probation commits a second offense that is more severe than the first, he or she may also be indicated, tried, and sentenced on that second offense. Probation may be revoked simply because the rules and conditions of probation have not been met, even if the offender has not committed a further crime.

Each probationary sentence is for a fixed period of time, depending on the seriousness of the offense and the statutory law of the jurisdiction. Probation is considered served when the offender fulfills the conditions set by the court for that period of time; he or she can live without interference from the state.

Probation Sentences

Probationary sentences may be granted by state and federal district courts and state superior (felony) courts. Probation has become an accepted and widely used sentence for adult felons and misdemeanants and for juvenile delinquents.

In some states, juries may grant probation as part of their sentencing power; or they may make recommendations to judges, which judges will usually follow if the case meets certain legally regulated criteria (for example, if it falls within a certain class of offenses as determined by statute).[28] Juries can recommend probation, but the judge has the final say in the matter and can grant probation at his or her discretion. In nonjury trials, probation is granted solely by judicial mandate.

In most jurisdictions, all juvenile offenders are eligible for probation, as are most adults. Some state statutes prohibit probation for certain types of adult offenders, usually those who have engaged in repeated and serious violent crimes such as murder or rape. Mandatory sentences also have made some offenders ineligible for probation.

The term of the probationary sentence may extend to the limit of the suspended prison term; or the court may set a time limit that reflects the sentencing period. For misdemeanors, probation usually extends for the entire period of the jail sentence. For felonies, probationary periods are likely to be shorter and more limited than the prison sentences would have been. The federal criminal code recommends that probation for felons last five years; juveniles are typically placed on probation for periods from six to 24 months. Some state court judges also may impose monetary fines when granting probation; this practice is commonly applied to white-collar crimes, by which an offender may have profited from an illegal business practice.

Some judges may wish to grant an offender probation only after the offender has sampled prison life, perhaps to emphasize that the rules of probation must be kept. Probation cannot be granted after the offender has actually been incarcerated (since this practice is known as parole), but a judge does have available several devices to allow institutionalizing a convicted offender for a limited period of time before probation. For example, when the offender is charged with a variety of offenses, the judge may impose a short jail term on one criminal count and probation on the others. In some state codes and in the federal criminal code, a jail term can actually be a condition of probation; this is referred to as **split sentencing.**

However, the granting of probation to follow a jail sentence is frowned upon by some experts, who believe that even a brief period of incarceration can mitigate the purpose of probation, which is to provide the offender with nonstigmatized, community-based treatment.

Probation Organizations

About 1,920 agencies nationwide list adult probation as their major function. At last tally, they supervise about 2,094,405 adult probationers, an increase of 6 percent over the preceding year.[29] During 1986, about 1.2 million people were placed on probation, and 1.14 million finished their probationary sentence; about 1,178 people per 100,000 population were on probation, or 65 percent of the correctional population.

Most probation agencies are organized as state-level agencies (56 percent); the remainder are organized at the county or municipal level of government.

About 30 states combine probation and parole supervision into a single state agency.[30]

There are arguments both for placing probation services under the supervision of individual courts and for creating statewide agencies. Local supervision makes probation more responsive to court discretion and helps judges get better information on the effectiveness of their decisions. Since the bulk of the probation department's work is in the local courts, it seems appropriate that the agencies should be organized at the county level of government.

Those who advocate large state probation agencies argue that probation is a correctional service and therefore should be part of the executive level of government.[31] Larger agencies can facilitate coordination for programs and staff, establishment of training programs, and distribution of budget. However, as of this writing, no one position prevails; probation remains organized at both the state and the local level.

Probation Services

After a person is convicted of a crime, the probation department investigates the case to determine the factors related to the criminality of the offender. Based on this presentence investigation, the department recommends to the sentencing judge whether the offender should be given eligibility for community release. In the event the offender is placed on probation, the investigation findings will be used as the basis for treatment and supervision.

If the offender is placed on probation, the department makes a diagnosis of his or her personality and treatment needs. Based on this evaluation, some offenders will be given little supervision, perhaps a monthly phone call or visit, while others will be maintained under close supervision and will receive intensive care and treatment.

The probation officer also participates in treatment supervision. Based on concepts of psychology, social work, or counseling, and on the diagnosis of the offender, the probation officer plans a treatment schedule that, it is hoped, will allow the probationer to fulfill the probation contract and make a reasonable adjustment to the community.

The treatment function is a product of both the investigative aspect and the diagnostic aspect of probation. It is based on the probation officer's perception of the probationer, including family problems, peer relationships, and employment background. Treatment may also involve the use of community resources. For example, a probation officer who discovers that a client has a drinking problem may help to find a detoxification center willing to accept the case, while a chronically underemployed offender may be given job counseling or training. Or, in the case of juvenile delinquency, a probation officer may work with teachers and other school officials to help a young offender stay in school. Of course, most cases do not (or cannot) receive such individualized treatment; some treatment mechanisms merely involve a weekly or biweekly phone call to determine whether a job is being maintained or school attended.[32]

Innovative Probation Services

Probation departments have attempted numerous innovative programs to service clients, including house arrest and electronic monitoring, intensive supervision, shock probation and split sentencing, volunteer workers, and restitution.

House Arrest and Electronic Monitoring. Because of extreme overcrowding in prisons and jails, many states are instituting sentences in which offenders who might normally be incarcerated are ordered to remain confined in their homes, typically under supervision of the county probation department. In more than 20 states, offenders also are being monitored by electronic devices which detect if they leave their home without permission. In other instances, probation officers, other monitors, or even computers call offenders to make sure they are at home.

The advantages of house arrest include: low cost; the fact that the offender can be allowed leave to maintain a job or treatment program; keeping families intact; protection of nonviolent offenders from the danger and stigma of prison; and the flexibility for the justice system to deal with particular types of offenders who have to be confined for only particular periods of time (for example, an individual who continually gets drunk on weekends). Those who oppose this approach maintain that it is a Big Brother-like intrusion of privacy, that it widens the net of social control, or that it is not serious enough punishment for the

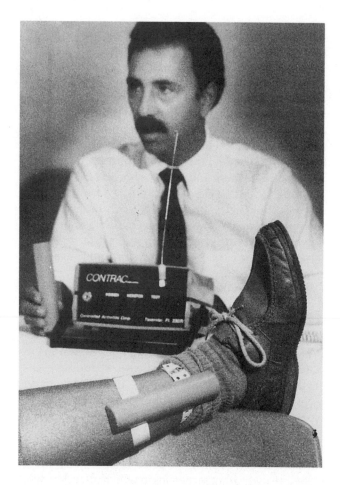

This electronic monitor can be worn on the arm or leg and keeps track of probationers sentenced to home-incarceration or work programs.

offenders who most typically receive it, such as drunk drivers.[33]

Intensive Probation Supervision.
As the cost of prison mounts and correctional institutions experience continued overcrowding, many jurisdictions are now turning to **intensive probation supervision,** or **IPS.** Under the IPS system, offenders who would ordinarily be sentenced to a term of incarceration are placed in the community under extremely close supervision of the probation staff. In an impressive review of IPS programs, **James Byrne** found that some required up to five or more contacts to be made each week while others were far less intrusive (2 contacts per month); drug and alcohol testing, restitution to the victim, mandatory curfew, and other control mechanisms were routinely employed.[34]

While most of the IPS programs are relatively new and are undergoing review, Georgia has successfully implemented an IPS program. An evaluation of the Georgia experience indicates that IPS saves quite a bit of money (almost $7,000 per client), relieves prison overcrowding (the correctional population declined 10 percent), and presents little additional danger to the community. Though 16 percent of the IPS clients were considered failures, less than 1 percent committed additional violent crimes; their recidivisim record compared favorably with conventional probationers and prison releasees.[35] In a national evaluation of IPS programs, Joan Petersilia of the Rand Corporation found that they were an inexpensive alternative to incarceration which did not jeopardize public safety.[36]

Shock Probation and Split Sentencing.
Shock probation has been used in a few states, such as Kentucky and Ohio.[37] Under this plan, offenders begin serving their prison sentence but, after a brief stay, may petition to serve the rest of their sentence in the community. **Split sentences,** used extensively by federal courts, enable the judge to give a probationary sentence but include a short prison stay as a condition of probation. Both systems operate under the belief that the shock of a prison stay will jolt the offender into conventional behavior. Several studies that have attempted to test the effectiveness of this approach have failed to indicate that it reduces recidivism. Critics argue that even a short prison stay can damage offenders and mitigate the purpose of probation.

Volunteers.
Since probation services are so widely used, the burden on individual probation officers is tremendous. It is not unusual for probation officers to maintain over a hundred clients. To meet this challenge, it has become commonplace for probation departments to employ paraprofessionals and volunteers in what might be considered regular line positions. Volunteers often make up a significant portion of probation department staffs. This practice is not without controversy. Volunteers and paraprofessionals can certainly make an important contribution, but their employment has not always been met with enthusiasm by regular probation staff members.

They are sometimes viewed as a threat to job security and as an excuse for legislatures to deny budgetary increases for probation services.

Restitution. Probation officers also have been assigned to operate court-based **restitution** programs. The restitution concept requires defendants to either pay back the victims of their crimes (monetary restitution) or serve the community to compensate for their criminal acts (community service restitution). The restitution concept received its impetus from federal funding, but the termination of support has caused ongoing programs to be incorporated into existing court structures, such as probation departments.[38]

Ordinarily, as mentioned, restitution programs require offenders to pay back victims of crime or serve the community as a condition of probation.[39] The process thus offers the convicted offender a chance to avoid a prison sentence or a more lengthy probationary period. Restitution also may be used as a diversionary device to offer some offenders the chance to avoid a criminal record altogether. In this instance, the judge continues the case "without a finding" while the defendant completes the restitution order; after the probation department determines the restitution has been made, the case is dismissed.

Some restitution programs, such as the Win-Onus program in Winona, Minnesota, and the EARN-IT program in Quincy, Massachusetts, have proven highly successful.[40] A national evaluation of juvenile restitution programs found that 87 percent of 12,000 probationers successfully completed their restitution orders and that 86 percent of the clients had no further contact with authorities because of new offenses.[41]

Probation Rules and Revocation

Each offender granted probation is given a set of rules to guide his or her behavior. Most jurisdictions have a standard set of rules, which include behaviors such as: (1) maintaining steady employment; (2) making restitution for loss or damage; (3) cooperating with the probation officer; (4) obeying all laws; and (5) meeting family responsibilities. Sometimes an individual probationer is given specific rules that relate to his or her particular circumstances, such as

the requirement to enroll in a drug treatment program.

If rules are violated, a person's probation may be **revoked** by the court, and the person either begins serving the sentence or, if he or she has not yet been sentenced, receives a prison sentence from the court. Revocation for violation of probation rules is called a **technical violation;** probation also can be revoked if the offender commits another offense.

In a series of cases, most importantly *Gagnon v. Scarpelli*, the Supreme Court has ruled that before probation can be revoked, the offender (1) must be given a hearing before the sentencing court, and (2) must be provided with counsel if there is a substantial reason for him or her to require the assistance of an attorney.[42]

Success of Probation

There is some question as to how successful probation actually is. That is, how often do probationers commit new crimes while they are under supervision? A federal survey found that 27 percent of people entering prison for the first time are on probation for a prior offense, and that 21 percent of all entering inmates are on probation.[43]

In a similar vein, Joan Petersilia and her colleagues at the Rand Corporation followed the careers of 1,672 California men granted probation for felony offenses.[44] They found that 1,087 (65 percent) were rearrested, 853 (51 percent) were convicted, and 568 (34 percent) were incarcerated. The researchers uncovered the disturbing fact that 75 percent of the new charges were for serious crimes, including larceny, burglary, and robbery; 18 percent were convicted on serious violent crime charges. They also found that about 25 percent of felons granted probation had personal and legal characteristics indistinguishable from people put in prison for the same original charge.

So, although probation remains the predominant criminal sentence, its success may be undermined by the pressure to keep the prison population down which results in probation being granted to serious felony offenders. The fact that it costs far less to maintain an offender in the community than in prison, combined with continued prison overcrowding, leads to constant economic pressure to grant probation to serious felony offenders.

Community-Based Institutions

Community-based institutions have come into prominence in the past twenty years; today, hundreds of community-based programs are operating around the country.

Community-based institutions can be classified into three types: halfway houses that serve as a bridge between prison and the community and hold inmates just before their release; community facilities that serve as an original treatment alternative for offenders who are judged to be in need of a structured environment but whose behavior does not warrant a prison sentence; and, finally, some facilities that house both types of clients.

The theoretical basis of community-based institutions is found on four major concepts:[45]

1. It is considered more humane to treat offenders in the community than in large, fortress-like prisons. The community-based institution can help integrate the offender back into society.
2. Community-based institutions are viewed as a way to divert offenders from the traditional prison system. When community institutions are used as the primary correctional measure, the offender is spared the stigma of the prison experience.
3. Community corrections also have been viewed as a more effective rehabilitation device than the prison. When the offender's ties with family, friends, job, and neighborhood are maintained, the dehumanizing effect of prison is avoided.
4. Community institutions are cost-effective, since the needs for high security and the large staff of the traditional prison are avoided.

Most community institutions are used to serve inmates before their release into society. Several different community corrections strategies have been employed recently. The traditional halfway house serves as a transitional setting between institution and community for selected inmates. An inmate is transferred to a halfway house just before being granted parole. He or she works during the day and usually receives counseling at night. The group living experience in the community helps prepare inmate for success when they are eventually released.

A more recent model is for offenders to serve their entire term within the halfway house setting. For example, Portland House, a private residential center in Minneapolis, Minnesota, operates as an alternative to county jail or state prison commitment for young adult felony offenders. Residents regularly receive group therapy and counseling on financial, employment, educational, family, and personal matters. With funds withheld from their earnings at work-release employment, residents pay room and board, family support, self-support, and income taxes.[46]

Despite attempts at innovation, nagging doubts persist about the overall effectiveness of community-based corrections. Conflict theorist Andrew Scull suggests that community-based corrections are simply a way of managing offenders at a lower cost than prison.[47] And John Hylton argues that they help widen the net: "Persons who were not subjected to control previously may now be controlled under the guise of community treatment."[48]

Thus, although many community-based correctional programs are still in operation, and new ones are being created, the jury is still out on their overall efficiency and effectiveness.[49]

JAILS

The jail, sometimes referred to as a house of correction, is a secure institution used to (1) detain offenders before trial if they cannot afford or are not eligible for bail, and (2) serve as an institution to house misdemeanant offenders sentenced to terms of one year or less, as well as some nonserious felons.

The jail is of European design. It originated in the sixteenth century and was used to house those awaiting trial and punishment. Jails were not used to house sentenced criminals, since at that time punishment was either by fine, exile, corporal punishment, or death.

Throughout their history, jails have been considered hellholes of pestilence and cruelty. In early English history, they were used to house offenders awaiting trial as well as vagabonds, debtors, the mentally ill, and assorted others. The cost of running the jail was paid by the prisoners themselves:

In 1748 the admission to Southwark prison was eleven shillings and four pence. Having got in, the prisoner had to pay for having himself put in irons, for his bed, of whatever sort, for his room if he was able to afford a separate room. He had to pay for his food, and when he had paid his debts and was ready to go out, he had to pay for having his irons struck off, and a discharge fee . . . The gaolers [jailers] were usually "low-bred, mercenary and oppressive, barbarous fellows, who think of nothing but enriching themselves by the most cruel extortion, and have less regard for the life of a poor prisoner than for the life of a brute."[50]

The American colonists adopted the European custom of detaining prisoners in jail. As noted previously, William Penn instituted the first jails to house convicted offenders while they worked off their sentence. The Walnut Street Prison, built in 1790, is considered the first modern jail.

Jail Populations

There has been a national effort to remove as many people from local jails as possible through the adoption of both bail reform measures and pretrial diversion. Nonetheless, jail populations have been steadily increasing, due in part to the increased use of mandatory jail sentences for such common crimes as drunk driving and the use of local jails to house inmates because of crowded conditions in state prisons.

There were approximately 275,000 people held in the nation's jails at the time of the last jail census (June 1986).[51] Whereas the number of jails has declined from a high of 4,037 in 1970 to about 3,500 today, the number of inmates has increased about 70 percent (from 160,683); thus, there is a trend toward fewer but larger jails.

Since 1983, about 8.3 million people have been admitted to jails annually, including about 7.5 million males and 800,000 females. Though the jail population is only 10 percent female, the number of women admitted to jails increased 80 percent over a eight-year period (1978 to 1986).

While the removal of juveniles from adult jails has long been a national priority, more than 90,000 youths are still admitted to adult jails each year. Similarly disturbing is the fact that minorities are disproportionately represented in the jail population; about 40 percent of jail inmates are black and 14 percent are Hispanic.

A federal survey of a jail inmates found that they were disproportionately young, single, minority males whose annual income was around $3,700; 60 percent had not finished high school.[52] One in four inmates had been financially dependent on welfare, Social Security, unemployment insurance, family, and friends rather than their own wages. This was particularly true of black female inmates, whose poverty level was extremely high. The survey also found a great many inmates were involved in daily drug use (40 percent). About 20 percent were under the influence of drugs at the time of their offense, and 25 percent reported being drunk.

In sum, the jail population reflects the social and economic factors typically associated with crime: poverty, lack of education, unemployment, and substance abuse.

Jail Conditions

Jail conditions have become a national scandal. Throughout the United States, jails are marked by violence, overcrowding, deteriorated physical conditions, and lack of treatment or rehabilitation efforts. Suicides are common, as are fires and other calamities.[53] Another problem is the housing together of convicted offenders and detainees. And, despite government efforts to end the practice, many juvenile offenders occupy cells within adult jail facilities. The Federal Jail Survey found that 27 percent of jails with large populations were under court order to improve conditions. The most common grievances were overcrowding (86 percent) inadequate recreational facilities and services (51 percent), and deficient medical services and facilities (41 percent).[54]

Some effort has been made to ameliorate jail conditions. The American Correctional Association has set up the Commission on Accreditation for Corrections, which has defined standards for health care, treatment, and visitations. A multistate pilot project has helped local facilities to improve conditions so they may be accredited by the commission.[55]

In a similar vein, a number of states have passed minimum standard acts to force local counties to improve their jail conditions. State funding is made available to areas that cannot comply with conditions because of budgetary problems.[56] When state efforts have not been sufficient, national agencies have sometimes helped. The National Institute of Corrections has established a national jail center in Boulder, Colorado, to develop training materials and hold workshops for jail personnel.

— CLOSED INSTITUTIONS: PRISONS —

The various state and federal governments maintain closed correctional facilities to house convicted felons. Usually called prisons or penitentiaries, these institutions have become familiar to most people as harsh, frightening places filled with dangerous men and women. San Quentin (California), Attica (New York), Statesville/Joliet (Illinois), Leavenworth (Kansas), and Pontiac (Michigan) are but a few of the large state and federal prisons made well known by films, books, or the media.

This section discusses types of correctional institutions, life and treatment in prison, and the prisoners' rights movement.

Types of Institutions

Of the more than 500 adult prisons operating in this country, the overwhelming majority are state institutions.[57] These prison systems are usually subdivided—according to the level of security they maintain and their inmate populations—into maximum-, medium-, and minimum-security institutions. There are approximately 150 **maximum-security prisons,** which are surrounded by high walls and have elaborate security measures and armed guards. They house inmates classified as potentially dangerous. The 225 medium-security prisons have similar protective measures but usually contain less violent inmates. Consequently, they are more likely to offer a variety of treatment and educational programs to their residents. The 182 minimum-security prisons operate without armed guards or walls; usually, they are constructed in compounds surrounded by a cyclone fence.

Minimum-security prisons usually house the most trustworthy and least violent offenders; white-collar criminals may be their most common occupants. Work furloughs and educational releases are encouraged,

and vocational training is of the highest level. Dress codes are lax.

Minimum-security facilities may employ dormitory living or have small private rooms for inmates. Prisoners are allowed much discretion in keeping with them personal possessions that might be deemed dangerous in a maximum-security prison. The major security measure in minimum-security institutions is the threat that an escape will lead to transfer to a more secure facility.

Prisoners in the United States

One of the most significant problems in the criminal justice system has been the meteoric rise in the prison population. The prison population has doubled between 1980, when 300,024 adults were incarcerated, and year-end 1987, when the number reached 580,000.[58] This is a continuation of a trend of sharp increases in the prison population, despite the stabilization in the crime rate and attempts to use alternatives to incarceration. The percentage of people sentenced to prison per 100 reported crimes, arrests, cleared crimes, and crimes reported by the National Crime Survey has increased substantially in the past few years. In 1980 there were 139 inmates per 100,000 population; by 1988 there were 228. This is further evidence of the influence of conservative, get-tough trends in the criminal justice system.

Because of this influx of offenders, the nation's prisons are operating at over 100 percent of capacity, even though thousands of prisoners are being held in local jails because of overcrowding.

Recognizing the dangers associated with overcrowding, courts have ordered a number of state jurisdictions to reduce their inmate populations. In order to address the situation, various state correctional authorities have been adopted and a number of jurisdictions are operating under court order to reduce overcrowding.

Profile of Prison Inmates

What are the personal characteristics of U.S. prison inmates? As would be expected, they reflect the same qualities that were found in the analysis of serious criminal behavior (Chapter 4).[59]

TABLE 17.1   Profile of Prison Inmates

Over four-fifths of state prison inmate were recidivists—they had previously been sentenced to probation or incarceration as a juvenile or adult. More than 60 percent had been either incarcerated or on probation at least twice; 45 percent, three or more times; and nearly 20 percent, six or more times.

Two-thirds of inmates in 1986 were serving a sentence for a violent crime or had previously been convicted of a violent crime. Most of these—55 percent of all inmates—had a current violent offense.

The 11 percent of inmates whose current offense was nonviolent but who had previously been convicted of a violent crime had the longest prior records of all recidivists—72 percent had three or more prior convictions.

More than half (53 percent) of all inmates were recidivists with a record of at least one violent conviction.

Of the one-third of inmates with no record of violence, 84 percent (29 percent of the total state inmate population) were recidivists. Only 5 percent of state prison inmates in 1986 were nonviolent offenders with no previous convictions. Over half of these were convicted of drug trafficking or burglary.

About 13 percent of the inmate population were first-time offenders in for a violent crime. Over half of these had been convicted of murder (including nonnegligent manslaughter) or robbery.

Just over a third (35 percent) of all inmates said they were under the influence of a drug at the time of their offense, and 43 percent said they were using drugs daily in the month before the offense.

More than half of inmates (54 percent) reported that they were under the influence of drugs and/or alcohol at the time of the offense.

Most of the victims of state prison inmates incarcerated for a violent crimes were male, about two-thirds were white, and over one-fourth were well known to the offender.

One-third of murderers and nearly half of those convicted of negligent manslaughter said their victims were well known to them. Similarly, a third of rapists and almost two-thirds of those sentenced for other types of sexual assault reported that their victims were well known to them.

SOURCE: Christopher Innes, *Profile of State Prison Inmates, 1986* (Washington, D.C.: Bureau of Justice Statistics, 1988), p. 1.

Inmates of state prisons are predominantly poor, young, adult males with less than a high-school education. Prison is not a new experience for them; they have been incarcerated before, many first as juveniles. The offense that brought them to prison was a violent crime or a burglary. Along with a criminal history, they have a history of drug abuse and are also likely to have a history of alcohol abuse. They are typically housed in a maximum- or medium-security prison, where they are likely to be sharing their living space with at least one other person.

There are other important characteristics of the incarcerated inmate population. Blacks are overrepresented, making up 47 percent of the inmate population. Hispanics represent only a small percentage of prisoners, but their numbers have increased to about 12.6 percent.

The largest group of inmates is aged 25 to 34 (46 percent); only 2.4 percent are over 55 years old. About 61 percent had not finished high school, and 31 percent were unemployed during the year before the arrest that led to their incarceration. Their median

income was far below the national average (60 percent earned under $10,000).

A majority of the state inmates had been regular drug users at some time in their lives. More than half indicated they were under the influence of drugs or alcohol when they committed their current crime. Table 17.1 contains more information on the typical prison inmate.

Prison Life: Males

Inmates in large, inaccessible prisons find themselves physically cut off from families, friends, and former associates. Visitors may find it difficult to travel great distances to visit them; mail is censored and sometimes destroyed. The prison is a "total institution" regulating dress, work, sleep, and eating habits.[60]

Inmates soon find themselves in a totally new world with its own logic, behavior, rules, and language. They must learn to live with the stress of prison life. According to Gresham Sykes, the major losses are goods and services, liberty, heterosexual relationships, autonomy, and security.[61] Prisoners find they have no privacy; even when locked in their own cells, they are surrounded and observed by others.

Inmates must adjust to the incentives prison administrators have created to promote security and control behavior.[62] One type of incentive involves the level of comfort provided the inmate. Those obeying rules are given choice work assignments, privileges, and educational opportunities. Those who flout prison rules may be segregated, locked in their cells, or put in solitary confinement (the hole).

Administrators also can control the amount of time spent in prison. Furloughs can be dispensed to allow prisoners the opportunity to work or visit outside the prison walls. Good-time credit can be extended to lower the minimum sentence. Parole decisions can be influenced by reports on inmates' behavior.

The inmate must learn to deal with sexual exploitation and violence in the prison. One position says that this phenomenon is a function of racial conflict; another holds that victims are targets because they are physically weaker and less likely to form cohesive defensive groups.[63] In one study, Daniel Lockwood found that inmate aggressors come from a street culture that stresses violence and that they continue to behave violently while in prison.[64]

To cope with sexual aggression, inmates can fight back to indicate that they are not people to be taken advantage of, or they can join cliques and seek out mutual protection from other inmates. Some seek transfers to a different cell block or prison, ask for protective custody, or simply remain in their cells all the time.

Part of inmates' early adjustment involves becoming familiar with and perhaps participating in the hidden, black-market economy of the prison—the **hustle.** Hustling provides inmates with a source of steady income and the satisfaction of believing they are beating the system.[65] Hustling involves sales of such illegal commodities as drugs (uppers, downers, pot), alcohol, weapons, and illegally obtained food and supplies. When prison officials crack down on hustled goods, it merely serves to drive the price up—giving hustlers a greater incentive to promote their black-market activities.[66]

Inmates also must learn to deal with the racial conflict that is a daily fact of life. Prisoners tend to segregate themselves and—if peace is to reign in the institution—stay out of each other's way. Often, racial groupings are quite exact; for example, Hispanics may separate themselves according to their national origin (Mexicans, Puerto Ricans, Colombians, and so on). Prisons represent one area in which minorities often hold power; as one sociologist, James B. Jacobs, observed, "Prison may be the one institution in American society that blacks control."[67]

Prisoners must learn to deal with their frustrations over getting a "rotten deal." They may find that some other inmates received far lower sentences for similar crimes. They may be turned down for parole and then observe that others with similar records are granted early release. There is some evidence that perceived discrimination in the distribution of rewards and treatment may contribute to dissatisfaction, maladjustment, and prison violence.[68]

Finally, as the inmate's sentence winds down and his parole date nears, he must learn to cope with the anxiety of being released into the outside world. During this period, inmates may question their ability to make it in an environment in which they have failed before. Have their families stood by them? Are they unwanted outcasts?

Thus, adapting to prison requires coping with a whole series of new conditions and personal crises. Failure to cope can lead to mental breakdown or suicide.

Traditional Male Inmate Society.   A significant element of the inmate's adjustment to prison is the encounter with what is commonly known as the **inmate subculture.**[69] One major aspect of the inmate subculture is a unique **social code,** unwritten guidelines that express the values, attitudes, and types of behavior that the older inmates demand of younger inmates. Passed on from one generation of inmates to another, the inmate social code represents the values of interpersonal relations within the prison.

National attention was first drawn to the inmate social code and subculture by Donald Clemmer. In his *The Prison Community,* Clemmer set out to present a detailed sociological study of life in a maximum-security prison.[70] Referring to thousands of conversations and interviews, as will as to inmate essays and biographies, Clemmer was able to identify a unique language (**argot**) that prisoners use. In addition, Clemmer found that prisoners tend to group themselves into cliques on the basis of such personal criteria as sexual preference, political beliefs, and offense history. He found that there were complex sexual relationships in prison and concluded that many heterosexual men will turn to homosexual relationships when faced with long sentences and the loneliness of prison life.

Clemmer's most important contribution may have been his identification of the **prisonization** process. This he defined as the inmate's assimilation into the existing prison culture through acceptance of its language, sexual code, and norms of behavior. Those who become the most "prisonized" will be the least likely to reform on the "outside."

Using Clemmer's work as a jumping-off point, some prominent sociologists have set out to explore more fully the various roles in the prison community. For example, in one important analysis entitled *The Society of Captives*, Gresham Sykes further defined prison argot and argued that prison roles exist because of the deprivations presented by the prison.[71] Later, writing with Sheldon Messinger, Sykes identified the following as the most important principles of the prison community:

- *Don't interfere with inmates' interests*—Within this area of the code are maxims concerning the serving of the least amount of time in the greatest possible comfort. For example, inmates are warned never to betray another inmate to authorities; grievances must be handled personally. Other aspects of the noninterference doctrine include "Don't be nosy," "Don't have a loose lip," "Keep off the other inmates' backs," and "Don't put another inmate on the spot."

- *Don't lose your head*—Inmates also are cautioned to refrain from arguing, quarreling, or engaging in other emotional displays with fellow inmates. The novice may hear such warnings as "Play it cool" and "Do your own time."

- *Don't exploit inmates*—Prisoners are warned not to take advantage of one another—"Don't steal from cons," "Don't welsh on a debt," "Be right."

- *Inmates are cautioned to be tough and not lose their dignity*—While rule two forbids conflict, once it starts an inmate must be prepared to deal with it effectively and thoroughly. Maxims include "Don't cop out," "Don't weaken," and "Be tough; be a man."

- *Don't be a sucker*—Inmates are cautioned not to make fools of themselves by supporting the guards or prison administration over the interest of the inmates—"Be sharp."[72]

Not all prison experts believe that the prison culture is a function of the harsh conditions existing in a total institution. In 1962, John Irwin and Donald Cressey published a paper in which they conceded that a prison culture exists but claimed that its principles are actually imported from the outside world.[73] In their *importation model*, Irwin and Cressey conclude that the inmate culture is affected as much by values of newcomers:

> *Many inmates come to any given prison with a record of many terms in correctional institutions. These men, some of whom have institutional records dating back to early childhood, bring with them a ready made set of patterns which they apply to the new situation, just as is the case with participants in the criminal subculture.*[74]

Irwin and Cressey found that the inmate world was actually divided into three groups, each corresponding to a role in the outside world. The *thief subculture* is made up of professional criminals who stick to themselves and always try to "do their own time." Members of the *convict subculture* try to obtain power in the prison and control others for their own needs. The *conventional subculture* is made up of inmates who try to retain legitimate elements of the outside world in their daily life (that is, they identify with neither of the deviant prison subcultures).

Although the debate between the prisonization and important models has not been concluded, there may actually be a middle ground between them. For example, Charles Thomas suggests that an inmate's preincarceration personal characteristics, such as social class, attitudes, and values, will significantly influence the way they assimilate to prison culture.[75] Consequently, the development of an inmate culture may contain elements of both prisonization and importation.

The New Inmate Culture. While the "old" inmate subculture may have been harmful because its norms and values insulated the inmate from change efforts, it also helped create order within the institution and prevented violence among the inmates. People who violated the code and victimized others were sanctioned by their peers. An understanding developed between guards and inmate leaders: the guards would let the inmates have things their own way; the inmates would not let things get out of hand and draw the attention of the administration.

The old system may be dying in most institutions or it may be already dead. The change seems to have been precipitated by the Black Power movement in the 1960s and 1970s. Black inmates were no longer content to fill a subservient role and challenged the power of established white inmates. As the Black Power movement gained prominence, racial tension in prisons created divisions which severely altered the inmate subculture. Older, respected inmates could no longer cross racial lines to mediate disputes. Predatory inmates could victimize others without fear of retaliation.[76] Consequently, more inmates than ever are being assigned to protective custody for their own safety.

Sociologist James B. Jacobs is perhaps the most influential expert on the changing inmate subculture. His research has helped him to conclude that the development of black and Hispanic power in the 1960s, spurred by the Black Muslim movement, significantly influenced the nature of prison life.[77] According to Jacobs, black and Hispanic inmates are much more cohesively organized than whites. Their groups are sometimes rooted in religious-political affiliations, such as the Black Muslims, groups created specifically to combat discrimination in prison, such as the Latin group La Familia, or in reformation of street gangs in prison, such as the Vice Lords, Disciples, or Blackstone Rangers in the Illinois prison system and the Crips in California. In California white inmates successfully organized, and there it is in the form of a neo-Nazi group called the Aryan Brotherhood. Racially homogeneous gangs are so cohesive and powerful that they are able to supplant the original inmate code with one of their own. Consider the oath taken by new members of Nuestra Familia (Our Family), a Latin gang operating in California prisons: "If I go forward, follow me. If I hesitate, push me. If they kill me, avenge me. If I am a traitor, kill me."

It is evident that future research on prison culture will begin to evaluate the role race plays in prison life, how inmate racism influences the "traditional" prisoner culture. This research is particularly important considering that it has been estimated that just four California gangs—Nuestra Familia, the Mexican Mafia, the Aryan Brotherhood, and the Black Guerilla Family—have reportedly killed 111 inmates and injured scores of others in the past eight years.[78] In fact, the situation is so bad and tensions so high that an authority as well respected as James Jacobs has suggested that it may be humane and appropriate to segregate inmates along racial lines in order to maintain order and protect individual rights. Jacobs believes that in some prisons, administrators use integration as a threat to keep inmates in line; to be transferred to a racially mixed setting may mean beatings or death.

Prison Life: Females

Women make up about 4.4 percent of the adult prison population. Usually, they are housed in minimum-security institutions more likely to resemble college dormitories than high-security male prisons.

Women in prison tend to be of three basic types, described by Esther Heffernan as: "the square," who is basically a noncriminal but who, in a fit of rage, may have shot or stabbed a husband or boyfriend; "the life," who is a repeat offender—shoplifter, prostitute, drug user, or pusher; and "the cool," who is part of the sophisticated criminal underworld. The square usually espouses conventional values and wants to follow the rules; the life rejects prison authority and is a rebel; the cool is aloof, manipulates the environment, and does not participate in prison life.[79]

Daily life in the women's prison community is also somewhat different from that in male institutions. For one thing, women usually do not present the immediate physical danger to staff and fellow inmates that many male prisoners do. For another, the rigid, antiauthority inmate social code found in many male institutions does not exist in female prisons. Confinement for women, however, may produce severe anxiety and anger, because they are separated from families and loved ones and unable to function in normal privacy. Unlike men, who typically direct their anger outward, female prisoners may revert to more self-destructive acts to cope with their problems. Female inmates are perhaps more likely than males to mutilate their own bodies and attempt suicide.

One common form of adaptation to prison employed by women is the surrogate family. This group contains masculine and feminine figures acting as fathers and mothers; some even act as children and take on the role of either brother or sister. Formalized marriages and divorces may be conducted. Sometimes, multiple roles are held by one inmate, so that a "sister" in one family may "marry" and become the "wife" in another.[80]

Correctional Treatment

Correctional treatment has been an integral part of prison life since Z. R. Brockway introduced it as part of the daily regime at the Elmira reformatory.

There are many approaches to treatment. Some, based on the medical model, rely heavily on counseling and clinical therapy. Others, reflecting interactionist theory, attempt to reintegrate the offender into the community; they rely on work release, vocational training, and other such programs. Although it is beyond the scope of this book to describe the vast number of correctional treatment programs, a few important types are discussed.

Therapy and Counseling. The most traditional type of treatment in prison involves psychological counseling and therapy. Counseling programs exist in almost every major institution. Some stress individual treatment with psychotherapy or other techniques. However, because of lack of resources, it is more common for group methods to be used. Some groups are led by trained social workers, counselors, or therapists; other reply on lay personnel as leaders.

Group counseling in prison usually tries to stimulate inmates' self-awareness and their ability to deal with everyday problems.[81] Since the group is a microcosm of the real world, containing winners, losers, toughs, straights, and others, successful adaptation to the group process is believed to be analogous to improving relationships with other social groups. Thus, by identifying roles and behaviors that occur within the group and uncovering the motivations underlying them, inmates learn to understand why they act as they do and how others react to their behavior.

A wide variety of innovative psychological treatment approaches have been used in the prison system: *behavior therapy* uses tokens to reward conformity and help develop positive behavior traits; *reality therapy* is meant to help satisfy individuals' needs to feel worthwhile to themselves and others; *transactional analysis* encourages inmates to identify the different aspects of their personalities and to be their own therapists; *milieu therapy* uses the social structure and processes of the institution to influence the behavior patterns of offenders.[82]

Educational Programs. The first prison treatment programs were educational in nature. A prison school was opened at the Walnut Street Prison in 1784. Elementary courses were offered in New York's prison system in 1801, and in Pennsylvania's in 1844. An actual school system was established in Detroit's House of Corrections in 1870, and Elmira Reformatory opened a vocational trade school in 1876.

Today, most institutions provide some type of educational program. At some prisons, inmates are given the opportunity to obtain a high-school diploma through general equivalency diploma (GED) programs. Other institutions provide an actual classroom education, usually staffed by full-time certified teachers or by part-time teachers who work at an institution after a full day's teaching in a nearby school.[83] Many institutions also offer college-level courses. A survey of prison education programs found that 96 percent of surveyed institutions had both basic education (basic literacy) programs and secondary education (high-school level) programs, 83 percent had postsecondary education (college level) programs, 89 percent had vocational (skilled job training) programs, and 44 percent had programs offering social education (life skills, consumer education, problem-solving skills).[84]

Vocational Rehabilitation. Most prisons operate numerous vocational training programs designed to help inmates develop skills to help them secure employment on their release. In the past, the traditional prison industries of laundry and license plate manufacture failed to provide skills that helped inmates secure employment upon release. Today, programs stress such marketable skills as dental laboratory work, computer programming, auto repair, and radio and television work.

Unfortunately, it is often difficult to obtain the necessary equipment to run meaningful programs. Therefore, many prisons have adopted **work furlough** programs to allow inmates to work in the community during the day and return to the institution at night.

In addition to work furlough programs, several state correctional departments have instituted

CLOSE-UP

Private Prisons

One significant development in the correctional field is the increased use of privately funded and privately run correctional institutions. The federal government has used private companies to run detention centers for illegal aliens who are being held for trial or deportation. One private firm, the Corrections Corporation of America, runs a federal halfway house, two detention centers, and a 370-bed jail in Bay County, Florida. On January 6, 1986, the U.S. Corrections Corporation opened the first private state prison in Marion, Kentucky, a 300-bed minimum-security facility for inmates who are within three years of parole. Today, more than 20 companies are trying to enter the private prison market, while three states have passed enabling legislation and more than 10 others are actively considering doing so. Table A describes the various forms private corrections may take.

Though privately run institutions have been around for a few years, their increased use may present a number of problems. For example, will private providers be able to effectively evaluate programs, knowing that a negative evaluation might cause them to lose their contract? Will they skimp on services and programs in order to reduce costs? Might they not skim off the "easy" cases and leave the hard-core inmate for state care? And will the need to keep business booming require widening the net to fill empty cells?

In addition to these problems, private corrections can run into opposition from existing sate correctional staff and management, who fear the loss of jobs and autonomy. Moreover, the public may be skeptical about the untested private concern's ability to provide security and protection.

There are also administrative problems in private corrections. How will program quality be controlled? In order to compete on price, a private facility may have to cut corners to beat out the competition. And there will be difficulty in determining accountability for problems and mishaps when dealing with a corporation which is a legal fiction and which protects its officers from personal responsibility for their actions. Legal problems can emerge very quickly: can privately employed guards patrol the perimeter and use deadly force to stop escape attempts?

Finally, the notion of running prisons for profit may be unpalatable to large segments of the population. However, the idea of private prisons is not very much different from a private hospital or college which distributes services also provided by the state. The issue which determines the future of privates corrections may be one of efficiency and cost-effectiveness, and not one of fairness and morality.

prerelease and postrelease employment services. Employment program staff members assess inmates' backgrounds to determine their abilities, interests, goals, and capabilities. They consult with clients to help them create job plans (which are essential to their receiving early release, or parole). They also help them successfully reintegrate placements in sheltered environments to help inmates bridge the gap between the institution and the outside world. Services include job placement, skill development, family counseling, and legal and medical attention.

Private Industry in Prisons.   A new version of vocational rehabilitation is the development of private industry in prison. This can take on many different forms, including private citizens who sit on prison industry boards; private vendors who market goods from prison industry; inmates who manufacture and market their own goods; private management of state-owned prison industry; franchising within the prison system, in which manufactured goods are marketed under license from a private firm; and privately owned industries on prison grounds which employ inmate labor.

Another approach is the **free venture** programs developed in the 1980s in Minnesota, Kansas, and other states.[85] The programs involve businesses set up by private entrepreneurs off prison grounds which contract with state officials to hire inmates at free-market wages to produce goods that are competitively marketed. Inmates can be fired by being sent back to the general population.

On paper, private industry in prison is quite attractive. It teaches inmates skills in usually desirable

Discussion Questions

1. How does a private prison differ from a private hospital or college?

2. Should inmates be allowed to profit from their business? Could they hire other inmates, or would this create a power struggle within the institution?

SOURCES: John Dilulio, *Private Prisons* (Washington, D.C.: U.S. Government Printing Office, 1988); Judith Hackett, Harry Hatry, Robert Levinson, Joan Allen, Koen Chi, and Edward Feigenbaum, *Contracting for the Operation of Prisons and Jails* (Washington, D.C.: National Institute of Justice, 1987); Joan Mullen, *Corrections and the Private Sector* (Washington, D.C.: National Institute of Justice, 1984); *Report to the Nation on Crime and Justice*, 2d ed. (Washington, D.C.: Bureau of Justice Statistics, 1988).

TABLE A   Private Prison Types

Contracting for services—A government agency enters into a contract with a private firm to provide a service. Contracts are used for food, laundry, or medical services for a correctional institution; education or vocational training for inmates; and staff training.

Prison Industries—A government agency enters into an agreement with a private firm to operate an industry or business within the prison using inmates as employees. As of January 1985, Sexton et al. identified 26 projects with private sector involvement in state-level prison industries, including hotel and motel telephone reservation systems located inside of prisons, through which inmates answer the phones and make reservations for customers who do not know they are talking to a prisoner; and factories installed in the prison and managed by private sector employees who supervise the prison inmate "factory workers." These factories manufacture various items, including office furniture and computer equipment.

Private sector financing of prison—A private firm provides the funds needed to build a correctional institution and signs a long-term agreement to lease the institution to the government. Mullen found that these financial arrangements were being seriously considered in a number of states in 1984 and had been used for a $30.2 million jail and sheriff's facility in Colorado, a $50 million jail in Philadelphia, a $5 million jail in Tennessee, and a jail and criminal justice training center in Los Angeles.

Private facility ownership and operation—A private firm locates a site, builds a prison (or remodels an existing structure), and runs the prison on a day-to-day basis under contract with the government. The government pays the firm for all expenses under a contract, in many cases being charged a daily fee for each inmate. This type of arrangement has been used by the federal government to house illegal aliens and youthful offenders, by a few local governments for jails, and by state and local governments for juveniles, halfway houses, and small minimum-security facilities. Despite the willingness of private corrections firms to operate large, maximum-security prisons, state governments have moved slowly in this area.

commercial areas, such as data processing. It increases employment opportunities on the outside in areas where the ex-offender can earn enough to forgo a life of crime. Various evaluations of the programs have given them high marks. However, private industry programs so far have used relatively few inmates. It is also questionable whether they could be applied to the general prison population, which contains many people with educational deficiencies and a history of substance abuse.

Another new approach is to have major corporations manage prisons for profit. The Close-Up entitled "Private Prisons" describes this program.

Conjugal Visits. The conjugal visit is another mode of treatment that has received renewed emphasis from correctional administrators. During conjugal visits, prisoners are regularly able to have completely private meetings with their spouses. The explicit purpose of the program is to grant inmate access to normal sexual outlets and thereby counteract the pains of imprisonment. Though it is a relatively new and infrequently used phenomenon, the conjugal visit has provoked much debate. Detractors view it as degrading. They also say it creates sexual tension among single prisoners who cannot share in the program, and may produce children who cannot be adequately supported by their parents. Supporters view it as a major development in maintaining normal relationships among incarcerated felons, and a mechanism for keeping families together.[86]

Coed Programs.   Another recent trend, one with strong historical roots, is the **"coeducation" prison.**

Since 1973, prisons housing both men and women have proliferated throughout the United States. Examples of coed institutions include the Renz Correctional Center in Cedar City, Missouri, established in 1975, and the Maine Correctional Center in South Windham, Maine, established in 1976.[87]

In all, it is estimated that in the federal prison system, 58 percent of females and 7 percent of males are in coed prisons; the figures for state systems are much smaller—9.7 percent of females and 0.53 percent of males.[88]

Generally speaking, the typical coed prison is a small, low-security institution, predominantly of one sex (either mostly male or mostly female), populated by nonviolent, carefully screened offenders. In most instances, males and females live in physically separate housing—either in different buildings or in separate cottages. Again, the purpose of this method is to provide a more normal environment for prison inmates.

Does Rehabilitation Work?   Despite the variety and number of treatment programs in operation, there is some question about their effectiveness. In their oft-cited research, Robert Martinson and his associates found that a majority of treatment programs were failures.[89] Martinson found in a national study that, with few exceptions, rehabilitative efforts seemed to have no appreciable effect on recidivism.

Martison's work was followed by efforts that found, embarrassingly, that some high-risk offenders were more likely to commit crimes after they had been placed in treatment programs than before the onset of rehabilitation efforts.[90] Even California's highly touted community treatment program, which matched youthful offenders and counselors on the basis of their psychological profiles, was found by Paul Lerman to exert negligible influence on its clients.[91]

These devastating reviews of correctional rehabilitation helped develop a more conservative view of corrections, which holds that prisons are places of incapacitation and punishment and should not be used for treatment. Current social policy stresses eliminating the nonserious offender from the correctional system, but at the same time increasing the sentences of serious, violent offenders. Thus, through the past decade it has become fashionable to disparage correctional rehab programs and to view the prison as a place of incapacitation only. The development of lengthy mandatory and determinate sentences to punish serious offenders and the simultaneous evolution of restitution, diversion, and pretrial release programs to limit the nonserious offender's interface with the system are demonstrable manifestations of this view.

While there are still criminologists such as Jerome Miller, Ted Palmer, Paul Gendreau, Francis Cullen, and Karen Gilbert who continue to challenge the "nothing works" philosophy, their voices are often drowned by a sea of professional and public opinion calling for longer sentences and high security rather than care and treatment.[92]

Prison Violence

One of the more significant problems facing prison administrators is the constant fear of interpersonal and collective violence. Hans Toch, an expert on violence, has said:

> Jails and prisons . . . have a climate of violence which has no free-world counterpart. Inmates are terrorized by other inmates and spend years in fear of harm. Some inmates request segregation, others lock themselves in and some are hermits by choice. Many inmates injure themselves.[93]

What are the causes of prison violence? Though there is no single explanation for either collective or individual violence, theories abound. One position holds that inmates are often violence-prone individuals who have always used force to get their own way. In the crowded, dehumanizing world of the prison, it is not surprising that they resort to force to exert their dominance over others.[94]

A second view is that prisons convert people to violence by their inhumane conditions, including overcrowding, depersonalization, and threats of homosexual rape. One social scientist, Charles Silberman, suggests that even in the most human prisons, life is a constant put-down and prison conditions threaten the inmates' sense of self-worth; that violence is a consequence of these conditions is not surprising.[95]

Still another view is that prison violence stems from mismanagement, lack of strong security, and inadequate control by prison officials.[96] This view has contributed to the escalated use of solitary confinement in recent years as a means of control. Also contributing to prison violence is the changing prison population. Younger, more violent inmates, who often have been members of teenage gangs, now dominate prison life. The old code of "do your own time" and "be a right guy" may be giving way to a prison culture dominated by gangs and their leaders, whose very nature breeds violence.

Sometimes prison violence generates large-scale rioting. The American Correctional Association gives a number of reasons for prison flare-ups: unnatural institutional environment; antisocial characteristics of inmates; inept management; inadequate personnel practices; inadequate facilities; insufficient constructive, meaningful activity; insufficient legitimate rewards; basic social values and unrest in the larger community; inadequate finances; and inequities and complexities in the criminal justice system.[97]

In an analysis of the similarities between the two worst prison riots of recent times, Attica in 1971 and New Mexico State in 1980, the following phenomena were observed:

- Prisoners felt they were not being treated like human beings
- Line officers were unprepared; they were not informed of plans and regulations at the prison
- Administrators lacked consistency; their policies lacked stability
- Legislators were insensitive to the needs of the penal system
- The public and media were unconcerned about the corrections system.[98]

Overcrowding and Violence. Another recent trend in prisons that may be associated with violence is the overcrowding caused by rapid increases in the prison population. Data from Texas indicate that a large increase in the inmate population, unmatched by creation of new space, was associated with increases in suicide, violent death, and disciplinary action rates. The largest prisons in Texas (with populations of over 1,600) demonstrated violence rates higher than the smaller prisons (800 or less).[99] Similar data from Oklahoma on crowding and violent deaths corroborate the Texas findings.

One explanation is that high population in an institution exerts a negative influence that is associated with violence.

Other recent research efforts have reached similar conclusions. Paul Paulus and his associates found that feelings of crowding and blood pressure rates increased in cells occupied by more than one person.[100] Edward Megargee found that crowding was associated with increased disciplinary infractions.[101] P. L. Nacci and his associates found that the federal correctional institutions that were most overcrowded also had the highest disciplinary infraction rates.[102]

Others disagree that prison overcrowding by itself can cause violence. For example, Sheldon Ekland-Olson and his associates found that the age of the prison population and not overcrowding was the factor producing violence; younger prisoners are the most likely to be violence-prone.[103] Despite this evidence, most studies do conclude that a violence-overcrowding link exists.[104]

It seems evident, then, that as the prison population continues its upward climb, unmatched by expanded correctional capacity, prison violence may increase. Though judges in some states have ordered the mandatory release of prisoners because of overcrowded conditions, the problem of overcrowding may become even more acute in future years. Consequently, prison administrators have attempted to reduce tension levels by creating inmate councils to help govern the institution (self-governance), and by creating grievance mechanisms so that inmates' complaints will be taken into account. Such measures have worked rather effectively in some institutions.

Corrections and the Rule of Law

For many years, the nation's courts did not interfere in the operation of the prison, maintaining what is called the **hands-off doctrine.** The court's reluctance to interfere in prison matters was based on (1) the belief that it lacked technical competence in prison administration, (2) society's general apathy toward the prison, and (3) the belief that prisoners' complaints involved privileges rather than rights.[105] Consequently, prisoners had no legal rights and were "slaves of the state."

The hands-off doctrine was lifted in the 1960s. General concern with civil and human rights, and increasing militancy in the prison population, and the reformist nature of the Warren Court created a climate conducive to reform.

The first area of chance came in the First Amendment right of freedom of religion. The Black Muslims, a politically active religious organization led by Elijah Muhammed of Chicago, had many adherents in the prison system. Using their legal and financial clout, the Black Muslims litigated claims that their followers were being denied the right to worship according to their faith. A series of Supreme Court cases upheld the Black Muslims' freedom of religion and opened the door to further issues of inmates' rights.[106]

Today, most litigation is brought under the federal Civil Rights Act (28 USC 1982), which states:

> Every person who, under color of any statute, ordinance, regulation, custom, or usage of any State or Territory subjects, or causes to be subjected, any citizen of the United States or other person within the jurisdiction thereof to the deprivation of any rights, privileges, or immunities secured by the Constitution and laws shall be liable to the party injured in an action at law, suit in equity or other proper proceeding for redress.

Although the Supreme Court has recently limited the methods by which inmates can seek release or redress, it has consistently upheld the rights of inmates to seek legal remedies. For example, in *Johnson v. Avery*, the Supreme Court upheld the right of legally trained inmates (jail house lawyers) to help fellow inmates prepare legal documents.[107] In *Gilmore v. Lynch*, the Court maintained that prisons must have an adequate law library and make it available to inmates.[108] Consequently, there has been a revolution in the area of prisoners' rights and in prisoners ability to seek help with their institutional problems. Some of the more important areas of prisoners' rights are briefly discussed below.

Freedom of Press and Speech.   The courts have ruled that inmates retain freedom of speech and press unless correctional authorities can show that it interferes with or threatens institutional freedom. For example, in *Procunier v. Martinez*, a court ruled that an inmate's mail could be censored only if there existed substantial belief that its contents would threaten security.[109] Similarly, in *Nolan v. Fitzpatrick*, a federal court upheld the right of prisoners to write to newspapers unless their letters discussed escape plans or contained contraband.[110] However, in *Saxbe v. Washington Post*, the right of an inmate to grant press interviews as limited, since the Supreme Court argued that such interviews would enhance the reputations of particular inmates and jeopardize the authorities' desire to treat everyone equally.[111]

Medical Rights.   After many years of indifference, inmates have been given the right to secure proper medical attention. To gain their medical rights, prisoners generally have resorted to class actions (suits brought on the behalf of all individuals governed in similar circumstances, in this case poor medical attention). In one such case, *Newman v. Alabama*, the entire Alabama prison system's medical facilities were declared inadequate. The court cited the following factors as contributing to inadequate care: insufficient physicians and nurses; reliance on untrained inmates for paramedical work; intentional failure to treat the sick and injured; and failure to conform to proper medical standards.[112]

In 1976, after reviewing the legal principles established over the preceding 20 years in cases such as *Newman v. Alabama*, the Supreme Court, in *Estelle v. Gamble*, clearly stated the inmate's right to have medical care.[113] Gamble had hurt his back in a Texas prison and filed suit to contest the type of treatment he had received, and also to question the lack of interest prison guard had shown in his case. Although the Supreme Court referred Gamble's cases to a lower court to determine whether he had actually been treated negligently, it laid down the following standard for judging future complaints:

> Deliberate indifference to serious medical needs of prisoners constitutes the "unnecessary and wanton infliction of pain," . . . proscribed by the Eighth Amendment. This is true whether the indifference is manifested by prison doctors in their response to the prisoner's needs or by prison guards in intentionally denying or delaying access to medical care or intentionally interfering with the treatment once prescribed.[114]

Lower courts will now decide, case by case, whether "deliberate indifference" actually occurred.

Cruel and Unusual Punishment and Overall Conditions.   Prisoners have long suffered severe physical punishments in prison, ranging from whipping to extended periods of solitary confinement. The courts have held that such treatment is unconstitutional when it:

- Degrades the dignity of human beings[115]
- Is more severe than the offense for which it has been given[116]
- Shocks the general conscience and is fundamentally unfair[117]

The courts also have ruled on the necessity of maintaining the general prison system in a humane manner. For example, in 1970 the entire prison system in Arkansas was declared unconstitutional, because its practices of overt physical punishment were ruled to be in violation of the Eighth Amendment.[118]

Two recent cases have been interpreted as signaling a slowdown in the Court's restrictions on oppressive prison conditions. In *Bell v. Wolfish* and *Rhodes v. Chapman*, the Supreme Court upheld the practice of double-bunking two or more inmates in a small cell (50 square feet):[119]

> *Conditions of confinement must not involve the wanton and unnecessary infliction of pain nor may they be grossly disproportionately to the severity of the crime warranting imprisonment . . . [but] conditions that cannot be said to be cruel and unusual under contemporary standards are not unconstitutional. To the extent that such conditions are restrictive and even harsh, they are part of the penalty that criminal offenders pay for their offenses against society.*[120]

While these cases have limited inmates' rights to better living conditions, a number of state cases, especially *Estelle v. Ruiz*, have put corrections departments on notice that overcrowding will not be tolerated and that no new inmates can be admitted to prison unless the number of inmates is reduced.[121]

Procedural Due Process.   Another critical element of prisoners' rights is in the area of procedural due process. This issue arises when the inmate is subject to disciplinary actions involving the loss of privileges,

good time, or parole. In the landmark case of *Wolff v. McDonnell*, the Supreme Court established these guidelines for disciplinary hearings:[122]

1. Advance written notice of the charges must be given to the inmate no less than 24 hours before the prisoner's appearance at the disciplinary committee hearing.
2. There must be a written statement by the fact-finders as to the evidence relied upon and the reasons for the disciplinary action.
3. The inmate should be allowed to call witnesses and present documentary evidence as defense if these activities will not jeopardize institutional control.
4. The inmate has no constitutional right to confrontation and cross-examination in prison discipline proceedings.
5. The inmate has no right to retained or appointed counsel, although substitute counsel, such as a staff member or another inmate, may be provided in certain cases.
6. The inmate has the right to have an impartial group conduct disciplinary hearings.
7. In regard to regulations governing inmate mail, the state may require that mail from an attorney to a prisoner be identified as such and that the attorney's name and address appear on the communication. In addition, as a protection against contraband, prison authorities may open mail in the inmate's presence.

Despite the liberalization of due process rights brought about by *Wolff*, the Court has limited such rights by denying inmates the right to counsel at parole hearings and at hearings to consider transfer to another institution. The legal rules of thumb appear to be (1) prisoners have a right to personal freedom as long as it cannot be construed as interfering with prison security; and (2) prisoners have procedural rights when something is to be taken from them that they already have, but relatively few legal rights when they are denied special privileges that other inmates may have obtained.

There seems to be little question that prisoners' rights law has been put on hold. A more conservative Court has cut back on granting additional rights, major changes may not be in the offing for years.

☰ CLOSE-UP

Recidivism of Young Parolees

A recent federal study examined the criminal careers of a sample of 3,995 youthful offenders (ages 17 to 22) for six years after they were released from prison. The study found that approximately 69 percent were rearrested for a serious offense; 53 percent were convicted for a new offense; and 49 percent returned to prison. Other findings are outlined below.

• Excluding violations of parole and probation, these parolees were rearrested for more than 36,000 new felonies or serious misdemeanors, including approximately 6,700 violent crimes and nearly 19,000 property crimes.

• Approximately 10 percent of the persons paroled accounted for 40 percent of the subsequent arrest offenses.

• About a fifth of the subsequent arrests occurred in states other than the original paroling state.

• An estimated 37 percent of the parolees were rearrested while still on parole.

• Recidivism rates were highest in the first two years after an offender's release from prison. Within one year, 32 percent of those paroled had been rearrested; within two years, 47 percent had been rearrested.

• Recidivism was higher among men, blacks, and persons who had not completed high school than among women, whites, and high-school graduates.

• Almost three-quarters of those paroled for property of-

fenses were rearrested for a serious crime, compared to about two-thirds of those paroled for violent offenses.

• Approximately a third of both property offenders and violent offenders were rearrested for a violent crime upon release from prison.

• The longer the parolee's prior arrest record, the higher the rate of recidivism—over 90 percent of the parolees with six or more previous adult arrests were rearrested, compared to 59 percent of the first-time offenders.

• The earlier the parolee's first adult arrest, the more likely the chances for rearrest—79 percent of those arrested and charged as an adult before the age of 17 were rearrested, compared to 51 percent of those first arrested at the age of 20 or older.

• Time served in prison had no consistent impact on recidivism rates—those who had served six months or less in prison were about as likely to be rearrested as those who had served more than two years.

Discussion Questions

1. Considering its failure rate, should parole be abolished?
2. Is parole for the benefit of the inmate or the institution?

SOURCE: Allen Beck and Bernard Shipley, *Recidivism of Young Parolees* (Washington, D.C.: Bureau of Justice Statistics, 1987).

PAROLE

The final component of corrections, parole is the planned release and community supervision of incarcerated offenders before the actual expiration of their prison sentences. It is usually considered to be a way of completing a prison sentence in the community and is not the same as a pardon; the paroled offender can be legally recalled to serve the remainder of his or her sentence in an institution if the parole authorities deem the offender's adjustment inadequate, or if the offender commits a further crime while on parole.

The decision to parole is determined by statutory requirement and usually involves the completion of a minimum sentence. Parole is granted by a state *parole board*, a body of men and women whose task it is to review cases and determine whether an offender has been rehabilitated sufficiently to deal with the outside world. The board also dictates what specific parole rules a parolee must obey. Some states with determinate sentencing statutes, such as Indiana and California, do not use parole boards but release inmates at the conclusion of their maximum term less accumulated good time. This is referred to as **mandatory release.**

Once community release has begun, the offender is supervised by a trained staff of parole officers who help the offender adjust to the community, help in the search for employment, and monitor behavior and activities to insure that the offender conforms to the conditions of parole.

Parolees are subject to a strict standardized or a personalized set of rules that guides their behavior and sets limits on their activities. If these rules are violated, the offender can be returned to the institution to serve the remainder of the sentence; this is known as a technical parole violation. Inmates released in determinate sentencing states can have part or all of their good time revoked if they violate the conditions of their release.

Parole also can be revoked if the offender commits a second offense; the offender also may be tried and sentenced for this subsequent crime. The Supreme Court has granted parolees due process rights similar to those of probationers at revocation hearings.

Parole is viewed as an act of grace on the part of the criminal justice system. It represents an actual manifestation of the policy of returning the offender to the community. There are two conflicting sides to parole, however; on one hand, the paroled offender is given a break and allowed to serve part of the sentence in the community; on the other hand, the sentiment exists that parole is a privilege and not a right, and that the parolee is in reality a dangerous criminal who must be carefully watched and supervised. The conflict between the treatment and enforcement aspects of parole has not been reconciled by the criminal justice system, and the parole process still contains elements of both orientations.

As of 1987, there were about 326,000 adults on parole in the United States, an increase of 9 percent over the previous year.[123] Despite the increased use of mandatory and determinate sentences, the number of parolees grew 32 percent between 1983 and the beginning of 1987. A total of 223,182 inmates were paroled in 1986, and 196,633 were discharged from supervision.

Parole Decision-Making

Most inmates become eligible for parole at the completion of their minimum sentence. The actual parole decision is made at a *parole grant hearing.* There, the full board or a selected subcommittee reviews information, may meet with the offender, and then decides whether the parole applicant has a reasonable probability of succeeding outside of prison. Candidates for parole may be chosen by statutory eligibility on the basis of time served in relation to their sentences. In most jurisdictions, the minimum sentence imposed by the judge regulates eligibility for parole; when no minimum sentence is set, parole eligibility is based on the policy of the board or the corrections department. Finally, in many jurisdictions, the good time an offender accumulates can serve to reduce the minimum sentence and therefore hasten eligibility for parole.

Each parole board works in a unique way and has its own administrative setup for reviewing cases. In some, the full board meets with the applicant; in others, only a few members are required. In some jurisdictions, a single board member can conduct a personal investigation and submit the findings to the full board for a decision.

What factors influence parole board decision-making?[124] Of primary concern is whether board members believe that the offender can make an adjustment in the community or that continued confinement would be more beneficial. Boards are also interested in whether offenders have paid their debt to society. Does the time served seem adequate to compensate for the seriousness of the crime? Have other inmates been treated similarly?

The parole board is also concerned with inmates' preparation to make it "outside." Do they have families who can help them? Jobs waiting? Have they taken vocational and educational training courses while in prison?

The parole board also considers the conditions existing within the penal institution. Is overcrowding a problem? Are the inmates tense because some recent parole requests have been turned down? What are the feelings of the correctional administrators about parole decisions?

To help parole decision-makers, parole prediction tables have been developed.[125] These tables correlate personal information on inmates who were released in the past with their rates of rearrest. The best-known predictive device is the Salient Factor Score Index, originally developed by members of the federal parole system. The salient factor score includes age, type of offense, prior parole revocations, history of heroin use, and employment background.[126]

☰ CLOSE-UP

AIDS and the Correctional System

A discussion of the correctional system today deserves mention of the problem of AIDS among the inmate population and the measures taken to combat its spread. The following information was taken from federal surveys on AIDS in correctional facilities.

What Is AIDS?

AIDS is caused by the Human Immunodeficiency Virus (HIV). It infects and destroys certain white blood cells, thereby undermining the body's ability to combat infection. One can be infected with HIV for years without ever developing symptoms of AIDS. However, infected persons can transmit the virus even though they may not have symptoms.

Opportunistic diseases include a particular type of pneumonia, malignancies, and a type of skin cancer. Persons who die from AIDS die from such opportunistic diseases, not from AIDS itself.

Other symptoms include fever, weight loss, diarrhea, and persistingly swollen lymph nodes. Patients with such symptoms, but not meeting the Centers for Disease Control definition of AIDS, are generally considered to have "AIDS-related complex" (ARC). Although the symptoms of ARC may be debilitating, they are generally not life threatening. To date, not all persons who have ARC have developed AIDS.

AIDS Cases among Correctional Inmates

As of October 1, 1987, there had been a cumulative total of 1,964 confirmed AIDS cases among inmates in seventy responding federal, state, and local correctional systems in the United States. There had been 1,320 cases in thirty-nine state and federal correctional systems. Thirty-one responding city and county jail systems reported 644 cases. Total AIDS cases in all responding American correctional systems thus increased from 766 to 1,964—or 156 percent—in the two years since the first survey and 59 percent in the one year since the second survey.

The growth in AIDS cases was slightly slower in correctional systems than in the population at large both between 1985 to 1986 and 1986 to 1987. Moreover, it should be noted that the National Institute of Justice (NIJ) survey results probably include some double-counting of cases—that is, individuals who were known to have AIDS while they were in county jail and then entered a state institution. In Canada, a cumulative total of two cases was reported by the federal system and thirteen cases by provincial systems.

The figures above are *cumulative* totals—that is, all cases reported since the correctional systems began keeping records. Thirty-nine state and federal systems in the United States reported 295 *current* cases of AIDS among inmates, while thirty-one responding city and county systems reported 126 *current* cases. There were four cases in Canadian systems as of October 1, 1987.

State and federal systems in the United States report that a cumulative total of 716 inmates have died from AIDS while in custody; responding city and county systems in the U.S. report 159 inmate deaths. Of 875 total inmate AIDS deaths in the United States, 346—or 40 percent—have occurred since the 1986 survey was taken. Canadian correctional systems report three deaths among inmates.

Sexual Activity, Intravenous Drug Abuse, and AIDS

Virtually all inmate AIDS cases are thought to be related to intravenous drug abuse or sexual activity. On average, correctional systems attributed two-thirds of their male cases to IV drug abuse and 43 percent to homosexual activity. Predictably, female cases were overwhelmingly (92 percent, on average) attributed to IV drug use. However, it is important to note that in some correctional systems, particularly those in the Middle Atlantic region, the percentage of all cases attributed to IV drug abuse is much higher than elsewhere; these are also among the systems with the largest number of inmate AIDS cases.

Correctional Management Issues: Education and Training

Because there is no vaccine or cure for the disease, education and training programs are the cornerstone of efforts to curb the spread of AIDS in prisons and jails, as well as in the population at large. Education and training programs also provide the opportunity to counteract misinformation, rumors, and fear concerning the disease. For example, the majority of systems responding to the questionnaire reported that inmates and staff worried about the possibility of contracting AIDS; many responses referred to fear of casual contact or types of contact not actually associated with transmission of the virus.

As a result, many correctional administrators feel strongly that education and training are not options but absolute requirements. Ninety-three percent of the responding jurisdictions currently offer or are developing AIDS educational programs for staff; 83 percent offer or are developing such programs for inmates.

Among respondents whose educational programs have operated for some time, the vast majority believe these programs to be effective in reducing the fears of staff and inmates. Several jurisdictions reported that timely educational efforts had successfully averted threatened job actions by correctional staff unions.

Correctional Policies on Antibody Testing

Only four state correctional systems (Nevada, Colorado, Iowa, and Missouri) have implemented or plan to implement mass screening programs for inmates; no city or county systems responding to the questionnaire have instituted or planned such programs. However, almost 90 percent of the responding jurisdictions do employ testing for more limited purposes. These include testing of risk-group members, testing in support of diagnoses of AIDS or ARC, testing in response to incidents in which the AIDS virus might have been transmitted, testing on inmate request, and testing carried out as part of anonymous epidemiological studies.

Correctional Housing Policies

One of the most critical and difficult decisions for correctional administrators is where to house and treat inmates with AIDS or ARC. Of course, medical considerations dictate many of these decisions. Most jurisdictions place inmates with confirmed diagnoses of AIDS in a medical facility either within the correctional system or in the community, although the duration of such hospitalization varies considerably.

Preventing the spread of AIDS within the prison and protecting affected inmates from intimidation and violence are important considerations. Other factors in treatment and housing decisions include availability and location of facilities able to provide appropriate care, costs of any new construction or renovations necessary to prepare special units, and staffing of any special AIDS units (correctional as well as medical). The key options are the following:

- Maintaining inmates in the general population
- Returning inmates to the general population when their illnesses are in remission
- Administratively segregating inmates in a separate unit or relying on single-cell housing
- Hospitalization; and
- Case-by-case determination of all housing and treatment decisions.

Two-thirds of the federal and state systems, and 70 percent of city and county systems have written policies in place or in development for managing inmates with AIDS or ARC. City and county jurisdictions are more likely to use segregation: 39 percent of responding city and county jail systems segregate all AIDS-related inmate categories, as opposed to only 16 percent of state and federal prison systems. Almost one-third of all responding systems have basic policies involving case-by-case determination of treatment and housing programs.

Medical Issues

Perhaps the highest priority in the correctional response to AIDS is providing timely, professional, and compassionate medical care to inmates who become ill with the disease. As in society at large, prompt detection and diagnosis are needed to minimize spread of the disease and alleviate the suffering of patients.

Legal Issues

Suits on the quality of correctional medical care may be brought on the basis of federal constitutional standards, state law, or common law. There are three constitutional principles relevant to correctional medical care.

First, under the Eighth Amendment, inmates are entitled to a safe, decent, and humane environment. Second, in *Estelle v. Gamble*, "deliberate indifference to serious medical need" was held to violate the Eighth Amendment protection against "cruel and unusual punishment." Finally, the constitutional guarantee of "equal protection of the laws" applies to correctional medical care cases, and particularly to cases involving AIDS inmates, because of the segregation issues.

Discussion Questions

1. Should inmates carrying the AIDS virus be separated from the general inmate population?
2. Should correctional administrators provide inmates with condoms?

SOURCE: Theodore Hammett, *AIDS in Correctional Facilities* (Washington, D.C.: National Institute of Justice, 1988); Hammett, *AIDS and the Law Enforcement Officer* (Washington, D.C.: National Institute of Justice, 1987); Hammett, *AIDS in Prison and Jails: Issues and Opinions* (Washington, D.C.: National Institute of Justice, 1986).

How Effective Is Parole?

Conservative thinkers criticize parole because it allows possibly dangerous offenders into the community before the completion of their sentence. Since parole decision-making relies on human judgment, it is quite possible for dangerous offenders, who should actually have remained inside a secure facility, to be released into society, while others who would probably make a good adjustment to the community are denied release.

The evaluation of parole effectiveness is still questionable, since various studies have produced conflicting results. For example, a study of a sample of over 104,000 parolees released between 1965 and 1970 indicated that success (lack of recidivism) was quite high. Rates of nonrecidivism ranged from 90.1 percent for homicide offenders to 64 percent for motor vehicle theft violators.[127] In every offense category, offenders with prior records had somewhat lower success rates than first offenders, though the differences were not enough to discourage the continued use of parole for recidivists.

Similarly, a three-year Bureau of Justice Statistics study of the parole experiences of the 64,000 people paroled during 1974 and 1975 found that only 25 percent had their parole revoked or were returned to prison before their parole ended.[128]

However, not all studies of parole effectiveness reach the same optimistic conclusions. A recent six-year follow-up of 1,806 federal releases (parolees and people whose sentences had expired) found that 1,129 cases (62.5 percent) were arrested at least once after release or had their parole revoked on a technical violation. In 738 cases (40.9 percent), more than one criminal arrest was recorded. All told, more than 2,788 separate criminal arrests were recorded.[129] In the Close-Up entitled "Recidivism of Young Parolees," further information on recidivism is presented which indicates that parole is less successful than might be desired.

Should Parole Be Abolished?   There have been many attacks on early release via parole, and there have been calls to eliminate the practice. The criticism leveled against parole is threefold:

1. The procedures that control the decision to grant parole are vague and have not been controlled by

due process considerations. Consequently, some inmates may be subject to the unfair denial of parole, while some who are underserving may benefit.

2. It is beyond the capacity of parole authorities either to predict who will make a successful adjustment on parole or to accurately monitor parolees' behavior in the community.

3. It is unjust to decide whether to release an individual from prison based on expectations of what the person will do in the future—there is no way of determining that accurately.[130]

Beyond these considerations, the parole process has been criticized as heightening the inmate's sense of injustice and powerlessness in the face of an omnipotent prison administration. As one prison expert, David Fogel, suggests:

Parole board decisions are also unreviewable and are not hammered out in an adversary clash; rather they are five to fifteen minute sessions with members frequently using a combination of whim, caprice, and arbitrariness.[131]

The indeterminate sentence, the heart of the parole process, is being replaced in many jurisdictions by mandatory, flat, and presumptive sentences (see Chapter 16), which severely limit parole eligibility. Maine has abolished parole completely; other states, like California, have retained parole as postrelease supervision for inmates who have completed their prison sentences. Monitored by the community release board, inmates can have their good time revoked for behavioral indiscretions and can therefore be returned to prison. Because of these changes, the percentage of inmates leaving prison on parole has declined dramatically; in 1977, 72 percent received parole, while in 1986 only 43 percent were paroled.[132]

It is likely that the abolition of parole may shift the burden of discretion from the prison authorities to the district attorney (who charges the defendants and conducts plea bargains), the judge (who sentences), and the prison authorities (who control good time violations). Of course, the inmates' sense of frustration might still remain; and sentencing disparity could still occur. Moreover, critics allege that abolishing parole would hurt prison discipline (except in states that maintained extremely liberal good time allowances of up to 50 percent of the prison sentence—almost an equivalent to parole). Despite these factors, the antiparole movement probably will continue in the years ahead, especially now that the federal government's new criminal code replaces parole with determinate sentences.

SUMMARY

Corrections involves the punishment, treatment, and incapacitation of convicted criminal offenders. Methods of punishing offenders have undergone many changes through history. At first, fines were levied to compensate the victims and their families for losses. Then, cruel corporal and capital punishments were developed. The mercantile system and the development of overseas colonies created the need for labor; so slavery and forced labor began to replace physical punishments. However, in the late eighteenth century, the death penalty began to be used once again.

Reformers pushed for alternatives to harsh, brutal, physical punishment. The prison developed as an alternative that promised to reform and rehabilitate offenders. However, early institutions were brutal places featuring silence, corporal punishment, work details, and warehousing of prisoners. Around the turn of the century, reformers began to introduce such measures as educational training and counseling for inmates.

Today, corrections can be divided into four components: community-based corrections, jails, prisons, and parole programs.

Many convicted offenders are treated in the community. Some are put on probation under supervision of local probation departments. If they obey the rules of probation, they are allowed to serve their sentences in the community. A new development is community-based correction facilities. These institutions allow the offender to remain in the community but live in a regulated environment. Some community institutions are used to house probationers who need a regulated living situation and intensive treatment. Others house prison inmates just before their release into the community. A third institution type allows inmates to serve their entire sentence in a community correctional facility. Despite their promise, community corrections methods generally have not experienced lower recidivism rates than traditional methods.

The jail is the second element of corrections. It houses misdemeanant offenders serving their sentences, and both felons and misdemeanants awaiting trial. The jail is a sore spot in the criminal justice system, because jails are usually old and dilapidated and lack rehabilitory programs.

Prisons are used to house convicted felony offenders. Recently, shifts in criminal justice philosophy and the passage of laws requiring mandatory and presumptive sentences have caused a large upswing in the U.S. prison population and consequent overcrowding.

Prisons are total institutions. Inmates must adjust to a new regime that controls every aspect of their lives. Prison is a violent, stressful place with its own unique subculture and language.

Various rehabilitation devices are used in the prison system, including counseling, educational programs, vocational training, conjugal visits, and coed prisons. However, critics charge that these methods do not seem to work. Consequently, the most recent philosophy to dominate the justice system holds that prisons are places of punishment and incapacitation and not treatment.

In the past 20 years, prisoners have been awarded some legal rights by the nation's courts. Today, their rights include medical treatment, freedom of religion, procedural due process, and correspondence with the media.

The fourth component of corrections is aftercare. About 43 percent of inmates are released on parole. Parole officers supervise inmates in the community while they complete their sentences. Recently, parole has been under attack; a number of states have actually abolished the practice. Flat and mandatory sentences without parole are viewed as promoting fairness and ending sentencing disparity.

KEY TERMS

parole	James Byrne
prison	shock probation
jail	split sentences
community-based	restitution
correctional institutions	revoked
halfway houses	technical violation

punishment

capital punishment

corporal punishment

Poor Laws

Society for Alleviating the
   Miseries of Public Prisons

Walnut Street Prison

Auburn system

Z. R. Brockway

penologists

split sentencing

intensive probation
   supervision (IPS)

maximum-security prisons

hustle

inmate subculture

social code

argot

prisonization

work furlough

free venture

conjugal visit

hands-off doctrine

mandatory release

NOTES

1. For a general discussion of this issue, see, Donald Newman, "In Defense of Prisons," *Psychiatric Annals* 4 (1974):6–17.

2. Graeme Newman, *The Punishment Response* (Philadelphia: J. B. Lippincott, 1978), p. 13.

3. Among the most helpful sources for this section are Benedict Alper, *Prisons Inside-Out* (Cambridge, Mass.: Ballinger, 1974); Gustave de Beaumont and Alexis de Tocqueville, *On the Penitentiary System in the United States and Its Application in France* (Carbondale, Ill.: Southern Illinois University Press, 1964); Orlando Lewis, *The Development of American Prisons and Prison Customs 1776–1845* (Montclair, N.J.: Patterson-Smith, 1967); Leonard Orland, ed., *Justice, Punishment and Treatment* (New York: Free Press, 1973); J. Goebel, *Felony and Misdemeanor* (Philadelphia: University of Pennsylvania Press, 1976); Georg Rusche and Otto Kircheimer, *Punishment and Social Structure* (New York: Russell and Russell, 1939); Samuel Walker, *Popular Justice* (New York: Oxford University Press, 1980); Graeme Newman, *The Punishment Response*.

4. Rusche and Kircheimer, *Punishment and Social Structure*, p. 9.

5. *Ibid.*, p. 19.

6. G. Ives, *A History of Penal Methods* (Montclair, N.J.: Patterson-Smith, 1970).

7. Leon Radzinowicz, *A History of English Criminal Law*, vol. 1 (London: Stevens, 1943), p. 5.

8. Graeme Newman, *The Punishment Response*, p. 139.

9. Walker, *Popular Justice*, p. 34.

10. Lewis, *Development of American Prisons and Prison Customs*, p. 17.

11. *Ibid.*, p. 29.

12. de Beaumont and de Tocqueville, *On the Penitentiary System in the United States*, p. 49.

13. Michel Foucault, *Discipline and Punish* (New York: Vintage Books, Random House, 1978).

14. *Ibid.*, p. 139.

15. *Ibid.*, p. 16.

16. David Rothman, *The Discovery of the Asylum* (Boston: Little, Brown, 1970).

17. Orland, *Justice, Punishment and Treatment*, p. 143.

18. *Ibid.*, p. 144.

19. Walker, *Popular Justice*, p. 70.

20. *Ibid.*, p. 71.

21. See, Z. R. Brockway, "The Ideal of a True Prison System for a State," in *Transactions of the National Congress on Penitentiary and Reformatory Discipline*, reprint ed. (Washington, D.C.: American Correctional Association, 1970), pp. 38–65.

22. This section relies heavily on David Rothman, *Conscience and Convenience* (Boston: Little, Brown, 1980).

23. *Ibid.*, p. 23.

24. *Ibid.*, p. 133.

25. See, generally, Jameson Doig, *Criminal Corrections: Ideals and Realities* (Lexington, Mass.: Lexington Books, 1983).

26. See, generally, Chris Eskridge, Richard Seiter, and Eric Carlson, "Community Based Corrections: From the Community to the Community," in Vincent Webb and Roy Roberg, eds., *Critical Issues in Corrections* (St. Paul, Minn.: West Publishing, 1981), pp. 171–203.

27. H. Allen, E. Carlson, and E. Parks, *Critical Issues in Adult Probation* (Washington, D.C.: U.S. Government Printing Office, 1979), p. 11.

28. George Killinger, Hazel Kerper, and Paul Cromwell, *Probation and Parole in the Criminal Justice System* (St. Paul, Minn.: West Publishing, 1976), p. 35.

29. Thomas Hester, *Probation and Parole, 1986* (Washington, D.C.: U.S. Department of Justice, 1987).

30. Allen, Carlson, and Parks, *Critical Issues in Adult Probation*, p. 47.

31. *Ibid.*

32. See, generally, Patrick McAnany, Doug Thomson, and David Fogel, *Probation and Justice: Reconsideration of Mission* (Cambridge, Mass.: Oelgeschlager, Gunn and Hain, 1984).

33. Ronald Corbett and Ellsworth Fersch, "Home as Prison: The Use of House Arrest," *Federal Probation* 49 (1985):13–17; Joan Petersilia, "Exploring the Option of House Arrest," *Federal Probation* 50 (1986):50–55.

34. James Byrne, "The Control Controversy: A Preliminary Examination of Intensive Probation Supervision Programs in The United States," *Federal Probation* 50 (1986):4–16. See also, Larry Travis, "Intensive Supervision in Probation and Parole," *Corrections Today* 46 (1984):34–40.

35. Billie Erwin and Lawrence Bennett, *New Dimensions in*

Probation: Georgia's Experience with Intensive Probation Supervision (IPS) (Washington, D.C.: National Institute of Justice, 1987).

36. Joan Petersilia, *Expanding Options for Criminal Sentencing* (Santa Monica, Cal.: Rand Corp., 1987).

37. Paul Friday, David Petersen, and Harry Allen, "Shock Probation: A New Approach to Crime Control," *Georgia Journal of Corrections* 1 (1973):1–13.

38. For a further analysis of restitution, see Larry Siegel, "Court-Ordered Victim Restitution: An Overview of Theory and Action," *New England Journal of Prison Law* 5 (1979):135–50.

39. Richard Maher and Henry Dufour, "Experimenting with Community Service: A Punitive Alternative to Imprisonment," *Federal Probation* 51 (1987):22–28.

40. Descriptive materials can be obtained from the EARN-IT Program, District Court of East Norfolk, 50 Chestnut Street, Quincy, MA 02169.

41. "Expanded Use of Financial Restitution Urged," *Justice Assistance News* 2 (August 1981):6.

42. Gagnon v. Scarpelli, 411 U.S. 778, 93 S.Ct. 1756, 36 L.Ed. 2d 655 (1973).

43. Lawrence Greenfield, *Examining Recidivism* (Washington, D.C.: Bureau of Justice Statistics, 1985).

44. Joan Petersilia, Susan Turner, James Kahan, and Joyce Peterson, *Granting Felons Probation: Public Risks and Alternatives* (Santa Monica, Cal.: Rand Corp., 1985).

45. Eskridge, Seiter, and Carlson, "Community Based Corrections," pp. 183–85.

46. This program is evaluated in E. Kim Nelson, Howard Ohmart, and Nora Harlow, *Promising Strategies in Probation and Parole* (Washington, D.C.: U.S. Government Printing Office, 1978), pp. 25–26.

47. Andrew Scull, *Decarceration: Community Treatment and the Deviant: A Radical View* (Englewood Cliffs, N.J.: Prentice-Hall, 1977).

48. John Hylton, "Rhetoric and Reality: A Critical Appraisal of Community Correctional Programs," *Crime and Delinquency* 28 (1982):341–73.

49. For example, see, Howard Kaplan and Joseph Meyerowitz, "Evaluation of a Halfway House: Integrated Community Approach in the Rehabilitation of Narcotic Addicts," *International Journal of Addictions* 4 (Winter 1969):65–66; James Beck, "An Evaluation of Federal Community Treatment Centers," *Federal Probation* 43 (1979):36–40.

50. Margaret Wilson, *The Crime of Punishment*, Life and Letter Series, no. 64 (London: Jonathon Cape Ltd., 1934), p. 186.

51. Bureau of Justice Statistics, *The 1986 Jail Census* (Washington, D.C.: U.S. Department of Justice, 1987).

52. Bureau of Justice Statistics, *Profile of Jail Inmates* (Washington, D.C.: U.S. Department of Justice, 1980).

53. See, generally, Daniel Kennedy, "A Theory of Suicide While in Police Custody," *Journal of Police Science and Administration* 12 (1984):191–200.

54. Bureau of Justice Statistics, *The 1986 Jail Census*, p. 3.

55. See note, *Jail Administration Digest* 3 (1980):4.

56. See note, *Jail Administration Digest* 2 (1979):6.

57. Bureau of Justice Statistics, *Prisons and Prisoners* (Washington, D.C.: U.S. Government Printing Office, 1982).

58. Bureau of Justice Statistics, *Prisoners in 1987* (Washington, D.C.: U.S. Department of Justice, 1988).

59. Christopher Innes, *Profile of Prison Inmates, 1986* (Washington, D.C.: Bureau of Justice Statistics, 1988).

60. See, Erving Goffman, "Characteristics of Total Institutions," in Leonard Orland, ed., *Justice, Punishment and Treatment* (New York: Free Press, 1973), pp. 153–58.

61. Gresham Sykes, *The Society of Captives* (Princeton, N.J.: Princeton University Press, 1958), pp. 79–82.

62. Nicolette Parisi, "The Prisoner's Pressures and Responses," in N. Parisi, ed., *Coping with Imprisonment*, pp. 9–16.

63. Daniel Lockwood, "The Contribution of Sexual Harassment to Stress and Coping in Confinement," in Parisi, ed., *Coping with Imprisonment*, p. 47.

64. Ibid.

65. Sandra Gleason, "Hustling: The 'Inside' Economy of a Prison," *Federal Probation* 42 (1978):32–39.

66. Ibid., p. 39.

67. "The Killing Ground," *Newsweek* (18 February 1980), p. 75.

68. Parisi, "The Prisoner's Pressures and Responses."

69. John Irwin, "Adaptation to Being Corrected: Corrections from the Convict's Perspective," in Daniel Glazer, ed., *Handbook of Criminology* (Chicago: Rand McNally & Co., 1974), pp. 971–93.

70. Conald Clemmer, *The Prison Community* (New York: Holt, Rinehart & Winston, 1958).

71. Sykes, *The Society of Captives*.

72. Adapted from Gresham Sykes and Sheldon Messinger, "The Inmate Social Code," in Norman Johnston, et al., eds., *The Sociology of Punishment and Corrections* (New York: John Wiley & Sons, 1970), pp. 401–408.

73. John Irwin and Donald Cressey, "Thieves, Convicts, and the Inmate Culture," *Social Problems* 10 (1962):142–55.

74. Ibid., p. 145.

75. Charles Thomas, "Prisonization or Resocialization? A Study of External Factors Associated with the Impact of Imprisonment," *Journal of Research in Crime and Delinquency* 10 (1973):18–20.

76. Paul Gendreau, Marie-Claude Tellier, and J. Stephen Wormith, "Protective Custody: The Emerging Crisis Within Our Prisons," *Federal Probation* 49 (1985):55–64.

77. James B. Jacobs, *New Perspectives on Prisons and Imprisonment* (Ithaca, N.Y.: Cornell University Press, 1983); idem., "Street Gangs Behind Bars," *Social Problems* 21 (1974):395–409; idem., "Race Relations and the Prison Subculture," in N. Morris and M. Tonry, eds., *Crime and Justice* (Chicago: University of Chicago Press, 1979), pp. 1–28.

78. Victor Cox, "Prison Gangs: Inmates Battle for Control," *Corrections Compendium* 10 (1986):1–9.

79. Esther Hefferman, *Making It in Prison: The Square, the Cool and the Life* (New York: Wiley, 1972).

80. Rose Giallombardo, *Society of Women: A Study of a Women's Prison* (New York: Wiley, 1966), pp. 165–89.

81. See, generally, G. Kassebaum, D. Ward, and D. Wilner, "Group Counseling," in N. Johnston and L. Savitz, eds., *Legal Process and Corrections* (New York: Wiley, 1982), pp. 255–70.

82. See, William Glasser, *Reality Therapy* (New York: Harper & Row, 1965); Richard Rachin, "Reality Therapy: Helping People Help Themselves," *Crime and Delinquency* 16 (1974):143–45; Eric Berne, *Transactional Analysis in Psychotherapy* (New York: Grove Press, 1961); Richard Nicholson, "Transactional Analysis: A New Method for Helping Offenders," *Federal Probation* 34 (1970):29–31; Gaylord Thorne, "Behavior Modification Techniques: New Tools for Probation Officers," *Federal Probation* 31 (1967):21–23; Ralph Schwitzgabel, *Street Corner Research* (Cambridge, Mass.: Harvard University Press, 1964); J. T. Saunders and N. D. Reppucci, "Reward and Punishment: Some Guidelines for Their Effective Application in Correctional Programs for Youthful Offenders," *Crime and Delinquency* 18 (1972):284.

83. Sylvia McCollum, "New Designs for Correctional Education and Training Programs," *Federal Probation* 37 (June 1973):6.

84. R. Bell, et al., *Correctional Education Programs for Inmates* (Washington, D.C.: U.S. Government Printing Office, 1979), pp. 18–19.

85. See, generally, Michael Fedo, "Free Enterprise Goes to Prison," *Corrections Magazine* 7 (1981):11–18.

86. Ann Goetting, "Conjugal Association in Prison," *Crime and Delinquency* 28 (1982):52–62.

87. J. G. Ross, E. Hefferman, J. R. Sevick, and F. T. Johnson, *Assessment of Coeducational Corrections* (Washington, D.C.: U.S. Government Printing Office, 1978).

88. *Ibid.*

89. D. Lipton, R. Martinson, and J. Wilks, *The Effectiveness of Correctional Treatment: A Survey of Treatment Evaluation Studies* (New York: Praeger, 1975).

90. Charles Murray and Louis Cox, *Beyond Probation: Juvenile Corrections and the Chronic Delinquent* (Beverly Hills, Cal.: Sage Publications, 1979).

91. Paul Lerman, *Community Treatment and Social Control* (Chicago: University of Chicago Press, 1975).

92. Francis Cullen and Karen Gilbert, *Reaffirming Rehabilitation* (Cincinnati: Anderson Publications, 1982).

93. Hans Toch, *Police, Prisons and the Problems of Violence* (Washington, D.C.: U.S. Government Printing Office, 1977), p. 53.

94. For a series of papers on the position, see, A. Cohen, G. Cole, and R. Baily, eds., *Prison Violence* (Lexington, Mass.: Lexington Books, 1976).

95. Charles Silberman, *Criminal Violence, Criminal Justice* (New York: Vintage Books, 1978).

96. See, Hans Toch, "Social Climate and Prison Violence," *Federal Probation* 42 (1978):21–23.

97. American Correctional Association, *Riots and Disturbances in Correctional Institutions* (Washington, D.C.: American Correctional Association, 1970), p. 1.

98. Sue Mahar, "An 'Orgy of Brutality' at Attica and the 'Killing Crowd' at Santa Fe: A Comparison of Prison Riots," in N. Parisi, ed., *Coping with Imprisonment*, p. 75.

99. Cited in G. McCain, V. Cox, and P. Paulus, *The Effect of Prison Crowding on Inmate Behavior* (Washington, D.C.: U.S. Government Printing Office, 1981), p. vi.

100. P. Paulus, V. Cox, G. McCain, and J. Chandler, "Some Effects of Crowding in a Prison Environment," *Journal of Applied Social Psychology* 5 (1975):86–91.

101. Edwin Megargee, "The Association of Population Density, Reduced Space, and Uncomfortable Temperatures with Misconduct in a Prison Community," *American Journal of Community Psychology* 5 (1977):289–98.

102. P. Nacci, H. Teitelbaum, and J. Prather, "Population Density and Inmate Misconduct Rates in the Federal Prison System," *Federal Probation* 41 (1977):26–31.

103. Sheldon Ekland-Olson, Dennis Barrick, and Lawrence Cohen, "Prison Overcrowding and Disciplinary Problems: An Analysis of the Texas Prison System," *Journal of Applied Behavioral Science* 19 (1983):163–76.

104. D. D'Atri, "Psychophysiological Response to Crowding," *Environment and Behavior* 7 (1975): 237–52; D. D'Atri and A. Ostfeld, "Crowding: Its Effect on the Elevation of Blood Pressure in a Prison Setting," *Preventative Medicine* 4 (1975):550–66; J. Freedman, *Crowding and Behavior* (San Francisco: Freeman, 1975).

105. National Advisory Commission on Criminal Justice Standards and Goals, *Volume on Corrections* (Washington, D.C.: U.S. Government Printing Office, 1973), p. 18.

106. See, for example, Cooper v. Pate, 378 U.S. 546 (1964).

107. Johnson v. Avery, 393 U.S. 483 (1969).

108. Gilmore v. Lynch, 319 F.Supp. 105 (N.D. Cal. 1970).

109. Procunier v. Martinez, 411 U.S. 396 (1974).
110. Nolan v. Fitzpatrick, 451 F.2d 545 (1st Cir., 1971).
111. Saxbe v. Washington Post, 41 L.Ed. 2d 514 (1974).
112. Newman v. Alabama, 349 F.Supp. 278 (M.D.Ala. 1974).
113. Estelle v. Gamble, 429 U.S. 97 (1976).
114. 97 S.Ct. 291 (1976).
115. See, for example, Trop v.Dulles, 356 U.S. 86, 78 S.Ct. 590, 2d 630 (1958); see also, Furman v.Georgia, 408 U.S. 238, 92 S.Ct. 2726, 33 L.Ed. 2d 346 (1972).
116. See, for example, Weems v. United States, 217 U.S. 349, 30 S.Ct. 544, 54 L.Ed. 793 (1910).
117. See, for example, Lee v. Tahash, 352 F.2d 970 (8th Cir. 1965).
118. 309 F. Supp. 362 (E.D. Ark. 1970); aff'd 442 F.2d 304 (8th Cir. 1971).
119. Bell v. Wolfish, 99 S.Ct. 1873–1874 (1979); Rhodes v. Chapman, 452 U.S. 337 (1981).
120. Rhodes v. Chapman.
121. Estelle v. Ruiz, 74–329 (E.D. Texas, 1980).
122. Wolff v. McDonnell, 418 U.S. 539 (1974).
123. Hester, *Probation and Parole, 1986*, p. 3.
124. See, generally, Vincent O'Leary and Joan Nuffield, *The Organization of Parole Systems in the United States* (Hackensack, N.J.: National Council on Crime and Delinquency, 1972).
125. See Peter Hoffman and Lucille DeGostin, "Parole Decision-Making: Structuring Discretion," *Federal Probation* 38 (1974):19–21.
126. Peter Hoffman and Barbara Stone-Meierhoefer, "Post-Release Arrest Experiences of Federal Prisoners: A Six Year Follow-Up," *Journal of Criminal Justice* 7 (1979):193–216.
127. Don M.Gottfredson, M. G. Neithercutt, Joan Nuffield, and Vincent O'Leary, *Four Thousand Lifetimes: A Study of Time Served and Parole Outcome* (Fort Lee, N.J.: National Council on Crime and Delinquency, 1973).
128. National Council on Crime and Delinquency, *Parole in the United States, 1979* (Washington, D.C.: U.S. Government Printing Office, 1981).
129. Hoffman and Stone-Meierhoefer, "Post-Release Arrest Experiences," p. 202.
130. Listed in Andrew Von Hirsch and Kathleen Hanrahan, *Abolish Parole?* (Washington, D.C.: U.S. Government Printing Office, 1978).
131. David Fogel, *. . . We are the Living Proof . . .: The Justice Model for Corrections* (Cincinnati: Anderson, 1979), p. 197.
132. Hester, *Probation and Parole, 1986*, p. 4.

EPILOGUE

There are many questions still to be answered about the nature, extent, cause, and control of crime. Nonetheless, as this text has demonstrated, criminologists have already developed a body of knowledge about criminality and criminal behavior. This epilogue highlights some of the most important facts contained in this text which help define the field of criminology.

Crime has been and always will be a significant social problem. Fear of crime has had a significant influence on the everyday behavior of the general public. Concern about crime has been channeled into gun ownership, citizen self-help groups, the purchase of crime protection devices, and other self-help measures.

Criminology is an essentially interdisciplinary field. Though most criminologists remain trained in sociology, there is little question that many contributions are being made in a broad variety of areas, including biology, psychology, and other natural and social sciences.

There are many criminological controversies. The field of criminology is not unified. As in other social sciences, there are significant disagreements among professional criminologists. Not surprisingly in a field dedicated to the study of a politically sensitive and controversial subject, there are opposing factions and subfactions. Consequently, there are many "solutions" offered to the control of crime.

There is a difference between crime and morality. Not all criminal acts are immoral; not all immoral acts are crimes. This social fact is important, because it is the foundation of a culturally relative definition of crime:

crime is a violation of societal rules of behavior as expressed by a criminal code created by people holding social and political power. Individuals who violate these rules are subject to sanctions by state authority, social stigma, labeling, and loss of status.

Most criminologists tie the definition of crime to the existing criminal law. Though there are separate schools of criminological thought, all agree that the criminal law defines crime. There are significant differences, however, over the development of the criminal law and its progression into its present form.

American criminal law has its origin in the British common law. The common law began in the eleventh century, when Norman judges began unifying the definition of criminal acts and consequent punishments.

The law is a dynamic entity constantly changing to reflect the spirit and morality of the times. While some crimes, mala in se, are constant, others mirror existing norms, public opinion, and popular causes. People who attempt to control the content of the criminal law are known as "moral entrepreneurs."

The criminal law is a multi-purpose concept. Included within the functions of the criminal law are social control, retribution, deterrence, order maintenance, and expression of the public will.

While the insanity defense is still quite controversial, it is actually used far less often than the public imagines. A number of states have moved to discontinue the insanity defense or restrict its use. Research indicates that relatively few cases end in a not guilty by reason of insanity (NGRI) decision. Moreover, those pleading insanity are often nonviolent offenders who spend many years in mental health institutions.

Legal reform movements have been extensive during the past decade.   Led by the federal government, many jurisdictions have overhauled their criminal codes. Among the targets are rape and drug and alcohol abuse laws. Criminal sentences have been modified with a tendency toward increasing uniformity.

The accuracy of crime data is still a major criminological issue.   The three main sources of crime data have been criticized on the grounds of validity. It is still uncertain how much crime exists, where it occurs, and who commits it.

Crime rates have stabilized.   After 20 years of rapid increase, crime rates stabilized in the mid-1980s. Recent hikes, though unexpected, may be more a result of increased reporting by victims than actual changes in the crime rate.

There are stable patterns in the crime rate.   Though the number and rate may vary, there are certain stable patterns in the crime rate. Over the years, crime is more likely to occur in large cities, during warm summer months, and on the west and east coasts.

The true crime rate is much greater than the official police statistics show.   The so-called "dark figures of crime" are offenses not reported to police authorities. Victim surveys indicate that more than 30 million crimes occur each year, while self-report surveys indicate that a significant portion of all youths engage in criminal activity.

The true relationship between class and crime has not been determined.   One of the great criminological debates has been fought over the association between class and crime. Self-report studies often fail to show that lower-class youths commit more crime than those in the upper- and middle-classes. However, the weight of the recent evidence seems to indicate an inverse relationship between class and crime exists.

Males are significantly more criminal than females.   Though criminologists warned of the "new" female criminal, this prediction has not been seen in the crime statistics. All three crime data sources indicate that crime is preponderantly a male-oriented phenomenon. The ratio between male and female arrests remains about 4 to 1 overall and 8 to 1 for violent crimes.

People commit less crime as they age.   Though this is another criminological controversy, there is little question that the crime rate is negatively associated with age. Some criminologists see chronic offenders as people who are immune to the aging out process; their crime rate is consistent throughout their life span.

The chronic offender has become the focus of significant criminological interest.   Since first being identified by Wolfgang, the career criminal has been the focus of significant criminological research. There is a growing consensus that a small portion of the criminal population commits a major portion of all serious criminal acts. Logically, it follows that if this group could be identified and incapacitated, then the crime rate would be dramatically lowered.

There is considerable similarity between the personal characteristics of victims and criminals.   Surveys show that the personal characteristics of victims are remarkably similar to those of criminals. Both criminals and victims tend to be teenagers, male, and urban residents. The usual times and places of criminal events and victimizations are also a close match.

The elderly are the least likely to become the victims of crime; teenagers the most likely.   While the public views senior citizens as being extremely vulnerable to predatory crime, victim surveys indicate that the most likely victims are teenage males.

The choice of routine personal activities significantly influences the likelihood of victimization.   The distribution of victimization in our society is not random. People can increase or diminish the likelihood of their being the victims of crime by changing their daily routine. For example, going out late at night to open public areas in large cities significantly increases the likelihood of becoming a victim of crime; staying at home decreases the chance of becoming a victim of predatory crime.

There is little conclusive evidence that perceptions of punishment can deter criminal activity.   While some research indicates a positive association between perceptions of punishment and a deterrent effect, there is no conclusive evidence that people who believe they will be punished if they commit crime are less likely to engage in criminal behavior.

There is some evidence that increasing legal sanctions can have a deterrent effect. Crime rates vary with such measures of legal sanctions as arrest rates, incarceration rates, and sentencing severity. Nonetheless, accurate measurement of the deterrent effects of legal punishment is extremely difficult.

There is little evidence that capital punishment can reduce the murder rate. While the general public approves of capital punishment, there is little if any research evidence that capital punishment can have either a short- or a long-term deterrent effect on the murder rate. There is evidence that use of the death penalty may encourage murder through a brutalization effect.

There is little conclusive evidence that a policy of incapacitation can effectively reduce the crime rate. Research shows that reducing the crime rate through a policy of incapacitation would result in an overloaded prison system without a significant influence on the crime rate.

While there is evidence linking biological factors to crime, current research methodology is not sufficient to draw firm conclusions. Some research studies show that convicted criminals may have physical characteristics which differentiate them from the general population. Nonetheless, there is insufficient evidence that physical or constitutional factors alone can influence criminality. However, the evidence needed to conclude that there is no association between physical and constitutional factors and crime is also deficient.

There is an association between observing violence and acting violently. Youths who have been the subject of violence at home or who observe it in the media are more likely to engage in personal acts of violence and aggression.

There is no conclusive evidence of a direct link between IQ and crime. While a number of studies show that delinquents and criminals have lower aggregate IQs than the general population, the relationship is at best indirect. Intelligence is related to poor school perfor-

mance and academic failure, which is directly associated with criminality.

Mentally ill people are no more likely to commit crime than members of the general population. The factors associated with criminality among the general population are identical to those in the population of mental hospitals. The mentally ill are no more likely to engage in crime than the mentally sound.

One emerging school of criminology finds that some people are likely to choose crime because of mental, physical, or constitutional factors. Criminal choice and behavior have been linked with personal characteristics. This association has sparked a great deal of debate and criticism among mainstream criminologists, who maintain crime is of social and not individual behavior.

Urban lower-class areas are the sites of teenage street gangs and high levels of predatory crime. There is general agreement among criminologists that people living in deteriorated inner-city areas are the most likely to experience conditions which result in increased crime rates.

Ecological conditions in deteriorated urban areas, and not the people living in them, are responsible for the high crime rates. Certain ecological areas maintain high crime rates regardless of the ethnic or racial composition of their residents. Stable rates implies that crime rates are a function of area and not resident characteristics.

Crime rates will be highest in areas whose residents in close proximity to one another have significant income and lifestyle differentials. Relative deprivation in lifestyle and income is linked to violent predatory crime rates.

Crime promoting inner-city cultural values are passed on from one generation to another. Cultural transmission can be seen today in the rebirth of gangs in New York and Los Angeles and in the active gang recruitment of young members.

Poor early socialization is a strong predictor of later criminality. People growing up in warm, nurturing households, who have strong attachments to their parents and learn conventional values, are the least likely to engage in crime and delinquency.

Youths growing up in deteriorated inner-city areas, who also maintain poor personal relationships with family and neighbors, and who associate with and learn from deviant peers will be the most likely to become involved in long-term criminal careers.   Integrated theories indicate cultural and personal behaviors interact to produce criminal tendencies.

There is little conclusive evidence that labeling by the criminal justice system is associated with criminality.   There is little direct evidence that being labeled by the justice system alone can cause a person to become enmeshed in a criminal career. Nonetheless, the relationship between chronic offending and labeling has yet to be determined.

Class conflict has had a significant impact on the development of law and justice.   Laws controlling lower-class activity, such as vagrancy and theft, can be traced to the use of power by members of the ruling classes to control the direction and content of the legal system.

A subculture of violence may exist, in which aggression and violence are socially acceptable cultural norms.   The subculture of violence is a feature of inner-city areas. Recent outbreaks of gang activity in Los Angeles and New York support this view.

Date rape has become all too common on college campuses.   Studies indicate that a significant number of college women have been the victim of sexual assaults by male companions whom they knew and trusted.

Change in the legal processing of rape cases has been slow in forthcoming.   While rape shield laws and other legal protections have been passed, there are significant state-by-state variations in the treatment of rape victims.

The serial killer has become recognized as a significant social problem.   While relatively few in number, the serial killer, who goes from victim to victim without apparent motive, is now recognized as a specific and dangerous crime type.

Millions of cases of child abuse, sexual abuse, and spousal abuse occur each year.   The family is considered an extremely violent institution. Reported incidents of child abuse have skyrocketed in the past few years.

Property crimes are often committed by professional criminals.   The professional criminal is one whose life revolves around theft, who is skilled in the ways of criminality, and who views him- or herself as a professional abiding by a set of rules and values.

White-collar crimes probably cause greater social harm than common street crimes.   While many Americans are afraid of burglars, muggers, and robbers, the losses due to their activities are actually overshadowed by the losses due to white-collar criminals.

White-collar crime is a multifaceted enterprise system.   While originally viewed as violations in the corporate world, the concept of white-collar crime today involves individual acts such as bribery, tax evasion, insider trading, swindles, embezzlement, and employee fraud.

There is a strong conceptual link between white-collar crime and traditional organized crime.   Both can be viewed as ongoing efforts by organizations and their personnel to profit by bending rules and regulations for the sake of profit and power.

The enforcement of white-collar laws has been improving.   While white-collar criminals are still often immune to punishment, the prosecution and punishment of white-collar criminals is being toughened. Nonetheless, prosecution efforts are often directed at common-law crimes, such as embezzlement and wire fraud, and not at large-scale corporate criminality.

Corporate crime may be a function of corporate culture.   The social and business climate within an organization can encourage white-collar crime in the same fashion that neighborhood culture and values can promote street crime.

Traditional organized crime structures are no longer operational.   The view of organized crime as a unified structure controlled by a few cohesive, ethnic "families" no longer seems valid. Today many groups compete side by side for profits, through the sale of illegal goods and services or the use of force to extort money from legitimate or illegitimate enterprises.

Despite increased federal enforcement pressure, organized crime continues to involve hundreds of billions of dollars annually. Criminal syndicates continue to maintain substantial control over the drug trade, gambling, union activity, and sex for profit, as well as infiltrating legitimate businesses.

There is significant evidence that observation of violence-oriented pornography may cause sexual violence and aggression. While the causal connection has not been absolutely determined, there is significant laboratory evidence that males exposed to violent pornography will subsequently act in a more aggressive manner and voice negative attitudes toward women.

Significant numbers of children are used in the sex for profit industry, including prostitution and pornography. One of the most disturbing aspects of public order crime is the use of children as prostitutes and in adult magazines and films. Each year, children as young as 10 are arrested on prostitution charges, and kiddie porn has become a staple of the obscenity business.

While the illegal drug trade continues to be a major social problem, the frequency of substance abuse seems to have stabilized. While media attention to the drug problem is at an all-time high, most research indicates that the number of addicts has remained stable for the past decade, while the prevalence of substance abuse among teenagers and the general public has declined. Even cocaine, the one substance whose use had been steadily increasing for over a decade, seems to have peaked in popularity. Nonetheless, drug use seems to be concentrated in inner-city urban areas, creating ecological pockets of high dependency.

There is an extremely strong association between drug use and crime. Every survey of known criminals has consistently shown that an overwhelming number were drug or alcohol abusers at the time of their arrest. This in itself is not conclusive evidence that drugs cause crime, since most criminals report drug use began after the onset of their criminal careers. Nonetheless, drugs seem to significantly amplify criminal activity.

Narcotics users go through abuse cycles ranging from infrequent to heavy usage. Narcotics use is not consistent over an addict's lifetime. Users drift between episodes of heavy use, in which drugs become their life, to periods of occasional use, when their narcotics addiction can be contained within elements of a conventional lifestyle.

Drug enforcement efforts may be doomed because enforcement success will drive up drug prices, making the importation of narcotics more lucrative and forcing users to commit more crimes to pay the higher prices. Drug enforcement efforts may be ineffective because of a Catch-22 situation: the lower the supply of drugs coming into the country, the more costly they become; higher costs mean more profits for successful dealers and force users to commit more crimes to support their habits. Focusing on the user is costly because of an overcrowded prison system and high recidivism rates. Drug education programs, if effective, could be the most realistic approach.

The criminal justice system is a vast, complex set of agencies which process millions of cases at a cost of about $50 billion a year. There are thousands of police, court, and correctional agencies, employing thousands of people and costing billions of dollars. Organized on the local, state, and federal levels, the justice system is charged with investigating crimes, identifying perpetrators, filing charges, trying cases, and correcting and punishing convicted offenders. There is also a parallel system of juvenile justice which deals with cases involving juvenile delinquents and status offenders.

The justice system can be characterized as operating with selective enforcement, great amounts of discretion, and individualized justice. While there is a formal system of justice involving the full range of rights and procedures including a jury trial, most cases are settled in an informal manner, in which a bargain is struck between the accused and agents of the justice system. Consequently, justice is often served on an individual level, with no two cases being dealt with exactly alike.

There is no single view or concept of justice which dominates the justice system today. There are a number of competing views of justice which exist simultaneously within the U.S. justice system. These include the crime control, nonintervention, rehabilitation, due process, radical, and justice models. Because different points of view abound, it is not surprising that the justice system has been criticized and divided.

The Supreme Court plays an important role in the day-to-day criminal justice process. From the activist leadership of Earl Warren in the 1960s to the more conservative stewardship of Chief Justices Burger and Rehnquist in the 1980s, the Supreme Court's decisions have shaped the way police search for evidence and make arrests. Courts conduct trials and correctional administrators operate their facilities.

There is little evidence that the police alone can deter crime. Empirical research indicates that police presence has little deterrent effect on crime.

Detectives solve relatively few crimes. Unlike their fictional counterparts, real-life detectives actually solve few crimes. Unless a crime is reported in progress, the chances of catching the perpetrator are relatively small.

The Supreme Court has loosened legal controls on police behavior. In recent years the Court has weakened the power of the exclusionary rule, liberalized search and seizure law, and granted a number of exceptions to the Miranda rule.

The police use of deadly force has been reduced. The number of civilians killed by police and the number of officers killed by civilians has declined in the past few years. Legal and administrative controls have been effective in reducing fatalities.

The courts routinely dispense bargain justice. Most cases end in plea bargains. However, the typical bargain is a guilty plea to the top charge filed.

Significant numbers of felony offenders are sentenced to probation. Despite charges that the American justice system is overly strict and punitive, research shows that many serious felons are granted probation sentences.

There has been a trend to reduce judicial discretion in sentencing through the creation of legislatively fixed sentences. While the indeterminate sentence is still widely used, the trend has been to create flat, mandatory, and other types of legislatively determined sentences.

The Supreme Court has upheld the legality of the death penalty despite challenges on the grounds that it is employed in a racially biased manner. Despite research indicating that the race of the victim often determines whether the prosecution will request the death penalty, the Court has ruled that racial bias must be proven in the case at hand in order for a capital sentence to be appealed.

The use of guidelines to limit judicial discretion has been expanding. Sentencing guidelines and bail guidelines are a relatively new development. Both their legality and effectiveness have become important policy issues.

The prison system has become vastly overcrowded. After many years of rapid population expansion, the inmate population today is over 600,000. Overcrowding has become one of the most important issues in corrections.

The use of probation has significantly expanded. Prison overcrowding and costs have made probationary sentences highly desirable. New forms of probation, such as intensive supervision and house arrest, should significantly expand probation's appeal.

The average time served in prison is considerably less than trial sentence. Good time, early release, and parole programs reduce the percentage of a prison sentence actually served. The longer the original sentence, the greater the reduction in time served.

Privatization programs are becoming a conspicuous trend in the correctional system. Privately run prisons and private industry in prisons are a relatively recent development. Their continued use and expansion will depend on evaluations of effectiveness, cost benefit, security, and impact on existing correctional institutions.

The effectiveness of the correctional system is still an open issue. Research indicates that far too many correctional clients recidivate within a few years of their release. The view that corrections can be used as a rehabilitation-oriented crime-reducing system has been superseded by focus on its incapacitative and punitive function.

GLOSSARY

absolute deterrent A legal control measure designed to totally eliminate a particular criminal act.

Academy of Criminal Justice Sciences A society which serves to further the development of the criminal justice profession and whose membership includes academics and practitioners involved in criminal justice.

accountability system A way of dealing with police corruption by making superiors responsible for the behavior of their subordinates.

actus reus An illegal act. The actus reus can be an affirmative act, such as taking money or shooting someone, or a failure to act, such as failing to take proper precautions while driving a car.

adjudication Determination of guilt or innocence; a judgment concerning criminal charges. Trial by jury is a method of adjudication. The majority of offenders charged plead guilty. Of the remainder, some cases are also adjudicated by a judge without a jury and others are dismissed.

administrative model Sentencing scheme in which control over sentence length is left to correctional authorities.

adversary system Procedure used to determine truth in the adjudication of guilt or innocence, which pits the defense (advocate for the accused) against the prosecution (advocate for the state), with the judge acting as arbiter of the legal rules. Under the adversary system, the burden is on the state to prove the charges beyond a reasonable doubt. This system of having the two parties publicly debate has proved to be the most effective method of achieving the truth regarding a set of circumstances. Under the accusatory, or inquisitorial, system which is used in continental Europe, the charge is evidence of guilt which the accused must disprove; the judge takes an active part in the proceedings.

aggressive preventive patrol A patrol technique designed to suppress crime before it occurs.

aging out Process in which the crime rate declines with age.

alien conspiracy theory The view that organized crime was imported by Europeans and that crime cartels restrict their membership to members of their own ethnic background.

American Society of Criminology Professional society of the criminological field.

anger rape A rape incident motivated by the rapist's desire to release pent-up anger and rage.

anomie A condition produced by normlessness. Because of rapidly shifting moral values, a person has few guides to what is socially acceptable behavior.

appeal Review of lower court proceedings by a higher court. There is no constitutional right to appeal. However, the "right" to appeal is established by statute in some states and by custom in others. All states set conditions as to type of case or grounds for appeal, which appellate courts may review. Appellate courts do not retry the case under review. Rather, the transcript of the lower court case is read by the judges, and the lawyers for the defendant and for the state argue about the merits of the appeal—that is, the legality of lower court proceedings instead of the original testimony. Appeal is more a process for controlling police, court, and correctional practices than for rescuing innocent defendants. When appellate courts do reverse lower court judgments, it is usually because of ''prejudicial error'' (deprivation of rights), and the case is remanded for retrial.

appellate courts   Courts which reconsider a case already tried in order to determine whether the measures used complied with accepted rules of procedure and were in line with constitutional doctrines.

arbitrage   The practice of buying large blocks of stock in companies which are believed to be the target of corporate buyouts or takeovers.

argot   Unique language which influences the prison culture.

arraignment   The step at which the accused is read the charges against him or her and is asked how he or she pleads. In addition, the accused is advised of his or her rights. Possible pleas are guilty, not guilty, nolo contendere, and not guilty by reason of insanity.

arrest   Taking of a person into the custody of the law, the legal purpose of which is to restrain the accused until he or she can be held accountable for the offense at court proceedings. The legal requirement for an arrest is probable cause. Arrests for investigation, suspicion, or harassment are improper and of doubtful legality. The police have the responsibility to use only reasonable physical force necessary to make an arrest. The summons has been used as a substitute to arrest.

arrest warrant   Written court order issued by a magistrate authorizing and directing that an individual be taken into custody to answer criminal charges.

Aryan Brotherhood   A white supremicist prison gang.

assembly line justice   The view that the justice process resembles an endless production line which handles most cases in a routine and perfunctory fashion.

atavistic   According to Lombroso, the primitive physical characteristics which distinguish born criminals from the general population; according to Lombrosian theory, characteristics of criminals which are throwbacks to animals or primitive society.

attainder   Loss of all civil rights due to a conviction for a felony offense.

Attorney General   Senior U.S. prosecutor and cabinet member who heads the Justice Department.

Auburn System   Prison system developed in New York during the nineteenth century which stressed congregate working conditions.

Augustus, John   The individual credited with pioneering the concept of probation.

authoritarian   A person whose personality revolves around blind obedience to authority.

bail   Monetary amount for or condition of pretrial release, normally set by a judge at the initial appearance. The purpose of bail is to ensure the return of the accused at subsequent proceedings. If the accused is unable to make bail, he or she is detained in jail. The Eighth Amendment provides that excessive bail shall not be required.

basic car plan   Patrol deployment system used in cities such as Los Angeles.

Beccaria, Cesare   Eighteenth-century Italian philosopher who argued that crime could be controlled by punishments only severe enough to counterbalance the pleasure obtained from them.

behaviorism   Branch of psychology concerned with the study of observable behavior rather than unconscious motives. It focuses on the relationship between particular stimuli and people's responses to them.

bill of indictment   A document submitted to a grand jury by the prosecutor asking them to take action and indict a suspect in a case.

blameworthiness   Amount of culpability or guilt a person maintains for participating in a particular criminal offense.

blue curtain   According to William Westly, the secretive, insulated police culture that isolates the officer from the rest of society.

booking   Administrative record of an arrest, involving listing offender's name, address, physical description, date of birth, employer, time of arrest, offense, name of arresting officer, etc. Photographing and fingerprinting of the offender are also part of booking.

bot   Under Anglo-Saxon law, the restitution paid by the offender to the victim.

bourgeoisie   In Marxist theory, the owners of the means of production; the capitalist ruling class.

broken windows   Term used to represent the role of the police as maintainers of community order and safety.

burglary   Breaking and entering into a home or structure for purposes of committing a felony.

capital punishment   Use of the death penalty to punish transgressors.

career criminal   A person who has repeated experiences in law-violating behavior and organizes his or her lifestyle around criminality.

challenge for cause   Removing a juror because of bias, having prior knowledge about a case, or for other reasons which demonstrate inability to render a fair and impartial judgment in a case.

chancery court   Created in fifteenth-century England to oversee the lives of high-born minors who were orphaned or otherwise could not care for themselves.

charge   In a criminal case, the specific crime the defendant is accused of committing.

Chicago Crime Commission   Citizens' action group set up in Chicago to investigate problems in the criminal justice system and explore avenues for positive change; the forerunner of many such groups around the country.

child abuse   Any physical, emotional, or sexual trauma to a child for which no reasonable explanation, such as an accident, can be found. Child abuse can also be a function of neglecting to give proper care and attention to a young child.

chronic juvenile offender   According to Marvin Wolfgang, a delinquent offender who is arrested five or more times before they are 18 and who stands a good chance of becoming an adult criminal; responsible for more than half of all serious crimes.

civil law   All law which is not criminal, including torts (personal wrongs), contract law, property law, maritime law, commercial law, and so on.

Civil Rights Division   Part of the U.S. Justice Department which handles cases involving violation of civil rights guaranteed by the U.S. Constitution and criminal justice code.

classical theory   Theoretical perspective suggesting that: (1) people have free will to choose criminal or conventional behavior; (2) people choose to commit crime for reasons of greed or personal need; (3) crime can be controlled only by fear of criminal sanctions.

classification   Procedure in which prisoners are categorized on the basis of their personal characteristics and criminal history and then assigned to an appropriate institution.

Code of Hammurabi   First written criminal code, developed in Babylonia about 2000 B.C.

coeducational prison   Institution which houses both male and female inmates, who share work and recreational facilities.

cognitive theory   Study of the perception of reality and the mental processes required to understand the world we live in.

cohort study   A study using a sample whose behavior is followed over a period of time.

common law   Early English law, developed by judges, which incorporated Anglo-Saxon tribal custom, feudal rules and practices, and the everyday rules of behavior of local villages. Common law became the standardized law in England and eventually formed the basis of criminal law in the United States.

community policing   Police strategy that emphasizes fear reduction, community organization, and order maintenance rather than crime fighting.

community treatment   Refers to the actions of correctional agencies which attempt to maintain the convicted offender in a community instead of a secure facility; includes probation, parole, and residential programs.

complaint   A sworn allegation made in writing to a court or judge that an individual is guilty of some designated (complained of) offense. This is often the first legal document filed regarding a criminal offense. The complaint can be made by the victim, the police officer, the district attorney, or other interested party. Although the complaint "charges" an offense, an indictment or information may be the formal charging document.

concurrent sentence   Prison sentences for two or more criminal acts which are served simultaneously or run together.

conduct norms   Behaviors which are expected of social group members. If group norms conflict with those of the general culture, individuals may find themselves described as outcasts or criminals.

conflict view   The view that human behavior is shaped by interpersonal conflict and that those who maintain social power will use it to further their own needs.

conjugal visit   A prison program that allows inmates to receive private visits from their wives for the purpose of maintaining normal interpersonal relationships.

consecutive sentence   Prison sentences for two or more criminal acts which are served one after the other or follow one another.

consensus view of crime   The belief that the majority of citizens in a given society share common ideals and work toward a common good, and that crimes are acts which are outlawed because they conflict with the rules of the majority and are harmful to society.

constable   Peacekeeper in early English towns; organized citizens to protect his territory and supervised the night watch to maintain order in the evening.

constructive intent   The finding of criminal liability for an unintentional act that is the result of negligence or recklessness.

constructive possession   In the crime of larceny, willingly giving up temporary physical possession of property but retaining legal ownership.

continuance   A judicial order to continue a case without a finding in order to gather more information, begin an informal treatment program, etc.

contract system (attorney)   Providing counsel to indigent offenders by having an attorney(s) under contract to the county to handle all (or some) indigent matters.

contract system (convict)   System used in the early twentieth century by which inmates were leased out to private industry to work.

convict subculture   Separate culture which exists in the prison which has its own set of rewards and behaviors. The traditional culture is now being replaced by a violent gang culture.

conviction   A judgment of guilt; a verdict by a jury, a plea by a defendant, or a judgment by a court that the accused is guilty as charged.

corporal punishment   Use of physical chastisement, such as whipping or electro-shocks, to punish criminals.

corporate crime White-collar crime involving a legal violation by a corporate entity such as price fixing, restraint of trade, waste dumping, and so on.

corpus dilecti The body of the crime made up of the actus reus and mens rea.

corrections Refers to the agencies of justice which take custody of an offender after conviction and are entrusted with treatment and control.

court administrator Individual who controls the operations of the courts system in a particular jurisdiction; may be in charge of scheduling, juries, judicial assignment, and so on.

court of last resort Court which handles the final appeal on a matter. The U.S. Supreme Court is the official court of last resort for criminal matters.

courtroom work group The view that all parties in the adversary process work together in a cooperative effort to settle cases with the least amount of effort and conflict.

courts of limited jurisdiction Courts which handle misdemeanors and minor civil complaints.

crime A violation of existing societal rules of behavior as interpreted and expressed by a criminal code created by those holding social and political power.

crime control Model of criminal justice which emphasizes the control of dangerous offenders and the protection of society. Its advocates call for harsh punishments which would act as a deterrent to crime, such as the death penalty.

crime fighter Police style which stresses dealing with hard crimes and arresting dangerous criminals.

Criminal Division Branch of the Justice Department that prosecutes criminal violations.

criminal justice process Decision-making points from the initial investigation or arrest by police to the eventual release of the offender and his or her reentry into society; the various sequential criminal stages through which the offender passes.

criminal law Body of rules which define crimes, set punishments, and mandate procedures in carrying out the criminal process.

criminal sanction Refers to the right of the state to punish a person if they violate rules set down in the criminal code. The punishments connected to commission of a specific crime.

criminology Scientific approach to the study of criminal behavior and society's reaction to it.

cruel and unusual punishment Physical punishment or punishment which is far in excess of that given to people under similar circumstances, and is therefore banned by the Eighth Amendment. The death penalty has so far not been considered cruel and unusual if it is administered in a fair and nondiscriminatory fashion.

cultural transmission Concept that conduct norms are passed down from one generation to the next so that they become stable within the boundaries of a culture; guarantees that group lifestyle and behavior is stable and predictable.

culture conflict According to Sellin, a condition brought about when rules and norms of an individual's subcultural affiliation conflict with role demands of conventional society.

culture of poverty The view that people in lower-class society form a separate culture with its own values and norms that are in conflict with conventional society; the culture is self-maintaining and on-going.

curtilage Fields attached to a house.

custodial convenience Principle of giving jailed inmates the minimum comforts required by law in order to keep down the costs of incarceration.

cynicism The belief that most actions are motivated solely by personal needs and selfishness.

deadly force Ability of the police to kill a suspect if they resist arrest or present a danger to the officer or the community. The police cannot use deadly force against an unarmed, fleeing felon.

decriminalize Reducing the penalty for a criminal act but not actually legalizing it.

defendant The accused in criminal proceedings; he or she has the right to be present at each stage of the criminal justice process except grand jury proceedings.

defense attorney Counsel and representative for the defendant in a criminal trial from arrest to final appeal.

degenerate anomalies According to Cesare Lombroso, the primitive physical characteristics which make criminals animalistic and savage.

deinstitutionalization Movement to remove as many offenders as possible from secure confinement and treat them in the community.

demystify Process by which Marxists unmask the true purpose of capitalist system's rules and laws.

desert-based sentences Principle of basing sentence length on the seriousness of the criminal act and not the personal characteristics of the defendant or the deterrent impact of the law; punishment based on what people have done and not on what others may do or what they themselves may do in the future.

desistance Process in which crime rate declines with age; synonymous with the aging out process.

detective Police agency or agent who is assigned to investigate crimes after they have been reported, gather evidence, and identify the perpetrator.

detention Holding an offender in secure confinement before trial.

determinate sentence Involves "fixed" terms of incarceration, such as three years' imprisonment. It is felt by many to be too restrictive for rehabilitative purposes; the advantage is that offenders know how much time they have to serve (when they will be released).

deterrence Act of preventing crime before it occurs by means of the threat of criminal sanctions.

deviance Behavior that departs from the social norm.

differential association According to Edwin Sutherland, the principle that criminal acts are related to a person's exposure to an excess amount of antisocial attitudes and values.

direct examination Questions of counsel's own (prosecution or defense) witness during a trial.

directed verdict Right of a judge to direct a jury to acquit a defendant because the state has not proven the elements of the crime or has not established guilt according to law.

discretion Use of personal decision-making and choice in carrying out operations in the criminal justice system. For example, police discretion can involve the decision to make an arrest; prosecutorial discretion can involve the decision to accept a plea bargain.

disposition For juvenile offenders, the equivalent of sentencing for adult offenders. The theory is that disposition can be more rehabilitative than retributive. Possible dispositions may dismiss the case, release the youth to the custody of parents, place the offender on probation, or send him or her to an institution or state correctional institution.

district attorney County prosecutor who is charged with bringing offenders to justice and enforcing the laws of the state.

diversion A noncriminal alternative to trial, usually featuring counseling, job training, and educational opportunities.

double bunking Practice of holding two or more inmates in a single cell because of prison overcrowding; upheld in *Rhodes v. Chapman.*

drift According to Matza, the view that youths move in and out of delinquency and that their lifestyles can embrace both conventional and deviant values.

drug courier profile A way of identifying drug runners based on their personal characteristics; police may stop and question people based on the way they fit the characteristics contained in the profile.

Drug Enforcement Administration (DEA) Federal agency which handles enforcement of federal drug control laws.

due process Basic constitutional principle based on the concept of the primacy of the individual and the complementary concept of limitation on governmental power; a safeguard against arbitrary and unfair state procedures in judicial or administrative proceedings. Embodied in the due process concept are the basic rights of a defendant in criminal proceedings and the requisites for a fair trial. These rights and requirements have been expanded by appellate court decisions and include (1) timely notice of a hearing or trial which informs the accused of the charges against him or her; (2) opportunity to confront accusers and to present evidence on one's own behalf before an impartial jury or judge; (3) presumption of innocence under which guilt must be proven by legally obtained evidence and the verdict must be supported by the evidence presented; (4) the right of an accused to be warned of constitutional rights at the earliest stage of the criminal process; (5) protection against self-incrimination; (6) assistance of counsel at every critical stage of the criminal process; and (7) the guarantee that an individual will not be tried more than once for the same offense (double jeopardy).

Durham Rule Definition of insanity which required that the crime be excused if it was a product of a mental illness; still used in New Hampshire.

economic crime An act in violation of the criminal law which is designed to bring financial gain to the offender.

economism Policy of controlling white-collar crime through monetary incentives and sanctions.

electroencephalogram (EEG) A device that can record electronic impulses given off by the brain, commonly called "brain waves."

embezzlement Type of larceny which involves taking the possessions of another (fraudulent conversion) which have been placed in the thief's lawful posses-sion for safekeeping. For example, a bank teller misappropriating deposits, or a stock broker making off with a customer's account.

enterprise syndicate An organized crime group which profits from the sale of illegal goods and services such as narcotics, pornography and prostitution.

entrapment Criminal defense which maintains that the police originated the criminal idea or initiated the criminal action.

exclusionary rule Principle that prohibits using evidence illegally obtained in a trial. Based on the Fourth Amendment "right of the people to be secure in their persons, houses, papers, and effects, against unreasonable searches and seizures," the rule is not a bar to prosecution, as legally obtained evidence may be available which may be used in a trial.

excuse A defense to a criminal charge in which the accused maintains he or she lacked the intent to commit the crime (mens rea).

ex post facto laws Laws which make an act criminal after it was committed, or retroactively increase the penalty for a crime. For example, an ex post facto law could change shoplifting from a misdemeanor to a felony and penalize people with a prison term even though they had been apprehended six months before; these laws are unconstitutional.

expressive crime A crime which has no purpose except to accomplish the behavior at hand, e.g., shooting someone, as opposed to shooting someone to create monetary gain.

false pretenses Illegally obtaining money, goods, or merchandise from another by fraud or misrepresentation.

Federal Bureau of Investigation (FBI) Arm of the Justice Department which investigates violations of federal law, gathers crime statistics, runs a comprehensive crime laboratory, and helps train local law enforcement officers.

felony A more serious offense which carries a penalty of incarceration in a state prison, usually for one year or more. Persons convicted of felony offenses lose such rights as the right to vote, hold elective office, or maintain certain licenses.

fence Buyer and seller of stolen merchandise.

flat, or fixed, sentencing Sentencing model which mandates that all people who are convicted of a specific offense and sent to prison must receive the same length of incarceration.

focal concerns According to Walter Miller, the value orientations of lower-class cultures whose features include the need for excitement, trouble, smartness, fate, and personal autonomy.

folkways Generally-followed customs which do not have moral values attached to them, such as not interrupting a person when they are speaking.

fraud Taking the possessions of another through deception or cheating, such as selling a person an antique which is known to be a copy.

free venture Starting privately-run industries in a prison setting in which the inmates work for wages and the goods are sold for profit.

functionalism A sociological perspective which suggests that each part of society makes a contribution to the maintenance of the whole; stresses social cooperation and consensus of values and beliefs among a majority of society's members.

general deterrence A crime-control policy that depends on fear of criminal penalties; measures, such as long prison sentences for violent crimes, are aimed at convincing the potential law violator that the pains associated with a crime outweigh its benefits.

good faith exception Principle of law which holds that evidence may be used in a criminal trial even though the search warrant used to obtain it is technically faulty, if the police acted in good faith and to the best of their ability when they sought to obtain it from a judge.

good time credit Time taken off a prison sentence in exchange for good behavior within the institution; for example, ten days per month; device used to limit disciplinary problems within the prison.

grand jury A group (usually comprised of twenty-three citizens) chosen to hear testimony in secret and to issue formal criminal accusations (indictments); also serves an investigatory function.

grass eaters Term used for police officers who accept payoffs when their everyday duties place them in a position to be solicited by the public.

greenmail Process by which an investor buys large blocks of a company's stock and threatens to take over the company and replace the current management. To ward off the threat to their positions, management uses company funds to repurchase the shares at a much higher price, creating huge profits for the corporate raiders.

guardian ad litem Court-appointed attorney who protects the interests of a child in cases involving the child's welfare.

habeas corpus See *writ of habeas corpus.*

habitual criminal statutes Laws which give long-term or life sentences for offenders who have multiple felony convictions.

halfway house A community-based correctional facility which houses inmates before their outright release so that they can gradually become acclimated to conventional society.

hands-off doctrine The judicial policy of not interfering in the administrative affairs of a prison.

hearsay evidence Testimony which is not firsthand but relates information told by a second party.

house of correction County correctional institution generally used for the incarceration of more serious misdemeanants whose sentences are usually less than one year.

hue and cry In medieval Britain, the policy of self-help used in villages demanded that everyone respond if a citizen raised a hue and cry for aid.

hundred   In medieval Britain, a group of one hundred families which had responsibility for order maintenance and the trying of minor offenses.

incapacitation   Policy of keeping dangerous criminals in confinement so that the risk of repeating their offense in society is eliminated.

indeterminate sentence   Incarceration with a stated minimum and maximum term; for example, a sentence to prison for a period of from three to ten years. The prisoner would be eligible for parole after the minimum sentence had been served. Based on the belief that sentences should fit the criminal, indeterminate sentences allow "individualized" sentences and provide for sentencing flexibility. Judges can set a high minimum to overcome the purpose of the indeterminate sentence.

index crimes   According to the FBI, the eight crimes which, because of their seriousness and frequency, have their reported incidence recorded in the annual Uniform Crime Reports: murder, rape, assault, robbery, burglary, arson, larceny, and motor vehicle theft.

indictment   Written accusation returned by a grand jury charging an individual with a specified crime after determination of probable cause; the prosecutor presents enough evidence (a prima facie case) to establish probable cause.

information   Like an indictment, a formal charging document. The prosecuting attorney fills out the information and files it in court. Probable cause is determined at the preliminary hearing, which, unlike grand jury proceedings, is public and attended by the accused and his or her attorney.

initial appearance   The step at which the arrested suspect is brought before a magistrate for consideration of bail. The suspect must be taken for an initial appearance within a "reasonable time" after arrest. For petty offenses, this step often serves as the final criminal proceeding, either through adjudication by a judge or a guilty plea.

inmate social code   Informal set of rules that govern inmates while in prison.

insider trading   Illegal buying of stock in a company based on information provided by another who has a fiduciary interest in the company such as an employee or an outside attorney or accountant hired by the firm for management or legal purposes. Federal laws and the rules of the Security and Exchange Commission require all profits acquired by insider trading be returned, and provide for fines and a prison sentence.

instrumental Marxist theory   The view that capitalist institutions such as the criminal justice system has (as their main purpose) the control of the poor in order to maintain the hegemony of the wealthy.

interactionist perspective   The view that perception of reality is significantly influenced by a person's interpretations of the reactions of others to similar events and stimuli.

interrogation   Method of accumulating evidence in the form of information or confessions from suspects by police; questioning, which has been legally restricted because of concern about the use of brutal or coercive methods and in the interest of protecting individuals against self-incrimination.

investigation   Inquiry concerning suspected criminal behavior for the purpose of identifying offenders or gathering further evidence to assist the prosecution of apprehended offenders.

jail   Usually part of the local police station or sheriff's office; used to detain people awaiting trial, to serve as a "lockup" for drunks and disorderly individuals, and for short-term confinement of offenders serving sentences of less than one year.

just desert   A philosophy of justice which asserts that those who violate the rights of others deserve to be punished; severity of punishment should be commensurate with the seriousness of the crime.

justice model   A philosophy of corrections which stresses determinate sentences, abolition of parole, and the view that prisons are places of punishment and not rehabilitation.

justification   A defense to a criminal charge in which the accused maintains that his or her actions were justified by the circumstances, and therefore the accused should not be held criminally liable.

juvenile delinquency Participation in illegal behavior by a minor who falls under a statutory age limit.

juvenile justice process Court proceedings for youths within the "juvenile" age-group that differ from the adult criminal process. Originally, under the paternal (parens patriae) philosophy, juvenile procedures are informal and nonadversary, invoked *for* the juvenile offender rather than *against* him or her; a petition instead of a complaint is filed; courts make findings of involvement or adjudication of delinquency instead of convictions; and juvenile offenders receive dispositions instead of sentences. Recent court decisions (*Kent* and *Gault*) have increased the adversary nature of juvenile court proceedings. However, the philosophy remains one of diminishing the stigma of delinquency and providing for the youth's well-being and rehabilitation, rather than seeking retribution.

Kansas City Study An experimental program that evaluated the effectiveness of patrol; found that the presence of patrol officers had little deterrent effect.

Knapp Commission Led the investigation into police corruption in New York and uncovered a widespread network of payoffs and bribes.

labeling Process by which a person becomes fixed with a negative identity, such as "criminal" or "excon", and is forced to suffer the consequences of outcast status.

male in se Crimes that are outlawed because they violate basic moral values: rape, murder, assault, robbery, and so on.

male prohibitum Crimes that are outlawed by statute because they clash with current norms and public opinion: tax laws, traffic laws, drug laws, and so on.

mandamus See *writ of mandamus.*

mandatory sentence Statutory requirement that a certain penalty shall be set and carried out in all cases upon conviction for a specified offense or series of offenses.

marital exemption The practice in some states of prohibiting the prosecution of husbands for the rape of their wives.

masculinity hypothesis The view that women who commit crimes have biological and psychological traits similar to those of men.

mens rea Guilty mind; the mental element of a crime or the intent to commit a criminal act.

middle-class measuring rods According to Cohen, the standards with which teachers and other representatives of state authority evaluate lower-class youths; because they cannot live up to middle-class standards, lower-class youths are bound for failure, which brings on frustration and anger at conventional society.

Miranda warning The result of two Supreme Court decisions (*Escobedo v. Illinois* [378 U.S. 478] and *Miranda v. Arizona* [384 U.S. 4361]) which require that a police officer inform individuals under arrest of their constitutional right to remain silent, to know that their statements can later be used against them in court, that they can have an attorney present to help them, and that the state will pay for an attorney if they cannot afford to hire one. Although aimed at protecting an individual during in-custody interrogation, the warning must also be given when the investigation shifts from the investigatory to the accusatory state, i.e., when suspicion begins to focus on an individual.

misdemeanor A minor crime usually punished by less than one year's imprisonment in a local institution, such as a county jail.

moral entrepreneurs People who use their influence to shape the legal process in ways they see fit.

motion Oral or written request asking the court to make a specified finding, decision, or order.

murder transaction The concept that murder is usually a result of behavior interaction between victim and offender.

National Crime Survey Ongoing victimization study conducted jointly by the Justice Department and Census Bureau which surveys victims about their experiences with law violation.

nolo contendere No contest; an admission of guilt in a criminal case with the condition that the finding cannot be used against the defendant in any subsequent civil cases.

nolle prosequi The term used when a prosecutor decides to drop a case after a complaint has been formally made. Reasons for a nolle prosequi include evidence insufficiency, reluctance of witnesses to testify, police error, office policy, and so on.

obscenity According to current legal theory, sexually explicit material lacking a serious purpose, which appeals solely to the purient interest of the viewer. While nudity per se is not usually considered obscene, open sex behavior, masturbation, and exhibition of the genitals is banned in many communities.

official crime Criminal behavior that has become known to the agents of justice.

opportunist robber Someone who steals small amounts or items when a vulnerable target presents itself.

parole Release of a prisoner from imprisonment subject to conditions set by a parole board. Depending on the jurisdiction, inmates must serve a certain proportion of their sentences before becoming eligible for parole. Upon determination of the parole board, the inmate is granted parole. Conditions of parole may require him or her to report regularly to a parole officer, to refrain from criminal conduct, to maintain and support family members, to avoid contact with other convicted criminals, to abstain from alcoholic beverages and drugs, to remain within the jurisdiction, etc. Violations of the conditions of parole may result in revocation of parole, in which case the individual will be returned to prison. The concept behind parole is to allow the release of the offender to community supervision, where rehabilitation and readjustment will be facilitated.

partial deterrent A legal measure designed to restrict or control, rather than eliminate, an undesirable act.

particularity Requirement that a search warrant state precisely where the search is to take place and what items are to be seized.

paternalism Male domination; a paternalistic family, for instance, is one in which the father is the dominant authority figure.

Pennsylvania System Prison system developed during the nineteenth century which stressed total isolation and individual penitence as a means of reform.

peremptory challenge Dismissal of a potential juror by either the prosecution or defense for unexplained discretionary reasons.

plea An answer to formal charges by an accused; possible pleas are guilty, not guilty, nolo contendere, or not guilty by reason of insanity. A "guilty" plea is a confession of the offense as charged. A "not guilty" plea is a denial of the charge and places the burden on the prosecution to prove the elements of the offense.

plea-bargaining Discussion between the defense counsel and the prosecution by which the accused agrees to plead guilty for certain considerations. The advantage to the defendant may be in the form of a reduction of the charges, a lenient sentence, or (in the case of multiple charges) dropped charges. The advantage to the prosecution is that a conviction is obtained without the time and expense of lengthy trial proceedings.

police discretion Refers to the ability of police officers to enforce the law selectively. Police officers in the field have great latitude to use their discretion in deciding whether to invoke their arrest powers.

police officer style Refers to the belief that the bulk of police officers can be classified into ideal personality types; popular style types include: supercops, who desire to enforce only serious crimes like robbery and rape; professionals, who use a broad definition of police work; service-oriented, who see their job as that of a helping profession;

avoiders or shirkers, who do as little as possible. The actual existence of ideal police officer types has been open to much debate.

population   All people who share a particular personal characteristic, e.g., all college students or all police officers.

positivism   Branch of social science which uses the scientific method of the natural sciences and which suggests that human behavior is a product of social, biological, psychological, or economic forces.

power rape   Rape motivated by the need for sexual conquest.

power syndicates   Organized crime groups which use force and violence to exhort money from legitimate businesses and other criminal groups engaged in illegal business enterprises.

praxis   Application of theory in action; in Marxist criminology, applying theory to promote revolution.

preliminary hearings   The step at which criminal charges initiated by an *information* are tested for probable cause; the prosecution presents enough evidence to establish probable cause, i.e., a prima facie case. The hearing is public and may be attended by the accused and his or her attorney.

pre-sentence report   Investigation performed by a probation officer attached to a trial court after the conviction of a defendant; contains information about the defendant's background, education, previous employment, family, defendant's statement concerning the offense, prior criminal record, interviews with neighbors or acquaintances, mental and physical condition (i.e., information that would not be made record in the case of a guilty plea or that would be inadmissible as evidence at a trial but could be influential and important at the sentencing stage), and so on. After conviction, a judge sets a date for sentencing (usually ten days to two weeks from date of conviction), during which time the pre-sentence report is made. The report is required in felony cases in federal courts and in many states, is optional with the judge in some states, and is mandatory in others, before convicted offend-

ers can be placed on probation. In the case of juvenile offenders, the pre-sentence report is also known as a social history report.

prison   State or federal correctional institution for incarceration of felony offenders for terms of one year or more.

probable cause   The evidentiary criterion necessary to sustain an arrest or the issuance of an arrest or search warrant; less than absolute certainty or "beyond a reasonable doubt" but greater than mere suspicion or "hunch"; a set of facts, information, circumstances, or conditions that would lead a reasonable person to believe that an offense was committed and that the accused committed that offense. An arrest made without probable cause may be susceptible to prosecution as an illegal arrest under "false imprisonment" statutes.

probation   A sentence entailing the conditional release of a convicted offender into the community under the supervision of the court (in the form of a probation officer) subject to certain conditions for a specified time. The conditions are usually similar to those of parole. *Note:* Probation is a sentence, an alternative to incarceration; parole is administrative release from incarceration. Violation of the conditions of probation may result in revocation of probation.

procedural law   Rules that define the operation of criminal proceedings; describes the methods that must be followed in obtaining warrants, investigating offenses, affecting lawful arrests, using force, conducting trials, introducing evidence, sentencing convicted offenders, and reviewing cases by appellate courts (in general, legislatures have ignored post-sentencing procedures). Given the substantive law, which defines criminal offenses, procedural law delineates how the substantive offenses are to be enforced.

proof beyond a reasonable doubt   The standard of proof needed to convict in a criminal case. The evidence offered in court does not have to amount to absolute certainty, but should leave no reasonable doubt that the defendant committed the alleged crime.

psychopath   Person whose personality is characterized by lack of warmth and affection, inappropriate behavior responses, and an inability to learn from experience. While some psychologists view psychopathy as a result of childhood trauma, others see it as a result of biological abnormality.

random sample Sample selected on the basis of chance so that each person in the population has an equal opportunity to be selected.

rationale choice The view that crime is a function of a decision-making process in which the potential offender weighs the potential costs and benefits of an illegal act.

relative deprivation Condition which exists when people of wealth and poverty live in close proximity to one another. Some criminologists attribute crime rate differentials to relative deprivation.

release on recognizance Nonmonetary condition for the pretrial release of an accused individual; an alternative to monetary bail, which is granted after determination that the accused has ties in the community, has no prior record of default, and is likely to appear at subsequent proceedings.

restitution Condition of probation in which the offender repays society or the victim of crime for the trouble or damage the offender caused; monetary restitution involves a direct payment to the victim as a means of compensation; community service restitution may be used in victimless crimes and involves volunteer work in lieu of more severe criminal penalties.

routine activities The view that crime is a "normal" function of routine activities of modern living. Offenses can be expected if there is a suitable target unprotected by capable guardians.

sadistic rape Rape motivated by the offender's desire to torment and abuse the victim.

sample A limited number of persons selected for study from a population.

schizophrenia Type of psychosis often marked by bizarre behavior, hallucinations, loss of thought control, and inappropriate emotional responses. There are different types of schizophrenia: catatonic, which characteristically involves impairment of motor activity; paranoid, which is characterized by delusions of persecution; and hebephrenic, which is characterized by immature behavior and giddiness.

self-report study Research approach that requires subjects to reveal their own participation in delinquent or criminal acts.

sentence Criminal sanction imposed by the court on a convicted defendant, usually in the form of a fine, incarceration, or probation. Sentencing may be carried out by judge, jury, or sentencing council (panel of judges), depending on the statutes of the jurisdiction.

Sherman Report National review of law enforcement education programs, which found that a liberal-arts-related curriculum was the most appropriate learning tool for police officers.

shield laws Laws designed to protect a rape victim by prohibiting the defense attorney from inquiring about her previous sexual relationships.

shire reeve In early England, the senior law enforcement figure in a county; forerunner of today's sheriff.

shock probation Sentence that involves a short prison stay to impress the offender with the pains of imprisonment before he or she begins a probationary sentence.

short-run hedonism According to Cohen, the desire of lower-class gang youths to engage in behavior which will give them immediate gratification and excitement, but which in the long run will be dysfunctional and negativistic.

Sir Robert Peel British Home Secretary, who in 1829 organized the London Metropolitan Police, the first local police force.

social disorganization Neighborhood or area marked by culture conflict, lack of cohesiveness, transient population, insufficient social organizations, and anomie.

special deterrence   Crime-control policy which suggests that punishment should be severe enough to convince previous offenders never to repeat their criminal activity.

specific intent   Intent to accomplish a specific purpose as an element of crime, e.g., breaking into someone's house for the express purpose of stealing jewels.

stare decisis   To stand by decided cases; the legal principle by which the decision or holding in an earlier case becomes the standard by which to judge subsequent and similar cases.

statutory law   Laws created by legislative bodies to meet changing social conditions, public opinion, and custom.

sting   Undercover police operation in which police pose as criminals to trap law violators.

stoopers   Petty criminals who earn their living by retrieving winning tickets which are accidentally discarded by race track patrons.

stop and frisk   Situation where police officers who are suspicious of an individual run their hands lightly over the suspect's outer garments to determine if the person is carrying a concealed weapon; also called a "patdown" or "threshold inquiry"; a search intended to stop short of any activity that could be considered a violation of Fourth Amendment rights.

stradom formations   According to the Schwendingers, adolescent social networks whose members have distinct dress, grooming, and linguistic behavior.

street crime   Illegal acts designed to prey on the public through theft, damage, and violence.

strict-liability crimes   Illegal acts whose elements do not contain the need for intent or mens rea; usually, acts that endanger the public welfare, such as illegal dumping of toxic wastes.

structural Marxist theory   The view that the law and justice system is designed to maintain the capitalist system and that members of both the owner and worker classes, whose behavior threatens the stability of the system, will be sanctioned.

subculture   Group that is loosely part of the dominant culture but maintains a unique set of values, beliefs, and traditions.

substantive criminal laws   A body of specific rules that declare what conduct is criminal and prescribe the punishment to be imposed for such conduct.

summons   Alternative to arrest, usually used for petty or traffic offenses; a written order notifying an individual that he or she has been charged with an offense. A summons directs the person to appear in court to answer the charge. It is used primarily in instances of low risk, where the person will be required to appear at a later date. The summons is advantageous to police officers in that they are freed from the time normally spent for arrest and booking procedures; it is advantageous to the accused in that he or she is spared time in jail.

surplus value   Marxist view that the laboring classes produce wealth which far exceeds their wages and goes to the capitalist class as profits.

team policing   Experimental police technique that employs groups of officers assigned to a particular area of the city on a twenty-four-hour basis.

technical parole violation   Revocation of parole because conditions set by correctional authorities have been violated.

thanatos   According to Sigmund Freud, the instinctual drive towards aggression and violence.

tort   Law of personal wrongs and damage; tort-type actions include negligence, libel, slander, assault, and trespass.

totality of the circumstances   A legal doctrine which mandates that a decision-maker consider all the issues and circumstances of a case before judging the outcome. For example, before concluding whether a suspect understood their Miranda warning, a judge must consider the totality of the circumstances under which the warning was given. The suspect's age, intelligence, and competency may be issues which influence their understanding and judgment.

transferred intent If an illegal, yet unintended, act results from the intent to commit a crime, that act is also considered illegal.

transitional neighborhood An area undergoing a shift in population and structure, usually from middle-class residential to lower-class mixed use.

Type I offenses Synonymous with index crimes.

Type II offenses All crimes other than index crimes and minor traffic offenses; the FBI records annual arrest information for Type II offenses.

venire Group called for jury duty for which jury panels are selected.

victimization survey A crime-measurement technique that surveys citizens in order to measure their experiences as victims of crime.

victimology Study of the victim's role in criminal transactions.

victim precipitated Describes a crime in which the victim's behavior was the spark that ignited the subsequent offense, e.g., the victim abused the offender verbally or physically.

voir dire Process in which a potential jury panel is questioned by the prosecution and defense in order to select jurors who are unbiased and objective.

waiver The act of voluntarily relinquishing a right or advantage; often used in the context of waiving one's right to counsel (e.g., Miranda warning) or waiving certain steps in the criminal justice process (e.g., the preliminary hearing); essential to waiver is the voluntary consent of the individual.

warrant Written order issued by a competent magistrate authorizing a police officer or other official to

perform duties relating to the administration of justice.

watch system During the Middle Ages in England, men were organized in church parishes to guard at night against disturbances and breaches of the peace under direction of the local constable.

wergild Under medieval law, money paid by the offender to compensate the victim and the state for a criminal offense.

white-collar crime Illegal acts that capitalize on a person's place in the marketplace; can involve theft, embezzlement, fraud, market manipulation, restraint of trade, and false advertising.

Wickersham Commission Created in 1931 by President Herbert Hoover to investigate the state of the nation's police forces; found that police training was inadequate and the average officer incapable of effectively carrying out duties.

work furlough A prison treatment program that allows inmates to be released to work in the community and return to prison on a daily basis.

writ of certiorari An order of a superior court requesting that the record of an inferior court (or administrative body) be brought forward for review or inspection.

writ of habeas corpus A judicial order requesting that a person detaining another produce the body of the prisoner and give reasons for his or her capture and detention; a legal device used to request that a judicial body review reasons for a person's confinement and the conditions of confinement; known as "the great writ."

writ of mandamus An order of a superior court commanding that a lower court or an administrative or executive body perform a specific function; commonly used to restore rights and privileges lost to a defendant through illegal means.

SUBJECT INDEX

NAME INDEX

TABLE OF CASES